T0388687

The Palgrave Handbook of Utopian and Dystopian Literatures

Peter Marks · Jennifer A. Wagner-Lawlor ·
Fátima Vieira
Editors

The Palgrave Handbook of Utopian and Dystopian Literatures

palgrave
macmillan

Editors
Peter Marks
University of Sydney
Sydney, NSW, Australia

Fátima Vieira
Department of Anglo-American Studies
Faculty of Arts
University of Porto
Porto, Portugal

Jennifer A. Wagner-Lawlor
Department of Women's, Gender,
and Sexuality Studies, and English
The Pennsylvania State University
University Park, PA, USA

ISBN 978-3-030-88653-0   ISBN 978-3-030-88654-7   (eBook)
https://doi.org/10.1007/978-3-030-88654-7

Cover illustration: @Maurice Rosenfeld/Getty Images

This Palgrave Macmillan imprint is published by the registered company Springer Nature
Switzerland AG
The registered company address is: Gewerbestrasse 11, 6330 Cham, Switzerland

ACKNOWLEDGEMENTS

This book is the result of immense effort from dozens of people around the world over several years. The editors would like to acknowledge the contributions of all the authors gathered in these pages, thanking them for their expertise, their labor, and their patience. We also want to give special thanks to the skilled and determined team who, whether proofreading, translating, or formatting, helped transform individual chapters into the finished volume. Our sincere gratitude, then, to Bethany Doane, Ben Eldridge, Raquel Jones, and Jo Watson; without your generosity and diligence the completed work would not exist. Thanks, too, to our long-suffering partners and families for their forbearance. Finally, at the risk of seeming self-indulgent, the editors would like to thank each other for the camaraderie, energy, and good humor that has sustained us through life changes, illnesses, and a global pandemic. Working in three separate continents and in three vastly different time zones provided immense challenges, but the volume resulting from our collective efforts is a small testament to the vitality and indeed the necessity of the utopian spirit.

CONTENTS

Editors and Contributors

About the Editors

Peter Marks is Emeritus Professor of English at the University of Sydney. As well as chapters and articles on George Orwell, Samuel Beckett, the literature of the 1930s, surveillance, and literary periodicals, he is the author of four books: *British Filmmakers: Terry Gilliam* (Manchester University Press, 2009); *George Orwell the Essayist: Literature, Politics and the Periodical Culture* (Continuum Books, 2011); *Surveillance: Eutopian and Dystopian Literature and Film* (Edinburgh University Press, 2015); and *British Literature of the 1990s: Endings and Beginnings* (Edinburgh University Press, 2018).

Jennifer A. Wagner-Lawlor is Professor of Women's, Gender, and Sexuality Studies, and English at Pennsylvania State University. She has published two monographs, *Postmodern Utopias and Feminist Fictions*, published by Cambridge University Press in 2013; she also has edited two essay collections, including *The Scandal of Susan Sontag* (Columbia University Press, 2009). She is author of dozens of book chapters and articles in *Utopian Studies, Feminist Studies* and *Contemporary Women's Writing*. She is a former president of The Society for Utopian Studies (SUS). Her current work looks at the cultural significance of plastic and plastic waste, and its impacts on environmental crisis. She has published several articles on *plaesthetics,* a term that incorporates the study of plasticity as a trope and the hermeneutics of plastic artifacts in literary and artistic texts.

Fátima Vieira is Professor of English at the University of Porto. She was the Chair of the Utopian Studies Society/Europe from 2006 to 2016. She is the Coordinator of the University of Porto's branch of CETAPS—Centre for English, Translation and Anglo-Portuguese Studies, where she has coordinated several funded projects on utopianism. She is the coordinator of the ARUS (Advanced Research in Utopian Studies) Postdoctoral program and of the Arus Digital Repository that hosts the Lyman Tower Sargent Bibliography on utopianism, with over 19,000 entries (arus.letras.up.pt). She is book review editor for the American journal *Utopian Studies,* for which she prepared two special issues to commemorate the 500th anniversary of Thomas More's *Utopia,* has edited 15 books—the most recent being *Food futures: ethics, science and culture* (Wagningen Academic Publisher, 2016) and *Dystopia (n) Matters: On the Page, on Screen, on Stage* (Cambridge Scholars, 2014) and contributed with over 100 articles for edited books and journals.

Contributors

Bill Ashcroft University of New South Wales, Sydney, NSW, Australia

Barnita Bagchi Utrecht University, Utrecht, Netherlands

Antonis Balasopoulos University of Cyprus, Nicosia, Cyprus

Kim Beauchesne University of British Columbia, Vancouver, Canada

Matthew Beaumont University College, London, UK

Quitterie de Beauregard Sorbonne Université, Paris, France

Liam Benison University of Porto, Porto, Portugal

Carlos Eduardo Ornelas Berriel University of Campinas, Campinas, Brazil

Artur Blaim University of Gdansk, Gdansk, Poland

Roland Boer Dalian University of Technology, Dalian, China

Andrew Byers Durham, NC, USA

Ildney Cavalcanti Federal University of Alagoas, Maceió, Brazil

Edward K. Chan Waseda University, Tokyo, Japan

Gregory Claeys University of London, London, UK

Claire P. Curtis College of Charleston, Charleston, SC, USA

Laurence Davis University College Cork, Cork, Ireland

Jacqueline Dutton University of Melbourne, Melbourne, Australia

Ainehi Edoro-Glines University of Wisconsin-Madison, Madison, WI, USA

Caroline Edwards Birkbeck, University of London, London, UK

José Eduardo Franco Aberta University, Lisbon, Portugal

Cristina Gil Polytechnic Institute of Setúbal, Setúbal, Portugal

Miguel Ramalhete Gomes University of Lisbon, Lisbon, Portugal

Brian Greenspan Carleton University, Ottawa, ON, Canada

Christian P. Haines Penn State University, University Park, PA, USA

Carrie Hintz Queen's College and The Graduate Center, City University of New York, New York City, NY, USA

Naomi Jacobs University of Maine, Orono, ME, USA

Francisco L. Lisi Universidad Carlos III de Madrid, Madrid, Spain

Etta M. Madden Missouri State University, Springfield, MI, USA

Maria Luísa Malato University of Porto, Porto, Portugal

Gonçalo Marcelo University of Coimbra, Coimbra, Portugal

Peter Marks University of Sydney, Sydney, NSW, Australia

Sam McAuliffe Goldsmiths, University of London, London, UK

Anne L. Melano University of Wollongong, Wollongong, NSW, Australia

Marie-Claire Phélippeau Former Editor of Moreana, Paris, France

David Pinder Roskilde University, Roskilde, Denmark

Gib Prettyman Penn State University, Fayette, PA, USA

Killian Quigley Australian Catholic University, Melbourne, Australia

Miguel A. Ramiro Avilés University of Alcalá, Madrid, Spain

José Eduardo Reis University of Trás-os-Montes e Alto Douro, Vila Real, Portugal

Peter Sands University of Wisconsin-Milwaukee, Milwaukee, WI, USA

Alessandra Santos University of British Columbia, Vancouver, Canada

Edson Luiz André de Sousa Federal University of Rio Grande do Sul, Porto Alegre, Brazil

Paola Spinozzi University of Ferrara, Ferrara, Italy

Adam Stock York St. John University, York, UK

Mikhail Suslov University of Copenhagen, Copenhagen, Denmark

Matt Tierney The Pennsylvania State University, State College, PA, USA

Brenda Tooley Grand Valley State University, Allendale, MI, USA

Fátima Vieira Department of Anglo-American Studies, Faculty of Arts, University of Porto, Porto, Portugal

Patrícia Vieira CES, University of Coimbra, Coimbra, Portugal; Georgetown University, Washington, DC, USA

Jennifer A. Wagner-Lawlor The Pennsylvania State University, University Park, PA, USA

Nathaniel Robert Walker College of Charleston, Charleston, SC, USA

Darren Webb University of Sheffield, Sheffield, UK

Phillip E. Wegner University of Florida, Gainesville, FL, USA

Introduction

Peter Marks, Fátima Vieira, and Jennifer A. Wagner-Lawlor

INTRODUCTION

Thomas More's *Utopia*, first published in Latin in 1516, was written for a small, intellectually elite audience, in a world where few people could read. The book's very title, subtly playing on the prefixes *eu* (good) and *ou* (no)—so that the island of Utopia that gives the book its name famously is the good place that is no place—could be appreciated fully only by people able to recognize such complexities and contradictions. To miss these provocative ambiguities was potentially to misunderstand the book itself, to believe among other things that More himself endorsed the conditions, practices, and philosophy said to exist on Utopia by Raphael Hythloday, who claimed to have visited the fantastic island. Hythloday (a name suggesting to the learned someone who was a "purveyor of nonsense") presents himself as a returned adventurer who had sailed with Amerigo Vespucci at the turn of the sixteenth century, asserting that he came across the island of Utopia somewhere in a Pacific Ocean then largely unknown to Europeans. Hythloday argues with

P. Marks (✉)
University of Sydney, Sydney, NSW, Australia

F. Vieira
Department of Anglo-American Studies, Faculty of Arts,
University of Porto, Porto, Portugal

J. A. Wagner-Lawlor
The Pennsylvania State University, University Park, PA, USA

P. Marks et al. (eds.), *The Palgrave Handbook of Utopian and Dystopian Literatures*, https://doi.org/10.1007/978-3-030-88654-7_1

More's doppelgänger and other real "characters" in the text itself that Utopia is far superior in organization, customs, and philosophy to the Europe they inhabit. The text More fashions out of this complex and intense debate is a sophisticated and consciously challenging blend of the real and imagined, the serious and absurd, a world of communal living and slaves, where materialism is scorned, mercenaries are hired, and where every house door opens automatically, so "there is nothing private anywhere" (More 2002, 42). In our world, where Mark Zuckerberg can comment that privacy is an outmoded concept, such a phrase has a dreadful power, but More was probing the degree to which his contemporaries might be willing to give up privacy for security or stability.

Built into *Utopia*'s DNA is the comparison of one world with another, a maneuver that generates much of the originating text's intellectual dynamism, activating arguments about the world conjured up by Hythloday in relation to the world its first readers inhabited. What is remarkable is that over 500 years later *Utopia* (now translated into dozens of languages in countless editions) still can perform this task, prompting readers in the twenty-first century to think critically about the world they inhabit in relation to a place imagined more than five centuries ago. The terms "utopia" and "utopian" have long been part of the lexicon of informed cultural and political debate, of brilliant and inspiring speculations, and of chilling forecasts. *The Palgrave Handbook of Utopian and Dystopian Literatures* aims to display this immense and still-active richness in its historical sweep and international reach, surveying and assessing the range of topics, critical thinking, and creative genius that continue to make the utopian and dystopian thinking vital to and invigorating in our world.

By definition, any artistic genre requires multiple examples produced over an extended time period by numerous figures. *Utopia* later came to be understood as inaugurating and naming a genre that has produced innumerable projections across subsequent centuries, including arresting sub-genres such as dystopias and anti-utopias. In this broader sense, *Utopia* and texts like it encouraged new ways of thinking, the adjective "utopian" extending the boundaries of the genre well beyond the literary world into other cultural forms and into social, political, and philosophical debate. Utopian thinking prompted people to construct actual communities on the bases of what their inhabitants understood as utopian principles. For some of its detractors, this potential "real world" application makes utopian thinking inherently programmatic and potentially repressive. The political philosopher John Gray, for example, in his polemical critique *Black Mass* (2007), likens utopian thought to apocalyptic religious zealotry, an "attempt to remake the world by force" (Gray 2007, 15). For other critics, such as Friedrich Engels in his essay "Socialism: Utopian and Scientific," (Engels, 1972) utopian thinking is hopelessly and indeed dangerously optimistic, distracting attention from harsh social and political realities that need addressing through the "scientific socialism" Engels himself advocated.

Against these nay-sayers are those who, in diverse ways, understand utopian thinking as productively critical of the world as it is, pointing creatively toward worlds still to be built. More than a century ago, in *A Modern Utopia*, H.G. Wells declared that "every generation will have its new version of Utopia" (Wells 1994, 220), while Ernst Bloch's three-volume *The Principle of Hope* (originally published in 1954) argued that a sense of the "not yet" is built into the human condition. Ruth Levitas argues in *Utopia as Method: The Imaginary Reconstitution of Society* that "the utopian experiment disrupts the taken-for-granted nature of the present. It creates a space in which the reader may, temporarily, experience an alternative configuration of needs, wants and satisfactions" (Levitas 2013, 4). Utopias are also flexible enough to allow that such possibilities are not achieved, that complex social dynamics are not fully resolved, that the "not yet" remains tantalizingly incomplete, and that that is not necessarily a bad thing. Indeed, for Lucy Sargisson, "Utopias will always fail.... They need to. They are no places. But they are important because they function to show us that radical thinking needs to be attempted; they deny that there are no alternatives" (Sargisson 2012, 39). Not for nothing did Ursula Le Guin, one of the genre's most brilliant and thought-provoking exponents, subtitle her novel *The Dispossessed* (1974) "An Ambiguous Utopia." That we could equally apply that subtitle to More's original text speaks to the inherent intellectual vitality, complexity, and playfulness of the genre as a whole. Few works first published in Latin half a millennium ago are even read today. Fewer still provide the basis for a dazzling array of planning, imagining, and debate exemplified by utopian texts in the intervening centuries.

As its title indicates, *The Palgrave Handbook of Utopian and Dystopian Literatures* concentrates on creative literature and the commentary on that literature. But it also contains focused chapters on vital cultural arenas such as film, animation, architecture, and the recent innovation of electronic gaming and web-based hyperutopias. The handbook strives to recognize and celebrate the current state of thinking on utopias and dystopias, to provide a guide to key creative and critical texts through history. But the sheer volume of primary and secondary material makes it impossible for any volume to be comprehensive—even one with over fifty chapters by scholars from around the globe. In devising the structure of the handbook, the editors were mindful of the need to deal with conceptual questions about the definition of utopia and its sub-genres, as well as to recognize the long historical narrative and vast geographical sweep of utopian projections, including extra-terrestrial worlds. They also took account of the amazing diversity of cultural, social, and political approaches and issues that have been enlivened by utopian responses and counter-responses. One necessary realization was that no volume could adequately cover the vivid immensity of the topic. Instead, the editors trust that the handbook can act as a richly informed guide and as a prompt for the vast audience of academics, students, and the intelligent public to whom it is addressed. Such readers are encouraged to use the handbook as a catalyst for creative and independent thinking, very much in the spirit of More's original work.

In that spirit (and as a counter to critics of utopias and of utopian thinking per se who see them as irredeemably reductive and rigid), there is no single perspective taken in these pages, no overarching or subterranean ideology hidden in its chapters. Contributors were allowed to demonstrate their own awareness and expertise and to express these without the imposition of a standardized jargon. In a similar way, the editors expect that few readers who pick up *The Palgrave Handbook of Utopian and Dystopian Literatures*, whether literally or virtually, will read it sequentially from cover to cover, instead following their own intellectual inclinations. We hope that exploring in this way they will inevitably venture down new paths, discovering fresh, illuminating territory for thought, study, and discussion. This open-minded approach recognizes overlaps between chapters as well as competing or even contradictory interpretations of primary and of secondary texts. But, in the spirit of Walt Whitman's "Song of Myself," where the question "Do I contradict myself?" receives the confident reply, "Very well then I contradict myself," *The Palgrave Handbook of Utopian and Dystopian Literatures* is large and contains multitudes.

The First 500 Years of Utopian and Dystopian Literature

When Thomas More forged the neologism *utopia*, he constructed a platform for the unlimited exercises of imagination that have become part of the identity matrix of Western societies. Over the centuries, literary utopias and utopianism exploded in different directions, but they never lost sight of the literary work that was at their origin. This happened because More did not just publish a book, but also proposed a new way of addressing problems. More was, in fact, a *founder* of a specific *discursivity*, as Michel Foucault says of Sigmund Freud and Karl Marx: like the Austrian psychoanalyst and the German philosopher, More produced "the possibilities and the rules for the formation of other texts"; he set up a discursive practice that is "heterogeneous to its subsequent transformations" (Foucault 1984, 114–116). This is why, when we look at contemporary utopian literature and coeval utopianism, or when we analyze every stage of their evolution, we notice a transformation of the utopian discursive practice while acknowledging its affiliation to the primeval text. The result is there is no such thing as an isomorphic utopianism.

From this perspective, although Utopia as a literary genre is to be defined in light of the structure, narrative framework, and fabulation strategies that characterize More's masterpiece, we need to consider how it has been influenced throughout the centuries by other literary genres—travel literature, romance, novel, autobiography, epistolary works, science fiction, and hyperfiction, among others—and by different worldviews. These influences have resulted in an evolution of the genre, a mark of its capacity to adapt to new times and tastes, which ensured its survival. Five centuries of variations on utopian possibilities have transformed utopian literature into a *site of memory*, as Pierre Nora defines it (1998): of countless alternatives and historical opportunities for transformation, in the case of utopian literature; of the human capacity to resist, oppose, and counteract, in the case of dystopian literature. This memory has pervaded the diachronic identity of Western societies, forming its connective structure and performing an autonoetic[1] function, i.e., providing societies with an awareness of what they are, how they are meant to (re)act, and what they are supposed to become.

Reporting on 500 years of utopian and dystopian literature with the aim of evincing the most meaningful evolutionary moments entails the creation of typologies that may sound artificial. It is with this awareness we offer an account of five centuries of utopias, highlighting, in each century, changes in how utopian and dystopian fiction relate to real/fictional space and time, how they focus on the interests of the community or of individuals, or how they range from idealizing society to proposing feasible ideas.

The Sixteenth and Seventeenth Centuries

The label "Renaissance Utopias" hides many particularities that may be arranged in five different groups to reflect changes in the utopian tradition. The first group is modeled after Thomas More's *Utopia*, from whence springs not only utopia as a literary genre but also what we would call the *idealistic strand* of utopian literature, concerned with philosophical concepts such as justice, and resting upon the idea that reason will engender the good society. Many names, such as William Godwin or William Morris, will join this strand over the centuries; in the eighteenth century, utopists will take it to a further stage, and imbue it with the conviction that human progress is possible. This was an idea More would never subscribe to, constrained as his views were by the unavoidable belief in Original Sin. The "authoritarianism" that characterizes the utopias of the sixteenth and the seventeenth centuries results, in fact, from the tension caused by Christian Humanism, which led utopists to believe that the progress of societies is possible—while human progress is unachievable. The recipe, then, for a good society, will be the creation of strict laws. That is why imagined communities are set on distant and unreachable islands, and once a "utopian recipe" is created, it is crystallized in time.

The first literary utopias do not offer, in fact, a blueprint for a possible future, but provide space for a critique of the present, evincing what needs to be changed. They are, in this sense, critical and speculative; the main question that worries utopists is the exploration of alternative ways of organizing society. Parallel to the *idealistic strand*, a *materialistic strand* is discernable, also crossing the centuries. Stemming from Francis Bacon's *New Atlantis* (1626), this strand extends its reach to Edward Bellamy's *Looking Backward* (1888), and toward the science fiction that pervades the second half of the twentieth century. What distinguishes Bacon from More is not just a whole century of political, economic, social, and religious changes, but also the conviction that science will bring about prosperity. While not relinquishing the power of reason, Bacon establishes that scientific progress can afford material prosperity and thus engender the good society; at the same time, his utopia hints at how science may also generate political and social unrest. This opens up a critical debate: are scientific and technological development to be seen as positive inspiration, or as potential threat?

Both of the types of literary utopias created by More and Bacon are clearly inflected by the tropes of Renaissance travel literature. Travel is in fact at the basis of utopian literature from the start: the discovery of new worlds led to the publication of reports on travel and on the exploration of distant places; discovery voyages led to imaginary voyages—and then to utopian thinking and utopian (Hartig and Soboul 1976, 165).

The third stage of the evolution of Renaissance utopias is to be found in Gerrard Winstanley's *The Law of Freedom* (1652) and James Harrington's *Oceana* (1656). In the turmoil of civil war and Oliver Cromwell's Protectorate, respectively, these utopias speculate on very concrete solutions: Winstanley calls for the economic liberation of the people from the landowners and for the establishment of non-hierarchical, communistic society, while Harrington, standing for the rights of the bourgeoisie, forges a plan for the instauration of a society based on a fair system of private property. Forging the ideal constitution thus becomes the focus of Renaissance utopian literature, as it will once more in the late eighteenth century.

The Restoration of the monarchy in 1660 seems to calm revolutionary aspirations. The few literary utopias that are then written (and form the fourth variety of Renaissance utopias) concentrate on idealizing the moral role of the king. But in the decades following the Restoration, another kind of utopian mode arises: no longer geared toward making concrete proposals, these texts turn to satire to prompt critical attention to controversial philosophical and religious matters. This is a historic moment of mutual influence between two utopian literary traditions, the French and English, as several French utopias are translated into English, and vice-versa. Examples of this utopian exchange are the *Histoires des Sevarambes* (1667–1669), by the French writer *Denis Varaisse d'Allais*, and *Les Aventures de Jacques Sadeur*, (France, 1676; England, 1693 as *A New Discovery of Terra Incognita Australis, or the Southern World*), by Gabriel de Foigny. These satirical texts take the utopian imagination to its limits, and find English counterparts in works such as *Gerania* (1675), by Joshua Barnes, or *The Blazing World* (1668), by Margaret Cavendish. This is a moment when utopian imagination scans the four corners of the globe, in an attempt to rejuvenate the genre (Trousson 1979, 96). Indeed, that imagination reaches beyond our globe, for as early as 1638 appear two utopias set on the moon. Francis Goodwin's *The Man in the Moone* and John Wilkins' *The Discovery of a World in the Moon* indicate that utopia's previous relation with space or time does not prevent the reader from entertaining these utopias as plausible or realizable, despite the technical impossibility of flying to the moon.

The fifth stage of Renaissance utopias will have a significant impact on eighteenth-century literary utopianism; bringing together all these influences, it will show an interest in fanciful settings and details as a way of enhancing critical thinking on contemporary matters. By the end of the seventeenth century, after the Glorious Revolution of 1688, the philosophical and political essay regains an important place among intellectuals; while these texts cannot be labeled as strictly utopian, they too will influence the next stages of the utopian literary tradition.

The Eighteenth Century

The English eighteenth century starts with a disconcerting anti-utopia, *The Island of Content* (1709), voicing scathing criticism of the idea of utopia itself, i.e., the aspiration to construct an ideal society, and to express the desire for a happier, freer, unregulated life. Although anti-utopias are not to be seen as variations of utopia as a literary genre, it is essential to note that they replicate their narrative framework to denounce the shortcomings, or even the danger, of longing for what will never happen.

Three types of literary utopias are discernable in the eighteenth century. The first type, the satirical utopia, predominates and is exemplified by Jonathan Swift's *Gulliver's Travels* (1726). In these utopias, the fictional space works as an inverted representation of the utopist's society, benchmarking what needs to be corrected. As most of the planet has already been explored, the author of the satirical utopia either invents spaces on our planet without any concern for the plausibility of their existence, or directs the imagination toward the moon, in the tradition of Goodwin's and Wilkins' utopias.

The second type of literary utopia is influenced by the ideas of human progress and perfectibility, both of which preside over the spirit of this century. Grand scientific discoveries affirm an optimistic worldview that transits to literary utopias. In England, the third Earl of Shaftesbury proposes in *Characteristics of Men, Manners, Opinions and Times* (1711) that the *educated man* (the Whig aristocrat) is capable of countering the human tendency to evil. But it is in France especially that the ideas of infinite human perfectibility and technological progress give birth to the conviction that the future is bound to bring about not only a fairer society, in terms of social justice, but also a society of material plenty. In France, these ideas inspire Louis-Sébastien Mercier to write *L'An 2440: Un Rêve s'il en fut jamais* (1771), which marks a significant deviation from the way utopias traditionally relate to space and time: no longer in a far place, but in Paris; no longer in a parallel (unreachable) time, but in the future. Mercier's utopia introduces the idea of causality: the future will only be brighter if we act now. It should be noted, however, that it will take almost a century for euchronias to be popular in the anglophone tradition.

The third type of utopia traverses the entire century and testifies to the permanence of the *idealistic strand* that Thomas More initiated while also denoting an evolution as regards the ideas of space and time. "A Description of 'New Athens' in 'Terra Australis Incognita'" (1720), by Ambrose Philips, describes the three-year pilgrimage by one-hundred-thousand Greek citizens in search of a place where they may enjoy liberties without danger. Likewise, *An Account of the First Settlement, Laws, Form of Government, and Police, of the Cessares, A People of South America* (1764), by James Burgh, reports on how the Cessarians traveled from Holland, where they lived under the permanent menace of a Spanish invasion, in pursuit of an area where they could realize a fairer society. The novelty of these utopias is that they bridge the gap between the utopias of the Renaissance, which describe a place without explaining how to reach it, and the socialist utopias of the nineteenth century, which not only describe the passage to utopia (the revolution) but also set it on national soil and evince its feasibility. The literary genre itself also evolves, incorporating the popular epistolary genre: *New Athens* is presented in the form of a letter addressed to a London esquire, while the account of *The Cessares* comprises nine letters signed by a Dutch explorer.

Later in the eighteenth century, after the American and French Revolutions, inspired by Thomas Paine's idea of the "new Adam" (i.e., the conviction that it is possible to start over) and by William Godwin's idea of a new, moral man, further developments are detected in this third strand of idealistic utopias. *Memoirs of Planetes, or a Sketch of the Laws and Manners of Makar* (1795), by Thomas Northmore, depicts a utopian society not at its final, crystallized stage, as was the case with Renaissance utopias, but open to further development, thus announcing the dynamic utopias of the nineteenth century. Furthermore, resting upon Godwin's idea of a most needed "revolution in opinion" (Godwin 2013), *Memoirs of Planetes* makes it clear that the change depends not on a set of strict laws but on an internalization of a set of moral values.

In many ways, the literary utopias of the eighteenth century prepare for the socialist utopias that will predominate next, but they also pave the way for the birth of the dystopias that will prevail in the first half of the twentieth century. The critical tone that pervades satirical utopias and the projection of utopia into the future are, in fact, the tools dystopia will need to transform utopia into a cautionary tale.

The Nineteenth Century

The turn from the eighteenth to the nineteenth century is marked by the desire to construct a *euchronia*, to make a "good time" into a historical reality. It is best summarized by Henri de Saint-Simon when he proclaims that the Golden Age lies not in the past but in the future (Saint-Simon 1814, 112). While Friedrich Engels disparaged the likes of Henri de Saint-Simon, Charles Fourier, and Robert Owen as "utopian socialists," none of those three actually produces a literary utopia. Still, their influence on the genre is perceptible in the conviction that the existing order is not immutable, and that it is the human being's responsibility to transform it. The space and the time for fulfilling social dreams are, they propose, in the *here and now*.

Although Marx and Engels, too, never published a literary utopia, their theories have an even more profound impact on the evolution of the utopian literary genre, as they redefine the very premise upon which euchronias are based. Mercier projects his utopia into the future, because he believes that a fairer society could be built by and for a more perfect human being. Marxist utopists see a promise in history itself. Furthermore, they believe that only when the economic, social, and political conditions are changed will the *new human being* be born. By subscribing to Marxist ideology, utopian authors of the nineteenth century imbued their work with an awareness of historicity. Moreover, they redefine the idea of progress as no longer a merely intellectual venture, but rather as a strong economic and moral project. In light of this idea, the utopian imaginary becomes both expansive, even global, in its purview; and it becomes dynamic, understood as setting forth a guiding principle.

The Marxist-euchronian perspective is no doubt what most impacts the utopian literary genre in the nineteenth century, forcing it to reconceptualize its relation to space (the national soil) and time (utopia will be established only after the revolution takes place). But the euchronia is not the only, or even the predominant, form of the time. The over 1,100 entries that Lyman Tower Sargent offers for the nineteenth century in his online *Utopian Literature in English: An Annotated Bibliography from 1516 to the Present* testify to the coexistence of a variety of perspectives. Although the list includes texts that go beyond utopia as a literary genre (also considering political and religious treatises, essays, poems, plays, and short stories, among other literary forms), we can see throughout the century how the *idealistic strand* that stems from More's *Utopia* persists. John Lithgow's *Equality – A Political Romance* (1802) is an excellent example of how the idea of an ordered society informs nineteenth-century utopianism. As the century goes by, euchronias—not necessarily in Marxist terms—take the utopian imagination further into the future. Some of these utopias are inspired by the theories of the utopian socialists, as is the case with William H. Graham's *Henry Russell; Or, The Year of Our Lord Two Thousand* (1846), which reports on an intentional community, based on Charles Fourier's socialist principles, that manages to establish itself worldwide. Other nineteenth-century euchronias are motivated by speculations regarding the role of technology in a future society, and by the early expressions of feminists who begin mobilizing for social reform, gender equality, and financial independence for women.

Alongside the idealistic strand, the *materialistic strand* finds its best expression in the euchronias that rest upon the idea that technology will bring about a society of plentiful resources, as in *Messages from Mars by the Aid of the Telescope Plant* (1892), by Robert Braine. Here, science and technology have solved all problems, and people now benefit from the discovery of the Elixir of Life. And many utopias of this time combine the idealistic and the materialistic strands. Such is the case with *Three Hundred Years Hence* (1836), by Mary Griffith, in which advances in technology make women's lives easier within the framework of a society where economic equality between men and women prevails. Another example is *1931; A Glance at the Twentieth Century* (1881) by Henry Hartshorne, in which technological breakthroughs are but an aspect of a far more advanced, democratic society.

The possibility of negative consequences from a shifting social landscape, brought about by technological developments and by the redefinition of the role of women, causes the satirical utopia to flourish again. Annie Denton Cridge's *Man's Rights; or How Would You Like It* (1870) is one notable example that exploits the satiric "reversal" trope of utopian fiction in order to critique the deep-seated—but, Cridge hopes, not irreversible—sexism of American society, and in particular, of the traditional division of labor. Several texts from this period tap into the familiar "dream-vision" structure of utopian writing to imagine a new life for women; Rosa Graul's *Hilda's Home: A Story of Women's Emancipation* (1897), for example, refers to the "dream-picture" painted in a speech made by the eponymous Hilda, who asks, "How can I dare to hope [this dream of a cooperative home] could ever be realized"; and wonders whether it is not "wrong-headed ... to be constantly sighing for still more" (Kessler 1995, 114). And in "A Divided Republic: An Allegory of the Future" (1887), Lillie Devereaux Blake imagines women finally having had enough, and leaving their homes *en masse* to create their own society out West. A predictable collapse of the abandoned men into untidiness, disorganization, and sexual frustration brings about their ultimate surrender. This sort of gender-reversal utopia, in particular, effectively highlights the systemic devaluation of women's bodies, minds, work, art ... the list goes on.

Utopia as a literary genre continues to rework its relationships to contiguous literary genres, such as the romance and the novel, and moves closer to science fiction. The many imaginary voyages to the Moon that are now published allow utopists to explore not only alternative social organizations but also the potential of technology from a different, speculative stance. According to Sargent's *Bibliography,* the last twelve years of the century feature 660 utopias and dystopias. Besides the feminist texts just mentioned, Edward Bellamy's *Looking Backward* (1888) and William Morris's *News from Nowhere* (1890) foster the debate on Fabian and socialist-communist proposals, respectively. Utopia as a literary genre is now, more than ever, a vehicle for the political debate; but it is also the moment when the difference between the *materialistic strand* represented by Bellamy and the *idealistic strand* represented by Morris becomes more striking: for Bellamy, technological development will ensure prosperity and bring about social order; for Morris, the Revolution is the *sine qua non* for a fairer society, and for a further development of the human being. In the twelve final years of the century, many utopias either support or contradict Bellamy's and Morris's proposals. The century also witnesses the rise of dystopia, with interesting narratives such as Richard Jefferies's post-apocalyptic *After London* (1885), where utopian possibilities can be discerned at the end of the book. Population control and eugenic concerns are also voiced by nineteenth-century utopias, dystopias, and anti-utopias—by men and women alike. But it is also in this period when H. G. Wells' unsettling novel, *The Time Machine* (1895), is published, announcing the shape of things to come in the first decades of the next century.

The Twentieth Century

The history of utopian and dystopian literature of the first half of the twentieth century is traditionally summed up through the reference to three main authors: H. G. Wells, Aldous Huxley, and George Orwell. These are, no doubt, the most interesting authors from a literary point of view, as they stood the test of time, but to consider only these three writers is to miss the subtleties and complexities of utopian literature of this period, which go beyond dystopian thinking.

Sargent's bibliography, which relies on a broad concept of literary utopianism, offers for the period 1900–1949 an impressive list: 364 titles in the 1900s; 281 in the 1910s; 303 in the 1920s; 416 in the 1930s; and 227 in the 1940s, totaling 1,581 texts. A careful analysis of every decade in this period will lead us to important landmarks and trends, only a few of which we can mention here: the essays in this *Handbook* help to fill out this history. Indeed, the legacy of this literary triumvirate overshadows at least two other critical strands: utopian writing by feminists, which as we have seen has already become a vehicle for political protest; and by writers of color.

Thus, one of the most important texts from the first quarter of the twentieth century is Charlotte Perkins Gilman's series, *Moving the Mountain* (1911), *Herland* in 1915, and its sequel, *With Her in Ourland* in 1916. Anticipated in her shorter "A Woman's Utopia" (1907) these were all essentially "self-published," appearing in the politically progressive *Forerunner*, which Gilman herself launched in 1909, writing the entirety of each monthly issue for the next seven years until the journal closed in 1916 under financial duress. According to Carol Farley Kessler's introduction to the much-needed anthology, *Daring to Dream: Utopian Fiction by United States Women Before 1950* (first published in 1984), Gilman's popularity among feminist critics stems from her "incisive [thinking] about gender, although not about sexual, racial, or class issues. Her fiction and essays are cut from one cloth in their consistent concern to explicate or expose gender practices" (Kessler 1995, 131). Despite the essentialist nature of her thinking on sex and gender, and her apparent "racism and elitism that readers must not ignore" (132), Gilman plays an important role in highlighting the need for women's education and economic independence *as a social good*. Other feminist texts in these early years included visions of communitarian and egalitarian living, interplanetary travel—in both directions: one woman-traveler visits an unknown planet on which men and women are equally responsible for child care; and a Venusian observer critiques the hierarchical gender relations on Earth.

The year 1932, which sees the publication of Huxley's *Brave New World*, is particularly fertile for utopian thinking. The list of utopian texts prepared by Sargent displays 49 titles, of which only 11 are truly dystopian, aiming to explore negative consequences of technological developments. Sargent also lists three satirical utopias, five ambiguous/flawed utopias, and 29 utopian texts offering positive views on social arrangements and on how technology can improve our lives. And if we look at the utopian texts written in 1949, the year of the publication of Orwell's *Nineteen Eighty-Four*, we will find that, out of the 22 texts published along the year, there are seven dystopias (mainly troubled by authoritarian governments and negative technological developments), two satirical gender-reversal dystopias (written by two male authors), four flawed/ambiguous eutopias/dystopias, and nine eutopias offering positive views on technological developments and communal ways of living. While utopian visions outnumber dystopian narratives, this does not mean that Huxley and Orwell do not reflect the spirit of their time. Their work registers a fear which is genuinely of the period: that technology can be used for the consolidation of the power of authoritarian governments. But we should also note that even Huxley, after publishing his dystopian *Brave New World*, writes *Island* (1960), a utopia that, in spite of its dystopian ending, suggests it is worth trying to construct a better society.

In between those years, 1932 and 1949, Katherine Burdekin's *Swastika Night* (1937) taps directly into anti-authoritarian fears for the future, and, just as significantly, also identifies the hypermasculine toxicity of such regimes. Interestingly, however, this is not Burdekin's first dystopian effort: *The End of This Day's Business* was completed in 1935, but was not published until 1989! In this quite riveting text, Burdekin imagines a female-ruled regime equally as hierarchical as the masculinist dystopia of the later, published novel—although in this text, one woman, herself a member of the ruling class, detects the flaws in the country's ethical and political systems—and breaks the law by educating her son out of the brutish existence expected for all males. As Daphne Patai writes in her excellent afterword to the novel's 1989 publication, Burdekin would

> [excoriate] women for imitating, in their own writings, men's sexual sadism. She attributes the antifeminism of many women's writings during this period to their habitual desire to placate men and their lack of self-esteem because they could only give life, not take it in battle. (Patai 1989, 174–175)

Nonetheless, Patai concludes, Burdekin displays no misandry or bitterness; "it is always with sadness, not with glee at having found men out" (175).

Nor should we overlook the disturbing satire of the African-American back-to-Africa movement in the early twentieth century, George S. Schuyler's

Black Empire, published serially from 1936 to 1938 in two parts: first, "The Black Internationale: A Story of Black Genius Against the World," followed by "Black Empire: An Imaginative Story of a Great New Civilization in Modern Africa." The two parts were published as a single volume only in 1991). The author (who originally published these stories under the pseudonym, Samuel I. Brooks) was a conservative critic of Marcus Garvey, head of the Universal Negro Improvement Association, and of the Black Star shipping line that Garvey helped create with the goal of eventually transporting African Americans back to the continent, and building up a global African economic system. Schuyler's rather outrageous and unsettling text depicts Garvey himself in the guise of a ruthlessly authoritarian yet charismatic savior, preposterously named Dr. Belsidus, who uses a form of aerial biological warfare to infect and exterminate the entire white race in America, and then uses this same flight technology to reunite the African diaspora on its home soil through a sort of reversed Middle Passage. For all its stylistic extravagance, which ironically signals the satiric nature of the author's intention, the novel nonetheless marks an early example of what we now call Afrofuturism, complete with then—speculative technologies such as solar power. Schuyler himself was sympathetic to pan-Africanism, even as he was deeply suspicious of self-proclaimed liberationist leaders like Marcus Garvey who, he seemed to suggest, were manipulative and Manichean in their reform practices. Like Burdekin, perhaps, Schuyler's abhorrence of fascism tainted his view of utopian possibility. Schuyler was not opposed to Garvey's ultimate goal of organizing the black race so that, as he wrote, "they can present united opposition to those who seek to continue their enslavement" (quoted in Hill and Rasmussen 1991, 275), but the very success of his publication at the time seemed only to verify a low view of the average citizen. To one P. L. Prattis (editor of *The Pittsburgh Currier*), Schuyler writes the following in 1937:

> I have been greatly amused by the public enthusiasm for "The Black Internationale," which is hokum and hack work of the purest vein. I deliberately set out to crowd as much race chauvinism and sheer improbability into it as my fertile imagination could conjure. The result vindicates my low opinion of the human race. (Hill and Rasmussen 1991, 200)

Nonetheless, *Black Empire* stands out as an early, if acerbic, example of black re-imaginings of race history and social-justice movement. The 1960s and the 1970s are marked by "ambiguous utopias," as Le Guin described her own *The Dispossessed* (1974). In fact, Le Guin stands as one of the great figures of the last 100 years of utopian and dystopian writing, her work touching on just about every theme mentioned thus far in this introduction, and then some: technology; interplanetary travel; authoritarianism; colonialism; gender and sexuality; history and historicity; the nature of dream and reality; the archival impulse of humanity; sustainability of not only environment but of culture; war; and freedom. The intellectual scope of her writing is extraordinary, sometimes drawing her into odd places from a literary point of view; but when her prose matches her vision, the result is profound and, without overstating the matter, almost mythological. Le Guin's writing is in one sense typical of the period, insofar as it carries a positive awareness that social and political arrangements will always have flaws, but also that these flaws leave space for improvement.

Utopias of the period between 1960 and 2000 are dynamic, open to social and political experimentation—and in fact Le Guin is only one of numerous important feminist utopian writers (though not all of them call themselves such): Suzy McKee Charnas (*Walk to the End of the World*, 1973); James Tiptree, Jr. [Alice Sheldon] ("The Girl Who Was Plugged In," 1973); Joanna Russ (*The Female Man*, 1975); Marge Piercy (*Woman on the Edge of Time*, 1976); Angela Carter (*The Passion of New Eve*, 1977); Doris Lessing (*The Making of the Representative for Planet 8*, 1982); Margaret Atwood (*The Handmaid's Tale*, 1985); Fay Weldon (*Darcy's Utopia*, 1992); Nicola Griffith (*Ammonite*, 1992); Octavia Butler (*Parable of The Sower*, 1993); Karen Tei Yamashita (*Tropic of Orange*, 1997); Nalo Hopkinson (*Brown Girl in the Ring*, 1998)—and many more. We do see separatist utopias—Wittig's *Les Guérillières* (1969), or the ambiguous vision of Sherri Tepper's *The Gate to Woman's Country* (1993), for example; but also the dystopic nightmare of Atwood's *The Handmaid's Tale*, the impact of which is very much with us, giving us contemporary texts such as *The Power* (2017) by Naomi Alderman, another gender-reversal dystopia.

A quick survey of names reveals the broadening range of voices—from Afro-futurists to indigenous to queer and gender-bending writers. For all their differences from one another, these texts share one thing: the effort to challenge and in many cases overturn what we know or think we know regarding just about everything having to do with human and, indeed, other-than- and more-than-human lives. The popularity and excellence of science fiction explodes with the fearlessness of authors' imaginations, and with the expansion of technological possibilities, including the modern versions of dreams and fantasy in the opening up of virtual planes of action. Science fiction and speculative writing by the likes of Robert Heinlein, Isaac Asimov, Philip K. Dick, Frank Herbert, J. G. Ballard, William Gibson, Kim Stanley Robinson, Ursula Le Guin, and so many more finally pulled that genre out of second- or third-rate literary status, and made it impossible for detractors *not* to see the narrative and speculative possibilities of writing intimately related to utopian/dystopian tropes of structure and critique. The "(other-)world-making" aspirations of these authors—whether of a utopian sensibility or not—have led readers to astonishing, queer places and non-places, and created pathways for writing in the new millennium. As Kim Stanley Robinson recently said, "Science fiction is the realism of our time" (Robinson 2020).

THE NEXT 500 YEARS OF UTOPIAN AND DYSTOPIAN LITERATURE

In fact, there has always been something "queer" at the heart of utopia. In its critical function to make strange normative idea(l)s and practices, to "think otherwise" and "desire differently," utopia's essential conundrum, its trafficking in the "real" and the "unreal," the abstract and the concrete, keeps destabilizing the ground under us—or dematerializes "the ground" altogether! The queerness of the concept of utopia lies in the essential plasticity of its forms and speculations, which is the source of the "strangeness" that characterizes the experience of any utopian/dystopian traveler-reader. To say this is finally to reject any "utopian blueprint" idea, which seems to have emerged from a fundamental simplification of what Sir Thomas More was onto in the first place.

Contemporary philosopher Miguel Abensour defines utopia as "*the various forms of alterity* to which the desire for freedom ... has given birth through the course of history": "Utopia may seem to tell a story about historical tendencies and ideologic propensities that direct history a certain way; but utopia is also a kind of disruption: [what matters is the] *orientation toward what is different, the wish for the advent of a radical alterity* here and now" (Abensour, 407). Thus, the crucial characterization of utopia as "the everreborn movement toward something indeterminate" through "a new struggle for alterity" (409). This "ever-reborn"-ness, accounting for utopia's historical "persistence," is a regenerative quality made possible by the conceptual plasticity of utopian and dystopian speculations, and their representational forms in literature. As symbolic forms of desire, whether individual or collective, utopian narratives capture what Abensour calls the essence of utopia, "this non-achievement of being, in its gap in relation to essence, [in which] persistence of utopia resides, the engine of enigmatic rebirth ... [that] derives its force from non-accomplishment" (2008, 409). To "demand the impossible," as utopia theorist Tom Moylan (1986) enjoins us, is to entertain the possibilities of other worlds, forms of speculative biologies and sexualities, new forms of cognition, of social repertoires, and of cultural practices. But also, in our so-called real world, we must entertain new narrative forms that can accommodate these (im)possible imaginative visions.

One etymology of "queer" (*twerkh*) reminds us that centuries before the word had any relevance to descriptions of gender or sexuality, it had simply to do with spatial oblique-ness or off-centeredness, its meaning gradually evolving to describe people or things that are odd, strange, peculiar, off-kilter, twisted. (The first known reference to a homosexual as a "queer" was in 1894, when John Douglas, the 9th Marquess of Queensberry and the nemesis of Oscar Wilde, established this word as a homophobic slur.) The queer horizons of utopian and dystopian literatures today are multi-directional, multi-perspectival, multi-dimensional, in both space and time: in other words, *emergent*. In a recent (2019) major study of contemporary British utopian literature, Caroline Edwards (also a contributor to this *Handbook*) refers to an "emerging caucus" (29) of contemporary texts that foreground the relationship of temporality to narrative, producing thereby a set of methodological horizons attuned to the writer's experience of contemporaneity and—more characteristically—*noncontemporaneity*. Today's utopian texts, Edwards argues, reflect a remarkably common perception of "the contemporary" as disjointed, or parallactic, or queer.

For this reason, the first decades of this twenty-first century represent a particularly robust period of experimentation and inventiveness. Edwards's method of analysis lets loose the play of evolving temporal dimensions and plastic narrative structuralizations. Such novels, she proposes, should be read

> as enacting "theories of their own," ... their interventions into contemporary political and philosophical discourse demonstrat[ing that fiction] reveals to us the possibility of redeeming our past miscalculations in a temporal ambit that is already alive with utopian futural alternatives. (Edwards 2019, 29)

Edwards's characterization of reading as productive in these ways is an appealing challenge to the reader, as it explicitly joins us to the project: that is, the reader is invited to think about reading itself as enacting those theories and involving us in that a critical practice. Our reading is directed, but within a narrative that is self-reflexive regarding its (our) movements "among narratology, formalism, post-structuralism, ecocriticism, post-secular readings, utopian thinking and philosophies of time" (25).

In addition to utopian and dystopian literatures' ongoing investigation of temporal frontiers—queer temporalities, broadly speaking—these texts continue to explore the possibilities of queer embodiment and ontological evolutions. For that matter, we can speak of the queerness of *dis*embodiment, as virtual beings are able to inhabit virtual worlds that are co-temporaneously as real as the one you are located in now. William Gibson's co-evolving subjects and landscapes come to mind: in *The Peripheral* (2014), for instance, we glimpse the grotesque adaptations of "the Patchers," who inhabit a sort of "eighth continent" of toxic plastic trash, the direct descendant of today's Great Pacific Garbage Patch; or, we wonder at the rather thrilling "living tattoos" that canvas the body of a skin-artist. These animate tattoos respond, as skin does, to changes in the artist's own environment, as if illustrating her own sensory experiences; yet they seem as well to respond to her *thoughts*, as well, representing a sort of a mindscape. China Miéville's and N.K. Jemisin's astonishing hybrid creatures, alt-speciations and Remades populate worlds that accommodate all manner of new strangenesses including, *contra* Margaret Atwood's Crakers (in *Oryx and Crake* (2004), from the MaddAddam trilogy), a newly emergent aesthetics made possible by the "glandular arts" of a Kepri (insectoid-human) sculptor in Miéville's *Perdido Street Station* (2001) in the *New Crobuzon* series. N.K. Jemisin's "stone-eaters" in *The Fifth Season* (2015) are one of the more astonishing of her inventions; appearing as literally stat-uesque beings in "our" world, they are made from, move through, and consume rocks. And, rarely, they can love and protect a human.

Similarly, post- and eco-apocalyptic imaginaries, by-now "standard" symp-toms of planetary dread, might seem to traffic in the inventive predictions of decadence and entropy. But in some authorial hands, severe historical disrup-tion also clears the way for something like a "post-normative" state of freedom, alongside the wreckage. Indeed, in a discussion of Miéville's theoretical clash with science-fiction theorist Darko Suvin on the future of utopian writing, Rhys Williams (2014) observes that Miéville's prose characteristically seeks "the novel's rejection of normative genres and its seeking for a new, satisfac-tory frame." Satisfactory, but necessarily temporary, as the narrative constantly presents "a dissolving of boundaries and the search for an escape—a Deleuzian *line of flight*—that does not lead back into the old tangle of thought but instead strives, as far as possible, *to break with the ground and articulation of that thought*" (2014, 629, emphasis added). Jeanette Winterson's *The Stone Gods* (2007) is another excellent example of this urge to "break with the ground," and to reject the old entanglements: while "everything is imprinted with what it once was," observes this novel's refrain, we can only evolve by pursuing escape—not from "the world" but from the "same old story" of that, our, world. In an essay from *Art Objects: Essays on Ecstasy and Effrontery* (1997), Winterson observes that we need not "give up reading nineteenth-century novels … What we must do is give up writing them" (191). Temporal linearity is defied by *The Stone Gods'* representation of temporality (as in others of her novels); temporal and spatial boundaries blur and fold backward and forward over vast distances in multiple directions and dimensions, effecting just the kind of *noncontemporaneity* that Edwards describes.

New speculative fiction takes up the investigation of embodiment and sexu-ality where James Tiptree, Jr., Ursula Le Guin, and Octavia Butler left off. There are clear implications for not only generic narrative structures but also for the nature of characterological subjectivities. In Nalo Hopkinson's *Midnight Robber* (2000), the narrator of the entire story turns out to be an about-to-born, neuronally "enhanced" (by epigenetic accident) child of paternal incest. This suggests a new direction entirely for not only the history of the African diaspora, already departed from Earth to inhabit a new, free planet; but also for the history of the trans- and post-human. Winterson's *Stone Gods* includes a spaceship crew member who is a *Robo Sapiens*, a product of the co-evolution of AI bots and *Homo Sapiens Sapiens*; genderless—but presumed by the human neuronormals to be female, and desired as such even though "she" insists that gender is irrelevant to the *Robo Sapiens*.

Moreover, each year brings forward new works by queer and trans authors whose world(ing)s explore levels of physical and psychological intimacy atyp-ical of traditional utopian texts. A 2017 anthology entitled *Meanwhile, Elsewhere: Science Fiction and Fantasy from Transgender Writers* (eds. Fitz-patrick & Plett) may be the first such publication to pointedly resist tropes that simply do not serve. While so much of utopian and dystopian literature is ultimately about survival, living on in some better way, the editors of *Meanwhile, Elsewhere* have a slightly different take:

> For a long time, trans people have been treated in science fiction and fantasy as part of the spectacle: either as an amazing future technology (people can *change sex!*) or as awful unlikely monsters. We hoped to challenge this by making a book of stories that allow room for the heroic everydayness of real trans people's lives, even among outer space or apocalypse, and we hope that it might, in a Janus-like fashion, act as both an escape from the current world and manual for your own possibilities. (Fitzpatrick and Plett 2017, 440)

While an eyebrow might be raised at the idea of wanting anything called a "manual" for such purposes, we can appreciate the statement's utopian resonances, and the several stories in the anthology that have engaged the utopian in repudiation of a trend in queer nihilism.

Queerness *itself* contains a utopian kernel, argues Amalia Ziv, beyond the envisioning of inclusive and hospitable utopian spaces. As utopia "reeducates" (230) the imagination, Ziv proposes, it twerks "resignifications of sex, gender and identity—and the cultural context in which some things and practices signify, and some don't." Such resignifications introduce *new* "repertoire[s] of cultural notions, narratives, and roles" (Ziv 2015, 230–231) and create not simply resistant readers, but reparative ones. Queer utopias can renew our attention to the harms impacting gender-nonconforming individuals in a systemically racist and heterosexist culture—and in doing so, lay bare the complicities that so many of us—perhaps all of us in the end—must practice, against somebody or something, to live more "easily." Lynne Copson and Avi Boukli (2020), working in the field of criminology, are particularly interested in how queer utopian literature offers ways of understanding difference, imagining "other-wise" and creating a practice that leads toward transformative change. Their attention to dismantling criminal justice and legal frameworks that disadvantage queer/trans folk leads them to argue that queer theory actually *is itself* a "concrete utopia" insofar as it "essentially concerns recognizing and reflecting the need to engage with the affective consequences of cultural abjection, humiliation, illness and political hopelessness" (512).

Queer utopianism's first proponent, José Esteban Muñoz, perhaps puts it best: queer utopianism, he argues, is "meant to serve as *something of a flight plan* for a collective political becoming" (Muñoz 2009, 189, emphasis added). "*Something of*" a plan—not a definitive route or plotting on a map, perhaps only an orientation or a tentative trajectory, inevitably open to revision or reimagining. "Something of" is by definition incomplete, a rough and always evolving sketch of speculative futures. Narratives that "take place" on virtual gaming or other cyber-platforms, as exemplified in Gibson's *The Peripheral*, take full advantage of the confusions of space and time, such that we scarcely know which world—the one now, then, or in the future; the "actual" or the "virtual" one—is the "real" one, or whether that question even matters.

Rumors announcing the death of utopia are, in short, very premature. For the next 500 years, what might we anticipate? Its broad thematics are likely to include the always-persistent ones: history, historicity, and narrative; nations, nationalisms, and post-national possibilities; coloniality and, especially, postcoloniality; dimensions of time and space; hauntology and abstract embodiments; alternative conceptions of modernities; the plasticity of form, and formal rupture; the resources of generic resistance; a continuous bothering (if not deconstruction) of the real/unreal, possible/impossible, good/bad, human/inhuman, nature/culture, divine/mundane sets of binary oppositions whose tensions inform both utopian and dystopian literatures. These themes are attached to frameworks shaped by ever-evolving utopian theories and generic motifs: tropes of "double-vision," cognitive mapping, speculative biologies, enhanced sensation, virtual spaces and possible futures, utopian desire and hope, becoming and identity, collective self-becoming, hospitality, alienation. The "truths" of humanity are anything but self-evident: but utopian and dystopian literatures are motivated by the search for further evidence that we *"might-could,"* as one says in parts of the U.S. south, find some better way.

Winterson, certainly among the most steadfastly passionate writers today, warns that "passion" itself, sexual or otherwise, is not "truth," and it is not art; but without a sense of passion, there will be neither truth nor art:

> In search of this truth, beyond the fear of the consequences of this truth, are *the flight-maps of art*. When truth is at stake, and in a society that desperately needs truth, we have to be wary of those side-tracks to nowhere that mislead us from the journey we need to make. There are plenty of Last Days sign-posts to persuade us that nothing is worth doing and that each one of us lives in a private nightmare occasionally relieved by temporary pleasure. Art is not a private nightmare, not even a private dream, it is a shared human connection that traces the possibilities of past and future in the whorl of now. It is a construct, like science, like religion, like the world itself. It is as artificial as you and me and as natural too. We have never been able to live without it, we have never been able to live with it. (Winterson 1997, 117)

China Miéville may be at once the most forward-looking and the most profoundly skeptical of contemporary speculative writers regarding the possibilities of utopia today. Deeply critical of its limits ("The utopia of togetherness is a lie" ["The Limits of Utopia," n.p.]), he acerbically asserts that under the spirit of capitalism (which "gets you coming and going") "we *live* in utopia; it just isn't ours. So we live in apocalypse too." *And yet*: At the same time, Miéville obdurately urges that utopia must remain vital. In fact, *utopia* must no longer be simply a noun. It must be a verb, an action word:

Is there a better optimism? And a right way to lose hope? It depends who's hoping, for what, for whom – and against whom. We must learn to hope with teeth.

We won't be browbeaten by demands for our own bureaucratized proposals. In fact there is no dearth of models to consider, but the radical critique of the everyday stands even in the absence of an alternative. We can go further: if we take utopia seriously, as a total reshaping, its scale means we can't think it from this side. It's the process of making it that will allow us to do so. It is utopian fidelity that might underpin our refusal to expound it, or any roadmap. *We should utopia as hard as we can.* Along with a fulfilled humanity we should imagine flying islands, self-constituting coraline neighborhoods, photosynthesizing cars bred from biospliced bone-marrow. Big Rock Candy Mountains. Because we'll never mistake those dreams for blueprints, nor for mere absurdities (Miéville 2015, italics added).

NOTE

1. *Autonoesis* derives from the Latin words *autos* (self) and *noesis* (cognition).

REFERENCES

Abensour, Miguel. 2008. Persistent Utopia. *Constellations* 15 (3): 406–421.

Atwood, Margaret. 2004. *Oryx and Crake.* New York: Knopf Doubleday.

Bloch, Ernst. 1995. *The Principle of Hope.* 3 vols. Cambridge, MA: The MIT Press.

Copson, Lynne, and Avi Boukli. 2020. Queer Utopias and Queer Criminology. *Crimology and Criminal Justice* 5: 510–522.

Edwards, Caroline. 2019. *Utopia and the Contemporary British Novel.* Cambridge, UK: Cambridge University Press.

Engels, Friedrich. 1972. Socialism: Utopian and Scientific. In *The Marx-Engels Reader*, ed. R. Tucker, 605–639. New York: Norton.

Fitzpatrick, Cat, and Casey Plett, eds. 2017. *Meanwhile, Elsewhere: Science Fiction and Fantasy from Transgender Writers.* Brooklyn, N.Y.: Topside Press.

Foucault, Michel. 1984. Des espaces autres. Hétéropie. Conférence au Cercle d'études architecturales. *Architecture, Mouvement, Continuité* 5: 46–49.

Gibson, William. 2014. *The Peripheral.* New York: Berkley Books.

Godwin, William. 2013. *An Enquiry Concerning Political Justice.* Oxford: Oxford University Press.

Gray, John. 2007. *Black Mass: Apocalyptic Religion and the Death of Utopia.* London: Allen Lane.

Hartig, Irmgard, and Albert Soboul. 1976. "Notes pour une histoire de l'Utopie en France, au XVIIe siècle". *Annales Historiques de la Révolution Française* 224: 161–179.

Hopkinson, Nalo. 2000. *Midnight Robber.* New York: Grand Central Publishing.

Kessler, Carol Farley, ed. 1995. *Daring to Dream: Utopian Fiction by United States Women Before 1950*. Syracuse: University Press.

Le Guin, Ursula. 1974. *The Dispossessed: An Ambiguous Utopia*. New York: Avon.

Levitas, Ruth. 2013. *Utopia as Method: The Imaginary Reconstitution of Society*. New York: Palgrave Macmillan.

Martin, Biddy. 1994. Sexualities Without Genders and Other Queer Utopias. *Diacritics* 24: 104–121.

Miéville, China. 2001. *Perdido Street Station*. New York: Del Ray.

Miéville. 2015. The Limits of Utopia. *Salvage* 1. https://salvage.zone/mieville_all. html. Accessed 9 December 2021.

More, Thomas. 2002. *Utopia*. Revised edition. ed. G. Logan and R. Adams. Cambridge: Cambridge University Press.

Moylan, Tom. 1986. *Demand the Impossible: Science Fiction and the Utopian Imagination*. London: Methuen.

Muñoz, José Esteban. 2009. *Cruising Utopia: The Then and There of Queer Futurity*. New York: New York University Press.

Nora, Pierre, ed., with Lawrence D. Kritzman. 1998. *Realms of Memory: Rethinking the French Past*. trans. Arthur Goldhammer. Chicago: University of Chicago Press,.

Oxford English Dictionary, *queer. "queer, n.2"*. *OED Online*. March 2021. Oxford University Press. https://www-oed-com.ezaccess.libraries.psu.edu/view/ Entry/156235?result=1&rskey=UGjk0R. Accessed 27 May 2021.

Patai, Daphne. 1989. Afterword. *The End of This Day's Business*. ed. Katherine Burdekin. New York: The Feminist Press. 159–190.

Robinson, Kim Stanley. 2020. The Corona Virus Is Rewriting Our Imaginations. *The New Yorker*, http://www.newyorker.com/culture/annals-of-inquiry/the-coronavirus-and-our-future. Accessed 26 June 2021.

de Saint-Simon, Henri. 1814. *De la reoganisation de la société européenne*. Paris: Égron.

Sargent, Lyman Tower. *Utopian Literature in English: An Annotated Bibliography from 1516 to the Present*. University Park, PA: Penn State Libraries Open Publishing, 2016 and continuing. https://doi.org/10.18113/P8WC77

Sargisson, Lucy. 2012. *Fool's Gold? Utopianism in the Twenty-First Century*. London: Palgrave Macmillan.

Schuyler, George S. 1991. In *Black Empire*. ed. Robert Hill and R. Ken Rasmussen. Boston: Northeastern University Press.

Trousson, Raymond. 1979. *Voyages aux pays de nulle part: Histoire littéraire de la pensée utopique*. Brussels: University of Brussels.

Wells, H.G. 1994. *A Modern Utopia*. London: Everyman.

Williams, Rhys. 2014. Recognizing Cognition: On Suvin, Miéville, and the Utopian Impulse in the Contemporary Fantastic Author(s). *Science Fiction Studies* 41 (3), 617–633.

Winterson, Jeanette. 1997. *Art Objects: Essays in Effrontery*. New York: Vintage.

Ziv, Amalia. 2015. *Explicit Utopias: Rewriting the Sexual in Women's Pornography*. Albany: SUNY Press.

Concepts

Utopia

Patrícia Vieira

INTRODUCTION: UTOPIAN TWISTS AND TURNS

Much has been written about the turn from utopia to dystopia in the twentieth century, a trend that seems to have deepened in the first decades of the new millennium.[1] Apart from a brief resurgence in utopian writings in the 1960s and 1970s, fueled by the counter-culture movements and political activism of those decades (Moylan 2000, xiv, 68; Booker 1994, 17), the past one hundred years or so have witnessed the rise of dystopianism as the predominant zeitgeist. True, this purportedly dystopian attitude hinges upon the definition of the term, a hotly contested territory that has given rise to a copious literature.[2]

If both utopia and dystopia can easily be distinguished from their literary cousin, science fiction, for their focus on social and political critique (Booker 1994, 19), the difference between the two former concepts is not easy to pinpoint.[3] Are dystopias primarily cautionary and reactive, telling us what not to do, while utopias are forward-looking, showing us the way onward? The separation between the two genres is not so clear-cut. To begin with, utopia shares the same goal as dystopia, namely, that of criticizing the negative features of a certain society by comparing it to another, fictional one. And, as Gregory Claeys points out, someone's utopia might well be someone else's dystopia (2017, 7). Many canonical utopias of the past have features

P. Vieira (✉)
CES, University of Coimbra, Coimbra, Portugal

Georgetown University, Washington, DC, USA

P. Marks et al. (eds.), *The Palgrave Handbook of Utopian and Dystopian Literatures*, https://doi.org/10.1007/978-3-030-88654-7_2

that most modern readers would clearly identify as dystopian: the strict social control in Thomas More's *Utopia* (1516); or the incipient eugenics of Tommaso Campanella's *City of the Sun* (1602), among countless other examples. This proximity between the two notions has led scholars to define dystopia as utopia's "shadow" (Kumar 2013, 19) or "alter ego" (Davis 2013, 23). Michael Gordin, Helen Tilley, and Gyan Prakash note that dystopia is not simply the opposite of utopia, i.e., an imagined society, which is completely unplanned or planned to be deliberately awful. Rather, dystopias are often utopias gone wrong or utopias that work only for a very limited segment of the population (Gordin et al. 2010, 1). In other words, utopias function by contrasting the status quo with a social arrangement that is perceived to be more perfect. Because they are already as good as can be, most utopias are static, the apex of a given civilization.[4] Dystopias, on the other hand, depict a society recognizably worse than another one that is used as a point of reference, and describe a situation that can, and often does, deteriorate even further as the plot unfolds.

It is worth pondering why the past century appears to have turned its back on utopianism and embraced instead various forms of dystopian thought and writings. Whence our seeming dislike for utopia that has led writers to prefer dystopianism as a more faithful reflection of our epoch? The excesses of imperialism and late-stage capitalism (Moylan 2000, xi), authoritarianism and despotism, the threat of nuclear annihilation, environmental degradation (Claeys 2017, 448ff), a weakening belief in the future and a conviction that meaningful change is no longer possible (Jameson 2010, 24) have been identified as some of the key culprits of the current dystopian outlook. To be sure, associating the move to dystopia with political events and tracing it to feelings of social malaise presupposes a link between fiction and reality that is far from uncontroversial. Yet, utopia and dystopia are preeminently political literary genres that hinge upon societal criticism and a desire for social change. It is therefore safe to assume that utopian and dystopian fiction and thought at least refract, if not reflect, the vicissitudes of collective existence and the spirit of the times.

The rejection of utopianism is often attributed to an intrinsic problem of utopia, which, according to a variety of thinkers, tends to lead to oppression.[5] British philosopher John Gray (2008), for instance, argues that utopias work as normative models used to justify violent acts perpetrated by religious or political groups and concludes that they necessarily lead to totalitarian political regimes.[6] The move away from utopia would be, according to this perspective, a response to the totalitarian horrors of the past century that posited a perfect, utopian society—the classless society of communism or the cohesive national community of Nazism, for example—as an end to be achieved no matter the human and environmental costs. But, as I argued in the Introduction to my coedited book *Existential Utopia* (2011), utopianism does not necessarily equate a transcendent, trans-historical ideal to be relentlessly pursued, sacrificing who- and whatever in the present to the altar of a higher value. Rather, utopias can operate intra-historically, forming pockets of resistance and/or opening paths away from what is into a more just polity. This is the sense of *existential* utopia, that is to say, an intra-temporal thought of new possibilities within everyday reality (Vieira and Marder 2011, xii).

Assuming that not all utopias necessarily drive us to totalitarianism, the purported contemporary dismissal of utopianism is also often blamed on the collapse of so-called grand narratives, most saliently the belief in human progress and secular perfectibility.[7] The confidence in the power of reason and science to usher humans into an era of peace and prosperity has certainly declined since its heyday in the Enlightenment. But more than a distrust in the human ability to build a better society to come, the move from utopia to dystopia seems to point to an uncertainty about what a good society is. The apparent failure of our utopian imagination betokens a failure in defining what a *eutopian* social arrangement would actually be. The difference between past- and present-day authors, then, is that the latter can only identify what bad polities look like. To put it differently, late modern thinkers are quick to diagnose the ills of our time but seem incapable to determine possible forms of cure.

What could be the reasons for this inability to imagine positive social scenarios? An easy scapegoat is the relativism often associated with the postmodern turn that marked the last decades of the past century. If there are no objective truths, so the familiar indictment of postmodernity goes, how are we to know right from wrong, good from ill, and so on? A more intellectually rigorous assessment of postmodern thought, however, would recognize that the situated knowledge it advocates is not equivalent to the anything-goes caricature of the movement painted by its detractors. Still, I would argue that our move away from utopianism is not entirely divorced from a postmodern frame of mind. I see the steady decline of utopia in the past century as going hand in hand with a questioning of humanity's place on the planet. It is not so much that we fail to conjure up a good society but, rather, that we are unsure as to whether human society as such is a good thing. In the rest of this chapter, I will discuss the turn from utopia to dystopia (and back) as a result of regarding humans on earth as a force that does more harm than good. In the next section, I consider the possibility of human extinction within the framework of utopian visions. The final section of the chapter turns to Margaret Atwood's MaddAddam trilogy (2004–2013) as a fictional example that plays out the prospect of a world in which humans have all but become extinct.

EXIT HOMO SAPIENS: UTOPIA WITHOUT US

Utopia, at least in its current form, came into being at the dawn of modernity with More's eponymous book from 1516, and utopianism, together with dystopia, has been entangled with valuations of what it means to be modern ever since. Many early dystopias were diatribes against the ideals of the Enlightenment or the French Revolution (Claeys 2017, 292ff) and this anti-modern streak of dystopianism continued well into the twentieth century, leading authors such as Moylan to consider that dystopia often "expresses a simple refusal of modern society" (2000, xii).

For those who espouse a utopian faith in modernization, the problem of contemporary society lies in an incomplete modernity, whose promise of rational socio-political organization and techno-scientific progress has not yet been completely fulfilled. Anti-modern thinkers, conversely, regard these very same developments as potentially leading to disaster. From the perspective of anti-modern thought, dystopias are not mere cautionary tales that highlight the excesses of modernity. Rather, modernity itself is dystopian and utopia would, in this view, amount to a retreat to a pre-modern, bucolic, pastoral, or Georgian way of life. Fredric Jameson sees a direct link between anti-modern ideology, embraced by writers and philosophers as varied as José Ortega y Gasset, T. S. Eliot, or Martin Heidegger, and the fear of a dystopian, overpopulated world. For Jameson, "[i]t is only in postmodernity and globalization, with the world population explosion, the desertion of the countryside, the growth of the megacity, global warming and ecological catastrophe," that the ills of our society were blamed upon "the scandal of multiplicity and of what is generally referred to as overpopulation, or in other words, the definitive appearance of the Other in multiple forms and as sheer quantity or number" (2010, 36). For anti-modern intellectuals, the various socio-political and economic problems we face can be traced back to "all those unknown others who constitute 'society' beyond one's immediate circle of acquaintances," a feeling that is then "concentrated in the fear or multiplicity and overpopulation" (36). Jameson sees in the images of soulless clones or of living-dead, brainless zombies an expression of the anti-modern, dystopian horror of the masses conservative thinkers regard as responsible for the decline of our civilization (36).

Utopian and dystopian takes on modernity and overpopulation are heavily indebted to eschatologically inflected modes of thinking that place an emphasis on the end of times as a Millenarian kingdom of peace and prosperity, a land of milk and honey for everyone, or on an apocalyptic vision of widespread death and destruction. Frank Kermode has rightly sounded a note of caution about the pitfalls of eschatology and of assuming that our polity stands in an extraordinary relation to the time to come. For Kermode, every age judges the crises of their society to be deeper or more significant than the ones of previous eras (2000, 93ff). Those who reflect upon the future tend to think that they live in the end of an era, at a critical juncture, and on the brink of period-defining events that often entail the annihilation of the entire human race. Both utopian and dystopian thought would therefore belong in a long line of reflections about crisis that would either herald a dramatic change for the better or result in a doomsday scenario.

What Kermode fails to mention as an issue that distinguishes more recent utopian or dystopian eschatological predictions from previous ones is that, in the past, eschatology involved the intervention of a divine entity that brought about the end of a fallen society. It is only in the twentieth century that humanity acquires the ability to effect change upon the entire human race through nuclear technology, genetic manipulation, and a dramatic modification of the biosphere. This is the meaning of secularism: humankind has now taken over the role of divinity as creator and destroyer of life. It is no coincidence that dystopianism appears to have accompanied the human capability to bring about a radical transformation of life on earth. For if previous generations could count on divine wisdom to make the right decision about the eschaton, humanity from the start of the nuclear age onwards had to reckon with the fact that decisions about the fate of the planet and all its inhabitants are in the hands of flawed beings, whose actions are, more often than not, grounded in self-interest.

Modernity, then, is inextricably linked to an exponential growth of human population, a development that cannot be attributed to the intercession of a transcendent entity but, rather, to a scientific approach to reality. Thomas Malthus infamously predicted that an incessant population growth would soon lead to widespread famine in his 1798 *Essay on the Principle of Population*, a situation that the so-called "Green Revolution," enabled by industrial agriculture relying heavily on fertilizers, pesticides, and machinery powered by fossil fuels, managed to avert (Bergthaller and Carretero González 2018, 5). For utopians, the escape from the worst anxieties surrounding overpopulation reinforces their belief in the promise of modernity; dystopian thinkers consider that it will only be a matter of time before such fears become reality.

What has up until recent years united both utopian and dystopian thought is a view of human disappearance from the face of the earth as an eminently negative development. From the Biblical episode of the flood that wiped out most of humanity, through concerns about exceeding the earth's carrying capacity, to images of deadly viruses spreading to the entire globe, the extinction of our species has been interpreted as *the* negative outcome of social crisis, which both utopian optimists and anti-modern dystopians wish to avoid. It is therefore unsurprising that threats to the survival of humankind became the center of many dystopian narratives from the mid-twentieth century onwards. Utopians are confident that human annihilation will be obviated by a deepening and expansion of modernity's project to all human beings. Anti-modern thinkers, while viewing overpopulation as a dystopian scenario, also shy away from pushing for the disappearance of humanity as such. For them, the extinction of humans would be a dystopia, caused precisely by the imbalances of modern life and by uncontrollable masses of people.

In the past few decades, there has been a subtle shift in the lines separating utopian and dystopian views on modernization and human population. For if dystopias express, from the inception of the genre, a renunciation of modernity, that rejection has of late transformed into a repudiation of humans as the agents who brought about modern life and its attendant evils. Such an assessment of humankind goes hand in hand with contemporary reflections on the Anthropocene, a geological era marked by human beings' lasting impact on the planet.[8] As Dipesh Chakrabarty (2008) argues, the distinction between human and natural history, as well as humanist accounts of modernity and globalization, collapses when we regard humans as a geological force. The unprecedented rate of anthropogenic changes to the earth, including the contamination of the oceans, soils, and atmosphere by industrial by-products and waste, the mass extinction of other species and global warming have led some thinkers to consider that the disappearance of *Homo sapiens* might be a positive development, if not for humans, then for the earth and all other living beings. From being regarded as an unintended, dystopian outcome of modernity-gone-wrong, human extinction has come to acquire utopian undertones.

Works like Alan Weisman's book *The World Without Us* (2007), together with films including *The Future is Wild* (2002), *Aftermath: Population Zero* (2008) and *Life after People* (2008 and 2010), invite us to imagine our planet without humans as an idyllic place where non-human beings thrive once again. If the recent Extinction Rebellion protests against climate change and human-induced ecological collapse precisely in order to prevent the human extinction that gives the movement its name, these other visions of the world without us regard extinction as a good thing. As Mark Jendrysik notes, this represents a mutation in eschatological, millenarian thought, in that such scenarios promise salvation to nature, not humanity; or better still, they promise salvation to nature *through* the absence of humans (Jendrysik 2011, 35). While Weisman's book and the above-mentioned films skirt the thorny issue of how the earth got rid of humanity in the first place, activist groups such as the Voluntary Human Extinction Movement call for people to abstain from reproduction to facilitate *Homo sapiens*'s gradual demise and prevent environmental degradation, while the even more radical anti-human Church of Euthanasia advises its followers to "Save the Planet, Kill Yourself."

Vincent Geoghegan summarily defines advocates of human extinction as "self-loathers," who "expend utopian energy anticipating the extinction of a humanity that is deemed to be a parasite on nature" and contrasts this stance with a self-critical perspective that would recognize human failings, all the while working toward the betterment of humankind (Geoghegan 2013, 46). Jendrysik agrees that thoughts of human extinction amount to a surrender to despair, since they imply giving up hope of ever attaining utopia (2011, 35). But, as Geoghegan himself acknowledges, there is a utopia of "humanity crushed" (Geoghegan 2013, 46). If humans are a blight on the planet, responsible for widespread destruction of their environment wherever they take root, then their extinction would amount to the only true utopia. It would entail a return to Arcadia or a Garden of Eden devoid of humans, a kind of renewed Genesis enabled by the sacrifice of the human species (Geoghegan 2013, 51). "Without man," writes Jendrysik, "the peaceable kingdom is established at last" and "[t]he end of history has finally arrived" (2011, 48). Human society is deemed beyond repair and the only way of achieving utopian aspirations is to do away with *Homo sapiens* altogether.

Utopia has made a comeback with a twist through the dream of a world without humans that is eerily peaceful and harmonious, reminiscent of utopian visions of Paradise. What does this conception of a human-free Eden mean for the tradition of utopian writings inaugurated at the outset of modernity? In the last section of this chapter, I discuss Margaret Atwood's MaddAddam trilogy in light of the utopian/dystopian imagination of a world with (almost) no humans.

USTOPIAN EXTINCTION: MARGARET ATWOOD'S MADDADDAM TRILOGY

Margaret Atwood's MaddAddam trilogy, which includes the novels *Oryx and Crake* (2003), *The Year of the Flood* (2009) and *MaddAddam* (2013), fictionalizes the emergence of new hominoid beings called the Crakers. They get their name from the game Extinctathon that their creator, a brilliant scientist called Glenn, used to play with his best friend Jimmy when they were adolescents. The game was about guessing the name of a species that had become extinct in the past fifty years and players had to choose an extinct animal as their codename. Glenn picked Crake, after the Australian Red-necked Crake, and thus the beings he genetically engineered were dubbed "Crakers." Ironically, though, and in spite of the origin of their name, the Crakers, far from being on the brink of annihilation, flourish in their post-Apocalyptic world. Humans are the ones who get extinct in the novels, by virtue of a virus that Crake releases embedded in the BlyssPluss sexual enhancement pill, which also promises protection against STDs and the prolongation of youth. After driving countless species to extinction, it is humans who endure an extinctathon—a marathon of extinction, a ton of human extinctions, a hecatomb—that leaves *Homo sapiens* reduced to a few scattered survivors.

At first glance, the eradication of almost all human beings, literally reduced to pulp, appears to be the ultimate dystopia. As Crake himself points out, "all it takes is the elimination of one generation" for the entire infrastructure of late modern society to come crumbling down (Atwood 2004, 261). Even if human know-how were somehow to be preserved, the few people who remained alive would not have the tools or be able to produce the energy to keep the machinery that moves the modern world going. And this collapse of life as we know is exactly what happens shortly after the virus hits. As Jimmy, one of the few survivors, reflects: "Strange to think of the endless labour, the digging, the hammering, the carving, the lifting, the drilling, day by day, year by year, century by century, and now the endless crumbling that must be going on everywhere. Sandcastles in the wind" (Atwood 2004, 50). Humans and the complex political structures and technology they created to mold reality to their needs rapidly vanish with their extermination.

And yet the novels do not depict the world without humans as an altogether bad thing. To be sure, as Paul Harland mentions, the few human survivors mourn the loss of their loved ones and of the way of life before the onset of the plague (2016, 583ff). But the overwhelming sense conveyed by the trilogy is that humankind had it coming. As the roommates of Jimmy's girlfriend put it: "Human society [...] was a sort of monster, its main by-products being corpses and rubble. It never learned, it made the same cretinous mistakes over and over, trading short-term gain for long-term pain" (Atwood 2004, 285). They go on to compare humanity to an enormous, life-destroying animal: "It [human society] was like a giant slug eating its way relentlessly through all the other bioforms on the planet, grinding up life on earth and shitting it out the backside in the form of pieces of manufactured and soon-to-be obsolete plastic junk" (285). Adam One, the leader of the radical environmentalist group God's Gardeners, also decries human behavior once he realizes the deadly virus is spreading: "It is not this Earth that is to be demolished: it is the Human Species. Perhaps God will create another, more compassionate race to take our place" (Atwood 2010, 508).

In the aftermath of the "Waterless Flood," the Biblically inspired name the Gardeners gave to the plague, a small number of humans is left to coexist together with the Crakers. Toby, a former member of God's Gardeners who is in charge of telling the hominoids stories through which they try to make sense of their origin and of the world around them, tellingly designates the years before the plague as chaos. The three MaddAddam novels move back and forth in time, describing the period before the annihilation of most humans as a world of out of kilter, dominated by rampant capitalism. The employees of large corporations lived in fortified compounds insulated from the majority of the population, who inhabited the lawless pleeblands. Climate change had caused massive droughts and large areas of the planet—Texas and the Mediterranean basin, for instance—had turned into deserts. Countless plants and animals had gone extinct, while unbridled genetic manipulation had given rise to bizarre crossbreeds, including rakunks, liobams, and pigoons, the latter designed with implanted human stem cells, in order to grow human organs for transplant. As Toby explains to the Crakers, "[t]he people in the chaos cannot learn. They cannot understand what they are doing to the sea and the sky and the animals. They cannot understand that they are killing them, and that they will end by killing themselves" (Atwood 2013, 353). Humans were engaged in relentless, widespread destruction of the earth and their demise is presented as an almost inevitable outcome of their actions and as a blessing for all other living beings.

Atwood is known for her engagement in environmentalist causes[9] and has spoken out against the toll our consumer-driven society and rapid population growth is exerting on the planet.[10] She writes that "[t]he rules of biology are as inexorable as those of physics: run out of food and water and you die. No animal can exhaust its resource base and hope to survive. Human civilizations are subject to the same law" (Atwood 2005, 322). It is telling that she does not regard the MaddAddam novels as works of science fiction, as they contain nothing that would be impossible in the present, at least in theory.[11] She prefers to use the term "speculative fiction," since the texts mention "nothing we haven't already invented or started to invent" (322). Rather, the narratives expand upon a conjecture, a "what if" question: "What if we continue down the road we're already on? How slippery is the slope? What are our saving graces? Who's got the will to stop us?" (323). Atwood regards her books as thought experiments. She does not see human extinction as particularly catastrophic, but merely as one of the possible outcomes of our way of life, one of the possible answers to the question of *Homo sapiens*'s future. As she remarks, Crake is, from a certain perspective "the most altruistic person around" (quoted in Bouson 2016, 348), since he is courageous enough to act in order to stop humanity's complete destruction of the biosphere.[12]

The (almost) post-human world after the plague is therefore not a somber wasteland but a place where an accelerated rewilding process is happening, as fauna and flora, including genetically modified species, quickly reconquer what were once bustling cities. The few humans left seem destined to perish and the survival of *Homo sapiens* lies in interbreeding with the Crakers. Toward the end of *MaddAddam*, several Craker–Human children are born who will carry at least part of the human genetic heritage forward. The Crakers themselves are presented as an alternative to humankind's destructiveness. Problematic as their origin certainly is—they were designed by a scientist and are therefore living proof of human hubris and desire to bend the rules of nature—they are painted in idyllic colors. Simple-minded, peace-loving, egalitarian, and friendly, they lack the racism, sexism, hierarchical social organization, and drive to exploit the environment that is the hallmark of humanity. They are vegetarian and able to digest raw plant material, which means that they have an almost endless source of nourishment at their disposal; are physically adapted to a significantly warmer climate (their skin smells of citrus, so as to repel insects, and is UV resistant); and their females come in heat once every three years, at which time they amicably mate with four males until they get pregnant, thus rendering jealousy obsolete. It is unclear which traits will live on in the Craker–human infants, but the new interbred community is likely to avoid some of the worst features of humankind.

The MaddAddam novels, often read as dystopias, are therefore only dystopic from the narrow perspective of humanity. From the point of view of the Crakers, or of the biosphere at large, the world after the Waterless Flood is significantly better than before. Atwood herself has noted that she does not believe in pure utopias or dystopias: "within each utopia, a concealed dystopia; within each dystopia, a hidden utopia" (2011, 82). She uses the word "ustopia" to describe the inevitable fusion of the two genres. "*Ustopia*," she writes, "is a word I made up by combining utopia and dystopia—the imagined perfect society and its opposite—because, in my view, each contains a latent version of the other" (82). The novels in the trilogy are ustopias because their utopian or dystopian outlook depends on whose perspective we adopt: that of the billions who perished in the Waterless Flood, of the human survivors, of the Crakers, of non-human beings, and so on. But the narratives are also *us*topias in that they invite readers to reflect about us, humans, as a species.

Does *Homo sapiens* deserve to live, or would the world really be better off without us? And is this a matter of choice, or has our fate already been sealed by the unintended, cumulative effect of our actions? Atwood leaves these questions open in her texts but makes it clear that the future of our planet hangs in the balance.

Utopia in the Anthropocene

An offshoot of modernity, utopia is based on a conception of human beings as rational individuals in charge of their lives and able to choose, as a group, how best to live them. By offering models of significantly better—or worse, in the case of dystopia—social arrangements, the genre presupposes that humans can decide how to organize themselves to either emulate superior polities or avoid the mistakes of bad ones.[13] Even the possibility of human annihilation through nuclear technology still had elements of choice. To be sure, no one could elect not to have a nuclear disaster such as Chernobyl, but people were able to determine not to start a nuclear war. This element of volition that is crucial to utopianism is all but absent from an understanding of humanity as a species. Humankind has certainly not decided to overpopulate the earth beyond its carrying capacity or give rise to global warming. By delivering themselves to unbridled expansion and modification of the planet to meet the needs of their growing numbers, humans irrationally undermine the conditions for their own survival. Can such a predicament devoid of volition still allow for utopian thought?

Atwood's MaddAddam trilogy prompts readers to assess humankind as a species. For scientist Crake, *Homo sapiens* is not worth saving and the future of humanity lies in the Crakers. "As a species we're doomed by hope, then," asserts Jimmy in one of the novels. Crake replies, in a continuation of the dialogue:

> "You could call it hope. That, or desperation."
> "But we're doomed without hope, as well," said Jimmy.
> "Only as individuals," said Crake cheerfully.
> "Well, it sucks."
> "Jimmy, grow up." (Atwood 2004, 139)

In a reiteration of the arguments adduced by utopia's detractors, Crake came to the conclusion that hope—the driving force of utopia—is the root cause of human destructiveness. Utopia realized, the Crakers are devoid of hope, in the same way as they experience no fear. The world of Crakers and Craker–humans enabled by Crake's release of the Waterless Flood plague is therefore a better version of human society. True, it came into being after one last act of human volition—the will of a mad scientist—but the novels suggest that humanity was doomed one way or the other. Crake's actions only sped up a process already well underway, creating a utopia of life without human life.

Conclusion: Utopia in the Anthropocene

What is, then, the role of utopian thought in the Anthropocene? For one, considering human beings not as rational individuals, fully able to determine all aspects of their lives, but as a species that is not insulated from its surroundings means an emphasis on the *topos* of utopia. A world without humans would be considered utopian exactly because humanity's systematic destruction of its environment, of the *topos* that is the planet we inhabit, would come to an end. Our ability to imagine the globe without *Homo sapiens* as utopian can also be seen as a coming of age of humans, who finally get over the narcissistic belief that they are god(s)'s gift to the earth, and realize that they turned out to be more of a curse. But a post-human world such as the one created by Crake is just one possible scenario, a "what if" among others. What if we give hope a chance after all? Can there still be a utopia that would include us humans in the mix? And what would be the role of such a utopian desideratum in the age of the Anthropocene?

Notes

1. Scholars agree that the twentieth century marked a shift from a predominantly utopian to a dystopian outlook. Keith Booker writes that "much of the history of recent utopian thought can be read as a gradual shift from utopian to dystopian emphases" (1994, 15). For Krishan Kumar, "it is mainly in the twentieth century that dystopia truly comes into its own" (2013, 19). Lyman Tower Sargent argues that "dystopia has been the dominant form of utopianism since around World War I" and goes on to add that "the twentieth century has quite correctly been called the dystopian century, and the twenty-first century does not look much better" (2013, 10).
2. Several designations have been used to describe a dystopia: anti-utopia, heterotopia, negative utopia, anti-utopia, and cacatopia, among others.
3. One can distinguish three broad tendencies in utopianism: utopian thought, utopian literature, and historically existing utopian movements. Dystopianism consists primarily of dystopian thought and fiction, even though several historical groups that preach an impending apocalypse have adopted some dystopian traits. In this chapter, I focus primarily on utopian/dystopian literature and thought, and will bracket a discussion of historically existing utopian/dystopian communities.
4. Mark Featherstone came up with the concept of "kinet utopia," or utopia of movement, to describe capitalist utopias, but saw this kind of utopias in a negative light (2017, 7).

5. Thinkers including Karl Popper, Isaiah Berlin, Leszek Kolakowski, Michael Oakeshott, and Friedrich Hayek believe that utopia leads to totalitarianism (Davis 2013, 23).

6. Gray makes this case in his ominously titled book *Black Mass. Apocalyptic Religion and the Death of Utopia* (2008).

7. As Kumar points out, the main targets of dystopia have been the grand narratives of modernity: "reason and revolution, science and socialism, the idea of progress and the faith in the future" (2013, 19).

8. The recent history of the term goes back to atmospheric chemist and Nobel Prize winner Paul Crutzen, who cowrote an article with Eugene Stoermer in 2000 arguing that, due to our extensive impact on the planet, the current geological period should be called the "Anthropocene:" the age of humans. See Robin et al. (2013).

9. Deborah Bowen summarizes some of Atwood's contributions to the environmentalist cause: "In 1995 she gave up her house in France after President Jacques Chirac resumed nuclear testing. In 2000 she donated a significant portion of her Booker Prize money to environmental groups; since 2006, Atwood and her partner Graeme Gibson, an avid birder, have been joint honorary presidents of the Rare Bird Club within BirdLife International; in the last ten years she has used her book tours to promote environmental activism, ensuring that travel on these tours is carbon–neutral, and particularly promoting shade-grown coffee, to protect the migratory songbirds of the forest canopy" (2017, 700).

10. As Atwood puts it: "We must slow our growth rate as a species or face a series of unimaginable environmental and human catastrophes" (cited in Bouson 2016, 342).

11. Atwood offers the following definition of science fiction: "I define Science Fiction as fiction in which things happen that are not possible today—that depend, for instance, on advanced space travel, time travel, the discovery of green monsters on other planets or galaxies, or which contain various technologies we have not yet developed" (2005, 85).

12. Jimmy also reflects upon Crake's motivations for releasing the virus: "Had he been a lunatic or an intellectually honourable man who'd thought things through to their logical conclusion? And was there any difference?" (Atwood 2004, 343).

13. The modern conception of humans as rational individuals is questioned from early on. Immanuel Kant, for instance, considered that humans worked toward the betterment of society almost in spite of themselves. By believing to act in their own self-interest, they were, in fact, promoting the cause of humanity and progress toward perpetual peace. This was also, mutatis mutandis, the idea behind Adam Smith's notion of the invisible hand, through which individual and often selfish decisions contributed to the well-oiled functioning of the market. Both of

these ideas, however, presupposed the existence of God, who guaranteed that the sum total of human actions led history (or the market) in the right direction. With the erosion of faith in a divine entity, history came to be perceived as the result of scattered decisions with no obvious greater purpose and determined by the limited understanding of the individuals who made them.

REFERENCES

Atwood, Margaret. 2005. *Curious Pursuits: Occasional Writing, 1970–2005*. London: Virago.

———. 2004. *Oryx and Crake*. New York: Anchor Books.

———. 2010. *The Year of the Flood*. New York: Anchor Books.

———. 2011. *In Other Worlds: Science Fiction and Human Imagination*. London: Virago.

———. 2013. *MaddAddam*. New York: Nan A. Talese/Doubleday.

Bergthaller, Hannes and Margarita Carretero González. 2018. Population, Ecology, and the Malthusian Imagination: An Introduction. *Ecozon@* 9 (1): 1–10.

Booker, Keith. 1994. *The Dystopian Impulse in Modern Literature: Fiction as Social Criticism*. Westport, Connecticut: Greenwood Press.

Bouson, J. Brooks. 2016. A "joke-filled romp" Through end Times: Radical Environmentalist, Deep Ecology and Human Extinction in Margaret Atwood's Eco-apocalyptic *MaddAddam* Trilogy. *The Journal of Commonwealth Literature* 51 (3): 341–357.

Bowen, Deborah. 2017. Ecological Endings and Eschatology: Margaret Atwood's Post-apocalyptic Fiction. *Christianity and Literature* 66 (4): 691–705.

Chakrabarty, Dipesh. 2008. The Climate of History: Four Theses. *Critical Inquiry* 35: 197–222.

Claeys, Gregory. 2017. *Dystopia: A Natural History. A Study of Modern Despotism, Its Antecedents, and Its Literary Diffractions*. New York: Oxford University Press.

Crutzen, Paul, and Eugene F. Stoermer. 2000. The 'Anthropocene'. In *The Future of Nature*. eds. Robin, Libby, Sverker Sörlin and Paul Warde. 2013, 483–490. New Haven: Yale University Press.

Davis, Lawrence. 2013. Dystopia, Utopia and Sancho Panza. In *Dystopia(n) Matters: On the Page, On Screen, On Stage*, ed. Fátima. Vieira, 23–27. Newcastle upon Tyne: Cambridge Scholars Publishing.

Featherstone, Mark. 2017. *Planet Utopia: Utopia, Dystopia and Globalization*. London and New York: Routledge.

Geoghegan, Vincent. 2013. Darkness and light. In *Dystopia(n) Matters: On the Page, on Screen, on Stage*, ed. Fátima. Vieira, 46–48. Newcastle upon Tyne: Cambridge Scholars Publishing.

Gordin, Michael, Helen Tilley, and Gyan Prakash. 2010. Introduction: Utopia and Dystopia Beyond Space and Time. In *Utopia/Dystopia: Conditions of Historical Possibility*, ed. Michael Gordin, Helen Tilley, and Gyan Prakash, 1–17. Princeton and Oxford: Princeton University Press.

Gray, John. 2008. *Black Mass: Apocalyptic Religion and the Death Of Utopia*. London: Penguin.

Harland, Paul. 2016. Ecological Grief and Therapeutic Storytelling in Margaret Atwood's *Maddaddam* Trilogy. *Interdisciplinary Studies in Literature and Environment* 23 (3): 583–602.

Jameson, Fredric. 2010. Utopia as Method, or the Uses of the Future. In *Utopia/Dystopia: Conditions of Historical Possibility*, ed. Michael Gordin, Helen Tilley, and Gyan Prakash, 21–44. Princeton and Oxford: Princeton University Press.

Jendrysik, Mark. 2011. Back to the Garden: New Visions of Posthuman Futures. *Utopian Studies* 22 (1): 34–51.

Kermode, Frank. 2000. *The Sense of an Ending: Studies in the Theory of Fiction*. Oxford and New York: Oxford University Press.

Kumar, Krishan. 2013. Utopia's Shadow. In *Dystopia(n) Matters: On the Page, on Screen, on Stage*, ed. Fátima. Vieira, 19–22. Newcastle upon Tyne: Cambridge Scholars Publishing.

Marder, Michael, and Patrícia Vieira. 2012. Introduction: Utopia, a Political Ontology. In *Existential Utopia: New Perspectives on Utopian Thought*, ed. Patrícia Vieira and Michael Marder, ix–xv. New York: Continuum.

Moylan, Tom. 2000. *Scraps of the Untainted Sky: Science Fiction, Utopia, Dystopia*. Boulder: Westview Press.

Sargent, Lyman Tower. 2013. Do Dystopias Matter? In *Dystopia(n) Matters: On the Page, On Screen, On Stage*, ed. Fátima. Vieira, 10–13. Newcastle upon Tyne: Cambridge Scholars Publishing.

Vieira, Patricia and Michael Marder, eds. 2011. *Existential Utopia: New Perspectives on Utopian Thought*. London: Continuum.

Anti-utopia

Artur Blaim

INTRODUCTION

The terminological and genealogical jungle surrounding the key concepts of utopian studies involving the central trinity of utopia–dystopia–anti-utopia is often accompanied by a multitude of derivative classificatory labels such as critical dystopia; satirical dystopia; counter-utopia; reverse utopia; negative utopia; cacotopia; etc. Together these constitute a complex socio-politico-literary-cultural agglomerate used for a variety of political and cognitive purposes. Unlike in the case of utopia, where there seems to be a general consensus as to its meaning, despite hundreds of superficially different but essentially similar definitions, dystopia and anti-utopia continue to be defined by diverse criteria ranging from genre conventions, through socio-political contexts, to authorial intentions and subjective reception by different readers.

Arthur O. Lewis, Jr. offered one of the first definitions of the anti-utopian novel when he identified it as a "work depicting a society that is officially 'perfect' but which is demonstrated to have flaws making it unacceptable to the author's – and presumably the reader's – point of view," observing that the "societies depicted in these novels have been called … reverse utopias, negative utopias, inverted utopias, regressive utopias, cacoutopias, dystopias, non-utopias, satiric utopias, and … nasty utopias" (1961, 27). The same approach appears in such classic studies of anti-utopian fiction as Chad Walsh's

A. Blaim (✉)
University of Gdansk, Gdansk, Poland

P. Marks et al. (eds.), *The Palgrave Handbook of Utopian and Dystopian Literatures*, https://doi.org/10.1007/978-3-030-88654-7_3

From Utopia to Nightmare (1962) or Mark Hillegas's *The Future as Nightmare: H. G. Wells and the Anti-Utopians* (1967). In countless other books, articles, and dictionary definitions, ranging from popular internet sites to such distinguished works as Vita Fortunati's and Raymond Trousson's *Dictionary of Literary Utopias*,[1] the two terms continue to be used as perfect synonyms, which manifests itself in statements like "a true anti-utopia, a dystopia" (Elliott 1970, 97); "anti-utopia (or, more neutrally, dystopia)" (Schäfer 1979, 97); "dystopia – or anti-utopia" (Ferns 1999, 78); "dystopias (sometimes termed 'antiutopias' or, more scatalogically, 'cacatopias')" (Pfaelzer 1984, 79); or "dystopia means a 'bad place' or 'anti-utopia'" (Abdelbaky 2016, 17).[2] In his popular introduction to the study of dystopia, M. Keith Booker defines dystopia as "a general term encompassing any imaginative view of a society that is oriented toward highlighting in a critical way negative or problematic features of that society's vision of the ideal" subsuming all other designations such as "negative utopia," "anti-utopia," "heterotopia," "cacotopia," and the like (1994, 22). Matthew Beaumont identifies anti-utopia with dystopia referring to "the anti-utopian, or dystopian, imagination" (Beaumont 2005, 131–132), but at the same time he introduces the term "cacotopia" to refer to the anti-communist writings forming "a sub-genre that specializes in apocalyptic images of the proletariat" (8) that originated in late nineteenth-century England as a result of reports of the Paris Commune.

The most elaborate conceptions of anti-utopia were proposed in terms of the literary-theoretical approach. The most ambitious attempt was made by Gary Saul Morson who, working within the Russian Formalist/Bakhtinian paradigm, conceptualizes anti-utopia as an anti-genre, the distinctiveness of which lies in the fact that the conventions it employs "establish a *parodic* relation between the anti-generic work and the works and traditions of another genre, the target genre"; the principal aim of the anti-genre is to discredit not a single work in the target genre, but the genre as a whole" (Morson 1981, 115–116).[3] Anti-utopia is "a didactic genre" that lays bare "the devices of another didactic genre in order to deprive those devices of their effectiveness," so as to reveal "the danger and folly of utopian lessons, but also the duplicitous strategies by which those lessons are taught" (Morson 1981,138). This account may give rise to some doubts. Although the first texts commonly regarded as anti-utopias appeared already in the eighteenth century—Jonathan Swift's *Gulliver's Travels* (1726), Samuel Johnson's *Rasselas* (1759), or less known anti-Jacobin works such as George Walker's *The Vagabond* (1799)[4]— they did not aim at parodying or questioning the automatized or ossified conventions of the genre.[5] Indeed, they were not particularly concerned with literary conventions at all.[6] Whenever early anti-utopian texts employed the conventions of the utopian genre, they did so only in order to question the very possibility of imposing any form of utopian order on the imperfect world marred by the Original Sin (*Gulliver's Travels*) or to point out the inherently negative consequences of the excess of everything pleasurable (*Rasselas*). More importantly, the classic anti-utopian works such as Yevgeny Zamyatin's

We (1924), Aldous Huxley's *Brave New World* (1932), or Ray Bradbury's *Fahrenheit 451* (1953), often regarded as providing the genre pattern for the anti-utopian genre, do not focus on parodying or ridiculing the conventions of utopian fiction. What they parody, ridicule, or reject are real-life "utopian" solutions and/or their consequences. The status of George Orwell's *Nineteen Eighty-Four* (1949) is even more complex[7] as it owes its anti-utopian status not to the fact that Oceania purports to be an ideal state or characterizes itself as such, but to implicit references to the totalitarian models implemented in the Soviet Union and Nazi Germany which, in terms of their own self-description, presented themselves as (potentially, or intentionally) ideal states and societies.[8]

Boris Lanin, who otherwise tends to identify anti-utopia with dystopia, attempts to formulate a normative poetics of the genre on the basis of contemporary Russian anti-utopian fiction in terms of Bakhtin's ideas of carnival and carnivalized literature. Its distinctive features include a rebel protagonist, extensive use of the motifs of illicit sex, heavy intoxication, and feasting, which, however, appear in a degenerate or distorted form characteristic of the officially sanctioned pseudo-carnival which constitutes "the core of anti-utopia." This pseudo-carnival is radically different from the traditional one as it is sustained by fear and "designed to exist for ever, for the end of the pseudo-carnival would signify the end of the authoritarian regime that has created and regimented it" (Lanin 2006, 405). The protagonist rebels against the norms imposed by the state and society so that "his personal, intimate life is sometimes the only way for him to express his own 'I'" (406). The state, on the other hand, "claims to be a divine power" giving "new names, with new meanings, to phenomena, objects and processes that we would recognize as part of the 'real' world" (407). The principal function of anti-utopia consists in offering a dramatized warning against "the possible negative course of history and against the negative, destructive tendencies in contemporary society" by pointing out "the absurdity of the negative features of human life today" while at the same time it constitutes a "dispute with utopia or with a utopian plan" (405).

FINDING THE BOUNDARIES

Another increasingly popular approach consists of an attempt to clearly demarcate the boundaries between anti-utopia and dystopia. This is done in a variety of ways. John Huntington understands anti-utopia in a very broad sense as "a type of skeptical imagining that is opposed to the consistencies of utopia-dystopia" and aims at criticizing the way of thinking that constructs a particular utopian structure rather than that structure itself. He argues further that "[i]f the utopian-dystopian form tends to construct single, foolproof structures which solve social dilemmas, the anti-utopian form discovers problems, raises questions, and doubts" (Huntington 1982, 123).

Lyman Tower Sargent defines anti-utopia as "a non-existent society described in considerable detail and normally located in time and space that the author intended the contemporaneous reader to view as a criticism of utopianism or of some particular eutopia" in contradistinction to dystopia, "a non-existent society described in considerable detail and normally located in time and space that the author intended the contemporaneous reader to view as considerably worse than the society in which that reader lived" (Sargent 1994, 9). Sargent's definitions and distinctions continue to be adopted, occasionally with minor modifications, by the majority of utopian scholars such as Frauke Uhlenbruch who employs the term "anti-utopia to refer to works that critique the utopian impulse, utopias, and their writers" (Uhlenbruch 2015, 193). Tom Moylan and Rafaella Baccolini in the introduction to *Dark Horizons* modify Sargent's distinction between dystopia and anti-utopia, by defining dystopia as "the textual form that critiques and rejects not only Utopia but also the political thought and practice that is produced and motivated by Utopia as a force of societal transformation," and so becomes "a textual expression of the historical, political position of Anti-Utopia" (Moylan 2000, 129). However, at the same time, they regard it as an autonomous form thematically and ideologically situated in the border zone between utopian and anti-utopian genres:

> Dystopias negotiate the social terrain of Utopia and Anti-Utopia in a less stable and more contentious fashion than many of their eutopian and anti-utopian counterparts. As a literary form that works between these historical antinomies and draws on the textual qualities of both subgenres to do so, the typical dystopian text is an exercise in politically charged form of hybrid textuality, or... "genre blurring." (Baccolini and Moylan 2000, 147)

Darko Suvin makes use of dystopia as an umbrella term comprising "simple" dystopia and anti-utopia:

> Anti-Utopia finally turns out to be a dystopia, but one explicitly designed to refute a currently proposed eutopia. It is a pretended eutopia - a community whose hegemonic principles pretend to its being more perfectly organized than any thinkable alternative, while our representative "camera eye" and value-monger finds out it is significantly less perfect than an alternative, a polemic nightmare. "Simple" Dystopia (so-called to avoid inventing yet another prefix to topia) is a straightforward dystopia, that is, one which is not also an anti-utopia. (Suvin 2003, 189)

For Phillip E. Wegner anti-utopia constitutes a subgenre of the negative utopia which "takes as the target of its critical estrangement not the histories of its present, but the desires and programs of the very generic institution from which it emerges" (Wegner 2002, 147–148). He makes a distinction between "the dystopia, the 'bad place'" and "a more generalized antituopia," with the former presenting "a critique of the limitations of a specific form of imagining place, the latter a rejection of this cognitive act altogether" (153).

Dohra Ahmad, who regards anti-utopia as a subgenre, defines it by contrasting it with dystopia ("a fictional representation of a place that, from the point of view of the narrator, is patently bad") and identifying it with negative utopia "a place that is not bad per se but functions exactly as it should, a place where most people are content with the utopian compromise to which they have implicitly consented." Although it is "essentially a utopian society," the author "portrays it as a horror, and judges the compromise not to have been worthwhile" (Ahmad 2009, 210).

Antonis Balasopoulos also views anti-utopias and dystopias as different modes of discourse considering "anti-Utopias as representations which do not restrict themselves to an 'internal' critique of Utopian visions but which move to a rejection of Utopianism from a position allegedly outside it" (Balasopoulos 2011, 60). He distinguishes five basic sub-categories of anti-Utopianism: satirical anti-Utopias ("which attack previous works or intellectual traditions by exposing them as impractically and unrealistically 'Utopian'"), dogmatic fictional anti-Utopias ("a Utopian vision associated either with a specific text or with a broader tradition is imagined as substantively realized, but with catastrophic results"), pre-emptive anti-Utopias ("texts that neither engage in the negation of the premises of Utopian texts or traditions nor deploy the device of catastrophic projections of the future," but "explicitly suggest that existing reality is, in substance, already Utopian, and hence, that continuing dissatisfaction with it is implicitly or explicitly illegitimate or even dangerous"), critical anti-Utopias ("works in the areas of philosophy, psychoanalysis and political theory… opposed to Utopianism, but without either upholding the desirability of the current social order or rejecting the prospects of radical social change") (Balasopoulos 2011, 61–63).

Alexandra Aldridge sees anti-utopia as a historical phenomenon accompanying utopia from its very beginning: "attacks in utopia or a spirit of anti-utopianism run parallel to the whole of what can loosely be called utopian thought," "the earlier critical term and its literal usage, the earlier form" (Aldridge 1984, 4, 8). As a "negative literary form" opposed to utopias and utopianism it belongs to an evolutionary chain whose main stages are: "satirical utopia, anti-utopia and the dystopian novel" that "with a certain amount of overlap can be said to have evolve in that order (Aldridge 1984, 16)." In other words, Aldridge regards anti-utopia as a transitional stage between satirical utopia and dystopia. As such, apart from being "a theoretical reaction to a theoretical idea," it is assigned certain characteristics that it shares with the other two genre variants: "a distaste for the social consequences of science and technology" and a lack of "the dark or apocalyptic strain" of dystopia (Aldridge 1984, 16).

Recently Aldridge's position has been reiterated by Demir Alihodžić, and Selma Veseljević-Jerković (2016), for whom "anti-utopian works date from about the mid to late nineteenth century and dystopian works are a twentieth century phenomenon" (Alihodžić & Veseljević-Jerković 2016, 44). Accordingly, "dystopia is more than just a direct attack on utopianism" being "a vehicle for social commentary and human introspection" aimed at exploring "the relationship between the possibilities inherent in human nature and the social constructs we have already devised or are capable of devising" (Alihodžić and Veseljević-Jerković 2016, 46). Comparing Aldridge's views to Morson's, they erroneously suggest that she regards dystopia as a subgenre of anti-utopia (Alihodžić and Veseljević-Jerković 2016, 45), whereas in fact, for Aldridge, both are simply interrelated but autonomous stages of the literary/ideological evolution.

David W. Sisk, somewhat eccentrically, extends the concept of anti-utopia to cover also competing utopias, arguing that "[m]any anti-utopian fictions depict pleasant societies," calling William Morris's *News from Nowhere*, one of "the numerous attacks mounted against Edward Bellamy Looking Backward" (Sisk 1997, 5).[9] He regards dystopia as "a much narrower descriptive term," arguing counterfactually, that "all dystopias are anti-utopias, but not all anti-utopias are dystopias," although at the same time he seems to view anti-utopia as a genre variant of dystopia: "dystopia as a genre encompasses a spectrum of works ranging from a few anti-utopias proper… through novels that create miserable societies without directly attacking utopian ideals" (Sisk 1997, 5). He also remarks, again providing no evidence, that "anti-utopian fiction may (or may not) address the existing problems of its writer's world, but dystopia must always do so" (6).

The distinction proposed by Sargent and followed in different ways by numerous other critics and scholars seems ultimately valid, although the commonly accepted implication that dystopia and anti-utopia constitute two distinct modes or genres—though potentially politically expedient—is cognitively questionable at best. Whereas dystopia is clearly the reverse of utopia in terms of the depicted world (a bad place as opposed to a good place) constituting the key distinctive formal feature of the two, their ideological functions may occupy different positions ranging from absolute identity (both may aim at criticizing the present state of affairs) to radical opposition, when the presentation of a bad place is intended to question a particular utopian proposal or utopianism in general. Unlike utopia and dystopia, granting an autonomous status to anti-utopia relies almost exclusively on thematic criteria or the critique of utopianism, whether explicit or implicit, rather than on a clearly defined set of distinctive features. Moreover, there is a fundamental difference in the possible mode of existence of utopia and dystopia on the one hand and anti-utopia on the other. Whereas it is possible to intentionally create a dystopia in the real world (*vide* Auschwitz or Gulag) or attempt to implement a utopian project (New Lanark, Oneida, kibbutzim, etc.), it is not possible to establish an anti-utopia, or become its citizen, although it is possible to use a verbal or visual representation of an empirically existing state as part of anti-utopian strategy (cf. the depictions of the West in the Soviet propaganda, or of the communist bloc in the Western media). After all, for anti-utopia, the only possible mode of existence is in the realm of discourse. In this context, the occasionally used term "dystopianism" may refer, at best, to phenomena of a completely different order from those denoted by the binary opposition of utopianism/anti-utopianism, both of which call for adopting a certain ideological stance or initiating some practical action, be that positive or negative.

Conclusion

All this leads to the conclusion that in order to avoid the proliferation of confusing and often contradictory definitions and the subsequent misreadings and misunderstandings, it would be more advantageous to use the term "anti-utopia" to denote a certain function or social use of a dystopian text explicitly or implicitly questioning/opposing particular utopian solutions or utopianism in general, rather than as an autonomous mode or genre.[10] Viewed in this way, the anti-utopian function is not attached to any specific genre conventions or literary devices such as typical plots, protagonists, or settings. In this respect, the element shared by such anti-utopian works as Jonathan Swift's *Gulliver's Travels* (1726), Samuel Johnson's *Rasselas* (1759), a farcical playlet *Heaven on Earth, or the New Lights of Harmony. An Extravaganza, in Two Acts* published by an anonymous author under the pseudonym of Peter Puffem (1825), Ann Dodd's *The Republic of the Future* (1887), E.M. Forster's *The Machine Stops* (1909), or Ayn Rand's *Atlas Shrugged* (1597) is the fictional world presented as an extremely bad place, regardless of whether in terms of its own self-description it projects the image of the best one possible or not. Moreover, by conceptualizing anti-utopia in terms of function, or use, the problem of the real author's intentions moves is abandoned in favour of answering the fundamental question concerning its reception in historically changing interpretive communities. Here, the history of the public and critical reception of Orwell's *Nineteen Eighty-Four* put to different uses at different times and from divergent ideological perspectives is highly instructive.

Finally, a few words might be said about the relationship between anti-utopias and utopias. For Krishan Kumar, anti-utopia constitutes a response to utopia, being its "malevolent and grimacing doppelgänger" (Kumar 1987, 99) or "distorted image, seen in a cracked mirror" (100). Fátima Vieira observes that without utopia anti-utopia "could never have come into existence as it shares its strategies and its narrative artifices," but used for opposite aims (Vieira 2010, 16). In this context, Fredric Jameson makes an important distinction between different kinds of negation of utopias arguing that "the 'unknowability thesis' whereby so radically different a society cannot even be imagined is a rather different proposition from the anti-Utopian one according to which attempts to realize Utopia necessarily end up in violence and totalitarianism" (Jameson 2005, 142). The anti-utopian rejection of the supposedly ideal or even perfect solutions, "a standard weapon in the armoury of the status quo" (Levitas & Sargisson 2003, 15), implies an alternative arrangement also seen as the best one possible, even if sometimes it only means the 'utopi-anizing' of the existing state of affairs. Corin Braga observes that "antiutopia can be defined as a reverse dual system, in which the negative pole belongs to a nightmarish elsewhere or elsewhen, the 'here' and the 'now' appearing, by contrast, as a positive, albeit imperfect pole, which is, in any case, preferable to the other pole" (Braga 2016, 10). In all such cases, the *status quo*, while neces-sarily imperfect (the imperfections assuming the role of anti-utopian elements), turns out to be the best one possible. Peter Fitting maintains that anti-utopia is "explicitly or implicitly a defence of the status quo" (Fitting 2010, 141).[11] A similar idea is anticipated by Frank and Fritzie Manuel: "If in the background of every utopia there is an anti-utopia, the existing world seen through the critical eyes of the utopia-composer, one might say conversely that in the back-ground of many a dystopia there is a secret utopia" (Manuel & Manuel 1979, 6).

The "utopianizing" procedure delineated above invests the real and/or its representation with the anti-utopian function by being defined in opposition to another utopia. Approaching the same issue from a different perspective, Wegner expresses doubts whether "anti-utopia is a position that any human being can inhabit for very long, and if such a pure form of an assault on the utopian imaginary exists," because "most anti-utopias on further inspection turn out to be … what Karl Mannheim calls 'conservative utopias,' a form of 'counter-utopian' thinking wherein 'not only is attention turned to the past and the attempt made to rescue it from oblivion, but the presentness and immediacy of the whole past becomes an actual experience'" (Wegner 2009, 123). Ultimately, anti-utopias and anti-utopianism can be seen not simply as a way of questioning utopianism as such, but as a way of replacing one particular utopia by another, in accordance with Ruth Levitas's suggestion that "[t]he struggle for the future is always the struggle between competing Utopias" (Levitas and Sargisson 2003, 26) and Fredric Jameson's observation that any form of active anti-utopianism will invariably "sooner or later reveal itself as a vibrant form of Utopianism in its own right" (Jameson 1994, 67).[12]

Notes

1. See, Vita Fortunati, and Raymond Trousson, 2000, *Dictionary of Literary Utopias*, Paris: Honoré Champion. The entry on anti-utopia simply refers to the entry on dystopia (180–185). See also Northrop Frye, Sheridan Warner Baker & George B. Perkins, 1985, *The Harper Handbook to Literature*, New York: Harper and Row. A similar defi-nition can be found here: "Greek for 'bad place': an anti-UTOPIA" (156).

2. The identification of dystopia and anti-utopia is powerful. See, for example, Zeynep Tuna Ultav, 2015, An Interdisciplinary Perspective for Reading Utopia versus Dystopia: "The Ultimate City" by J.G. Ballard, AIZ ITU Journal of the Faculty of Architecture 12 (2): 173–184. Ultav

even misquotes Kumar, replacing the term "anti-utopia" used in the original text (100) with "dystopia": "dystopia is formed by utopia and lives parasitically on it" (1).

3. The idea of anti-utopia as an anti-genre predominates among Russian scholars. See, for example, R.R. Galiullin, 2013, The Genre of Utopia/Anti-Utopia in the Tatar Literature at the Beginning of the XX Century, The World of Scientific Discoveries 11: 261–268. See also, Chris Ferns, 1999, Narrating Utopia: Ideology, Gender, Form in Utopian Literature. Liverpool: Liverpool University Press. Ferns is one of the few Western critics who share Morson's view in regarding anti-utopia as a reaction against the traditional utopia which "both parodies and subverts the traditional utopian model as a means of satirizing and warning against some of the more alarming trends in contemporary society" (15). At the time he identifies anti-utopia with dystopia. See finally, Fredric Jameson, 2005, Archaeologies of the Future: The Desire Called Utopia and Other Science Fictions, London & New York: Verso. Jameson offers a radically different and politicized reading of Morson's theory (176–179).

4. See M.O. Grenby, 2001, The Anti-Jacobin Novel. British Conservatism and the French Revolution, Cambridge: Cambridge University Press; April London, 2000, Novel and History in Anti-Jacobin Satire, The Yearbook of English Studies 30: 71–81; and April London, 2004, Radical Utopias: History and the Novel in the 1790s, Eighteenth-Century Fiction 16: 783–802.

5. Some critics such as consider Bishop Hall's Mundus Alter et Idem (1607 [1605?]) as the first anti-utopia. However, although Hall clearly makes use of the devices of literary utopia, his aim is to construct "perfect" dystopian worlds governed by particular vices, and not to parody the utopian conventions, or particular utopias. \See: Krishan Kumar (1987), Elizabeth McCutcheon (2015), and Nicole Pohl (2010).

6. See, Chloe Houston, 2007, Utopia, dystopia or anti-utopia? Gulliver's Travels and the Utopian mode of discourse, *Utopian Studies* 18: 425–442. Houston argues that Swift is primarily concerned with parodying the utopian conventions in Gulliver's Travels: "Gulliver's Travels is neither a utopia, nor a dystopia, nor even an anti-utopia (as it has variously been read); rather, it contains images of and interactions with ideas of utopia and dystopia which reflect its engagement with the utopian mode and qualify it as simultaneously utopian and dystopian" (8).

7. See, Gregory Claeys, 2016, Dystopia: A Natural History. Oxford: Oxford University Press. Claeys offers a comprehensive account of the critical debate around Orwell's Nineteen Eighty-Four.

8. See, Gregory Claeys, 2010, The Origins of Dystopia: Wells, Huxley and Orwell, in The Cambridge Companion to Utopian Literature, ed. Gregory Claeys, 107–132, Cambridge: Cambridge University Press.

Claeys argues convincingly that Nineteen Eighty-Four was not intended by its author as an anti-utopia (2010, 107).

9. A similar case is mentioned by Fredric Jameson in Archaeologies of the Future, when he discusses Samuel Delany's Trouble on Triton: "the novel has… generally been read as a Utopian answer to another Utopia, rather than as an anti-Utopia of the more familiar Cold War type" (144–145).

10. See, Artur Blaim, 2013, Hell upon a Hill: Reflections on Anti-utopia and Dystopia, in Dystopia(n) Matters: On the Page, on Screen, on Stage, ed. Fátima Vieira, 80–91, Newcastle upon Tyne: Cambridge Scholars Publishing. I originally proposed this way of understanding anti-utopia.

11. Cf., Bronisław Baczko, 1989, Utopian Lights: The Evolution of the Idea of Social Progress, trans. Judith L. Greenberg, New York: Paragon House. Baczko argues that "anti-utopia is not necessarily an apologia for the established order," but sometimes even offers "a more radical and more bitter critique of the present than any utopia," compromising the present "with and by means of the utopias that it produces" (330–331).

12. See Ruth Levitas, 2013, Utopia as Method: The Imaginary Reconstitution of Society, Houndmills: Palgrave Macmillan. Levitas offers a critical analysis of contemporary anti-utopianism (7–19).

References

Abdelbaky, Ashraf. 2016. A Perfect World or an Oppressive World: A Critical Study of Utopia and Dystopia as Subgenres of Science Fiction. *IJELLH International Journal of English Language, Literature and Humanities* 4: 17–33.

Ahmad, Dohra. 2009. *Landscapes of Hope. Anti-Colonial Utopianism in America*. Oxford: Oxford University Press.

Aldridge, Alexandra. 1984. *The Scientific World View in Dystopia*. UMI Research Press.

Alihodžić, Demir and Selma Veseljević-Jerković. 2016. *The Boundaries of Dystopian Literature: The Genre in Context*. Tuzla: OFF-SET d.o.o.

Baccolini, Raffaella and Tom Moylan. 2003. Introduction. Dystopia and Histories. In *Dark Horizons: Science Fiction and the Dystopian Imagination*, ed. Raffaella Baccolini and Tom Moylan, 1–12. London and New York: Routledge.

Baczko, Bronisław. 1989. *Utopian Lights: The Evolution of the Idea of Social Progress*. trans. Judith L. Greenberg. New York: Paragon House.

Balasopoulos, Antonis. 2011. Anti-utopia and Dystopia: Rethinking the Generic Field. In *Utopia Project Archive, 2006–2010*, ed. Vassilis Vlastaras, 59–67. Athens: School of Fine Arts Publications.

Beaumont, Matthew. 2005. *Utopia Ltd. Ideologies of Social Dreaming in England 1870–1900*, Leiden: Brill.

Blaim, Artur. 2013. Hell Upon a Hill: Reflections on Anti-utopia and Dystopia. In *Dystopia(n) Matters: On the Page, on Screen, on Stage*, ed. Fátima. Vieira, 80–91. Newcastle upon Tyne: Cambridge Scholars Publishing.

Booker, M. Keith. 1994. *The Dystopian Impulse in Modern Literature: Fiction as Social Criticism*. Westport: Greenwood Press.

Braga, Corin. 2016. From Eden to Utopia: A Morphology of the Utopian Genre. *Journal for the Study of Religions and Ideologies* 15: 3–32.

Claeys, Gregory. 2010. The Origins of Dystopia: Wells, Huxley and Orwell. In *The Cambridge Companion to Utopian Literature*, ed. Gregory Claeys, 107–132. Cambridge: Cambridge University Press.

Claeys, Gregory. 2016. *Dystopia: A Natural History*. Oxford: Oxford University Press.

Dodd, Ann Bowman. 1887. *The Republic of the Future, Or, Socialism a Reality*. New York: Cassell & Co.

Elliott, Robert C. 1970. *The Shape of Utopia. Studies in a Literary Genre*. Chicago & London: University of Chicago Press.

Ferns, Chris. 1999. *Narrating Utopia: Ideology, Gender, Form in Utopian Literature*. Liverpool: Liverpool University Press.

Fitting, Peter. 2010. Utopia, Dystopia and Science Fiction. In *The Cambridge Companion to Utopian Literature*, ed. Gregory Claeys, 135–153. Cambridge: Cambridge University Press.

Fortunati, Vita, and Raymond Trousson. 2000. *Dictionary of Literary Utopias*. Paris: Honoré Champion.

Forster, E.M. 1909. The Machine Stops. *Oxford and Cambridge Review* 8: 83–122.

Frye, Northrop, Sheridan Warner Baker, and George B. Perkins. 1985. *The Harper Handbook to Literature*. New York: Harper and Row.

Galiullin, R.R. 2013. The Genre of Utopia/Anti-Utopia in the Tatar Literature the Beginning of the XX Century. *The World of Scientific Discoveries* 11: 261–268.

Grenby, M.O. 2001. *The Anti-Jacobin Novel. British Conservatism and the French Revolution*. Cambridge: Cambridge University Press.

Hillegas, Mark. 1967. *The Future as Nightmare: H. G. Wells and the Anti-Utopians*. New York: Oxford University Press.

Hall, Joseph. 1607. *Mundus alter et idem siue Terra Australis ante hac semper incognita longis itineribus peregrini academici nuperrime lustrata auth: Mercurio Britannico*. London: Francofurti: Humphrey Lownes.

Houston, Chloe. 2007. Utopia, Dystopia or Anti-utopia? Gulliver's Travels and the Utopian Mode of Discourse. *Utopian Studies* 18: 425–442.

Huntington, John. 1982. Utopian and Anti-Utopian Logic: H. G. Wells and His Successors. *Science-Fiction Studies* 9: 122–147.

Huxley, Aldous. 1932. *Brave New World*. London: Chatto & Windus.

Jameson, Fredric. 1994. *The Seeds of Time*. New York: Columbia University Press.

———. 2005. *Archaeologies of the Future: The Desire Called Utopia and Other Science Fictions*. London & New York: Verso.

Johnson, Samuel. 1759. *The Prince of Abissinia: A Tale*. London: R. and J. Dodsley, W. Johnston.

Kumar, Krishan. 1987. *Utopia and Anti-Utopia in Modern Times*. Oxford: Basil Blackwell.

Lanin, Boris. 2006. Imagination and Carnival in Russian Utopia and Anti-utopia. *Caietele Echinox* 10: 405–420.

Levitas, Ruth, and L.M. Sargisson. 2003. Utopia in Dark Times: Optimism/Pessimism and Utopia/Dystopia. In *Dark Horizons: Science Fiction and the Dystopian Imagination*, ed. Raffaella Baccolini and Tom Moylan, 13–27. New York & London: Routledge.

Levitas, Ruth. 2013. *Utopia as Method: The Imaginary Reconstitution of Society*. Houndmills: Palgrave Macmillan.

Lewis, Arthur O., Jr. 1961. The Anti-Utopian Novel: Preliminary Notes and Checklist. *Extrapolation: A Science-Fiction Newsletter* 2: 27–32.

London, April. 2000. Novel and History in Anti-Jacobin Satire. *The Yearbook of English Studies* 30: 71–81.

———, April. 2004. Radical Utopias: History and the Novel in the 1790s. *Eighteenth-Century Fiction* 16: 783–802.

Manuel, Frank E., and Fritzie P. Manuel. 1979. *Utopian Thought in the Western World*. Cambridge, MA: Harvard University Press.

McCutcheon, Elizabeth. 2015. Reimagining the Aftermath of the Fall. Three Dystopian/Utopian Narratives in Jacobean England. *Moreana* 52: 201–202.

Morson, Gary Saul. 1981. *The Boundaries of Genre: Dostoevsky's Diary of a Writer and the Traditions of Literary Utopia*. Austin: University of Texas Press.

Moylan, Tom. 2000. *Scraps of the Untainted Sky: Science Fiction, Utopia, Dystopia*. Boulder: Westview Press.

Orwell, George. 1949. *Nineteen Eighty-Four*. London: Secker & Warburg.

Pfaelzer, Jean. 1984. *The Utopian Novel in America 1888–1896: The Politics of Form*. Pittsburgh: University of Pittsburgh Press.

Pohl, Nicole. 2010. Utopianism after More. In *The Cambridge Companion to Utopian Literature*, ed. Gregory Claeys, 51–78. Cambridge: Cambridge University Press.

Puffem, Peter [pseud.]. 1825. *Heaven on Earth, or the New Lights of Harmony. An Extravaganza, in Two Acts*. Philadelphia, PA.

Rand, Ayn. 1957. *Atlas Shrugged*. New York: Random House.

Sargent, Lyman Tower. 1994. The Three Faces of Utopianism Revisited. *Utopian Studies* 5: 1–37.

Schäfer, Martin. 1979. The Rise and Fall of Antiutopia: Utopia, Gothic Romance, Dystopia. *Science Fiction Studies* 6: 287–295.

Sisk, David W. 1997. *Transformations of Language in Modern Dystopias*. Westport CT: Greenwood Press.

Suvin, Darko. 2003. Theses on Dystopia 2001. In *Dark Horizons: Science Fiction and the Dystopian Imagination*, ed. Raffaella Baccolini and Tom Moylan, 187–201. New York & London: Routledge.

Tuna Ultav, Zeynep. 2015. An Interdisciplinary Perspective for Reading Utopia versus Dystopia: "The Ultimate City" by J.G. Ballard. *AIZ ITU Journal of the Faculty of Architecture* 12 (2): 173–184.

Swift, Jonathan. 1726. *Travels into Several Remote Nations of the World. In Four Parts. By Lemuel Gulliver, First a Surgeon, and then a Captain of Several Ships*. London: Benjamin Motte.

Uhlenbruch, Frauke. 2015. *The Nowhere Bible: Utopia, Dystopia, Science Fiction*. Berlin: Walter de Gruyter GmbH.

Vieira, Fátima. 2010. The Concept of Utopia. In *The Cambridge Companion to Utopian Literature*, ed. Gregory Claeys, 3–27. Cambridge: Cambridge University Press.

Walker, George. 1799. *The Vagabond. A Novel*. London: Printed for G. Walker.

Walsh, Chad. 1962. *From Utopia to Nightmare*. New York: Harper & Row.

Wegner, Phillip E. 2002. *Imaginary Communities: Utopia, the Nation, and the Spatial Histories of Modernity*. Berkeley & Los Angeles: University of California Press.

Wegner, Phillip E. 2009. *Life between Two Deaths, 1989–2001. US Culture in the Long Nineties*. Durham & London: Duke University Press.

Zamyatin, Yevgeny. 1924. *We*. trans. Gregory Zilboorg. New York: E. P. Dutton.

Dystopia

Gregory Claeys

INTRODUCTION

The word *dystopia* apparently first appears in English, spelt as *dustopia*, in 1747, with the spelling *dystopia* occurring the following year, describing "an unhappy country."[1] Its next prominent usage was by the leading liberal social theorist John Stuart Mill, who in an 1868 speech called Britain's treatment of Ireland "too bad to be practicable," and its proponents "cacotopians" (after the Greek, bad place), or dys-topians. The term did not begin to circulate widely, however, until the late twentieth century. In 1952 Glenn Negley and J. Max Patrick termed it "the opposite of *eutopia*, the ideal society." In the late twentieth and early twenty-first centuries, it has usually been taken to describe two phenomena: real societies which had sunk into despotism, particularly the totalitarian regimes produced by Nazism and Stalinism; and the literary refractions of such developments. Such societies typically seek to enslave parts of their population and to keep much of the rest in a constant state of fear in order to maintain order. Widespread alienation, paranoia, scapegoating and enemy-creation typifies most such regimes. The principle of fear had been used to characterize despotisms in some early analyses in political theory, notably by Montesquieu in *The Spirit of the Laws* (1748). Group psychology is another important methodological starting point for the subject. So is the literature on historical and imaginary apocalypses of various types.

G. Claeys (✉)
University of London, London, UK

P. Marks et al. (eds.), *The Palgrave Handbook of Utopian and Dystopian Literatures*, https://doi.org/10.1007/978-3-030-88654-7_4

In the first half of the twentieth century, three texts emerged to define the dystopian genre (or sub-genre, if we take it to be a subset of utopian literature): Yevgeny Zamyatin's *We* (1924), Aldous Huxley's *Brave New World* (1932), and George Orwell's *Nineteen Eighty-Four* (1949). The popularity of the genre dates from the Cold War, and a "dystopian turn" in literature appears evident by the 1960s, and certainly by the beginning of the twenty-first century, when utopian writing became overwhelmed by the outpouring of dystopian texts. At least one classic text appeared in the later period, Margaret Atwood's *The Handmaid's Tale* (1986). Works of dystopian fiction sometimes appear as counterfactual "future histories," which project narratives from the present into the future. They are often combined with technological and scientific projections of various kinds and are sometimes described as a subset of science fiction.

THE DEVELOPMENT OF A TRADITION

As a literary genre, dystopian fiction has antecedents in various forms of satire, as early as Aristophanes' "Parliament of Women" (c. 390 BCE), and including Joseph Hall's *Mundus Alter et Idem* (1605). In the eighteenth century it is notably exemplified in this form in the fourth voyage of Jonathan Swift's *Gulliver's Travels* (1726), where a life lived according to the principles of reason is portrayed. This indicates that the genre has functioned as an anti-utopian device at various points; that is, as a means of indicating the degree to which the pursuit of utopia, usually defined as the ideal society, results in its opposite, a dystopian condition, often because of some combination of sin, stupidity, folly, and malevolence. Such devices have often been used to indicate the potential limits of social and political reform. From this viewpoint the earliest literary dystopias occur already at the time of the French Revolution, when *A Trip to the Island of Equality* (1792) satirizes the egalitarian republican principles of the most famous tract appearing in English during the French Revolution debate, Thomas Paine's *Rights of Man* (1791–1792). A second important instance of the genre which appeared slightly later was John Reeves' *Publicola. A Sketch of the Times and Prevailing Opinions, from the Revolution in 1800 to the Present Year 1810* (1810), where Paine was again the key target.

The first major upsurge of dystopian literature occurred thereafter as a consequence of the immense popularity of Edward Bellamy's *Looking Backward 2000–1887* (1888). Bellamy's modernist vision of the future portrayed a highly regulated, technologically centered, and largely urban society. Here all are educated to age 21, then serve for twenty-four years in the labor army. Some variation in employment is possible, but evasion of this duty is not, and those who shirk their responsibilities face being "sentenced to solitary confinement on bread and water" (Bellamy 2009, 75). (In the second edition this was rephrased to "cut off from all human society.") Critics asserted that

Bellamy's collectivism implied authoritarian politics and military-style regimentation, opening up the possibility of corruption and an anti-democratic political regime. Other texts of this period, like Jack London's *The Iron Heel* (1908), portray the existing society, dominated (as it was) by great Trusts or corporate monopolies, and ever more prone to plutocracy, and degenerating steadily into what we would today term dystopia.

Another leading theme, which develops quite independently in this period, is anxiety about the role increasingly played by machinery in human society, and its potential to overwhelm its creators. In mainstream social theory such prospects had been floated by, among others, Adam Ferguson in the eighteenth century, and Karl Marx in the mid-nineteenth. In utopian/dystopian literature, a chapter entitled "The Book of the Machines" in Samuel Butler's *Erewhon* (1872) provides the first major projection of machines evolving, as humanity had evolved from apes, into a higher form of intelligence. By the turn of the century "metal monsters" known as "muglugs" were being described as having taken over most of human labor (in William Wallace Cook's *A Round Trip to the Year 2000*, 1925, first published in *Argosy* in 1903). Already, thus, the Frankenstein motif, one of several growing out of the prehistory of dystopian thought, was being rendered more realistic and applied to machines as well as organic beings.

The Bolshevik Revolution of October 1917 provided the greatest impetus to the specifically anti-collectivism literary dystopia. Although its author had been associated with the Bolsheviks after 1905, Zamyatin's *We* describes a society a thousand years in the future dominated by an "instinct of unfreedom" in which all citizens wear identical uniforms adorned with their numbers. All are "one of" the group, follow the routine of the Table of Hourly Commandments, and live in full sight of one another in glass buildings, curtains being drawn only during Sexual Days, for which pink coupons are issued by the Sexual Bureau, which aims at eugenically-defined mating. The hero, D-503, engages in illicit sex and contemplates fleeing beyond the Green Wall, where trees and animals proliferate. He cannot escape, however, and by a fantasiectomy has his imaginative propensities removed. The novel combines three of the great themes subsequently definitive of many dystopian texts: a satire on collectivist despotism and the suppression of individuality by the group; an assault on the embrace of machine-like ideals and tendencies; and a vision of the great modern dilemma as the pursuit of pleasure and happiness versus the desire for freedom.

That such themes would come to define such a large part of the negative experience of humanity in the twentieth century represents a remarkable prophecy. Lenin's political police, the Cheka, was founded in December 1917, and the systematic extermination first of opponents of the regime, including anarchists, social democrats, and all servants of the former Tsar, proceeded apace. With Stalin's ascent to power in the late 1920s, the finger of suspicion pointed ever more widely. During the Great Terror of 1937–1938 some 680,000 were executed. Much of the population lived under constant fear throughout this epoch, indeed down to Stalin's death in 1953. Some twenty million are estimated to have died through torture, execution, or overwork in the vast system of concentration camps known as the Gulag. During the 1930s a rival totalitarian system was introduced by Adolf Hitler in Germany, which resulted in the murder of some six million Jews in the Holocaust, most notably in the death camp of Auschwitz, and in deaths of more than twenty million in Eastern Europe and the USSR after Germany's invasion in 1941. Such regimes, based on the principle of fear, the isolation of individuals from one another, and the cultivation of deliberate distrust through paranoia and misinformation, coupled with widespread surveillance of the population, can be characterized as dystopian. By implication eutopia, the good place, can be defined in terms of the maximization of trust, friendship, solidarity, sympathy, and enhanced sociability among the members of a given group, so long as these qualities are compatible with toleration, individuality, a respect for personal dignity and rights, and the need for privacy. But these qualities may not extend to an entire given population, and a dystopia for the many may well coincide with a eutopia for the few.

ALDOUS HUXLEY'S *BRAVE NEW WORLD* (1932)

Of the two main literary dystopias of the twentieth century, the first, Aldous Huxley's *Brave New World*, precedes Hitler's rise to power, though Bolshevism is one target of the novel. Huxley also takes up another theme rarely associated with satires on Bolshevism, however: eugenics. This had been alluded to or indeed centrally definitive of a number of post-Darwinian Victorian utopias/dystopias, some of which adopt eugenics proposals with great enthusiasm from what would today also be called a left-wing perspective.[2] It was the leading theme in H. G. Wells's *The Island of Doctor Moreau* (1896), in which a vivisectionist creates "beast-men" out of animals, again extending the Frankenstein motif. Huxley brilliantly systematizes such themes, though not without ambiguity, for his sympathy for certain types of eugenic engineering remained throughout his life. In the year 632 After Ford (AD 2495), the world is governed by ten Controllers, and divided into five castes, Alphas, Betas, Gammas, Deltas, and Epsilons. The Controllers are Alpha Plus intellectuals, bred from a single egg. The rest are cloned, as we would say today, as many as 17,000 from a single egg. They are then conditioned through propaganda, hypnopedia (sleep teaching), and other devices, including Solidarity Services which encourage ecstatic release, to be satisfied with their lot in life.

This satisfaction is reinforced by identification with the larger group. The disappearance of marriage and family life mark one element of the regime's collectivism. Private affection is actively discouraged: "When the individual feels, the community reels" (Huxley 2007, 81). Mandatory promiscuity lessens the risk of individual emotional attachment, as in Zamyatin. The workload is light, some seven and a half hours a day. Amusements like the "Feelies," a more tactile form of cinema, ensure the hedonistic bent of the society is satis-fied. A drug named *soma* alleviates all worries, but anxieties do nonetheless exist, and in an ill-fated play based on the novel, Huxley made it clear that the threat of *soma* withdrawal was a keen source of discomfort for the population. Consumption of commodities is encouraged: "Ending is better than mending. The more stitches, the less riches" (2007, 42). Huxley was good with slogans and had a keen sense of the power of advertising in modern life. Yet the new world has of course its share of misfits. A number of key characters revolt, and much of the plot revolves around a contrast between the new world and the old, exemplified by the character John, an inhabitant of a savage reserva-tion where some still live in primitive circumstances. John stands for freedom, which he conceives in terms of God, poetry, danger, freedom, goodness, sin, "the right to be unhappy," and "to grow old and ugly and impotent" (2007, 212). The new world has eliminated such risky prospects and is "blissfully ignorant of passion and old age" (2007, 194).

Some of this satire is directed at Wells, and some at Bolshevism. But much of it centers on the dominant ethos of capitalist modernity as such, compulsive consumption, and an obsession with pursuing individual happiness. Huxley's satire is so well contrived that modern students on a first reading, certain in their identification with the Alpha Plus caste, are often unsure as to whether the combination of cradle-to-grave welfare and free sex and drugs can be construed as dystopian at all. We can be certain of Huxley's contempt for the shallow hedonism which defines the new world. Yet he had little sympathy for the savage alternative. In 1946 he reflected that "The Savage is offered only two alternatives, an insane life in Utopia, or the life of a primitive in an Indian village, a life more human in some respects, but in others hardly less queer and abnormal," adding that if he had the chance to write the book anew, he "would offer the Savage a third alternative": "Between the Utopian and the primitive horns of his dilemma would lie the possibility of sanity—a possibility already actualized, to some extent, in a community of exiles and refugees from the Brave New World, living within the borders of the Reservation" (Huxley, 2004, 6). Here "economics would be decentralist and Henry-Georgian, poli-tics Kropotkinesque and cooperative. Science and technology would be used as though, like the Sabbath, they had been made for man, not (as at present and still more so in the Brave New World) as though man were to be adapted and enslaved to them" (Huxley 2007, xlii–xliv). To some degree this vision was fleshed out in Huxley's last work, *Island* (1962).

George Orwell's *Nineteen Eighty-Four* (1949)

Compared to Huxley's great work, the central text in the dystopian tradition leaves little doubt or sense of authorial ambiguity in the minds of most readers. Orwell's *Nineteen Eighty-Four* represents the culmination of the author's development as a socialist with anarchist sympathies from the late 1930s, when he fought briefly against Franco during the Spanish Civil War and became a convinced anti-Stalinist as a consequence. Preceded by the brilliant short satire on the failure of the Russian Revolution, *Animal Farm* (1945), Orwell's novel is both a dystopia and, in part, a satire on some types of utopianism, where Wells is a target who stands for a particularly modernist vision of utopia. Characteristically an alienated outsider, Orwell came to fear the left's embrace of a machine-dominated world as much as that of its opponents and came to believe that both shared much of this in common. Already in *The Road to Wigan Pier* (1937) he warned that many socialists viewed "mechanical progress, *as such*, with enthusiasm," but that this vision would end in a world with "no disorder, no loose ends, no wildernesses, no wild animals, no weeds, no disease, no poverty, no pain—and so on and so forth. The Socialist world is to be above all things an *ordered* world, an *efficient* world" (Orwell 1959, 188). Yet Orwell, exultant at Labour's victory in the 1945 General Election in Britain, would remain a socialist to the end of his life.

This fact ensures that interpretations of his key work remain contradictory, contentious, and often highly politicized. Those who view the novel only in terms of its central themes and narrative structure often maintain that Orwell's evident refusal to offer any "hope" in the text illustrates a resolute pessimism as well as an anti-Marxist bias in particular. Those, however, who read the book contextually, with an eye to Orwell's political pronouncements throughout the period of its composition, usually allow that any such critique of Stalinism does not represent a break with socialism, or utopianism, as such. The narrative, admittedly, bears out a bleak reading of the work's central themes. Its anti-hero, Winston Smith, lives in London, now a city in Oceania, ruled by a Party whose ideology is defined as Ingsoc, which was originally inspired by English socialism. Oceania is constantly at war with Eurasia and Eastasia, and conditions of life are bleak for the majority of "proles," even for the Inner Party, to which Winston belongs as an employee of the Ministry of Truth whose task is to rewrite newspapers to accord with the latest shift in the party line. Only for the Inner Party is this regime worthwhile, and they cling to power, using the ubiquitous telescreen, or two-way television, to observe members of the Party, and a ruthless secret police to suppress all dissidence.

For reasons that are never made clear, Winston chooses to rebel against the system, first by buying a diary, then by commencing an affair with Julia, another Outer Party member, conducting it, finally, in a secret room above an antique shop. Much of this episode, along with Winston's contact with an organization supposedly dedicated to overthrowing the system, turns out to have been stage-managed by the police. Winston is caught, he and Julia are tortured, and in the end he loves Big Brother, the possibly fictional symbol of the regime's power. Along the road we are given a lengthy explanation as to how the regime originated, in the book-within-the-book, Emmanuel Goldstein's *The Theory and Practice of Oligarchical Collectivism*, which owed much to the writings of James Burnham, though in the novel it appears that this too has been composed by the police.

The central passages of the novel engage with Orwell's main theme, the lust for power, and the pervasiveness of totalitarian ideals among the British middle classes who are the chief object of the satire. Yet Orwell's text is more telling still. Besides the more obvious critique of Stalinist collectivism in particular, it contains a subtle account of group psychology, in which the sublimation of the erotic plays a central role, and which is hinted at in an earlier essay, "Notes on Nationalism" (1945). It also expounds at length on Orwell's central worry, that the idea of objective truth was fast disappearing, replaced by mere propaganda. This theme, so obviously relevant to our own era of "fake news," has assured the novel's continuing popularity long after the threat of Soviet totalitarianism disappeared. The accusation that Orwell exaggerated the cruelty of Stalinism has however also disappeared in light of historical research from Solzhenitsyn onwards, which has revealed both the scale of murder and destruction in the regime and the pervasiveness of fear it inspired. Reality, in fact, turns out to be much more terrifying than fiction.

Dystopia After Orwell

The seventy years since the appearance of *Nineteen Eighty-Four* have witnessed a series of developments in the dystopian fictional genre. A few anti-totalitarian works rose to respectable levels of literary attainment, among which David Karp's *One* (1953) is notable. One of the most successful post-war works was B.F. Skinner's *Walden Two* (1948), which portrays a small-scale community imbued with behaviorist psychological principles. Here positive reinforcement of a kind experimented with by early socialists like Robert Owen, who rejected punishment as a tool of social engineering, successfully guides a thousand rural colonists. During much of the subsequent decade, however, fear of nuclear war produced several notable works. Works like Bernard Wolfe's *Limbo '90* (1953), Walter Miller's *A Canticle for Leibowitz* (1959), Mordecai Roshwald's *Level 7* (1959), and Pat Frank's *Alas, Babylon* (1959) spell out the anxiety of the Cold War epoch, when annihilation was a very real possibility.

At the same time, dystopia was also conceived as potentially emanating from several other sources. By the early 1950s, it was already evident that computers would play a prominent role in any future. They come to control the world in a number of novels of this period, notably Kurt Vonnegut's *Player Piano* (1952). Warnings of the potential and malevolent predominance of great multinational corporations are already present in this period, for instance in Frederick Pohl and Cyril Kornbluh's *The Space Merchants* (1953). The possibility that middle-class American society would produce an increasingly oppressive conformity of thought analogous to some forms of totalitarianism was explored in various works, notably Ray Bradbury's *Fahrenheit 451* (1953). As in Huxley, a central theme here is the obsessive hedonism of modern Americans, for whom "Fun is everything" (94) and "slippery stuff like philosophy or sociology" (91) only produce melancholy. Thus, the proclamation that "We must all be alike" (88) with "everyone *made* equal" (88) rather than having been created equal comes to symbolize the egalitarianism of capitalist modernity, rather than its totalitarian counterpart.

In this period two new key themes also emerge. The specter of global over-population gains prominence as we reach the 1960s with works like Anthony Burgess's *The Wanting Seed* (1962), Harry Harrison's *Make Room! Make Room!* (1966), John Brunner's *Stand on Zanzibar* (1968), and Max Ehrlich's *The Edict* (1971). The specter of environmental catastrophe, while present in some early novels, moves to center stage in J. G. Ballard's *The Drowned World* (1963), where solar flares cause rising ocean levels, and in John Brunner's *The Sheep Look Up* (1972) and other works. Epidemics provide the background to a number of post-apocalyptic novels in this period, notably Doris Lessing's *The Memoirs of a Survivor* (1974). The potential centrality of robots to human life appears in several works which border on, or are usually classified as, science fiction in this period, notably Philip K. Dick's *Do Androids Dream of Electric Sheep?* (1968). The persistence of male oppression of women looms large in Sally Gearhart's *The Wanderground: Stories of the Hill Women* (1978). The most famous contemporary feminist dystopia is Margaret Atwood's *The Handmaid's Tale* (1986), which portrays a Christian fundamentalist dictatorship in which the red-robed handmaids cater to the needs of their commanders. (A notable forbearer and critique of Nazism in particular is Katherine Burdekin's *Swastika Night*, 1937).

In the early twenty-first century, the themes of the preceding half-century reappear in various combinations. Ecological disaster is virtually a given after the 1990s, even in novels centrally concerned with other themes, as Marge Piercy is with human/mechanical identity and the challenges of Artificial Intelligence in *He, She and It* (1991). The emerging *eminence grise* of this period has doubtless been Margaret Atwood. Three novels, *Oryx and Crake* (2003), *The Year of the Flood* (2009), and *MaddAddam* (2013), collectively referred to as the MaddAddam trilogy, unite themes of environmental catastrophe, corporate dictatorship, the perils of scientific and technological progress, cloning, and mass society. The coincidence of the election of Donald Trump as President of the United States in 2016, which the evident racism, misogyny, and Christian fundamentalist intolerance which this both fed upon and reinforced, gave a tremendous impetus to Atwood's works (and Orwell's too), with *A Handmaid's Tale* becoming a highly successful television adaptation in 2017. While Atwood includes science fiction elements in her works, her insistence that these derive as closely as possible from feasible developments from existent science and technology demarcates her writing from science fiction as such. This self-conscious methodological positioning has been named the "Atwood principle" (Claeys 2016, 287). Another trend in the early 2000s has been the increasing tendency for post-apocalyptic novels not to engage with any serious reflections on the causes of humanity's decline. Popular accounts like Cormac McCarthy's *The Road* (2006) and Jim Crace's *The Pesthouse* (2007) fall into this category. The accidental elimination of much of the planet's population through pandemics is also central to novels like Emily St. John Mandel's

Station Eleven (2014). Another tendency has been the emergence of Young Adult Dystopias, sometimes first appearing as films, in which teenage heroes and heroines typically do battle with the forces of evil, usually emerging victorious. The genre typically engages with every stage of modern technological development, with Dave Eggers's highly successful *The Circle* (2013) taking up the theme of internet surveillance as productive of a potential universal social, emotional, and psychological transparency, a trope which takes us back to Orwell and indeed to Thomas More's original formulation of the ideal.

Controversies and Debates

Modern dystopian fiction thus moves from a concentration on satirizing Bolshevik collectivism in the 1920s–1940s to a broader interest in the prospective dangers of mass conformism in notionally liberal democracies and an increasing focus, in the later twentieth century, on the problems of nuclear war, environmental collapse, and the predominance of various forms of technology over humanity.

As the genre of dystopian fiction has grown into prominence, a number of central theoretical controversies have come to the fore. The first and most obvious, perhaps, is the definition of the genre itself. Dystopias are often characterized as inverted or negative utopias, or anti-utopias, on the supposition that they aim to satirize the failure of utopian aspiration in real life. As we have seen, this is an adequate reflection on the first wave of dystopian fiction, the reaction to Bellamy's *Looking Backward*. However, many later twentieth- and twenty-first-century works also satirize liberal democratic societies or portray post-apocalyptic scenarios where the cause of universal catastrophe is not explicitly named. Here dystopia is a state or condition characterized by malevolence, fear, social and political breakdown, and disorder. The clarity of the genre is muddied further by the routine introduction of science fiction elements. Often this is in service of perpetuating a particular political regime (as in Huxley and Orwell), while also serving to expose the threat of potential technological developments (usually computers, robots, nuclear power, and now the internet). Moreover, it is clear that many novels in the field more widely (including utopias) portray both elements of utopia and dystopia simultaneously, or a sequence of passage from, or reversion to, one or the other. Small groups may benefit from what is for the majority a dystopia, giving us the impression that one person's utopia may well be another's dystopia.

Pockets of resistance to dystopian regimes are thus portrayed in novels from at least the 1930s. These are sufficiently common that defining them as "critical dystopias," because they indicate the potential for regime change in the novel, seems as pointless as the denomination of "critical utopias," which undermines any sense of the complexity of the genre. Many literary utopias present themselves critically in relation to specific embodiments of the utopian tradition, for instance Thomas More with Plato and Christianity, or William Morris's *News from Nowhere* in relation to Bellamy. Such variants and thematic intermixtures of utopia and dystopia are in fact quite common throughout the tradition, from at least the Bellamy period onwards (Bellamy's own *Equality*, 1897, permitted the obstinate to withdraw to reservations). All dystopias are "critical" even when they do not explicitly outline a utopian alternative within the text itself, in the sense of engaging with the preceding tradition and consciously innovating within it. As an analytic category, thus, the "critical dystopia" does not stand up to historical scrutiny, much less one which indicates a trend in reaction of Orwell.

A second definitional and genre-related problem stems from the anti-totalitarian thrust of many works from Zamyatin through Orwell and into the later twentieth century. Though there is some consensus, no settled definition of totalitarianism exists, and the much greater knowledge of the phenomenon at the end of the twentieth century invalidated or greatly challenged some hypotheses of the earlier period. (Thus, Solzhenitsyn and some account of Pol Pot's Kampuchea must be used to supplement Hannah Arendt's classic account, *The Origins of Totalitarianism*, 1951). Many on the political left long rejected any application of the term *totalitarianism* to the USSR, preferring its confinement to Nazi Germany and fascism. This view is completely untenable. Attempts to dismiss the value of Orwell's and other novels for their refusal to offer "hope" to the reader of the overthrow of totalitarian regimes are similarly misguided. This is generally derived from a perspective associated with the German philosopher Ernst Bloch, who has made major contributions to the interpretation of utopia. But too often it results in concerns which are chiefly propagandistic and hortatory, rather than heuristic, and which echo that facile optimism which was the official ideology of "real existing socialist" regimes and capitalist societies alike, and which thus denies the legitimacy of any "pessimistic" interpretation of reality.

Thirdly, parallel to the problem as to whether we can consider small groups as embodying "utopia," as opposed to nations or at least much larger groups, the term "dystopia" must be applicable to larger rather than smaller numbers. Societies in which localized breakdown, immorality, and violence are portrayed, like Anthony Burgess's *A Clockwork Orange* (1962), which has been called an "inverted utopia," thus challenge the genre's definition. Nonetheless the fact that utopias have often been set on islands in the midst of non-utopian seas, literally as well as figuratively, indicates that this is not an insuperable problem. Pockets or enclaves of both utopian and dystopian space might be identified within many or most societies, where the norms and rules governing behavior vary extremely from those of most of the rest of the society. (Michel Foucault's concept of "heterotopia" is sometimes employed to express such possibilities.) This can also be conceived in terms of specific moments in time, the euchronia as "good time" being potentially contrasted to the "dyschromia" or bad time, though the terminology requires further exploration. This question also raises the further issue of group, and especially crowd, psychology as a starting point for the study of the subject, and the potential oppression of individuals and suppression of individuality by groups, as the central theme of the tradition. This seems to have been the direction in which Orwell was moving in the last five years of his life. An approach derived from social identity theory, which stresses the group component in individual identity, is accordingly a plausible starting point in this field.

Fourthly, and related to the function of some dystopian texts as anti-utopias, one of the central themes to emerge in the secondary literature has been the issue as to whether the ideal society involves complex regulation to assure security from want, longevity, and the diminution of anxiety; or whether such regulation, by reducing freedom of choice, including the freedom to make serious mistakes, eliminates a vital element requisite for a fully human life. This is a central theme for Zamyatin, Huxley, Skinner, and many other writers in this field. If conditioning can produce highly virtuous behavior, whereas free will leads us frequently to sin and error, the argument runs, then we should prefer virtue to freedom. And surely we do prefer it anyway, given the fact that all education and indoctrination amounts to conditioning, more or less self-consciously. And then there is the possibility that we embrace obedience to strong rulers more or less naturally and willingly. While Skinner came down, as we have seen, on the side of conditioning, and reinforced his original case in *Beyond Freedom and Dignity* (1971), many other authors have taken an opposite view, notably Huxley, whose character of John the savage embodies the desire for "freedom," and Anthony Burgess, who attacked Skinner as proposing the death of autonomous man. Similarly, the rebels in Ira Levin's *This Perfect Day* (1970), rendered docile by state-induced drug treatments which leave them permanently smiling, nonetheless long for "true freedom" (142) and given up "efficiency—in exchange for freedom" (120). Thus, to leading twentieth-century critic George Kateb, "The way of sin, the way of experience, the way of loss of innocence, must be the way by which the generally virtuous character is formed. This is the way of the world; this is the way that Utopia eschews; but this is the better way" (Kateb 1972, 186–7). Such discussions at least indicate the perennial, indeed the increasingly pressing, relevance of the genre.

NOTES

1. This account broadly follows that presented in my *Dystopia: A Natural History* (Oxford University Press, 2016). As in this work, most of the generalisations presented here are based on the Anglo-American literary tradition.

2. See the introduction to my *Late Victorian Utopias* (6 vols, Pickering & Chatto, 2008), vol. 1, pp. ix-xxxi.

REFERENCES

Bellamy, Edward. 2009. ed. Matthew Beaumont. *Looking Backward*. Oxford Classics.

Claeys, Gregory. 2016. *Dystopia: A Natural History*. Oxford: Oxford University Press.

Huxley, Aldous. 2007. *Brave New World*, ed. Margaret Atwood and David Bradshaw. New York: Vintage Books.

Kateb, George. 1972. *Utopia and its Enemies*. New York: Schocken Books.

Levin, Ira. 1970. *This Perfect Day*. New York: Random House.

Orwell, George. 1959. *The Road to Wigan Pier*. London: Secker & Warburg.

Critical Dystopia

Ildney Cavalcanti

Introduction: The Rise of the Critical Dystopia

From its initial elaborations in the 1980s to the more systematic critical attention of the early 2000s and still echoing in the present, the concept of the
critical dystopia[1] has emerged and been explored in relation to a shift in
the structural elements noticeable in dystopian narratives—more specifically
of (but not limited to) the literary type—thus providing a useful framework
to work through specific issues related to poststructuralist trends and reading
positions in a context of escalating social, economic, and environmental pressures. Although the term dystopia was coined in the eighteenth century,[2] its
usage became widespread after the publication of the classical dystopian novels
by Yevgeny Zamyatin (*We*, 1924), Aldous Huxley (*Brave New World*, 1932),
Katherine Burdekin (*Swastika Night*, 1937), and George Orwell (*Nineteen
Eighty-Four*, 1949), which accompanied the gradual dwindling of the utopian
ideals of modernity and progress resulting from the harshly violent and authoritarian political events (at times, reaching peaks of genocidal dictatorships
and totalitarian states), the devastating wars, and the environmental disasters which punctuated the last century. After the utopian resurgence of the
human rights, anti-racist, feminist, and ecological activism of the 1960s and
1970s, and following the logic of worldwide hegemonic neoliberal capitalist
and increasingly transnational tendencies that have characterized the decades
since then, economic, social, and ecological crises have erupted at an alarming

I. Cavalcanti (✉)
Federal University of Alagoas, Maceió, Brazil

P. Marks et al. (eds.), *The Palgrave Handbook of Utopian and Dystopian
Literatures*, https://doi.org/10.1007/978-3-030-88654-7_5

pace. In literature, it was during such crises that a distinct dystopian new wave emerged, requiring a different way of reading: the critical dystopia. This, in turn, triggered critics' attention to an examination of its traces. Living in the first decades of the new millennium, we have witnessed still another invasion of history and of contemporary discourse by dystopias,[3] as they reach an unprecedented peak in popularity: not only has dystopia penetrated history, but it has also turned into a major vehicle for our hopes and fears, mainly in its literary and filmic configurations. This exploration of the critical dystopia examines its emergence in scholarship and what distinguishes this mode from its classical predecessor, as we probe the meanings of the term *critical* as a distinguishing trace presented from different perspectives in the field of Utopian Studies. This is followed by a contextualization of the concept by examining Atwood's *The Handmaid's Tale* as a critical dystopia, and by observing recent deployments of the concept.

EXPANDING DYSTOPIA: REVISITING THE GENRE IN ITS CRITICAL TURN

In the second half of the last century, the usage of the word dystopia to define a narrative form portraying an alternative space–time in which social evils were highlighted was current in Anglophone literary criticism. The chronology of the form was further established and some of its contours delineated in a 1983 essay by Beauchamp, who aptly named the predecessors of the twentieth-century classical dystopias *proto-dystopias*. In the 1990s, a key move prompting the scrutiny of a renewed dystopian narrative dynamics, beyond its classical manifestation, was proposed in Lyman Tower Sargent's 1994 revision of his own taxonomy of utopian forms: "we need to think more seriously about the possibility of a 'critical dystopia'" (9). Foregrounding works like Marge Piercy's *He, She and It* (1991), which set eutopias alongside dystopias and "undermine all neat classification schemes" (7), the critic stressed the need to rethink the concept of the dystopia in terms of its critical successor, despite the oxymoronic[4] quality of the term. His insight is inspired by Tom Moylan's conceptualization of the "critical utopia," a category used to describe a new direction in utopian writing in the 1970s:

> The new novels negated the negation of utopia by the forces of twentieth-century history: the subversive imaging of utopian society and the radical negativity of dystopian perfection is preserved; while the systematizing boredom of the traditional utopia and the cooptation of utopia by modern structures is destroyed. Thus, utopian writing in the 70 s was saved by its own destruction and transformation in the 'critical utopia'. (*Demand*, 10)

Starting from this theoretical step, Sargent, thus, triggers a rich conversation regarding the critical dystopia in its complex blending of eutopian and dystopian traces, a dialogue that, having started before the publication of his essay, gained momentum following his incitement in "The Three Faces."

A shift toward transgression of the clear-cut binary views (the eutopia *versus* dystopia dichotomy) then takes place. Centered upon such renewed perception of the literary dystopias and working to consolidate the category theoretically, scholars then built different analytical approaches to the critical dystopias. Works along these lines—some of which predate Sargent's call—include Søren Baggesen (1987), Constance Penley (1986), Jenny Wolmark (1994), Ildney Cavalcanti (1999), and Raffaella Baccolini (2000). Baggesen expresses discontent with the reductionist opposition between the eutopian and the dystopian modes in writing, and suggests a distinction between "utopian" and "dystopian pessimism"[5] found in specific dystopian texts, thus constructing a more complex reading protocol. Penley, in turn, uses the term "critical dystopia" to define a futuristic narrative which "locates the origins of future catastrophe in decisions about technology, warfare and social behavior that are being made today," (116) thus requiring more complex responses from readers when faced with issues such as the exploration of subjectivities beyond the human/machine binary. From a perspective informed by feminism, Wolmark, Cavalcanti, and Baccolini further examine what they call critical dystopias in light of the interweaving of genre and gender. The contradictory subject positions available in a postmodern world, as well as issues involving identity and difference, are highlighted in Wolmark's readings. As she analyzes works by Octavia Butler, Gwyneth Jones, C.J. Cherryh, Vonda McIntyre, Suzy McKee Charnas, Sally Miller Gearhart, Sheri Tepper, Pamela Sargent, Margaret Atwood, Pat Cadigan, Rebeca Ore, Marge Piercy, and Elisabeth Vonarburg, Wolmark evidences the dissolution of the boundaries between utopia and dystopia at work in postmodernist fictions, an argument that clearly echoes Baggesen's. Alongside this analytical path, and providing readings of works by Marge Piercy, Doris Lessing, Suzy McKee Charnas, Lisa Tuttle, Suzette Elgin, Margaret Atwood, and Margaret Elphinstone, Cavalcanti, in turn, elaborates her understanding of the feminist critical dystopia, with "critical" referring to three factors: "the negative critique of patriarchy brought into effect by the dystopic principle; the textual self-awareness not only in generic terms with regard to a previous utopian literary tradition (in its feminist and non-feminist manifestations), but also concerning its own constructions of utopian 'elsewheres'"; and "in the sense that the feminist dystopias [...] may have a crucial effect in the formation or consolidation of a specifically critico-feminist public readership" (9). From a different perspective, against conclusive generic boundary demarcations, and looking at fictions by Katherine Burdekin, Margaret Atwood, and Octavia Butler, Baccolini (2000) finds in some structural generic intersections themselves—of the dystopia, the epistolary novel, the diary, and the historical novel—the *loci* of opposition as well as the opening for utopian elements. Some shared assumptions among these critics regarding the critical dystopia are: the coexistence of both utopian and dystopian traces in the works analyzed, brought into effect by a stance of militant (or utopian) pessimism[6]; the cognitive mapping of historical evils, balanced by a textually inscribed counter-narrative move of resistance; a high degree of textual self-reflexivity that strongly relies on genre self-awareness, genre blurring as well as other shared metafictional strategies (such as the emphasis on linguistic tensions and on storytelling); the activation of a utopian function regarding readers' critical response and consequent political positioning; recurring traces of gender sensitivity and class and race awareness.

Such studies paved the way for the publication of the most comprehensive examination in the realm of the critical dystopias: Tom Moylan's *Scraps of the Untainted Sky – Science Fiction, Utopia, Dystopia* (2000). This volume focuses on fictions produced in the late 1980s and 1990s[7]—Kim Stanley Robinson's *Gold Coast* (1988), Octavia Butler's *Parable of the Sower* (1993), and Marge Piercy's *He, She and It* (1991)—and provides a major source for the study of the critical dystopia because, besides minutely surveying previous scholarship on literary dystopianism, it synthesizes the concept and aligns the new dystopias with some of the formal delineations of sf—mainly their encounters with popular and feminist sf and cyberpunk—without losing sight of the very specific historical contexts in which they were engendered. Drawing from and recycling the studies mentioned above, Moylan weaves critical threads that allow him to argue that these fictions "represent a creative move that is both a continuation of the long dystopian tradition and a distinctive new intervention" (*Scraps*, 188); and that this "textual mutation [...] self-reflexively takes on the present system and offers not only astute critiques of the order of things but also explorations of the oppositional spaces and possibilities from which the next round of political activism can derive imaginative sustenance and inspiration" (xv). One of the most original points in his theoretical elaboration is his argument that "the dystopian genre has always worked along a contested continuum between utopian and anti-utopian positions: between texts that are emancipatory, militant, open, and 'critical' and those that are compensatory, resigned, and quite 'anti-critical'" (188), an idea developed from Baggesen's notions of "utopian" and "dystopian pessimism."[8] Thus, for Moylan, the critical dystopian continuation of a tradition is realized in narratives that "negotiate the social terrain of Utopia and Anti-Utopia in a less stable and more contentious fashion than many of their eutopian and anti-utopian counterparts. As a literary form that works between these historical antinomies and draws on the textual qualities of both subgenres to do so, the typical critical dystopian text is an exercise in a politically charged form of hybrid textuality, or what Raffaella Baccolini calls "'genre blurring'" (*Scraps*, 147). Insofar as he provides an extensive overview of the genre, Moylan's volume remains a key text for an understanding of the concept in that it sheds light on the iconic and discreet levels of difference regarding the classical and the critical dystopias.

ATWOOD'S *The Handmaid's Tale* AS A CRITICAL DYSTOPIA

For a closer examination of the concept, I focus on Margaret Atwood's *The Handmaid's Tale* (1985), one of the texts that has most frequently been read in alignment with this trend.[9] Atwood's novel is recognizably one of the most popular dystopias of the twentieth century, having had an immense impact on a feminist readership due to its powerful rendering of a violent and militarized theocratic state in which women are stratified according to their social roles and submitted to all men, as well as to other women of higher rank. The major narrative voice is that of Offred, who belongs to the class of the handmaids: women who, being still fertile after environmental problems have rendered most of the adult population barren, have had their humanity negated and been dispossessed to serve as surrogate mothers to the children of the elite: "We are two-legged wombs, that's all: sacred vessels, ambulatory chalices" (*The Handmaid's Tale*, 128). The novel has been awarded important prizes and adapted into a film, an opera, a movie show, a graphic novel.[10] Its sequel, *The Testaments*, came out in 2019. It has reached renewed popularity lately, especially in response to the re-emergence of the extremist right-wing political wave noticeable all over the world in the past decades, as well as a consequence of worldwide reach of streaming shows in our time. It offers, thus, an appropriate choice of text to illustrate the concept of the critical dystopia.

As early as 1989, in one of the initial surveys of feminist utopianism, Bartkowski called readers' attention to a renewed mode in the rhetoric of hope—after the global changes that marked the ideology of the New Right—that had rendered the earlier rhetoric of the feminist utopias of the 1970s and early 1980s naive. In her analysis, she argues for the ambivalent quality of Atwood's dystopia and points out, with reference to Offred's speech, that there is "hope in the register of an enslaved female voice in fiction" (*Feminist utopias*, 135). This evidences her perception of the oscillation between the utopian and anti-utopian poles negotiated by the critical dystopias, but still without naming the category (which would happen later). Actually, in a similar direction, Wolmark remarks the following: "As a critical dystopia, *The Handmaid's Tale* is not concerned to portray the inevitability and awfulness of a future in which patriarchy has become fully totalitarian. Instead, the kind of extrapolation used in the novel alerts us to the necessity to rethink the forms which contemporary gender relations take" (*Alien and Others*, 107).[11] She stresses the narrator's memories of her life in the pre-Gilead regime (the time equivalent to the historical period of the novel's publication, marked by the cultural backlash in face of the increasing impact and achievements regarding the feminist policies of the previous decades), which are then juxtaposed by the narration of Offred's "present" (the "future" for contemporary readers in the mid-1980s), living in "reduced circumstances" (*The Handmaid's Tale*, 8). For Wolmark, this narrative detail "suggests that ambivalence toward feminism on the part of women has in part been responsible for the ascendency of the repressive politics of the New Right" (105). Some of the women had actually supported—or been indifferent to, as was Offred's case—the rise of an extremist and dominant masculinity. While opening space to provoke some negative feminist criticism (if one thinks of the reading position of a feminist subject eager for role-models), this strategic use of narrative voice helps build the political consciousness of the necessary resistance in the face of conservative agendas. Contextualizing the novel from our contemporary moment, its continued impact is evident in readers' responses via cultural criticism and public manifestations all over the world.[12] Besides street activism, reader responses to feminist sf have also taken creative routes, as is the case of imaginactivism, detailed by Haran in relation to Octavia Butler's and Starhawk's fictions (Imaginativismo, 33).

Corroborating Wolmark's point, Baccolini and Cavalcanti, in their turn, also consider gender-marked traces in Atwood's work and further probe its feminist critical quality by focusing on the novel's critique of patriarchal culture—whose exaggerated portrayal is a trace of its satirical vein—and on its self-reflexive and metafictional qualities, but do so from different, but interrelated, perspectives. While Baccolini stresses genre blurring as a subversive strategy explored by Atwood, Cavalcanti explores the tensions in the uses of language in the novel's three diagetic blocks—Offred's narration, the historical notes and the novel as a whole through its extradiegetic level: that is, its heterodiegetic prism or "public" narration. Their readings similarly stress the narrative strategies of genre blurring and multifocal perspective as the formal qualities that allow for a categorization of *The Handmaid's Tale* as a critical dystopia. For Baccolini, an "impure" text is more likely to allow for a "multi-oppositional" stance (Gender and Genre, 18); Cavalcanti, in her turn, considers that Offred's space *of* and *off* narration (situated beyond the novelistic frame) inscribes, at the same time, a utopian "elsewhere" in which the feminist subject can articulate, by means of her "recorded" narration, her desires and fears, as well as the paradoxical semiotic condition regarding utopia's "absent presence" (*Articulating*, 185). Interestingly, Moylan reads the novel as a transitional work, situated between the classic and the critical dystopia (*Scraps*, 2000); whereas the feminist readings argue for its critical quality.

(Re)Deploying the Concept: From Genre to Mode

While Moylan highlights that the fictional works he defines as critical dystopias are "distinct products of their time and express the political and aesthetic conditions of that time" (he is referring to the US culture in the 1980s and 1990s, as well as to the conservative turn in the Thatcher–Reagan–Gorbachev era), his theories have been instrumental for (re)thinking utopianism far beyond that specific context.

Prompted by these ideas, academics have produced a body of criticism that has helped crystalize the concept, as well as extend its reach.

Illustrative of this trend are the critical texts collected in Baccolini and Moylan's *Dark Horizons: Science Fiction and the Dystopian Imagination* (2003)—which functions as a sister volume to *Scraps*—and Vieira's *Dystopia(n) Matters – On the Page, on Screen, on Stage* (2013), which stretch the possibilities of reading the critical dystopias regarding the *corpus* studied and the context of production, furthering the understanding that this theoretical framework need not be limited to the boundaries of a specific literary genre. This critical work embraces cultural expressions (such as films, plays, and histories, to name some) which have been produced and circulate in different formats and *media*, in myriad contexts and experiences. A survey of the topic shows that scholars have recycled the concept flexibly in order to shed light on publishing genres as varied as graphic novels, video games, metal music, TV series, artistic experiments,[13] besides the mainstream and popular sf narratives in the form of novels and short stories. In general, this scholarship follows the major analytical moves outlined above insofar as they deal with a dystopian mode that is no longer characterized by the closure observed in the classical dystopian form, suggesting an oppositional stance and an opening up of a horizon of hope. In the face of the range of cultural media that has appeared, reading protocols have been updated and are no longer fully dependent on the generic structural traces initially studied as characteristic of the critical dystopian literary fictions and film. Writing precisely about this point in her introduction to *Dystopia(n) Matters*, Vieira emphasizes "the operability of the concept of critical dystopia" (7) when she assesses the multifaceted ways in which the contributors (re)activate it in their critical pieces. Thus, it seems clear that, despite still being operable in regard to the literary genre, reading approaches to the critical dystopia have moved in the direction of a critical dystopian mode, inscribed in different artistic and cultural forms.

Conclusion: The Critical Dystopia Meets Intersectionality, Decoloniality, and the Anthropocene

If totalitarianism, or imaginative surrender to its inevitability, somehow lies at the core of the upsurge of classical dystopias; as does late corporate capitalism and the backlash at that of critical dystopias, a note remains to be made concerning the reconfigurations of dystopian expressions in response to the recent critical moves provoked by the intersectional, decolonial, and anthropocene-informed views debated in the arenas of feminism, gender and queer studies, ecocriticism, critical race studies, and others, Margaret Atwood's *MaddAddam* trilogy (2003–2013), Cormac McCarthy's *The Road* (2006), Jeanette Winterson's *The Stone Gods* (2007), Kim Stanley Robinson's *New York 2140* (2017) are among the narratives that have fuelled the debate. Responding to our contemporary imaginaries, these fictions have sharpened readers' perceptions by dramatizing the depiction of apocalyptic, post-apocalyptic, eco-catastrophic, technoscientific, and posthumanist themes in our century. As expected, such dystopian reconfigurations have brought about reflections on the possibility of derivational successors to the critical dystopias. However, despite some contentions in favor of a "third turn" in the history of dystopias,[14] the arguments raised so far have not justified any important theoretical maneuvers in relation to this narrative mode, that still provides a picture of the darkest possibilities regarding social, political, and environmental issues, without losing the spark of hope for a better space–time. Finally, it should be stressed that, due to its sharply critical edge, the critical dystopian mode still offers contemporary literature, film, art, and other media an opportunity to intervene in respect of the concrete problems in the contemporary world (issues including social injustice, climate change, species extinction, gender regulations, and racial prejudice). In his major study of the emergence of "new maps of hell," Moylan appropriately remarks that "dystopian stories of violent and unjust societies can [...] provide a creative take on the problems of the current social order as well as on possibilities for political moves against and beyond it" (*Scraps*, 145). Thus, reassessing the critical dystopia from our (still) dark times may provide ways of "staying with the trouble," to use Haraway's expression, in order to not only survive, but to anticipate politically just and ecologically balanced space-times.

NOTES

1. Also named *flawed dystopia* (Suvin 2003), *open dystopia* (Baccolini and Moylan 2003), *transgressive utopian dystopias* (Mohr 2007).
2. Cf. Chuanacháin 2013.
3. Cf. Vieira ed. 2013; Claeys 2017.
4. In his problematization of the terminology to be used in its definition, Sargent questions the plausibility of the critical dystopia and, because all dystopias are "critical," whether "it is simply an oxymoron" (The three faces, 9). However, grammatically speaking, the usage of the term suggests a doubling, a building in of redundancy, or the addition of a meta-level of critique.
5. Moylan proposes "utopian" and "anti-utopian pessimism" as a more effective designation. Cf. his argumentation in *Scraps*, 153–154.
6. Cf. note 4 above.
7. Moylan positions Atwood's *The handmaid's tale* as a predecessor to the critical dystopia (*Scraps*, 188). And in their introduction to *Dark Horizons*, Baccolini and Moylan state that Atwood's novel "directly drew on the classical dystopian narrative even as if it interrogated its limits and suggested new directions" (3). From my own perspective, this interrogation marks in itself the work's critical quality.

8. Moylan prefers the designation "anti-utopian pessimism" for the latter, in order to avoid confusion, since both types of pessimism are present in dystopian narrative.

9. *See*, for example, readings by Wolmark (1994), Cavalcanti (1999, 2000), Baccolini (2000), Mohr (2005, 2007, using "transgressive utopian dystopia," instead of "critical dystopia," but to ta similar effect), Tolan (2007), Cojocaru (2015), Van de Neste (2018).

10. The novel won the 1985 *Governor General's Award* and the first *Arthur C. Clark Award* in 1987. Among the many prizes awarded to the TV series are four 2017 Emmy awards and two 2018 Golden Globes. For its adaptations, cf. *The Handmaid's Tale* film, directed by Volker Schlöndorf, 1990; the opera, composed by Poul Ruders to a libretto by Paul Bentley, premiered in Kopenhagen on March, 6, 2000; the TV series, produced by Bruce Miller, Hulu streaming released on April, 26, 2017; the graphic novel, art and adaptation by Renée Nault, published by Doubleday, 2019.

11. This point gets very close to Penley's, discussed above, thus helping construct one of the meanings of "critical" as that element which activates a conscious reader response.

12. The handmaid's outfit has become a sign of feminist resistance: "People all over the world are wearing red cloaks and white bonnets to protest various injustices, particularly regarding women's rights" (*New Media*).

13. Although examples are too many to be listed here, the following illustrations, drawn from publications in English and in Portuguese, will do as a sample: Taylor (2006) listens to the recorded texts of the metal bands VOLvod and Fear Factory, whose style she names "cyber metal," for their preoccupation with technology in subject matter and in sound, arguing that they "represent prime examples of the critical dystopia in metal music"; Loy examines Allan Moore and David Lloyd's *V for Vendetta*, besides other narrative genres, in his *Anarchy in Critical Dystopias: An Anatomy of Rebellion* (2008); Schulzek (2014) "explores the capacity of video games and virtual worlds to function as critical utopias or dystopias"; Cavalcanti (2015) approximates multimedia artist Vik Muniz's experiment that resulted in the photography series "Pictures of Garbage" to the critical dystopian strategies. Lopes (2018) approaches *Black Mirror* from the perspectives of the canonical and the critical dystopias and, by looking specifically at the episode "Nosedive," stresses that the critically dystopian trace in that episode lies in the effect it may trigger upon the audience.

14. *See*, for instance, Chang (2011) for commentaries on the insufficiency of the concept of the critical dystopia for reading contemporary dystopian fictions. On a contrary move, Jennings (2013) and Fortunato (2018) still activate it in their readings.

References

Atwood, Margaret. 1986. *The Handmaid's Tale*. Boston: Houghton Mifflin Company. [1985]

Baccolini, Raffaella. 2000. Gender and Genre in the Feminist Critical Dystopias of Katherine Burdekin, Margaret Atwood and Octavia Butler. In *Future Females, the Next Generation: New Voices and Velocities in Feminist Science Fiction*, ed. Marleen Barr, 13–34. Boston: Rowman and Littlefield.

Baccolini, Raffaella, and Tom Moylan, eds. 2003. *Dark Horizons: Science Fiction and the Dystopian Imagination*. London: Routledge.

Baggesen, Søren. 1987. Utopian and Dystopian Pessimism: Le Guin's *The Word for World is Forest* and Tiptree's "We Who Stole the Dream". *Science Fiction Studies* 14: 34–43.

Bartkowski, Frances. 1989. *Feminist Utopias*. Lincoln and London: University of Nebraska Press.

Beauchamp, Gorman. 1983. The Proto-Dystopia of Jerome K. Jerome. *Extrapolation* 24.2: 170–181.

Cavalcanti, Ildney. 1999. *Articulating the Elsewhere: Utopia in Contemporary Feminist Dystopias*. PhD thesis. Glasgow, University of Strathclyde.

———. 2015. Da Terra Desolada ao Deslocamento da Utopia: As Mobilidades do Experimento de Vik Muniz. 2015. In *Os Retornos da Utopia: Histórias, Imagens, Experiências*, ed. Alfredo Cordiviola and Ildney Cavalcanti, 211–234. Maceió, Edufal.

———. 2000. Utopias of/f Language in Contemporary Feminist Dystopias. *Utopian Studies* 11 (2): 152–180.

Chang, Hui-Chuan. 2011. Critical Dystopia Reconsidered: Octavia Butler's *Parable* Series and Margaret Atwood's *Oryx and Crake* as Post-apocalyptic Dystopias. *Tamkang Review* 41: 2.

Chuanacháin, Deirdre. 2013. *Utopianism in Eighteenth-Century England*. PhD thesis. University of Limerick.

Claeys, Gregory. 2017. *Dystopia: A Natural History*. Oxford: Oxford U. P.

Cojocaru, Daniel. 2015. *Violence and Dystopia: Mimesis and Sacrifice in Contemporary Western Dystopian Narratives*. Newcastle upon Tyne: Cambridge Scholars Publishing.

Fortunato, Pedro. 2018. Representações Utópicas e Distópicas na Trilogia *MaddAddam*, de Margaret Atwood. MA thesis. Universidade Federal de Alagoas.

Haran, Joan. 2018. Imaginativismo: explorações do impulso utópico dos feminismos da ficção científica e do ativismo do/a leitor/a/escritor/a. *Revista Morus – Utopia e Renascimento* 13, 29 June 2019. http://www.revistamorus.com.br/index.php/morus/article/view/336/310

Jennings, Hope. 2013. A Repeating World: Redeeming the Past and Future in the Utopian Dystopia of Jeanette Winterson's *The Stone Gods*. *Interdisciplinary Humanities* 27 (2): 132–146.

Lopes, Juliana. 2018. Is There Any Way Out? *Black Mirror* as a Critical Dystopia of the Society of the Spectacle. *Via Panoramica: Revista de Estudos Anglo-Americanos* 7 (2): 85–94.

Loy, Taylor Andrew. 2008. *Anarchy in Critical Dystopias: An Anatomy of Rebellion*. M.A. Thesis. Virginia Polytechnic Institute and State University.

Mohr, Dunja M. 2007. Transgressive Utopian Dystopias: The Postmodern Reappearance of Utopia in the Disguise of Dystopia. *ZAA* 55 (1): 5–24.

———. 2005. *Worlds Apart? Dualism and Transgression in Contemporary Female Dystopias.* Jefferson and London: McFarland & Coompany Inc.

Moylan, Tom. 1986. *Demand the impossible: Science fiction and the utopian imagination.* New York and London: Methuen.

———. 2000. *Scraps of the Untainted Sky: Science Fiction, Utopia.* Dystopia: Boulder, Westview Press.

New Media Activism Insights. 2018. The Handmaid's Tale-Inspired Protests. http://wpmu.mah.se/nmict182group7/the-handmaids-tale-inspired-protest/. Accessed 29 June 2019.

Penley, Constance. 1986. Time Travel, Primal Scene, and the Critical Dystopia. In ed. Annette Kuhn, *Alien zone: Cultural Theory and Contemporary Science Fiction Cinema.* London and New York: Verso.

Sargent, Lyman Tower. 1994. The Three Faces of Utopianism Revisited. *Utopian Studies* 5 (1): 1–37.

Schulzke, Marcus. 2014. The critical power of virtual dystopias. *Games and Culture.* 9 (5): 315–334 (July).

Taylor, Laura. 2006. *Metal Music as Critical Dystopia: Humans, Technology and the Future in 1990s Science Fiction Metal.* PhD diss.: Brock University.

Tolan, Fiona. 2007. *Margaret Atwood - Feminism and Fiction.* Amsterdam, Rodopi.

Van de Neste, Tara. 2018. Female dystopias as a Warning. 29 June 2019 https://lib.ugent.be/fulltxt/RUG01/002/479/035/RUG01-002479035_2018_0001_AC.pdf

Vieira, Fátima., ed. 2013. *Dystopia(n) Matters: On the Page, on Screen, on Stage.* Cambridge Scholars Publishing: Newcastle upon Tyne.

Wolmark, Jenny. 1994. *Alien and Others: Science Fiction, Feminism and Postmodernism.* New York: Harvester Wheatsheaf.

Historical Contexts

Prefigurations

Francisco L. Lisi

INTRODUCTION

Thomas More's invention of the word *utopia* points to the book's fictional character. No actual political effect was intended. Over its long reception history, the word achieved a much broader meaning, including standing for political projects and vague aspirations of justice and freedom. In this chapter, I take it as a consciously fictional narration of an ideal state in which justice and the negation of the individual interests are at the heart of the social organization. That organization is the product of human politics and not the result of divine action; rather, it is based on human knowledge and labor. As a countermodel of existing realities, it is supposed to be realizable for human beings. Therefore, it has to be strictly distinguished from simply paradisiac tales such as the existence of a Cockaigne, where human labor is non-existent and extraordinary geographical and climatic conditions make life easier.[1] While utopia proper belongs to modernity, there were significant antecedents, which paved the way for *Utopia*'s extraordinary impact in the political thought of western civilization.

F. L. Lisi (✉)
Universidad Carlos III de Madrid, Madrid, Spain

P. Marks et al. (eds.), *The Palgrave Handbook of Utopian and Dystopian Literatures*, https://doi.org/10.1007/978-3-030-88654-7_6

GREEK DESCRIPTIONS OF MODEL STATES

We know several descriptions of model states existing in Greece during the fifth and fourth centuries B.C. They emerged as a result of the discussion about the best form of political regime, whose first written testimony occurs in Herodotus (3: 80–82). In the epitaph, which Thucydides puts in Pericles' mouth, the politician gives also an idealized version of the Athenian constitution (2: 34–46). According to Pericles, in Athens rules an egalitarian democracy that fosters happiness, virtue, justice, and freedom among his citizens. Pericles' speech has probably the goal of praising the Athenian model in opposition to other views like Xenophon's *Lacedaemonian Constitution* or the anonymous *Athenian Constitution*, which, originating in oligarchic circles, praised the Spartan political regime and reviled democracy. The works coming from the oligarchic circles projected an image of Sparta as an ideal political regime that contributed to the enormous prestige accorded the Lacedaemonian system, especially after its victory in the Peloponnesian war. The idealization of the oligarchic regimes can be observed in the preserved title of Critias' work, *Measured Constitutions* (*politeiai emmetrai*; DK 88 [81] A 22). In Athens, both parties, oligarchs, and democrats, considered the Solonian constitution the best possible organization of a state. It was called the "constitution of the fathers" (*patrios politeia*). Plato's *Menexenus* and Isocrates' *Panathenaicus* are two examples of many of the esteem the intellectuals felt for it. The political system of old Athens is for Plato good (*kale*). He characterizes it as an aristocracy called democracy. It is "an aristocracy with a good reputation by the multitude" (*Menexenus* 238d). These encomia should not be mixed with texts nearer to our present notion of utopia: the descriptions of existing political systems and projects of reform of the existing constitutions. Many works are now lost, while Epimenides, Critias and Thrasymachus and the Pythagoreans wrote descriptions of existing constitutions. Two examples of such writings are transmitted in the *corpus Xenophonteum*: the Athenian and the Lacedaemonian constitutions.

The first concrete mention of projects of reform for achieving the best possible constitution is transmitted by Aristotle's *Politics*. Their main goal was to avoid revolts in the city through an order more just. Phaleas of Chalcedon proposed a system, which equalized the citizen's goods through marriage according to which the rich had to pay dowry (II 7, 1266a, 39-b5) The second basic factor for reaching equality was, for Phaleas, education (b 32–33). Aristotle also mentions another important social reformer, Hippodamus of Miletus (7, 1267b, 22–1268a15), who wrote a treatise *On Constitution*. His project planned a city of 10,000 inhabitants divided into three categories: artisans, peasants, and warriors. The country was also divided into three parts: sacred (devoted to the gods), public (for maintaining the warriors) and private (attributed to the farmers). He proposed also a reorganization of the penal code and a democratic system, in which the citizenship participated in the election of the magistrates. The main goal of both reform projects is the establishment of justice among citizens. They represent the first testimony of the use of political art as an instrument for the improvement of human life.

To this group, we should add Plato's social projects presented in the *Republic* and the *Laws*. Plato considered Callipolis, the city described in the *Republic*, as the social embodiment of the form of justice. Its population was divided into two main classes, producers and warriors. The latter was selected and educated to defend the independence of the city against foreign enemies and to respect communal norms. From them emerged the best individuals, who were to receive the highest education and arrive at the contemplation of the highest Form, the Idea of the Good. After numerous proofs, they had to overcome the last and most important one when they turned fifty years old: the exercise of absolute power over five years. If they demonstrated a just and equilibrate exercise of power, they were definitively incorporated in the circle of the ruling philosophers. The members of the ruling class in all their spheres (warriors and philosopher-kings) do not have any property and live like a family practicing communism, sharing all properties, women and children included. This is an aristocratic system, where a philosopher exercises absolute power during an undetermined period. The idea of absolute communism had a major impact on the history of utopian thought, even if the sharing of women and children was not accepted during the period in which Christendom predominated.[2]

Magnesia,[3] described in Plato's *Laws*, accepted private property and a more balanced scheme of power, a mixture of democracy, oligarchy, and monarchy, in which the oligarchic is predominant. At the top of the structure, Plato puts an institution, the nocturnal council, which exercises the functions of the philosopher-kings in the *Republic*. The basis of the community is now the family and there is a strict regulation of the relations of property that is not private, but familiar. The polis is constituted by 5040 households divided into four classes according to their wealth. Possession of gold or silver is not allowed and only a kind of money without value outside Magnesia is permitted for making possible the exchange with the foreigners working as artisans or practicing commerce on the market. The institutions are similar to the existing in the Greek city-states, especially at Athens, albeit Magnesia is conceived as a preponderantly Dorian colony.

Callipolis and Magnesia follow the reformist tradition of the political thinkers of the classical world. They are models of the best possible organizations of a typical Greek institution, the polis, and neither have nor pretend to have a universal character. The same is true of Aristotle's constitution described in the seventh and eighth book of the *Politics*. Unfortunately, this constitution has been preserved in a fragmentary form, since the eighth book is interrupted at the beginning. In the seventh book, Aristotle discusses the theoretical principles which are the foundation of the best state. His proximity to Plato's *Laws* is evident in most of the details. He also proposes an aristocratic state where the warriors and the so-called "deliberative part" constitute the ruling city.

Peasants, artisans, and workers do not share governance (VII 9, 1328b24–1329a39). As in Plato's *Laws*, the land workers are slaves (10, 1330a25–9). In other aspects, however, Aristotle introduces innovations, stressing the advantages of the proximity to the sea and the utility of a city wall. The eighth book is devoted to education. Aristotle follows the traditional Platonic view which distinguishes between two kinds of education, one general and other more specialized. It is likely that he also provided a more "philosophical" education for the rulers.

A Platonic dialogue describing two states nearer to our concept of utopia occurs in the *Critias*, probably one of the main sources of inspiration for the utopian genre. The *Critias* is also a supposed fragmentary text because it interrupts abruptly just at the moment when the main speaker begins to tell the story of the war between Athens and Atlantis.[4] Both cities were the expression of the best possible state ruled by humans. The Athenians were direct survivors of the people living in the period of Cronos when men were immediately ruled by gods (*Critias* 109d; cf. *Statesman* 269c–274e1). Athens had the political structure described in the *Republic*. Nevertheless, the most interesting case for the utopian tradition is Atlantis, the disappeared island ruled by the descendants of Poseidon. The country had extraordinary conditions and a rich and extensive territory from which they administrated their maritime empire. Their aggression lasted for a long period since they menaced Europe's and especially Athens' freedom. The latter had to face Atlantis for preventing their own and Europe's slavery.

THE HELLENISTIC DESCRIPTIONS
OF IDEAL POLITICAL REGIMES

After the city lost its independence as an autonomous political organization, reform projects of the political circumstances continued to be an object of philosophical reflection among the Stoics, as it is shown by the works with the title *Republic* written by Zenon and Chrysippus. According to Plutarch, Zenon wrote his *Republic* against Plato's dialogue (*On the Stoics Self-Contradictions* 8, 1038 f. = SVF I 260). The few testimonies preserved of Zenon's writing do not let us know very much about its substance. It seems that it was a project praising the universal common-law (SVF 262), but which could be followed only by the best people (*spoudaioi*; SVF I 222). It is not clear whether Zenon defended a universal state because in the much-debated fragment 262 only the existence of a common natural law is expressed with certainty. Between the second half of the fourth and the first half of the third century B.C. appeared many writings describing travels to distant countries where marvelous people lived. These works are usually grouped in a literary genre, the *staatsroman*, which sometimes is identified with the genre of utopia. The genre definition of the *staatsromans* is blurred given that not only stories about idealized civilizations usually are included in it, but also political projects without any relation to the literary genre of roman, such as Plato's *Republic* or

Laws. To these could be added writings that their authors considered historical works as is the case with Xenophon's *Cyropaedy* or Theopompus' *Meropis*, written around 300 B.C.[5]

EUHEMERUS' SACRED HISTORY

Nearer to our former definition of utopia comes the description of a city on the island of Panchaea in Euhemerus' *Sacred History*. Through Diodorus Siculus, we have Euhemerus' account of the voyage he made to the Arabic countries following the order of the Macedonian King Cassander (305-ca 298 BCE). That Diodorus read and took excerpts from Euhemerus' book can be concluded from his testimony (6: 1: 11) and from an indirect testimony that attributes to Euhemerus the theology in the same book and chapter.[6] In its present state, the text cannot be considered a fragmentary quotation, but rather an abstract whose style and content were adapted by Diodorus Siculus. The texts present many structural inconsistencies that occasioned misinterpretations. From Diodorus' presentation of life in Panchaea it is not clear whether the text refers to the whole island or mainly to the city of Panara.[7] I am convinced that the description is related only to Panara, the main city of Panchaea. The city was the only one on the island which had an independent structure of government consisting of three archons elected for a period of a year and governing about all issues except in the decisions on death penalties, which were decided by the priests (5: 42: 5). Apparently, Diodorus has disregarded some important parts of Euhemerus' texts, since at 45: 2 he interrupts the geographical description of the island beginning at 41: 1 and returns to its political organization. He has now forgotten Panara and mentions three important cities on the island, Hyparkia, Dalis, and Oceanis (45: 2). The following text seems to adapt better as a continuation of the former description of the temple of Zeus Trifylius which crowned the exposition of the political regime at Panara.[8] The society now described is a community of warriors using old war techniques (45: 2) divided into three classes. The priests are now the leaders with power for deciding litigations and all public issues. They constitute the highest class together with the artisans. The members of the second class are the farmers. The third class is composed of the warriors and the herdsmen. Both farmers and herdsmen give their production to the priests who distribute it among the population and keep the double portion for themselves (45: 5). As von Pöhlmann rightly observed more than 100 years ago, there is no common property in the described *politeia*.[9] They possess private houses and gardens; only the production is shared by the whole population and is distributed according to what the classical Greeks would call "geometrical justice." Although they do not have money, the garments and sumptuous way of life of the priests clearly show the stratification of society and suggest the existence of private property.

Diodorus Siculus preserves the abstract of another writer of fantastic voyages to marvelous territories, Jambulus. There is no other mention of this author, except a fleeting reference in Lucianus' *True Stories* (1: 3: 3–8).[10] His story of the Islands of the Sun has given rise to a wide hermeneutic phantasy, from its supposed abolition of the contradiction between hand and intellectual work (in terms very similar to the Marxist view)[11] to its consecration as the quintessence of a supposed Greek utopian tradition.[12] This story has been compared to Plato's *Critias*.[13] The text was probably written between the second and the first century B.C.[14] Diodorus' abstract (2: 55–60) suggests that Jambulus' book was mainly the description of his vicissitudes told in the first person including a description of at least one marvelous land.[15] After a voyage of four months from Ethiopia, Jambulus and his travel companions arrive in a group of islands dwelled on by humans of a very superior nature (56: 2–6). The nature of the island is also marvelous. The climate is benign (56: 7–57: 1). The land is fertile and with plenty of exotic and edible fruits and animals as well as abundant water (57: 2–3, 58: 2–5, 59: 1–4). They have a temperate way of life, organized in family and groups of no more than 400 houses (57: 1). They live mainly in the meadows, sharing their goods and alternating in the necessary work. They have writing, education, and practice at least one kind of knowledge, astrology (57: 3). About their social organization, we read only that the communities are organized as a family, where women are shared and the children are raised together trying to avoid their parents recognizing their sons. The result is a great unity of the social structure. The leadership is exerted by the oldest member of the community in a kind of absolute monarchy (58: 5). The leader commits suicide when he reaches 150 years and is succeeded by the oldest man in the community. Crippled and unworthy members of the community are eliminated. Nothing is said about the existence of slavery. These are the scarce data given by Diodorus' presentation. It belongs probably to a short story in a collection of marvelous adventures. The account has echoes of the Greek tradition of the abolition of the family and the sharing of women, who are considered the property of the men.

From the Terrestrial City to the Celestial One

The Roman elites were strongly influenced by Greek culture. However, the individualism and practical sense of the Roman people seem to have prevented a deep impact of the fictional stories forged by the Greeks on the Latin culture. Ennius had composed a book entitled *Euhemerus* which probably was a translation or an adaptation of Euhemerus' work.[16] It is obvious that in Rome, especially in the classical and Augustan era, there were echoes of the Greek myths of a paradisiac time under the rule of Saturnus/Cronus.[17] Greek bucolic poetry had a wide impact on Roman literature of the period. However, the description of a past or future epoch of happiness cannot be considered utopian in a proper sense. Romans looked to their past as an example of good governance. This is the case of Cicero's *Republic* and *Laws*, which tried to emulate Plato's homonymous dialogues. Cicero did not propose an idea of a society not yet existing, but rather the re-establishment of the old Roman order, the incarnation of natural law. His works aim at proposing a concrete reform of the Roman republic. He does not believe they are the picture of a utopian world, but are a concrete plan for the reformation of the existing corruption through the reinstatement of the ancient order. Rome is the expression of the best possible political order and there was no place for ideal polities,[18] at least among the Roman and Greek elite. Nevertheless, there was the irruption of oriental religions, and especially of Judaism and Christendom, which contributed to the expansion of a new kind of fiction: the arrival of a new paradisiac era at the end of time.

The fall of Rome in 410 opened a crisis and the traditional forces saw the defeat as a consequence of abandoning the traditional gods and embracing Christendom as the official religion of the Empire. In the early fifth century, the bishop of Hippo, Aurelius Augustine, wrote a work destined to become a cornerstone of the Western thought, the *City of God against the Pagans*. Augustine opposed the corrupted terrestrial city of the followers of error and Devil to the celestial one of the followers of Christ. At the end of time in the Last Judgement, the members of the terrestrial city will be punished and the Christians will be recompensed in the celestial kingdom after the end of the world (Books 21 and 22). Augustine's work cannot be considered a utopia, but it shows a tendency central to the Middle Age: the hope for a better world at the end of time caused the general expectation of the Last Judgement and the Paradise, the real better world beyond this world.[19] Nevertheless, the ancient Greek tradition of projecting marvelous cities to the limits of the known world continues in some stories as the letter of Prester John, bishop of a supposed capital of India, inhabited by very faithful Christians (Zarncke 1879, 24f.). Prester John's version of the life in Hulna is a projection of the life in Paradise in this world as the insistent mention of the river Physon shows.[20] Similar is Joachim's of Fiore prophecy about the Third Empire, Age or State where humanity would live in an eternal state of grace. According to Joachim, the monks will lead the society in the Third Age and will be the depositories of the divine grace.[21] These ideas cannot be considered utopias in a proper sense, according to the definition we have adopted in this study. They are prophecies, not utopias.[22] In the Middle Ages the versions of a better epoch were connected to the reign of a particular ruler.[23] However, the existence of a good ruler, whose happy time ended with his death, cannot be considered a utopia.

Conclusion

All the texts and intellectual movements we have considered can be characterized as pre-figurations of the utopian genre, in so far as they exhibit many features that occur in Thomas More's book. Nevertheless, the English High Lord Chancellor created the new genre by applying his ironical distance, initiating something that would be immensely influential in Modern Europe.[24]

The hypothesis defended in this chapter affirms that the literary genre of utopia is a typical phenomenon of the modern age and cannot be projected to the different descriptions of better circumstances, which occurred before the publishing of Thomas More's book in 1516. The deep impact of *Utopia* in the history of political ideas shows a new human attitude. This implies technological and scientific progress that makes real the possibility of creating the events for attaining a better world.[25] For that, a new vision of history was necessary.

Acknowledgements I thank the revisers and editors of the book for their help in the form and content of this chapter.

Notes

1. For the difference between Cockaigne and modern utopia, cf. Frantisek Graus, 1967, Social Utopias in the Middle Ages. *Past & Present* 38: 9 f; and Moses Finley, 1967, Utopianism Ancient and Modern, in *The Critical Spirit. Essays in Honor of Herbert Marcuse*, ed. Kurt H. Wolff and Barrington Moore Jr., 3–20, Boston: Beacon Press, 6 f.
2. See Mario Vegetti, ed., 1998/2007, Platone, *La Repubblica. Traduzione e commento a cura di M. V.* Tracassa, Napoli: Bibliopolis.
3. See Friedrich Kleinwächter, 1891, *Die Staatsromane. Ein Beitrag zur Lehre vom Kommunismus und Socialismus*, Wien. Contrary to Kleinwächter's opinion (28–32), Plato's *Laws* are not a *staatsroman*, simply because they do not describe a political community in the fiction as actually existing. The same can be stated concerning Callipolis (cf. 36–41), which is only a very vague description of a political structure. Callipolis, contrary to Magnesia, does not even have a specific location. See also Christopher J. Bobonich, 2002, *Plato's Utopia Recast. His Later Ethics and Politics*, Oxford: Oxford University Press. The above criticism is also valid for all the attempts to characterize both works as a utopia, as Bobonich does.
4. There are many hypotheses about the actual reason for the abrupt interruption of the story. Some scholars believe that during the transmission of the text the missing parts were lost. Others think that Plato could not finish the text before his death. Finally, some suppose that the interruption is intentional because Plato did not like to expose Athenian infractions just on the feast of the patron goddess of the city.
5. As is the case in, for example, Kleinwächter (1891).
6. In spite of the general agreement that the text is a direct quotation of Euhemerus' book, no indication of it can be found in the story told by Diodorus. We do not know whether it is a paraphrase, a quotation or an excerpt. Therefore, Honigman's (2009) reconstruction of Euhemerus' book is not based on Diodorus' testimony. On the reception of Euhemerus among the historians cf. Brown (1946).

7. Cf. Marek Winiarcyzk, 2013, *The* Sacred History *of Euhemerus of Messene*. Beiträge zur Altertumskunde 312. Berlin: De Gruyter. Contrary to Winiarcyzk's claim, *abasileutos* cannot mean "not subject to any authority."

8. Also, the three archons are now forgotten, but it does not need to be contradictory to the former description of the political reality in Panara, which was very incomplete.

9. Contrary to Winiarcyzk's opinion (2013, 74), the Greek text does not allow us to suppose the existence of communism.

10. Cf. Widu-Wolfgang Ehlers, 1985, Mit dem Sudwestmonsum nach Ceylon. Eine Interpretation der Iambul-Exzerpte Diodors. *Würzburger Jahrbücher für die Altertumswissenschaft* N. F. 11: 74.

11. Cf. Robert Von Pöhlmann, 1925, *Geschichte der sozialen Frage und des Sozialismus in der antiken Welt*, 2nd edition, München: C. H. Beck'sche Verlagsbuchhandlung: II. 305–324. This influential view was followed by Ernst Bloch 1959, *Das Prinzip Hoffnung*. Suhrkamp Taschenbuchwissenschaft 3, Frankfurt a. M.: Suhrkamp, 568–569. For an accurate criticism of von Pöhlmann's view, cf. Ehlers (1985, 81–82). Bloch's book produced an inadmissible extension of the concept of utopia as it can be observed e.g. in Flashar 1974, Koch 1979 and Bichler 1984, among many others. In such approaches, the distinction between utopia and practical political projects is completely lost as it happens, as, for example, in Diego de Brasi, 2007, Platone, padre dell'utopia? *Les Études Classiques* 79: 207–226.

12. Winston 176.

13. Cf. Jesús Lens Tuero and Pedro Pablo Fuentes González, 2000, Iamboulos, in *Dictionnaire des philosophes Antiques* 840–853, III, Paris: CNRS Éditions, 847, 849.

14. Cf. David Winston, 1976, Iambulus "Islands of the Sun" and Hellenistic Literary Utopias, *Science-Fiction Studies* 3 (3): 219.

15. Winston's (1976, 219–221) attempt to reconstruct and organize the supposed structure of the writing is not only unconvincing but also methodologically wrong. See also, Erwin Rohde, 1900. *Der griechische Roman und seine Vorläufer*, 2nd edition, Leipzig: Breitkopf und Härtel; and Ehlers (1985). Rohde's (243n1) interpretation of Diodorus' abstract is much more convincing than Ehlers (75–76). Diodorus respected neither the style nor the structure of Iambulus' book.

16. Cf. Lactantius, *Divine Institutions* 1: 13.

17. As it is the case of Virgil's fourth Eclogue or Ovid's *Metamorphoses* 1: 80–112.

18. See, Frank E. Manuel and Fritzie P. Manuel, 1960, *Utopian Thought in the Western World*. Cambridge, MA: The Belknap Press, 21.

19. About the significance of the belief in the Paradise in Middle Age, cf. Graus (1967, 4 f).

20. The Physon was one of the rivers of Paradise.

21. See, Matthias Riedl, 2004, *Joachim von Fiore. Denker der vollendeten Menschheit*. Epistemata. Würzbuger Wissenschaftliche Schriften. Reihe Philosophie, 361, Würzburg: Königshausen & Neumann; Matthias Riedl, 2012, A collective Messiah: Joachim of Fiore's Constitution of Future Society, *Mirabilia* 14: 57–80.

22. Riedl (2012, 58).

23. Graus (1967, 15–17). [ditto].

24. More's ironical distance can already be observed in the title of his book A little, true book, both beneficial and enjoyable, about how things should be on the new island Utopia.

25. Cf. Finley (1967, 12–14). However, Finley's distinction between ancient and modern utopias does not agree with the definition adopted here.

References

Bichler, Reinhold. 1984. Zur historischen Beurteilung der Griechischen Staatsutopie. *Gräzer Beiträge* 11: 179–206.

Bloch, Ernst. 1959. *Das Prinzip Hoffnung*. Suhrkamp Taschenbuchwissenschaft 3. Frankfurt a. M.: Suhrkamp.

Bobonich, Christopher J. 2002. *Plato's Utopia Recast: His Later Ethics and Politics*. Oxford: Oxford University Press.

de Brasi, Diego. 2007. Platone, padre dell'utopia? *Les Études Classiques* 79: 207–226.

Brown, Truesdell S. 1946. Euhemerus and the Historians. *The Harvard Theological Review* 39 (4): 259–274.

Ehlers, Widu-Wolfgang. 1985. Mit dem Sudwestmonsum nach Ceylon. Eine Interpretation der Iambul-Exzerpte Diodors. *Würzburger Jahrbücher für die Altertumswissenschaft* N. F. 11: 73–84.

Finley, Moses I. 1967. Utopianism Ancient and Modern. In *The Critical Spirit. Essays in Honor of Herbert Marcuse*, ed. Kurt H. Wolff and Barrington Moore Jr., 3–20. Boston: Beacon Press.

Flashar, Helmut. 1974. *Formen utopischen Denkens bei den Griechen*. Innsbrucker Beiträge zur Kulturwissenschaft. Dies philologici Aenipontani H. 3. Innsbruck: Institut für Sprachen und Literatur.

Graus, Frantisek. 1967. Social Utopias in the Middle Ages. *Past & Present* 38: 3–19.

Honigman, Sylvie. 2009. Euhemerus of Messene's and Plato's Atlantis. *Historia* 58 (1): 1–35.

Kleinwächter, Friedrich. 1891. *Die Staatsromane. Ein Beitrag zur Lehre vom Kommunismus und Socialismus*. Wien.

Koch, Michael. 1979. Zur Utopie in der alten Welt. In *Auf den Weg gebracht: Idee und Wirklichkeit der Gründung der Universität Konstanz. Festschrift für Kurt Georg Kissinger*, 399–417. Konstanz: Universität Konstanz.

Lens Tuero, Jesús, and Pedro Pablo Fuentes González. 2000. Iamboulos. In *Dictionnaire des philosophes Antiques*, 840–853. III, Paris: CNRS Éditions.

Manuel, Frank E., and Fritzie P. Manuel. 1960. *Utopian Thought in the Western World*. Cambridge, MA: The Belknap Press.

Riedl, Matthias. 2004. *Joachim von Fiore. Denker der vollendeten Menschheit.* Epistemata. Würzbuger Wissenschaftliche Schriften. Reihe Philosophie, 361. Würzburg: Königshausen & Neumann.

———. 2012. A Collective Messiah: Joachim of Fiore's Constitution of Future Society. *Mirabilia* 14: 57–80.

Rohde, Erwin. 1900. *Der griechische Roman und seine Vorläufer*, 2nd ed. Leipzig: Breitkopf und Härtel.

Vegetti, Mario, ed. 1998/2007. Platone, *La Repubblica. Traduzione e commento a cura di M. V.* Tracassa. Napoli: Bibliopolis.

———. 2013. *The* Sacred History *of Euhemerus of Messene.* Beiträge zur Altertumskunde 312. Berlin: De Gruyter.

von Pöhlmann, Robert. 1925. *Geschichte der sozialen Frage und des Sozialismus in der antiken Welt*, 2nd ed. München: C. H. Beck'sche Verlagsbuchhandlung.

Winston, David. 1976. Iambulus "Islands of the Sun" and Hellenistic Literary Utopias. *Science-Fiction Studies* 3 (3): 219–227.

Zarncke, Friedrich. 1879. Der Priester Johannes. Erste Abhandlung enthaltend Kapitel I, II und III. *Abhandlungen Der Sächsichen Akademie Der Wissenschaften Zu Leipzig, Philologisch-Historisch Klasse* 17: 826–1028.

Pöhlmann (1925). Geschichte der sozialen Frage und des Sozialismus in der antiken Welt. 2nd. Ed. München: C. H. Beck'sche Verlagsbuchhandlung.

The Renaissance

Marie-Claire Phélippeau

INTRODUCTION

Until the Renaissance the human mind did not imagine the possibility of radical progress in the societies of people on earth. It tended to see the future of humanity in returning cycles and definite salvation in the afterlife, at best. With the development of printing in Europe and the "discovery" by European explorers of a new continent on the far side of the Atlantic, with the end of feudal societies and the unmistakable path toward capitalism, Europeans reappraised their position in the universe, exploring and enjoying the expanded world they now encountered. New interests developed, which would later be gathered under the term "humanism"; they included the rediscovery and interpretation of the original classical texts of European antiquity, and a novel freedom in literary and artistic creativity. Renaissance Europeans were slowly breaking free from their dependence on religion and asserting their own dignity, even if that dignity was deemed to be God-given. The world as experienced by Europeans in the Renaissance suddenly became of interest again, and the belief that European society could be improved gained traction. It became possible to locate the New Jerusalem somewhere on the earth. This chapter considers Thomas More's *Utopia* as exemplary of this new way of thinking about society and about the world more generally. And this larger

M.-C. Phélippeau (✉)
Former Editor of Moreana, Paris, France

91

P. Marks et al. (eds.), *The Palgrave Handbook of Utopian and Dystopian Literatures*, https://doi.org/10.1007/978-3-030-88654-7_7

sense is critical to the ongoing relevance of Utopia, for although it demonstrates many characteristics of Renaissance thinking, it also challenges that thinking in imaginative ways.

With many rhetorical precautions, this is exactly what Thomas More attempted. Pretending an old sailor had told him about a perfect island he had discovered in the antipodes, More wrote the dialogue he had with that sailor and called the emblematic island Utopia. The irony inherent in More's fiction leaves the reader uncertain of the actual existence of the island, but much better informed about the need for reform of his own society when compared to that ideal commonwealth where its citizens live in a happy, generous, and tolerant community. More's *Utopia* (1516) was a seminal text, although (as other chapters in this volume acknowledge) we can easily find classical sources in Plato's *Republic*, Lucian of Samosata, Cicero's various writings, and Saint Augustine's *City of God*. That said, *Utopia* stands as the basis of all the utopias imagined, whether written or actually created and experienced after that. More wrote his *Utopia*—or rather his *Libellus vere aureus*—,[1] in Latin in 1516, in response to his friend Erasmus's *Praise of Folly*—*Encomium Moriae*—which exposed the corruption and nonsense of their contemporary society, and whose title was a pun on More's name, since Erasmus's title could be read either as Praise of Folly or Praise of More. In his ideal republic, More imagined a land whose geography was remodeled into a fortified island by Utopus, its founder, in order to make it impregnable. Safe inside their protected shores, Utopians worked hard at devising the best possible form of government, in order to offer education, equality, and well-being to all the citizens. Therefore, Utopia is to be understood as the result of the best effort of man to live on earth, despite the inherent difficulties humans usually encounter on our planet. Utopia is not Cockaigne, that mythical land of plenty imagined in medieval times, but rather an island in the middle of nowhere, where happiness and abundance are only due to the wisdom, virtue, and common efforts of its inhabitants.

Utopia is ideal indeed. It must be read as a model, the tentative blueprint of what a society could be if men were wise enough to organize their lives with priority given to fraternity and sharing rather than personal possession. However, More is realistic and knows that man is finally driven by passions and self-interest, and while he presents his Utopia with much humor, his skepticism is unmistakable. His character Morus ends the book with these words: "I freely confess that in the Utopian commonwealth there are very many features that in our own societies I would wish rather than expect to see" (More 2002, 107). Hence his joco-serious attitude in his choice of words, which contemporary humanists were invited to decipher. Most Utopian names are oxymorons, affirming and negating at the same time. If the ideal island is called *U-topia*, it is to be deciphered as *U-topos* meaning in Greek "Nowhere," to which is added a pun with *Eu-topia*, meaning the "Good Place." And the reader is told, in the opening poem that "Good Place by rights it should be called." The main city of the isle of Utopia is Amaurot, meaning "the city in the clouds" or "the mirage city," through which flows the Anhydrid, the no-water river. More's rhetorical language, based on irony, litotes, and paradoxes, is there to point to the illusion he is creating in his *Utopia*, so readers may understand that what they are reading does not actually exist but is shown (in a blurred picture) as a possible and desirable alternative to their existing world. In doing so, More invented what in time would become a literary genre, a type of tale in which the reader may dream of a better world and also believe in that world. This first example of a utopia, therefore, is not a chimera, but a possible world, accessible to us if we put enough effort in to build it.

Thomas More divided his *Utopia* into two parts, called Book I and Book II. The reader has to wait until Book II to discover the island of Utopia. More chose to add a first part only after he had imagined his ideal commonwealth, perhaps in an effort to emphasize the moral, political, and social aim of his work. Book I presents the narrator of the account of Book II, placing him in a contemporary scene. The first vernacular translations often forgot Book I altogether, focusing on the ideal island only, which were more to the taste of many a Renaissance reader, curious to hear about new exotic lands that explorers such as Christopher Columbus and Amerigo Vespucci had visited. However, More's *Utopia* cannot be fully understood unless all its elements are united. Book I greatly adds to the verisimilitude of the tale: it describes the meeting between Morus and his friend Peter Giles in Antwerp; these are real people meeting in existing places. Giles acquaints Morus with one Raphael Hythloday, an old sailor who had joined the Amerigo Vespucci expeditions of the late fifteenth and early sixteenth centuries, and "was Vespucci's constant companion on the last three of his four voyages" (More 2002, 10). Famously, Vespucci's first name would provide the basis for the name "America," perhaps the most visible sign of the massive expansion of European knowledge that marked the Renaissance. Just as importantly for the rhetorical strategies of *Utopia*, Vespucci (unlike Hythloday) actually existed. If we add that a number of letters written by More's humanist friends are also part and parcel of the book, we realize the author's intention: tricking his readers into believing he was actually narrating a true story.

Book I continues with the first part of Raphael's account, where he insists he has met with the most virtuous and the wisest people of the earth when he happened to discover one faraway island. Before he describes Utopia, Raphael recalls a conversation he had had one evening at Cardinal Morton's house in England and this is the occasion for an exposition of many of the social ills that England was suffering from in More's time: expeditive justice, poverty, inequality, the ruin of poor peasants forced to leave their lands taken over by sheep owners. Thus, *Utopia* is never simply the account of a marvelous land in a part of what Europeans labeled "The New World" that the returned traveler Hythloday wishes to describe and exalt. The reader reads about problems in the contemporary Renaissance world, such as the scandal of enclosures, for example. More made this system infamous by calling the sheep "man-eaters," since the excessive interest in raising sheep for the wool, which would be advantageously traded in Flanders, turned the small peasants into jobless roamers on the roads of the kingdom. What could they do but steal to survive, and then be hanged as thieves? The structure of *Utopia* thus ensures that beyond Hythloday's extremely positive and extended take on the virtues of Utopia the place, More exposes a number of topics of current concern to him during the table conversation. These range from a discussion on the appropriateness of entering the service of a king for an enlightened subject such as Raphael Hythloday, to various travel accounts to exotic lands endowed with astonishing laws and customs. Only after this focus on questions that exercised at least some Renaissance thinkers does More engage in the more formal description of Utopia and its institutions.

When Book II opens, Raphael monopolizes the dialogue, as the reader is taken with the narrator's enthusiasm at describing the marvel of Utopia. Starting with its geography, Raphael opens with: "The island of the Utopians is two hundred miles across in the middle part" (More 2002, 41), dimensions which compare with England. He goes on describing it as "crescent-shaped, like a new moon" (41), and explains how difficult it is to sail between the horns of the crescent, since the bay inside hides many dangerous shallows which only a local pilot can manage. Thus the stress is placed on the inaccessibility of the island before the narrator reveals a little of the Utopians' history: "their land was not always surrounded by the sea. But Utopus, who conquered the country and gave it its name [...] had a channel cut fifteen miles wide where the land joined the continent, and thus caused the sea to flow around the country" (42). The man-made island is emblematic of a utopia, in that it claims its isolation from a polluted environment, as the result of a deliberate human decision. Good government must be secured by human action rather than merely by tradition. Raphael Hythloday is then free to expose the marvelous organization of Utopia. "There are fifty-four cities on the island, all spacious and magnificent, entirely identical in language, customs, institutions and laws" (43). The repetition of the same pattern meant beauty, harmony, plus equality of course, in that early modern context. As for the Utopian institutions, they are meant to preserve equality, justice, and well-being. Raphael describes the joy of Utopia's citizens at sharing the same meals in the common halls, at mixing generations at the dinner table, organizing festivities every month, and the overall impression should be one of familial joy. Utopians live in a fraternal community, exchanging children with other families in order to maintain a balanced ratio, and moving to another city if their city becomes overcrowded while another is sparsely populated. Utopians want to share each other's way of life, therefore "every ten years they exchange the houses themselves by lot" (46) and they also regularly leave their town homes to work in farms in the country and vice versa.

What stunned More's Renaissance readers the most was that Utopians have abolished private property and the use of money. Money and possession are considered elements of corruption, leading to greed, pride, and vanity and their absence helps the citizens not to fall into these traps. The basic principle is sharing the goods according to everyone's needs. All that is produced by each household is brought to a common warehouse and "the head of every household looks for what he or his family needs, and carries off what he wants without any sort of payment or compensation" (More 2002, 55). The narrator, foreseeing the Renaissance reader's reaction, adds: "Why should anything be refused him? There is plenty of everything, and no reason to fear that anyone will claim more than he needs" (55). He concludes: "Thus the whole island is like a single family" (59). That principle conditions the world of work too, "for where money is the measure of everything, many vain and completely superfluous trades are bound to be carried on simply to satisfy luxury and licentiousness" (51). Hence absence of money means the satisfaction of the basic human needs, such as food, dress, and shelter for all, but also no privilege, no fancy, or occasion for vice. Therefore, all Utopians dress alike in simple undyed linen or wool according to the season, and there are no taverns or brothels which would give occasions of debauchery. These radical suggestions are meant to provoke the initial Renaissance readers of *Utopia* and they succeed in so doing. In fact, they have continued to provoke, inspire, and alarm readers in the centuries since. It is part of the genius of More's creation that the text is a Renaissance thought experiment that has far outlived the Renaissance. While it provides a vivid sense of at least some of the concerns of Renaissance society, it also speaks beyond its moment and indeed well beyond the European context in which it appears. Temporally, geographically and conceptually, *Utopia* exceeds its brief.

Another Renaissance concern More deals with that remains current is labor. Work is the basic social link between Utopians, and communal work is described as a source of joy. Farming is "the one job at which everyone works, men and women alike, with no exception" (More 2002, 48), thus "they allot only six hours to work" the narrator explains, since this suffices "to provide not only enough but more than enough of the necessities and even the conveniences of life" (51). The good Utopians fight idleness, a fault severely punished in their island and yet observed everywhere else in the world. Indeed, in all other countries more than half the population does not work, Raphael remarks, since women do not have a job, and "there is a great lazy gang of priests and so-called religious. Add to them all the rich, especially the landlords, who are commonly called gentlemen and nobles" (51). The centrality and power of religion in the Renaissance is given its due; even in Utopia they need priests and scholars. Those who are naturally oriented toward studying usually combine manual and intellectual work but they may be allowed to become full-time scholars if they demonstrate outstanding talents. It is among them that the higher administrators and the priests are recruited. Readers may wonder at the paradox of such a cryptic text, which praises Utopian priests who are allowed not to work while denouncing the practice as a fault in other countries. But the organization of labor on Utopia allows for some leniency, given that "since almost all the rest of the populace is neither idle nor engaged in useless trades, it is easy to see why they produce so much in such a short working day" (52). Well before the full flowering of capitalism, More's text hints at how efficiency might transform the conditions and output of labor.

A number of oddities come with the imagination of any new type of Commonwealth, even a fictional one. To his Renaissance contemporaries, More must have appeared a revolutionary in imagining in *Utopia* such moral practices condemned by Christianity as divorce and euthanasia. Both however are presented by More as the result of a compassionate attitude, typical of the Utopians who base their ethics on nature. The narrator also offers this explanation: the naturally good Utopians are ignorant of the Revelation which brought Christianity to other parts of the world. However, as soon as the European navigators bring to their island the message of their own religion, the Utopians readily recognize its truth and are anxious to become Christians too. Their sense of compassion seems to extend to all humans and animals but there are oddities there too. They take exceptional care of the sick and the more fragile, and protect their sense of compassion by entrusting the slaughtering of animals to bondsmen, who operate outside the walls of their cities. "The Utopians feel that slaughtering our fellow creatures gradually destroys the sense of compassion, the finest sentiment of which our human nature is capable" (More 2002, 55). We also discover there are slaves in Utopia and that equality is paradoxically reserved for the best citizens. Repeatedly, More's projections work to unsettle Renaissance commonplaces and certainties. So, for example, Utopia is so sure that it has devised the best form of commonwealth on earth that it generously proposes to annex territories on the nearby continent, creating Utopian settlements "wherever the natives have plenty of unoccupied and uncultivated land" (54). At the dawn of European colonial expansion across the Atlantic and beyond, "foreigners" are expected to be thankful for being colonized and are invited to live under Utopian laws. Should they not yield to Utopia they are driven out of their land, "and against those who resist them," Utopians wage war, an action deemed "perfectly justifiable" given that these people should be ashamed to leave "their land idle and waste" (54). Given that Hythloday's leader, Amerigo Vespucci, had only recently returned from the New World, we might see this attitude as remarkably prescient of self-serving arguments repeatedly used by Europeans over the next few centuries as they brutally imposed colonial rule over huge areas of the globe.

Although the Utopians are said to "utterly despise war as an activity fit only for beasts" (More 2002, 85), More devotes a long chapter to military practices, including the Utopian insistence on the participation of women in military training. As with so many aspects of *Utopia*, this example appears radically out of step with prevailing Renaissance attitudes, and indeed would still be a controversial move in many parts of the globe. Readers are informed that Utopians go to war "only for good reasons": to protect their land, to drive invading armies from the territories of their friends, or to liberate an oppressed people, in the name of compassion and humanity. Whenever lives are at risk or real cruelty is deemed necessary, they prefer to use mercenaries, as they are "ashamed when their forces gain a bloody victory" (86). Rather than fighting they prefer offering gold or using ruse, and they employ secret agents to end a war more quickly and avoid combat. To that effect, they store great quantities of gold, a metal which they train their citizens to despise by using it for making chamber-pots, children's baubles, and slave chains. But when war becomes a patriotic affair, everyone becomes involved, including wives and children who support their husbands and fathers by standing at the rear of the battlefields. Prisoners of war are brought to Utopia to become slaves, but Utopians take pride in treating their slaves better than elsewhere. Indeed, they keep slaves and bondsmen on their island and slavery is one of the punishments of bad or criminal behavior.

These peaceful people with their strong work ethic do not exclude pleasure in their lives, far from it. Their Epicurean position is implicit when Raphael Hythloday observes that "they seem rather too much inclined to the view which favours pleasure, in which they conclude that all or the most important part of human happiness consists" (More 2002, 65). Moreover the debate about true and false pleasures is something the Utopians are fond of. Thus do they share a common philosophy which they are happy to reveal to their visitor who reports that "by pleasure they understand every state or movement of the body or mind in which we find delight according to the behests of nature. They have good reason for adding that the desire is according to nature" (69). Of course pleasures which lead to sins of pride, idleness, or debauchery are labeled false pleasures, since they eventually cause pain or ruin. The wisdom of Utopians is constantly at work in order to maintain the right balance in that field, hence their love of philosophical discussions, a natural inclination which is fostered by their enlightened education.

Behind Utopian practices Renaissance readers could not fail to discover a possible remedy to the ills of their respective societies. However one must never forget the amusement Thomas More took in devising what he called "my little fancy." He pretends to imitate Plato's *Republic* when, in the opening poem, he declares: "Now I compete with Plato's state." He can even be said to parody Plato's dialogues, especially the *Banquet*, by presenting his account in the form of a philosophical debate taking place during meals. But More is not to be taken seriously all the time. The irony he uses to mock the Utopians, as well as his contemporary fellows, brings him closer to the Greek satirist Lucian of Samosata, some of whose works he and Erasmus had earlier translated with delight together. When it comes to truly dreaming of a possible heaven on earth, then Augustine's *City of God* is the obvious reference, as it nourished More's religious meditation during his younger years. After all, Augustine's New Jerusalem is depicted as the ideal city on earth, made of wise and religious citizens who live in the faith of the love of God. Thomas More lectured on the *City of God* in his early twenties in a London church. He was already familiar with the dream of a perfect world which he shared with his audience. But in 1516, with his *Utopia*, More shunned the role of preacher, choosing instead literature, and amusing himself with coined names, Greco-Latin play on words and unheard-of solutions to the ills of his maddened world. His aim was to awake the consciences of his contemporary readers by proposing the picture of a new world which was both fascinating by its novelty and appeal and yet not totally impossible.

The first edition of *Utopia* was printed in Louvain in 1516 by Thierry Martens and was an immediate success, the use of Latin making it accessible to all learned people throughout Europe. It was followed by three other Latin editions: Paris in 1517, then Basel in March and November 1518. It is interesting to note that each new edition gave a different overall impression, as printers did not choose the same paratexts or the same order for the letters framing the actual account.[2] When *Utopia* started being translated into vernacular languages, the intention clearly changed with the times, and very often Book I and the paratexts disappeared altogether. The vernacular editions began with the German translation in 1524, followed by the Italian in 1548, the French in 1550, and the English only in 1551. By then, Europe, with the Reformation especially, had become a different place and *Utopia* was read more as a fantastic travel account than as a treatise of political philosophy, the term "utopia" being gradually understood as a chimera or impossible dream. However the genuine dream of a better world, of a *eutopia*, never ceased to exist and it even gave birth to actual experiments in various parts of the world.

Utopias After *Utopia*

New utopias followed in various languages, with the common aim of denouncing a state of things that needed reform. This could be achieved either through mockery, derision, or serious planning. In the same sixteenth century, French author François Rabelais, launched his saga of Pantagruel and Gargantua, two bawdy giants presented as the new kings of Utopia. In the *Tiers Livre* (1546) when Pantagruel embarks on a new venture, taking his Utopians to colonize Dipsodie, there is no doubt that readers at the time would have understood the ludicrous complicity with More's *Utopia*. Barthélemy Aneau (1510–1561), who contributed to the translation of *Utopia* into French, also produced his own work of fiction, *Alector* (1560), which described the rather dystopian city he called Orbe, presented as a translation from a Greek account. After Thomas More, a number of European writers were driven to a serious reflection of the idea of *res publica*. Among them is French thinker Jean Bodin (1530–1596) who was greatly influenced by More's *Utopia* which he quotes in the first book of his *Six Livres de la République*, published in 1577. Bodin discreetly worked at promoting religious tolerance, and was instrumental in bringing about the text of the Edict of Nantes (1598), which gave rights to the French Protestants and ended the Wars of Religion under Henri IV. Like More, Bodin defends the idea that laws should be as few as possible in a republic, but he reasons that, if happiness is indeed the result of virtue, his experience has proved that, in a happy republic, nothing is more imperiled than virtue itself.[3] In Poland, Krzysztof Warszewicki (1543–1603) also known as Christophorus Varsevicius, produced *De optimo statu libertatis* in 1598, where he defends the concept of liberty in a monarchy.

Interesting responses to *Utopia* were the concrete experiments which were carried out in various parts of the world. In Italy in the 1580s, the fortified town of Sabbionetta was built in the province of Mantua at the heart of the Po valley, with the double aim of resisting the Spanish conquest and preserving a humanist ideal. But the most successful utopian experiment of the sixteenth century was certainly carried out in Michoacán, Mexico, by Vasco de Quiroga (1488–1565) with his *Pueblos hospitales* where, as early as 1531, native Americans were made to live in communities based on the Utopian principles of equality and communism. We may recall also the fight led by Bartolomé de Las Casas (1474–1566) in favor of the Indians, as well as the Jesuit *reducciones* established in Paraguay later. In all these the common denominator is the attempt to enforce Utopia's idea of individual liberty, communal living, and absence of private property.

At the turn of the century, a new ideal, taking technological progress into account, became gradually visible in the works of idealists. With Tommaso Campanella's *Civitas solis*, in 1604, science and astrology were at the center of his imagination of the *City of the Sun*. Francis Bacon also relied heavily on science in his *New Atlantis* (1627) where all sorts of agricultural and mining experiments were carried out to improve the material welfare of the citizens. However, religion remained at the core of the story, in both works, as a guarantee of virtue, the necessary element of all successful communities. Although mixed with esoteric flavor it had also been the case with *Christianopolis*, the work of the German author Johannes Valentinus Andreae in 1619. In 1641, a utopian fiction borrowing from Thomas More's *Utopia* its dialogic form and its name *Macaria*, an island visited by Raphael Hythloday in More's *Utopia* —was long regarded as Samuel Hartlib's work before being now attributed to Gabriel Plattes. From the long list of Utopians inspired by More in the first half of the seventeenth century, we may also name Gerrard Winstanley, who, with his pamphlet *The New Law of Righteousness* in 1649, took up the fight against the enclosures which Thomas More had denounced in Book I of *Utopia*.

CONCLUSION

Today's appreciation of Thomas More's *Utopia* is less philosophical and more literary. Focus on More's rhetoric has led to a finer understanding of More's intention in writing what remains a cryptic book, not the blueprint of a possible society, yet not totally a piece of science fiction either.[4] New translations of More's work have appeared in any number of languages, taking the latest literary research into account, with the aim of restoring the original flavor of More's irony, litotes,[5] and paradoxes. These actions have not reduced *Utopia* to an historically distant document, but, like a restored painting, have recreated its original vividness. *Utopia* remains one of the few texts published in its time still read widely in the twenty-first century, not just as a window back to the imaginative projections of a subtle and stimulating thinker, but also a prompt to the assessment of contemporary societies, and how they might be criticized and improved. Due to its paradoxes and ambiguities, modern readers might label the work a dystopia, but this possibility only emphasizes the complexity, vivacity, and provocativeness of More's creation. New generations will continue to fashion new judgments, each one a testament to the astonishing suggestiveness of this enduring Renaissance text.

NOTES

1. The first Latin title was *Libellus vere aureus nec minus salutaris quam festivus de optimo reip[ublicae] statu, deque noua insula Vtopia,* Louvain, Thierry Martens, 1516.
2. This is discussed in McCutcheon, "More's *Utopia* and its Parerga (1516–1518)."
3. See Teller, "Thomas More dans *La République* de Jean Bodin." Teller ends his article thus: "A l'heure du grand 'Essor de la philosophie politique' (P. Mesnard), les références faites volontairement à l'*Utopie* attestent l'attrait qu'exerce sur les esprits les plus musclés et les têtes les mieux faites, Thomas 'Le More.'"
4. See for instance McCutcheon, *My Dear Peter: The Ars Poetica and Hermeneutics for More's "Utopia.";* Fox, *Utopia: An Elusive Vision;* Baker-Smith, *More's Utopia.*
5. See McCutcheon, "Denying the Contrary: More's Use of Litotes in the *Utopia.*" A Festschrift on More's *Utopia* in Honour of Edward Surtz, S.J.

REFERENCES

Baker-Smith, Dominic. 2000. *More's Utopia.* Toronto: University of Toronto Press, The Renaissance Society of America.

Fox, Alister. 1993. *Utopia: An Elusive Vision.* New York: Twayne Publishers.

McCutcheon, Elizabeth. 1971. Denying the Contrary: More's Use of Litotes in the *Utopia.* A Festschrift on More's *Utopia* in Honour of Edward Surtz, S.J. *Moreana* 31–32 (November): 107–121.

———. 1983. *My Dear Peter: The Ars Poetica and Hermeneutics for More's "Utopia."* Angers: Moreanum.

———. 2015. More's *Utopia* and Its Parerga (1516–1518). *Moreana* 52 (201–202): 133–148.

More, Thomas. 2002. *Utopia,* ed. George M. Logan and Robert M. Adams. Cambridge: Cambridge University Press.

Teller, Emile V. 1970. Thomas More dans *La République* de Jean Bodin. *Moreana* 27–28: 103–106.

The Eighteenth Century

Brenda Tooley

Introduction

What is utopian writing? How do we recognize a piece of writing as being within the tradition or genre of utopian writing? In this brief survey of eighteenth-century utopian writing in western Europe, I begin by acknowledging the elusive aspects of this act of categorization. Some texts fit securely within the category of utopian writing, invoking prior examples of utopian literature by working within a tradition of speculation about the good society or dwelling upon concerns shared by prior instances of utopian writing. Many texts do not fit so easily into the category but appear to readers today to be connected in some way—utopian adjacent, one could say—with utopian elements or themes. So, we can look to a variety of genres of writing, from scholarly to journalistic, philosophical to political to scientific, popular to polemical to poetic even, to locate instances of utopian speculation. The production of political, philosophical, and scientific writing for learned audiences spurs theorizations about "the good society" that in turn inform, reflect, and respond to major political and social events within the period we now call the Enlightenment. Popular fiction, and particularly the new genre of The Novel (i.e., the formally realistic novel with contemporary settings and complexly psychologized characters) captures and responds to the extension of educational opportunities to girls and women, the growing purchasing and

B. Tooley (✉)
Grand Valley State University, Allendale, MI, USA

P. Marks et al. (eds.), *The Palgrave Handbook of Utopian and Dystopian Literatures*, https://doi.org/10.1007/978-3-030-88654-7_8

political power of the middle class, and the expansion of British and European markets and commercial enterprise into urban centers and non-European locations. Utopian writing, in short, takes place within the contexts of the advance of European colonialism, emerging industrialized labor formations, and revolutionary movements in Europe and America.

With the emergence of the novel as a form in western Europe (and particularly within the English-speaking part of it), the "blueprint" utopia gives way to utopian narratives that envision change, introducing plot, and thus conflict. Eighteenth-century utopian literature develops narrative trajectories, introduces complex characters, begins to explore more fully than previous texts how one gets from here to there, and examines what happens within a well-designed society to the individuals who inhabit it. Novels begin featuring "boutique utopias," small enclaves of intentionally gathered people—often women's societies, or, more generally, literary representations of intentional communities centered upon shared resources and healthful living.

Utopian Themes Within Eighteenth-Century Philosophical Writing

I will group critical approaches to utopian writing of the eighteenth century into two sets. The first set focuses on continuities with earlier utopian writing and philosophical speculation regarding the good society, or the "best possible world." These critics and literary historians are perhaps best exemplified by the magisterial overview of utopian literature, Frank and Fritzie Manuel's scholarly accomplishment in *Utopian Thought in the Western World* (1979), which explores the development of utopian writing with a focus on major authors of the western canon. The Manuels open their discussion of utopias in the eighteenth century by noting that the *Encyclopédie* does not include "utopia" as a term in its entries. In the authors' view, the eighteenth century produced no outstanding instances of utopian literature, although elements of utopian speculation inform significant texts, both literary and philosophical, throughout the century. Instead, they identify "five rather different positions on utopia": the philosophical; the Rousseauistic; the popular; the theoretically communist or collectivist; and the sexually libertine (414). The Manuels' survey did help to place utopian literature within the stream of the "history of ideas" of (western) civilization, and thus also helped to shape a small but growing discursive community of scholars, such as the Society for Utopian Studies in the U.S. and the Utopian Studies Society in Europe, who began to take utopian writing seriously from an academic point of view.

Of course, recognized classics of utopian writing (More; Bacon) were influential in shaping the eighteenth-century speculation about the good society, introducing themes and images of egalitarian welfare structures and celebrating the value of organized, and well-funded, scientific inquiry. According to the influential contemporary utopian scholar Gregory Claeys, in "some instances, too, utopian tracts led to liberal and humanitarian thinking about individual rights, at least a century and sometimes two in advance of their times" (Claeys 2012, xi; see also Claeys 2000 and 2010). But according to the Manuels, philosophical speculation in the eighteenth century did not result in the production of notable utopian texts as such. Diderot and his fellow philosophes viewed history as cyclic, and were thus skeptical of visions of infinite perfectibility, preferring a pragmatic approach to ameliorating social ills through the interventions of an enlightened ruler. That said, the philosophes arguably had an underlying utopian motive for their project. "There is a sense in which a utopian idea … lay behind the whole ambitious enterprise: the belief that a small band men of good will, learned and moderately zealous, through the propagation of ideas … could serve as leaven to raise the general consciousness of their society" (Manuel and Manuel 1979, 21).

Subsequent freedom movements of colonized and enslaved people were anticipated in Condorcet's work (Manuel and Manuel 1979, 503). Still, the concept of an equality of different cultures and polities was alien to his thought. "The progressists had so absolute a faith in the objective validity of their scientific utilitarian civilization that its universal propagation as a perfect good was never questioned for a single moment. The Europocentrism of the liberal idea of progress exemplified by Condorcet became one of its more naive though deep-rooted preconceptions" (Manuel and Manuel 1979, 504).

Jean-Jacques Rousseau (1712–1778) turns from the civilizing and humanizing projects of the philosophes to a celebration of the innocence and virtue of "the primitive." Before Rousseau, European writing on the topic tended to juxtapose the concepts of primitive nobility derived from classical literature with accounts of actual colonialist encounters, "project[ing] their terrors of the wild and of the unknown primitive, as well as their hopes for a less repressive, freer way of life—sometimes on the same page" (Manuel and Manuel 1979, 426). Rousseau, as well as popular novelists who created tales of newly discovered utopian lands (often exoticized as sexually unconstrained), built upon the myth of the "noble savage" and a pristine primitive society, in contrast to their present social environments. Rousseau never wrote a utopia as such, but his works are suffused with sketches of, and meditations upon, the ideal society, and he was conversant with classical and seventeenth-century utopian writing. Rousseau addresses questions often raised in utopian writing regarding the ideal social unit; the relationship of an ideal world to history and eternal time; the relationship of the sexes, of need and desire; the place of the individual within the common/communal; and the "state of nature" versus contemporary society (Manuel and Manuel 1979, 439).

Eighteenth-century writing that includes elements of utopianism within its philosophical and political projects also incorporates a belief in progress that in turn leads to significant change in how stories about utopias are shaped: the achieved utopia rather than the discovered utopia. Two currents worked simultaneously here—the sense of decline and decadence and the more hopeful sense of progress, discovery and improvement. According to Manuel and Manuel, "[i]t is only in the latter part of the eighteenth century that the debate on the idea of progress, on the utopia of the good future time, was joined in earnest" (1979, 455). This concept of collaborative human effort toward a better society opened the door to new narrative structures for utopian fiction: the euchronia narrative. Rather than the discovery of a lost society, the explorer in these narratives encounters utopia in a future time. Edward Bellamy's *Looking Backward* (1888) is often credited with the "awakened sleeper" trope, but Louis-Sébastien Mercier's novel *L'An 2440* (1770) presents a utopian Paris with wide boulevards and friendly pedestrians, "where reason and utility reigned supreme" and "science and learning and diligence were esteemed and everyone was happy" (Manuel and Manuel 1979, 459). Futurity becomes an increasingly important trope.

While the Manuels' tome does acknowledge a new focus of utopian speculation on gender relations and marital structures, and on the revolutionary fervor that fueled the French Revolution, what they miss is the emergence of women's voices and of the intertwining of utopian blueprint elements with the narrative trajectories of the formally realistic novel. The novel's complexly "new" and increasingly popular form, thanks to increasing literacy and an audience of readers with disposable income, is a turning point in the history of the genre.

Utopian Speculation in Eighteenth-Century Novels, Satires, and Philosophical Romances

Christine Rees' 1996 *Utopian Imagination and Eighteenth-Century Fiction* sets out a nuanced survey of British utopias produced in the century, with careful critical attention paid to popular utopian writing. She makes connections between utopian writing and other forms of eighteenth-century fiction: the travel tale (Daniel Defoe's *Robinson Crusoe* [1719] and other narratives of island discoveries); utopia and satire (Jonathan Swift's *Gulliver's Travels* [1726]); "domestic utopias" (Henry Fielding's *Joseph Andrews* [1742] and *The History of Tom Jones* [1749], Samuel Richardson's *Clarissa* [1748] and *Sir Charles Grandison* [1753]); women's utopias (Mary Astell's *A Serious Proposal to the Ladies* [1694 and 1697] and *Reflections upon Marriage* [1700]; Sara Scott's *Millenium Hall* [1750]) and Mary Hamilton's *Munster Village* [1778]); and the philosophical tale (Samuel Johnson's *The History of Rasselas, Prince of Abissinia* [1759]). Rees concludes that eighteenth-century utopian writing incorporates a "much enhanced role" for "the individual consciousness" in the portrayal of utopian encounters: "what would it be like to encounter or inhabit utopia as an individual human being conditioned in specific ways by gender, class, education and culture—is constantly addressed by eighteenth-century writers" (Rees 1996, 71).

Rees coins the term "domestic utopia," which, she argues, develops in conjunction with a new focus on private life in the emerging genre of the realist novel:

Eighteenth-century writers are [at the midpoint of the eighteenth century] developing the conceptual strain in utopian literature which represents the family unit both as a political paradigm and as a structure of social well-being, the growing point of the moral commonwealth. In doing so, they often merge this concept of domestic semi-autonomy and self-sufficiency with the Horatian ideal: the satisfactions of an independent country property large enough to be self-sufficient, but small enough to be under the proprietor's eye. (1996, 179)

She identifies the convergence of various genres of writing as a strength of eighteenth-century utopian speculation; varying forms, including satire and the novel, political philosophy, and fantasies of travel to the moon all contribute to its robustness. This position contrasts with the Manuels', who see this mélange of narrative possibilities as negative. Rees explores it instead as a positive feature of eighteenth-century writing, a kind of discursive heteroglossia: "The techniques of inset narrative and debate offer a mainstream novelist the means of admitting utopian discourse into his or her fiction, but also cordoning it off at the same time" (1996, 184).

Let us look at the interweaving of satire, the philosophical tale and utopia, with the help of Rees' astute critical lens on Samuel Johnson's *The Prince of Rasselas* (1759). "Politically, [Samuel Johnson] is very conscious of the central utopian problem—how to translate planning into action" (Rees 1996, 243). Johnson's exploration does not take as its premise the attainability of utopia, the setting out of a blueprint of an established (and just now discovered) ideal society. Instead, his tale exhibits the difficulty of putting large-scale plans into action: "Johnson doubts not just the efficacy but the relevance of political institutions, real or imaginary, when it comes to improving the quality of human life" (Rees 1996, 243). *Rasselas* is skeptical about the very possibility of utopia. "There is an underlying consistency in Johnson's suspicion of such visionary schemes. His case against them rests on two simple observations: First, that they wouldn't work, and, second, that they're largely irrelevant to human wellbeing" (Rees 1996, 244). This skepticism, however, is not a dismissive impatience that leaves the tradition of utopian speculation to one side. Instead, the author explores it, pulling apart its inconsistencies and insufficiencies. Johnson's fascination with imagination informs his understanding of the impetus behind the creation of utopias. Rees explains: "Perhaps no eighteenth-century writer has more acute insight into what it is in human psychology that impels us to invent utopias in the first place. ... However, ironically, the very impulses that produce utopian constructs ensure that these constructs are unstable and unrealizable. The need for variety, novelty, in a word, change, is deeply ingrained in the human psyche, so that a state of permanent happiness in this world is impossible" (244). Nonetheless, Rees concludes, "the occupation and development of the mind is profoundly pleasurable, so that inventing utopia is far more satisfying than living in it would be" (244).

Thus the emphasis on education in *Rasselas*. Johnson points out the need for comparison, the desire for change, and the likelihood that satiety leads to dissatisfaction. In particular, education—so often a fundamental component of utopian life—leads not to integration into the community, but to separation from it. Thought and imagination, which lead to utopian conceptualization, write change out of the imagined utopia. Johnson's protagonist Imlac is a version of More's Hythlodaeus, but a Hythlodaeus "who has never found his utopia" (Rees, 252). Rasselas, the questing prince, and Nekayah, his sister, leave utopia to discover "a choice of life" through encounters in the outside world, reversing the usual order of the utopian narrative. After the episode of the astronomer, who imagines he can control the weather and agonizes about how best to benefit all of mankind, the three young people who are the central figures in the story renounce their own fantasies: Nekayah, the aristocratic pastoral; Pekuah, the fantasy of ultimate power; and Rasselas, the dream of "a perfect government." Rees counters Paul Fussell's argument that the three central characters' future plans at the novel's conclusion (in which "nothing is concluded") reveal an underlying "secret lust for power over others" (Fussell, 1971, 241); Rees points out that both beneficent motives and a desire for power "seem to me to be genuine and inseparable: together, they explain a great deal about the psychology of utopian imagination" (Rees 1996, 264).

A second deeply valuable emphasis within current critical studies of eighteenth-century utopian writing is a focus on women's education and women's communities within eighteenth-century utopian texts. As innovations in technology, commerce, and education emerge during the course of the century, new questions and new narrative shapes emerge; in this century, utopias appear that are not a matter of discovery, but of purposeful creation. Might a society, or a subset of a society, create a utopia in the midst of the present flawed society? Ever more frequently as the century goes on, the answer is a qualified yes.

According to Rees, women's utopian fiction in this period defines itself against precedents established by male writers; these authors must have asked themselves, "given the all too evident constraints on women in the 'real' world, what does the utopian tradition have to offer beyond fantasy and wish-fulfillment?" (1996, 205). What is possible for women in the eighteenth century is not the creation of universal schemes, but boutique experiments, and these are only available to women with sufficient means to acquire education and property. "For women, there is virtually no opportunity to exercise power that doesn't derive from property and privilege, and, unsurprisingly, their utopian fictions reflect this fact of life" (Rees 1996, 205). Women writers who do experiment with utopian fictions often extend access to their imagined utopia via charitable outreach to women without the means to gain it on their own, by providing educational opportunities and inclusion in sheltered communities. Women utopists certainly found inspiration in earlier utopias, particularly those focused on education and structured like well-funded universities—"Women can claim the right as scholars and scientists to enter the male preserve of the House of Solomon, but that right doesn't emancipate their sex "as a whole" (Rees, 207).

As Gary Kelly outlines in the excellent editorial preface to the Broadview edition of Sarah Scott's *Millenium Hall* (1762), this novel "creates a utopian vision of gentry capitalism reformed according to bluestocking feminism. … It outlines a program to reform economic, social, and cultural relations at a time of major political change in Britain, centered on the domestic effects of the Seven Years War with France, the coronation of the young monarch George III, and attendant changes at the centre of power and patronage" (Scott [1762] 1995, 26). The structure of this fiction is the "discovered utopia," wherein two male travelers happen upon the utopian estate as they seek assistance following an accident on the road. The narrator, the older of the two men (structuring his tale as a letter to a male friend), describes the history and functioning of Millenium Hall in its social, cultural, economic, and religious aspects; the narrative is interspersed with dialogue and recounted histories of some of the participants in Millenium Hall society. By the end of the narrative, the utopian traveler is persuaded to establish his own version of Millenium Hall on his estate. Kelly points out that

> the descriptions and the 'histories' alternate throughout the text, and together they link the oppression of women to oppression of other powerless social groups under the unjust systems of intertwined paternalism, patronage and patriarchy. *Millenium Hall* shows how representatives of one set of the oppressed - women - have reformed this system to provide properly for the dispossessed and powerless of several kinds, including women. (Scott [1762] 1995, 28)

Mrs. Maynard is the main "speaker" on behalf of the estate, explaining the structure and governance of the estate to the visitors. Kelly explains, "The implied plot takes up these [embedded] plots to suggest that their protagonists were driven to build the utopian world of *Millenium Hall* as a refuge for themselves and other women like themselves, extended to other social groups marginalized by the same unjust economic and social practices of the dominant culture" (Scott [1762] 1995, 29). This makes the static form of the discovered utopia host to incipient narratives of a created utopia, although we do not witness the utopia in the process of construction.

Scott's novel provides a good example of a boutique or pocket utopia. It also shows up the dependency of such utopian enclaves on a larger and much less secure world:

> The Hall is given its nickname by the male narrator and not by its female proprietors or lower-class dependents. … Furthermore, as the "histories" of the proprietors show, the Hall is a refuge from the world … The proprietors have gained their utopia through exceptional moral and intellectual qualities and the conventionally feminine virtue of fortitude—the ability to withstand the oppression of courtly patriarchy, and thus to transcend it. On the other hand, they also gain their utopia by providential means—an unexpected inheritance, a lucky discovery, a fortunate friendship. (Kelly's preface in Scott [1762] 1995, 31–32)

Like other instances of utopian enclaves (for example, the good convent in Ann Radcliffe's *The Italian* [1797]), the sheltering community requires and depends upon the world beyond it, not simply as a defining contrast, but as the society that makes it possible:

> Women's utopianism in the early modern period and the eighteenth century is concerned with the establishment of an "intersubjective space" … This literature serves as a site for experimentation with alternative ideas of community, government, nation state, kinship, status, notions of home and family, gender and sexuality—in short, a complex political and social agenda. What emerges is not a uniform vision but utopian narratives that struggle with the dual operation of resisting ideology and producing oppositional practice. (Pohl and Tooley 2007, 8)

This novel, with its complex interweaving of privileged patronage and inclusive sanctuary, has a parallel in history: Sarah Scott's sister attempted to offset the ill effects upon workers of the capitalist improvements she and her husband implemented in their mines and other properties in the north of England (Kelly's preface in Scott [1762] 1995, 34). Scott's utopia echoes this "self-interested philanthropy": "The feminized, Christian economy of *Millenium Hall* is designed to promote similar ends, and to redress the wrongs of women. … The Hall's proprietors achieve their aims by detaching gentry capitalism from courtliness and patriarchy—male-dominated cultures—and re-attaching it to femininity and Christianity" (Kelly's preface in Scott [1762] 1995, 34–35).

FICTIONS OF UNINHABITED ISLANDS AND OTHER UTOPIAN SPACES

The influential and schematically productive excursus on the development of the novel in English, Michael McKeon's *The Origins of the English Novel 1600–1740* (1987), offers an insightful and provocative way to approach instances of utopian (and satirically dystopian) writing in the eighteenth-century century. McKeon posits two intersecting axes that structure the development of the formally realistic novel in eighteenth-century Britain: *questions of truth* enable explorations of veracity and verisimilitude in narrative; *questions of virtue* enable explorations of the ways in which good characters are rewarded (or not) for their honesty and abilities. The questions that the emerging form of the novel explores are also questions utopian writing explores: what is a good society? For whom? How do we know? How well does the world accord with individuals' perceptions of merit and truth—and how does one capture this in narrative form? Explains McKeon: "[The novel] attains its modern, 'institutional' stability and coherence at this time because of its unrivaled power both to formulate, and to explain, a set of problems that are central to early modern experience. These may be understood as problems of categorial instability, which the novel, originating to resolve, also inevitably reflects" (McKeon 1987, 20).

These instabilities include *generic* categories (especially in the novel's incorporation of romance, travel narrative, and journalistic tropes), gender categories, and moral categories; and are reflected through the novel's articulation of both epistemological and ontological confusions:

> Questions of truth and questions of virtue concern different realms of human experience, and they are likely to be raised in very different contexts. Yet in one central respect they are closely analogous. Both pose problems of signification: What kind of authority or evidence is required of narrative to permit it to signify truth to its readers? What kind of social existence or behavior signifies an individual's virtue to others? (McKeon 1987, 20)

McKeon traces a process of exploration and reaction that occurs in dialogic exchanges between naive romance, progressive realism, and skeptical, conservative reaction, which query the truth-effects of realism, while weaving in the imaginative resources of romance. Thus, the cultural instabilities of the eighteenth century, analogized in the structuring of plot and the development of character, are ironically, "the enabling foundation of the eighteenth-century novel" (22).

Utopian concerns about the good life take on a new form with the development of the formally realistic novel. What does this mean for utopian conceptions of "the good life," on the one hand, for individual members of a community as well as for the "commonwealth" of community itself; and on the other, for the disruptive aspect of a changing economic and social complex? In McKeon's formulation, "romance idealism" posits a simple identification of archetypal truth and the satisfying adventures and closures of plot, of the fit between truth and story's outcome. The increasingly realistic mode of the novel form, however, offered a new way to tell a story, with "naive empiricism" signaling truth through quantitative completeness in description; and an answering "extreme skepticism" challenging the truth content of quantitative completeness (indeed, of the concept of descriptive completeness as such, as description requires selection of detail). In parallel, an "aristocratic ideology" positing a simple fit between a protagonist's station and character is challenged by the new novel's "progressive ideology" which opens narratives with the attractive discomfort of status inconsistency, or the lack of fit between the protagonist's station in life and her or his character. In the formally realistic novel, a protagonist of middle-class or lower-class origins receives recognition, after various trials and challenges, of his or her just due. This in turn evokes a response by writers operating out of a conservative ideology that finds the self-serving narratives of lower-class "virtue rewarded" to be unconvincing, at best.

Can utopia be found, or made, in narratives that use the elements of formal realism to explore questions of truth and virtue? Even the first major author of realist fiction, Samuel Richardson, questions his own earlier and massively successful plot device of virtue rewarded (in *Pamela* [1740]), when he writes *Clarissa* (1748), and moves his heroine's reward beyond the world entirely: "In reserving this heroine's [Clarissa's] reward for heaven, Richardson evinces the darker, conservative apprehension that the essence of utopia is that it is not to be found in this world" (McKeon 1987, 418).

This question is best answered by looking at Daniel Defoe's *Robinson Crusoe* (1719) and Jonathan Swift's *Gulliver's Travels* (1726). An important focus in critical literature on utopian writing in the eighteenth century is the complexity of colonial utopianism, or utopian colonialism. Whereas Thomas More's *Utopia* provides a vision of a wanderer who discovers an advanced society that provides a glimpse into a better, healthier, happier world (Bacon's utopia offers the same sort of encounter), subsequent utopian narratives borrow colonizing language and presume the authority and centrality of European culture. The newly discovered island is empty, available for development of the utopian society (or inhabited by individuals who "need" European leadership). The wanderer encounters not advanced civilizations from which he may learn but a *tabula rasa* upon which he can build a society better than, but also drawn from, home. As many have pointed out, discovery of new lands by European explorers provides the framework for adventure tales that contain episodes of encounter with utopian societies (Manuel and Manuel 1979, 432). In most robinsonades, the escapades and loose plotting that end with the hero's eventual success in society overshadow the glimpses of utopia; the pointed purpose of earlier utopias as evoking in their readers an increased understanding of contemporary society in juxtaposition with the ideal is seldom if ever central to the popular fictions of Robinsonian adventures.

The novel that founded this strain of popular fiction is far more complex than its imitators. In the first of what are actually several novels in a series of Crusoe's adventures, questions of truth and questions of virtue are deeply intertwined in ways that prompt questions about the creation of utopia within a narrative shaped by a singular voice speaking about an unfolding and ever-deepening self-understanding acquired through experiences that are framed as truth:

> epistemology is so inextricably embedded in narrative substance that it may feel artificial to separate questions of truth from questions of virtue; but the distinction can be made. It is clear enough that Defoe's claim to historicity oversees the narrative's formal procedures. If it is complicated by the island, the journal, and the temporal dislocations of God's society and the power of imagination, that is because Defoe gives to the notion of the true history of the individual so intimate and introspective a form that it comes close to looking more like self-creation. (McKeon 1987, 336–337)

In striking contrast, Gulliver never gains the self-knowledge or the material rewards of Crusoe, although he also experiences alienation from his home and encounters with others who challenge his sense of self, conveyed through a voice of psychologized self-awareness. "The success of the younger son in Defoe's narrative depends on his ability to internalize providence and to naturalize his appetites; less sympathetically, we might say that he learns how to project this desire and then to forget that he has done it. Gulliver never attains that comfort" (McKeon 1987, 340). Showing every evidence of being a discovered utopia within his journey, Gulliver's Houyhnhnm Land is ultimately profoundly inaccessible to him, its inhabitants entirely alien. Swift asks us to consider the possibility that we could find a utopia that is nonetheless inimical to human life, impossible to adopt or transport. In the end, Gulliver famously finds his former family and mates entirely repulsive and, well, bestial: "Gulliver ends radically at odds with himself, violently repudiating his own human nature yet spurned by that other nature with which he has learned to identify so closely" (McKeon 1987, 340–341).

Crusoe finds himself as he makes a life with remnants of the wrecked ship on what he takes to be a deserted island, bringing another person into the circle of "his" society, renaming and subjugating him in doing so. Gulliver, however, is never able to accommodate himself to any of the societies he encounters, either as commanding presence or as abject prisoner and servant—except within the society of the intelligent race of horses, the Houyhnhnms. Ironically, that final stop on Gulliver's travels makes him unable to accommodate himself to his own contemporary society when he returns. Gulliver's narrative has the same markers of realistic fiction as Crusoe's: specificity of detail; obsessive self-awareness; the apparent humility of an "actual report." But readers are held at a distance by the details recounted; by the many prompts within the fiction that tell us Gulliver is an unreliable narrator; by the carefully crafted satiric presentation of contemporary European, and specifically British, society. In light of the utopian tradition of the traveler's experience of the good society, Jonathan Swift's narrative, every bit as fully as Thomas More's, prompts readers to see through the interstices of the travel narrative to the underlying commentary upon society and, perhaps, to point out the inaccessibility of the good society that forms the foundation for the contrast.

Defoe's *Robinson Crusoe* therefore stands out as an innovation that incorporates elements of utopian speculation not because it returns to a lost clarity of structure as a utopian novel, but because it introduces elements of individualized psychology expressed in narrative that contain the seeds of the novels of Samuel Richardson that are soon to come. The so-called robinsonade, which features the establishment of a utopian society by a castaway on almost uninhabited island, is a motif quickly taken up by other European writers. This narrative offers the prospect of a wholesome society emerging from primitive conditions, given, of course, the importation of European knowledge and practical customs via a resourceful, inventive protagonist.

Conclusion

Utopian speculation of the eighteenth century draws, of course, upon the utopian writing of previous centuries. Utopian writing responds, in this century as always, to the concerns and interests of authors and their envisioned audiences. It is shaped by contemporary forms of imagination, political and philosophical communities and contentions, literary forms, and practical (or what are perceived to be practical) innovations. Distinctive features of utopian speculation in this century emerge with the development of the realist novel and its psychologically complex protagonist, whose inward life and unfolding personal development provide the central subject matter. Other emergent features of eighteenth-century utopia include the emergence of boutique, enclave, or pocket utopias that are situated within, dependent upon, and resistant to a flawed but enabling exterior world; women's writing and women's readership; the increase in number of educational initiatives by and for women; and, late in the century, representations of planned pocket societies designed to ameliorate the living conditions of laborers in particular situations of gentry-owned industries.

References

Claeys, Gregory. 2000. *Restoration and Augustan British Utopias*. Syracuse: Syracuse University Press.

———. 2010. *The Cambridge Companion to Utopian Literature*. Cambridge: Cambridge University Press.

———. 2012. *Utopias of the British Enlightenment*. Cambridge: Cambridge University Press.

Fussell, Paul. 1971. *Samuel Johnson and the Life of Writing*, 1st ed. New York: Harcourt, Brace, Jovanovich.

Johnson, Samuel. (1759) 1990. *The History of Rasselas, Prince of Abissinia*, ed. G.J. Kolb. New Haven: Yale University Press.

Manuel, Frank E., and Fritzie P. Manuel. 1979. *Utopian Thought in the Western World*. Cambridge: Harvard University Press.

McKeon, Michael. 1987. *The Origins of the English Novel 1600–1740*. Baltimore: Johns Hopkins University Press.

Pohl, Nicole, and Brenda Tooley, eds. 2007. *Gender and Utopia in the Eighteenth Century: Essays in English and French Utopian Writing*. Farnham: Ashgate.

Rees, Christine. 1996. *Utopian Imagination and Eighteenth-Century Fiction*. Harlow: Longman Group.

Scott, Sarah. (1762) 1995. *Millenium Hall*, ed. Gary Kelly. Peterborough: Broadview Press.

Swift, Jonathan. (1726) 1960. *Gulliver's Travels*, ed. Louis Landa. Houghton-Mifflin, Riverside.

The Early Nineteenth Century (1800–1850)

Peter Sands

Introduction

The nineteenth century, particularly in the United States, sees the great flowering of utopian literature and alternative living experiments. Things start to pick up after 1850, and the last quarter of the century is particularly full of utopian writing and social schemes. But the first half holds literary historical treasures as well, with around 190 literary utopias published in English, and many of the century's more than 100 communal living experiments beginning before 1850. A standard bibliography such as Lyman Tower Sargent's *Utopian Literature in English: An Annotated Bibliography from 1516 to the Present*, describes approximately 150 utopias between 1800 and 1850, including poetry, political tracts, and early utopian fiction. The present essay owes much to Sargent's bibliography and his "Themes in Utopian Fiction in English Before Wells" (Sargent 1976). Additional important early bibliographical work appears in Kenneth Roemer's *American Utopian Literature (1888–1900): An Annotated Bibliography*, later expanded as part of his *The Obsolete Necessity: America in Utopian Writings, 1888–1900* (Roemer 1976), and his essay in *The Cambridge Companion to Utopian Literature* (Roemer 2010). Many of the texts they describe, such as one of the first modern utopias written by an American woman, Mrs. Mary Griffith's *Three Hundred Years Hence* (1836), prefigure both science-fictional and utopian literature of the latter half of the century. In England and France, Robert Owen's many

P. Sands (✉)
University of Wisconsin-Milwaukee, Milwaukee, WI, USA

P. Marks et al. (eds.), *The Palgrave Handbook of Utopian and Dystopian Literatures*, https://doi.org/10.1007/978-3-030-88654-7_9

essays and books, Saint-Simon's political and scientific works, Étienne Cabet's *Voyage en Icarie* (The Voyage to Icaria, 1840), and Charles Fourier's *Théorie des Quatre Movements et de Destinées Générales* (1808), inspired utopian social experiments in the United Kingdom, Europe, and the New World, including New Harmony in 1825, Oneida in 1848, the Amana Colonies in 1855, and lesser-known or smaller experiments, such as Brook Farm in 1840, memorialized by Nathaniel Hawthorne in *The Blithedale Romance* (1852). This essay surveys the texts in historical context and relationship to utopianism broadly defined, before discussing contemporary treatments of the period. The essay then presents readings of several exemplary texts, particularly from the United States, which largely set the terms for the genre as it developed into utopia, dystopia, critical utopia, critical dystopia, and other contemporary forms later in the nineteenth and through the twentieth century.

Utopian texts of the second half of the century participate in the broad revolutionary ferment of 1848 and beyond in both Europe and the United States. But utopian literary texts also predate the second-half wave in the century. Consider, for instance, Percy Shelley's 1817 poem *Laon and Cythna; or, The Revolution of the Golden City: A Vision of the Nineteenth Century* or his 1819 poem, *The Masque of Anarchy*, both of which engage the possibility of a utopian and egalitarian society and are in response to the contemporary political situation in England and Europe. In 1807 Joel Barlow published *The Columbiad*, a revision of his eighteenth-century epic poem; the text is explicitly utopian about the past and future of the Americas. Throughout the Atlantic world prior to 1850 the developing industrial and scientific revolutions, the economic depression of 1807–1814, the Second Great Awakening of 1800–1840, changing views on slavery and women's rights, and challenges to existing forms of government such as the US and French Revolutions and the Haitian Revolution of 1791–1804 are part of a trans-Atlantic conversation about the possibility of alternatives. And US utopias before the Civil War, including the earliest American movement toward the gynotopias of the latter half of the century, illustrate ways the early Republic is itself an expression of utopianism. No less an authority than Gordon S. Wood (2015, 229) writes that "[t]he republican revolution was the greatest utopian movement in American history. The revolutionaries aimed at nothing less than a reconstitution of American society [...]. They sought to construct a society and governments based on virtue and disinterested public leadership and to set in motion a moral movement that would eventually be felt around the globe." As Spiller et al. (1974, 215) write in *The Literary History of the United States*, "as much as during the eighteenth century, it was, in the early years of the nineteenth, still a Utopian land, or rather a land where Utopias became realities." The founders of the United States literally wrote into being an alternative to their present; in that sense, early nineteenth-century literary texts participate in both legal and literary developments that Robert A. Ferguson (1984, 8) identifies as "contrasting visions of the republic and a dialectic in post-Revolutionary searches for national identity that pitted millennial utopianism against common law theory." Thus, as in other eras, utopias of the period address themselves to labor, education, women's rights and roles, economics, and the transition from the mostly monarchical and agrarian eighteenth-century societies of both the Old World and the New to the new political organizations and industrial and urban societies of the later nineteenth century and the present.

Contemporary Critical and Theoretical Debates

There is not a great deal of scholarship on specifically utopian literary texts in English for the period 1800–1850, excepting a small but steady stream on late eighteenth- and early nineteenth-century social reformers such as Robert Owen of New Lanark in the United Kingdom and communitarian experiments in the United States. Scholarship on early American literature tends to be on the sparse side, and has been for some time, as occasionally noted in the influential annual *American Literary Scholarship*; early American utopian literature does not occupy a prominent place in either critical theoretical or literary critical discourses, partly because the corpus of texts is relatively small and partly because the bulk of literary critical work on early American literature is more focused on texts and practices more typical of the general late eighteenth and early nineteenth century, such as the continuing formal development of the novel and the quickly rising print culture in the Atlantic world. In the American context that means the political and essayistic texts of the Revolutionary and early Republic periods, the circulation of Anglo and European literary texts in the colonies and early republic, and the rise of American literary and belletristic writing by native-born or transplanted Americans.

This is not to say that there are no formally utopian texts in the period, but rather that there is a more prominent utopianism—embodied in the texts of the Declaration of Independence, the Articles of Confederation, and the US Constitution as documenting the imagination and execution of the alternative—and a less prominent set of actual utopian fictions, essays, and poems. And this leaves aside the utopian impulse animating actual communitarian experiments in both the colonies and the early United States. Sargent notes that communes had appeared in North America as early as 1663, and that the Plymouth colony itself can be read as a kind of "communitarian experiment" (Sargent 1976, 278) All of which is to say that the utopia, whether strictly defined as Sargent does in "The Three Faces of Utopia Revisited" as "a non-existent society described in considerable detail and normally located in space and time" (Sargent 1994, 9) or more loosely as others have done, is present across multiple genres and forms of expression, and might best be looked at through the lens of utopianism. Sargent defines utopianism as "social dreaming" in the same work, but it would be fair to say that the two-word definition does not quite capture the sense of utopianism as an attitude, feeling, or affect in texts which are not full-blown or centrally created as utopias but which instead carry the sense of possibility or Not-Yetness derived from Bloch's work on utopia in *The Principle of Hope* and *The Spirit of Utopia*. Another way to put this is that "utopia is the expression of the desire for a better way of living" (Levitas 1990, 8) which is how Ruth Levitas begins her essential exploration of the utopian impulse in *The Concept of Utopia*. As Levitas notes, the tendency toward focusing on formal elements of texts as determining whether they are utopias elides their content and function to no good end, and de-emphasizes the processual character of utopianism, a thought captured by that ancient conservative Noah Webster, when he wrote that "a fundamental mistake of the Americans has been that they considered the revolution as completed when it was just begun" (Webster 1789, 214)[1] Consider, finally, that significant works of abolitionist or emancipationist literature depend for their narrative power on an imagined alternative, a society not built on slavery. In that vein, a text such as Martin Delany's unfinished 1859 novel, *Blake, or the Huts of America*, which imagines a slave revolution in response to the Fugitive Slave Act, or Frederick Douglass's 1845 autobiography *Narrative of the Life of Frederick Douglass, an American Slave*, are also arguments for that imagined other world.

As with the relative paucity of critical work on utopias and utopianism in literature of the period 1800–1850, contemporary theoretical work on utopian literature is generally not framed through or for the study of early American or contemporaneous English texts. In the English case, there is of course scholarship on early nineteenth-century texts, but the relative paucity of significant formal utopias in the period means that much of the scholarship—on Shelley's poems of anarchy and utopia, e.g.,—is not utopian studies scholarship per se. Exceptions appear, as in the scholarship on Mary Shelley's 1826 *The Last Man*, a postapocalyptic novel, but on the whole, neither literary critical nor theoretical work as a rule addresses the utopian works of the period, in part because the years immediately after 1850 provide more grist for the scholar's mill. The perceptive and readable Peter Ruppert spends no time at all writing about English or American utopias or utopians of the period, and the more expansive and encyclopedic work of the Manuels devotes a mere 114 pages of their nearly 900 to the period, and that centered around Saint-Simon, Fourier, and Owen, rather than on literary texts, and in the service of their broad historical overview of "utopian propensities."[2] This is not to say that influential theoretical work such as Fredric Jameson's and his student Philip Wegner cannot be applied to the study of the period, but that their exemplars and concerns do not generally or directly address, say, Symzonia. Important critical work on women's writing and writing by enslaved persons either picks up the thread later in the century or does not focus on utopianism. It is more common to find historical work, such as Richard Slotkin's (1973) myth-and-symbol studies of the American Frontier or Leo Marx's *The Machine in the Garden* (1964), addressing themselves to pastoral or other versions of the national imaginary that are at least utopias-adjacent. Again, more focused critical and theoretical attention is paid to the founding documents of the American experiment. For instance, Ferguson's classic *Law and Letters in American Culture* explores the broad interplay between and among legal writing, essays, fiction, and other forms of prose and dramatic expression (as well as in the case of Joel Barlow, poetry), which necessarily involves the (unnamed, unacknowledged) utopianism animating early American literature and culture. Ferguson's third chapter takes its title from the Preamble to the US Constitution: "To form a more perfect union," a phrase that perfectly encapsulates both the intent of the Framers and the utopianism which runs throughout the idea of America.

Other important critical work regularly addressed in *American Literary Scholarship* reads African-American, Native American, and women writers; in the case of abolitionist work, the strain of utopianism—the imagination of a world freed of slavery and organized thus on a completely different social, economic, and racial model—remains largely unremarked but ripe for critical reading. An enterprising scholar might make much of both recovery work and of reading into a utopian studies framework narratives of slave uprising from prior to 1850.

READINGS OF SPECIFIC TEXTS

Utopian texts of the early nineteenth century have about them more of the romance than the novel, in that they are filled with stock characters, but they also have about them the peculiar form of the genre: didactic dialogue wars with didactic exposition for primacy, both at a scope and vision far removed from the coming interiority of fiction later in the century. Consider, for instance, John Lithgow's *Equality—A Political Romance*, published in Philadelphia in 1802. The text is an anticapitalist tract that engages with the economic downturn of the early Republic and imagines a lifelong equitable distribution of resources and responsibilities, at least for men. It does not thrill with character or plot development.

Responses to economic crisis were not the only venue for utopian and alternative imaginaries, however. In the same decade, Washington Irving included the satirical short "The Men of the Moon," in his *Knickerbocker's History of New York* (1809). In that story, a trenchant take on colonial abuse of indigenous peoples, Irving imagines an invasion by "Lunatics," a green-skinned race from the Moon who take over Earth and confine humanity to what are thinly disguised reservations. The moon as a site of alternative or imagined societies was fairly popular in early nineteenth-century fiction, as well as the subject of a treasure of early cinema a century later, *Le voyage dans la Lune* (1902) by Georges Méliès; in many cases the setting on the moon is a clear synecdoche for colonial or imperial outposts on Earth.

The most widely known early American utopia is *Symzonia: A Voyage of Discovery*, an 1820 novel fictionalizing the theories of the explorer John Cleves Symmes but published under the pseudonym Jonathan Seymour and sometimes tentatively attributed to Nathaniel Ames, a sailor and nautical writer. *Symzonia* is a hollow-earth novel depicting a society inside the planet. This society of preternaturally white-skinned people is free of violence and illness, Christian, and in many ways a counterpoint to the colonial and violent society of the nineteenth century. It ends with the Symzonians banishing their American discoverers when they learn of the violence and illness plaguing surface-dwelling society. *Symzonia* is an important source text for Edgar Allan Poe's *The Narrative of Arthur Gordon Pym of Nantucket* (1838), which also posits a hollow-earth society populated by a race of small, completely white-skinned people. Poe's short novel, the only full-length fiction published in his lifetime, is not a fully developed utopia but, in addition to being a lost-at-sea adventure considered an important source for *Moby-Dick*, presents an encounter with a degenerate dark-skinned surface-dwelling lost tribe—through whose territory the narrator must pass to reach the white utopian society inside the hollow earth[3]; the latter an imagined alternative to American society very much in the vein of *Symzonia*.

Less known but perhaps more important is Mrs. Mary Griffith's *Three Hundred Years Hence*, published in 1836, and the only text of consequence prior to 1850 treated in Carol Farley Kessler's *Daring to Dream: Utopian Fiction by United States Women Before 1950* (1995). This is widely considered the first utopia by an American woman, but primacy might arguably go to Eliza Winkfield's *The Female American* (1767) if its provenance were more certain. Griffith was a writer of prose sketches, horticultural works, and science texts, publishing in both learned journals and popular press. *Three Hundred Years Hence* originally appeared in *Camperdown; or, News from Our Neighbourhood*, a collection of sketches, before being rediscovered and reissued on its own in 1950 as a recovered work of early science fiction, and again in 1975 with a preface by the important science fiction editor David Hartwell. In Griffith's novel, protagonist Edgar Hastings, a Quaker, falls asleep and is buried under his own collapsed house in 1835. The burial somehow preserves him in a state of suspended animation; he awakens in 2135. A fairly standard utopian narrative dialogue between Hastings and a representative of the future society reveals its contours and limns the sociopolitical world of the early republic through implicit and sometimes direct comparison and reference. The text anticipates Edward Bellamy's better-known 1888 novel, *Looking Backward*, in its suspended-animation time-travel device and several other particulars. Griffiths argues for gender equality in property ownership, contracting, education, and ability to work, but she divides men and women according to traditional gender roles and limits the kinds of employments most women seek to those traditionally assigned to women, with some exceptions, as in the case of small businesses owned and operated by women in the public markets. She imagines a collective reliance on social goods, education, equitable distribution of wealth, and a very limited role for the state and relative limits on the military, and presents a laundry list of governmental goals and functions toward the socialist end of the political spectrum—a kind of libertarian socialism. The rest of the novel outlines much that would tend toward in some sense a feminist viewpoint but she clearly preserves as proper societal structures which maintain the different status and role of women, while rejecting this differentiation as necessarily creating a second-class status for women. She is willing to forgo the Quaker dress of her 1835 setting, preferring apparently that of 1780 (a significant year, since in 1789 the Constitution is ratified, and a woman of 1780 would be a woman of the first decade of the American Republic as Griffith understood it). In that, perhaps she is saying that the Quakers, with their theological and political divisions that she discusses briefly, represent the potential division of American life over similar or analogous disputes. She takes as inevitable that the country will change—will send the slaves to Liberia; will modernize technologically and will remove much of the drudgery, uncertainty, and danger from occupations; will take as a matter of course the responsibility of the state to shepherd and guide society through regulation and laws; and that women will come into their own as citizens, while retaining divisions between men and women based on their physical natures and distinct sensibilities. Thus, particularly in the context of early US political formations and its actual development over the past 185 years, hers was a radical vision of the community of goods somehow combined with a system of private capital and property that maintained mostly economic social divisions while somehow also creating a more egalitarian and safety-conscious society. Moreover, its fundamental expectation of equitable distribution of education, wealth, and opportunity was largely standard in later US utopias, and against which dystopian texts appearing after 1850, particularly texts trenchantly addressing actual inequities of class and gender might be measured. Such exploration of gender and labor equity became a standard center for utopian and dystopian fictions. For instance, consider an even more obscure example of a utopian text of the period addressing women's rights, "A New Society," published in 1841 by Betsey Guppy Chamberlain in *The Lowell Offering*, an organ for publishing writing by women mill workers. Chamberlain is sometimes also identified as a Native American writer, but there is no definitive evidence either way on that question. Her text imagines gender equity and equitable economic treatment of labor in the form of a manifesto.

Not long after Griffith, the French writer Étienne Cabet published *Voyage en Icarie* (1840), a communist utopia the Manuels (1979, 376) refer to as the "most-popular nineteenth-century exemplar" of the "flat, two-dimensional utopian model" employed by most texts between Thomas More and the French Revolution. Cabet's utopia replaced capitalism with worker's cooperatives and was popular enough that, hounded by problems in Europe and England, Cabet founded two utopian communes in the United States in 1848, the same year that Marx and Engels published *The Communist Manifesto*.[4] Cabet's work is often considered alongside the other major influence on communal experiments, Charles Fourier, who between 1808 and 1837 published several works that led to the formation of "phalanxes," or cooperative utopian communities, particularly in North America.[5] While not strictly a literary text, his *Théorie des quatre mouvements et des destinées générales* (*Theory of the Four Movements*) is a wildly speculative and surreal vision of humanity's future organization and evolution. Fourier's ideas sparked around 300 communal experiments, including the famous one at Brook Farm in Massachusetts, from his stay at which Nathaniel Hawthorne wrote *The Blithedale Romance* (1852). As Sean Wilentz (2005, 721) notes, "various utopian writers," including those associated with Fourierism in the early nineteenth century, attached themselves to movements such as the National Reform Association dedicated to creating economic equality through land ownership in the hopes "that the wage slave would be freed." Even earlier in the century, Owenites had attempted to put Robert Owen's ideas into practice in the famous community at New Harmony, Indiana. New Harmony lasted only a short time but inspired as many as twenty others in the United States and England (Pitzer 1997, 9). Those who occupied the intentional communities enacting the ideas of Fourier, Cabet, Owen, and others, believed they were "engaged in building the society of the future on the principle of association" (Spiller et al. 1974, 646). Parallel and sometimes overlapping religious, but similarly utopian communities, such as those of the Mormons and Hutterites, appear throughout the early years of the century.

In addition to the texts which fall under ordinary definitions of utopian literature, a number of novels in the period, such as *Pym*, use utopian tropes or utopianism but are not strictly utopias. A major example would be Herman Melville's first novel, *Typee: A Peep at Polynesian Life*. The young Melville fictionalized his own and others' experiences at sea, centering on the captivity of a young deserter in the Marquesas. While often read as an adventure story, and particularly as a story of cannibalism among Pacific Islanders, it is also a utopian meditation on the alternative organization of society by indigenous peoples versus European and US colonial and genocidal ambitions globally and on the North American continent. An odder document largely ignored in the writer's corpus is James Fenimore Cooper's *The Crater* (1847). H. Daniel Peck (1988, 250) thinks of it as the "first true allegorical novel" in American literature, and says that it "represents symbolically the course of America's empire—its past, present, and future." A shipwrecked sailor makes use of an island created by volcanic eruption to "develop and colonize" the land, which ultimately is destroyed by a second eruption not long after the sailor, Mark Woolston, is deposed by sociopolitical forces running counter to Cooper's conservative and class-based politics, mirroring those in the United States of the time. *The Crater* begins with a short discussion of the value of imagined worlds for understanding the actual, and a claim that the novel's events might be read as "a timely warning" (Cooper 1885, 2–5). It ends with a stentorious lecture on the folly of humans who "forget our origin and destination, substituting self for that divine hand which can alone unite the elements of worlds..."; in other words: be wary of imagining alternatives to divinely ordered political life.

CONCLUSION

While the early nineteenth century did not produce as many utopias as the second half, it remains a worthwhile period for study and critique. For instance, such texts as Jane Sophia Appleton's "Sequel to the 'Vision of Bangor in the Twentieth Century,'" and the text to which it responds, Edward Kent's "A Vision of Bangor in the Twentieth Century," are frequently presented as the polar opposites that they are—Kent's treatment of women prompting Appleton's rejoinder. On their own they are interesting artifacts of their times, with Appleton predicting a temperance-society of colonialism American patriarchy encompassing the whole hemisphere, built on traditional gender roles and freed from the apparent curse of writing. Appleton, succinctly summarized by Darby Lewes in her *Gynotopia: A Checklist of Nineteenth-Century Utopias by American Women*, counters with a vision more like Griffiths: gender parity but not sameness, financial independence for women, and, startlingly, a retreat from political life by women because "order and beauty" have been restored and their input is no longer needed. Kent, at the time governor of the US state of Maine, envisions the elimination of both slavery and socialism and dismisses the possibility of women participating in government as ridiculous because of their distraction by fripperies. Appleton replies with a vision of a post-conflict world, communal eating, and cooperative labor, and the emancipation of women from patriarchy and politics. Perhaps needless to say, the two visions, minor responses to the revolutions and economic upheavals of the late eighteenth century and early nineteenth, remain locked in combat today.

NOTES

1. Cited in Wilentz, *The Rise of American Democracy: Jefferson to Lincoln*, 10.
2. See Manuel and Manuel, *Utopian Thought in the Western World*; Ruppert, *Reader in a Strange Land: The Activity of Reading Literary Utopias*.
3. On hollow-earth fictions, *see* Fitting, *Subterranean Worlds: A Critical Anthology*.
4. For this and other utopian living experiments, *see* Pitzer, *America's Communal Utopias*.
5. See Guarneri, *The Utopian Alternative: Fourierism in Nineteenth-Century America*.

REFERENCES

American Literary Scholarship. 1963. Durham, NC: Duke University Press.
Appleton, Jane Sophia. 1848. Sequel to the "Vision of Bangor in the Twentieth Century". In *Voices from the Kenduskeag*, 243–265. Bangor: David Bugbee.

Barlow, Joel. 2008. *The Columbiad*. [Miami, Fla.]: Wolf Den Books.

Bellamy, Edward. 2003. *Looking Backward, 2000–1887*. Peterborough, ON, Canada: Broadview.

Bloch, Ernst. 1986. *The Principle of Hope*, trans. Neville Plaice, Stephen Place, and Paul Knight. Cambridge, MA: MIT Press.

———. 2000. *The Spirit of Utopia*. Stanford, CA: Stanford University Press.

Cabet, Étienne. 2003. *Travels in Icaria*. Syracuse: Syracuse University Press.

Chamberlain, Betsey Guppey. 1841. *A New Society. The Lowell Offering; A Repository of Original Articles*, Written Exclusively By Females Employed in the Mills (Lowell, MA) 1: 191–192.

Cooper, James Fenimore. 1885. *The Crater; or, Vulcan's Peak, a Tale of the Pacific*. New York: J. W. Lovell.

Delany, Martin Robison, and Jerome J. McGann. 2017. *Blake or, the Huts of America: A*. Corrected. Cambridge, MA: Harvard University Press.

Douglass, Frederick, and Scott C. Williamson. 2021. *Narrative of the Life of Frederick Douglass, an American Slave*. Macon: Mercer University Press.

Ferguson, Robert A. 1984. *Law and Letters in American Culture*. Cambridge, MA: Harvard University Press.

Fitting, Peter. 2004. *Subterranean Worlds: A Critical Anthology*. Middletown, CT: Wesleyan University Press.

Fourier, Charles. 1967. *Théorie Des Quatre Mouvements Et Des Destinées Générales*. Paris: J.-J. Pauvert.

Griffith, Mary. 1975. *Three Hundred Years Hence*. Boston: G. K. Hall.

Guarneri, Carl. 1991. *The Utopian Alternative: Fourierism in Nineteenth-Century America*. Ithaca, NY: Cornell University Press.

Hawthorne, Nathaniel, and Richard H. Millington. 2011. *The Blithedale Romance: An Authoritative Text, Contexts, Criticism*. New York: W. W. Norton.

Irving, Washington. 1959. *Knickerbocker's History of New York*. New York: F. Ungar.

Kent, Edward. 1848. A Vision of Bangor, in the Twentieth Century. *Voices from the Kenduskeag*. Bangor: David Bugbee.

Kessler, Carol Farley, ed. 1995. *Daring to Dream: Utopian Fiction by United States Women Before 1950*. Syracuse, NY: Syracuse University Press.

Levitas, Ruth. 1990. *The Concept of Utopia*. Syracuse, NY: Syracuse University Press.

Lewes, Darby. 1989. Gynotopia: A Checklist of Nineteenth-Century Utopias by American Women. *Legacy* 6 (2) (Fall): 29–41.

Lithgow, John. 1802. Equality—A Political Romance. *The Temple of Reason* (Philadelphia, PA) 2: 17–23.

Manuel, Frank E., and Fritzie P. Manuel. 1979. *Utopian Thought in the Western World*. Cambridge, MA: Harvard University Press.

Marx, Leo. 1964. *The Machine in the Garden; Technology and the Pastoral Ideal in America*. New York: Oxford University Press.

Peck, H. Daniel. 1988. Cooper and the Writers of the Frontier. In *Columbia Literary History of the United States*, ed. Emory Elliott, Martha Banta, and Houston A. Baker, 240–261. New York: Columbia University Press.

Pitzer, Donald E. 1997. *America's Communal Utopias*. Chapel Hill: University of North Carolina Press.

Poe, Edgar Allan, Frederick S. Frank, and Diane Long Hoeveler. 2010. *The Narrative of Arthur Gordon Pym of Nantucket*. Peterborough, ON: Broadview Press.

Roemer, Kenneth M. 1971. American Utopian Literature (1888–1900): An Annotated Bibliography. *American Literary Realism* 4 (3): 227–254.

———. 1976. *The Obsolete Necessity: America in Utopian Writings, 1888–1900*. [Kent, Ohio]: Kent State University Press.

———. 2010. Paradise Transformed: Varieties of Nineteenth-Century Utopias. In *The Cambridge Companion to Utopian Literature*, ed. Gregory Claeys, 79–106. Cambridge: Cambridge University Press.

Ruppert, Peter. 1986. *Reader in a Strange Land: The Activity of Reading Literary Utopias*. Athens: University of Georgia Press.

Sargent, Lyman Tower. 1976. Themes in Utopian Fiction in English Before Wells. *Science Fiction Studies* 3 (3): 275–282.

———. 1994. The Three Faces of Utopianism Revisited. *Utopian Studies* 5 (1): 1–37.

———. 2016. Utopian Literature in English: An Annotated Bibliography from 1516 to the Present. http://openpublishing.psu.edu/utopia/. Accessed 13 June 2021.

Shelley, Mary Wollstonecraft. 2019. *The Last Man*. Mineola, New York: Dover Publications.

Shelley, Percy Bysshe. 1817. *Laon and Cythna; or, the Revolution of the Golden City: A Vision of the Nineteenth Century. In the Stanza of Spenser*. n.p.

———. 1990. *The Masque of Anarchy 1832*. Oxford, England; New York: Woodstock Books.

Shelley, Percy Bysshe, and Anahid Nersessian. 2016. *Laon and Cythna: Or, the Revolution of the Golden City*. Peterborough, ON: Broadview Press.

Slotkin, Richard. 1973. *Regeneration Through Violence: The Mythology of the American Frontier, 1600–1860*. Hanover, NH: Wesleyan University Press.

Spiller, Robert Ernest, Thomas Herbert Johnson, and Richard M. Ludwig, eds. 1974. *Literary History of the United States*. New York: Macmillan.

Symmes, John Cleves [Capt. Adam Seaborn, pseud.]. 1974. *Symzonia; Voyage of Discovery*. NY: Arno Press.

Webster, Noah. 1789. *An American Selection of Lessons in Reading and Speaking*. Philadelphia: Young and McCulloch.

Wilentz, Sean. 2005. *The Rise of American Democracy: Jefferson to Lincoln*. New York: Norton.

Winkfield, Eliza. 2014. *The Female American*, ed. Michelle Burnham and James Freitas. Tonawanda, NY: Broadview Press.

Wood, Gordon S. 2015. *The American Revolution: Writings from the Pamphlet Debate*. New York: Library of America.

The Late Nineteenth Century (1848–1899)

Matthew Beaumont

Introduction

In one of a series of articles entitled "What the People Read," printed in the English periodical the *Academy* in 1898, "A Wife" is asked whether she likes "novels about the future." How does she respond? "She pondered a moment, wrinkling her brows," the anonymous author of this informative piece on the popular reading habits of the time comments, in distinctly condescending tones, before reporting her answer: "'Well, I can't say that I exactly *like* them', she said; 'but one has to read them, because everyone talks about them'" (Anonymous 1898, 293).

H.G. Wells first published *The War of the Worlds* in book form in 1898, and the popularity of his "scientific romances" in the second half of the 1890s is no doubt the immediate reason for the apparently ingenuous confession of the "Wife" interviewed or invented for the purposes of the article in the *Academy*. Novels about the future had however proved a commercially viable phenomenon for publishers throughout the previous decade; indeed, women novelists, some of whom were feminists chafing precisely against being identified as no more than wives, were increasingly the authors as well as readers of utopian fiction. The most decisive shift, in terms of the regeneration or reinvention of the utopian genre, took place from 1888. This was the year in which Edward Bellamy's utopian blockbuster *Looking Backward, 2000–1887* first appeared in the United States. Bellamy's novel of the future, especially popular

M. Beaumont (✉)
University College, London, UK

P. Marks et al. (eds.), *The Palgrave Handbook of Utopian and Dystopian Literatures*, https://doi.org/10.1007/978-3-030-88654-7_10

in its second edition, sold some 200,000 copies in the United States during its first year in print. In Britain, where the *Review of Reviews* reported sales of some 100,000 copies by 1890, it was almost as successful. There, the first generation to have benefitted from the limited achievements of the Elementary Education Act of 1870 formed an enthusiastic readership for its visions of a democratic, egalitarian future. The "Bellamy Library of Fact and Fiction," a series of cheap, pocket-sized books curated by the British publisher William Reeves over the course of the 1890s, catered to precisely this constituency. Its sixpence edition of *Looking Backward* included both an index of ideas and an additional chapter comprising a précis of the book's politics.

In addition to attracting hundreds of thousands of readers, from the working as well as middle classes, the book inspired hundreds of writers. Or its commercial success did. Some of these marketed themselves as direct responses to Bellamy's utopia. In 1890 alone, for instance, *Looking Further Backward*, *Looking Backward and What I Saw*, and *Looking Further Forward* all appeared in print. Others, most famously William Morris's *News from Nowhere*, initially serialized in 1890, adopted a slightly more oblique relationship to *Looking Backward*. Beyond the Anglosphere, meanwhile, the economist Theodor Hertzka's *Freeland: A Social Anticipation* (1889) rapidly sold tens of thousands of copies in its German edition, earning its author the sobriquet "the Austrian Bellamy." The years from 1888 to 1898—when Bellamy, the accidental leader of a not insubstantial political movement associated with the Populists, finally died of tuberculosis—were utopian fiction's *anni mirabili*. By then, more than 500,000 copies of *Looking Backward* had been sold in the United States, and it was well on its way to becoming only the second novel published there, after *Uncle Tom's Cabin* (1852), to sell a million copies. "Taking the test of direct intellectual influence," the sober-minded English economist J.A. Hobson attested in a useful survey of "The Utopian Romance" in 1898, "we must account 'Looking Backward' one of the most important literary events of the century" (Hobson 1898, 179). Readers' romance with the "utopian romance" probably faded from this point on. If 1898 marked the publication of Wells's *War of the Worlds*, a distinctly dystopian "novel about the future," then it also marked the publication of Ebenezer Howard's *To-Morrow: A Peaceful Path to Real Reform*, a conspicuously pragmatic program for what came to be called the "garden-city movement."

Innumerable utopian and anti-utopian fictions, then, appeared at the *fin de siècle*, above all in Britain and the United States, but also in Europe, Japan, and Russia. If this was a time of imperial expansion, as the names of these countries imply, when the most economically or militarily powerful nation-states were committed to extending their colonial borders in order more effectively to compete with one another in the increasingly cut-throat capitalist marketplace, then it was a time too in which, to paraphrase a formulation from one of H. Rider Haggard's contemporaneous novels of colonial adventure, these same nations, not least through the increasingly profitable fiction industry, dramatically extended the "empire of the imagination" (Haggard 1998, 161). As imperialists expropriated spaces and marketplaces that had hitherto been the preserve principally of native peoples, especially in Africa and parts of Asia, opening them up to commercial opportunities that ruthlessly served the nation-states they represented, so journalists, novelists, and social commentators of all stripes colonized a temporality that had previously remained relatively resistant to the political imagination: the future. The utopian tradition that commenced with Thomas More's *Utopia* (1516) had generally located the ideal society it posited in unmapped space. Bellamy and his imitators relocated it to a relatively far-distant future. This appealed to readers in an epoch shaped both by an acute sense of historical expectation, at once optimistic and pessimistic, and a deepening suspicion that, because of the pace of imperial expansion, the opportunities for peopling the planet's unmapped space with utopian possibilities were rapidly disappearing. In the political imagination, there was a scramble for the future. As the Freethinker George William Foote put it in 1886, a couple of years before the explosion of utopian fiction initiated by *Looking Backward*, "at the present day, social dreams are once more rife" (Foote 1886, 190).

The explosion of utopian thinking in the later nineteenth century, the most striking symptom of which was probably the popularity of "novels about the future," must then be seen in part as a consequence of the development of this phase of imperialism. But various other, more proximate historical developments, related to the reorganization of capitalism along inter-imperial lines, helped determine the phenomenon. The third quarter of the nineteenth century, roughly between the revolutions across Europe in 1848 and the brief achievement of the Paris Commune in 1871, was a period in which, aside from its innately competitive character, the industrial capitalist system seemed comparatively stable, in contrast to the *fin de siècle*. These were fairly affluent decades for the manufacturing middle classes; and the working classes, for their part, benefitting in certain limited, temporary respects from this situation, as well as bruised by the defeats of the late 1840s, adopted a broadly defensive, as opposed to openly confrontational, relationship to capitalism. The demise of Chartism in Britain, and the assimilation of its political energies to the middle-class movement for electoral reform, is exemplary in this respect. This kind of accommodation between labor and capital, albeit uncomfortable, did not lead to the kind of contradictory, unstable social conditions in which the utopian imagination is habitually stimulated. As the historian E.H. Carr once neatly put it, "the failures and disillusionments which followed the revolutions of 1848 created a climate unpropitious to Utopias" (Carr 1969, 15). From the end of the 1840s to the beginning of the 1870s, an era of social and economic stabilization, capitalism seemed for the first time not merely militant but triumphant. And there are, in consequence, relatively few utopian fictions from this time (Nathaniel Hawthorne's *Blithedale Romance* (1852) is perhaps the exception that proves the rule, since it is a retrospective, and openly nostalgic, account of his time at Brook Farm, the Transcendentalist community in Massachusetts, in 1841).

The events of the early 1870s challenged this fragile settlement. Perhaps the most dramatic development, in this respect, was the irruption, in the aftermath of the Franco-Prussian conflict, of the Paris Commune. Before the brutal suppression of this brief experiment in proletarian democracy, when more than 15,000 Parisians were killed by French troops led by General Thiers, the Commune opened up the prospect, horrifying or inspiring depending on the onlooker's politics, of a post-capitalist future. For the first time since 1848, "the spectre of revolution once again irrupted into a confident capitalist world," as Eric Hobsbawm put it (Hobsbawm 1962, 248). Furthermore, the effects of this political shock to the European ruling class, apparent in the United States as well as throughout the continent and in Britain, were reinforced by the series of economic recessions that defined capitalism in the epoch of the Great Depression, so-called, from approximately the early 1870s to the early 1890s. As a result, the bourgeoisie "was a little less confident than before, and its assertions of self-confidence therefore a little shriller, perhaps a little more worried about its future" (Hobsbawm 1962, 308). These socio-economic conditions, in contrast to those of the third quarter of the nineteenth century, were distinctly propitious to utopias, to use Carr's terms. As Wells remarked in an article on "Utopias" in 1939, overstating or simplifying the matter only slightly, "the more disturbed men's minds are, the more Utopias multiply" (Wells 1980, 198). Women's minds, too. From the spiritualist and suffragist Annie Denton Cridge's *Man's Rights; or, How Would You Like It?* (1870) to Charlotte Perkins Gilman's famous *Herland* (1915), via Mary E. Bradley Lane's feminist science fiction *Mizora: A Prophecy* (1880–1881), women's battles for social, sexual, and political equality were increasingly reflected in novels about the future.

The economic recessions and the political ructions of the late nineteenth century, which included struggles for women's as well as workers' rights, created a culture characterized both by anxiety and expectancy. "Expectancy belongs by nature to a time balanced uneasily between two great periods of change," the English social reformer C.F.G. Masterman claimed at the turn of the century: "on the one hand is a past still showing faint survivals of vitality; on the other is the future but hardly coming to birth" (Masterman 1905, xii). This perception that an uncertain present was parturient with an unknown future was a pervasive feature of the *fin de siècle*. From the early 1870s, indeed, there were both hopes and fears that this future, more or less apocalyptic, might take the form either of the collapse of capitalism or the realization of socialism, or both together. These fantasies were first refracted, via a convenient coincidence, through the differing visions of an alternative future articulated in two or three popular and influential fictions that appeared on the scene almost simultaneously in early May 1871, at the height of the Paris Commune. On the 1st of May, George Chesney published *The Battle of Dorking* (1871), a scare-mongering account of a Prussian invasion of the

South coast of England, in *Blackwood's Magazine*; and Edward Bulwer-Lytton published *The Coming Race* (1871), a novel which imagined an innately aristocratic people whose inventive use of a formidable subterranean energy source called Vril has enabled them to build an alternative civilization that ultimately threatens to colonize the entire earth. On that same day, Samuel Butler deposited the manuscript of *Erewhon* (1872), his Swiftian satire of Victorian society, which is centered on the fantastical, if prophetic idea that machines might acquire consciousness, with his editor at Chapman and Hall. "The last four or five years," testified one well-informed librarian in 1873, in his "Bibliography of Utopias and Imaginary Travels and Histories," "have been remarkably fruitful in works of a Utopian character." He identified "the new political influences resulting from the late Franco-Prussian war"—that is, the Paris Commune—as one of the principal reasons for this (Presley 1873, 22).

These three fictions, by Chesney, Bulwer-Lytton, and Butler, each of which in different ways proved influential in the subsequent development of the utopian or dystopian novel, were not of course direct responses to the Paris Commune. But they resonated nonetheless in the climate of anxiety and expectancy fostered at a time when, under the pressure of increasing, if intermittent, economic and political setbacks for the ruling class throughout Europe and in the United States, the narrative of progress that, in ideological terms, framed and justified the expansion both of capitalism and imperialism, came to seem comparatively implausible. Readers of *The Coming Race*, for example, especially ones with a sense of contemporary developments on the continent, or memories of the so-called Hungry Forties, probably recognized the figure of an angry, politically resurgent working class in the terrifying sight the hero glimpses as he first inadvertently penetrates the underground society of the Vril-ya: "a vast and terrible head, with open jaws and dull, ghastly, hungry eyes" (Bulwer-Lytton 1871, 10). So, no doubt, did readers of *The Time Machine* (1895), in which Wells portrays the cannibalistic Morlocks as troglodytic descendants of the industrial proletariat, a quarter of a century later. Gustave Flaubert, it seems, was not the only member of the European middle class to feel traumatized by what he apparently referred to as the "Gothicity" of the Paris Commune (quoted in Jellinek 1937, 417). Indeed, numerous commentators on the revolution unfolding in France in 1871 underscored its ominous, if not catastrophic, implications for the future of civilization itself. For instance, one article on "The English Working Classes and the Paris Commune," published in *Fraser's Magazine* in 1871, after the Communards' cataclysmic defeat, argued that "the Commune has only been scotched, not killed," and that "its essential elements are left alive, and they will breed and brood." The "spirit that in France took the name of Communism," it concluded, is "stalking abroad," and, "if not exorcised, will mean social disturbance, and may come to mean social destruction."

These fears determinately shaped the dystopian imagination that, intimately tied to the utopian imagination of this period, emerged in the late nineteenth century. They are palpable, for example, in the anti-communist fantasies that, openly functioning as propaganda, shaped a number of short stories and novels published in the aftermath of the Commune. Among these "cacotopias," as they might be called, *The Commune in London* (1871), by Samuel Bracebridge Hemyng, the author of some twenty romances and boys'-own adventure novels, is particularly vivid in its presentation of ruling-class anxiety (see Beaumont 2005, 129–168). Subtitled a "Chapter of Anticipated History," and purporting to record events that take place some "Thirty Years Hence," it portrays an English working class stirred into insurrection by the cumulative effects of a Reform Bill, a German invasion like the one pictured in such detail by Chesney, and an imminent economic depression (Hemyng 1871). It thus took the temperature of the times rather efficiently, even if it apparently remained unconscious of the fact that these circumstances were precisely the preconditions of its own disproportionately feverish politics. *The Commune in London* thus joined *The Battle of Dorking* in establishing a template for dystopian fiction of the late-Victorian era, one to which even *The War of the Worlds*, in spite of Wells's more liberal attitudes to the working class, is indebted in several of its evocations of social destruction. From the second half of the 1880s, when social disturbances in Britain and the United States took the form of labor demonstrations that, on occasion, led to the police physically attacking workers with nothing short of fatal consequences, this "pattern of expectation" once more seemed eminently viable as a form of fiction (see Clarke 1979). Charles Gleig's *When All Men Starve* (1898), for example, articulates its paranoid anxieties about Britain's imperial decline through images of a rebel force that, goaded by bread shortages caused in part by a costly naval conflict against the combined forces of France, Germany, and Russia, massacres some 6000 policemen.

Gleig's novel is almost as critical of the aristocratic and plutocratic classes, which combine to form "a rotten edifice of money-bags," as it is of the proletarians it presents as a "great surging mob of yelling devils"—though its portrait of the former, predictably, isn't quite as visceral in its anger as his portrait of the latter (Gleig 1898, 181, 183). In directing its polemic simultaneously at the decadent ruling class and the insurgent working class, *When All Men Starve* is representative of many of the utopian as well as cacotopian or dystopian novels published in the 1880s and 1890s. These often attacked both capitalism, at least in its most economically inefficient and socially divisive forms, and communism, especially when the administrative solution they proposed to the socio-economic and political crisis of the time involved some relatively anemic program of social-democratic reform. Bellamy's *Looking Backward* is exemplary, if not paradigmatic, in this respect. Its "Nationalist" politics, as he called them, were premised on the conviction that, in order to end the inequalities of class society, a highly centralized nation-state needed, in the interests of democracy, to control all aspects of production and consumption currently monopolized by competing capitalist corporations. As both "the great business crisis of 1873" and the "labor troubles" of the late 1880s indicated, according to Bellamy's narrator, "the relation between the workingman and the employer, between labor and capital, appeared in some unaccountable manner to have become dislocated" in the late nineteenth century (Bellamy 2007, 9–10). Some kind of social solution that might render the operations of capital less competitive, less counterproductive, so to speak, and that might in consequence appease and pacify the working class, was therefore imperative. *Looking Backward* thus represented a utopian projection of one of the most prevalent tendencies in the capitalist economics of the time, namely the "development of the great private monopolies," as William Morris trenchantly put it (Morris 1994, 421).

But "Nationalism" also constituted an attempt to cleanse its vision of social reform from associations with the more militant or red-blooded versions of anti-capitalist politics then fighting for attention. In the late 1880s, and above all in the aftermath of the Haymarket Affair, when eight innocent anarchists were charged with murder because an explosion detonated at a peaceful demonstration in Chicago in 1886 killed more than a dozen people, the term "socialism," let alone the terms "anarchism" and "communism," trailed incendiary associations that linked it to violent revolutionism. In a letter to the novelist William Dean Howells, who was himself to publish a utopian romance, entitled *A Traveler from Altruria* (1892–1893), Bellamy observed with some disgust that the term socialism "smells to the average American of petroleum, suggests the red flag, with all manner of sexual novelties, and an abusive tone about God and religion" (quoted in Morgan 1944, 374). Like most middle-class people at this time, from whose ranks were recruited most authors of utopian fiction, he feared both monopolistic capitalist corporations and the more militant socialist associations that opposed them. An article that appeared in the English periodical *The Leisure Hour* in 1889, the year *Looking Backward* was published in Britain, articulated a similar position when it argued against "all attempts to reconstruct society by sudden and forcible means," such as the ones associated with "communism and anarchy," and emphasized that "in England there are many thoughtful men who know that, in order to avoid social revolution, social reforms are called for" (Anonymous 1889, 52).

Looking Backward's narrative pivots on the time-traveling adventures of its hero, an aristocratic Bostonian called Julian West (whose surname, tellingly, evokes the pioneer spirit and, to some extent, the imperial aspirations summarized in the proverbial injunction, "Go West, young man, and grow up with the country"). West falls asleep one night in 1887, thanks to the intervention of a fashionable hypnotist, and wakes up in the year 2000—he is the Rip Van Winkle of the *belle époque*. As Bellamy's time traveler discovers, with an increasing willingness to see the social and political prejudices of his class overturned, the United States has evolved, through a gradual and orderly process, into a rationally planned, democratic society in which corruption and competition are a distant memory:

> The industry and commerce of the country, ceasing to be conducted by a set of irresponsible corporations and syndicates of private persons at their caprice and for their profit, were intrusted to a single syndicate representing the people, to be conducted in the common interest for the common profit. The nation, that is to say, organized as the one great business corporation in which all other corporations were absorbed; it became the one capitalist in place of all other capitalists... (Bellamy 2007, 33)

In spite of its inspiring effect on the late nineteenth-century socialist movement, then, twenty-first century Boston constitutes not a socialist society but, paradoxically enough, a classless capitalist one—capitalism without competing capitals. Production and consumption, for their part, are administered on ruthlessly efficient, rationalistic lines in Bellamy's utopia. Labor, for example, is organized according to the "principle of universal military service" into an "industrial army" (Bellamy 2007, 36). This type of scientific management, comparable to the roughly contemporaneous innovations of the apostle of business rationalization F.W. Taylor, is the archetypal social arrangement at the center of Bellamy's utopian blueprint. It is, however, the dynamics of consumption, not production, that conducts what Italo Calvino might have called *Looking Backward*'s "utopian charge" (Calvino 1987, 247). There are, strikingly, no accounts of labor processes in the novel; but, as befits a romance written during the ascendency of consumer capitalism, there is instead a lavish description of West's trip, with his utopian host's attractive daughter Edith, "an indefatigable shopper," to the department store that stands resplendent in twenty-first century Boston (Bellamy 2007, 59–60). This is a "vast hall full of light" from which the commodities themselves, available via a streamlined system of "pneumatic transmitters," have been discreetly erased, like the labor process itself. Aestheticized consumption, not militarized production, is at the core of utopian desire for an alternative future in *Looking Backward* (Bellamy 2007, 63).

Morris's *News from Nowhere*, the most significant riposte to *Looking Backward*, is an idiosyncratic Marxist critique of both the productivist and consumerist aspects of Bellamy's novel. Subtitled "An Epoch of Rest," it is an immensely influential utopian fiction in its own right, in part because of its Ruskinian vision of communist society, which has proved especially appealing to readers more conscious than Bellamy's admirers of the environmental destruction caused by industrial methods of production; in part because of the seductive dreaminess of its prose, which makes Bellamy's far more functional literary style, at its most forceful in the more polemical passages, seem flat and lifeless by comparison. Morris, who reviewed *Looking Backward* in 1889, did not dismiss the political importance of the book he subsequently rebutted, tempting though this must have seemed to him. Indeed, he insisted that it "is one to be read and considered seriously." But he feared, realistically enough, that it might be "taken as the Socialist bible of reconstruction," and that, as such, its gradualist, reformist politics, which implied that capitalism would inevitably evolve into a kinder, contradiction-free version of itself, were likely to mislead its readers and contribute to a fundamental misunderstanding about socialism (Morris 1994, 425). Morris's polemical review, published in *Commonweal*, the organ of the Socialist League, which he had established with Eleanor Marx among others, concluded that "a machine-life is the best which Mr Bellamy can imagine for us on all sides" (Morris 1994, 423).

Morris's own utopian fiction, in consequence, celebrates an artisanal as opposed to mechanical economy. In its portrait of a communist society of the future, *News from Nowhere* takes care to reconstruct economic and social relations that are nothing like those that prevail in the late nineteenth century. If it dramatizes processes of production and consumption that are manifestly shaped by pre-capitalist precedents, as in Morris's characteristically medievalist description of the time traveler purchasing an ornamental pipe in a shop, then it also outlines the unalienated conditions that might prevail in an essentially post-capitalist community. Each lovingly individuated, highly ornamented commodity, in Morris's communist society, is the product of pleasurable labor governed by the laws not of exchange-value but use-value (Morris 1912, 217). In this way, Morris sought to exceed the ideological conditions that, in the utopian thinking of social reformists such as Bellamy, let alone more conservative-minded contemporaries, set the limits to what can be imagined. He sought to upset the "class anthropomorphism," to use Roland Barthes' formulation, that he blamed for Bellamy's failure to imagine a future radically different from the present (Barthes 1997, 29).

Morris's utopia, like Bellamy's, like every lesser author's utopia from the second half of the nineteenth century, represents an attempt, at least in part, to probe or test, if not finally to escape, the limits of the social and political imaginary of their time. In this respect, utopian fiction is innately self-reflexive. It explores, in more or less sophisticated ways, more or less successfully, its own conditions of possibility; and the conditions of impossibility, so to speak, of its various visionary dreams. The founding commitment of utopian fiction, in fact, is to historicize its own present, which it posits as the identifiable past of the future it invents. The opening sentences of Wells's *The War of the Worlds* are representative in this respect because they compelled the novel's contemporary readers to grasp the present, in historical terms, as the prehistory of an apocalyptic future:

No one would have believed in the last years of the nineteenth century that this world was being watched keenly and closely by intelligences greater than man's and yet as mortal as his own; that as men busied themselves about their various concerns they were scrutinised and studied, perhaps almost as narrowly as a man with a microscope might scrutinise the transient creatures that swarm and multiply in a drop of water. [...] At most terrestrial men fancied there might be other men upon Mars, perhaps inferior to themselves and ready to welcome a missionary enterprise. Yet across the gulf of space, minds that are to our minds as ours are to those of the beasts that perish, intellects vast and cool and unsympathetic, regarded this earth with envious eyes, and slowly and surely drew their plans against us. (Wells 2005, 7)

Brilliantly, these sentences also comprise a decisive critique of the logic of colonialism, especially insofar as Britain embodied this logic in the late nineteenth century. For if Wells portrays the late nineteenth century as merely the prelude to the apocalypse, he portrays the Earth as little more than some overpopulated, socially primitive geographical territory that, because of its complacency and insularity, is fatally susceptible to the sophisticated imperial ambitions of Mars. The clinical gaze of the Martians thus both replicates that of the imperialist ruling class in nations like Britain, as it extends its surveillance over land it intends to annexe; and distills the archetypal perspective of utopian fiction, the purpose of which is in part to fix the present time as objectively as possible.

One might speculate that the "Wife" cited in the *Academy* experienced an unsettling but possibly not unpleasurable thrill on reading these lines and suddenly intuiting that her class, her species even, was secretly being observed by a hostile and predatory power; and that the future was not necessarily set to be no more than an uncomplicated, potentially endless extension of the present, as some of her more complacent contemporaries, secure in their sense that the late nineteenth century represented the acme of civilization, rather naively imagined as the twentieth century, in all its destructiveness, emerged from its predecessor.

The utopian and dystopian fiction that proliferated so rapidly, and with such popularity, in the final quarter of the nineteenth century, was the product of contradictory historical conditions in which, to a hitherto unprecedented extent, the capitalist system seemed to many commentators not only inherently unstable but, it was not impossible, moribund. At this time, various anarchist, communist and social-reformist political currents, building in some cases on the utopian socialism of the earlier nineteenth century, surfaced at the edges of the mainstream to challenge the hegemony of capitalism, at least in its prevailing form. These competing ideologies generated numerous opportunities, on the part of journalists, novelists, and political activists of one kind or another, for reconceiving the future, whether this entailed relatively mild-mannered, gradualist adjustments to the current organization of society, as in the case of Edward Bellamy, or more revolutionary change, as in the case of William Morris. H.G. Wells, in his remarkable scientific romances of the 1890s, gave especially vivid, indeed apocalyptic expression to both the hopes and fears of what might be thought of as the most productive generation since the time of Thomas More to turn to the utopian form as a means of articulating their political imagination.

REFERENCES

Anonymous. 1889. The Social Revolution Achieved; What Then? *The Leisure Hour* 38: 51–53.

———. 1898. What the People Read XI.—A Wife. *Academy* 53: 294–294.

Barthes, Roland. 1997. Martians. In *The Eiffel Tower and Other Mythologies*, trans. Richard Howard, 27–29. Berkeley: University of California Press.

Beaumont, Matthew. 2005. *Utopia Ltd.: Ideologies of Social Dreaming in England, 1870–1900*. Leiden: Brill.

Bellamy, Edward. 2007. *Looking Backward, 2000–1887*, ed. Matthew Beaumont. Oxford: Oxford World's Classics.

Bulwer-Lytton, Edward. 1871. *The Coming Race*. Edinburgh: Blackwood.

Calvino, Italo. 1987. *The Uses of Literature*, trans. Patrick Creagh. New York: Harcourt.

Carr, E.H. 1969. Editor's Introduction. In *The ABC of Communism*, ed. N. Bukharin and E. Preobrazhensky, trans. Eden and Cedar Paul, 13–52. Harmondsworth: Penguin.

Clarke, I.F. 1979. *The Pattern of Expectation, 1644–2001*. London: Jonathan Cape.

Foote, G.W. 1886. Social Dreams. *Progress* 6: 189–194.

Gleig, Charles. 1898. *When All Men Starve: Showing How England Hazarded Her Naval Supremacy, and the Horrors Which Followed the Interruption of Her Food Supply*. London: Lane.

Hemyng, Bracebridge. 1871. *The Commune in London; or, Thirty Years Hence: A Chapter of Anticipated History*. London: Clarke.

Hobsbawm, E.J. 1962. *The Age of Capital, 1848–1875*. London: Weidenfeld & Nicolson.

Hobson, J.A. 1898. Edward Bellamy and the Utopian Romance. *Humanitarian* 13: 179–189.

Jellinek, Frank. 1937. *The Paris Commune of 1871*. London: Gollancz.

Masterman, C.F.G. 1905. *In Peril of Change: Essays Written in Time of Tranquillity*. London: Fisher Unwin.

Morgan, Arthur E. 1944. *Edward Bellamy*. New York: Columbia University Press.

Morris, William. 1912. *News from Nowhere*. In *The Collected Works of William Morris*, vol. 16. London: Longmans Green.

———. 1994. Looking Backward. In *Political Writings: Contributions to Justice and Commonweal, 1883–1890*, ed. Nicholas Salmon, 419–425. Bristol: Thoemmes Press.

Presley, James T. 1873. Bibliography of Utopias and Imaginary Travels and Histories. *Notes and Queries* 12: 22–23.

Rider Haggard, H. 1998. *She*, ed. Daniel Karlin. Oxford: Oxford World's Classics.

Wells, H.G. 1980. Utopias. In *H.G. Wells's Literary Criticism*, ed. Patrick Parrinder and Robert M. Philmus, 117–121. Brighton: Harvester Press.

———. 2005. *The War of the Worlds*, ed. Patrick Parrinder. Oxford: Oxford World's Classics.

The Twentieth Century

Adam Stock

INTRODUCTION

In 1962, Frankfurt School theorist Theodor Adorno stated that paradoxically, "numerous so-called utopian dreams—for example, television, the possibility of traveling to other planets, moving faster than sound—have been fulfilled. However … they all operate as though the best thing about them had been forgotten" (quoted in Bloch 1988, 2). The twentieth century could have been characterized by social development and scientific promise, but was instead defined by militarism, genocide, and inequality. For Adorno, the closer the "proximity of utopia" became the more people committed to keeping the world as it was, turning against utopia as an "attainable possibility" (quoted in Bloch 1988, 4). This chapter uses utopian and dystopian literature to unpick the tensions Adorno identifies between technological promise and material political reality. I begin by showing how developments in biological science affected changing conceptions of the body politic and embodied experience. I then discuss responses to totalitarianism and mid-century industrial warfare. Next, I argue utopian expression was important for decolonial movements in the postwar era, while self-reflexive *utopian* critiques of literary utopia's limitations emerged in the 1970s grounded in ecological opposition to capitalism. Yet with the end of the Cold War in the 1990s, I conclude that an anti-utopian globalization narrative of individualist consumerism heralded the new digital age.

A. Stock (✉)
York St. John University, York, UK

P. Marks et al. (eds.), *The Palgrave Handbook of Utopian and Dystopian Literatures*, https://doi.org/10.1007/978-3-030-88654-7_11

BIOLOGICAL DETERMINISM

Late nineteenth-century literary naturalism emphasized detailed observation and privileged the scientist's perspective as a (supposedly) detached observer. In *Anticipations of the Reaction of Mechanical and Scientific Progress upon Human Life* (1901) H. G. Wells used naturalist techniques to produce utopian prophecies with claims to scientific determination. In Wells' vision an intellectual and financial elite develops to establish a rational and enlightened World State. In it the health, physical and intellectual abilities of individuals will advance through application of scientific knowledge, via a selective breeding program grounded in the biological science of eugenics.

Wells' use of eugenics responds to contemporary social Darwinian fears about working-class "degeneration." A similar logic is at work in Charlotte Perkins Gilman's *Herland* (1915), where three men find a long-lost country inhabited by pathogenic women. As a positivist social scientist, Gilman treated her utopia as "an entirely experimental realm—a place for creating new social conditions and for testing new ideas," according to Brian Lloyd (1998, 95). While Gilman stresses the social utility and historical necessity of female equality, she treats race as equally "natural" and necessary, pointedly emphasizing Herland women are of "Aryan stock, and were once in contact with the best civilization of the old world" (1999, 55). Throughout the novel the binary between natural and unnatural behavior for women is rigorously maintained through a maternity cult.

Eugenics debates continued in the 1920s, grounded in colonialist white supremacism. In 1924 Bertrand Russell published *Icarus, or the Future of Science*, a response to his friend J. B. S. Haldane's *Daedalus, or Science and the Future* (1923), which had prophesized that within two hundred years in vitro human reproduction would be universal (Haldane and Dronamraju 1995, 41–42). Russell was more sanguine about science. He predicted the cost of eugenic improvement to average intelligence would be damage to "exceptional intelligence" and warned the adoption of birth control by "the white races" would decrease the birth rate "at a time when uncivilized races are still prolific and are preserved from a high death-rate by white science" (Russell 1925, 49, 46). Haldane's wife Charlotte responded with the novel *Man's World* (1926), focusing on women's future experiences of reproductive technologies. Judith Adamson argues Charlotte Haldane's "distrust of scientific hubris and her feminism turned what she had begun as a utopian experiment into a powerful dystopia" (1998, 55). In it, white women are categorized by biological capability and white men are ranked by intelligence, while non-whites are attacked via race-specific chemical warfare. The novel is pointedly ambiguous about whether such genocide is desirable, but the very idea of a racially-specific biological weapon essentializes historically contingent processes of racialization.

EMBODIMENT, THE BODY POLITIC, AND MASS POLITICAL MOVEMENTS

In the early twentieth century then, inter-related developments in biology, political thinking, and the social sciences led to utopian literature's long-standing concern with embodiment becoming an obsession. In dystopias the treatment of physical human bodies was used to critique the Enlightenment goal of conquering nature as inevitably ending in the dominance of individual human beings. For example, E. M. Forster's story "The Machine Stops" (1909) depicts a future in which "it was a demerit to be muscular" (Forster 1954, 109). In Yevgeny Zamyatin's dystopia *We* (first published in translation, 1924), appearance and behavior within the "green wall" enclosing the novel's totalitarian OneState is tightly regulated, right down to the number of chews per mouthful of petroleum-derived food (Zamyatin 1999, 21, 102). The novel satirizes the mass production techniques of Fordism and "scientific management" pioneer Frederick Winslow Taylor, and likewise rejects Russian Bolshevism's authoritarian attitude toward individual spontaneous action. A resistance (The "Mephi") lives beyond the wall and organizes collectively in favor of freedom of movement. For David Bell, the text "rejects [the] closure" of the totalitarian "OneState" without creating its own utopian alternative in the sense of a social and political *place* (Bell 2017, 4).

Karel Čapek's four act drama, *R.U.R.* (1920) critiques the post-Enlightenment nation-state from a different angle. Chiefly remembered for coining the term "robot" (from the Czech *robota*, meaning "forced labor"), in the play Rossum's Universal Robots are put to work as cannon fodder, servants, and manual laborers. While it is unclear by the play's end whether they will ever successfully reproduce themselves (the robotic "life" creating formula is lost during the uprising), rebellious robots do learn to form the attachments of romantic love. The ending frames two robot lovers as a new Adam and Eve.[1] As Alfred Thomas points out, this "ostensibly 'happy ending'" seems to foreshadow that of Thea von Harbou and Fritz Lang's (1927) dystopian film *Metropolis* (Thomas 146). Here, the answer to political problems of a class-based, gendered society is revealed through its epigram and final intertitle, reading "the mediator between head and hands must be the heart!" The statement refers to rapprochement between the city's architect and the appointed head of the workers—that is, a mediation between capital and labor. As for the heart, the image of the body politic it recalls is folded within the visual context of a Christian symbolic schema, making it the sacred heart of Christ. Within its historical context of crisis-stricken Weimar Germany, the film favors social democratic values with an unmistakably Christian flavor.[2]

Through concern with embodiment, these dystopias critique the state as a regulator of life processes. This is even more explicit in Aldous Huxley's *Brave New World* (1932), in which the World State regime reproduces its hegemony via means including eugenic ex-vitro reproduction, behaviorist psychological conditioning, and state promoted recreational use of the blissful narcoleptic drug *soma*. In Huxley's World State sensual and sexual pleasure and the consumption of consumer goods is elevated to the status of religious practice. The state controls its population via the regulation of life processes from conception, gestation, and birth, through childhood development and education, healthcare, recreation, and death to produce a population of what Michel Foucault would later term "docile bodies" (Babaee et al. 2013, 490). Ronja Tripp also leans on Foucault, highlighting the "biopolitics" of control when, "actions and reactions are... regulated by the state, which has a strong interest in manipulating the body politic into the perfect consumer, a mark of the economic totalitarianism of this society" (2015, 37), promoting regime stability above all else.

The Rise of Totalitarianism

Huxley's novel of totalitarian "stability" was published amid the tumult of rising totalitarianism. As Andy Croft notes, "The 1930s was an especially rich period in the development of utopian and dystopian writing in Britain" (1984, 186). Gregory Claeys charts some of the forgotten chauvinist, anti-socialist, and pro-imperialist British and French dystopian fictions from the early twentieth century up to WWII (2016, 7), but Croft argues that by the mid to late 1930s, "it was *anti-fascism* above all that informed the majority of non-realist fiction" (1984, 186). An important example of such writing can be found in the novels of Katharine Burdekin.

In *Proud Man* (1934), Burdekin reverses the usual journey of the visitor to the land of Utopia; here the Utopian comes to visit present-day London instead. Burdekin's narrator, an unnamed "Person" from a genderless and classless utopian future, travels back in time via a dream to learn about the "subhumans" who are "half conscious" and "cannot apparently exist without their societies being divided" by sex and class (1985, 17). In Burdekin's utopian politics, heterodox socialism was a pre-condition for spiritual growth and a reconfiguration of gender and sexuality.[3] These commitments drive her dystopia *Swastika Night* (1937), set in a far-future world split between German and Japanese feudal empires where women are kept like cattle in cages for reproductive rape, Jews have been wiped out, Christians are racialized as social outcasts, and male homosexuality is the only form of love sanctioned. Burdekin highlights the centrality of misogyny and racial myths to Nazi ideology through conditions that produce a population not only lacking knowledge of how to resist, but also the skills and historical knowledge to conceptualize how the world might be made differently. Only the protagonist, who learns the forbidden historical truth about the pre-Nazi past, has the imaginative capacity to conceive of femininity and female autonomy.

THE GREAT UPHEAVAL

Future global warfare was an object of anxiety in utopian and especially dystopian works throughout the twentieth century. Conflicts in the 1930s, from the Spanish Civil War to the Italian invasion of Abyssinia, gave a flavor of the atrocities to be expected in looming global conflict. The early years of World War II were marked by attempts to historicize the conflict in allegorical texts like Rex Warner's *The Aerodrome* (1940) and Storm Jameson's *Then We Shall Hear Singing* (1942). By the War's end, concern was with the immediate future: whether (as in Aldous Huxley's *Ape and Essence* [1948]) it would be global catastrophe and barbarism, or present opportunities for the sort of small experimental community behaviorist psychologist B. F. Skinner depicts in his utopia *Walden Two* (1948).

George Orwell's *Nineteen Eighty-Four* (1949) is a text full of contradictions, generating prodigious levels of debate and influencing wider political discourse. It is the quintessential dystopian genre text, though it employs tropes and conventions from romance, gothic, and horror. The style, as Philip Wegner contends, is indebted to Wellsian naturalism, but as Patricia Rae argues, it shows the influence of literary modernism (Wegner 2002, 189; Rae 1997, 196–220). Tom Moylan notes Orwell himself "regarded his work as a utopian attack on what he saw as anti-utopian historical tendencies," and yet "the book tends to outstrip itself in its pessimistic virtuosity" (1986, 162, 163). The book influenced a spate of notable 1950s dystopian novels. Many of these critiqued postwar consumer capitalism in the US, such as Kurt Vonnegut's critique of the automated industry, *Player Piano* (1952); Ray Bradbury's classic jeremiad against the "dumbing down" of culture and an atmosphere of anti-intellectualism, *Fahrenheit 451* (1953); and Frederik Pohl and C.L. Kornbluth's growth-limit dystopia *The Space Merchants* (1953). One nearly ubiquitous element of such dystopias (including Orwell's) is the destructive presence of nuclear weapons. Science fiction was a mode attuned to answer questions about the consequences of the nuclear age and the rise of the Cold War, and it began to shape wider political discourse.

The 1950s was a decade of both Western anxiety and triumphalism. Films like *Invasion of the Body Snatchers* (1956) demonstrated this through their depictions of the "good life" and freedom embodied in the postwar order through material abundance and the heteronormative white middle-class family structure, set against the unfree regimentation of the USSR. The irony that this illustrated the paranoid "Red Scare" gripping US politics since the late 1940s did not escape writers like John Wyndham, whose post-nuclear holocaust dystopia *The Chrysalids* (1955) follows a witch-hunt for mutants by a puritanical religious society. Nevertheless, American pundits and politicians alike hailed prosperity. Peter Fitting notes this was "to some extent an illusion as many citizens were excluded from the American Dream: African Americans of course, as well as women and the poor" (to which we may add minoritized groups including LGBTQ+ and indigenous people) (2010, 142).

Before the end of the decade, civil rights groups were already amassing wide support, and many of the conditions that gave rise to 1960s countercultures were in place. Moylan argues "Utopian expression became a major element of the oppositional projects of the postwar decades" (2000, 68) and utopianism is certainly present in Frantz Fanon's anti-colonialism, the late Pan-Africanism of Malcolm X, and the millenarian rhetoric of Martin Luther King. Yet in the same historical moment, a form of hyper-technological utopianism was central to military-industrial projects such as the Space Race. Moreover, popular texts like Anthony Burgess's imaginative *A Clockwork Orange* (1962) continued the strong tradition of right-wing dystopias critiquing social change and social democratic politics.

UTOPIA, COLONIALISM, AND DECOLONIZATION

These divergent uses of utopianism point to how from Thomas More's *Utopia* (1516) onward utopianism has been important to envisioning colonialism. As Sargent shows, for European colonial settlers in North America and the Antipodes migration was often driven by hardship and poverty. Colonies promised a better life, whatever their reality (Sargent 2010, 200–201). For indigenous populations, however, colonization was experienced as dispossession and even genocide. For example, by 1900 the genocide of an estimated ten million Congolese by the forces of Leopold II of Belgium was well underway, and in 1904 Germany attempted the total extermination of Hettero and Namaqua tribes in Namibia (German South West Africa).[4]

Within Europe, the widespread Jewish experience of antisemitism in the nineteenth century, symbolized by the *cause célèbre* of the Dreyfus Affair in France (1894–1906), led to calls by an initially small number of Jews to establish a Jewish state. Theodor Herzl, who convened the first Zionist Congress in 1897, wrote the utopia *The Old-New Land* (1902). Its strange mix of "socialist and anarchist aspects" alongside classist, "orientalist and colonialist tropes" was inspirational to the fledgling movement (Dayan-Herzbrun 2012, 96). In colonial India, meanwhile, the Muslim, feminist educationalist Rokeya Sakhawat Hossain (also known as Begum Rokeya) wrote the anti-colonial short story "Sultana's Dream" (1905). The material absence of the British is a pre-condition to this utopian imaginary, but the literary history of western utopias remains an important intertextual reference point. Barnita Bagchi locates Rokeya within an Indian women's movement that fought for education, suffrage, and independence. "Sultana's Dream" codes both colonialism and nationalism as masculine, and "the driving force behind the success of the utopian feminist country of Ladyland is women's education," through which the women overcome "male militarism" (Bagchi 2012, 171).

Anti-colonial utopianism can be found in many texts (whether or not formally utopias) in the interwar years, from the poetry of Irish modernist William Butler Yeats (e.g. "The Second Coming" [1933]) to the didactic closing section of Mulk Raj Anand's slice-of-life novel about a Dalit teenager,

Untouchable (1935), in which alongside independence, the importation of (existing, western) sanitation technology is touted as hastening an end to caste-based discrimination. After the War, utopian imaginaries frequently played a role in decolonial politics, and as Sargent notes "the greatest growth of utopianism… came with postcolonialism and images of independence and a better life free from colonial domination" (2010, 215). Nicholas Brown however cautions that these utopian impulses function critically, hinting "at an as yet unimaginable future" rather than supplying positive visions (2005, 22). He reads the critical force of utopian impulses in the work of writers such as Ngugi wa Thiong'o and Chinua Achebe by placing their works in dialogue with modernists including James Joyce and Wyndham Lewis. In the US, meanwhile, musician Sun Ra starred with his "Arkestra" in the 1974 film *Space is the Place*, in which (playing a version of himself), he finds a planet on which to establish "a colony for black people… on the other side of time," a place of "altered destiny." Sun Ra is often credited as a founder of Afrofuturism, an Afrodiasporic approach to cultural production which creates, in Kodwo Eshun words, "temporal complications and anachronistic episodes that disturb the linear time of progress" and thereby resists Eurocentric historical narratives of modernity (2003, 297).

CRITICAL UTOPIAS, ECOLOGY, AND POSTMODERNISM

By the 1970s radical writers tried a variety of strategies to reclaim utopian values from the limits they acknowledged in the western utopian tradition. Ursula K. Le Guin's novel *The Dispossessed* (1974), subtitled "An Ambiguous Utopia," is set between an authoritarian capitalist planet of soaring inequality named Urras that reproduces the "three worlds" system of Cold War international relations and an independent anarcho-syndicalist settler colony on its moon of Anarres. *The Dispossessed* dramatizes the practical and political struggles of a utopian society facing resistant forces from both within and without. Tom Moylan groups it with novels such as *The Female Man* by Joanna Russ (1975), Marge Piercy's *Woman on the Edge of Time* (1976), and Samuel Delany's *Triton* (1976) in a subgenre he calls "critical utopia." These texts work through the genre's historical connections to colonialism and patriarchy, "reject[ing] utopia as blueprint while preserving it as dream" (1986, 83).

Such texts typically share ecological concerns. Although there is a rich history of arcadian and ecological values in utopian literature, Lisa Garforth points out that the "green" values of pre-twentieth-century utopian writers like More, Thoreau, Kropotkin, and Morris do not constitute "an unbroken countermelody to modernity's technocentrism and expansion." Rather, as with Huxley's *Island* (1962) and Ernest Callenbach's *Ecotopia* (1975), "they are constantly reinvented in response to changing historical contexts" (2018, 17). Like much science fiction of the nuclear age, ecological utopias built on and subsequently informed scientific discourse. For example, biologist Rachel Carson's bestselling nonfiction book *Silent Spring* (1962) opens with an extended vignette of an apocalyptic American landscape destroyed by the chemical DDT. The book led to a successful campaign to ban DDT, and inspired dystopias of environmental degradation.

Garforth examines reports such as *The Limits to Growth* (1972) which argue that "social and natural processes at the global scale are locked together" in closed feedback loops, and "world population and industrial systems were growing exponentially" (2018, 33). These led to several global initiatives to consider more sustainable modes of living, and an expansion of the work of environmental sciences. Yet the rise of the New Right in the 1970s and application of neoliberal economics in states such as Chile following Pinochet's 1973 coup (backed by the CIA) attacked the nation-state as a regulator for constraining growth. The ascendency of this ideology owes much to "structural weaknesses within the global economy," which as Alexander Beaumont notes include "the 1973 oil crisis, the near bankruptcy of New York city in 1975 and the UK's application for a $3.9 billion bailout from the International monetary Fund in 1976" (2018, 273). Paradoxically then, structural economic crisis occurred alongside the realization that economic growth based on exploitation of finite natural resources is ultimately unsustainable, yet macroeconomic policy shifted from managed growth toward financialization.

In literature, the new critical utopian fiction acknowledged the capture and commodification of utopia itself by (neo-colonial) capitalism, while at a broader cultural level there was a shift from modernist strategies toward those of postmodernism. In the 1980s cyberpunk dystopias began to work through some of these contradictions. William Gibson's *Neuromancer* (1984) highlights the cost of exponential economic growth through its depiction of "the sprawl" connecting cities on the Eastern seaboard of the US, a mega-urbanization trope reminiscent of the dystopian metropolis of Mega City One in the British comic serial *Judge Dredd*.[5] At cyberpunk's most bombastic, Neal Stephenson's *Snow Crash* (1992) links globalized finance and the franchise model of expansion not only to ecological fears, but successively to organized crime, religious cults, migration fears, and the AIDS crisis. Cyberpunk typically engaged with social experiences of post-industrial urban spaces of decline using hard-boiled protagonists wearing gleaming mirror shades. But the shift to the virtual world also marked a shift in the cycle of (re-)production and consumption, and for writers like Gibson and Stephenson digital reproduction does not fulfill the promise of transcending resource limits of a finite planet.

Alongside (male-dominated) cyberpunk, feminist novels including Margaret Atwood's *The Handmaid's Tale* (1985), Octavia Butler's *Xenogenesis* trilogy (1987–1989) and *Parable of the Sower* (1993) contribute to what Baccolini and Moylan identify as a "dystopian structure of feeling" (2003, 4). *Dawn* (1987), the first *Xenogenesis* novel, opens with the working-class Nigerian-American protagonist Lilith Iyapo awaking in a magically transformed future among aliens who have rescued her from global nuclear war. The aliens live in eco-utopian harmony with each other, but as rescuers they are no Samaritans. The novel problematizes the forced removal of a woman of color from the place of her birth, who is made to participate in an unequal "gene trade" through intrusions into her body and claims on her fertility. Using parallels with the history of American slavery, the novel deals with historical and contemporary trauma by estranging it through a future perspective.

THE POST-COLD WAR YEARS

Observing the spread of elements of "consumerist Western culture" around the globe, in 1989 neoconservative Francis Fukuyama declared "the end point of mankind's ideological evolution and the universalization of Western liberal democracy as the final form of human government" (3). Fukuyama follows in the intellectual footprints of mid-twentieth century anti-utopians like Karl Popper and Isaiah Berlin, who associated the "blueprints" of utopian visions with totalitarian violence. In the wake of the dissolution of the Soviet Union and the Warsaw Pact, Lois Lowry's 1993 Young Adult novel *The Giver* follows similar logic. The novel acts as precursor to the wave of post-millennial YA dystopias that became multimillion-dollar franchises. In it, teenage protagonist Jonas' colorless world, "isn't fair" because "there aren't any choices! I want to wake up in the morning and *decide* things!" (127) His rebellion is essentially motivated by a desire for freedom to consume as he chooses. Lowry's didactic Bildungsroman exemplifies a post-Cold War approach to consumer capitalism in which choice itself becomes a political value so that paradoxically means *themselves* are the ends. The only substantive goal left for political economy under this logic is to find ways to deliver public services within a market system, where provision of choice trumps quality or accountability.

By the closing years of the twentieth century, many of the utopian technological dreams of the century's early years such as space travel, flight, and even test tube babies, had long been achieved. As this chapter has shown, the traditional form of the utopian novel had likewise been largely superseded, both artistically and politically, while utopian and dystopian ideas began to proliferate across new types of media from comic books to video games. By now dystopian and utopian literature often blended into other genres and looked beyond the limits of the western utopian tradition. Nalo Hopkinson's *Brown Girl in the Ring* (1998) for example, blends post-apocalyptic science fiction, dystopia, magical realism, and Afro-Caribbean myth in its depiction of marginalized communities in a post-collapse Toronto. The novel's resolution depicts a self-supporting community which is invested in the flourishing of all members. Looking back on the twentieth century through utopian literature reveals the shifts in dominant historical understandings of the human body, its imbrication with the natural world, science and technology, and global change. It shows us how colonial logic and both anti- and decolonial resistance continued to shape cultural production and political action. Finally, it can help to pinpoint how the great upheavals of an age marked by global conflict, radical economic change, and aesthetic novelty were understood, critiqued, and questioned in popular culture.

NOTES

1. See Alfred Thomas, 2007, *The Bohemian Body: Gender and Sexuality in Modern Czech Culture*, Madison: University of Wisconsin Press, 142–152.
2. See Paul March-Russell, 2015, *Modernism and Science Fiction*, London: Palgrave Macmillan, 4–5; 79–80.
3. See Elizabeth English, 2015, *Lesbian Modernism: Censorship, Sexuality and Genre Fiction*, Edinburgh: Edinburgh University Press.
4. See Adam Hochschild, 2006, King Leopold's Ghost: A Story of Greed, Terror and Heroism in Colonial Africa, London: Pan; Jeremy Sarkin, 2011, Germany's Genocide of the Herero: Kaiser Wilhelm II, His General, His Settlers, His Soldiers, Rochester, NY: Boydell & Brewer.
5. Created by John Wagner and Carlos Ezquerra, *Judge Dredd* began life in British comic *2000 A.D.* and appeared as a comic strip in *The Daily Star* from 1981. It has been the basis of two feature films and many graphic novels.

REFERENCES

Adamson, Judith. 1998. *Charlotte Haldane: Woman Writer in a Man's World*. London: Macmillan.

Anand, Mulk Raj. 2014. *Untouchable*. London: Penguin.

Babaee, Ruzbeh, Wan Roselezam Wan. Yahya, and Shivani Sivagurunathan. 2013. Manifestation of Biopower in Aldous Huxley's *Brave New World*. *Advances in Natural and Applied Sciences* 7 (5): 489–497.

Baccolini, Raffaella, and Tom Moylan. 2003. Introduction: Dystopia and Histories. In *Dark Horizons: Science Fiction and the Dystopian Imagination*, ed. Raffaella Baccolini and Tom Moylan, 1–12. New York: Routledge.

Bagchi, Barnita. 2012. Ladylands and Sacrificial Holes: Utopias and Dystopias in Rokeya Sakhawat Hossain's Writings. In *The Politics of the (Im)Possible: Utopia and Dystopia Reconsidered*, ed. Barnita Bagchi, 166–178. Los Angeles: Sage.

Beaumont, Alexander. 2018. Dystopia and Euphoria: Time-Space Compression and the City. In *British Literature in Transition, 1980–2000: Accelerated Times*, ed. Berthold Schoene and Eileen Pollard, 273–288. British Literature in Transition. Cambridge: Cambridge University Press.

Bell, David M. 2017. *Rethinking Utopia: Place, Power, Affect*. New York: Routledge.

Bloch, Ernst. 1988. *The Utopian Function of Art and Literature: Selected Essays*, trans. Jack Zipes and Frank Mecklenburg. Cambridge, MA: MIT Press.

Brown, Nicholas. 2005. *Utopian Generations: The Political Horizon of Twentieth-Century Literature*. Princeton, NJ: Princeton University Press.

Burdekin, Katharine. 1985. *Swastika Night*. New York: The Feminist Press.

———. 1993. *Proud Man*. New York: The Feminist Press.

Butler, Octavia. 1989. *Xenogenesis: Dawn; Adult Rites; Imago*. New York: Warner.

Čapek, Karel. 1999. *R.U.R.* In *Čapek Four Plays*, trans. Cathy Porter and Peter Majer. London: Bloomsbury.

Carson, Rachel. 1965. *Silent Spring*. London: Penguin.

Claeys, Gregory. 2016. *Dystopia: A Natural History*. Oxford: Oxford University Press.

Croft, Andy. 1984. Worlds Without End Foisted Upon the Future—Some Antecedents of Nineteen Eighty-Four. In *Inside the Myth: Orwell: Views from the Left*, ed. Christopher Norris, 183–216. London: Lawrence and Wishart.

Dayan-Herzbrun, Sonia. 2012. Palestine: Land of Utopias. In *The Politics of the (Im)Possible: Utopia and Dystopia Reconsidered*, ed. Barnita Bagchi, 95–105. Los Angeles: Sage.

English, Elizabeth. 2015. *Lesbian Modernism: Censorship, Sexuality and Genre Fiction*. Edinburgh: Edinburgh University Press.

Eshun, Kodwo. 2003. Further Considerations of Afrofuturism. *CR: The New Centennial Review* 3 (2): 287–302.

Fitting, Peter. 2010. Utopia, Dystopia and Science Fiction. In *The Cambridge Companion to Utopian Literature*, ed. Gregory Claeys, 135–153. Cambridge: Cambridge University Press.

Forster, E.M. 1954. *Collected Short Stories*. Harmondsworth: Penguin.

Fukuyama, Francis. 1989. The End of History? *The National Interest* 16: 3–18.

Garforth, Lisa. 2018. *Green Utopias: Environmental Hope before and after Nature*. Cambridge: Polity.

Gibson, William. 2016. *Neuromancer*. London: Gollancz.

Gilman, Charlotte Perkins. 1999. *The Yellow Wall-Paper, Herland, and Selected Writings*, ed. Denise D. Knight. London: Penguin.

Haldane, J.B.S., and Krishna R. Dronamraju. 1995. *Haldane's Daedalus Revisited*. Oxford: Oxford University Press.

Hochschild, Adam. 2006. *King Leopold's Ghost: A Story of Greed, Terror and Heroism in Colonial Africa*. London: Pan.

Hopkinson, Nalo. 2012. *Brown Girl in the Ring*. New York: Grand Central.

Hossain, Rokeya Sakhawat. 2007. *Sultana's Dream' and 'Padmarag*. New Dehli: Penguin.

Le Guin, Ursula K. 2002. *The Dispossessed: An Ambiguous Utopia*. London: Gollancz.

Lloyd, Brian. 1998. Feminism, Utopian and Scientific: Charlotte Perkins Gilman and the Prison of the Familiar. *American Studies* 39 (1): 93–113.

Lowry, Lois. 2014. *The Giver*. London: HarperCollins.

March-Russell, Paul. 2015. *Modernism and Science Fiction*. London: Palgrave Macmillan.

Metropolis. 2010. Directed by Fritz Lang. London: Eureka Entertainment.

Moylan, Tom. 1986. *Demand the Impossible: Science Fiction and the Utopian Imagination*. New York: Methuen.

———. 2000. *Scraps of the Untainted Sky: Science Fiction, Utopia, Dystopia*. Boulder, CO: Westview.

Rae, Patricia. 1997. Mr. Charrington's Junk Shop: T. S. Eliot and Modernist Poetics in Nineteen Eighty-Four. *Twentieth-Century Literature* 43 (2): 196–220.

Russell, Bertrand. 1925. *Icarus, or The Future of Science*. London: Keegan Paul, Trench, Trubner & Co.

Sargent, Lyman Tower. 2010. Colonial and Postcolonial Utopias. In *The Cambridge Companion to Utopian Literature*, ed. Gregory Claeys, 200–222. Cambridge: Cambridge University Press.

Sarkin, Jeremy. 2011. *Germany's Genocide of the Herero: Kaiser Wilhelm II, His General, His Settlers, His Soldiers*. Woodbridge, Suffolk; Rochester, NY: Boydell & Brewer.

Space Is the Place. 1974. Directed by John Coney, written by Sun Ra. North America Star System. Film.

Stephenson, Neal. 1993. *Snow Crash*. London: Penguin.

Thomas, Alfred. 2007. *The Bohemian Body: Gender and Sexuality in Modern Czech Culture*. Madison: University of Wisconsin Press.

Tripp, Sonja. 2015. Biopolitical Dystopia: Aldous Huxley's *Brave New World* (1932). In *Dystopia, Science Fiction, Post-Apocalypse: Classics—New Tendencies—Model Interpretations*, ed. Eckart Voigts and Alessandra Boller, 29–45. Trier: WVT Trier.

Wegner, Phillip E. 2002. *Imaginary Communities: Utopia, the Nation, and the Spatial Histories of Modernity*. Berkeley, CA: University of California Press.

Wells, H.G. 1902. *Anticipations of the Reaction of Mechanical and Scientific Progress upon Human Life and Thought*. London: Chapman & Hall.

Zamyatin, Yevgeny. 1999. *We*, trans. Mirra Ginsburg. New York: EOS HarperCollins.

The Twenty-First Century

Matt Tierney

INTRODUCTION

In April 2000, Toni Morrison charted a task for the humanist university for the decades ahead. She gave voice to what seems the most tolerable version of utopian thinking today, enunciating a vision for a struggle against exploitation in which failure appears likely, yet that must proceed anyway, because the price of doing nothing is still greater than the price of failure. In order to "reignite wider and more variable notions of virtue, civitas, response-ability, and freedom," Morrison told the crowd at Princeton's Center for Human Values, academics need not repeat the tired justifications for humanities research. Rather than trumpet compromised virtues of citizenship or professionalization, she argued, intellectuals can "speculate instead on a future where the poor are not yet, not quite, all dead; where the under-represented minorities are not quite all imprisoned" (2001, 278). This is utopianism. Dreaming neither of a different world nor of a kind of human life that leaves behind all its impediments, Morrison dreams instead of this world, the actual world, where these impediments are only marginally transformable by the humans they affect. Her utopianism is in the stubborn insistence, against all available evidence, that some people might remain alive and free, despite rapacious capitalism and state-authorized white supremacy. This chapter juxtaposes two kinds of utopianism, both endemic to this century: on one side, visions of another world than this one, committed to a total transformation of human

M. Tierney (✉)
The Pennsylvania State University, State College, PA, USA

P. Marks et al. (eds.), *The Palgrave Handbook of Utopian and Dystopian Literatures*, https://doi.org/10.1007/978-3-030-88654-7_12

relations with each other and with human-made machines; and on the other side, visions of this world lived otherwise than according to the rules of accumulation and violence.

Utopia or Nothing

The twenty-first century seems a strange time to talk about utopia. Climate collapse appears imminent, and the continuing rise in sea levels will likely soon flood financial centers after which economic collapse may follow closely behind. For the eschatologically inclined, increasingly severe storms and earthquakes, mass extinctions and mass migrations give reason to forecast an end to human activity, and even to terrestrial life. For the rest of us, the future remains hard to plan for, as imaginations struggle to pose affirmative visions for anything at all that could come next. But as Morrison argues, we have to do it anyway, or else "some other regime or ménage of regimes will do it for us, in spite of us, and without us" (278). This obdurate imaginative struggle is only one version of utopianism. Most extant utopianisms are more committed to oppression, marginalization, and the accrual of wealth. Nevertheless, alternative utopianisms have managed to sustain themselves (in spite of a likely and constant failure) on sociopolitical difference, mutual care, and active critique.

Morrison's utopianism has its precedents. Among these, a century ago, self-described literary radical Randolph Bourne protested U.S. entry into the First World War. Bourne's complained that liberal intellectuals had lent their tacit support to an imperialist war machine. Under the ideological cover of pragmatist thought, he determined, these intellectuals had transformed a good-faith philosophical inquiry into a craven realpolitik of collaboration with their obvious enemies. In the 1917 essay "A War Diary," Bourne lamented: "what then is there really to choose between the realist who accepts evil in order to manipulate it to a great end … and the Utopian pacifist who cannot stomach the evil and will have none of it? Both are coerced. The Utopian, however, knows that he is ineffective and that he is coerced" (1917, 535). Bourne is like many on today's left, disappointed in their weathered alliance with liberals: insubstantial friends too willing to plead the side of markets and nation-states against planetary movements for freedom; more eager to endorse pluralist ideals of inclusion than revolution toward large-scale social restructuring; and too open to elusive fantasies of "just war." Bourne concluded: "it is only 'liberal' naïveté that is shocked at arbitrary coercion and suppression" (541).

Likewise queer anarchist novelist and public poet Paul Goodman, in his 1962 book *Utopian Essays and Practical Proposals*, later decried any utopian plan built on principles of uniformity. Peace for Goodman, as for Morrison and Bourne, would never arise from perfected conditions of consensus. It would arise instead from an analysis or negation of imperfect conditions, and an advocacy for those excluded. This analysis or negation, for Goodman, is explicitly utopian, but it is diverse in its aims, local in its practice, and non-totalizing. Such utopianism would hope to supplant both the enforced consensus and the technologies of its enforcement:

> In our era, to combat the emptiness of technological life, we have to think of a newform, the conflictful community … Is such a model improvable and adaptable to cities and industrial complexes? Can widely differing communities be accommodated in a larger federation? How can they be encouraged in modern societies? These are utopian questions. (22)

Like Bourne who had seen utopianism as a radical imagination conducted without the illusion of freedom or effectivity, and predicting Morrison who would see that a utopian society as one that saves its most vulnerable from the threat of its most predatory, Goodman situates his utopianism at the point where philosophical ideals must enter the world of worlded activity. The question is not how to produce agreement among dissenting parties, nor even to produce a public square for safe disagreement, but rather how to scale up a discursive practice—conflict—that gets results.

This practical but anti-pragmatist line of thought, from Bourne to Goodman, finds its apogee in Toni Morrison. In 1976, in response to a speech by James Baldwin, Morrison announced her commitment to unreasonableness: "Our past is bleak. Our future dim. But I am not reasonable … I prefer not to adjust to my environment. I refuse the prison of 'I' and choose the open spaces of 'we'" (246). This unreasonable attitude, plural but not pluralist, offers a rejoinder to the consensus of despair that defines this present. Straggling utopians in the bad twenty-first century, by contrast to liberals and pragmatists, may acknowledge that the world is as it is, and that it is unlivable, and oppose the unlivability of the world anyway, while telling conflictful stories because they cannot afford to tell other stories or no stories at all. Whatever is, in short, is untenable. This perspective is not alone that of Twentieth century literary radicals, and neither does it only persist into Morrison's late work. For contemporary media critic Claire L. Evans, in her role as lead singer for the electropop band YACHT, utopia is similarly the least-worst available material for any subsequent political project: "We all know when we wake up / That this is all we get. // This is all we get: /… / utopia utopia utopia utopia" (YACHT 2011); while for another electropop band, Katie Stelmanis's Austra, utopia must be fought for and defended by any means: "It might be fiction but I see it ahead … // Utopia: / like a hunter with teeth, / there's nothing I wouldn't do" (Austra 2017).

Current perspectives on utopia all exploit a basic ambiguity in Thomas More's book of that name, between eutopia, a good place, and outopia, a no-place. As Ruth Levitas famously notes: "The pun has left a lasting confusion around the term utopia, and one which constantly recurs like a familiar but nonetheless rather troublesome ghost" (2010, 3). Yet as Lewis Mumford wrote eight decades before her, it is precisely by dwelling with this ghost, in the oscillation between these poles ("between eutopia and nothing—or rather, nothingness"), that the utopian endeavor becomes recognizable, as a world-view or a world-plan that must always be pursued as an escape from nihilistic practicability, and that should therefore not be shoehorned into a market-ready program for action (1922, 268). There do remain utopians who, because they are utopians, commit to the inadequacy of available political techniques (YACHT's "this is all we get"), the certainty that a hard fight will require hardened fighters (Austra's "hunter with teeth"), and the conviction that any worthwhile utopianism will be practiced collectively and to the benefit of all (Morrison's "open spaces of 'we'"). This worthwhile utopianism is premised on the risky work of organization and research, the fierce acquisition and employment of political knowledge, and the tacit acknowledgment that the most radical or ethical actions may entail compromise and produce limited effect. This modified utopianism is not the only kind, and by its own admission it sits among the least successful of totalizing planetary visions.

Digital Utopia

Digital utopianism, by contrast, has proven very effective. The association of high technology with social transformation does not begin with computation but has instead repeatedly emerged since the industrial revolution, upon the invention of each ostensibly (or actually) epochal machine. Each new form of telecommunication and cultural distribution has been associated with a narrative of planetary respatialization to rival the absurd Borgesian map of an empire that is the size of the empire (Borges 1998, 325). Before these, however, the newspaper, magazine, novel, motion picture, train, and automobile had already arrived, each with a set of associated hopes, fears, and cultural shifts. This problem has been formalized by literary counter-histories of the last 20 years, with particular force in Colson Whitehead's first two novels—*The Intuitionist* (1999), about elevators; and *John Henry Days* (2001), about trains and steam drills—and in William Gaddis's posthumous last novel—*Agapē Agape* (2002), about player pianos. When satellite and cable networks emerged in the final third of the last century, certain medium-specific and world-historical promises could again be heard muttering through the wires. Applying this experimental literary method to the digital age are such grand-scale novels as Richard Powers's *Plowing the Dark* (2000), a darkly conceptual book concerning penality and virtual reality; Louisa Hall's *Speak* (2015), a *longue durée* counter-history of artificial intelligence; and Tim Maughan's *Infinite Detail* (2019), a plurivocal narration of both mainstream and revolutionary strains in computational thinking, as well as devastation in which they (and much else) shall end. But these are studies, not enactments, of digital utopianism.

Digital utopians, faced with obstacles to human fulfillment that might once have been overcome through some kind of laborious human activity, now picture amelioration only by technological means. According to Richard

Barbrook and Andy Cameron over two decades ago, that Silicon Valley confidence amounts to a "Californian Ideology"—enough in touch with the soul and intellect to cultivate personal virtues, enough in touch with the wallet to get rich. Barbrook and Cameron write:

> Promoted in magazines, books, TV programmes, Web sites, newsgroups, and Net conferences, the Californian ideology promiscuously combines the free-wheeling spirit of the hippies and the entrepreneurial zeal of the yuppies. This amalgamation of opposites has been achieved through a profound faith in the emancipatory potential of the new information technologies. In the digital utopia, everybody will be both hip and rich. (45)

This ideal of freedom through machines, liberation from inconvenience, access to full connectivity, and flexible work hours is what has legitimized world-shaping by digital capitalism, from cryptocurrency to the gig economy. Interrogating these clustered attitudes and promises have been many works of contemporary fiction, often novels about life in and around the computing industry, like Ellen Ullman's *The Bug* (2003), Hari Kunzru's *Transmission* (2005), Thomas Pynchon's *Bleeding Edge* (2013), and Dave Eggers's *The Circle* (2013).

Digital utopianism belongs peculiarly to the end of the prior century and the beginning of this one. Its roots are in *Wired*, a magazine founded in 1993 as a mouthpiece for the burgeoning computer industry. Founded to share product information and celebrate the faculty of human inventiveness, while also gearing up for an imminent boom in speculative investment, *Wired* perfected a purified form of the Californian Ideology at the same time that it ground out optimistic clichés to justify already-existing practices, while also ginning up enthusiasm among venture capitalists. One much-cited article, appearing in 1994, touted the ingenuity of so-called "extropians." Not to be confused with extopians (those from an outside-place), extropians are the advocates of extropy, the opposite of entropy, whose digital engagements have taken them away from randomness and toward order. As explained in *Wired* by Ed Regis, a transhumanist science writer:

> The general Extropian approach ... is a philosophy of boundless expansion, of upward and outwardness, of fantastic superabundance. It's a doctrine of self-transformation, of extremely advanced technology, and of dedicated, unmovable optimism. Most of all, it's a philosophy of freedom from limitations of any kind. (104)

Regis's article appears in *Wired* not because the extropian experience was typical, but because it illustrated the perceived potential of computation and biotechnology to overhaul civil society, and indeed to alter the terms of human existence. In the words of Jedediah Purdy's influential analysis of extropianism, entitled "The God of the Digerati": "Extreme as they are, the Extropians are representative lunatics ... Nearly every issue of *Wired* includes a lionizing portrait of a trail-blazing go-it-alone entrepreneur, delivered in tones that would make Ayn Rand blush" (1998, 87).

The apparent paradox at the heart of Silicon Valley—what Barbrook and Cameron pinpoint as the desire to be both entrepreneurial and freewheeling—is in fact a kind of alibi generator spinning in perpetual motion. The high-tech industry has built massive server farms that damage local ecologies in unpredictable ways, yet these are ignored or forgiven because the supposed "nature" of the digital revolution is to shift toward order and ephemerality, and away from disorder and materiality. Social media produces new venues for violent speech, yet this speech is taken to be a flaw rather than a feature of otherwise progressive forms of mediated connection. The tech industry produces new forms of exploitative labor in the extraction of rare-earth minerals and the sweatshop assembly of computational devices, yet still it trumpets the arrival of post-industrial flexibility among those who buy and use those devices. A few billionaires center around themselves an unprecedented wealth even while advocating a decentralized kind of order, a network. But the latter is not the kind of decentralization that an anarchist like Goodman would advocate. Instead, it is decentralization as the pursuit of "freedom from limitations of any kind": a procedure by which multinational capitalists seem to transcend the bounds of their location, applying new-built tools to the task of expropriating influence from national and financial capitals.

This libertarian decentralization was influentially criticized by philosopher of technology Langdon Winner in the same year that Barbrook and Cameron's essay appeared. Winner concluded that the politics of *Wired* were utopian:

> Again and again we hear of redemption supposed to arrive through the Computer Revolution, Information Society, Network Nation, Interactive Media, Virtual Reality—the label changes just often enough for prophets to discover yet another world-transforming epoch in the works ... This cyber-libertarian worldview draws heavily upon the fizzing bromides of technological utopianism. (1995, 19)

The utopianism in question is an aspect of late technological modernity as such. Built on emancipatory claims for trains and industrial automation it enters its maturity in the age of computers. As Winner's mention of redemption would suggest, technological revolutions are less political or scientific than religious. Under the sign of utopianism, technology is less an applied science than an applied belief; and it is this belief that legitimates a totalizing vision of a fetishistic and predatory culture. The narrator of Jarett Kobek's polemical novel *i hate the internet* thus apostrophizes the very city of San Francisco:

> You have bequeathed to us a vision of the billionaire in a hooded sweatshirt and you have created an environment in which no one will acknowledge the idiotic theater of a billionaire in a hooded sweatshirt! You have taken the last true

good thing, the initial utopian vision of the Internet, and you have perverted it into a series of interlocking fiefdoms with no purpose other than serving advertisements. (Kobek 2016, 267)

As a form of governance, digital utopianism is often called by the very pre-digital name of technocracy. Technocracy, as a consequence, takes two dissimilar meanings. In terms of its coinage, technocracy is a rule by experts and demands efficiency not only from industrial production but also from political and social processes. For engineer William Henry Smyth, credited with coming up with the idea in 1919, technocracy involved "organizing and coordinating the Scientific Knowledge, the Technical Talent, the Practical Skill, and the Man Power of the entire Community: focusing them in the National Government, and applying the Unified National force to the accomplishment of a Unified National Purpose" (Smyth 1921, 13). It is in this sense, the labor of skilled specialists working together to reduce error and find common cause, that giants of US liberalism from Woodrow Wilson to Barack Obama and Elizabeth Warren have rightly been called technocrats. Yet even so, as industrial and then post-industrial machines have obtained more central roles in social processes, technocracy has named rule by those who know how to build, use, and maintain the machines. This means not only that experts with "Talent" or "Skill" can gather political power, but rather that experts in some fields more than others—in telecommunication and biotechnology, say—find themselves in control of large-scale political and financial systems. Silicon Valley is in this way not just home to libertarian and hyper-capitalist ideologues. It is also, and at once, home to some of the most influential and wealthy people in the world, whose influence and wealth have been accumulated on the force of a utopian mythos. So whereas, once upon a time, technocracy might have involved experts in law or planning, increasingly it refers only to those who know how to mobilize computers and computational systems.

Technocracy, given these two definitions, can be said to have two distinct utopian afterlives. From its original sense, as the rule by experts, technocracy results in the utopias of bureaucracy itself. What is bureaucracy, after all, except a composite of highly siloed sites of expertise, striving to work perfectly in isolation, while also finding harmony in tandem? David Graeber has written about the cost to life under such white-collar circumstances, where the struggle for workplace efficiency gets bound up with the struggle for human dignity in conditions of contemporary capitalism: "Bureaucracies are utopian forms of organization. After all, is this not what we always say of utopians: that they have a naive faith in the perfectibility of human nature and refuse to deal with humans as they actually are?" (Graeber 2015, 48). There is no way to live bureaucratically and realistically at the same time, it follows, and the idealistic impulse is so thoroughgoing under capitalism that societies have repeatedly chosen bureaucracy over reality. The costs of this choice are high, "where bureaucracy has been the primary means by which a tiny percentage of the population" (Graeber 2015, 205). From the seemingly new and sensible modernist arrangement by which experts run the show, there emerges something thoroughly familiar: old-fashioned accumulation of wealth and control.

In its second utopian afterlife, where technocracy names an accrual of political power by a computer industry, technocracy is an aspect of political and economic globalization. When the world is said to have been globalized, what is meant in part is that the world is accelerated and bound together by technologically enabled communicative practices that exert a determined effect on human relation. The utopian dimensions of this electronic "global village," to use Marshall McLuhan's popular phrase, were definitively dismissed by cultural critics in the late 1960s, including Marxist literary and political theorist Raymond Williams's withering review in 1967. Yet this presumption, that the world is reshaped and sped up by electronic means, remains very much in force outside of scholarship, with effects not only on media theory and practice but also on the conduct of finance, diplomacy, and military policy. For example, speaking to new graduates of the Columbia School of International and Public Affairs in 2018, Amina Jane Mohammed identified the task of the United Nations, of which she is Deputy Secretary-General, with the connective function of Facebook or Twitter:

> Social media offers the opportunity to reach across borders and to join our efforts with others in the same country or around the world, through campaigns, non-governmental organizations and other online communities. We now live in a global village, and the United Nations is the global Town Hall. (Mohammed 2019)

With McLuhan's phrase, Mohammed thus equates the real-life activity of diplomacy with the confessional activity of life as conducted online. Political procedures that purportedly operate outside of the models of national and commercial exchange are thus said to be rebuilding themselves according to those very models.

Left philosophers and social theorists have not ceased to chart the effects of utopian attitudes that stem from tech industry practice. Fred Turner is the historian most associated with the phrase "digital utopianism," having influentially noted that a foundational commitment to capitalist accumulation is often disavowed in the conduct of digital culture but remains at the heart of things. In a criticism of Barbrook and Cameron, Turner writes that "analysts of digital utopianism have dated the communitarian rhetoric surrounding the introduction of the Internet to what they have imagined to be a single, authentically revolutionary social movement that was somehow crushed or co-opted by the forces of capitalism" (Turner 2006, 34). But according to Turner, the political culture of Silicon Valley is not a betrayal of core leftist principles. Instead, early computationalist thought always owed more to a less progressive politics of consciousness and communalism. By failing to see how this latter conservatism informs their imaginary, Turner writes: "contemporary theorists of digital media have often gone so far as to echo the utopians of the 1990s" (Turner 2006, 34). Even left activists, argues Jen Schradie, have absorbed the utopianism that, as Turner shows, has planted roots not in the struggles for freedom but instead in the institutions of moneyed individualism. "The neoliberal market-based system itself is what prevents equality in digital politics," argues Schradie: "The connections across citizenship, class, the state and the economy are inextricably linked to neoliberalism" (Schradie 2015, 79). This imbrication of digitality and society leads to a near-inevitable result: digital activism ends up repeating the dicta of neoliberalism rather than undermining them. This said, because digital capitalism is capitalism, its utopianism has been most successful in the global application of financial and geomilitary might.

David Golumbia has argued influentially that the practice of high-frequency trading (HFT) has grown from libertarian hopes for computational immateriality, but has in fact resulted in an all-too-material decrease of freedom. Golumbia writes:

> Despite the widespread rhetoric that computerization inherently democratizes, the consequences of the introduction of HFT are widely acknowledged to be new concentrations of wealth and power, opacity rather than transparency of information flows, and structural resistance to democratic oversight and control. (Golumbia 2013, 278)

More insidiously, it is not only in the cause of peace or wealth that the world-shrinking digital language of "reaching across borders" is employed. It is a short distance between a world in which communities or accounts are connected with less loss of data, for instance, and a world in which drones may fly into target zones more quickly and drop bombs with less "collateral damage." (The inconvenient truth that drones fly with less prompting and less legislative supervision, and therefore result in more death not less, is understood to be a failure of decision rather than an aspect of the device or a flaw in its utopian promise.)

Despite their obvious and numerous differences, digital capitalism, neoliberal internationalism, and militarist nationalism are thus bound up in a shared ensemble of utopian motifs—speed, losslessness, and world-shrinking togetherness—that is specifically tied to the development of industries of computation and telecommunication. When there appears no political outside to their operation, these industries are treated like a force of nature. Like the auto industry in the Obama era, they are too big to fail. Yet they are also taken to have no size at all, no density, and no mass. Indeed, in what Djelal Kadir calls "a metamorphosis of global monopoly and planetary hegemony," the fetish for immateriality and transcendence is among the utopian visions guiding both neoimperialist war and computerized markets. Kadir expounds:

> Capital is no longer just territorial but constantly extra-territorial…made possible by the most advanced teletechnologies and their digital algorithms that recognize no state sovereignty or national frontiers other than those declared to lie within the perimeters of the homeland and the aegis of its homeland security that extends beyond all frontiers. (2019, 159)

Ascendant economic and technological utopianisms are not discontinuous with the rise of neoimperialist militarization. To the extent that both proceed by unmooring familiar ethnonational spatial markers and building outopian "no-places" (and, depending on whom you ask, eutopian 'good places') where formerly there were real places, these twin formations manifest as one. This pairing does not exclude a simultaneous rise in ethnonationalist utopias either, as these latter have prospered and multiplied under the spatial regimens of computation and neoimperialism, for which imaginary and ideological forms of filiation are far more important than mere borders. Borders meanwhile obtain renewed significance as a symbols of police authority. Unshackled to solely earthly concerns, borders license the adjudication not only of national citizenship and police jurisdiction but also the presumption of (im)morality and (in)humanity that inhere to these practices.

Chastened Utopia

When Toni Morrison speculates in 2000 about a possible world where some of the poor are not dead and some of the under-represented are not in prison, she proceeds from two assumptions. First, it should not be too much to ask from each other that humans stop constructing new institutions for confining, excluding, or killing people who are already disadvantaged by existing power structures. Second, from all appearances, it actually is too much to ask. Every structure for habitation, and every metric for thriving, has as its warrant the maintenance of health and wealth for those who are already healthy and wealthy. In her final lectures, Toni Morrison made explicit her stakes in revoking this warrant, whereby utopianism can only benefit those whose lives are, by contrast to the objects of their violence, already utopian. For Morrison, "in this world of tilted resources, of outrageous shameless wealth-squatting, hulking, preening itself before the dispossessed, the very idea of plenty, of sufficiency, as utopian ought to make us tremble" (276). Why tremble? Because "plenty should not be regulated to a paradisiacal state, but to normal, everyday, humane life" (2019, 276).

Either the present is unprepared for utopian thinking, because it has failed to produce conditions for planetary well-being. Or else quotidian "humane life," as the refusal of any exceptional "paradisiacal state," is the only viable utopia: a utopia against utopias, a utopia of minimal conditions for mutual care. This is also what Gerald Vizenor, in 2008, calls an "aesthetics of survivance" and defines as "a responsible presence of natural reason" by which "to outlive, persevere" (19). Survivance for Vizenor, like unconfinement and plenty for Morrison, "is an active sense of presence over absence, deracination, and oblivion" and "the continuance of stories … [as] renunciations of dominance, detractions, obtrusions, the unbearable sentiments of tragedy, and the legacy of victimry" (1). These ideals of survivance and sufficiency could be called, following theorist Tom Moylan, "critical utopias," a label that applies to any utopia that would pose a meaningful rejoinder both to naive idealism and to right-wing reaction, as well as to the forms of social and political violence that they enable, as "a diagnostic and critical account of the totality" of contemporary society, and a "literary strategy that is more attuned to the process of social negation and transformation of the existing society in the name of those who are oppressed by it" (2002, 269). In critical utopianisms are echoed Paul Goodman's demand for a "conflictful community" and Randolph Bourne's admission that a utopian thinker must accept "that he is ineffective and that he is coerced"; yet as well, they echo Toni Morrison's demand that life-preserving thought proceed to imagine or invent worlds, or else some "ménage of regimes will do it for us."

Historian Jackson Lears has called this sort of utopianism a "chastened utopianism" (Lears 2000, 39). Built outward from humility, even from exhaustion, chastened utopia is a utopia that would be "sober in its acknowledgement of ineradicable evil, yet capable of indignation and hope" (39). On this view, there is nothing wrong with utopia that will not be solved by an orientation toward ethical means rather than totalizing ends. To acknowledge utopian activity as ineffective, but then to go through with it anyway, is not to court quixotism. Rather, it is to admit that the utopian image or narrative is not alone sufficient to change the world. Political life can be acknowledged as coercive without equating utopia with the mere reaction to external pressures. A chastened utopia need only observe that the tools for unsanctioned radical thought are inherited from the very apparatuses and institutions that are tasked with sanctioning and then to act on that observation.

A chastened utopia, furthermore, is not just a critique of other utopias; it can also make space for what anthropologist Athena Athanasiou calls "utopian thinking as critique." Like Moylan's critical utopia, Athanasiou's utopia-as-critique may gesture "beyond the reification of the existing present and toward interstitial and liminal qualities of making time (and taking one's time) otherwise in the interlocking realms of ethics, politics, and aesthetics" (2020, 269). That is to say, this kind of utopia, generating an oppositional understanding of the world's normal and normative topoi, takes shape between and against regulatory temporalities, between and against disciplinary operations and political spheres. Moreover, as sound and performance theorist Jayna Brown insists, opposition need not be the only mode of relation to take shape through this "unfinished and never fully attainable" utopianism (Brown 2021, 16). Brown urges rather that conflict is only one mode among many possible modes, and "that instead of thinking of processes of change as necessarily based in a binary of opposition and antagonism, we can consider the possibility for processes of becoming that involve multiple forms of relations—cooperative, desirous, sometimes conflictual—between multiple elements" (Brown 2021, 19).

This composite perspective is a radical vision perhaps most recognizable to many in critical theory as an extension, or correction, of what Fredric Jameson intends in his major contribution to utopian thinking. For Jameson, in a paradigmatic 1982 essay reprinted in his 2007 book about science fiction, if it is not possible to tell convincing stories about a world that works properly, it at least remains possible to tell stories about that impossibility: "the true vocation of the utopian narrative begins to rise to the surface—to confront us with our incapacity to imagine Utopia … in the interrogation of the dilemmas involved in their own emergence as utopian texts" (Jameson 2007, 156). This kind of utopian thinking is a dance at the edge of the known world, naming those tendencies (decolonization perhaps, or Marxism) that have freed more people than they have confined, while noting which factors (capitalist or authoritarian accumulation, say) have inhibited this freedom through violence or coercion. Where Jameson leaves off, on the knife's point of textual play, critical and chastened utopians of the twenty-first century have picked up.

CONCLUSION

Morrison's insistence on utopian critique, in the existing world rather than the imagined alternative world, thus serves as a rejoinder to Jameson. Compellingly too, the sociologist Avery Gordon finds Jameson too closely identifying utopia with the narrativization of other worlds, aside from this world. Gordon writes that "there can be no utopian thinking under this presumptive segregation" between the real world and the better world, and that by contrast, "to treat the utopian as a way of conceiving and living in the here and now, is to accept that, like us, it is inevitably entangled with all kinds of deformations and ugly social habits" (Gordon 2018, 65). Resonating with perspectives that range from Bourne and Goodman to Morrison to Moylan and Lears to Athanasiou and Brown, Gordon draws explicitly on the novelist-theorist Toni Cade Bambara, whose *The Salt Eaters* conceives a mode of utopian living in the here and now. Adopting a historicist rather than an essentialist position, Gordon seeks ways to draw on fundamental and long-standing practices of subsistence and mutual care. Life was not always like this. It used to be like something else, perhaps something far worse. But even so, human beings survived at odds with the forces that would dehumanize them. Utopianism thus emerges as a way to tell "stories of living otherwise with the degradations of exploitation, racism, authoritarianism," and "stories of living better than all that" (Gordon 2018, 41). Utopia as no-place or good-place becomes utopia as this-place, but lived unreasonably, in a posture of defiance or difference, a conflictual or cooperative posture, in the face of what makes this-place unlivable.

References

Athanasiou, Athena. 2020. At Odds with the Temporalities of the Im-possible; or, What Critical Theory Can (Still) Do. *Critical Times* 3 (2): 249–276.

Austra. 2017. Utopia. *Future Politics*. Domino Recording Company.

Bambara, Toni Cade. 1980. *The Salt Eaters*. New York: Random House.

Barbrook, Richard, and Andy Cameron. 1996. The Californian Ideology. *Science as Culture* 6 (1): 44–72.

Borges, Jorge Louis. 1998. *Collected Fictions*, trans. Andrew Hurley. New York: Viking.

Bourne, Randolph. 1917. A War Diary. *The Seven Arts* 2: 535–547.

Brown, Jayna. 2021. *Black Utopias: Speculative Life and the Music of Other Worlds*. Durham, NC: Duke University Press.

Eggers, Dave. 2013. *The Circle*. New York: Knopf.

Gaddis, William. 2002. *Agapē Agape*. New York: Penguin.

Golumbia, David. 2013. High-Frequency Trading: Networks of Wealth and the Concentration of Power. *Social Semiotics* 23 (2): 288–299.

Goodman, Paul. 1962. *Utopian Essays and Practical Proposals*. New York: Random House.

Gordon, Avery. 2018. *The Hawthorn Archive: Letters from the Utopian Margins*. New York: Fordham University Press.

Graeber, David. 2015. *The Utopia of Rules: On Technology, Stupidity, and the Secret Joys of Bureaucracy*. Brooklyn, NY: Melville House.

Hall, Louisa. 2015. *Speak*. New York: HarperCollins.

Jameson, Fredric. 2007. *Archaeologies of the Future: The Desire Called Utopia and Other Science Fictions*. New York: Verso.

Kadir, Djelal. 2019. Imperium Century XXI. In *Empires and World Literature*, ed. Piero Boitani and Irene Montori, 149–162. Milan: Edizioni AlboVersorio.

Kobek, Jarett. 2016. *I Hate the Internet*. New York: We Heard You Like Books.

Kunzru, Hari. 2005. *Transmission*. New York: Plume.

Lears, Jackson. 2000. Techno-Utopia? *Tikkun* 15 (1): 39.

Levitas, Ruth. 2010. *The Concept of Utopia*, 2nd ed. Oxford: Peter Lang.

Maughan, Tim. 2019. *Infinite Detail*. New York: Farrar, Straus, and Giroux.

Mohammed, Amina Jane. 2019, May 16. Deputy Secretary-General's Commencement Speech at George Mason University. https://www.gmu.edu/news/2019-05/amina-j-mohammed-speech-spring-commencement-2019. Accessed 11 June 2021. Web.

Morrison, Toni. 1976. Response. In *The Nature of a Humane Society: A Symposium on the Bicentennial of the United States of America*, ed. H. Over Hess, 240–246. Philadelphia, PA: Fortress Press.

———. 2001. How Can Values Be Taught in the University? *Michigan Quarterly Review* 40 (2): 273–278.

———. 2019. *The Source of Self-Regard: Selected Essays, Speeches, and Meditations*. New York: Knopf.

Moylan, Tom. 2002. Utopia, the Postcolonial, and the Postmodern. *Science Fiction Studies* 29 (2): 265–271.

Mumford, Lewis. 1922. *The Story of Utopias*. New York: Boni and Liveright.

Powers, Richard. 2000. *Plowing the Dark*. New York: Farrar, Straus, and Giroux.

Purdy, Jedediah. 1998. The God of the Digerati. *The American Prospect* 37 (5): 86–90.

Pynchon, Thomas. 2013. *Bleeding Edge*. New York: Penguin.

Regis, Ed. 1994. Meet the Extropians. *Wired* 2 (10): 102–108, 149.

Schradie, Jen. 2015. Silicon Valley Ideology and Class Inequality: A Virtual Poll Tax on Digital Politics. In *Handbook of Digital Politics*, ed. Stephen Coleman and Deen Freelon, 67–84. Cheltenham, UK: Edward Elgar Publishing.

Smyth, William Henry. 1921. *Technocracy, First and Second Series*. Reprinted from the Gazette. Berkeley, CA.

Turner, Fred. 2006. *From Counterculture to Cyberculture: Stewart Brand, the Whole Earth Network, and the Rise of Digital Utopianism*. Chicago: University of Chicago Press.

Ullman, Ellen. 2003. *The Bug*. New York: MacMillan.

Vizenor, Gerald. 2008. Aesthetics of Survivance: Literary Theory and Practice. In *Survivance: Narratives of Native Presence*, ed. Gerald Vizenor, 1–24. Lincoln, NE: University of Nebraska Press.

Whitehead, Colson. 1999. *The Intuitionist*. New York: Anchor Books.

———. 2001. *John Henry Days*. New York: Doubleday.

Winner, Langdon. 1995. Peter Pan in Cyberspace. *Educom Review* 30 (3): 18–20.

YACHT, 2011. *Shangri-La*. DFA Records.

Aesthetic Forms and Genres

Narrative

Jennifer A. Wagner-Lawlor

INTRODUCTION

While what we call "utopian thinking" can be identified throughout history and in every culture, the concept of utopia is itself a specifically modern one. Fátima Vieira describes the invention of Utopia as "a new idea, a new feeling that would give voice to the new currents of thought that were then [in the sixteenth century] arising in Europe" (2010, 4). These currents include a new "confidence in the human being's capacity … not yet a capacity to reach a state of human perfection (which would be impossible within a Christian world-view …) but at least an ability to arrange society differently in order to ensure peace" (2010, 4). The "humanistic logic" of this optimism is reflected in the imperialist explorations of the Renaissance. More had read the travel accounts of Amerigo Vespucci, Christopher Columbus, Angelo Poliziano, and others, and his *Utopia* models itself on these discovery narratives, mimicking the scientific objectives of explorers' anthropological and cartographic representations—not to mention the economic and imperial objectives of such travel to *terrae incognitae*. But inventiveness of utopian *narrative*, as a form of literary technology, lies in its acknowledgment of not only logic and rationality in support of a "humanistic" logic of organization and order but also of the imagination and of something called "hope."

Utopian narrative has enjoyed a long and productively complex history since its invention by lawyer, social philosopher, and statesman Sir Thomas

J. A. Wagner-Lawlor (✉)
The Pennsylvania State University, University Park, PA, USA

P. Marks et al. (eds.), *The Palgrave Handbook of Utopian and Dystopian Literatures*, https://doi.org/10.1007/978-3-030-88654-7_13

More (1478–1535). The origin of the word and concept are well-known: the word *utopia* is a neologism based on an aural and typographical pun: *u* + *topos* could be heard as either *eu-* (Gr., good) or *ou-* (Gr., non) + *topos* (Gr., place): a good place that is "no place." Utopian thinking is a form of speculation, a "what-if" imaginary place that would be "good" comparatively speaking—if it existed. And "what-if" it did … how to describe that place? The effectiveness of More's narrative is that he takes advantage of a travel-narrative convention already associated with the advance of knowledge and the expansion of what is "real" or "true" about the world. More's innovation is to adapt the process of speculation ("what-if" we were to discover a society that is different and … "good"?) and to a narrative form that presents that speculative process as itself an education, a leading-out of what is known to something not known: people, places, laws, mores, habits, ways of working, playing, and being. More's educated readership would recognize the paradigm of travel, discovery, and observation as the reader/listener is drawn toward the "entertainment" of a strange or new idea different from one's common experience. J. C. Davis is correct, however, in suggesting that the "semantic territory of islands, oceans, and voyages" (2008, has had a flattening effect based in the very familiarity of the voyage and "tour-guide" paradigm, with the narrator arriving and finding himself (usually male) led around the place, and reporting back in an anthropological manner. Indeed, several modern texts identify the traveler-narrator as a professional anthropologist. From a narratological point of view, this has meant that the question of literary form tends to be secondary to the descriptive representation of a utopian society in any given text. The sociological nature of utopian description and the anthropological sensibilities of the typical "utopian traveler" have favored more generalized histories of utopian thought. Krishan Kumar's *Utopia and Anti-Utopia in Modern Times* (Kumar, 1987) is exemplary: while basing his argument on five well-known utopian texts, from *Looking Backward: 2000–1887* (Edward Bellamy, 1888) to *Walden Two* (B. F. Skinner, 1948), this sociologist understands the texts per se as vehicles for a specific line of socio-historical content. The interest is not on getting there so much as it is on *being* there, although as Davis and others point out, utopian narrative frequently ends with a return "home" that leaves the narrator-traveler feeling anywhere from disoriented to nearly insane. The narrative frequently ends in a whimper, not a bang—when it is precisely the eruption of movement against a flawed society that seems most obviously needed. Rarely do we hear about the Revolution—and the blueprint model for utopian speculation has long been critiqued for its *political* ineffectiveness.

What gets left out of such readings as Kumar's, however, is attention to resources offered by the very "literariness" of the texts: metaphor and other tropes; characteristics of form and structure; precisely the active(ist) resources of "the literary." The relatively recent claims of a "new activist formalism" are pertinent, insofar as it might reorient our view of the history of utopian narrative toward a "productive rather than merely reflective" concept of literary form (Levinson 2007, 563). To view the textuality and critical formalism of utopian narrative from this perspective illuminates the most radical feature of utopian texts: the essential indeterminacy of utopian content. This is precisely what Davis worries about; similarly, Ruth Levitas observes that in our late-modernity period "it is no longer possible to say anything about the nature of utopia itself, but only the communicative processes by which it may be negotiated. Thus the only kind of utopia which is possible is the processual and communicative" (1990, 37). Levitas seems to view this as a "reduction" of the capacities of utopian thought. From a narratological point of view, however, the opposite is the case. In the section that follows, I argue that More's formal inventiveness in creating a dialogic and open-ended narrative for the representation of Utopia builds in the processual and indeed the *anticipatory* motif of utopian thinking that would become so important a dimension in later centuries.

COGNITIVE MAPPING

The neologism *utopia* does not itself connote anticipation or futurity, but alterity. Etymologically there is no connection to the "good time": the term *euchronia* comes later, expanding the horizons of utopian journeying from near to remote futures. More's *Utopia* never leaves the author's "present" at all; King Utopus' island may be distant geographically from sixteenth-century London but is not temporally so. The first-edition frontispiece, a topographical map of the imaginary island, mimics the cartographic paraphernalia of Renaissance explorers' accounts as they skirted the shores of unmarked coastlines, and hazarded incursions into land interiors and into communities of previously unknown peoples. The implication is that commonwealth of Utopia "exists" in the here and now, however distant it may be from the British islands. The first time-travel utopian narrative, by some accounts, does not appear until the eighteenth century.

But More's originary utopian text does capture the *anticipation* of Europe's mastery of land and sea, as well as its exploitation of found resources (including slaves, which are present in Utopia). One of the (perhaps) unforeseen consequences was the discovery as well of developed peoples and cultures radically different from anything Europeans had seen before. The concept of utopia, the book *Utopia*, and every utopian narrative written since then is "context specific," as Vieira says; but to speak more emphatically, each is *situated* historically and politically, geographically, and temporally. More's narrative's situatedness is embodied, moreover, in not one but three figures: the traveler/narrator, Raphael Hythloday; the listener, "More"[1] himself; and Peter Giles, their common acquaintance. The relationship is frequently overlooked, and yet it is key to pinpointing a crucial aspect of the anticipatory structure of utopian narrative *qua* narrative. Utopia is a *story* that must be told.

The centrality of the dialoguic relationality is manifest in the framed narrative as a formal trope that is characteristic of the utopian genre. The utopian narrative's embedded structuring is fundamental, moreover, to its task of opening up a space for speculation. While the framed narrative would become a common device of the novelist, the novel as such did not yet exist in the English tradition. Thus in *Utopia*, it is remarkable that "More" simply runs into friend Peter Giles, who in turn insists that he and one Raphael Hythloday meet one another, to More's immediate reluctance and impatience. This "interruption" is one of the generic traits of utopian narratives, a kind of "shock-event" (to use a currently popular, dystopian Trump-era term): in many cases, the discovery of utopia in any given text is accidental. Ships get blown off course (*Gulliver's Travels*, 1726); carriages break down (*Millennium Hall*, 1762); the utopian narrator falls down a hidden crevice (*The Coming Race*, 1871); or falls asleep, and "wakes up" either somewhere else or at some other time (*News from Nowhere*, 1890). Marge Piercy's Connie, in *Woman at the Edge of Time* (1985) is visited by an apparition from the future, who "transports" her to Mattapoisett: the standard utopian "guide" comes to her first, reversing the usual order of things.

Arriving at a utopia always takes the narrator by surprise, over-taken (*surpris*) by an encounter with the strangeness of the place. In that suspended moment of surprise the narrator recognizes that they cannot "read" the scene: they are returned to a kind of epistemological childhood or state of "innocence," in the etymological sense of *not knowing*. The "tour" that forms the central action of the utopian text is itself an extended experience of what Suvin calls, in his important 1979 study of science-fiction narrative, *cognitive estrangement*. This extremely important critical term concisely clarifies not only the specific functioning or "operation" of the utopian narrative—that is, precisely to "make strange" both the epistemological and ontological assumptions of the utopian visitor. But the presence of the guide initiates what is in effect a form of therapeutic re-education. If that term sounds possibly threatening, that would not be wrong: some utopian travelers balk at being confronted with a way of being and knowing that appears to highlight not only the worst aspects of their "home country" but sometimes even what they had thought to be its best aspects. In Gilman's *Herland*, for instance, there are three travelers, representing a range of responses from wholesale idealization of the Herland culture (Jeff), to rabid and ultimately violent opposition (Terry), to measured, thoughtful critique of both Herland and "Their-land" (Vandyke). Accommodating oneself to new forms of ontology and epistemology takes persuasion, even in the face of "clear evidence." There is a *lot* of talking and debating in utopian novels.

This ethical motive may be More's most critical challenge to the reader who engages the utopian narrative: like the utopian traveler who must learn to read cultural signs and a new landscape, the reader will be internally debating pros and cons. Laurence Davis correctly proposes that what we readers are doing is to "[interpret]" (Davis 2001, 78). "More" himself, having listened to Hythloday's report, judges much in Hythloday's story to be "quite absurd" (hence his name, which translates from Greek as "nonsense purveyor"); but being the philosophical sophisticate and court officer that he is, "More" is at least intrigued enough by alternative ways of thinking about society to learn more. The text eventually closes with a more tempered assessment: while there is much he cannot agree with in this Utopia "More" nonetheless appreciates aspects of that society that he himself "might wish for" (*optarim*) if not actually hope for (*uerius quam sperarim*) (More 2003, 308–309). He leaves open the possibility of "an other time" [*aliud tempus*], in which "I will be [Lat. *fore*] thinking further [*altius cogitandi*, with altius also suggesting 'at a higher level'] and conferring more fully" [*uberius*, a word also suggesting productivity] with Hythloday. The Latin word *fore* is the less common form of the future infinitive of *esse* (to be); and in the way that narrative has of entangling forms of temporality, therefore, "More" leaves with the persistent hope of a future memory: an anticipation. This hope is, to echo philosopher and semiotician Jacques Derrida (1930–2004), the "trace" of a utopian encounter with difference; as such it also "repeatable," since a trace of difference will always be nonidentical to itself. Difference and repetition: these are the twin polarities of utopia's narrative temporality. All that can be anticipated of the trace is its repeatability: the simultaneity of protention (in anticipation) and retention (the "irreducibility of the always-already-there") (Derrida 1977, 66). Without that tension, utopia is reduced again to the blueprint model: it is static, unchanging in its perfection and non-repeatability. But that is not the utopia we want: we want change, evolution, history—not an end-time.

ANTICIPATORY DYNAMICS

As Oscar Wilde reminds us, "A map of the world that does not include Utopia is not worth even glancing at, for it leaves out the one country at which Humanity is always landing. And when Humanity lands there, it looks out, and, seeing a better country, sets sail. Progress is the realization of Utopias." Thus are the temporalities of utopian narrative translated, according to Mark Currie, "into spatial relationships or differences": "The Derridean concept of *différance* seemed to qualify the structural model of difference by allowing time back into the analysis of meaning: *différance* carried with it a temporal as well as a spatial meaning" (Currie 2004, 53). Utopian narrative models a structuralization of *différance*, and understanding its structure in this way clarifies the fragile tethering of utopian tropes of spatiality and temporality. Darko Suvin gave his own name to this narratological structure: *the novum* (Suvin 1979). Suvin's framework for talking about this narrative mechanism is neo-Marxian and so inherently historical. But the *novum* marks more than something that is "new" or "innovative": these are the descriptors of a "capitalist practice" that "eventually [perfects] an image of time rigidified into an exactly delimited, quantifiable continuum filled with quantifiable 'things'" (Suvin 1979, 84), such that time is converted to "the equivalent of money and thus of all things" (ibid., 73). Suvin seeks a transformative kernel with the function of "de-alienating human history" (84) from the mystifications derived from capitalism's false equivalencies.

The *novum* represents "a really radical novelty such as a social revolution and change of scientific paradigm" (81) that generates the "possibility of something [truly] new" (81–82). Quoting Ernst Bloch directly, Suvin argues that the only consistent novelty is one that constitutes an open-ended system, "which possesses its *novum* continually both in itself and before itself as befits the unfinished state of the world, nowhere determined by any transcendental supraworldly formula" and thus "eschew[ing] any final solutions" (quoted in Suvin 2010, 88). The novum is generative, based not in "any transcendental supraworldly formula" (Suvin 1979, 82) but in the open-ended deferral of final form: not simply a figuration of difference but of an open-ended and generative *structuralization* of difference.[2] Therefore, "as befits the unfinished state of the world," the achievement of the *novum* is its non-achievement. Miguel Abensour's excellent analysis of utopia's "persistence" derives from this essential nonclosure: "[utopia's] non-coincidence between what was projected and what has come about throws us back into a new struggle for alterity. ... The persistence of utopia, we see, is due not so much to the repeated pursuit of a determinate content as to the *ever-reborn* movement toward something indeterminate ... Not to assign it a goal to desire but *to open a path for it*" (Abensour 2008, 407; emphasis added). Utopian narrative is itself a figuration of a process of *non*-fulfillment; it is not the narrative of perfectibility or the arrival at the New Jerusalem. Insofar as utopia is understood as a site of "permanent struggle" or critique, then it "gives birth to ... a stubborn impulse toward freedom and justice" (ibid., 407). The blueprint model that suggests that utopia is a desire for "perfection" and an end to change is actually inconsistent with utopian narrative's particular task: not simply to "educate desire," but as Fredric Jameson argued in an earlier, more optimistic mode, to activate "a learning to desire, the invention of the desire called utopia in the first place" (Jameson 1996, 90).

To return to More's *Utopia*, the importance of the novum's role in a utopian narrative re-emphasizes the importance of the reader/listener. In this sense Levitas' negative definition of utopia is right: it is impossible to describe the nature of utopia *except as a process and as a communication*. That is, utopia must *be* a story or narrative: construction of an alternative space–time, the experience of which the narrator relates to an-other in an encounter that itself begins again, in that other, the surprise of onto-epistemologic disruption, cognitive estrangement, and (re)mapping. The task of the narrative is to re-attune the listener to the possibilities of difference: the learning to desire, and thus to speculate and, even, to anticipate. The task of utopian narrative is to teach every reader how to see and think otherwise, such that "new and constructive ways to disclose aspects of the world" (Rouse 2009, 202) might emerge: or at the very least be imagined.

In his "Introduction to the ontology of anticipation," Roberto Poli grounds this ontology in the temporal: "the future [is] part of a *structured story* whose past and present are at least partially known" (2010, 769; emphasis added). Two kinds of stories we tell about the future are *forecasting* and *scenario-building*; but Poli distinguishes those perspectives from an "anticipation viewpoint": "the future can be better confronted by opening our minds and learning to consider different viewpoints," thus "preparing for the unforeseeable novelties awaiting us in the future." Poli's definitions correspond to utopia's ongoing structuralization of "an other time" and place, and to utopian literature's narratological methods of exploring the future in the present. The notion of propensies is central to anticipation theory, based in the work of Karl Popper (1990): "Just like a newly synthesized chemical compound, whose creation in turn creates new possibilities for new compounds to synthesize, so all new propensities always create new possibilities. And new possibilities tend to realize themselves in order to create again new possibilities. Our world of propensities is inherently creative" (20) as we anticipate a "better world, even while remaining attuned to unpredictable accidents and disruptions marking encounters with alterity" (Poli 2010, 773). Contravening the achievements of the hardened systems of present-day ideological formation, speculation destabilizes the self-identity of the "as is" (*speculum*) in favor of the "as if," the projecting out of possibility. The shapes and shades emerging from speculation are, in a word, *anticipations* with the potential to disrupt "the system." Thus the aptness of Roberto Poli's statement that the "main assumption of [a]nticipatory systems" is that "[f]uture states may determine present changes" (Poli 2017, 176). Anticipatory systems are speculative in nature—epistemically ungrounded, but not groundless: where rationality falls short, imagination and perceptual intuition rise, and disrupt.

In the context of utopian narrative, the self-reflexivity of this definition is highly suggestive. Robert Rosen's "predictive" anticipatory system is not mere replication. For at a certain point, a self-replicating system no longer "needs" the anticipatory. The system simply becomes what it is, in a logical tautology. I take Rosen's notion of "a system containing a predictive model of itself" (Rosen 1985) to mean something closer to (*re)generation*, a "living" system as it were that recognizes its own propensity to evolve. According to Mihai Nadin, a predictive model also means acknowledging the animation of the present by anticipation (Nadin 2010, 4). This may be a more radical reading than Rosen intends, but his formulation points toward a way of understanding the resilience of the concept of utopia, and the persistence of utopian, dystopian, and speculative literatures. The reiterative nature of utopia *is* its fictional realization again and again *as* a work of literature, artwork, and speculative philosophy.

The regenerative germ of utopian visioning explains why the genre of utopian narrative is so long-lived, resilient, and generative of other closely related subgenres of fiction, such as science fiction or fantasy literature. The task of utopia is to generate a "predictive model of itself"; that is, a figuration of utopia's generative possibilities *as narrative*. The "predictive model" of utopian narrative aligns with models of anticipation that acknowledge the essentially contingent nature of historical temporality: utopian speculation cannot *predict*, but it can *propose*, place something before us. The speculative *what-if* presumes the potentialities and possibilities offered by alterity and difference, *whether in the future or the past*. But most important is that there be "some other time" for dialogue, for the telling of the story. If anything is "predictive" in this narrative model, it is its speculative nature. The sensibility cultivated through speculative standpoint makes possible a configuration of history that is neither simply linear nor cyclical, but a complex temporality that is represented by the symbolic form of utopia's generic framed or embedded narrative. It is a structured story weaving and reweaving threads, parallel lines of memories *as well as* parallel lines of anticipation or hopeful imagining. This is the work of speculative fiction, to invent ways to intervene that are not always just a disruption but an evolution.

JEANETTE WINTERSON'S *THE STONE GODS*

British author Jeanette Winterson is keenly attuned to the temporal complexities not only of anticipation but of a kind of self-generative novelty that structures future forms of utopian narrative. *The Stone Gods* (2007) is a novel all about the repeatability of stories and events, constructed of multiple stories of adventure, risk and romance, genesis, and apocalypse. This highly allusive text interweaves narrative threads from the most familiar literary texts: fairy tales; the *Bible*; *Robinson Crusoe*; Captain Cook's *Journals*; the historical romances of Sir Walter Scott; the travel tales of Joseph Conrad; lines from the love poetry of Shakespeare, Herrick, Wyatt, T. S. Eliot, and Donne's "The Sun Rising"; contemporary science fiction from Joanna Russ's *The Female Man* (1975), and Marge Piercy's *He, She and It* (1993) to Atwood's speculative fiction. Characteristically, the novel also alludes to Winterson's own work. These threads are so tightly woven into the line of this novel that its form functions as an echo chamber, inter- and intratextually.

Indeed, "Echo" is a central trope in the novel—as is storytelling. The crew of a spaceship investigating the sighting of a new Earth-like planet are already at work creating the history of this signal event. The spaceship crew creates a beautiful fable, "the way all shipcrew tell stories" (Winterson 2009, 50), describing a series of planets, each a version of Earth—and each one a possible future, or a possible past, each a place "real and imaginary. Actual and about to be" (39). In particular, they describe "a planet called Echo": "*It doesn't exist. It's like those ghost-ships at sea, the sails worn through and the deck empty ... It passed straight through the ship and through our bodies, ... Then it was gone, echoing in another part of the starry sky, always, 'here' and 'here' and 'here', but nowhere. Some call it Hope*" (51). In a following episode a further iteration of the novel's refrain records the sailors' discovery of a nameless planet: "*Chanc'd upon, spied through a glass darkly, drunken stories strapped to a barrel of rum, shipwreck, a Bible Compass, a giant fish led us there, a storm whirled us to this isle. In this wilderness of space, we found ....*" (51). Once ("once upon a time, once upon a time like the words in a fairytale" [52]) this planet held oceans, cities, and life, "naked and free and optimistic" (52); and while in days past it was "a world like ours" (56), now it is a "bleached and boiled place" with "no future" (52), a "white-out"—as if its story itself had been erased. Below the charred surface is an "elephant's graveyard," in which, presumably, everything is remembered. In this Dantesque space are the "carcasses of planes and cars" trapped in an endless cycle of melting down and re-forming: "This was the inferno, where a civilization has taken its sacrifices and piled them to some eyeless god, but too late" (52). The captain of the spaceship asserts that this white planet is "where we used to live" (55), a potential image of our own contemporary world. While "Hope" is about to be actualized in the voyage to Planet Blue, the narrator, fearing "a repeating world—same old story" (49), wishes that this planet "could sail through space" toward a place, and time, beyond human reach, "where the sea, clean as a beginning, will wash away any trace of humankind" (22).

This trope of a repeating history, possibly "a suicide note," possibly "a record of our survival" (Winterson 2009, 39), is mirrored by the narratological structure of the novel, which fissures into multiple temporal planes: the Near-Future; the Past (eighteenth century); the Farther-Future; the Prehistoric (the time of the dinosaurs, 65 million years ago); the Present. In each of these temporal planes a recurrent figure named Spike appears. In one plane she is an evolving form of humanity called the *Robo-Sapiens*; she is also a (male) member of Capt. Cook's Easter Island voyage; a contemporary woman who proposes sending a message, *forward in time*: "Now … [the *Robo Sapiens*] was coding something different—for the future, whenever that would be. 'A random repeat, bouncing off the moon. One day, perhaps, maybe, when a receiver is pointed in the right direction, someone will pick this up. Someone, somewhere, when there is life like ours'" (82)—when and if history repeats itself on a planet "some call Hope." As she sends the signals Spike remarks on the paradox of past and future: "Everything is imprinted for ever with what it once was." Although "you [mankind] made a world without alternatives" (65), she points out, the quantum universe is "neither random nor determined. It is potential at every second. All you can do is intervene" (62).

Even a man-made apocalypse is a kind of intervention: whether random or not, events create the conditions for a future not possible before. These "time-bridges" are characteristically signaled in this novel by the appearance of portals of one sort or another, not an edge, over which one either stands or falls, but a "liminal opening" (Winterson 2009, 146): a gate; a door; or, a story, the "true" kind that "lie[s] open at the border, allowing a crossing, a further frontier." And the protagonist, "Billie," looks for those open portals to her past, revealing "imprints from everything [she] once was," but also portals to the future, all her possible futures: "The final frontier is just science fiction—don't believe it. Like the universe [a 'memory of our mistakes'], there is no end" (87). Billie reiterates her hope offered by stories, not those with "a beginning, a middle and an end, but … [the ones] that began again, … that twisted away, like a bend in the road" (87): "True stories are the ones that lie open at the border, allowing a crossing, a further frontier" (87). The instant when "time became a bridge" (80) is her paradigmatic chronotype.

Toward the end of *The Stone Gods*, such a bridge suddenly stretches out—and again, it takes the form of a story—*this story*. A present-day figure who is clearly "Winterson herself," finds a manuscript lying on a coach seat in the London Underground, with the title, *The Stone Gods*. Reading at random, Billie-"Winterson" thinks it's perhaps a dissertation on the Easter Islands; or, no, "a love story ... maybe about aliens. I hate science fiction" (Winterson 2009, 119). In a wonderfully metafictional moment, the manuscript suddenly becomes something else. The (current-day) narrator reveals to her companion Spike that the manuscript is one she had previously lost, leaving it on a seat of Circle Line train, only to have it return now: "I had a strange sensation, as if this were the edge of the world and one more step, just one more step ..." (147). In handing it to Spike, she drops it, its unnumbered pages are "shuffled as a pack of cards." She decides then to leave it Underground: no matter how she might originally have put the pages together, every person who finds it will create the story they want, or need: "A message in a bottle. A signal. ... A repeating world. Read it. Leave it for someone else to find. The pages are loose—it can be written again" (203).

This is the key to utopia's literary nature: while things are imprinted with what they always were, there can always be *another story*, generated by both the memory of the past, and the anticipation of the future. Following the More paradigm, once more: as with the *Utopia*, *The Stone Gods* leaves off, incomplete. But there is the *anticipation* that it will be found, lost and found by someone else, in a different time. Once again, the utopian narrative form reveals its resilience and plasticity: the very existence of such a narrative antic-ipates the (now-absent) presence of an other: a new reader/listener, whose encounter with such a strange text of other worlds may generate yet another text. Works of utopian literature constitute *strategy* for incorporating what Mihai Nadin calls "anticipatory dynamics." The great value of a specula-tive utopian narrative is that whether it takes us forward, backward, or in place temporally, the speculation *historicizes the present* in ways that clarify not only the influence of the past in the future but also the *confluence* of future possibilities, where our horizons may lie.

NOTES

1. When referring to the author, I write More; when referring to the char-acter of More who appears in Utopia, I designate his fictional status by writing "More."
2. Note the difference between the words structure and structuralization, the former referring to a completed, hardened form, and the latter to the process of becoming a structure.

REFERENCES

Abensour, Miguel. 2008. Persistent Utopia. *Constellations* 15 (3): 406–421.

Currie, Mark. 2004. *Difference*. London: Routledge.

Davis, J.C. 2008. Going Nowhere: Travelling to, Through, and from Utopia. *Utopian Studies* 19 (1): 1–23.

Davis, Lawrence. 2001. Isaiah Berlin, William Morris, and the Politics of Utopia. In *The Philosophy of Utopia*, ed. Barbara Goodwin, 56–86. London: Frank Cass.

Derrida, Jacques. 1977. *Of Grammatology*. Baltimore: The John Hopkins University Press.

Jameson, Fredric. 1996. *The Seeds of Time*. New York: Columbia University Press.

Kumar, Krishan. 1987. *Utopia and Anti-Utopia in Modern Times*. Oxford: Blackwell.

Levinson, Marjorie. 2007. What Is New Formalism. *PMLA* 122 (2): 558–569.

Levitas, Ruth. 1990. *The Concept of Utopia*. Syracuse: Syracuse University Press.

More, Thomas. 2003. *Utopia*. London: Penguin Classics.

Nadin, Mihai. 2010. Anticipation and Dynamics: Rosen's Anticipation in the Perspective of Time. *International Journal of General Systems* 39 (1): 3–33.

Poli, Roberto. 2010. An Introduction to the Ontology of Anticipation. *Futures* 42: 769–776.

———. 2017. *Introduction to Anticipation Studies*. New York: Springer.

Popper, Karl. 1990. *A World of Propensities*. London: Thoemmes.

Rosen, Robert. 1985. *Anticipatory Systems*. Oxford: Pergamon Press.

Rouse, Joseph. 2009. Standpoint Theories Reconsidered. *Hypatia* 24 (4): 200–209.

Suvin, Darko. 1979. *Metamorphoses of Science Fiction: On the Poetics and History of a Literary Genre*. New Haven: Yale University Press.

———. 2010. *Defined by a Hollow: Essays on Utopia, Science Fiction and Political Epistemology*. Bern: Peter Lang.

Vieira, Fátima. 2010. The Concept of Utopia. In *The Cambridge Companion to Utopian Literature*, ed. Gregory Claeys, 3–27. Cambridge: Cambridge University Press.

Winterson, Jeanette. 2009. *The Stone Gods: A Novel*. New York: Mariner Books.

Science Fiction

Caroline Edwards

INTRODUCTION

The production of utopian and satirical romances in the Early Modern period was inspired by accounts of European travelers and the non-Europeans they encountered, and forms a major part of science fiction's pre-history. The strange utopian societies glimpsed in Thomas More's *Utopia* (1516), Francis Bacon's *New Atlantis* (1627), Cyrano de Bergerac's *The Other World: Comical History of the States and Empires of the Moon* (1657), Margaret Cavendish's *The Description of a New World, Called The Blazing World* (1666), and Jonathan Swift's *Gulliver's Travels* (1726) facilitate what John Rieder (2008) calls a "disturbance of ethnocentrism" (2). This colonial context plagues both utopian literature and science fiction, and yet is also the crucible in which ideas of *political alterity*—what Darko Suvin (1979) famously termed "cognitive estrangement"—are woven into narratives of strange new technologies and alien landscapes. In this chapter, I will trace the relationship between utopia and science fiction along this axis of alterity, suggesting that what unites these historically divergent kinds of narrative is their use of an estranging perspective to imagine that better worlds are possible.

C. Edwards (✉)
Birkbeck, University of London, London, UK

P. Marks et al. (eds.), *The Palgrave Handbook of Utopian and Dystopian Literatures*, https://doi.org/10.1007/978-3-030-88654-7_14

SWISS CHEESE UTOPIAS: SUBTERRANEAN WORLDS

Popularized by various amateur scientists and writers since the seventeenth century, the theory of the "hollow Earth" inspired a number of exotic travel narratives in the eighteenth and nineteenth centuries. Many of these fictions used their exotic belowground locations to reflect upon possible utopian worlds within the earth's core. H. G. Wells's contemporary C. J. Cutliffe Hyne, for example, drew on the late-Victorian sub-genre of the Lost World story in *Beneath Your Very Boots: Being a Few Striking Episodes from the Life of Anthony Merlwood Haltoun, Esq* (1889), imagining an underground utopia of ancient Celts, whose technological capabilities are superior to those of their compatriots above. Hyne's narrative draws on the pseudoscience of what Pierre Versins calls the "Swiss cheese" model of hollow Earth theory: richly detailed visions of subterranean worlds cavernous enough to contain mountains, oceans, and entire civilizations (Fitting 2004, 9). Perhaps the best-known late-nineteenth-century hollow Earth story is Edward Bulwer-Lytton's *The Coming Race* (1871). The unnamed American narrator falls through a British mineshaft and discovers the Vril-ya: a highly developed underworld civilization whose scientific and technological progress are centuries in advance of the narrator's own cherished institutions of American democracy and European culture. This progress has been made possible by the discovery, and harnessing, of Vril: an infinitely renewable energy source that is described as being something like electricity, but also like magnetism or galvanism.

However, Bulwer-Lytton's sketch of a utopian realm of perfect peace and longevity is not the most interesting feature of *The Coming Race*. Rather, it is the novel's Darwinian thought experiment about a technologically and biologically superior race that has captivated readers since the novel's publication. Having learned about the existence of human civilization above ground, the narrator's conjecture that the Vril-ya will surely venture to the surface and become "our inevitable destroyers" gives the novel its title and an ominous note of forewarning (Bulwer-Lytton 2007, 129). After the publication of Darwin's *Origins of the Species* (1859), the imagination "of a strange new species was no longer a mere literary conceit invented for didactic purposes or for entertainment" as had been the case with Jonathan Swift's creatures in *Gulliver's Travels*, for example. Rather, as Frank E. Manuel and Fritzie P. Manuel (1979) note, "it became a reasonable possibility in the portrayal of future animal destiny" (774). This inspired a number of Darwinian futurist novels that extrapolated distant states of biological development: a theme most famously encapsulated in H. G. Wells's division of the human race into subterranean laboring Morlocks and effete, upperworld Eloi in *The Time Machine* (1895). The Vril-ya thus come to represent both an existential threat to mankind in the form of a superior culture as well as a fascinating embodiment of American and British expansionism at a time of colonial expansion, situating the novel as an exemplary work of imperial Gothic.

More alarming still, for Bulwer-Lytton's late-nineteenth-century readership, the superiority of Vril women over their hapless menfolk leveled a
warning to smug patriarchy about its assumed continuance. This gender role
reversal is the central tenet of another influential hollow Earth narrative: Mary
E. Bradley Lane's *Mizora: A World of Women* (1880–1881). Mizora's balmy
Italianate climate, lush orchards and flower gardens, and advanced technology
all bear the hallmarks of the utopian kingdom; while its sophisticated mechanization of domestic labor has done away with "the toil that we know, menial,
degrading and harassing" (Lane 1999, 21). Mizoran society is exclusively
female, having developed parthenogenesis (self-reproduction) as a refinement
of natural law—described in curiously botanical terms, like some kind of horticultural experiment. It is also exclusively Aryan, occupied by a beautiful race of
celibate blonde-haired women. When she asks what happened to the country's
dark-haired women, Vera is bluntly told that "[w]e eliminated them" (92).
Lane's vision of utopian eugenics in the white maternal state of Mizora thus
contributes to a racist American discourse of social Darwinism that drew on
spurious and highly racialized scientific research into phrenology, craniometry,
and skin color, revealing what Toni Morrison (1992) has called the "impenetrable whiteness" of nineteenth-century American literature, that reasserts
itself after encountering a black subject.

EUCHRONIAS: THE NEXT HISTORICAL
STAGE OF INDUSTRIAL DEVELOPMENT

As nineteenth-century scientific and technological progress accelerated the
pace of industrial development in countries such as America, Great Britain,
France, and Germany, writers increasingly imagined waking up in the future
to see their dreams of utopian socialism fulfilled. The genre evolved from
narratives set "elsewhere" to narratives set "elsewhen" and the *euchronia* (a
term credited to Charles Renouvier's coinage in *Uchronie* [1876]) emerged
as a dynamic mode of utopian literature that envisaged history as inevitably
leading toward teleological progress. The earliest euchronias date back to
eighteenth-century France and the period leading up to, and following, the
French Revolution. Louis-Sébastien Mercier's proto-science-fictional *L'An
2440, rêve s'il en fut jamais* (translated as *Memoirs of the Year Two Thousand
Five Hundred*, published in Holland in 1771 and translated in 1797) is set
732 years in the future, a time when "[i]t seems as if our reason has been
enlarged in proportion to the immeasurable space that has been discovered
and traversed by the sight" (Mercier 1974, 153). As a bestselling work of
pre-revolutionary French political speculation, *L'An 2440* inspired several
later French euchronias that explored the consequences of utopian socialism
and futuristic technologies. J. J. Grandville's illustrated vision in *Un autre
monde [Another World]* (1843), for instance, fictionalizes Charles Fourier's
utopian system of factory production in an extended parody of utopian
socialism's cult status, populating his utopia with surreal animal hybrids and

talking vegetables—satirizing the natural world from which Fourier argued man had become estranged. In *Le Monde tel qu'il sera* [*The World As It Shall Be*] (1846), Émile Souvestre suggested that highly technologized euchronian futures could just as easily deliver a world of complete commodification. Meanwhile, with its hidden levers and seemingly sentient lighting systems Souvestre's fully mechanized house of the future provides an entertaining farce that also articulates a genuine fear of automation.

The increasing automation of manufacture posed a problem for late-nineteenth-century utopian writers in North America. While it undoubtedly delivered a world free from back-breaking drudgery, workers were less enthusiastic about "celebrat[ing] the very machines that often put them out of work and strengthened the powers of the rich" (Roemer 1976, 110). Indeed, the sudden proliferation of American utopian novels (many of which were also euchronias) in the 1880s and 1890s offered readers utopian parallel worlds that responded directly to events of the day—including increasingly militant industrial action as exemplified in the Pullman railroad workers' strike, the Homestead Steel Strike, and the Haymarket Square Riot. Workers' strikes set the scene for the most iconic of all the late-nineteenth-century euchronias: Edward Bellamy's *Looking Backward, 2000–1887* (2007). Having gone to sleep in the 1880s, the protagonist Julian West is struck by the city's calm sense of order and quiet productivity in the year 2000. Nineteenth-century monopoly capitalism, as West's utopian hosts patiently explain, was a necessary historical stage in the evolution toward state socialism; and Bellamy's extended reverie on the mechanics of warehouse storage and distribution (involving a lot of pneumatic tubes) is designed to persuade the reader of capitalism's gross waste of energy and resources.

The euchronia also proved to be an effective form in which to imagine women's emancipation. More than 50 years before Bellamy's novel, Mary Griffith had used the euchronia to project an American future in which women have achieved equality in her novella *Three Hundred Years Hence* (1836). "As soon as [women] were considered of equal importance with their husbands," the utopian traveler is told, "all of the barbarisms of the age disappeared" (Griffith 2017, 40). Meanwhile, Elizabeth Burgoyne Corbett's late-Victorian novel *New Amazonia: A Foretaste of the Future* (1889) offers a female-centered vision of scientific achievement in a euchronian future Ireland. Corbett's utopian vision was grounded in the real-life example of the all-woman government of Oskaloosa, Kansas. Full automation has released women into public life in Anna Bowman Dodd's epistolary novella *The Republic of the Future; or, Socialism a Reality* (1887). "One sees [women] everywhere," the male narrator marvels, "in all the public offices, as heads of departments, as government clerks, as officials, as engineers, machinists, aeronauts, tax collectors, filling, in fact, every office and vocation in civil, political and social life" (Dodd 2012, 37–38).

RED PLANET, RED FLAG: MARTIAN UTOPIAS

Where euchronias imagined utopian societies 100s of years into the advanced industrial future, another strand of fin-de-siècle utopian literature strove to envisage perfected worlds beyond the edges of the mapped cartographic universe. Giovanni Schiaparelli's announcement in 1878 that he had observed linear features he called *canali* (the Italian word for channels, which became misconstrued as "canals") on the surface of Mars spurred a sudden interest in the red planet and boosted popular appetite for planetary astronomy, as well as inspiring a number of writers to set their utopian narratives among sentient alien races. The earliest notable Martian utopia is Percy Greg's *Across the Zodiac: The Story of a Wrecked Record* (1880), which features an ideal scientific society. Any ideas contrary to the material sciences (such as religious faith) have been declared "utterly fatal to the progress of the race" and refusing to accept the infallibility of science is an offense punishable by incarceration in a lunatic asylum (Greg 2015, 36). Rev. Wladislaw Somerville Lach-Szyrma's *Aleriel, or A Voyage to Other Worlds* (1883) similarly gives imaginative heft to the Renaissance belief in the inhabitation of planets in the solar system and uses its Martian perspective to expound a Darwinian account of evolution on an interplanetary scale. The eponymous figure of Aleriel, a winged alien traveler from Venus, shocks the narrator with his withering dismissal of London, questioning late-Victorian colonial triumphalism from the estranging perspective of a sophisticated interplanetary learnedness: "He evidently sincerely pitied us, pitied London, pitied England" (Lach-Szyrma 2018, 23).

Alice Ilgenfritz Jones and Ella Merchant's novella *Unveiling a Parallel: A Romance* (1893) employ the Martian utopia to envisage an overhaul of nineteenth-century gender relations. The utopian guide's sister, Elodia, is a banker and notable civic leader with financial interests in the railways, steam liners, mining, and manufacturing. To the male narrator's horror, she exhibits a variety of masculine behaviors: getting drunk at her club on champagne and discussing politics, reading the papers, smoking a pipe, enjoying women's boxing, and having illegitimate children whom she financially supports but doesn't raise. "She amused herself with us [men]," he notes, "just as I have seen a busy father amuse himself with his family for an hour or so of an evening" (Jones and Merchant 1893, 38). In addition to revealing the hypocrisies of American patriarchal culture, the text treated its fin-de-siècle readers to the estranging vision of clean electric power. We find a similarly unearthly experience of pollution-free utopian society when Leonid travels to Mars in Alexander Bogdanov's *Krasnaya Zvezda* [*Red Star*] (1908). Martian utopias appealed to many Russian writers of the fin-de-siècle period and into the early 1900s and 1910s, and Bogdanov's influential novel sketches a Bolshevik utopia forged through a highly developed scientific culture that has perfected factory management. Bogdanov's Martian factory is "completely free from smoke, soot, odors and fine dust" and is powered not by "the crude force of fire and steam, but the fine yet even mightier power of electricity" (Bogdanov 1984, 63).

THE LIMITATIONS OF THE LITERARY UTOPIA

If the utopian science fiction enjoyed an impressive golden age during the fin-de-siècle and into the early years of the twentieth century, the traumatizing experience of World War I and subsequent rise of fascism leading to the Second World War dampened writers' optimism in the relationship between techno-logical and social progress. As Tom Moylan (1986) writes in his influential study *Demand the Impossible: Science Fiction and the Utopian Imagination*, the anti-capitalist movements that underpinned and informed utopian narratives—socialism, the trades union movement, anarchism, syndicalism—had largely been co-opted or crushed by the 1920s and, as a result, "utopian writing came upon hard times" (7–8). Dystopian visions predominated from the 1930s to the 1950s and utopian science fictions only re-emerged as a vital literary and political impulse with the radical social movements of the late 1960s and early 1970s. Moylan introduced the term "critical utopia" to describe the messy utopian societies that remediated this experience of political activism, focusing upon the agonistic pluralism necessary to the *process* of utopian trans-formation, rather than *systemic* visions of perfected worlds. Moylan's examples included the embedded utopias of Whileaway in Joanna Russ' *The Female Man* (1987), the ramshackle pastoralism of Marge Piercy's futuristic Mattapoisett in *Woman on the Edge of Time* (2000), the gritty urban city-state on Neptune's eponymous moon in Samuel Delany's *Triton* (1992), and Ursula Le Guin's barren lunar world in *The Dispossessed* (1974). Of these science fictions, Le Guin's novel is most self-consciously engaged with literary genre of utopia (it is subtitled *An Ambiguous Utopia*). The protagonist, Shevek, is a cele-brated theoretical physicist visiting the capitalist ("propertarian") world of Urras from its moon, Anarres. Several 100 years before the novel's action, Anarres was given to anarchist settlers who have lived in strict seclusion ever since. Shevek's visit to the wealthy nation of A-Io on Urras causes a schism in Anarres, revealing the colony's worker-led anti-intellectualism and insularity as calcifying into a bureaucratic state structure. "It is not all … all milk and honey, on Anarres," Shevek reveals (Le Guin 2002, 235). Moylan (1986) notes that Le Guin refuses to present her utopia as some Edenic post-scarcity vision of abundance and plenty: "It's as though Le Guin combined the Oklahoma dust bowl of the 1930s with the ecology of the high desert of the southwest and set up a utopia to scratch out its existence within this unpastoral environment" (96).

Le Guin's unlikely lunar utopia thus overcomes the stilted guided tours we encounter in traditional literary utopias and early science fiction *Voyages extraordinaires* to reveal a radically transformed egalitarian world that is only gradually revealed to the reader, in analeptic chapters that complement the action within the present. This novelistic structure refuses the linear quest narrative inherited by utopian fictions from early modern travelogs and exotic tales of pelagic adventure and, in so doing, elides the implicit colonialism that has plagued the genre. Naomi Mitchison's *Memoirs of a Spacewoman* (2011) similarly challenges the latent imperialism often found in science fictions that journey into extra-terrestrial or euchronic utopian worlds. As Jane Donawerth (1997) notes, "We have only to remember all the times that Captain Kirk in the 1960s *Star Trek* violently interfered to save the humanoids or the democrats, to realize that Mitchison is criticizing the plots of traditional science fiction as ideology that justifies imperialism" (32). Set centuries in the future, the novel's protagonist Mary is a scientist and interstellar traveler whose research is advanced, not in order to gain mastery over nature, but rather to live alongside it in harmony with alien species and the ecosystem.

A World of Women: Feminist Separatist Utopias

If feminism was a significant political influence on the formal experimentation of "critical utopias," elsewhere it produced a vigorous dialog about separatist utopian narratives. The rediscovery in the 1970s of Charlotte Perkins Gilman's forgotten utopian novels energized a period of utopian feminist production, while also bestowing an uncertain and difficult legacy for narratives of separatist communities. Originally serialized in Gilman's self-published magazine *The Forerunner*, *Herland* (1915) was almost entirely forgotten until Ann J. Lane edited and reissued a new edition of the story for the Women's Press in 1979, which led to spirited discussions of the novel among feminists throughout the 1980s. Gilman's unambiguously eugenicist story of Aryan utopians, in which the "lowest types" are bred out of existence through highly controlled reproduction, amounts to what Judith A. Allen (2009) calls "an ignoble legacy, contaminated by class bias, racism, ethnocentrism, and anti-Semitism" (xiv).

If the problematic utopianism of *Herland* is a product of first-wave American feminism, then Monique Wittig's *Les Guérillères* (1971) offers a more dynamic (but no less violent) separatist world that responds directly to second-wave French feminism and the women's liberation movement. Considered the first significant lesbian utopian novel, Wittig's text eschews Gilman's antiseptic asexuality and elevation of the status of motherhood (albeit, recast as a collective responsibility) in favor of an erotic free play of non-reproductive sexual relations. With her examination of non-biological motherhood and fluidly amorous lesbianism, Suzy McKee Charnas' *Motherlines* (1989) combines elements of these two science-fictional precursors. The utopian sequel to her dystopian novel *Walk to the End of the World* (1974), *Motherlines* features a postapocalyptic lesbian society of "Riding Women," whose relationship with their horses extends to bestial insemination in an elaborate mating ritual between genetically modified women whose reproductive systems can only be triggered by stallions' sperm. Like Moylan's critical utopias, Charnas' novel complicates the traditional literary utopia. Although they enjoy a hard-won freedom, the lesbian separatist communities of *Motherlines* (of which the peripatetic Riding Women are just one group) barely tolerate one another, live in fear and suspicion, and remain at war with the patriarchal male societies they have escaped from.

Several lesbian utopian science fictions of this period imagine essentialized postapocalyptic or extra-terrestrial worlds in which high-tech urban environments are coded as masculine while the ravaged rural landscapes are feminine: the rural Hillwomen in Sally Miller Gearhart's *The Wanderground: Stories of the Hill Women* (1978) leave the cities to live in nature, reproducing via a mystical process of "ovular merging," while the part-alien women in Katherine V. Forrest's *Daughters of a Coral Dawn* (1984) quit Earth altogether, escaping 1970s patriarchal repression to found a lesbian space colony called Maternas. Similarly, Joan Slonczewski's *A Door into Ocean* (1986) depicts a matriarchal utopian society living underwater on a moon planet, Shora.

APOCALYPTIC AND ANTI-CAPITALIST SCIENCE FICTION

In the period of neoliberal capitalism, we find utopian communities imagined not as the final inevitable historical stage of evolutionary development but, rather, hidden in near- and distant-future worlds that are often dystopian or postapocalyptic. Environmental crisis and anthropogenic climate change are central to these utopian science fictions and often deliver the post-capitalist future, literalizing Fredric Jameson's (2003) famous quip that "it's easier to imagine the end of the world than the end of capitalism" (76). Ursula K. Le Guin's *Always Coming Home* (1985) is an early example of a novel that employs a postapocalyptic narrative framework to explore the utopian possibilities of life after capitalism. Le Guin's resistance to any straightforward presentation of rural California in the distant future formally enacts her desire to move utopian thinking away from the European, masculinist principles of colonial appropriation and its legitimating framework of Enlightenment rationalism (Le Guin 1989). This reorientation of the utopian impulse away from euchronian industrial development is shared by Starhawk, a prominent ecofeminist, neopagan activist, and occult practitioner whose novel *The Fifth Sacred Thing* (1993) examines a utopian response to catastrophic climate change. Set in what used to be called San Francisco, after the collapse of the United States, the novel depicts an ecotopian society of small-scale, self-sufficient permaculture, solar-powered gondolas, and community governance.

Another significant work that anticipated the ecological turn, which has characterized twenty-first-century utopian science fiction, is Kim Stanley Robinson's "Mars" trilogy (1992–1996). The epic scale of Robinson's trilogy enables him to explore the messiness of the revolutionary process in an intergalactic context and, taken together, the three novels provide an extended meditation on the enactment of utopia. Approaching the red planet for the first time, the colonists gaze upon their new world "in all its immense potential: *tabula rasa*, blank slate. A blank red slate. Anything was possible, anything could happen—in that sense they were … perfectly free. Free of the past, free of the future, weightless in their own warm air" (Robinson 1993, 108).

By explicitly framing science fiction's quest to chart the expanding frontiers of the extra-terrestrial New World as an act of imperialism, *Red Mars* responds to this central problem of the utopian literary tradition. Ever since King Utopus colonized Abraxa and its people in More's *Utopia*, the genre has endured a problematic relationship with colonial appropriation. Weaving between multiple points of view chapters, competing ideas of Martian colonization start to crystallize over the course of *Red Mars*. The "reds" want to respect and preserve the alterity of the austere Martian ecosystem, while the "greens" advocate a high-tech program of terraforming to construct a fecund, productive world. These opposing camps embody alternative ideas of utopia: the traditional, *systemic* model of large-scale architectural blueprints and bioengineering versus the critical, *processual* approach of ongoing deliberation.

With its multinational mining companies and high-rise urbanization, Robinson's Mars trilogy unambiguously critiques the sociopolitical context of its time: 1990s globalization and neoliberal finance capitalism. Robinson's critique is shared by a number of contemporaneous works of utopian science fiction in the late 1990s and early 2000s, including Iain M. Banks' space opera "Culture" series (1987–2012), which began with the publication of *Consider Phlebas* in 1987, Ken MacLeod's *Star Fraction* and subsequent "Fall Revolution" series (1995–1999), Brian Aldiss' *White Mars; or, The Mind Set Free* (2000) (written in collaboration with the physicist Roger Penrose) and China Miéville's *Iron Council* (2005), the third novel in his Bas-Lag trilogy. Taking this critique to its logical conclusion and completing the revolution of work depicted in late-nineteenth-century socialist euchronias, Cory Doctorow's *Walkaway: A Novel* (2018) imagines a post-scarcity utopia made possible by 3D printing in which the workers walk away from capitalism into a gift economy of barter and exchange. Doctorow's utopian critique of neoliberal capitalism responds directly to the Global Financial Crisis of 2007–2008 and gives voice to an Occupy-era generation of under- and unemployed millennials; a revolutionary subject that is similarly referenced in Robinson's recent flood fiction, *New York: 2140* (2017), which imagines the political overthrow of bloated finance capital. What is most striking about Robinson's near-future vision of New York is not, in fact, the apocalyptic rise in sea levels but the utopian possibilities of this postcarbon landscape: roads have been appropriated for habitat corridors, skyscrapers boast rooftop farms and wine is even being produced in the Flatiron building's picturesque vineyard (Robinson 2017, 133, 380).

ECOLOGICAL UTOPIAS FOR THE ANTHROPOCENE

Responding to increasingly fractious political times, Phoebe Wagner and Brontë Christopher Wieland's edited collection *Sunvault: Stories of Solarpunk and Eco-Speculation* (2017) brings together short fiction, poetry, and artwork animated by recent movements such as Black Lives Matter, Occupy Wall Street, and the green movement. Scavenging among the ruined remains of depopulated cities and broken machinery, the narrator of Lavie Tidhar's (2017) short story "The Road to the Sea" observes that "humans only ever deluded themselves that they were the ruling species of this world" (137). This post-anthropocentric perspective enacts the unquestionably utopian gesture of redressing centuries of human arrogance that assumed the superiority of the rational Western (male) subject over the natural world, and enacted colonial dispossession by practising a logic that assimilated the non-Western with the animal, the uncultivated and the uncivilized. We find a similarly post-anthropocentric focus in Nalo Hopkinson's *Midnight Robber* (2000). The teenage protagonist Tan-Tan encounters the utopian, healing properties of the mysterious elephantine daddy tree, after she has crossed over from the high-tech world of Toussaint into the primitive alternate reality of the New Half-Way Tree. Described as being "wide as a village," the daddy tree helps Tan-Tan adapt to life among the sentient non-human culture of the douen and negotiate her own traumatic situation as a victim of incest and rape (Hopkinson 2000, 187, 219).

This blending of the utopian and the ecological is also a key feature of Tade Thompson's debut *Rosewater* (2016), the first novel in the "Wormwood" trilogy, which features a mysterious alien biodome that transforms a dusty Nigerian backwater region. The biodome's regenerative powers attract pilgrims, while its fungal communicative network grants a small number of people psychic abilities that the repressive Nigerian state co-opts. Thompson's novel is a slick science fiction adventure narrative, but it also contains a small utopian community known as Lijad, which is explicitly described as a kind of journey rather than a static location. The novel's protagonist Kaaro is told: "don't see this place like a village. Think of it as a vehicle" (Thompson 2016, 295–296). The microtopian community of the Lijad literalizes the utopian impulse that H. G. Wells argued must be the central premise of utopian narratives in *The Modern Utopia* (1905). Confronting the authoritarian tendencies of so-called "static" utopias, Wells (2005) wrote, "the Modern Utopia must be not static but kinetic, must shape not as a permanent state but as a hopeful stage leading to a long ascent of stages" (11). A similar ecological focus informs Nnedi Okorafor's *Lagoon* (2014), which imagines an alien invasion as experienced by a series of point of view characters, including non-human protagonists such as a tarantula, a swordfish, and an omniscient spider-narrator (a retelling of the trickster storyteller Anansi in West African folklore). Okorafor's alien ambassador Ayodele combines Yoruba myths of shapeshifters with the ecological conscience of an environmental activist. As she announces to the Nigerian president, "We do not seek your oil or other resources. We are here to nurture your world" (Okorafor 2014, 113). Among her other accomplishments, Ayodele repurposes the bodies of dead soldiers are into a plantain tree, cleans the sea of pollutants and restores diverse marine life, and convinces the president to replace the Nigerian oil industry with green (alien) technology.

The rise of the far-right in recent years, which led to the presidency of Donald Trump (2016–2020) and has brought xenophobic ideas into mainstream political discourse in numerous democracies around the world, has informed an increasing number of dystopian visions in literature. A notable reaction against the contemporary fascination with dystopia is Ada Palmer's debut novel *Too Like the Lightning* (2017), the first in the Terra Ignota series. Palmer, a Renaissance historian at the University of Chicago, imagines an ecotopian future for Earth almost 500 years from now. Palmer's ecotopian vision responds to the Wellsian tradition of optimistic visions of technological and industrial development, while also reflecting upon questions of ecological balance. Palmer differentiates between novels that depict perfected utopian worlds and works that reflect upon the *process of utopian world-building*. Terra Ignota, she explains, "is using utopia and commenting on utopia without being a utopia" (Palmer 2015).

Conclusion

Despite the apparent vogue for dystopian narratives, utopian science fictions remain a crucial political resource in which to critique the present and offer estranging narrative realities in which, to borrow the slogans from Mai 1968, *another world becomes possible*. As N. K. Jemisin (2018) similarly reflects in her short story "The Ones Who Stay and Fight" from the collection *How Long 'til Black Future Month?*, while Utopia remains might be thought of as "a fairy tale, a thought exercise," it is also a necessary antidote to the "barbaric America" of the reader's present (6). The black utopian subjects of Um-Helat reject the logic that sexism, racism, and homophobia are natural and inevitable social ills: a daring narrative gesture in contemporary American politics that reveals the ongoing importance of the utopian impulse in science fiction.

References

Aldiss, Brian. 2000. *White Mars; or, The Mind Set Free: A 21st-Century Utopia*. London: Sphere.

Allen, Judith A. 2009. *The Feminism of Charlotte Perkins Gilman: Sexualities, Histories, Progressivism*. Chicago: University of Chicago Press.

Banks, Iain M. 1988. *Consider Phlebas*. London: Orbit.

Bellamy, Edward. 2007. *Looking Backward, 2000–1887*, ed. Matthew Beaumont. Oxford: Oxford University Press.

Bogdanov, Alexander. 1984. *Red Star: The First Bolshevik Utopia*, ed. Loren R. Graham and Richard Stites, trans. Charles Rougle. Bloomington: Indiana University Press.

Bulwer-Lytton, Edward. 2007. *The Coming Race*. London: Hesperus Classics.

Charnas, Suzy McKee. 1989. *Walk to the End of the World and Motherlines*. San Francisco: The Women's Press.

Corbett, Elizabeth Burgoyne. 1889. *New Amazonia: A Foretaste of the Future*. London: Tower Publishing Company.

Delany, Samuel. 1992. *Triton*. London: Grafton.

Doctorow, Cory. 2018. *Walkaway: A Novel*. London: Head of Zeus.

Dodd, Anna Bowman. 2012. *The Republic of the Future; Or, Socialism a Reality*. London: Forgotten Books.

Donawerth, Jane. 1997. *Frankenstein's Daughters: Women Writing Science Fiction*. New York: Syracuse University Press.

Fitting, Peter, ed. 2004. *Subterranean Worlds: A Critical Anthology*. Middletown: Wesleyan University Press.

Gilman, Charlotte Perkins. 1979. *Herland*, ed. Ann J. Lane. New York: Pantheon Books.

Grandville, J.J. 2011. *Un Autre Monde, Un Autre Temps*. Milan: Cinisello Balsamo.

Greg, Percy. 2015. *Across the Zodiac: The Story of a Wrecked Record*. San Francisco: CreateSpace.

Griffith, Mary. 2017. *Three Hundred Years Hence*. Seattle: CreateSpace.

Hopkinson, Nalo. 2000. *Midnight Robber*. New York: Grand Central Publishing.

Hyne, C.J. Cutliffe. 1889. *Beneath Your Very Boots: Being a Few Striking Episodes from the Life of Anthony Merlwood Haltoun, Esq*. London: Digby and Long.

Jameson, Fredric. 2003. Future City. *New Left Review* 21: 65–79.

Jemisin, N.K. 2018. The Ones Who Stay and Fight. In *How Long 'til Black Future Month?* 1–13. London: Orbit.

Jones, Alice Ilgenfritz, and Ella Merchant. 1893. *Unveiling a Parallel: A Romance*. Boston: Arena Publishing.

Lach-Szyrma, Wladislaw Somerville. 2018. *Aleriel, Or a Voyage to Other Worlds*. London: Forgotten Books.

Lane, Mary E. Bradley. 1999. *Mizora: A World of Women*. Lincoln: University of Nebraska Press.

Le Guin, Ursula K. 1989. A Non-Euclidean View of California as a Cold Place to Be (1982). In *Dancing at the Edge of the World: Thoughts on Words, Women, Places*, 80–100. New York: Grove Press.

———. 2002. *The Dispossessed: An Ambiguous Utopia*. London: Gollancz.

MacLeod, Ken. 2001. *The Star Fraction*. London: Tor.

Manuel, Frank E., and Fritzie P. Manuel. 1979. *Utopian Thought in the Western World*. Cambridge: The Belknap Press of Harvard University Press.

Mercier, Louis-Sébastien. 1974. *Memoirs of the Year Two Thousand Five Hundred*, trans. William Hooper. New York: Garland Press.

Miéville, China. 2005. *Iron Council*. London: Macmillan.

Mitchison, Naomi. 2011. *Memoirs of a Spacewoman*, Revised ed. London: Kennedy & Boyd.

Morrison, Toni. 1992. *Playing in the Dark: Whiteness and the Literary Imagination*. Cambridge: Harvard University Press.

Moylan, Tom. 1986. *Demand the Impossible: Science Fiction and the Utopian Imagination*. New York: Methuen.

Okorafor, Nnedi. 2014. *Lagoon*. London: Hodder & Stoughton.

Palmer, Ada. 2015. Thoughts on the Cover for *Too Like the Lightning. Ex Urbe* (blog), September 24. http://www.exurbe.com/?p=3402. Accessed 26 Apr 2018.

———. 2017. *Too Like the Lightning*. London: Head of Zeus.

Piercy, Marge. 2000. *Woman on the Edge of Time*. London: The Women's Press.

Rieder, John. 2008. *Colonialism and the Emergence of Science Fiction*. Middletown: Wesleyan University Press.

Robinson, Kim Stanley. 1993. *Red Mars*. London: HarperCollins.

———. 2017. *New York: 2014*. London: Orbit.

Roemer, Kenneth. 1976. *The Obsolete Necessity: America in Utopian Writings, 1888–1900*. Kent: The Kent State University Press.

Russ, Joanna. 1987. *The Female Man*. Boston: Beacon.

Souvestre, Émile. 2004. *The World as It Shall Be*, ed. I.F. Clarke, trans. Margaret Clarke. Middletown: Wesleyan University Press.

Starhawk. 1993. *The Fifth Sacred Thing*. New York: Bantam Books.

Suvin, Darko. 1979. *Metamorphoses of Science Fiction: On the Poetics and History of a Literary Genre*. New Haven: Yale University Press.

Thompson, Tade. 2016. *Rosewater*. London: Orbit.

Tidhar, Lavie. 2017. The Road to the Sea. In *Sunvault: Stories of Solarpunk and Eco-Speculation*, ed. Phoebe Wagner and Brontë Christopher Wieland, 137–142. Nashville: Upper Rubber Boot Books.

Wagner, Phoebe, and Brontë Christopher. Wieland, eds. 2017. *Sunvault: Stories of Solarpunk and Eco-Speculation*. Nashville: Upper Rubber Boot Books.

Wells, H.G. 2005. *The Modern Utopia*, ed. Gregory Claeys and Patrick Parrinder. London: Penguin.

Wittig, Monique. 1971. *Les Guérillères*, trans. David Le Vey. London: Peter Owen.

Young Adult (YA) Fiction

Carrie Hintz

INTRODUCTION

Contemporary dystopian writing for young adults has added significantly to the utopian literary tradition. These works might be read as a "gateway" to the mainstream utopian tradition for young readers, introducing them at an early age to modes of speculative thought and to political thinking. The young child who reads Lois Lowry's *The Giver* (1993)—with its controlled society devoid of color, memory, or genuine emotion—will be able to recognize similar themes later in his or her reading life when encountering the blissed-out, docile citizens of Aldous Huxley's *Brave New World* (1932). Yet utopian and dystopian books for children and young adults function as more than introductions to the mainstream utopian and dystopian canon; they are shaped by our cultural understanding of what young people need for their development.

Childhood is itself often constructed as a utopia, with much of the writing for younger children lying within the pastoral tradition. Adolescence, in contrast, is considered a time of turmoil and self-discovery: ideal for exploring the kinds of social and political issues literary dystopias raise, such as questions of political discord, social chaos, or authoritarian control. Many young adult dystopias, in fact, have a distinct kinship with the *Bildungsroman* (or

C. Hintz (✉)
Queen's College and The Graduate Center,
City University of New York, New York City, NY, USA

P. Marks et al. (eds.), *The Palgrave Handbook of Utopian and Dystopian Literatures*, https://doi.org/10.1007/978-3-030-88654-7_15

coming-of-age) tradition. The process of attaining maturity means an engagement with the corruptions of society, imagined as a breaking of innocence. Roberta Seelinger Trites (2000), in her foundational work on young adult literature, *Disturbing the Universe: Power and Repression in Adolescent Literature*, argued that the signature attribute of young adult literature is a young person's engagement with the ways in which forces of power shape subjectivity. Whereas "children's literature often affirms the child's sense of Self and her or his personal power ... in the adolescent novel, protagonists must learn about the social forces that have made them what they are" (Trites 2000, 3). This is abundantly true of dystopian novels that dramatize an adolescent's burgeoning understanding of the constraints that face them as young adults.

Whether young adult dystopias actually inspire social and political transformation is an ongoing critical debate. Some critics have read young adult dystopias as inviting young people to get involved in political and public life; others see them as popular works that might offer a vicarious experience of a nightmarish society but not much else in the way of critical reflection. The works themselves are aligned with popular genres such as romance and adventure, which can have a dampening effect on their radical potential,[1] but might also harbor unexpected political and affective possibilities. Young adult dystopias might be most notable—in an age of mediated communication and experience—for offering a vision of direct sensation and experience reminiscent of the Romantic movement's emphasis on feeling and connection. Another cultural phenomenon that seems to fuel these works is an emphasis on youth rebellion, which dovetails with our cultural expectations of adolescence as a rebellious time. A major cultural function of young adult dystopias, then, might be to portray political change and turmoil as difficult but also exhilarating.

From Childhood to Adolescence

Nikolajeva describes children's literature (distinguishing it from young adult literature) as "optative," or reflecting a vision of childhood "not as it is, but as adult authors remember it, as they wish it were or had been and might be in the future, and not least what they wish, consciously or subconsciously, that young readers should believe it is" (Nikolajeva 2014, 33). This is not to say that all children's literature is in this utopian mode. Children's literature, even for the very young, is capable of delivering the sober visions that compromise the ideal nature of much utopian writing. At the same time, many children's books are set in nurturing pastoral spaces, such as Frances Hodgson Burnett's *The Secret Garden* (1911), or within enchanted idyllic or safe spaces like Winnie-the-Pooh's Hundred-Acre Wood. When utopian children's literature moves from the natural environment to the world of human creation, there is often an emphasis on the power of the imagination to shape its own realities and to render the world more welcoming and habitable. One work in this vein is Paul Fleischman and Kevin Hawkes's *Weslandia* (1999), where

Wesley, a socially isolated young boy, invents his own country, including his own staple crop. In many ways, *Weslandia* embodies the utopian impulse—the dream of a better world—through its protagonist's imaginative control and consummate ease. Many secondary worlds are meant to embody a world that is better than our own, as we see, for example, in L. Frank Baum's Oz as a contrast to the harshness of Kansas, or J. R. R. Tolkien's serene and ethereal Rivendell. The association of children with utopianism carries a number of cultural assumptions (or cultural fantasies) unrelated to the actual experiences of children. One is that childhood is a state of bliss.

Young adult dystopias, in contrast, can be read as a forthright challenge to the utopian model of childhood as a protected and happy space. It is no coincidence that in Lois Lowry's *The Giver* (1993), one of the works that inaugurated the current "boom" in young adult dystopias, the protagonist Jonas first becomes aware of the lies and suppressive nature of his society at age 13. What appears to be a cozy, loving culture is revealed to be a cruel and heartless one, literally so since its citizens lack emotions of any kind. In engineering a world without color, emotion, or historical memory, the long-ago founders of Jonas's world sought to shelter people from all conflict and all upheaval, in a way reminiscent of the protections that are—at least theoretically—offered to children.

Young adult dystopias, then, dramatize a rejection of the powerlessness of childhood. This can be seen in the well-honed survival skills of the hero or heroine of dystopian fiction, forced to grow up quickly in dire circumstances. The young adult dystopia is not just about dire conditions; more often than not, it is also about no longer being able to imagine safe conditions. When Jonas begins to endure the memories of his society from the Giver of Memory—a difficult process for him—his first impulse is to reject the responsibility: "Jonas did not want to go back. He didn't want the memories, didn't want the honor, didn't want the wisdom, didn't want the pain" (Lowry 1993, 152). The young adult dystopia represents a lamentable end to childhood. At the same time, adolescents can also find the dystopia's challenge to the protections of childhood exciting. Kate Behr points to this aspect of children's literature more generally when she notes that a child reader of the *Harry Potter* series "is actively trying to lose his/her innocence" (2005, 114).

Generalizing about Young Adult dystopias can be challenging, since they vary in style, tone, and relationship to the dystopian genre. Some are near-future dystopias; others take place in a future very far away. Sheer survival in the face of poverty and scarcity is a concern of many young adult dystopias, extending a long tradition in children's literature. Anne Boyd Rioux points out, for example, that Jo March, the protagonist of Louisa May Alcott's *Little Women* (1868–1869), shares with *The Hunger Games*' Katniss Everdeen a need to provide for her family. Jo does so with her pen, Katniss with her bow: "Like Jo, [Katniss] is primarily concerned with providing for her family in her father's absence and especially looks out for a younger sister who needs her protection" (Rioux 2018, 206–207). We might also read the many young adult dystopias dealing with scarcity as a fantasy of self-sufficiency, a shift in role from being nurtured like a child to taking on a leadership role.

Many Young Adult dystopias represent an effort to fight authoritarianism. Cory Doctorow's *Little Brother* (2008) is a near-future dystopia; it imagines the aftermath of a terrorist attack on San Francisco's Bay Bridge. The adolescent protagonist Marcus, arbitrarily detained with some of his friends by the Department of Homeland Security, fights the surveillance state that has emerged in the wake of the attack and uses technology as a means of mobilizing his peers, keeping them informed of the government's activities, and strategically disrupting the DHS's surveillance efforts. *Little Brother* celebrates youth culture and adolescent activism—particularly through the character's innovative hacking of the electronic tools of the security state using machines adapted from gaming technology.

Sharp dystopian satire, much of it sardonic in tone, reaches out to the cultural construction of the adolescent who tends to view the established order with a jaundiced eye. M. T. Anderson's *Feed* (2002) imagines a far future where the Internet is literally wired into people's heads, offering a continuous stream of vapid entertainment and shopping opportunities, as the natural environment grows ever more degraded. The adolescent characters, with the exception of a single character who received the feed later in life, accept this world without question even as hideous lesions, a by-product of the feed, appear on their young bodies. The insipid slang of its characters adds to the book's absurdity, ultimately creating a sense of longing for a lost world of literacy and reflection; the main character, Titus, frequently employs the empty phrase "da da da" to share his observation and thoughts. Libba Bray's *Beauty Queens* (2011) is another young adult dystopia that uses humor to good effect, when a group of beauty pageant contestants crashes on a desert island and divides into two teams: "Sparkle Pony" and "Lost Girls," a kind of demented *Lord of the Flies.* In the words of Bridgitte Barclay, *Beauty Queens* uses the pageant system as a "dystopian subculture that exaggerates pressures of beauty and perfection to critique real-world dominating systems impacting women" (Barclay 2014, 142). As the Beauty Queens move away from performing for others, however, they gain an increased sense of their own identity: "Maybe girls *need* an island to find themselves. Maybe they *need* a place where no one's watching them so they can be who they really are" (Bray 2011, 177).

The fact that so many dystopian heroines are women distinguished by their courage and power—like Katniss Everdeen or *Divergent*'s Tris Prior—has provoked appraisals of the Young Adult dystopia as a feminist form. Sara K. Day, Miranda A. Green-Barteet, and Amy L. Montz study rebellious women in young adult dystopias:

> The dystopian mode provides girls—who continue to be constructed as passive and weak within much of Western culture—with the means to challenge the

status quo, even as many of these works remain invested in elements of romance that may be seen as limiting girls' agency. While these girls and their forms of rebellion may not always succeed and may even inadvertently reaffirm the very heteronormative ideals they subvert, these characters occupy the role of active agent rather than passive bystander. (2016, 4)

Katherine R. Broad is particularly interested in the role of romance in limiting girls' agency. She reads the ending of *The Hunger Games* series and its resolution of Katniss's story critically: "The series' conclusion in an epic heroine defaulting to a safe, stable, and highly insular heterosexual reproductive union—a union so much like the social and sexual status quo of our own world—raises questions about just what has been transformed by Katniss's harrowing fight" (Broad 2013, 125). At the same time, some critics see radical potential in the romance elements of young adult dystopias. Lisa Manter and Lauren Francis discover "sororal desire" in the book: "In concentrating her romantic energies on Prim and Rue, Katniss subverts heteronormative expectations and thus challenges the view that romance must be by nature conservative" (2017, 287). Perhaps the kinds of human bonds and alliances we see in these works are not so much constrained by the convention of popular romance, but actively facilitated by it.

The popularity of young adult dystopias has provoked a great deal of speculation about why young adult dystopias have emerged as the cultural force they are. There was in fact an earlier, and smaller, wave of young adult dystopian fiction in the 1980s connected to nuclear war, a preoccupation of that period (Ames 2013, 8; Hintz and Ostry 2003, 12). Accounts in the popular press focus on the pressures of a contemporary generation coping with the threat of global warming, the surveillance society, social media pressures, and school shootings. As I will discuss later in this essay, a number of these works engage directly or indirectly with climate emergency. Many critics have traced young adult dystopias to the concerns of 9/11. Melissa Ames notes that the "post 9/11 climate has contributed to the popularity of these YA dystopias as they present fictional fear-based scenarios that align with contemporary cultural concerns" (2013, 4). Ames sees young adult dystopias as capable of providing a "safe space to wrestle with, and perhaps displace, the fears they play upon— fears that are set and, not unimportantly, *resolved* amidst the comfortable narrative threads of young adult narratives, coming-of-age rituals, identity struggles, romantic love triangles, and so forth" (7). Ames points here to the sometimes-surprising mix of intimate coming-of-age themes and wider political questions that characterizes the young adult dystopia genre. However, many young adult dystopias might be read as refusing to provide "comfort," which is particularly true of some of the recent dystopias like *Orleans* or *The Marrow Thieves*, both of which offer quite a bracing and painful vision of coming-of-age.

Rebellion

Some young adult dystopias are able to provide commentary on present social conditions or to extrapolate to the future in the time-honored dystopian mode of offering a "warning." Yet the cultural work enacted by most young adult dystopias may lie most fully in the affective impact of their portrayal of youth rebellion and thorough social change. With their emphasis on sensual experience, youth leadership, and rebellion, young adult dystopias are in many ways a reinvention of some of the affective modes we associate with Romanticism, including the feeling of being unmoored from conventions and needing to create a more improvisatory way of living.

In assessing the impact of young adult dystopias on their readers, both young adults and adults, it might be useful to collect first-person accounts of their emotional impact. Neil Gaiman's reaction to *Little Brother* is a case in point:

> I think it'll change lives. Because some kids, maybe just a few, won't be the same after they've read it. Maybe they'll change politically, maybe technologically. Maybe it'll just be the first book they loved or that spoke to their inner geek. Maybe they'll want to argue about it and disagree with it. Maybe they'll want to open their computer and see what's in there. I don't know. It made me want to be 13 again right now and reading it for the first time, and then go out and make the world better or stranger or odder. (Gaiman 2007)

Gaiman's response to *Little Brother* encompasses both the conviction that Doctorow's work is transformative and a capacious sense of what that transformation could mean—from a recognition of one's "inner geek" to a more resistant reading that wants to "argue with" the book. There is no question in his mind, however, that the book will affect its readers. Some of this is based on the heady and timely-for-its-era treatment of national security issues, but it is probably more deeply bound up with the idea of a young person who confronts the pleasures and perils of a wider world for the first time.

We see a love of heightened experience throughout the young adult genre, even in a dystopian satire like M. T. Anderson's novel *Feed* (2002). *Feed*'s characters could not be more apathetic, as we see in the book's famous first line, spoken by the protagonist Titus: "We went to the moon to have fun, but the moon turned out to totally suck" (Anderson 2002, 3). Indifference and *ennui* are some of Anderson's targets in *Feed*, as is a consumer culture that has utterly extinguished any thought, as we see in protagonist Titus's meditation on corporate control:

> Of course, everyone is like, *da da da, evil corporations, oh they're so bad*, we all say that, and we all know they control everything. I mean, it's not great, because who knows what evil shit they're up to. Everyone feels bad about that. But they're the only way to get all this stuff, and it's no good getting pissy

about it, because they're still going to control everything whether you like it or not. (Anderson 2002, 48–49)

This indifference is hard to pierce; it could be argued that due to its root-edness in the nihilism of its protagonist, the book never manages to offer a positive alternative to rampant consumerism. Yet witness Titus's first encounter with his love interest, Violet, as he witnesses her drinking juice on the moon: "She just opened her mouth and pushed it out with her tongue. The juice came out of her lips as if it was being extracted real careful by a rock-star dentist who she loved. Her eyes were barely open, and it came out in lo-grav/no-grav as a beautiful purple wobble" (Anderson 2002, 18–19). This enrap-tured moment of vicarious pleasure points to an unspoken—and ultimately utopian—yearning for a life lived in connection with others. Even the ways in which *Feed*'s teenagers use recreational drugs or go "into mal" by manipu-lating their feeds to create a drug-like high, indicates their love for heightened states and their discontent with the banalities of their quotidian existence. This is all the more pronounced because of the amount of technological mediation in *Feed:* the characters no longer talk "in the air" but only chat through their feeds. Here again we see a cultural ideal of adolescence as fueled by passionate feeling; the young adult dystopias produced for this audience both respond to the need for heightened emotion and create it.

YOUNG ADULT DYSTOPIAS, RACE, AND QUEER SEXUALITY

If young adult dystopias are imagined as responding to the cultural and political growth of adolescents, we need to be attentive to the ways they represent—or do not represent—all adolescents. Mary Couzelis speaks to the silence of many dystopian works on questions of racial difference and the under-representation of people of color:

> By maintaining narrative silence about this contemporary issue, these novels perpetuate the hegemonic status quo of pretending race does not matter, which only privileges the dominant race. If these utopian/dystopian novels are to critique current society, then the ideologies about race and class privilege must be exposed. (2013, 132)

In this vein, Suzanne Roszak argues that young adult dystopias "echo current issues of race and ethnicity without naming them as such" (2016, 61). Roszak compares Veronica Roth's young adult book *Divergent* (2011) to Sandra Cisneros's *The House on Mango Street* (1984), with both examining "the construct of the divided city, depicting segregation as a component of social inequality, control, and injustice, while also analyzing the distinct ideolog-ical values in which physically demarcated and separated communities can be steeped" (Roszak 2016, 62). In Cisneros's realistic work, her protagonist

Esperanza deals with the "de facto segregation of her economically marginalized Chicana/o community from wealthier white neighbors and their inhabitants" (Roszak 2016, 63). *Divergent*'s postapocalyptic Chicago is divided into five "factions"—with "Erudite" representing intelligence, "Amity" representing social harmony and so on. Uneven resources and poverty are a problem for Roth's society just as they are on Cisneros' Mango Street, with the "Abnegation" faction living in poverty due to its devotion to serving others. Roszak acknowledges that Roth's vision of a divided city allows for critical thinking about nonhierarchical social arrangements:

> By creating these implicit parallels and encouraging young readers to culti-vate general values such as tolerance of difference and nonhierarchical thinking, dystopian young adult fiction can indirectly draw attention to and attempt to help eradicate the racial injustice that they do not acknowledge directly. (Roszak 2016, 61)

Yet the indirection with which Roth treats racialized injustice—the metaphorical qualities of its vision of inequity—also misses "potent opportunities for witnessing, allyship, and social resistance" (Roszak 2016, 62). *Divergent* offers a supple consideration of difference, yet race is elided because it is never acknowledged. To Roszak, Cisneros can offer more opportunities for "witnessing, allyship, and social resistance" because her portrayal of racialized poverty is infinitely more specific and politically located.

Roszak ultimately advocates for bringing *Divergent* and *House on Mango Street* into a critical conversation, largely to bring the omissions of *Divergent* into relief. At the same time, it would be a mistake to dismiss the speculative power of *Divergent* and other speculative fictions entirely, as Roszak in fact notes: they might still have a powerful role in introducing young people to political thinking in the abstract, a structure of thought that can then be turned to more concrete questions in the political sphere.

Despite the many elisions in the genre to date, some recent young adult dystopias tackle inequality, racism, youth disenfranchisement, queer sexuality, and the exploitation of women with refreshing directness. Tehlor Kay Mejia's *We Set the Dark on Fire* (2019) speaks in an all-too-timely fashion about the devastating effect of the harsh enforcement of borders. *We Set the Dark on Fire* is set in Medio, a divided country where the desperate poor live close to the wall of a bordertown. Latinx heroine Daniela Vargas, born into poverty and smuggled across the wall as a child by her parents, uses forged identity papers and becomes part of the elite. She attends the Medio School for Girls, which trains promising young womens to become one of two wives to men of the elite: the Primera, valued for the intellectual and managerial skills that will help her husband advance his career, and the Segunda, whose destiny is to bear a child and to act as an object of desire for her husband as well as indulging his emotional needs. Like the many post-*Handmaid's Tale* young adult dystopias (see, e.g., Philpot 2012), *We Set the Dark on Fire* is concerned with women's control over their own bodies and destinies. Daniela is chosen as a Primera, and her school nemesis Carmen as a Segunda. As events unfold, however, both women end up working on behalf of the rebel group La Voz: a movement that seeks to bring down the status quo in Medio. Carmen is revealed to be an immigrant from over the wall herself. The two women fall in love and begin a sexual relationship, in one of the only depictions in young adult dystopia of queer sexuality: a lesbian bond that is threatening to the strict patriarchal system of Medio. The book, therefore, offers an intersectional vision of power and resistance, tackling questions of race, class, sexuality, and solidarity between women.

Cherie Dimaline's *The Marrow Thieves* (2017) is set in a far future Canada ravaged by global warming and hurricanes, earthquakes, and tsunamis. The survivors, traumatized by these events, have lost all power to dream, except for North America's Indigenous people, who carry the capacity for dreaming within their bone marrow. Inuit, Métis, and First Nations peoples are hunted for this marrow and the healing serum it can produce by the government of Canada's Department of Oneirology. They are brought by "Recruiters" to marrow-harvesting factories modeled on the real-world atrocities of Residential Schools, boarding schools to which thousands of Indigenous children were forcibly located in the nineteenth and twentieth centuries. A group of Indigenous people work to elude the Recruiters and build community in the face of this relentless persecution. As Shannon Ozirny (2017) writes, "The brilliance here is that Dimaline takes one of the most well-known tropes in YA—the dystopia—and uses it to draw explicit parallels between the imagined horrors of a fictional future with the true historical horrors of colonialism and residential schools."

Two works set in postapocalyptic New Orleans can be seen as attempts to engage with environmental racism: Paolo Bacigalupi's *Ship Breaker* (2010) and Sherri L. Smith's *Orleans* (2013). In the world of *Ship Breaker*, the polar ice caps have melted, leaving New Orleans underwater, with a local economy revolving around the salvaging of copper and other valuable materials from washed-up oil tankers. Nailer, the fifteen-year-old protagonist of *Ship Breaker*, is a member of "light crew" who also copes with the brutish violence of his drug-addicted, alcoholic father. Saba Pirzadeh notes how Bacigalupi's novel exposes the ways in which "the institutionalization of environmental racism coerces poor people (both adults and children) into working in highly contaminated and toxic conditions, regardless of the danger to their health or safety" (2015, 211).

Sherri L. Smith's *Orleans* is set in 2056, when a series of hurricanes has racked the gulf area, unleashing a Delta Fever that affects people with different blood types differently, which sparks a grisly trade in human blood trafficking. A quarantine has sealed the borders of the American South: "all borders will be sealed" (Smith 2013, iv). In Smith's book, the Northern States (or "Outer States") literally abandon the South in a way that evokes the government neglect of poor people and people of color in our time. The first hurricane mentioned is Hurricane Katrina, which reminds readers of the ways in which people of color were disproportionately affected by Katrina. Fen de la Guerre is a woman of color raising a child in Orleans, and Daniel is a scientist who, with good intentions, travels from the Outer States to Orleans to try and find a cure for Delta Fever, discovering that the Institute for Post-Separation Studies that was supposed to find the cure never actually intended to do so, and was only going to study the blood tribes for the benefit of the Outer States. Micah-Jade Coleman appraises the importance of *Orleans* as follows:

> While racial injustice has long been famously addressed by YA fiction, and while contemporary YA dystopias display the disorder of capitalism run amok and profound classism, Smith's *Orleans* connects all these issues under the canopy of climate change and, with her ecofeminist perspective, adds gender and race as major factors for consideration. The result is a rich and thorough lesson on environmental injustice, which is inextricably linked to the problem of the North/South divide. (2016, 28)

Conclusion

Coleman's notion of "connection" rings true for *Orleans*, as well as for *Ship Breaker*, *We Set the Dark on Fire*, and *The Marrow Thieves*. Recent work that harnesses the power of dystopian speculation with a bold consideration of the class, race, and gender dimensions of climate crisis (and other political crises) may represent a new stage in our understanding of the needs of adolescent readers. This change signals not only a movement away from the construction of childhood innocence but also an increased commitment to engaging with the global challenges of our time. Whether they inspire or potentially dampen social and political transformation remains an ongoing debate.

Note

1. For some appraisals of the innate conservatism of the genre, see *Contemporary Dystopian Fiction for Young Adults: Brave New Teenagers*, ed. Balaka Basu, Katherine R. Broad, and Carrie Hintz, 117–159. New York: Routledge.

References

Ames, Melissa. 2013. Engaging "Apolitical" Adolescents: Analyzing the Popularity and Educational Potential of Dystopian Literature Post 9/11. *The High School Journal* 97: 3–20.

Anderson, M.T. 2002. *Feed*. Cambridge: Candlewick Press.

Barclay, Bridgitte. 2014. "Perpetually Waving to an Unseen Crowd": Satire and Process in *Beauty Queens*. In *Female Rebellion in Young Adult Dystopian Fiction*, ed. Sara Day, Miranda A. Green-Barteet, and Amy Montz, 141–156. New York and London: Routledge.

Behr, Kate. 2005. "Same-as-Difference": Narrative Transformation and Intersecting Cultures in *Harry Potter*. *Journal of Narrative Theory* 35 (1): 112–137.

Bray, Libba. 2011. *Beauty Queens*. New York: Scholastic.

Broad, Katherine R. 2013. "The Dandelion in the Spring": Utopia as Romance in Suzanne Collins's *The Hunger Games* Trilogy. In *Contemporary Dystopian Fiction for Young Adults: Brave New Teenagers*, ed. Balaka Basu, Katherine R. Broad, and Carrie Hintz, 117–130. New York: Routledge.

Coleman, Micha-Jade. 2016. Decolonizing the YA North: Environmental Injustice in Sherri L. Smith's *Orleans*. Master's Thesis, University of Southern Mississippi.

Couzelis, Mary J. 2013. The Future Is Pale: Race in Contemporary Young Adult Dystopian Novels. In *Contemporary Dystopian Fiction for Young Adults: Brave New Teenagers*, ed. Balaka Basu, Katherine R. Broad, and Carrie Hintz, 131–144. New York: Routledge.

Day, Sara, Miranda A. Green-Barteet, and Amy Montz, eds. 2016. *Female Rebellion in Young Adult Dystopian Fiction*. New York and London: Routledge.

Gaiman, Neil. 2007. Changing Planes, Saturday, December 22, 2007 (blog post). http://journal.neilgaiman.com/2007/12/changing-planes.html. Accessed 11 July 2019.

Hintz, Carrie, and Elaine Ostry, eds. 2003. *Utopian and Dystopian Writing for Children and Young Adults*. New York and London: Routledge.

Lowry, Lois. 1993. *The Giver*. New York and Boston: Houghton Mifflin Harcourt.

Manter, Lisa, and Lauren Francis. 2017. Katniss's Oppositional Romance: Survival Queer and Sororal Desire in Suzanne Collins's *The Hunger Games* Trilogy. *Children's Literature Association Quarterly* 42 (3): 285–307.

Nikolajeva, Maria. 2014. *Reading for Learning: Cognitive Approaches to Children's Literature*. Amsterdam: John Benjamins Publishing Company.

Ozirny, Sharon. 2017. Review: Heather Smith's *The Agony of Bun O'Keefe*, Cherie Dimaline's *The Marrow Thieves* and S.K. Ali's *Saints and Misfits*. *The Globe and Mail*, September 22.

Philpot, Chelsey. 2012. The New Handmaids. *Slate*. http://www.slate.com/articles/arts/books/2012/06/young_adult_novels_and_abortion_megan_mccafferty_s_thumped_anna_carey_s_eve_dan_wells_partials.html. Accessed 17 May 2021.

Pirzadeh, Saba. 2015. Children of Ravaged Worlds: Exploring Environmentalism in Paolo Bacigalupi's *Ship Breaker* and Cameron Stracher's *The Water Wars*. *ISLE: Interdisciplinary Studies in Literature and Environment* 22(2): 203–221.

Rioux, Anne Boyd. 2018. *Meg, Jo, Beth, Amy: The Story of Little Women and Why It Still Matters*. New York: W.W. Norton.

Roszak, Suzanne. 2016. Coming of Age in a Divided City: Cultural Hybridity and Ethnic Injustice in Sandra Cisneros and Veronica Roth. *Children's Literature* 44: 61–77.

Smith, Sherri L. 2013. *Orleans*. New York: Putnam Juvenile.

Trites, Roberta Seelinger. 2004. *Disturbing the Universe: Power and Repression in Adolescent Literature*. Iowa City: University of Iowa Press.

Apocalyptic Visions

Gib Prettyman

INTRODUCTION

Visions of systemic collapse and its aftermath permeate early twenty-first-century cultural forms from popular entertainment to theoretical discourse. Peter Paik (2017) calls postapocalyptic fiction "arguably the defining genre of the contemporary period." Yet this remarkable outpouring also belongs to a history of continuous apocalyptic thought stretching back millennia. The cultural persistence of apocalyptic thought, the inherent provocations of apocalyptic representations, the magnitude of the latest boom, and the sense that the postapocalyptic is historically different have prompted many to study the phenomenon. This essay focuses on intersections of utopianism and apocalyptic visions as seen through contemporary anglophone fiction. Sometimes this convergence is relatively explicit, describing utopian or proto-utopian communities blooming in the wake of a catastrophically altered Earth. More frequently, postapocalyptic narratives incorporate utopian, dystopian, or anti-utopian elements in ambiguous and fragmented ways. But even in the absence of overt utopian representations, postapocalyptic fictions as a speculative form often generate utopian longing in indirect ways, so that even texts as bleak as Cormac McCarthy's *The Road* invite reading for utopian significance (see, e.g., Jergenson 2016).

G. Prettyman (✉)
Penn State University, Fayette, PA, USA

203

P. Marks et al. (eds.), *The Palgrave Handbook of Utopian and Dystopian Literatures*, https://doi.org/10.1007/978-3-030-88654-7_16

NARRATIVE FUNCTIONS

At first blush, of course, apocalypse and utopia seem polar opposites. Rhetorically, apocalypse signifies catastrophic possibilities and utopia signifies triumphant ones. Materially, apocalyptic destruction would represent the failure of secular human history, while utopian achievements would represent the apotheosis of human cultural ambitions. Together they mark the ultimate fork in the road, a teleological crux whose imagined paths diffract retrospective significance on human history generally and the present moment particularly.

However, these rhetorical opposites also have much in common, beginning with significant formal similarities. The ancient Greek term for apocalypse signified "revelation," referring not only to prophesized destruction but also to promised "heaven on earth." Traditional apocalyptic narratives described obliterated human institutions replaced by final divine justice. Their form thus parallels traditional utopian narratives, which imagined a "utopian break" whereby existing society would be replaced by its utopian alternative. In fact, Fredric Jameson (2005, 231–233) gives us reason to view contemporary postapocalyptic stories as attempts to "think the [utopian] break itself" (Canavan 2012, 139).

In addition to imagining decisive breaks in human history, the decisive conclusions of traditional apocalyptic and utopian narratives produce what Frank Kermode (2000) calls the "sense of an ending." Reflecting on the intellectual persistence of apocalypticism, Kermode labels such stories "concord-fictions" (Kermode 2000, 58) and identifies their function to be "sense-making" (39), arguing that humans "need, and provide, fictions of concord" (59). Traditional utopian narratives project sense-making endings by envisioning radically better societies just as traditional apocalyptic narratives do by prophesizing divine justice and meaning. Kermode argues that the "pattern" (10) of apocalyptic ending is reassigned by each generation to approaching historical events, thereby ascribing narrative order onto lived uncertainty. The fact that apocalypse is repeatedly "disconfirmed without being discredited" indicates the power of the form: "when we refuse to be dejected by disconfirmed predictions we are only asserting a permanent need to live by the pattern rather than the fact, as indeed we must" (Kermode 2000, 8, 11). Utopian endings too were disconfirmed repeatedly by history without the pattern being discredited. However, living "by the pattern rather than the fact" eventually generated enough contradictions to fundamentally alter contemporary apocalyptic and utopian narratives and to provoke self-conscious assessments of each form's historical functions.

Utopia and apocalypse also share more specific narrative functions that enable them to work together. Especially if we follow Mark Bould's lead and "take 'utopia' primarily to refer to literature that speculates about social organization and transformation, including satires and dystopias that exaggerate rather than negate elements of their real-world context" (Bould 2015, 84), then it becomes easier to see why postapocalyptic speculations produce potentially utopian negations and exaggerations. Both genres traditionally function as narrative frameworks for scrutinizing existing society in fundamental ways, and indeed for imagining it away. Visions of apocalyptic destruction also have clear affinities with dystopian narratives and the terms are sometimes used interchangeably to describe contemporary works.

Of course, apocalypse and utopia also differ significantly, and their contemporary forms differ substantially from their traditional forms. Most importantly, utopian narratives typically privilege human agency whereas traditional apocalyptic prophecies assert divine rule. The disconfirmation of apocalyptic prophecies thus seems fundamentally different from disconfirmation of utopian projections, even if they reflect similar attachment to living "by the pattern," since the former requires continued religious faith while the latter requires reinterpreting history. But this distinction blurs because most contemporary postapocalyptic narratives lack a millennial framework and most contemporary utopian narratives lack confident endings. Contemporary forms of both apocalypse and utopia are therefore similarly marked by lost faith in the sense of an ending, with awareness of lost faith becoming an element of their altered forms.

Kermode, well aware of this historical development in the apocalyptic tradition, nevertheless sees persistent patterns of sense-making in which "[w]e achieve our secular concords of past and present and future, modifying the past and allowing for the future without falsifying our own moment of crisis" (Kermode 2000, 59). Interestingly, Kermode describes secular concord-fictions as "treating the past (and the future) as a special case of the present" (59), much like contemporary speculative fictions. As Connor Pitetti notes, "the narrative paradigms we use to stabilize and structure the experience of history are [now] most explicitly articulated in science fiction and related literary genres" (Pitetti 2017, 438). In addition to formal and functional similarities between traditional apocalypse and utopia, then, the conspicuous absence of confident millennial or utopian endings in their altered contemporary forms opens similar speculative space. Bould reminds us that utopian speculations "are to be understood as discourses about change—as fluid evocations of possibility rather than static plans for a perfected world. Combining pessimism of the intellect with optimism of the will, they aspire to a world better than the unhomely ruin we continue daily to make" (Bould 2015, 84). The increasing familiarity with "unhomely ruin" that sparks stories of secular apocalypse also brings aspirations for a better world into sharper focus. "Paradoxically," as Jameson notes, the "increasing inability to imagine a different future enhances rather than diminishes the appeal and also the function of Utopia" (Jameson 2005, 232).

CONTEMPORARY DEBATES

Contemporary criticism of literary intersections between utopia and apocalypse primarily assesses the generic effects and historical implications of postapocalyptic fictions. If traditional apocalyptic narratives make meaning by their sense of an ending, how do we use representations (to use James Berger's phrase) "after the end?" (1999, xi). When apocalyptic stories no longer promise heaven on earth, what draws us to them, and what utopian functions could they serve? If utopian narratives need to imagine apocalyptic collapse, what does that say about utopianism in our historical moment? Can apocalyptic stories provide energy to utopian aspirations, or do they indicate a fundamental inability to imagine effective alternatives?

Like postapocalyptic fictions themselves, these questions involve overt sense-making about our historical moment. In 1965, Kermode cited postmodern challenges to narrative as motivation for his reflections on apocalyptic sense-making. "[W]e had our paradigmatic fictions," he declared, but these "no longer serve," and "[t]he recognition, now commonplace, that the writing of history involves the use of regulative fictions, is part of the same process" (Kermode 2000, 42–43). Combined with historical traumas like the Holocaust and philosophical provocations like Existentialism, anti-narratives like the *nouveau roman* struck Kermode as threats to meaning-making in general. Ironically, he narrativized those fears by placing them within an ongoing cultural tradition of apocalyptic sense-making, reassuring his audience that there were natural limits to anti-narrative experimentation and that fears of postmodern meaninglessness were merely the latest in a continuous history of apocalyptic forecasts. Even in 1999, in a new epilogue written at "the approach of the millennium," Kermode insisted that there is "nothing new" about apocalyptic fears experienced in a world with nuclear weapons (Kermode 2000, 181). Every age, he argued, feels just as vividly the "terrors and apprehensions" of apocalyptic thoughts and "if anything is needed to give additional substance to our anxieties, the world, at whatever period, will surely provide it" (182).

Few contemporary observers share either Kermode's confidence that nothing is different now or his reductive treatment of "the world" as imaginative fodder for "our" subjective anxieties. In the Anthropocene, global climate change, pandemic diseases, ecological devastation, and mass extinction of species reveal the planet-wide material effects of human thoughts and actions. Interestingly, however, we do still discuss these issues in terms of concord-fictions such as apocalypse and utopia. What sense-making do postapocalyptic narratives perform or attempt? What do they suggest about their historical period? What do they reveal about narrative sense-making in general?

Debates begin with definitions of "postapocalyptic." Loosely, the term describes stories told during or after any widespread catastrophe or breakdown. Scholars often imply historical or generic categorization, as in "postapocalyptic imagination," without specifying definitions. More explicit definitions focus on how the postapocalyptic relates to traditional apocalypse or how it is historically and theoretically unique. Especially given Kermode's emphasis on endings, uncertain divisions between "apocalyptic" and "postapocalyptic" beg questions about historical sense-making and prompt some critics to propose careful distinctions between these two narrative modes. Pitetti, for example, argues that the decisive breaks of apocalyptic narratives provide reassuring historiographical structure, while postapocalyptic narratives "blur before/after distinctions" and "draw attention to the necessarily indeterminate nature" of history and the future (2017, 438). He therefore argues that "[a]s critical terms, postapocalypse and postapocalyptic are more productively understood as marking a conceptual distinction from apocalyptic narrative, rather than a temporal succession" (Pitetti 2017, 447). Teresa Heffernan further insists that the apocalyptic mode includes traditional religious revelation, leaving postapocalyptic texts to focus on "the implications and repercussions of living in a world that does not or cannot rely on revelation as an organizing principle" (Heffernan 2008, 7). Berger uses the same distinction to ignore "apocalyptic thinking or millennialism" and focus instead on representations of "aftermaths and remainders" and "how to imagine what happens after an event conceived of as final" (Berger 1999, xii). Such approaches, based on formal distinctions, tend to be more literary. When critics privilege the sense-making of traditional apocalypse, they also locate reliable meaning in the past—or, as in Kermode's analysis, within reassuringly continuous cultural traditions.

Definitions of the postapocalyptic on its own terms typically emphasize characteristic historical problems and consider how the genre relates to those problems. Here a crucial touchstone is the apparent inability to imagine alternatives to global capitalism. In these readings, pronouncements like Francis Fukuyama's "the end of history" and Margaret Thatcher's "no alternative" to capitalism describe a new state of foreclosed political outcomes. As a familiar expression holds, it is now "easier to imagine the end of the world than to imagine the end of capitalism" (see Canavan 2012, 138). Mark Fisher argues that this expression "captures precisely" the "widespread sense that not only is capitalism the only viable political and economic system, but also that it is now impossible even to imagine a coherent alternative to it" (2009, 2). Fisher demonstrates how capitalism "seamlessly occupies the horizons of the thinkable" (8), producing the sense of inescapability that he labels "capitalist realism" and others call "cynical reason" (see Jameson 2010, 30). Critics often use "postapocalyptic" to signify this historical endlessness and inescapability. Phillip Wegner contends that "the apocalypse represented in [postapocalyptic] narratives" is characteristically "a pseudo-event, and the world that is figured in the text simply a continuation or repetition of the reigning status quo" (Wegner 2014, 94). A slightly different argument holds that "catastrophe has become the precondition for the establishment of utopia, both as the compelling threat that demands a plausible response to impending annihilation and as the necessary event that apocalyptically clears the ground for new modes of living" (Beck and Dorrian 2014, 132). As Gerry Canavan explains, "apocalypse is the only thing in our time that seems to have the capacity to shake the foundations of the system and 'jumpstart' a history that now seems completely moribund—the only power left that could still create a renewed, free space in which another kind of life might be possible" (Canavan 2012, 139). As these critics emphasize, using apocalypse to imagine alternatives to capitalism is problematic at best.

Ecological catastrophe is an intricately related historical touchstone. Building on his observation that apocalypse may be used to imagine the end of capitalism, Canavan notes "the unexpected utopian potency lurking within our contemporary visions of eco-apocalypse," because "though apocalypse might appear at first glance to assert the impossibility of significant change in our social relations ... the radical disruption of history offered by eco-apocalypse is, in fact, a dialectical reassertion of both the possibility and the necessity of such change" (Canavan 2012, 139). Here again, as he and others detail, utopian fantasies involving eco-apocalypse are deeply problematic. In terms of agency, or "the politics of apocalypse," Kim Stanley Robinson notes that excessively pessimistic stories can make readers feel powerless, while excessive optimism implies no need to act (Canavan 2012, 155; Rohn 2007). Adeline Johns-Putra observes the "representational contradictions" raised by global climate change, which is "everywhere because it is a global problem that has become a mainstay of our collective cultural life, but nowhere because it is knowable and solvable only at a remove, through the mediation of science and the machinery of politics" (Johns-Putra 2014, 127). As Brent Bellamy and Imre Szeman detail, even "science faction" texts that imagine Earth after the complete extinction of humans, like Alan Weisman's *The World Without Us* (2007), produce political implications that contradict their authors' ecological intentions (Bellamy and Szeman 2014, 193).

Debates about modernism and postmodernism constitute another common context for defining the postapocalyptic. Heather Hicks argues that twenty-first-century novels "use the conventions of postapocalyptic genre fiction to interrogate the category of modernity," unlike the "postmodern formal experimentation" of earlier novels (Hicks 2016, 2). She sees this engagement as belonging to Jameson's "narrative category" of modernity as opposed to "the profound experimentation, fragmentation, indeterminacy, and mysticism" of postmodernism (Hicks 2016, 5). Hicks notes that Jameson's term is from his *A Singular Modernity* (2013, 40). At the same time, she notes, these contemporary novels interrogate the ambiguities of "modernism beyond salvage" (Hicks 2016, 1). By contrast, Berger suggests that different forms of postapocalypse are "characteristic" of modernity and postmodernity and that "representations of post-apocalypse" sometimes "blur these distinctions and categories" (Berger 1999, 8–9). Many critics follow Jameson's political assessment that "[t]he problem to be solved is that of breaking out of the windless present of the postmodern back into real historical time, and a history made by human beings" (quoted in Canavan 2014, 14).

Whether essentially modern or postmodern, most critics judge postapocalyptic stories to be politically problematic at best. Some dismiss postapocalyptic tropes as too easy, too overused, or too popular to produce genuine utopian insights. Ursula Heise (2015) argues that telling stories of "postapocalyptic wastelands" is "losing its political power" by becoming "familiar and comfortable." As Fisher notes, would-be rebellious cultural forms "don't designate something outside mainstream culture; rather, they are styles, in fact *the* dominant styles, within the mainstream" (Fisher 2009, 9). More specifically, apocalypse also enacts fantasies of escape from present-day political complexities in ways similar to the "world reduction" that Jameson observes in utopian texts (Jameson 2005, 271). Jameson notes that imagining away multinational corporations and fragmenting into small pastoral communities are examples of "historical regression and the attempt to return to a past that no longer exists" (2010, 37). Moreover, such nostalgia is symptomatic of an inability to "think of an impending future of size, quantity, overpopulation, and the like, except in dystopian terms" (37). Paik, too, finds fantasies at work in apocalyptic fictions but interprets them from an anti-utopian "realist" perspective, arguing that "a realist depiction of a transformed world … is one that does not omit the horrors that accompany its foundations" (Paik 2010, 22). By means of "fantastic realism," apocalyptic texts "confront us with the harsh truths evaded or repressed by liberal and progressive thought" (Paik 2010, 19). Where critics like Canavan emphasize the utopian longing represented by "active fantasy" that "the nightmare of exploitation, and our own complicity in these practices, might somehow be stopped, despite our inability to change" (2014, 14), Paik sees "the lure of a posthistorical salvation" as "repressed religion" used to deny "the workings of power" (2010, 22).

More narrowly, scholars contest the utopian implications of postapocalyptic fictions by examining their characteristic subjects. For example, Hicks notices repeated engagements with the story of Robinson Crusoe, arguing that they allow authors to reimagine the colonial roots of modernity. Postapocalyptic landscapes also replicate "first contact" stories that were apocalyptic for so many indigenous peoples. Hicks argues that "the texts present the new world after the apocalyptic event as a simulacrum of the 'New World' once 'discovered' by European explorers, and they inlay their narratives with a palimpsest of colonial and post-colonial signifiers" (2016, 18) such as the unpalatable metaphor of capitalism as cannibalism in *Cloud Atlas*: "[t]he weak are meat, the strong do eat" (Mitchell 2004, 503). Where Hicks sees these Robinsonade elements as fodder for insightful literary treatments, however, Heise (2015) sees escapism: "What really counts is that the characters, in their break from the corruptions of the past, no longer have to deal with things like crowded cities, cumbersome democracies, and complex technologies." Crusoe scenarios strike her as vehicles for familiar "survivalist scenarios," do-it-yourself "maker culture," and other "untiring attention to routines of everyday life."

In addition to invoking colonial encounters with "New Worlds," Canavan notes the "tight relationship between fantasies of apocalypse and fantasies of the frontier—the notion that after the end of civilization the entire world becomes again free and open land, to be once again molded and 'tamed' by heroic individuals" (2012, 141). Self-conscious retellings of such plots invite reflection on the relationships between modern "civilization" and systemic violence, including genocide. At the same time, the nested histories of *Cloud Atlas* emphasize a question that Paik finds to be suggested by many postapocalyptic narratives: "Would the act of salvaging modernity ultimately restart an historical process that leads inescapably to conquest and colonization?" (Paik 2017). Heise (2015) reads the MaddAddam trilogy (Atwood 2003, 2009, 2013) this way, arguing that "[f]or all of its indictments of the mayhem and death obsession of the old society, the new society of the MaddAddam trilogy relies on exclusion by violence, at both the micro- and macroscales," and "this basic plotline" makes it "doubtful" that the ending "promises any world better than the one whose demise the trilogy has staged."

By imagining the dissolution of society, postapocalyptic narratives similarly spotlight questions of "human nature," allowing authors like Atwood and Octavia Butler to investigate the virulence of sexual violence, dehumanization, and abusive power. In addition to highlighting injustices, Claire Curtis reminds us that postapocalyptic representations of human nature "take up the primary query of political philosophy: the deliberation over the conditions under which we would like to live" that lead to particular models of the social contract (2010, 8). John Beck and Mark Dorrian argue that "[w]ithin many of the darkest imaginings of a world on the threshold of annihilation, a yearning for renewal through containment and control can be discerned" (2014, 133). Human irrationalities are similarly spotlighted, raising questions of how we use non-rational forms of knowing the world and how that relates to sociopolitical contexts. As a character in Cory Doctorow's *Walkaway* implores, "the inability to see reason is a species-destroying crossroads and we're *at it now*" (2017, 197, original emphasis). Butler's *Parable* novels simultaneously explore religion as a threatening form of fundamentalism and as a source of potential social change and cohesion. Where many critics see disconcerting influences of "New Age" spirituality, Clarence Tweedy (2014) argues that the *Parable* novels (1994, 1998) "continue the tradition of Black theology's call for civic responsibility and social activism." Novels like *Station Eleven* (2014) and *Cloud Atlas* (2004) explore transhistorical human uses of art and esthetics, including storytelling itself.

All of these topics bring us back to ongoing debates about genres and their uses for historical sense-making. Berger views late-twentieth-century postapocalyptic visions as nightmares: "The study of the post-apocalyptic world is a study of symptoms and of representations that partly work through and partly act out the past that haunts them" (1999, xv). Hicks argues that recent postapocalyptic texts engage historical issues relatively realistically and directly, producing "remarkably rich, provocative narratives by affixing layers of imaginative detail, intertextual reference, and historically specific critique onto the framework provided by the post-apocalyptic form" (2016, 8). Like Pitetti, she associates this more direct engagement with "genre science fiction" (5), reminding us of related historical efforts to define the loss of faith in paradigmatic utopian fictions by invoking concepts like "critical utopia" and "critical dystopia" (see Moylan 2000, 2014). Wegner suggests that we might profitably consider the term "critical post-apocalypse" for texts that escape the dominant nostalgia of postapocalyptic narratives (2014, 94). Alternatively, Heise (2015) views postapocalyptic fictions as contemporary examples of the traditional genre of dystopia. While Hicks disagrees that the dystopian tradition fully explains postapocalyptic texts, she notes that Heise's distrust of "repetition and cliché" is itself related to the "still nascent discussion about the increasing centrality of genre fiction to twenty-first-century anglophone literature" (2016, 8, 19). Hicks speculates that the pleasures of generic repetition may themselves be "the utopian component that has unified [apocalyptic] material for so long" (21). For critics like Heise, such generic pleasures, if true, represent esthetic and political failure.

These debates show how complexly apocalypse and utopia intertwine with questions of genre and its historical functions, whether those functions are symptomatic, esthetic, philosophical, or material. Arguably these divergent critical judgments all share the same absent and potentially utopian referent: where, how, or if hope for a better future can be found.

NARRATIVE LABORS AND NARRATIVE MATTERING

One way to pursue these debates without simply repeating them is to explore more precisely the materiality of narrative labors represented in and by postapocalyptic fictions. As Heise explains, "by scaling up the human" to planetary levels, the Anthropocene "undermines concepts of human individuality and sociality that have to date informed the way in which the stories of human pasts and futures are told" (2019, 278). And in addition to telling stories differently, we need to interpret them differently. To put it simply, we must work toward ecological precision about the human uses of narrative sensemaking that Kermode observed and for which intersections of utopia and apocalypse produce such provocative examples.

Focusing on the situated materiality of narrative resonates with theoretical responses to the Anthropocene. McKenzie Wark, for example, proposes a strategic reorientation to "low theory" gleaned from the "labor point of view" as opposed to elusive and illusory "high theory" that would somehow encompass all perspectives and material conditions (2015, xvi–xxi, 218). As Wark notes, "critical theory can become hypocritical theory if it attempts to dominate other forms of knowing from other modes of collective experience" (14). Instead, Wark suggests that we focus on particular sites of interpretive labors, each of which has its own material challenges, methods, products, and by-products. Reorienting to low theory in this way "changes the object of theory from nature in the abstract to the practices in which it is encountered and known" (18). Wark's strategy of "low theory" draws in part on

Karen Barad's (2007) articulation of "agential realism," one of the primary theoretical inspirations of new materialisms. Barad, too, focuses on particular sites where perceptions of the world are produced, and she attempts to demonstrate with scrupulous precision the complex "intra-actions" involved. Describing scientific experiments that deploy an "apparatus" designed to measure a specific aspect of "matter," she details the entangled processes of "mattering" (132–185). "Realism," Barad explains, "is not about representations of an independent reality but about the real consequences, interventions, creative possibilities, and responsibilities of intra-acting within and as part of the world" (37). These theories address a major challenge of thinking ecologically: refining techniques for perception, description, and narration that allow us to grasp accurately the material complexities connecting embodied actions and global processes.

In the Anthropocene, then, narratives are key techniques for such "mattering." Instead of trying to assess the functions of texts or genres as a whole, however, we can focus on their more localized instances of mattering with particular narrative labors. By means of apocalyptic and utopian techniques (among others), postapocalyptic narratives engage specific aspects of global systems from particular labor points of view. From this orientation, for example, the postapocalyptic world reduction, which many critics mistrust as suspiciously easy, can be seen as a specific apparatus for initiating narrative perceptions. In Barad's terms, it performs an "agential cut" in the phenomena that constitute reality (140). The apocalyptic break fictively cuts into global totalities, opening spaces for narrative labors on particular topics—very much like traditional utopian literature pours over quotidian details of its imagined worlds.

Doctorow's 2017 novel *Walkaway* nicely illustrates material uses of apocalyptic and utopian techniques from labor points of view. The novel situates its explicitly utopian speculations within a slowly unfolding social collapse. The enduring business-as-usual society is referred to as "default," but "more people than ever … don't have any love for the way things are" (129). The North American heartland is a patchwork of "blighted zones and small default towns with stores and people living like civilization would endure forever" (183), while the ultra-privileged "zottarich" live in fortified compounds and continue to accumulate wealth and power with cancerous intensity (36). Dispossessed and disillusioned people become "walkaways," leaving behind their old lives and forming ad hoc communities in brownfields, abandoned factories, or roadside waystations. Because "[d]efault had produced an endless surplus of sacrifice zones, superfund sites, no-man's-lands and dead cities" (238) which are all potentially "fungible," walkaways rely on an ethos of non-scarcity, collective scavenging, and what Wark would call "hacker" deployments of technological skills (Wark 2015, 27). The story unfolds through episodic but intimate walkaway perspectives, with only an impressionistic historical arc.

Instead, the narrative spotlights specific efforts to produce hope and effective political principles in the midst of repeated creation and destruction of walkaway communities.

These stories of small transient communities explore utopia in Bould's (2015) sense of "fluid evocations of possibility" rather than outlining systems or institutions. In fact, the novel actively undermines totalizing theorizations and stories. As one character says, "I'm suspicious of any plan to fix unfairness that starts with 'step one, dismantle the entire system and replace it with a better one,' especially if you can't do anything else until step one is done. Of all the ways that people kid themselves into doing nothing, that one is the most self-serving" (Doctorow 2017, 38). In this light, the novel's lack of decisive apocalyptic plot seems a conscious effort to challenge what it labels "self-serving bullshit" (182)—stories used to satisfy self-perceptions and self-interests. Walkaways relentlessly test each other for self-serving bullshit in public arguments, eventually learning to call bullshit on their own thoughts.

Characters also drill down into systemic injustices by challenging specific narratives about human nature. Contemplating the novel's representative zottarich plutocrat, walkaways note that

[h]is beliefs don't start with the idea that it's okay to kid yourself you're a special snowflake who deserves more cookies than all the other kids. It starts with the idea that it's *human nature* to kid yourself and take the last cookie, so if he doesn't, someone else will, so he had better be the most lavishly self-deluded of all, the most prolific taker of cookies. (39, original emphasis)

The analysis reveals a particular instance of the recursive relationship between individual stories and collective stories. More materially, it uses this insight as a technique to bore into an intractable impediment using competing stories, easily available for collective political use. The plutocrat in turn scolds his walkaway daughter by asserting the narrative of capitalist realism: "what good do you think it does to turn your back on reality? You can't wish inequality away" (199). The novel's intentionally apocalyptic and utopian narrative labors include contesting such stories in their lived particularity and producing competing stories that others can use. These labors resist being extrapolated to postmodern relativisms (everyone tells themselves stories, everything is just a fiction) or to paralyzingly encompassing definitions of reality. In Wark's terms, they pursue "an alternative realism" that "sticks close to the collaborative labors of knowing and doing" (2015, xxi).

Confirming the pattern of salvage that Hicks identifies in other postapocalyptic novels, the walkaways salvage abandoned landscapes, resources, and means of production: "so here we are on the world's edge, finding our own uses for things" (Doctorow 2017, 129). These "things" have become worthless in terms of capitalist markets but remain sources of collective abundance in material terms. Here are more examples of narrative "mattering," familiar and yet vexing: the essentially fictional contexts of markets and laws produce paradoxical material outcomes of worthlessness and private property. These fictions also demonstrate "gamification," ignoring reality to focus on game-playing with the rules, with the result that "every incentive distorted into titanic frauds that literally left structures in ruins, rotten to the mortar" (Doctorow 2017, 84). Here, too, walkaways work to produce narratives that define "normal" in competing ways. "These days," they observe, "it's not about armed conflict, it's war of norms, which of us is normal and who are the crazy radicals" (330). Global capitalist systems are not illusory despite being fictional, nor are utopian alternatives powerless because they are fictional; on the contrary, "[t]he root of *credit* was *credo*: belief" (365). Narratives are material tools used in particular labors at specific sites and the "mattering" they perform necessarily produces some realities and excludes or discards others. As another character says, "there are as many walkaway philosophies as there are walkaways, but mine is, 'the stories you tell come true'" (66).

In particular, the novel experiments with how narrative labors generate hope. "If your ship goes down in the middle of the open water," a walkaway explains, "you don't give up and sink." Although "[r]ealistically speaking … you're a goner," still "you tread water until you can't kick another stroke." Such acts are not "optimistic," but rather "hopeful" or "at least not hope-empty." By means of instrumental stories like this, the characters choose to "exercise" or "perform" hope, which is "all you can do when the situation calls for pessimism. Most people who hope have their hopes dashed. That's realism, but everyone whose hopes weren't dashed started off by having hope. Hope's the price of admission" (Doctorow 2017, 215–216). Such hope is explicitly not generated from the sense of an ending: "Victory isn't a thing that walkaways will ever have." Like exercising hope, "[w]alking away isn't victory, it's just not losing" (329). Similarly, this attenuated hope as "the price of admission" is only one possible kind produced by postapocalyptic techniques, and any of them might turn out to be "[p]erfect self-serving bullshit, rationalizing the least-frightening action as the most prudent" (271).

The "unspeakable secret" that Wark notes about climate change no doubt pertains to all global crises that fuel contemporary postapocalyptic visions: "nobody really wants to think about it for too long" because it "seems like helplessly watching some awful train derailment career in slow motion" (2015, xvi). By "thinking about it," Wark means doing the painstaking work of rational thought. By comparison, audiences willingly use other cognitive processes to engage with postapocalyptic fictions, even though they imaginatively embrace disaster and jump ahead to "what-if?" stories. Clearly such stories can produce a range of material effects including escapist fantasies, self-serving bullshit, or capitalist realism. But as *Walkaway* demonstrates, postapocalyptic techniques can also produce "alternate realisms" and emphasize the material uses of narrative from labor points of view. To view the Anthropocene through this lens, Wark argues, is to "take this world-historical moment to be one in which to reimagine what the collective efforts of everyone who labors could make of the world, and as a world" (2015, 83). It suggests collective production of histories from labor points of view and the intra-active mattering of narrative perceptual apparatuses. At the same time, this viewpoint is a reminder to pursue strict ecological precision about the intra-active processes of narrative mattering, strict psychological precision about narrative cognition, and strict material precision about how human uses of "living by patterns" accord or do not accord with the natural world and with "living by the fact."

CONCLUSION

The profusion of near-future postapocalyptic narratives and critical debates about the contemporary status of utopia and apocalypse seem to confirm Kermode's insight that "concord-fictions" treat the past and the future as special cases of the present. However, while these fictions indeed continue to salvage recognizable patterns of narrative pleasures and existential compensations, we cannot afford to perpetuate Kermode's laconically literary view of apocalyptic threats, or of history, or even of storytelling itself. Utopian-inflected novels like *Walkaway* or Robinson's *The Ministry for the Future* (2020) represent urgent efforts at specific, accurate, and efficacious narrative mattering in the face of evident apocalyptic horizons, and these efforts must not be overlooked in our search for encompassing generic and historical judgments. As Canavan (2020) decisively concludes in his review of Robinson's novel, "the terms are clear: if you're reading this, you are the Ministry for the Future. Get back to work."

REFERENCES

Atwood, Margaret. 2003. *Oryx and Crake*. New York: Doubleday.
———. 2009. *The Year of the Flood*. New York: Doubleday.
———. 2013. *MaddAddam*. New York: Doubleday.
Barad, Karen. 2007. *Meeting the Universe Halfway: Quantum Physics and the Entanglement of Matter and Meaning*. Durham: Duke University Press.
Beck, John, and Mark Dorrian. 2014. Postcatastrophic Utopias. *Cultural Politics* 10 (2): 132–150. https://doi.org/10.1215/17432197-2651738.
Bellamy, Brent, and Imre Szeman. 2014. Life After People: Science Faction and Ecological Futures. In *Green Planets*, ed. Gerry Canavan and Kim Stanley Robinson, 192–205. Middletown: Wesleyan University Press.
Berger, James. 1999. *After the End: Representations of Post-Apocalypse*. Minneapolis: University of Minnesota Press.
Bould, Mark. 2015. The Futures Market. In *The Cambridge Companion to American Science Fiction*, ed. Gerry Canavan and Eric Carl Link, 83–96. Cambridge: Cambridge University Press.
Butler, Octavia. 1994. *Parable of the Sower*. New York: Grand Central Publishing.
———. 1998. *Parable of the Talents*. New York: Grand Central Publishing.

Canavan, Gerry. 2012. Hope, but Not for Us: Ecological Science Fiction and the End of the World in Margaret Atwood's *Oryx and Crake* and *The Year of the Flood*. *Literature Interpretation Theory* 23: 138–159.

———. 2014. Introduction: If This Goes On. In *Green Planets*, ed. Gerry Canavan and Kim Stanley Robinson, 1–21. Middletown: Wesleyan University Press.

———. 2020. Of Course They Would: On Kim Stanley Robinson's *The Ministry for the Future*. *Los Angeles Review of Books*. https://lareviewofbooks.org/article/of-cou rse-they-would-on-kim-stanley-robinsons-the-ministry-for-the-future/. Accessed 24 Mar 2021.

Curtis, Claire P. 2010. *Postapocalyptic Fiction and the Social Contract: We'll Not Go Home Again*. Lanham: Lexington Books. ProQuest Ebook Central. Accessed 9 Apr 2021.

Doctorow, Cory. 2017. *Walkaway*. New York: Tom Doherty Associates.

Fisher, Mark. 2009. *Capitalist Realism: Is There No Alternative?* Winchester: Zero Books.

Heffernan, Teresa. 2008. *Post-Apocalyptic Culture: Modernism, Postmodernism, and the Twentieth-Century Novel*. Toronto: University of Toronto Press.

Heise, Ursula K. 2015. What's the Matter with Dystopia? *Public Books*. https://www. publicbooks.org/whats-the-matter-with-dystopia/. Accessed 24 Mar 2021.

———. 2019. Science Fiction and the Time Scales of the Anthropocene. *ELH* 86 (2): 275–304. https://muse.jhu.edu/. Accessed 14 Mar 2021.

Hicks, Heather J. 2016. *The Post-Apocalyptic Novel in the Twenty-First Century: Modernity Beyond Salvage*. New York: Palgrave Macmillan.

Jameson, Fredric. 2005. *Archaeologies of the Future: The Desire Called Utopia and Other Science Fictions*. London: Verso.

———. 2010. Utopia as Method, or the Uses of the Future. In *Utopia/Dystopia: Conditions of Historical Possibility*, ed. Michael D. Gordin, Helen Tilley, and Gyan Prakash, 28–53. Princeton: Princeton University Press. ProQuest Ebook Central. Accessed 18 Mar 2021.

———. 2013. *A Singular Modernity: Essay on the Ontology of the Present*. London: Verso.

Jergenson, Casey. 2016. "In What Direction Did Lost Men Veer?": Late Capitalism and Utopia in *The Road*. *The Cormac McCarthy Journal* 14 (1): 117–132. https:// muse.jhu.edu/. Accessed 12 Mar 2021.

Johns-Putra, Adeline. 2014. Care, Gender, and the Climate-Changed Future: Maggie Gee's *The Ice People*. In *Green Planets*, ed. Gerry Canavan and Kim Stanley Robinson, 127–142. Middletown: Wesleyan University Press.

Kermode, Frank. 2000. *The Sense of an Ending: Studies in the Theory of Fiction with a New Epilogue*. Oxford: Oxford University Press. Kindle Edition.

McCarthy, Cormac. 2006. *The Road*. New York: Vintage.

Mitchell, David. 2004. *Cloud Atlas*. New York: Random House.

Moylan, Tom. 2000. *Scraps of the Untainted Sky: Science Fiction, Utopia, Dystopia*. Boulder: Westview.

———. 2014. *Demand the Impossible: Science Fiction and the Utopian Imagination*, ed. Raffaella Baccolini. Oxford: Peter Lang.

Paik, Peter Y. 2010. *From Utopia to Apocalypse: Science Fiction and the Politics of Catastrophe*. Minneapolis: University of Minnesota Press.

————. 2017. Recycling Apocalypse: A Review of Heather J. Hicks, *The Post-Apocalyptic Novel in the Twenty-First Century: Modernity Beyond Salvage*. *Postmodern Culture* 27 (3). https://muse.jhu.edu/. Accessed 3 Feb 2021.

Pitetti, Connor. 2017. Uses of the End of the World: Apocalypse and Postapocalypse as Narrative Modes. *Science Fiction Studies* 44 (3): 437–454.

Robinson, Kim Stanley. 2020. *The Ministry of the Future*. New York: Orbit.

Rohn, Jennifer. 2007. Interview with Novelist Kim Stanley Robinson. http://www.lablit.com/article/208. Accessed 12 Mar 2021.

St. John Mandel, Emily. 2014. *Station Eleven*. New York: Alfred A. Knopf.

Tweedy, Clarence W., III. 2014. The Anointed: Countering Dystopia with Faith in Octavia Butler's *Parable of the Sower* and *Parable of Talents*. *Americana: The Journal of American Popular Culture, 1900 to Present* 13 (1). ProQuest.com. Accessed 15 Feb 2021.

Wark, McKenzie. 2015. *Molecular Red: Theory for the Anthropocene*. London: Verso.

Wegner, Phillip E. 2014. *Shockwaves of Possibility: Essays on Science Fiction, Globalization, and Utopia*. Oxford: Peter Lang.

Weisman, Alan. 2007. *The World Without Us*. New York: Picador.

Utopian Realism

Sam McAuliffe

I

Over the course of its history as a distinct discursive form with its own code of conventions, the distribution of categories that provide the utopian text with its frame has undergone a "transformation," and this has modified in turn the relation that this particular mode of discourse holds to its referent. The claim is made by Bloch at the outset of his discussion with Adorno on "the contradictions of utopian longing":

> At the very beginning Thomas More designated utopia as a place, an island in the distant South Seas. This designation underwent changes later so that it left space and entered time. Indeed, the Utopians, especially those of the eighteenth and nineteenth centuries, transposed the wishland more into the future. In other words, there is a transformation of the topos from space into time. With Thomas More the wishland was still ready, on a distant island, but I am not there. On the other hand, when it is transposed into the future, not only am I not there, but utopia itself is also not with itself. This island does not even exist. But it is not something like nonsense or absolute fancy; rather it is not *yet* in the sense of a possibility; *that* it could be there if we could only do something for it. Not only if we travel there, but *in that* we travel there the island utopia arises out of the sea of the possible – utopia, but with new contents. (Adorno and Bloch 1988, 3)

S. McAuliffe (✉)
Goldsmiths, University of London, London, UK

P. Marks et al. (eds.), *The Palgrave Handbook of Utopian and Dystopian Literatures*, https://doi.org/10.1007/978-3-030-88654-7_17

Once it is conceived of in temporal terms, utopia becomes a projection. Located in a future to come, the world to which it makes reference concerns reality not as it is, but as it could be. Since, however, this future has not yet come to pass, and since it cannot come to pass in accordance with the present that acts as a support for its manifestation, it follows that utopia is just as readily characterized by its current inexistence. In the present it can only appear at a distance from itself, inaccessible and unattainable, consigned to a state which leaves it, with respect to itself, *nowhere*: "utopia itself is... not with itself." And yet, as Bloch also suggests here, having acceded to expression a utopian projection draws this possible future closer. By giving a definite shape to "the being of What-Is-Not-Yet," it demonstrates that the present's given form is not definitive, that it has "the potential to become otherwise" (*der Potenz das Anders-Werdenkönnen*). With this "transformation of the topos from space into time," the referential function of utopian discourse therefore finds itself recast: the possibility to which its projection gives expression acquires a degree of reality it would not otherwise have had, were it to have remained unexpressed. Utopia becomes a discursive practice that precipitates the actualization of its referent, through the act of reference itself, and it is this that constitutes its specificity in relation to all other forms of fiction-making. "Not only if we travel there, but *in that* we travel there the island utopia arises out of the sea of the possible..." (Bloch 1989, 3).

Throughout *The Principle of Hope* (published in three volumes between 1954 and 1959), Bloch's engagement with this tendency makes repeated use of a particular concept, the features of which are delineated most sharply in the context of aesthetics. The concept is that of *Vor-Schein*, pre-appearance.[1] It is this that confers upon an aesthetic representation its utopian aspect, making the work of art appear as if "lit by a world which is not yet there" (Bloch 1986–1995, 2: 811; 1985, 950).[2] On its account, an intimation of the future to come is able to appear in all its irreducibility, *here and now*, ahead of time and in advance of its actuality. As Bloch is keen to stress, this phenomenon draws the category of appearance or semblance (*Erscheinung*) away from its recognized meaning in classical aesthetics. The work of art formed in accordance with this configuration is neither an "idealistic correction" of reality nor the latter's "mere reproduction" in its given state (2: 809; 947). Rather, by opening up a perspective onto the tendencies and latencies traversing reality as a still ongoing, unfinished process, it traces the trajectory along which whatever is represented finds itself propelled forward, carried beyond its recognizable form, and thereby *viewed ahead*, under a horizon that extends beyond the present's own. What allows pre-appearance to be told apart from the mere semblance [*Schein*] or illusion [*Illusion*] that it admittedly always risks being confused with is the unbroken contact it maintains with this "future-laden definiteness [*eine zukunfttragende Bestimmtheit*] in the real itself" (1: 235; 271). In other words, it draws out of reality its *real possibility*, which Bloch defines as follows: "real possibility is the categorical In-Front-of-Itself of material movement considered as a process; it is the specific regional character of reality itself, on the Front of its occurrence… there is no true realism without the true dimension of this openness" (1: 237; 274). This is what makes the work of art anticipatory in nature. Its "claim to truth" is measured less by adequation or verisimilitude, than the degree of pressure it is able to exert on reality through anticipation:

> And the answer to the aesthetic question of truth is: artistic appearance is not only mere appearance, but a meaning [*Bedeutung*], cloaked in images and which can only be described in images, of material that has been driven further, wherever *the exaggeration and fantasising represent a significant pre-appearance, circulating in turbulent existence itself, of what is real* [*wo die Exaggerierung und Ausfabelung einen im Bewegt-Vorhandenen selber umgehenden und bedeutenden Vor-Schein von Wirklichem darstellen*], a pre-appearance which can specifically be represented in aesthetically immanent terms … Pre-appearance is this attainable thing itself because the métier of *driving-to-the-end occurs in dialectically open space*, in which any Object can be aesthetically represented. (1: 214–215; 247. Emphases in original)

When, much later in the same work, Bloch takes up the question once more, he adds that "art drives world-figures, world-landscapes, without them being destroyed, to their entelechetic limit: only the aesthetic illusion detaches itself from life, whereas the aesthetic pre-appearance is precisely one because it stands itself in the horizon of the real" (2: 809–810; 948). This is the framework within which it becomes possible to discern in Bloch's aesthetics a re-formulation of the discursive properties, functions, and operations associated with the term *realism*. The framework of utopia alters what can be expected from this particular signifying practice. Above all this alteration concerns what Bloch refers to in this section of the text as the realist *demand* (*Forderung*): namely, the effort to secure through exactitude of reference a maximum degree of correspondence between the real and its representation; to recover in and through representation reality in its entirety. "How legitimate Homer's realism is, a realism of such exact fullness that almost the whole of Mycenean culture can be visualized from it… Such precision and reality is undoubtedly peculiar and essential to all great literature" (1: 214; 245–246).

Now, it is precisely this demand which increasingly comes to appear in a different light in *The Principle of Hope*: "Realism in art is no descriptive or explanatory stock-taking, but it holds up, in an activating way, a mirror of immanent anticipation, it is tendential-utopian realism [*tendenzhaft-utopischer Realismus*]" (2: 811; 950). The referential function of the realist text remains in effect, but re-directed toward an entirely new end. Reference is reconfigured as a capacity or a power, to draw out and drive forward, and its exercise affects a change in reality itself. It becomes a means of *activation*. In this sense the relation between the real and its representation is inverted. The reality represented by this realism is not in place in advance of its representation *but is elicited through it*. What is reproduced in discourse is at the same time produced in reality, in the mode of "immanent anticipation." Here Bloch offers a way of thinking through a question that will later be posed by Barthes: "Why not test the 'realism' of a work by examining not the more or less exact way in which it reproduces reality, but on the contrary the way in which reality could or could not effectuate the novel's utterance?" (Barthes 1989, 136).

Making realistic depiction a means of anticipation, a mirror that catches in its reflection the lineaments of what is to come, can only be achieved by dissociating realism from the "surface [*flache*] empiricism" by which Bloch suggests it has been progressively subsumed. Such empiricism only ever makes contact with the world in a reified form. Arbitrarily cutting into "the flow of the real," it "keeps a firm hold on individual moments of process and anchors them as facts." By erroneously treating this isolated abstraction as the entity's definitive form, it represents the latter without the horizon which belongs to it as a "process-reality" (*Prozeßwirklichkeit*): "the perspective of grovelling empiricism and the naturalism that corresponds to it in aesthetic terms... never advances from the establishment of what is factual to the exploration of what is essentially happening" (Bloch 1986–1995, 1: 222; 1985, 256).[3]

A "tendential-utopian realism": what would this look like in practice?

1. Paul Scheerbart's *Glass Architecture* (1914) could certainly be said to belong to this genre.[4] The vision it sets forth, of a built environment in which glass would be the primary if not exclusive material of construction, envisages a redetermination of the very frameworks through which lived experience is channelled. "The new environment, which we must create, must bring us a new culture" (Scheerbart 1972, 41). On account of its fundamental property—*its transparency*—the expanded use of this material would give rise to new forms of dwelling and new forms of sociality, on account of the singular regime of proxemics it makes possible (glass architecture "takes away the closed character of the rooms in which we live" [41]). At the same time, Scheerbart always presents this vision from the standpoint of real possibility. For example, the text offers entirely practical instructions for the realization of this new world. As a "simple and convenient" (44) first step, all existing buildings should immediately be fitted with a glass veranda, which would very quickly supplant the building of which it is an appendage. "So the veranda continues to grow; in the end it emancipates itself from the main building, and may become the main building itself. To promote this evolution of the veranda will be the chief task of every glass architect" (44). From this relatively inauspicious start, nothing less than "the transformation of the earth's surface" should be expected (71). "One thing leads to another, and to stop the process is unthinkable" (44). This is what it means to view the real in terms of its horizon, to take a material and drive it further through its portrayal.

2. Gabriel Tarde's *Fragment of Future History* (1896), initially published in English as *Underground Man* (1905), also cultivates a realism of this type. The novel envisages a future age in which the world has been exposed to the catastrophe of "solar apoplexy" (Tarde 2004, 52). With the sun having permanently weakened, the surface of the earth is no longer habitable and what remains of humanity is sent downwards: "let us withdraw to the interior of our planet ... let us bury ourselves in order to rise again, and ... let us carry with us into our tumb, all that is worthy to survive of our previous existence" (Tarde 2004, 86). But underground existence is not simply suffered. On the contrary, it lays the ground for an "undreamt-of recovery" (Tarde 2004, 142), humanity learning to utilize the distinct properties of the new milieu in which it now finds itself. For example, the Underground gives rise to "a modern architecture so profoundly original that no one could have predicted it," an immense network of unbroken interconnection which founds a new organization of spatiality and a new distribution of human relations: a "true social revolution" (Tarde 2004, 122). "For the modern architect the interior alone exists, and each work [habitation] is linked on to those which have gone before. None stands by itself. They are only an extention and ramification, one of another, an endless continuation..." (Tarde 2004, 128). Transparency of glass, extensivity of earth: each of these utopian projections attain its consistency by recognizing a tendency lying latent in material reality itself. Each presents a vision of matter on the basis of its "future-laden properties" (Bloch: "matter is the site of the conditions according to whose stipulations entelechies reveal themselves" (1986–1995, 1: 207; 1985, 236)). However fantastic these future worlds appear, however far the element of "exaggeration and fantasising" in them is carried, their respective lineaments remain derived from and determined by concrete reality. They are instances of what Bloch calls "founded [*fundiertem*] appearance" (1: 216; 249).

There does remain a further feature of Bloch's aesthetic configuration to consider here. The *"dialectically open space"* that the utopian work presides over has as its condition the future defined as an expanse (*Weite*), the horizon of which finds itself ceaselessly pushed backward. If "everything real passes over into the Possible at its processual Front," if "Mobile, changing, changeable Being, presenting itself as dialectical-material, has this unclosed capability of becoming, this Not-Yet-Closedness both in its ground and in its horizon" (1: 196; 225–226), this is only insofar as the future lies before it as something inexhaustible: "a world... would not be in the least changeable without the enormous future" (1: 223; 257). But here a tension begins to make itself felt. Whenever the work of art drives something forward into this expanse, this movement is not undertaken indiscriminately but in view of the represented entity's end, its "entelechetic limit": the work is *a portrayal of the tendency and latency of its Objects occurring* in the manner of the *pre-appearance driven to an end*" (2: 809; 947). Were it to be attained, this end would mark the definitive fulfilment of the entity—its "immanent perfection," Bloch says—making it that after which nothing further could be expected; an attainment of the *Ultimum* (1: 203; 233). In this sense, pre-appearance presents the future of the thing *but also* the thing without future. By bringing this end into view, a restriction is imposed on the "open space" that allows this end to be approached in the first place.[5] No doubt Bloch is perfectly aware of this aporia. "The motto of aesthetically attempted pre-appearance runs along these lines: how could the world be perfected without this world being exploded and apocalyptically vanishing, as in Christian-religious pre-appearance" (1: 215; 248). This end is both the condition of the model of representation instituted by Bloch here, but also its unrepresentable limit.[6]

II

The future understood as a question with which realist discourse is brought face to face as a matter of necessity at a particular phase in its development, and especially insofar as this question is given its shape by the context of utopia, is also a central concern of a short text written by Elias Canetti in 1965, "Realism and New Reality" ("Realismus und neue Wirklichkeit").[7] At its outset, the realist enterprise is defined as "a method of gaining reality for the novel. *Total* reality, it was important not to exclude anything from this reality, whether for aesthetic or for bourgeois moral conventions," Canetti then asking himself under what conditions it would be possible to produce such a work *today*. "Could those of us who are after the same goal, though as people of our era, and who regard themselves as modern realists – could we employ the same methods?" (Canetti 1979, 55; 1981, 72). The question is necessary because the extent to which reality has been transformed since this method's progressive development over the latter half of the previous century is "enormous." What is it, then, that characterizes "modern reality" under-stood as something that lacks all contiguity with all that has gone before? On the one hand, Canetti argues, it has become more abundant: "a lot more exists now, not only numerically, there are many more people and things; but a far greater immensity exists in quality as well. The old, the new, and the different flow in from everywhere" (Canetti 1979, 55, 72). On the other, it has become more precise: "The sector of 'approximate' activity and knowledge is rapidly shrinking... Reality is departmentalized, subdivided, and can be grasped down to its minutest units from many directions" (57–58, 75). And yet, while these tendencies show a divergence with past reality, it is nevertheless possible to anticipate their development on the latter's basis. This is not the case with the final phenomenon that holds Canetti's attention here. From the perspective of what was, its occurrence will have been entirely unforeseeable. As such it constitutes an absolute break with the period it distinguishes itself from. This change concerns, so Canetti claims, "the reality of the future" (*die Wirklichkeit des Kommenden*), the author tending to refer here not to *die Zukunft* but *das Kommende*: the forthcoming, that which is on the verge of coming about. He writes:

> The future exists quite differently from ever before, it is approaching more swiftly and it is being consciously brought about. Its dangers are our most intrinsic work; but so are its hopes. The reality of the future has split: on the one side, annihilation [*Vernichtung*]; on the other, the good life. Both are simultaneously active, in the world, in ourselves. This split [*Spaltung*], this double future, is absolute, and there is no one who could ignore it. Everyone sees a

dark and a bright shape [*Gestalt*] at once, approaching him at an oppressive velocity. One may hold either shape at bay to see only the other, but both are persistently there. (Canetti 1979, 58; 75–76)

It is particularly this double aspect of the future, actively wished and actively feared, that distinguishes our century's reality from that of the previous one... The aspect of the future is totally different [*Der Aspekt des Kommenden ist ein von Grund auf anderer*], and one can say without exaggeration that we are living in a period of the world that does not have the most important thing in common with the period of our grandfathers: its future [*Zukunft*] is not a whole thing anymore, it is split in two. (59; 77)

This, then, is the fundamental feature of present-day reality for Canetti: its future has come apart. Henceforth it is something that bears down upon the present in two distinct forms, *at one and the same time*. In Bloch's terms, it is as if the horizon at reality's outer edge no longer coheres as one. These two shapes are not only irreconcilable but incompossible, mutually exclusive to the extent that the actuality of either would constitute the radical negation of the other. This is why the split is absolute. Yet because neither side outweighs the other, because their degree of viability is in each case absolutely the same, in the extremity of their difference they become locked in a relation of co-implication; incompossible *and yet* concomitant. "One may hold either shape at bay to see only the other, *but both are persistently there*."

Something of this situation can be approached through the framework provided by *The Principle of Hope*; at least up to a point. To conceive of process-reality in terms of its Not-Yet-Closedness is to establish that change-ability (*Veränderlichkeit*) is a fundamental feature of its constitution. This, after all, is what the real's "capability-of-becoming-other" signifies. But whenever such change is on the point of coming to pass, this liminal moment introduces an element of "uncertainty" into the process, since the outcome of this change cannot be secured in advance. If reality always "has something advancing and breaking out at its edge" (Bloch 1986–1995, 1: 197; 226), there is nothing to guarantee that this will not be to reality's detriment; a change "for the worse." "The disaster character [*Unheilscharakter*] of the Possible thus mili-tates against the above-mentioned salvation character [*Heilscharakter*], hope character of the Possible, which lies no less powerfully in the changeability of a situation" (1: 233; 268).

A light shape and a dark shape. In each case, Canetti has a definite project in mind. On one side of the split, there lies utopia. At this historical juncture utopian projection has acquired an unparalleled power (*Stoßkraft*): "Every-where on earth, in the most diverse forms, utopias are about to come true... There is no utopia that could not be materialized" (Canetti 1979, 58; 1981 76). This power installs utopia as a means of placing "the enormous sum total of reality that has come down to us" (59) on a different trajectory, re-directing the line of extension along which process-reality is unfolding. "Utopias are sliced up into segments and then tackled as plans stretching over a given number of years" (58). And yet, Canetti insists, it is precisely the effort undertaken to implement such plans that brings the future's other form into view. "But let us not forget," he writes,

> that there are very different kinds of utopias and that all of them are active at the same time. Social, scientific-technological, national utopias strengthen each other and chafe each other. They protect the continuance of their realization by developing weapons to intimidate. One knows what these weapons are like. Their actual use would turn against the user with no less force. Everyone senses this dark side of the future, which may come true. (59; 76–77)

On one side of the split, utopia, on the other side, destruction, total, and without limit.[8] Dark accompanies light as its shadow. This shadow is cast not in spite of what utopia promises but because of it. And the stakes of this situation are further compounded once it is acknowledged that this "oppressively close, unrelenting threat" (59) would in actuality amount to the irrevocable withdrawal of any further future. This contingency is described by Blanchot, writing one year earlier than Canetti, in the following way: "Today there is the atomic bomb; humanity can destroy itself; this destruction would be radical; the possibility of a radical destruction of humanity by humanity inaugurates a beginning in history; whatever happens, whatever precautionary measures there may be, we cannot go backward" (Blanchot 1997, 101). Here "the disaster character of the Possible" acquires a disconcerting new sense, because it now concerns an event that would foreclose all other possibilities.[9] And yet however much this circumstance constitutes an historical beginning for Canetti this alone does not exhaust the specificity of modern reality, which rests with the fact that such destruction appears inextricably bound up with its absolute antithesis. The standpoint of modern reality is traversed by both possibilities at once, the light and the dark, never one without the other, and its modernity consists in being inscribed within or exposed to this double bind.[10]

All this has significant implications for any discourse charged with representing reality. How would the referential function of this discourse be administered in view of this situation? In *Aesthetic Theory* (2002) Adorno develops one possible answer to this question. He does so, moreover, from the very same standpoint as Canetti, with reference to the modern epoch as "an age in which the real possibility of utopia – that given the level of productive forces the earth could here and now be paradise – converges with the possibility of total catastrophe." He continues: "In the image of catastrophe, *an image that is not a copy of the event but the cipher of its potential*, the magical trace of art's most distant prehistory reappears under the total spell, as *if art wanted to prevent the catastrophe by conjuring up its image*" (33; my emphases). The nuclear event, the instantiation of this "total catastrophe," can only be referred to in an anticipatory form, as having not yet happened.[11] As with Bloch's utopian realism, then, referentiality is reoriented toward the future. But in this instance its function becomes apotropaic. It is deployed as a means of warding off the event in question, whose possibility it nevertheless acknowledges; its aim is to maintain the event in its inexistence, preventing it from passing across the threshold from possibility into actuality. As such this model of representation can be considered the precise inverse of the one informing Bloch's, for which reference is also anticipatory, but as a means of activation.

Approached along these lines, one of the fundamental paradoxes encompassing utopian realist discourse at this particular juncture is that the "double future" it is tasked with representing demands two distinct models of referentiality, the respective operations of which cannot be brought into correspondence with one another. To draw the light side of the future nearer on the one hand, to keep the dark side of the future at bay on the other. It is this that the realist text must bring to expression, as Canetti's closing words indicate:

> Presumably, one or several of the aspects of our reality, such as I have briefly described, must emerge in the novel of our times; otherwise one could hardly call it realistic. It is now up to our conversation to determine the extent to which this has already happened or could still happen. (Canetti 1979, 59; 1981, 77)

Ultimately, then, what this understanding of the future gives us to think is a form of writing, the realism of which would rest with the capacity to approach its object against the background of these two fundamentally antagonistic realities, the light and the dark, its standpoint having found a way to let itself be marked by the alternation between them.

NOTES

1. The term appears in a variety of forms in English translations of Bloch's work. See, Jack Zipes, 1998, Introduction: Toward a Realization of Anticipatory Illumination, in *The Utopian Function of Art and Literature: Selected Essays*, ed. Ernst Bloch, trans. Jack Zipes and Frank Mecklenburg, Cambridge, MA: MIT Press, xi–xliii. Here, for example, Zipes renders it as "anticipatory illumination," and proceeds to provide an account of the concept's relation to the wider German aesthetic tradition (xxxiii–xxxvi).

2. Quotations from this work refer to the English translation first (volume: page number), followed by the German original. The following editions have been consulted: Ernst Bloch, 1986–1995, *The Principle of Hope*, 3 vols, trans. Neville Plaice, Stephanie Plaice, and Paul Knight, Cambridge, MA: MIT Press; Original edition: Ernst Bloch, 1985, *Das Prinzip Hoffung*, Frankfurt: Suhrkamp.

3. Bloch's critique here shares several points of affinity with the Brechtian effort to derive a different sense from the literary form in question and the intention to practice this form differently (that is to say, *politically*). See Bertolt Brecht, 2003, Notes on the Realist Mode of Writing,

in *Brecht on Art and Politics*, ed. Tom Kuhn and Steve Giles, trans. Laura Bradley, Steve Giles, and Tom Kuhn, London and New York: Bloomsbury, 242–262. Here, Brecht claims that "a realist perspective is one which studies the dynamic forces, a realist mode of action is one which sets the dynamic forces in motion" (260). See also Fredric Jameson, 2013, *The Antinomies of Realism*, London and New York: Verso. Jameson identifies similarly competing visions of the realist enterprise in his study of the form: on the one hand, a realism "absolutely committed to the density and solidity of what is," this amounting to "a professional endorsement of the status quo"; on the other, a realism of tendency, concerned with the "transformation of being… somehow implicit in being itself" (215–216).

4. In fact Scheerbart does make a brief appearance in *The Principle of Hope*, in the section 'Buildings which depict a better life, architectural utopias' (2: 736; 861).

5. See also Elizabeth Grosz, 2001, Embodied Utopias: The Time of Architecture, in *Architecture from the Outside: Essays on Virtual and Real Space*, Cambridge, MA: MIT Press, 131–150. Grosz's stringent critique of the utopian tradition is focused on a similar tendency: "utopia, like the dialectic itself, is commonly fantasized as the end of time, the end of history, the moment of resolution of past problems." What does this mean? In short, "While a picture of the future, the utopic is fundamentally that which *has no future*" (137–138). For her, the viability of a utopian projection rests on its ability to resist this closure so that the future it envisages keeps open the possibility of another future in turn.

6. An analysis of the same configuration can be found in Hans Magnus Enzensberger, 1982, Two Notes on the End of the World, in *Critical Essays*, ed. Reinhold Grimm and Bruce Armstrong, New York: Continuum, 233–241: "without catastrophe no millennium, without apocalypse no paradise" (234; 240–241).

7. Quotations refer first to the English translation, and the original text subsequently. The following editions have been consulted: Elias Canetti, 1979, Realism and New Reality, in *The Conscience of Words*, trans. Joachim Neugroschel, New York: Seabury Press, 55–59; Original edition: Elias Canetti, 1981, Realismus und neue Wirklichkeit, in *Das Gewissen der Worte*, Frankfurt am Main: Fischer Taschenbuch Verlag, 72–77.

8. See, Elias Canetti, 1978, *The Human Province*, trans. Joachim Neugroschel, New York: Seabury Press. Canetti's notebooks confirm that this thesis concerning *die Wirklichkeit des Kommenden* is conceived in direct response to the deployment of the atomic bomb, the first appearance of what he refers to there as the "double-tongued future" explicitly tied to the date "August 1945" (66–67).

9. See, Fredric Jameson, 2005, *Archaeologies of the Future: The Desire Called Utopia and Other Science Fictions*, London and New York:

Verso. One could envisage something like a new political imperative emerging in response to this circumstance, of the sort described by Jameson when he writes: "Perhaps indeed we need to develop an anxiety about losing the future... a fear that locates the loss of the future and futuricity, of historicity itself, within the existential dimension of time and indeed within ourselves" (233).

10. A systematic study of this double bind would have to account for the fact that once the light and the dark are conjoined in this way, the "actively wished" and the "actively feared" become increasingly difficult to tell apart. See Michael S. Roth, 2012, Trauma: A Dystopia of the Spirit, in *Memory, Trauma and History: Essays on Living with the Past*, 87–103, New York: Columbia University Press. For Roth, the context in which the implications of this tendency are best understood is that of trauma: "The terrain demarcated by the concept of trauma has become a crucial form of negative utopia of the late twentieth and early twenty-first century... In this discourse the negative of utopia is not pointing toward a state of affairs that we would all strive mightily to avoid but rather to a state of affairs that we might intensely desire. Dystopia is the utopia you must be careful not to wish for" (87–88).

11. See, Jacques Derrida, 1984, No Apocalypse, Not Now (Full Speed Ahead, Seven Missiles, Seven Missives), trans. Catherine Porter and Philip Lewis, *Diacritics* 14 (2): 20–31. Writing a generation later on this point, Derrida argues: "It [nuclear war] has never occurred, itself; it is a non-event... The terrifying reality of the nuclear conflict can only be the signified referent, never the real referent (present or past) of a discourse or a text. At least today apparently... [hence] it has existence only through what is said of it, only where it is talked about" (23).

References

Adorno, Theodor W. 2002. *Aesthetic Theory*, ed. Gretel Adorno and Rolf Tiedemann, trans. Robert Hullot-Kentor. London: Continuum.

Adorno, Theodor W., and Ernst Bloch. 1988. Something's Missing: A Discussion Between Ernst Bloch and Theodor W. Adorno on the Contradictions of Utopian Longing. In *The Utopian Function of Art and Literature: Selected Essays*, ed. Ernst Bloch, trans. Jack Zipes and Frank Mecklenburg, 1–17. Cambridge, MA: MIT Press.

Barthes, Roland. 1989. *Sade, Fourier, Loyola*, trans. Richard Miller. Berkeley and Los Angeles: University of California Press.

Blanchot, Maurice. 1997. The Apocalypse Is Disappointing. In *Friendship*, trans. Elizabeth Rottenberg, 101–108. Stanford: Stanford University Press.

Bloch, Ernst. 1986–1995. *The Principle of Hope*, 3 vols, trans. Neville Plaice, Stephanie Plaice, and Paul Knight. Cambridge, MA: MIT Press. Original edition: Bloch, Ernst. 1985. *Das Prinzip Hoffnung*. Frankfurt: Suhrkamp.

———. 1989. *The Utopian Function of Art and Literature: Selected Essays*, trans. Jack Zipes and Frank Mecklenburg. Cambridge, MA: The MIT Press.

Brecht, Bertolt. 2003. Notes on the Realist Mode of Writing. In *Brecht on Art and Politics*, ed. Tom Kuhn and Steve Giles, trans. Laura Bradley, Steve Giles, and Tom Kuhn, 242–262. London and New York: Bloomsbury.

Canetti, Elias. 1978. *The Human Province*, trans. Joachim Neugroschel. New York: Seabury Press.

———. 1979. Realism and New Reality. In *The Conscience of Words*, trans. Joachim Neugroschel, 55–59. New York: Seabury Press. Original Edition: Canetti, Elias. 1981. Realismus und neue Wirklichkeit. In *Das Gewissen der Worte*, 72–77. Frankfurt am Main: Fischer Taschenbuch Verlag.

Derrida, Jacques. 1984. No Apocalypse, Not Now (Full Speed Ahead, Seven Missiles, Seven Missives), trans. Catherine Porter and Philip Lewis. *Diacritics* 14 (2): 20–31.

Enzensberger, Hans Magnus. 1982. Two Notes on the End of the World. In *Critical Essays*, ed. Reinhold Grimm and Bruce Armstrong, 233–241. New York: Continuum.

Grosz, Elizabeth. 2001. Embodied Utopias: The Time of Architecture. In *Architecture from the Outside: Essays on Virtual and Real Space*, 131–150. Cambridge, MA: MIT Press.

Jameson, Fredric. 2005. *Archaeologies of the Future: The Desire Called Utopia and Other Science Fictions*. London and New York: Verso.

———. 2013. *The Antinomies of Realism*. London and New York: Verso.

Roth, Michael S. 2012. Trauma: A Dystopia of the Spirit. In *Memory, Trauma and History: Essays on Living with the Past*, 87–103. New York: Columbia University Press.

Scheerbart, Paul. 1972. *Glass Architecture; Alpine Architecture*, ed. Dennis Sharp, trans. James Palmes and Shirley Palmer. London: November Books.

Tarde, Gabriel. 2004. *Underground (Fragments of Future Histories)*, trans. Cloudesley Brereton. Updated Liam Gillick. Brussels: Maîtres de Forme Contemporains; Dijon: Presses du reel.

Zipes, Jack. 1988. Introduction: Toward a Realization of Anticipatory Illumination. In *The Utopian Function of Art and Literature: Selected Essays*, ed. Ernst Bloch, trans. Jack Zipes and Frank Mecklenburg, xi–xliii. Cambridge, MA: MIT Press.

Cinema

Peter Marks

Introduction

Men were first filmed walking on the moon in 1902; specifically in Georges
Méliès twelve-minute fantasy *Le Voyage dans la Lune*. Méliès's playful
creativity set him apart from his chief cinematic rivals, the more Auguste and
Louis Lumière, whose pioneering recording of a train arriving at a station
(1895) advertised the startling capacity of the new medium to document
reality. These advances in early cinema had a radical impact on the history
of painting and photography, and on notions of reality; the Lumiere films
labelled their films "Actualities." Méliès more quickly recognized the fantastical possibilities of cinema, creating hitherto impossible scenarios and effects.
In *Le Voyage* a group of scientists is shot by cannon to the lunar surface,
hitting The Man in the Moon in the eye in what remains one of cinema's
iconic moments. Jules Verne's *From the Earth to the Moon* (1865) and H.G.
Wells's *The First Men in the Moon* (1901) were two famous literary precursors, but Méliès's exuberant visual representation of the trip, as well as of
the lunar environment and its supposed creatures, promoted cinema's ability
to present captivating visions of other worlds. Given that a cannon capable of
firing a capsule to the moon *still* does not exist, films like *Voyage* also promised
to present audiences with visions of "the future." This chapter explores how
filmmakers since Méliès have created a corpus of utopian and dystopian movies
that continue to instruct, thrill and warn.

P. Marks (✉)
University of Sydney, Sydney, NSW, Australia

P. Marks et al. (eds.), *The Palgrave Handbook of Utopian and Dystopian
Literatures*, https://doi.org/10.1007/978-3-030-88654-7_18

The birth of cinema coincided with a new century when the utopian visions characteristic of the nineteenth century began to be eclipsed by dystopian threats. As Raffaella Baccolini and Tom Moylan note: "In the twentieth century, the dark side of Utopia—dystopian accounts of places worse than the ones we live in—took its place in the narrative catalogue of the West and developed in several forms throughout the rest of the century" (Baccolini and Moylan 2003, 1). In that same century, cinema rose from relatively crude beginnings to a popular and hugely influential artform, quickly developing new ways of presenting characters, setting, perspective and narrative. Yet the relative expense and the industrial, collaborative filmmaking process, coupled with the rapid rise of Hollywood to cultural and economic dominance over the industry (for which there is no literary equivalent), has meant that film can too easily be dismissed as cheap mass entertainment. Cinema on this reading is incapable of or uninterested in dealing with complex ideas or of mounting substantive critiques of the status quo. Tellingly, utopian scholars have noted a relative absence of utopian films, Peter Fitting admitting that "there is no accepted body of utopian films and no accepted definition. In fact, few films come to mind when the subject [what is a utopian film?] is raised" (Fitting 1993, 1). Subsequent researchers have expanded the catalogue of utopian films, but dystopian films remain the prevalent form. And as Gregory Claeys suggests, in the contemporary world "film is, for many, the primary entry point into dystopia" (Claeys 2017, 492). The modern dominance of dark literary forecasts holds true for cinema.

For all the obvious connections and overlaps between literature and film, the latter by its nature allows for more detailed and large-scale visual representation of societies and spaces. Hence the power of early films such as *Metropolis* (1927), *Things to Come* (1935) and *Lost Horizon* (1937), or more recent works such as *Avatar* (2009) and *Blade Runner 2047* (2017), to conjure up finely detailed and immersive worlds for mass audiences to contemplate and critique. Spectacle can come at the expense of depth, especially in terms of characterization, Claeys arguing that "dystopia and cinema are a marriage made in Heaven, for both are in love with high drama, exaggeration and special effects" (Claeys 2017, 491). This explains his view that the "purpose" of fictional film "is primarily entertainment rather than edification" (490), though the same argument could be made about much fiction. The superficiality of at least some speculative films might be seen to accord with H.G. Wells' critique in *A Modern Utopia* (1905):

> Their common fault is to be comprehensively jejune. That which is the blood and warmth and reality of life is largely absent; there are no individualities, but only generalised people.... [with] characterless buildings, symmetrical and perfect cultivations..... This burthens us with an incurable effect of unreality, and I do not see how it is altogether to be escaped. (Wells 2005, 4)

But Wells here is lambasting literature, not film, *A Modern Utopia* being but one of his many attempts to overcome the shortcomings he detected in literary versions of the genre. Wells' undeniable capacity to create relatively "real" characters in "unreal" situations—Martian invasions, invisible men, parallel planets—allowed him to overcome the faults he detected in others. Little wonder that his novels have generated myriad adaptations—though not yet, it is worth noting, of *A Modern Utopia*.

The adaptation of Wells' utopian text *The Shape of Things to Come* (1933) as the film *Things to Come* (1936) and Frank Capra's 1937 film version of James Hilton's novel *Lost Horizon* (1933) makes Fitting's very short list of unambiguously utopian films. Even here, Fitting makes a distinction between utopian films in themselves and films that are adaptations of utopian novels, adding that "there are almost no films of the classics of the utopian tradition" (Fitting 1993, 1). By this perhaps he means such classics in English language works as *Utopia, Erewhon, Looking Backward, News from Nowhere* and *Herland*. That same paucity is not true in the case of dystopian films, Fitting recognizing that there are "numerous versions of dystopian classics" (Fitting 1993, 2)—he references *Nineteen Eighty-Four, Brave New World, A Clockwork Orange* and *The Handmaid's Tale*. This imbalance might simply reflect the dominance of dystopian literature generally in the first century of cinema. It could also speak to the sort of distinction delineated by Artur Blaim and Ludmiła Gruszewska-Blaim, that in a utopia "the journey of the main protagonist to a utopian country assumes an educational, rather than adventurous or sentimental character, hence the prevalence of descriptive and explicatory modes in utopian narratives" (Blaim and Gruszewska-Blaim 2015, 8–9). They add that "[d]ue to the amicable guidance on the part of utopians, the process of knowledge acquisition can be depicted as orderly and systemic, which helps the reader easily follow and admire the beauty and logic of the utopian condition" (9). By contrast, the dystopia "adopts different principles of text construction: it foregrounds narrativity at the expense of descriptiveness, and favours plot rather than setting" (10). The journey motif is a standard utopian maneuver, the new arrival often receiving a long explication of the history, organization and working of the utopia land. Claeys suggests that this educative function in part distinguishes literature from film, but that function also necessarily slows the development of plot that Blaim and Gruszewska-Blaim recognize as a central component of dystopian literature—and of most films. To adapt Wells' critique of literary utopias, long explications of utopian (or dystopian) principles and processes in a film, as opposed to a novel, risk boring audiences primed for the visual richness and vivid action associated with cinema.

UTOPIAN FILMS

Fitting's focus on *Things to Come* and *Lost Horizon* as rare examples of utopian films illuminates "the visual nature of film and its difference from the literary" (1993, 1). He notes that both films were made in the 1930s, "a moment of both heightened utopian activity and of a belief in technology's ability to build a better world" (2). Fitting suggests that "the two films devote relatively little space to the representation of a new society" and that while

> the spectator takes away strong visual impressions of these utopian communities, there are very few details of what actually constitutes the future society, unlike what we usually learn from a written utopia. In *Things To Come* details about the society are replaced by a futuristic look.... [while in *Lost Horizon*] the look of utopia owes more to the 'lost civilisation' tradition. (2)

The visual differences between these films, one futuristic in its later sections, the other timelessly idyllic, strongly suggest their distinct attitudes. *Lost Horizon* ends with an idealistic British diplomat, Robert Conway, fleeing the contemporary world to return to the tranquil perfection in Shangri-La, hidden somewhere in Tibet. *Things to Come* concludes with a massive Space Gun firing a shell that will take adventurous humans on a return trip to the moon, a precursor for further exploration. The Wellsian hero Oswald Cabal declares that humans must conquer the mysteries of space and time, and explore the universe: "All the universe or nothing. Which shall it be... ? Which shall it be?" (1:33:55–1:34:03). *Things To Come* illustrates Wells' obsession with technological advance. The film bore only a passing resemblance to the original text, itself less a novel than a creative treatise. John Hammond reads the film as presenting a "stoic vision of man's destiny," explaining however that Wells disliked the finished product

> intensely, finding it "pretentious, clumsy and scamped." By telescoping and oversimplifying his ideas the film merely strengthened the notion he was enthusiastic for material progress per se; its underlying message of the dangers of war and national solitary sovereignty was lost in a futuristic vision of a soulless cosmopolis. (Hammond 1993, xxxvii)

The film on this description seems to exemplify precisely the flaws Wells had diagnosed in *A Modern Utopia* three decades earlier. In fact, the "soulless cosmopolis" that for some represented a modernist "Wellsian" utopia occupies only the last half hour of the 94-minute film. *Things To Come* opens in the representative "Everytown" in the near-future year of 1940, with the world on the brink of war. Where the pessimistic engineer John Cabal fears conflict, warning that "if we don't end war, war will end us" (6:30–6:33), his naively positive friend "Pippa" Passworthy downplays the danger. The subsequent war proves Cabal right, dragging on destructively for decades, with society breaking down. By 1970 Everytown has been reduced to rubble, survivors living a semi-feudal existence under the thuggish "Boss." Wells' own fears of the inevitable consequences of a world not ruled by a rational, centralized government are evident in the degraded physical and political environment of Everytown.

Wellsian hope is personified in the figure of John Cabal, a name that resonates with Wells' belief in the necessity of a ruling intellectual elite, called "Samurai" in *A Modern Utopia*. Cabal has survived and (now an old man) arrives by futuristic plane to announce the existence of a sophisticated organization of engineers and mechanics, "Wings Over the World," which he trumpets as "The Brotherhood of Efficiency and The Freemasonry of Science." After a one-sided battle in which the technically superior Wings Over the World squadron crushes the Boss's out-dated air force, Cabal announces "the rule of the Airmen, and a new life for mankind" (1:04:05–1:04:09). He and his cohorts revitalize Everytown as a twenty-first-century metropolis, shown in an extended montage (1:04:29–1:11:24) that incorporates cutting-edge film technology and futuristic designs to rival Kubrick's much later *2001: A Space Odyssey*. Everytown is completed in 2036 (the centenary of the film's release), embodying the now-dead John Cabal's utopian dream. His descendant, Oswald Cabal, even more certain of the benefits of science and technology, leads the ruling Council. But Wells includes dissenting voices including a descendent of Passworthy who timidly questions the need for endless progress, and the stentorian craftsman, Theotocopulos, who demands a world without progress, arguing that instead "the object of life is happy living" (1:19:00–1:19:03). His explicitly rabble-rousing speech, beamed to a public square on a giant transparent screen, moves some of the population to attempt to destroy the Space Gun. Where Cabal sees this technology as fundamental for the heroic exploration of space, Theotocopulos opposes the notion of eternal progress it symbolizes. Cabal's vision triumphs, his triumphant concluding speech prophesying humankind's ultimate conquest of space. In a world where the plane was barely three decades old, such speculation was remarkably forward-thinking. Competing characters debate the virtues of such thinking, but the uplifting finale underpins the film's fundamentally positive perspective.

If *Things To Come* put its faith in technology still to be invented, Shangri-La, the utopian idyll of Frank Capra's *Lost Horizon*, suggests the benefits of a simpler past. The action begins in a recognizably boisterous 1930s, in this case in China, where a group of Westerners attempt to escape a local rebellion. Robert Conway, a brilliant diplomat and charismatic leader, facilitates their flight on the final plane which includes a small group including his brother George; the terminally-ill pessimist Gloria; Lovett, an eccentric paleontologist, and a cynical fraudster, Barnard. Unbeknownst to them, the plane has been hijacked and is flown toward Shangri-La. Although it crashes short of its destination, a rescue party led by a mysterious emissary, Chang, brings the survivors to the secret world of Shangri-La, hidden in a valley surrounded by mountains. Before the narrative begins, title cards address the audience directly:

> In these days of wars and rumors of wars haven't you ever dreamed of a place where there was peace and security, where living was not a struggle but a lasting delight? Of course you have. So has every man since Time Began. Always the same dream. Sometimes he calls it Utopia. Sometimes the Fountain of Youth. Sometimes merely "that little chicken farm." (1:15–1:42)

Where the eventual utopia of Wells' Everytown lies a century in the future, *Lost Horizon* suggests that utopia already exists. Or rather, that the conditions for something like Shangri-La do not require destructive wars, advanced technology and prolonged reconstruction, but the activation of the human predilection for utopia and an awareness of the damage inflicted by current systems of thought and social organization. Shangri-La is a bucolic paradise rather than a hi-tech metropolis (it has no electronic communication with the outside world). Its guiding principle is not progress but kindness.

The narrative structures of the two films accentuate their different approaches to the presentation of the respective utopias and their appeal to audiences. *Things to Come* follows sequentially from war-threatened present, through dark interlude to a relatively brief climatic triumph in the Everytown of 2036. After the initial escape flight, most of the screen time in *Lost Horizon* is spent in Shangri-La itself, as the survivors overcome their initial suspicions and bewilderment and (except for George Conway) develop as human beings, learning to love life in a world without greed, brutality and desire, one that values beauty, culture and community. One consequence of this utopian life is that people age far more slowly, living for hundreds of years. Despite these benefits, George never overcomes his negative assessment, finding a confederate in Shangri-La's Maria. He convinces his reluctant brother to leave with them, but beyond the pristine environment Maria ages rapidly, George goes mad with this revelation and dies, and Robert forges on alone back to "civilization." There, after telling his fantastic tale to a British diplomat named Gainsford, he escapes back to Shangri-La. Gainsford, questioned in London by his fellow civil servants as to if he believes in Conway's seemingly fantastic tales, replies emphatically: "Yes. I believe it because I want to believe it.... Here's my hope that we all find our Shangri-Las" (2:05:44–2:06:10). Even the bureaucrat actively embraces the film's utopian spirit. As they raise a toast, Capra cuts to a final shot of an exhausted but exultant Conway approaching the mountain pass that leads back to Shangri-La, as bells ring out in celebration. While both films end on an upbeat note, their utopian versions are distinct, almost contradictory. Wells puts faith in technology, while *Lost Horizon* suggests that utopias are less technological transformations than places of revamped consciousness. The extended screen time spent in the alluring vistas as well as the lengthy arguments presented by Chang and others are designed to convince the film's viewers of Shangri-La's subtle virtues. The film proved a critical success (winning two Oscars), its lasting value registered later when it was added to the National Film Registry for work that is "culturally, historically, or aesthetically significant." *Things to Come* and *Lost Horizon* do not, of course, exhaust the possibilities of utopian films, and though they both were produced in the 1930s, they suggest distinctiveness rather than uniformity, valuably exemplifying different arguments for utopian worlds, and providing compelling representations of very different types of good place.

World War II and the onset of the Cold War laid waste to most notions of global utopias. *Things to Come* had explicitly posited such a war, prophesying a period of barbarity and then a technology-driven renewal. But the increasingly polarized world was closer to the vision of Orwell than of Wells. In the absence of the latter's benevolent world government, political and ideological conflicts dominated. The consumerism of the 1950s (primarily in the United States) and the explosion of youth culture in the 1960s more generally in the West allowed for elements of hope and prosperity to incubate, but nuclear arms races, and proxy wars fought on dubious grounds around the globe provided insurmountable barriers to global flourishing. The fifties could be understood less as a consumerist paradise than as a decade of numbing conformity, exposed in films such as *The Invasion of the Bodysnatchers* (1956), while the counterculture of the sixties, for all its youthful energy, could not stop the Vietnam War or challenge the dominance of global superpowers. Films that initially seem set in futures such as the "perfect world of total pleasure" portrayed in the twenty-third-century domed city of *Logan's Run* (1976) are exposed as delusions designed to hide the reality (in this instance) that all inhabitants must die at the age of 30 to sustain the society. *Logan's Run* attacked the materialism, hedonism and ageism of the seventies, exemplifying the trope redeployed in films such as *Gattaca* (1997), *The Truman Show* (1998) and *The Island* (2005) in which an apparent utopia is revealed as a dystopia from which the newly awakened protagonist must escape. Like *Things to Come* and *Lost Horizon*, these films displayed cinema's unrivalled power to present vivid, multidimensional representations of attractive worlds that bedazzle their characters and audiences (at least initially).

Spike Jonze's *Her* (2013) is rare among modern films in presenting and exploring what is essentially a non-threatening if somewhat bland utopia. The film posits a near-future Los Angeles whose environment is pleasant and whose people are materially prosperous and seemingly happy, a far cry from the hellish 2019 Los Angeles portrayed in *Blade Runner* (1982). Wealth and ease hide, however, the reality that in a technologically advanced world human emotions and interactions have become artificial. *Her*'s lonely protagonist, Theodore Twombley, cannot connect emotionally, so purchases an AI operating system that promises to function as a companion. The film explores the reality behind the utopian veneer of social media, exploring how technology has damaged meaningful personal interaction. The film plays with questions of human and AI identity and the possibility of emotional interaction between the two. Many films exploring these themes (*Blade Runner*, *AI*, and *Ex Machina* among them) present dystopian worlds in which one group threatens the other, sometimes with extinction. *Her* takes a different approach, allowing the AIs to evolve quickly alongside and then well beyond the humans. They then leave *en masse* to engage in higher forms of existence, without harming the humans who created them. The film ends with Theodore and the love interest hiding in plain sight, Amy, contemplating a future where human-to-human interaction might rekindle, including her own relationship. *Her* ends gently, Theodore and Amy suggesting the possibility that humans might recapture and express the genuine emotions that the film makes clear are more important than material comforts. Utopia lies in genuine human interaction rather than in Wellsian technology.

Many dystopian films depict environmentally degraded if not entirely exhausted environments. Perhaps this century's most influential environmental documentary film to date, *An Inconvenient Truth* (2006), painted a dystopian scenario if changes are not made. One welcome alternative to the depressingly catalogue of environmental disaster films is Damon Gameau's low-budget documentary *2040* (2019) which asks what the planet will look like in the eponymous year, when Gameau's young daughter Velvet will be an adult. Sincere but never po-faced, open-minded and inventive, *2040* styles itself an exercise in fact-based dreaming. The film is underpinned by interviews with experts and practitioners from several countries and contains short statements from young children who offer their thoughtful, surprising and often amusing assessments of the current state of the world and of their hopes and fears. In finding current responses to such problems as energy use and distribution, transport, food production and consumption, population and pollution, Gameau limits himself to what is currently available, asking the question: "What would be the world of 2040 look like if we just embraced the best of what already exists?" The film moves back and forth between the world of 2019 and that of 2040, where a fictional older version of his daughter exists in a world transformed for the better (and in which Gamerau, made up to look the age he will be in 2040, self-deprecatingly plays the role of embarrassing dad). Against the overwhelming diet of dire predictions that can induce pessimistic resignation, *2040* presents a fact-based argument for hope in the future given action in the present. With cruel irony, the film was released in the run-up to the Covid-19 pandemic that kept people out of cinemas, so that its practical optimism did not receive the critical attention the film deserved.

Dystopian Films

The norm among films has been far darker. Claeys ends his detailed account of the history of literary dystopias on the prudently negative note that "they warn us against and educate us about real-life dystopias.... pessimism has its place" (Claeys 2017, 501). The prevalence of dystopian films in the century when film came of age has not abated in the twenty-first century. Again, this is unsurprising, given the multinational reach of terrorism, financial insecurity, pandemics, the prospect of technological tsunamis, the rapid rise of a surveillance culture and the planetary threat of climate disaster. Yet, just as both *Things to Come* and *Lost Horizon* contained dystopian elements (particularly the prospect of war that haunted the 1930s), some early dystopian films contained utopian aspects, or attempt to reconcile dystopian and utopian impulses.

One of the earliest and still one of the most influential of these, Fritz Lang's *Metropolis* (1927), presents a world separated into an elite, who thrive in materialist splendor high above the workers who toil below as subterranean slaves. The film visually contrasts the modernist utopian spaces of a high-tech metropolis (a model for films such as *Blade Runner*) with the dangerous and monotonous world the workers inhabit. The freedom and sensuality of elite life requires a slave class, their dehumanization suggested emblematically by the uniforms they wear, their expressionless faces, and their programmed movements, performed in unison to the tireless rhythms of machines they ostensibly control. Lang exposes the brutalizing effect of the relatively new Taylorized industrial processes, and *Metropolis* excoriates the oppressive pleasure-seekers who rule Metropolis. Various subplots (including a mad scientist, the sensuous female robot Maria and her saintly human equivalent, as well as a scion of the elite who revolts against the system) complicate the inevitable conflict between the downtrodden and their putative masters, but the film ends with the reconciliation of competing factions and the prospect of a better future for all. Despite the positive finale, the film's emotional power lies in its critical depiction of the dehumanizing effects of emerging ways of life, whether it be bleak uniformity, oppressive technology or empty hedonism. Charlie Chaplin would refashion some of these elements to darkly satiric effect in *Modern Times* (1936), in which the Tramp, having become essentially a human robot on an assembly line, is literally drawn into the machine. Chaplin's brilliant physical comedy plays on the fear of humans being turned into robots, while Lang's Maria suggests the possibility of a robot becoming human, or of being indistinguishable from a human.

The potentially porous line between human and non-human proved a rich and multidimensional theme in the work of Philip K. Dick, whose hyper-productive output and capacity to illuminate new possibilities in vivid cinema-friendly terms mark him as the late-twentieth-century equivalent of H.G. Wells. Writers and directors have freely adapted Dick's work into some of the most visually arresting and thought-provoking dystopias, perhaps most effectively in *Blade Runner*. Director Ridley Scott presents a vision of environmental disaster, constant surveillance and junk consumerism where most people have left the planet now under threat from android replicants who are increasingly difficult to tell from actual humans. The threat of various forms of not-quite-humans constitutes a recurring theme in dystopian films, from the advanced robots of the film version of *Westworld* (1973), the incessant killers in *The Terminator* series or the sentient machines in *I, Robot*. These films speak in different ways to anxieties about human control. In *Ex Machina* (2014), this theme is explored through the all-too-common example of the sexually alluring robot (instigated in *Metropolis* and replicated in the various *Blade Runner* films), although in *Ex Machina* heterosexual male fantasies are critically scrutinized and the male protagonists are brutally killed off by the "female" robot who escapes captivity to the "real world" beyond.

The massively successful *Matrix* franchise (inaugurated in 1999) takes the anxiety about the divide between humans and technology even further, projecting a future in which humans are merely biological batteries for intelligent machines. In this instance, the machines create the alternative reality, the Matrix, which, given the actual hellish condition of the planet, is relatively utopian, even if a ruse to dupe and exploit human energy. The *Matrix* films to date have brilliantly utilized film's capacity to create plausible representations of hyperreal places in order to investigate the nature of perceived reality, challenging the audience's willingness to suspend disbelief and to accept the world as it seems. Presenting a small group of humans who come to understand the truth of the dystopian reality and fight against odds to resist it, the *Matrix* films follow the dystopian tradition that sees illuminated rebels fighting against oppressive systems that others fail to comprehend, or have accommodated to passively. Collectively, such films visualize the massive and accelerating impact of technology over the little more than a century and a quarter since films first appeared.

Surveillance embodies another form of potentially oppressive technological advance. In *Minority Report* (2007), based on a 1956 Philip K. Dick novella, murders in Washington DC have been eliminated because a system of psychics and advanced surveillance can read the minds of those merely thinking of committing the crime. The notion of arresting people before they commit a crime had particular resonance in a post-9/11 world. In the earlier satire, *The Truman Show* (1998), surveillance is monetized entertainment for a mass audience who have watched the television show's protagonist, Truman Burbank, since birth. Growing up in the faux-50s utopia of Seahaven (in fact, a giant set peopled by actors) Truman initially is unaware of his situation. Once he finds out, he escapes to the grim contemporary world beyond the set, swapping artificial utopia for reality. By contrast, in *Gattaca* (1997), genetic surveillance from birth imposes a form of biological apartheid. The genetically elite "Valids" live a utopian life that potentially allows them access to space exploration, while the genetically inferior "InValids" are reduced to service roles. The supposed InValid Vincent Freeman assumes the identity of a crippled Valid, Jerome Morrow, proving through force of will that he is capable of overcoming whatever genetic deficiency he has been assigned statistically at birth. In films such as these, protagonists struggle to assert their individuality and their capacity to overcome or undermine totalizing systems of control.

The more recent fear of environmental catastrophe invigorates many dystopian films. Humanity's degrading of the environment sometimes results in utopian enclaves separated from the dystopian world beyond or below. A stimulating early example is *Soylent Green* (1973) a police procedural film set in a twenty-first century in which overpopulation and pollution have degraded the planet, and in which the plankton-based food of the film's title sustains a population divided into the privileged few and the beleaguered many. In fact, because of the sullied oceans, there is no plankton; Soylent Green is made out of people, meaning humans have survived unwittingly as cannibals. Environmental degradation is a strong possibility for the infertility of women in both *The Handmaid's Tale*, a disappointing 1990 film adaptation of Margaret Atwood's classic novel, and *Children of Men* (2008), Alfonso Cuaron's riveting update of P.D. James's 1992 novel. In the latter, cities are polluted and crowded, though the countryside offers some form of haven. Britain has walled itself in from the outside world, but the reality that the human race must inevitably die out has produced widespread chaos and torpor (suicide is supported by a government program). The birth of a new child offers hope, but the film ends with the fate of that child unresolved. Any positive future depends on unlikely odds. Depleted environments dominate the Young Adult subgenre of dystopian films (including *The Hunger Games*, *Divergent* and *Maze Runner* series) in which youthful protagonists battle adult authority in oppressive worlds left to or imposed upon them. It says much for possibilities nascent even in the bleakest environments, though, that the final scene of *The Hunger Games* tetralogy has the still-youthful Katniss Everdeen and Peeta Mellark together in an idyllic meadow with their young children. Even in darkest worlds, the natural environment offers at least the glimpse of a utopian alternative.

CONCLUSION

Film quickly became the mass art form of the twentieth century, producing vivid narratives that captured and helped shape the hopes, dreams and fears of global audiences. While many films derived from literary sources, film itself proved a medium well-suited to conveying utopian and dystopian projections to a global audience experiencing immense and often alarming changes and challenges. Dystopian images, from the powerfully seductive female robot of *Metropolis* and Chaplin's *Tramp* within in the cogs of a huge machine, through to the dark landscape of *Blade Runner* and Arnold Schwarzenegger's Terminator, have seared themselves in the minds of billions of spectators. Utopian films have been far less prevalent, as befits a time transformed by often brutal forces: Shangri-La can seem like an escape from reality rather than a realistic and achievable goal. It might seem a critique of the medium that its predominant mode is dystopian. Or we might take this as a positive, recognizing that films presenting dystopian futures warn spectators about dangerous social forces, nascent problems, conceptual blind spots, traps and dead ends. And in presenting arresting and resilient individuals, from Linda Connor in *The Terminator* to Katniss Everdeen in *The Hunger Games*, from Neo, Trinity and

Morpheus in *The Matrix* to Truman Burbank in *The Truman Show*, among countless others, film has played a crucial role in critically evaluating modern society and in suggesting creative options for better worlds.

REFERENCES

Anderson, Michael (dir.). 1976. *Logan's Run*. MGM.

Baccolini, Raffaella, and Tom Moylan, eds. 2003. *Dark Horizons: Science Fiction and the Dystopian Imagination*. London: Routledge.

Blaim, Artur, and Ludmila Gruszewska-Blaim. 2015. On Utopia, Adaptation and Utopian Film Analysis. In *Mediated Utopias: From Literature to Cinema*, ed. Artur Blaim and Ludmila Gruszewska-Blaim. Oxford: Peter Lang.

Capra, Frank (dir.). 1937. *Lost Horizon*. Columbia Pictures.

Chaplin, Charles (dir.). 1936. *Modern Times*. Charles Chaplin Productions.

Claeys, Gregory. 2017. *Dystopia: A Natural History, A Study of Modern Despotism, Its Antecedents, and Its Literary Diffractions*. Oxford: Oxford University Press.

Fitting, Peter. 1993. What Is a Utopian Film? An Introductory Taxonomy. *Utopian Studies* 4: 1–17.

Fleischer, Richard (dir.). 1973. *Soylent Green*.

Gameau. Damon (dir.) 2019. *2040*. Good Things Productions.

Garland, Alex (dir.). 2014. *Ex Machina*. Universal Pictures.

Hammond, John. 1993. Introduction. In *The Shape of Things to Come*, ed. H.G. Wells, xxxi–xxxix. London: Everyman.

Jonze, Spike (dir.). 2013. *Her*. Annapurna Pictures.

Lang, Fritz (dir.). 1927. *Metropolis*. UFA.

Méliès, Georges (dir.). 1902. *Le Voyage dans la Lune*. Star Film.

Menzies, William Cameron (dir.). 1936. *Things to Come*. London Film Production.

Scott, Ridley (dir.). 1982. *Blade Runner*. The Ladd Company.

Weir, Peter (dir.). 1998. *The Truman Show*. Paramount Pictures.

Wells, H.G. 1933. *The Shape of Things to Come: The Ultimate Revolution*. London: Dent.

———. 2005. *A Modern Utopia*. London: Penguin.

Comics, Manga and Graphic Novels

Miguel Ramalhete Gomes

INTRODUCTION: THE UTOPIAN AND THE GRAPHIC

The conjunction of text and static image was a feature of the utopian genre from its inception, namely in the detailed woodcut map of Thomas More's *Utopia*, and especially with the addition of further visual aids in the 1518 Basel edition.[1] This early connection between utopianism and visual culture means that narratives told through a sequence of images were already a privileged site for the development of the utopian and the dystopian imagination. Indeed, by the twentieth century, comics were telling highly sophisticated narratives through the combination of word and image. They offered a medium for spectacular visual experimentation which was often inexpensively distributed in newspapers and magazines. On the one hand, comics could show utopia in narrative sequences of images, without needing to be as verbose as literary utopias; on the other hand, they could do so cheaply, unlike film.

By exploring the budding genre's formal limits, comics' authors quickly made use of the potentialities of architectural fantasy and the detailed exploration of fantastic urban spaces, as developed in illustrations from previous centuries. But comics have also been said to contain "little utopias of disorder" (Bukatman 2011, 11). Bringing together an exploration of dream worlds (*Little Nemo*), of Cockayne (*Li'l Abner*; cf. Sargent 2015, 34), of science fiction (*Buck Rogers* and *Flash Gordon*) and of other places (*Tarzan*; cf.

M. R. Gomes (✉)
University of Lisbon, Lisbon, Portugal

P. Marks et al. (eds.), *The Palgrave Handbook of Utopian and Dystopian Literatures*, https://doi.org/10.1007/978-3-030-88654-7_19

Savramis 1987), early comics began to apply utopian or dystopian world-building systematicity to flesh out newspaper strips, Sunday comics and finally individual albums. The dystopian theme is, however, much more prevalent in comics than utopia: although panoramic visions of advanced societies are a frequent feature of SF or superhero comics, adventure stories depend on some form of conflict, hence the greater frequency of dystopian worlds or times (Lefèvre 2016).

Comics has become a global language with important intersections into other forms of mass popular culture, such as film and gaming. Its study has, in the meantime, critically come of age and comics are rightly considered to be an artistic medium (cf. Groensteen 2007; Petersen 2011; Smith and Duncan 2012). The medium's international reach and remarkable popularity were also due to the development of major national or regional styles and conventions. Comics have only been around since the late nineteenth century, but the sheer number of comics dealing with utopia and dystopia is already overwhelming. The following sections will therefore focus on three major traditions, each originating in a specific national context, but having gone on to become global phenomena[2]: Franco-Belgian *bande dessinée*; Japanese manga, with parallel developments in anime; and Anglo-American comics, from superhero comics to the graphic novel. Nevertheless, because each is a complex historical system—ranging from different magazines privileging specific subgenres and demographics to self-contained albums and their auteurs—they can only be represented here by a limited number of examples.[3]

FRANCO-BELGIAN BANDE DESSINÉE: TECHNOLOGICAL OPTIMISM, SATIRE, AND DYSTOPIAN SF

One early and influential euchronia in comics is *Zig et Puce au XXIe siècle* (1935), by Alain Saint-Ogan (cf. Baroni 2015). However, as Nicolas Tellop (2017) explains, it was the technological optimism surrounding the Expo 58 in Brussels that can be said to have profoundly characterized an important moment in the history of Franco-Belgian comics, with their depiction of a simple, well-organized society barely recovered from the ravages of World War II but untouched yet by the historical processes of decolonization and counterculture. This miniature model world inhabited by boys and men, which nowadays has been so ideologically challenged (cf. Miller 2007), can be found in the *Spirou* stories of Franquin, the *Blake & Mortimer* albums of Edgar P. Jacobs and the style of Hergé. This belief in progress was not without its own satirical, anti-utopian moments, as when technology fails (or works too well) in *Spirou*, or in more complex iterations, as when Blake and Mortimer, in *L'énigme de l'Atlantide* (1955–1956, 1957), travel to the underground society of Atlantis, which, having survived the cataclysm narrated by Plato, has managed to become a futuristic superpower unknown to the world, only to be ultimately ravaged by civil war.

On the other hand, Pascal Lefèvre (2016) has contended that there is a tendency for dystopian or post-apocalyptic scenarios in Franco-Belgian comics, especially from the 1960s onwards. These tend to be future dystopias—such as Jacobs' *Le Piège diabolique* (1960–1961, 1962), where Mortimer travels to the year 5060 and finds a post-atomic-war society organized as an ant colony—and extra-terrestrial dystopias; Lefèvre exemplifies with the Terango albums of Greg's *Luc Orient* series (1967–1994), and one might add several albums of Pierre Christin and Jean-Claude Mezieres' *Valerian* (1967–).

Later postmodernist takes on dystopia in French comics reveal a tougher vision of the future, combined with a much more exacerbated satirical dimension. These exist alongside softer versions of the utopian theme: *Simon du Fleuve* (1976–1989), by Claude Auclair, represents a post-apocalyptic rural communitarian utopia; in *Achille Talon et l'archipel de Sanzunron* (1987), Greg's protagonist flees from a money-driven society to an archipelago where money does not exist, a utopia which he then proceeds to ruin by reinventing banking; and *En pleine guerre froide* (1984), by Jean-Louis Floch e Jean-Luc Fromental, compiles in postmodernist fashion a series of colorful and disconcerting utopias and dystopias.

The 1980s would, however, be marked by a superior dystopian achievement, *The Incal* (1980–1988), by Alejandro Jodorowsky and Jean Giraud, better known as Mœbius, which introduced readers to the "Jodoverse", or "Metabarons Universe". Jodorowsky wrote several prequels, sequels and spin-offs, whereas Mœbius also did his own explorations of breath-taking utopian and dystopian vistas in *The Airtight Garage* and *The World of Edena*. *The Incal* tells the story of John Difool, a detective who moves around a space-opera universe, in which extreme capitalist consumerism and postmodern spectacle—the public face of an authoritarian and oligarchical empire ruthlessly secured by the military power of the Metabarons and the cult of the Technopriests—are the object of incessant satire. *The Incal* could still allow for mystical reconciliation and for the redeeming force of love; other forays into the genre, by Philippe Druillet (*Les six voyages de Lone Sloane*), by Chantal Montellier (*1996*), and especially by Enki Bilal, have been much darker. After explorations of the theme of utopia in three albums drawn by Bilal and written by Pierre Cristin, namely *La ville qui n'existait pas* (1977), dealing with the impossibility of realizing a theory or an illusion, which can never coincide with whatever is actually constructed (cf. Saouter-Caya 1985, 77), Bilal authored the three parts of *The Nikopol Trilogy* (1980–1992), the first part of which, *La Foire aux immortels*, depicts a fascist dictatorship in 2023 France, where women are imprisoned in underground clinics for purposes of reproduction. This grotesquely misogynistic regime is toppled and replaced by a revolutionary government, which, with its uniform reddish haircuts and talk of ideological models, is an improvement, but a satirically undercut one (cf. Iung 2018, 13–23). Bilal's work would go on to show an increasing attention to ecological catastrophe.

Documentary accounts in comic book form of real intentional communities complement such wildly satirized imaginary worlds. Two examples are *La Communauté* (2008 and 2010), by Yann Benoît et Hervé Tanquerelle, about a community formed in the wake of the countercultural movement of May 1968, and *L'essai* (2015), by Nicolas Debon, about an anarchist colony founded in 1903 in the French Ardennes. They testify to the persistent interest in real utopianism in the wake of decades of dystopian visions.

The Post-Apocalyptic Imagination of Manga and Anime

To consider the role of utopia and especially of dystopia in manga and anime can be a daunting task, since, although mixed with optimism about technological advances, the apocalyptic imagination has quite understandably played a decisive part in post-war Japanese culture. One unavoidable author is Osamu Tezuka (cf. Power 2009), whose *Mighty Atom* (known in the West as *Astro Boy*) was serialized from 1952 to 1968; its animated version, starting in 1963, was the first Japanese animation to use the style now associated with anime. Mighty Atom was an android boy living in "a futuristic city-state called the 'Atom continent'", which soon became "the symbol of Japan's postwar pursuit of a new, peaceful type of high technology" (Schodt 2007, 19, 120).

The theme of nuclear energy and weapons is a common one in Japanese SF manga, and nuclear disasters are a frequent narrative device. Variations of this theme became darker and more pessimistic throughout the 1980s. Katsuhiro Otomo's *Akira* (1982–1990, with an anime version directed by Otomo himself in 1988) became a watershed moment in manga (cf. Klausner 2015; de la Iglesia 2018). It took place in Neo-Tokyo, nearly four decades after a mysterious nuclear explosion that devastates Tokyo and initiates World War III. Developing around a number of adolescents and children with technologically induced superpowers, the second half of the story takes place in the city's ruins, in a post-apocalyptic failed state named The Great Tokyo Empire, whose first action is the appropriation of foreign aid and expulsion of American and United Nations military. Interestingly, once Akira and Tetsuo, the superhuman figures behind The Great Tokyo Empire, disappear and foreign forces return, these are once more expelled and once more in the name of empire. This time, however, this is done by the teenager protagonists of the story, who declare that any external intervention beyond mere aid—including intervention by the Japanese government—will be considered an interference in internal affairs. This imperial theme strikes an ominous note, thoroughly explored by the body horror of the unstable figure of Tetsuo, but it is counterbalanced by its appropriation by a group of disaffected teenagers. As Susan J. Napier has put it regarding the 1988 version of *Akira*, "Tetsuo's monstrousness can thus be coded in ideological terms as a reflection of Japan's own deep-seated ambivalence at this time, partly glorying in its new identity but also partly fearing it" (2005, 40).

Otomo would return to the post-apocalyptic genre in *The Legend of Mother Sarah* (1990–2004), while other manga, such as the equally popular *The Ghost in the Shell* (1989–1990, with an anime version from 1995), by Masamune Shirow, developed the technological sublime patent in *Akira* and especially its cyberpunk aesthetic. Exploring the idea of what it means to have a cybernetic body, *The Ghost in the Shell* was set in a violent future in which technological advances affecting the notion of identity and consciousness are shown to be both fragile and deeply challenging (cf. Orbaugh 2006; Stoddard 2010).

The world of anime has also yielded several utopias and dystopias,[4] namely in Hideaki Anno's *Neon Genesis Evangelion* anime (1995–1996), which pits *mechas* (giant robots) against alien invaders in the post-apocalyptic and futuristic city Tokyo-3. But the most productive anime from the point of view of Utopian Studies is the work of Hayao Miyazaki (cf. Napier 2018), whose films for Studio Ghibli have revealed an impressive combination of artistic quality and box-office success in Japan and abroad, especially since *Princess Mononoke* (1997) and *Spirited Away* (2001).[5] His *Nausicaä of the Valley of the Wind* (1984) is a post-apocalyptic SF story with a strong ecological message, whereas *Laputa: Castle in the Sky* (1986) offers a variation of the theme of ancient technology being resurrected for destructive purposes; the destruction of nature by civilization is one of Miyazaki's returning themes, from *Princess Mononoke*'s questioning of the forces of progress to literalized allegories of river pollution in *Spirited Away*. Yet, his repeated figuration of flying devices reveals a fascination with the technology of flight and an avoidance of technophobia. A holistic approach can also be found at work in his detailed and infinitely imaginative worldbuilding, so that his worlds are often versions of the ecotopia, threatened, destroyed or potentially redeeming (cf. Liou 2010; Wegner 2014, 257ff.).

SUPERHERO WORLDBUILDING AND GRAPHIC NOVEL DYSTOPIAS

North American comics, dominated by the secular mythology of the superhero as a god among humans, bring different emphases to the utopian and the dystopian theme. The classical formula of superhero comics posits a conflict between villains who want to radically change the world—sometimes by destroying it, but also by attempting to rule it or to painfully alter aspects of it—and superheroes who manage to preserve it (cf. Veitch and Kulcsar 2018; Hatfield et al. 2013). This conservative perspective therefore tends to understand radical change and utopian blueprints as inherently dystopian and it therefore deems villains those who do not conform.

There are, however, exceptions to this rule, usually referring to utopias or dystopias that already exist and that do not depend on changing society: these include utopias in hiding (the city of the Inhumans, for example), alien worlds (such as Jack Kirby's New Genesis and Apokolips), future worlds that have benefited from the presence of superheroes (in the *Legion of Super Heroes*), and, above all, heterotopian enclaves, such as the Savage World, the island of Genosha and the X-Men's School for Gifted Youngsters. The School's safe environment, alluding to LGBT struggles, became increasingly inclusive during Chris Claremont's classic stint—while including several dystopian threads, such as the "Days of Future Past" (1981) story—to the point that its celebration of plurality became a battleground for competing utopian projects in Grant Morrison's *New X-Men* (2001–2004). In *New X-Men*, the theme of utopia and of the failure of its dreamers—either too ambitious or too timorous—finds expression in a student rebellion, whose leader protests that Utopia keeps being promised but never really arrives. As Mark Singer has put it, "Morrison has taken the narrative constraints faced by any never-ending, corporate-owned serial – the impossibility of establishing any permanent change to the status quo or bringing the series to a definitive ending – and turned them into indictments of the protagonists' failures to change their society" (2012, 173).

Morrison was, however, writing in the aftermath of a revolution in superhero comics, initiated by Alan Moore's *Miracleman* (1982–). In the wake of increasingly violent comics, such as Judge Dredd (1977–), who distributes instant justice in the future dystopia of Mega-City One, Alan Moore revived a 1950s British comics hero and, in what later became known as superhero revisionism (cf. Hyman 2017), explored what would realistically happen to such a character, with the powers of a god, in the 1980s. Moore's realism meant that the final manifestation of the main villain, Nemesis, was an act of shockingly illustrated genocide set in London, from which no there was no going back. This triggers Miracleman's decision to do what only villains had done before him: to take the construction of utopia into his own hands (cf. Wolf-Meyer 2003). As James Chapman explains, Miracleman and his companions "destroy all nuclear weapons, restructure the global economy, restore the ozone layer and eradicate disease and poverty. The outcome is a benevolent dictatorship of super beings" (Chapman 2011, 193). Issue #14 leaves the title character gazing at his completed utopia and wondering why there should be people in it who do not want to be perfect in a perfect world. Though plagued by copyright issues, Neil Gaiman and Mark Buckingham added a small number of issues to the serialization, later collected under the title *The Golden Age* (1992), in which they explored what ordinary life is like in an extraordinary utopia. Purposefully reducing the presence of Moore's godlike protagonists to a minimum, it showed that couples were still separated, and teenagers still defied the system, whereas utopia came with unexpected practical challenges, namely what to do with former spies, suspicious of a world alleging that it had no more need for them.

Partly due to a complicated publication history, *Miracleman* made a smaller impact than Moore's later revisionist take on the superhero mythology: *Watchmen* (1985–1987). Admittedly, *Watchmen* was the result of a much more impressive creative effort on the part of Moore and Dave Gibbons, reimagining an alternate reality in which vigilantes had been around since the influential first appearance of Superman in *Action Comics*, in 1938. In the 1980s, at the height of the Cold War and the threat of atomic annihilation, one such "hero" decides to unite the world, by making it believe it has been savagely attacked by an imaginary alien enemy: bringing about the utopia of global peace is once more done at the cost of genocide, this time in New York. Even though the critical dystopia of *Watchmen* is replaced by a eutopia at the end, this is a flawed utopia, since it "poses the fundamental question of what cost we are willing to pay or require others to pay to achieve a good life" (Sargent 2003, 226; cf. Gomes 2013).

Variations of godlike superheroes behaving like villains and forcefully bringing about their idea of utopia became more common in comics, with such variants as *Superman: Red Son* (2003), by Mark Millar, which imagines what would have happened if the space capsule containing baby Superman had fallen in the Soviet Union, instead of in the US. Superman becomes a communist superhero and by the end of the story has become the nearly global ruler of a totalitarian dystopia (Lewis 2010, 619).

The revisionist approach to superheroes has often been associated with a new form: the graphic novel. This canonical "upgrade" of the medium of comics from popular culture into a format associated with what is today the most popular and most respected of literary forms, the novel, has normally come with suggestions of a greater literary density, even though, like nineteenth-century novels, many graphic novels were first published in serial form (cf. Baetens and Frey 2014; Tabachnick 2017). One such example, Alan Moore and David Lloyd's *V for Vendetta* (1982–1990), also came with a more direct intertextual engagement with the genre of the dystopia: in it, an anarchist terrorist brings down a fascist dictatorship in 1990s Britain, in what was the very near future at the time of writing, while taking revenge of his former abusers.

V for Vendetta's originality and impact cannot be overestimated. It is still probably the comic book that most people first associate with the genre of dystopia. This is also due to its afterlife, in James McTeigue's 2005 film adaptation and in the adoption of V's Guy Fawkes mask in hacking actions by Anonymous and street protests by Occupy. Although V's mask went on to become a political symbol, the depiction of the fascist regime was deeply unglamorous, instead emphasizing its racist, sexist and homophobic brutality, as well as the degradation and banality of the fascist mind. *V for Vendetta* was also Moore's form of cultural resistance to Thatcherite ideology (cf. Gray 2010; Di Liddo 2009, 111ff.). Its poetic, intertextual, and psychological density also set it apart from a medium that was still associated with easy commercial profit, while aligning it with a very British version of the dystopian, post-apocalyptic story, with clear links to Orwell and Huxley.

Moore's use of a wealth of literary allusions and quotations, mixing high and low cultural references in a medium associated with mass culture, and especially his development of the dystopian literary tradition made *V for Vendetta* a favorite object of Utopian Studies (cf. Paik 2010; Garlington 2012;

Vanderbeke and Vanderbeke 2015). The story's open ending, in the immediate aftermath of complete governmental breakdown, is ambiguous as to what will follow, but has been interpreted as a hopeful anarchist revolution (cf. Moffett 2016), whereas the film version considerably toned down Moore's anarchism and converted V into a liberal freedom fighter more in tune with less ambiguous Hollywood revolutionaries.

GRAPHIC META-UTOPIAS

As a conclusion, it is worth returning to Franco-Belgian BD, namely to what is perhaps the most accomplished approach to worldbuilding in comics, the series *The Obscure Cities* (*Les Cités Obscures*), by François Schuiten and Benoît Peeters, begun in 1983. The sheer variety and mass of utopian, dystopian, anti-utopian and uchronian material in the history of comics find its apex in this series. Based on an extensive knowledge of the tradition of utopian and dystopian literature and cinema, and making use of uchronias, retro-futurism, parallel worlds, and generic hybridity, the series *The Obscure Cities* merits individual attention.

Ever since *Murailles de Samaris* (1983), Schuiten and Peeters have published some thirty objects, including conventional comics albums, illustrated stories, a film and all manners of hybrid documents which present themselves as coming from within this fictional world: a library report (*L'Archiviste*, 1987); a facsimile of a newspaper (*L'Echo des Cités*, 1993); even a large tourist guide, which describes several of the Obscure Cities in remarkable detail (*Le Guide des Cités*, 1996). The main albums of the series comprise a complex web of interrelated stories which revolve around the exploration of urban or constructed spaces.

The series is not simply a utopia, a dystopia or even their critical versions, although individual cities could be characterized in terms of each of these categories; the catalogue of a 2019–2020 exhibition around *The Obscure Cities* at La Maison d'Ailleurs, a museum of science fiction, utopias, and extraordinary journeys in Yverdon-les-Bains (Switzerland), appropriately organized essays by François Rosset and Marc Atallah around the poles of utopia and dystopia (Atallah 2019). Ultimately, the series can be best understood as a graphic meta-utopia, since it is "highly self-reflexive as a study about the possibilities and problems of the genre and its variants, constructing itself out of the immense field of utopian literature and thinking" (Gomes 2007, 100). Schuiten and Peeters include frequent references and allusions to Kafka, Calvino, Borges, and especially Jules Verne, whose visions of the future help to shape a parallel world with the nineteenth-century ambience of retro-futuristic dreams. This universe composed of the anachronic scraps of European utopias is also the closest thing in comics to Thomas More's combination of humanistic erudition, satire and authorial obfuscation: the albums' erudite and often abstruse references are playful, and grand urban blueprints are always a page away from being debunked; like classical utopias, the stories of *The Obscure*

Cities often present themselves as real, or allude to passages linking these cities to the real world, while at the same time inquiring about the always fragile nature of the reality of their world.

Its overriding interest in architecture and urban planning allows for detailed experimentation with different architectural styles which are holistically projected onto urban landscapes in a manner that would have been impossible for organically developed European cities: from the Art Nouveau of Xhystos to the fascist architecture of Urbicande, the architect and the urbanist combines in the totalitarian figure of the "urbatect". While often self-referential to the point of solipsism, the series also responds to its authors' world, focusing, for instance, on the infamous process of "Brusselisation", that is, the indiscriminate construction of modernist high-rise buildings in older neighborhoods of Brussels around the late 1950s, as in the album *Brüsel* (1992).

The recent republication of all the original albums and surrounding material in four substantial tomes in a French edition by Casterman (2017–2019) suggests that the series may have reached its end, although Schuiten and Peeters continue to collaborate. The publication in 2020 of the first book-length overview of the entire series by the important critic Jan Baetens, *Rebuilding Story Worlds*: The Obscure Cities *by Schuiten and Peeters*, also demonstrates the continuing resonance and depth of the series, with chapters dedicated to worldbuilding, storytelling technique, genre, transmediality, and politics, among others. As an illustration of its unsystematic openness, Baetens proposes that "The underlying visual model of *The Obscure Cities* is not that of the jigsaw puzzle, which presupposes an existing totality and the possibility to achieve a complete view of it, but that of the mobile, more particularly that of an incomplete or multiplying mobile" (Baetens 2020: 92). Information on the series has also benefited from the unceasing labors of enthusiastic readers.Information on the series has also benefited from the unceasing labors of enthusiastic readers, namely in the establishment of an online repository, "Altaplana" where fans and critics have continued Schuiten and Peeters' work of mapping the world of *The Obscure Cities*: https://www.altaplana.be/en/start. After more than a century, the field of utopian and dystopian comics thus seems far from being exhausted and developments of its imaginary places may, therefore, be expected even beyond the utopian vistas on the double-page spread.

CONCLUSION

Although little over a century old, comics in their various historical forms and national iterations have tapped into the potentialities of the early interaction between word and image in Thomas More's *Utopia* and proved to be one of the most creative outlets for the utopian and dystopian imagination. In order to address both continuities and particularities, this chapter has abstained from a global approach and has considered instead three major traditions which have tended to dominate the field: Franco-Belgian *bande dessinée*, Japanese manga and anime, and Anglo-American comics, specifically superhero comics and the graphic novel. These allow one to trace a parallel and mutually influenced development responding to a mixture of technological optimism and post-apocalyptic anxiety in the post-war years, later tempered by an increasingly satirical and sceptical view of utopian worldbuilding. Together they contribute to what is already an impressive canon of graphic utopias and dystopias with representatives in every one of the three traditions considered here, namely in the work of Jodorowsky and Moebius, Enki Bilal, Katsuhiro Otomo, Hayao Miyazaki, Alan Moore, and culminating in François Schuiten and Benoît Peeters' *The Obscure Cities*, probably the most accomplished expression of the form of the graphic utopia. Comics' almost effortless traversal of the already porous boundaries between artistic expression and mass culture has secured their position as one of the most imaginative modes of utopian and dystopian storytelling and image-making; their vitality and expansiveness thus seem to be as never-ending as their future dreamscapes.

NOTES

1. I would like to gratefully acknowledge the help of my friend and colleague David Pinho Barros, from the University of Porto, who gave me several precious suggestions at the beginning of my research for this chapter.
2. The fluidity between these traditions becomes clearer if we notice that, for instance, Katsuhiro Otomo, the author of *Akira*, was visually influenced by the work of Mœbius; Otomo would go on to influence Frank Miller, the author of, among other things, the post-apocalyptic graphic novel *Ronin* (1983–1984). See Mazur and Danner (2014, 174–201).
3. It is unfortunately not possible to offer an adequate account of the global variety outside of these major traditions (including the world of *fumetti*, *manhua*, *manhwa*, webcomics, etc.) in this limited space.
4. The journal *ImageTexT: Interdisciplinary Comic Studies* includes a thematic issue (5.2) on "Anime and Utopia", at http://imagetext.eng lish.ufl.edu/archives/v5_2/.
5. For an online bibliography of Miyazaki's work, see https://sites.google. com/site/miyazakibib/.

REFERENCES

Atallah, Marc, ed. 2019. *MONDES imPARFAITS: Autour des Cités Obscures de Schuiten et Peeters*. Yverdon-les-Bains: Les Impressions Nouvelles/Maison d'Ailleurs.
Baetens, Jan, and Hugo Frey. 2014. *The Graphic Novel: An Introduction*. Cambridge: Cambridge University Press.
Baetens, Jan. 2020. *Rebuilding Story Worlds: The Obscure Cities by Schuiten and Peeters*. New Brunswick: Rutgers University Press.

Baroni, Raphaël. 2015. L'exploration temporelle comme modalité du voyage imaginaire dans la bande dessinée franco-belge (1930–1980). *Image [&] Narrative* 16 (2): 96–113.

Bukatman, Scott. 2011. Little Utopias of Disorder. *American Art* 25 (2): 11–14.

Chapman, James. 2011. *British Comics: A Cultural History*. London: Reaktion Books.

de la Iglesia, Martin. 2018. Has *Akira* Always Been a Cyberpunk Comic? *Arts* 7 (3): 1–13.

Di Liddo, Annalisa. 2009. *Alan Moore: Comics as Performance, Fiction as Scalpel*. Jackson: University Press of Mississippi.

Garlington, Ian. 2012. R for Reappropriation: The Function of Utopia in the Superhero Narratives of Alan Moore. *Osaka Literary Review* 50: 67–84.

Gomes, Miguel Ramalhete. 2007. The City and the Plan: Schuiten and Peeter's Graphic Meta-Utopias. *Spaces of Utopia: An Electronic Journal* 4: 88–105. http://ler.letras.up.pt.

———. 2013. "Nothing Ever Ends": Ending Dystopian History in Watchmen. In *Dystopia(n) Matters: On the Page, on Screen, on Stage*, ed. Fátima. Vieira, 270–279. Newcastle upon Tyne: Cambridge Scholars Publishing.

Gray, Maggie. 2010. "A Fistful of Dead Roses…". Comics as Cultural Resistance: Alan Moore and David Lloyd's *V for Vendetta*. *Journal of Graphic Novels and Comics* 1 (1): 31–49.

Groensteen, Thierry. 2007. *The System of Comics*, trans. Bart Beaty and Nick Nguyen. Jackson: University Press of Mississippi.

Hatfield, Charles, Jeet Heer, and Kent Worcester (eds.). 2013. *The Superhero Reader*. Jackson: University Press of Mississippi.

Hyman, David. 2017. *Revision and the Superhero Genre*. New York: Palgrave Macmillan.

Iung, Olivier. 2018. *La Trilogie Nikopol. Du Réalisme aux Imaginaires chez Enki Bilal*. Éditions PLG.

Klausner, Sebastian. 2015. Ōtomo's Exploding Cities: The Intersection of Class and City in Ōtomo Katsuhiro's Works Before, During, and After the Bubble Economy in Japan. *Writing Visual Culture* 6: n.p.

Lefèvre, Pascal. 2016. L'utopie en question(s) dans la bande dessinée francophone de Belgique (1945–1989). *Textyles* 48. https://doi.org/10.4000/textyles.2669.

Lewis, Jacob. 2010. Superman: Red Son. In *Encyclopedia of Comic Books and Graphic Novels. Volume 2: M–Z*, ed. M. Keith Booker, 617–619. Santa Barbara; Denver; Oxford: Greenwood.

Liou, Anthony. 2010. The City Ascends: Laputa: Castle in the Sky as Critical Ecotopia. *ImageTexT: Interdisciplinary Comic Studies* 5 (3). http://imagetext.english.ufl.edu/imagetext/archives/v5_2/lioi/.

Mazur, Dan, and Alexander Danner. 2014. *Comics: A Global History, 1968 to the Present*. London: Thames & Hudson.

Miller, Ann. 2007. *Reading* bande dessinée*: Critical Approaches to French-language Comic Strip*. Bristol; Chicago: Intellect.

Moffett, Paul. 2016. U for Utopia: The Dystopian and Eutopian Visions in Alan Moore and David Lloyd's *V for Vendetta*. *Journal of Graphic Novels and Comics*. https://doi.org/10.1080/21504857.2016.1233894.

Napier, Susan J. 2005. *Anime from Akira to Howl's Moving Castle: Experiencing Contemporary Japanese Animation*. New York: Palgrave Macmillan.

———. 2018. *Miyazakiworld: A Life in Art*. New Haven, CT: Yale University Press.

Orbaugh, Sharalyn. 2006. Frankenstein and the Cyborg Metropolis. The Evolution of Body and City in Science Fiction Narratives. In *Cinema Anime: Critical Engagements with Japanese Animation*, ed. Steven T. Brown, 81–111. New York: Palgrave Macmillan.

Paik, Peter Y. 2010. *From Utopia to Apocalypse: Science Fiction and the Politics of Catastrophe*. Minneapolis; London: University of Minnesota Press.

Petersen, Robert S. 2011. *Comics, Manga, and Graphic Novels: A History of Graphic Narratives*. Santa Barbara: Praeger.

Power, Natsu Onoda. 2009. *God of Comics: Osamu Tezuka and the Creation of Post-World War II Manga*. Jackson: University Press of Mississippi.

Saouter-Caya, Catherine. 1985. Pour ou contre l'utopie: La réponse des protagonistes de la B.D. utopique. *Canadian Woman Studies/les cahiers de la femme* 6 (2): 77–79.

Sargent, Lyman Tower. 2003. The Problem of the "Flawed Utopia": A Note on the Costs of Eutopia. In *Dark Horizons: Science Fiction and the Dystopian Imagination*, ed. Raffaella Baccolini and Tom Moylan, 225–231. New York: Routledge.

———. 2015. The American Cockaigne from the Sixteenth Century to the Shmoo and Beyond. *Utopian Studies* 26 (1): 19–40.

Savramis, Demosthenes. 1987. Religion et bandes dessinées: Tarzan et Superman sauveurs. *Social Compass* 34 (1): 77–86.

Schodt, Frederik L. 2007. *The Astro Boy Essays: Osamu Tezuka, Mighty Atom, and the Manga-Anime Revolution*. Berkeley: Stone Bridge Press.

Singer, Mark. 2012. *Grant Morrison: Combining the Worlds of Contemporary Comics*. Jackson: University Press of Mississippi.

Smith, Matthew J., and Randy Duncan (eds.). 2012. *Critical Approaches to Comics: Theories and Methods*. New York; London: Routledge.

Stoddard, Matthew. 2010. Contested Utopias: Ghost in the Shell, Cognitive Mapping, and the Desire for Communism. *ImageTexT: Interdisciplinary Comic Studies* 5 (2). http://imagetext.english.ufl.edu/imagetext/archives/v5_2/stoddard/.

Tabachnick, Stephen E. (ed.). 2017. *The Cambridge Companion to the Graphic Novel*. Cambridge: Cambridge University Press.

Tellop, Nicolas. 2017. *L'Anti-Atome. Franquin à l'Épreuve de la Vie*. Éditions PLG.

Vanderbeke, Dirk, and Marie Vanderbeke. 2015. Graphic Dystopia. *Watchmen* (Moore/Gibbons, 1986–1987) and *V for Vendetta* (Moore/Lloyd, 1982–1989). In *Dystopia, Science Fiction, Post-Apocalypse: Classics—New Tendencies—Model Interpretations*, ed. Eckart Voigts and Alessandra Boller, 201–220. Trier: Wissenschaftlicher Verlag Trier.

Veitch, Adam, and Laszlo Kulcsar. 2018. Malthus Meets Green Lantern: Comic Book Representation of Malthusian Concerns. *Journal of Graphic Novels and Comics*. https://doi.org/10.1080/21504857.2018.1431798.

Wegner, Phillip E. 2014. *Shockwaves of Possibility: Essays on Science Fiction, Globalization, and Utopia*. Oxford/Bern: Peter Lang.

Wolf-Meyer, Matthew. 2003. The World Ozymandias Made: Utopias in the Superhero Comic, Subculture, and the Conservation of Difference. *The Journal of Popular Culture* 36 (3): 497–517.

Gaming

Brian Greenspan

Introduction

Games have always figured in utopian narratives as emblems of transformed social relations. Just as utopian narratives from every period feature fictional representations of games, so actually existing games often include utopian or dystopian storylines and themes. Digital games remediate and intensify many features of utopian societies from novels and films, including their speculative technologies, communal orientation, and playfully provisional attitude, along with their characteristic boredom and inevitable failures. Some games even encourage the formation of persistent communities of gamers that play by different social rules, challenging dominant notions of reality through their gameplay, and demonstrating that other worlds are possible. The subject of utopian gaming can be approached by examining the games that appear in utopias, the traces of utopian dreaming found within games, and intentional gaming communities with utopian characteristics.

Games in Utopia

Although utopias are often described as overly earnest and dull, games and play have played a vital role in utopian narratives since the genre's origin. More's Utopians play two kinds of games

B. Greenspan (✉)
Carleton University, Ottawa, ON, Canada

P. Marks et al. (eds.), *The Palgrave Handbook of Utopian and Dystopian Literatures*, https://doi.org/10.1007/978-3-030-88654-7_20

not unlike our chess; the one is between several numbers, in which one number, as it were, consumes another; the other resembles a battle between the virtues and the vices... But the time appointed for labour is to be narrowly examined... (2005, n.p.)

The second of these games could be read as an epitome of *Utopia* itself, a rhetorical game in which vice "secretly undermines virtue" (Book II) through verbal ironies, litotes, and other "not unpleasant" figures (Greenblatt 2005, 132). Games can thus be understood as part of *Utopia's* broader economy of verbal, semiotic, and conceptual *play*.

In shifting abruptly from the topic of Utopian games to that of labor, More's discourse establishes an antinomy that continues to structure the place of games and gaming within utopian discourse. For Philip Abbott, More's description of utopian entertainments "struggles between games as play and games as indoctrination," as the "utopian playfulness" evidenced in More's "joking, punning, bantering, even trickery" is balanced against *Utopia's* earnestness in seeking out solutions to real-world problems (2004, 53, 48ff.). Ever since, utopian authors have attempted to resolve this antinomy: William Morris's *News from Nowhere* (1890), for example, anticipates an artisanal society in which all labor is transformed into play (Abbott 2004, 54).

Utopian games more typically remain distinct from the domain of work, while working to emblematize the transformed social relations of the utopian society. In Bellamy's *Looking Backward: 2000–1887* (1888), professional athletics have been replaced by teams of young men from trade guilds who compete in yachting races and other athletic games. The games played by the female inhabitants of Charlotte Perkins Gilman's femtopia *Herland* (1915) strike her male narrator as "more like a race or a – a competitive examination, than a real game with some fight in it"; yet, one resident of Herland receives the male interlopers more like "an intent boy playing a fascinating game than... a girl lured by an ornament" (1998, 14, 28). Games in *Herland* are thus aligned with post-patriarchal forms of play that trouble the male narrator's assumptions regarding gender differences, the first step in a utopian "education of desire" (Levitas 1990, 106–130). Imaginary games are often used in this way to emblematize the educated desires of utopian societies, from the cathartic blood sport in Callenbach's *Ecotopia* (1975) to the horseback games inspired by American indigenous cultures in Ursula K. Le Guin's *Always Coming Home* (1985).

Whereas Morris imagined the overcoming of industrial capitalism through a return to artisanal craft, others tie the transformation of labor to the continued advance of post-industrial technologies. In his philosophical dialogue *The Grasshopper*, Bernard Suits argues that "the total implementation of computerized automation" will create a society free not just of labor, but of all "instrumental necessities"—governance, art, morality, science, sex, love, and friendship (1984, 8–9). Suits predicts that his hypothetical utopians, having no necessary activities to fulfill, will turn to games to introduce challenges and avoid boredom (8). Moreover, any activity they do perform will perforce become a game, which the Grasshopper defines as "the voluntary attempt to overcome unnecessary obstacles" (Suits 2014, 55). Suits imagines a ludic social life beyond exploitative labor relations, the inverse of "gamefication." In some ways, his playful dialogue echoes the fanciful vision of Charles Fourier's utopian phalanstery, in which "everything one might understand as children's play became, within this system, their impetus to work" (Pearson 2002, 32).

If, for Suits's Grasshopper, Utopia is that condition in which all of reality has become a game, mistaking reality for a game leads directly to *dystopia* in other fictional scenarios. Ernest Cline's speculative novel about future gaming, *Ready Player One* (2011), revolves around a fictional virtual gaming platform called the OASIS, which exemplifies Suits's vision of "a highly technical, computerized, environment where travel, adventure, and interpersonal relationships are all perfected and available every moment" (Nordstrom 2016, 248). For Justin Nordstrom, The OASIS "is simultaneously utopian and dystopian – as it enhances education and ignites a player's imagination on one hand, and leads to abandonment of the world's pressing needs on the other" (246). Orson Scott Card's *Ender's Game* (1985) is the story of future cadets who train using military strategy video games that turn out to be command and control for an intergalactic war. The protagonist sacrifices his game pieces to win the battle, resulting in actual genocide and a pyrrhic military victory. Card's novel anticipated the U.S. Military's adoption of the first-person shooter *America's Army* (2002) as a training simulation.

The young adults in Karen Lord's *The Galaxy Game* (2015) compete at "wallrunning" (Lord 2015, 30) a sport played vertically on a game Wall engineered with differential gravity. The players eventually discover that the empathic abilities that allow team members to move in concert on the Wall also enable a new interplanetary form of travel, in which numerous people move between worlds as "a collective consciousness, a temporary colony organism" (Lord 2015, 279). As in *Ender's Game*, the narrative's central game turns out to be a deceptively important vehicle of interstellar colonial struggle. These fictional games reflect the tendency of actually existing digital games to function as "*paradigmatic media of Empire*," in Hardt and Negri's sense of a global capitalist network, exploiting the free labor and cognitive capital of gamers (Dyer-Witheford and de Peuter 2009, xv; emphasis in original). At the same time, Nick Dyer-Witheford and Greig de Peuter argue that digital games are training grounds within which "multitudinous" (xxiii) resistance can emerge, allowing those working in creative, communicative, and informational fields to form alliances capable of evading and exploiting the networks of capital.

Utopia in Games

Just as utopian narratives have always included games, so countless card, board, and role-playing games have borrowed fictional worlds and motifs from Verne, Wells, Herbert, *Star Wars*, or *Dr. Who*. Digital games likewise remediate narratives from the utopian megatext, transforming them in the process. Tracy Fullerton's *Walden: A Game* (2017) is an interactive adaptation of Thoreau's 1854 idyll that preserves the contemplative spirit of the original through the unlikely medium of a first-person adventure game. Players learn to live off the land around the cabin at Walden Pond, fishing or planting beans, and watching the exquisitely rendered foliage around them turn with the seasons, occasionally reading excerpts from Thoreau's letters and manuscripts. With a state-of-the-art game engine to realistically render the natural environment and gameplay that privileges contemplation over kinetic action, Fullerton's *Walden* remediates the contradictions of Thoreau's own experiment in living, which trumpeted civil disobedience and Transcendentalist self-reliance even as it reproduced the comforts and values of bourgeois society. The game reminds us that, "in the era of communicative capitalism" when even our games reinforce the virtues of workplace productivity, "the most radical action might be a kind of passivity" (Thorne 2018, 176).

Games are rarely content to reside in utopian equilibrium for very long, however, tending more often to adapt dystopian narratives and themes. Other Ocean Interactive's *The War of the Worlds* (2011) is based loosely upon H.G. Wells's eponymous novel about a Martian colonization of earth and its cinematic adaptation. A single-player, side-scrolling platformer set in 1953, it evokes the feel of early arcade games, complementing the retro-aesthetic of its Wellsian source material. Another homage to a classic dystopia, Osmotic Studios's *Orwell: Keeping an Eye on You* (2016), uses a bureaucratic interface to simulate the experience of working for a near-future surveillance state known as The Party. Like so many utopian narratives, *Orwell* blurs the line between work and play, enlisting the user to sort through archived emails and news clippings in order to identify alleged members of a terrorist network. That "uncovering" terrorists (in fact framing innocent citizens, as the player comes to realize) should be as easy as triaging email or ranking forum posts from one's desktop forces reflection on the role of social media networks in spreading viral panic and perpetrating state-sanctioned violence.

Compulsion Games's *We Happy Few* (2018) also alludes to *1984*, right down to the redacted newspaper headings, along with other classic dystopian novels and films. The game is set in an alt-historical 1960s Britain devastated by the War, in which all citizens consume a hallucinogen called "Joy" that prevents them from seeing the reality of their world. As in Philip K. Dick's story "Faith of our Fathers," drugs are a novum that estrange the operations of the ideological state apparatus, but sobriety alone does not guarantee demystification. This clever use of game mechanics to encode ideological interpellation recalls the first-person shooter *Bioshock* (2007), which manipulates its own rules in order to undermine the user's agency over their avatar and the game world, in a mockery of Ayn Rand's anti-utopian pursuit of individual rights and happiness. Its parody of motifs and designs from numerous utopian and dystopian novels, films, and TV shows "self-consciously critiques the notion of utopia itself," functioning as a *critical dystopia* (Aldred and Greenspan 2011, 484).[1] *Bioshock* even critiques utopian programs to improve human nature itself through technology, a dangerous dream allegorized by any game that allows players to customize their avatars.

These visions of utopias gone wrong remind us that all utopias must inevitably fail—although in so doing, as Fredric Jameson has argued, they reveal the contradictions of capitalism that prevent us from imagining another world entirely (Jameson 2005, 232–233). Games challenge written utopias for the title of "the art of failure," as Jesper Juul puts it (2013), as repeated failure is an inevitable part of gameplay, a result of the obstacles that games put in the path of their users. Some games by "indie" designers even thematize failure in their design, such as Pippin Barr's *Sisyphus: The Game* (2010) or *The Artist Is Present* (2011), games so nearly unplayable that they allegorize the "surplus repressions" that prohibit creativity and play in capitalist societies (Marcuse 1955, 35).

The inevitable failures of utopias might in part explain why dystopian games far outnumber those with obvious utopian thematics. Yet, even the most hopeless or apocalyptic games introduce utopian novums at the level of system, interface, algorithm, and mechanics, offering images of abundance, of energy, of open and honest communication, and above all, community, a utopian surplus that stimulates hope for another world, as Richard Dyer has argued of other popular entertainments (Dyer 1977). In single-player games like Ubisoft's *Assassin's Creed* (2007) franchise, open community is symbolized by the porous and clearly mapped city, replete with authentically rendered crowds of non-player characters (NPCs). Of course, not all simulated communities are utopian. The goal of *State of Emergency* (2002), Rockstar's game based loosely on the 1999 WTO protests in Seattle, is to incite a riot in a shopping mall. The game's mechanics, however, do not emulate the activities or scale of the alter-globalization movement. Its countless NPCs operate as individuals or small cadres, not as a community, gathering only to shoot or be shot by player characters, but never to organize, occupy, or change the game's world-state in meaningful ways. Just as fictional narratives with manifestly utopian content might not be utopian in orientation, so games with utopian thematics often involve gameplay mechanics that reinforce agonistic relations and individualist wishful thinking, rather than communal modes of "will-full thinking" and dreaming (Levitas 2013, 86–88).

Mitigating against the boredom of "grinding" and the inevitable failures of gameplay are the rewards associated with world-building, which falls under the mode of gaming that Roger Caillois classifies as *mimicry* (1961, 13). In *Katamari Damacy* (2004), the player rolls a sticky ball around the landscape, collecting branded consumer goods until the ball grows so massive that it becomes a star, a new totality born out of capitalist waste. More realistic digital games like *Minecraft* (2011), *Caesar* (1992), and *SimCity* (1989) allow users to build towns, cities, or entire nations, directing the process of historical development through a map-based interface. Ted Friedman argues that such games are not utopias, but *utopian simulations* with the potential to actualize the "aesthetic of cognitive mapping" that Jameson proposes as a means of comprehending social space under transnational capitalism (Friedman 1999, n.p.). If *SimCity* offers any cognitive map, however, it is one charting not the trade routes of late capitalism, but the gift economies of online gaming communities. Ever since the release of the urban renewal kit (SCURK) with *SimCity 2000*, users have customized and shared their cities, some even modelling them after Callenbach's *Ecotopia* or George Miller's dystopian *Mad Max* universe in the attempt to present imaginary solutions to the real obstacles people face in their everyday negotiation of urban spaces and cyberspaces alike. This kind of "architectural" world-building is essential to what Ruth Levitas calls the Imaginary Reconstitution of Society (IROS), and a necessary step for moving beyond the sublime of utopian failure to effect concrete change in the world (2013, 124).

Utopian Gaming Communities

If a game is the overcoming of unnecessary obstacles, then the "overcoming of obstacles to movement" in particular resides at the "core of the utopia of open space" in role-playing videogames (RPGs) (Hourigan 2003, 56). Ben Hourigan shows that fantasy games such as *Neverwinter Nights* (1991) or *The Legend of Zelda* (1996) enact a dialectical movement between the structured space of utopian society and the empty virtual space of movement, process, and play. Some gamers even translate this ludic, allegorical movement into the real world by modding, hacking, or pirating games, resisting "capitalist or analogous forces that seek to restrict movement," and anticipating the move into a future utopian space beyond the control of capital (58–60). For many gaming communities, virtual movement has real consequences. The Gathering of Uru was a group of gamers who became "refugees" after their game server was shut down, and moved *en masse* to a new platform, as Celia Pearce documents. Although forged in a virtual world, their community was strong enough to survive a forced migration, and many went on to develop real-world, life-long relationships (Pearce 2011).

If single-player games offer images of community, multiplayer games often function as platforms for building communities. Persistent-world Massively Multiplayer Online Role-Playing Games (MMORPGs) encourage membership in teams, guilds, or nations that arguably have much in common with conventional Intentional Communities, or real-life utopian "experiments in community" (Sargisson and Sargent 2004, 6, 159). Challenging the myth of the isolated and anti-social gamer, T. L. Taylor emphasizes the intensely social and collective orientation of gamers in her ethnography of the MMORPG

EverQuest (1999–), which "is constructed through the joint practices of designers, publisher, world managers, and players... [forming a] collective construction of the space across multiple actors" (2006, 133). Taylor points to examples of gift-giving, property sharing, trust, and communal support among *EverQuest* gamers, noting that interpersonal networks are extended beyond the game to various paratexts, sites, and practices "that constitute the social world of the game... the collection of message boards, databases, comics, fan art and stories, and even game modifications that contribute to players feeling a bond and connection" (57). It is this constant crossing of the boundary between the game and the world, the virtual and the real, that makes the game—and perhaps all games—so compelling (Taylor 2006, 153).

Others have argued that MMORPGs allow users to explore the protocols governing digital networks generally, blurring the lines between sanctioned and disruptive behavior, between social and technical regulation, and between real and virtual interactions. *World of Warcraft* (2004), for instance, allows friendly in-world interactions, structured collaborations, and random acts of kindness (such as kill assists and buffs), while permitting creative exploits with no purpose beyond having fun, like dances and slumber parties, along with antagonistic, anti-communal actions (like spamming, ganking, or corpse camping) (Nardi and Harris 2006, 149–158). Taylor notes that the collective creation involved in MMORPGs does not always manifest as recreation: in considering how laborious grinding can be fun for gamers, she asks, "might we imagine a space in which our games at times are not always 'fun' and, conversely, our labor can be quite pleasurable?" (2006, 88–89).

In fact, virtual game worlds rarely offer clear expressions of utopian desire: "the very act of creating an immaterial utopian space at the same time inscribes a whole vocabulary of algorithmic coding into the plane of imagination that thereby undoes the play of utopia in the first place" (Galloway 2006b, n.p.). For Alexander Galloway, the utopian dimension of fantasy role-playing games like *Warcraft* resides mainly in the offer of escape to "*a world without signifiers,*" a pre-capitalist space devoid of brand names, logos, and "unnecessary ornamentation" (Galloway 2006b, 114; emphasis in original). Such nostalgic visions of pre-capitalist society might operate only as a compensatory fantasy: the farm simulator game *Stardew Valley* (2016), for instance, provides a "picture of a lost era of tightly knit villages where humans lived in organic harmony with nature... [that] placate[s] a need for a collective and organized past as an alternative to contemporary chaos" (Bown 2018, 41–42).

Crucially, it is not only the player character or avatar who moves through the virtual world of these games, but the actual player who overcomes obstacles by traversing the game's many layers of representation and control. Just as More's utopia enables a form of *spatial play* in which various city plans and social settings overlap, conflict, and negate each other (Marin 1984), so digital games tell stories that unfold in overlapping and contradictory environments, both diegetic (e.g., cut scenes and heads-up displays) and extra-diegetic (e.g., maps, inventories, and other interface controls) (Galloway 2006a, 6ff.). Such traversals are an essential part of Alternate Reality Games (ARGs) that add a second defamiliarizing layer to the player's real-world environment, much as *Assassin's Creed* or Marge Piercy's *Woman on the Edge of Time* (1976) create estrangement by alternating between temporal settings. ARGs blend real life with "live-action role-playing games... [plus] mobile games, flash mobs, and improvised street performances. They use the real world as a platform, appropriating existing media infrastructures, both analog and digital, to lure willing players into the game through phone calls, faxes, newspapers, postcards, emails, and live events that hint at the shape of another universe within our own" (Greenspan 2015, n.p.) The ARG *Year Zero* (2007), developed to promote a concert tour by the industrial rock band Nine Inch Nails, used puzzles and clues hidden within the record album to lead astute fans into a fictional shadow-world of government conspiracy, perpetuated through clandestine answering services, dark websites, and flash drives. As Alex Hall argues, the game's dystopian trappings concealed a utopian impulse that went "beyond merely keeping hope alive" to "encourage the kind of action necessary to move closer to the new social system through game-specific, diegetic action while simultaneously inspiring greater attention to real-world issues" (Hall 2009, n.p.). Like MMORPGs, ARGs demand a degree of networked, communal interaction from their players that printed novels and films can only represent. Jane McGonigal even argues that ARGs can help us to "fix reality" by "stok[ing] our appetite for engagement, pushing and enabling us to make stronger connections – and bigger contributions – to the world around us" (McGonigal, 10). In Blochian terms, McGonigal suggests that ARGs like Ken Eklund's *World Without Oil* (2007), a collaborative simulation of a post-petroleum world, can bridge the gap between merely compensatory *abstract* utopias of personal fulfillment and *concrete* utopias of lasting social change (Levitas 1990, 88–90).

Yet, *Year Zero* was ultimately a marketing campaign, a reminder that while ARGs may encourage collaboration and active consumption, they are simultaneously complicit in multinational entertainment industries. The game industry's relation to the global "military-industrial-media-entertainment network" (Dyer-Witheford and de Peuter 2009, xv) has been foregrounded by the rising popularity of "indie" games designed by small studios or independent developers, games that "invite us to focus on the complexities of the ways that games are made and on the micro-economics and idiocultures of game production and consumption" (Simon 2013, 3). In *Utopian Entrepreneur* (2001), the confessions of an indie feminist videogame designer, Brenda Laurel takes up the question of whether utopian game developers can coexist with capitalist markets from a feminist perspective. Laurel co-founded Purple Moon, a company "devoted to making interactive media for little girls" (Laurel 2001, 1), before it succumbed to speculative capital and the internet bubble. Despite this financial failure, Laurel's experience gave her "faith in the power of popular culture to shape values and inform citizenship, influencing both public and private institutions" (10).

Many indie games explore themes that directly oppose capitalism or state violence. Neil Farnan's *Utopoly* (2017) is a collaborative hack of the Parker Brothers board game *Monopoly* that rewrites the original game's goal of acquiring wealth and property in a wage-based economy; while Lucas Pope's *Papers, Please* (2013) puts users in the role of an immigration officer policing the border between the fictional dystopias of East and West Grestin, confronting them with impossible ethical choices that are anything but fun. Yet, by reimagining "work and laborious activity as a form of satiric play" that interrogates "the growing relationship between gaming, governance, economics, and social relations," Pope's game sustains a horizon of hope in the manner of a critical dystopia (Benn 2018, 160, 168). Still, the category of "indie games" might only authorize a form of precarious labor that ultimately reinforces exploitative industrial relations. Stephanie Boluk and Patrick Lemieux argue that commercial videogames—indie or otherwise—might not be games at all: "When did *player* become a code word for *customer*?" (2017, 8) They accuse Suits's utopian dialogue of "relegat[ing] the radical potential of games to a speculative horizon rather than a historical practice," arguing instead that the only actual game is the *metagame*, a form of play that takes commercial games as raw material and, in the process, "ruptures the logic of the game, escaping the formal autonomy of both ideal rules and utopian play" (7).

CONCLUSION

By rupturing the artificial autonomy of both games and utopias, metagaming asserts their potential to concretely transform the material world in the here and now. Challenging the myth of the isolated and anti-social gamer, online and transmedia games are intensely social and collective creative forms, demanding a degree of networked, communal interaction from their players that printed novels and films can only represent. Digital games allow users to inhabit utopias and dystopias in ways that other media cannot, shifting utopian critique from the allegorical to the virtual dimension. They simulate the Imaginary Reconstruction of Society, inviting users to participate in the communal process of world-building, and to premediate imaginary solutions to real problems. Many mainstream game titles critique state violence and capitalism, while indie games challenge exploitative labor relations in their very model of production. Even the most apocalyptic dystopian games introduce a utopian surplus that awakens repressed hopes for a better world. While gamers will doubtless think of additional game titles, franchises, developers, platforms, genres, national traditions, and communities that do just that, a comprehensive survey of such an ancient and pervasive activity as gaming would be an undertaking of Blochian scope. I only hope that this brief account might provide a framework for further consideration of the many intersections of gaming and utopia.

NOTE

1. On the critical dystopia, see Tom Moylan, 2000, *Scraps of the Untainted Sky: Science Fiction, Utopia, Dystopia*, Boulder: Westview Press, 183–199.

REFERENCES

Abbott, Philip. 2004. Utopians at Play. *Utopian Studies* 15 (1): 44–62.

Aldred, Jessica, and Brian Greenspan. 2011. A Man Chooses, a Slave Obeys: *BioShock* and the Dystopian Logic of Convergence. *Games and Culture* 6 (5): 479–496.

Barr, Pippin. 2010. *Sisyphus: The Game*. Web: https://www.pippinbarr.com/2010/07/31/sisyphus-the-game.

———. 2011. *The Artist Is Present*. Web: http://www.pippinbarr.com/games/theartistispresent/TheArtistIsPresent.html.

Bellamy, Edward. 2008 [1888]. *Looking Backward, 2000–1887*. Urbana, IL: Project Gutenberg. https://www.gutenberg.org/ebooks/624. Accessed 3 June 2019.

Benn, Adam. 2018. Trading Frames: Interface Operations and Social Exchanges in Video Games. Ph.D. dissertation, Carleton University.

Blizzard Entertainment. 2004. *World of Warcraft*. Blizzard Entertainment. Microsoft Windows; Mac OS.

Boluk, Stephanie, and Patrick Lemieux. 2017. *Metagaming: Playing, Competing, Spectating, Cheating, Trading, Making, and Breaking Videogames*. Minneapolis: Minnesota University Press.

Bown, Alfie. 2018. *The Playstation Dreamworld*. Cambridge: Polity Press.

Caillois, Roger. 1961. *Man, Play and Games*, trans. Meyer Barash. New York: Free Press of Glencoe.

Callenbach, Ernest. 1975. *Ecotopia: A Novel*. Toronto: Bantam Books.

Card, Orson Scott. 1985. *Ender's Game*. New York: T. Doherty Associates.

Cline, Ernest. 2011. *Ready Player One*. New York: Random House.

Compulsion Games. 2018. *We Happy Few*. Gearbox Publishing. Linux; Microsoft Windows; PlayStation 4; Xbox One.

Dick, Philip K. 1967. Faith of Our Fathers. In *Dangerous Visions*, ed. Harlan Ellison, 172–203. New York: Doubleday.

Doyle W. Donehoo/The United States Army/Unreal Engine 3. 2002. *America's Army*. 4.0. The United States Army. Windows.

Dyer, Richard. 1977. Entertainment and Utopia. *Movie* 24: 2–13.

Dyer-Witheford, Nick, and Greig de Peuter. 2009. *Games of Empire: Global Capitalism and Video Games*. Minneapolis: University of Minnesota Press.

Eklund, Ken. Independent Television Service (ITVS) Interactive. 2007. *World Without Oil*. Transmedia.

Farnan, Neil. 2017. *Utopoly: A Utopian Design Game*. Public Seminar. http://www.publicseminar.org/2017/12/utopoly. Accessed 11 May 2018.

Friedman, Ted. 1999. The Semiotics of SimCity. *First Monday* 4 (4–5). https://journals.uic.edu/ojs/index.php/fm/article/view/660/575#f5. Accessed 11 June 2019.

Fullerton, Tracey/USC Game Innovation Lab/. 2017. *Walden: A Game*. USC Games. Microsoft Windows.

Galloway, Alexander R. 2006a. *Gaming: Essays on Algorithmic Culture*. Minneapolis: University of Minnesota Press.

———. 2006b. Warcraft and Utopia. *CTheory.net*. Accessed 9 June 2021.

Gilman, Charlotte Perkins. 1998. *Herland*. Mineola, NY: Dover.

Greenblatt, Stephen. 2005. *Renaissance Self-Fashioning: From More to Shakespeare*. Chicago: University of Chicago Press.

Greenspan, Brian. 2015. Don't Make a Scene: Game Studies for an Uncertain World. *Digital Studies/Le champ numérique*. https://www.digitalstudies.org/articles/10.16995/dscn.35. Accessed 22 November 2017.

Hall, Alexander Charles Oliver. 2009. "I Am Trying to Believe": Dystopia as Utopia in the *Year Zero* Alternate Reality Game. *Eludamos: Journal for Computer Game Culture* 3 (1): 69–82. Web: https://www.eludamos.org/index.php/eludamos/article/view/vol3no1-8/111. Accessed 8 June 2021.

Hourigan, Ben. 2003. The Utopia of Open Space in Role-Playing Videogames. *Proceedings of MelbourneDAC*, 53–62. Melbourne: University of Melbourne.

Impressions Games. 1992. *Caesar*. Sierra On-Line. Web.

Irrational Games. 2007. *Bioshock*. 2K Games. Microsoft Windows; Xbox 360.

Jameson, Fredric. 2005. *Archaeologies of the Future: The Desire Called Utopia and Other Science Fictions*. London: Verso.

Juul, Jesper. 2013. *The Art of Failure: An Essay on the Pain of Playing Video Games*. Cambridge, MA: MIT Press.

Laurel, Brenda. 2001. *Utopian Entrepreneur*. Cambridge, MA: MIT Press.

Levitas, Ruth. 1990. *The Concept of Utopia*. Syracuse, NY: Syracuse University Press.

———. 2013. *Utopia as Method: The Imaginary Reconstitution of Society*. New York: Palgrave Macmillan.

Lord, Karen. 2015. *The Galaxy Game*. New York: Del Rey.

Marcuse, Herbert. 1955. *Eros and Civilization*. Boston: Beacon Press.

Marin, Louis. 1984. *Utopics: The Semiological Play of Textual Spaces*, trans. Robert A. Vollrath. New York: Humanity Books.

Maxis. 1989. *SimCity*. Electronic Arts. Amiga; Macintosh.

McGonigal, Jane. 2011. *Reality Is Broken: Why Games Make Us Better and How They Can Change the World*. New York: Penguin Books.

Mojang. 2011. *Minecraft*. Mojang. Windows; OS X; Linux.

More, Thomas. 2005 [1516]. *Utopia*. Urbana, IL: Project Gutenberg. https://www.gutenberg.org/ebooks/2130. Accessed 3 June 2019.

Morris, William. 2007 [1890]. *News from Nowhere; Or, an Epoch of Rest*. Urbana, IL: Project Gutenberg. https://www.gutenberg.org/ebooks/3261. Accessed 3 June 2019.

Moylan, Tom. 2000. *Scraps of the Untainted Sky: Science Fiction, Utopia, Dystopia*. Boulder: Westview Press.

Namco. 2004. *Katamari Damacy*. Namco. PlayStation 2.

Nardi, Bonnie, and Justin Harris. 2006. Strangers and Friends: Collaborative Play in World of Warcraft. CSCW'06, 149–158. Banff, Alberta: ACM.

Nordstrom, Justin. 2016. 'A Pleasant Place for the World to Hide': Exploring Themes of Utopian Play in *Ready Player One*. *Interdisciplinary Literary Studies* 18 (2): 238–256.

Osmotic Studios. 2016. *Orwell: Keeping an Eye on You*. Fellow Traveller. Windows; OS X; Linux; Android; iOS.

Other Ocean Interactive. 2011. *The War of the Worlds*. XBLA. Xbox 360; PlayStation 3.

Pearce, Celia. 2011. *Communities of Play: Emergent Cultures in Multiplayer Games and Virtual Worlds*. Cambridge, MA: MIT Press.

Pearson, Maeve. 2002. All Their Play Becomes Fruitful: The Utopian Child of Charles Fourier. *Radical Philosophy* 115: 29–39.

Piercy, Marge. 1976. *Woman on the Edge of Time*. New York: Fawcett Crest.

Pope, Lucas. 2013. *Papers, Please*. 3909 LLC. Microsoft Windows; OS X; Linux; iOS; PlayStation Vita.

Sargisson, Lucy, and Lyman Tower Sargent. 2004. *Living in Utopia: New Zealand's Intentional Communities*. New York: Ashgate.

Simon, Bart. 2013. Indie, eh? Some Kind of Game Studies. *Loading...* 7 (11): 1–7.

Suits, Bernard. 1984. Games and Utopia: Posthumous Reflections. *Simulation and Gaming* 15 (1): 5–24.

———. 2014. *The Grasshopper: Games, Life and Utopia*. Peterborough, ON: Broadview Press.

Taylor, T.L. 2006. *Play Between Worlds: Exploring Online Game Culture*. Cambridge, MA: MIT Press.

Thorne, Sarah. 2018. The Shape of Games to Come: Critical Digital Storytelling in the Era of Communicative Capitalism. Ph.D. dissertation, Carleton University.

Ubisoft Montreal. 2007. *Assassin's Creed*. Ubisoft. PlayStation 3; Xbox 360; Microsoft Windows.

VIS Entertainment. 2002. *State of Emergency*. Rockstar Games. PlayStation 2.

Deaftopias

Cristina Gil

Introduction

In a footnote in *Seeing Voices*, neurologist and author Oliver Sacks mentions the novel *Islay* published three years before, by Douglas Bullard, which explores the idea of building a Deaf[1] town (Bullard 2013 [1986]; Sacks 1989). Sacks applied the term "fantasy" and not "utopia" to describe his serendipitous finding, though it has since been described as a Deaftopian novel. The theoretical concept of Deaftopia is intentionally flexible, encompassing both utopian and dystopian Deaf-led manifestations and discourses, which are not only a contribution to, but also embedded within the Deaf Mythomoteur,[2] a theoretical framework composed of pivotal concepts for Sign Language Peoples, or SLPs (Gil 2019).[3] Deaftopian representations are diverse, encompassing an expression of ideals, worldmaking (Goodman 1978) and allusions to desired spaces; typically, everyone speaks sign language, showcasing the realm of the visual, of Deaf agency and representativity, and projecting a safe space for "the People of the Eye"[4] and their diverse identities. A place where Deaf Cultures are cherished. Other Deaftopian discourses are highly critical of the many

This chapter is based on a doctoral research funded by the scholarship PD/BD/128194/2016 from the Portuguese Foundation for Science and Technology.

C. Gil (✉)
Polytechnic Institute of Setúbal, Setúbal, Portugal

P. Marks et al. (eds.), *The Palgrave Handbook of Utopian and Dystopian Literatures*, https://doi.org/10.1007/978-3-030-88654-7_21

forms of audistic oppression: the pathologizing of Deaf bodies (Lane 1992; Solomon 2014); the exercise of eugenics and control of the right to be born; and dysconscious audism, among other examples. Therefore, Deaftopias fall into the categories of transgressive utopias and critical utopias, and function as a method[5] for critically engaging with Deaf History and the colonial legacy. These cultural productions also promote opportunities for reflection and dialogue narratives and discourses, thus raising awareness about the volatile future of Deaf Culture and the sustainability of signed languages and SLPs (Pabsch 2016). This is particularly important as Deaf people worldwide have been perceived as pathologized bodies requiring life-long rehabilitation and therapies to enforce body normativity, which is associated with a hearing body (Freire 1970 [1968]; Foucault 1978, 2003 [1963]). This biological reductionism and other discriminatory practices persist to this day toward Deaf Culture and toward signed languages, which are not granted equal status or legal recognition in society. Therefore, narratives produced by and concerning the oppressed realities of SLPs play an important role in the ongoing process of decolonizing oppressed peoples (Wa Thiong'o 1994 [1987]; Rutheford 1993; Ladd 2003; Gil 2020). To hearing audiences, SLP narratives can also increase cultural awareness, such as the richness of signed languages, and the ways in which Deaf Culture contributes to human diversity.

SLPs' cultural productions vary in media, ranging from artworks to performances, novels, poems, films, political manifestos. Deaftopias often are about the creation of Deaf Spaces as safe places that can be found in intentional communities or shared sign communities, temporary places like congresses, Deaflympics, or the spaces of a Deaf association/club (Haualand et al. 2015). The SLPs' shared ideals can also be projected through activism and legal lobbying for Deaf Rights and the preservation of signed languages and Deaf Culture (Veditz 1913). Deaftopian narratives are highly critical and express their dissatisfaction with current realities (Gil 2020); however, they also display efforts toward the mapping of the future (Wegner 2002) and identify the clashes of idiorrhythms that both hearing and Deaf people can identify by living together (Barthes 2013). Finally, they express the desire to replace what is unsatisfactory (Bloch 2009 [1918]) and critique the colonial oppression, biopower oppression, right to be born, right to exist, right for SLPs, aiming toward the decolonization of the Deaf mind (Gil 2020).

Signed languages have endured significant and diverse forms of oppression, not only in the education of D/deaf children, but also in terms of language accessibility policies and language status in society. This has improved over the last decades of the twentieth century, after important breakthroughs in the field of signed language linguistics that scientifically demonstrated that sign languages are full-fledged languages. However, SLPs, Deaf collectives, signed languages and Deaf Cultures have for centuries dealt with challenges and serious threats. These threats have materialized in different forms: the supporters of Oralism, a practice that defends the exclusive teaching of spoken languages to D/deaf people, and hindering signed languages; the eugenics movement, which prohibited D/deaf people from getting married and having children, and enforced sterilization and extermination. This threat of extinction has been held over Deaf people on several occasions and in several countries, as during the Third Reich; or in the thought of Alexander Graham Bell in the United States (Ryan and Schuchman 2002; Greenwald 2006, 2007).

DEAFTOPIA IN THE UNITED STATES

The best-known example of Deaftopian fiction is *Islay*, a novel by Douglas Bullard published in 1986. Bullard was a Deaf author who wrote about Deaf characters and a richly allusive Deaf Culture. The novel's style is satirical, critical of both hearing and Deaf people, condemning polarization and essentialism. *Islay* tells the story of Lyson C. Sulla, a Deaf man who dreams of building a Deaf state in the United States. We follow the protagonist as he travels the country Vieira (2010) seeking financing and allies in his endeavors to create a place for Deaf people, fully accessible in sign language. Every space is built to ease visual communication and address any other type of accessibility issue.

When he was networking to build Islay, Lyson searched for Deaf-led businesses, Deaf priests, Deaf lawyers, and others, in order to accurately portray the internal networks that exist in some Deaf communities. Lyson is particularly interested in the importance of Deaf spaces and Deaf architecture (Bauman 2014), the theory of which is grounded on the importance of visual input, accessibility, and information availability for Deaf people. Deaftopia architecture stresses the strategic placement of windows, glass elevators, floor materials that are either reverberation-conductive or absorbing (depending on the room's function), and visual warning technology that replaces alarms or doorbells. These practical details in the novel highlight hearing culture's total disregard of Deaf people's needs. Generally speaking, Lyson imagines a world in which the frictions between hearing and Deaf people are allayed. The protagonist comes up with a strategy of devising very specific dynamics in his town, reshaping the notion and distancing it from the dynamics of a hearing cluster. The existing Deaf school in *Islay*, for example, reads like a description of a maximum-security prison. Signs or even gestures like pointing are strictly forbidden. Hearing aids must be worn at all times, children can only speak when spoken to and must sit on their hands except when they are required to use them to eat. Lyson's distress when visiting the school puts forth a critique of the D/deaf education policies that exert diverse forms of oppression on signed languages.

Islay is still relevant today as a critique that contributes to the several ongoing discussions among SLPs on lack of opportunities, lack of agency and political and societal representation available to Deaf people, as well as the critique to Oralism in D/deaf education. Lyson imagines a community that lacks the constant friction between the different cultures and languages and solves their struggles of living together by turning the town into a Deaf-led place. There are several references to real-world conditions, such as Reaganomics (the economics of Ronald Reagan, 1981–1989, 40th President of the United States), familiar car brands as Datsun, Mercedes, Renault, and Lincoln, and especially familiar for the Deaf readers—the TTY. These references in the narrative (Bruner 1991) increase the feeling of verisimilitude, conveying it as possible, attainable (Ryan 2013 [2012]), and credible, which increases our connection not only toward the causes defended by the protagonist, but to the Deaf community's cause. The readers' empathy also increases toward Lyson Sulla who, for all his clumsiness as he navigates the hearing world, is also a subversive force, as he gradually attains his great goals (Peters 2000).

A peculiar feature to highlight in *Islay*, is that Bullard decided to graphically depict American Sign Language (ASL), spoken language, and TTY interactions distinctively. For ASL the author used italics following some of the ASL grammar features, for TTY capital letters were used, and the remaining text in traditional typeface. This is a visual engaging strategy to stress the different communication modalities, but also to include both Deaf signing reader as well as the hearing and deaf non-signer reader.

Another piece of Deaftopian American literature is *Mindfield* by John F. Egbert, a novel that also takes place in the United States. A terrorist cell develops a bioterrorist weapon that spreads spinal meningitis, resulting in a deafness pandemic. At first, technology seems to come to the rescue, but given the scale of the events, the North American government turns to the American Deaf community to learn how to cope with this new normal. The novel opens on a dystopian scene, with the pandemic affecting everyone and with no solution in sight. However, solutions develop from the input and perspectives of the Deaf community. The population undergoes such transformations that what is presented originally as such a social and medical tragedy suddenly ceases to be one, in light of a final, Deaf-friendly utopian framework.

Deaftopia in the United Kingdom

From the United Kingdom comes another Deaf Literature fictional narrative: the novel *Milan* written by Nick Sturley, who describes himself as a "profoundly Deaf British Sign Language (BSL) user and has Usher which is a visual condition" (Sturley 2003, 234). *Milan* is a dystopian science-fiction narrative that tells the story of Milan, a villain that transforms the entire British Deaf community into hearing people—with the exception of two survivors, who must save the community while fighting three Matrix-inspired hunters who are Milan's lackeys. We are introduced to the *SignWorld* where figures from Deaf History, including De L'Épée and Laurent Clerc, are members of a council designed to defend signed languages and Deaf Culture. The readers' knowledge of Deaf Culture can be a valuable addition to fully grasping the nuances that Sturley introduces. For the unfamiliar hearing reader, it might be a surprise to learn that turning Deaf people into hearing people is a dystopian event and that Deaf people pursue the goal of remaining as they are: as fulfilled Deaf people. Another example of an "insider" cultural reference is the title of the novel, which is not only the name of the villain, but also a reference to the International Congress of Educators of the Deaf, which took place in the city of Milan in 1880. This event had severe consequences in the usage of signed languages in the education of D/deaf children and had great impact on the lives of Deaf people on a global scale at the time of its occurrence and for generations to come, extending its impact until today.

Another British example is the serialized novel entitled *In the Mystic Land of Silence—A Strange and Weird Tale of Adventures in Unknown Lands* written by Ernest J.D. Abraham, who also signs as an anagram as his *nom de plume*, Tsenre Maharba J.D. The story's sixteen chapters appeared in three periodicals: *The British Deaf-Mute and Deaf Chronicle*; *The Bolton Review*; and *The Lancashire Review*. It tells the tale of an English Deaf young boy called Henry Dunbar (at times the name changes to Harry Dunbar) who is traveling with his father, a Captain of an old merchant ship. When Henry's father dies, he continues the trip with his guide Akalabo, but Henry is kidnapped and finds himself in a place where everyone uses sign language beyond the Tibetan mountains. "These mysterious people have tongues, but speak not; ears, but hear not. They converse by signs" (Abraham and Tsenre 1892, 14). The plot then turns into a romantic story and it is Edmund, the son of Henry, who finds the manuscript that tells this story.

Short Stories in the United States

The short story format has also been popular for Deaf writers, and we will briefly describe four thought-provoking examples: "Vibrating Mouth" by John Lee Clark, and "Understanding" by Kelsey Young, both part of the anthology *Tripping the Tale Fantastic—Weird Fiction by Deaf and Hard of Hearing Writers* (2017). "The Sonic Boom of 1994" by Mervin D. Garretson is found in the anthology, *Another Handful of Stories: Thirty-Seven Stories by Deaf Storytellers* (1984), and "A Brave New World" by Lawrence Newman in *I Fill this Small Space—The Writings of a Deaf Activist* (2009).

"Vibrating Mouth" by John Lee Clark tells the story of Laurent Clerc who is a leader and a protector of Deaf people. The character's name is inspired by the real Laurent Clerc, a French Deaf Teacher who co-founded the first American school for the Deaf with Thomas Hopkins Gallaudet in Hartford, Connecticut in 1817. The story of how Laurent Clerc came to the United States has been told and retold and elevated to the same status of a myth of origin of a nation. The story undergirds the theoretical framework of the Deaf Mythomoteur (Gil 2019), aimed at the empowerment of SLPs.

In "Vibrating Mouth," Clerc warns the reader about the oppressors, the "Mouthies," who are described as non-human. "Vibrating Mouth" is a dystopian narrative with a pungent critique concerning cochlear implants in babies, speech therapy, policies of rehabilitation in D/deaf education. It concerns the several axes of colonial oppression through Oralism, biopower, and biopolitics exerted upon the lives of Deaf people throughout history.

"Understanding" by Kelsey Young presents both Deaftopian and sci-fi features. The narrative shows a different universe, rich in Deaf Historical references. Planet Eyeth is a Deaf colony planet with different countries named Pegasus, Fence, and Milan. The concept of "Eyeth/EYETH" is recurrent in Deaf Literature and visuature (Peters 2000) and will be further explored below. In the story, the Lanners are the inhabitants from Milan, where Bell University is located, thus these are all referents to an oral-based environment as "Manual isn't allowed in Milan" (Young 2017, 166). The 1880 Milan Congress enforced Oralism and prohibited signed languages, having Alexander Graham Bell as a leader of a eugenics movement who authored several works on how to control the "deaf variety of human race" (Bell 1884).

The protagonist of "Understanding" is Bryant, a young student to whom signs come naturally. He has an almost perfect audiogram but auditory/verbal agnosia. To have information available in a visual format is preferential for Bryant, who finds it very difficult to follow the oral method. Therefore, Bryant moves to "Fence" in search of a place that would allow for such visual means of communication and learning, which were impossible in "Milan." Young tackles the issues in intra-community hierarchies, the diversity of forms of communication, the educational needs and preferences and exposes how institutions disregard the diversity of D/deaf people.

"The Sonic Boom of 1994" by Mervin D. Garretson is originally visuature but has also been transliterated into English.[6] It tells the story of a Concorde plane that hit the sound barrier, causing a sonic boom which left all people in the United States deaf. Like in "Mindfield," the Deaf community stepped in to provide council to the American government and the White House, establishing a protocol with NAD (the National Association of the Deaf) to teach American Sign Language at a national level. The NAD president later becomes President of the United States and everyone ends up signing, which is by definition a Deaftopian ending.

"A Brave New World" by Lawrence Newman does not resemble the plot of Aldous Huxley's novel of the same title, however repetition of the same title suggests a particular purpose. Huxley's *Brave New World* (2006 [1932]) describes a futuristic perfect society living in peace while grounded in the engineering industry and consumerism. This society has a rigid class system and succeeds at alienating individual and collective consciousness by focusing on the technology that maintains this "happiness." Deaf people are a majority and hearing people the minority. We understand that there are adaptations toward the hearing minorities, but hearing people are prohibited from using their speech, and education is conducted strictly through signs. The President of the United States is a fifth-generation Deaf man. Hearing people have their own associations created in order to accommodate hearing inclusion in society. There is an overall patronizing attitude toward hearing people who thrive to be dentists, lawyers, and other white-collar employment positions. Newman exposes the audism and the difficulties that the Deaf collectives have struggled with for centuries: inequalities, grievances, and severe flaws in education, in employment, and in society in general. Perhaps Newman is inviting the reader to consider how accommodated and adjusted Deaf people have become in the light of their oppression. Newman's satirical short story not only invites hearing audiences to consider the life of Deaf people, but also encourages Deaf people to take the lead in the decolonization of the Deaf mind.

As previously mentioned, visuature is a literary text in any sign language and it comprises several typologies, including VV (Visual Vernacular), ABC poetry, and signed songs. Two short stories that appear in American Sign Language are examples of fictional visuature with Deaftopian features. "Planet Way Over Yonder," by Stephen M. Ryan,[7] explores the story of a Deaf boy who starts to explore the skies with a telescope, despite discouragement. He decides he wants to explore space, studies innumerable books, and ends up building a rocket. In a single-crew rocket, he lands on a breathable, walkable planet where he discovers everyone is using sign, information is visual, and technology is not sound-based. This is planet Eyeth. This is a wordplay using the words "ear" and "eye" in opposition: *Earth*, where communication relying on auditory abilities is prevalent, and *Eyeth*, where visual communication and signed languages prevail. The signplay between EYETH and EARTH is also present in ASL.

In Eyeth, the inversion element comes into play, making hearing people a minority. The main character sees public protests demanding a "hearing president now!" which is a clear historical reference to the Deaf President Now movement that occurred in the United States. The inversion of society is a common trope in utopian/dystopian fiction. In brief, DEAF PRESIDENT NOW or DPN is a famous demonstration that occurred at Gallaudet University's campus in March 1988 and had an international impact. The school's entire Deaf community, from students, to faculty, to alumni gathered to protest, demanding a Deaf president for the university and focusing on rights which needed to be achieved in order to make the institution Deaf-led (Christiansen and Barnartt 2003; Gannon 2009). Gallaudet University is a singular place for Deaf students with a majority of Deaf faculty members, and it has been called by many a Deaf Space, the closest many come to a "Deaf utopia" or "Deaf mecca" (Gil 2020). Gallaudet students' movement to achieve their demands, in a victory for Gallaudet's future, inspired American and worldwide activism for Deaf rights.

"Bleeva—The Narrative of Our Existence" by Benjamin Bahan, also known as Ben Bahan, has Deaftopian features, as it takes the audience into an imaginary scenario with pivotal contributions from SLPs' history and legacy—full of Deaf Cultural references, inviting viewers to reshape their understanding of human diversity and reconsider the valuable asset of Deaf people in our world. This visuature piece articulates the concept of Deaf Gain, a perspective that focuses on how Deaf Culture, signed languages, and therefore, Deaf people, enrich our human diversity and give valuable contributions to our world (Bauman and Murray 2014). "Bleeva—The Narrative of Our Existence" is yet to be published, and although Bahan has been known to have performed it from time to time, we need to wait for official publication in order for it to be consistently available to all viewers.[8] "Bleeva" is accompanied by a visual art composition and is performed by the author in American Sign Language. The plot gathers in a witty allusive eloquence several fictional theories with actual facts from Deaf History, Deaf Studies research, and Deaf Cultures and puts forth an explanation as to why Deaf people exist on Earth and where they come from.

CONCLUSION

All of the examples presented in this chapter have consistent features such as references concerning Deaf Culture and signed languages, as well as projections of utopian ideals and dystopian forewarning of the dangers that SLPs are facing. Space limitations do not allow us to include Deaftopian filmic narratives, but suffice it to say that there are also many that engage the same themes we have covered. Deaftopian narratives convey not only Deaf people's and SLPs' desires for utopian futures, but also their dystopian fears, forewarning the dangers to be faced if we do not reflect upon our own existence. These Deaftopian fictional narratives offer discourses of resistance and counternarratives that outline paths toward the decolonization of Sign Language Peoples and Deaf people. Deaftopias advocate for Deaf agency and representation, aiming to protect Deaf bodies and their right to be born and exist. They also advocate for the importance of Deaf spaces, Deaf cultural heritage and the vital need for policies for the protection of signed languages (De Meulder, et al. 2019). They remind us all of the importance of SLPs' networks (Wrigley 1996; Jankowski 1997; Ladd 2003, 2013). Many more examples can be found around the world as Deaf-led cultural productions are expanding, not only in the United States and the United Kingdom, but also in other non-western countries. This is a field of Utopian Studies that has scarcely been touched—and that has important contributions for the future of the field—as well as for Sign Language Peoples and Deaf Studies.

NOTES

1. The uppercase "D" stands for an ethnic cultural and linguistic group as one would write "Black," "Women," or "Native American" people. Accordingly, the lowercase "d" is used to refer to people who do not identify themselves as culturally Deaf, and do not use signed languages and communicate using spoken languages, thus identifying themselves with the culture of the hearing majority. The usage of "D/deaf" intends to refer to both groups or undefined.

2. The Deaf Mythomoteur is a concept that articulates DEAFHOOD (Ladd 2003), DEAF WORLD (Lane et al. 1996), DEAF WAY (Erting et al. 1994) and DEAF GAIN (Bauman and Murray 2014). This is grounded in the Mythomoteur by Armstrong (1982) articulated with Barthes (1957) and Anderson (1991 [1983]), thus serving as a lever towards the empowerment of Sign Language Peoples and Deaf Human Rights (Gil 2019).

3. Sign Language Peoples (SLPs) is a term that stands for the collective that uses signed languages (Batterbury et al. 2007), a designation deflecting from the pathological conceptualizations thrown upon Deaf individuals and collectives for centuries, and centred on Deaf Culture, signed languages and their consequent cultural productions.

4. "The People of the Eye" is a famous expression by George Veditz, a Deaf American Leader and activist for Deaf Culture and Sign Language preservation (1861–1937) (Veditz 1912 [1910], 22).

5. Sargisson (1996), Levitas (2010, 2013), Moylan (2014).

6. It was not possible to access the ASL original, therefore this analysis is on the transliteration into English.

7. There is no agreement about authorship of the tale of EYETH, it is a visuature piece that has been told by many Deaf storytellers and circulates in the American Deaf Community. For reference, this analysis is based on 1991's Stephen M. Ryan's version.

8. I was fortunate to watch the performance by Ben Bahan on Gallaudet University campus, in Washington, DC on November 5, 2018.

REFERENCES

Abraham, Ernest J.D., and J.D. Maharba Tsenre. 1892–1898. "In the Mystic Land of Silence—A Strange and Weird Tale of Adventures in Unknown Lands"/"In the Mystic Land of Silence—A Romance". *The British Deaf-Mute and Deaf Chronicle* Vol. II, no. 13 & Vol. IV, no. 37–46: 5–6, 12–15, 22, 26–27, 36–37, 45–46, 52, 55, 70, 84, 89–90, 108, 140, 154, 171, 188. *The Bolton Review* Vol. I: 380. *The Lancashire Review* Vol. II: 30–32, 62, 94–95.

Anderson, Benedict. 1991 [1983]. *Imagined Communities: Reflections on the Origin and Spread of Nationalism.* London: Verso.

Armstrong, John A. 1982. *Nations Before Nationalism.* Chapel Hill: University of North Carolina Press.

Bahan, Benjamin. 2018. *Bleeva—The Narrative of Our Existence*, Live Performance November 5. Washington, DC: Gallaudet University.

Barthes, Roland. 1991 [1957]. *Mythologies.* New York: Noonday Press, Farrar, Straus & Grioux.

———. 2013. *How to Live Together: Novelistic Simulations of Some Everyday Spaces.* New York: Columbia University Press.

Batterbury, Sarah C. E., Paddy Ladd, and Mike Gulliver. 2007. Sign Language Peoples as Indigenous Minorities: Implications for Research and Policy. *Environment and Planning A: Economy and Space* 39 (12): 2899–2915.

Bauman, Hansel. 2014. DeafSpace: An Architecture Toward a More Livable and Sustainable World. In *Deaf Gain: Raising the Stakes for Human Diversity*, ed. H-Dirksen L. Bauman and Joseph J. Murray, 375–401. Minneapolis: University of Minnesota Press.

Bauman, H-Dirksen L., and Joseph J. Murray (eds.). 2014. *Deaf Gain: Raising the Stakes for Human Diversity*. Minneapolis: University of Minnesota Press.

Bell, Alexander Graham. 1884. *Memoir Upon the Formation of a Deaf Variety of the Human Race*. Washington, DC: National Academy of Sciences. University Microfilms International.

Bloch, Ernst. 2009 [1918]. *The Spirit of Utopia*. Meridian, CA: Stanford University Press.

Bruner, Jerome. 1991. The Narrative Construction of Reality. *Critical Inquiry* 18 (1): 1–21.

Bullard, Douglas. 2013 [1986]. *Islay: A Novel*. Washington, DC: Gallaudet University Press.

Christiansen, John B., and Sharon N. Barnartt. 2003. *Deaf President Now! The 1988 Revolution at Gallaudet University*. Washington, DC: Gallaudet University Press.

Clark, John Lee. 2017. Vibrating Mouth. In *Tripping the Tale Fantastic—Weird Fiction by Deaf and Hard of Hearing Writers*, ed. Christopher Jon Heuer, 76–79. Minneapolis: Handtype Press.

De Meulder, Maartje, Joseph J. Murray, and Rachel L. McKee (eds.). 2019. *The Legal Recognition of Sign Languages: Advocacy and Outcomes Around the World*. Bristol: Blue Ridge Summit: Multilingual Matters.

Egbert, John F. 2006. *Mindfield*. Lincoln, Nebraska: iUniverse, Inc.

Erting, Carol J., Robert C. Johnson, Dorothy L. Smith, and Bruce D. Snider (eds.). 1994. *The Deaf Way: Perspectives from the International Conference on Deaf Culture*. Washington, DC: Gallaudet University Press.

Foucault, Michel. 1978. *The History of Sexuality*. New York: Pantheon Books.

———. 2003 [1963]. *The Birth of the Clinic—An Archaeology of Medical Perception*. London: Routledge.

Freire, Paulo. 1970 [1968]. *A Pedagogia do Oprimido*. Rio de Janeiro. Paz e Terra.

Gannon, Jack R. 2009. *The Week the World Heard Gallaudet*. Washington, DC: Gallaudet University Press.

Garretson, Mervin D. 1984. The Sonic Boom of 1994. In *Another Handful of Stories: Thirty-Seven Stories by Deaf Storytellers*, coordinated by Barbara Kannapell and Roslyn Rosen, ed. Ivey B. Pittle and Roslyn Rosen, 51–54. Washington, DC: Division of Public Services, Gallaudet College.

Gil, Cristina. 2019. The Deaf Mythomoteur. In *Línguas de Sinais: Cultura Educação Identidade*, ed. Isabel Sofia Calvário Correia, Pedro Balaus Custódio, Ronaldo Manassés, and Rodrigues Campos, 75–92. Lisboa: Ex-Libris.

———. 2020. Deaftopia: Utopian Representations and Community by the Deaf. Ph.D. dissertation, Portuguese Catholic University.

Goodman, Nelson. 1978. *Ways of Worldmaking*. Indianapolis: Hackett Publishing Company.

Greenwald, Brian H. 2006. Alexander Graham Bell Through the Lens of Eugenics, 1883–1922. Ph.D. dissertation, George Washington University.

———. 2007. Taking Stock: Alexander Graham Bell and Eugenics 1883–1922. In *The Deaf History Reader*, ed. John Vickrey van Cleve, 136–152. Washington, DC: Gallaudet University Press.

Haualand, Hilde, Per Koren Solvang, and Jan-Kåre Breivik. 2015. Deaf Transnational Gatherings at the Turn of the Twenty-First Century and Some Afterthoughts. In *It's a Small World—International Deaf Spaces and Encounters*, ed. Michele Friedner and Annelies Kusters, 47–56. Washington, DC: Gallaudet University Press.

Huxley, Aldous. 2006 [1932]. *Brave New World*. New York: Harper Perennial.

Jankowski, Katherine A. 1997. *Deaf Empowerment: Emergence, Struggle, and Rhetoric*. Washington, DC: Gallaudet University Press.

Ladd, Paddy. 2003. *Understanding Deaf Culture in Search of Deafhood*. Clevedon, England; Buffalo: Multilingual Matters.

———. 2013. Sign Language Peoples and the Significance of Recognition of Deaf Cultures. Presentation at the Digiti Lingua: A Celebration of British Sign Language and Deaf Culture, The Royal Society, London, February 28.

Lane, Harlan. 1992. *The Mask of Benevolence: Disabling the Deaf Community*. New York: Knopf.

Lane, Harlan, Richard Pillard, and Ulf Hedberg. 2011. *The People of the Eye: Deaf Ethnicity and Ancestry*. New York; Oxford: Oxford University Press.

Lane, Harlan, Robert Hoffmeister, and Benjamin J. Bahan. 1996. *A Journey into the Deaf-World*. San Diego, CA: Dawn Sign Press.

Levitas, Ruth. 2010. *The Concept of Utopia*. Ralahine Utopian Studies. Bern, Switzerland: Peter Lang.

———. 2013. *Utopia as Method—The Imaginary Reconstitution of Society*. Hampshire: Palgrave Macmillan.

Moylan, Tom. 2014. *Demand the Impossible: Science Fiction and the Utopian Imagination*, ed. Raffaella Baccolini. Oxford: Peter Lang.

Newman, Lawrence R. 2009. A Brave New World. In *I Fill This Small Space—The Writings of a Deaf Activist*, ed. David. J. Kurs, 224–226. Washington, DC: Gallaudet University Press.

Pabsch, Annika. 2016. Sign Language Legislation as a Tool for Sustainability. In *Sign Language, Sustainable Development, and Equal Opportunities—Envisioning the Future for Deaf Students*, ed. Goedele A. M. De Clerck and Peter V. Paul, 161–189. Washington, DC: Gallaudet University Press.

Peters, Cynthia. 2000. *Deaf American Literature: From Carnival to the Canon*. Washington, DC: Gallaudet University Press.

Rutheford, Susan. 1993. *A Study of American Deaf Folklore*. Linstok Press Dissertation Series. Linstok Press.

Ryan, Donna F., and John S. Schuchman. 2002. *Deaf People in Hitler's Europe*. Washington, DC: Gallaudet University Press.

Ryan, Marie-Laure. 2013 [2012]. Possible Worlds. In *The Living Handbook of Narratology*. https://www.lhn.uni-hamburg.de/node/54.html. Accessed 12 June 2021.

Ryan, Stephen M. 1991. Planet Way Over Yonder. In *ASL Storytime*, vol. 5. Washington, DC: Gallaudet University. Video Cassette.

Sacks, Oliver. 1989. *Seeing Voices: A Journey into the World of the Deaf*. CA: University of California Press.

Sargisson, Lucy. 1996. *Contemporary Feminist Utopianism*. London: Routledge.

Solomon, Andrew. 2014. Deaf. In *Far from the Tree: Parents, Children and the Search for Identity*. London: Vintage Books.

Sturley, Nick. 2003. *Milan*. Victoria, BC: Trafford.

Veditz, George. 1912 [1910]. *Proceedings of the Ninth Convention of the National Association of the Deaf and the Third Worlds Congress of the Deaf*. Philadelphia: The Philocophus Press.

———. 1913. *The Preservation of Sign Language*. National Association of the Deaf. http://videocatalog.gallaudet.edu/?video=2520.

Vieira, Fátima. 2010. The Concept of Utopia. In *The Cambridge Companion to Utopian Literature*, ed. Gregory Claeys, 3–27. UK: Cambridge University Press.

Wa Thiong'o, NGugi. 1994 [1987]. *Decolonising the Mind: The Politics of Language in African Literature*. Harare, Zimbabwe: Zimbabwe Publishing House.

Wegner, Phillip. 2002. *Imaginary Communities: Utopia, the Nation, and the Spatial Histories of Modernity*. Berkeley: University of California Press.

Wrigley, Owen. 1996. *The Politics of Deafness*. Washington, DC: Gallaudet University Press.

Young, Kelsey. 2017. Understanding. In *Tripping the Tale Fantastic—Weird Fiction by Deaf and Hard of Hearing Writers*, ed. Christopher Jon Heuer, 157–173. Minneapolis: Handtype Press.

Micronations and Hyperutopias

Fátima Vieira

Introduction

The entry for "How to Start Your Own Country," from wikiHow, "the most trusted how-to site on the internet," takes us on a 15-step journey to start our own micronation (wikiHow 2021, n.d.). The recipe is simple and has widespread application, and is available in several languages from many other websites related to nation-building: first, we look at our own country and decide what aspects should be preserved or changed; then we make our plans, we invent names for the nation, the capital, the language, and create a flag, an anthem, a state seal and other symbols; we find land that has not been claimed by existing countries, conquer a micronation, or explore the sea or the virtual world; we invite our friends—like-minded people—and establish a government, a constitution, an economy, decide a title for ourselves and the other citizens (is the micronation a kingdom, a principality, a republic?...); we present ourselves to the other imaginary nations, engage in diplomatic relations, and try not to get conquered by a stronger community. This chapter explores worlds that are inventing themselves.

F. Vieira (✉)
Department of Anglo-American Studies, Faculty of Arts,
University of Porto, Porto, Portugal

P. Marks et al. (eds.), *The Palgrave Handbook of Utopian and Dystopian Literatures*, https://doi.org/10.1007/978-3-030-88654-7_22

279

MICRONATIONS

The internet is bursting with imaginary countries in all languages, often described on websites constructed with online drag and drop tools. The questionable aesthetics and reduced functionalities of these websites indicate that, as a rule, they are created by adventurous people with no formal training in computing or design. The high degree of similarity between the maps adopted by recent micronations reveals that they are all resorting to the same fantasy map tools and probably watching the same tutorials.[1] It seems as though the internet has been invaded by worldbuilders—eager to share the wonders of their imagination though technically unskilled. But are these amateurs aware of the fact that while they are describing the geography, ethnography, politics, religion, and education of their imagined countries they are modelling their worlds after Thomas More's literary utopia? Most of the time, they are not.

Over recent years, micronations have become a powerful pedagogical tool for simulation and scenario-based learning. Salto-Youth, for instance, a "network of seven Resource Centers working on European priority areas within the youth field" (Salto-Youth, n.d.), created The Intercultural Fiesta on Imaginary Countries and Cultures, a tool for intercultural learning via creativity. In the same way, books such as Kathy Ceceri's *Micronations: Invent Your Own Country and Culture with 25 Projects* (2014) were written for class activities, indicating grade level and text complexity according to the Guided Reading Levels and Lexile measures. In one way or another, the various pedagogical tools and books related to the invention of micronations raise awareness about the functioning of a nation, inviting students to research different forms of democracy, reflect on rights, laws, and rules, and fostering discussion on themes such as inclusion and the environment; they nurture curiosity, creating spaces for experimentation and collective decision-making; and they promote active citizenship and cooperation, orienting the school community toward realizing projects in real life. Nevertheless, the word "utopia" is seldom used, and even when it is, with no reference to Thomas More, the father of worldbuilding. Pan-Utopia 2100 is an exception in this respect.

Pan-Utopia 2100 was presented in 2010 by ILCML,[2] a research center of the University of Porto, as an interactive utopia meant to provide students with a "forum for reflecting on the future" and "designing an alternative society set on an imaginary island." The site invited schools to form a "League of Utopian Schools" and offered pedagogical resources with a section on the concepts of utopia and utopianism.[3] While investing in their exercise of collective imagination (each class was expected to present its own utopia), students were very much aware of the link between their narratives and Thomas More's *Utopia*. Not a word on micronations was then uttered—and perhaps it is because of this that students always thought that what they were writing were Utopias, which were then published on the internet. Another word was used instead to describe what they were doing: writing *hyperutopias*. We will return to the topic of *hyperutopias* later.

Outside the school system, micronations proliferated so much at the turn to the twentieth century that Lonely Planet published, in 2006, *Micronations: The Lonely Planet Guide to Home-Made Nations*,[4] presenting it as a "fully illustrated, humorous mock-guidebook to the nations that people create in their own backyards—most of which can be visited" (LibraryThing, n.d.). Online micronations are nowadays aggregated in leagues, associations and a variety of organizations. According to LOSS—the League of Secessionist States—micronations go by different names: "ephemeral states, imaginary states, model nations, counter-countries and unrecognized states" (LOSS, n.d.). Some micronation sites highlight the differences that separate them from imaginary countries; the features that are normally evoked are their eccentric and ephemeral nature, and their unrecognized claim of sovereignty over some physical territory,[5] but in recent years the virtual space of the internet has been persistently explored and claimed as well.[6] Another aspect has to do with the (quite often difficult) diplomatic relations micronations establish with each other. In fact, many micronation associations were created to provide these microstates with opportunities to establish alliances.[7] The MicroFreedom (2021) website reminds us that micronations can take different forms: they may be "a collection of brave souls trying to establish a new country; a group of people claiming sovereignty from an existing government; a model country that exists solely as work of fiction, or just for fun; a tiny jurisdiction that has escaped the notice of major powers." The site offers a dynamic vision of worldbuilding: 39 "Distinguished Micronations"; "14 Emerging Micronations"; and 243 "Defunct." This last number gives full expression to the ephemeral nature of online micronations which renders the very scarce literature on them quickly obsolete.[8]

As a rule, the Home Page of a micronation's site offers an explanation about its statute. Karnia-Ruthenia's (2020) site clarifies for its visitors: "A constitutional Monarchy claiming lands in America and Europe, we are not a simulation or a game, but we are a real, functioning micronation. If you join us, the Emperor and the People will chart the course for your future in a common effort to build and maintain our great nation." The site is structured like a blog with five main sections: "About" (History, Structure, Symbols, Culture); "News" (written in journalistic style); "Geography"; "Monarchy" (Dynasty, Emperor, Nobility); "More" (Military, Government, Diplomacy). The Home Page also displays sections for requesting online citizenship, challenging visitors to contribute to the nation by taking on the role of a journalist, a diplomat, an economist, or a senator, and suggesting that the Emperor may even make him a nobleman. Although the website is in English, one can find information about the nation in different languages elsewhere on the internet. *Courrier Micronational*, an online publication on micronations, offers a study allegedly written by "King-Emperor Oscar de Karnia-Ruthenia" (2020)[9] and translated into French "by Prince Emanuel de Bérémagne"[10] (testifying to knowledge exchange between the nations), while the Karnia-Ruthenia official website forwards the visitor to a rather dynamic Facebook page that includes posts in Portuguese and in English and displays an address in São Paulo, Brazil. A post dated 18 April 2021 reveals that a new census has been released: "Brazilians become the majority among citizens (22.3%), the most declared ethnicity among citizens is Caucasian (71.6%), Catholicism remains the predominant religion (40.8%), and increases the number of men (79%)."[11]

Cases of Micronations congregating citizens from all over the world and with information in different languages are not rare.[12] The most celebrated example is perhaps that of The Holy Empire of Reunion/O Sacro Império de Reunião, which, when it was created in 1997, displayed a version in English and in Portuguese.[13] From 1999 on, only the Portuguese version was regularly updated. For two decades, it thrived on the internet as an active, participatory, and democratic micronation. It basically ceased its activity in 2018, as its Facebook page indicates[14]; in that year, the "Emperor" declared to the main television network of Réunion (the real, macronation in the Indian Ocean that is an overseas department and region of France) that his micronation had 100,000 citizens from all over the world.[15] He then disclosed that, right from the start, the micronation was all about discussing ideal models and putting them into written speeches—thousands of pages arguing for different views on a better world. The section on "Micronationalism" provides relevant information on the history and heterogeneity of the micronational movement, as well as on micropatriology, a "scientific discipline that studies micro-states, micro-nations and separatist movements in general."[16] This section also identifies the theoretical references of the Holy Empire of Reunion, among which Fabrice O'Driscoll's *Ils ne siègent pas à l'ONU* (They do not sit on the United Nations, 2000). An interesting chapter concerns "Projeto Alvorada" (the Sunrise Project); the text describing the project, published about one decade after the creation of the Holy Empire, calls for the energy and the creativity of its citizens to be channeled toward a further development of micronationalism, which implies a renovation of the ideas and a deeper investment in diplomatic initiatives with other micronations (Sacro Império de Reunião, n.d.). Although it is an imperialistic nation, Reunion aims at promoting democratic modes of organization. As we can read on its website, in Reunion "every individual is a public person; everything he writes and says is heard and taken into account by the other subjects (citizens) through an official list of messages (e-mails) named CHANDON" (Sacro Império de Reunião, n.d.). This is no doubt a good example of how a micronation is revealed to the real world.

Sometimes the relation to the real world is more direct—quite often through humorous criticism. The Aerican Empire is a good example of a project that started as a joke. Founded in 1987 by the Canadian Eris Lis and his friends, the micronation claimed sovereignty over the solar system—quite often over invented planets; however, with the advent of the internet, it engaged in diplomatic relations with other micronations, which forced the Aerican community to more clearly define its ideal forms of organization. Its website reflects an investment in documents regarding foreign affairs but also the Constitution of the micronation. Humor is transversal to all of this imaginary country—and the object of its criticism as well. The "Hillary Clinton Act" is a good example of this: "A citizen of any colony may run for a senate seat in another colony provided that if said citizen wins he or she must move to the colony he or she represents."[17] Many of the sections are simply silly: the nation's official religion is Silinism, that worships the Great Penguin, and one of the most important ministries is the Ministry of Silly Things 3000 that monitors "silliness in the Empire, as well as holidays, celebrations, events, and more" (Aerican Empire, n.d.). What most obviously emanates from this micronation, however, is a fascination for Sci-Fi and for pure invention. These seem to be good reasons for Aerican communities across the world to meet not only online, but also by attending physical events. The website has an online shop that sells Aerican-related items, most of which bear the nation's icon: the Canadian flag with a smiley face covering up the maple leaf. For a reasonable price visitors may buy mugs, t-shirts, stickers, and towels, among other items.[18] Aericans first began issuing coinage as early as 2009, stamps in 2015 and banknotes in 2017. The first passport was issued in 2007.

The Principauté d'Aigues-Mortes (Principality of Dead-Eagles) also started as a joke, a parody of the Principality of Monaco. Created in 2011, it soon engaged the local community of Camargue, France, in an alternative movement that inspired local artisans and contributed to the socio-cultural and economic development of the region. In 2017, the Principality launched its own currency to support local trade and crafts. Nowadays, it serves the city through an association—LOUPAM—that enables the Principality to organize events which are meaningful, in different ways, to the community (Principauté d'Aigues-Mortes 2020).

Other micronations have been founded out of cries of protest. Such was the case with the Gay and Lesbian Kingdom of the Coral Sea Islands, established in 2004 as a symbolic protest by a group of gay rights activists based in Australia, demanding that the government recognize same-sex marriages. The micronation created a flag, stamps, and other symbols. It was dissolved in 2017 when Australia legalized gay marriage.[19]

Cyber Yugoslavia is also a subversive response to the problems Yugoslavs suffered from the disintegration of the Socialist Federal Republic of Yugoslavia. Arguing that its citizens had lost their country in 1991 and have been ever since citizens of Atlantis, this micronation offers passports to any individual, regardless of his/her nationality: "If you feel Yugoslav, you are welcome to apply for CY citizenship, regardless of your current nationality and citizenship." Cyber Yugoslavia thus challenges the idea of nationhood normally associated with micronations[20]; and this explains why its Constitution is translated into 18 languages (plus Cyber Yugoslavian, an obviously invented language). The playfulness of the idea of a counter-state also emanates from the Constitution that establishes, in its first article, that the text is always open to be changed: "Changes on the Constitution are suggested on citizen's personage page (interactive passport). Every citizen has the right to suggest a change to the Constitution. This suggestion can only be accepted or rejected if the majority of the population of CY agrees, through a Method of public vote" (Cyber Yugoslavia 1999).

There are many other micronations that position themselves as counter-states, standing for values that do not predominate in real societies, but that also have the very clear objective of having an impact on citizens' real life. The Grand Duchy of Flandrensis' website, for instance, is very clear regarding its political program: "As an environmental nonprofit organization we use micronationalism to raise on [sic] a creative manner awareness for climate change and Antarctica" (Flandrensis, n.d.). Claiming to have 729 citizens of 71 nationalities (and zero inhabitants), the Flandrensis sees as its responsibility "to protest against organizations or countries who harm the Antarctic environment and to support the ones who want to transform Antarctica into one protected maritime area" (ibid.).

Although they create a world very much of their own, with original flags, anthems, coats of arms, stamps, national currency, and even merchandise, and are clearly part of a much wider game as they associate with other micronations in alliances and confederations, making a considerable investment in diplomatic relations, the truth is that the micronations we find today on the internet are, in their vast majority, very different from the ones that abounded during the three final decades of the twentieth century, claiming sovereignty over a physical space (however small and most impracticable for a whole community to live in). With the advent of the internet, micronations gained, in fact, a global expression, contradicting the national/local vocation of the first fictive experiments. Inscribed on the global space of the internet, current micronations subscribe to Peter Ravn Rasmussen's (Prince of Corvinia) idea that what binds a nation together is its "shared cultural heritage," its "linguistic coherence" and the "sense of identification" it provides its members, an experience that does not necessarily imply the existence of a physical territory.[21] Furthermore, micronations have allowed for the formation of virtual communities of like-minded people who go on to meet outside the cyberspace.[22] This feeling of community results from the active engagement of the citizens: the longest-lasting micronational experiments are the ones that manage to ensure the involvement of its members in the construction of the nations' identity.[23] This idea fully matches the reality of our community networks, that are of a truly rhizomatic nature.

Hyperutopias

It has always struck me as self-evident that micronations and utopias belong to the same family; the silence on this not-so-distant relationship has puzzled me for the past two decades. It has most certainly to do with the fact that the first statement that a micronation ever makes is about the reality of its existence (in spite of the impracticality or non-existence of its territoriality); in fact, this is part of the game—micronations always challenge us to accept this paradox.

But are we not faced with a similar paradox when reading More's *Utopia*, whose very name indicates that it is a *non-place*? It is true that there are two other aspects that need to be taken into consideration when we are thinking of the relation between utopias and micronations: the active engagement of micronations with each other (often of a warmongering nature), and the collective engagement of a community of worldbuilders. But don't we feel, while reading a utopian text, that it engages in a conversation with other texts within the same tradition? At times, the conversation between texts is more evident, as is the case with William Morris's *News from Nowhere* (1890) responding to Edward Bellamy's Fabian vision in *Looking Backward* (1888), or with the meta-utopian *A Modern Utopia* (1904), in which H.G. Wells considers both individual and collective preceding utopian visions. On the other hand, the very nature of utopianism has changed over the last decades— Miguel Abensour (2013, 205–206) called it the *new utopian spirit*: it is now experimental, fragmentary (in the sense that it invests in the creation of "small utopias"), and results from a collective imagination exercise. These traits, that we can find in the pragmatical utopianism that has become characteristic of French activism in particular,[24] inevitably affected utopia as a literary genre.

The reason why, in my perspective, we do not think of micronations as literary utopias is because we still have, as a single point of reference, printed literary utopias. We need, then, to contemplate what will happen to utopia if we transpose it to the internet. I am not referring, naturally, to literary texts published in PDF format, or the equivalent, but rather to texts that adopt the new hypertextual language that characterizes electronic literature.

The hypertext has become an instrument and a platform for literary experiments, as the new modalities for artistic and literary creation not only interfere with the way text is presented but also with the way meaning is conveyed (Cordeiro 2004). In hypertextual fiction (or hyperfiction) readers are faced with blocks of text they are supposed to assemble by clicking on links; these will forward them to other (multimodal) documents belonging to the same assemblage. By creating their own paths through these blocks of text, readers thus take on a performative role. In some way, they become the authors of those particular (unrepeatable) paths. The hypertext thus relies on the idea of the construction of narrative in an open (cyber) *space* through the linkage of *fragments*, presenting this process as a collaborative and positive one. In this way, it gives expression to our contemporary experience of life, as we no longer live—as Michel Foucault (1984) has contended and Edward Soja (1999) repeatedly elaborated on—in the era of time (which informed euchronia) but in the era of space, of the dispersed, of the juxtaposed, of the simultaneous, in which events, more than in their diachronic dimension, are to be understood synchronously, by the extension and possibilities that are constantly crossing them (Soja 1999, 11). But what will a literary utopia published on the internet, resorting to hyperfiction conventions (i.e., a hyperutopia), look like? Pretty much like an online micronation.

Bergonia, a Website constructed by Joe Cometti, is a very good example of a hyperutopia.[25] At first glance, it looks like an ordinary site on the internet. Cometti has thus resorted to a strategy similar to More's to confer verisimilitude on his narrative: More built his narrative on the model of travel literature; Cometti uploaded his imaginary country to the internet, closely following the models set by sites of real countries. One should also evoke the analogies that can be established between the sea voyages of Raphael Hythloday and the common metaphor of the internet as a sea of information. By sailing on a sea that mixes real and unreal information, the internet user discovers the site of a country named Bergonia; and like the Portuguese sailor, who, coming ashore on the island of Utopia, explored the streets, chatted with the natives and tried to understand their customs, so the modern sailor of the internet meticulously explores the imaginary country of Bergonia, following a road made of hyperlinks. In fact, one of the main differences between *Utopia* and *Bergonia* lies in the higher level of autonomy that the latter confers on the reader—which results, however, from the fact that we are not talking about printed fiction, but about hyperfiction.

By visiting Bergonia, the Internaut reader will encounter the most important themes of utopian literature. Bergonia is a Democratic Republic, consisting of 31 states, which justifies the variety of languages and cultures that characterizes this country. The respect for the Other seems to be a constant in this society in all aspects of its organization: Bergonia is a country populated by tolerant and friendly people, a society that is capable of welcoming the differences and making them productive. Respect for the Other also implies the desire to get to know the culture of the Other by learning the Other's language; that is the reason why Bergonia is a multilingual society. On the site, the political organization of Bergonia is carefully described: a decentralized democratic socialism prevails in the country. The investment in the creative imagination of a history for Bergonia also led the author to describe the revolution which resulted in the implementation of the current political system, which in turn brought about the establishment of a new economy, presenting mixed solutions, but mainly based on a cooperative system and aimed at respecting ecological concerns. Libertarian socialist law is the organizing principle of this society, whereas a remarkable spirit of tolerance presides over the sociability of an unusual religious heterogeneity. The site carefully describes the simple life of the Bergonians, what they wear and where they live, their gastronomy and all kinds of recreation; the invention of a likely historical past drew Cometti to pre-historical times, compelling him to invent the history of the evolution of the different Bergonian languages and even of the different features of each race.

We can thus find in Bergonia's seemingly never-ending feast of imagination a utopia that is, in the way it operates, very similar to the traditional literary utopias. In truth, if in the Morean text the reader is introduced to a world where the frontiers between the real and the unreal are blurred, in Bergonia's case the utopian imagination is founded on a serious study, on the part of the author, of the historical evolution of various civilizations. Behind the invention of several languages, religions, and races, lies thorough research in the fields of Anthropology, Linguistics, Sociology, Political Philosophy, Geography and the History of Religions. This oscillation between invented and real referents performs in Bergonia—as indeed in the utopian literature in general—the function of promoting a very explicit political, economic, and social message. On the site, we can find hyperlinks to other sites on the internet that the utopist found to be of some relevance. Although these are quite different in nature, they all have in common the fact that they describe political organizations that really exist and that contest the established political and social order in the USA. Oscar Wilde's assertion that a map without utopia is not worth looking at, used by Cometti as an epigraph for the "About US" section, clearly also inscribes Bergonia in the utopian tradition.

CONCLUSION

Because *Bergonia* directly resorts to utopian works and tropes, the reader inevitably takes it as a hyperutopia. However, there are not many differences between the structure of Cometti's Website and the structure of Micronations, as a comparison between *Bergonia* and *The Holy Empire of Reunion*, for instance, would reveal. It is true that what distinguishes Micronations is the fact that they are the product of collective imagination, but there is nothing in the utopian genre establishing that utopias need to be written by one author only. I believe that the reason we do not immediately accept online Micronations as an evolution of literary utopianism has to do with the fact that their literary quality is not evident. However, this is the very nature of cyberspace: as Alain Finkielkraut has noted, the internet promotes a discourse that is entirely levelled, an "exuberance without hierarchies" (Finkielkraut 2002, 24). This applies both to micronations and hyperfiction, as all authors, professionals, or amateurs, are given the same exact right to publish online: cyberspace is now the public *agora* where everyone is entitled to speaking. The fact that new drag and drop storytelling software is getting more accessible and affordable everyday clearly contributes to this democratizing of the cyberspace. However, as Paul Soriano (2002, 55) has argued, it is not the communication device that creates the *agora*: a public space needs a common language and culture, in other words, like-minded people, to construct community. The question that needs answering, in the framework of a century bursting with micronational imagination, is: what will the result be of all these collective exercises of imagination? Are we finally training the generations of creative, collaborative, and participative minds we need to change the world? Is utopia at last performing its catalyzing mission?

Notes

1. There are many online tutorials for the creation of maps of imaginary countries. Adobe Photoshop, for instance, seems to be an easy tool for creating fantasy maps (*see* e.g. https://www.youtube.com/watch?v=plF 8mdhANMM).

2. Instituto de Literatura Comparada Margarida Losa.

3. *See* http://panutopia.oxys.pt/. This version of PAN-UTOPIA was updated in 2016 and invited students to reflect on the importance of food by creating an "Alimentopia." The theme of the previous version (2010–2014), no longer available online, was broader, and mainly built on a previous project (2005–2009) called Eurotopia, which challenged students to imagine what Europe will be like in the year 2100. More than 5000 students participated in these projects.

4. The book, written by John Ryan, George Dunford, and Simon Sellars, was also published in the same year under the title *Micronations: The Lonely Planet Guide to Self-Proclaimed Nations*.

5. *See*, for example, *Micronations: A Brief History*, an anonymous online book published in 2011. Available at: https://pdfcoffee.com/micro-nations-pdf-free.html.

6. *See* Frédéric Lasserre, "Les hommes qui voulaient être rois. II. Sociologie des États privés".

7. The Organisation de la microfrancophonie (Microfrancophone Organization), for example, was created in 2016 to favor inter-micronational harmony. *See* http://www.microfrancophonie.org.

8. Reading Stephen Mihm's article "Utopian Rulers, and Spoofs, Stake Out Territory Line," published in *The New York Times* in May 2000 is quite an experience, as many of the sites mentioned are no longer available.

9. Available at: http://www.courriermicronational.com/infos/actualites/oscar-de-karnia-ruthenia-une-etude-sur-le-micronationalisme.html.

10. My translation from the French publication.

11. Available at: https://www.facebook.com/karniaruthenia/.

12. A good example of this is the Principality of Surland, established in 2015 to "spread science, education, culture." The site is available in both French and English: https://surlandgouv.wixsite.com/surlandgouv.

13. Today only a few sections of the English version of the site are available.

14. *See* https://www.facebook.com/reuniao/. The Holy Empire of Reunion's Webpage displayed only two posts in 2019 and three in 2020; no posts for 2021.

15. *See* https://www.facebook.com/reuniao/videos/626100674454747. This is quite an interesting video, recorded when the "Emperor", aged 39, visits the island for his honeymoon.

16. *See*   http://www.reuniao.org/projeto4.0/micr_micropatriologia.htm (my translation). According to the website, there were reports as early as 1973 of an international association of Micropatriology, directed by Frederick W. Lehmann.

17. Available at: http://www.aericanempire.com/clintonact.html. Adopted into law: 10/18/01.

18. *See* the Aerican Empire "Souvenir Shop." Available at: https://www.cafepress.com/aerica.

19. *See* https://comicro.fandom.com/wiki/Gay_and_Lesbian_Kingdom_of_the_Coral_Sea_Islands. The original website is no longer available online.

20. As is the case with The Empire of Atlantium, which presents itself as "a Global Sovereign State" informing us, in the FAQs section, that "The primacy legitimacy of Atlantium should be determined by its de facto existence as represented by its community of Citizens—wherever they happen to be distributed geographically—and its operation institutions—and not on the basis of assertions of territorial imperium " (https://www.atlantium.org/faq.html).

21. For more information on these ideas, *see* http://www.reuniao.org/projeto4.0/micr_micropatriologia.htm. *See also* http://www.corvinia.org.

22. As one can read on the website of the Holy Empire of Reunion, many couples first met on the Website, and then married and had children: http://www.reuniao.org/projeto4.0/imperio.htm (my translation).

23. The Empire of Atlantium's Website indicates that citizens may "explore business or trade opportunities, promote open discussions, debate policy positions, or provide practical, material or in-kind support as their level of motivation and circumstances allow" (https://www.atlantium.org/faq.html).

24. *See* Roudaut, *L'Utopie. Mode d'emploi*, esp. pp. 12, 20–21.

25. www.bergonia.org.

References

Abensour, Miguel. 2013. *Utopiques II. L'Homme est un animal utopique*. Paris: Sens&Tonka.

Aerican Empire. n.d. MST3K. http://www.aericanempire.com/bst.html. Accessed 25 June 2021.

Ceceri, Kathy. 2014. *Micronations: Invent Your Own Country and Culture with 25 Projects*. Illustrated by Chad Thompson. White River Junction: Nomad.

Cordeiro, Andreia. 2004. O que é o hipertexto electrónico e de que forma altera a organização e a utilização dos textos? *DigLitWeb: Digital Literature Web*. http://www.ci.uc.pt/diglit/DigLitWebCdeCodiceeComputadorEnsaio07.html.

Cyber Yugoslavia. 1999. Constitution of CY (English). http://www.juga.com/constitution/const_eng.htm. Accessed 25 June 2021.

Driscoll, Fabrice. 2000. *Ils ne siègent pas à l'ONU*. Paris, Toulon: Presses du Midi.

Finkielkraut, Alain. 2002. Fatal Liberdade. In *Internet: O Êxtase Inquietante*, ed. Alain Finkielkraut and Paul Soriano, 9–33. Lisbon: O Século.

Flandrensis. n.d. Who are we. https://flandrensis.com/about/who-are-we/. Accessed 25 June 2021.

Foucault, Michel. 1984. *Foucault Reader*, ed. Paul Rabinow. London: Penguin.

Karnia-Ruthenia. 2020. Structure. http://karnia-ruthenia.org/about/structure-and-name/. Accessed 25 June 2021.

de Karnia-Ruthenia, Oscar. 2020. Oscar de Karnia-Ruthenia: Une Étude sur le Micronationalisme. *Courrier Micronational*, September 8. http://www.courriermicronational.com/infos/actualites/oscar-de-karnia-ruthenia-une-etude-sur-le-micronationalisme.html.

Lasserre, Frédéric. 2012. Les hommes qui voulaient être rois. II. Sociologie des États privés. *Cybergeo: European Journal of Geography/Revue Européene de Géographie*. https://journals.openedition.org/cybergeo/25385.

LibraryThing. n.d. Micronations: The Lonely Planet Guide to Self-Proclaimed Nations. https://www.librarything.com/work/1675880. Accessed 25 June 2021.

LOSS. n.d. What Is the LOSS? http://www.theloss.org/. Accessed 25 June 2021.

MicroFreedom. 2021. What Is a micronation? https://travisdmchenry.wixsite.com/microfreedom. Accessed 25 June 2021.

Mihm, Stephen. 2000. Utopian Rulers, and Spoofs, Stake Out Territory Online. *The New York Times on the Web*, May 24. https://archive.nytimes.com/www.nytimes.com/library/tech/00/05/circuits/articles/25nati.html.

PAN-UTOPIA. n.d. Pan-Utopia 2100: An Interactive Utopia. http://panutopia.oxys.pt/. Accessed 25 June 2021.

Principauté d'Aigues-Mortes. 2020. Laissez-nous nous presenter. https://www.principaute-aigues-mortes.com/. Accessed 25 June 2021.

Roudaut, Sandrine. 2018. *L'Utopie. Mode d'emploi. Modifier les comportements pour um monde soutenable et désirable*. Rezée: La Mer Salée.

Ryan, John, Georges Dunford, and Simon Sellars. 2006. *Micronations: The Lonely Planet Guide to Home-Made Nations*. London: Lonely Planet.

Sacro Império de Reunião. n.d. Informações Gerais. http://www.reuniao.org/projeto4.0/saiba.htm. Accessed 25 June 2021.

———. n.d. Projeto Alvorada. http://www.reuniao.org/projeto4.0/micr_alvorada.htm. Accessed 25 June 2021.

Salto-Youth. n.d. About SALTO-YOUTH. https://www.salto-youth.net/about/. Accessed 25 June 2021.

Soja, Edward. 1999. *Postmodern Geographies: The Reassertion of Space in Critical Social Theory*. London: Verso.

Soriano, Paul. 2002. O Zero-Um e o Infinito: Um Humanismo sem Homem? In *Internet: O Êxtase Inquietante*, ed. Alain Finkielkraut and Paul Soriano, 35–67. Lisbon: O Século.

wikiHow. 2021. How to Start Your Own Country. https://www.wikihow.com/Start-Your-Own-Country. Accessed 25 June 2021.

wikiHow. n.d. Main Page. https://www.wikihow.com/Main-Page. Accessed 25 June 2021

Political Theories and Practices

Humanism

Carlos Eduardo Ornelas Berriel

Introduction

There is a deep connection between Humanism and the emergence of utopia as a literary genre. More's *Utopia* is often understood as an inherently Humanist work concerning the rationale of the State and the real-life, historical exercise of politics. Humanism falls into a broad category of ethics which affirms how morality—and consequently value and dignity—depends on what is common to men in their condition, thus refuting transcendent paradigms. Humanism's foundations lie in Ancient Greek considerations of human existence that can be found in works of Hellenic theater. It also benefitted from Roman philosophical literature, notably the works of Cicero (106 BCE–43 BCE) and Seneca (4 BCE–65 CE). Humanism understands human nature as essentially cultural, its resurgence in the Renaissance a consequence of the historicization of thinking by the Ancients through the discovery of lost texts, the study of architectural monuments, the analysis of ancient languages, the "imitation" of Ancient thinking, the comparative confrontation with their present and its defense, and the return to nature and reality. The rise of modern philology allowed Humanists, influenced by Petrarch (1304–1374), to evaluate the genetics of the manuscripts found. Cicero's concept of *Humanitas*, which re-emerges in this period, is understood in terms of civilization, culture, education, discipline, and training. The making of a human

C. E. O. Berriel (✉)
University of Campinas, Campinas, Brazil

© The Author(s), under exclusive license to Springer Nature
Switzerland AG 2022
P. Marks et al. (eds.), *The Palgrave Handbook of Utopian and Dystopian Literatures*, https://doi.org/10.1007/978-3-030-88654-7_23

is the simultaneous development of independent thought, free reason, critical thinking, individual work, and research. These principles were cultivated through the ancient ideal of broad-based education and training, or Paideia. The restored Ancient intellectual universe becomes the Humanist model of knowledge. Renaissance humanism, then, took Athens and Rome as sources of cultural and political inspiration. Greco-Roman everyday life was valued as the reference point for fulfilled experience in Italian Renaissance city-states, especially Florence and Rome (see Baron 1988). Cultural relativity or the consciousness felt by Humanists to "live" simultaneously in two histories, their own and that of Antiquity, allowed the foundation of History as science, not merely as a chronicle. A consequence of this new knowledge was that Humanists no longer understood themselves as products of a pre-existing nature, but were instead the authors of their own selfhood. The emergence of Utopia, a place constructed by independent-minded humans, depends on that understanding. This chapter explores the early development of Humanism and its ongoing relevance to utopian thinking in our own time.

PICO DELLA MIRANDOLA AND ERASMUS OF ROTTERDAM

In this atmosphere of philosophical Humanism, Pico della Mirandola (1463–1494) in the *Oration on the Dignity of Man* (*Oratio de Hominis Dignitate*, 1486) asserts that humans are the authors of their own existence, analogous to the architect endowed with infinite, though imperfect, creative ability. This allows for infinite self-perfecting (also found in the Augustinian tradition). Starting from the creation myth, Pico imagines that God, having fashioned the world and its non-human life forms, decided to create humankind as the exemplar of his work. God decided that humankind would not have a defined nature, nor a precise place to live, in as much as, completely free to choose, humankind would find the most satisfactory position. Humans stand in contrast to the natural world ruled by fixed and immutable laws ascribed by God, being just as capable of falling to the level of beasts as they are to cleave their spirit to the divine. According to Pico, humankind would have possibilities of growth and improvement, of transforming the world and the self. The dignity of humanity consists not in *being*, but in *becoming*, the latter something fundamentally different from the "becoming" of natural things. Not surprisingly, the *Oratio* is often considered a Humanistic manifesto, and it is possible to speculate that there is no bourgeois ethics without it. Critically, Thomas More translated Pico's work, as did Erasmus of Rotterdam. Considered the foremost exponent of so-called Christian Humanism, Erasmus (1466–1536) combined both Classic and Patristic models in his observations on contemporary political and ethical problems—the Reformation, the consolidation of nation-states, the New World. Like Pico della Mirandola, Erasmus formulated a theory according to which every human being is sovereign of their own consciousness and, therefore, of their own actions (*Diatribe de Libero Bítrio, The Freedom of the Will*, 1524). Thus, philosophical Humanism came to elaborate a theory of humankind—on their constitution, their place in the cosmos, their Divine relations and destiny, and their roles in a community. The nature-culture dialectic that arises from the analysis of the relationship between the individual and the cosmos, the macrocosm and the microcosm, reveals in Humanism the insurmountable relationship between the two terms, as well as the tension and the recurring risk of favoring one to the detriment of the other.

UTOPIA

It could be said that the utopian genre was born under a promising star: individual existence and social living are seen by Humanism as historical and therefore malleable. The conception, developed by social praxis, that humankind could be accountable for its own destiny, suggested the existence of universally valid criteria that could and should be met by everyone, so that a standard, a guide, a rule, a code emerged for different sector of human activity. This was a time of manuals, thesauruses, and treatises, explaining everything from the creation of a successful ruler, as in *The Prince* by Niccolò Machiavelli (1513), or the perfect courtier, as with Baldassare Castiglione's *The Book of the Courtier* (1528), down to the perfect manners at table, recommended by Giovanni Della Casa in *The Rules of Polite Behavior* (1558). *Utopia* might be seen in this environment as representing the perfect republic. Yet from the outset, the title has been understood in a variety of ways, including (but not limited to) supposedly perfect societies. *Utopia* in time came to be seen as the prototype of a literary genre that continues to evolve and unfold in numerous manifestations, always reflecting the conditions and problems of the respective utopist. To More and his contemporary Humanists, the term "utopia" carries a range of semantic possibilities: non-reality; the project of an ideal state; the ideal of virtue; something with no possibility of realization; the function of a critical norm. The utopian genre as it develops synthesizes this initial complex dynamism between tradition and reformation that marked Renaissance Humanism. While belief in social perfectibility, intrinsic to Christianity, preceded the genesis of *Utopia*, More's text indicated that society was incomplete, but that this incompleteness had a solution based on reason. The influence of Plato is evident, but *Utopia* would also combine economic and ethical perspectives, which could suggest an anti-capitalistic basis for living. Additionally, the historicization and denaturalization of human subjectivity are linked to Humanism's secularization of nature, through the emergence and transmission across Europe of modern scientific methods and discoveries, developed and debated by people such the Englishman Francis Bacon (1561–1626), the Italian Galileo Galilei (1561–1626) and the Frenchman René Descartes (1596–1650).

More's *Utopia*, then, can be seen as a cultural symptom of the interstice between feudalism and capitalism, the work of a humanist and statesman who identifies the advent of the monetary economy as the source of the festering social ills of sixteenth-century England. Consequently, that type of economy is absent in his fictitious state. The abolition of private property, the dignification of labor (mandatory for all inhabitants of Utopia), the uniformity of education and dress codes, the food consumed in the community, and an austere life—all derive from the traditional praise of Christian confessional poverty. The perspective of More (and other early utopists) is based on subordinating economy to ethics, creating the model of a society not governed by necessity, but by Christian charity. This parallel world also is designed to maximize the output of work through superior technique and organization, communal participation, and the humanizing of labor. These factors suggest *Utopia* as a special style of political fiction, one that unites the ethical and economic perspectives in one body of work, with structural elements reminiscent of the primitive Greek community.

HUMANISM: A CONCEPT IN TRANSITION

The concept of Humanism has always been in a state of flux, reflecting, at any given time, the demands of an ever-changing world. With the *Essays* of Michel de Montaigne (1533–1592) Humanism begins to be defined by self-investigation (with its prefatory admission: "*je suis moi-même la matière de mon livre*"; "I am the subject of my book"). There is often an encounter with alterity and an engagement with history and culture from the Ancients. Montaigne's approach, for example, allows him to understand and value cannibals for their rites and virtues, their nature and their acknowledged culture (*Essais*, 1580–1588). By contrast, Gottlieb Leibniz (1646–1716) in *Théodicée* (1710), explores how God can allow evil to occur in the world. Leibniz's thought assumes a single ruling point—the supreme monad, which is God. For Leibniz, the consequence of this approach is the perception of our world as the best that is possible, which makes for a "divine utopia." For humanists who have absorbed the thesis that original liberty is capable of elevating humankind toward the divine, Leibniz's ideas represent an extraordinary challenge. The essays that make up that study argue that even in the most astonishing and grotesque of environments there may be enough reasons why God—always aware of how much evil would worsen our world—has chosen to create this universe. Thus, if humankind gazes on the totality of creation with the eyes of the Spirit, they should understand that it would not be possible to create anything better than the existing world. One consequence of this is that the reason for any earthly utopia created by humans is dismissed.

Utopia emerges in the history of modern thought as full of productive contradictions and semantic potential. It has been understood negatively, as immature, pre-political, unrealistic, petit-bourgeois; and positively, as potentially and successfully combining ethics and political practice. The history of the evaluative and/or semantic variations of utopia has been thoroughly studied by Hans-Gunther Funke in "*Il termine utopia attraverso i secoli*" ("The Term Utopia through the Centuries"). Utopias have been accused of promoting outdated notions of a new society, for not considering "human realities" such as ambition and the desire for power, and for lagging behind breakthroughs in the sciences and social engineering. From another angle, though, the revolutionary utopian spirit has been criticized as self-defeating, in that in a "perfect" society there would be no revolutions, change, or progress.

The changing nature of utopia has raised an extraordinary array of questions about social organization and process, one reason for its richness as a field of study. English poet and naturalist George Crabbe (1754–1832), for example, believed that utopias laid claim to eternity, in that achieving utopia would lead to the end of History. Less dramatically, the French author, poet, and statesman Alphonse de Lamartine (1790–1869) proposed the notion that "utopias are often only premature truths," a maxim later quoted by Karl Mannheim in his *Ideology and Utopia* (Mannheim 1936, 203). And yet the term "utopianist" was also used as a negative label to criticize early nineteenth-century socialists such as Robert Owen (1771–1858) in England, and the Frenchmen Henri Saint-Simon (1760–1825), Charles Fourier (1772–1837), and Pierre-Joseph Proudhon (1809–1865). In these disputes, the "utopianist" position was contrasted with the "scientific socialism" proposed by Karl Marx and Friedrich Engels. The concept of socialism as espoused by Owen, Fourier and the like was considered utopianist for disregarding the importance of the class struggle as the most efficient way to realize the revolution. Instead, such figures argued for gradual change, an approach seen by their detractors as a passive and therefore unrealistic attempt to reconfigure the economic and political structure of capitalist society. By not objectivizing political power, these detractors believed, the failure of the utopianists was inevitable. But this denunciation of utopian socialism would not prove fatal, being only one of myriad arguments and counterarguments that have energized political and social thinking over the last few centuries.

Humanism and Utopia: Modern Trends

In terms of Humanism, writers from diverse backgrounds in the last hundred years have proposed a range of definitions of utopia, its nature and prospects. So, the Spanish philosopher José Ortega y Gasset (1883–1955) considered that reality, like a landscape, had infinite perspectives, all equally true and authentic: the false perspective claims to be the only one available. Karl Mannheim (1893–1947) in *Utopia and Ideology* and other works, argued that the term utopia could be applied to any thought process that is stimulated not by reality, but by concepts, such as symbols, fantasies, dreams, and ideas, that in a broader sense are non-existent: they correspond to a spiritualization of politics. Utopias could possess a dual aspect, according to Max Horkheimer (1895–1973): they simultaneously serve as a critique of what is and a representation of what they should be. For Ralf Dahrendorf (1929–2009), attempting to achieve utopia, to accomplish the impossible, drives itself to totalitarianism, as only through the use of terror can the appearance of a conquered paradise be constructed. Looking back through history, the Italian philosopher and historian Norberto Bobbio (1909–2004) proposed that the eras with the greatest utopian spirit—the late Renaissance and late Enlightenment—were the eras with the most severe disruption to the social contract. During these periods, Bobbio argued, the natural desire for reform was not yet supported by a profound enough social transformation to allow the theorist to shift from abstract speculation of a new society to concrete social reform. At the same time, in works such as *Left and Right: The Significance of a Political Distinction*, Bobbio notes that

> the persistence of the utopian ideal in the history of mankind. . .is incontrovertible proof of the fascination that the egalitarian ideal exercises in all people in all countries and in all times, along with the ideals of liberty, peace and affluence (The Land of Plenty). (Bobbio 1996, 64)

And yet he was also aware, as in his 1989 *New Left Review* article "The Upturned Utopia," written as communist regimes collapsed or were being put under unprecedented stress, that at least one utopian experiment in the real world had failed (Bobbio 1989).

Bobbio's fellow Italian, the theologian Sergio Quinzio (1927–1996), suggested that we now know that utopias exist only while the unhappiness of their deferral persists, only to die once they are realized. Pioneer of utopian studies Raymond Ruyer (1902–1987) in works such as *L'Utopie et les utopies* (1950) judges the utopian method as an exercise and a game concerning the possibilities of reality. André Lalande (1867–1963) considers utopia a process that consists of representing a state of fictitious things realized in a concrete manner, either to assess the consequences that this would entail, or to demonstrate that these consequences would be beneficial. What is striking about these pronouncements is their variety and the fact that active critical thinking about utopias continued into modern times as an enlivening and positively contentious form of political and philosophical speculation. Revealingly, in his work *Existentialism is a Humanism* (1946), a key text of the then-emerging existential movement, the politically-engaged philosopher Jean-Paul Sartre (1905–1908) writes: "Man is not only that which he conceives himself to be, but that which he wills himself to be, and since he conceives of himself only after he exists, just as he wills himself to be after being thrown into existence, man is nothing other than what he makes of himself" (Sartre 2007, 22). Sartre seems to revisit, in modern terms and with due skepticism about religion, Pico della Mirandola's Renaissance suppositions about Humanism.

Georg Lukács (1885–1971) was the most outspokenly Humanist among the influential Marxists of the twentieth century. Even though he rejected the utopian proposal as a pathway to revolution in the mold of the utopian socialists, Lukács would develop the intensely revolutionary-charged "utopia-form" concept within his aesthetic theory. The concept seeks to reconcile the subject and the object, that is, what is and what should be, which must be homogenized and become one through the mediation of the form, in order to overcome the metaphysical disjunction created by the chasm between people and the world. This ideal can only be achieved at the vanishing point of History, given that such conciliation is in itself unattainable. Utopia is therefore a precondition of the art form, as the movement contained in its achievement consists of an opposition to the given reality. Nevertheless, the possibility of reconciling what is and what should be is put forth as a fundamental condition for the realization of the artistic form: "Art as utopia-form is and continues to be the anticipation of the not-yet-existent ideal model" (Lukács 1973, xxxiii). When the category of the form, in achieving the artistic object, fulfills its function of utopia-form, the user subject experiences, in the aesthetic object, the creation of "a perfect world that in its immediate sensorial reality soothes all pain and suffering, overcomes so much, in the true sense of the word, that infinite happiness—that gushes from it more than it remains within—frees itself" (Lukács 1973, 269). Aesthetic enjoyment takes on an equally utopian character, comprising a moment of suspension in the day-to-day life of the receiver, as in that moment of aesthetic enjoyment the subject and the artwork are removed from the continuous and sprawling temporal-historical flux that is daily life. In this way, both man and art may be transported to another, utopian dimension, in which subjects incorporate into themselves the utopian reality created in each artwork. By being removed from the historical continuum in the moment of aesthetic reception, the work of art takes on an existential character: "always 'new' because it is already 'old' at the time of birth, and located beyond historical time because it is born from it, and returns to it continuously" (Lukács 1973, 271). For each new work that is created, a new world, different in every way from other worlds that have already been created, ideally also comes into being. Despite these new worlds not being similar to those that preceded them or the worlds that, ideally, have yet to be created in the future, they all carry in them the possibility of becoming objects of *Erleben* (lived reality), in the sense that the receiving subject can recall at some times the hidden archetypal images of all existing things in the world, and at others, the creation legends of the world and the marvels of creation. This is an idea central to Lukács's aesthetic theories: artworks as humanity's memory, a memory which is evoked by the aesthete when he comes into contact with the art object.

Lukács's *History and Class Consciousness: Studies in Marxist Dialectics* (1923) excited his friend Ernst Bloch (1885–1977), who, in the 1920s, shared with Bertolt Brecht, Theodor W. Adorno and Walter Benjamin the hope of the imminent advent of communism. Influenced by the artistic avant-garde and a utopian stream of Marxist thought, Bloch saw in the desperate crisis of his era the end of a decrepit world, and simultaneously the harbinger of the imminent change that placed humanity's ontological dimension in the future. The ontology of "not-yet being" is central to Bloch's discussion in his *The Spirit of Utopia* (2018), one that would become a leitmotif of his argument. His book *The Principle of Hope* (1954–1956) is a sort of phenomenology which describes diverse forms and experiences of what Bloch calls "anticipatory consciousness," in other words, the consciousness of humanity when, moved by desire and hope, it anticipates the future. Through his work, Bloch presented utopia's positive function, the ability to bring reality into the light of day by way of the critical instrument, to act as a real compelling force of History, to enable the affirmation of law over force. Founding his political design "on the possible," Bloch declares his utopia-related project "utopian," making use of the imagination that renders the impossible possible—in the near future. Humanity becomes a project, a projection in the direction of a better future. Humans would live solely facing the future, the momentum leading them to expand "man's horizon." Humanity is called to project itself, to change the world and itself, an act that is accomplished in the utopian space.

Herbert Marcuse (1898–1979) was a proponent of Marxist Humanism and an analyst of Marx's early writings. In his work, *One-Dimensional Man* (1964), Marcuse expressed his skepticism regarding the possibilities of the liberation of humanity, due to the fact that advanced industrial society seemed to him to be one-dimensionally totalitarian. Within technology itself would lie an instrument for imposing new forms of control and social cohesion, more comfortable and therefore more effective. The improvement in the standard of living, thanks to the technological progress achieved by an affluent society, has become a vehicle of repression, having generated the obsessive desire to produce and consume and rendering obtuse the potential for resistance and opposition to the system. Thanks to the standardization of cultural values, flattened by the existing social order, an apparent forfeit of freedom can be observed, one that does not upset the ruling interests; quite the opposite, it ensures and reinforces the continuance of repression. In modern democracies, tolerance coincides with permissiveness, stemming from the assumption that no one person holds the truth. So, the subject of these choices must be the collective, supposedly made up of individuals capable of choice. With society acting as a total manager of the existence of individuals, the truth is that the opposite effect comes about; that is, generalized conformity. The type of thought corresponding to this scenario is one-dimensional, as it merely reproduces the existing reality and becomes incapable of opposition and critique.

Marcuse rebukes the more prevalent trends of twentieth-century philosophy, which to him are pragmatism, neo-positivism, and analytical philosophy. In them, the truth of a theory is at the mercy of the observation of empirical facts, or the level of success found in conforming to them: truth depends on usefulness, and, as a consequence, reason and language lose the ability to transcend facts and the prevailing reality, becoming subordinate to them instead. However, in his view, the purpose of philosophy is to rouse a great rejection of society as it exists and to keep the possibility of other ways of being alive, staying faithful to the universal content of concepts: the concepts of beauty or freedom, for example, contain all the beauty and freedom that have yet to be realized. Formulated in this way, it becomes possible to understand things in light of their potential and prospects. Marcuse therefore places fundamental importance on the imagination, which is independent of factual data and able to consider an object even in its absence. "All power to imagination" would become the slogan of revolt for the student unrest of May 1968. More than the working class, which seems to him more ingrained in the system and identified with its values, Marcuse designates the students, the third world guerilla fighters, the marginalized groups such as black people and immigrants, and the urban subproletariat as potential revolutionary subjects, as long as they ally themselves with other organized oppositional forces within society. In *The End of Utopia* (1967), Marcuse propounds the need for liberation from all forms of repression that had existed until then, a liberation he saw in the historical experience of these new protest and revolt movements, with their righteous violence against the establishment. *One-Dimensional Man* ends with a quote from Walter Benjamin: "It is only for the sake of those without hope that hope is given to us" (Marcuse 1991, 261). The radical attack on technological society contained within this work did not survive more rigorous testing, nor the trial of facts.

But in his 1969 *Essay on Liberation*, Marcuse displays a significant shift in perspective and new confidence in the utopia of a liberated society. The time had come to relaunch the concept of utopia in its full subversive and creative force. "What is denounced as 'utopian' is no longer that which has 'no place' and cannot have any place in the historical universe, but rather that which is blocked from coming about by the power of the established societies" (Marcuse 1969, 13). A new way of conceiving a technological society is expressed in a passage of this work:

> Is it still necessary to state that not technology, not technique, not the machine are the engines of repression, but the presence, in them, of the masters who determine their number, their life span, their power, their place in life, and the need for them? Is it still necessary to repeat that science and technology are the great vehicles of liberation, and that it is only their use and restriction in the repressive society which makes them into vehicles of domination? (Marcuse 1969, 13)

In this essay, Herbert Marcuse expands on the new possibilities of human liberation: subtracting man from the machine which enforces his servitude by fulfilling his needs. In this state, liberation would become the natural environment of an organism no longer able to conform to the competitive demands of wellbeing, nor capable of tolerating the aggression and ugliness of the lifestyle imposed on him by the establishment.

Conclusion

Arising out of the social, political, and philosophical transformations of the Renaissance, Humanism as a way of conceptualizing reality and humanity's place in that reality has proved remarkably varied and resilient. From the outset, Humanist thinkers no longer understood themselves as products of a pre-existing nature. Instead, they saw themselves as the authors of their own selfhood, the architects of the world they inhabited. Neither that self nor that world could be perfect, and as this chapter has shown, no one set of ideas would be prevail. But the striving for something new, something better, something essentially human would energize some of history's most provocative thinkers and writers, from Pico della Mirandola and Thomas More to Ernst Bloch and Herbert Marcuse and beyond. Five centuries after its emergence, Humanism remains a prompt for critical thinking and imaginative projection.

REFERENCES

Baron, Hans. 1988. *In Search of Florentine Civic Humanism: Essays on the Transition from Medieval to Modern Thought*. NJ: Princeton University Press.

Bloch, Ernst. 1985. *Das Prinzip Hoffnung: in fünf Teilen*. Frankfurt am Main: Suhrkamp Verlag.

———. 2018. *Geist der Utopie: Erste Fassung*. Frankfurt am Main: Suhrkamp Verlag.

Bobbio, Norberto. 1989. *The Upturned Utopia*. New Left Review, 1/177, September-October: 37–39.

———. 1996. *Left and Right: The Significance of a Political Distinction*. Cambrdige: Polity Press.

Castiglione, Baldassare. 1981. *Il Libro del Cortegiano*. Torino: UTET.

Erasmus of Rotterdam. (*Diatribe de Libero Bitrio*, 1524).

Funke, Hans-Gunther. 2003. Il termine utopia attraverso i secoli. In *Dall'Utopia all'Utopismo – Percorsi Tematici*, ed. Vita Fortunati, Raymond Trousson, and Adriana Corrado. Napoli: CUEN.

Leibniz, Gottfried. 2018. *Theodicy Essays: On the Goodness of God, the Freedom of Man and the Origin of Evil*. Morrisville: LULU Press.

Lukács, Georg. 1970. *Geschichte und Klassenbewusstsein: Studien über marxistische Dialektik*. München: Luchterhand.

———. 1973. *Filosofia dell'arte - Primi scritti sull'estetica 1912–1918*, vol. 1, trad. L. Coeta. Milano: SugarCo Edizioni.

Machiavelli, Niccolò. 1979. *Il Principe*. Milano: Feltrinelli Editore.

Mannheim, Karl. 1936. *Ideology and Utopia*. Chicago: International Library of Psychology, Philosophy and Scientific Method.

Marcuse, Herbert. 1969. *An Essay on Liberation*. London: Penguin.

———. 1991. *One-Dimensional Man: Studies in Ideology of Advanced Industrial Society*. New York: Routledge.

Mirandola, Giovanni Pico della. 1987. *Oratio de hominis dignitate*. Brescia: Editrice La Scuola.

Ruyer, Raymond. 1950. *L'Utooie et les utopies*. Paris: P.U.F.

Sartre, Jean-Paul. 2007. *Existentialism Is a Humanism*, trans. Carol Macomber. New Haven; London: Yale University Press.

Eugenics

Claire P. Curtis

INTRODUCTION

Utopian accounts imagine better worlds, better ways of living, and in doing so critique the contemporary societies of the respective authors. In some utopian accounts, the better world imagined is achieved through eugenic procedures chosen to improve people: better people, better world. The inverse is true in other utopian accounts: better world, better people.

Utopia and eugenics both intersect (often misleadingly) with the idea of perfection. Each is concerned with the idea of making better and how that process might be understood. Often (but not always), "making better" includes a focus on science and/or technology: how might we engineer a better society, or a better human? But where eugenics tends toward confidence about such engineering, utopia does not. Eugenics and utopia share the prefix *–eu*, meaning good. When Thomas More coined the word *utopia* he was playing with the contrasting prefix *–u*, meaning none (eutopia/utopia is the good place that is no place). While utopia has embedded in its very definition a concern or even skepticism about the idea of the good (even if it is simply that the good is not realizable), the term eugenics has no such skepticism. Eugenics is a utopian exercise. There are a number of eugenic utopias that use eugenic practices to facilitate a blueprint utopia.[1] But utopia need not include eugenic practice.

C. P. Curtis (✉)
College of Charleston, Charleston, SC, USA

© The Author(s), under exclusive license to Springer Nature Switzerland AG 2022
P. Marks et al. (eds.), *The Palgrave Handbook of Utopian and Dystopian Literatures*, https://doi.org/10.1007/978-3-030-88654-7_24

This entry is organized into four sections, the first setting out some of the broad issues in addressing eugenics and utopia. The next three sections outline the relationship between eugenics and utopia. First, I take up the eugenic utopia, where the practice of eugenics is central to the utopian imagining. Second, I consider utopian accounts that include some form of eugenic practice, but emphasize the changing of external conditions, rather than the improvement of humans. Third, I question the posthuman in utopia as a potential eugenic manifestation.

EUGENICS AND UTOPIA

Francis Galton coined the word "eugenics" in 1883 but, as with Thomas More coining "utopia" before him, the idea of eugenics preceded the term. Eugenics is the practice of improving humans through manipulating reproductive practices, (mirroring ways in which people breed cattle or dogs). Eugenic practice is divided into "positive" eugenics that encourages certain people to breed for desired characteristics or "negative" eugenics that uses techniques like sterilization to remove the possibility that some will reproduce.[2] Eugenic practice neither began nor ended with the Nazi Final Solution. Eugenics predates World War II and lasted afterward, although rarely with the term "eugenics" attached. In the United States, coerced sterilization campaigns against prisoners and those deemed to be intellectually disabled were justified as forms of eugenics. In the early twenty-first century, ethicists distinguish between "authoritarian" and "liberal" eugenics, which some also refer to as neo-eugenics.[3] Eugenics is not simply an off/on phenomenon. The practice of eugenics exists along a continuum.

Extreme and state-sponsored actions are not the total of eugenics. At one end of the eugenics continuum are state-sanctioned genocidal actions for the purpose of eradicating a gene pool. At the other end of the spectrum might be something like one individual's choice to take prenatal vitamins. Liberal eugenics advocates for parental choice, which might include a choice to abort after a prenatal diagnosis or the choice to implant embryos only after genetic testing (preimplantation genetic diagnosis, PGD).[4] Where on the continuum might we then consider the following non-exhaustive list of interventions: prenatal care, statutes banning first cousin marriage, genetic counselors, long-acting reversible contraception as a condition of prison sentencing, and selective abortion? Additionally, how do these practices fit within particular utopian imaginings?

Further, it is not simply the degree of intervention that is relevant, but also the reasoning behind and the conditions under which interventions take place. For example, at the end of Ursula K. Le Guin's utopian novel *The Dispossessed* (1974), Earth is described as "a planet spoiled by the human species" (Le Guin 1994, 347). Preserving human life on the planet required radical measures: "Total control over the use of every acre of land, every scrap of metal, every ounce of fuel. Total rationing, birth control, euthanasia, universal conscription into the labor force. The absolute regimentation of each life toward the goal of racial survival" (348). Do the conditions of Earth so described demand eugenic interventions for survival? What would those same interventions look like absent such conditions?

Finally, one might object to eugenic practices because of the consequences of such practices. For example, what if eugenic practices produce a radical divide between the enhanced and the unenhanced? In the film *Gattaca* (1997), people are divided into the "valids" and the "in-valids" based on their propensity toward genetic disease or decline. The main character is an in-valid who uses the DNA of another to rise through the ranks and achieve a place on the deep space exploration team. So, is the film arguing against eugenics; eugenics as a practice of capitalism; or the social consequences of the unequal application of genetic modification (and thus genetic discrimination)?

Recognizing that eugenics falls on a continuum and that objections to eugenics do not always focus on the fact of eugenics itself, but instead on the consequences of eugenics, clarifies how to think about the relationship between eugenics and utopia. The focus on improvement and the expectation that such improvement can be produced through human ingenuity is certainly part of a classical utopian mindset. While many utopias utilize eugenic practices as central to their utopian purpose, there are plenty of other utopian imaginings that eschew the improvement of human beings as a central feature. Eugenics is a procedure; utopia is a principle. The question is the degree to which eugenics becomes a procedure used within the principle of utopia. Utopian authors may well believe that humans will be better (to one another) absent conditions of want, fear, violence, and deprivation, and a utopian might desire those changes to the conditions under which humans live to be permanent, but that is not sufficient for the eugenicist.

EUGENIC UTOPIAS

Patrick Parrinder asks "can we imagine a better society without imagining, and wishing to create, better people?" (1997, 1); Julian Savulescu asserts, "To be human is to be better. Or, at least, to strive to be better" (2005, 39). Savulescu's enthusiasm about humans becoming better and the moral obligation to enhance is mirrored in the eugenic utopias of Plato and Charlotte Perkins Gilman.

Eugenic utopias include eugenic procedures as an essential feature of the utopia. Starting from Plato we see an overt eugenicism that is crude in practice but absolutely clear in intent. While the purpose of the *Republic* (380 BCE) is to define and defend a theory of justice, the method Plato uses to reveal this definition is to create an ideal city (*kallipolis*). The key to this city being an example of justice is ensuring that everyone do the job for which they are supposedly "naturally suited." Some are by nature suited to rule and must be educated to fulfill that role. Likewise, with those who are suited to defend the city and those suited to produce goods for the city. To reliably achieve this end Plato highlights not only a strict education system but also total control over reproduction. Plato outlines a system of reproduction that is based on a rigged lottery where philosopher rulers will choose which guardians will have sex with one another so that "the best men should mate with the best women in as many cases as possible, while the opposite should hold of the worst men and women; and that the offspring of the former should be reared, but not of the latter, if our flock is going to be an eminent one" (2004, V, 459e).

This eugenic intent is further highlighted when Plato clarifies the negative eugenic consequence, infanticide, for any child born that is visibly imperfect or from the issue of unsanctioned reproductive sex. In addition, in Book VIII, when Plato indicates that the kallipolis will inevitably fail he sees the inevitable failures in his reproductive system as the key to the failures of the ideal city ("fail to ascertain periods of good fertility... so they will sometimes beget children when they should not" [VIII, 546b]). Plato's ideal city does not simply include eugenics, rather it is that this eugenic system is crucial to the ideal character of the kallipolis as Plato understands it.

This kind of certitude that creating a radically better system requires eugenic reproductive practices is also evident in utopias at the end of the nineteenth century with the rise of the eugenics movement. Christina Lake offers a comprehensive survey of feminist interest in family structure, reproduction and human improvement: "Their primary purpose was not simply establishing equality for women, but imagining a better world where values often associated with women, such as love, morality, chastity and spirituality, could be achieved through evolutionary advances" (2018, 1280). Charlotte Perkins Gilman was active in the eugenics movement and *Herland* (1914) reflects the idea of human improvement, albeit using a non-reproducible eugenic procedure.[5]

Based on the practice of parthenogenesis after the loss (through war and natural disaster) of the men of the community, the narrator notes that "very early they recognized the need of improvement... and devoted their combined intelligence to that problem – how to make the best kind of people" (1998, 51). This desire to birth the best women coincides with the realization that the exponential growth of their population (every woman giving birth to five daughters) was not sustainable. The women decide on "a period of 'negative eugenics'" (59). Beyond this collective decision to limit their numbers, they also focus on producing better children, noting that those with "bad qualities" alongside a sense of "social duty" were willing to forego motherhood, while a "few of the worst types were ... unable to reproduce" (70). Described by Van, the narrator, as "Conscious Makers of People," the women of Herland are adamant about the necessity of eugenic practices.[6]

These women extend their eugenic breeding practices to plant and animal life, eliminating larger mammals, breeding cats who will not kill songbirds, and replacing all trees with fruit and nut-bearing ones. The country is described as a giant garden and the focus for both human and non-human life is a purposefully bred existence that will serve the well-being of the whole.[7] This holistic approach to eugenics, its practices not limited only to humans, should extend to all of nature, return in the post and transhuman eugenics of the twentieth and twenty-first centuries (discussed below).

Aldous Huxley's *Brave New World* (1969) offers the dystopian version of this focus on purposefully "making" people. Despite Huxley's own enthusiasm for eugenics, the novel's dystopian nature is precisely connected to the use of eugenics.[8] The familiar division of people into castes, the specific breeding of people with different abilities to fulfill different tasks, and the mindset that connects the progress of the world presented with the reproductive practices outlined illustrates a eugenic dystopia that may well criticize the extremes to which the One State has gone without criticizing the particular eugenic practices at play.

Utopias with Modified Eugenic Practice

The above examples all include eugenic practices that are central to the utopian principles of the communities created. Absent those eugenic practices, the utopian community would cease to be utopian. Not so for the examples discussed here. In this section, there are utopias that include some form of eugenic practice, but that practice is not central to the utopian imagination. Additionally, these practices are less extreme than the control over reproduction seen in the eugenic utopias.

Thomas More's eponymous utopia (1516) is an interesting example here. While More's island of Utopos includes some minimal claims of eugenic thinking—for example, the presentation of potential spouses naked prior to any match in order to identify any flaws—there is little indication that More's *Utopia* is interested in improving the human population over generations. While the Utopians have used "scientific methods" to increase the fertility of the land ("by careful cultivation they correct the deficiencies of the soil" [1965, 99]), there is little sense that such techniques are applied to humans. The potentially eugenic consequences of choosing a spouse are emphasized centuries later in Edward Bellamy's *Looking Backward* (1887). Instead of viewing your partner naked, Bellamy notes that the mere fact of choosing one's spouse would improve humanity over time. Julian West, the visitor from the nineteenth century, notes of Boston in the year 2000: "Human nature itself must have changed very much." Dr. Leete, however, responds in the negative, asserting simply that "the conditions of human life have changed, and with them the motives of human action" (1996, 29).

Both More and Bellamy include eugenic practices while also arguing for changed conditions for human living. More notes that "cheerfulness, peace of mind, [and] freedom from anxiety" follow when "the Utopian can feel absolutely sure that he, his wife, his children, his grandchildren, his great-grandchildren, his great-great-grandchildren.... will always have enough to eat and enough to make them happy" (1965, 128–129). Freedom from anxiety about the well-being of those that you love may not be the most common eugenic procedure, but it surely counts as a kind of improvement for the experience of being human. This method for improving human life resists the focus on changes in reproductive practices while still advocating for radical changes.

Distinguishing between changing the world in which humans live, and changing humans themselves is mirrored in today's disability studies literature. This growing literature concerns the social model of disability wherein disability comes from the experience of living in a society built for some bodies and not others. The disability question is important to raise when thinking about eugenics and utopia. Is there a place for bodily difference along the eugenics continuum? Does the eugenics continuum imply a continuum absent disability? One can certainly interpret More and Bellamy on changing the conditions of human life to include the kinds of changes that would diminish disability. Additionally, both More and Bellamy write utopias that mention people with disabilities as a part of the human population (and not a problem to be solved). Rosemarie Garland Thompson (2012) equates utopia with eugenic thinking. But utopian texts do not wholly confirm her claim.

Marge Piercy's feminist utopian classic, *Woman on the Edge of Time* (1976), includes the practice of eugenics alongside an argument about the limits of that practice. In the novel, children are purposefully created and produced out of a planned mix of genes and gestated externally. This reproductive method is justified both to ensure the equality of men and women and as a method for purposeful gene mixing. On the latter point, the novel includes a debate over the relative degree of genetic intervention. The two positions represented by the "Shapers" and the "Mixers" mirror contemporary debates around reprogenetics. In Piercy's novel, the Shapers favor genetic intervention, where the Mixers seek to intervene only to "spot problems" (1976, 226). The Mixers describe their position by claiming that "we don't think people can know objectively how people should become" (226). The Shapers are interested in epigenetic interventions that will enhance selected traits. While the discussion between the two sides is presented briefly, the primary characters side with the Mixers and the novel itself reflects the principle that society should not predetermine one's future.

Even with the claim that we cannot know "how people should become," the novel presents a utopian society that is eugenic. *Woman on the Edge of Time* does not embrace eugenics in the way that either Gilman or Plato do; instead, the novel represents a point on the eugenic continuum away from total coercive control but nevertheless far from individual choice. The Shaper/Mixer debate reflects an openness to the disability concerns and the existential questions raised by Jurgen Habermas concerning preimplantation genetic diagnosis (2003).[9]

Eugenics, Enhancement, and the Posthuman

The relationship between eugenics and utopia depends, clearly, on the utopian vision, but also on the understanding of eugenics. What is the nature of human improvement? How is it to be brought about? Under what conditions? The previous two sections illustrate, in the first section, that utopias depend on clear eugenic practices controlled centrally. The second section looks at utopias that use eugenic techniques which are either not centralized or are not coercive. Contemporary utopias that explore posthuman imaginings reflect the same range: enthusiastic eugenic utopian posthumanism and more skeptical explorations of the approaching posthuman era.

The question of the relationship between posthuman imaginings and eugenics goes alongside recognition of changes in the techniques of potential eugenic practices. Eugenicists prior to the late twentieth century sought to control and manipulate typical forms of human reproduction. With the advent of reproductive technologies including in vitro fertilization, surrogacy, cloning, and preimplantation genetic diagnosis, current proponents of neo-eugenics utilize a broader array of techniques. These techniques raise questions about the degree to which advocacy for the posthuman is eugenic. What is the role of the human in the arguments for enhancement and augmentation? Utopian novels are one place to consider answers to these questions about the role of embodiment in being human; the issue of lifespan; and the melding of the human and the machine.[10]

Nick Bostrom identifies transhumanism as a movement that "[evaluates] the opportunities for enhancing the human condition and the human organism opened up by the advancement of technology" (2005, n.p.). This enhancement can take a number of forms, although increasing the human life span is a key component. Bostrom's notion of enhancement is clearly eugenic, although he is going in a different direction than either Plato or Gilman (or other earlier eugenic utopians). His argument for transhumanism is less interested in a centrally organized shift to mandated reproductive practices and more in a kind of free form exploration of the boundaries of the human and beyond (biohacking is included in here, though it is usually not reprogenetic). The Bostrom position is not only eugenic but also utopian. It is given fictional energy in Cory Doctorow's *Walkaway* (2017), which considers the notion of "better" from multiple perspectives: economic, social, and moral. Alternatively, Octavia Butler's Xenogenesis trilogy, collected as *Lilith's Brood* (2000), and Kim Stanley Robinson's *2312* (2012) both imagine a critical utopian future where bodily change is not wholly tied to the idea of enhancement or species improvement.[11]

Doctorow's *Walkaway* engages the eugenic question and the link between eugenics and a utopian world in a variety of ways. On the one hand, the novel is critiquing a form of capitalist eugenics that restricts betterment to those with the money and access to purchase the technology. On the other hand, the novel is fully comfortable with using science and technology to better people and to better the world, as long as access is open to all. *Walkaway* expresses a clear enthusiasm for the possibilities of technology: "But the most important thing about that breakthrough isn't what we can do now that we didn't used to be able to do – it's *the fact that we are making progress*" (Doctorow 2017, 300). This claim is made in reference to the idea of "upload," transferring one's consciousness to a network of computers, but the principle of "making progress" permeates the novel, and fuels its utopian imagining.

The conversations around upload and between those who have been uploaded and those who have not illustrated a transhumanist obsession: avoiding death, "[n]ot just the ability to come back from the dead, but the ability to rethink what it means to be alive" (128). The technology of upload is scarcely questioned; most of the novel's moral concerns involve either access to upload or scanning and uploading someone without their consent. While those who have been uploaded struggle to come to terms with what they are experiencing, the novel ends on a purely eugenic and utopian note, where uploads are downloaded into new, pristine, grown bodies. But even in this happily ever after ending there is a Bellamy-like undercurrent—*how* you think about the technologies, and the possibilities of living under different conditions, are what matter most. "You got the world you hoped for or the world you feared – your hope or your fear made it so" (89).

Kim Stanley Robinson's *2312*, as with *Walkaway*, is concerned with the consequences of technology and access to improvements when only those with means can benefit. While the novel focuses on a group of "spacers" whose access appears to be free and open, those characters consider the access to such enhancements of those still on earth: "The wealthiest lived as if they were spacers on sabbatical, mobile and curious, actualizing themselves in all ways possible, augmenting themselves – genderizing – speciating – dodging death, extending life" (2012, 360). For the spacers, genetic intervention is the norm. The novel *2312* also raises the question of whether every change is necessarily an improvement. While *2312* does not clarify how and when such decisions are made, people are presented with variations in their size (smalls, talls), their gender (gynandromporph, androgyn), and other more idiosyncratic choices. The novel also notes that a spacer returns to Earth, "not one whit wiser, or even more intelligent" (2012, 86).

Where *Walkaway* presents characters who are enthusiastic about engineering and uploading humans, *2312* includes a main character, Swan, whose choices to alter her body are both wholly her own and potentially problematic. Described by a former partner as becoming "some kind of post-human thing, or at least a different person," Swan replies, "it would be stupid not to do the good things when you can, it would be *anti*human" (109). Swan is not talking about progress here. She is simply reflecting her own desire to experiment. Swan is identified by others as a "new thing" but her newness is certainly not presented as a model for the species. *2312*, like *Woman on the Edge of Time*, seems more interested in the utopian possibilities of changing the conditions under which we live. But where *Woman on the Edge of Time* treats eugenics with a brief discussion of the kinds of interventions pursued, *2312* includes a considered debate on the idea of augmentation and the limits of the human.

What contemporary utopias include that many classical utopias ignored are clear arguments for and against their own eugenic impulses. Whether the eugenic impulse is central to the organization of the community or simply an additional feature of that society, contemporary utopian accounts want to critically engage with this eugenic impulse. What does it mean to think about the improvement of human beings? Utopian imagining need not be limited to the dogmatically eugenic. These texts are useful as ethicists, scientists, and theorists consider new reproductive technologies. Dorothy Roberts uses the language of utopia to argue for a resistant mindset that does not reject the possibility of using technology, but does reject current uses "in service of a neoliberal agenda": "I can also imagine a new utopia arising from feminists' radical resistance .... that is emboldened by new alliances – joining reproductive justice with antiracist, disability rights, and [with] economic justice movements that recognize their common interest in contesting a race-based reprogenetic future" (2009, 800). A critical assessment of the role that different modes of eugenics might play in utopian imaginings opens a space for thinking about how improving human beings can and should work toward creating a better world.

CONCLUSION

Utopian texts, particularly in the twentieth century and beyond, are skeptical about their utopian imaginings. This skepticism might extend to any eugenic practices that utopian imagining includes. Eugenic practices are not so skeptical. We might be skeptical about those practices, but eugenics is a confident practice for human betterment. Some utopias share that confidence and include eugenic practices as central to their utopian vision, as in Plato's *Republic* and Charlotte Perkins Gilman's *Herland*. Other texts include debates over the extent and value of such eugenic practices, for example, Marge Piercy's *Woman on the Edge of Time*. Posthuman imaginings provide a different kind of window into purposeful human alteration that may or may not be tied to the idea of improvement.

NOTES

1. See, for example, Timothy Murphy, 2018, Physiology Is Destiny: The Fate of Eugenic Utopia in the Fiction of H.P. Lovecraft and Olaf Stapledon, *Utopian Studies* 29: 21–43; Patrick Parrinder, 2015, *Utopian Literature and Science: From the Scientific Revolution to Brave New World and Beyond*, New York: Palgrave Macmillan; David A. Kirby, 2008, The Devil in Our DNA: A Brief History of Eugenics in Science Fiction Films, *Literature and Medicine* 26: 83–108; Dana Seitler,

2003, Unnatural Selection: Mothers, Eugenics Feminists, and Charlotte Perkins Gilman's Regeneration Narratives, *American Quarterly* 55: 61–88; John S. Partington, 2003, H.G. Wells' Eugenic Thinking of the 1930s and 1940s, *Utopian Studies* 14: 74–81.

2. This language of positive and negative is sometimes inverted, particularly when talking about fetal interventions, where 'positive' means active interventions to enhance genetically and 'negative' means therapeutic intervention for disease prevention.

3. See, Jurgen Habermas, 2003, *The Future of Human Nature*, Cambridge: Polity Press; Nick Bostrom, 2005, Transhumanist Values. https://nickbostrom.com/ethics/values.pdf. Accessed 29 June 2019.

4. For more on contemporary reproductive technologies and eugenics, see Paul Lombardo, 2011, *A Century of Eugenics in America: From the Indiana Experiment to the Human Genome Era*, Bloomington: Indiana University Press; Nikolas Rose, 2007, *The Politics of Life Itself*, Princeton: Princeton University Press.

5. See, Seitler, 2003; Sharon Lamp and W. Carol Cleigh, 2011, A Heritage of Ableist Rhetoric in American Feminism from the Eugenics Period, in *Feminist Disability Studies*, ed. Kim Q. Hall, 175–189, Bloomington: Indiana University Press.

6. Another feminist novel that uses manipulated reproduction to try and achieve desired results is: Sheri Tepper, 1988, *The Gate to Woman's Country*, New York: Doubleday.

7. *Herland* is one of the most discussed texts among utopia scholars for thinking about the relationship between eugenics and utopia. See, for example, Christina Lake, 2018, Eugenics in Late 19th Century Feminist Utopias, *American Journal of Economics and Sociology* 77: 1277–1312; Stephanie Peebles Tavera, 2018, Her Body, *Herland*: Reproductive Health and Dis/topian Satire in Charlotte Perkins Gilman, *Utopian Studies* 29: 1–20; Andrew Christensen, 2017, Charlotte Perkins Gilman *Herland* and the Tradition of the Scientific Utopia, *Utopian Studies* 28: 286–304; Egan, Kristen R. 2011. Conservation and Cleanliness: Racial and Environmental Purity in Ellen Richards and Charlotte Perkins Gilman. *Women's Studies Quarterly* 39: 77–92.

8. See, Joanne Woiak, 2007, Designing a Brave New World: Eugenics, Politics, and Fiction, *The Public Historian* 29: 105–129.

9. See Jurgen Habermas, 2003, *The Future of Human Nature*, Cambridge: Polity Press. Habermas shares the concern of the Mixers described by Piercy. He is concerned about parents making decisions about who a child is going to be, and highlights the distinction between "the grown and the made" (52).

10. These issues are also raised in contemporary utopian literature. See, for example: Margaret Atwood, 2003, *Oryx and Crake*, New York: Nan A. Talese; Kazuo Ishiguro, 2005, Never *Let Me Go*, London: Faber and Faber; Paolo Bacigalupi, 2009, *The Windup Girl*, San Francisco:

Nightshade Books. See also Marie Ferreira, 2011, Toward a Science of Perfect Reproduction? Visions of Eugenics in Contemporary Fiction. In *Restoring the Mystery of the Rainbow: Literature's Refraction of Science* and Evie Kendal, 2015. Utopian Visions of "Making People": Science Fiction and Debates on Cloning, Ectogenesis, Genetic Engineering, and Genetic Discrimination Additionally one might consider the posthuman in a more literal form: the utopian imagining of a world without people. See, Mark S. Jendrysik, 2011, Back to the Garden: New Visions of Posthuman Futures, *Utopian Studies* 22: 34–51.

11. The Xenogenesis trilogy includes: *Dawn* (1987), *Adulthood Rites* (1988) and *Imago* (1989). Butler's trilogy is complicated on this point of bodily change not being tied to the idea of enhancement as it considers a truly posthuman future, one where humans must reproduce with an alien species for any kind of survival. The link between these novels and the idea of eugenics and disability are explored in Claire Curtis, 2015, Utopian Possibilities: Disability, Norms, and Eugenics in Octavia Butler's Xenogenesis, *Journal of Literary & Cultural Disability Studies* 9: 19–33; Naomi Jacobs, 2003, Posthuman Bodies and Agency in Octavia Butler's Xenogenesis, in *Dark Horizons: Science Fiction and the Dystopian Imagination*, eds. Raffaella Baccolini and Tom Moylan, 91–111. New York: Routledge.

REFERENCES

Atwood, Margaret. 2003. *Oryx and Crake*. New York: Nan A. Talese.

Bacigalupi, Paolo. 2009. *The Windup Girl*. San Francisco: Nightshade Books.

Bellamy, Edward. 1996. *Looking Backward*. New York: Dover Publications.

Bostrom, Nick. 2005. Transhumanist Values. https://nickbostrom.com/ethics/values.pdf. Accessed 29 June 2019.

Butler, Octavia. 2000. *Lilith's Brood*. New York: Grand Central Publishing.

Christensen, Andrew. 2017. Charlotte Perkins Gilman *Herland* and the Tradition of the Scientific Utopia. *Utopian Studies* 28: 286–304.

Curtis, Claire. 2015. Utopian Possibilities: Disability, Norms, and Eugenics in Octavia Butler's Xenogenesis. *Journal of Literary & Cultural Disability Studies* 9: 19–33.

Doctorow, Cory. 2017. *Walkaway*. New York: Head of Zeus and Tor Books.

Egan, Kristen R. 2011. Conservation and Cleanliness: Racial and Environmental Purity in Ellen Richards and Charlotte Perkins Gilman. *Women's Studies Quarterly* 39: 77–92.

Ferreira, Marie Aline. 2011. Toward a Science of Perfect Reproduction? Visions of Eugenics in Contemporary Fiction. In *Restoring the Mystery of the Rainbow: Literature's Refraction of Science*, ed. Valeria Tinkler-Villani and C.C. Barfoot, 395–415. Amsterdam, Netherlands: Brill.

Garland Thomson, Rosemarie. 2012. The Case for Conserving Disability. *Journal of Bioethical Inquiry* 9: 339–355.

Gattaca. 1997. Directed by Andrew Niccol. Columbia Pictures.

Gilman, Charlotte Perkins. 1998. *Herland*. New York: Dover Publications.

Habermas, Jurgen. 2003. *The Future of Human Nature*. Cambridge: Polity Press.

Huxley, Aldous. 1969. *Brave New World*. New York: Perennial Library, Harper and Row.

Ishiguro, Kazuo. 2005. *Never Let Me Go*. London: Faber and Faber.

Jacobs, Naomi. 2003. Posthuman Bodies and Agency in Octavia Butler's Xenogenesis. In *Dark Horizons: Science Fiction and the Dystopian Imagination*, ed. Raffaella Baccolini and Tom Moylan, 91–111. New York: Routledge.

Jendrysik, Mark S. 2011. Back to the Garden: New Visions of Posthuman Futures. *Utopian Studies* 22: 34–51.

Kendal, Evie. 2015. Utopian Visions of "Making People": Science Fiction and Debates on Cloning, Ectogenesis, Genetic Engineering, and Genetic Discrimination. In *Biopolitics and Utopia: An Interdisciplinary Reader*, ed. Patricia Stapleton and Andrew Byers, 89–117. New York: Palgrave Macmillan.

Kirby, David A. 2008. The Devil in Our DNA: A Brief History of Eugenics in Science Fiction Films. *Literature and Medicine* 26: 83–108.

Lake, Christina. 2018. Eugenics in Late 19th Century Feminist Utopias. *American Journal of Economics and Sociology* 77: 1277–1312.

Lamp, Sharon, and W. Carol Cleigh. 2011. A Heritage of Ableist Rhetoric in American Feminism from the Eugenics Period. In *Feminist Disability Studies*, ed. Kim Q. Hall, 175–189. Bloomington: Indiana University Press.

Le Guin, Ursula. 1994. *The Dispossessed*. New York: Harper Voyager.

Lombardo, Paul. 2011. *A Century of Eugenics in America: From the Indiana Experiment to the Human Genome Era*. Bloomington: Indiana University Press.

More, Thomas. 1965. *Utopia*. London: Penguin Books.

Murphy, Timothy. 2018. Physiology Is Destiny: The Fate of Eugenic Utopia in the Fiction of H.P Lovecraft and Olaf Stapledon. *Utopian Studies* 29: 21–43.

Parrinder, Patrick. 1997. Eugenics and Utopia: Sexual Selection from Galton to Morris. *Utopian Studies*, 8 (2).

Parrinder, Patrick. 2015. *Utopian Literature and Science: From the Scientific Revolution to Brave New World and Beyond*. New York: Palgrave Macmillan.

Partington, J.S. 2003. H.G. Wells' Eugenic Thinking of the 1930s and 1940s. *Utopian Studies* 14: 74–81.

Piercy, Marge. 1976. *Woman on the Edge of Time*. New York: Ballantine Books.

Plato. 2004. *Republic*, trans. CDC Reeve. Indianapolis: Hackett Books.

Roberts, Dorothy. 2009. Race, Gender, and Genetic Technologies: A New Reproductive Dystopia? *Signs* 34: 783–804.

Robinson, Kim Stanley. 2012. *2312*. New York. Orbit.

Rose, Nikolas. 2007. *The Politics of Life Itself*. Princeton: Princeton University Press.

Savulescu, Julian. 2005. New Breeds of Humans: The Moral Obligation to Enhance. *Reproductive BioMedicine Online* 10 (S1): 36–39.

Seitler, Dana. 2003. Unnatural Selection: Mothers, Eugenics Feminists, and Charlotte Perkins Gilman's Regeneration Narratives. *American Quarterly* 55: 61–88.

Tavera, Stephanie Peebles. 2018. Her Body, *Herland*: Reproductive Health and Dis/topian Satire in Charlotte Perkins Gilman. *Utopian Studies* 29: 1–20.

Tepper, Sheri. 1988. *The Gate to Woman's Country*. New York: Doubleday.

Woiak, Joanne. 2007. Designing a Brave New World: Eugenics, Politics, and Fiction. *The Public Historian* 29: 105–129.

Marxism

Antonis Balasopoulos

Introduction

The case of the relationship between, on the one hand, "utopia" and "utopianism" as ways of naming the imagining of a social ideal and the tendency of thought to orient itself toward the desirable and the possible, and, on the other, "Marxism" as a corpus of theoretical texts, an ensemble of convictions and a set of political practices, is a reminder both of the importance of clear and precise definitions and of the difficulty of attaining them in matters of the human and the social sciences. For this relationship is often not defined unambiguously even within the limits of a single text or the corpus of a single author; and it is certainly divergently imagined when a broader array of writings is taken into consideration. I will here entirely omit consideration of the question of utopia's and utopianism's response to Marxism; I will content myself to remark that it is itself considerably complex. For there are, within literary history, utopias that are partly amenable to a Marxist framework of thinking, others that are consciously Marxist in nature, and still others that are either indifferent or actively hostile to Marxist ideas. Likewise, though "utopianism" as a tendency and Marxism as an ensemble of theoretical concepts, subjective convictions and political practices are very often thought as fellow travelers, there are ways in which "utopianism" can lead to the rejection of specific aspects of Marxist theory and practice, sometimes, though not always, claiming to do so from within Marxism itself.[1]

A. Balasopoulos (✉)
University of Cyprus, Nicosia, Cyprus

P. Marks et al. (eds.), *The Palgrave Handbook of Utopian and Dystopian Literatures*, https://doi.org/10.1007/978-3-030-88654-7_25

What follows, then, is an attempt to present a concise and synoptic exposition of the other side of the relationship, that which pertains to Marxism's response to both utopia and utopianism. Of course, "Marxism" is also, even at first glance, a complex object of study, not only because it involves the triadic configuration of texts, convictions and practices, but also because it evolves historically, with the rise of "post-Marxism" in the work of Ernesto Laclau and Chantal Mouffe (1985) constituting an important and consequential development for the last two decades of the twentieth century and the first two of the twenty-first.[2] I will only be able to address this last period briefly in my conclusion, however; the main body of the essay will break down the historical terrain into three parts: the "classical" period of Marx and Engels's own writings, roughly from the *Economic and Philosophic Manuscripts* of 1844 until *The Civil War in France* in 1871; the cross-pollination of classical Marxism and certain elements of anarchist or quasi-anarchist thought after the Paris Commune, particularly regarding the ideas of *pleasure* and of *leisure* or freedom from labor; and, finally, twentieth-century Marxist re-visions of the meaning of "utopia" from a Marxist standpoint, from Ernst Bloch to Louis Marin, Fredric Jameson and Henri Lefebvre.

The Classical Matrix

In early 1873, Wilhelm Liebknecht informed Frederick Engels of his intention to publish a "social and political library" (Engels 1989, 671) that would begin with Thomas More's *Utopia* and extend to a number of his and Karl Marx's works. The project did not materialize, but the fact that it was imagined in the first place is indicative of the complications that attend to the relationship between Marxism and the broader tradition of utopia. At the time of his response to Liebknecht, Engels was vague about his own position on the matter of this relationship: "you have plenty of time before you get from the *Utopia* to us," he replied to Liebknecht; "better look after the intermediate links first" (Engels 1989, 477). Even so, the response suggests that he was not averse to the idea of Marxism as the endpoint of an evolutionary continuum whose origin would be More's *Utopia* and whose intermediate stages would involve the utopian socialism of Owen, Fourier, and Saint-Simon. This (Hegelian) idea, of Marxism as a properly dialectical—rather than one-dimensionally destructive—overcoming of a utopian legacy that it simultaneously preserves, negates, and raises to a higher level is of seminal significance to the matter at hand.

But the spectrum of possible interpretations of classical Marxism's relation to utopia in the classical period is not exhausted in the schema of the evolutionary continuum. It ranges from viewing Marxism as an "anti-utopian utopianism" (Lukes 1984, 155) or as an "accidental" utopianism with clear anti-utopian intentions (Webb 2000, 109–137), to interpreting it as an "anti-humanist" utopianism (Paden 2002, 85ff.), as ambivalent utopianism (Geoghegan 2008, 39–54), and finally, as utopianism plain and simple, whether this is polemically intended as a critique of classical Marxism itself (Coby 1986, 22–32), or as a rejection of the "scientific" elements of Marxism in favor of the 'utopian' ones (Lovell 2004, 630–638; Claeys 2018, 231–240).

In general, and irrespectively of which interpretive path one takes, it is arguable that the corpus of classical Marxism understands "utopia" and the "utopian" in three fundamental ways: first, and least interestingly, as a pejorative synonym for the unrealizable, naïve and illusive; secondly, as a legacy that productively questions bourgeois economic and political theory at the same time that it needs to be questioned itself on a number of grounds; and thirdly, as a disavowed but arguably appropriate name for certain vital dimensions of Marxism's own "positive" content, namely of its humanist envisioning of non-alienated labor and companionate social being, or what Darren Webb has described as "the dream of the whole man," the vision of "the all-round individual" and the "ontological necessity of labor" (2000, 109–137).

Eschewing reference to the strictly polemical and pejorative uses of the word 'utopia' in the classical Marxist tradition, it is important to note two features that pertain to the second and most extensive of its rules of engagement, that of a historical materialist critique of utopian means, ends and presuppositions. First, no matter how intense such criticism may be, there is also a consistent trend of *anti-anti-utopianism* within the writings of Marx and Engels—a vigilance regarding the reactionary character of facile contempt for the insights contained in utopian thought. Thus, Engels attacks Eugen Dühring for his vulgar disrespect toward Owen, Saint-Simon, and Fourier, observing venomously:

In comparison with the basic conceptions even of the 'idiot' Fourier's most recklessly bold fantasies; in comparison even with the paltriest ideas of the 'crude, feeble, and paltry' [Owen] — Herr Dühring, himself still completely dominated by the division of labor, is no more than an impertinent dwarf. (1987, 279)[3]

Likewise, Marx (referring to himself in the third person) attacks Proudhon for heaping "coarse insults on the utopian socialists and communists whom Marx honored as the forebears of modern socialism" (Marx 1989, 326),[4] while noting, with clear approbation, that their utopias "contain the presentiment and visionary expression of a new world" (1987, 326).[5]

Secondly, though there are a number of moments where Marx and Engels evoke "science" and the "scientific" in opposition to "utopia" and the "utopian," this is by no means a neatly binary opposition. As Marx notes in a passage of vital significance in *The Poverty of Philosophy* (1847):

these theoreticians are merely utopians who, to meet the wants of the oppressed classes, improvise systems and go in search of a regenerating science. But in the measure that history moves forward, and with it the struggle of the proletariat assumes clearer outlines, they no longer need to seek science in their minds; they have only to take note of what is happening before their eyes and to become its mouthpiece. So long as they look for science and merely make systems, so long as they are at the beginning of the struggle, they see in poverty nothing but poverty, without seeing in it the revolutionary, subversive side, which will overthrow the old society. From the moment they see this side, science, which is produced by the historical movement and associating itself consciously with it, has ceased to be doctrinaire and has become revolutionary. (Marx, 1976, 177–178)

Clearly, the master opposition here is not at all that of "science" versus "utopia." What is rather involved is the difference between a science based on the cerebration of abstract systems and one drawing on immediate historical experience; between "doctrinaire" and "revolutionary" science.

If anti-anti utopianism and the slippery nature of any presumed opposition between utopianism and "science" (in the sense, at least, of scientific positivism and empiricism that the term involved in the nineteenth century) are the two principal mitigators of Marx and Engels's often vociferous critique of utopian socialism, the affirmative ethical content of Marxism, especially the envisioning of non-alienated being and of an overcoming of the division of labor, as well as the references to the free association of independent producers and to the abolition of the opposition between town and country, constitute basic reasons why it is impossible to view Marxism as in any straightforward manner "anti-utopian."[6] In the *Economic and Philosophical Manuscripts* of 1844, Marx accordingly envisions "communism" as "the *genuine* resolution of the conflict between man and nature and between man and man," while the supersession of private property is expected to lead to "the complete *emancipation* of all human senses and attributes" (1992, 348, 352). What Krishan Kumar has described as a vision that is more "dazzling" than anything in "serious utopian literature" (quoted in Webb 2000, 71) also involves the positing of "the need of society" as an end in itself and hence the ideal of a life ruled not by naked need but by "[c]ompany, association, conversation" (Marx 1992, 365); the abolition of the compulsion involved in the division of labor, so that "nobody has one exclusive sphere of activity but each can become accomplished in any branch he wishes" (Marx and Engels 1976, 47); the envisioning, even as a theoretical hypothesis, of "a community of free individuals, carrying on their work with the means of production in common, in which the labor power of all the different individuals is consciously applied as the combined labor power of the community" (Marx 1996, 89)[7]; and the assertion that "the abolition of the antithesis between town and country is no more and no less utopian than the abolition of the antithesis between capitalists and wage-workers" (Engels 1988b, 384).

Though I would agree with Darren Webb that utopian socialism cannot quite be said to have provided Marx or Engels with any concrete positive program (2000, 63–68), it is difficult to completely disentangle classical Marxism from the broader legacies of utopianism, whether these are positively or negatively appraised. Perhaps the issue has been best put by T.I. Oizerman, who presents "the overcoming of utopianism by Marxism as an uncompleted historical process." It is not simply that, as Oizerman puts it, Marxism "preserves the inadequately expressed truths, the confused anticipations of the future, and the penetrating critique of capitalism" (Oizerman 2001, 73) contained in the utopian socialists themselves. Rather, the incompleteness of utopianism's "overcoming" by Marxism can be viewed as constitutive to the extent that one queries the construction of actual historical processes in terms of unequivocal linearity and teleology—two of the aspects of nineteenth-century "scientism" that are now likely to be perceived as most crudely ideological. The encounter between Marxism and utopia is in this sense neither a narrative of triumphant transition from childhood to maturity nor one of misrecognition, failure, or catastrophe; it is an open-ended adventure whose political and artistic results have often been both surprising and invigorating.

UNDER THE SHADOW OF THE COMMUNE

Erupting, seemingly out of nowhere, in the Spring of 1871, the Paris Commune was just such a surprising and invigorating challenge for the founders of Marxism—at once a verification of Marx's expectation that "the social revolution of the nineteenth century cannot draw its poetry from the past, but only from the future" (Marx 1979, 106) and a refutation of the doctrinaire rejection of the revolutionary potential inherent in Proudhonist and anarchist thought. As is well known, Marx embraced the Paris Commune despite his initial skepticism, famously observing that the proletariat has no "ready-made utopias to introduce" but must forge its path "through a series of historic processes, transforming circumstances and men" (1986a, 335).

To the extent, however, that it drew its poetry from the future, the Commune also reintroduced a utopian imaginary that Marx had believed definitively overcome by the historical process. For it must be observed that the entire humanist strain on alienation, the division of labor and species being within Marxism was silently premised on the idea "that labor becomes an 'essential' need as the result of the proletariat's own practical activity" (Webb 2000, 128) and is thus the fundamental prerequisite for the self-realization of the human being. By "acting on the external world and changing it," the worker, Marx had posited, "changes his own nature," thus actualizing "his slumbering powers" (1996, 187). The Commune, on the other hand, privileged an imaginary in which the older, even pre-capitalist utopian ideals of freedom from compulsion, leisure, and the pleasures of association—the language of "communal luxury and future splendors" (Ross 2015, 39, 58–59)—prevailed.

The tension between these two positions is perhaps nowhere more pointedly clear than in the pamphlet Marx's son-in-law, Communard, and founder of French Marxism, Paul Lafargue, was to publish from prison in 1883: *The Right to Be Lazy: Being a Refutation of the 'Right to Work' of 1848*. Lafargue's tract begins poignantly, by quoting Thiers, the grand villain of the repressions of Spring 1871, and his promotion of a philosophy that would teach "man that he is here to suffer" rather than "enjoy" (1904, 3). Indeed, Lafargue argues, the assault of the productivist ethos of the bourgeoisie on the prole-tariat has been so intense and unrelenting that it has succeeded in making the "furious mania for work" (5) an element of working-class morality, thus contributing actively to the workers' physical ruination, mental stagnation and political submission. The task of "revolutionary Socialists," therefore, is to "proclaim that the earth will cease to be a valley of tears for the workers, that in the Co-operative Commonwealth… human passions will have free play," so that workers can begin to "practice the virtues of laziness" (4, 32)—the enjoy-ment of modest Epicurean pleasures in eating and drinking well, the leisurely cultivation of the mind, the bliss of bodily health and vigor.

Far from being a solitary eccentricity, Lafargue's defense of the "right to laziness" should be viewed as strongly anticipatory of post-World War II devel-opments in Western Marxism, including, quite clearly, Herbert Marcuse's *Eros and Civilization* (1955),[8] aspects of the thought of the Situationist movement in 1960s France (particularly the work of Raoul Vaneigem),[9] as well as the concept of the "refusal of work" in Italian Operaismo and autonomism in the 1960s and 70s.[10] But, in another sense, it also highlights, by way of contrast, a link between classical Marxism and classical utopianism that is certainly not canceled out by Marx and Engels's reservations about the utopian socialists: their shared distaste for idleness, which they both tend to view as synonymous with ruling-class parasitism. Conversely, and at the other end of the spectrum, the anarchist elements which Lafargue and the Paris Commune incorporated within the process of "social dreaming" seem rather to correspond to what J.C. Davis has usefully distinguished from the utopia and termed Arcadia. Indeed, Lafargue's entire line of argumentation presupposes and evokes the two fundamental pillars of the Arcadian tradition, namely that nature "is gener-ously benevolent rather than hostile to man" and that "men's desires… are assumed to be moderate" (Davis 1981, 22).[11]

The parallels between Lafargue's polemic against the deification of labor and what is arguably the most influential Marxist literary utopia of the nine-teenth century, William Morris's *News from Nowhere* (1890), are multiple and striking: if Lafargue had an active if brief role in the Paris Commune (Marx 1986b, 397), Morris, after his late-life conversion to socialism and subsequent mobilization within the Socialist League, "emerged as one of the foremost British supporters of the memory of the Paris Commune" (Ross 2015, 61); if Lafargue's work has been, despite his founding role within French Marxism, far more resonant for anarchism (Derfler 1991), Morris's novel was praised, despite his own overt criticism of anarchism, by no less prominent an anarchist than Piotr Kropotkin, as "perhaps the most thoroughly and deeply Anarchistic conception of future society that has ever been written" (cited in Morris 2002, 347)[12]; and if Lafargue seems to have been accordingly chastised for deviance from orthodoxy by the founders of Marxism,[13] so was Morris (Thompson 1976, 785–786).

It is well known that *News from Nowhere* was largely occasioned by Morris's sense of distaste for the philistinism he sensed in Edward Bellamy's popular socialist utopia, *Looking Backward* (1888). It is perhaps less often noticed that Morris's 1889 critique is largely occasioned by his rejection, in ways that are highly evocative of Lafargue, of the detachment of industrial productivity from actual human needs.[14] For Morris, who explicitly references Lafargue's 1887 *Commonweal* article at the beginning of his novel,[15] Bellamy's bourgeois vision of utopian socialism produces the impression of "a huge standing army, tightly drilled, compelled by some mysterious fate to unceasing anxiety for the production of wares to satisfy every caprice, however wasteful and absurd" (Morris 2004, 356). In Morris's novel, on the other hand, leisure, the cultivation of the aesthetic sense, the pursuit of pleasure, joy and convivial sociability prevail over the fetishization of productivity, which, like Lafargue, Morris suspected of being responsible for the accumulation of idle capital and the drive to imperial expansion.[16] Writing under the long shadow of the Commune's brief glimpse at utopian realization, Lafargue dreams of the "old earth, trembling with bliss" and with the stirrings of a "new world" once the workday has been drastically reduced (1904, 41); while Morris concludes his novel, tellingly subtitled "An Epoch of Rest," with the injunction of the visionary denizens of utopian England to "build up little by little the new day of fellowship, and rest, and happiness" (2004, 228).[17]

CRISIS AND BEYOND: THE TWENTIETH CENTURY

Unlike the nineteenth century, which is dominated by the Hegelian idea of relying on the "movement of history," Alain Badiou remarked, the twentieth aimed to "confront History, to master it politically." For Badiou, this means that "what fascinated the militants of the twentieth century" was no longer "glorious tomorrows" but "the real, even in its horror" (2007, 15, 19). The consequences of this shift are twofold, and to a certain extent distributed evenly across the two halves of the twentieth century: in the first half, the dominant tendency is for utopianism to take a back seat to the actual work of revolutionary struggle. Utopias are still being written, of course, even if it is to a significant extent the East that provides their most fertile setting: in the decade following the Russian revolution of 1917, Richard Stites notes "an enormous blossoming of revolutionary science fiction," much of it utopian in character, and amounting to a total of about two hundred works (1984, 14). Alexander Bogdanov's *Red Star* and *Engineer Menni*, written in 1907 and 1912, respectively, represent particularly influential instances of the cross-pollination between science fiction, utopia and revolutionary Marxism in the years following Morris's epoch-making (and Commune-inspired) focus on armed struggle and concrete revolutionary dynamics in *News from Nowhere*. But it is tempting to also consider, as both Stites and Fredric Jameson note in different contexts, that there is a relationship of antagonism between utopianism and revolution such that "periods of pre-revolutionary ferment" no longer allow the utopian imagination "free play," while, on the contrary, "reality paralysis," the sense that revolution is either no longer imminent or has failed, could be particularly productive of flights of utopian speculation (Jameson 2004, 44; and see Stites 1984, 6).

Be that as it may, the institutionalization of Socialist Realism after 1932 and the party and state repression of the *avant garde* aesthetics of the turbulent 1920s spelled a sharp decline in the actual production of Marxist utopias. It is arguable, on the other hand, that state revolution and the Soviet Union tend to play a large role in the increasing hegemony of *dystopias*, beginning with Yevgeni Zamyatin's *We* (1921), and extending seminally to George Orwell's *Animal Farm* (1945) and *Nineteen Eighty-Four* (1949). After Orwell and after official "de-Stalinization" in the USSR, it would prove as difficult for Marxist *literary* utopias to emerge as during the heyday of Socialist Realism in the 1930s and early 1940s. Essentially, the relationship between Marxism and utopia after World War II tended, to the extent that it existed at all, to become a *hermeneutic* rather than a *generative* one. I will here briefly touch upon three of the main hermeneutic contexts within which the encounter between Marxism and utopia would prove fruitful and influential.

The first of these is the work of what has loosely been termed the Frankfurt School, wherein we might wish to distinguish between the negative utopianism and secularized Messianism of thinkers like Walter Benjamin and Theodor W. Adorno[18] and the sustained Marxist rehabilitation of utopia in the work of Ernst Bloch, particularly in his magnum opus, *The Principle of Hope* (1954–1959). The significance of Bloch's contribution, as Douglas Kellner and Harry O'Hara have noted, lies in his effort to correct the attenuation, within so-called "orthodox" Marxism, of the positing of alternatives capable of mobilizing the dreams and passions of the exploited and oppressed, and—relatedly—in the attempt to move beyond the analytical limits of a "mechanical, non-dialectical, economistic sort of dogmatic Marxism" (1976, 13). The rehabilitation of utopia, then, is the other side of the restoration of "telos" within Marxism: human emancipation, dis-alienation, all-round development. To this goal, Bloch mobilizes a "positive hermeneutic" (Jameson 1974, 119–120), one aiming to excavate, uncover and restore to consciousness the entire scope of forms of the "utopian impulse" (Jameson 2005, 2–3), of "prefigurations of a liberated and non-alienated condition" (Kellner and O'Hara 1976, 15) contained within the archive of human culture, from fairytales to cinema, from architecture to philosophy, and from religion to technology. Ultimately, we might argue, Bloch's life-long intervention worked to restore the question of utopia as a central one for Marxism via a double gesture of at once insisting on the necessity of Hegelian dialectic (hence the Blochian preoccupation with subjective and objective [Bloch 1995a, 148], cold and warm streams in Marxism [205–210], abstract and concrete utopia [17–18, 146, 157, 197, 204–205, 221–223][19]) and of infusing Marxism with a bold measure of Heraclitean ontology (the world as existing in a constant process of becoming) (Kellner and O'Hara 1976, 23; Levitas 1990, 14, 17, 19) and Aristotelianism (not only in terms of the importance of entelechy and teleology but also in that of the privileging of potentiality over actuality) (Kellner and O'Hara 1976, 23).

The publication, in 1973, of Louis Marin's *Utopiques: Jeux d' espaces* (translated as *Utopics: Spatial Play* in 1984) demonstrates once again the generative and unpredictable impact of what Badiou would call evental rupture on the Marxist engagement with utopia. Marin, whose engagement with the questions of ideology and with the triad of Imaginary, Symbolic and Real attests to both a Lacanian and an Althusserian influence on his thought, notes the seminal importance of "May 1968" on the conception of the work, since that event "is directly linked to the question of utopia… in its more universal nature as a revolutionary festival" (1984, 3). Despite his references to Bloch, however,[20] Marin's work marks a sharp departure away from the humanist and broadly philosophical character of Bloch's engagement and toward the textual and formal emphases of semiotics and the post-structuralist critique of language and representation that were emerging in France and the Western academic world shortly before, and for a while after, May 1968.[21] For Marin, accordingly, utopia is not an "impulse" but a "practice," whose concrete product is above all *a text*. It is "a discourse, but not a discourse of the concept"; rather, it is "a discourse of the figure," of "a particular figurative mode," whose most prominent feature is, for Marin, "the neutral," the space of thought that "sits somewhere between yes and no, false and true, but as the *double of figure, the ambiguous representation, the equivocal image of possible synthesis and productive differentiation*" (Marin 1984, 8).

This unprecedented and pioneering analysis owed a considerable debt to semiotician Algirdas Julien Greimas, whose own study of the cognitive import of narrative structures seems to derive from medieval exegeses of a distinction first introduced by Aristotelian logic—that between contradiction and contrariety.[22] It allowed Marin insight into the complex levels of play between contradictory propositions or modalities within the utopic text, of which More's founding text furnished the fundamental example. "Utopia" is now transformed from an expression of innate human aspirations for emancipation into a machine for the systematic articulation of ideological and structural antinomies and hence into a map of the limits of the thinkable within a historical moment (which, in More's case, Marin understood very much in terms of the Marxist narrative of transition from late feudalism to early capitalism).

This combination of the strengths of semiotic and structural analysis quickly attracted the attention of Marxist literary and cultural critic Fredric Jameson, who, after writing an extensive review of Marin's work in 1977, would deploy the so-called Greimasian semiotic rectangle in a broad variety of studies of utopia, from his *Political Unconscious* (1981) to his *Archaeologies of the Future* (2005).[23] Running through them like a thread is an entirely new conception of the link between utopia and the impossible. Rather than a sign of utopia's impracticality or naivete (as it was in the polemical uses of the word "utopia" in classical Marxism), impossibility becomes an indication of the utopian text's success via failure, its ability to probe the limits of the conceivable within determinate historical, political, social and economic conditions. "Utopia's deepest subject, and the source of all that is most vibrantly political about it, is precisely our inability to conceive it" (Jameson 1988, 101), Jameson wrote in 1977, adding in 1982:

> the political function of the utopian genre … is to bring home, in local and determinate ways and with a fullness of concrete detail, our constitutional inability to imagine Utopia itself: and this, not owing to any individual failure of imagination but as the result of the systemic, *cultural and ideological closure* of which we are all in one way or another prisoners. (2005, 289; emphasis added)

What Michael Gardiner, among others, has called "everyday utopianism" (2013, 20), especially its articulation in the theoretical work of Henri Lefebvre, is both equally a product of the turbulent energies of May 1968[24] and a return to earlier preoccupations in the history of the encounter between Marxism and utopia. If it is clear that Lefebvre's project of a "critique of everyday life" is fundamentally inspired by the early, humanist Marx and by his critiques of alienation and the division of labor (Brenner and Elden 2009, 10; Gardiner 2013, 120–121), it also bears noting that this project consists in the revalorization of the revolutionary impetus of Romanticism (including, prominently, the moment of Morris, of the Romantic become revolutionary) (Gardiner 2013, 19–20; Coleman 2013, 350), as well as in the critique of both the classical Marxist obsession with labor and productivity (Gardiner 2013, 122; Lefebvre 2009, 206–207) and of the commodification and betrayal of its opposite number, the dream of 'rest' and creativity-enhancing leisure (Gardiner 2013, 123–125, 127). Whereas the line of interrogation undertaken by the encounter of Marxism with structuralism and semiotics privileges a negative hermeneutic that draws attention to ideological closure, the approach to "everyday utopianism" consists in reclaiming the value of individual and collective *autopoiesis*, the power to remake and reshape life beyond any pre-posited *telos*. "Utopia," Lefebvre would assert, "is not an 'eschatology', a theory that the process of becoming might be brought to an end" (Lefebvre 2002, 73); for, as Nathaniel Coleman puts it, for Lefebvre reality itself is never complete (Coleman 2013, 356). Rather, the very category of totality, Lefebvre argued, needs to be rethought, particularly in light of the blatant falsification of classical Marxist expectations as to the defeat of capitalism and the triumph of socialism: positing the existence of a system is something both necessary and dangerous, both productive and disabling, for theoretical thought (Lefebvre 2002, 185). If utopia, like Marxism, is to retain its relevance for the present—and for Lefebvre, this is necessary (1995, 92; 2002, 38, 41, 241)—it must do so by valorizing the immanent potential within every here and now, by becoming a "method" for restoring agency and possibility to life as it is in the present:

Only a kind of reasoned but dialectical use of utopianism will permit us to illuminate the present in the name of the future, to criticize bourgeois or socialist everyday life …. The possible has ceased to be abstract … it is no longer a question of one leap into the distant future over the head of the present and the near future, but of exploring the possible using the present as a starting point … the possible and the utopian method can no longer be synonymous with foresight, prophecy, adventurism or the vague consciousness of the future. … [W]e must use utopian method experimentally, looking ahead to what is possible and what is impossible, and transforming this hypothetical exploration into applicable programs and practical plans. (Lefebvre 1995, 357, 360)

CONCLUSION

Although, as I have noted above, a literary utopianism in dialogue with Marxism seemed for some time to become a virtual impossibility, particularly after the institutionalization of "socialist realism" in the Soviet Union and the mass catastrophe of World War II throughout Europe, the global resonance of May 1968 did not remain confined in the field of literary and cultural criticism. Initially conceived as a project in the period from the late 1960s to the early 1970s though it arrived on the scholarly scene more than a decade later, Tom Moylan's *Demand the Impossible* (1986) diagnosed, as part of its own milieu of formation and emergence, the rise, within US Science Fiction, of a new wave of utopian literary production with a largely anti-capitalist and anti-authoritarian character. For Moylan, this resurgence, which spoke to the existence of a "struggle to make a better world" at a time of "oppositional, indeed utopian, feeling" (2014, x, xii), involved both formal and ideological shifts. Moylan influentially termed the texts he engaged with "critical utopias," to the extent that they all tended to challenge the teleological, blueprint-based, and "closed" horizons of earlier utopian fictions (including state-socialist ones) in conjunction with a tendency to question Marxist orthodoxy regarding the status of the proletariat as the privileged subject of social change or centralized statism as the social-organizational ideal.

The publication, a year before Moylan's study was finally published, of Laclau and Mouffe's *Hegemony and Socialist Strategy* (1985), tends to telescope two discrete historical moments that share both similarities and differences; on the one hand, Laclau and Mouffe were addressing a conjuncture of left-wing defeat in the West in the early years of neoliberal governance in the advanced capitalist core, unlike Moylan, whose study emerged out of a far more optimistic and forward-looking global moment; on the other, there is, both in the authors Moylan examines (Joanna Russ, Ursula K. Le Guin, Marge Piercy and Samuel Delany) and in Laclau and Mouffe's reappropriation of the notion of hegemony in a late classical Marxist like Gramsci, a shared interest in the problem of negotiating horizontal alliances between different sectors of disenfranchised or disempowered populations, created not merely by relations of class dominance but also by ones of racial, gender and sexual exclusion and oppression.

Part of the irony generated by the telescoped publication history of the two texts involves the fact that the historical conditions of the 1980s that mobilized Laclau and Mouffe were already generating a new turn toward the dystopian horizon (Moylan would address this both at the level of literary form and that of political theory and practice in his *Scraps of the Untainted Sky*, as well as in the collection he co-edited with Rafaella Baccolini, *Dark Horizons: Science Fiction and the Dystopian Imagination*). Today, even though dystopian modalities remain dominant, the cross-pollination between varieties of post-Marxism and critical utopia has continued to engender a number of important literary interventions. Authors like Kim Stanley Robinson (see his *Mars Trilogy*) or China Miéville (see his *Iron Council*) have persisted in making the case for the importance of a complex and difficult romance between forms of (post-) Marxist critique and the utopian imagination, not only because they share the anti-capitalist sensibilities of the "critical utopists" of the New Left and its allies in the late 1960s and early 1970s, but also because they bring literary production in active dialogue with the theoretical preoccupations that breathed new life into the study of utopia from a Marxist or Marxisant standpoint after 1968.[25]

NOTES

1. On this issue, see Domenico Losurdo, 2003, History of the Communist Movement: Failure, Betrayal, or Learning Process? *Nature, Society, and Thought* 16 (1): 33–58.
2. This is not to imply that there are no precursors to a decisively "post-Marxist" outlook, from the work of Herbert Marcuse in the 1950s and 60s to *Tel Quel* in France.
3. See also Frederick Engels, 1987, Anti-Dühring, in Marx & Engels, *Collected Works*, Vol. 25, London: Lawrence & Wishart, 31, 252, 253–254, 302–303.
4. Similarly, Marx defends Fourier's "socialist sentimentality" against Proudhon's "presumptuous platitudes" in an 1846 letter to Annenkov (in Marx & Engels, *Collected Works*, Vol. 38. London: Lawrence & Wishart, 1982, 104).
5. See also Frederick Engels, 1988a, Supplement of the 1870 Preface to the *Peasant War in Germany*, in Marx & Engels, *Collected Works*, Vol. 23, London: Lawrence & Wishart, 630.
6. Even in the case of an epigone of the Marxist tradition like Georges Sorel the issue remains complex, both because Sorel's anti-utopianism does not involve rejection of the need to imagine a better future and because it supplements a rejection of utopian aspects in Marxism itself. See Antonis Balasopoulos, 2020, Georges Sorel and Critical Anti-Utopianism, *Revista Polis* 8 (4): 1–16.
7. See also Karl Marx, 1985, Instructions for the Delegates of the Provisional General Council, in Marx & Engels, *Collected Works*, Vol.

20, London: Lawrence & Wishart, 190; and 1986a, The Civil War in France, in Marx & Engels, *Collected Works*, Vol. 22, London: Lawrence & Wishart, 335.

8. See Herbert Marcuse, 1962, *Eros and Civilization: A Philosophical Inquiry into Freud*, New York: Vintage Books, esp. 117–26, 127–43.

9. See Raoul Vaneigem, 2001, *The Revolution of Everyday Life*, trans. Donald Nicholson-Smith, London: Rebel Press, esp. 52–56; and 1984, *The Book of Pleasures*, trans. John Fullerton, Seattle: Left Bank Books.

10. See Patrick Cunninghame, 2005, Autonomia in the 1970s: The Refusal of Work, the Party and Power, *Cultural Studies Review* 11 (2) (September): 77–94; and Nicola Pizzolato, 2017, A New Revolutionary Practice: Operaisti and the 'Refusal of Work' in 1970's Italy, *Estudos Históricos* 30 (61) (May–August): 449–464.

11. See also Paul Lafargue, 1904, *The Right to Be Lazy: Being a Refutation of the 'Right to Work' of 1848*, trans. Harriet E. Lothrop, Terre Haute: Standard Publishing, 4, 6–7, 23, 37.

12. On Morris's relations to anarchism, see his own 1979 Socialism and Anarchism in *Political Writings of William Morris*, ed. A.L. Morton, London: Lawrence & Wishart, 209–213; Michael Holzman, 1984, Anarchism and Utopia: William Morris's *News from Nowhere*, ELH 51 (3): 589–603; and Ruth Kinna, 2012, Anarchism, Individualism and Communism: William Morris's Critique of Anarcho-Communism, in *Libertarian Socialism: Politics in Black and Red*, ed. Alex Prichard et al., 35–56, Houndmills: Palgrave Macmillan.

13. See Fredrick Engels's (1992) well-known remark that Marx was so little impressed by French Marxism that he proclaimed that he is not a Marxist, in Letter to Eduard Bernstein, 2–3 November 1882, in Marx & Engels, *Collected Works*, Vol. 46, London: Lawrence & Wishart, 356; and his (2001) words to Lafargue in the letter of 11 May 1889, in Marx & Engels, *Collected Works*, Vol. 48, London: Lawrence & Wishart: "We have never called you anything but 'the so-called Marxists' and I would not know how else to describe you" (312).

14. See Lafargue, *The Right to Be Lazy*, 20, 22, 26–28, 36.

15. Lafargue's "The Morrow of the Revolution" (1887) argued that "the end of the social revolution is to work as little as possible and to enjoy as much as possible" (n.p.). Morris's novel opens thus: "there had been one night a brisk conversational discussion, as to what would happen on the Morrow of the Revolution." See *News from Nowhere and Other Writings*, London: Penguin, 2004, 43. See also Owen Holland, 2017, *William Morris's Utopianism: Propaganda, Politics and Prefiguration*, Houndmills: Palgrave Macmillan, 159.

16. See Lafargue, *The Right to Be Lazy*, 20–22; and Morris, *News from Nowhere and Other Writings* (2004), 125–126.

17. On the differences between Lafargue and Morris's approach to labor, see Holland, *William Morris's Utopianism*, 158–159, 257; and Morris, Useful Work Versus Useless Toil, in *Political Writings of William Morris*, 86–108.

18. See Ilan Gur Ze'ev, 1999, "Walter Benjamin and Max Horkheimer: From Utopia to Redemption", *The Journal of Jewish Thought and Philosophy*, 8 (1): 119–155; Michael Löwy, 1992, *Redemption and Utopia: Jewish Libertarian Thought in Central Europe, A Study in Elective Affinity*, trans. Hope Heaney, London: Athlone Press, esp. 71–94; and Mattias Martinson, 2014, "Adorno, Revolution, and Negative Utopia", in *Jewish Thought, Utopia, and Revolution*, ed. Elena Namli et al., Leiden: Brill/Rodopi, 33–48.

19. See also Ernst Bloch, 1995, *The Principle of Hope*, Vol. 3, trans. Neville Plaice, Stephen Plaice, and Paul Knight, Cambridge: MIT Press, 968, 1048, 1053, 1365–1370.

20. See for example Louis Marin, 1984, *Utopics: Spatial Play*, trans. Robert A. Vollrath, Atlantic Highlands: Humanities Press, xvii–xix.

21. I am thinking here, among others, of the conference that introduced post-structuralism in the US, "The Language of Criticism and the Sciences of Man," held at Johns Hopkins in 1966 and hosting Derrida, Barthes, Lacan and de Man, among others.

22. On the distinction, see Jean-Yves Beziau, 2016, Disentangling Contradiction from Contrareity via Incompatibility, *Logica Universalis* 10: 158; and Fredric Jameson, 1987, Foreword to A.J. Greimas, *On Meaning: Selected Writings in Semiotic Theory*, trans. Paul J. Perron and Frank H. Collins, Minneapolis: University of Minnesota Press, xiv.

23. See Fredric Jameson, 1988, Of Islands and Trenches: Neutralization and the Production of Utopian Discourse in *The Ideologies of Theory: Essays 1971–1986*, vol. 2, Minneapolis: University of Minnesota Press, 75–101; and Philip Wegner, 2014, *Periodizing Jameson: Dialectics, the University, and the Desire for Narrative*, Evanston: Northwestern UP, esp. xxv–xxvii, 183–203.

24. On the impact of 1968 on Lefebvre's thought see Michael Gardiner, 2013, *Weak Messianism: Essays in Everyday Utopianism*, Oxford: Peter Lang, 127–128; and Neil Brenner and Stuart Elden, 2009, State, Space, World: Lefebvre and the Survival of Capitalism, in *State, Space, World: Selected Essays*, Henri Lefebvre, ed. Neil Brenner and Stuart Elden, Minneapolis: University of Minnesota Press, 6–7, 14–15, 38–39.

25. Robinson studied with Fredric Jameson at the University of California in San Diego in the 1970s; Miéville, who is a political activist and literary critic as well as a creative writer, completed a Ph.D. thesis on Marxism (published in paperback in 2006 as *Between Equal Rights: A Marxist Theory of International Law*, Chicago: Haymarket Books) and in 2009 coedited *Red Planets: Marxism and Science Fiction*, Middletown, CT: Wesleyan University Press.

References

Badiou, Alain. 2007. *The Century*, trans. Alberto Toscano. Cambridge: Polity.

Balasopoulos, Antonis. 2020. Georges Sorel and Critical Anti-Utopianism. *Revista Polis* 8 (4): 1–16.

Beziau, Jean-Yves. 2016. Disentangling Contradiction from Contrariety via Incompatibility. *Logica Universalis* 10: 157–170.

Bloch, Ernst. 1995a. *The Principle of Hope*, vol. 1, trans. Neville Plaice, Stephen Plaice, and Paul Knight. Cambridge: MIT Press.

———. 1995b. *The Principle of Hope*, vol. 3, trans. Neville Plaice, Stephen Plaice, and Paul Knight. Cambridge: MIT Press.

Bould, Mark, and China Miéville. 2009. *Red Planets: Marxism and Science Fiction*. Middletown, CT: Wesleyan University Press.

Brenner, Neil, and Stuart Elden. 2009. State, Space, World: Lefebvre and the Survival of Capitalism. In *State, Space, World: Selected Essays*, Henri Lefebvre, ed. Neil Brenner and Stuart Elden. Minneapolis: University of Minnesota Press.

Claeys, Gregory. 2018. *Marx and Marxism*. London: Pelican.

Coby, Patrick. 1986. The Utopian Vision of Karl Marx: Contradicting Logic and History. *Modern Age: A Conservative Review* 30: 22–32.

Coleman, Nathaniel. 2013. Utopian Prospect of Henri Lefebvre. *Space and Culture* 16 (3): 349–363.

Cunninghame, Patrick. 2005. Autonomia in the 1970s: The Refusal of Work, the Party and Power. *Cultural Studies Review* 11 (2): 77–94.

Davis, J.C. 1981. *Utopia and the Ideal Society: A Study of English Utopian Writing 1516–1700*. Cambridge: Cambridge University Press.

Derfler, Leslie. 1991. *Paul Lafargue and the Founding of French Marxism, 1842–1882*. Cambridge: Harvard University Press.

Engels, Frederick. 1987. Anti-Dühring. In *Collected Works*, Karl Marx and Frederick Engels, vol. 25, 5–312. London: Lawrence & Wishart.

———. 1988a. Supplement of the 1870 Preface to the *Peasant War in Germany*. In *Collected Works*, Karl Marx and Frederick Engels, vol. 23. London: Lawrence & Wishart.

———. 1988b [1872–3]. The Housing Question. In *Collected Works*, Karl Marx and Frederick Engels, vol. 23, 317–391. London: Lawrence & Wishart.

———. 1989. Letter to Wilhelm Liebknecht, February 12, 1873. In *Collected Works*, Karl Marx and Frederick Engels, vol. 44, 477. London: Lawrence & Wishart.

———. 1992. Letter to Eduard Bernstein, November 2–3, 1882. In *Collected Works*, Karl Marx and Frederick Engels, vol. 46, 353–357. London: Lawrence & Wishart.

———. 2001. Letter to Paul Lafargue, May 11, 1889. In *Collected Works*, Karl Marx and Frederick Engels, vol. 48, 312–314. London: Lawrence & Wishart.

Gardiner, Michael. 2013. *Weak Messianism: Essays in Everyday Utopianism*. Oxford: Peter Lang.

Geoghegan, Vincent. 2008 [1987]. *Utopianism and Marxism*. Oxford: Peter Lang.

Holland, Owen. 2017. *William Morris's Utopianism: Propaganda, Politics and Prefiguration*. Houndmills: Palgrave Macmillan.

Holzman, Michael. 1984. Anarchism and Utopia: William Morris's *News from Nowhere*. *ELH* 51 (3): 589–603.

Jameson, Fredric. 1974. *Marxism and Form: Twentieth-Century Dialectical Theories of Literature*. Princeton: Princeton University Press.

————. 1987. Foreword to A.J. Greimas. In *On Meaning: Selected Writings in Semiotic Theory*, trans. Paul J. Perron and Frank H. Collins. Minneapolis: University of Minnesota Press.

————. 1988. Of Islands and Trenches: Neutralization and the Production of Utopian Discourse. In *The Ideologies of Theory: Essays 1971–1986*, vol. 2, 75–101. Minneapolis: University of Minnesota Press.

————. 2004 The Politics of Utopia. *New Left Review* II (25): 35–54.

————. 2005. *Archaeologies of the Future: The Desire Called Utopia and Other Science Fictions*. London: Verso.

Kellner, Douglas, and Harry O'Hara. 1976. Utopia and Marxism in Ernst Bloch. *New German Critique* 9 (Autumn): 11–34.

Kinna, Ruth. 2012. Anarchism, Individualism and Communism: William Morris's Critique of Anarcho-Communism. In *Libertarian Socialism: Politics in Black and Red*, ed. Alex Prichard et al., 35–56. Houndmills: Palgrave Macmillan.

Kropotkin, Piotr. 2003. From an Obituary Notice in Freedom, November 1896. In *News from Nowhere*, William Morris, ed. Stephen Arata, 347. Lancashire: Broadview.

Lafargue, Paul. 1887. The Morrow of the Revolution. https://www.marxists.org/archive/lafargue/1887/morrow.htm. Accessed 9 June 2021.

————. 1904. *The Right to Be Lazy: Being a Refutation of the 'Right to Work' of 1848*, trans. Harriet E. Lothrop. Terre Haute: Standard Publishing.

Laclau, Ernesto and Chantal Mouffe. 1985. *Hegemony and Socialist Strategy: Towards a Radical Democratic Politics*. London and New York: Verso.

Lefebvre, Henri. 1995. *Introduction to Modernity*. Trans. John Moore. London and New York: Verso.

Lefebvre, Henri. 2002. *Critique of Everyday Life*, vol. II, trans. John Moore. London: Verso.

Levitas, Ruth. 1990. Educated Hope: Ernst Bloch on Abstract and Concrete Utopia. *Utopian Studies* 1 (2): 13–26.

————. 2009. The Worldwide and the Planetary. In *State, Space, World: Selected Essays*, ed. Neil Brenner and Stuart Elden, 196–209. Minneapolis: University of Minnesota Press.

Lovell, David. 2004. Marx's Utopian Legacy. *The European Legacy* 9 (5): 629–640.

Löwy, Michael. 1992. *Redemption and Utopia: Jewish Libertarian Thought in Central Europe, A Study in Elective Affinity*, trans. Hope Heaney. London: Athlone Press.

Lukes, Steven. 1984. Marxism and Utopianism. In *Utopias*, ed. Peter Alexander and Roger Gill, 153–167. London: Duckworth.

Marcuse, Herbert. 1962. *Eros and Civilization: A Philosophical Inquiry into Freud*. New York: Vintage Books.

Marin, Louis. 1984. *Utopics: Spatial Play*, trans. Robert A. Vollrath. Atlantic Highlands: Humanities Press.

Martinson, Mattias. 2014. Adorno, Revolution, and Negative Utopia. In *Jewish Thought, Utopia, and Revolution*, ed. Elena Namli, Jayne Svenungsson, and Alana M. Vincent, 33–48. Leiden: Brill/Rodopi.

Marx, Karl. 1976 [1847]. The Poverty of Philosophy. In *Collected Works*, Karl Marx and Frederick Engels, vol. 6, 105–212. London: Lawrence & Wishart.

————. 1979. The Eighteenth Brumaire of Louis Bonaparte (1851–2). In *Collected Works*, Karl Marx and Frederick Engels, vol. 11, 99–197. London: Lawrence & Wishart.

———. 1982. Letter to Pavel Vasilyevich Annenkov, December 28, 1846. In *Collected Works*, Karl Marx and Frederick Engels, vol. 38, 95–106. London: Lawrence & Wishart.

———. 1985 [1867]. Instructions for the Delegates of the Provisional General Council. In *Collected Works*, Karl Marx and Frederick Engels, vol. 20, 185–194. London: Lawrence & Wishart.

———. 1986a [1871]. The Civil War in France. In *Collected Works*, Karl Marx and Frederick Engels, vol. 22, 307–359. London: Lawrence & Wishart.

———. 1986b. Letter to the Editor of *The Sun*, Charles Dana, August 25, 1871. In *Collected Works*, Karl Marx and Frederick Engels, vol. 22, 396–399. London: Lawrence and Wishart.

———. 1987. Letter to Ludwig Kugelmann, October 9, 1866. In *Collected Works*, Karl Marx and Frederick Engels, vol. 42, 325–326. London: Lawrence & Wishart.

———. 1989. Note on the *Poverty of Philosophy*. In *Collected Works*, Karl Marx and Frederick Engels, vol. 24, 326–327. London: Lawrence & Wishart.

———. 1992. Economic and Philosophical Manuscripts. In *Early Writings*, 279–400. Harmondsworth, Middlesex: Penguin.

———. 1996 [1867]. Capital, Vol. 1. In *Collected Works*, Karl Marx and Frederick Engels, vol. 35. London: Lawrence & Wishart.

Marx, Karl, and Frederick Engels. 1976. The German Ideology. In *Collected Works*, Karl Marx and Frederick Engels, vol. 5. London: Lawrence & Wishart.

Miéville, China. 2006. *Between Equal Rights: A Marxist Theory of International Law*. Chicago: Haymarket Books.

Morris, William. 1979a. Useful Work Versus Useless Toil. In *Political Writings of William Morris*, 86–108. London: Lawrence & Wishart.

———. 1979b. Socialism and Anarchism. In *Political Writings of William Morris*, ed. A.L. Morton, 209–213. London: Lawrence & Wishart.

———. 2002. *News from Nowhere*. Ed. Stephen Arata. Lancashire: Broadview Press.

———. 2004. *News from Nowhere and Other Writings*. London: Penguin.

Moylan, Tom. 2014 [1986]. *Demand the Impossible: Science Fiction and the Utopian Imagination*. Oxford: Peter Lang.

Oizerman, T.I. 2001. Marxism and Utopianism. *Russian Studies in Philosophy* 39 (4): 54–79.

Paden, Roger. 2002. Marx's Critique of the Utopian Socialists. *Utopian Studies* 13 (2): 67–91.

Pizzolato, Nicola. 2017. A New Revolutionary Practice: Operaisti and the 'Refusal of Work' in 1970's Italy. *Estudos Históricos* 30 (61): 449–464.

Ross, Kristin. 2015. *Communal Luxury: The Political Imaginary of the Paris Commune*. London: Verso.

Stites, Richard. 1984. Fantasy and Revolution: Alexander Bogdanov and the Origins of Bolshevik Science Fiction. In *Red Star: The First Bolshevik Utopia*, Alexander Bogdanov, ed. Loren R. Graham and Richard Stites, trans. Charles Rougle, 1–16. Bloomington: Indiana University Press.

Thompson, E.P. 1976. *William Morris: Romantic to Revolutionary*. New York: Pantheon Books.

Vaneigem, Raoul. 1984. *The Book of Pleasures*, trans. John Fullerton. Seattle: Left Bank Books.

———. 2001 [1967]. *The Revolution of Everyday Life*, trans. Donald Nicholson-Smith. London: Rebel Press.

Webb, Darren. 2000. *Marx, Marxism and Utopia*. Aldershot: Palgrave.

Wegner, Philip. 2014. *Periodizing Jameson: Dialectics, the University, and the Desire for Narrative*. Evanston: Northwestern UP.

Ze'ev, Ilan Gur. 1999. Walter Benjamin and Max Horkheimer: From Utopia to Redemption. *The Journal of Jewish Thought and Philosophy* 8 (1): 119–155.

Anarchism

Laurence Davis

Introduction

One of the hallmarks of the utopian tradition is its capacious pluralism and diversity. There are many different varieties of utopia, representing a wide range of ideological traditions. This chapter examines the relationship between the anarchist and utopian traditions, focusing especially on the political significance of their intersection.

The essay argues that anarchist utopianism manifests certain distinctive ideological features which, together, suggest a revolutionary, realistic, and grounded utopian alternative to the dominant statist, growth-oriented, abstractly rationalist, and perfectionist utopian traditions. The plan for the chapter is as follows: first, I introduce the theory and practice of anarchism, and clear up some common misconceptions about it; second, I elucidate anarchism's utopian dimensions; and third, I identify some of the key features of the anarchist utopian tradition that distinguish it from other more well-known and better-understood varieties of utopianism, and that make it particularly politically relevant in a time of global political, economic, and ecological crisis such as our own.

L. Davis (✉)
University College Cork, Cork, Ireland

333

P. Marks et al. (eds.), *The Palgrave Handbook of Utopian and Dystopian Literatures*, https://doi.org/10.1007/978-3-030-88654-7_26

ANARCHISM

Anarchism is one of the most vital impulses of contemporary radical politics, a heterodox way of seeing and being in the world that provides an ideological framework for understanding and acting upon some of the most pressing problems of our times. Evidence of anarchism's recent resurgence may be found in the decentralized networks of the global Occupy and European *Indignado* movements; the Arab revolutions of 2011 and their utopian surplus (Verikas 2002), from Rojava to Egypt; worldwide anti-austerity and anti-capitalist mobilizations; interconnected alter-globalization struggles from Latin America to Asia, Africa, and the Middle East; deep green ecological and climate justice campaigns led by small farmers and indigenous peoples in the global South; anti-fascist coalitions and campaigns from Greece to the United States; student struggles from Chile to Quebec and the United Kingdom; and countless experiments in cooperative production and distribution, alternative media and art, social libertarian forms of education, practices of egalitarian collective living, and self-consciously political expressions of non-conforming sexualities and gender identities. Fired by the conviction that it is possible to create another world far better than the one we currently inhabit, those now inspired by anarchist ideas and ideals have refused to acquiesce to the prevailing consensus that there is no alternative to a way of life based on domination and hierarchy.[1]

Yet for all this resurgent political energy, anarchism remains the most widely misunderstood modern political ideology. Intelligent and well-informed accounts are a rarity in the mainstream academic literature, and inquiry into the subject, as one contemporary philosopher of anarchism has observed accurately, is typically greeted by colleagues "with prejudicial incredulity, condescension, and even hostility—beyond the normal ignorance of the over-specialized" (McLaughlin 2007, 14). Many analysts muddle matters with false, simplistic, or misleading claims about anarchism. Here I will briefly consider two that are particularly relevant to an accurate understanding of anarchist utopianism: first, the claim that anarchists are opposed to organization; and second, the assertion that anti-statism is the defining feature of anarchist ideology.

The first of these claims, that anarchists are opposed to organization, is a myth. Its persistence in the popular mind derives in part from unreflective repetition, and in part as well from an understandable confusion of terms. As the historian of anarchism George Woodcock points out, the original Greek word *anarche* means merely "without a ruler," and thus the English term *anarchy* can be used in a general context to mean either the negative condition of unruliness or the positive condition of being unruled because rule is unnecessary for the preservation of order (Woodcock 1962, 10). It is with this latter sense of the term that anarchists identify, ever since the French political thinker Pierre-Joseph Proudhon proudly adopted the insignia in 1840.

Organization is thus entirely compatible with anarchism, so long as it is not hierarchical and/or coercive.

The second claim, that anti-statism is the defining feature of anarchist ideology, is reductive and hence also misleading. The state is indeed a primary target of anarchist criticism, insofar as it is the paradigmatic "archist" institution, distinguished above all by its claim of a monopoly on the legitimate use of force in a given territory. However, anarchists have traditionally struggled against a wide range of regimes of domination, from (to cite but a few examples) capitalism, patriarchy, heterosexism, the war system and the domination of nature to colonialism, slavery, fascism, white supremacy, and certain forms of organized religion. Moreover, there is no reason to believe that a future stateless world would necessarily be one entirely free of all forms of domination. On the contrary, the evidence of history suggests that every victory in the never-ending struggle against oppression and injustice creates a new situation with its own new and unpredictable problems and demands. It follows that while anti-statism has been, and for the foreseeable future will likely continue to be, a core defining feature of anarchist ideology, it is not (as some have misleadingly claimed) its "defining" feature. Indeed, as John Clark reminds us, it would be a mistake to define anarchism in terms of its relation to *any* one social institution, no matter how important it may be (Clark 1984, 122).

What, then, lies at the core of anarchist ideology, if not anti-statism and opposition to all forms of organization? The core of anarchism, I suggest, is the belief that society can and should be organized without hierarchy and domination. While anarchist ideas may be traced back thousands of years to the Taoists in ancient China, anarchism first emerged as a coherent political ideology in the late eighteenth century. It developed primarily in opposition to centralized states and industrial capitalism, and by the end of the nineteenth century was a mass revolutionary movement attracting millions of adherents worldwide.

ANARCHISM AND UTOPIANISM

Over time anarchists have generated a rich variety of visions of social life structured according to principles other than hierarchy and domination. While these visions range from the predominantly individualistic to the predominantly communitarian, features common to virtually all include an emphasis on self-management and self-regulatory methods of organization, voluntary association, decentralized federation, and direct democracy. In short, anarchists desire a decentralized society, based on the principle of free association, in which people will manage and govern themselves. Such a society, anarchists contend, is the one best suited to maximizing the values of liberty, equality, and solidarity.

Considering the anarchist tradition as a whole, it is fair to say that most anarchists have been ambivalent about the concept of utopia. On the one hand, they wish to avoid being tarred with the negative connotations of the term associated with influential liberal and Marxist anti-utopian criticisms of utopia, particularly the suggestion that utopian imagination necessarily represents a form of apolitical and anti-historical abstraction from the existing reality. Hence the frequent emphasis in anarchist writing on its grounding in existing libertarian tendencies in society, and its anti-perfectionist commitment to endless experimentation and open-ended social and political change. On the other hand, anarchists clearly recognize that while some things are indeed impossible, others are "impossible" only because humanly created institutions make them so. Hence the need for anarchist utopian thought experiments and experiments in living that expose the partiality of currently dominant perceptions of reality, and thus facilitate free choice from among a fuller range of practical social alternatives (Davis 2009, 2).

The work of the anarchist revolutionary Peter Kropotkin (1842–1921), one of anarchism's leading lights, nicely illustrates this ambivalence. As Kropotkin accurately observed, Anarchy does not come from the universities, or scientific researches, or any system of philosophy developed by an intellectual elite. Rather, it originated among the multitude, as a creative and constructive revolutionary social movement of the people, who elaborated common-law institutions in order to defend themselves against a dominating minority. But no sooner had the anarchist movement sprung up than it began to work out a general expression of its principles, and the theoretical and scientific basis of its teachings. At the same time, it worked out its own ideal, for "no struggle can be successful if…it has no definite and concrete aim" (Kropotkin 2014a, 180). This ideal was "utopian" in the sense that it challenged dominant conceptions of realism, yet it was neither impractical nor dogmatically rigid. Rather, and here Kropotkin makes an interesting observation relevant to contemporary debates about the "recuperation" of anarchism and utopia, insofar as the anarchist ideal emerged out of and continues to be informed by popular struggle, it retains its political utility and avoids the worst features of prescriptive academic utopias drafted by "desk-bound utopians" (Kropotkin 2014b, 508). Like Marx, Kropotkin repeatedly criticized "a priori" utopias (Kropotkin 1910) drafted by those who wished to produce "ready-made recipes for political cooking" (Kinna 2016, 132). Unlike Marx, however, Kropotkin resisted the temptation to throw out the baby of utopianism along with the bathwater of its more abstractly idealist variants. For example, in his 1913 Preface to *How We Shall Bring About the Revolution*, by Émile Pataud and Émile Pouget, Kropotkin emphasized the need for books that will enable the mass of the people to form for themselves a concrete idea of what it is that they desire to see realized in a near future, sketches that will show in their main lines what the coming Revolution proposes to realize. Such books should not be regarded as gospels to be accepted in their entirety or left alone, but rather as suggestive proposals intended to refine aspirations and demonstrate the feasibility of a masterless society. Indeed, Kropotkin proceeds to reference his own book *The Conquest of Bread* as one such attempt to sketch a Communal Utopia (Kropotkin 1913, 557–560).

Stepping back from Kropotkin's work to again consider the anarchist tradition as whole, it makes little sense to dismiss outright the claim that anarchism is a utopia. Rather, it is far preferable from an analytical point of view simply to acknowledge the utopian aspect of anarchism, while simultaneously observing that it is a utopia of a particular kind. More specifically, the anarchist utopia is an example of what I have elsewhere termed a "grounded" utopia (Davis 2012), or one that emerges organically out of, and contributes to the further development of, historical movements for grassroots social change. Emphatically not fantasized visions of perfection to be imposed upon an imperfect world, such utopias are an integral feature of that world, representing the hopes and dreams of those consigned to its margins. Part and parcel of dynamic and open-ended processes of struggle, and grounded in immediate everyday needs, grounded utopias challenge dominant conceptions of reality not by measuring them against the transcendent ethical standard of a fixed vision of an ideal society, but by opening a utopian space for thinking, feeling, debating and cultivating the possibility of historically rooted (and thus historically contingent) alternative social relations.

The grounded utopianism of anarchism is evident in an almost endless variety of social practices in human history, from cooperative egalitarian tribal traditions and anarchistic millenarian movements to ecological communities, movements for the liberation of women, and the radically libertarian moments of many of the world's great revolutions (Clark 2009, 23). Far from being a utopia in the common-sense understanding of the term as an unachievable ideal of impossible perfection, anarchism is an eminently practical ideology that has already "lifted a huge load of human misery" (Ward 2004).

In Spain in the 1930s, for example, anarchists not only resisted the rise of fascism in the form of a military coup and insurrection by General Francisco Franco, they also undertook a social revolution that transformed the lives of millions. Over the course of three years (1936–1939), in the midst of civil war and despite the opposition of all the Spanish political parties and foreign powers including Nazi Germany, Mussolini's Italy and Stalinist Russia, rank-and-file anarchists among the workers and peasants spearheaded an unprecedented, large-scale social experiment in agricultural and industrial collectivization. Millions of workers and peasants took control of the land and the factories and began to work them without bosses, capitalist managers, landlords, or the authority of the state. By the end of 1936 some three million men, women and children were living in rural and urban collectives based on the principle of self-management. Many of these collectives abolished money and instituted economic equality in accordance with the communist principle "From each according to his or her ability and to each according to his or her needs." They built schools and hospitals and made significant advances in eradicating illiteracy and providing essential medical services. They coordinated their activity through free association in regional federations and increased production and communal wealth despite the shortage of labor created by the war effort. In place of formal representative democracy, they implemented a grassroots form of participatory democracy in which every member of the community proposed, discussed, planned, and implemented major initiatives which affected their lives. In some of the rural collectives, women who had previously been oppressed by illiteracy, poverty, male dominance, and organized religion took on positions of responsibility and led the struggle to challenge the destructive roles of church and state in intimate life. A number of women organized an autonomous revolutionary women's group within the anarchist ranks, the 30,000-strong *Mujeres Libres* (Free Women), and campaigned for full gender equality, free sexual unions, and the free availability of information about sexuality and birth control.[2]

In their fictional guise, anarchist utopias have proven to be a particularly fruitful source of imaginative reflection about the possibilities and limits of anarchy. In works such as Joseph Déjacque's *L'Humanisphère, Utopie anarchique* (1858), Aldous Huxley's *Island* (1962), Ursula K. Le Guin's *The Dispossessed: An Ambiguous Utopia* (1974) and *Always Coming Home* (1985), Robert Nichols' four-volume *Daily Lives in Nghsi-Altai* (1977–1979), and Starhawk's *The Fifth Sacred Thing* (1993) and *City of Refuge* (2016), fiction writers have brought their formidable artistic talents to bear on the creative challenge of depicting a functioning anarchist society.[3] What makes these works particularly interesting from the perspective of students of political ideologies are the ways in which they engage the reader in complex dialogue about what is, what might be, and the relationship between the two. They are thus neither purely escapist fantasies nor narrowly didactic constructions meant to secure the reader's unquestioning assent to a particular socio-political agenda. Rather, in their most artistically sophisticated forms, they are thought experiments that invite readers to participate in a time-sensitive journey of the utopian imagination complete with fundamental moral conflict, meaningful choice, and continuing change, by the end of which they may return to the non-fictional present with a broader perspective on its latent emancipatory possibilities (Davis 2012, 137).

To focus on but one especially notable example, in her science-fiction novel *The Dispossessed*, Ursula K. Le Guin manages the remarkable feat of detailing the texture of everyday life in an anarchist utopian society. Moreover, as the subtitle of the book ("An Ambiguous Utopia") suggests, she does so in a way that both, on the one hand, foregrounds the dynamic and value-pluralist relationship between this ambiguously utopian world and our own and, on the other, critically interrogates the anarchist ideology that so deeply inspires and informs the narrative. The result is an exceptionally thoughtful and powerfully imagined work of art that dramatizes one of the most important, if frequently neglected, features of anarchist ideology: its capacity for reflective self-correction and perpetual recreation.[4]

Anarchist Utopianism and the Political Uses and Abuses of Utopia

In her pioneering study of the utopian tradition, *Journey through Utopia*, first published in 1950, Marie Louise Berneri argues that two main trends manifest themselves in utopian thought throughout the ages. One, she suggests, seeks the happiness of humankind through material well-being, the sinking of individuality into the group, and the greatness of the State. The other, while demanding a certain degree of material comfort, consider that happiness is the result of the free expression of individual personality and must not be sacrificed to an arbitrary moral code or the interests of the State. Whereas the former ("authoritarian utopias") resemble nothing so much as a "lifeless machine" and are chiefly responsible for the anti-utopian attitude prevalent among contemporary intellectuals, the latter ("anti-authoritarian utopias") gave us utopias where people were free from both physical and moral compulsion, where they worked not out necessity or a sense of duty but because they found work a pleasurable activity, where love knew no laws and where everyone was an artist. In short, they were "the living dreams of poets" (Berneri 1987, 2–3, 8, 317).

Contemporary scholars of utopia have drawn comparable distinctions and reached similar conclusions. For example, in his helpful but relatively neglected study *Narrating Utopia: Ideology, Gender, Form in Utopian Literature* (1999), Chris Ferns distinguishes between "Utopias of Order" and "Utopias of Freedom." While his conclusions are ambivalent—he acknowledges the extent to which even many of the more libertarian utopias remain constrained by the limitations of the traditional or dominant utopian narrative paradigm—he also argues, with particular reference to Piercy and Le Guin, that utopia is "still capable of pointing the way, however hesitantly, toward something new" (Ferns 1999, 236). It does so, in part, he suggests, by experimenting with novel narrative frameworks that serve to foreground the relationship between utopia and the reality from which it stems—yet to which it proposes a *historically conditional* radical alternative.

These conclusions are confirmed and developed considerably in more recent scholarly studies of the relationship between the anarchist and utopian traditions. In 2009, for example, Ruth Kinna and I published the first collection of original essays to explore the relationship between the anarchist and utopian traditions, and in particular the ways in which their long historical interaction from the Warring States epoch of ancient China to the present time has proven fruitful for emancipatory politics (Davis and Kinna 2009). Among the most notable findings of the work is that nearly all the anarchist or anarchistic utopias examined are open, dynamic, and organically linked to actual social practices. There is a consensus among the contributors that in stark contrast to the rationally fixed and transcendent utopias associated with escapism and/or domination, the largely anti-perfectionist and antiauthoritarian utopias they examine do not represent a form of abstraction from the world. On the contrary, such utopias are focused, first and foremost, on transforming the present as part of an organic process in which already existing historical tendencies are actively engaged with, nurtured, and built upon. Most of them call into question modern conceptions of progress and recall the organic communities of the premodern past and the dissident present to inspire and inform contemporary libertarian struggles for a more humane future. They affirm the reality and worth of those natural and cultural forces that are the devalued and rejected "other" of civilized domination, and in their non-literary forms frequently exemplify a prefigurative form of direct-action politics demonstrating that libertarian utopias are not only eminently desirable but also immediately realizable.

The practical political implications of the above analysis are, I contend, profound. From the point of view of contemporary grassroots social movements seeking to reclaim democratic control over the conditions of their existence in a context of market globalization, ecological collapse, and resurgent xenophobia and fascism, transcendent utopian imagination or theory is of little value. This is because it depicts or conceptualizes a static vision of society in which change seems neither desirable nor possible. It thus reproduces the dichotomous division between the actual and the real, on the one hand, and the impossible and the ideal, on the other that it seeks to challenge, and so disempowers those who engage in dissident politics precisely in order to reject predetermined assumptions about what should be desired and what can be attained.

By contrast, the grounded utopian politics of anarchism speaks directly to the needs of a wide range of grassroots social movements, insofar as the contemporary anarchist movement and its associated political culture and ideas have emerged out of or in close association with these wider movements, and informed their ongoing development.[5] With the decline of Marxism as the hegemonic ideology on the Left, anarchism has arguably emerged as the leading revolutionary movement of the twenty-first century. However, its status as a source of inspiration for contemporary revolutionary politics is very different from that formerly occupied by Marxism. Commenting on precisely this point, the anarchist anthropologist David Graeber notes that whereas different schools of Marxism tend to be named after Great Thinkers (e.g., Leninists, Maoists, Trotskyites, Gramscians and Althusserians), anarchists like to distinguish themselves by what they do, and how they organize themselves to go about doing it. This does not mean, he hastens to add, that anarchists are or must be against theory. Rather, the point is that while anarchism clearly has need of the tools of intellectual analysis and understanding, it does not need what he calls "High Theory," that is, theory intended to determine the correct historical analysis of the world situation, so as to lead the masses along in the one true revolutionary direction. Anarchist-inspired groups generally tend to embrace a form of "Low Theory," characterized by Graeber as a non-vanguardist means of grappling with real, immediate questions that emerge from a transformative or revolutionary project. Importantly, this distinctive variety of practice-grounded anarchist theorizing presumes and indeed values diversity of sometimes incommensurable perspectives (Graeber 2004, 4–9).

While there is an element of caricature in Graeber's analysis, which he acknowledges, and there is a great deal of potential complementarity between anarchism and Marxism (Prichard et al. 2012), his brief discussion of some of the distinguishing features of anarchist and Marxist theory usefully highlights yet another core feature of anarchist ideology that is frequently overlooked or misunderstood by its more critical expositors. Anarchists believe that there should be an ethically consistent relationship between the means of social change and the ends. Whereas many Marxists would maintain that it is acceptable that "tactics contradict principles," because the ends justify the means, anarchists insist that means must match ends because they help shape them (Van der Walt 2011), and are in fact ends in the making. Hence the traditional anarchist opposition to organizational forms such as the political party, whether of a liberal democratic or Leninist variety.[6] Hence also the anarchist preference for "direct action," defined by Uri Gordon as "action without intermediaries, whereby an individual or a group uses their own power and resources to change reality in the desired direction, intervening directly in a situation rather than appealing to an external agent (typically the state) for its rectification" (Gordon 2009, 269).

This important feature of anarchism is reflected as well in its distinctive, and distinctively intertwined, conceptions of utopia and revolution. Unlike both Plato's utopia(s) and Marx's "scientific socialism," the anarchist utopia is not an end-state model but has the commitment to constant experimentation and flux built into it (Suissa 2009, 243). Crucially, for anarchists, the means to an end are in constant interplay with it, and the anarchist utopia, far from being a fixed point in the distance, is always a part of present activity insofar as it arises in the course of that activity, is employed to give it adding meaning and direction, and is continually revised as new activities occasion new consequences (Suissa 2009, 246). In political terms, this rejection of the means-ends dichotomy translates critically into an aversion to both blueprint utopias and millenarian conceptions of revolution, and positively into a form of revolutionary politics akin in some ways to the Zapatista philosophy of "walking, we ask questions."

Finally, and I will close with this point, anarchist utopianism manifests a distinctive temporality with significant political ramifications. Much current scholarship exploring the relationship between anarchism and utopianism rightly emphasizes the present-tense orientation of contemporary anarchist utopian aspirations.[7] From this perspective, anarchist utopianism is not a rigidly fixed rational projection of a perfected society of the future to be realized once and for all "after the revolution," but a present-day process and a potential dimension of everyday life. Anarchist utopianism is, in short, profoundly shaped by the principle of prefiguration, which inspires anarchists to try to create a new world in the shell of the old by inhabiting, to the greatest extent possible, social relations that approximate their ideals for society as a whole.

True so far as it goes, this line of analysis tends to overlook the *temporally extended* nature of the present moment toward which anarchist aspirations are oriented. As the life and work of the temporal physicist Shevek in Le Guin's *The Dispossessed* demonstrates so dramatically, time may be understood as a correlation of future, past, and present in which past and future *coexist* with the present *conjointly*. From this perspective, past and future are always found intertwined with the present, and actions undertaken in the present are necessarily entrained in a temporal trajectory that extends into the past and future (Davis 2005). It follows that anarchism is as much about the re-enactment of the possibilities of the past as it is an ideology focused on the present, or indeed the future. Moreover, historical time is no longer conceived as continuous and homogeneous, the present is no longer understood as the linear result of the past, and historical testimonies and memories are pregnant with living dreams for another and better life (Liakos 2007).

This distinctive anarchist temporality, which historically has coexisted with and simultaneously countered the temporality of Western modernity (Konishi 2013), suggests potential resonances between anarchist, indigenous, feminist, and postcolonial utopian politics. As Kahala Johnson and Kathy Ferguson have observed, state time and settler time bracket anarchism and indigeneity as untimely, albeit in different ways. Indigenous thinkers are discounted in hegemonic time as hopelessly nostalgic for a pristine but lost past, while anarchists are dismissed as optimistic for a perfect but impossible future. Yet anarchism and indigeneity share an insistence on confounding the dominant historical narrative about what has been and what is possible (Johnson and Ferguson 2019). This is an important element of postcolonial utopian literature as well. As Bill Ashcroft has documented in his helpful survey of utopianism in postcolonial literature, one of the key features of postcolonial texts, particularly those from Africa and the Caribbean, is a transformed conception of time that regards it as layered and interpenetrating, spiraling rather than linear. By conveying experience itself as a palimpsest of different orders of reality, as in the Aboriginal Dreaming, the postcolonial novel can convey a different knowledge of time, specifically knowledge of the "broken" time of the traumatized colonial subject. Like anarchist utopianism, it can also help us to reimagine revolution, not only as a revolt against the failures of the past but as a revolving or spiraling into the future (Ashcroft 2017). In sum, while scholarship on the subject is still in its infancy,[8] the resonances between anarchist, indigenous, feminist, and postcolonial utopianisms suggest both promising paths for future research and the basis for important political alliances, with potentially revolutionary implications.[9]

CONCLUSION

In this chapter I examined the relationship between the anarchist and utopian traditions, focusing especially on the political significance of their intersection. First, I introduced the theory and practice of anarchism and cleared up some common misconceptions about it. Second, I elucidated the ideology's utopian dimensions and maintained that, notwithstanding the great diversity in the anarchist tradition, those who advocate for it tend to share a vision of the good society as one that is decentralized and based on the principle of free association, in which people manage and govern themselves. I also argued that, notwithstanding the pronounced ambivalence in the anarchist tradition toward the concept of utopia itself, anarchism may be regarded as a utopia of a particular kind, namely a "grounded utopia" that is emphatically not a fantasized vision of perfection to be imposed on an imperfect world but an integral part of that world representing the hopes and dreams of those consigned to its margins. Third, I identified some of the key features of the anarchist utopian tradition that distinguish it from other more well-known and better-understood varieties of utopianism, and that make it particularly politically relevant in a time of global political, economic, and ecological crisis such as our own. I emphasized anarchism's distinctive conceptions of time and revolution and concluded the analysis on a somewhat unexpected note by observing important resonances or affinities between anarchist, indigenous, feminist, and postcolonial utopianisms. My open-ended conclusion is that these affinities suggest both promising paths for future research and the ideological basis for important political alliances with potentially revolutionary implications.

NOTES

1. The following account of anarchism draws on the much fuller discussion in my contribution to the 4th edition of *Political Ideologies: An Introduction*, ed. Vincent Geoghegan and Rick Wilford. See Laurence Davis, 2014, Anarchism, in *Political Ideologies: An Introduction*, ed. Vincent Geoghegan and Rick Wilford, 213–238, Abingdon and New York: Routledge.
2. See on the Spanish Revolution Ackelsberg (2004), Dolgoff (1974), Leval (1975), Mintz (1982), Orwell (2001), Peirats (1990), Richards (1983).
3. For fuller bibliographies see www.acratie.eu/. Last accessed 9 Apr 2021; and Margaret Killjoy, 2009, *Mythmakers and Lawbreakers: Anarchist Writers on Fiction*, Oakland and Edinburgh: AK Press.
4. More in-depth analysis of these points may be found in *The New Utopian Politics of Ursula K. Le Guin's* The Dispossessed, ed. Laurence Davis and Peter Stillman, 2005, Lanham, MD: Lexington Books.
5. As Uri Gordon has accurately observed in his book *Anarchy Alive!* (Pluto Press, 2008), the chief roots of today's anarchist networks and ideas may

be found in processes of intersection and fusion among non-explicitly anarchist radical social movements since the 1960s, including the radical, direct-action end of the ecological, anti-nuclear and anti-war movements, and of movements for women's, black, indigenous, LGBT+ and non-human animal liberation. One of the many interesting questions raised by this anarchist revival around the turn of the millennium is its relationship to the so-called "classical anarchist tradition," strongly rooted in a working-class and libertarian socialist milieu.

6. See, on anarchist opposition to the Leninist political party, Benjamin Franks, 2006, *Rebel Alliances: The Means and Ends of Contemporary British Anarchisms*, 212–218, Oakland and Edinburgh: AK Press and Dark Star.

7. See, for example, the chapters by Newman and Gordon in Davis and Kinna (2009).

8. See, for example, Taiaiake Alfred, 2005, *Wasáse: Indigenous Pathways of Action and Freedom*, Toronto: University of Toronto Press; and Jacqueline Lasky, 2011, Indigenism, Anarchism, Feminism: An Emerging Framework for Exploring Post-Imperial Futures, in *Affinities: A Journal of Radical Theory, Culture, and Action* 5 (1), ed. Glen Coulthard, Jacqueline Lasky, Adam Lewis, and Vanessa Watts. Special Issue on Anarch@Indigenism, 3–36.

9. There are numerous historical examples of such political alliances, which have tended to survive at the margins of the colonial capitalist world, and which suggest emergent alternatives to its racialised and gendered transcendent utopia of global resource extraction. For example, in Bolivia in the early twentieth century anarcho-syndicalism found resonance within Indigenous communities, offering social alternatives and models of political organising that challenged the "winner take all" approach of extractive industries. Working-class and Indigenous women, especially, found new means of empowerment through anarcho-syndicalist groups. The submerged anarcha-feminist Indigenous history in Bolivia also includes the *cholas*, or Indigenous women in the local market spaces of La Paz, who sold and bartered within complex marketplace economies operating outside the rules and structures of capitalism, and who actively worked against normative structures of gender and sexuality. This radical genealogy has, in turn, inspired contemporary anarcha-feminist groups such as Mujeres Creando, whose members collectively authored the remarkable 2011 grounded utopian document "The Feminist Political Constitution of the State: The Impossible Nation We Build as Women," an anarcha-feminist Indigenous rejoinder to then President of Bolivia Evo Morales' Plurinational Constitution, written from the perspective of "indigenous women, whores, and lesbians." See, on these subjects, Macarena Gómez-Barris, 2017, *The Extractive Zone: Social Ecologies and Decolonial Perspectives*, Ch. 5, Durham and London: Duke University Press; and María Galindo, and Mujeres Creando, 2011,

The Feminist Political Constitution of the State: The Impossible Nation We Build as Women, trans. Abigail Levine. Available in English translation at http://hemi.nyu.edu/hemi/en/emisferica-111-decolonial-gesture/galindo?format=phocapdf. Last accessed 9 Apr 2021.

REFERENCES

Ackelsberg, Martha. 2004 [1991]. *Free Women of Spain: Anarchism and the Struggle for the Emancipation of Women*. Edinburgh and Oakland: AK Press.

Alfred, Taiaiake. 2005. *Wasáse: Indigenous Pathways of Action and Freedom*. Toronto: University of Toronto Press.

Ashcroft, Bill. 2017. *Utopianism in Postcolonial Literatures*. London and New York: Routledge.

Berneri, Marie Louise. 1987. *Journey Through Utopia*. London: Freedom Press.

Clark, John. 1984. *The Anarchist Moment: Reflections on Culture, Nature and Power*. Montreal and Buffalo: Black Rose.

———. 2009. Anarchy and the Dialectic of Utopia. In *Anarchism and Utopianism*, ed. Laurence Davis and Ruth Kinna, 9–32. Manchester: Manchester University Press.

Davis, Laurence. 2005. The Dynamic and Revolutionary Utopia of Ursula K. Le Guin. In *The New Utopian Politics of Ursula K. Le Guin's* The Dispossessed, ed. Laurence Davis and Peter Stillman, 3–36. Lanham, MD: Lexington Books.

———. 2009. Introduction. In *Anarchism and Utopianism*, ed. Laurence Davis and Ruth Kinna, 1–8. Manchester: Manchester University Press.

———. 2012. History, Politics, and Utopia: Toward a Synthesis of Social Theory and Practice. In *Existential Utopia: New Perspectives on Utopian Thought*, ed. Patricia Vieira and Michael Marder, 127–140. New York and London: Continuum.

———. 2014. Anarchism. In *Political Ideologies: An Introduction*, ed. Vincent Geoghegan and Rick Wilford, 213–238. Abingdon and New York: Routledge.

Davis, Laurence, and Ruth Kinna (eds.). 2009. *Anarchism and Utopianism*. Manchester: Manchester University Press.

Davis, Laurence, and Peter Stillman (eds.). 2005. *The New Utopian Politics of Ursula K. Le Guin's* The Dispossessed. Lanham, MD: Lexington Books.

Dolgoff, Sam (ed.). 1974. *The Anarchist Collectives: Workers' Self-Management in the Spanish Revolution 1936–1939*. Montreal: Black Rose Books.

Ferns, Chris. 1999. *Narrating Utopia: Ideology, Gender, Form in Utopian Literature*. Liverpool: Liverpool University Press.

Franks, Benjamin. 2006. *Rebel Alliances: The Means and Ends of Contemporary British Anarchisms*. Oakland and Edinburgh: AK Press and Dark Star.

Galindo, María, and Mujeres Creando. 2011. *The Feminist Political Constitution of the State: The Impossible Nation We Build as Women*, trans. Abigail Levine. Available in English translation at http://hemi.nyu.edu/hemi/en/emisferica-111-decolonial-gesture/galindo?format=phocapdf. Last accessed 9 Apr 2021.

Gómez-Barris, Macarena. 2017. *The Extractive Zone: Social Ecologies and Decolonial Perspectives*. Durham and London: Duke University Press.

Gordon, Uri. 2008. *Anarchy Alive! Anti-Authoritarian Politics from Practice to Theory*. London and Ann Arbor: Pluto Press.

———. 2009. Utopia in Contemporary Anarchism. In *Anarchism and Utopianism*, ed. Laurence Davis and Ruth Kinna, 260–275. Manchester: Manchester University Press.

Graeber, David. 2004. *Fragments of an Anarchist Anthropology*. Chicago: Prickly Paradigm.

Johnson, Kahala, and Kathy E. Ferguson. 2019. Anarchism and Indigeneity. In *The Palgrave Handbook of Anarchism*, ed. Carl Levy and Matthew S. Adams, 697–714. Houndmills: Palgrave Macmillan.

Killjoy, Margaret. 2009. *Mythmakers and Lawbreakers: Anarchist Writers on Fiction*. Oakland and Edinburgh: AK Press.

Kinna, Ruth. 2016. *Kropotkin: Reviewing the Classical Anarchist Tradition*. Edinburgh: Edinburgh University Press.

Konishi, Sho. 2013. *Anarchist Modernity: Cooperatism and Japanese-Russian Intellectual Relations in Modern Japan*. Cambridge, MA and London: Harvard University Asia Center.

Kropotkin, Peter. 1910. Anarchism. In *The Encyclopaedia Brittanica*, 11th ed. Available online at http://dwardmac.pitzer.edu/anarchist_archives/kropotkin/britannia anarchy.html. Last accessed 9 Apr 2021.

———. 1913. Preface to *How We Shall Bring About the Revolution*. In *Direct Struggle Against Capital: A Peter Kropotkin Anthology*, ed. Iain McKay. Oakland and Edinburgh: AK Press.

———. 2014a. Modern Science and Anarchism [1912]. In *Direct Struggle Against Capital: A Peter Kropotkin Anthology*, ed. Iain McKay, 180. Oakland and Edinburgh: AK Press.

———. 2014b. Revolutionary Government [1882]. In *Direct Struggle Against Capital: A Peter Kropotkin Anthology*, ed. Iain McKay, 180. Oakland and Edinburgh: AK Press.

Lasky, Jacqueline. 2011. Indigenism, Anarchism, Feminism: An Emerging Framework for Exploring Post-Imperial Futures. *Affinities: A Journal of Radical Theory, Culture, and Action* 5 (1), ed. Glen Coulthard, Jacqueline Lasky, Adam Lewis, and Vanessa Watts. Special Issue on Anarch@Indigenism, 3–36.

Leval, Gaston. 1975. *Collectives in the Spanish Revolution*. London: Freedom Press.

Liakos, Antonis. 2007. Utopian and Historical Thinking: Interplays and Transferences. *Historein* 7: 20–57.

McKay, Iain (ed.). 2014. *Direct Struggle Against Capital: A Peter Kropotkin Anthology*. Oakland and Edinburgh: AK Press.

McLaughlin, Paul. 2007. *Anarchism and Authority: A Philosophical Introduction to Classical Anarchism*. Aldershot: Ashgate.

Mintz, Jerome. 1982. *The Anarchists of Casas Viejas*. Chicago and London: University of Chicago Press.

Newman, Saul. 2009. Anarchism, Utopianism, and the Politics of Emancipation. In *Anarchism and Utopianism*, ed. Laurence Davis and Ruth Kinna, 207–220. Manchester: Manchester University Press.

Orwell, George. 2001. *Orwell in Spain*. London: Penguin Books.

Peirats, José. 1990. *Anarchists in the Spanish Revolution*. London: Freedom Press.

Prichard, Alex, Ruth Kinna, Saku Pinta, and David Berry (eds.). 2012. *Libertarian Socialism: Politics in Black and Red*. Houndmills: Palgrave.

Richards, Vernon. 1983. *Lessons from the Spanish Revolution (1936–1939)*. London: Freedom Press.

Suissa, Judith. 2009. 'The Space Now Possible': Anarchist Education as Utopian Hope. In *Anarchism and Utopianism*, ed. Laurence Davis and Ruth Kinna, 241–259. Manchester: Manchester University Press.

Van der Walt, Lucien. 2011. Counterpower, Participatory Democracy, Revolutionary Defence: Debating Black Flame, Revolutionary Anarchism and Historical Marxism. *International Socialism: A Quarterly Journal of Socialist Theory*: 130. Available online at www.isj.org.uk/?id=729. Last accessed 9 Apr 2021.

Varikas, Eleni. 2002. The Utopian Surplus. *Thesis Eleven* 68: 101–105.

Ward, Colin. 2004. *Anarchism: A Very Short Introduction*. Oxford: Oxford University Press.

Woodcock, George. 1962. *Anarchism: A History of Libertarian Ideas and Movements*. New York: Meridian.

Labor

Peter Sands

Introduction

Labor and labor history are integral to utopianism, or social dreaming of an
alternative to the present. The very concept of labor—of work—is part of
the firmament of the utopian imagination, inseparable from its core: "the
arrangement of productive activity is so central to almost any conceivable
polity that utopian thinkers have tended to treat it extensively" (Grey and
Garten 2002, 9). Work, whether artisanal or industrial, domestic or commercial, infuses human activity and aesthetic figurations of the social; a genre built
on consideration of human sociality is by its very nature always already also
about human labor. Utopia and labor are forever in symbiosis. Indeed, by
some reckoning, the concept of a labor force as part of a system of production arises at roughly the same time as the idea of utopia, if we date "utopia"
from More's *Utopia* in 1516. Of course, some utopian works address the labor
question more directly than others, and some theoretical approaches in particular are most concerned with labor, but the labor question is never far from the
utopian imagination. Labor is generally inclusive of the people, the activities,
and the skills and effort involved in production. In this sense, it encompasses
both the economic formulation of production—the outputs versus the inputs
from a given firm or company—but also the workers themselves, the things
they do, and the specialized knowledge or abilities they apply. Some might
generally define labor as the human resources involved in production. It is

P. Sands (✉)
University of Wisconsin-Milwaukee, Milwaukee, WI, USA

P. Marks et al. (eds.), *The Palgrave Handbook of Utopian and Dystopian
Literatures*, https://doi.org/10.1007/978-3-030-88654-7_27

possible, as well, to even more generally remove such financialized senses from the discussion and speak of labor as being human activity, and particularly human activity toward the ends of satisfying basic needs and participating in any form of exchange economy. This chapter briefly touches on labor in significant or canonical works of utopian literature in political philosophy and fiction, addresses the contemporary relationship of utopian studies and labor, and presents short readings of exemplary fictions from the late nineteenth century to the present to illustrate some of the themes—full employment, equitable distribution, education for professions and trades, gender roles, and the role of the state—that have appeared so frequently in utopian literature's engagement with human labor.

To be sure, all forms of human social organization implicate labor in some way—the labor of living from day to day, or the freedom from labor in the presence of plenty, the relationship of the laborer to her work, the hierarchy between management or rulers and workers, the tension between the realization of individual human potential and the need for individuals to be parts of a collectivity that may necessarily run roughshod over its parts. Arendt (1998) distinguishes between labor and work—between *animal laborans* and *homo faber*—but in practical terms, the two are largely conflated; in more recent years "labor" is a shorthand for work done under the control of a managerial class. Utopian fiction in particular, as a form intended to both edify and alter the reader, has traditionally focused quite closely on labor and labor relations as foundational to both the society under critique and the imagined form of the alternative. This is true whether the text remains at the level of the quotidian, considers different essential relationships of scale and kinds of labor, or embraces revolutionary principles in response to contemporary outrages. Thomas More's *Utopia* (1516) discusses labor at length in Book II, Raphael Hythloday's discourse describing Utopian society and life. Much earlier, Plato's *Republic* (ca. 380 BC), is often credited with the conceptualization of the division of labor in society. Recent political work across the spectrum often addresses utopia and utopianism with respect to labor, as part of its consideration of the centrality of work to human life.

Utopian fiction from its heyday in the nineteenth century to the present almost always concerns itself directly with labor. Indeed, Lyman Tower Sargent's bibliography of utopian literature in English lists 137 entries from 1638 to the present with a keyword of "labor," 47 with "industry," 27 with "job," 32 with "employment," ten with "manual," 19 with "worker," and six with specific reference to "labor union." It would be difficult to find a utopian novel that does not address labor in some fashion; even tales of a land of plenty such as Cockaigne are best understood as describing an inverse relationship to the realities of daily labor. To look at another example familiar to many readers, the central preoccupation of the major utopian novel of the nineteenth century, Edward Bellamy's *Looking Backward* (1888), is labor. Violent uprising by labor in response to violent suppression by oligarchy drives Ignatius Donnelly's dystopian response to Bellamy, *Caesar's Column* (1890).

Across the Atlantic, William Morris's *News from Nowhere* (1890), imagines an artisanal culture of non-alienated labor as a direct counterpoint to Bellamy's corporate socialist unionism. In the twentieth century, touchstone dystopias such as *Brave New World* and *1984* both take labor and workers as central concerns.

Labor in all senses figures prominently in both fictional utopias and other forms of utopian expression, not least because of the emphasis on the social in utopian thought. Lyman Tower Sargent's (1994, 3) baseline definition of utopianism in "The Three Faces of Utopianism Revisited" is social dreaming. Krishan Kumar (2003, 66ff.) is perhaps a bit more insistent on a strict limitation of utopianism to forms of ideal cities or societies drawn either from a spatial tradition traceable to the Greeks or a temporal tradition traceable to millennial Christianity. One might argue that Bloch's (1986, 142 passim, 882ff.) lengthy drawing-out of the distinction between abstract and concrete utopianism, the movement from daydream to action in the real, is a theoretical explication of the need to put in the labor to work toward the anticipatory consciousness, the Not-Yet. In any case, the tendency of the utopian to think in terms of societal blueprints that specify details of human work right down to the trash schedules has been oft-noted, perhaps most famously by Fredric Jameson in several essays, the bulk of which are collected in his *Archaeologies of the Future*. Indeed, work in all its forms is central to the organization of society, which exists in part to satisfy basic human needs for food and shelter, as well as those needs beyond the basic; labor or work is thus central to the concerns of the utopian thinker, for to organize society is to organize work, or in chiastic inversion, to organize work is to organize society.

CONTEMPORARY CRITICAL THEORY AND DEBATES

The past thirty years have seen the steady publication of new critical theoretical works on utopia, including the widely known and densely theoretical work of Fredric Jameson, the sociological and Blochian work of Ruth Levitas, and regular literary critical engagement around utopias of particular historical periods, authors, or particular genres and subgenres. And, as with the literary utopia generally, most of the critical work on utopia at least implicitly engages with labor. For instance, the recently reissued *Journey Through Utopia* (2019; originally published 1950) by Mary Louise Berneri devotes more index entries to labor than any other topic. But there is also a significant body of work that more or less specifically engages with labor and utopia, dating back to the rise of modern sociology and labor-focused economic writing, as the 1880 publication by Engels of *Socialism: Utopian and Scientific* indicates by its very title. Engels, of course, repudiates the utopianism of Saint-Simon, Fourier, and Owen as being for "all humanity at once" rather than specifically "representative of the interests of [the] proletariat" (Engels 1977, 33). Mid-twentieth-century works such as Laslett's *Labor and the Left: A Study of Socialist and Radical Influences in the American Labor Movement, 1881–1924*

(1970), Grob's *Workers and Utopia: A Study of Ideological Conflict in the American Labor Movement 1865–1900* (1969), and Braverman's *Labor and Monopoly Capital: the Degradation of Work in the Twentieth Century* (1974; 25th anniversary reissue 1998) also engage utopia with varying levels of granularity. For instance, Laslett's (1970, 63) historical investigation of the failure of socialism to take strong root in American unions, for instance, really only mentions Bellamy as an aside in which he notes that the Nationalist clubs and other forms of socialism were not widely taken up by trade-unionists at the time. Grob (1969, 187) notes that "the years between the Civil War and the turn of the century were indeed crucial ones for the American labor movement," without noting that the same period is also the time of greatest utopian literary production. Earlier, he notes that labor in the middle of the nineteenth century was introducing a series of movements that taken together was "a means of escaping from reality through supporting a comprehensive program of social reform that would introduce, if not the millennium, then certainly a form of utopia" (Grob 1969, 6). In context, his reference to "escaping from reality" is less a denigration of utopianism than another way of speaking about an imagined alternative among adherents of "reform unionists," or those who preceded the more pragmatic trade-unionists, who were "little interested in plans for social reform" (Grob 1969, 9). In other words, for Grob, the utopian-minded reform unionists were in conflict with the pragmatic trade-unionists in much the same dynamic as idealists versus realists in political theory or international relations. As Fran Shor (1997, xiii–xvi) notes, these same dynamics in the United States were participating in a larger, cross-national conversation about the possibility of another, better world for labor, as embodied in the Second International of 1889 in Paris.

More to the present moment, recent works such as Peter Frase's *Four Futures* (2016), Rutger Bregman's *Utopia for Realists* (2017), and Nick Srnicek and Alex Williams's *Inventing the Future: Postcapitalism and a World without Work* (2015), directly address the application of utopian thinking to problems of labor and inequality in the present. Additional works, such as Jonathan Crary's *24/7* (2013), Jenny Odell's *How to Do Nothing* (2019), Brian O'Connor's *Idleness: A Philosophical Essay* (2018), David Graeber's *The Utopia of Rules* (2015) and *Bullshit Jobs* (2018) address themselves to the conflict between work and human potential by exploring alternatives to participation in an increasingly work-dominated late capitalism, not unlike the earlier exhortation to self-exploration and expression as a form of protest against the need to constantly labor as a worker contributing to the expansion of someone else's capital, Paul Lafargue's *The Right to Be Lazy* (1898). In sociology, Erik Olen Wright's *How to be an Anti-Capitalist in the Twenty-First Century* (2019) and his related works in the Real Utopias project (2006, 2007), explicitly address what Wright (2010, x) identifies as a "focus on specific proposals for the fundamental redesign of different arenas of social institutions rather than" "grand designs" or incremental reforms. Wright's work is notable for its gentle insistence on forms of market socialism that acknowledge possible roles for capital markets but still develop "institutional designs that would increase social empowerment over the economy" in the form of increased participation by labor in economic matters (Wright 2010, 265). It is thus possible to say that because so much of work on work, on utopia, on dystopia, on economic approaches to things, on things themselves, and even on sub-areas such as food, water, fuel, and so forth arguably also touch on labor, it would be impossible to identify a particular debate or set of debates as the most important with respect to utopia and labor. But two significant works in addition to those listed above bear inclusion in any such discussion of contemporary debates, *Utopia and Organization* (2002), and Fredric Jameson's *An American Utopia* (2016).

The first is not widely cited but does directly address questions of work and labor with explicit reference to utopia. *Utopia and Organization* (2002), was compiled by the editorial board of *The Sociological Review*, one of the older and more prestigious journals in the field, and which early on published Durkheim, Du Bois, Mannheim, H. G. Wells, and others. *Utopia and Organization* directly addresses itself to the utopian—imagination of the alternative—dimension of organizations and organizational thinking, highlighting the consequences of imaginal choices: "different forms of hierarchy, legitimacy, codification of rules, processes of selection and socialization, distribution of resources, spatial and temporal arrangements, can result in organizations as different as a monastic order or a city-state, a feminist co-operative or a multinational corporation" (Parker 2002, 2). The introductory essay by Martin Parker goes on to observe that "[n]owadays, however, it seems that there are an increasing number of people who believe that most of these alternatives should be consigned to the dustbin of history." It is a form of the acknowledgment that the so-called "realists" dominate and dismiss other forms of being in and imagining the world, one that plays out in international relations, state politics, and so on down to the local levels of human interactions. As Parker (2002, 4) goes on to say, "a pro-market managerialism which is utopian in form gets naturalized and justified at the same time that discussions of other ways of thinking about organizing are closeted as curios." His argument is essentially that the tomes and predictions of futurologists and captains of industry are treated as data-driven experts when they publish "modestly unimaginative visions of utopia" that emphasize the needs of corporate and industrial masters for particular kinds of societal organization, including labor.

The second significant contemporary engagement with the labor question directly in relation to utopia is the polemic *An American Utopia: Dual Power and the Universal Army*, by Fredric Jameson. It is most assuredly in the vein of a post-work future; that is, it is a vision of what the world might be like when automation and rejection of artificial scarcity and austerity combine to create conditions under which a new relationship between and among work, workers, and the world might be forged. An unusual book, it presents an argument for a society modeled at least in part on the industrial army of Edward Bellamy, using the conceit of compulsory national military service, but at the same time freeing people from much of the drudgery that characterizes work or labor today. Accompanying essays, especially that by Kathi Weeks, elucidate and articulate Jameson's vision of an industrial army in which all Americans would perform national service, but at fewer hours per week and day, with a guaranteed income, and all in order to free them for what Weeks (2016, 249) identifies as "ample room for a vision of free-unscripted and unaccountable-time to develop on its basis." Jameson (2016, 96) ends with the claim that "a universal militarization permits the organization of a minimum of necessary production sufficient to satisfy the multiple needs of a given population, from food and housing to education and medical treatment, thereby liberating a free time unexpected and unplanned for in Darwinian evolution and the natural world." This is the world in which the rejection of speed-up or domination of life by work advocated by Crary, Odell, and others becomes the fully automated luxury communism of Aaron Bastani's (2019) manifesto of that name.

Specific Texts

The earliest American utopia by a woman writer, Mrs. Mary Griffith's *Three Hundred Years Hence* (1836), is preoccupied with the nature and distribution of labor throughout the American society she envisions from her own vantage point in the Early Republic. Griffith spends much of her text expounding theories of education grounded in those of Fellenberg, a Swiss theorist of education and agriculture who advocated for a combination of traditional school learning with trades and crafts, as well as education for both boys and girls. In other words, a system for producing a literate but technically capable workforce of both sexes. Her utopia describes a United States in which such equity has come to pass for the most part. Other utopian texts maintain labor's centrality to the social enterprise, but certain texts give particular attention to the problems of labor and can be exemplars for readers interested in thinking labor through a utopian lens. Three important nineteenth-century texts—Bellamy's *Looking Backward* (1888), Donnelly's *Caesar's Column* (1890), and Morris's *News from Nowhere* (1890), are crucial to thinking labor through utopia and vice-versa. More recent novels by Ursula K. Le Guin, Kim Stanley Robinson, and Cory Doctorow, are other exemplars, and interested readers could easily find their way into other utopian texts: what are *The Circle* (2014) or its Canadian counterpart *The Affinities* (2016) if not meditations on the convergence of the surveillance society, social media, and labor?

The late nineteenth century saw the beginning of labor-centered movements in Europe and significant labor-related strife in the United States, beginning at least with the 1848 revolutions in Europe and labor strikes, anarchist activity, and other near-uprisings in the United States, a trend that certainly continued through the New Deal and into the postwar economic consensus in the twentieth century. In literary history, the end of the nineteenth century saw a sudden flowering of utopian fiction, particularly in the

United States. Chief among those works, indeed the second-best-selling novel of the century, was Edward Bellamy's *Looking Backward, 1988–1888*. Set largely one hundred years into the future, but beginning in 1887, Bellamy's novel depicts a country transformed into an industrial army, *Looking Backward* is the definitive utopian text of the labor movement in the late nineteenth-century United States, not because it expresses ideas that were widely taken up by labor, as noted by Laslett, but because it both expressed a growing concern for the roles of labor and capital and was widely embraced as a vision of a radical future in which the centrality of industrialized work was embraced and developed.

Bellamy's novel depicts a United States in which a peaceful revolution has erased class friction and reorganized the country into a single industrial army; the entire nation is organized completely and entirely around labor. In Bellamy, the entire nation is organized as a corporation designed to maximize utility and profit. It was a popular vision, even if it did not sway trade-unionists completely: "Within a year of its publication in 1888, *Looking Backward* sold a quarter of a million copies in the United States alone... It was the best-selling novel in nineteenth-century America after *Uncle Tom's Cabin*, and the second novel in American literature to sell a million copies. It was trans-lated... into every major language in the world" (Kumar 1987, 133). On the other hand, because of its panopticism and insistence on subordinating all aspects of society to economic productivity, Northrop Frye saw it as "a sinister blueprint of tyranny" (Frye 1965, 327). In Bellamy, the system for produc-tion and distribution of material goods is described generally as "divided" into ten departments, creating a "vast" machine, "so logical in its princi-ples and direct and simple in its workings, that it all but runs itself" (Bellamy 2003, 151). It is also apparent in the following: "The national organization of labor under one direction was the complete solution of what was, in your day and under your system, justly regarded as the insoluble labor problem. When the nation became the sole employer, all the citizens, by virtue of their citizenship, became employees, to be distributed according to the needs of industry" (Bellamy 2003, 80). Two significant responses to Bellamy bear mention: Ignatius Donnelly's *Caesar's Column* and William Morris's *News from Nowhere*. Donnelly's novel is among the first true dystopias, and depicts a labor uprising and war of all-against-all that ends in a global paroxysm of violence and societal collapse; it was written in response to Bellamy's vision of a peaceful transition to a socialist order. Morris similarly wrote *News from Nowhere* in response to Bellamy, but where Bellamy's revolution leads to a giant, corporate industrial army, and Donnelly's leads to apocalypse, Morris's leads to a pastoral utopian socialism of un-alienated craft and labor.

Contemporary utopian fiction tends strongly toward the dystopian, but there are notable examples from the last fifty years of utopian works that directly engage with labor. Probably the most famous is Ursula K. Le Guin's *The Dispossessed* (1974). There, Le Guin presents three models of society: on the planet Urras one that is a synecdoche for the United States and the West and another that is a synecdoche for the Soviet Union. On Urras's moon, Anarres, a third society, is modeled after anarchism. Of particular note is the Division of Labor office on Anarres, a mechanism by which Le Guin illustrates how an anarchist economy might operate. A full discussion of the ways the three societies mirror the geopolitics of the 1970s and present Le Guin's anarcho-communism as a possible, but not untroubled, the alternative appears in Tom Moylan's *Demand the Impossible* (1986). In Kim Stanley Robinson's *Pacific Edge* (1988), published a little more than a decade later, the near-future depicted showcases the consequences of worldwide, radical degrowth. The United States and the rest of the world have come to an agreement to slow growth and development, to shrink the size of economies and personal wealth, and to make fundamental choices about energy use, travel, calories, and other aspects of human life that necessitate a smaller and slower footprint. International travel and communication have not ceased. Space travel and exploration continue. But lifestyles, homes, public and private spaces, and the rhythms of daily life have all been slowed down as part of a conscious recognition that the world has finite resources and better choices for a sustainable present and future can be made. Moreover, rather than large industrial and corporate operations providing most of the work opportunities, corporate size and personal income have been capped, and hours of labor reduced, with—in the Orange County setting of most of the novel—an attendant increase in community-service labor to ensure the continuation of basic civic functions and infrastructure. In some ways, *Pacific Edge* depicts the transition period that in *Looking Backward* is in the past of the narrative: the time during which the consolidation of the nation or world into an alternative social schema occurs. But in Bellamy, all corporations eventually merge into one giant corporation, which becomes the nation, while in Robinson the world enacts size and business limits on corporations; both novels play out the consequences of those choices by focusing on the implications for labor. More recently, Cory Doctorow's *Walkaway* (2017) depicts a near-future North America, an anarchic society liberated by technology from the demands of labor we experience today; people essentially work when they want to, although this practice of walking away from society is in conflict with a corporation-dominated mainstream society still. Doctorow envisions wild disparities in wealth but also a gift economy made possible by automation and post-scarcity, as well as a social movement away from meaningless forms of labor. If Robinson and Doctorow can be said to be representative of the utopian mode, their vision is one of un-alienating labor and recentering of the value of work in society.

Finally, film is acknowledged as a difficult medium for utopian fiction, particularly for a lay audience which associates utopia with perfection or an ideal society, hardly a prescription for the necessary kinesis of the moving image. But film has frequently engaged with utopianism, if defined more accurately as the desire or imagination of a possible alternative, and it has often done so through narratives concerned with labor. Fritz Lang's *Metropolis* (1927), one of the earliest full-blown science fiction films, is unabashedly utopian: it depicts an alternative future society torn between the head and the hand, or between management and labor. Its famous Moloch sequence of workers death-marching into the maw of the industrial beast is one of the indelible images of early twentieth-century depictions of alienated and disposable labor. Another significant early SF film of utopia is Cameron Menzies's *Things to Come* (1936), an adaptation of H.G. Wells's epoch-spanning history of the future *The Shape of Things to Come* (1933); both of which center labor issues and culminate in a technocratic utopia. A much more recent film, Alex Rivera's *Sleep Dealer* (2009) envisions a near-future Mexico in almost total subservience to a completely fenced-off United States, which remains dependent on the labor of brown bodies but independent of the actual bodies through telepresence. Rivera's film riffs on the labor consequences of the 1994 North American Free Trade Act (NAFTA), the ever-present *maquiladoras* of northern Mexico, and the rapidly developing global flows of information and labor enabled by the internet and its constant insertion into everyday lives and labor. It is a trenchant critique of the exploitation of labor in the Global South by the Global North.

References

Arendt, Hannah. 1998. *The Human Condition*. Chicago: University of Chicago Press.

Bastani, Aaron. 2019. *Fully Automated Luxury Communism: A Manifesto*. London and New York: Verso.

Bellamy, Edward. 2003. *Looking Backward, 2000–1887*. Peterborough, ON, Canada: Broadview.

Berneri, Marie Louise. 2019. *Journey Through Utopia: A Critical Examination of Imagined Worlds in Western Literature*. Oakland, CA: PM Press.

Bloch, Ernst. 1986. *The Principle of Hope*, trans. Neville Plaice, Stephen Place, and Paul Knight. Cambridge, MA: MIT Press.

Braverman, Harry. 1998. *Labor and Monopoly Capital: The Degradation of Work in the Twentieth Century*. New York: Monthly Review Press.

Bregman, Rutger, and Elizabeth Manton. 2017. *Utopia for Realists: How We Can Build the Ideal World*. New York: Little, Brown and Company.

Crary, Jonathan. 2013. *24/7: Late Capitalism and the Ends of Sleep*. London and New York: Verso.

Doctorow, Cory. 2017. *Walkaway*. New York: Tor.

Donnelly, Ignatius. 1890. *Caesar's Column: A Story of the Twentieth Century*. Chicago: F. J. Schulte.

Eggers, Dave. 2014. *The Circle*. New York: Vintage Books.

Engels, Friedrich. 1977. *Socialism, Utopian and Scientific*. Westport, CT: Greenwood Press.

Frase, Peter. 2016. *Four Futures: Visions of the World After Capitalism*. London and New York: Verso.

Frye, Northrop. 1965. Varieties of Literary Utopia. *Daedalus* 94: 323–347.

Graeber, David. 2015. *The Utopia of Rules: On Technology, Stupidity, and the Secret Joys of Bureaucracy*. Brooklyn: Melville House.

Grey, Christopher, and Christina Garten. 2002. Organized and Disorganized Utopias: An Essay on Presumption. In *Utopia and Organization*, ed. Martin Parker, 9–23. Oxford, UK and Malden, MA: Blackwell.

Griffith, Mary. 1975. *Three Hundred Years Hence*. Boston: G. K. Hall.

Grob, Gerald N. 1969. *Workers and Utopia: A Study of Ideological Conflict in the American Labor Movement, 1865–1900*. Chicago: Quadrangle Books.

Jameson, Fredric. 2005. *Archaeologies of the Future: The Desire Called Utopia and Other Science Fictions*. New York: Verso.

———. 2016. *An American Utopia: Dual Power and the Universal Army*. New York: Verso.

Kumar, Krishan. 1987. *Utopia and Anti-Utopia in Modern Times*. Oxford, UK and New York, NY: Blackwell.

———. 2003. Aspects of the Western Utopian Tradition. *History of the Human Sciences* 16 (1): 63–77.

Lafargue, Paul, and Harriet E. Lothrop. 1898. *The Right to Be Lazy: Being a Refutation of the "Right to Work" of 1848*. New York: International Publishing.

Laslett, John H. M. 1970. *Labor and the Left; a Study of Socialist and Radical Influences in the American Labor Movement, 1881–1924*. New York: Basic Books.

Le Guin Ursula, K. 1974. *The Dispossessed: An Ambiguous Utopia*. New York: Harper & Row.

Morris, William, and Krishan Kumar. 1995. *News from Nowhere, or, an Epoch of Rest: Being Some Chapters from a Utopian Romance*. Cambridge, England and New York, NY, USA: Cambridge University Press.

Moylan, Tom. 1986. *Demand the Impossible: Science Fiction and the Utopian Imagination*. New York: Methuen.

O'Connor, Brian. 2018. *Idleness: A Philosophical Essay*. Princeton: Princeton University Press.

Odell, Jenny. 2019. *How to Do Nothing: Resisting the Attention Economy*. Brooklyn, NY: Melville House.

Parker, Martin. 2002. *Utopia and Organization*. Oxford, UK and Malden, MA: Blackwell.

Robinson, Kim Stanley. 1988. *Pacific Edge*. New York: ORB.

Sargent, Lyman Tower. 1994. The Three Faces of Utopianism Revisited. *Utopian Studies* 5 (1): 1–37.

Shor, Francis Robert. 1997. *Utopianism and Radicalism in a Reforming America, 1888–1918*. Westport, CT: Greenwood.

Srnicek, Nick, and Alex Williams. 2015. *Inventing the Future: Postcapitalism and a World Without Work*. Brooklyn, NY: Verso Books.

Weeks, Kathi. 2016. Utopian Therapy: Work, Nonwork, and the Political Imagination. In *An American Utopia*, ed. Slavoj Žižek, 243–265. New York: Verso.

Wilson, Robert Charles. 2016. *The Affinities*. New York: Tor Books.

Wright, Erik Olin. 2006. Compass Points: Towards a Socialist Alternative. *New Left Review* 41: 93–124.

———. 2007. Guidelines for Envisioning Real Utopias. *Soundings* 36: 26–39.

———. 2010. *Envisioning Real Utopias*. London and New York: Verso.

———. 2019. *How to Be an Anticapitalist in the Twenty-First Century*. London and Brooklyn, NY: Verso.

Race

Edward K. Chan

INTRODUCTION

During my research for this contribution I became immersed in simply searching for utopian texts that deal with race. The first place I searched was Lyman Tower Sargent's invaluable online annotated bibliography.[1] What I have tried to do is build a simple sub-bibliography listing utopias that deal with race in some way based on information I could find on each text and reading as many as possible.[2] The goal is certainly neither to be comprehensive nor exhaustive; rather, it's merely a starting place for those looking into the issue of race in utopias (primarily in English), and also to give myself some kind of overall picture of how race has been treated in mostly anglophone utopian literature. My hope is that others will find absences or inappropriate inclusions and continue to revise the list. Though not online and dynamic, I offer it as an ongoing project and in this article provide brief commentary on specific texts. I also discuss the scholarship on race as a subfield of utopian studies.

Given language restrictions, I will unfortunately focus mostly on anglophone literature, though I will try to indicate non-anglophone texts where possible. Furthermore, I will cover eutopia (the good place) and dystopia, both of which generally fall under the more general term "utopia."

E. K. Chan (✉)
Waseda University, Tokyo, Japan

P. Marks et al. (eds.), *The Palgrave Handbook of Utopian and Dystopian Literatures*, https://doi.org/10.1007/978-3-030-88654-7_28

LITERATURE

To begin with, we should acknowledge that, in a sense, notions of race could be said to appear in many early Western utopias that involve "whiteness" as the prevailing, if unspoken, monoracial identity. This goes back to the early texts that define the Western tradition such as Plato's *Republic* (360 BCE), about which at least one scholar presumes that the inhabitants of the ideal city are all one "race"—that is, Greek, to the extent that people from different national groupings are racialized (Klosko 1991, 9). Early modern and Enlightenment utopias are influenced by the "discoveries" of different lands and peoples by European exploration, and so there is a notion of racial difference that could apply to some of these faraway locations. Complicating matters is the fact that ideas of race that we are familiar with today were only starting to coalesce in this period.[3] While More's imaginary island of Utopia is located somewhere in the New World, "[t]he locale of More's society is almost incidental to the social structure that he describes" (Goodey 1970, 18). Thus, the racial identity of the Utopians and any racial difference from Europeans is somewhat moot, and we could imagine some kind of presumed whiteness of the inhabitants (Campbell 2017, 407). Those who dwell in Campanella's *La Città del Sole* (1623) are derived from India, but again, this seems to be unimportant, and functions as a sort of placeholder for white Europeans to imagine the practices applying to themselves. Jumping forward to the US in the nineteenth century, Bellamy's *Looking Backward* (1888) famously avoids the issue of race.[4] This is also true of B. F. Skinner's *Walden Two* (1948, see Day 1999).

As the sub-bibliography shows, issues of race and racial difference (in all their many guises) have appeared in many texts throughout utopian literature. I divide utopias that deal with race into five categories: (1) eutopias that try to address race in a positive way, (2) utopias that involve the discovery of a lost race that is racially different from white explorers in the sense that they are neither white nor some variation of European people,[5] (3) racial dystopias and utopian satires, (4) intentionally and actively *racist* utopias (usually emanating from some form of white supremacy), and (5) colonial/postcolonial utopias. For each of these categories, I briefly describe a few representative texts that deal substantively with race, especially those that have not received much commentary. However, in the sub-bibliography I have included a fuller list of utopias that address race in some fashion, in order to sketch the larger parameters of each category, which sometimes overlap.

Before moving on to describe the categories, let me note that a number of recent anthologies have also pushed the issue of race to the forefront in speculative/science fiction: *Dark Matter: A Century of Speculative Fiction from the African Diaspora* (2000), *So Long Been Dreaming: Postcolonial Science Fiction and Fantasy* (2004), *Walking the Clouds: An Anthology of Indigenous Science Fiction* (2012), *Octavia's Brood: Science Fiction Stories from Social Justice Movements* (2015), the "People of Colo(u)r Destroy" special issues (2016) on science fiction (*Lightspeed* magazine) and fantasy (*Fantasy* magazine), *Global*

Dystopias (2017) and its companion pieces in *Boston Review, New Suns: Original Speculative Fiction by People of Color* (2018), *A People's Future of the United States* (2019), *The Dystopian States of America* (2020), and *Love After the End: An Anthology of Two-Spirit & Indigiqueer Speculative Fiction* (2020). Many of the pieces in these and other volumes push the boundaries of what we consider utopia, for example, shifting the narrative emphasis to questions of identity rather than the eutopic or dystopic world itself.

Racial Eutopias

These texts deal with race in a positive way, even though marked by racist logics that are contemporaneously status quo to the author. Thanks to the work of many scholars interested in African-American speculative fiction, there has been growing commentary on a core of African-American utopias: Sutton E. Griggs's *Imperium in Imperio* (1899), Edward A. Johnson's *Light Ahead for the Negro* (1904), and W. E. B. Du Bois's *Dark Princess* (1928).[6] Also in the US tradition, there are a string of well-known critical utopias dealing substantively with race that emerged in the 1970s, particularly Samuel Delany's *Triton* (1976) and Marge Piercy's *Woman on the Edge of Time* (1976). Octavia Butler's Xenogenesis trilogy (1987–1989, reprinted as *Lilith's Brood* in 1989) is debatably *eu*topian, but is, for me, at least one that is ambiguous and features a diversity of characters, not to mention the potential allegorical figuration of racial difference in the Oankali aliens. Kim Stanley Robinson's Mars trilogy also grapples with issues of race as the characters try to construct eutopia on Mars.

Next, I will briefly discuss some texts that don't often receive commentary. In this category, various strategies are used to achieve racial eutopia, such as collapsing racial differences by putting them under a larger national or world-state identity, or even appealing to a broad "humanity" as a way to erase racial difference. In the US, one example based on national identity is Jane Ellis's "A Vision of Our Country in the Year Nineteen Hundred" (1858), a short piece by an Oberlin College student. The narrator falls asleep in a chair and imagines herself in the future of 1900 and describes the many changes that have taken place, including the US having expanded to cover both North and South America. It is a true eutopia without poverty, prejudice, or crime, and with many innovations in technology and travel. In relation to race, the narrator claims, "Our republic was the home of persons of every tribe and tongue. With the Chinese, a people so jealous and reserved, a free and friendly intercourse had been established."[7]

An example of a world-state eutopia is the English-born Australian writer Edward William Cole's predictions of the future in "Federation of the World Inevitable before the Year 2000" (1886). Although racist by today's standards—"All savage and barbarous races will be subjugated by more advanced nations, civilized, and then, like grown-up children, allowed the rights of equals" (Cole 1886, 2)—Cole at least believed in the eventual unity and equality of all races. In 1890, he published the fifty best essays submitted in a contest on his notion of a federation of the world, both for and against. The winning essay explains that "The immediate purpose of Federation is to bring some degree of order out of this venerable chaos. Its final object is the abolition of all distinctions of race, lineage, language, religion, and mode of government; the welding of mankind into one homogeneous family…" (Edmonds 1890, 11). This strategy of a world state as a way to bring together different races and cultural groups also occurs in H. G. Wells's more prominent *A Modern Utopia* (1904/5).

We see an example of racial separation—however distasteful or even impossible this might be—as the path to racial eutopia in Paschal Beverly Randolph's *After Death, or Disembodied Man* (1868), which describes a complex system of levels in the afterlife based on nineteenth-century notions of racial hierarchy and polygeny (the theory of separate and multiple human racial origins), even though he was African-American (Randolph 1886, 48, 100).

More famously, Ernest Callenbach's *Ecotopia* (1975) "solves" the racial problem by creating separate areas within Ecotopia dedicated to African-Americans (Oakland), Chinese Americans (Chinatown), and other separate enclaves for various ethnic groups (Callenbach 1975, 164).

Another strategy is interracial relationships or artificial ways of creating a mixed-race population. This can particularly be found in Dorothy Bryant's *The Kin of Ata Are Waiting for You* (1971), in which individual residents present an array of mixed phenotypical traits, and perhaps most famously in Piercy's *Woman on the Edge of Time* (1976), where racial traits are mixed into the population artificially.[8]

There is also a string of short utopian pieces that deserve commentary. For each, solving the racial problem is only one of many concerns. Henry Hartshorne's *1931: A Glance at the Twentieth Century* (1881), while overbearingly Christian-centric, evinces several socially progressive ideas including women's suffrage, racial representation in the government by African-Americans and American Indians, and proclaims that "[a]ll prejudice of race, in fact, has now very much disappeared, and is looked back upon as a preposterous error of the past."[9] In Welsh writer Margaret Haig Rhondda's essay "The World As I Want It" (1935), the call for racial equality represents the third out of four pillars: a world "[i]n which neither race nor class nor sex nor marriage nor any other irrelevant consideration forms any kind of stumbling block to full economic, political, and social status and opportunity" (Rhondda 1935, 243).

Pelican Lee's "Santa Fe in 2028" (2008) is a multidimensional eutopia showing the intersections of many progressive eutopian themes like world peace, absence of poverty, local/sustainable food economies, openness to LGBTQ+ issues, and a dynamic multicultural/multiracial coexistence symbolized in an image of Black kids riding bikes with Asian kids (Lee 2007, 2008, 126).

Lost-Race Utopias

One well-known lost-race utopia dealing with race is James Hilton's *Lost Horizon* (1933), in which a group of white people discovers the Asian Shangri-La. Here, I will describe Australian writer Henry Crocker Watson's *Adventures in New Guinea* (1876, pseud. Crocker) about a French sailor lost at sea and stranded in New Guinea, where he encounters an indigenous tribe of people who accept him as one of their own. The people are described as "negroes," though in an illustration in the book, they appear more as "Malay."[10] He marries a native woman for which they must dye his skin darker to be like their own, though he eventually becomes white again. His native wife "was not black by any means, she was fairer than any of the Orangwŏks, and they were usually of a dark olive complexion" (Crocker 1876, 158), thus making her an acceptable romantic interest for the narrator. At one point during the narrative, the narrator states about one of the native priests that "[h]e, I suspect, fully understood that white men were superior to black men" (64). Not surprisingly, racial ideas were carried by European explorers to these distant lands.

Racial Dystopias and Utopian Satires

Here, we confront the largest category: dystopias and utopian satires that critique racism and either inherently or obviously have a progressive posture toward racial justice. Some of the most prominent include Katherine Burdekin's *Swastika Night* (1937) in which Nazis dominate the world, John A. Williams's *Sons of Darkness, Sons of Light* (1969) portraying a racial conflict, Walker Percy's *Love in the Ruins* (1971) featuring both racial conflict and separatism, Nadine Gordimer's *July's People* (1981) portraying race war, pieces in Jewelle Gomez's *July's People* (1991) dealing with race and eco-disaster, Walter Mosley's *Futureland* (2001) featuring dystopias depicting racial discrimination, and Philip Roth's *The Plot Against America* (2004) treating antisemitism and Nazism. Here too, Delany and Butler have made important contributions. Delany's masterwork *Dhalgren* (1975) is a surreal postapocalyptic epic. Butler's noted dystopias are the Parable series (1993/1998) and arguably *Lilith's Brood* (with qualifications mentioned above)—in each of which race is a substantial factor. Another prominent writer, Nalo Hopkinson weaves elements of Afro-Caribbean culture into her dystopian *Brown Girl in the Ring* (1998).

Based on the sub-bibliography, certain themes stick out, though because of reasons of space I am unable to discuss them all here: racial invasion/takeover, racial conflict/civil war/revolution,[11] racial separatism, straightforward racism,[12] the past/present as dystopia, genocide,[13] eugenics,[14] anti-immigration, and antisemitism.[15]

Racial Invasion/Takeover

Racial invasion/takeover often appears in rac*ist* utopias and is often associated with Asians (particularly in Australian literature), but Vachel Lindsay's "The Golden-Faced People" (1909) is a complex nonracist example. The story appears as a typical "yellow peril" tale in which the white narrator dreams that the Chinese have taken over the US and put white people at the bottom of the racial hierarchy. In this allegory, however, Lindsay was trying to critique the American racial hierarchy, picturing whites in the place of Blacks and the Chinese in the place of whites—this estrangement meant to point out the arbitrary nature of racial oppression. The story's ending, at which point the narrator has awoken, starkly puts us back into the actual racial violence of the times with the lynching of four men: a "Chinaman" (with whom the narrator had gotten into an argument and who had struck him with a broom at the beginning of the story), a Japanese man (for whose lynching no reason is given), a Greek man (who innocently hadn't kept "out of the way," and anyway Greeks are "an awful ignorant people"), and a "n-----" (who *may* have been "too free with his lip") (Lindsay 1914, 41–42).

Racial Separatism

As discussed above, racial separatism also appears in eutopias. Indeed, racial separation has been deployed in terms of both racism (e.g., apartheid, US racial segregation, and particularly white supremacist texts)—as we see in the fourth category—and racial justice (e.g., black nationalism, Harriet Beecher Stowe's abolitionism). However, racial separatism also appears frequently in dystopia. An interesting recent example is Ben Peek's *Black Sheep* (2007), in which cities with ubiquitous surveillance have been strictly divided by race, and a Japanese immigrant in "Asian-Sydney" violates the law against multiculturalism and is punished by having his skin turned alabaster white to mark him as a criminal "Assimilate."

Past/Present as Dystopia

I'm somewhat hesitant to include texts that deal with the actual past or present as racial dystopias, since they aren't primarily imagining another society steeped in racism, but rather the racist societies we already have or have had. Yet, after reading Tananarive Due's "The Reformatory" (2017a), I have become persuaded that at least some of these texts should indeed be included as racial dystopias, such as Octavia Butler's famed *Kindred* (1979). Due's short story, which takes place at a reform school for boys in Florida in 1950, depicts a whipping of a young African-American boy in such powerful detail that it's, as she terms it in an interview (2017b), "very visceral for the reader." Overall, the brutal treatment of the young black boys brings the dystopic environment of slavery into the twentieth century.

Anti-Immigration

Immigration has historically been both racialized and used for scapegoating. There are more dystopias about immigration in texts that are intentionally and actively racist (my fourth category); however, we also see the plight of immigrants in nonracist dystopian terms as well. Not surprisingly, since the 2016 election of Trump and his fixation on border walls and the "problem" of immigration, with parallel sentiments in Europe, this issue has once again become central. Lizz Huerta's "The Wall" (2019) responds to this by imagining the realization of Trump's campaign promise and the resulting dissolution of "the empire" to the north of the wall and the world on the Mexican side of the wall. Tunnels constructed by drug lords belie the imagined impenetrability of a border wall, and "runners" and "crossers" repeatedly defy its myth of containment. As the first-person narrator states, in a way that could also count as postcolonial, "[t]he difference between the now defunct United States of America and Mexico is that the USA started as a settler state, decimating the indigenous population. Spaniards made babies. Those babies made Mexico, fucked up but brown and proud" (Huerta 2019, 51).

Racist Utopias

Racist utopias are generally connected to some form of white supremacy; however, some might argue that extreme forms of black nationalism (especially in relation to antisemitism) or even Japanese ethnonationalism could also be considered racist. Nevertheless, racism in the West most often expresses itself in terms of white racism. While we encounter texts that express a sort of status quo racism of the times in previous categories, this one focuses on texts that exhibit an intentional and actively racist viewpoint. Key texts that fit this mold but are not generally considered in relation to utopia include Thomas Dixon's *The Clansman: A Historical Romance of the Ku Klux Klan* (1905) as well as the many recent manifestos written by what I call "white power" mass murderers, such as Anders Breivik, Dylann Roof, and Brenton Tarrant: all diagnosing a contemporary dystopia for white people and urging race war to bring about white eutopia. The 1973 French dystopia *Le Camp des Saints* about an "invasion" of Europe by nonwhite immigrants has gained recent notoriety, being embraced by high-profile Trump advisors like Steve Bannon and Stephen Miller.

I've discussed some recent, white racist *eu*topias elsewhere,[16] so here I will briefly discuss a racist dystopia: Australian-born South African Leonard Flemming's "And So It Came to Pass" (1924). It begins with a white farmer hearing about a scientist predicting the end of humankind. He begins to imagine what people will write in the future: "The last historians of that period state that the beginning of the end of mankind came when the White races were completely exterminated and the Black and Yellow races ruled" (Flemming 1924, 26). The narrator is then magically swept into the future to witness this reversal firsthand: a Black king, whites working as servants to

Blacks, rewards for the Blacks who steal the most sheep, and ultimately the "Great War of the Blacks" bringing humankind to its end. The story expresses the fear of racial invasion (of which there are many examples from Australia), inversion of the racial hierarchy, and reversal of roles.

Colonial/Postcolonial Utopias[17]

As mentioned above regarding dystopias based on the past or present, there is good reason to treat at least some historical narratives as dystopias. Thus, something like Bartolomé de las Casas' *A Short Account of the Destruction of the Indies* (1552) might feasibly qualify as a dystopian narrative describing the colonization of the Americas.[18] Gloria Anzaldúa's *Borderlands/*La Frontera (1987) exemplifies the intersection of several identities including queer and Chicana combined with a powerful eutopian desire from within the postcolonial border between Mexico and the US. It brings together cultural history (chapter 1), cultural anthropology (chapter 2), a reclamation and adaptation of mythology (chapters 2 and 3), a self-reflexive meditation on the act of writing and the "life" of narrative (chapter 6), a cultural-political manifesto (chapter 7), poetry (the second half of the book, but also scattered throughout), and finally a theory of utopia (the entire book, but especially chapters 4 and 7). While being all these things, the book's strongest identity is as a utopian vision, especially through the figure of the new *mestiza* who embodies an intersectional eutopian identity.

SCHOLARSHIP

Many scholars, including myself, have noted the historical absence of research on the relation between race and utopia; however, there has been a steady, albeit rather small, stream of studies over the years from the early 1960s until the 2000s,[19] after which the subfield started expanding significantly. Much of this work I've referred to throughout the discussion of the literature above. Some recent books treating race and utopia include Alex Zamalin's *Black Utopia: The History of an Idea from Black Nationalism to Astrofuturism* (2019), Verena Adamik's *In Search of the Utopian States of America: Intentional Communities in Novels of the Long Nineteenth Century* (2020), and Duncan Bell's *Dreamworlds of Race: Empire and the Utopian Destiny of Anglo-America* (2020). Zamalin traces the complex thread of "Black utopia" from Martin Delany through to Octavia Butler, while insisting that each emanation responds to its historical moment. Adamik delves into the fundamental link between American national identity and utopia in a range of texts from the late eighteenth-century to the early twentieth, including *Imperium in Imperio* and *The Quest of the Silver Fleece*, noting that these texts are not descriptive utopias but rather representations of utopian practice. Bell explores what he calls the "racial utopianism" built into the idea of an Anglo-American union at the turn of the twentieth century that would have consolidated the global dominance of Anglo-Saxonism.

Part of the motor driving the recent interest in race and utopia is the growing interest in the relationship between race and science fiction and more particularly Afrofuturism, the broad aesthetic movement of artistic/intellectual works in many media from Africa and the African diaspora.[20] In embracing the technofuture, Afrofuturism often promotes a eutopian mindset (a good example, though it's not literature per se, would be the lyrics of Sun Ra's 1973 song "Space Is the Place" or his opening monologue in the 1974 film *Space Is the Place*). Afrofuturism has also inspired other racialized minorities, such as in what Catherine Ramírez calls "Chicanafuturism" (which later inspired a broader "Latinofuturism"),[21] "Indigenous Futurism,"[22] and even "Asian Futurism," which because of the shadow of techno-Orientalism must strive to incorporate agency for Asian cultural producers.[23] These movements expand utopia into music, film/video, comics, and visual art. The energy inaugurated by the recent interest in Afrofuturism and these other movements seems to promise much work to be done by creators and scholars exploring the intersection between race and utopia.

NOTES

1. https://openpublishing.psu.edu/utopia/. To find utopias that deal with race, I used several search terms: "race," "racial," "racism," "racist," "multicultural," "pluralism," "yellow peril," "Africa," "Asia," "survivalist," "Nazi," "KKK"/"Ku Klux Klan," "genocide," "colonial"/"postcolonial," "Jew," "Native America," "indigenous," and "anti-Semitic." This was supplemented with other texts I am aware of but are not listed in the database.

2. The sub-bibliography is available at https://drive.google.com/drive/folders/1QaiRCMTjYm9v5E__8MwZp4fsn44WKJmq?usp=sharing.
Here, I only include bibliographic information for literary and scholarly texts cited directly; for literary texts referred to in a general way, please see the sub-bibliography.

3. Though I'm no expert in this period, the following seem useful starting places: Kim F. Hall's *Things of Darkness: Economies of Race and Gender in Early Modern England* (1995), Ania Loomba and Jonathan Burton's *Race in Early Modern England: A Documentary Companion* (2007), the special issue of *Shakespeare Quarterly*, ed. Peter Erickson and Hall (2016), and Urvashi Chakravarty's "The Renaissance of Race and the Future of Early Modern Race Studies," *English Literary Renaissance* 50, no. 1 (2020). Useful general histories of race include Michael Banton's *Racial Theories* (1987/1998), Nell Irvin Painter's *The History of White People* (2010), George M. Fredrickson's *Racism: A Short History* (2015), and Ibram X. Kendi's *Stamped from the Beginning: The Definitive History of Racist Ideas in America* (2016).

4. See Strauss (1988). There is some minimal mention of racism in Bellamy's *Equality* (1897).

5. An example of the latter is Elton R. Smilie's *The Manatitlans* (1877, pseud. Smile), which includes a search for "a white race of great beauty" in South America (3).

6. Other texts include Du Bois's *Quest of the Silver Fleece* (1911) and "The Comet" considered alongside the poem "A Hymn to the Peoples" (1920), the latter two of which only gesture toward racial eutopia at the end, as well as Frances Harper's *Iola Leroy* (1892), which, while clearly expressing utopian hope, does not have a detailed description of racial eutopia. Schuyler's important books *Black No More* (1931) and *Black Empire* (1937–1938) could be read as eutopian, if not for their heavily satiric and anti-utopian bent. For a comprehensive overview of African-American utopias, see Sargent's "African Americans and Utopia" (2020)—here, I avoid texts discussed there.

7. Ellis, Kindle loc. 1385.

8. See Edward K. Chan, *The Racial Horizon of Utopia*, Ch. 3.

9. Hartshorne, Kindle loc. 46–51.

10. Crocker, the illustration appears between pages 50 and 51.

11. See Tal, Bould (2007, 2010), Tabone, and Sargent, "African Americans and Utopia."

12. One interesting text in this category is Fritz Leiber's *A Specter Is Haunting Texas* (1968/1969), in which eight-foot white Texans have taken over most of what used to be the US and subjugate the Mexican population.

13. Sargent describes two works by Carl Lee Shears (pseud. Saggittarus) that imagine schemes to kill all or as many African Americans as possible: *Count-Down to Black Genocide* (1973) and *The Last Days of the Sunshine People* (1978, play); see both the bibliography and his article.

14. An example is Milo Hastings' *City of Endless Night* (1919), set in a pre-Nazi eugenic Germany confined in a multi-leveled Berlin.

15. The example I would have used here is David Samuel Levinson's *Tell Me How This Ends Well* (2017), which interweaves a kind of ambient antisemitism throughout the narrative, as American society falls apart.

16. See Edward K. Chan, "The White Power Utopia."

17. See Booker, Pordzik, and Smith. I have decided not to include texts that describe native dictatorships in the wake of colonization.

18. It could also be a racial dystopia about genocide.

19. See Chan and Ventura, "Introduction: Articulating Race and Utopia," for references to some of this work.

20. Much has been written, but here are some starting points: the 2007 special issue in *Science Fiction Studies* (vol. 34, no. 2), edited by Mark Bould and Rone Shavers; Ytasha L. Womack's *Afrofuturism: The World of Black Sci-Fi and Fantasy Culture* (2013); *Afrofuturism 2.0* (2016), edited by Reynaldo Anderson and Charles E. Jones; and the

2020 special issue in *Extrapolation* (vol. 61, nos. 1–2), edited by Isiah Lavender and Lisa Yaszek.
21. See Ramírez (2004) and Merla-Watson (2019).
22. See Lempert (2014) and Hunt (2018).
23. See Dawn Chan (2016).

References

Adamik, Verena. 2020. *In Search of the Utopian States of America: Intentional Communities in Novels of the Long Nineteenth Century.* Cham: Palgrave Macmillan.

Bell, Duncan. 2020. *Dreamworlds of Race: Empire and the Utopian Destiny of Anglo-America.* Princeton: Princeton University Press.

Booker, M. Keith. 1995. African Literature and the World System: Dystopian Fiction, Collective Experience, and the Postcolonial Condition. *Research in African Literatures* 26 (4): 58–75.

Bould, Mark. 2007. Come Alive by Saying No: An Introduction to Black Power SF. *Science Fiction Studies* 34 (2): 220–240.

———. 2010. Revolutionary African-American Sf Before Black Sf. *Extrapolation* 51 (1): 53–81.

Callenbach, Ernest. 1975. *Ecotopia.* Berkeley: Banyan Tree.

Campbell, Jane MacRae. 2017. Dress, Ideology, and Control: The Regulation of Clothing in Early Modern English Utopian Texts, 1516–1656. *Utopian Studies* 28 (3): 398–427.

Chan, Dawn. 2016. Asia-Futurism. *Artforum* 54 (10). https://www.artforum.com/print/201606/asia-futurism-60088.

Chan, Edward K. 2016. *The Racial Horizon of Utopia: Unthinking the Future of Race in Late Twentieth-Century American Utopian Novels.* Bern: Peter Lang.

———. 2019. The White Power Utopia and the Reproduction of Victimized Whiteness. In *Race and Utopian Desire in American Literature and Society*, ed. Patricia Ventura and Edward K. Chan, 139–159. Cham: Palgrave Macmillan.

Chan, Edward K., and Patricia Ventura. 2019. Introduction: Articulating Race and Utopia. *Utopian Studies* 30 (1): 1–7.

Cole, Edward William. 1886. Federation of the World Inevitable Before the Year 2000. https://www.dropbox.com/s/8vw682ox9m1xumd/Federation%20of%20the%20World%20Inevitable%20Before%20The%20Year%202000%20-%20EWC.pdf?dl=01886.

Crocker, Rev Henry. 1876. *Adventures in New Guinea: The Narrative of Louis Trégance, a French Sailor, Nine Years in Captivity Among the Orangwòks, a Tribe in the Interior of New Guinea*, ed. and with an intro. The Rev. Henry Crocker. London: Sampson Low, Marston, Searle, & Rivington. https://books.google.co.jp/books?id=uvcbo3Z2fEMC&hl=ja&source=gbs_book_other_versions&pli=1.

Day, Susan X. 1999. *Walden Two* at 50. *Michigan Quarterly Review* 38 (2): 247–259.

Due, Tananarive. 2017a. The Reformatory. In *Global Dystopias*, ed. Junot Díaz. Kindle, loc. 1465–1760. Cambridge: MIT Press.

———. 2017b. History Is a Dystopia. Interview by Avni Sejpal. *Boston Review*, November 16. http://bostonreview.net/PODCAST-LITERATURE-CULTURE-ARTS-SOCIETY/TANANARIVE-DUE-HISTORY-DYSTOPIA.

Edmonds, Thomas. 1890. Essay 1: In Favor. In *Cyclopedia on the Federation of the Whole World: Fifty Prize Essays by Fifty Australasian Writers*, First Series, ed. Edward William Cole. Melbourne: E. W. Cole Book Arcade. https://www.ewcole.com/publication/federation-of-the-world/.

Ellis, Jane. 1858. A Vision of Our Country in the Year Nineteen Hundred. In *The Western Literary Magazine, and Journal of Education, Science, Arts, and Morals*, ed. George Brewster, 81–84. Columbus, OH: George Brewster and Kindle.

Flemming, Leonard. 1924. And so It Came to Pass. In *A Crop of Chaff*, 26–31. Pietermaritzburg, South Africa: Natal Witness.

Goodey, Brian R. 1970. Mapping 'Utopia': A Comment on the Geography of Sir Thomas More. *Geographical Review* 60 (1): 15–30.

Hartshorne, Henry. 1881. *1931: A Glance at the Twentieth Century*. Philadelphia: E. Claxton and Kindle.

Huerta, Lizz. 2019. The Wall. In *A People's Future of the United States: Speculative Fiction from 25 Extraordinary Writers*, ed. Victor LaValle and John Joseph Adams, 49–61. New York: One World.

Hunt, Dallas. 2018. 'In Search of Our Better Selves': Totem Transfer Narratives and Indigenous Futurities. *American Indian Culture and Research Journal* 42 (1): 71–90.

Klosko, George. 1991. 'Racism' in Plato's *Republic*. *History of Political Thought* 12 (1): 1–13.

Lee, Pelican. 2007–2008. Santa Fe in 2028. *Sinister Wisdom* 72: 125–128.

Lempert, William. 2014. Decolonizing Encounters of the Third Kind: Alternative Futuring in Native Science Fiction Film. *Visual Anthropology Review* 20 (2): 164–176.

Lindsay, Vachel. 1914 [1909]. The Golden-Faced People. *The Crisis* 9 (1): 36–42. https://www.marxists.org/history/usa/workers/civil-rights/crisis/1100-crisis-v09n01-w049.pdf.

Merla-Watson, Cathryn. 2019. Latinofuturism. In *Oxford Research Encyclopedia*, published April 26. https://oxfordre.com/literature/view/10.1093/acrefore/9780190201098.001.0001/acrefore-9780190201098-e-648.

Pordzik, Ralph. 2001. *The Quest for Postcolonial Utopia: A Comparative Introduction to the Utopian Novel in the New English Literatures*. New York: Peter Lang.

Ramírez, Catherine S. 2004. Deus ex Machina: Tradition, Technology, and the Chicanafuturist Art of Marion C. Martinez. *Aztlan* 29 (2): 55–92.

Randolph, Paschal Beverly. 1886 [1868]. *After Death, or Disembodied Man*. Toledo: Randolph Publishing.

Rhondda, Margaret Haig. 1935. The World as I Want It. *The Forum and Century* 93 (4): 243.

Sargent, Lyman Tower. 2020a. African Americans and Utopia: Visions of a Better Life. *Utopian Studies* 31 (1): 25–96.

———. 2020b. *Utopian Literature in English: An Annotated Bibliography from 1516 to the Present*. University Park, PA: Pennsylvania State University. https://openpublishing.psu.edu/utopia/.

Smile, R. Elton. 1877. *The Manatitlans, or a Record of Scientific Exploration in the Andean La Plata S. A.* Buenos Ayres: Calla Derécho, Imprenta De Razon. https://www.google.co.jp/books/edition/The_Manatitlans_Or_A_Record_of_Recent_Sc/QGnRAAAAMAAJ?hl=en&gbpv=0.

Smith, Eric D. 2012. *Globalization, Utopia, and Postcolonial Science Fiction: New Maps of Hope*. London: Palgrave Macmillan.

Strauss, Sylvia. 1988. Gender, Class, and Race in Utopia. In *Looking Backward, 1988–1888: Essays on Edward Bellamy*, ed. Daphne Patai, 68–90. Amherst: University of Massachusetts Press.

Tabone, Mark. 2019. Black Power Utopia: African-American Utopianism and Revolutionary Prophesy in Black Power-Era Science Fiction. In *Race and Utopian Desire in American Literature and Society*, ed. Patricia Ventura and Edward K. Chan, 59–78. Cham: Palgrave Macmillan.

Tal, Kali. 2002. That Just Kills Me: Black Militant Near-Future Fiction. *Social Text* 20 (2): 65–91.

Zamalin, Alex. 2019. *Black Utopia: The History of an Idea from Black Nationalism to Afrofuturism*. New York: Columbia University Press.

Biopolitics

Christian P. Haines

INTRODUCTION

At first glance, Jeff VanderMeer's *Southern Reach* trilogy has little to do with
the genre of utopian literature. Far from imagining the good place, it narrates
the cycles of an alien ecosystem—"Area X"—threatening to consume the
Earth. It is a zone in which identity gives way to "transformations": "Transformations were taking place here, and as much as I had felt part of a 'natural'
landscape on my trek to the lighthouse, I could not deny that these habi-
tats were transitional in a deeply *unnatural* way" (VanderMeer 2014, 160).
These sentences from the trilogy's first book, *Annihilation*, have more in
common with H. P. Lovecraft's "The Colour Out of Space" than Thomas
More's *Utopia*. Like Lovecraft, VanderMeer blurs the line between the natural
and the unnatural through descriptions of uncanny figures and landscapes,
and also like Lovecraft, Vandermeer seems more interested in showing how
people, society, and the environment unravel than in charting their progress. If
VanderMeer's trilogy belongs to the genre known as weird fiction, it is because
it exhibits, to quote Mark Fisher, "a fascination for the outside, for that which
lies beyond standard perception, cognition and experience" (Fisher 2016, 8).
It gravitates toward "that *which does not belong*"; it "brings to the familiar
something which ordinarily lies beyond it, and which cannot be reconciled
with the 'homely' (even as its negation)" (Fisher 2016, 10–11). In contrast to
the sense of coming home (*Heimat*) that Ernst Bloch associates with utopia,

C. P. Haines (✉)
Penn State University, University Park, PA, USA

P. Marks et al. (eds.), *The Palgrave Handbook of Utopian and Dystopian
Literatures*, https://doi.org/10.1007/978-3-030-88654-7_29

weird fiction emphasizes a sense of "wrongness," the feeling of being absorbed by an unearthly earth.

What differentiates VanderMeer's fiction from Lovecraft's, however, is its utopianism. VanderMeer offers a reflexive twist on the weird, stepping back from the dialectic between attraction and repulsion in Lovecraft (a dialectic all too often synonymous with racism and xenophobia) to ask *why* these strange encounters throw human beings into disarray. Along with other practitioners of the New Weird, VanderMeer dwells in the transformative potential of encounters with the alien.[1] The protagonist of *Annihilation* (2014) doesn't flee from Area X. Instead, she surrenders to the infection she has contracted from the alien landscape: "It is just beginning, and the thought of continually doing harm to myself to remain human seems somehow pathetic" (Vander-Meer 2014, 194). The disintegration of personhood becomes positive in the sense of being transformative. The human parameters of the self give way to something larger and messier, something whose shape cannot be predicted in advance. VanderMeer's trilogy embodies a biopolitical utopianism: a practice of imagining radical otherness less as another place than as the warping of a body or the mutation of a species.

This chapter argues that biopolitical utopianism is a conceptual and aesthetic register more than a genre. It travels across the boundaries between genres, renewing the utopian imagination by shifting its focus from space to flesh. The literary works participating in this kind of utopian practice defy the opposition between utopia and dystopia, upending the commonplace tale according to which the utopian fictions of the sixteenth through nineteenth centuries give way to the dystopian ones of the twentieth and twenty-first. These texts are less interested in differentiating good from bad than in using bodies as figures for radical social transformation. In short, utopia becomes less a matter of the good place than of life, transformed utterly.

FROM SPACE AND PLACE TO BODY AND PRACTICE

The dominant critical narrative regarding utopian literature has been of rise and decline: born in the sixteenth century with Thomas More's *Utopia*, it continued through the nineteenth century only to decline in the twentieth century, with visions of a brighter future giving way to the dystopian fables of Huxley, Orwell, and Zamyatin. Although there is truth to this tale—dystopian fiction does begin to proliferate in the twentieth century and continues to do so into the present—it conceals a more complex drama in which utopian visions flicker to life even in the most dismal situations. The field of utopian studies has challenged this reductive story in numerous ways. Raymond Williams points out that works like Ursula K. Le Guin's *The Dispossessed* (1974) reinvent utopianism as a "restless, open, risk-taking experiment," overcoming "the corrosive cynicism of the dystopian mode" (2006, 211–212). In contrast, Tom Moylan (2000) argues that dystopian fictions are actually the heirs to utopian fiction, with their critiques of worlds gone awry meant to stoke the hope that change is still possible. For his part, Fredric Jameson (2005) has suggested that utopian fiction has seen another renaissance, this time in a federalist form. Works such as Kim Stanley Robinson's *Mars* trilogy (1992–1996) imagine a plurality of radically different social worlds instead of a singular one, and in doing so, suggest that utopia names less a state of ultimate fulfillment than a laboratory in which to test out new social forms. These perspectives share the conviction that the history of utopia frustrates linear narrative, that its story has multiple beginnings, rebirths, and endings.

Much of the energy in utopian studies has gone into analyzing utopian fiction's renewal in spatial terms. At the same time, another tradition of utopianism, going back at least to Ernst Bloch's three-volume *The Principle of Hope* (1986) has charted the vicissitudes of the utopian imagination in terms of embodied subjects. This tradition has looked to social, cultural, and political practices that constitute concrete anticipations of other worlds. In doing so, it frequently frames utopia in gestural terms, showing how the coming of another social world takes shape through the arrangements of bodies. In other words, this strand of utopian criticism shifts the focus from space and place to body and practice. This tradition includes work on intentional communities, such as Lucy Sargisson's *Utopian Bodies and the Politics of Transgression*. Sargisson eschews the reduction of intentional communities to "attempts to create the concrete utopia: Heaven on Earth," instead redefining utopia as a set of practices that are "internally subversive," "flexible and resistant to permanence and order," and "intentionally and deliberately utopian" (2000, 1–2). Utopia names an open-ended process of debate and experimentation. Sargisson focuses on green, or ecologically oriented, communities in Britain. Although she does not deny the significance of physical space in her analyses, she also does not privilege space over other expressions of utopia. This methodological choice stems from the fact that for many of the communities Sargisson studies, it is the "process of living" that constitutes the object of social and political change (63). Summarizing her interviews of participants in these communities, Sargisson writes: "In these communities, pragmatism combines with idealism. They share a desire for a sustainable lifestyle.... Sustainable human relations are also aspired to, and here co-operation, sharing and respect are keywords in the interview transcripts" (Sargisson 2000, 50). The inhabitants of these communities turn utopianism into a reflexive practice through which bodies transgress the status quo and invent new values for living.

It is tempting to read this turn from space and place to body and practice as a turn from the imaginary to the real, but doing so would ignore the complicated relationship between reality and imagination on which utopia thrives. Even in the context of intentional communities, what makes utopia utopian is the way it stretches the limits of reality, blurring the lines between the possible and the impossible, projecting figures of life that break with the order of things. From this perspective, there is an ontological equality between utopian literature and utopian social practice, meaning that the one is no less real than the other. As Ruth Levitas argues, it might be better to understand utopia as a method instead of an object, what she describes as "the Imaginary Reconstitution of Society" driven by "the desire for being otherwise, individually and collectively, subjectively and objectively" (Levitas 2013, xi). Levitas categorizes the appearance of utopia into three categories—archaeological, architectural, and ontological—each of which is defined by the questions on which they focus. For this chapter, it is the ontological category that matters most, because it echoes biopolitics in

> address[ing] the question of what kind of *people* particular societies develop and encourage. What is understood as human flourishing, what capabilities are valued, encouraged and genuinely enabled, or blocked and suppressed, by specific or potential social arrangements: we are concerned here with the historical and social determination of human nature. (Levitas 2013, 153)

When biopolitics asks after utopia, it does so in the same manner as Levitas's ontological mode, though with the crucial caveat that for biopolitics, utopia will always come down to bodies and populations and to their potential to be otherwise.

Utopia and Biopolitics

In a 1966 radio address, "The Utopian Body,"[2] Michel Foucault speaks of utopia as the "contrary of the body." If utopia is a longed-for place over the horizon, the body, in contrast, is "irreparably here, never elsewhere" (Foucault 2010, 9). Foucault's initial claim is that imagining utopia means "erasing the body" (13). The implication seems to be that utopia is a kind of transcendence; it neglects the messy realities of bodily life in favor of an airy paradise. However, Foucault reverses course in the same address, arguing that utopia and the body are actually intertwined: "I was very wrong earlier to say that utopias were turned against the body and meant to efface it: they are born of the body itself and are perhaps subsequently turned against it" (14). This reversal depends on Foucault's reevaluation of the body's material presence. In analyses of bodily practices, including tattooing, dance, and religious rituals, Foucault complicates the equation between embodiment and simple self-presence. Instead, he contends that these practices demonstrate that the body "is *always* elsewhere, it is linked to all the elsewheres of the world, and to tell the truth it is elsewhere than in the world" (17). It is "the degree zero of the world, there where paths and spaces cross the body is nowhere: it is, at the heart of the world, this little utopian core through which I dream, I speak, I put forward, I imagine, I perceive things in their place and I also deny them through the indefinite power of the utopias that I imagine" (18).

Like utopia, the body's presence and potentiality depend on a constitutive dissonance—they *are* only insofar as they *are not*. Utopia and the body realize themselves by escaping from determinate positions in the world. They are twin nowheres, blurring immanence and transcendence in what Pierre Macherey has called "an immanence of the beyond" (Macherey 2011, 10, translation mine). In sum, Foucault suggests that the body is both the source of utopia—its point of origin, its material foundation—and its object—its point of application. To imagine utopia is therefore to draw on and draw out a body's capacity for transformation.

Foucault's "Utopian Body" puts his theory of biopolitics in a different perspective. At first glance, Foucault's conceptualization of "biopower" as constitutive of life seems to imply little room for radical change, let alone utopianism. If modern power "fosters" life, if it fabricates bodies and populations, as he writes in the first volume of the *History of Sexuality*, then how can life encounter the radical otherness of utopia? (1990a, 138). Foucault's project of describing power as a constructive force would appear at odds with the utopian imagination's particular combination of negativity (the critique of the status quo) and positivity (the imagining of new social worlds). Foucault, however, preserves a gap between power and life: "It is not that life has been totally integrated into techniques that govern and administer it; it constantly escapes them" (1990a, 143). Although there is no strict opposition between power and life, life can nonetheless transform itself into something that breaks with arrangements of power. It is this potentiality for becoming other that allows Foucault to write lines that echo the speculations of science fiction:

> [W]e need to consider the possibility that one day, perhaps, in a different economy of bodies and pleasures, people will no longer quite understand how the ruses of sexuality, and the power that sustains its organization, were able to subject us to that austere monarchy of sex. (Foucault 1990a, 159)

Given that for Foucault, sexuality is nearly synonymous with the modern exercise of power, and power suffuses the most minute details of everyday life, "a different economy of bodies and pleasures" can only be understood as a completely new social system. Foucault does not just insist on life's ability to escape specific power relations, he also insists on the utopian possibility of creating new worlds.

This desire for utopia is not an anomaly in Foucault's work. It's evident when he describes the gay liberation movement as "hav[ing] to invent from A to Z, a relationship that is still formless, which is friendship: that is to say, the sum of everything through which they can give pleasure" (Foucault 1989, 309). Or when he sums up ancient Cynicism by saying that the cynic "transposes anew the idea of an *other* life [a life of voluntary poverty, a life of rejecting social norms] into the theme of a life whose otherness must lead to the change of the world. An *other* life for an *other* world" (Foucault 2012, 287). Foucault even describes his motivation for analyzing sexuality and power in utopian terms:

> It was curiosity – the only kind of curiosity, in any case, that is worth acting upon with a degree of obstinacy: not the curiosity that seeks to assimilate what is proper for one to know, but that which enables one to get free from oneself. (Foucault 1990b, 8)

What emerges in these quotations is a thinker for whom utopia names the passage from one form of life to another. More precisely, Foucault rearticulates utopia as a practice of self-transformation that brings about the coming of another world: "An *other* life for an *other* world" (Foucault 2012, 287).

This utopian vector in biopolitics suggests that biopolitics should not be reduced to an analysis of power *over* life, because there is also a power *of* life. The politics of life itself includes a creative force of expression through which another social world might emerge. A number of philosophers and cultural critics have elaborated on the utopian possibilities of biopolitics. Antonio Negri, for instance, elaborates an affirmative biopolitics in which state and capitalist forms of governance are always subject to the creative powers of the multitude. In his work with Michael Hardt, he draws a distinction between biopower (power over life) and biopolitics (power of life), arguing that the latter always exceeds the former and that biopower can only ever capture a portion of the vital force of society. This surplus of life over power takes on a utopian quality when Hardt and Negri describe it as the promise of a future that breaks free from the past:

> We can recognize, however, that there is the unbridgeable gap that separates the desire for democracy, the production of the common, and the rebellious behaviors that express them from the global system of sovereignty.... We can already recognize that today time is split between a present that is already dead and future that is already living – and the yawning abyss between them is becoming enormous. In time, an event will thrust us like an arrow into that living future. (Hardt and Negri 2004, 358)

The utopian dimension of this longing for a living future becomes explicit in Negri's *Insurgencies: Constituent Power and the Modern State*, where he defines utopianism as an ongoing practice in which social potential overcomes present-day arrangements of power: "It ["democracy"] is a disutopia – that is, the sense of an overflowing constitutive activity, as intense as utopia but without its illusion, and fully material" (Negri 1999, 14). The "dis" in "disutopia" does not imply a rejection of utopia. Instead, it signifies the becoming immanent of utopia, the transformation of utopia into a matter of life.

Nor has this utopian biopolitics confined itself to political theory. Cultural and literary critics such as José Esteban Muñoz, Elizabeth Freeman, Jasbir Puar, Dana Luciano, and Alexander Weheliye have outlined different ways in which life overcomes social inertia. Muñoz's *Cruising Utopia: The Then and There of Queer Futurity* is the most explicit, redefining queerness as a "structuring and educated mode of desiring that allows us to see and feel beyond the quagmire of the present.... Queerness is essentially about the rejection of a here and now and an insistence on potentiality or concrete possibility for another world" (Muñoz 2009, 1). Muñoz finds this queer potentiality in dance halls, performance art, and literature. In each case, utopia is less a fixed place at which to arrive than a feeling—a vibe, a hum, a shudder—through which the future flirts with the present. This utopian performativity is, to use Muñoz's terminology, "not quite here but always in process, always becoming, emerging in difference" (Muñoz 2009, 112). In contrast, Weheliye's intervention into biopolitical theory might almost be described as dystopian. His account of modern racism rewrites the story of biopower as the barring of blackness from humanity. From this perspective, biopolitics is an effect of racism, and if an affirmative biopolitics is possible, it is only through a reckoning with the historical fact of racialized bondage. However, Weheliye's project of "disarticulat[ing] the human from Man," of reinventing what it means to be human in non-racist terms, is utopian in its own right (Weheliye 2014, 32). Weheliye finds potential for radical change in historical suffering. The impossibility of assimilating the pain of bondage into the liberal humanist terms of inclusion or tolerance becomes the demand for an entirely new foundation of social life:

> [S]uffering appears as utopian erudition.... Where dominant discourse seeks to develop upgrades of the current notions of humanity as Man, improvements are not the aim or product of the imaginaries borne of racializing assemblages and political violence; instead they summon forms of human emancipation that can be imagined but not (yet) described. (Weheliye 2014, 126–127)

Weheliye and Muñoz thus gesture toward the horizon of biopolitics: not just the transformation of a body but the reinvention of what it means to be human. This horizon is utopian, because it implies the conversion of impossibility into possibility—an immanent beyond—and because its temporality is that of the not-yet—futurity not as the extension of the present but as the arrival of something unprecedented.

LIFE, LITERATURE, UTOPIA

In literature, biopolitics and utopia intersect not as a genre but as a way of writing: a representational practice through which life becomes not just political but fluid and strange. As Davide Tarizzo argues (following in Foucault's footsteps), the modern reinvention of life as biology makes the body a temporary lodging for life:

> Each form-of-life is reduced to the precarious and transitory expression of a force-of-life, of a blind and hungry will to exist, of a 'silent and invisible violence which in the night devours' all living beings after having brought them into existence. (Tarizzo 2017, 4)

Biopolitics takes this Darwinian historicization of life for granted, treating life not as fixed forms but as the raw material of governance. Literature has had to reckon with both the fluidity of modern life and its ever-present exposure to power. Although literature and biopolitics should not be conflated, there nevertheless exists a writing practice that cuts across genres and social relations, a practice dedicated not only to dissecting modern forms of life (critique) but also to imagining the possibility of living differently (utopianism).

VandeerMeer's *Annihilation* exemplifies this biopolitical utopianism. As discussed previously, the novel follows a group of scientists into an alien ecosystem—Area X—that has made itself home on the Florida coast. The expedition falls apart as its members become fascinated by the strange life forms in Area X. This fascination leads the protagonist, known simply as the biologist, to abandon her humanity in favor of a process of change that has already taken root in her body. The novel foreshadows this mutation of human form when the expedition encounters "the tower," a tunnel into the earth covered in words composed of "fruiting bodies" (25). The biologist cannot pin down the meaning of this written form of life. (She discovers its source, a creature described as "the Crawler," but that only makes things more mysterious, more ominous.) She can only compare the writing to the behavior and structure of fungi, an analogy whose truth seems borne out when she breathes in its spores, becoming infected with the strange life of Area X. *Annihilation* is the story of an alien message that communicates itself through bodily transformation. As the biologist describes it,

> It creates out of our ecosystem a new world, whose processes and aims are utterly alien – one that works through supreme acts of mirroring, and by remaining hidden in so many ways, all without surrendering the foundations of its *otherness* as it becomes what it encounters. (191)

Area X does not stage a simple encounter between self and other, instead it rearticulates the self *as* other, in a process not unlike the transmission of a virus. The biologist becomes something more than human, and the concept of life becomes less rigid, less tied to preexisting organic forms.

Vandermeer's fiction is biopolitical, because it raises questions about the social and historical parameters of the human, but his work seldom examines specific political structures. In contrast, China Miéville's New Crobuzon novels, especially *The Scar* (2002) and *Iron Council* (2004), offer pointed critiques of capitalism and criminal punishment. Perhaps most striking are his fantastic figures, the "Remade," whose bodies have been "carved by science and thaumaturgy into a new shape, in punishment for some crime" (Miéville 2002, 25). One character, for example, has the lower half of her body replaced with steam-powered treads, while another has the tentacles of a marine creature grafted to his chest. These modifications are done in a manner that not only permanently marks their subjects as outcasts but also leaves them with lingering pain. In *Iron Council*, the Remade, conscripted as slave labor for the construction of a transcontinental railroad, organize into a revolutionary force. Their state-sanctioned mutilations serve as a shared badge of oppression, a kind of readymade class consciousness enabling their political mobilization. In *The Scar*, a novel set aboard a floating pirate colony, remaking becomes a utopian possibility when one character, Tanner Sacks, undergoes a voluntary transformation for the sake of being able to breathe underwater:

> But the chirurgeon had gently explained that some of the procedures were fundamental; some would involve the reconfiguration of his insides from the tiniest building blocks up. He could not move while the atoms and particles of his blood and lungs and brain found their ways along new pathways and met in alternative combinations. (Miéville 2002, 167)

The surgical reconstitution of Tanner is a biopolitical figure for utopia. It involves the remaking of life in a "fundamental" manner, so that what is utopian in the novel is less the setting than the inhabitants who occupy it. In short, Miéville reimagines utopia in Marxist and biopolitical terms as the remaking of working-class life.

China Miéville and Jeff VanderMeer show how utopianism can thrive outside of utopian fiction proper, but they are not the only writers demonstrating the symbiosis between biopolitics and utopia. A great deal of contemporary science fiction, especially by women of color, has shown how utopia might be less a wished-for place than an ongoing process of social and biological change. Octavia Butler's Xenogenesis trilogy, for example, examines the racialized and colonial boundaries of modern conceptions of humanity by imagining futures in which humans and aliens reproduce as a new species. More recently, N. K. Jemisin's Broken Earth trilogy investigates the complex relationship between the human species and the planet by imagining a group of humans capable of practicing a kind of geological magic ("oregeny"), as well as a humanoid species known as "Stone Eaters," created by humans long ago as a means of extracting the planet's energy. Jemisin tropes on the genre of post-apocalyptic fiction by asking what it would mean if the end of the world were periodic instead of punctual. The prologue of *The Fifth Season* (2015)—the trilogy's first novel—reads:

> This is what you must remember: the ending of one story is just the beginning of another. This has happened before, after all. People die. Old orders pass. New societies are born. When we say 'the world has ended,' it's usually a lie, because *the planet* is just fine. (Jemisin 2015, 14)

The "fifth season" is the name for periodic geological upheavals that cause life on the Stillness—the trilogy's ironic name for earth—to become almost unlivable. People survive fifth seasons, but only by abandoning customs, breaking taboos, becoming a different kind of species. These periods of upheaval are not strictly cyclical, however, because the only guarantee across periods is the expectation of another season with all the radical change it will bring. In other words, the only fundamental truth in Jemisin's universe is the utter contingency of life.

The narrative structure of the trilogy not only reinforces this truth, it also frames it in utopian terms. Jemisin uses ambiguity surrounding the identities of the narrator and the characters, as well as of the time of narration, to emphasize individual and social change. In the first novel, the narrative appears to tell the stories of three different characters—Damaya, Syenite, and Essun—only to reveal that these are not different characters but different moments in one and the same character's life. This life is characterized by discontinuity more than linear development, however: the three proper names represent breaks between one mode of existence and another, rather than phases in a singular trajectory. These breaks are traumatic, marked by painful separations and loss, but the narrator suggests that they are also what make life more than an inert passage through time:

> Perhaps you think it wrong that I dwell so much on the horrors, the pain, but pain is what shapes us, after all. We are creatures born of heat and pressure and grinding, ceaseless movement. To be still is to be … not alive. (Jemisin 2015, 361)

This equation of life with painful change takes on a historical scope in the trilogy's last novel, which reveals that the Stone Eaters are a species that were scientifically engineered for the sake of being instruments of energy extraction. Put differently, Jemisin literalizes modern scientific racism by transforming her trilogy from fantasy fiction about different "races" (analogous to J. R. R. Tolkien's humans, hobbits, and orcs) into science fiction involving slavery, oppression, and the technological manipulation of life. It is not possible to recount the entirety of Jemisin's narrative here, but it is worth noting that the fantasy land of the Stillness emerged from an act of revolution—a revolt by the Stone Eaters against the masters who created them, which resulted in knocking the moon out of orbit, thus changing the meteorological and geological conditions of Earth. Jemisin thus reframes biopolitics so that it includes a planetary horizon. In doing so, she renews the utopian impulse by literalizing its imagination of new worlds. What if utopia were literally the process of creating a new Earth?

Conclusion

This chapter shows that utopian literature might be understood in a broader sense than genre: it might also name literary efforts to imagine new ways of living. This understanding is biopolitical insofar as it wrestles with the mutual imbrication of life and power. Although biopolitics can be pessimistic, bemoaning life's reduction to an instrument of the state or capitalism, it can also be hopeful—it can dream up new kinds of bodies, it can flirt with vibrant futures, it can imagine alien earths. Taken together, then, utopia and biopolitics constitute a method—an optimistic practice—devoted to reading for another life and another world.

NOTES

1. On the New Weird as a genre or literary movement, see Ann and Jeff VanderMeer, eds., 2008, *The New Weird*, San Francisco: Tachyon Publications.
2. All translations mine, from the original French.

REFERENCES

Fisher, Mark. 2016. *The Weird and the Eerie*. Repeater Books.

Foucault, Michel. 1989. Friendship as a Way of Life. In *Foucault Live: Collected Interviews, 1961–1984*, ed. Sylvère Lotringer, 308–313. New York: Semiotext(e).

———. 1990a. *The History of Sexuality*, vol. 1, trans. Robert Hurley. New York: Vintage.

———. 1990b. *The Use of Pleasure*, trans. Robert Hurley. New York: Vintage.

———. 2010. Le corps utopique. In *Le Corps Utopique, Les Hétérotopies*, 7–20. Paris: Éditions lignes.

———. 2012. *The Courage of Truth: Lectures at the Collège de France, 1983–1984*, ed. Frédéric Gros, trans. Graham Burchell. New York: Picador.

Hardt, Michael, and Antonio Negri. 2004. *Multitude: War and Democracy in the Age of Empire*. New York: Penguin Books.

Jameson, Fredric. 2005. *Archaeologies of the Future: The Desire Called Utopia and Other Science Fictions*. London: Verso.

Jemisin, N.K. 2015. *The Fifth Season*. London: Orbit Books.

Levitas, Ruth. 2013. *Utopia as Method: The Imaginary Reconstitution of Society*. New York: Palgrave Macmillan.

Macherey, Pierre. 2011. *De l'utopie!* Paris: De l'incidence éditeur.

Miéville, China. 2002. *The Scar*. New York: Del Rey.

———. 2004. *Iron Council*. New York: Del Rey.

Moylan, Tom. 2000. *Scraps of the Untainted Sky: Science Fiction, Utopia, Dystopia*. Boulder: Westview Press.

Muñoz, José Esteban. 2009. *Cruising Utopia: The Then and There of Queer Utopia*. New York: New York University Press.

Negri, Antonio. 1999. *Insurgencies: Constituent Power and the Modern State*, trans. Maurizia Boscagli. Minneapolis: University of Minnesota Press.

Sargisson, Lucy. 2000. *Utopian Bodies and the Politics of Transgression*. New York: Routledge.

Tarizzo, Davide. 2017. *Life: A Modern Invention*, trans. Mark William Epstein. Minneapolis: University of Minnesota Press.

VanderMeer, Jeff. 2014. *Annihilation*. New York: FSG Originals.

VanderMeer, Ann, and Jeff VanderMeer (eds.). 2008. *The New Weird*. San Francisco: Tachyon Publications.

Weheliye, Alexander. 2014. *Habeus Viscus: Racializing Assemblages, Biopolitics, and Black Feminist Theories of the Human*. Durham: Duke University Press.

Williams, Raymond. 2006. Utopia and Science Fiction. In *Culture and Materialism*, 196–212. New York: Verso Books.

War

Andrew Byers

INTRODUCTION

War and society's preparation for it have been presented variously as utopian and dystopian visions, ranging from nightmarish scenarios that reveal existential destruction and must be avoided at all cost, to a kind of utopia that envisions mastery of war and military victory as a kind of fantasy. Utopian and dystopian writers have explored their hopes and fears about war, sometimes even redesigning imaginary societies to reflect ideas about how society might best prepare itself for the prospect of war, beginning with Thomas More's critique of sixteenth-century Europe in *Utopia* (1516). To More, the Utopian ideal might be pacifism and peace, but preparation for war—as a deterrent for it, if nothing else, through the idea of peace through strength—was still necessary. Others, including the creators of the genre of invasion literature of the 1870s through 1914, which began with "The Battle of Dorking" (1871) that presented a fictional invasion of Britain, have crafted dystopias specifically to warn of future conflicts, often urging social and military transformations of entire nations in order to prepare for, or head off, such conflicts. But while a few utopias have been intended to be places entirely free of conflict and war (e.g., Shangri-La or Big Rock Candy Mountain), most have not placed pacifist societies as the ideal. Militaristic utopias, including some Cold War utopian visions, like that of Cold War strategist Herman Kahn, in *On Thermonuclear War* (1960), have presented the mastery of war, even nuclear war, as a kind

A. Byers (✉)
Durham, NC, USA

P. Marks et al. (eds.), *The Palgrave Handbook of Utopian and Dystopian Literatures*, https://doi.org/10.1007/978-3-030-88654-7_30

of utopia. While many of these depictions are motivated by fear—fears of military defeat, societal destruction, or technological transformation—others romanticize war, or fetishize and fantasize about it.

Thomas More's *Utopia*, Militarism, and Just War

Thomas More's *Utopia* seems an appropriate place to begin a discussion of how war and warfare have been depicted in utopian literature. Here, More offers a number of critiques of war and its effects on society, unsurprisingly, given the state of war-torn Europe in the sixteenth century. More notes that "most princes apply themselves more to affairs of war than to the useful arts of peace...they are generally more set on acquiring new kingdoms, right or wrong, than on governing well those they possess" (2012, Book I, 36–37). He goes on to describe the folly of territorial conquest, and its deleterious effects on the conquering society, arguing that the cost of conquest "was equal to that by which it was gained... the conquered people were always... in rebellion" and the conquerors

> were obliged to be incessantly at war... and consequently could never disband their army; that in the meantime they were oppressed with taxes... their blood was spilt for the glory of their king without procuring the least advantage to the people, who received not the smallest benefit from it even in time of peace. (Book I, 42)

This is a grim but not inaccurate portrait of a continent torn apart by the constant warring of rival rulers.

More does not restrict his criticism to princes, but also levels it against professional soldiers, especially during peacetime, noting that "soldiers often prove brave robbers, so near an alliance there is between those two sorts of life." He uses the example of France to describe a country plagued by too large an army: "for the whole country is full of soldiers, still kept up in time of peace (if such a state of a nation can be called a peace)" (Book I, 42). In part, More's critique partly concerns the widespread militarism emerging from such a significant emphasis on the military, and partly on the costs of maintaining such a force during peacetime—he cites the fates of Rome and Carthage as cautionary tales of empires ruined by the need to maintain standing armies and engage in endless wars (Book I, 43).

Of the Utopians, More describes a society that sought to avoid war if at all possible, noting that they "detest war as a very brutal thing," believing that "there is nothing more inglorious than that glory that is gained by war" (Book II, Their Military Affairs, 152) but More makes clear that Utopia was not a pacifist society that had forsaken war, merely one that looked to war as a last resort for resolving conflicts while also seeking to mitigate the costs of war on society. More tells us that the Utopians used their vast wealth to hire foreign mercenaries in the event of war, which seems to be one possible solution for the need to maintain large standing armies that would absorb vast resources during peacetime (Book II, Their Wealth, 111–112).

But the Utopians do not leave war entirely to others in their hire; Utopian men and women alike engage in military exercises during peacetime so that "in cases of necessity, they may not be quite useless" (Book II, Their Military Affairs, 153). They do not, however, rely on conscripts, but rather have an all-volunteer force: "When they draw out troops of their own people, they take such out of every city as freely offer themselves, for none are forced to go against their wills" (Book II, Their Military Affairs, 160). The Utopians also have a remarkably progressive view on the issue of women in combat, reflecting their relatively egalitarian society:

> But as they force no man to go into any foreign war against his will, so they do not hinder those women who are willing to go along with their husbands; on the contrary, they encourage and praise them, and they stand often next their husbands in the front of the army. (Book II, Their Military Affairs, 161)

All Utopians, then, are ready for war at all times. The Utopians, More explains,

> do not rashly engage in war, unless it be either to defend themselves or their friends from any unjust aggressors, or, out of good nature or in compassion, assist an oppressed nation in shaking off the yoke of tyranny. They, indeed, help their friends not only in defensive but also in offensive wars. (Book II, Their Military Affairs, 153)

In terms of the Utopians' goals in war, More says,

> The only design of the Utopians in war is to obtain that by force which, if it had been granted them in time, would have prevented the war; or, if that cannot be done, to take so severe a revenge on those that have injured them that they may be terrified from doing the like for the time to come. (Book II, Their Military Affairs, 155–116)

This is a society that engages in what we might describe as an interventionist foreign policy, in support of allies and to promote its values abroad, while mostly seeming to follow the precepts of the Just War tradition.[1]

In combat, the Utopians are not interested in the mass slaughter of their enemies. "When they have obtained a victory, they kill as few as possible, and are much more bent on taking many prisoners than on killing those that fly before them" (Book II, Their Military Affairs, 163). Additionally,

> If they agree to a truce, they observe it so religiously that no provocations will make them break it. They never lay their enemies' country waste nor burn their corn, and even in their marches they take all possible care that neither horse nor foot may tread it down, for they do not know but that they may have use for it themselves. They hurt no man whom they find disarmed, unless he is a

spy. When a town is surrendered to them, they take it into their protection; and when they carry a place by storm they never plunder it, but put those only to the sword that oppose the rendering of it up, and make the rest of the garrison slaves, but for the other inhabitants, they do them no hurt; and if any of them had advised a surrender, they give them good rewards out of the estates of those that they condemn, and distribute the rest among their auxiliary troops, but they themselves take no share of the spoil. (Book II, Their Military Affairs, 164–165)

This was decidedly unusual wartime behavior during More's day, with the right of plunder and the taking of spoils one of the chief rewards of military victory throughout the Middle Ages and early modern period.[2] All told, More's vision for how the Utopians think about and conduct war represents a significant departure from how warfare was conducted in More's time, but he does not lay out a pacifist vision for society; on the contrary, More envisions war and the preparation for it as an ever-present part of human life.

FEARS OF ARMAGEDDON

Fears of future wars and conquest spawned an entire new genre of "invasion literature" that is usually said to begin in 1871 with the publication of "The Battle of Dorking" by George Tomkyns Chesney, which depicts a fictional invasion of Great Britain by Germany. Works in the genre almost always involve a future invasion by an enemy power that is usually successful due to inadequate military preparation and social and political weakness, often introduced by pacifists. In other cases, the invasion would eventually be defeated after strenuous national efforts and significant loss of life. But why did fictional military invasions become such a popular topic in popular literature starting in the early 1870s? The defining event seems to have been the Franco-Prussian War (1870–1871), in which Prussia invaded and rapidly defeated France, capturing Paris and imprisoning the French Emperor Napoleon III, through a series of rapid offensive operations that shocked all of Europe. Like many of his contemporaries, British military officer George Tomkyns Chesney was alarmed by this turn of events. "The Battle of Dorking" begins by depicting a sudden defeat of the British Royal Navy at sea, which serves as a prelude to the massive amphibious invasion of Great Britain by German armies, which quickly defeat the few remaining British regulars and some hastily assembled volunteers. The story then fast-forwards fifty years in time, showing a Britain still in ruins and a subject nation of the German empire. Chesney was clear that his intent in writing "The Battle of Dorking" was to wake up the British nation to the transformation in the nature of war and changing geopolitics; he was worried that Britain would be destroyed by what he perceived as its complacency and materialism, urging political, economic, and military reform and modernization (Moorcock 1975, 6–8).

The invasion literature genre was most popular in Great Britain, though there were numerous entries in France, Germany, the United States, and elsewhere, many written by active-duty or retired military officers. By 1914, over 400 invasion-themed novels or short stories had been penned, many achieving best-seller status. The best known may be H. G. Wells's *The War of the Worlds* (1898), which bears some similarities to "The Battle of Dorking," even referencing that town, though it depicts an England invaded not by the Germans but by invaders from Mars (Clarke 1992, 85–87). Wells also wrote *The War in the Air* in 1907, depicting invasions of the United States by Germany and the "Confederation of Eastern Asia," a conglomeration of China and Japan. The war leads to massive campaigns on land, at sea, and in the air, with the end result being a world war that leads to the destruction of all major cities around the globe, a massive financial panic that destroys the world's economy, a global pandemic, and the complete collapse of human civilization. The idea of invasion, military defeat, and subsequent subjugation by outside powers clearly captured the imaginations of publics around the world. Many of these works were used in public policy debates by advocates of increased military spending, weapons development, and preparation for future war, usually couched as a means of deterring such a fictional invasion from taking place in the real world.

Stephen Southwold, writing as "Miles," who penned *The Gas War of 1940* (published in 1931) encapsulated the central thesis of many of these works of invasion literature:

> Man has created a peril which he must at all costs avoid. That peril is the perfection of instruments of destruction. If man cannot so adapt himself, shall I say re-make himself, so that he can live in amity with man, he is lost. (quoted in Clarke 1992, 159)

Southwold describes successful German blitzkriegs against Poland and France; the two countries are invaded, their populations killed via aerial bombardment, enormous columns of tanks, and massive poison gas attacks. After the fall of France and Poland, London itself is also destroyed. Other governments around the world collapse, pandemics sweep through the world's surviving urban areas, and a militaristic Germany is left in control of what little is left of human civilization. In this case, the great powers were unable to find a way to live in peace with their rivals, and thereby brought about their destruction via the new military technologies that had become increasingly prevalent.

The genre did not fade away at the end of World War II, and even received a boost during the Cold War, when the Red Scare and fears of Communist subversion brought renewed fears of military invasion, nuclear war, and clandestine takeover. Here we might point out a number of works depicting overt, conventional invasions of the United States by Communist forces, including *Invasion USA* (1953), *Point Ultimate* (1955), *Red Dawn* (1984), and *Amerika* (1987), among others, as well as numerous other works focusing on the horrors of nuclear war, including *On the Beach* (1959), *Alas, Babylon*

(1959), and *The Day After* (1983). A number of other Cold War-era works used science fictional elements to detail clandestine infiltration and subversion of American society by foes bent on enslaving it, including Robert A. Heinlein's *The Puppet Masters* (1951) and Jack Finney's *The Body Snatchers* (1955), the latter of which was depicted on film four times, in 1956, 1978, 1993, and 2007.

FANTASIES OF WAR

Not all who have written about the future of war have done so with trepidation. In 1864 French novelist Victor Hugo wrote to the French balloonist Nadar that the invention of the airplane might mean the end of war. The invention of aircraft, Hugo said, would bring about:

> the immediate, absolute, instantaneous, universal and perpetual abolition of frontiers. Armies would vanish, and with them the whole business of war, exploitation and subjugation. It would be an immense peaceful revolution. It would mean the liberation of mankind. (quoted in Clarke 1992, 4)

Despite Hugo's hopes, science and technology did not bring about an end to war. Hugo was not alone in this hopeful view, however; in 1915 Orville Wright predicted that "The aeroplane will prevent war by making it too expensive, too slow, too difficult, too long drawn out." Two years later, still in the midst of the First World War, Wright stated that he and his brother "thought governments would recognize the impossibility of winning by surprise attacks and that no country would enter into war with another of equal size when it knew that it would have to win by simply wearing out its enemy" (quoted in Briggs 2003, np). This hope too would prove unfounded, with the Second World War two decades later demonstrating new and ever more destructive forms of warfare.

But not all writers of even apocalyptic visions of future wars have feared them; some have actually relished the prospect. Two strands of this kind of thinking emerge. The first, perhaps articulated most clearly in the aftermath of the First World War, sought to extrapolate the technological trends of that war and prophesy a kind of utopia in which a nation might embrace military technological change and use newly developed military capabilities to dominate rival powers. In this sort of thinking, war might be perceived as a way of unifying the nation or improving the nation's position on the world stage by, for example, invading a rival power and eliminating that nation as a geopolitical competitor. War might also prove to be a means of seeking glory or adventure, or demonstrating one's manhood through combat.[3]

A second strand of thinking about the desirability of future war arose in the writings of the so-called defense intellectuals of the early Cold War (Kaplan 1983), some of whom suggested that rather than fearing the prospect of nuclear war, the United States might instead seek to master nuclear weapons and use them in coldly rational, calculating kinds of ways to manage and even win future nuclear wars. This was an idea tied to a hope for techno-utopias and perhaps even a kind of technological fanaticism, which, as historian Michael Sherry has described, is the "pursuit of destructive ends expressed, sanctioned, and disguised by the organization and application of technological means" (Sherry 1987, 251–252). Both strands of thinking are worth exploring further.

The Italian strategist Giulio Douhet, often referred to by enthusiasts as the "prophet of air power," is one of the clearest examples of a thinker who envisioned future war as a kind of technological utopia.[4] Douhet argued that the airplane offered a revolutionary new military capability that made land-bound military forces of decidedly secondary importance. Defense against airplanes would be nearly impossible, Douhet believed; airplanes offered an unstoppable offensive potential. The air force capable of bombing its opponent's own air force into extinction could achieve command of the air, and with that, overall victory. Air-dropped conventional munitions and chemical weapons deployed against "vital centers" (cities and industrial centers) would break the enemy populace's will by imposing such vast destruction and loss of life that the enemy would be forced to capitulate (Douhet 1998, 57). As World War II demonstrated, Douhet's fantasy of defeating an enemy via strategic bombing—and therefore obviating the need for an army or navy, or long, drawn-out military campaign—did not come to fruition. But with the detonation of the first atomic weapons, and perhaps again beginning in the 1990s through the use of long-range precision-guided munitions, air power might again be said to play a more dominant role in war, with many of Douhet's ideas still clearly underpinning contemporary air power theory (Gilbert 1992). Nation-states and societies have proved far more resilient and adaptable to the loss of critical infrastructure and damage inflicted on it by the air. However, they usually respond to attacks like those imagined by Douhet by rallying around their flag and continuing to resist the enemy, as the U.S. military's post-9/11 drone campaigns throughout the greater Middle East have demonstrated.

Michael Sherry's *The Rise of American Air Power* (1987) serves as a useful adjunct to Douhet in his analysis of the rise of U.S. strategic bombing capabilities and the decision to employ atomic bombs against Japan. Sherry has argued that the American use of strategic bombing and the adoption of the nuclear weapon as the ultimate weapon of war were not simply products of technological or even strategic development. Sherry blamed the decision on what he describes as technological fanaticism, which led American strategic planners to pursue the massive destruction of Japan through a reliance on long-range strategic bombers and the atomic bomb. This destruction was seldom described as the desired end (securing victory over Japan was), but in practice, the ends and means of strategic bombing became blurred. Alternative methodologies for gaining victory were ignored in favor of strategic bombing, though other means might have proven more efficient and effective. Technological fanaticism had its origins in the nature of strategic bombing itself, which promised tremendous results for relatively low costs; the physical distancing of targeteers from their targets enabled by air war; and American self-identity and a conception of its (racialized) enemies. It is this last factor—the racial hatred for the Japanese and the denial of their shared humanity—that Sherry argues made possible the decisions to annihilate Japanese cities first through conventional strategic bombing then through the use of the atomic bomb.[5]

This technological fanaticism and embrace of future war as a utopian concept—rather than a dystopian one—continued through the Cold War, which may be somewhat surprising, given that the Cold War, and the advent of the nuclear age, also brought new existential fears about the potential of war to bring about the complete collapse of human civilization. But with the creation of the American national security state and the rise of prominent defense intellectuals and technocrats, war and its attendant fears became a phenomenon or practice that could be managed and perhaps even mastered.

One of this new breed of Cold War defense intellectuals was Herman Kahn of the RAND Corporation, a key defense think tank in the 1960s, whose most well-known work was entitled *On Thermonuclear War*, which mathematician James R. Newman described as "a moral tract on mass murder: how to plan it, how to commit it, how to get away with it, how to justify it" (1961, 197). The most well-known response to Kahn was Stanley Kubrick's darkly satirical *Dr. Strangelove or: How I Learned to Stop Worrying and Love the Bomb* (1964), with the eponymous Dr. Strangelove said to have been based largely on Kahn. Louis Menand described Herman Kahn as

> the heavyweight of the Megadeath Intellectuals, the men who, in the early years of the Cold War, made it their business to think about the unthinkable, and to design the game plan for nuclear war—how to prevent it, or, if it could not be prevented, how to win it, or, if it could not be won, how to survive it. The collective combat experience of these men was close to nil; their diplomatic experience was smaller. Their training was in physics, engineering, political science, mathematics, and logic, and they worked with the latest in assessment technologies: operational research, computer science, systems analysis, and game theory. The type of war they contemplated was, of course, never waged, but whether this was because of their work or in spite of it has always been a matter of dispute. (2005)

Kahn and his colleagues believed that nuclear war was not only possible but that it was winnable, and expended vast amounts of ink detailing various scenarios for such a victory. *On Thermonuclear War*'s first chapter includes a table entitled "Tragic But Distinguishable Postwar States," detailing the numbers of the dead in various scenarios—ranging from a mere two million dead to one hundred sixty million dead—along with the amount of time required for full economic recuperation, with time spans of one year to a century. Kahn poses the question "Will the survivors envy the dead?" at the bottom of that table (1961, 34). It is critical to understand that Kahn believed the answer to that question was no. Kahn explained that

> despite a widespread belief to the contrary, objective studies indicate that even though the amount of human tragedy would be greatly increased in the postwar world, the increase would not preclude normal and happy lives for the majority of survivors and their descendants. (quoted in Menand 2005, np)

As ludicrous or insensitive as that assumption may be, Kahn's point was the unless Americans accepted the premise that nuclear war was survivable, even under harsh and undesirable conditions, then nuclear deterrence would be meaningless. Without a willingness to accept the consequences of engaging in nuclear war, deterrence would fail; the enemy must believe that the other side would tolerate the deaths of, say, twenty million citizens in order for deterrence to hold. But it is no surprise that while Kahn (and RAND's) ideas had many supporters within the defense establishment, the American public generally found this cold-blooded set of rationalizations of life during and after a nuclear war to be not merely provocative, as Kahn may have intended, but actively repugnant. It is no small thing to accept the prospect that something as catastrophic as nuclear war might be manageable, and entered into rationally. But such was the thinking of consummate Cold Warriors like Kahn, who imagined a future in which nuclear war and the terrible losses and tragedies that it might bring would be reasonable.

CONCLUSION

It is clear that many of the literary depictions of future war have been motivated by fear: fears of militarism, military defeat by a nation's enemies, the annihilation of an entire society, or transformation of the very nature of war itself that might bring about terrible possibilities. These depictions have often been crafted and presented to their audiences with the intent of shaping public thought or policy debates; for example, to cause a nation to embark on a path of defense modernization, or to take note of a particular threat that another nation may present. But not all such depictions have arisen from fear: others have romanticized or fantasized about the prospect of future war—perhaps relishing the prospect of laying low a nation's enemy in time of war or presenting an opportunity to achieve a military victory—or conceiving of war as a phenomenon that could be managed and rationally entered into. In short, war and society's preparation for it have been presented variously as utopian and dystopian visions, ranging from nightmarish scenarios that risk existential destruction and must be avoided at all cost, to a kind of utopia that envisions mastery of war, and victory, as a kind of military fantasy.

NOTES

1. See Michael Walzer, 2015, *Just and Unjust Wars: A Moral Argument with Historical Illustrations*, 5th edition, New York: Basic Books.
2. See Geoff Mortimer, 2002, *Eyewitness Accounts of the Thirty Years War*, Houndmills, Basingstoke, and Hampshire: Palgrave.
3. As examples of some of these ideas, see H. Irving Hancock's four-volume "The Invasion of the United States" series published in 1916.
4. See Tami Davis Biddle, 2002, *Rhetoric and Reality in Air Warfare: The Evolution of British and American Ideas About Strategic Bombing, 1914–1945*, Princeton: Princeton University Press; and John Buckley, 1999, *Air Power in the Age of Total War*, Bloomington: Indiana University Press.
5. See also John Dower, 1986, *War Without Mercy: Race and Power in the Pacific War*, New York: Pantheon Books.

REFERENCES

Biddle, Tami Davis. 2002. *Rhetoric and Reality in Air Warfare: The Evolution of British and American Ideas About Strategic Bombing, 1914–1945*. Princeton: Princeton University Press.

Briggs, Johnathon E. 2003. Wrights Saw Airplanes as Tools of Peace. *The Baltimore Sun*, April 20.

Buckley, John. 1999. *Air Power in the Age of Total War*. Bloomington: Indiana University Press.

Clarke, I.F. 1992. *Voices Prophesying War: Future Wars, 1763–3749*, 2nd ed. Oxford: Oxford University Press.

Douhet, Giulio. 1998. *The Command of the Air*, trans. Dino Ferrari. Washington, DC: U.S. Air Force History and Museums Program.

Dower, John. 1986. *War Without Mercy: Race and Power in the Pacific War*. New York: Pantheon Books.

Gilbert, Silvanus T., III. 1992. *What Will Douhet Think of Next? An Analysis of the Impact of Stealth Technology on the Evolution of Strategic Bombing Doctrine*. Montgomery: Maxwell: United States Air Force Air University School of Advanced Airpower Studies.

Hancock, H. Irving. 1916. *The Invasion of the United States; or, Uncle Sam's Boys at the Capture of Boston*. Philadelphia: Henry Altemus Company.

Kahn, Herman. 1961. *On Thermonuclear War*. Princeton: Princeton University Press.

Kaplan, Fred. 1983. *The Wizards of Armageddon*. Stanford: Stanford University Press.

Menand, Louis. 2005. Fat Man: Herman Kahn and the Nuclear Age. *The New Yorker*, June 27.

Moorcock, Michael (ed.). 1975. *Before Armageddon: An Anthology of Victorian and Edwardian Imaginative Fiction Published Before 1914*. Suffolk: W. H. Allen.

More, Thomas. 2012. *Utopia*, ed. Stephen Duncombe. Wivenoe and New York: Minor Compositions.

Mortimer, Geoff. 2002. *Eyewitness Accounts of the Thirty Years War*. Houndmills, Basingstoke, and Hampshire: Palgrave.

Newman, James R. 1961. Review of *On Thermonuclear War* by Herman Kahn. *Scientific American* 204: 197–204.

Sherry, Michael S. 1987. *The Rise of American Air Power: The Creation of Armageddon*. New Haven: Yale University Press.

Walzer, Michael. 2015. *Just and Unjust Wars: A Moral Argument with Historical Illustrations*, 5th ed. New York: Basic Books.

Postcolonialism

Bill Ashcroft

INTRODUCTION

Postcolonial and Utopian studies emerged in the late 1980s but have had very little to do with each other, with some notable exceptions. While visions of a postcolonial utopia of the Thomas More variety have been extremely rare, the function of utopianism has been central to the decolonizing impetus of postcolonial literatures. In this, Ernst Bloch's insistence on the utopian function of art and literature is a key theoretical foundation. But just as different colonies experienced colonialism differently, so the forms of utopianism vary from region to region: from the African habit of employing memory as a basis for future thinking; to the building of contemporary Indian literature on the anti-nationalist utopianism of Tagore and Gandhi; to the centrality of Aztlan in Chicano visions of the future; to the function of an archipelagic consciousness in the Caribbean; to the conception of Oceania as a vision of Pacific society; to the vision of settler colonies in creating a "better England." All these demonstrate the rich diversity of utopian thinking in postcolonial creative production. In many respects the vision of a different kind of future society is integral to the transformative impetus of postcolonial consciousness, making postcolonial literatures a natural site for utopian thinking.

The theorizing of postcolonial utopianism is a recent phenomenon, the gestation of which may be traced to the year 1989 when *The Empire Writes Back* was published, and the year after the Utopian Studies Society was

B. Ashcroft (✉)
University of New South Wales, Sydney, NSW, Australia

397

P. Marks et al. (eds.), *The Palgrave Handbook of Utopian and Dystopian Literatures*, https://doi.org/10.1007/978-3-030-88654-7_31

formed. Despite this coeval emergence, it was some decades before postcolonial critics began to see the importance of utopian thinking to the insurgent temperament of postcolonial writers and intellectuals. It became obvious that the utopian spirit was a core feature of postcolonial cultural production because the vision of a transformed future was central to its quest for freedom and political independence. Utopias and utopian thinking arise from all cultural traditions, but postcolonial utopianism offers a particularly intense rhetoric of the future characterized by its engagement with imperial power.

In his *Utopia and Anti-Utopia in Modern Times* (1987) Krishan Kumar argues that "so far as I have been able to establish, nothing like the western utopia and utopian traditions exist in any non-western or non-Christian culture" (1987, 424). But this has appeared increasingly questionable: Ralph Pordzik produced *The Quest for Postcolonial Utopia* in 2001 and more recently Jacqueline Dutton and Lyman Tower Sargent produced a volume of *Utopian Studies* (2013) on "Utopias from Other Traditions" that revealed the rich and widespread presence of utopianism in other cultural traditions. Around the same time Sargent, Ashcroft, and Kesler produced an issue of *Spaces of Utopia* dedicated to postcolonial utopianism (2012). Ashcroft published the first comprehensive analysis—*Utopianism in Postcolonial Literatures*—in 2017.

Kumar may be correct in one respect: the distinctive feature of postcolonial orientations to the future is the dominance of *utopianism* over *utopia*. Certainly individual utopias occur from time to time in the literature, particularly in the settler colonies, but the predominant dynamic is the belief in the possibility of social change, and the postcolonial vision of utopia has been dominated by the persistent belief in a transformed future. The need for the utopian turn in postcolonial studies lay in the habit of some postcolonial analyses to see the colonial engagement with imperial power as locked into a simple anti-colonialism. Postcolonial utopianism arises from an unrecognized but powerful reality: that successful resistance is transformative, and transformation rests on the belief in an achievable future (Ashcroft 2001).

The pre-independence utopias of soon-to-be-liberated postcolonial nations provided a very clear focus for anti-colonial activism in British and other colonies. While they were not always depicted in the literature, the independent nation was a widely imagined utopia for anti-colonial activism. But this appeared to suffer a rapid demise once the goal of that activism was reached and the sombre realities of post-independence political life began to be felt. The utopian nationalist dreams of the anti-colonial liberation struggles were doomed to disappointment, bound, as the newly independent nations were, to the political structures of the colonial state and a political system largely incompatible with cultural realities. Yet the literature that flourished after independence, although it had its full share of critical anger about post-independence regimes, and more than its share of gaoled writers, nevertheless developed a hope in the future that could not be quenched.

Ernst Bloch's privileging of art and literature is well known, and literature is important in postcolonial studies because it is the seedbed of postcolonial theory itself. For Bloch the fact that the *raison d'être* of art and literature is the imaging of a different world is the source of their utopian function—what he calls their *Vorschein* or "anticipatory illumination." The anticipatory illumination is the revelation of the "possibilities for rearranging social and political relations to produce *Heimat*, the *home* that we have all sensed but have never experienced or known." "It is *Heimat* as utopia… that determines the truth content of a work of art" (Zipes 1989, xxxiii). *Heimat* becomes the utopian form in postcolonial writing that replaces the promise of nation. It may lie in the *future* but the promise of *Heimat* transforms the present.

Indian poet Meena Alexander explains something of the ambivalence of *Heimat*. When traveling to join her father, seconded to the Sudan from India after the Bandung conference, she turned five aboard ship.

> I still think that birthday on the deep waters of the Indian Ocean has marked me in ways utterly beyond my ken. It has left me with the sense that home is always a little bit beyond the realm of the possible, and that a real place in which to be, though continually longed for can never be reached. It stands brightly lit at the edge of vanishing. (2009, 2)

Home is always on the horizon, always up ahead. But at the same time poetry and place are bound up together. "If poetry is the music of survival," she says, "place is the instrument on which that music is played, the gourd, the strings, the fret" (2009, 4). When home becomes detached from place, the implication is that the music of poetry flourishes by producing different worlds—worlds that offer the horizon of the future, the horizon of *Heimat*.

VARIETIES OF POSTCOLONIAL UTOPIANISM

African Literature and Remembering the Future

The link between memory and the future runs deep in postcolonial writing. While utopias are often set in the future, utopianism cannot exist without the operation of memory. The polarity between past and future often seems insurmountable in European philosophy. For Plato, says Bloch, "'Beingness' is 'Beenness'" (8) and he admonishes Hegel for whom the concept of Being overwhelmed *becoming*. The core of Bloch's ontology is that "Beingness" is "Not-Yet-Becomeness": "From the anticipatory, therefore, knowledge is to be gained on the basis of an ontology of the Not-Yet" (Bloch 1986, 13). "In postcolonial writing it does this through what Édouard Glissant calls a prophetic vision of the past," an access to cultural memory that defines the future outside of any prescription provided by national history (Glissant 1989, 64).

Memory is deployed in African utopianism to contest the dominance of Eurocentric history. Hegel's notorious abolition of Africa from his *Philosophy of History* is well known.[1] When colonial societies are historicized, they are brought into history, mapped, named, organized, legislated, inscribed. But at the same time they are kept at history's margins. There are two ways in which the reinvention of African history has proceeded in literature: On the one hand we find a history that *interpolates* the master discourse of European history, engaging it on its own terms, a method powerfully represented in the later novels of Ayi Kwai Armah. Most commonly associated with the work of Chiekh Anta Diop in the 1970s (Diop 1974), the concept of Pharaohnic Africa is adopted enthusiastically by Armah in novels such as *KMT: In the House of Life* (2002).

On the other hand, we find the positing of a different *kind* of history, a history that might disregard the boundaries between "myth" and memory, a history that subverts the tyranny of chronological narrative. This is the history offered by Ben Okri in *The Famished Road* (1991), *Infinite Riches* (1998), and *In Arcadia* (2002). Okri generates a utopianism through an exuberant language that provides a richly utopian view of the capacity of the African *imaginaire* to re-enter and reshape the modern world. It is not merely a hope for African resurgence, but a vision of Africa's transformative potential.

Re-writing the Indian Nation

For most critics, and possibly for most readers, contemporary Indian literature entered a decisive, cosmopolitan, and globally popular phase with the publication of *Midnight's Children* in 1981. However, the "Rushdie revolution" may be seen to be a continuation of a deep vein of anti-nationalist Indian utopianism most prominent in the writings Rabindranath Tagore and Mohandas Gandhi. The irony of this is that both Tagore and Gandhi have become nationalist icons, and in Gandhi's case, sanctified almost as a national deity. Yet it is their insurgent *anti-national* philosophy that best survives in the contemporary novel. *Midnight's Children* won the Booker Prize in 1981, and we can follow the trajectory of subsequent Indian Booker Prize winners, the inheritors of Rushdie's prize-winning revolution, to understand how India came to be "re-written:" Arundahti Roy's *The God of Small Things* (winner in 1997), Kirin Desai's *The Inheritance of Loss* (2006), Aravind Adiga's *The White Tiger* (2008) and a novel that perhaps more than any others demonstrates the direction of Indian writing: the expatriate Hari Kunzru's *Transmission* (2004).

Nationalism, and its vision of a liberated nation, has still been extremely important to anti-colonial literature because the idea of *nation* has so clearly focused the utopian ideals of independence, and perhaps nowhere more so than in the early decades of twentieth-century India. Nevertheless, in Tagore we find the trenchant position of the earliest and most widely known anti-nationalist. For Tagore, there can be no good nationalism; it can only be what he calls the "fierce self-idolatry of nation-worship" (Tagore 2005, 39)—the exquisite irony being that his songs were used as Bengali, Bangladeshi, and Indian national anthems. Tagore's warning against the model of European nationalism was unmistakable. "Nationalism is a great menace," he says, "It is a particular thing which for years has been at the bottom of India's troubles"

(2005, 87). Tagore's skepticism about nationalism was a bi-product of his utopian vision. He railed against the teaching that "idolatry of the Nation is almost better than reverence for God or humanity" (2005, 83). Tagore's utopianism is nowhere more evident than in his belief in the spiritual potential of human society for openness and acceptance.

Gandhi's vision of *Hind Swaraj* (1909) is one of the most potent forms of utopianism in modern times, and was, as we have seen, a very different vision of "home rule" than that perceived by most politicians. *Hind Swaraj* is interesting because it was able to achieve what Fanon thought nationalism could not do: mobilize the "innermost hopes of a whole people" (Fanon 1963: 148). It is arguable that Nehru's modern industrial socialist nation could not have been established without the utopia of *Hind Swaraj*. But paradoxically this vision, so critical in the birth of Indian nationalism, was anti-nationalist, anti-Enlightenment, and anti-modern. Indeed, Gandhi's vision of Hind Swaraj was as far from the modern capitalist state as could be imagined. "Home rule" conceived an India outside any version of the modern nation state—an India much closer to Ernst Bloch's conception of *Heimat* than to the modern idea of nation (as indeed was Tagore's). This paradox emerges in Partha Chatterjee's foundational *Nationalist Thought and the Colonial World* (1986), which exposes the ambivalent relationship between utopian thinking and nation building and the actual process by which utopian thinking may evolve, or "degenerate," into an organized nation-state machine.

But when we examine the extent to which the post-Rushdie novel continues the resistance to the idea of the nation state, three themes appear: first is the continuation in different ways of the condemnation of class and economic injustice. In Gandhi this was most prominent in his condemnation of untouchability, but the philosophy of *Khadi*, or self-sufficiency, was at the same time a program of economic equality and a critique of capitalism. Second is the critique of the bounded nation state itself, a critique that blossoms in Indian writing in the metaphor of borders and continues the spirit of both Tagore's and Gandhi's anti-state philosophies. The third characteristic of the contemporary novel is its movement outward from "Home" into the "World." Both the actual mobility of writers and the exogenous way Indian consciousness interpolates the economic, cultural, and literary world in these novels suggests a trajectory that will continue through this century.

Aztlan and the Chicano Nation

The disillusion with the utopian dream of national independence is clear in Africa and India. But a very different utopian function emerges when a people with no hope of a separate nation state imagines a nation as a people rather than a structural entity. This is the case of the Chicano people in the United States who frame their culture with both ethnic and geographic location around the utopian concept of Aztlán.[2] At the First Chicano National Conference in Denver in 1969, the conference manifesto, called *El Plan Espiritual de Aztlán*, encapsulated for the first time the hopes, political aspirations, and cultural identity of the Chicano people. It gave birth, or rebirth, to the myth of Aztlán, the sacred Aztec homeland, a myth that has had an incomparable effect on the Chicano sense of identity and national purpose.

Remarkably, although the myth is many centuries old, it was virtually forgotten among Chicanos before 1969. A Chicano nation state exists "Nowhere" because it can never come about. But the identification of the myth of Aztlán with both the Chicano people and the Southwest of the US meant that the concept of an ethnic nation became prominent in Chicano consciousness. Aztlan became the focus of the journal *Aztlan* from 1968 and of novelists such as Rudolfo Anaya in *Heart of Aztlan* (1976). Aztlán occupies a "real," although fluid, site based in the unbounded space of the borderlands. As such it is describable by Foucault's term *heterotopia*. The reality of the Chicano nation, supported as it is by the Aztlán myth, offers the model of a space that, according to Foucault's sixth principal of heterotopias, has "a function in relation to all the space that remains" (1967: 27). While these may represent the fruits of an imperial utopianism they differ greatly from the utopianism that began to be generated in postcolonial literatures.

The issue of Chicano land, Chicano space, raises the associated issue of Chicano colonization and why we are justified in seeing Chicano resistance as a postcolonial movement. The border between the United States and Mexico is one of the longest between any two countries, some 3000 km from Tijuana-San Ysidro to Brownsville-Matamoros. In 1846 the US provoked Mexico to war, the result of which was the invasion of Mexico and the annexation of Texas, New Mexico, Arizona, Colorado, and California. The border fence that now divides the U.S. and Mexico was created, in effect, on February 2, 1848 when the treaty of Guadalupe Hidalgo, annexing those states, left 100,000 Mexican citizens on the US side. The borderlands therefore carry a meaning dense with history, belonging, and cultural identity. If we consider the borderlands to include all the territories taken from Mexico it is an extensive region, a space of intense interaction, a contact zone like no other. For Gloria Anzaldúa the U.S.–Mexican border is a "1950 mile long open wound" (1988, 193). It is not just a border, but "running down the length of my body / staking rods in my flesh" (193). It splits Chicano identity in a way that must be continually overcome in the vision of Aztlán.

THE CARIBBEAN: ARCHIPELAGO OF DREAMS

The Caribbean, that complicated and unruly invention of empire, devastated and impoverished by the sugar industry, often seen to be crime-ridden and dysfunctional, has become one of the most vibrant examples of postcolonial transformation. Conceived in what Kamau Braithwaite calls the "catastrophe" of slavery, the region has produced some of the most powerful examples of literary and cultural self-fashioning. The habit of postcolonial critics to focus on the catastrophe of colonization is deeply ingrained, and resistance its *cause célébre*. But this focus overlooks the radical hope, the belief in the future, that underpins the region's ebullient capacity for creative invention. The strategies developed in the Caribbean to reshape self and society, strategies based on a critique of the history of slavery and its consequences, offer some of the most powerful examples of utopian thinking by enacting a belief in radical transformation. What gives this transformative urge its force and scope is what may be called an "archipelagic consciousness," a sense of the vibrant multiplicity of the region that embeds itself in every individual cultural production.

Creative expression has had a central role in this process of cultural transformation (Zipes 1989, xxxiii). Caribbean literature, owing to its radical creolization of the English language, has been at the forefront of the innovative production of Caribbean culture and thus has been a major factor in the region's capacity for future thinking. The anticipatory illumination in art and literature reveals the "possibilities for rearranging social and political relations to produce *Heimat*"—a place beyond nation, perhaps even beyond time, but a home given its unique character by the concept of the archipelago (Zipes 1989, xxxiii).

Archipelagos are not simply the "other" of continents; they challenge the polarity of "Old World" and "New World," of sea and land, of island and continent, and indeed, go so far as to challenge binary thinking itself. The concept of the archipelago has become prominent in cultural geography (see Ashcroft 2016). Stratford et al. (2011, 15) claim that of the three sets of topological relations in island studies, land and water, island and continent/mainland, and island and island, the last is greatly under theorized. The significance of this is that such relations affect cultural discourse.

The salient question here is: How is archipelagic thinking directed toward the future, and how does it generate hope rather than simple opposition? The utopian dimension of such thinking comes about through the appropriation and transformation of inheritances of all kinds, both inheritances from colonial culture and those from other islands. Seen in this light, "thinking with the archipelago" offers us a clue to the Caribbean capacity for fluidity, multiplicity, and transformation in everything from language and literature to history and myth, including effects such as carnival, politics, religion, folklore, and food. This way of thinking is inevitably transformative, exogenous, and creative, confirming both the hope for the future and the capacity of that imagined future to critique the present. When we see how writers such as Derek Walcott, Kamau Brathwaite, Wilson Harris, Martin Carter, Édouard Glissant think with the archipelago, we see how the transformative processes of creolization and its cultural effects occur.

THE PACIFIC ISLANDS: OCEANIC HOPE

The Caribbean archipelago has been perhaps the most fertile and resourceful generator of postcolonial future thinking. But there is a similar orientation to the Not-Yet-Become in another island region: the Pacific. The history of this region differs greatly from that of the Caribbean. Here the indigenous people maintain a continuous connection to an Oceanic past, in contrast to the slave society's severance from an African (or Asian) homeland. Yet both share the same need for identification with something larger, whether geographically, historically, or imaginatively, and this takes form in both regions in a regional, archipelagic consciousness. In the Pacific this utopian dimension has come to be recognized as "Oceania," an ingenious redefinition of the significance of islands that had seemed tiny, insignificant, and marginal. Oceania is not only itself the name for a utopian formation, but also of a particular attitude toward time, one within which the remembrance of the past becomes a form of forward thinking that embeds itself in a vision of the achievable—a concrete utopia. *Oceania* owes its very meaning to the persistent reality of the crosscurrents of time and space in the region.

Albert Wendt's article "Toward a New Oceania" claimed, "I belong to Oceania—or, at least, I am rooted in a fertile part of it and it nourishes my spirit, helps to define me, and feeds my imagination" (1976, 49).

> So vast, so fabulously varied a scatter of islands, nations, cultures, mythologies and myths, so dazzling a creature, Oceania deserves more than an attempt at mundane fact; only the imagination in free flight can hope—if not to contain her—to grasp some of her shape, plumage, and pain. I will not pretend that I know her in all her manifestations (1976, 49).

For him it was a vision created and nurtured above all by art and literature. "In their individual journeys into the Void, these artists, through their work, are explaining us to ourselves and creating a new Oceania" (1976, 60).

Epeli Hau'ofa first picked up Wendt's vision in 1993 in an essay entitled "Our Sea of Islands" (Hau'ofa 1993), which reversed the bleak denigration of island nations by a simple change of perspective. Rather than "islands in a far sea," they could be regarded as "a sea of islands." Island nations may be tiny, but the history, myths, oral traditions, and cosmologies of the people of Oceania constituted a world that was anything but tiny—it was a vast space, a space of movement, migration, of immensity and longevity. The difference is reflected in the names—"Pacific Islands" and "Oceania." One denotes small, scattered bits of land, the other "connotes a sea of islands with their inhabitants" (Hau'ofa 1993, 92), a world in which people moved and mingled unhindered by the boundaries of state, culture, or ethnicity. This moving world, which seems to have been confined, constricted, and striated by the various boundaries of modernity, is the world of Oceanic hope, the world of the future.

SETTLER COLONIES: CREATING A NEW WORLD

While utopian communities have been established on various occasions in the postcolonial world, usually based on religious and communitarian principles, the settler colonies are distinctive in the utopian drive that propelled people to settle. Throughout the British Empire in particular, settlers fleeing the rigid class structures and economic inequality of Britain saw the colony offering a new start to free settlers. As one emigrant put it in a letter home, "Eight hours is a day's work. That is the best of this country. We go to work at 8 a.m., and leave at 5 p.m. A man is a man, and not a slave" (Sargent 2001, 6). But the escape from class was not matched by an escape from the civilizing mission. In the words from a poem by Thomas Campbell (1858), the immigrant's anticipation is

> To see a world, from shadowy forests won,
> In youthful beauty wedded to the sun;
> To skirt our home with harvests widely sown,
> And call the blooming landscape all our own,
> Our children's heritage, in prospect long. (1874, 249)

But if this start was not always as completely utopian as some texts hoped, it was an improvement for most settlers, and settler colonies demonstrated more purely utopian writing than any other colonized country. In Australia alone Lyman Tower Sargent lists 243 utopian works—both eutopias and dystopias—up to 1999 (Sargent 1999).

By the mid-nineteenth century the dystopian perception of the Antipodes was strongly augmented by a sense of its potential for the British race. In 1852, Samuel Sidney saw it as "a land of promise for the adventurous ... a home of peace and independence for the industrious ... an El Dorado and an Arcadia combined" (1852, 17). James Anthony Froude, in *Oceana, or, England and Her Colonies* (1886), envisaged a global commonwealth of English-speaking colonies in which the words of "Rule Britannia" would come true. Colonists would "become the progenitors of a people destined to exceed the glories of European civilization, as much as they have outstripped the wonders of ancient enterprise" (Froude 2010, 429). Consequently, the settler colonies have never been able to escape the civilizing mission bequeathed to them by British imperialism.

A disillusion with colonial utopia was a consequence of the economic inequality that came with capitalism. William Lane, whose ironically titled *The Working Man's Paradise* was written to help fund the families of shearers and bush workers charged with conspiracy after the 1891 shearer's strike, led a migration to a utopian settlement called New Australia in Patagonia. Disillusioned and unemployed, many bush workers saw the strike's failure as the end of their hopes for an egalitarian, workers' Australia. When Lane proposed starting anew in South America, over 2000 prospective colonists signed up immediately. Perhaps the most famous recruit was poet Mary Gilmore who stayed at New Australia from 1895 to 1902 (Whitehead 2003). But like most utopian communities, New Australia could not manage the problem of power and collapsed under Lane's authoritarian rule. Disillusioned with the class hypocrisy of nationalism, the utopians left, only to be disillusioned in turn by New Australia.

Conclusion

While these different regions demonstrate the rich diversity of utopian thinking in postcolonial literatures, they also reveal that future thinking is always about the present—about a critique of imperial power and a determination to change the present. Where postcolonial thinking turns away from imperial utopia is by *reconceiving the present*, specifically the place *of* the present and place *in* the present. Whether African, Indian, Chicano, Caribbean, Oceanic, or even settler colonial, these literatures offer a different way of being in the present: their utopian energy is directed at resistance to the tyranny of history by the promise of a transformation of society "here and now." The largely uncelebrated and often unrecognized power of postcolonial utopianism offers much to the modern field of utopian studies. In the end postcolonial literature reveals one of Ernst Bloch's most resonant declarations: hope may be disappointed, but it can never be destroyed.

Notes

1. "The Negro, as already observed, exhibits the natural man in his completely wild and untamed state. We must lay aside all thought of reverence and morality-all that we call feeling-if we would rightly comprehend him; there is nothing harmonious with humanity to be found in this type of character… At this point we leave Africa, not to mention it again. For it is no historical part of the World; it has no movement or development to exhibit" (1956, 99).
2. *Chicano* derives from a tribe of the Aztecs known as *Mexicas*. In time references to the tribe in the Nahua language as *Mexicanos* led through contraction and pronunciation to the present spelling and pronunciation *Mexicas, Mexicano, Xicano, Chicano*.

References

Alexander, Meena. 2009. Migrant Memory. In *Poetics of Dislocation*, 4–40. Ann Arbor: University of Michigan Press.
Anaya, Rudolfo. 1976. *Heart of Aztlán*. Berkeley: Editorial Justa.

Anzaldua, Gloria. 1988. The Homeland Aztlán / El Otro Mexico. In *Aztlán: Essays on the Chicano Homeland*, ed. Rudolfo Anaya and Francisco A. Lomelli, 191–204. Albuquerque: University of New Mexico Press.

Armah, Ayi Kwai. 2002. *KMT: In the House of Life*. Popenguine, Senegal: Per Ankh.

Ashcroft, Bill. 2001. *Post-Colonial Transformation*. London: Routledge.

———. 2016. *Utopianism in Postcolonial Literatures*. London: Routledge.

Ashcroft, Bill, Gareth Griffiths, and Helen Tiffin. 1989. *The Empire Writes Back: Theory and Practice in Post-Colonial Literatures*. London: Routledge.

Bloch, Ernst. 1986. *The Principle of Hope*, 3 vols. Translated by Neville Plaice, Stephen Plaice and Paul Knight. Minneapolis: University of Minnesota Press.

Campbell, Thomas. 1858. Lines on the Departure of Emigrants for New South Wales. In *The Complete Poetical Works of Thomas Campbell with a Memoir of His Life*, 256–258. Boston: Phillips, Sampson, and Company.

Chatterjee, Partha. 1986. *Nationalist Thought and the Colonial World: A Derivative Discourse*. Minneapolis: University of Minnesota Press.

Desai, Kirin. 2006. *The Inheritance of Loss*. London: Penguin.

Diop, Chiekh Anta. 1974. *The African Origin of Civilization*, trans. and ed. Mercer Cook. Chicago: Lawrence Hill.

Dutton, Jacqueline, and Lyman Tower Sargent (eds.). 2013. Special issue, *Utopias from Other Cultural Traditions: Utopian Studies* 21 (1): 1–161.

Fanon, Frantz. 1963. *The Wretched of the Earth*, trans. Constance Farrington. New York: Grove Press.

Froude, James Anthony. 2010. *Oceana, or, England and Her Colonies*. Cambridge: Cambridge University Press. First published 1886.

Gandhi, M.K. 1909. *Hind Swaraj [Home Rule]*. Ahmedabad: Navjivan.

Glissant, Édouard. 1989. *Caribbean Discourse: Selected Essays*, trans. J. Michael Dash. Charlottesville: University Press of Virginia.

Hau'ofa, Epeli. 1993. Our Sea of Islands. In *A New Oceania: Rediscovering Our Sea of Islands*, ed. Eric Waddell, Vijay Naidu, and Epeli Hau'ofa, 2–16. Suva: The University of the South Pacific in Association with Beake House.

Hegel, George Wilhelm Friedrich. 1956. *The Philosophy of History*. New York: Dover.

Kumar, Krishnan. 1987. *Utopia and Anti-Utopia in Modern Times*. Oxford: Blackwell.

Kunzru, Hari. 2004. *Transmission*. London: Penguin.

Lane, William. 2009. *The Working Man's Paradise*. Sydney: Sydney University Press.

Okri, Ben. 1991. *The Famished Road*. London: Jonathan Cape.

———. 1998. *Infinite Riches*. London: Phoenix House.

Pordzik, Ralph. 2001. *The Quest for Postcolonial Utopia: A Comparative Introduction to the Utopian Novel in the New Literatures in English*. New York: Peter Lang.

Roy, Arundhati. 1997. *The God of Small Things*. London: HarperCollins.

Rushdie, Salman. 1981. *Midnight's Children*. Harmondsworth: Penguin.

Sargent, Lyman Tower. 1999. Australian Utopian Literature: An Annotated, Chronological Bibliography 1667–1999. *Utopian Studies* 10 (2): 138–173.

———. 2001. Utopianism and the Creation of New Zealand National Identity. *Utopian Studies* 12 (1): 1–18.

Sargent, Lyman Tower, Bill Ashcroft, and Corina Kesler (eds.). 2012. Special Issue, *Postcolonial Utopianism: Spaces of Utopia* 2 (1): 1–17.

Sidney, Samuel. 1852. *The Three Colonies of Australia: New South Wales, Victoria, South Australia: Their Pastures, Copper Mines & Gold Fields*. London: Ingram, Cooke, & Co.

Stratford, Elaine, Godfrey Baldachino, Elizabeth McMahon, Carol Farbotko, and Andrew Harwood. 2011. Envisioning the Archipelago. *Island Studies Journal* 6 (2, November): 113–130.

Tagore, Rabindranath. 2005. *Nationalism*. Delhi: Rupa & Co.

Wendt, Albert. 1976. Towards a New Oceania. *Mana Review* 1 (1): 49–60.

Whitehead, Anne. 2003. *Bluestocking in Patagonia: Mary Gilmore's Quest for Love and Utopia at the World's End*. Sydney: Allen & Unwin.

Zipes, Jack. 1989. Introduction: Toward a Realization of Anticipatory Illumination. In *The Utopian Function of Art and Literature: Selected Essays*, by Ernst Bloch, xi–xliii, trans. Jack Zipes and Frank Mecklenburg. Minneapolis: University of Minnesota Press.

Human Rights

Miguel A. Ramiro Avilés

INTRODUCTION

The various forms of expression of utopian thought (literature, philosophy, politics, architecture, arts) are an invitation to build a fairer society (Sargent 1994, 1). This invitation has been answered by urban planners making cities safer, by scientists or technology engineers working to improve the quality of life, by political philosophers demanding rights for all human and non-human beings. This chapter focuses on the relationship between utopia and the idea of justice, opening with three approaches to this relationship. The first approach is to consider the relations between two emancipatory ideals promising a fairer (more just) future: namely, utopia and *human rights*. The second approach looks at the material characteristics of various models of an ideal society, determining which conditions are essential for even a discussion, much less a flourishing, of human rights. The third approach is more philological, determining when the language of rights appears expressly in literary utopias. Each approach throws into relief the *historical* character of both utopian thought and human rights discourse. Although Thomas More invented the word "utopia" and discussed some of the issues fundamental to demands for rights, not until the eighteenth-century Enlightenment do literary utopias reflect the *language* of rights, as bourgeois revolutions feed on

M. A. Ramiro Avilés (✉)
University of Alcalá, Madrid, Spain

P. Marks et al. (eds.), *The Palgrave Handbook of Utopian and Dystopian Literatures*, https://doi.org/10.1007/978-3-030-88654-7_32

a series of political texts that take the form of literary utopias. Upending the ideological formations of the *Ancien Régime*, these texts displayed possibilities for a completely new political and social imaginary.

HUMAN RIGHTS AS THE ULTIMATE UTOPIA

We are living in the age of rights (Bobbio 1991), our *ultimate* utopia, because

> When people hear the phrase "human rights," they think of the highest moral precepts and political ideals … a set of indispensable liberal freedoms, and sometimes more expansive principles of social protection. … The phrase implies an agenda for improving the world, and bringing about a new one in which the dignity of each individual will enjoy secure international protection. It is a recognizably utopian program: for the political standards it champions and the emotional passion it inspires, this program draws on the image of a place that has not yet been called into being. (Moyn 2010, 1)

As a materialization of a certain theory of justice (Rawls 1999a), human rights are closely connected to utopian thought because both are centered in an emancipatory ideal that has not yet been realized (Bloch 1986). The conjuncture of the concepts of utopia and of human rights can allow a vision, at least, of what a better living condition might look like once the social problems besetting human lives are solved. Utopia and human rights become intertwined conceptually at a moment of idealization—the Enlightenment, for instance—in a phase prior to the positivization phase or generalization phase (Peces-Barba 1995). The idealization of rights phase, following Karl Mannheim, would be an utopian moment that aims to transform "reality" as constituted through the formal institutions of government (Mannheim 1993).

To claim recognition of new rights, to extend the number of persons who are entitled to exercise them, is to reinforce the mechanisms guaranteeing rights; and to implement those rights poses a challenge to a current regime. And, to stay with Mannheim, if the claims that constitute the utopian moment were achieved, *that* concrete ideological moment would generate a new utopian moment. The history of the twentieth century, of course, shows that the ontological presuppositions upon which human rights have been based since the Enlightenment (human dignity, freedom, equality, fraternity) have not been achieved yet, and are still projected for the future, fuelling political actions and decisions. Utopian thought and human rights both exhibit a kind of gap between theory (the projected achievement of human rights justice) and practice (the disaster of its implementation). This gap is "the best expression of postmodern cynicism" (Douzinas 2000, 221) because the utopian universality of rights undergoes legal castration through its limitation, so that the prefigured beautiful future based on human rights will never come to be (Douzinas 2000, 235). The implementational disaster opens the door to *dystopia*, rather than creating an *eutopia* or "good place" (Kumar 1987,

100). Reality will never be *eutopia* as long as human rights remain limited; and human rights justice will always demand social transformation. Dystopias that are analyzed in terms of human rights are warnings about the dangers that certain political decisions can pose; but, following Tom Moylan, dystopias can also remind us that all is not lost (Moylan 2000, 156).

The ambiguity typical of utopian literature's presentation of its political proposals (Stillman 2001) means that some *eutopias* can also be regarded as *dystopias*, since every imagining of a perfection, of a paradise on earth, comes with a price in the form of a *limitation* of rights and freedoms, at least for some. We see this to be the case with the environmental fable by Ernst Callenbach in *Ecotopia* (1975), because the achievement of a sustainable society implies that the government can limit the options of (at least some of) the men and women who live there. William Weston, the journalist who travels to this new society of Ecotopia, argues for a public policy that sounds inescapably paternalistic, an approach that has anathema to political liberalism since John Stuart Mill's *On Liberty* (1859). In Ecotopia, we learn:

> [P]robably our greatest economies were obtained simply by stopping production of many processed and packaged foods. These had either been outlawed on health grounds or put on Bad Practices lists.
>
> This sounded like a loophole that might house a large and rather totalitarian rat. "What are these lists and how are they enforced" I asked.
>
> Actually, they aren't enforced at all. They're a mechanism of moral persuasion you might say. But they're purely informal. They're issued by study groups from consumer co-ops. Usually, when a product goes onto such a list, demand for it drops sharply. The company making it then ordinarily has to stop production, or finds it possible to sell only in specialized stores. (Callenbach 1990, 20–21)

Normative texts at the origin of liberal democracy, such as the *Declaration of Rights of Man and Citizen* of 1789, can also be the genesis of *dystopias*. Olympe de Gouges' recognition of this is why she wrote her *Declaration of Rights of Woman and Citizen*, since the 1789 declaration had excluded women from the possession of natural rights that should be universal. As this exclusion remained unremedied by 1870, Annie Denton Cridge wrote *Man's Rights; or, How Would You Like It*, showing an imagined utopic society for women—if not for men:

> Last night I had a dream, which may have a meaning. I stood on a high hill that overlooked a large city ... As I stood there, wondering what manner of city it was, its name, and the character of its inhabitants ... and lo! everywhere the respective duties of man and woman were reversed ... the women, and only women, were the lawmakers, judges, executive officers, &c., of the nation; that every office of honor and emolument was filled by women; that all colleges and literary institutions, with very few exceptions, were all built for women, and only open to women, and that men were all excluded. (Cridge 1995, 5, 13)

Utopian texts can be interpreted as dystopian, when rights and freedoms are completely absent, and when the state has become an all-powerful and omnipresent Leviathan (Claeys 2017). Such interpretations bind utopian thought to tyranny, violence, and totalitarianism (Berlin 1996; Avineri 1962; Popper 1947) because utopia "will lead to the end of history, politics and change (Sargisson 2007, 27). There is not, however, an inevitable connection between utopian thought and tyranny, violence and totalitarianism (Goodwin 1980), because perfection is not a defining feature of all utopias. Utopias are rarely static ... the glimpsed eutopias are dynamic worlds in which change and flux continue" (Sargisson 2007, 30–31). Secondly, according to Paul Ricoeur, utopia and ideology complement one other so that depending on the model of ideal society chosen, there will be greater affinity with the basic postulates of a specific political ideology (Ramiro Aviles 2005). The existence of fascist utopias cannot be ruled out (Coupland 1998) but it should not be forgotten that the status of rights, freedoms, and obligations, are recurrent themes through the history of utopian thought. In their literary utopias, authors beginning with More discuss the limits of the action of the state or the freedom from arbitrary domination: what we today call human rights (Ramiro Avilés 2022). And human rights are irreconcilable with a *closed society* "in which the only personal intervention is a judicious adjustment to dominant ideas and the exploitation of given and inescapable structures to the subject's advantage" (Douzinas 2000, 223). Human rights are characteristic of an *open society* and they have a place in utopias because both concepts (human rights and utopia) can be understood as aspects of a democratic, experimental, and future-oriented process that has no end (McKenna 2001).

If an optimal form of government as described in literary utopias seems ambiguous we should ask whether we are dealing with an *eutopia* or a *dystopia*, and what the criteria for making that determination are. These criteria should not flatten the ambiguity typical of the utopian form, but rather call for readers to take part in interpretation. But if, since the Enlightenment human rights have been considered the cornerstone of a well-ordered society (Rawls 1999b), then we can already anticipate a determined institutional response, based on the legitimacy of a particular dominant power or regime, and on the legitimacy of its exercise of power. Thomas Paine stresses both forms of political legitimacy in his book *The Rights of Man* (1790), as a response to Edmund Burke's attack on the political changes introduced by the French Revolution. Paine argues that the only legitimate origin of power is contractual, and that the only legitimate exercise of power is that which is limited:

> The fact therefore must be that the individuals themselves, each in his own personal and sovereign right, entered into a compact with each other to produce a government: and this is the only mode in which governments have a right to arise, and the only principle on which they have a right to exist. ... [T]he power produced from the aggregate of natural rights, imperfect in power in the

individual, cannot be applied to invade the natural rights which are retained in the individual. (Paine 1987, 218, 220)

These criteria may help us assess whether a literary utopia, especially a post-Enlightenment one, can be described as *eutopia* or *dystopia*. Thus, what we might find repellent about the society described by George Orwell in *Nineteen Eighty-Four* (1949) is the illegitimacy of both the origin and the exercise of power to which Winston Smith is subjected in his daily life. The outcome would be similar if these legitimacy criteria were applied to the solution proposed in Susan George's *The Lugano Report* (1999), were we to question the way certain international corporations claim and (self)legitimize both the origin and exercise of their power in a globalized world. George performs a satirical X-ray of the kind of society that might be advocated by an expert class—based upon a fictional report that clearly reflects today's society:

> This Report is to be for the eyes of the Commissioners alone ... this Report is to remain confidential, an assurance which has allowed us to proceed with utmost frankness ... The group unreservedly share the premise of the Commissioning Parties: a liberal, market-based, globalised world system should not merely remain the norm but the triumph in the twenty-first century. (George 1999, xiii, xiv, 3)

Even the description in Charlotte Perkins Gilman's *Herland*'s matriarchal society might arouse discomfort, since neither all men nor all women today would recognize that the current social system needs reforms to achieve greater equality between the sexes. In Gilman's Herland the meaning of femininity is redefined: "These women, whose essential distinction of motherhood was the dominant note of their whole culture, were strikingly deficient in what we call 'femininity.' This led me very promptly to the conviction that those 'feminine charms' we are so fond of are not feminine at all, but mere reflected masculinity" (Gilman 2009, 60). These examples show how three pressing issues—the tension between security and freedom; the equitable distribution of wealth; the claims of feminism—are resolved—if "ambiguously," in literary utopias. Critically, the ambiguity typical of the utopian literature allows the reader to see that there is not necessarily agreement on the specific content or meaning of rights and freedoms.

MODELING RIGHTS IN A DIFFERENT IDEAL SOCIETY

In *An Inquiry Concerning the Principles of Morals* (1751) David Hume points out that the principle of justice is useful to society only if human beings are situated in certain circumstances, neither of extreme abundance, nor of extreme need; neither of perfect moderation and humanitarianism, nor of complete rapacity and malice. He begins by suggesting we reflect on a situation in which a profuse abundance of all external conveniences are fully provided to every individual, without anyone exerting any industry. Hume concludes that in such a state "the cautious, jealous virtue of justice would never once have been dreamed of. For what purpose make a partition of goods, where every one has already more than enough? Why give rise to property, where there cannot possibly be any injury? ... Justice, in that case, being totally USELESS, would be an idle ceremonial" (Hume 1993, 21). He is describing a certain utopian trope: an image of a society without want, as in the legendary lands of Cockaigne and Arcadia (Davis 1981, 20–26). These stories ask the reader to consider the consequences of a scarcity of material goods available to people, and the need to moderate appetites. In such a society as Arcadia, humans are freed from the tyranny of needs: what needs they have been satisfied, and in any case their needs are reduced to a minimum. The reform these models implicitly propose entails the disappearance of society, economy, politics, and law, as people return to a primitive state of nature, with no cares about ownership of things, with no power relations, and with no conflicts requiring resolution by magistrates (Ramiro Aviles 2002, 95–158). In such a society, it is pointless to consider materializing the idea of justice through a pact to protect property rights.

Hume goes on to propose a situation in which "the mind is so enlarged, and so replete with friendship and generosity, that every man has the utmost tenderness for every man, and feels no more concern for his own interest than for that of his fellows" such that "the whole human race would form only one family"; where all would lie in common, and be used freely, without regard to property (Hume 1993, 21–22). Two models for such a society are named by J. C. Davis as a "Perfect Moral Commonwealth" and as "Millenium" (Davis 1981, 26–36); in either, there would be simply no use for a concept of justice, as they are based on the reform of human nature, either through education, or through an evolution generated by a transcendental force.

Furthermore, in these descriptions of the ideal society, as the necessary requirements for the liberal idea of an underpinning social contract basis are not satisfied, the transfer to the state of the natural right to self-protection is not necessary. If a society in which the state and the Law, as conceived by political liberalism, are unnecessary and, therefore, pose no threat to people's aspirations or limit their freedom of action, that ideal has been achieved. Those institutions that become unnecessary will not transform, but simply disappear. Legal *anomia* is achieved, since the State and its laws are irrelevant. There may be some kind of rule in these models of ideal society, but that rule will not be through legal, but rather moral precepts, or the result of customs (Ramiro Avilés 2002, 233–254). Members of that society need not claim or protect their natural rights, as classic contractualist authors do.

The fifth model of an ideal society is that of Utopia (Davis 1981, 38–40), characterized by maintaining the state and the Law as key elements in the construction of the best form of republic (Ramiro Aviles 2001, 234–244). Formal institutions of government, such as a property system to ensure fair distribution of scarce goods, and a justice system controlling behavior, must be established. This model does assume that authority and liberty are antithetical; during the sixteenth and seventeenth centuries, Davis notes, "in terms of civil liberty a congruence between liberty and law was sought in order to defend the subject from will and power ... That the essence of freedom was to live under known rules and not to be subject to the arbitrary wills of other men was a commonplace formulation of the seventeenth century well before John Locke gave his own utterance to it" (Davis 1993, 28). It is in relation to this ideal society model, which is linked to the struggle for the rule of law, that the post-Enlightenment debate over human rights makes sense. This model preserves the state and the Law as essential elements in the construction of the ideal society, and is therefore the only one in which the liberal idea of rights might have a place. It acknowledges that natural rights, the immediate precursors of what we know today as human rights, are limits on the action of the state. In the original liberal version, these limits will be negative and take the form of restrictions (actions that the State cannot perform) whereas in the welfare state version, they will be positive and take the form of interventions (actions that the state cannot fail to carry out).

The neoliberal vision of the role of the law and state, founded on works such as *Anarchy, State and Utopia* by Robert Nozick (1990) or *Road to Serfdom* by Friedrich Hayek (1945), builds a type of society in which it is difficult to talk about people's rights given the growing social "uberization" of labor relations, economic transactions, and models of consumption. The regressive movement of the state and of the law in relation to labor relations turns workers into *fake small entrepreneurs* who freely decide to reach agreements for the provision of services, ceasing to be wage earners, as if the "labour force" or "work capacity" were the same as "work." The legal protection provided by the Labor Law has been forfeited in pursuit of an alleged greater freedom.

The Language of Rights in Literary Utopias from Thomas More to the Enlightenment

The struggle for the rule of law, the limits to state action, resistance to tyranny, the right to vote, the humanization of criminal law, religious tolerance, and the issue of private property are all topics that shape the history of human rights (Peces-Barba 1995). They are debates of the Enlightenment, which are included in the first constitutions and declarations of rights of the late-eighteenth century, such as the *Declaration of Rights of Man and Citizen* of 1789 or the *Bill of Rights* of 1791.

The European enlightenment was the turning point at which rights became one of the standard topics in descriptions of ideal societies. Until the Enlightenment, literary utopias do not include a theory about universal natural rights or a solemn declaration of the rights, liberties, and duties of the citizens who inhabit the imaginary societies. However, *Utopia* and the books following this law-based utopia model contain the prerequisites for a rights-based society, the existence of laws, judgment based on authority, and some sort of coercive sanction (Davis 2010, 42). More's *Utopia* describes a political society governed by a range of laws and institutions imposed and administered by a centralized authority (Sargent 1982, 89–90). These laws and institutions control many aspects of people's lives (how they can dress, whether they can travel, the length of their working day) and are able to inflict punishments, including the death penalty, for breaches of these codes. The presence of a centralized authority and a legal system means that a discussion of rights is critical, since rights are to be considered as limits on the action of the state.

A number of these issues (struggle for the rule of law, liberty of conscience, the humanization of criminal law, property rights, and resistance to oppression) can be traced back to More's text, *Utopia* (Ramiro Avilés 2022). Between 1689 and 1776, "rights that had been viewed most often as the rights of a particular people – freeborn English men, for example - were transformed into human rights, universal natural rights, what the French called *les droits de l'homme* or the 'rights of man'" (Hunt 2007, 21–22). It was therefore in France that the use of the term *droits de l'homme* became widespread, especially after Jean-Jacques Rousseau included it in his *Social Contract* (1762) (Hunt 2007, 23–25). During the English and French Enlightenment we find descriptions of ideal societies in which the language of rights is included. English utopias of the Enlightenment, such as those attributed to James Burgh (*An Account of the First Settlement, Laws, Form of Government, and Police, of the Cessares, A People of South America* [1764]), Thomas Northmore (*Memoirs of Planetes, Or a Sketch of the Laws and Manners of Makar* [1795]) and William Hodgson (*The Commonwealth of Reason* [1795]); and French utopias of the Enlightenment, including Diderot's *Supplément au voyage de Bougainville* (1772), Étienne-Gabriel Morelly's *Le naufrage des isles flottantes, ou Basiliade du célèbre Pilpaï* (1753), and Louis-Sébastien Mercier's *L'An 2440. Rêve s'il en fut jamais* (1786), contain the first descriptions of ideal societies in which law and the state remain key elements and include Enlightenment philosophy about the "rights of man" (Ramiro Avilés 2022).

Burgh's *An Account of the First Settlement* for example deploys the language of rights and covers the most common political issues of the time, in order to propose the best form of government. Burgh tells how the Dutch explorer Vander Neck hoped to find a society with "a form of Government, as would be productive of the most beneficial and salutary consequences to every individual ... by securing to them the delightful enjoyment of their civil and religious liberties, under the government of laws founded upon justice, goodness, wisdom, and equity" (Burgh 1994, 77). Following the classic patterns of contractualism, those who found that new society met as an assembly to approve the form of government and the laws of the new commonwealth, "We then held a general assembly, in which the form of government and all the laws of our state, (drawn up some time before by Mr. Alphen and myself) were read and carefully considered, ... the whole assembly expressed their approbation of them and all who were above 21 years of age sign'd them; expressing thereby their submission to them, and by that means became entitled to all the privileges of citizenship. Then to prevent any disputes on our arrival at the desired country, all the citizens proceeded to the election of the magistrates" (Burgh 1994, 82–83). The chosen form of government was mixed "to secure our rights and liberties, to preserve a due balance, and keep a happy medium between the tyranny of arbitrary monarchy, the factions of aristocracy, and the anarchy, licentiousness, and wild tumults of a democracy" (Burgh 1994, 88). The author concludes that it would be difficult to "find a better form of government, where the liberty and happiness of every individual is more carefully consulted; where every tendency to vice and licentiousness is more effectually discouraged; and where more care is taken of the right education of the children, upon which the welfare of posterity greatly depends. What alterations may hereafter be introduced among us, when the present generation is dead … I cannot say. But happy will it be for our children, if they steadily pursue the same plan" (Burgh 1994, 136).

In France, Louis Sébastian Mercier published *L'An 2440*. The new society puts into practice Rousseau's political ideas. It is "a well-ordered society" in which fair laws have been enacted that recall "the natural equality that must reign among men" (2016, 58). In this new society, "freedom of the press gives the true measure of civil liberty" (79). The procedural system has been reformed so that lawyers do not defend the wicked (99) and criminal law has been humanized through the proportionality of penalties to crimes (100). The conquest of this new society causes people to become humans again and stop being slaves (115). The new system of government is neither monarchical, nor democratic, nor aristocratic but "reasonable and made for all men." The laws are an expression of the general will (251). In so far as no one is above the law (255), the good of the state has been reconciled with the good of individuals (257).

CONCLUSION

Given the historical nature of human rights, the terms of debates will expand. At any historical juncture, societies build their own utopia in reaction to specific injustices or specific problems. There is a blood-relationship between utopian thought and human rights that is as inevitable as it is impossible. Both project a new social order that is not real because the future is never made once for all. The impossibility of fully satisfying the demands of human rights offers the chance to extend the limits of the social by means of the literary form of utopias to project a future society in which there is a government with greater legitimacy both in origin and in exercise. Dystopia will be there too, indicating the path that should not be taken as it leads to servitude. The utopias presage a future social order, in which the human being is never degraded, enslaved, abandoned, or despised; a future that has yet to be achieved, and perhaps never will be.

References

Avineri, Shlomo. 1962. War and Slavery in More's *Utopia*. *International Review of Social History* 7: 260–290.

Berlin, Isaiah. 1996. *Four Essays on Liberty [1969]*. Oxford: Oxford University Press.

Bloch, Ernst. 1986. *The Principle of Hope*, vol. 1 [1959], trans. N. Plaice, S. Plaice, and P. Knight. Cambridge, MA: MIT Press.

Bobbio, Norberto. 1991. *L'età dei diritti*. Torino: Einaudi.

Burgh, James. 1994. An Account of the First Settlement, Laws, Form of Government, and Police, of the Cessares: A People of South America [1764]. In *Utopias of the British Enlightenment*, ed. Gregory Claeys, 71–136. Cambridge: Cambridge University Press.

Callenbach, Ernest. 1990. *Ecotopia: A Novel* [1975]. Berkeley: Bantam.

Claeys, Gregory. 2017. *Dystopia: A Natural History*. Oxford: Oxford University Press.

Coupland, Philip M. 1998. The Blackshirted Utopians. *Journal of Contemporary History* 33 (2): 255–272.

Cridge, Annie Denton. 1995. Man's Rights; or, How Would You Like It [1870]. In *Daring to Dream: Utopian Fiction by United States Women Before 1950*, 2nd ed., ed. Carol F. Kessler, 5–60. Syracuse: Syracuse University Press.

Davis, J.C. 1981. *Utopia and the Ideal Society: A Study of English Utopian Writing 1516–1700*. Cambridge: Cambridge University Press.

———. 1993. Formal Utopia/Informal Millennium: The Struggle Between Form and Substance as a Context for Seventeenth-Century Utopianism. In *Utopias and the Millennium*, ed. K. Kumar and S. Bann, 17–32. London: Reaktion Books.

———. 2010. El pensamiento utópico y el discurso de los derechos humanos: ¿Una conexión útil? In *Los derechos humanos: La utopía de los excluidos*, ed. M.A. Ramiro Avilés and P. Cuenca Gómez, 39–62. Madrid: Dykinson.

Diderot, Denis. 2002. *Supplément au voyage de Bougainville* [1772]. Paris: Gallimard.

Douzinas, Costas. 2000. Human Rights and Postmodern Utopia. *Law and Critique* 11: 219–240.

Gilman, Charlotte Perkins. 2009. *Herland* [1915]. *The Yellow Wall-Paper, Herland, and Selected Writings*. London: Penguin.

Goodwin, Barbara. 1980. Utopia Defended Against the Liberals. *Political Studies* 28 (3): 384–400.

Hayek, Friedrich A. 1945. *The Road to Serfdom*. London: George Routledge & Sons.

Hodgson, William. 1994. The Commonwealth of Reason [1795]. In *Utopias of the British Enlightenment*, ed. Gregory Claeys, 199–247. Cambridge: Cambridge University Press.

Hume, David. 1993. *An Enquiry Concerning the Principles of Moral* [1751]. Indianapolis: Hackett.

Hunt, Lynn. 2007. *Inventing Human Rights: A History*. New York: Norton.

Kumar, Krishan. 1987. *Utopia & Anti-Utopia in Modern Times*. Oxford: Basil Blackwell.

Mannheim, Karl. 1993. *Ideología y Utopía* [1929]. México: Fondo de Cultura Económica.

McKenna, Erin. 2001. *The Task of Utopia: A Pragmatist and Feminist Perspective*. London: Rowen & Littlefield.

Mercier, Louis S. 2016. *El año 2440. Un sueño como no ha habido otro* [1786]. Madrid: Akal.

More, Thomas. 1964. *Utopia* [1516], ed. E Surtz. New Haven: Yale University Press.

Morelly, Étienne-Gabriel. 1972. *Le naufrage des isles flottantes, ou Basiliade du célèbre Pilpaï* [1753]. Paris: Hachette.

Moylan, Tom. 2000. *Scraps of the Untainted Sky*. Boulder: Westview.

Moyn, Samuel. 2010. *The Last Utopia: Human Rights in History*. Cambridge, MA: Harvard University Press.

Northmore, Thomas. 1994. Memoirs of Planetes, Or a Sketch of the Laws and Manners of Makar [1795]. In *Utopias of the British Enlightenment*, ed. G. Claeys, 137–197. Cambridge: Cambridge University Press.

Nozick, Robert. 1990. *Anarquía, Estado y Utopía* [1974]. México: Fondo de Cultura Económica.

Orwell, George. 1999. *Nineteen Eighty-Four* [1949]. London: Penguin.

Paine, Thomas. 1987. Rights of Man [1790]. In *The Thomas Paine Reader*. London: Penguin.

Peces-Barba, Gregorio. 1995. *Curso de derechos fundamentales*. Madrid: BOE.

Popper, Karl. 1947. Utopia and Violence. *Hibbert Journal* 46: 109–116.

Ramiro Avilés, Miguel A. 2001. The Law Based Utopia. *The Philosophy of Utopia*, ed. B. Goodwin, 225–248. London: Frank Cass.

———. 2002. *Utopía y Derecho. El sistema jurídico en las sociedades ideales*. Madrid: Marcial Pons.

———. 2005. Ideología y Utopía: Una aproximación a la conexión entre las ideologías políticas y los modelos de sociedad ideal. *Revista De Estudios Políticos* 128: 87–128.

———. 2022. Human Rights and/in *Utopia*. In *Oxford Handbook of Thomas More's Utopia*, ed. C. Shrank and P. Withington. Oxford: Oxford University Press.

Rawls, John. 1999a. *A Theory of Justice* [1971]. Cambridge, MA: Harvard University Press.

———. 1999b. *The Law of Peoples*. Cambridge, MA: Harvard University Press.

Sargent, Lyman Tower. 1982. Authority and Utopia: Utopianism in Political Thought. *Polity* 14: 565–584.

———. 1994. The Three Faces of Utopianism Revisited. *Utopian Studies* 5: 1–37.

Sargisson, Lucy. 2007. The Curious Relationship Between Politics and Utopia. In *Utopia, Method, Vision*, ed. T. Molin and R. Baccolini, 25–46. Bern: Peter Lang.

Stillman, Peter. 2001. Nothing Is, but What Is Not": Utopia as Practical Political Philosophy. In *The Philosophy of Utopia*, ed. B. Goodwin, 9–24. London: Frank Cass.

Animal Rights

José Eduardo Reis

INTRODUCTION

In *The New Ecological Order* (1995), the French philosopher Luc Ferry identifies three discrete trends of reflection and discussion, each underpinned
by a particular theorization of the relations that link living beings and the
environment. In a characterization of what he terms the "three ecologies,"
Ferry stresses the differential epistemological structure that each exhibits in
their respective attempts to infuse humanism with a greater degree of critical thinking and thereby transcend its long-term tendency toward dogmatism.
According to Ferry, the first of these ecological philosophies has long remained
wedded to an essentially anthropocentric perspective that affirms the duty
of humans to legally protect nature as long as the survival of the species is
not threatened as a result. The third position advocates the establishment
of a globally applicable "natural contract" that recognizes all beings and
phenomena of nature—animal, vegetable, and mineral—as subjects of law.
For Ferry, however, the question of animal rights can be located in a second
ecology that lies between the anthropic and ecocentric extremes of the conceptual continuum. Its radical utilitarian postulate of achieving the maximum
possible welfare rescinds the rights of the human being to exercise uncon-
tested sovereignty and hegemony over nature, and extends legal rights and
guarantees based on moral considerations to the whole animal kingdom, but
not, as the ecocentric vision advocates, to nature in its entirety.

J. E. Reis (✉)
University of Trás-os-Montes e Alto Douro, Vila Real, Portugal

P. Marks et al. (eds.), *The Palgrave Handbook of Utopian and Dystopian
Literatures*, https://doi.org/10.1007/978-3-030-88654-7_33

With the aim of renewing humanistic values and the Enlightenment principle of the human right to autonomy, Ferry declares his support for the first of the three ecologies (the only one he deigns to describe as "democratic"), criticizing all ecological movements inspired either by utilitarianism or by ecocentricity, reserving, in the latter case, his gravest condemnation for so-called "Deep Ecology."[1] One cannot conclude, however, that Ferry denies the existence of an ecological turning point, let alone rejects the human duty to preserve the environment and to assign rationally grounded rights to the entire phenomenology of nature. Rather, his theoretical perspective stresses the need to revisit and renew the doctrinal assumptions of humanism and, by doing so, develop a truly democratic conception of ecology that is immune to totalitarian ideologies. Consequently, it is from the perspective of "non-metaphysical humanism" (1995, xxix) that Ferry reflects on animal rights, designating the aforementioned philosophical positions on ecology as "Cartesian," "republican and humanist," and "utilitarian," respectively (28). The Cartesian tradition reduces all nonhuman beings to mere automata, to mechanical entities devoid of either any index of intelligence or sensory attribute, subject only to the laws of motion unless employed as instruments subordinate to the human will. The humanist and republican position, especially that informed by Rousseau and Kant, ascribes to the human being—hitherto considered as only the holder of rights—the duty not to inflict unnecessary suffering on animals. Finally, the utilitarian vision, by transcending "the supreme principle of anthropocentric humanism" (28), confers moral dignity on nonhuman animals.

ANIMAL RIGHTS AND UTOPIA: THE EPISTEMOLOGICAL BREAK

In the course of positing his typology of ecological thinking, Ferry refers to the 1894 monograph *Animal Rights Considered in Relation to Social Progress,* written by the English polymath and social reformer Henry Salt. Salt deploys Bentham's philosophical innovations to set out the major themes of what would become "zoophile literature": (i) recognition of the legal dignity of all animals both domestic and wild; (ii) repudiation of their suffering and death for the purposes of human sustenance or in laboratory experiments; (iii) rejection of hunting and sports that violate their physical integrity, and; (iv) denunciation of the use of their body parts (skin, fur, feathers, and so on) as ornaments and garments. The monograph's title subtly evokes the utopian impulse in Salt's political and social thinking. Bypassing predominantly sentimentalist and philanthropic positions, Salt identifies human feeding practices as culturally and ideologically determined, and on ethical and rational grounds proposes a vegetarian diet that avoids the suffering and death of animals. He does not, however, infer a principle that is logically demonstrable and irreducible, as is the case with the contemporary philosopher Peter Singer (to whose argument we will return later) who extends and generalizes *jus animalium* to the complex and diverse universe of sentient beings.

In his multifaceted reflection on animal rights Salt fashions his own utopian rationality out of the arguments advanced in both idealist philosophy and in campaigns for moral and civic improvement. First, he invokes Schopenhauer's critique of a Cartesian rationalism that denied the existence of any moral agency between humans and nonhumans, and Darwin's acknowledgment, on phylogenetic grounds, of psychomotor similarities between superior primates and humans. Then, in a critical reinterpretation of the Darwinian thesis of natural selection through the struggle for life, Salt adapted the method used in *Mutual Aid* (1902) by the Russian anarchist Peter Kropotkin of placing the universal principles of cooperation and solidarity on an equal footing with those of competition and conflict. Thus, just as the Russian revolutionary thinker argued that in human society and history "sociability is as much a law of nature as mutual struggle" (Salt 1894, 20), Salt believed it was possible to advocate a "consistent position towards the rights of men and of the lower animals alike, and to cultivate a broad sense of universal justice (not 'mercy') for all living things" (21). It is worth recalling that Kropotkin's natural law of sociability reflects the "broadest principles of universal compassion" (3), the evolution of which Salt traces in a brief genealogy of the ethical-philosophical origins of animal rights, focusing on the works of the "humanitarian philosophers of the Roman empire" (2) Seneca, Plutarch, and Porphyry, the Renaissance authors Erasmus and More, and in particular the Enlightenment scholars Voltaire and Rousseau, inspirers of the "great Revolution of 1789" (3).

In his suggestively titled fifth chapter "Sport or Amateur Butchery," Salt explicitly quotes More's *Utopia* (1516) and goes on to denounce the cruelty of hunting and of other sporting practices involving animals that the unthinking idol of tradition has legitimized. Moreover, his evocation of the French Revolution provides a nexus of correlation between earlier calls for greater human, women's and animal rights and—with remarkable utopian foresight, given the ideological conjuncture in which he was writing—their eventual attainment. Salt notes the determining role of the French Revolution in the formation of the concept of civic and moral rights as expressed by Thomas Paine in his *Rights of Man* (1791) and Mary Wollstonecraft in *A Vindication of the Rights of Woman* (1792) that challenged the very principles of authority and hierarchy. To these titles he adds a third, *The Vindication of the Rights of Brutes*, published anonymously in 1792 but attributed to the Platonist Thomas Taylor, who, in a malicious attempt to ridicule Wollstonecraft's thesis, eventually provided "a notable instance of how the mockery of one generation may become the reality of the next" (Salt 1894, 4). Salt's reforming drive and animal rights activism goes hand in hand with his commitment to advocating for the replacement of culturally dominant dietary habits and leads him to champion the ethical cause of vegetarianism. Tinged with Enlightenment utopianism, his "rationalist, socialist, pacifist and humanitarian" vision of the world (Hendrick 1977, 1) can already be detected in the last essay of his earlier collection, *A Plea for Vegetarianism & Other Essays* (1886), and is also reflected in the penultimate chapter of his later work, *The Logic of Vegetarianism: Essays & Dialogues* (1906). Their respective titles ("Vegetarianism and Social Reform" and "Vegetarianism as Related to Other Reforms") indicate that in order to accomplish the just and benign transformation of an unequal and iniquitous capitalist society, an answer to the "Great Food Question" will have to be found and made to cohere with the diverse solutions to all of its other complex problems (Salt 1886, 111).

Linking the integral emancipation of human beings to the emancipation of women, the so-called inferior races and all nonhuman animals, Salt, having censured "the blindness which can see in unity and kinship ... only difference and division between the human and the non-human race" prescribes the cure: a progressive broadening of our rational and humanitarian consciousness that would foster a growing sense that the lower animals are closely related to us, and therefore possess rights (1906, 105). For Salt, the necessary and sufficient conditions for vegetarianism reside in the moral equivalence between human and nonhuman animals: "just as there is no human rights where there is slavery, so there is no animal rights where there is eating of flesh" (Salt, 1906, 109). Salt challenges the dominant paradigm, foregrounding the moral sphere and shifting the emphasis in the debate from regulating animal welfare on sentimental grounds to affirming their legal rights on ethical grounds, so much so that the sociologist Keith Tester felt able to conclude that Salt's theoretical contribution was nothing less than an "epistemological break in modern knowledge" (Tester 2015, 149). Undertaken on the basis of the recognition that human and nonhuman animals are only variations of the same vital principle in their discrete qualities, Salt's thinking made it possible to overcome the anthropocentrism that for too long had promoted a dualistic and antinomic view of animals. It also gave him hope that a kind of ecocentric utopia could evolve, in which "the broadest principle of universal benevolence" was applied, corresponding to his almost messianic conviction that "the great republic of the future will not confine its beneficence to man" (Salt 1894, 90).

Animal Rights and the Utopian Function

In "Outlines of a Better World," an encyclopedic inventory of the myriad forms that hope may assume, Ernst Bloch demonstrates how utopia functions as a means of representing ideals and archetypes that presage concrete future possibilities. For Bloch, the "utopian function" (1995, 144) of the social dreamer's imagination operates not so much to compensate for what has disappeared, but to project into the future what has already manifested itself in the past as myth or symbol, ideally imagined, intuited or experienced by our predecessors. Thus, Salt's ecocentric and zoophilic utopian "Great Republic" presages the materialization of the archetypal "Golden Age, Paradise ... as something expected in the Some Day of time," to use Bloch's words (1995, 98). By making explicit the heuristic value or concrete functionality of utopia, it is possible, for example, to understand how the initial fragment of the poem

Metamorphoses, in which Ovid imagines a mythical time when human sustenance was assured without recourse to animal sacrifice. While obviously not
having the same thematic scope or sharing the same formal intention as Salt's
monograph, it might be read from a Blochian perspective as heralding an
ideal zoophilic republican order and as rehearsing the thesis that the rights of
all animals—human and nonhuman—should be placed on an equal footing.
Ovid's depiction of the innocent vegetarianism of the Golden Age where
"Men were content with nature's food enforced, and strawberries on the
mountain side and cherries and the clutching bramble's fruit, and fallen acorns
from Jove's spreading tree" (Ovid, 1986, Book I, verses 104–107), corresponds to the biblical image of Paradise, with human and nonhuman creatures
coexisting in harmony on a frugivorous diet. A careful reading of Genesis
reveals that the description of the Garden of Eden corresponds to an ecocentric eutopia in which animals, while not granted rights as such, nevertheless
enjoy the grace inherent in the divine act of the creation of life. Moreover,
after the expulsion there is a shift from an initial frugivorous diet (Gen. 1:29)
to an omnivorous one, as if the ontological fall represents a breaking of the
order as originally conceived, and as if the moral frailty of humans mutates
into a boundless capacity for violence against nature that expressed itself, in
particular, in an unbridled willingness to survive at the expense of the animal
kingdom.

Regardless of the dominant Judeo-Christian views on the ontological status
of nonhuman animals, it is worth noting that in the introduction to *A New
System of Vegetable Cookery*, a vegetarian manual first published anonymously
in 1821, the reader is recommended to practice "abstinence from animal
foods," an injunction that can be seen as an operationalization of the function of utopian knowledge, as envisaged and explicated by Bloch. The author,
identified only as "A Lady" in the second edition of 1829, was in fact Martha
Brotherton, a member of the English Bible Christian Church, a congregation
inspired by Swedenborgian mysticism. Drawing selectively on biblical quotations, and ignoring the ambiguities of the Holy Book's dietary prescriptions,
Mrs. Brotherton emphasizes those passages that have a potentially vegetarian
interpretation, and seemingly implies that the rejection of a carnivorous diet
is a precondition for restoring the world to an Edenic state ordered along
Christian lines. While, in her view, meat-eating endorses—indeed requires—
animal cruelty and promotes poor health and early death among humans,
"[o]n the contrary, vegetable food clears the intellect, preserves innocence,
[and] increases compassion and love" to the extent that the vegetarian diet can
even be regarded as "the most effectual means of reforming mankind" (1812,
4, 14). Indeed, the proselytizing activities of this singular British Christian
religious denomination in favor of a diet without animal protein directly and
actively contributed to the founding of the English Vegetarian Society in 1847.
Thus ethical vegetarianism, founded on respect for animal life and as advocated
from a Christian perspective by Martha Brotherton, functions as a determining

force in the foundation of an ideal human order, rather than operating, in the manner of Henry Salt's exhortations, as a merely contributory factor.

From different paths of knowledge, diverse historical conjunctures, varied cultural traditions, and discrete political circumstances, the "utopian function"—the imagining and promotion of a common general good that progressively embraces all living beings—manifests itself through discursive strategies each indelibly marked by the author's particular intellectual profile and talents. One such strategy, that of irony, is a rhetorical device used abundantly by Thomas More in his *Utopia*, and amply employed by the seventeenth-century French writer Cyrano de Bergerac in *The Comical History of the States and Empires of the Worlds of the Moon and Sun* (1657). Cyrano, an Epicurean philosopher who believed that all forms of life deserve respect, constructs a plot replete with comic irony, in which a human narrator (who shares the author's name) recounts his extraterrestrial adventures, including his arraignment before an avian court on charges of "being a Man" (Bergerac 1687, 117). The irony of this denunciation of humanity's hegemony and totalitarian arrogance in regard to all other creatures is to be found in the way in which the above-mentioned scene provides a mirror image of mankind's assumed judicial superiority. But here it is not the human who judges other living creatures—as has historically been the case in pre-modern France, where legal proceedings were occasionally brought against farm animals, vermin, and household pests—but the human being who is allegorically judged by birds in the "Court of Nature." Put another way, rather than the received wisdom that the paragons of traditional thinking purvey, in which humanity is the "Lord of Nature" and holds sway over the whole animal world, Cyrano, by recognizing that all sentient animals have the right to life, is driven by the utopian function in critical and proto-ecocentric thought to denounce and satirically deconstruct the perverse effects of an anthropocentric conception of the world. In response to the pious and trite arguments of a jay—the human's defence council—he, as a representative of humankind, is placed under scrutiny and accused of overweening violence and disruptive behavior toward all of creation. He so persistently violates the order of Creation that the avian prosecutor asks rhetorically whether humanity's very existence is not a mistake of which nature herself should repent:

> I think, Gentlemen, it never was yet doubted, but that all Creatures are produced by our common Mother, to live together in Society. Now if I prove, that Man seems to be Born only to break it; shall I not make it out, that he going contrary to the end of his Creation, deserves that Nature should repent herself of her work? (Bergerac 1687, 118)

Hence the prosecutor's assertion that it can be legitimately concluded that the murderous and voracious conduct of humans is barbaric because it is contrary to the principle of equality between species. Notwithstanding the fact that humanity had ceased to practice it, the principle was nonetheless a constituent principle of the republican regime, the very same that prevailed on the island of Utopia as described by More and that in this allegory can be read as the political equivalent of the Golden Age or of Paradise in its original form.

ANIMAL RIGHTS AND ANIMAL LIBERATION

It is precisely the principle of equality that provides the fundamental premise on which the Australian philosopher Peter Singer bases his argument in his now classic text on animal rights and animal studies, *Animal Liberation* (1975). Singer uses arguments of a rationalist nature to present and develop the core of his thesis in favor of animal liberation. In line with utilitarian moral thought, he extends to the world of "non-human animals" the principle that no prejudice nor any social and ideological discrimination "based on [an] arbitrary characteristic like race or gender" should be accepted (Singer 2002, xxii). By analogy with the terms used to identify socially discriminatory attitudes such as racism and sexism, he adopts the term "speciesism" (which he acknowledges is not a felicitous one) to designate "a prejudice or attitude of bias in favor of the interests of one's own species and against those of members of other species" (6). Basically, Singer argues that just as it is ethically unacceptable that a higher degree of intelligence should confer on one human being the right to use another of his kind for his own benefit, there is no sound moral basis for humans to use animals for their own ends. Singer thus extends the basic moral utilitarian principle of "equal consideration of interests" to animals, arguing that the prerequisite for defining "interest" is precisely the capacity to suffer and to enjoy happiness. "The capacity for suffering and enjoyment is, however, not only necessary but also sufficient for us to say that a being has interests—at an absolute minimum, an interest in not suffering" (7). The moral principle of according all creatures' interests equal consideration therefore relates directly to the issue of the moral status of animals which, in turn, raises the question of their rights. However, it should be made clear—and this is where the philosophical argument becomes more complex—that, *grosso modo,* the extent to which we recognize animal rights will vary in scope and depth according to which of the following three interpretations we adopt: (a) that which springs from our attributing only a *minimum* moral status to an animal's self-interest in not suffering (what we might call the "animal rights" argument regarding moral status); (b) an intermediate position deriving from our acceptance that equality of interests exists between *all* creatures (that is, the "interest-based" argument); and (c) the most radical interpretation, according to which animal rights must be protected at all costs, even if this is disadvantageous to human beings (what has been called the "utility-trumping" argument). In order to deal with questions that, on a purely theoretical level, can lead to existential anxieties that are aberrant if not altogether specious—such as having to decide between two animals, one human and one nonhuman, knowing that by saving one the other will die—rationalist and anti-speciesist advocates of animal rights are obliged to adopt a position in which human and nonhuman interests are considered to be unequal. This is achieved by applying a "sliding scale of unequal interests" that in fact combines two distinct scales: first, a phylogenetic one that ranks living creatures according to the stage of complexity their evolution has reached, privileging those that most closely resemble the human species; second, a scale in which moral consideration ranges from a maximum (accorded to the human being) to a minimum (attributed to non-sentient beings).

Nevertheless, it has to be recognized that all this theoretical endeavor, all these attempts to put onto the agenda of Western ethics the senseless animal suffering brought about by our consumption of animal-based protein, are little more than a updating of an old anti-speciesist, utopian perspective. This was constantly voiced both underground and in parallel to the hegemonic speciesist perspective, and manifested itself as a call for the voluntary and conscious adoption of a nutritional regime that does not contravene nonhuman animals' fundamental interest in not suffering. It is therefore quite natural that a theme of this importance—translated into a demand for a better life for all—be appropriated by a heterodox imaginary or by some anticipatory utopian consciousness. In lieu of a conventional conclusion, in the reflections below the influence of Zen Buddhism on twentieth century English and American literature is examined through the lens of animal rights.

CONCLUSION: ANIMAL RIGHTS AND THE MINDFUL UTOPIA OF THE PRESENT: A LITERARY EXAMPLE

His now somewhat dated exegesis, *Zen in English Literature and Oriental Classics* (1942 [1941]), was the first of a set of monographs on Zen that the Orientalist Reginald Horace Blyth wrote for an English readership. It influenced, in some cases marginally and in others more decisively, some of the early works by leading Anglo-American authors—notably Aldous Huxley, and the Beat Generation writers Gary Snyder, Jack Kerouac, and Allen Ginsberg—in which an anticipatory utopian literary consciousness could be discerned. Blyth's volume offers a unique and idiosyncratic model of comparativist hermeneutics and critical reflection that draws on examples from a number of discrete cultural fields, providing support and elucidation for those studying non-attachment "mindfulness" as pursued and experienced in the annals of the traditional spiritual practice of Zen Buddhism.[2] Though Blyth's essay develops the many facets of non-attachment in great detail to illustrate the presence of full consciousness conveyed by literature, the author marshals other evidence and examples to support the development of his argument. One of the themes he takes up is consciousness in terms of the respect we should accord nonhuman animal life. Confessing that his interest and commitment to Zen Buddhism was awakened by his love of animals, Blyth seeks to establish the vital relationship between love for sentient creatures and spiritual discipline, insisting that freeing ourselves from the evil that humans often inflict on them can only be achieved if an enlightened consciousness—made present by the utopian imaginary—treats all of them, regardless of the species to which they belong—in a manner that transcends the illusion of self and insists on "an undivided, uninterrupted, whole-hearted, instinctive action" (Blyth 1942, 396) of indiscriminate sympathy for its existence.

Touching first on the ontological and ethical status of nonhuman animal life in different religious traditions and in ancient and modern thought, Blyth then dwells on the oriental doctrine of "ahimsa" (non-killing) and its place in Jain and Buddhist spirituality, seeking to go beyond a sentimental and therefore limited appreciation of the animal world and demand that we consciously and indiscriminately accord any form of sentient life the "whole-hearted instinctive action" it deserves. Blyth resorts to humor on at least three occasions to stress his argument: (i) when he appeals to his readers to "Consider the rats of the sewer, how they fight and squeal," or to "Consider the bacteria of typhus how they grow and multiply," he is paraphrasing the words of Christ (403); (ii) when he asks why it was that the Lord Buddha held up a flower and not "a cheese-rind or an old boot" (403), he is referring to the story of Siddhartha Gautama's so-called silent teaching[3]; (iii) and when he quotes a stanza from the poem "Bird" by the English metaphysical poet Henry Vaughan—"For each enclosed spirit is a star / Enlightening his own little sphere / Whose light, though fetched and borrowed from far / Both mornings makes and evenings there"—only to add that the same sentiment should apply to "centipedes, tapeworms, fungus and all the rest" (403). By using such a provocative and deliberately disconcerting tone, Blyth seeks to formulate a comprehensive truth in which the idealized representation of nature can be reconciled with the demystifying conception of nature as a cruel reality that is often hostile to the human condition. "If," he writes bitterly, "our attitude towards Nature, especially towards animals, is false, nothing can be true for us, or we for truth" (403). For Blyth, one of the most consistent expressions of this "truth" is the equanimity we should display toward all sentient creatures, including insects which, though often proving to be tenacious disruptors of the well-being of the dominant human species, nevertheless fulfil their destiny in the unfathomable order of universal creation. The haiku "I am sorry, my house is so small, / But practice your jumping, / Please, Mr. Flea!" (409), by the Japanese poet Issa (1763–1828), is one example. Another is a poem with a lesser dramatic effect, "Listening to the Insects," by the Chinese poet Po Chū-I (772–847), who was known in Japan as Hakurakuten: "Long is the night: unseen amid the gloom, the voices of insects. / It is the gathering rain, the darkness of autumn. / Do they dread that in my despair I shall sleep / my last sleep? / Their insistent voices deepen, they come nearer, and yet / more near" (407). In these poets' expressions of concern and appreciation for insects, Blyth sees a manifestation of the "Buddha nature," or of a fully developed consciousness devoid of personal preferences or value judgments, and guided by the recognition that love has an all-encompassing, leveling, and comprehensive effect. If, as is the case in the common representation of nature, sentient beings are what they are as a result of the judgments by which humans measure them, then on the plane of Zen consciousness, they are what they are in their pure and necessary existence, with no need for whys and wherefores, and entirely in conformity with the Buddha's understanding that all is well and is "Good [sic] without comparison or difference" (411). From the Zen perspective, Blyth argues that this is the difference between being and not being fully conscious (that is, enlightened or unenlightened), a distinction he illustrates toward the end of his reflection on the presence in English and Eastern literature of the Zen spirit in our understanding of the animal world:

> [J]ust as the hard horny hands of the young farmer do not become soft even though he falls in love with the gentle village maiden, so the man who is insensitive to the affection and charm of dogs, remains so after his enlightenment. Only, the use of his hard hands, the use of his hard mind, changes, since in both, self has decreased in quantity and importance, and other things correspondingly and inevitably increase in value and significance. What a strange emotion I feel when a man pats my dog on the head and says, with a smile, "I don't like dogs very much!". (411)

In many respects, reflecting on animal rights requires us to make an intellectual journey during which philosophical questions are continually summoned up—primarily ethical and ontological ones, but also those of a cultural, sociological, and political nature—which, due to their breadth and depth, intersect the multiple dimensions of ideal consciousness and utopian pragmatism. The widening of the notion of rights to nonhuman animals can and should be debated but it must be subjected, as it is by its most qualified defenders, to critical examination. Nevertheless, achieving true animal rights may ultimately coincide with the ontological possibility that is repeatedly referred to in the Bible, namely that humanity would return to the life it once had in Paradise and/or that all living beings would finally be reconciled. Could it be that the achievement of equality of rights for all sentient creatures is one of the "symbol-intentions of the Absolute" that Bloch identifies in his *Principle of Hope* and that he considered central to our attainment of the *summum bonum* or "highest good" (1995, 305)?

Acknowledgements The author would like to thank Chris Gerry for his contribution on the English editing of this essay.

NOTES

1. The term "Deep Ecology" refers to the ecocentric environmental movement founded by the Norwegian philosopher Arne Naess in 1972, in opposition to the anthropocentric current in ecology which emphasized structural reforms in both the political and economic spheres. See Timothy Clark (2011), Literature and the Environment. Cambridge: Cambridge University Press, 23.

2. In the context of Western culture and cognitive psychology, "mindfulness" designates an ancient meditative practice originally accreted to the Buddha's teachings, with a view to cultivating a mental attitude of non-discrimination and non-rejection in place of an attachment to wishes, beliefs, and preconceived ideas.
3. See Reps and Senzaki (1994 [1957], 173–174).

References

Bergerac, C. 1687. *The Comical History of the States and Empires of the World of the Sun*. trans. A. Lovell, A. M. London. Printed for Henry Rhodes, next door to Swan-Tavern, near Bride Lane in Fleet-Street.

Bloch, Ernst. 1995. *The Principle of Hope*. trans. Neville Plaice, Stephen Plaice, and Paul Knight. Cambridge: MIT Press.

Blyth, R.H. 1942. *Zen in English Literature and Oriental Classics*. Tokio: Hokuseido Press.

Brotherton, Martha. 1812. *A New System of Domestic Cookery by a Lady*. London: S. Hamilton.

Clark, Timothy. 2011. *Literature and the Environment*. Cambridge: Cambridge University Press.

Ferry, Luc. 1995. *The New Ecological Order*. trans. Carol Volk. Chicago: University of Chicago Press.

Hendrick, George. 1977. *Henry Salt: Humanitarian, Reformer and Man of Letters*. Urbana: University of Illinois Press.

More, Thomas. 1989 [1516]. In *Utopia* (p. 73). ed. George Logan and Robert M. Adams. Cambridge: Cambridge University Press.

Ovid. 1986. *Metamorphoses*. trans. A. D. Melville. Oxford: Oxford University Press.

Reps, Paul & Nyogen Senzaki, comp. & trans. 1994 [1957]. *Zen Flesh and Zen Bones*. Boston: Shambala.

Salt, Henry. 1886. *A Plea for Vegetarianism and Other Essays*. Manchester: The Vegetarian Society.

———. 1894. *Animals' Rights Considered in Relation to Social Progress*. New York & London: Macmillan & Co.

———. 1906. *The Logic of Vegetarianism*. London: George Bell and Sons.

Singer, Peter. 2002 [1975]. *Animal Liberation*. New York: Harper Collins.

Tester, Keith. 2015. *Animals and Society: The Humanity of Animal Rights*. London: Routledge.

Food

Etta M. Madden

Introduction

By showing us how societies could be organized to feed everyone adequately
and efficiently, utopias suggest that hunger, agro-ecological devastation and
domestic drudgery are neither inevitable nor eternal.

–Warren Belasco, *The Future of Food*.

We can't expect our food of the future to be produced only by traditional
farming families in rural areas.

–Will Allen, *The Good Food Revolution*.[1]

More than a decade ago, food historian and theorist Warren Belasco summed
up a view of utopian food practices that could have been written almost
anytime during the last two centuries, if not before. Belasco's touchstones
of scarcity, environmental distress, and gender and class labor issues associated
with food production have been commonplaces of utopian and dystopian literature since at least the time that Thomas More coined the term "utopia" in his
satirical literary account in 1516. Additionally, however, as this chapter demonstrates, an important topic that Belasco leaves out is the place of commensality,
or eating together. A few years after Belasco's book appeared, food activist

E. M. Madden (✉)
Missouri State University, Springfield, MI, USA

Will Allen embraced community building through shared consumption. At the same time Allen acknowledged that food production methods must change. These topics in Allen's book demonstrate that utopian foodways are about more than physical sustenance. Meeting nutritional needs is essential, but it is only one part of the social dreaming that literature presents. Whether utopian or dystopian, the literature promotes social change in almost all aspects of eating practices.

Utopias of Abundance

The earliest stories of utopia, predating printed literature, include tales of abundance without human intervention. Labor was unnecessary for alimentary fulfilment. Without technology—spades, hoes, knives, or fires—humans lived surrounded by fruits of the earth and at peace with animals, whether in the Eden myth of the biblical Genesis or in Greek literature collected by Athenaeus. In the Middle Ages, such tales of the west came to be labeled the Cockaigne, or Cokaygne, from the Middle English or Old French for "plenty." As one medieval poem explains:

> In Cokaygne we drink and eat
> Freely without care and sweat,
> ...
> There no lack of food or cloth,
> There no man or woman wroth.
> ...
> All is sporting, joy and glee,
> Lucky the man that there may be.
> There are rivers broad and fine,
> Of oil, milk, honey and of wine
> ...
> Every man takes what he will,
> As of right, to eat his fill.
> All is common to young and old,
> To stout and strong, to meek and bold."[2]

Such visions of abundance likely emerge from contexts of scarcity and represent the desires of people at the bottom of the social hierarchy.[3] By the sixteenth century such dreams build upon scarcity appeared in Thomas More's *Utopia*, the imaginary civilization whose name, drawn from two Greek words, designates both "good place" and "no place." Food scarcity, abundance, and commensality play significant roles in More's literary creation.

From Scarcity to Equality?

More's first food references appear within the context of production, poverty, and greed, as his characters, the traveler Raphael Hytholoday, More, and More's friend Peter Giles discuss the contrasting lives of those in England and those on the imaginary island, Utopia, which Hytholoday has visited. Rampant crime in England—especially theft—and the overtaxed prison system are the result of poverty, begat by greed. The first cause of these crimes is pastureland having been raped by grazing livestock, grown ever more numerous due to already-wealthy landowners' selfish desires. The now non-arable land tracts, ever-increasing in size, have reduced the amount of grain and other foods raised to feed the hungry. Hunger feeds the theft. If peoples' basic nutritional needs are met, the account argues, other social ills will disappear.

In Utopia, by contrast, food production occurs through a rotation of people through commonly owned fields. Rather than being assigned ownership or laboring at birth, due to social class, everyone rotates through production. Those more inclined to bookish practices may opt out of physical labor, but this decision is one of inclination rather than class. Hytholoday also adds pictures of idyllic consumption at table. Meals are both entertaining and educational—all pleasant, daily enjoyment.

Yet during the pleasant common consumption, women are excluded from the main tables. Although there is neither "head table" nor age segregation, as younger people learn from the older people through their modeled manners and conversation, women are marginalized. They sit with the extremely young children, who will need constant attention and assistance. More's pictures of utopian foodways fail to address inequities associated with gender difference, even as they provide a social leveling for food production so that consumption is more equitable.

In fact, an hierarchical approach infiltrates other aspects of food production and consumption in Utopia, specifically with references to "slaves" (criminals and some people taken in war), women and children. Women do the final preparation, cooking, and "ordering" of the tables. And slaves do the dirty work of animal slaughtering, part of the regular food production, which occurs outside the city walls for hygiene reasons. The hierarchy, then, extends to dominance over non-human life as well. Although there are references to people who abstain from flesh for religious purposes, most consume animals and their by-products. In fact, an incubator for eggs—the only reference to technological innovation—indicates the mass production and consumption of either eggs or chickens.

In More's *Utopia* there are no simple pills that people ingest in order to *not* spend time at table, and there are no devices that radically simplify food production in the kitchen. By the nineteenth-century industrial revolution, however, literary works and social experiments would include visions of technological progress that would alleviate aches and pains associated with food production and consumption as they addressed equality and scarcity.

Individual and Communal Visions: Secular and Sacred

On the heels of More's work, other visions suggested social structures that would revise political monarchies and religious institutions. Some advocated alternative communities with a spiritual inclination, while others espoused secular views and a more individualized approach. Literature associated with these reforms often provided guidelines or rigid strictures for food practices. Some envisioned a Cartesian dualism that separated mind and spirit from body, giving them freedom to eat whatever they liked or required that they "deny the flesh" any pleasures, such as rich food, meat, and alcohol. Some advocated a nostalgic pastoralism, reaching back with a simplistic back-to-land and closer-to-nature approach that associated "progress" and "civilization" with a human "fall from Eden."

One example of this type of regressive vision emerged in Thomas Morton's sixteenth-century satire, *New English Canaan*, which glorified indigenous Americans and their eating habits for English readers. The indigenous people were "not served in dishes of plate with sauces to procure appetite," Morton explained. They had no need of such stimuli. Instead, "the rarity of the aire" and "the medicinable quality of the sweete herbes" contributed to healthy digestion.[4] Benjamin Franklin would similarly idealize eating and drinking with a satirical voice in his autobiography, which modeled individual success as a means of building the healthy social organism. He advocated "temperance," vegetarianism, and water-drinking for their contributions to moral and economic success. Morton's and Franklin's ideals continued in the nineteenth century with authors such as Henry David Thoreau, who supported a vegetarian life. He wrote of consuming animal flesh, coffee and even tea, as manifestations of human "abdomen" desires.[5] For Sylvester Graham, as for Thoreau, the simple diet was associated with spirituality. Graham's diet, consisting of vegetables and whole grains (including what later came to be known as the "Graham cracker"), also excluded alcohol, tea, and coffee.

Believed to suppress fleshly desires, Graham's diet appealed to the communal, celibate Shakers, formally named the United Society of Believers in Christ's Second Appearing. They had journeyed to the North American colonies in part because of their founder Ann Lee's visions of fertile abundance. Growing from a group surviving by the good will of others in the eighteenth century to producers of agricultural and artisanal products such as cider, which they marketed and sold widely in the nineteenth century, the Shakers experimented with food practices. When the Graham diet was introduced, however, complaints arose among habituated meat eaters and drinkers of Shaker cider as well as among the cooks, who had to learn new methods of serving the community. The practice was short-lived, although their commensality was not.[6]

Even secular communal groups, such as one imagined by imprisoned French revolutionary, Étienne Cabet, had highly regulated food practices. As

Cabet's *Voyage in Icaria* explained, the community established laws based on "good" and "bad" qualities in foods, noting which were "necessary, useful and agreeable" as well as "the most suitable ways of preparing each" and regulating the production and distribution of those deemed "good." Meal times and locations of "common dinners" with music, flowers, and ample and delicious foods contributed to the equitable distribution in this fictional utopia.[7] After the work's appearance, a community of *citoyens* calling themselves Icarians gathered to adhere to these ideals and emigrated from France to parts of the US.

The Icarians' practices likely did not live up to Cabet's ideals. Other nineteenth-century literary works note the gaps between the ideal and real, moving them into the category of dystopia that would explode as a genre in the twentieth century.[8] For example, Louisa May Alcott's autobiographical *Transcendental Wild Oats* (1873) and Nathaniel Hawthorne's *Blithedale Romance* (1852) point, respectively, to issues of scarcity when pastoral nostalgia triumphs over technology and to ongoing gendered labor distinctions. Alcott's satirically conveyed memories of childhood in her father's short-lived Fruitlands community in western Massachusetts in 1843 include an initial "frugal" meal of "roasted potatoes, brown bread and water, in two plates, a tin pan, and one mug." As one leader explained, "Neither sugar, molasses, milk, butter, cheese, nor flesh" were to be consumed; "nothing is to be admitted which has caused wrong or death to man or beast." The Transcendentalist community, elevating the spiritual over the material, would not use animals to plow, nor would they eat root vegetables. Such beliefs posed a challenge to women in the kitchen as well as to men tending the fields.[9]

Hawthorne's novel, based on his time just outside Boston at the experimental Brook Farm, presents a circle of previous city dwellers eating at a rustic supper table, where the narrator pretends to be satisfied with simple fare, such as "bread and buttermilk" at a common kitchen table rather than the after-dinner sherry and cigars, taken in his private room, that he has left behind. Yet in this imagined utopian community, the women labored with domestic chores. As the tragic heroine Zenobia explains, "To bake, to boil, to roast, to fry, to stew –... these, I suppose, must be feminine occupations for the present." It is "a pity," the narrator explains, "that the kitchen, and the house-work generally, cannot be left out" of the community's "system."[10] Literary utopias later in the century, especially those written by women, would begin to depict technological escapes from such dystopian labor.

Pastoral Nostalgia and Technological Visions

Utopian food visions of the last century and a half may be organized into two categories: those romanticizing technological progress and others idealizing pastoral regress. For example, in the late nineteenth century, Mary Bradley Lane's *Mizora* (1880–1881), a feminist utopia, advocated for scientific productions such as synthetic meat and "dairy" products and even bread made from the stone waste of marble quarries. Lane's women also used science to alter color, flavor, longevity, and seeds. This emphasis on technology was more typical of the period than "outlier," pastoral views such as William Dean Howells's, *A Traveler from Altruria* (1894), which decried urban filth and poverty. Many works in the vein of Lane's celebrated "technological agrarianism," which linked scientific advancement to positive results instead of negative ones. Similarly, in Charlotte Perkins Gilman's well-known *Herland*, although the vegetarian women eat healthily of their own fruits and nuts, they are not ignorant of grafting and other scientific interventions that sustain them.[11] While Lane's and Gilman's all-female worlds may seem highly speculative and unattainable, Edgar Chambless's *Roadtown* (1910) more realistically bridges the "the relationship between nature and technology, city and countryside." Within his fictional landscape, food travels fewer miles and humans labor less in its production. From farm, to table, to disposal, to cleanup—food moves only a short distance. All three authors capture "'the needs of the individual biological body'" and "'our fundamental connection with the environment'" as well as "our indebtedness to science and technology.'" That is, while utopian literature may be dichotomized into "natural/artificial" or "pastoral/technological" binaries, the realities are not so. Most food production entails even simple technology—such as knife or fire.[12]

Nonetheless, the binaries have remained. For example, in H. G. Wells's *The Food of the Gods* (1904), Boomfood produces larger chickens but also creates "giant humans." Harry Harrison's *Make Room! Make Room!* (1966) includes "Soylent Green," made from "recycled motor oil, plankton, white blubber and algae." The novel's film version, which took the name of the food, includes "recycled dead humans" in the mix.[13] Two elements of this inventive food product merit note. First, these elements might be classified as waste products by many in the world's civilized cultures. Yet white blubber, algae, and plankton are important nutrients for some ethnic groups and species. Second, with its vibrant color which generally signifies healthy life, Soylent Green here takes on the opposite connotation. The tale upends western expectations of good food into dystopian food.

A more recent work that plays off the "Soylent Green" tradition, juxtaposing the natural and the technological, is Robin Sloan's *Sourdough*, which features the blended all-in-one nutritive shake, the Slurry. Like Hawthorne's and Alcott's works, the narrative could be called a utopian satire, or a dystopian vision set in a very real place—the San Francisco Bay area. In Sloan's imaginative account, the Slurry reduces all need for shopping and cooking. The highly branded and marketed "meal" allows inventive programmers of Silicon Valley to stay at work while they eat. Yet the narrator heroine fulfils her otherwise vacuous life as a programmer by learning to bake bread from an ancient strain of sourdough, while also falling in love with one of the men who has transported the vibrant yeast across space and time, from its ancient, pastoral "home" halfway around the globe. Sloan's *Sourdough* illustrates not only the pastoral-technological tension but also that food is much more than nutrition alone. It is connected to memories, traditions, people, and place. Simple organisms such as yeast draw from their local environment, combine themselves with grain, dairy products and like to create unique flavors in bread, cheese, wine, and beer. Consuming such foods and even producing them signifies connections with others across space and time.

Hospitality & Commensality: Food as "Bridge" in Speculative Fiction and Film

These familiar elements of shared meals and carefully crafted "homemade" foods tap into the nostalgia of relationships and care, combining them with a hopeful vision of what might be maintained in the future. Even in the imaginary worlds of some recent films, where food production has otherwise drastically changed, the "traditional" and the nostalgic lie side by side with the futuristic. In the Matrix and China Miéville's *Perdido Street Station*, for example, "the narrative function of familiarizing the unfamiliar" occurs in an otherwise strange setting through known cultural practices, such as a shared meal or baking cookies. Even if the food is unfamiliar, the practice of sharing it becomes "a bridging substance" in a world of estrangement.[14]

Food plays a similar role in speculative fiction of the last two decades. In women's literature, in particular, the hospitality of welcoming a stranger winds through such works as Toni Morrison's *Paradise* (1998), where a "convent" full of victimized women are soothed by shared food. Connie, the community's new "great mother" figure, prepares bountiful spreads that feed bodies as well as souls. The town's communal Oven "no longer functions to feed anyone," but the convent's kitchen and cook offer food to "anyone who walks in, no matter what she is hungry for."[15] Food becomes more than a means of survival. Morrison's shared meals, more nostalgic and less futuristic than some feminist speculative fiction, remind readers that even while foodways change, the relationships built by commensality remain essential. The novel's final scene, where two characters lie in each other's arms amidst a trash-littered beach, highlights the bonding and bridging as most important, even when consumption and waste are realities of the surrounding world.

Samuel Delany's "Driftglass" (1966) also foregrounds food production, consumption, and commensal bridge-building amidst a world of destruction and waste. As the title suggests, the tale's through line is beauty made from waste and destruction. Scraps of colored glass collected from the seaside sand stand in synecdochically for the main character Cal's life and body. Damaged by an earlier work accident on the coast of a Brazilian fishing village, Cal represents creatures who appear altered and not fully human, as Delany creatively imagines genetic modification. The tale describes how corporations modify humans considered less valuable into creatures with gills and an added third eye that serves as an underwater lens. These "amphimen" are able to work under the water for extended periods, laying a giant cable to provide power for oil wells, "undersea mines and farms," all to advance society. While the techno-logical progress is destroying individuals physically, even while it "improves" them for supposed social good, it fragments families and communities. But Delany suggests they might be restored partially through empathy and gift exchange centred upon food.

Cal, for example, had spent his first ten "formative" years in a farming collective in Denmark. He now exhibits his communal concerns in this fishing village halfway around the world. In a gesture of empathy, he offers a gift of food and builds an emotional bridge with the young, beautiful, and emotion-ally wounded Ariel. She "husbands"—like a sheep herder or vine tender—the "deep down creatures" being unsettled by the Marine Reclamation Division, whose workers are laying the underwater cable. Ariel extends a gift to Cal by inviting him to a big beach bonfire, celebrating with cooking and feasting prior to the laying of the cable that Cal had tried to lay when his damaging accident occurred. The women fry shrimp netted by the Brazilian village's long-time fishermen. Later, they grill a gigantic fish that the younger hero Tork spears. In collective effort, other fishermen bring the bound creature to the surface. The communal meal elicits empathy and nostalgia for feasting with friends and family and for fresh, local food, even as it places the scene in the midst of tragic environmental destruction brought on by technological advances.

The shared meals provide a contrasting image of hope in an otherwise story of despair. The story's final lines focus on the much older and disfigured Cal inviting the young and beautiful Ariel into his home for a local avocado "better than any they grow in California." He also offers her a cup of tea—a gesture that marks this moment as one bridging tradition and nostalgia with the freshness of the present. Even if read as misogynistic—an older male taking advantage of a younger and emotionally vulnerable female—the scene captures the commensality and gift giving that mark the tale as hopeful. Hope reigns when creatures acknowledge each others' emotional and physical needs with empathy.

Margaret Atwood illustrates similar food themes in her MaddAddam trilogy, as the volumes present technological crises emblematic of dystopian life. People eat SecretBurgers and drink Happicuppas while pigoons and rakunks roam the earth. The second volume, *The Year of the Flood*, especially reflects these topics. Set twenty-five years after a decimating viral flood has wiped out almost all humans and forced a few to figure out survival strategies, the book culminates with a symbolic evening "feast"—almost void of food and drink. The date is the Feasts of Saint Julian's and All Souls, a traditional celebration that evokes for the heroine Ren a wave of memories of world-making, when children would "glean" garbage to create their own "Cosmos." Now Ren and survivors Toby, Amanda, Jimmy and two considered their enemies, the Painballers, sit around a fire, fortunate to be alive. Toby has concocted "a soup from… leftovers of the rakunk," wild mustard greens, and "dried botanicals." Normally not flesh eaters, they ask forgiveness of the animal for preparing to consume it. Toby has given Amanda water with honey and herbs to fight her dehydration, she has fed Jimmy a spoon of honey to ease the pain of his fever, and she serves the soup to everyone—even the enemy Painballers who have brutalized Amanda. All six share from the two cups they have, as Toby asks them to forget the past and to "be grateful for this food." Ren forgives Jimmy, who "broke her heart," and helps him drink. After passing the cups, the survivors hear "the sound of many people singing," approaching through the darkness.[16]

Atwood's volume ends, then, not simply with food scarcity—gleaning what wild greens there are and consuming technologically created species—but with survival through willingness to cook, to share, and to forgive. The circle of six expands into a larger circle—not with the "people" they expect, but another species that exemplifies a future world of change. These final pages are not an ending then but the beginning of the third volume, presenting the close relationship between utopian hope and dystopian despair. They remind readers that the hope only exists and persists with visions that revise such dualistic views of good and evil, acceptable and unacceptable, food and people, animals and humans. Such simple binaries do not sustain survival. In an even more optimistic move, Atwood gave the third book in the series a hopefulness through interspecies communication, scenes of eating and storytelling, and egg symbolism, which also plays an important role in *The Handmaid's Tale* (1985). The egg represents breakfast, "reproduction and sustainability," all signs of hope for a new day and a new future.[17]

MEMOIRS, NON-FICTION AND SYMPOSIA: PAST, PRESENT, AND FUTURE

Outside these fictional worlds, many memoirs, non-fiction works, conferences, and symposia of the last two decades have emphasized utopian food practices with a nostalgic desire for shared meals and local production, even while acknowledging the necessity for embracing change. For example, Michael Pollan's numerous books and Barbara Kingsolver's *Animal, Vegetable, Miracle: A Year of Food Life* (2007) ring with "social dreaming" as the authors advocate for changes in food practices.[18] Perhaps more radical than Kingsolver or Pollan, former professional athlete Will Allen advocates for a "good food revolution" that employs new technologies of production. His work, partially memoir, partially prophetic jeremiad, taps nostalgically into memories of his mother's and his stepfather's traditions of self-sustenance in the South and the urban metropolis of D.C. in the Jim Crow era as he glorifies their hearty work ethic and sharing of meals. They contributed to his successes as a professional athlete and salesman for Proctor and Gamble as well as his more recent triumphs with Growing Power, a venture that cultivates young people's self-esteem while grounding them in urban agriculture. The organization imagines new futures by generating nutrients through food waste. Organic compost is the "black gold" that feeds the soil and generates energy.[19] Through urban compost collection and fish production in barrels and tanks, within a closed system, Growing Power does much more than cultivate plants. It is also about cultivating individuals within communities.

These non-fictional works illustrate the enthusiasm of gatherings such as "Utopian Appetites," the twenty-first Symposium of Australian Gastronomy, where more than a hundred speakers from around the globe discussed topics ranging from Persian cookbooks to Kiwi communities, "from medieval manuscripts to space food."[20] Within this wide-ranging discussion of utopian foodways, keynote speaker Robert Appelbaum explained that any single past vision, such as More's satirical Utopia, "was not a blueprint for the future." In fact, "Good food, the raising of it, the preparing of it, the serving it, the consuming of it,... is a form of utopia constantly in danger of degenerating into false consciousness, of becoming an enterprise of escapism and self-delusion, rather than a confrontation with the world as it is." Contemporary themes of "environmental sustainability, equitable food distribution, rejiggering the role of food production networks in global warming"–all central to utopian and dystopian literature—call us to confront the world as it is, so as to sustain some hope for the future.[21]

NOTES

1. Belasco, The Future of Food, 98; Allen, The Good Food Revolution, 187.
2. From A. L. Morton, *The English Utopia*, quoted in Claeys and Sargent, 72–73.
3. Lyman Tower Sargent, "The American Cockaigne," applies A. L. Morton's argument to mid-twentieth century songs and comics which include fantastic images of abundance, sung and read by a populous in the United States who had been deprived of much during the Great Depression and in the Jim Crow south.
4. Morton, New English Canaan, 117.
5. Franklin, *Autobiography*, 17, 49–51; Thoreau, *Walden*, 258–65.
6. Etta Madden and Martha Finch, *Eating in Eden*, 13, 21.
7. Quoted in Claeys and Sargent, *Utopian Reader*, 223–24.
8. Claeys, *Dystopia*, 3–4.
9. Alcott, *Transcendental Wild Oats*, 31, 33–39.
10. Hawthorne, *Blithedale Romance*, 48.
11. Belasco, 107. Teresa Botelho provides a summary of this dichotomy, as Belasco describes it, 31.
12. Botelho, 31. She draws from Jean P. Ritzinger, Speculative Visions and Imaginary Meals: Food and the Environment in (Post-Apocalyptic) Science Fiction Films. *Cultural Studies*, Vol. 22, Nos. 3–4: 369–90, 2008, 371.
13. Botelho, 30.

14. Botelho, 25–26. She cites Paul Atkinson, 11, Eating Virtue, in *The Sociology of Food and Eating: Essays on the Sociology and Significance of Food*. Ed. Anne Murcott, Aldershot, Gower: 9–17.
15. Jennifer A. Wagner-Lawlor, *Feminist Fictions*, 142.
16. Atwood, *Year of the Flood*, 428–31; Atwood, *MaddAddam*.
17. Boyd, Ustopian Breakfasts, 162.
18. Madden, Eating Ideally, 14–15.
19. Allen, *The Good Food Revolution*, 221.
20. Jacqueline Dutton and Kelly Donati, Utopian Appetites, 6.
21. Appelbaum, Concepts of Utopia, 37, 42.

References

Alcott, Louisa May. 1873. In *Transcendental Wild Oats: A Chapter from an Unwritten Romance*, ed. Carlisle, 23–62. Massachusetts: Applewood.

Allen, Will. 2012. *The Good Food Revolution: Growing Healthy Food, People, and Communities*. New York: Penguin.

Appelbaum, Robert. Concepts of utopia, concepts of food. In *Utopian Appetites*, ed. Jacqueline Dutton and Kelly Donati, 37–44. https://www.sag23covidium.com/_files/ugd/1e614b_a3e6c02cca2542448b13150be06c70c3.pdf

Atwood, Margaret. 2009a. *The Year of the Flood*. 2010. New York: Anchor Books.

———. 2009b. *MaddAddam*. Toronto: McClelland and Stewart.

Belasco, Warren. 2006. *Meals to Come: A History of the Future of Food*. Berkeley: University of California Press.

Botelho, Teresa. 2017. "Eating the Stones of the Earth": Romancing the scientific production of food in technological utopias, *Cadernos de Literatura Comparada*. 36: 23–42. https://doi.org/10.21747/21832242/litcomp36a1. Accessed 11 Feb 2018.

Boyd, Shelley. 2015. Ustopian breakfasts: Margaret Atwood's MaddAddam. *Utopian Studies* 26 (1): 160–181.

Claeys, Gregory. 2018. *Dystopia: A Natural History*. Oxford: Oxford University Press.

Claeys, Gregory, and Lyman Tower Sargent, eds. 1999. *The Utopia Reader*. New York: New York University Press.

Delany, Samuel. 1966. Driftglass. In *Aye, and Gomorrah*, 2003, ed. Samuel Delany, 102–121. New York: Random House.

Dutton, Jacqueline and Kelly Donati, eds. Forthcoming. Utopian Appetites: Proceedings of the 21st Symposium of Australian Gastronomy Utopian Appetites 2–5 December 2016 Melbourne, Australia. https://www.sag23covidium.com/_files/ugd/1e614b_a3e6c02cca2542448b13150be06c70c3.pdf

Franklin, Benjamin. 1986. *The Autobiography*. New York: Penguin.

Hawthorne, Nathaniel. 1852. *The Blithdale Romance*. 1996. Boston: Bedford/St. Martin's.

Kingsolver, Barbara. 2007. *Animal, Vegetable, Miracle: A Year of Food Life*. New York: HarperCollins.

Madden, Etta. 2015. Eating ideally: Production, consumption, commensality, and cleanup. *Utopian Studies* 26 (1): 2–18.

Madden, Etta and Martha Finch, eds. & intro. 2006. *Eating in Eden: Food and American Utopias*. Lincoln: University of Nebraska Press.

More, Thomas. 1516. *Utopia*. 2003. New York: Penguin.

Morton, A.L. 1952. *The English Utopia*. London: Lawrence & Wishart.

Morton, Thomas. 1637. *New English Canaan*. 1883 ed. Boston: Prince Society. https://Archive.org/details.newenglishcanaan00morton. Accessed 3 June 2019.

Sargent, Lyman Tower. 2015. The American Cockaigne from the Sixteenth Century to the Shmoo and Beyond. *Utopian Studies* 26 (1): 19–40.

Sloan, Robin. 2017. *Sourdough*. New York: MCD.

Thoreau, Henry David. 1854. *Walden*. 1983. New York: Penguin.

Wagner-Lawlor, Jennifer A. 2013. *Postmodern Utopias and Feminist Fictions*. Cambridge: Cambridge University Press.

Natural and Built Spaces

Environment

Anne L. Melano

Introduction

"Environment," in a general sense of the characteristics of a place, has been
a theme within utopian works from their earliest appearance. The arcadia or
idealized pastoral has placed landscape at the centre of its utopian desire since
at least Virgil (37 BC) and Theocritus (c. 280–240 BC). Thomas More's
Utopia (1516) was written against the injustices of the enclosures of the
commons, and William Morris's *News from Nowhere* (1890) sought to reverse
the impact of industrialization on the living world. From the 1970s a growing
awareness of ecological harm was among the socio-political issues which drew
new responses from the utopian imagination in the novels that Tom Moylan
has grouped as "critical utopias" (2014). Utopia in the early twenty-first
century grapples with questions of climate change and species loss in Kim
Stanley Robinson's *New York 2140* (2017) and other works.[1]

We might now even ask if "utopia" can continue to be defined in purely
human terms. Arguably, utopia's "better place" now calls for not only human
flourishing but for planetary, multispecies flourishing. The concept of an
ecological utopia, in particular, suggests we must consider a utopia's orientations to the more-than-human world, to use David Abrams's term (1996).

A. L. Melano (✉)
University of Wollongong, Wollongong, NSW, Australia

447

P. Marks et al. (eds.), *The Palgrave Handbook of Utopian and Dystopian
Literatures*, https://doi.org/10.1007/978-3-030-88654-7_35

The "more-than-human" includes not only biological life in the form of plants and animals, but also winds and weather, landforms and soils, rivers and mountains, the biosphere and the seasons, "the surrounding powers of earth and sky" (Abrams 1997, 7, 22, 71).

As awareness of ecological harm in the second half of the twentieth century has intensified to awareness of crises in the twenty-first, relations with the more-than-human world have become a focus of the utopian imagination (Garforth, 2018, 20–21). The result has been a profound shift in orientation, described here through the various modes of "care" which ground utopia's relations with more-than-human others. Qualitatively different forms of care are observable in utopian works, including before and after the various industrial revolutions and accompanying a growing awareness of planetary crises.

THE "NOWHERE" THAT IS SOMEWHERE, SOMEWHERE GREEN

A literary utopia that describes its locale, however thinly sketched or impossibly located, is a nowhere that is somewhere. When relations with place are described "in some detail," (Sargent, 1994, 7) a utopia will inevitably speak to the hopes and desires, fears and griefs which relate to the world beyond its bounds. Of course, these utopian concerns are historically mediated (Williams 1978, 206), so that the appearance of green or ecological utopias reflects anxieties and hopes related to specific "social-natural problems and dilemmas" and how these are framed (Garforth 2018, 8). Utopian anxiety in ecological utopias is largely directed at the forces impoverishing the biosphere, whether framed as industrialization, consumerism or capitalism itself, and whether with or without technology as the source or the magnifier.[2] Utopian hope is invested in a re-orientation to the "more-than-human" world, where landscape is reinhabited and human–environment relations are reimagined.

Karen Warren (2000, 108), the ecofeminist philosopher, argues that "the appropriateness or suitability of any ethical principle or practice in a given context is determined, at least in part, by considerations of care." In charting utopia's orientations of environmental care through the categories of *absence, utility, regard, co-existence,* and *provisioning,* I offer here a line of sight rather than a utopian typology; as only an indirect account is taken of human social-systemic relations or of specific fears and desires. However, this approach highlights some aspects of the shifts to the "critical utopias" of the late 1960s and 1970s (Moylan 2014), and from there to more recent environmental utopias represented by Kim Stanley Robinson's *Mars* works (1994–1999), *2312* (2012) and *New York 2140* (2017), and Margaret Atwood's *Maddaddam* trilogy (2003–2013).

LITERALLY "NOWHERE," AND OTHER ABSENCES

The *absence* of the more-than-human can describe an "unsituated" utopia. Utopia's relations to environs are not always represented: examples are heavens and hells, phantasmagorical and virtual worlds. Iain M Banks's *Surface Detail* (2010), for example, includes a world that is both a hell and is located in virtual space. There is also a question mark around eutopian fantasy fictions which, although ostensibly located and inhabited, are "historically unanchored" as Darko Suvin (2000, 222–3) describes them, through their "movement into a different and radically simplified, *expurgated* Otherwhere." This is not always true, as Suvin acknowledges: some fantasy eutopias, such as Ursula K Le Guin's eutopian Isle of Gont in her *Earthsea* volumes, are rich in their complex appraisal of both human and more-than-human relations (Suvin 2000, 211). Le Guin herself argues persuasively for their relevance: "What fantasy often does that the realistic novel generally cannot do is include the nonhuman as essential" (Le Guin 2009, 40).

The presence and absence of animals within Le Guin's *Earthsea* cycle provide an interesting case. While she famously revisions gender power relations in the later *Earthsea* books, those novels can also be read as reprising human–animal relations. The goats that Ged herds as a small boy in the first volume *A Wizard of Earthsea* (1968) are not individuated but are merely arcadian markers or subjects on whom he demonstrates his nascent strength as a mage. However, by the final books goats are individually present, in complex relations with Ged including as a source of wisdom (Le Guin 1990, 200; [2001] 2002, 35–36). The world-destroying threat of her final volume *The Other Wind* (2001) can be perceived as a wrong that elite male power has wrought, but also as an interrogation of human exceptionalism (Le Guin 2002, 225–8, 236–9). *Earthsea*'s future is imperilled through the creation of a realm called "the dry land" for the ever-more-numerous human dead. The analogy to overpopulation and colonization of more-than-human space is clear. When "the dry land" reaches crisis point, its dystopian wrongness is identified by its animal absence (44). For eutopia to be restored, human claims to dominance must be demolished and metaphysical space returned to dragons, which we might interpret allegorically as a return of space to the more-than-human world.

In dystopian science fiction, the absence of the more-than-human can also provide a powerful commentary on systemic harm. In Le Guin's *The Dispossessed* (1974), the Terran ambassador's disclosure seemed a shocking one: "My world, my Earth, is a ruin. A planet spoiled by the human species. ... There are no forests left on my Earth" (1975, 287). By 2009 this idea was all-too familiar when James Cameron's Jake in *Avatar* offered: "See the world we come from. There's no green there. They killed their mother."[3] The absence of the more-than-human can also contribute to curious forms of placelessness; the endless vista of enmeshed pods in which Neo awakes in Lana and Lilly Wachowski's *The Matrix* (1999) and the near-total absence of biological life in

Cormac McCarthy's *The Road* (2006) are examples. "In *The Road* … it is not nature but nothingness, represented by the omnipresent ashes, that encroaches on civilized society as well as on nature," Inger-Anne Søfting (2013) notes. Dystopia's nowhere is everywhere. Zygmunt Bauman (2003, 20, 23) has theorized placelessness as a characteristic of late capitalism or "liquid modernity," where elites inhabit "no geographically fixed *topoi*," feel no responsibility for earth-bound others struggling for survival, and have no interest in the future.

USE-VALUE, EUTOPIAN LIMITS, AND DYSTOPIAN COMMODIFICATION

An orientation of care for the more-than-human can be anthropocentric, based mainly on *utility* or use-value. That is to say, other species or ecosystems might be valued and cared for mainly for their material return in the form of food, transport, or materials. Some ecological possibilities can be located even within an anthropocentric "utility." A commitment to observing limits may be present, even if designed to preserve human futures. Plato sets this out from the beginning in the *Republic* (c. 386–367 BC). His narrator Socrates describes a small *polis* which he calls the "true and healthy" city. Its people are adequately dressed, eat well of simple foods, live in harmony and trade peacefully with other cities, and do "not produce [children] beyond their means, being cautious of the twin dangers of poverty and war" (Plato 1979, 44). However, this simple life is rejected by Socrates' listeners, so he models another, a larger, "spoiled city" with a greater variety of foodstuffs, trades, and possessions. The larger city understands limits but is determined to exceed them, accepting the inevitability of war over resources (44–45).

Garrett Hardin (1993) argues that a worldview of limits was widely shared until around 1600, when science seemed to promise all limits could be transcended. Thomas More's *Utopia* (1516) and Francis Bacon's *New Atlantis* (1627) mark that shift. In More's *Utopia* as in the *Republic* population is either moderated or growth gives rise to questions of limits which must be resolved by taking up others' uncultivated land, if necessary using warfare (More 1999, 51, 54, 63). In Bacon's *New Atlantis*, a new boundlessness made possible by science is envisaged and celebrated: "The end of our foundation is the knowledge of causes, and secret motions of things; and the enlarging of the bounds of human empire, to the effecting of all things possible" (Bacon 2010, 50). Raymond Williams notes that More's and Bacon's texts offer "permanent alternative images" (Williams 1978, 206) of socio-economic organization. More's land and resources must be located and are finite. Bacon's text has the more-than-human world, including soils, plants, animals, lightning, caves, and oceans, as an endless treasure-trove of knowledge to be unlocked (Bacon 2010, 50ff.).

An orientation of mere utility might be more difficult when living in close proximity to the more-than-human. Animals, even if kept for their use-value, can speak back and make their presence felt and their needs evident. As

Le Guin noted, relations with the more-than-human are more likely to be present in fantasy fiction, which we might attribute in part to fantasy's often pre-modern, rural settings.

Yet proximity does not necessarily shift relations beyond utility. In Le Guin's *The Word for World is Forest* (1972), the Terran military are destroying an entire planet by harvesting its resources, with the Indigenous inhabitants kept in their camp pens for use as servants and slave labor. Claire G Coleman offers a powerful use of "estrangement arising out of an alternative historical hypothesis" (Suvin's description of utopia (2010, 30)), and a searing indictment of British colonialism in her dystopian *Terra Nullius* (2017) where we learn the despised "Natives," who are viewed by the settlers as "not … people at all," are Terrans (Coleman 2017, 5). *Terra Nullius* places us all into servitude of alien colonizers who see nothing of beauty or value in the landscape around them unless it serves productive capacity. Val Plumwood (2009, 119) goes as far as to describe modernity as characterized by this "reductive materialism" which "reduces non-human forms to 'mere matter', emptied of agency, spirit and intelligence."

Utopian Ecopoiesis: Regard for the More-Than-Human

Regard includes forms of care that Jennifer A. Wagner-Lawlor has described as valuing, attentive, aesthetic, or even affectionate (2016, 654–55). For Tim Morton aesthetics "performs a crucial role, establishing ways of feeling and perceiving (2007, 2–3)" but it can be caught up in the "poetics of sensibility." In its stronger forms, based on sympathetic observation, it can be closely aligned to an ecological ethic and offer the potential to reduce harm within relations of utility, or to ground more active forms of care (Cook 2008). Wagner-Lawlor suggests that "an economy of regard" stands in contrast to "an economy of purpose" in human–environmental relations (2013, 195). In its weaker form, regard includes the desire to inhabit landscape primarily for its picturesque or nostalgic qualities.

In the literary genre of arcadia, or utopian pastoral, *regard* was both poetic and spiritual. Several of Theocritus's *Idylls* are also more or less realistic portrayals of daily life in an idealized community which included care for animals and synergistic relations between people and animals, and an appreciation of the beauty of the more-than-human world.[4] Arcadia as a literary form was re-energized in the Renaissance, but its possibilities as situated utopia were eroded, as "step by step, living tensions are excised, until there is nothing countervailing, and selected images stand as themselves: not in a living but in an enamelled world," Williams (1973, 16–18) writes. Regarding the shepherds of Philip Sidney's *Arcadia* (1590 and 1593), Levin (1970, 95) writes that "they are merely a chorus in the background," and we might see this as equally true of its more-than-human figures. Sidney's poiesis barely registers an actual, living, more-than-human world.

A strong form of poetic regard is associated with the Romantic period. Tim Morton describes how the Romantics' insistence on an affective connection to Nature emerges at "the moment at which the capitalism that now covers the earth began to take effect" (Morton 2007, 4, 10). By 1854 Henry David Thoreau was able to draw on its energies in *Walden: or, Life in the Woods*, a eutopian account of place, intensely situated in and with the more-than-human. Thoreau (2007, 315) describes intimate encounters with the more-than-human, more so than of human sociality: "Instead of calling on some scholar, I paid many a visit to particular trees." In one astonishing passage, Thoreau discerns the fractal nature of the world and perceives the human as merely a part of the pattern (Thoreau 2007, 472). *Walden* exemplifies Kate Rigby's suggestion that ecopoiesis can not merely draw us in but also "send us forth" not merely through celebration but by bearing witness to harm and "responding with tones of grief, protest, accusation, or exhortation" (Rigby 2004, 438, 439). Greg Garrard (2012, 55) finds "the sojourn at Walden Pond is clearly designed to make possible a revaluation of modernity, if not its outright rejection."

By the late nineteenth century, William Morris was sufficiently dismayed by the spread of the "dull squalor of civilization" to ask "Was it all to end in a counting-house on the top of a cinder-heap ...?" (Morris 1984 [1894], 244). He sought to imagine an alternative future, one which brought together socialism, aesthetics and a closely observed, affective sympathy for the more-than-human inherited from the Romantics (Abensour 1999, 126–7). The result was his utopian novel, *News from Nowhere* (1890), in which *ecopoiesis* and love of place are exceptionally strong. Abensour describes how the "Morrisean utopia" marks a new stage of utopianism, one which seeks not to offer a schema or plan but to "educate desire" and to deconstruct those "visible or hidden centres ... that are at the origin of the reversal and transformation of humankind and of the domination of nature" (1999, 158). One of the ways that Morris reimagines utopia beyond utility is through a rejection of a human/nature divide:

> Clara: "Was not their mistake once more bred of the life of slavery that they had been living? – a life which was always looking upon everything, except mankind, animate and inanimate – 'nature', as people used to call it – as one thing, and mankind as another. It was natural to people thinking in this way, that they should try to make 'nature' their slave, since they thought 'nature' was something outside them." (Morris 1995 [1890], 186–187)

In the twentieth century, the "critical utopias" all reimagine relations with the more-than-human, their *ecopoiesis* is strong and all are accompanied by forms of care that exceed mere regard. Yet perhaps a critique could be made of Ernest Callenbach's *Ecotopia* (1975) as its return to a frontier consciousness (Katerberg 2008, 130)[5] leads at times to a restored more-than-human but at others to the merely picturesque: a tree-adorned city and a forest which functions as backdrop for hunting or wargames. Indeed, the more-than-human as merely picturesque can be a marker of dystopia in twenty-first century texts. In Neill Blomkamp's film *Elysium* (2013) the wealthy enclave on the orbital station is adorned with well-watered trees and green spaces, while the Earth itself is a parched and dusty landscape of industrial pollution and grime.

Contradictions can arise in eutopia when an ecological ethos leads its citizens to reject consumerism and extraction industries, leaving us wondering what might be the means of producing their "force barges," trains, or bicycles.[6] Paula Arcari et al. (2020) warn that projects to create multispecies environments can be accompanied by forms of disregard that "off-stage" the commodification of other animals, or fail to note detriments to ecosystems elsewhere. Fredric Jameson's comment, discussing utopia's attempt to dis-alienate labor, applies equally to its attempt to dis-alienate the more-than-human world: "aesthetic theories seem to shadow Utopian ones at every turn, and to make themselves available for plausible resolutions of otherwise contradictory Utopian dilemmas" (2007, 152).

CO-EXISTENCE: DWELLING-WITH AND RE-GREENING

Co-existence with the more-than-human world is a utopian orientation similar to Gary Snyder's (1987, 28) concept of "reinhabitation." He describes paying serious attention to who lives in a locale already, to systems and energies and how they interconnect, to limits, to communication, to consideration of who came before and who might come after. Co-existence involves forms of care that recognize the "conativity" (Mathews 2011, 369) of the more-than-human members of an ecological community, Freya Mathews's term for self-realizing subjects or systems. It ensures human practices allow for their space and sustenance, and refrain from taking from systems in ways that are heedless of other species. For Morton (2013, 128), co-existence is "what ecology profoundly means. We coexist with human lifeforms, nonhuman lifeforms, and non-lifeforms, on the insides of a series of gigantic entities with whom we also coexist: the ecosystem, biosphere, climate, planet, Solar System." Indigenous traditions encompass ideas of co-existence in highly developed ways. Within Western modernity, co-existence can be expressed as actions such as setting aside or protecting forests or other habitat, as well as ethical remediation, in the form of returning or restoring habitat to non-human others. In Morris's *News from Nowhere* care includes a re-greening of London, the releasing of a tributary of the Thames from its culvert, and the freeing of birds from gamekeepers (Morris 1995 [1890], 177–8). This is a radical shift in utopia; it is an active, programmatic commitment to co-existence with the more-than-human, anticipating aspects of twentieth century ecological movements by many decades (O'Sullivan 1990). What Abensour (1999, 146, 150) describes as "a new being-in-the-world, and a new living-together" applies equally to Morris's more-than-human vision as to his social vision.

In the group of novels that Tom Moylan theorizes as critical utopias, co-existence features strongly, encompassing relations of care with the more-than-human as well as human relations of difference. He notes that these are "profoundly shaped" by feminism (Moylan 2014, 10–11). Marge Piercy's *Woman on the Edge of Time* (1976) includes in decision-making meetings an "Earth Advocate" who "speaks for the rights of the total environment," as well as an "Animal Advocate" (Piercy 1984, 151). Several of the critical utopias have projects to care for the world through its re-greening. On Le Guin's planet Anarres in *The Dispossessed* a major reforestation project involves work that is hard, exhausting and unhealthy, in dust that causes constant coughing, yet the creation of green life brings intense, spiritual joy (Le Guin 1975, 46–7, 50). Re-greening is central to Ernest Callenbach's *Ecotopia* (1975), with a "mighty boulevard" in the heart of San Francisco reduced to a mere two lanes, the remainder "planted with thousands of trees" (Callenbach 2004, 11). The town of El Modena in Robinson's *Pacific Edge* (1990) also has a project to tear up the streets, and *Woman on the Edge of Time* involves dismantling toxic buildings (Piercy 1984, 240; Robinson 1995, 2). *Pacific Edge* creates green private spaces, working against the human culture/external nature dualism to build homes that can accommodate more-than-human others (Robinson 1995, 107).

Although Morris's *News from Nowhere* includes a reference to habitat and foregrounds restorative work (1995 [1890], 177), and Charlotte Perkin Gilman's *Herland* (1915) has botany and forestry,[7] the critical utopias have a more developed understanding of inter-meshed ecological systems. The outdoor education in *Ecotopia* includes the study of ecology, so that "a six-year-old can tell you all about the 'ecological niches' of the creatures and plants he encounters in his daily life" (Callenbach 2004, 35–6). Callenbach's stable-state economics in *Ecotopia* is a particularly significant socio-political response, offering a radically different vision to that of growth capitalism (ibid., 18). Several texts emphasize recycling, with Piercy's *Women on the Edge of Time* explicitly connecting this to an orientation of care for more-than-human needs:

> "Many of my generation … suspect the Age of Greed and Waste to be… crudely overdrawn. But to burn your compost! To pour your shit into the waters others downstream must drink! That fish must live in! Into rivers whose estuaries and marshes are links in the whole offshore food chain!" (Piercy 1984, 55)

Marius de Geus (1999, 20–21) describes several of the critical utopian works, as well as More's and Thoreau's, as ecological "utopias of sufficiency" as differentiated from technological "utopias of abundance." Their deliberate turn toward scarcity and away from technology is due to a consideration of the more-than-human, as well as human needs, complicating what J C Davis (1981, 21, 36) called "the collective problem" of how to allocate the limited satisfactions available in the face of potentially unlimited human desires. A turn away from technology is not complete, however; most adopt Morris's solution of having some technology for onerous work, or using technology for certain utopian purposes, such as ecology and agriculture, and celebrate medical or ecological innovations.[8] Jameson (2007, 152–3) comments that "the separation of the theme of technology and invention from the 'ugliness' of factory and industrial work" acts as a kind of *deus ex machina* for utopias.

Several of the critical utopias draw elements from Indigenous cultures, as Piercy's utopian guide acknowledges, "We learned a lot from societies that people used to call primitive. Primitive technically. But socially sophisticated" (Piercy 1984, 125). A major utopian work by Le Guin, *Always Coming Home* (1985), draws further away from technology than the critical utopias, and closer to the life practices of Indigenous peoples. An orientation of co-existence is strong in her work, and in her utopian commentary where she claims the organic over the machine, and a Cree principle of "I go backward, look forward" over the endless pursuit of capitalist growth (Le Guin 2016).

Provisioning in the Anthropocene

Provisioning is a form of care that strives actively to assist more-than-human others in the Anthropocene. Examples include offering food and water sources, routes or dwelling spaces, and biotechnological interventions such as vaccinations or genetic modification. Provisioning answers Tim Morton's challenge of providing for planetary life in a world where no part lies untouched or unaltered by human activity, actual or planned (Morton 2013, 88). This aspect of care is associated with living in the time "after nature." It assumes that the time of ethical letting-be, which relied on the regenerative systems of "nature" and its refuges, has passed (Haraway 2015, 160). Garforth describes the shift in utopia "after nature" as one where "the world we have made and must inhabit is a messy, dynamic assemblage of the natural, the technological and the human. There is no room for the nature that has been crucial to those green visions and ecological discourses that since the late 1970s have appeared to hold out the best hope for alternatives to a destructive and instrumental modernity" (Garforth 2018, 138). Donna Haraway (2015, 160) comments that, "Maybe, but only maybe, and only with intense commitment and collaborative work and play with other terrans, flourishing for rich multispecies assemblages that include people will be possible."

In Robinson's *Mars* works (1994–1999), local attention to species and biotic systems is presented as *ecopoiesis* in a new sense of creating ecologies, made possible through sciences which make life accessible to creative shaping. At the same time, the self-organizing quality of life is acknowledged and celebrated (Robinson 1994, 91–92). Mars is transformed to a green planet. Much of its surface has life created anew and its past history erased, reversing Morris and the critical utopias. Yet, like the earlier utopias, the *Mars* series is propelled forward by an image of a verdant, living world, and smaller, more contained human settlements than those of populous Earth. In Robinson's *2312* (2012), the hollowed-out asteroids populated by Terran species and the final release of animals to re-wild the Earth are an exuberant form of provisioning, one that embraces rather than rejects the possibilities of technology. Robinson's *Aurora* (2015) returns to restoration and remediation in the final pages where the failed interplanetary colonizers join a community committed to renewing Earth's beaches. In his *New York 2140* (2017), a major character travels the world in her blimp *Assisted Migration* to pick up animal populations and move them as the climate changes.

Provisioning is now a feature of science as well as of utopia. Scientists increasingly discuss "intervention ecology" as an alternative to "restoration" or "conservation" ecologies. Intervention ecology "covers a wide range of active interventions in ecosystem dynamics that are increasingly required in order to ensure the continuation of ecosystem service provision" (Hobbs et al. 2011). Ecological politics, science, public policy, and technology are present throughout Robinson's fiction, and are wearying and effortful, but nonetheless utopian, forms of world-care. Tom Faunce's *Split by Sun* (2019) also highlights a struggle to achieve scientific and political responses to climate issues, centred on artificial photosynthesis as a form of "biomimicry." His attention to more-than-human others is focused on plants and the ecosystems of insects and animals they support (Faunce 2019). Milner and Burgmann (2020, 48) locate science and politics as the main forms of utopian hope in their *Climate Change and Science Fiction*, where they catalogue and theorize a growing number of climate fiction novels which offer a planetary perspective on the Anthropocene.

Margaret Atwood's "ustopian" trilogy *Oryx and Crake* (2003), *The Year of the Flood* (2009), and *Maddaddam* (2013) has several darkly ironic examples of provisioning.[9] The novels open in a world of climate change, corporatization, and bioengineering. Scientist Crake creates genetically modified, post-human "Crakers" as more viable human sub-species. To make room for them, he releases a deadly virus that wipes out most of the existing human population (Atwood 2003, 305, 346). Although the Crakers are initially provided with care by his friend Jimmy, this is later reversed when they are released from the compound and provision Jimmy by catching him a fish each week (100). "Pigoons" created by former corporations from both human and pig genetic material survive in the post-virus world, and initially seem a threat to the few surviving humans. However, by the end of the trilogy an alliance has been formed between the pigoons, Crakers, and human survivors (Atwood 2015, 268ff.). For Tom Moylan, "alliance politics" is a source of hope in both the 1970s critical utopias and the critical dystopias of the late twentieth and twenty-first centuries (Moylan 2014, 188, 194; Baccolini and Moylan 2003, 237). Atwood's is an alliance where the human, more-than-human, and post-human are equal partners. Gerry Canavan reads Atwood's texts as expressive of hope in the face of the enclosure of capitalism. He notes that ecological utopia now asserts its "radical break" through the allegory of a post-apocalyptic future: "The entire *world* would end first—and even that might not be enough" (Canavan 2012, 138).

Conclusion

Utopia might well be located in "no-place," but its environs are often closely described. Unless it is a purely human heaven or hell, these will include more-than-human others. When we look closer, we see that a range of interactions are possible between utopia and these others, reflecting utopia's ecological and socio-political assumptions, hopes, or anxieties. One way to conceptualize these interactions is through their orientations of care.

Arcadia has offered an intensely aesthetic and spiritual *regard* for more-than-human others. William Morris extended utopia's liberatory potential in a transformed landscape which offered an alternative vision to the excesses of the second industrial revolution. The critical utopias from the 1960s onwards further developed this responsive revaluing. These utopias drew on Indigenous and ecological knowledges and the energies of environmental activism. Revitalizing a sense of reverence and regard for the more-than-human, they also created conditions of *co-existence*, including practices to restrain consumption and repair ecologies. However, in recent decades, post-human/post-natural utopias have had to confront worsening conditions and the deepening crises of the Anthropocene, including climate change. Insofar as a human/nature divide and a fractured politics have worked to make biospheric systems of exchange largely invisible, these utopias have attempted to reverse that absence. They confront planet-wide crises and explore new forms of world-care that include *provisioning*.

Arguably, we must now actively extend Ruth Levitas's concept that utopias "explore and bring to debate the potential contents and contexts of human flourishing" to include the more-than-human (Levitas 2013, xi). The re-situating of human environments within a more-than-human world, not only in utopian fiction but also within ecology itself, offers a richer set of possibilities in which we might find new sources of hope.

Notes

1. For a comprehensive study of climate change texts, both dystopian and eutopian, *see* Milner and Burgmann (2020), *Science Fiction and Climate Change: A Sociological Approach*.
2. See e.g. de Geus, Ecological Utopias: Envisioning the Sustainable Society, 20–21; Canavan 2014, 14.
3. At 2 h 3 min.
4. *See* especially Idyll VII, "The Harvest-Home."
5. Trains and bicycles replace fossil fuel vehicles in many eutopian works; force-barges appear in Morris (1995, 168).
6. The forestry and ecology of *Herland* is directed overwhelmingly at human utility: [1915]1979, 105.
7. *See* Piercy 1984, 53; Le Guin 1975, 158; Morris 1995, 168.

8. "Ustopia" is Atwood's coinage: "a word I made up by combining utopia and dystopia – the imagined perfect society and its opposite – because, in my view, each contains a latent version of the other" (Atwood, "The Road to Ustopia," *The Guardian*, 15 October 2011).

REFERENCES

Abensour, Miguel. 1999 [1982]. William Morris: The Politics of Romance. In *Revolutionary Romanticism: A Drunken Boat Anthology*, ed. M. Blechman, 125–161. San Francisco: City Lights.

Abrams, David. 1997. *The Spell of the Sensuous: Perception and Language in a More-Than-Human World*. New York: Vintage Books.

Arcari, Paula, F. Probyn-Rapsey, and H. Singer. 2020. When Species Don't Meet: Invisibilized Animals, Urban Nature and City Limits. *EPE: Nature and Space*. https://doi.org/10.1177/2514848620939870.

Atwood, Margaret. 2003. *Oryx and Crake*. London: Bloomsbury.

———. 2015 [2013]. *Maddaddam*. London: Bloomsbury.

Baccolini, Raffaella, and Tom Moylan. 2003. *Dark Horizons: Science Fiction and the Dystopian Imagination*. London and New York: Routledge.

Bacon, Francis. 2010 [1627]. *New Atlantis*. Nashville: Watchmaker.

Banks, Iain M. 2011 [2010]. *Surface Detail*. New York: Orbit/Hachette.

Bauman, Zygmunt. 2003. Utopia with No Topos. *History of the Human Sciences* 16 (1): 11–25.

Blomkamp, Neill, dir. *Elysium*. 2013. Sony Pictures.

Callenbach, Ernest. 2004 [1975]. *Ecotopia*. Berkeley (CA): Banyan Tree Books.

Cameron, James, dir. *Avatar*. 2009. Twentieth Century Fox.

Canavan, Gerry. 2012. Hope, But Not for Us: Ecological Science Fiction and the End of the World in Margaret Atwood's *Oryx and Crake* and *The Year of the Flood*. *LIT: Literature Interpretation Theory* 23 (2):138–159.

———. 2014. Introduction: If This Goes On. In *Green Planets: Ecology and Science Fiction*, ed. G. Canavan and K.S. Robinson, 141–221. Middletown (CT): Wesleyan University Press.

Coleman, Claire G. 2017. *Terra Nullius*. Sydney: Hachette Australia.

Cook, Barbara J. 2008. Multifaceted Dialogues: Toward an Environmental Ethic of Care. In *Women Writing Nature: A Feminist View*, ed. B J Cook. Lanham (MD) and Plymouth: Lexington/Rowman & Littlefield.

Davis, J.C. 1981. *Utopia and the Ideal Society: A Study of English Utopian Writing 1516–1700*. Cambridge, New York and Melbourne: Cambridge University Press.

de Geus, Marius. 1999 [1996]. *Ecological Utopias: Envisioning the Sustainable Society*, trans, P Schwartzman. Utrecht: International Books.

Faunce, Tom. 2019. *Split by Sun*. London, Singapore and New York: World Scientific.

Garforth, Lisa. 2018. *Green Utopias: Environmental Hope Before and After Nature*. Cambridge and Polity.

Garrard, Greg. 2012. *Ecocriticism*, 2nd ed. Oxford and New York: Routledge.

Gilman, Charlotte Perkins. 1979 [1915]. *Herland*. London: The Women's Press.

Haraway, Donna J. 2015. Anthropocene, Capitalocene, Plantationocene, Chthulucene: Making Kin. *Environmental Humanities* 6: 159–165.

Hardin, Garrett. 1993. *Living Within Limits: Ecology, Economics, and Population Taboos.* Oxford and New York: Oxford University Press.

Hobbs, Richard J., et al. 2011. Intervention Ecology: Applying Ecological Science in the Twenty-first Century. *BioScience* 61 (6): 442–450.

Jameson, Fredric. 2007 [2005]. *Archaeologies of the Future: The Desire Called Utopia and Other Science Fictions.* London and New York: Verso/New Left Books.

Katerberg, William H. 2008. *Future West: Utopia and Apocalypse in Frontier Science Fiction.* Lawrence (KS): University Press of Kansas.

Le Guin, Ursula K. 1979 [1968]. A Wizard of Earthsea. In *The Earthsea Trilogy.* Harmondsworth: Penguin.

———. 1976 [1972]. *The Word for World is Forest.* New York: Berkley/G P Putnam's Sons.

———. 1975. *The Dispossessed.* St Albans (UK): Panther/Granada. First published 1974, with some editions subtitled "An Ambiguous Utopia."

———. 1986 [1985]. *Always Coming Home.* London: Victor Gollancz.

———. 1990. *Tehanu: The Last Book of Earthsea.* New York: Atheneum.

———. 2002 [2001]. *The Other Wind.* London: Orion.

———. 2009. The Critics, the Monsters, and the Fantasists. In *Cheek by Jowl*, 27–43. Seattle: Aqueduct Press.

———. 2016. A Non-Euclidean View of California as a Cold Place to Be. In *Utopia by Thomas More.* London and New York: Verso. 1982 as a lecture; published 1989; additional notes 2016.

Levin, Harry. 1970 [1969]. *The Myth of the Golden Age in the Renaissance.* London: Faber and Faber.

Levitas, Ruth. 2013. *Utopia as Method: The Imaginary Reconstitution of Society.* Basingstoke: Palgrave Macmillan.

Mathews, Freya. 2011. Towards a Deeper Philosophy of Biomimicry. *Organization & Environment* 24 (4): 364–387.

McCarthy, Cormac. 2006. *The Road.* New York: Alfred A Knopf.

Milner, Andrew, and J.R. Burgmann. 2020. *Science Fiction and Climate Change: A Sociological Approach.* Liverpool: Liverpool University Press.

More, Thomas. 1999 [1516]. Utopia. In *Three Early Modern Utopias: Utopia, New Atlantis, The Isle of Pines*, ed. S. Bruce. Oxford: Oxford University Press.

Morris, William. 1995 [1890]. *News from Nowhere.* Cambridge: Cambridge University Press.

———.1984 [1894]. How I Became a Socialist. In *Political Writings of William Morris*, ed. A. L. Morton, 6–241. London: Lawrence and Wishart.

Morton, Timothy. 2007. *Ecology Without Nature: Rethinking Environmental Aesthetics.* Cambridge (MA) and London: Harvard University Press.

———. 2013. *Hyperobjects: Philosophy and Ecology After the End of the World.* Minneapolis and London: University of Minnesota Press.

Moylan, Tom. 2014 [1986]. *Demand the Impossible: Science Fiction and the Utopian Imagination.* 2nd ed. Bern: Ralahine/Peter Lang.

O'Sullivan, Patrick. 1990. The Ending of the Journey: William Morris, News from Nowhere and Ecology. In *William Morris and News from Nowhere: A Vision for Our Time*, eds. S. Coleman and P. O'Sullivan, 169–181. Hartland: Green Books.

Piercy, Marge. 1984 [1976]. *Woman on the Edge of Time.* London: The Women's Press.

Plato. 1979 [(c. BC386–367]. *The Republic*, trans. R Larson. Wheeling (IL): Harlan Davidson.

Plumwood, Val. 2009. Nature in the Active Voice. *Australian Humanities Review* (46): 113–129.

Rigby, Kate. 2004. Earth, World, Text: On the (Im)possibility of Ecopoiesis. *New Literary History* 35 (3): 427–442.

Robinson, Kim Stanley. 1995 [1990]. *Pacific Edge*. London: HarperCollins.

———. 1994 [1993]. *Green Mars*. London: HarperCollins.

———. 2013 [2012]. *2312*. New York: Orbit.

———. 2015. *Aurora*. London: Orbit.

———. 2017. *New York 2140*. London: Little, Brown & Co/Hachette UK.

Sargent, Lyman Tower. 1994. The Three Faces of Utopianism Revisited. *Utopian Studies* 5 (1): 1–37.

Snyder, Gary. 1987. Reinhabitation. *Earth First!* 8 (23 September): 28.

Søfting, Inger-Anne. 2013. Between Dystopia and Utopia: The Post-Apocalyptic Discourse of Cormac McCarthy's *The Road*. *English Studies* 94 (6): 704–713.

Suvin, Darko. 2000. Considering the Sense of "Fantasy" or "Fantastic Fiction": An Effusion. *Extrapolation* 41 (3): 209–248.

Suvin, Darko, 2010 [1973]. Defining the Literary Genre of Utopia: Some Historical Semantics, Some Genology, a Proposal, and a Plea. In *Defined by a Hollow: Essays on Utopia, Science Fiction and Political Epistemology*, 17–47. Bern: Ralahine/Peter Lang.

Theocritus. 1912 [c. 280–240 BC]. Idylls. In *The Greek Bucolic Poets*, ed J. M. Edmonds. Cambridge (MA): Harvard University Press.

Thoreau, Henry David. 2007 [1854]. *Walden: Or, Life in the Woods*. Edison (NJ): Castle Books.

Virgil. 1960 [37 BC]. *The Eclogues*, trans. C S Calverley. New York: The Heritage Press.

Wachowski, Lana and Lilly Wachowski, dirs. 1999. *The Matrix*. Warner Bros.

Wagner-Lawlor, Jennifer A. 2013. *Postmodern Utopias and Feminist Fictions*. Cambridge: Cambridge University Press.

———. 2016. Regarding Intimacy, Regard, and Transformation Feminist Practice in the Art of Pamela Longobardi. *Feminist Studies* 42 (3): 649–688.

Warren, Karen J. 2000. *Ecofeminist Philosophy: A Western Perspective on What it Is and Why it Matters*. Lanham (MD) and Oxford: Bowman & Littlefield.

Williams, Raymond. 1973. *The Country and the City*. London: Chatto & Windus.

———. 1978. Utopia and Science Fiction. *Science Fiction Studies* 5 (3): 203–214.

Space

Phillip E. Wegner

It is no coincidence that the modern genre of the utopia emerges in the early sixteenth century with the celebrated work by Thomas More, *De Optimo Reipublicae Statu Deque noua insula Utopia libellus uere aureus, nec minus salutaris quam festiuus* (*The Best State of a Commonwealth and the New Island of Utopia, A Truly Golden Handbook, No Less Beneficial than Entertaining*) (1516) that introduces into Europe simultaneously a new word, genre, and conceptual problematic. This is because More's late-feudal world found itself in the first throes of the traumatic upheavals and sometimes violent dissolutions of older traditional organizations of social and cultural life, processes so marvelously captured in Karl Marx's phrase "*Alles Ständische und Stehende verdampft*" (or in the classic translation, "all that is solid melts into air") (Marx and Engels 1989, 16; Marx and Engels 1978, 476): the long revolution of creative destruction and recomposition, of de- and reterritorialization of the social and cultural body that we have now come to understand as a central aspect of the experiences of modernization and modernity. This chapter explores the fundamental role the genre of utopia plays in thinking what I term in *Imaginary Communities* (2002) the "spatial histories of modernity" (Wegner 2002, 3). Utopia offers a vitally important technology for imagining space anew, an aspect of the practice whose importance continues into our increasingly global or planetary present. Recognizing this dialectic will also

P. E. Wegner (✉)
University of Florida, Gainesville, FL, USA

P. Marks et al. (eds.), *The Palgrave Handbook of Utopian and Dystopian Literatures*, https://doi.org/10.1007/978-3-030-88654-7_36

help grasp in more productive ways the long and complex history of this significant genre.

Early in his landmark *Archaeologies of the Future* (2005), Fredric Jameson suggests that there are "two distinct lines of descendency from More's inaugural text: the one intent on the realization of the Utopian program, the other an obscure yet omnipresent Utopian impulse finding its way to the surface in a variety of covert expressions and practices" (Jameson 2005, 3). The latter, the utopian impulse, predates More's invention of the term and is concerned with utopia as ontology, what Ernst Bloch names the "principle of hope" (*Prinzip Hoffnung*), the deeply human desire for positive change in our world. Jameson suggests such an impulse involves an open-ended and "protean investment in a host of suspicious and equivocal matters"—among them, "liberal reforms and commercial pipedreams," "political and social theory," and "the individual building" (Jameson 2005, 3–4). The utopian impulse is also at the basis of the allegorical hermeneutic developed by Bloch and further refined by Jameson, which aims to tease out the manifestations of utopia found on the planes of "the body, time, and collectivity" (4).

The first line of descent, the utopian program, Jameson identifies as "systemic" or totalizing in orientation, involving an utter break with the status quo, whether such a process of transformation unfolds according to the imaginaries of what Karl Mannheim terms the millenarian, progressive, conservative, or communist-socialist mentalities.[1] Jameson further maintains,

> Totality is precisely this combination of closure and system, in the name of autonomy and self-sufficiency and which is ultimately the source of [Utopia's] otherness or radical, even alien, difference.... [I]t is precisely this category of totality that presides over the forms of Utopian realization: the Utopian city, the Utopian revolution, the Utopian commune or village, and of course the Utopian text itself. (Jameson 2005, 5)

As Jameson's list makes evident it is in the various faces of the utopian program that the deeply spatial nature of utopia becomes most readily apparent.

In order to understand this connection, we need to dispense with the commonplace understanding of "space" as something fixed, static, and exterior to ourselves. The pioneering French social theorist Henri Lefebvre maintains that the emergence of any social formation occurs through a particular "(social) production of (social) space:" a space that is produced by and through human actions, and which is thus "constituted neither by a collection of things or an aggregate of (sensory) data, nor by a void packed like a parcel with various contents, and... is irreducible to a 'form' imposed upon phenomena, upon things, upon physical materiality" (Lefebvre 1991, 26–7). According to Lefebvre, such a space is deeply historical, any apparent stability at best short-lived and contingent. Indeed, *all* spaces are contradictory, conflicted, and subject to change.

Lefebvre further maintains that any collective space is constituted through a dialectic of what he terms "spatial practices," "representations of space," and "spaces of representation," each associated with a specific cognitive mode: respectively, the "perceived," the "conceived," and the "lived" (Lefebvre 1991, 53) The first, spatial practices, involve the most abstract processes of social production, reproduction, and cohesion, all of which we "perceive" through the formalized axioms of the sciences. The third, spaces of representation, which we re-present to ourselves through art, encompass the "lived" space of the individual's embodied experience and the signs, images, and forms that give it shape and significance. Finally, the concrete structuration of social space that Lefebvre refers to as spatial practice, space organized into a system, as well as our lived everyday experiences of space emerge over the course of time in a large part as the result of the creative processes involved in representations of space. Of the practices that constitute such representations, Lefebvre notes,

> conceptualized space, the space of scientists, planners, urbanists, technocratic subdividers and social engineers, as of a certain type of artist with a scientific bent – all of whom identify what is lived and what is perceived with what is conceived. (Lefebvre 1991, 38)

For Lefebvre representations of space are conceived by architects, urban planners, social engineers, communalists, and revolutionaries—and to his list we should add the creators of utopias.

In its deep imbrication with representations of space, the genre of utopia looks at once backward and forward. On the one hand, utopia, like its kin genre of the travel narrative, finds its roots in the older tradition of the romance, which Jameson elsewhere notes.

> is precisely that form in which the worldness of world reveals or manifests itself, in which, in other words, world in the technical sense of the transcendental horizon of our experience becomes visible in an inner-worldly sense. (Jameson 1981, 112)

On the other hand, utopia is one of the most significant forerunners of a modern science fiction, whose "distinctiveness... as a genre has less to do with time (history, past, future) than with space" (Jameson 2005, 313). For this reason, when science fiction becomes a pre-eminent narrative technology for conceiving space, Darko Suvin names utopia "the socio-political subgenre of SF" (1988, 38).

Building on Lefebvre's insights, the geographer Neil Smith develops another notion crucial for understanding the spatial thinking that takes place in the utopia: what Smith terms "scaled spaces" (Smith 1993, 89). Smith argues for the necessity when addressing any cultural phenomenon of taking into account its embeddedness in a number of different "nested" spatial contexts:

body, home, community, city, region, nation, and globe. Smith concludes, "By setting boundaries, scale can be constructed as a means of constraint and exclusion, a means of imposing identity, but a politics of scale can also become a weapon of expansion and inclusion, a means of enlarging identity" (Smith 1993, 114).

It is precisely such an enlargement of identity that takes place in More's *Utopia*. In his groundbreaking semiological study, *Utopiques: jeux d'espace* (1973), Louis Marin meticulously traces the ways *Utopia* develops a figuration, a pre-conceptual conceiving or "speaking-picture," of a social reality that "has not yet found its concept" (Marin 1984, 163). This reality is European capitalism, which will remorselessly sweep away, melting into air, all older ways of organizing and living social and cultural life. At the same time, as I demonstrate in *Imaginary Communities*, More's text contributes to the development of the radically new spatial scale known as the *nation-state*.

More's figuration of this spatial form occurs during Raphael Hythlodaeus's narration of the "birth" of Utopia:

> As the report goes and as the appearance of the ground shows, the island once was not surrounded by sea. But Utopus, who as conqueror gave the island its name (up to then it had been called Abraxa) and who brought the rude and rustic people to such a perfection of culture and humanity as makes them now superior to almost all other mortals, gained a victory at his very first landing. He then ordered the excavation of fifteen miles on the side where the land was connected with the continent and caused the sea to flow around the land. (More 1965, 113)

By digging the trench that creates the insular space (*insula Utopia*), Utopus marks a border where there had previously existed only an indistinct frontier between "neighboring peoples," a disjunctive act of territorial inclusion as well as exclusion that Anthony Giddens defines as foundational for the development of the spatial practices of the modern nation-state: "Borders, in my view, are only found with the emergence of nation-states" (1987, 50). The historical originality of such a representation of space is indicated in the double-meaning at play in Hythlodaeus's closing statement, "Now I have described to you, as exactly as I could, the structure of that commonwealth [*Reipublicae*] which I judge not merely the best but the only one which can rightly claim the name of a commonwealth" (More 1965, 237). Utopia, as a figure of an England transformed, is not only the one place that could lay the claim to being ordered in the interest of the "public good"—the older definition of the Latin *respublica* or its subsequent English translation "a common weale"—but also already a "commonwealth" as the term would subsequently be defined as a synonym for the nation-state.

Utopus himself—for whom there is no place in the community— performs the role of the absolutist monarch in the real history of the formation of the nation-state: the monarch serves as a vanishing mediator, dissolving the power of the feudal estates and Roman Catholic Church and clearing the space for the emergence of a new kind of centralized social, political, and cultural authority. At this crucial historical juncture, the interchange between the imaginary community of Utopia and what Benedict Anderson famously terms the "imagined community" (1986) of the nation-state works to instantiate the latter spatial practice in its distinctly modern form. Moreover, as Sarah Hogan (2018) more recently bears out, More's fiction and many of the most significant utopias that follow in its wake also figure the spatial practices of imperialism that will be of such vital importance to the first European nation-states.

All subsequent utopian fictions stand in one fashion or another as responses to More's founding text. As the nation-state becomes increasingly accepted as the "natural" form of the social and cultural totality, the majority of utopian fictions to appear in the subsequent three and a half centuries follow More's lead and take this spatial scale as the necessary one on which to conceive new ways of being in the world. However, in the first century following the publication of *Utopia*, two alternative conceptualizations of space emerge that will also have a marked impact on later utopian imaginings. The first is represented by the Italian Domincan friar Tomasso Campanella's *La città del Sole* (*City of the Sun* [1602]). Like More, Campanella was deeply influenced by Plato's *Republic* and employed the open-ended dialogue form throughout his text. However, unlike More and as the title of his work indicates, Campanella repeats Plato's older spatial scale of the city. This choice of this spatial scale also reflects the fact that the Italian city-states—especially during what Giovanni Arrighi terms the "long fifteenth-sixteenth century," the first "systemic cycle of accumulation" dominated by Genoese finance capital and Iberian military power—offer what seems to be a viable alternative to the spatial practices of the fledgling nation-state (1994, 109–126).

While history rules on the side of More and the nation-state, the spatial scale posited by Campanella would prove vitally important to a wide variety of the utopian programs that emerge in the nineteenth and twentieth centuries, especially in the architectural and urban planning realms. These include, among others, Charles Fourier's *phalanstère* (1822), Ebenezer Howard's Garden City (1898), Tony Garnier's *Cité industrielle* (Industrial City) (1904), Job Harriman's *Llano del Rio* (1914), Le Corbusier's *Ville radieuse* (Radiant City) (1930), and Rem Koolhaas's Manhattanism (1978). Although these various conceptualizations of space would have marked impacts on spatial practices in terms of both the intentional communities modeled on them and in later urban reforms, efforts to delink from the worlds in which they exist retreat from the systemic and totalizing spatial program inaugurated by More. The reasons for such a retreat will be touched on momentarily.

The other spatial scale that will play a prominent role in the subsequent history of utopia is to be found in one of the first texts to reply directly to More's *Utopia*: François Rabelais's carnivalesque *La vie de Gargantua et de Pantagruel* (1532–1564). In Rabelais's Second Book (1532)—as with

Utopia, Rabelais's second book is composed before his first (1534)—More's island nation of Utopia is explicitly invoked on a number of occasions; and Rabelais's Third Book (1546) opens, "After having completely conquered the land of Dipsodia, Pantagruel transported there a colony of Utopians to the number of 9,876,543,210 men, not including women and small children" (1955, 289). Even more significantly, the final seven chapters of The First Book outline a community in the Abbey of Thélème that responds to that conceived in More's *Utopia*. Although the scale of the community recalls the significance in More's development of the genre of his first-hand knowledge of monastic communities, it is the contrasting vision of everyday life, experienced first and foremost on the spatial scale of the sensuous body, that will constitute Rabelais's most lasting legacy: "All their life was regulated not by laws, statutes, or rules, but according to their free will and pleasure. They rose from bed when they pleased, and drank, ate, worked, and slept when the fancy seized them" (159).

Rabelais's text inaugurates a significant dialectic that will continue throughout the genre's history. In one of the founding essays of the transdisciplinary practice of utopian studies, Lyman Tower Sargent identifies two strands of imagining ideal worlds that predate More's founding texts, which he terms "the utopia of human contrivance or the city utopia" and "utopias of sensual gratification or body utopias." Sargent locates the paradigm of the former in Plato's *Republic* and *Laws* and the latter in the various Land of Cockaigne fables that flourish in the medieval period (1994, 10–11).[2] With More's and Rabelais's texts these two strands are brought into coordination, and a similar dialectic will be enacted again in such couples as Edward Bellamy's "utopia of human contrivance" (Sargent 1994, 10–11), *Looking Backward, 2000–1887* (1888) and William Morris's pastoral "epoch of rest," as he puts it in *News from Nowhere* (1890); and later between Ursula K. Le Guin's *The Dispossessed: An Ambiguous Utopia* (1974) and Samuel Delany's *Trouble on Triton: An Ambiguous Heterotopia* (1976). Moreover, Rabelais's critical response to More's text will play a significant role in the development in the late nineteenth century of that even more consequential reply to utopia, the *dystopia*.

The scale of conceptualizing perceived and lived space established by More and his followers comes into crisis in the latter part of the nineteenth century. The first inklings of such a turning point are evident in the most influential utopia of the late nineteenth century (and arguably one of the most influential utopias after More), Bellamy's *Looking Backward*. In *Imaginary Communities*, I map out Bellamy's meticulous efforts to neutralize the threats offered by various "agents of disorder"—among others, Indians, radical industrial labor activists, immigrants, and tramps—to a "tenuous national unity that had been so recently forged with the conclusion of the Civil War" (Wegner 2002, 70–72). At the same time, Thomas Peyser (1998) shows how Bellamy's narrative gives one of the earliest expressions to the dynamics of what the British journalist W. T. Stead will label in his eponymously titled book, *The Americanization of the World; or The Trend of the Twentieth Century* (1901).

This crisis in the utopia's spatial imaginary will become even more explicit in the next few decades. For example, in his great Russian revolutionary-period utopia, Красная звезда (*Red Star*) (1908), Alexander Bogdanov has one of his characters meditate on the consequences of the bounding of the utopian program within the totality of the nation-state:

If this happens, the individual advanced countries in which socialism triumphs will be like islands in a hostile capitalist and even to some extent precapitalist sea. Anxious about their own power, the upper classes of the nonsocialist countries will continue to concentrate all their efforts on destroying these islands. They will constantly be organizing military expeditions against them, and from the ranks of the former large and small property-holders in the socialist nations themselves they will be able to find plenty of allies willing to commit treason. It is difficult to foresee the outcome of these conflicts, but even in those instances where socialism prevails and triumphs, its character will be perverted deeply and for a long time to come by years of encirclement, unavoidable terror and militarism, and the barbarian patriotism that is their inevitable consequence. This socialism will be a far cry from our own. (1984, 113–14)

Even more directly, H. G. Wells proclaims in *A Modern Utopia* (1905):

No less than a planet will serve the purpose of a modern Utopia. Time was when a mountain valley or an island seemed to promise sufficient isolation for a polity to maintain itself intact from outward force.... But the whole trend of modern thought is against the permanence of any such enclosures. We are acutely aware nowadays that, however subtly contrived a State may be, outside your boundary lines the epidemic, the breeding barbarian or the economic power, will gather its strength to overcome you.... A state powerful enough to keep isolated under modern conditions would be powerful enough to rule the world, would be, indeed, if not actively ruling, yet passively acquiescent in all other human organizations, and so responsible for them altogether. World-state, therefore, it must be. (1967, 11–12)

Wells here gives voice to the question that will increasingly dominate the genre: how might we conceive of utopia on a truly global or planetary spatial scale?

As I suggested above, in the utopian imaginaries developed by some architects and urban planners we witness a retreat from the genre's totalizing program. Similarly, both the nativism and racism evident in populist utopias ranging from Ignatius Donnelly's *Caesar's Column: A Story of the Twentieth Century* (1890) to Charlotte Perkins Gilman's *Herland* (1915) and "pocket utopias" such as the Shangri-La of James Hilton's *Lost Horizon* (1933) serve as defensive or nostalgic responses to the increasingly global nature of perceived space. However, even later pocket utopias, such as Aldous Huxley's final novel, *Island* (1962)—which, as Robert C. Elliott already intuits in his landmark *The Shape of Utopia* (2013 [1970], Ch. 7), prefigures the revival of the utopian imaginary that will occur in the late 1960s and early 1970s—warn of the dangers involved in any effort to conceive of utopia on a spatial scale below that of the globe.

Bellamy's moment also would witness the development of another powerful response to the utopia in the practice of the dystopia. The utopias of Bellamy, Morris, and others emerge as a negation of a then dominant literary naturalism, with Bellamy's narrator in *Looking Backward* specifically decrying the "profound pessimism of the literature of the last quarter of the nineteenth century" (1960, 194). The dystopia in turn emerges as a negation of the literary utopia's negation of naturalism, resulting in an original form that incorporates naturalism's thoroughgoing pessimism about both the present and human potential and projects this into carefully wrought imaginary other, alternate, or future worlds.[3] As is made evident in one of the most influential of the early dystopias—Yevgeny Zamyatin's Мы (*We*) (1921), a major inspiration for both Aldous Huxley's *Brave New World* (1932) and George Orwell's *Nineteen Eighty-four* (1949)—the target of many of these dystopias will be "the utopia of human contrivance" (Sargent, 1994, 10–11) developed in the line of fictions extending from More through Bellamy. Moreover, in its figures of the Mephi people—those living beyond the walls of the novel's carefully regulated glass city—and the "infinite revolution," *We* offer glimpses of future utopias conceived at once on the spatial scales of the body and the globe.[4] However, other dystopias, most prominently among them being Orwell's *Nineteen Eighty-four*, will turn the critical energies of the dystopia toward what Mannheim identifies in *Ideology and Utopia* (1929) as a "conservative" utopianism, dominated by a nostalgia for the older spatial practices and lived spaces, Orwell's "Golden Country," of the nation-state.[5]

Although the dystopia will remain deeply influential throughout the post-World War Two period, and has taken on a renewed significance in the last few decades, it in turn gave rise to the new form of fiction that Tom Moylan and Peter Fitting name the "critical utopia" (Moylan 2014; Fitting 1979). These texts play a fundamental role in developing more expansive and inclusive utopian representations of space. Moylan argues:

> A central concern in the critical utopia is the awareness of the limitations of the utopian tradition, so that these texts reject utopia as a blueprint while preserving it as a dream. Furthermore, the novels dwell on the conflict between the originary world and the utopian society opposed to it so that the process of social change is more directly articulated. Finally, the novels focus on the continuing presence of difference and imperfection within utopian society itself and thus render more recognizable and dynamic alternatives. (2014, 10)

The landmark texts in this tradition—among others, Le Guin's *The Dispossessed*, Joanna Russ's *The Female Man* (1975), Marge Piercy's *Woman on the Edge of Time* (1976), and Delany's *Trouble on Triton*—not only call into question the classical utopia's assumption concerning the naturalness of the scale of the nation-state, they draw upon on the resources of feminist thought to bring a renewed attention within the tradition to the scale of the body.

Jennifer A. Wagner-Lawlor highlights the ways subsequent feminist utopian fictions—by, among others, Rajah Alsanea, Margaret Atwood, Octavia Butler, Angela Carter, Doris Lessing, Fatima Mernissi, Shahrnush Parsipur, Susan Sontag, and Jeanette Winterson—contribute to the development of a truly global conception of space in their emphasis on forms of community forged through a recognition of difference and an enactment of hospitality. For example, in her discussion of Toni Morrison's great historical novel-cum-utopia, *Paradise* (1997), Wagner-Lawlor observes,

> what Morrison offers... is a vision of *hospitality* centered in a particular and robust notion of love. In important ways, Morrison's speculation builds off of earlier feminist utopian vision, but she exceeds her predecessors in her frank insistence on the inclusion of all outsiders, including the reader, in that communal vision. (2013, 137)[6]

Similarly, in the early years of the twenty-first century, Michael Hardt and Antonio Negri's *Empire* trilogy (2000–2009) conceives of new forms of global belonging in their deeply spatial figure of the "multitude;" and Judith Butler explores original utopian figures of "kinship" and "family," which replace "the blood tie as the basis for kinship with consensual affiliation" and thereby "provide a critical perspective by which the very terms of livability might be rewritten, or indeed, written for the first time" (2000, 55, 74).[7]

Other contemporary utopias—to take only two of the most well-known examples, Kim Stanley Robinson's monumental Mars trilogy (1993–1996) and its "sequel," *2312* (2012); and Ken MacLeod's Fall Revolution quartet (1995–1999)[8]—develop original global figures of utopian space. Jameson concludes the first part of *Archaeologies of the Future* with a meditation on the necessary form of such a "new global Utopia" (224). Jameson maintains that we need to imagine such.

> autonomous and non-communicating Utopias—which can range from wandering tribes and settled villages all the way to great city-states or regional ecologies—as so many islands: a Utopian archipelago, islands in the net, a constellation of discontinuous centers, themselves internally decentered. (Jameson 2005, 221)

Jameson further suggests "if it were not so outworn and potentially misleading a term, federalism would be an excellent name for the political dimensions of this Utopian figure, until we have a better one" (224).

Given the need for such a form, it comes as no surprise that a number of the other most significant recent utopias—Nalo Hopkinson's *Midnight Robber* (2000), Tobias S. Buckell's Xenowealth series (2006–2012) and *Arctic Rising* (2012), and Karen Lord's *The Best of All Possible Worlds* (2013)—are composed by writers originally hailing from the Caribbean. Indeed, in her acknowledgments, Lord states, "The Caribbean is to me the new cradle of humanity. It was easy for me to imagine an entire planet just like it, with people from every corner of the world" (2013, 306).[9] At the same time, these texts and others like them take up the pressing challenges posed by a planetary-scaled climate change. One of Robinson's characters in *2312* exclaims of the Earth, "The place is trashed, they're cooked, they need to do it. In effect Earth needs terraforming as much as Venus or Titan!" (357)[10] It is precisely such a terraforming—inspired by efforts like Robinson's to conceive new spatial practices and lived spaces appropriate to emerging realities—that lies at the heart of the most significant contemporary utopias.

NOTES

1. *See* Karl Mannheim (1936), *Ideology and Utopia: An Introduction to the Sociology of Knowledge*, trans. Louis Wirth and Edward Shils, New York: Harcourt Brace Jovanovich. I (2002) discuss Mannheim's ideas in more detail in *Imaginary Communities: Utopia, the Nation, and the Spatial Histories of Modernity*, Berkeley: University of California Press, Ch. 6.
2. For a recent survey of medieval utopianisms, *see* Karma Lochrie (2016), *Nowhere in the Middle Ages*, Philadelphia: University of Pennsylvania Press.
3. For further discussion of the origins of the dystopia, *see* Phillip E. Wegner (2009), *Life between Two Deaths, 1989–2001: U.S. Culture in the Long Nineties*, Durham, N.C.: Duke University Press, Ch. 5; and Wegner (2014), "British Dystopian Novel from Wells to Ishiguro," in *The Blackwell Companion to British* Literature, eds. Bob DeMaria, Heesok Chang, and Samantha Zache, New York: Blackwell, 454–470.
4. For further discussion, *see* Wegner, *Imaginary Communities*, Ch. 5.
5. For further discussion, *see* ibid., Ch. 6.
6. For more on Butler's Paradise, *see* Phillip E. Wegner (2014), *Shockwaves of Possibility: Essays on Science Fiction, Globalization, and Utopia*, Oxford: Peter Lang, Ch. 3.
7. I discuss Butler's insights for reading utopian fictions in *Life between Two Deaths*, Ch. 8.
8. For more on MacLeod's quartet, *see* Wegner, *Shockwaves of Possibility*. Ch. 8.
9. For further discussion, *see* Phillip E. Wegner (2020), *Invoking Hope: Theory and Utopia in Dark Times*, Minneapolis: University of Minnesota Press, Ch. 7.
10. For further discussion, *see* Wegner, *Invoking Hope*, Ch. 7.

References

Arrighi, Giovanni. 1994. *The Long Twentieth Century: Money, Power, and the Origins of Our Times*. New York: Verso.

Bellamy, Edward. 1960. *Looking Backward, 2000–1887*. New York: New American Library.

Bogdanov, Alexander. 1984. *Red Star: The First Bolshevik Utopia*, ed. Loren R. Graham and Richard Stites, trans. Charles Rougle. Bloomington: Indiana University Press.

Butler, Judith. 2000. *Antigone's Claim: Kinship Between Life and Death*. New York: Columbia University Press.

Elliott, Robert C. 2013. In *The Shape of Utopia*, ed. Phillip E. Wegner. Oxford: Peter Lang.

Fitting, Peter. 1979. The Modern Anglo-American SF Novel: Utopian Longing and Capitalist Cooptation. *Science Fiction Studies* 6 (1): 59–76.

Giddens, Anthony. 1987. *The Nation-State and Violence*. Berkeley: University of California Press.

Hogan, Sarah. 2018. *Other Englands: Utopia, Capital, and Empire in an Age of Transition*. Stanford: Stanford University Press.

Jameson, Fredric. 1981. *The Political Unconscious: Narrative as a Socially Symbolic Act*. Ithaca: Cornell University Press.

———. 2005. *Archaeologies of the Future: The Desire Called Utopia and Other Science Fictions*. New York: Verso.

Lefebvre, Henri. 1991. *The Production of Space*, trans. Donald Nicholson-Smith. Oxford: Blackwell.

Lochrie, Karma. 2016. *Nowhere in the Middle Ages*. Philadelphia: University of Pennsylvania Press.

Lord, Karen. 2013. *The Best of All Possible Worlds*. New York: Del Rey.

Mannheim, Karl. 1936. *Ideology and Utopia: An Introduction to the Sociology of Knowledge*, trans. Louis Wirth and Edward Shils. New York: Harcourt Brace Jovanovich.

Marin, Louis. 1984. *Utopics: The Semiological Play of Textual Spaces*, trans. Robert A. Vollrath. Atlantic Highlands, NJ: Humanities Press International.

Marx, Karl, and Friedrich Engels. 1989. *Manifest Der Kommunistischen Partei*. Berlin: Dietz Verlag. English edition: Marx, Karl, and Friedrich Engels. 1978. Manifesto of the Communist Party. In *The Marx-Engels Reader*, ed. Robert C. Tucker, 469–500. New York: Norton.

More, Thomas. 1965. Utopia. In *The Yale Edition of the Complete Works of St. Thomas More*, Vol. 4, ed. Edward Surtz and J.H. Hexter. New Haven: Yale University Press.

Moylan, Tom. 2014. *Demand the Impossible: Science Fiction and the Utopian Imagination*, ed. Raffaella Baccolini. Oxford: Peter Lang.

Peyser, Thomas. 1998. *Utopia and Cosmopolis: Globalization in the Era of American Literary Realism*. Durham: Duke University Press.

Rabelais, François. 1955. *Gargantua and Pantagruel*, trans. J. M. Cohen. New York: Penguin.

Robinson. Kim Stanley. 2012. *2312*. New York: Orbit.

Sargent, Lyman Tower. 1994. The Three Faces of Utopianism Revisited. *Utopian Studies* 5 (1): 1–37.

Smith, Neil. 1993. Homeless/global: Scaling places. In *Mapping the Futures: Local Cultures, Global Change*, ed. Jon Bird, et al., 87–119. New York: Routledge.

Suvin, Darko. 1988. *Positions and Presuppositions in Science Fiction*. Kent, OH: The Kent State University Press.

Wagner-Lawlor, Jennifer A. 2013. *Postmodern Utopias and Feminist Fictions*. Cambridge: Cambridge University Press.

Wegner, Phillip E. 2002. *Imaginary Communities: Utopia, the Nation, and the Spatial Histories of Modernity*. Berkeley: University of California Press.

———. 2009. *Life between Two Deaths, 1989–2001: U.S. Culture in the Long Nineties*. Durham, N.C.: Duke University Press.

———. 2014. British Dystopian Novel from Wells to Ishiguro. In *The Blackwell Companion to British Literature*, ed. Bob DeMaria, Heesok Chang, and Samantha Zache, 454–470. New York: Blackwell.

———. 2014. *Shockwaves of Possibility: Essays on Science Fiction, Globalization, and Utopia*. Oxford: Peter Lang.

———. 2020. *Invoking Hope: Theory and Utopia in Dark Times*. Minneapolis: University of Minnesota Press.

Wells, H.G. 1967. *A Modern Utopia*. Lincoln: University of Nebraska Press.

Architecture

Nathaniel Robert Walker

INTRODUCTION

It is extremely difficult to construct a comprehensible vision of utopia without contending with architecture. For millennia, architecture and utopian dreaming have walked hand-in-hand, occasionally locking their steps and moving as one. This intimate bond has proven so powerful for two key reasons: first, human beings as we know and recognize them on Earth possess fragile bodies, and in the words of Nathaniel Coleman, "any Utopia that shelters corporeal beings requires a setting attuned to its specific objectives," which invariably include keeping people alive and comfortable (Coleman 2011, 1). The second reason for this long partnership is that utopian dreaming is inherently, as Lyman Tower Sargent argued, "social dreaming" (Sargent 1994, 3). Our instinctive longing for companionship and the inherent limitations of the human mind and body mean that any utopia built for one person only, in nonnegotiable perpetuity, must necessarily transform its single citizen into either a prisoner or a god. Togetherness is intrinsic to the human condition, and architecture sets many of the basic terms of human relationships by, for example, delineating private and public space, facilitating movement, and creating a common immersive environment of aesthetic and functional experience. One might say that the cultural, economic, political, and other intangible fabrics of human society make up their "software," while architecture—including buildings, infrastructure, and modified landscapes—is the "hardware" that

N. R. Walker (✉)
College of Charleston, Charleston, SC, USA

P. Marks et al. (eds.), *The Palgrave Handbook of Utopian and Dystopian Literatures*, https://doi.org/10.1007/978-3-030-88654-7_37

accommodates those fabrics, helping to characterize and perpetuate them in the process, and therefore becoming a crucial instrument of reform. Until human beings no longer dwell in bodies, and until they all become natural and committed sociopathic hermits, architecture will always be the gateway to utopia.

An exploration of the long-intertwined histories of utopia and architecture reveals a great deal about both. Even if one begins at the beginning, so to speak, with the world's diverse array of mythological and religious gardens of paradise, one finds early utopian architectural stirrings, particularly in acts of enclosure and connection (Giesecke and Jacobs 2012). It was also in deep antiquity, and in concert with these garden dreams, that prophets and philosophers first offered visions of an ideal earthly life built by humans in great cities, where the founding acts of architectural design and construction were put forward as the catalyzing agents of redemption. Yet, there is a tension, historically, between the tree and the column; at times, the divine garden and the human city have been placed in rhetorical opposition to one another, while in other times, people hoped to see them embrace. The Renaissance in Europe brought revolutionary new literary visions of redeemed cities, carrying ancient religious ideas forward while also engaging in intense new speculation on science and the future. The notion of the happy, healthy, virtuous city was challenged and forever transformed when that scientific future arrived, however, and industrial towns became roaring engines of modern utopian speculation, in large part by synthesizing, as a potent but volatile fuel for human imaginations, rising faith in scientific and technological progress with growing horror at the social and architectural outcomes of that progress. The ongoing literary reaction from this painful collision is arguably the source of the present state of utopian discourse, which seems to tilt so decisively toward the despair of dystopia, where architecture becomes evil. There are, however, still glimmers of hope on the horizon, and it seems that architecture and utopia, though their increasingly tentative steps may falter, have not finished their journey together just yet.

A Match Made in Heaven: Gardens and Architecture

While utopias traditionally take place in our mortal world and depend on human agency for their creation, paradises tend to be otherworldly and divine in origin and character. The two concepts are different but they are deeply related, and it is impossible to understand utopian architecture without first considering the sacred green places that preceded and gave birth to it. In many societies, paradise has often been described as a painless, deathless world of field and flower, bird, and bower—a great garden brought to a state of exquisite perfection by the same sacred forces that set creation in motion. Myth and religion have had to contend with the evident distances in space or time between the happy garden and our present life of turmoil, suffering, toil, and death. This is where we see architecture intersecting with the garden in early and important ways: opening it up to welcome the most blessed members of the human family and walling it off to prevent its defilement. Paradise has thus been described for many centuries as a *hortus conclusus*, or an enclosed garden; even the word "paradise" derives from the ancient Persian word *pairidaëza*, which means "walled garden" or "enclosed park." These walls are consistently very high.

In ancient China, the complex philosophical and religious matrix of Daoism incorporated prehistoric myths about magical places and beings into its quest for natural harmony and, ultimately, immortality (Bauer 1976; Little 1988; Loewe 1994). Sacred stories told of distant, mountainous islands in the eastern sea, where deathless beings known as *xian*, or "Transcendants," lived in breezy palaces and fragrant gardens, drinking wine and joining cranes and dragons in flight. In the western Kunlun Mountains, Queen Xiwangmu held immortal court in a great palace enveloped by a grove of peach trees that, once every thousand years, offered the fruit of immortality. For the rare occasions in which uninvited guests managed to traverse her mystical mountains, Xiwang-mu's garden was surrounded by a high wall. Some Daoist adepts in the Chinese Empire worked in temples, libraries, mountain retreats, and other rarefied spaces in the hopes of reaching the state of worshipful enlighten-ment that provided passage to these realms, but the closest that most people could hope to get was reading about or viewing representations of these faraway paradises in poetry and painting, or else summoning their moun-tainous, watery, flowery forms in beautiful gardens of rock, pond, and blossom (Keswick et al. 2003, 46–51).

A poet named Tao Qian (also known as Tao Yuanming) pushed back against this elite mysticism, creating one of the first politically charged utopian visions in the process. In 421 AD, during a particularly troublesome period of the Eastern Jin dynasty, he wrote *The Peach Blossom Spring*, which told of a secluded mountain village of simple homes and working fields where a cluster of normal humans had achieved great happiness through kindness, contentment, and other virtues, leading to harmony with each other and the natural forces of the world. They were protected from external enemies and the corruption of urban imperial culture by a secret, disappearing tunnel that sealed their world from outsiders. The ephemeral beauty of peach blossoms enveloped their little village, but they did not seek the fruit of immortality and had no desire for palaces or formal gardens. Tao Qian's vision of a utopia of rustic farms struck quite a contrast with the luxurious enclaves of Xiwangmu or the eastern isles, but even his imaginary village required a wall, of sorts, in order to stay safe and pure (Chiang 2009; Walker 2013).

In the opposite hemisphere, many different cultural groups in ancient Mesoamerica developed concepts of a divine, immortal "flower world" or "flowery road" that welcomed the deceased into a "paradise of gardens" or "Spirit Land" defined by happiness, health, and colorful natural beauty (Hill 1992, 119, 127–128). For the Maya, the apotheosis of great kings and queens into divine inhabitants of the flower world was facilitated after death by their transformative ascent up a spiritual "flower mountain," which had an architectural counterpart in the urban temple pyramid tombs, ritually inscribed with sacred hieroglyphs, that bridged the divide between the earthly and the heavenly, the living and the dead (Taube 2004). Ancient Egyptians, too, created enormous works of funereal architecture, also covered in writing, to open and perpetuate exchanges between realms of creation. Their land of the dead took multiple forms, but at its happiest it was the "Field of Reeds," a green and watery place of "bliss, peace, and eternal plentitude." This was represented, or at least evoked, in large sacred gardens near the city of Memphis, as well as smaller gardens connected to many noble tombs (Assmann 2005, 221–2, 233). It was difficult for human souls to reach the "isle of the blessed," however, as they had to memorize the incantations written in the Book of the Dead and negotiate the hazards of the dark underworld to "emerge from the shielded gateway" and step into the eternal garden (Assmann 2005, 127). There were many differences among the paradises of Asia, America, and Africa, but they were consistently understood as floral heavens shut off from quotidian human existence by walls, gates, impassable mountains, tumultuous oceans, or vast expanses of sky—only by building bridges in the form of great temples and tombs could one hope to reach their unfading blossoms, while tantalizing windows on them were fashioned in spoken or written word, painted image, and in the planting of real, tangible, if also mortal, gardens on earth.

From the Middle East came the most enduringly influential accounts of enclosed garden paradises, and these were paired with cities in narratives offering distinct turns toward human-built architectural utopias as alternatives to or collaborators with divine natural paradises. Among the oldest mythical precincts of peace and immortality was the Mesopotamian island of Dilmun; this was associated with the real island of Bahrain, where tens of thousands of tombs attest to the ancient belief that a spiritual garden of divine happiness could be accessed from that place (Delumeau 5, Lamberg-Karlovsky 1982, 45–50). The Epic of Gilgamesh, considered by many to be the oldest example of narrative literature to survive into the present, draws upon the legend of Dilmun in its tale of the great King of Uruk who, seeking immortality, traverses ferociously guarded mountains passes and dark tunnels until he "finds himself in a garden of jewels" (George 1999, 70). He then reaches an island paradise only to fail in his quest; but when the dejected king arrives home, he takes comfort in the lasting fame he will earn through the grand, monumental architecture of his city: "Climb Uruk's wall and walk back and forth! Survey its foundations, examine its brickwork! .... A square mile is city, a square mile date-grove…half a square mile the temple of Ishtar" (George 1999, xxxiv, 99). This would have been of great significance to listeners and readers in Mesopotamian cities like Uruk, Ur, and Babylon: the gardens of immortality were ultimately inaccessible, but the architecture of a strong, well-ordered, garden-filled, splendid, and sacred city was the second-best thing, offering a semblance of eternal life, wrought by human hands, in the form of enduring glory—this is perhaps the first glimpse of utopia.

There are important parallels and differences with the Epic of Gilgamesh in the peerlessly influential story of creation and corruption shared, in whole or in part, by the Abrahamic traditions. According to the Book of Genesis, the primordial cradle of humanity was the Garden of Eden, which God planted with fruitful trees and watered with a river that divided into four branches (Genesis 2:8–10). The first woman and man dwelled there in happiness and safety until they chose to eat the forbidden fruit from the "the tree of the knowledge of good and evil," and were henceforth banished from the garden, which was walled off from them forever (Genesis 2:16–17, 3:6–24). Not long after, one of their sons murdered his brother and was banished even further. He fled to the east and invented architecture, among other things, and established Enoch, the first city—hardly an auspicious beginning for urban life (Genesis 4:1–17). After his descendants grew proficient in architectural technology, they decided to pile their bricks and mortar into "a city, and a tower with its top in the heavens," to "make a name for ourselves" (Genesis 11:1–9). God thwarted the arrogant Tower of Babel by instantaneously fracturing the human language into different tongues. Genesis thus presents an excruciating multiplicity of failures: banishment from the divine garden was followed by the collapse of the human city, and with it any cultural unity and social cohesion. Subsequent biblical discussions of cities like Nineveh and Sodom are persistently pejorative, and glimmers of goodness are brief and dim.

There is one outstanding exception: Jerusalem, where the Jewish temple facilitated rapprochement between God and humanity. When that city was periodically sacked by earthly enemies such as the Babylonians or the Romans, prophecies foretold the happy triumph of the New Jerusalem, which would sparkle as God rebuilt "your foundations with sapphires....your pinnacles of rubies, your gates of jewels" (Isaiah 54:11–12). The Book of Ezekiel foretold that when the leaders of Israel divided the land equally among the tribes, put an end to unjust rule, and reconstructed the temple according to God's specifications, a river would burst forth from its foundations, restoring the desert wastes to bountiful life, and sustaining marvelous trees that heal and nourish everyone, even the foreigners who flock there from many nations (Ezekiel 40:1–47:22). The Christian Book of Revelation echoed elements of this prophecy, but instead of placing the construction of the New Jerusalem in human hands, it foretold the city's descent from heaven as a sparkling, geometrically perfect piece of architecture "like a very rare jewel, like jasper, clear as crystal," and made of "pure gold, clear as glass" (Revelation 21:11, 18). It, too, featured a river flanked by restorative trees (Revelation 23:1–3).

These joyful urban prophecies, in which a redeemed city ushers in a restored garden, reverses the sad trajectory of history as recounted in Genesis. The role of human agency is not clear, however—in Ezekiel, the New Jerusalem is a pseudo-utopian enterprise, with human political reform and architectural construction precipitating God's gift of a renewed garden, but in Revelation, both the city and the garden are iridescent miracles. For centuries, people of faith have debated these visions and wondered whether it was the duty of the devout to actively build an earthly utopia or to patiently wait for a heavenly paradise, with important writers like Augustine of Hippo coming down firmly in favor of the latter in his influential 427 AD book *The City of God* (Walker 2020, 18–34). In later works of utopian literature, the rich and ambiguous relationship between the sacred garden and the human city was repeatedly revisited.

The works of classical poets and philosophers, especially Plato, also fed the imaginations of those who hoped to restore humanity to a Golden Age or to summon Elysium, which were the names that the Greeks and Romans, respectively, affixed to their godly gardens of immortal peace and joy. Plato's account of Atlantis bore striking resemblance to the narrative coupling of Eden and Babel, as a divine, enclosed, happy little grove on a secluded island was slowly corrupted as it transformed into a bustling city of metallic architecture, marvelous bridges and tunnels, constant commerce, and an arrogant desire to conquer the world. Accordingly, Atlantis irked the gods and was undone by their wrath. On the other hand, Plato insisted that powerful cities of happiness and harmony could be created if virtue was protected. He formulated a rigidly hierarchical social and political order that would exert perfect control over almost all human activity, especially the arts and crafts that gave form to the city and its culture and, consequently, helped shape the minds of its citizens. Architecture must, Plato argued, be ruthlessly regulated. In *The Laws*, he argued that all homes should be built with such "evenness and uniformity" that the whole city would take on "the appearance of one house" (Plato 1988, 167). In *The Republic*, he insisted that architects should study the finest and most divine qualities of nature, looking to music and "the condition of our bodies and of all things that grow," so that they can decode the fundamental character of harmony, gracefulness, order, beauty, and other virtues, and then apply them to the art of building. The results would be incredible: "our young can live in a healthy environment, drawing improvement from every side, whenever things which are beautifully fashioned expose their eyes or ears to some wholesome breeze…and lead them imperceptibly, from earliest childhood, into affinity, friendship and harmony with beauty of speech and thought" (Plato 2000, 91–92). This idea would prove perennially compelling to those who would build utopias.

The Middle Ages have often been described as a "barren period in the history of utopian thought" (Kumar 1978, 11). This is still debated, but the list of imaginative, ideal literary architectures from this period does seem comparatively small, with the medieval Irish wanderer St. Brendan's breathtaking description of pure crystal churches on mystical paradise islands in the western sea perhaps the most remarkable (Barron and Burgess 2005, 225). This time saw the steadily accelerating magnificence of medieval Christian cathedrals, in which the New Jerusalem was evoked with stone, garden, and glass in heavenly Augustinian terms (Helms 2002; Meyer 2003; Doquang

2018), and the proliferation of gorgeous Islamic gardens summoning the presence of Eden with peerless power (Thacker 1997, Barrucand and Bednorz 2002), but literary utopian speculation would only fully resurge in the Renaissance, as part of the reclamation of ancient arts and philosophies. Then, Plato's recipe for a naturally derived, divinely attuned city with the power to mold its inhabitants was recalled and intertwined with ongoing debate on the meaning of the biblical prophecies to animate a great explosion of utopian visions in Europe, written and disseminated to drive reform in the real world. Visionaries at this time would also detect, in the stormy light of religious conflict and natural science then growing on the horizon, premonitions and reflections of their hopes for the future in the botanical mysteries of the lost Eden and the soaring form of Babel, the glistening metal structures of Atlantis and the pure crystal of the New Jerusalem. The gates of the garden may finally be reopening, it was believed, and they promised to lead to cities of health, happiness, and luminous splendor.

Urban Fabrics Woven and Torn Asunder

When Thomas More published *Utopia* in 1516, London was already beginning to swell into an unmanageable mess due to agricultural reforms displacing countless peasants who poured into the city's streets and slums in search of work; this infuriated him, but he still had faith in the possibilities of urban life. His Utopia was, like so many of the secluded paradises that came before, located on a faraway, isolated island, but this was no natural place—the wise but mortal King Utopus had cut his peninsular realm off from the outside world by digging a great ocean channel through its neck. He also planned the island's fifty-four virtually identical, carefully gridded cities, where every block of homes "looketh like one large house," as Plato had suggested, and all citizens rotate from one communal apartment building to another, and sometimes to the cultivated garden countryside, so that they can love and improve the whole of the realm (More 1808, 60). The architecture of Utopia had evolved over time in a manner that suggests More was already theorizing a kind of technological progress: "…their houses were at first low and mean…with mud walls, any kind of timber, and thatched with straw. At present their houses are three storys high, faced with stone, plaster, or brick….Their roofs are flat, and they lay on them a kind of cheap plaster, which will not take fire, yet resists weather better than lead. Abounding in glass, they glaze their windows…" (More 1808, 61). To a person living in Tudor England, three-story homes with flat, plastered roofs and an abundance of glass would have sounded bizarrely wonderful. The Utopians also planted magnificent gardens in the courtyards of their shared homes, presenting a picture of orderly, egalitarian, technologically advanced, airy, clean, and verdant urban life that would have presented a sharp contrast with disorderly, unequal, often ramshackle, smoky, muddy London.

The Reformation followed the publication of More's happy vision of great garden cities, and many utopian books were published in the dramatic, even apocalyptic conflict that followed. Most drew upon all of the precedents discussed thus far: Eden and Babel, the New Jerusalem, Plato's ideal Republic and Atlantis, and More's *Utopia*, as well as visually entrancing proposals for geometrically perfect cities by Renaissance architects like Filarete and Francesco di Giorgio Martini (Rosenau 1959; Argan 1970, 9–29; Eaton 2002, 40–68). The Catholic friar Tommaso Campanella described his *City of the Sun*, a circular city of science where a Platonic hierarchy would watch over citizens as they effortlessly acquired a perfect knowledge of nature thanks to the scientific displays that covered every wall, while the Protestant clergyman Johann Andreae published *Christianopolis*, another perfectly ordered city, where industry and education were segregated into different quadrants and all citizens benefitted from clean, rational, simple homes cleansed by a tidy sewer system and cheered by the glow of streetlighting (Walker 2020, 46–58). These and other visions of this time, such as Francis Bacon's *New Atlantis* and Denis Vairasse's *The History of the Sevarites*, had much in common, including ubiquitous urban gardens. They also shared a faith that the emerging power of natural science would enable Christians to end the crisis of the Reformation and usher in the promised era of happiness foretold in the Bible, when the redeemed city would facilitate the reclamation of Eden, or what Bacon called the "Great Instauration" (Tuveson 1949; Manuel and Manuel 1979, 205–412).

This happy outcome was not, however, forthcoming, and religious skepticism began to rise amid the flames and smoke of the vicious and intractable Reformation conflict, while science continued to fuel speculation on the future. By the late 1700s, the wheels of industry began to turn in Britain, churning out immense wealth even as it submerged the working poor in unplanned urban slums with their attendant filth, disease, and squalor. Utopian visions for a radical new future once again rapidly proliferated, often tied to radical proposals for socialist political reform. Architecture was routinely put forward as a crucial means to redemption, but visions of utopian cities became increasingly rare, especially in the English-speaking world, where many reformers came to believe that science and technology would enable humans to disperse their New Jerusalems in a sprawling suburban landscape. These utopian dreamers promised to imbed every towering, garden-roofed apartment building and every robotically staffed crystal cottage in Edenic verdure, fresh air, and endless sunshine, while flying carriages and pneumatic tubes connected happy, modern people to scattered centers of production, consumption, and culture (Walker 2020). Jane Loudon even imagined homes that were also railway carriages, so that one could live in the suburbs of London on Thursday and then, with the flip of a few switches, take your entire household to the beach on Friday (Loudon 1828, 140–141). From Charles Fourier's proposal for industrial pleasure palaces laced through with glass arcades to Robert Owen's vision of walled garden settlements punctuated by glasshouses and steam-engine chapels, rural and suburban utopian schemes proliferated in the 1800s, and many people tried to build them. Some nineteenth-century utopian visionaries, like Étienne Cabet and James Silk Buckingham, proposed architectures that fused futuristic elements like mechanization, metal, and glass with cosmopolitan ornaments and forms from around the world, preparing to fulfill Ezekiel's prophecy that all of the nations would gather at the sparkling New Jerusalem, undoing the curse of Babel. With the arrival of popular science-fiction novels like Edward Bulwer-Lytton's *The Coming Race* of 1871 and Edward Bellamy's *Looking Backward 2000–1887* of 1888, utopian architectures and landscapes began to materialize in the minds of millions of readers around the world, who could close their eyes and imagine exchanging their brick terrace homes on sooty, tubercular streets for a hygienic, electrified villa of artificial stone with a vast garden sheltered by an aluminum-framed dome glistening with synthetic diamond panes. These earnestly written, politically charged futuristic utopias had demonstrable impacts on real urban planners and architects like Ebenezer Howard and Frank Lloyd Wright (Walker 2020; Watson 2017), contributing to the birth and proliferation of the modern suburb as well as modernist architecture.

As the twentieth century passed its middle decades, however, it seemed to many that the promise of a technological utopia had not only been broken but had also proven extremely dangerous. The movement to abandon traditional, human-scaled cities for endless, totally mechanized suburban landscapes had disastrous unintended consequences, resulting in dysfunctional, ecologically devastating, unhealthy, unattractive non-places; meanwhile, the technologically obsessed tenets of modernist architecture conspired with humanity's natural tendencies toward mediocrity to produce alienating structures and districts that were especially harmful to the marginalized people left behind in decaying, neglected cities. Dystopian books and films like *Metropolis, Brave New World, 1984, Clockwork Orange,* and *Blade Runner* proliferated in the 1900s and early 2000s, pointing accusing fingers at the hubris of our modern Towers of Babel by filling the vacuous halls of monstrous mega-structures with abusive corporations and governments, and cloaking chasm-like streets with impenetrable pollution swirling in the radioactive glare of teeming swarms of vehicles. Modern architects have worked, with mixed success, to confront the criticism in these dystopias, with one reform-minded book tellingly entitled *Back from Utopia: The Challenge of the Modern Movement* (Henket and Heynen 2002).

Conclusion

Outside of government propaganda or corporate advertising, utopian visions with optimistic architectures are rare in today's cynical world. Among the few to truly capture the public's imagination is the science-fiction African kingdom of Wakanda from the *Black Panther* comic books, brought vividly to life in the 2018 film of the same name. Mostly envisioned by the African-American production designer Hannah Beachler, its Golden City was explicitly designed to put "people before technology" (Flatow 2018, n.p.). The great capital had its fair share of gleaming skyscrapers, but it also incorporated many traditional architectural materials and ornaments, parks and gardens, and pedestrian streets of real urban density and human scale. It offered, in short, a sophisticated utopian urbanism that merged the timeless with the modern, the organic with the high-tech in a way unknown in most recent utopias and, for that matter, most architecture schools. In the process, it offered a vision of African sophistication and elegance that millions of people around the world found redemptive; it also, probably unconsciously, evoked the ancient longing to harmoniously interweave a flourishing Eden with a sparkling New Jerusalem. Perhaps utopia still has the power to beckon us—perhaps we can still set out to return to the lost garden, if we first retrace our steps to the city and get back to building together.

References

Argan, Giulio C. 1970. *The Renaissance City*. New York: George Braziller.

Assmann, Jan. 2005. *Death and Salvation in Ancient Egypt*, trans. David Lorton. Ithaca, New York: Cornell University Press.

Barron, W.R.J., and Glyn S. Burgess. 2005. *The Voyage of Saint Brendan: Representative Versions of the Legend in English Translation*. Exeter: University of Exeter Press.

Barrucand, Marianne and Achim Bednorz. 2002. *Moorish Architecture in Andalucia*. Cologne: Taschen.

Bauer, Wolfgang. 1976. *China and the Search for Happiness: Recurring Themes in Four Thousand Years of Chinese Cultural History*, Trans. Michael Shaw. New York: Seabury Press.

Chiang, Sing-Chen Lydia. 2009. Visions of happiness: Daoist utopias and Grotto Paradises in early and Medieval Chinese Tales. *Utopian Studies* 20 (1): 97–120.

Coleman, Nathaniel. 2011. Introduction: Architecture and Utopia. In *Imagining and Remaking the World: Reconsidering Architecture and Utopia*, ed. Nathaniel Coleman, 1–26. Oxford: Peter Lang.

Doquang, Mailan S. 2018. *The Lithic Garden: Nature and the Transformation of the Medieval Church*. Oxford University Press.

Eaton, Ruth. 2002. *Ideal Cities: Utopianism and the (Un)Built Environment*. New York: Thames and Hudson.

Flatow, Nicole. 2018. *The Social Responsibility of Wakanda's Golden City*. Bloomberg City Lab. https://www.bloomberg.com/news/articles/2018-11-05/how-hannah-beachler-built-black-panther-s-wakanda. Accessed 18 Mar 2021.

George, Andrew, trans. 1999. The Epic of Gilgamesh: The Babylonian Epic Poem and Other Texts in Akkadianu and Sumerian. London: Penguin Books.

Giesecke, Annette and Naomi Jacobs. 2012. Nature, Utopia, and the Garden. in *Earth Perfect? Nature, Utopia and the Garden*, ed. Annette Giesecke and Naomi Jacobs, 6–17. London: Black Dog Publishing.

Helms, Mary W. 2002. Sacred landscape and the early Medieval European Cloister: Unity, Paradise, and the Cosmic Mountain. *Anthropos* 97 (2): 435–453.

Henket, Hubert-Jean and Hilde Heynen. 2002. *Back from Utopia: The Challenge of the Modern Movement*. Rotterdam: 010 Publishers.

Hill, Jane H. 1992. The Flower World of Old Uto-Aztecan. *Journal of Anthropological Research* 48 (2): 117–144.

Keswick, Maggie, Charles Jencks, and Alison Hardie. 2003. The Chinese Garden: History, Art, and Architecture. Third edition. New York: Rizzoli.

Kumar, Krishan. 1978. *Utopia and Anti-Utopia in Modern Times*. Oxford: Basil Blackwell.

Lamberg-Karlovsky, C. C. 1982. Dilmun: Gateway to Immortality. Journal of Near Eastern Studies 41 (1): 45–50.

Little, Stephen. 1988. *Realm of the Immortals: Daoism in the Arts of China*. Cleveland: Cleveland Museum of Art in cooperation with Indiana University Press.

Loewe, Michael. 1994. *Ways to Paradise: The Chinese Quest for Immortality*. Taipei: SMC.

Loudon, Jane. 1828. *The Mummy! A Tale of the Twenty-Second Century*, vol. 1. London: Henry Colburn.

Manuel, Frank E., and Fritzie P. Manuel. 1979. *Utopian Thought in the Western World*. Cambridge, Massachusetts: Harvard University Press.

Meyer, Ann R. 2003. *Medieval Allegory and the Building of the New Jerusalem*. Cambridge: D.S. Brewer.

More, Thomas. 1808. In *Memoirs of Sir Thomas More, with a new translation of his Utopia*, ed. Arthur Cayley. London: Cadell and Davis.

Plato. 1988. *The laws of Plato*, trans. Thomas L. Pangle. Chicago: University of Chicago Press.

———. 2000. *The Republic*, trans. Tom Griffith. Cambridge University Press.

Rosenau, Helen. 1959. *The Ideal City: Its Architectural Evolution*. London: Routledge and Paul.

Sargent, Lyman Tower. 1994. The three faces of Utopia Revisited. *Utopian Studies* 5 (1): 1–37.

Taube, Karl A. 2004. Flower Mountain: Concepts of life, beauty, and paradise among the Classic Maya. *RES: Anthropology and Aesthetics* 45: 69–98.

Taube, Karl A. Flower Mountain: Concepts of Life, Beauty, and Paradise among the Classic Maya. RES: Anthropology and Aesthetics 45: 69–98.

Thacker, Christopher. 1997. *The History of Gardens*. Berkeley: University of California Press.

Tuveson, Ernest Lee. 1949. *Millennium and Utopia: A Study in the Background of the Idea of Progress*. Berkeley: University of California Press.

Walker, Nathaniel Robert. 2013. Reforming the Way: The Palace and the Village in Daoist Paradise. *Utopian Studies* 24 (1): 6–22.

———. 2020. *Victorian Visions of Suburban Utopia: Abandoning Babylon*. Oxford University Press.

Watson, Joseph M. 2017. Topographies of the Future: Urban and Suburban Visions in Edward Bellamy's Utopian Fiction. *Planning Perspectives* 32 (4): 639–649.

Urbanism

David Pinder

Introduction

What can be learned from the literatures of utopian urbanism for making better futures? How might rediscovering writings, images, and experiments in utopian urbanism from earlier periods help to ignite current imaginations and address global challenges? These questions are posed by Mike Davis in his essay, "Who will build the ark?": "Tackling the challenge of sustainable urban design for the whole planet, and not just for a few privileged countries or social groups, requires a vast stage for the imagination," he writes. "It presupposes a radical willingness to think beyond the horizon of neoliberal capitalism toward a global revolution that reintegrates the labor of the informal working classes, as well as the rural poor, in the sustainable reconstruction of their built environments and livelihoods." He adds: "Of course, this is an utterly unrealistic scenario, but one either embarks on a journey of hope, believing that collaborations between architects, engineers, ecologists, and activists can play small but essential roles in making an *alter-monde* more possible, or one submits to a future in which designers are just hireling imagineers of elite, alternative existences" (Davis 2018, 220).

Davis's text will be returned to later for it speaks to a central concern of this chapter, which is about the significance of utopian perspectives on urbanism and processes of urbanization not only historically but also for addressing current issues. At a time when capitalist urbanization processes have both

D. Pinder (✉)
Roskilde University, Roskilde, Denmark

P. Marks et al. (eds.), *The Palgrave Handbook of Utopian and Dystopian Literatures*, https://doi.org/10.1007/978-3-030-88654-7_38

intensified and extended in ways that some commentators have termed "planetary" (Lefebvre 2003; Brenner 2014), it is vital to ask critically about the futures being forged *and* foreclosed. What might be the role of utopian imaginations in outlining and constructing other possible urban worlds? How has utopian literature intertwined with and informed urban theory and practice, including planning? How does it speak to ambitions to transform urban spaces and life, including those commonly presented as unrealistic or impossible? What has recently become of utopian urbanism, and of how and why is so much urban thought dystopian?

Utopias have, since Plato and St Augustine, often been imagined in the form of the city. "The city always held the promise of utopia, the intimation that it be the spatial form in which a harmonious and wholesome society could take shape, as the emanation of a civic, rational, or holy order," notes literary scholar Lieven Ameel: "And as often the city has been associated with the opposite: with the failure of such an order to take hold, and with the sense that an imminent end-time could upend the social and cultural fabric of humankind in the form of its perhaps most celebrated cultural artefact" (Ameel 2016, 785).[1] In the text that inaugurates the literary genre in 1516, Thomas More's island of Utopia is adorned with fifty-four "large and well built" cities (More 2016, 73). Private property and money are abolished, houses are integrated with well-cultivated gardens, and spaces are open to a surveillant gaze. In utopian literature since then, urban forms frequently embody as well as become means for instilling harmony, stability, rationality, and equality. If that is the case for literary utopias conjuring alternative urban worlds in other spaces or times, it also speaks to utopian impulses underpinning urban plans and schemes intended to deliver a good life.

Utopian dreams are often shadowed by dystopian counterparts, however, whether that is through projecting their heavens against contemporary hells, or through themselves turning dark. There is further suspicion or even conviction from some quarters that utopias harbor an inherently dystopian core. The historian and urbanist Lewis Mumford argues that attributes such as fixation, regimentation, and standardization enter into the conception of the utopian city by the ancient Greeks. They then continue, whether overtly or in more disguised forms, through apparently more democratic modern urban utopias, such that "utopia merges into the dystopia of the twentieth century" (Mumford 1965, 277). Many critics have certainly attacked urban utopias for their supposedly controlling and authoritarian cast, which is based around fixing processes within a spatial form. While extensive debate surrounds how to read More's *Utopia*, the harmony and virtue of his urban spaces are maintained not only by a strong external border but also by restrictions on movement and the omnipresent ordering gaze where "all men live in full view, so that they are obliged both to perform their ordinary task and to employ themselves well in their spare hours" (More 2016, 93).

This chapter starts with the dark horizons of contemporary urbanization as rendered in dystopian literature and film. But noting the utopian impulses that underly critical dystopias, attention then turns more directly to utopian perspectives. Influential strands of utopian urbanism emerged during the late nineteenth and early twentieth centuries across literature, planning, and architecture in response to the problems of capitalist urbanization and in the belief that transforming urban spaces and life went together, with the production of new urban spaces seen as embodying and, in some cases, as the key for enabling a new urban life. Narratives of modern urbanism commonly tell of the demise and dismissal of such utopianism in the later twentieth century. But how might such stories be revisited? What utopian figures haunt them and how they might speak critically to different conditions today?

Dystopian Urbanism and Dark Futures

Fire, flood, drought, plague, pollution, nuclear attack, invading hordes, marauding monsters: they are only among the many varied means through which the destruction of urban settlements has been imagined and portrayed as part of wider narratives of social collapse (Davis 1998). Urban catastrophism has escalated in regions of the Global North since the turn of the century in response to a range of growing fears about the future (Urry 2016), with climate change and recently pandemic particularly prominent. But, as historian Gyan Prakash notes, "noir urbanisms" more generally have varied and influential histories, being characterized not just by "their bleak mood but also their mode of interpretation, which ratchets up a critical reading of specific historical conditions to diagnose crisis and catastrophe" (Prakash 2010, 1). Dystopian texts specifically place us "directly in a terrifying world to alert us of the danger that the future holds if we do not recognise its symptoms in the present" (2).

Dark urban futures are central in much science fiction. In canonical films such as *Metropolis* (1927) and *Blade Runner* (1982), it has been noted how "the architecture of the dystopian cityscape functions as a synecdoche for the wider catastrophe that has overcome their respective populations." In these cases, "the city *is* the dystopian novum, the shape of the prior catastrophe encoded deep within its social and architectural forms" (Milner 2004, 267). Urban crises from the 1970s and their rooting in the capitalist economy found responses and diagnoses not only in the development of critical urban theories of the time associated with David Harvey, Manuel Castells, and others but also in the speculative fiction of so-called "new wave" science fiction (Latham 2009). Over the following two decades, urban and social theorists drew inspiration in particular from the cyberpunk science fiction of William Gibson, Octavia Butler, and others to grapple with dystopian landscapes they saw as emergent under processes of neoliberalization, including their privatization, fortification, militarization, and spatial apartheid. Mike Davis (1998, 361–362), for example, in his writings on Los Angeles and its "ecology of fear", refers approvingly to these authors' use of "disciplined extrapolation to explore the dark possibilities of the near future," and favorably contrasts their accounts to the more familiar dystopian imagery of *Blade Runner*. The influences also run the other way, with Gibson in his novel *Virtual Light* acknowledging the influence of Davis's earlier writings on that city and specifically his accounts of the privatization of its public spaces (Gibson 1994, 351–352).

The turn by urban and social analysts to the fictional worlds of cyberpunk was associated with a wider *fin-de-millennium* pessimism and a "general loss of visions of utopian transcendence and hope in a better future" (Burrows 1997, 235). Since then, there has been extensive debate about the critical significance of dystopian perspectives for addressing urban questions. The fatalistic and disempowering nature of dystopian narratives is often commented upon where there seems no hope or potential to challenge the dark realities in which the reader or viewer is immersed. Literary dystopias may be understood as reproducing dominant narratives that there are no alternatives to current conditions and hence as *anti-utopian*. Within urban studies, planning and policy, dystopian perspectives often replay long-standing, anti-urban prejudices about cities as calamitous sources of social ills, as seedbeds of deprivation and disorder, with a languishing and dangerous "underclass" on to which bourgeois fantasies and desires are projected (Baeten 2002). These perspectives, too, are often anti-utopian, serving to naturalize problems and warn off efforts to tackle their roots.

At the same time, dystopian narrative forms have been widely deployed among urban critics to highlight the hellishness of current conditions so as to galvanize improvements, from nineteenth-century reformers confronting the dark sides of industrial cities to chroniclers of contemporary "slums." Some dystopian texts, in their efforts to critique developments through nightmarish presentations, retain utopian impulses. That is particularly the case with "critical dystopias" that critics identified as emerging from the late 1980s and 1990s as a number of SF writers and film-makers turned to dystopian narratives to explore utopian possibilities in dark times. They combine pessimism about current trends with resistance to closure, maintaining a horizon of hope through opening spaces of contestation and opposition (Baccolini and Moylan 2003). They thus renew links between utopia and imagination during a period of neoliberal capitalism and militarism when both were under assault. It is to the significance of utopian urban imaginations that I turn in the remainder of this chapter.

NEW SPACES AND NEW LIVES

"Surely I had never seen this city nor one comparable to it before." So announces Julian West, the wealthy narrator of Edward Bellamy's *Looking Backward 2000–1887* (1888), on awakening in Boston in the year 2000 and being taken to a rooftop. One evening in 1887 he had sought to overcome his insomnia by retreating from the city's noise to his underground sleeping chamber, and by being placed in a trance. Now, stretching in all directions at his feet, he finds miles of broad streets, grand public buildings, and tree-filled open squares where "statues glistened and fountains flashed in the late afternoon sun" (Bellamy 2007, 22). Spatial and social organization have been so transformed that he believes his slumber might have been for a thousand years. He learns from his host how surplus wealth, no longer lavished in private luxury, is now more popularly directed to "the adornment of the city, which we all enjoy in equal degree" (25). Industrial production and distribution have been reorganized along collective and rational lines, efficiently marshaled through the application of a national "industrial army" so as to overcome scarcity, to avoid waste, and to deliver the material conditions of a centralized and egalitarian socialist society.

As one of the most influential literary utopias of the modern period, which soon sold hundreds of thousands of copies worldwide, Bellamy's book was part of a remarkable flourishing of utopian writing in the last decades of the nineteenth century, particularly in Britain and North America (Beaumont 2009). This was in a context of economic and political instability that was marked by capitalist crises, heightened unemployment, working-class discontent, and a search for alternatives to the existing capitalist order. Early in the book West repeatedly references "labor troubles" and "almost incessant" strikes, and he conveys a common perception that society is approaching "a critical period which might result in great changes." Some of his contemporaries predict "impending social cataclysm" (Bellamy 2007, 9–11). The attention of commentators and reformers around this time was also increasingly turning to the unhealthy, overcrowded, impoverished, and potentially explosive conditions of what poet James Thomson designated in 1880 as "the city of dreadful night." Their concerns are echoed in Bellamy's passages on the destitution and wretchedness of contemporary Boston. But it was particularly his projected solution, in which capitalism is reordered without revolution, and in which a well-planned and smokeless metropolis replaces urban disorder, that led to many readers eagerly debating, organizing, and seeking to apply its lessons.

Among them was Ebenezer Howard who recounted being "carried away" on his first reading, and who took inspiration for developing his own utopian proposals in *Tomorrow: A Peaceful Path to Real Reform* (1898). Revised as *Garden Cities of Tomorrow* (1902), this in turn became one of the most influential books in the development of urban planning. Howard often recounted the significance of utopian literature for his thinking. He attested specifically to how reading Bellamy made him realize as never before "the splendid possibilities of a new civilization based on service to the community and not almost exclusively on self-interest," and how it left him determined to help "bring a new civilization into being."[2] Co-operation, cohesion, and harmony were central concerns behind his attempts to bring together town and country, which he saw as restoring a natural spatial as well as social order. The smoke-lessness of Bellamy's Boston is echoed in Howard's most visionary diagram labeled "Group of slumless, smokeless cities." Howard became more wary of the rigid and authoritarian elements of Bellamy's depiction of society as a "great Brotherhood," especially on reading William Morris's riposte in *News from Nowhere* (1890). The former pictured society "in the terms of a Mechanic, or at least in the terms of an Administrator and Law Giver," Howard commented, while Morris was "a poet, full of imagination." He nevertheless valued both "prophets" for their contrasting depictions of order and freedom.[3]

Bellamy attracted support from other planners and architects. Some, in turn, apparently influenced the more spatially specified suburbanized vision that he depicted in his less celebrated sequel *Equality* (1897). Frank Lloyd Wright directly acknowledged the influence of that latter book and included excerpts in promotional materials for his decentralized vision of Broadacre City in the 1930s (Watson 2017). The intertwining of utopian fiction and modern urban planning remains under appreciated, most often noted in relation to prominent individuals. The significance of a "veritable tidal wave" of less famous but popular Victorian writings that tackled problems of industrial urbanization by advancing contrasting visions for "dispersed garden living" has nevertheless recently gained recognition, especially in terms of the formation of "the modern suburban dream." Based neither on returning to the past nor on fundamentally challenging present social structures to remake the future, these reassuringly presented "a new kind of modernity that would offer its happy, healthy, virtuous residents all the pleasures of industrial society with none of the pain" (Walker 2020, 2–3).

Amid dramatic transformations and contradictory experiences of the early twentieth century, much European modernist and avant-garde literature and art became preoccupied with "an 'unreal city' between the extremes of hope and dread, between a distant Utopia and imminent Apocalypse" (Timms 1985, 7). Futurists, expressionists, constructivists, and others contributed to the ferment from which developed another strand of utopian urbanism around the Modern Movement in architecture and planning. Aligning itself with and seeking to advance modernization, this found its most influential expressions in the urban schemes of Le Corbusier during the 1920s and 1930s. Despite significant differences, Howard and Le Corbusier shared assumptions that reorganizing urban space was key to delivering a new civilization. Tackling current urban problems required the constitution of ordered alternatives. Their dreams of order were intended to circumvent the need for revolutionary change. Le Corbusier made this explicit when, having famously asked rhetorically "Architecture or revolution?", he replied: "Revolution can be avoided" (Le Corbusier 1946, 289).[4] Their utopianism was, in this sense, similar to that of Bellamy and other reformist social dreamers around his time whose utopian fictions attempted to resolve the social contradictions of the period. While in certain respects critical stimulants, their utopias also functioned as what Matthew Beaumont terms "a vaccination against the germ of revolution." In the face of insurgent energies from below, they were—to use a term he takes from Marx—"sedative" (Beaumont 2009, 70, 79).

Deaths and After-Lives of Utopian Urbanism

The same year that Julian West awakens from his deep sleep, the geographer David Harvey published *Spaces of Hope* in which he invokes Bellamy in relation to a bleak account of contemporary urban inequalities and injustices. Focusing on his then home city of Baltimore, Harvey highlights the concentrations of poverty, unemployment, homelessness, abandoned houses, and ill-health. More affluent residents meanwhile flee to exclusionary suburbs, or increasingly ex-urbs and gated communities. What disturbs him are not only the disparities of wealth and power within its uneven geographical development but also the apparent lack of fundamental alternatives. Corporate and big money interests, including the media, work relentlessly to naturalize the "free market." Attempts to find alternatives are suppressed or dismissed as utopian in the pejorative sense of fanciful, impossible, or even dangerous. Harvey is reminded of Ernst Bloch's comment, originally made in conversation with Adorno, that there is "a very clear interest that has prevented the world from being changed into the possible" (Harvey 2000, 258). He compares the situation with that of a hundred years before:

> Where is that inspiring vision of the sort that Bellamy provided? It is, alas, all too fashionable in these times to proclaim the death of Utopia, to insist that utopianism of any sort will necessarily and inevitably culminate in totalitarianism and disaster. Naturally enough, our urban problems, when seen through the lens of such cynicism, seem intractable, immune to any remedy within the grasp of us mere mortals. (Harvey 2000, 257–258)

The reference to Bellamy may seem surprising given the criticisms of his reformist vision by radicals since Morris. Harvey's rhetorical point, however, is to contrast the significance then accorded to Bellamy's utopia and the energies that it inspired, especially among those seeking to improve urban conditions, with the denigration of utopias a century on. Claims about the death of utopia certainly became widespread in the late twentieth century with the collapse of really existing state-based alternatives to capitalism and the rise of neoliberalism. In relation to urbanism, they rest more specifically on narratives concerning the disastrous consequences of earlier utopian perspectives and their efforts to modernize urban spaces especially following the Second World War. Images of urban destruction—both of the devastation that large-scale urban renewal required and of the purportedly broken results, most notoriously in the form of the Pruitt-Igoe housing estate in St Louis, demolished in 1972—helped critics to establish (highly questionable) equations between utopianism, modernism, and failed authoritarianism so as to justify their jettisoning. There is no space here to revisit such debates with their common villains and set pieces although Harvey indicates grounds for a more materialist analysis than those typically offered when he notes that many of the problems from efforts to realize utopias of "spatial form," such as those discussed above, flow not from the forms themselves but from the social processes mobilized to materialize them (ibid., 171–173). Howard's compromises with powerful forces so as to build garden cities, and the consequent dilution or loss of his social agenda, constitute such a case.

None of this is to say that utopian urbanism as such has come to an end. Harvey intersperses his account of Baltimore with photographs whose captions testify to its continued but "degenerate" forms (a term he takes from Marin [1984]). They include the "bourgeois utopia" of suburban sprawl; the "developer utopia" of waterfront spectacle; the "yuppie utopia" of gentrified industrial buildings; the "privatopia" of gated communities; and the "utopian nostalgia" of commercialized new urbanism (Harvey 2000, 139–172). He also refers to shopping malls of the form prototyped locally by developer James Rouse before the construction of his pavilions at the harbor. Whereas Louis Marin uses the term "degenerate utopia" to refer to the way that Disneyland glosses over contradictions and perpetuates rather than critiques the fetish of commodity culture, Harvey generalizes to argue that we are now surrounded by multiple degenerate utopias that "instantiate rather than critique the idea that 'there is no alternative,' save those given by the conjoining of technological fantasies, commodity culture, and endless capital accumulation" (168).

To these examples might be added many other recent urban projects worldwide, including those associated with "fantastic architecture" (Sargisson 2012) and "smart cities," the latter described as "the new urban utopias of the twenty-first century" (Datta 2015, 4). Drawing out critically their utopian dimensions and asking whose interests they serve are important for understanding as well as intervening in how they shape urban imaginaries and possibilities. That is even more important when their utopianism resists being so named and presents itself as an inevitable realism, a point that applies more generally to the degenerate utopianism of neoliberalism, the class basis and contradictions of which when spatially materialized are exposed with particular perspicuity by Harvey. But how to revivify utopian imaginations that can contest new "realisms"? How might utopianism go beyond offering enclaves for the privileged and serve to challenge the frameworks of capitalist urbanization? "'No alternative, no alternative, no alternative' echoes in my mind," writes Harvey, following a dispiriting walk through Baltimore. "It pummels me into sleep where a whole host of utopian figures return to haunt me in a restless dream" (Harvey 2000, 258). What might be learned from such figures?

REVOLUTIONARY AWAKENINGS AND TRAJECTORIES

In an often-overlooked appendix to *Spaces of Hope* entitled "Edilia," Harvey adopts the same literary device as Bellamy of sleeping into a transformed reality. The year is now 2020. Global environmental crises, pandemics, deepening inequalities, and a stock market crash have precipitated revolution. A collective movement led by women calling themselves "The Mothers of Those

Yet to be Born" has dismantled power hierarchies and systems of violence and exploitation. Habitation, decision-making, interaction, and exchange are collectively arranged across a variety of organizational units and scales. This social and spatial organization is intended to be well-ordered and planned to ensure life chances for all while also being porous and open to encourage diversity, social engagement, and self-realization. Urban structures are adapted for more collective living with formerly separate houses connected by puncturing walls or new linking structures. Urban gardens provide spaces of intense cultivation as well as socialization. Technological innovation is centered on relieving labor and benefitting all. Transportation is slow and free. In an act that recalls More's *Utopia*, money is abolished, in this case through refunctioning computerized banking systems to enable the bartering of goods and services.

Many readers, more attuned to Harvey's social and spatial theory, appear to be unsure how to read these pages. Harvey meanwhile admits to his own ambivalence—is this a dream or a nightmare?—and subtitles it "Make of it what you will." The switch in register no doubt throws some. But the greater difficulty, which Harvey reflects upon, lies with the already discussed suspicion commonly surrounding utopias as such. To analyze utopian perspectives on urban and geographical questions is one matter. But to present a utopia, even as a dream? Yet even as "no alternative" was echoing in Harvey's mind, cries for alternatives were increasingly being raised around the world. His book appeared at a time when neoliberal orders were being shaken and when global movements, some anti-capitalist in form, were insisting that another world *is* possible (Smith 2001). Discerning a few years later the recovered vitality of utopia as a political slogan among elements of the "post-globalized Left," Fredric Jameson argued that the significance of the utopian form in this context lies particularly in its *refusal* of the common debilitating belief that alternatives to capitalism are impossible and inconceivable. It is "a representational meditation on radical difference, radical otherness, and on the systemic nature of the social totality" (Jameson 2005, xii). The utopian imagining of future urban worlds, from this perspective, is less about planning spaces to come than it is about estranging and historicizing those of the present.

An operation of estrangement is vividly apparent in the last chapter of Bellamy's *Looking Backward* when the narrator, now in the year 2000, dreams he is back in nineteenth-century Boston. Attesting to the power of the vision of the future city "to make the real Boston strange," he is shocked by the "squalor and malodorousness of the town." He is soon reeling from its "glaring disparities," which previously had seemed to him "a matter of course," and "yet more from the entire indifference which the prosperous showed to the plight of the unfortunate" (Bellamy 2007, 182). He professes that "scales had fallen from my eyes" (ibid., 189). As Beaumont observes, the "utopian dream of the future and the dystopian nightmare of the present" are here inseparable. They are central to how Bellamy defamiliarizes the nineteenth-century present and renders it "both perceptible and representable" (Beaumont 2012, 46, 48). When Harvey imagines awakening in Baltimore, he similarly turns critically to his nightmarish present and to the need to remake it. He notes that the contents of his dream might seem "outrageously and outlandishly foreign to our contemporary ways," not to mention disturbing, but they leave lingering a range of imagined scenarios of what could be (Harvey 2000, 280). Also significantly returning through his dream is a figure that Bellamy sought to banish and that has been ever further outcast in recent times, and yet whose connections with utopia and the concept of totality run deep: that of revolution (Wegner 2007; Smith 2001).

Troubled by elements of Bellamy's tale and also recognizing that any utopia must be a product of its time, Morris (1889, 195) once worried about readers taking it as "the Socialist bible of reconstruction." It is difficult to imagine anyone doing the same of Harvey's dream, not least given how he undercuts such readings himself.[5] Edilia nevertheless arises from his efforts in earlier chapters of *Spaces of Hope* to chart a path for spatial and social change through building a "spatio-temporal" or "dialectical utopianism." This aims to transcend the difficulties he identifies of utopias based either on spatial form (where fixing space is meant to secure social processes) or on process (where questions of space and closure are evaded). Focusing on present conditions and possibilities, it seeks to point "towards different trajectories for human uneven geographical developments" (Harvey 2000, 196). Harvey recognizes the impossibility of defining some ideal end state. But at the same time, beyond the critical function of utopias in challenging ideological closure, he asserts the need for them to embody choices and provide direction.

POSSIBLE URBAN WORLDS

Harvey has long acknowledged his indebtedness to literature for his critical studies of the histories of capitalist urbanization. He has also discussed, in relation to Raymond Williams's novels, the distinctive affordances of fiction for handling in open ways the situated choices, tensions, and possibilities involved in historical–geographical change (Harvey 1996, 27–29).[6] His interest in science fiction indeed extends back to contributing to the magazine *New Worlds* in the mid-1960s, then edited by Michael Moorcock. It is therefore not surprising that, in outlining the principles of spatio-temporal utopianism, he turns to the exploration of "possible worlds" in literature and specifically to the reworking of the utopian genre by writers such as Ursula Le Guin, Marge Piercy, and Kim Stanley Robinson whose novels are more concerned with process, struggle, and the dialectics of making new worlds than with the presentation of a stable vision (Harvey 2000, 189–191). While finding such literature suggestive, however, he argues it is insufficient for addressing political and social transformation, and he soon returns to engaging with political economy and social-ecological relations as he highlights the closures and commitments inherent in materializing spaces. There is a need to become "insurgent architects," he suggests, not afraid to plunge into the unknown while pushing "human possibilities to their limits" (ibid., 255).

Yet a utopianism that takes seriously urban questions, such as that advanced by Harvey, needs to reckon with past writings, imaginaries, and experiments in urbanism. This includes considering figures that haunt current practices, from both dominant utopian traditions and those that have been suppressed, distorted, or absorbed into ends different from their own. While Harvey criticizes utopias of spatial form for how they lock in social processes in ways that are often authoritarian, he also notes how they embody "spatial play" (another term he takes from Marin). This invites us to consider how feminist, socialist, anarchist, ecological, and other radical urban texts and practices imagine and create spatial forms that open up possibilities for different ways of living and relating. Harvey's own broad categorizations of utopias, while allowing him to highlight significant contradictions and difficulties in how they become materialized, tend to skate over such distinctive histories and positions. Focused on developing conversations about alternatives, he is also no doubt wary of trusting "dead dreams resurrected from the past". He argues that the search to achieve "a just and ecologically sensitive urbanization process under contemporary conditions" must construct its "own poetry" (Harvey 1996, 438). However, insight and potential sustenance can be drawn from critically revisiting earlier writings and projects. Among them is the similarly dialectical utopianism developed by Henri Lefebvre, whose focus on the critique of everyday life and emphasis on urban experimentation and invention within the present is also, in its own ways, continuously pushing possibilities against what is held to be "impossible" (Pinder 2015).

CONCLUSION

There is value in returning to forms of modernist utopian urban experimentation, in particular, and asking again not only why many projects failed but also what might be salvaged from their efforts to conjoin spatial and social change. With respect to efforts by "left modernist" artists, architects, and planners to revolutionize urban space and social relations, for example, Owen Hatherley (2008, 13) highlights their usefulness as "a potential index of ideas". He argues that "they can they still offer a sense of possibility which decades of being told that 'There is No Alternative' has almost beaten out of us." In the context of contemporary climate crisis and global warming, Mike Davis (2018, xxiii) further advocates recovering specifically "those extraordinary discussions - and in some cases concrete experiments - in utopian urbanism that shaped socialist and anarchist thinking between the 1880s and the early 1930s." He stages a debate with himself in which he first presents a "pessimistic" case, in which urbanization is recognized to be a key contributor to carbon emissions, and in which hopes for averting catastrophe through co-ordinated international policy seem all but lost. But he then advances a counter-position that takes inspiration from earlier utopian ecological critiques of modern cities and from debates about socialist urbanism before they were suppressed, whether by Stalinism or by capitalist social democracy. He suggests their emphasizes on the affinities between social and environmental justice, and on public affluence over private wealth, offer pointers for how urbanization might be reimagined and remade as its own solution. He does not pretend to resolve the debate. He is nevertheless clear that, given current crises, "impossible" solutions are the only viable "realism." He asserts: "The *alter monde* that we all believe is the only possible alternative to the new Dark Ages requires us to dream old dreams anew" (Davis 2018, xxiii).

Notes

1. *See also* Frye (1965).
2. Howard, untitled and unpublished talk in 1926, Howard Papers D/EHo F18, Hertfordshire Archives and Local Studies.
3. Howard, unpublished manuscript for a talk on 22 August 1909, Howard Papers D/EHO F3/10/1–12. *See* Pinder (2005, Chapter 2).
4. *See* Pinder (2005).
5. Although it has inspired, among others, architecture design studios (for example, Troiani 2013).
6. On such affordances more widely, *see* Salmela et al. (2021).

References

Ameel, Lieven. 2016. Cities utopian, dystopia, and apocalyptic. In *The Palgrave Handbook of Literature and the City*, ed. Jeremy Tambling, 785–800. London: Palgrave Macmillan.

Baccolini, Raffaella, and Tom Moylan, eds. 2003. *Dark Horizons: Science Fiction and the Dystopian Imagination*. London: Routledge.

Baeten, Guy. 2002. Hypochondriac geographies of the city and the new urban dystopia. *City* 6 (1): 103–115.

Beaumont, Matthew. 2009. *Utopia Ltd: Ideologies of Social Dreaming in England 1870–1900*. Chicago: Haymarket Books.

———. 2012. *The Spectre of Utopia: Utopia and Science Fictions at the Fin de Siècle*. Bern: Peter Lang.

Bellamy, Edward. (1888) 2007. *Looking Backward 2000–1887*. Oxford: Oxford University Press.

Brenner, Neil, ed. 2014. *Implosion/Explosion: Towards a Theory of Planetary Urbanisation*. Berlin: Jovis.

Burrows, Roger. 1997. Cyberpunk as social theory: William Gibson and the sociological imagination. In *Imagining Cities*, ed. Sallie Westwood, 235–247. London: Routledge.

Datta, Ayona. 2015. New urban utopias of postcolonial India: "Entrepreneurial urbanization" in Dholera smart city, Gujarat. *Dialogues in Human Geography* 5 (1): 3–22.

Davis, Mike. 1998. *Ecology of Fear: Los Angeles and the Imagination of Disaster*. London: Verso.

———. 2018. *Old Gods, New Enigmas: Marx's Lost Theory*. London: Verso.

Frye, Northrop. 1965. Varieties of literary utopias. *Daedalus* 94 (2): 323–347.

Gibson, William. 1994. *Virtual Light*. New York: Bantam Books.

Harvey, David. 1996. *Justice, Nature and the Geography of Difference*. Oxford: Blackwell.

———. 2000. *Spaces of Hope*. Edinburgh: Edinburgh University Press.

Hatherley, Owen. 2008. *Militant Modernism*. Winchester: Zero Books.

Jameson, Fredric. 2005. *Archaeologies of the Future: The Desire Called Utopia and Other Science Fictions*. London: Verso.

Latham, Rob. 2009. The urban question in new wave SF. In *Red Planets: Marxism and Science Fiction*, ed. Mark Bould and China Miéville, 178–195. London: Pluto.

Le Corbusier. (1923) 1946. *Towards a New Architecture*, trans. Frederick Etchells. London: Architectural Press.

Lefebvre, Henri. (1970) 2003. *The Urban Revolution*, trans. Robert Bonanno. Minneapolis: Minnesota University Press.

Marin, Louis. (1972) 1984. *Utopics: The Semiological Play of Textual Spaces*, trans. Robert Vollrath. Atlantic Highlands, NJ: Humanities Press.

Milner, Andrew. 2004. Darker cities: Urban dystopia and science fiction cinema. *International Journal of Cultural Studies* 7 (3): 59–79.

More, Thomas. (1516) 2016. *Utopia*. London: Verso.

Morris, William. 1889. Looking backward. *Commonweal* 5 (180): 194–195.

Mumford, Lewis. 1965. Utopia, the city and the machine. *Daedalus* 94 (2): 271–292.

Pinder, David. 2005. *Visions of the City: Utopianism, Power and Politics in Twentieth-Century Urbanism*. Edinburgh: Edinburgh University Press.

———. 2015. Reconstituting the possible: Lefebvre, utopia and the urban question. *International Journal of Urban and Regional Research* 39 (1): 28–45.

Prakash, Gyan. 2010. Introduction: Imaging the modern city, darkly. In *Noir Urbanisms: Dystopic Images of the Modern City*, ed. Gyan Prakash, 1–14. Princeton: Princeton University Press.

Salmela, Markku, Lieven Ameel, and Jason Finch, eds. 2021. *Literatures of Urban Possibility*. London: Palgrave Macmillan.

Sargisson, Lucy. 2012. *Fool's Gold? Utopianism in the Twenty-First Century*. London: Palgrave Macmillan.

Smith, Neil. 2001. New geographies, old ontologies. *Radical Philosophy* 106: 21–30.

Timms, Edward. 1985. Introduction: Unreal city – theme and variations. In *Unreal City: Urban Experience in Modern European Literature and Art*, ed. Edward Timms and David Kelley, 1–12. Manchester: Manchester University Press.

Troiani, Igea. 2013. Eco-topia: "Living with nature" in Edilia, Iceland. *Journal of Architectural Education* 67 (1): 96–105.

Urry, John. 2016. *What is the Future?* Cambridge: Polity.

Walker, Nathaniel. 2020. *Victorian Visions of Suburban Utopia: Abandoning Babylon*. Oxford: Oxford University Press.

Watson, Joseph. 2017. Topographies of the future: Urban and suburban visions in Edward Bellamy's utopian fiction. *Planning Perspectives* 32 (4): 639–649.

Wegner, Philip. 2007. Here or nowhere: Utopia, modernity, and totality. In *Utopia Method Vision: The Use Value of Social Dreaming*, ed. Raffaella Baccolini and Tom Moylan, 113–129. Bern: Peter Lang.

Home

Jennifer A. Wagner-Lawlor

INTRODUCTION

The connections between "utopia-making" and architectural master-building are obvious, in the general sense that both represent human aspirations in terms of the control and manipulation of space. But it is a complex relation that remains poorly theorized as it relates to space and gender. This is no new topic certainly; architecture has from time immemorial thought about women's spaces and men's spaces; how, when, why, and where such spaces are to be organized and articulated. But that hardly explains that organization, that articulation, and this of course is where feminism intervenes. As feminist philosopher Elizabeth Grosz observes, the very concept of architecture is linked to a phallogocentric effacement of the female and the feminine, in line with Western culture's insistence on the neutrality of masculinist knowledge production.[1] Thus, like philosophical and scientific discourse, architectural discourse does not acknowledge that effacement despite a by-now commonplace understanding of space, built and not, as gendered. And yet to do so could open up architectural discourse—and practice—to what she calls "modes of inhabitation" that could revolutionize the field; more modestly, feminist architectural theory might, Grosz hopes, help architects understand how buildings themselves "change," through an unacknowledged material agency. "What sort of metamorphoses," she asks, "does structure undergo

J. A. Wagner-Lawlor (✉)
The Pennsylvania State University, University Park, PA, USA

P. Marks et al. (eds.), *The Palgrave Handbook of Utopian and Dystopian Literatures*, https://doi.org/10.1007/978-3-030-88654-7_39

when it's already there? What sorts of becomings can it engender?" (Grosz and Eisenman 2001, 6).

Feminist critics and historians have teased out the cultural fantasies that are the foundation of the fetishized house-as-home, and the elision of the woman's story in the cultural demarcation of the house as the proper domain of woman, while that very same space "belongs" to, and is in fact ultimately the domain and property of, the man. In this essay, I trouble "the story" that distinguishes "house" (as man's castle, or country estate) and "home" (as woman's production of "family") by thinking of that distinction in terms of the fetish. The fetishizing of "the house" obscures—as fetishes are designed to do—the fantasy that being a "home-maker," properly empowers woman, leaving "master-building" and/as utopia-making to the appropriation of man. Leslie Kane Weisman proposes therefore that we turn to feminist speculative and science fiction for thought experiments that can mark the limits of social, domestic, and psychic spaces of a world (or rather of a world-view) structured by an assumption of essential difference. Citing the work of Ursula Le Guin, Joanna Russ, Marge Piercy, and others, Weisman points at "fictional communities [… within which] sexual, economic, family, and male/female relationships are artfully redesigned" (Weisman 1994, 167).

Cultural narratives attributing women's empowerment to the management of a feminized economy are grounded in the conception of a two-sphere "home economics." And the recurring image of a house as a site for cultural contestation can be traced from the beginning of women's intervention in the utopian literary tradition. Such representations assist us in (re)thinking and incorporating the notion of difference into utopian literary and architectural spaces. They offer imaginary stages on which curiosity and critique can trouble compliance, and scenarios of transgressing walls and borders can anticipate experiences that might emerge from such experiments. Indeed, the persistent attention to woman's place in the home *and* outside of it organizes the very plot of numerous feminist speculative narratives. Reading the two-spheres cultural narrative in terms of fetish production, I argue that the house-as-fetish-object in these textual narratives tells two stories at once. Alongside the (fairy-tale) story that "appreciates" the value of home-making and the virtues of "whistling while we work" (for no pay), feminist utopian narratives imagine a home constructed on a different foundation, and embodying "articulations" of space (Ahrentzen et al. 1989) more hospitable to women and others.

WOMAN-HOUSES AND UTOPIA

In a provocative essay on the entangled relationships of "WOMEN/UTOPIA/FETISH" Carol Thomas Neely theorizes the production of fetishes as "emerg[ing] out of clashes of cultural values at particular historical moments; each ambivalently resists and incorporates these clashes" (Neely 1994, 59). Neely's reading proposes that Utopia is itself analogous to a fetish object, designed to protect against these threats [e.g., the "large threats" of "geographical, political or sexual outsiders"]; her striking characterization of the symbolic form of the utopia-making and fetishmaking is worth quoting at length:

> The utopian place and the fetish object protect against these threats through disjunction, substitution, replication, assemblage. They are characterized by being bounded and specularized, by their irreducible materiality or territoriality, and by narrativity. But they are not, of course, just alike. The fetish is a no-thing, a material object that is here and no there, made a good thing by fetishizing. Utopia is a no-place, a there that is not here, fashioned as a perfect place by its maker. ... A fetish is a story masquerading as an object," [Stoller] and a classic utopia is a "speaking picture," or "a tension between description and narrative." For their makers, these spoken objects and places acknowledge and "neutralize" the contradictions they are built on. (Neely 1994, 59)

This is, I propose, analogous to architecture's fetishizing of "house as home," and the contradictory story that feminist critics of architecture would mount; note that Neely even incorporates the language of building and foundations. I am particularly interested in women writers' appropriation of a conventional image of the "feminine" home, usually stone in fact, a point to which I will return. Women living in these houses do not seek a better floorplan that arranges space in a different way, just to fulfill a particular, "happier" lifestyle. These "woman-houses" characteristically take shape in the rupture of an idealized family life; and come to represent a *de*fetishizing of the traditional home and its gendered economics.

What these woman-houses "mean" first, is safety. What becomes of more interest is, how a space can accommodate what needs to happen to women, and men, to make a space live differently, to discover how to desire differently, and how not just to desire a different thing. What these texts seek is a portal of possibility. To focus on the significance of the house in feminist utopian and science fiction might seem a retrograde path for feminist movement; but regarded as a response to a psychic formation, the only real way out is through. Weisman observes "the house has been inextricably associated with women, especially women's bodies. References to the house as a 'birthplace,' a 'cozy nest,' a 'sheltering womb,' and a 'vessel for the soul' are widespread in most cultures. Caves, the earliest dwellings, were 'nature's womb'"; and literature in general, she adds, is "full of images of the house as a 'maternal womb.'" (Weisman 1994, 17) Such references point toward our cultural narrative of autochthonous human origins, molded from the earth to inhabit a mythic space of original innocence. Our Western version of mythic narrative, in which masculine hands shape the clay and a masculine spirit quickens it, famously effaces any female role in procreation. And continuing on in that narrative, housing per se (as well as clothing, labor) becomes necessary only after the Fall "brought about" by Eve. A postlapsarian "territorial imperative" stands as a compensatory recovery of what was lost; that same imperative is fundamental to the "[management of] personal identity by establishing the spatial and psychological boundary between self and other" (Weisman 1994, 22). The figure of the house stands at the point of tension between those two imperatives, as the outward movement of the first is accompanied by the second, inward movement toward protective control of one' s "own(ed)" space and everything inside it.

Weisman expected from feminist speculative fiction the promise of breaking from a masculinist ecology of domination, and of developing alternative liberatory buildings. Weisman seems disappointed with the results so far: while appreciating the visions of gender justice that feminist fictions offer, she observes that "built space [in those fictions] is rendered vaguely if at all" (Weisman 1994, 167). Given her own argument regarding the fetishization of the house in terms of the woman's body, Weisman might have read that vagueness in another way. The narratives' downplaying of the particularities of design and decoration of built spaces might be a resistance to the realist novel's mania for precise architectural renderings of imagined homes, with their inventories of furnishings and implied values thereof. Included in that inventory would also be the family itself—wife, sister (unmarried), children (hopefully at least one boy), and other human property whose "value" is given only in relation to the male owner. That resistance might highlight a feminist interest in the ecology of a house as a spatial figure for social relationships, rather than its home economy. The persistent trope of a "woman-house," however vague, might be better understood as an inversion of the fetishized house, the space of the woman-house recovering what a masculinist cultural hegemony has obscured: a woman-house where women can *be* "at home." In the speculative counterspace of the woman-house can be imagined a radically "other" principle for social organization, an alternative model of economy, and a notion of community based not on exclusion and ownership, but on inclusion and communalism.

The persistence of the house image initially seems straightforward enough. They are safe houses, retreats, havens from the abuses of a hostile environment organized around patriarchal domination and, always, potential violence, the very fear of which is a kind of force field that keeps women contained. To define the significance of "the house" at the center of these feminist fictions solely in terms of sanctuary, however, is clearly unsatisfactory from a feminist point of view. The house is invested with more than just the promise of a "home" in terms of safety, comfort, stability, familiarity, normality— indeed normativity. In fact, the feminist "woman-house" in utopian literature does not denote stability in any passive sense. Even as these houses are described as a kind of asylum giving physical and emotional shelter to social outcasts the contemporary woman-house transcends that function. More than a dwelling where such persons experience freedom from fear, from harassment and mistreatment, exploitation and oppression, the house demarcates spaces, both inside and out, where the criminally female can experience "freedom to." An early example of a utopian woman-house appears in Sarah Scott's 1762 novel, *Millenium Hall*. From the perspective of connecting utopian and architectural or built space, what is striking about this house, as with the examples of woman-houses that follow, is its sighting, and siting. This literary work is read as a proto-feminist revision of a labor regime emerging from England's cultivation of a gentry capitalism, and Nicole Pohl (2006), Gary Kelly (1995), and others have teased out the significances of a country house appearing within a feminist social and economic imaginary that challenges a masculinist one. Like many utopian narratives, the novel interweaves various perspectives on the discovered community. The first point of view we see is, appropriately enough, that of the men who seek shelter from the rain there, at the invitation of one of the house employees, after their carriage has broken down. Their "perspective" is represented before the narrative proper begins: the novel's original frontispiece shows three men at a break in the forest trees, revealing the country house in the distance. Notably, only two of three men are depicted. Presumably the narrator, the third of the party, is standing behind, and it is his perspective here, as in the narrative itself, that we are given. He, like the other two shown here, is rendered "motionless" by the "charm" of this "fairy land." Time also seems to go into suspense, or at least "steals away insensibly" (Scott 1995, 58). The composition of the frontispiece demarcates the "wilderness" of the travelers' route from the enlightened clarity of the vista toward the house and beyond; it marks too the marginality of these "intruders" (as the narrator calls themselves) standing (Satan-like) at the very edge of "this earthly paradise" (58). These ideal(ized) descriptions of the temporal and spatial setting are typical of the scenario these feminist narratives set up which stress, among other things, the ecological relationships of humankind, space, and (land)scapes.

Scott's male visitors anticipate those who approach Charlotte Perkins Gilman's *Herland*, displaying a curiosity regarding the very possibility of female commun(al)ity in "so uncommon a society" (Scott 1995, 58) and so hospitable a mansion. As in Herland, the park-like spaces around Millenium Hall are "well peopled" with a diversity of animals who "seem to have forgot all fear, and rather to welcome than fly those [including humans] who come amongst them" (Scott 1995, 59). This principle of unity in diversity is reiterated within a "preserve" (69) housing diverse individuals who are either physically disabled or "deviant"—the so-called "monsters" who were frequently displayed as "public spectacles." Their deviations of form and ability are enumerated, one by one, by the Hall mistress. In a surprising anticipation of today's linkage of feminism and disability studies around critiques of the normative body, the Hall's founding women clearly identify (with) these monsters as kin in their sufferance of grievous abuse at the hands of "mankind." The women's hospitality toward the "poor wretches" permits the recovery of body and of mind; the Hall is a hospital that becomes a permanent hotel. Several years on, these individuals no longer fear and even welcome strangers, like the narrator's party, into their private community.

The protective, intentional obscurity of such a "charmed" community means that care must be taken for it to remain so. Utopian narratives almost always find a way of highlighting the community's "exclusiveness," often by siting it in a protected space: in a walled garden (Eden-like); in the middle of an ocean (*Utopia* [More]); deep in the woods (*Millenium Hall* [Scott]); surrounded by un-scalable mountains (*Herland* [Gilman, 1915]) or underground (*The Coming Race* [Bulwer-Lytton, 1871]); on other planets (*Midnight Robber* [Hopkinson, 2000], *Parable of the Talents* [Butler, 1995]). The inhabitants of such spaces often allude to the need to defend their land from intruders. More recent representations of architectural "safe havens" hardly offer more promising levels of trust among women and men. In E.M. Broner's *Weave of Women* (1978), there are two houses: the first, the Home for Jewish Wayward Girls, a halfway house for young street prostitutes; the second, the so-called stone house. One woman lives there permanently—but there are another eleven, of various nationalities, religions, ethnicities, professions, ages, voices, who find their way there. Together they work to cultivate the kind of affiliation and hospitality their own original homes lacked. Both the home and the stone house are endlessly hassled by local politicians and government bureaucrats, the former as a physical blight on the neighborhood, entirely on account of who lives there, and the latter on account of the women's growing politicization. The stone house is eventually emptied of its inhabitants on the authority of the local government, and the women in turn are forced to take up residence elsewhere, moving just over the borders of Jerusalem proper to the unclaimed spaces of the desert, where they settle once again, defying the traditional fetishization of "the house" as "home," the contents of which belong to the (male) owner. As the mild Mrs. Mancel from Millenium Hall observes, women should not be forced into the "Procrustes' bed" laid for her—"But is not almost every man a Procrustes?" (Scott 1995, 72).

As feminist philosophers[2] have intervened in traditional and masculinist conceptions of hospitality, feminist writers mount a parallel investigation into a paradoxical state of comfort and discomfort, even danger, of being "at home" within a culture inhospitable to women. Margaret Atwood's *The Handmaid's Tale* (1985), with characteristic authorial irony, shows us both sides of the utopian fetish of the home: in Gilead, no woman owns anything, and for handmaids the Commander's house is—despite the rhetoric of "freedom from" rather "freedom to"—as treacherous a place to be as anywhere. These fictions (categorized as u/dystopian fiction, or science fiction, or sometimes both) offer something more radical. They concern themselves not simply with the formation of a feminist subjectivity via a particular modeling of and by feminist epistemology; nor simply with the delineation of "new rules" of an alternative just community that would ameliorate material conditions. The importance of the house is the arrival at its threshold: the interaction that leads to the moment of coming inside. The stone house, I propose, emerges as a figuration not of any conventional sense of house and home, but of radical hospitality.

With the shadow of Jerusalem's Wailing Wall as the backdrop to their lives, Broner's women discover, within the house, the possibility of rewriting traditional ritual, and engaging in the invention of creative rituals that resist patriarchal "management" of household and female identity alike. The stone house is a touchstone for the women as each explores ideological tensions and contradictions in all manner of spaces-private, public, domestic, sacred, forbidden, political, national(istic). As in Millenium Hall, each woman is carefully distinguished from the other, while once again the actual details of "built space" are few. But unlike the earlier novel, these women are not content to stay hidden in their pocket utopia. Everything that happens to each one resonates within a highly politicized context, and the women's dedication to contributing their own voices and perspectives is celebrated in each chapter's invention of a new ritual, sometimes parodic of patriarchal Jewish rituals, sometimes entirely new. Marilyn French notes that the rituals are fully conceived yet always open to new forms of participation with whoever wishes to participate, are rich in words and "sensuous detail ... so that their communal life is embedded in both the material world and the realm of the imagination" (French 1985, xv). As the women strengthen their identities both as individuals and as a community, their activities, protests, and increasingly feminist movement mobilize them against gender injustice, as well as corollary social injustices.

This motif of feminist movement as mobilization is also effectively articulated in Shahrnush Parsipur's *Women Without Men* (1989), in which five variously abused women leave their homes in urban Tehran, and end up, one by one, at the door of another stone house, this one in the suburb of Karaj. The house is presided over, spiritually, by Mahdokht, a woman of Karaj so disabled by fear of sex that she decides to "[plant] herself" in the family's country house, which will become, "with a little touching up, ... a paradise." The first woman to arrive at the for-sale house wishes to buy it and does not mind the "shameful" (according to Mahdokht's family) human tree on the property. Instead, this buyer, Farrokhlaqa, accepts Mahdokht "as she is." Thereafter, each stranger-woman arriving at the doorstep is similarly "accepted as she is." This hospitality contrasts starkly with the inhospitable nature of the houses of the fathers, husbands, brothers, and pimps who have aggressively, often violently, defined and/or defiled these women. The navigations of these women are not only geographical, but also spiritual, mirroring the allegorical nature of Islamic narratives in which "the soul [of a male or female person], represented as and personified by a woman, wanders along the narrow difficult path that leads to the beloved" (Schimmel 1997, 25) or to a heavenly paradise. The house and garden enclosed are more like "way stations" along a path toward a utopic hospitality. Whether literally mobile or only imaginatively so, each woman's traveling toward and within such spaces are figurations of a liberatory *process*, one not necessarily (in fact, rarely) achieved. Inside the women's space, the importance of cooperation and affiliation are emphasized within an evolving *oikos* that is not a closed-loop economy, but an open one, always emerging, in which the women who enter can investigate who they might really be, and what it means.

AT HOME SOMEWHERE, AND NOWHERE

Toni Morrison's masterpiece, *Paradise* (1998), is also directly concerned with "making a place" for others; more abstractly, it too is about the imperative for accepting "difference" (whether of race, gender, or class), the unfamiliar, even the hostile subject coming from "elsewhere," into one's home. In remarks following the novel's publication Toni Morrison provocatively claims that "all paradises in literature and history and ... in our minds and in all the holy books" are "special places that are fruitful, safe, gorgeous and defined by those who can' t get in. ... [A]ll paradises, all utopias are designed by who is not there, by the people who are not allowed in" (Morrison 1999). Thus Morrison identifies what she sees as utopia's deepest flaw: its inhospitableness. *Paradise* is yet another instance of a feminist utopian narrative with the image of "the house" as a sheltering, safe, and free place, at its heart.

Like the stone houses mentioned above, the Convent outside Ruby, Oklahoma is also located beyond bounded and ordered society, on the margin of "civilization," in the "middle of nowhere" (Morrison 1999, 44–45). The extraordinary nature of this "big stone house" is its explicit figuration of utopian desire at its most embodied and indeed sexualized, containing "in itself" both the phallic and the wom(b)anly. The Convent's spectacular detailing, including sculpted busts with jutting nipples, faucets with knobs like breasts, and spouts like penises, are all "obvious echoes of [the original owner's] delight" (Morrison 1999, 71). The eroticization of every useful and useless thing in this house effectively fetishizes not just the sexual body but the very desire for it. Like the stone house in Karaj, this stone house becomes open, hospitable to, "any true thing": it is occupied first by a brotherhood of fellow embezzlers and outlaws; second, by a sisterhood of Catholic nuns whose more godly desires include housing and educating "native" girls from America and overseas, all outcasts of colonial intrusion; then finally, by the contemporary assemblage of women who follow the nuns' footsteps in their own way: "[t]hey took people in—lost folk or folks who needed a rest" (Morrison 1999, 11). The very layout of the Convent denotes erotic desire, with the house's "glowing tip" (72) visible from outside, and walls of its womb-like basement found inside. Not only does the image of sexual body/-ies animate the very form of the structure, but also, in its "emergence and symbolic character," the house embraces diverse outcasts and strangers from contemporary American life, and encourages among its inhabitants, as well as among Ruby citizens and us, the readers, "questions about sexuality and gender [that] lie at [postmodernism's] heart" (Siebers 1995, 8). The orientation of the novel's plot around the Convent also suggests the possibility that Morrison is offering a vision of hospitality that is intimately connected with utopia and with a particular, nonmasculinist version of it.

Thus it is no accident that Ruby's Oven, reconstructed from its original setting in a post-Reconstruction town called Haven, no longer functions to feed anyone but the "warming flesh" (104) of surreptitious young lovers. In contrast, the center of Convent life remains its kitchen, where anyone who walks in is welcome to what she is hungry for: "Left alone Mavis expected the big kitchen to lose its comfort. It didn't. In fact she had an outer-rim sensation that the kitchen was crowded with children–laughing? Singing?–two of whom were Merle and Pearl [her dead infants]" (Morrison 1999, 41). Like Mavis, Gigi arrives at the stone house and is immediately "ravenous" (37); Pallas too arrives "starved" (177). When the young wanderer Pallas arrives, and judges this place "free of hungers" thanks to its "blessed malelessness, like a protected domain" (177), she is excited at the possibility that "she might meet herself here-an unbridled, authentic self … in one of this house's many rooms" (177). She might discover what she desires, rather than what others desire of her. Many of Ruby's own women will travel "out there" at the blue horizon, "minus invitation or reproach," for food, medicinal potions, and the comfort. At least one Ruby woman understands what the Convent women learn, that "[t]he only way to change the order … was not to do something differently but to do a different thing. Only one possibility arose—to leave her house and step into a street she [Sweetie] had not entered in six years" (125). Sweetie arrives with the last of the wandering women, welcomed equally, fed whatever they needed, and set to any work that would teach them that "[i]n this place every true thing is okay" (38).

This open attention to truth is at the heart of the Convent's hospitality, which "[n]ever saw a stranger inside here before" (Morrison 1999, 43). Travelers there found "a swept world. Unjudgmental. Tidy. Ample. Forever" (48), supported by a vision of the "living God" in living men and women alike, and by the "endless work" of loving. Thus the novel's "flaunting parody" (279) is not the behavior of the women but of the men, who demonize all difference, even among their own. The amplitude of vision Ruby once enjoyed has narrowed to a single point, and the space offered for a "true home" is not "some fortress you bought and built up and have to keep everybody locked in or out" (213). There is nothing about the Convent that does not become tainted by the men's suspicions of it, but the trajectory of the building's history moves the other way: what was once an embezzler's fortress, built for defense against its owner's terror of an invasion by the law, has become a "real home" (213) to those with a desire to lower defenses, and to belong, "your own home," like the one "where if you go back before your great-great-grandparents, past theirs, and theirs, past the whole of Western history, past the beginning of organized knowledge …" (213). This is why the Convent women turn over the womb-like basement to the enactment of a new world celebrating a vision in which welcome and hospitality, rather than suspicion and defense, are offered: "'If you have a place [urges the Convent leader, Connie] … that you should be in and somebody who loves you waiting there, then go. If not stay here and follow me.'" No one left, "as each of the women came to realize in no time at all … that they could not leave the one place they were free to leave," with its "sweet, unthreatening old lady who seemed to love each one of them the best … a perfect landlord who charged nothing and welcomed anybody" (262). This is not a home-making, in our trivialized sense, but housekeeping in the most ethical sense.

In this way begins a kind of ritualistic rebirthing on the floor of that womb-like basement, during which each woman—as in *Millenium Hall*, *A Weave of Women*, and *Women without Men*—tells a story of the abusive past bringing her to the Convent's door. This ritual of so-called "loud dreaming" is frightening at first for these women whose presumed sins are always being (pre)judged (Morrison 1999, 244); after the first session, "exhausted and enraged, they rise and go to their beds vowing never to submit to that again but knowing full well they will. And they do," as they all learn to "step easily into the dreamer's tale" (264) explore the dark memories of abuse and betrayal together. Eventually they "[have] to be reminded of the moving bodies they wore, so seductive were the alive ones below," where the demons of the world "out there" are exorcised. Willing followers of Connie's generous god, they themselves are "revised" or transfigured in such a way the neighbors can't help but notice a "sense of surfeit; the charged air of the house, its foreign feel and a markedly different look in the tenants' eyes-sociable and connecting when they spoke to you … their adult manner; how calmly themselves they seemed … no longer haunted. Or hunted either, she might have added. But there she would have been wrong" (265–266).

The central irony of the novel is that the only truly communal decision made by vain, divided and duplicitous males of Ruby is the one to mount a "home invasion" at the Convent and exterminate the women, to punish "the mutiny of the mares" (Morrison 1999, 308). In the aftermath of the attack, neither shame, guilt nor anger is acknowledged, and the Reverend Richard Misner, a moderate and thoughtful cleric from "outside," disbelieves most of the obviously mendacious accounts he hears of the attack. Misner reminds the sole repentant murderer that it is the "Lack of forgiveness. Lack of love" (303) that has doomed Ruby's men, and a refusal of hospitality, born of the conviction that every approach of one person to another is motivated by some form of enmity. In refusing this stance, Rev. Misner is the only man who is rewarded with a special invitation, a vision, offered as well to his partner Anna: "It was when he returned that they saw it. Or sensed it, rather, for there was nothing to see. A door, she said later. 'No, a window,' he said, laughing. What did a door mean? What a window? Focusing on the sign rather than the event; excited by the invitation rather than the party. They knew it was there. Knew it so well they were transfixed for a long moment before they backed away and ran to the car" (303). Both petrified and jubilant at this vision, this invitation "beckons" from another dimension, "toward another place–neither life nor death–but there, just yonder, shaping the thoughts he did not know he had." Shaping, in other words, the next utopian horizon, "Out There," that will offer "the splendor" that's invisible to that congregation, but "lying in wait" (307).

Paradise empties the fetishized woman-home by in essence removing the walls. This trace of a house is a literal "floating signifier," proposing more than just an "open floor-plan" that will only obscure and maintain entrenched relationships based on "home economics." But the appearance and disappearance of some form of portal—whether door or window or a shape that is undefinable—"invites" us into a space where the economic is superseded by the ecologic; where floorplans that function to define space are superseded by dis-located gestures toward a free-floating space; where designs and plans are continuously imagined and reimagined, as new "paths and connections" make themselves known, or can be perceived. The novel holds out an imaginary space that, in a hopeful postmodern twist, engages the reader in the possibilities of fluid, intersubjective affiliations where the education of desire can take place. As Morrison concludes regarding novels generally, there is "something in it [writing, reading a novel] that enlightens, something in it that opens the door and points the way" (Morrison 2016, 341).

CONCLUSION: POINTING THE WAY

Working toward a mobile architecture of hospitality, if you will, feminist speculative texts offer the promise of other social imaginaries, another vision of community, often founded on a set of temporary affiliations rather than on fixed identities and ideologies. Thus the very notion of architecture should, as Liz Grosz proposes, not efface the feminine, but come face to face with it as an alternative to the imperatives of property and ownership of now only the structure itself, but every item, including people, inside it. There is a nomadic impulse at work in many of these texts: a utopian woman-house must be plastic, adaptable, not a blueprint of either utopia or of home, but an ongoing structuralization. It must be designed with an open door, pointing the ways.

NOTES

1. Etymonline.com reveals that the very word *architect* is coded masculine: our word comes from Greek *arkhitekton* "master builder, director of works," from *arkhi-* "chief" (see *archon*) + *tekton* "'builder, carpenter,' from PIE root *teks- 'to weave,' also 'to fabricate'". The *archon* is "one of the nine chief magistrates of ancient Athens, 1650s, from Greek *arkhon* 'ruler,' ...noun use of present participle of *arkhein* 'Be the first,' thence 'to begin, begin from or with, make preparation for;' also 'to rule,...' from PIE *arkhein- "to begin, rule, command," a "Gk. verb of unknown origin, but showing archaic Indo-European features ... with derivatives *arkhe*, 'rule, beginning,' and *arkhos*, 'ruler'".
2. For example, see Irina Aristarkhova's *Hospitality and the Matrix* (2011).

REFERENCES

"architect", 2021. *Etymonline.com*, https://www.etymonline.com/search?q=architect.

"archon", 2021. *Etymonline.com*, https://www.etymonline.com/word/archon#etymonline_v_16964.

Ahrentzen, Sherry, et al. 1989. Space, time, and activity in the home: A gender analysis. *Journal of Environmental Psychology* 9: 89–101.

Aristarkhova, Irina. 2011. *Hospitality and the Matrix*. New York: Columbia University Press.

Atwood, Margaret. 1985. *The Handmaid's Tale*. New York.

Broner, Esther. 1978. *A Weave of Women*. Indiana University Press, 1985.

Bulwer-Lytton, Edward. 2005. *The Coming Race*. Middletown, CT: Wesleyan University Press.

Butler, Octavia. 2019. *Parable of the Talents*. New York: Grand Central Publishing.

French, Marilyn. 1985. Introduction. In *A Weave of Women*, ed. E. M. Broner. Bloomington: Indiana University Press, ix-xv.

Gilman, Charlotte Perkins. 2014. *Herland*. [1915]. New York: Signet.

Grosz, Elizabeth, and Peter Eisenman. 2001. *Architecture from the Outside: Essays on Virtual and Real Space*. Cambridge, MA: The MIT Press.

Hopkinson, Nalo. 2000. *Midnight Robber*. New York: Warner.

Kelly, Gary, ed. 1995. Introduction: Sarah Scott, Bluestocking Feminism, and Meillenium Hall. In *Millenium Hall* (1762). Peterborough, ON: Broadview.

Morrison, Toni. 1998. Conversation with Elizabeth Farnsworth, PBS NewsHour, March 9, 1998. https://www.pbs.org/newshour/show/toni-morrison. Accessed 14 June 2021.

———. 1999. *Paradise*. New York: Plume.

———. 2016. Rootedness: The Ancestor as Foundation (1984). In *I Am Because We Are: Readings in Africana Philosophy*, ed. Fred Lee, and Jonathan Scott Lee, Hord, 1984. Amherst: University of Massachusettes Press.

Neely, Carol Thomas. 1994. WOMEN/UTOPIA/FETISH: Disavowal and Satisfied Desire in Margaret Canvenish's new Blazing World and Gloria Anzaldua's Borderlands/La Frontera. In *Heterotopia*, ed. Tobin, Siebers. Ann Arbor: University of Michigan Press.

Parsipur, Sharnush. 2012. *Women Without Men*. New York: The Feminist Press.

Pohl, Nicole. 2006. *Women, Space and Utopia, 1600–1800*. Burlington VT: Ashgate.

Schimmel, Annemarie. 1997. *My Soul is a Woman: The Feminine in Islam*. New York: Continuum.

Scott, Sarah. 1995. In *Millenium Hall* [1762]. Ed. Gary Kelly. Peterborough, ON: Broadview.

Siebers, Tobin. 1995. *Heterotopia: Postmodern Utopia and the Body Politic*. Ann Arbor: University of Michigan.

Weisman, Leslie Kane. 1994. *Discrimination by Design*. Chicago: University of Illinois Press.

Oceans

Killian Quigley

INTRODUCTION

Utopian literatures and utopian thoughts have always manifested complex and intimate relations with oceans. Salt waters carry ships, passengers, and cargoes to so-called "new" lands and ferry feelings, imaginations, and metaphors toward the horizons of the known, or what Ernst Bloch called the "sea of the possible" (1988, 3). In certain respects, then, maritime movements are among the more utopian energies in existence. At the same time, waters are not places (*topoi*) fit for human habitation—however closely we may live *with* them, we cannot long survive *in* them—and they resist such forms of "terrestrial ontology" as comprehend the world in terms of "bounded zones and emplaced points of power and knowledge" (Steinberg and Peters 2015, 253). But if this tension implies that oceanic utopia, or "aquatopia," contains an irresolvable contradiction, that contradiction may actually underscore the suitability of seas for utopian imaginings. Utopia's original meaning is, after all, "non-place," and the meaning of place is perhaps never so insoluble as it is on, and under, the waves. This chapter briefly analyzes some important currents in (mostly) Western histories of aquatopic literature, paying special attention to the displacing nature of voyaging and the imbrications of marine utopism and maritime imperialism. Ultimately, I will turn to the unique histories, lives, processes, and possibilities of the *under*sea, which may prove not only aesthetically but ethically salubrious for navigating our ocean futures.

K. Quigley (✉)
Australian Catholic University, Melbourne, Australia

P. Marks et al. (eds.), *The Palgrave Handbook of Utopian and Dystopian Literatures*, https://doi.org/10.1007/978-3-030-88654-7_40

Aquatopia: Accounting for Watery Place

In 2013, an exhibition called *Aquatopia: The Imaginary of the Ocean Deep* showed at Nottingham Contemporary, an art gallery in central England. "Aquatopia" was a neologism, a fusing of a Latin term for water with a Greek one for place. It is a word that, from some vantages, ought to apply to our entire world, not just its abyssal regions. "How inappropriate," the writer Arthur C. Clarke is supposed to have said, "to call this planet Earth when clearly it is Ocean" (quoted in Lovelock 1990, 102). Clarke was apparently thinking of how the surface of the globe looks from outer space, an element that, like water, human beings cannot inhabit without substantial assistance. So however inappropriate "Earth" may be, the word's currency is not surprising: calling the world "Ocean" might minimize its humanity. *Aquatopia*'s curator, Alex Farquharson, suggests just as much when he describes marine zones as so much "profoundly non-human space" (2013, 6).

If oceans, in the main, are fundamentally not anthropic, then a discussion of marinal utopia seems to set out from a fundamental contradiction. Utopism, explains Fátima Vieira, is always essentially preoccupied by the "social concerns" of human communities (2010, 7). With "regard to their content," averred Bloch, "utopias are dependent on social conditions" (1988, 3). These concerns and conditions involve, and have always involved, the sea, especially among Earth's (or Ocean's) multifarious littoral societies. At the same time, a thorough accounting for oceanic place has to move beyond shores, bays, and even continental shelves, and beneath ships, surfaces, and photic zones, to spaces that mostly lie past "state borders," "legal protection," and indeed "cultural imaginaries" (Alaimo 2013, 50). Human cultures, like the human bodies that partly make them up, trend terrestrial. What business, then, do utopian projections really have with, on, and in salt waters?

One answer, of course, is a very, very great deal. So-called utopian literatures have been thoroughly sea-beaten since, and arguably since long before, the lawyer, author, and martyr Thomas More invented a Portuguese traveler named Raphael Hythlodaeus. In *Utopia* (1516), Hythlodaeus is said to have sailed with Amerigo Vespucci, to have reached and made a study of an extraordinary island, and to have returned to Europe to share his learning—and so to critique the institutions of More's England. With his Urtext of Western utopianism, More both drew upon the conventions of maritime writing and affirmed the centrality of humanist inquiry for the genres of Western seagoing. In other words, without the realities, records, and literatures of the maritime, the literary tradition that, over four centuries later, continues to claim *Utopia* as its root never comes to exist. And without the utopian tradition, narratives of voyaging shed one of their most influential and enduring frames.

It is worth emphasizing straightaway that this exchange also entails an important, and most generative, irony. By taking to sea, utopian writing installed the persons of the voyager and the sailor, and the reputations for slipperiness and superstition adhering thereto, at the heart of this kind of story. For just one among countless examples of this connection, think of the Ancient Mariner's shipmates, in Samuel Taylor Coleridge's "The Rime of the Ancient Mariner" (1798). Confronted by the Mariner's killing of the albatross, and by the mercurial sailing conditions that follow the deed, the other sailors struggle to reckon what they witness. Grasping to interpret things in terms of causality, they first castigate the Mariner—"'Ah, wretch!' said they"—when the weather worsens. When it subsequently improves, so, unthinkingly, does their estimation of the deed—"'Twas right,' said they" (Coleridge 1900, 7). This interpretive muddle tinges the whole of the ensuing enterprise, and any attempt at summarizing Coleridge's poem, with etiological, and so moral, ambivalence. As Jonathan Lamb has shown, this kind of uncertainty is constitutive of, not incidental to, European voyage narratives, particularly in the South Seas. Maritime testimonies of *terra* (and *aqua*) *incognita* incline less toward Enlightenment "universality" than toward "extravagant and utopian singularity," paradoxically reproducing the not-knowing that they are supposed to have replaced with reliable truths (Lamb 2001, 113).

In other than edifying ways, therefore, ocean matters and ocean movements helped establish the preconditions of utopian imagining, and utopism has reciprocally framed many writers' and readers' understandings of what it means to ply the briny. Many, but by no means all: the novelist Epeli Hau'ofa's sense of the Pacific as a networked "sea of islands" is just one example of oceanic orientations that predicate themselves on something other than alienating distance and difference (Amimoto Ingersoll 2016, 16). It bears stressing that utopian (and related) literary traditions in the West, particularly as genealogized with and through *Utopia*, represent a contingent assemblage of marine sensibilities. That assemblage has been neither monolithic nor unchanging, but is substantially underwritten by an impression of coastlines as the meeting places of discontinuous, and frequently antagonistic, lands and waters (Corbin 1988, 47). As a growing body of research and creative practice, owing particularly to the works of non-Western scholars and writers, makes clear, such an impression must not be mistaken for simply natural (Amimoto Ingersoll 2016; DeLoughrey 2007; Mack 2011; Marshall 2017; Shewry 2015; Te Punga Somerville 2017).

The following sections forego any pretensions to a comprehensive account of marine utopia in favor of a partial consideration of some of its primary energies, especially but not only as expressed by Western traditions. For an organizing principle, they linger with the idea of "aquatopia" and consider how, and to what ends, writers have made sense of watery place. By referring to deep seas as "space," Farquharson suggests that aquatopia amounts, paradoxically, to a negation of *topos*, or place. This is not trivial, because place is often a marker of ontological sophistication—of progress from a state of indefinition to one of what the geographer Jeffrey Sasha Davis calls "discursive-material formation" (2005, 610). Aquatopia, then, would appear to invalidate itself—if a place is watery, then it is *not* a place—and in this way (and, I am arguing, not coincidentally), it is a lot like utopia, which technically denotes a "non-place" (Vieira 2010, 4). Seas are unusually energetic collaborators in topological speculation, partly because they tend to tolerate no speculation's settling.

CHARTING UTOPIAN SEAS: THE PROMISE AND PROBLEM OF WAVES

For More's *Utopia*, and for many voyage stories, oceans play rich and contradictory roles. On the one hand, they are essential vectors for the movements that drive narrative: movements, for example, of ships, communities, economies, ideologies, artifacts, and so on. On the other hand, because oceans are rarely regarded as innately expressive and meaningful, they do not normally function as distinct narrative destinations. That is to say, maritime utopia relies *on* the sea but usually points, ultimately, *beyond* it, in a relationship that has to be regarded as at least partly exploitative. It is a relationship that, as the historian Jeff Bolster has explained, can have far-reaching, and tangibly deleterious, implications for oceanic ontology. Because the sea is too frequently figured "as a two-dimensional, air-sea interface," Bolster writes, waters are regularly reckoned, wrongly, as existing "outside of history" (2012, 7). When understood as bare means, and not as ends in themselves, oceans facilitate displacement from one terrestrial place and time to other terrestrial places and times, making them crucial facilitators of, but not necessarily integral participants in, utopian imagining.

Oceans are manifestly in flux and reflux. Saying as much need not entail affirming any absolute distinction between unchanging ground and inconstant waters—as John Muir realized, in *My First Summer in the Sierra* (1911), "everything is flowing—going somewhere, animals and so-called lifeless rocks as well as water" (316). Liquid materialities are notable, nonetheless, for troubling the idea of location as firmly fixed in space and time. As the geographers Philip Steinberg and Kimberley Peters explain, marine mobilities frustrate an understanding of environment as "a space of discrete points between which objects move." Instead, it only makes sense to talk about oceanic "place" if place is understood in terms of "flows and continual recomposition," as well as the absence of a "static background" (2015, 257). At sea, therefore, no part of a poetic or aesthetic relationship, whether of subject-object, speaker-addressee, character-setting, or otherwise, ever achieves complete stability.

By emblematizing and enacting perpetual motion, oceans conduce to idealizations of freedom, discovery, and reinvention, forms of what Steve Mentz describes as a Western "cultural fantasy" of the sea (2009, 998). As Margaret Cohen shows, such fantasy has long been active among the "saltwater genres" of European "sea fiction," and has a key counterpart in early modern legal theory (2010, 11, 59). In the first half of the seventeenth century, a high-stakes juridical debate ensued over the possibility of regarding bodies of water as territorial extensions of land. With *Mare Liberum* (1609), the lawyer and scholar Hugo Grotius argued that the seas were free from conventional sovereignty, constituting a global "commons" that peoples, nations, and empires were entitled to access without impediment (Price 2017, 46). For Peter Goodrich, Grotius's was a fundamentally "poetic" act of legal imagining, and it is not difficult to see how by defining oceans as accessible to anyone with the power to access them, *Mare Liberum* helped establish waters as invaluable collaborators in expansive literary dreaming (2018, 210). Political dreaming, too: in fiction and in fact, from pirate Captain Misson's "Libertalia" to the Nore mutineers' "Floating Republic," ships and seas have inspired and enabled radical experiments in social thought and practice (Cohen 2010, 94–96; Hoare 2017, 340).

A free and fluxible sea mobilizes all variety of utopian conjurings. In *Elements of the Philosophy of Right* (1820), G.W.F. Hegel reflected on the aquatic "element of flux, danger, and destruction," which carries navigators beyond "the soil," and so beyond "the limited circle of civil life," to find and forge new forms of relation (1952, 151). Hegel could have been thinking of Margaret Cavendish's generically ambitious feminist utopia, *The Description of a New World, called the Blazing-World* (1666), wherein a young woman sails toward the North Pole, beyond the limits of the known, to discover an unheard of realm. Soon after her arrival, the heroine becomes empress of the Blazing-World, and so the personification of Cavendish's ambition to become "Authoress of a whole world" through the use of "the Rational parts of Matter." Cavendish's utopian poetics is inextricable from her investigations into natural philosophy, and *Blazing-World* is in part a fictive alternative to the masculinist community—"some few men in a little Boat"—of the Royal Society of London for the Improving of Natural Knowledge, which had been established in 1660 (1668, 159).

Or Hegel could have been thinking of Daniel Defoe's *Robinson Crusoe*, first published anonymously in 1719. With *Crusoe*, arguably the most important island fiction in the history of European literature, the problems and possibilities of self-determination—of what Ian Watt called the "myth of modern individualism" (1996, 180)—come into focus. Defoe, who manifested a spirit of eager, if not always efficacious, entrepreneurship, was playing to an expanding market for printed fictions, as well as a widening fascination for ostensibly verisimilar voyage narratives. In this instance, his source material was the story of Alexander Selkirk, a sailor who was marooned on Juan Fernández Island, in the South Seas, from 1704 to 1709. *Crusoe*'s quasi-utopia, which dramatizes moral and civil virtue at the level of a single person, remains a landmark in the development of novelistic form, and reflects the fact that oceans, which have given rise to some of the more collaborative occupations in the history of human labor, have also prompted potent fantasies (and nightmares) of total individuation. Such asocial topologies run along a lengthy affective spectrum, from the Ancient Mariner's terrible solitude—"Alone, alone, all all alone/Alone on the wide wide Sea" (Coleridge 1900, 15)—to the popular whimsies of BBC Radio's *Desert Island Discs* (1942–present).

Transcending Hegel's "limited circle of civil life" could entail rendering oneself permanently unsuitable *for* that circle. Alfred Tennyson's "Ulysses" (1842) figures its protagonist as totally and irretrievably ensnared by the ambiguities of voyaging. When Ulysses, reflecting on his long and meandering journey home from Troy, declares that "all experience is an arch wherethro'/Gleams that untravell'd world, whose margin fades/For ever and for ever when I move," he is describing not just a passion but a kind of pathology. Reencountering his wife and son at home in Ithaca, Ulysses is complimentary—his heir is "blameless," "decent"—but also callous, and incapable of imagining a place for himself within his prior domain. To be aquatopic, here, is to live out terrestrial emplacement's contrary state, to "sail beyond the sunset, and the baths/Of all the western stars, until I die" (Tennyson 1868b, 265–267). With "The Lotos-Eaters" (1833), another riff on Homer's *Odyssey*, Tennyson attends not to Ulysses but to his soldiers, as they languidly ponder whether to continue their seafaring or to choose exile in Lotusland. Ironically, the exhausted and intoxicated fighters show significant perceptivity when they anticipate an alienating return to the places and people they formerly knew: "For surely now our household hearths are cold:/Our sons inherit us: our looks are strange:/And we should come like ghosts to trouble joy" (1868a, 147). Under the influence of the lotus, the soldiers' reason and motivation may be compromised, but—especially with "Ulysses" in view—they also come to seem insightful critics of the phenomenally displacing, or dis-topic, ramifications of their maritime journeys.

Islands and oceanic transits have been rich resources for not only metaphysical ponderings but imperial mongerings. James Grainger's *The Sugar-Cane*, from 1764, sets its scene among the Caribbean's "sea-girt isles" picturesquely dotting the "unadorned bosom of the deep" before homing in on Saint Christopher Island, nowadays part of the federation of St. Kitts and Nevis (1766, 12). Grainger's language, here, borrows from John Milton's *Comus* (1637), where Neptune, Roman god of the sea, is described as wielding "Imperial rule" over not only waters but gem-like islands (1782, 6). The citation is apt, because Grainger's poem, which depicts St. Christopher as a cane-growing utopia, is a vigorous defense of British maritime imperialism. Through possessions like St. Christopher, which it acquired through the treaty of Utrecht (1713), Britain has confirmed its position as "sole empress of the main." So doing, it has also acquired the mantle of Christopher Columbus, who reported visiting St. Christopher in 1493, and whom Grainger extols for having braved "storms," "monsters," and "new forms of death/In a vast ocean, never cut by keel" (1766, 13, 134).

Columbus's keel cutting the sea is analogous, in *The Sugar-Cane*, to the action of the "hoe," and of other implements besides, in the orderly cultivation of island soil. Those implements are worked, mostly, by enslaved persons— "Afric's sable progeny"—whose proper management is, disturbingly, another of Grainger's central subjects (1766, 3, 22). At St. Christopher, the making of imperial place is enacted through the labor of unfree persons, in tandem with the doctrine of enlightened agricultural improvement, which Richard Drayton called a species of "secular utopia" (2000, 87). Importantly, this place-making also functions through imperialism's vital, and vitally ambivalent, relationship with the ocean. Grainger's sea behaves like what Siobhan Carroll calls an "atopia," a space that is paradoxically both essential for the development of "imperial ideologies" and an obstacle to "imperial ambitions" on account of its "resistance to cultivation and settlement" (2015, 6). In the final pages of Grainger's poem, empire is articulated and anticipated as an essentially marine project: the "flaming scroll / Which Time unfolds" foretells that, "if Wisdom guide the helm" of her affairs, then "Britannia, Neptune's favourite queen" will "ever triumph o'er the main." That triumph involves not only making successful use of the sea, but of transcending its ontology, as the "art" of improvement "transforms the savage face" of the land, and so confirms its distinction from the "wild interminable waste of waves" (1766, 22, 107, 151). Aquatopia, then, is simultaneously empire's primary object and empire's opposite—both the core of imperial consciousness and the condition that consciousness yearns to supersede.

Utopia Submerged: Transmogrification, Terror, and Radical Possibility

What of those realms that lie under surf and swell, subaqueous zones where, as Matthew Arnold had it, "great whales come sailing by,/Sail and sail, with unshut eye,/Round the world for ever and aye?" (1857, 163). Arnold's "The Forsaken Merman" (1849) is one instance of a persistent and arguably transcultural, fascination with submarine regions as spaces where terrestrial order, identity, and temporality muddle and metamorphose. In an anthology of classical Japanese poetry known as the *Man'yōshū* (eighth–ninth c.), the story of Urashima of Mizunoé describes a fisher who becomes betrothed to the daughter of the Sea God and moves with her to a submarine "Land Everlasting." As if foreshadowing "The Forsaken Merman," Urashima's story involves a magical submerged "palace" where the happy couple "might have lived, both he and she,/Never growing old, nor dying,/Until the end of time" (Bates 2005, 67). They might have done so, that is, if Urashima had not, like Margaret in Arnold's poem, been drawn by vague but irresistible forces back to land.

Beneath the foam, suggest these literatures, it is possible to encounter the ontological opposite of all things grounded, natural, and known. When Nathaniel Hawthorne wrote his elegiac ballad for drowned seamen, "The Ocean" (1825), he idealized the undersea as a place free from topside "fury," "guilt," and "care" where the bodies of the lost remain "young," "bright," and "fair," as if they were transformed, through supernatural preservation, into angels (1834, 34).[1] This recalls the spirit Ariel's song, in William Shakespeare's *The Tempest* (1611), possibly the most famous European rendering of the depths' processual uniqueness. In some alluring lines, Ariel crafts a fictional account of a drowning:

> Full fathom five thy father lies;
> Of his bones are coral made;
> Those are pearls that were his eyes:
> Nothing of him that doth fade,
> But doth suffer a sea-change.
> Into something rich and strange. (1864, 19)

Ariel's dupe is Prince Ferdinand, whose father Alonso, King of Naples, is supposed not to have survived the play's titular storm. What is distinctive about the notion is not that Alonso is dead but that in dying how and where he has, his body has not undergone the kind of fading that decease is meant to involve. Instead, like Hawthorne's sailors, Alonso has transmogrified, his body attaining permanence through the negation of identity, the passage from a certain "him" to a "something" else. At five fathoms, or about thirty feet, under water, operates an aquatopia that situates by rendering the familiar unknown.

The enriching and estranging of stuff in submerged space, as drowned bodies and wrecked ships, is an enduring leitmotif of oceanic imaginings and owes, of course, to actual metamorphoses upon drowned matter. As early as the sixteenth century, such metamorphoses inspired not just ecstatic fancy but scientific speculation, not to mention actual salvage diving (Von Mallinckrodt 2018, 305). The protagonist of Thomas Heyrick's lengthy Pindaric immersion, *The Submarine Voyage* (1691), meanders the world's waters after being transformed by Neptune (encountered earlier in this essay via *Comus* and *The Sugar-Cane*) into a dolphin. Special care is taken to detail a visit to "th' Palace o'th' *Atlantian* Kings," where the royal quarters of the mythical inundated island, first recorded by Plato in *Timaeus* and *Critias*, are claimed to have "by accession of Sea-Treasure Nobler grown." Here, the poem explains, "*Atlantis* doth a Conquest boast,/Which i'th' uncertain Sea/Hath from all Change Exemption got,/And's plac'd beyond the Reach of Destiny" (22, 34, 36).

Unsurprisingly, if one kind of submarine poetics imagines submersion as ennobling, another kind projects a distinctly different, overtly dystopian, vision. Heyrick's contemporary Thomas Burnet, natural philosopher and author of *A Sacred Theory of the Earth* (1684), posited the planet's terrestrial regions as comprising the habitable detritus left in the wake of waters that had "shattered earthly paradise" in the course of the Noachian flood. In this account, *terra firma* was, in the fulness of its "youth and blooming nature," utterly contiguous, uninterrupted by "gaping channels" or other impediment to its "smoothness" (1816, 76). Accordingly, the fulfillment of Burnet's teleology sees the seas vanishing at the end of the human era; this is desiccation as revelation (Roman 2019, 44). As Mentz has observed, the "utopian" phantasm of a time when "there will be no more sea" was substantially influential for early modern literatures in the West (2009, 1001). And a broad sense of oceans as embodying the primitive, unformed, and deforming, as the chaotic antitheses of orderly creation, is one that has never stopped exerting its pull, whether to terrible or idealizing ends.

"The ocean," mused Henry David Thoreau, "is a wilderness reaching round the globe, wilder than a Bengal jungle, and fuller of monsters, washing the very wharves of our cities and the gardens of our sea-side residences" (1987, 128). By rendering the sea a threatening (and Orientalized) alien, *Cape Cod* (1865) commits the sort of "terracentrism" that, as Marcus Rediker and others have argued, contributes to that persistent and deleterious dualism of cultivated, historied earth and watery wasteland (2013, 115). At the same time, the idea that oceans are full of "monsters" connotes the lurking presences of not only leviathans and giant squid but ghosts and other specters, things temporarily hidden but always on the verge of uncanny return. This was not lost on Thoreau himself, who reflected that "There is no telling what" the sea "may not vomit up. It lets nothing lie" (1987, 78). Aquatopia, on this view, denotes a region that is not so much antithetical to land, and to human society, as it is a repository of the repressed that has never fully submitted to occlusion.

One of the more remarkable marine hauntings of any era comes from the contemporary legend of Drexciya, an underwater aquatopia said to host a society of submarine persons descended from pregnant enslaved women murdered by drowning in the Atlantic Ocean. In his poem "Middle Passage" (1945), Robert Hayden called the Atlantic transit a "Voyage through death" (248). For Drexciya's mythologists, who include the path-breaking electronic music group of that name, the painter Ellen Gallagher, the rappers Lupe Fiasco and clipping., the writer Rivers Solomon, and the graphic novelists Abdul Qadim Haqq and Dai Sato, it is possible to reimagine the victims of that voyage in terms of unprecedented forms of life and of humanity. In the liner notes to Drexciya's 1997 album *The Quest*, a figure identified only as "The Unknown Writer" wonders whether the Drexciyans were "spared by God to teach us or terrorise us." "Do they walk among us?" the writer continues. "What is their Quest?" (quoted in Eshun 2013, 142–143) With Drexciya, aquatopia achieves an extraordinary exemption—what Fredric Jameson might call a "radical break or secession" (2005, 232)—from standard structures of space, time, and being, a non-place of such oceanic richness and strangeness that it seems poised to unsettle the Earth.

Conclusion: Aquatopia Rising?

As waters warm, ice sheets sublimate, and seas rise, our planet is becoming "more oceanic" (DeLoughrey 2017, 33). This is one compelling reason to think seriously about how oceans are seen to make, and to unmake, places and spaces. At Plaquemines Parish, in southeast Louisiana, Elizabeth Kolbert has reported recently that the United States' National Oceanic and Atmospheric

Administration is actively retiring "place-names" as lands become submerged. After inundation, *terra firma* disappears from view, and so do the words that help give it form: advancing waters, writes Kolbert, leave "no there there anymore" (2019). Kolbert's haunting phrase acknowledges the losses, of place and in place, that coastal communities (human and otherwise) everywhere have been enduring. But ironically, it also echoes the fictions of *aqua nullius*— of waters as undifferentiated spaces—that have underwritten just those transits, extractions, and imperialisms that have hastened anthropogenic warming and exacerbated environmental injustices (DeLoughrey 2010, 704). Consequently, argues Elizabeth DeLoughrey, "new ocean imaginaries" are emerging, and are needed yet (2017, 34). It is hoped that a brief and partial history of aquatopia has contributed to their reckoning, as well as their making.

NOTE

1. I derive the date of first publication for "The Ocean" from George Monteiro's research into printings and reprintings of Hawthorne's poem (2012, 106–107).

REFERENCES

Alaimo, Stacy. 2013. Violet-Black: Ecologies of the Abyssal Zone. In *Aquatopia: The Imaginary of the Ocean Deep*, ed. Alex Farquharson and Martin Clark, 50–56. Nottingham Contemporary and London: Tate Publishing.

Amimoto Ingersoll, Karin. 2016. *Waves of Knowing: A Seascape Epistemology*. Durham, NC and London: Duke University Press.

Arnold, Matthew. 1857. The Forsaken Merman. In *Poems*, 3rd ed., 161–168. London: Longman, Brown, Green, Longmans, & Roberts.

Bates, Evan (ed.). 2005. Urashima of Mizunoé. In *Japanese Love Poems: Selections from the Manyōshū*, 66–68. Mineola: Dover Publications, Inc.

Bloch, Ernst. 1988. Something's Missing: A Discussion between Ernst Bloch and Theodor W. Adorno on the Contradictions of Utopian Longing. In *The Utopian Function of Art and Literature: Selected Essays*, trans. Jack Zipes and Frank Mecklenburg, 1–17. Cambridge and London: The MIT Press.

Bolster, W. Jeffrey. 2012. *The Mortal Sea: Fishing the Atlantic in the Age of Sail*. Cambridge and London: The Belknap Press of Harvard University Press.

Burnett, Thomas [*sic*]. 1816. *The Sacred Theory of the Earth*. London: T. Kinnersley.

Carroll, Siobhan. 2015. *An Empire of Air and Water: Uncolonizable Space in the British Imagination, 1750–1850*. Philadelphia: University of Pennsylvania Press.

Cavendish, Margaret. 1668. The Epilogue to the Reader. In *The Description of a New World, Called The Blazing-World*, 159–160. London: A. Maxwell.

Cohen, Margaret. 2010. *The Novel and the Sea*. Princeton and Oxford: Princeton University Press.

Coleridge, Samuel Taylor. 1900. *The Rime of the Ancient Mariner*. Boston, MA: L. C. Page and Company.

Corbin, Alain. 1988. *Le territoire du vide: L'Occident et le désir du rivage*. Paris: Aubier.

Davis, Jeffrey Sasha. 2005. Representing Place: "Deserted Isles" and the Reproduction of Bikini Atoll. *Annals of the Association of American Geographers* 95 (3): 607–625.

DeLoughrey, Elizabeth. 2007. *Routes and Roots: Navigating Caribbean and Pacific Island Literatures*. Honolulu: University of Hawai'i Press.

———. 2010. Heavy Waters: Waste and Atlantic Modernity. *PMLA* 125 (3): 703–712.

———. 2017. Submarine Futures of the Anthropocene. *Comparative Literature* 69 (1): 32–44.

Drayton, Richard. 2000. *Nature's Government: Science, Imperial Britain, and the 'Improvement' of the World*. New Haven, CT and London: Yale University Press.

Eshun, Kodwo. 2013. Dreciya as Spectre. In *Aquatopia: The Imaginary of the Ocean Deep*, ed. Alex Farquharson and Martin Clark, 138–146. Nottingham and London: Tate Publishing.

Farquharson, Alex. 2013. Aquatopia: The Imaginary of the Ocean Deep. In *Aquatopia: The Imaginary of the Ocean Deep*, ed. Alex Farquharson and Martin Clark, 6–11. Nottingham and London: Tate Publishing.

Goodrich, Peter. 2018. *Aquatopia*: Lines of Amity and Laws of the Sea. In *Morality and Responsibility of Rulers: European and Chinese Origins of a Rule of Law as Justice for World Order*, ed. Anthony Carty and Janne Nijman, 201–221. Oxford: Oxford University Press.

Grainger, James. 1766. *The Sugar-Cane: A Poem*. London.

Hawthorne, Nathaniel. 1834. The Ocean. In *The Mariner's Library or Voyager's Companion*, 34. Boston, MA: C. Gaylord.

Hayden, Robert E. 1945. Middle Passage. *Phylon* 6 (3): 247–253.

Hegel, Georg Wilhelm Friedrich. 1952. *Hegel's Philosophy of Right*, ed. Thomas Malcolm Knox. Oxford: Oxford University Press.

Heyrick, Thomas. 1691. *The Submarine Voyage*. Cambridge, MA: John Hayes.

Hoare, Philip. 2017. *RISINGTIDEFALLINGSTAR*. London: Fourth Estate.

Jameson, Fredric. 2005. *Archaeologies of the Future: The Desire Called Utopia and Other Science Fictions*. London and New York: Verso.

Kolbert, Elizabeth. 2019. Louisiana's Disappearing Coast. *The New Yorker*, April 1. https://www.newyorker.com/magazine/2019/04/01/louisianas-disappearing-coast.

Lamb, Jonathan. 2001. *Preserving the Self in the South Seas, 1680–1840*. Chicago,IL and London: University of Chicago Press.

Lovelock, James E. 1990. Hands up for the Gaia hypothesis. *Nature* 344 (6262): 100–102.

Mack, John. 2011. *The Sea: A Cultural History*. London: Reaktion.

Marshall, Virginia. 2017. *Overturning Aqua nullius: Securing Aboriginal Water Rights*. Canberra: Aboriginal Studies Press.

Mentz, Steven. 2009. Toward a Blue Cultural Studies: The Sea, Maritime Culture, and Early Modern English Literature. *Literature Compass* 6 (5): 997–1013.

Milton, John [*sic*]. 1782. *Comus. A Mask*. Edinburg: Apollo Press.

Monteiro, George. 2012. Nathaniel Hawthorne's Verse: A New Poem, Unrecorded Printings, and Some Puzzles. *Nathaniel Hawthorne Review* 38 (1): 105–110.

Muir, John. 1911. *My First Summer in the Sierra*. Boston, MA and New York: Houghton Mifflin Company.

Price, Rachel. 2017. Afterward: The Last Universal Commons. *Comparative Literature* 69 (1): 45–53.

Rediker, Marcus. 2013. Hydrarchy and Terracentrism. In *Aquatopia: The Imaginary of the Ocean Deep*, ed. Alex Farquharson and Martin Clark, 106–116. Nottingham and London: Tate Publishing.

Roman, Hanna. 2019. The logic of the invisible: Perceiving the submarine world in French Enlightenment geography. In *The Aesthetics of the Undersea*, ed. Margaret Cohen and Killian Quigley, 42–53. London and New York: Routledge.

Shakespeare, William. 1864. *Shakespeare's Tempest*, ed. J. M. Jephson. London: Macmillan and Co.

Shewry, Teresa. 2015. *Hope at Sea: Possible Ecologies in Oceanic Literature.* Minneapolis and London: University of Minnesota Press.

Steinberg, Philip, and Kimberley Peters. 2015. Wet Ontologies, Fluid spaces: Giving Depth to Volume Through Oceanic Thinking. *Environment and Planning D: Society and Space* 33: 247–264.

Tennyson, Alfred. 1868a. The Lotos-Eaters. In *Poems*, 19th ed., 142–149. London: Edward Moxon & Co.

———. 1868b. Ulysses. In *Poems*, 19th ed., 265–267. London: Edward Moxon & Co.

Te Punga Somerville, Alice. 2017. Where Oceans Come From. *Comparative Literature* 69 (1): 25–31.

Thoreau, Henry David. 1987. *Cape Cod.* New York: Penguin.

Vieira, Fátima. 2010. The Concept of Utopia. In *The Cambridge Companion to Utopian Literature*, ed. Gregory Claeys, 3–27. Cambridge: Cambridge University Press.

Von Mallinckrodt, Rebekka. 2018. Exploring Underwater Worlds: Diving in the Late Seventeenth-/Early Eighteenth-Century British Empire. In *Empire of the Senses: Sensory Practices of Colonialism in Early America*, ed. Daniela Hacke and Paul Musselwhite, 300–322. Leiden and Boston, MA: Brill.

Watt, Ian. 1996. *Myths of Modern Individualism: Faust, Don Quixote, Don Juan, Robinson Crusoe.* Cambridge: Cambridge University Press.

Moons and Planets

Maria Luísa Malato and Jennifer A. Wagner-Lawlor

Introduction

Historically, utopias on celestial bodies were comparable to utopias located on other distant or hidden places, such as undiscovered islands or underground worlds. The sheer inaccessibility of moons and planets for most of the human existence made them fertile landscapes for the imagination. Many chapters in this volume concentrate on the contemporary period, which introduced us to many famous planetary elsewheres, including: many works by "the dean of science fiction writers," Robert Heinlein's *Rocket Ship Galileo* (1947), *Red Planet* (1949), or *The Moon is a Harsh Mistress* (1966); Kim Stanley Robinson's *Mars Trilogy* (*Red Mars* 1992; *Green Mars* 1993; *Blue Mars* 1996); *Galileo's Dream* (2009); *Aurora* (2015), *2312* (2012), and others; Octavia Butler's *Parable(s) of the Sower* (1993) and *Talents* (1998); Joanna Russ's *And Chaos Died* (1970) and *The Two of Them* (1978); and so many more up to this very day, in which space travel and settlement gives imaginative space not only to "hard" science-fiction scenarios but also to Afrofuturist speculation, queer utopias, postcolonial futures of deterritorialization, and reterritorializing, in a different way.

M. L. Malato (✉)
University of Porto, Porto, Portugal

J. A. Wagner-Lawlor
The Pennsylvania State University, University Park, PA, USA

© The Author(s), under exclusive license to Springer Nature Switzerland AG 2022
P. Marks et al. (eds.), *The Palgrave Handbook of Utopian and Dystopian Literatures*, https://doi.org/10.1007/978-3-030-88654-7_41

This chapter looks backward in order to look forward; that is, backward into those times when travel to celestial bodies was technically impossible, except through the sort of creative leaps typical of utopias generally. It says much about the imaginative possibilities opened up by the very possibility of leaving earth, that connections to extraterrestrial bodies are created centuries before any vehicle was able to lift human beings into the air (Nicolson 1948; Trousson 1975; Guadalupi and Manguel 1982; Boia 1987; Parrett 2004). And whereas descent into caves might connote the autochthonic primitive, the retrograde, or, after Freud, repression, the ascent to other planets connotes human ingenuity and rationality, a disciplined use of technology, "progress," and sublimation. Literary utopias with "outer-space" settings can interrogate, *in extremis*, the boundaries and presumptions of a genre that frequently establishes itself at the razor's edge: in order to assess the value of one world, it discredits the other; in order to speak to the truth, it promises to lie; in order to speak of the Earth, it distances itself from this very planet. The imagining of space settlements emphasizes reflects back to us the way spatial and temporal distortions and changes often activate earth-bound utopias. In 1686, one character from Fontenelle's *Entretiens sur la pluralité de mondes* (*Conversations on the Plurality of Worlds*) observes that those who know the most about a planet are not its inhabitants, but their spectators (de Fontenelle 1852, 63). That is, an acute and fresh observation of Earth needs a perspective from elsewhere—the moon, the planets, another dimension of space–time. We cannot separate this reflection about "plural worlds" (Fontenelle), from the one about "possible worlds" (Suvin 2010, 111): both multiplicity and possibility are essential to the utopian genre.

(In)Definiteness

The geographical location of a utopian place derives from the contrast between a real place, well known by narrator and audience, and a distant, unknown place where the habitus of our everyday cannot be presumed. Such a contrast is modeled from the very outset of "utopia" itself—that is, by the two books of Sir Thomas More's *Utopia*. More's Utopia is certainly an earthly domain; but early, extraterrestrial utopian imaginaries appear in dreams or through imaginary travel, without which, of course, one could not leave the earth. The moon and planets are therefore, for most of history, forms of a *virtual* place. An early example of travel beyond our world is Lucian of Samosata's *A True Story* (c. 200 AD) which, while not exactly a "utopia," anticipates the idea that one could travel *to* somewhere else. Thomas More knew this text, and followed Lucian, in not trying to describe a perfect society, not caring if things described by him are impossible, and underlining from the beginning its fictional and fanciful *ethos*. Lucian bases his world precisely on the ambiguity of that razor's edge between reality and fantasy, and has Philosophy and History talk with Poetry. Lucian cites texts that inspire him: Homer's epic poems (wherein Ulysses narrates his adventures to the brutish Phaeacians);

the story of Ctesias who, in speaking of the Indies mixes fictional and "real" narratives; and the story of Iambulus, who had knowledge of certain Islands of the Sun to the east, reportedly inhabited by a wise and happy people. Not by chance is the narrator-character of *A True Story* part of a group of men who, thirsting for knowledge, embark on an adventure without an established direction. It is no coincidence that, when a storm hurls the boat to the Moon, these sailors mistake the Moon for an island on Earth. The rivers, the seas, the forests, and the mountains look the same as on Earth—though its inhabitants, the Lunars, are formed fantastically differently from humans. Lucian's narrative is not precisely a utopia, but it lingers over the wonders of the Moon—one of which is the absence of much human conflict: the battle of the sexes does not exist, as there are no women; and the existence of rich and poor people does not imply a different quality of life, but only a different level of ostentation. There is also some type of immortality: as the Lunars age, they become smoke, a sort of dematerialized presence. Thirst and hunger are apparently unknown (dew is enough for survival), as is hunger (since they feed on the steam produced by roasted batrachians). The Lunars, therefore, produce no bodily wastes.

There underlies the generic development of utopian narratives a journey that in some ways reflects, inversely, an earlier narrative: the philosophical myth of the cavern, or Plato's Cave. The narrative is, invariably, based on a grievance with, or by, humankind. This grief is symbolically brought to its limit by a storm, an illness; or some state of delusion that might resemble, or actually threaten, death. To see this situation from the perspective of a stranger makes possible a kind of rebirth, in the discovery of the potentialities forgotten by those living under this death-in-life (Malato 2014). The (eventual) narrator travels outside his known locale, to this elsewhere of different habits and ways, and then returns (usually) with a provable story of an improbable journey. Rhetorically, the narrator tries to convince, and not just persuade, their readers of the need to change both their logical, often instrumentalist ways of thinking, and above all, their ethical ways of thinking and behaving, directed by the certainty of a "universal" good.

Certainly, the principles of the eighteenth-century Enlightenment present such a scaffolding for utopian constructions. Although it is set on Earth, Thomas Northmore's *Memoirs of Planetes* (1795) imagines the cosmic reform of interplanetary utopias (Claeys 2012, 137–198). Planetes [*sic*] is the name of the reformist politician in the novel, signaling the universality of such utopian values as freedom, fraternity, and equality, for every human being, on this or any other planet. No doubt Northmore read Rousseau's *On the Social Contract*, published three years before his own book; they concur that human oppression is born of ideological constraints that can be altered by individual and/or collective will. Francis Godwin's 1638 *The Man in the Moone* is clearly another model for Northmore's text, as Godwin's revolutionary principles are evoked right at the beginning of *Memoirs of Planetes*: "It's a well-known principle of morality, says Mr. Godwin, that he who proposes perfection to himself, though he will inevitably fall short of what he pursues, will make a more rapid progress than he who is contented to aim only at what is imperfect" (Northmore 1795, n.p.). Contrary to those who might despise utopias, Northmore sees them as inevitable, even when they take a religious formulation.

FACT, FICTION, AND SCIENCE

Unsurprisingly, the validation of "universal" principles of the French Revolution on Earth is attractive to many utopian writers. Utopias on the moon or on other planets, more so than utopias on Earth, presuppose a vast plan of creation in which human beings stop being the center of the universe to become objects in orbit, as are moons and planets. More's Utopia in this aspect is a reflection of the Modern Age and its cosmic heliocentrism. As Raymond Trousson argues: "It was the Renaissance, with Thomas More, which declared its confidence in an earthly destiny and in a salvation based on man's own efforts rather than transcendence grace" (Trousson 2000, 544). Finding out that we are just another orbiting rock among others prompts a substantial conceptual shift. Consequently, the contingent nature of dogma and ideology is Godwin, Bergerac, and Voltaire, a common premise on the Moon, on Mars, and on Sirius. On other planets, moral perfectibility is often linked to intellectual or scientific perfectibility. Utopias located on other planets often serve the purpose of precisely announcing scientific-philosophical innovations. As such, scientific knowledge seems to emphasize the volitional nature of the utopian genre. Most of the utopias on other celestial bodies written during the sixteenth and seventeenth centuries were written by scientists, or by authors intending to disseminate scientific knowledge.

If we find, in these celestial utopias, the scientific validation of heliocentrism, we must also emphasize that science is a synonym for tolerance toward other points of view. But as Galileo Galilei learned from "real" experience, such narratives, factual or fictional, could be considered heretical at worst or inconvenient at best. Many authors of these extraterrestrial utopias publish them anonymously or leave these texts to be published posthumously. Physicist Johannes Kepler's *Somnium* is written in 1608 to explain his heliocentric theory but as a dream in the mouth of a student. This fiction is published posthumously in 1634, the same year (perhaps not coincidentally) in which Francis Hicks' English translation of Lucian's *A True Story* is published. Soon after, Francis Godwin publishes *The Man in the Moone* (1638) but without claiming authorship. Its narrative is credited to a Spanish adventurer with legal problems, one Domingo Gonsales, who claims to have made contact with inhabitants from the Moon.

Similarly, only after the author's death in 1655 did Cyrano de Bergerac's *Histoire Comique contenant Les Etats et Empires de la Lune* (*The Other World: Comical History of the States and Empires of the Moon*) appear, in 1657. This edition was followed by *Histoire Comique contenant Les Etats et Empires du Soleil* (*The Other World: Comical History of the States and Empires of the*

Sun), in 1662. The protagonist, Cyrano or Dyrcona (an anagram of Cyrano d'), meets Domingo Gonsales, the pseudo-author of Godwin's fiction, on the Moon. William Poole calls it a "Lucianic utopia-cum-moon-voyage" and suggests that it influenced H. G. Wells' *The First Men in the Moon* (2003, 12–13), dealt with later in this chapter, fiction, on the Moon. Finally, we must mention that these books coexist with Francis Bacon's *New Atlantis* (1627), perhaps the first to champion the development of science as a means of achieving utopian perfectibility.

FROM THE FLYING MAN TO THE *SUPERVIATOR*

For humans to reach celestial bodies by means other than dreams and fantasies, they must in some sense, and by some mechanism, fly. The development of balloons in the late seventeenth and early eighteenth century made the flight more possible for actual humans than ever before. In M. de Listonai's *Le Voyageur Philosophe dans un pays inconnu aux habitants de la Terre* (*The Philosophical Voyager in a land unknown to the inhabitants of the Earth*, 1761), the protagonist embarks for the Moon on a flying machine, prophesying that soon humankind would learn to fly. New times were announced, according to the author, by the attempts of Francesco Terzi and Bartolomeu de Gusmão (Rosset 2016, 1370). Francesco Terzi's hollow sphere (1670); Bartolomeu de Gusmão's airship, "Passarola" (1709); Desforges' "dirigible" (1779); and the second flight on the Montgolfier brothers' hot air balloon (1783), witnessed (according to reports from that time) by half of Paris' population, suggested exciting new possibilities. Not long after, manned hot air balloons were flown.

In the utopias of the second half of the eighteenth century we find a greater number of flying characters (Lynn 2010). And Voltaire's *Micromégas* (1751) records the first visit of extraterrestrials to Earth, made by two giant philosophers, one from Sirius and the other from Saturn. They are still mythical beings, but already distant from, say, the hippogriffs of Ariosto's *Orlando Furioso* (1516): there is a growing plausibility in these flying beings thanks to the progress of science. The wings that allow men to fly are elaborate mechanisms, more plausible than Godwin's Gansas. Still in a fantastic register, one should note Marie Anne de Roumier-Robert's *Voyages de Milord Ceton dans les sept planets* (*Lord Seton's Voyage Among the Seven Planets*) (1765–1766). Admittedly, they have little to do with the utopian thinking: they stem, largely, from astrology, which associates planets to certain vices and virtues. In *The Life and Adventures of Peter Wilkins* (1751), by Robert Paltock, the protagonist mates with a "gawry," a flying woman he discovers in a cave of the South Pole, then object of sea explorations. It should be noted that, in utopias on celestial bodies, women who fly are rare: confined to their traditional function as wives and mothers, they do not seem to have special roles in utopias, even on other planets (Baccolini 2000, 698–705).

As the public experiences with hot air balloons occur (through the demonstrations from the Montgolfier brothers, Lunardi, Blanchard, Robertson, and the like), the Moon becomes a recurrent theme in poetry, romances, opera. Carlo Goldoni's libretto, *Il mondo della Luna* (*The World of the Moon*), would serve as inspiration to composers such as Galuppi, Avondano, Paisiello, Astarita, and Haydn. The discovery of Australia and the exploration voyages of the Indian and the Pacific Oceans by the new scientific explorers (examined elsewhere in this volume) feed the imagination of those who read utopias, with the philosophical evocations and provocations sometimes being well evident. *A Voyage autour du monde* (*Voyage Round the World*) (1771), by Bougainville, seems to inspire some utopian reflections about the Moon. As the philosopher from Fontenelle's *Entretiens* observes, the imagination of the utopian spaces on other planets seems to depend on the perception of the planet Earth. Consequently, during the nineteenth century, immediately after the European exploration of places on Earth new to them, the literary importance of planets increases. Edgar Allen Poe's 1840s "Appendix" to his short story, a fictive voyage to the Moon entitled "The Unparallelled Adventure of One Hans Pfaall," is, according to Maurice Bennett, "the precursor to contemporary science-fiction works recounting astronautical adventures" with a significative difference: "All the works which came before 'Hans Pfaall' concerned themselves with public questions: with the state of science, with philosophy, with manners and mores. Pfaall, however, flees precisely to escape from these things, which to him have become insupportable" (Bennett 1983, 137). Times are changing.

In *Les Chants Modernes* (1855), Maxime du Camp laments the situation of dreamers: "Je suis fâché pour les rêveurs, le siècle est aux planètes et aux machines" ("I'm sorry for the dreamers. The century belongs to planets and machines") (Camp 1860, 29). Utopian literary texts will prove that "the dreamers" are adaptable: they are increasingly interested in the possibility of flying to other planets. The 1840 text *Voyage en Icarie* (*Travels in Icaria*) would enjoy such success that it leads to a new political movement. Several years later after the publication of *Voyage*, in his journal *Le Populaire*, Cabet posts this plea: "Allons en Icarie" ("Let Us Go to Icaria"). The announcement constituted the beginning of a collective movement that may have involved as many as a million of people. Cabet's Icaria was not to be located on the Moon, not even in his dreams; but the movement presupposed the boldness of human flight and a "planetary utopia" (Mattelart 1999).

Modern Horizons: Taking Flight

Jules Verne's *Robur, le Conquérant* (*Robur the Conqueror*) (1886), foresees to a great extent the technological opportunities offered by air travel. In 1865, Verne's *De la Terre à la Lune* (*From the Earth to the Moon*), draws from his thorough work of scientific documentation (which will serve as the screenplay for the film *A Trip to the Moon*, by Georges Méliès, in 1902) and the readings he makes of Poe's book. Neither Verne nor Poe are utopian minds: the inevitability of leaving paradise and having to rebuild it weighs upon Adam's desire. In both, art anticipates life, turns the fantastic believable, and the utopian dystopian. The reaction to a strategic of H. G. Wells' (a writer who was a member of the Fabian Society) is the best proof of it. Wells' books, such as *The First Men in the Moon* (1901), create the necessary plausibility so the listeners of *The War of the Worlds* (1898) panic in the face of the possibility of the Earth being invaded by aliens, when, forty years later, Orson Welles read it on the radio, in 1938.

The development of aviation in the twentieth century largely reproduces the fascination with and fears of flight experienced a hundred years earlier (cf. Pagetti 2000). But the age of flight also introduced a democratic world that encouraged the limits of borders, and a fascist world that watch everything and everyone. The wars of 1914–1918 and 1939–1945 paradoxically fuel the resurgence of the utopian spirit in a dystopic world (Guthke 2003). The destruction and the horror would be so devastating that, to the survivors, to rise from the ashes would be the only thing possible. International organizations place their hopes on a world government, such as the League of Nations (1919–1946), on a universal language such as Esperanto, on the 1948 *Universal Declaration of Human Rights. The New Moon* (1918), by Oliver Onions, is sub-entitled "a Romance of Reconstruction." José Nunes da Matta's (1921) *História autêntica do planeta Marte* (*A True History of the Planet Mars*) imagines a world government, a common language, a hybrid race, a eugenic society. The eugenics movement was represented by three major international congresses (1912, 1921, and 1932), and was proposed as a boon to societal health, and political hope. Matta does, however, protest the abuses of eugenics by the German Nazi party, even before the Second World War. The darkness of the Holocaust's eugenic dimension once known, extraterrestrial utopias come to reflect its vicious operation. In Pierre Boulle's *La Planète des Singes* (*Planet of the Apes* 1963) the evolution of the species, on Earth as on the planet Soror, leads to the replacement of the human species by apes.

The gentle giants of *Micromégas* are long gone. The history of utopia on other planets is overtaken by the history of science fiction. During the Cold War, *The Dispossessed* (1974), by Ursula K. Le Guin, imagines two planets fighting, one in the image of the United States of America and the other in the image of the Soviet Union. In a conclusion, utopia on other planets seems right: utopia always speaks, after all, about the planet Earth. As Fontenelle's character would say, to see the Earth from another planet is the best way to see it.

A Few Contemporary Examples

The teleology of the conventional novel supports the genre's original conservatism; its plot is a form of anticipation, as the reader sees the hero approach (re)integration into the social order. In utopian literature, conclusions are characteristically *in*conclusive, open, speculative. If anything is "predictive" in this narrative model, it is of that speculative nature. The sensibility cultivated through a "speculative standpoint" (Wagner-Lawlor, 2013) makes possible a configuration of history that is neither simply linear nor cyclical, but a complex temporality that is represented by the symbolic form of utopia's generic framed or embedded narrative. It is a structured story weaving and reweaving threads, parallel lines of memories *as well as* parallel lines of anticipation or hopeful imagining. This is the *work* of speculative fiction, to invent ways to intervene that are not always just a disruption but an evolution.

The essay begins with a list of some more contemporary texts, but there continues to be a steady stream of planetary visions: Nalo Hopkinson's *Midnight Robber;* N.K. Jemisin's stunning civilizational trilogies, including *The Inheritance Trilogy* (2015) and *The Broken Earth Trilogy* (2014); China Miéville's *Embassytown* (2011); Jeanette Winterson's *The Stone Gods* (2009); which is briefly interpreted at the end of the chapter; Nicola Griffith's *Ammonite* (1992); Emma Newman's *Planetfall* (2015), Sue Burke's *Semiosis* (2018) and *Interference* (2020)—to add one more is to miss another. A number of While British author Jeanette Winterson is not typically associated with planetary voyage literature, she is an explorer of her own deep-space visions of desire, and the domain of eros (2009, mentioned also in the NARRATIVE entry). *The Stone Gods'* framing story places a crew of astronauts, including a sentient, genderless robot, investigating the sighting of a new Earth-like planet are already at work creating the history of this signal event. The spaceship crew creates a beautiful fable, "the way all ship crew tell stories" (Winterson 2009, 50), describing a series of planets, each a version of Earth—and each one a possible future, or a possible past, each a place "real and imaginary. Actual and about to be" (39). In particular, they describe "a planet called Echo":

> It doesn't exist. It's like those ghost-ships at sea, the sails worn through and the deck empty … It passed straight through the ship and throughout bodies, and the strange thing that happened was the bleach. It bleached our clothes and hair, and men that had black beards had white. Then it was gone, echoing in another part of the starry sky, always, 'here' and 'here' and 'here', but nowhere. Some call it Hope. (Winterson 2009, 51)

In a following episode of the fable, however, a further iteration of the novel's refrain records the air sailors' discovery of a nameless planet: "Chanc'd upon, spied through a glass darkly, drunken stories strapped to a barrel of rum, shipwreck, a Bible Compass, a giant fish led us there, a storm whirled us to this isle. In this wilderness of space, we found …" Once ("once upon a time like the words in a fairytale") this planet held oceans, cities, and life, "naked and free and optimistic"; and while in days past it was "a world like ours" (Winterson 2009, 56), now it is a "bleached and boiled place" with "no future" (52), a "white-out"—as if its very history has been erased.

Below the planet's charred surface is an "elephant's graveyard," in which, presumably, everything is remembered. In this Dantesque space are the "carcasses of planes and cars" trapped in an endless cycle of melting down and re-forming: "This was the inferno, where a civilization has taken its sacrifices and piled them to some eyeless god, but too late" (Winterson 2009, 52). The captain of the spaceship asserts that this white planet is "where we used to live" (55), possibly referring to an image of our own contemporary world. As they voyage to the new Planet Blue, the narrator, fearing "a repeating world—same old story" (49), wishes that this ruined, white planet "could sail through space" toward a place and time beyond human reach, "where the sea, clear as a beginning, will wash away any trace of humankind" (22).

In Nalo Hopkinson's *Midnight Robber* it is white supremacy that is washed away on a new planet inhabited by the descendants of the African diaspora, leaves behind, in this Afro-futurist utopia. Unfortunately, there are still a few unscrupulous ones among the population, who are exiled to a prison planet for the most serious crimes. A young girl finds herself there with her disgraced father, where she herself, serially raped by her father, finally kills him. There, she is saved and brought back to both physical and spiritual healthy by an indigenous population of bird-like creatures, with a sophisticated culture and language all their own. Like many traditional utopias, this one too keeps itself hidden and protected, almost in plain sight—but up in the trees, while they accommodate these new "settlers." Differently gendered worlds too are featured—although it is difficult to name one that supercedes Ursula Le Guin's queer evolution of sex, gender, and sexuality in *The Left Hand of Darkness* and other tales.

Perhaps the farther the utopian traveler and the reader has to go to find hope—to another planet, in another galaxy, or another dimension altogether—is simply a measure of the extent that we need to find Utopia on the map, and a strategy for finding a vehicle that will take us there. These writers believe we already have that vehicle: the story-telling and image-making of literature itself, which can take a reader anywhere our horizons may lie.

References

Baccolini, Raffaela. 2000. *Woman, Dictionary of Literary Utopias*, 699–705. Paris: Honoré Champion.

Bennett, M.J. 1983. Edgar Allan Poe and the Tradition of Lunar Speculation. *Science Fiction Studies* 10: 2.

Boia, Lucian. 1987. *L'exploration imaginaire de l'espace*. Paris: La Découverte.

Boulle, Pierre. 1963. *Planet of the Apes*. Paris: Éditions Julliard.

Butler, Octavia. 1993. *The Parable of the Sower*. New York: Four Walls Eight Windows.

———. 1998. *The Parable of the Talents*. New York: Seven Stories Press.

Camp, Maxime du. 1860. *Les Chants Modernes*. Paris: Lib. Nouvelle.

Claeys, Gregory. 2012. *Utopias of the British Enlightenment*. Cambridge, MA: University Press (Online).

de Fontenelle, B.B. 1852 (1686). *Entretiens sur la pluralité des mondes*. Paris: Didier.

Godwin, Francis [anon]. 1638. *The Man in the Moone or a Discourse of a Voyage Thrither*. London: John Norton.

Griffith, Nicola. 1992. *Ammonite*. New York: Del Rey.

Guadalupi, Gianni, and Alberto Manguel. 1982. *Manuale dei Luoghi Fantastici*. Milano: Rizzoli.

Guthke, Karl S. 2003. Nightmare and Utopia. Extraterrestrial worlds. *Early Science and Medicine* 8: 173–195.

Hopkinson, Nalo. 2000. *The Midnight Robber*. New York: Grand Central Books.

Jemisin, Nora K. 2014. *The Inheritance Trilogy*. New York: Orbit Books.

———. 2015. *The Broken Earth Trilogy*. New York: Orbit Books.

Le Guin, Ursula. K. 2017. *The Hainish Novels and Stories* [Including the Novels *Rocannon's World, Planet of Exile, City of Illusions, The Left Hand of Darkness, The Dispossessed, The Word for World Is Forest, The Telling*]. New York: Library of America.

Lynn, Michael R. 2010. *The Sublime Invention. Ballooning in Europe*. London: Pickering & Chatto.

Malato, Maria L. 2014. *L'Histoire véritable de la planète Mars. Pour une morphologie de l'étranger et du voyage interplanétaire*, Carnets APEF, 2.ème série, n.º 1 (Online).

Mattelart, Armand. 1999. *Histoire de l'utopie planétaire : De la cité prophétique à la société globale*. Paris: La Découverte.

Nicolson, Marjorie Hope. 1948. *Voyages to the Moon*. New York: Macmillan.

Onions, Oliver. 1918. *The New Moon: A Romance of Reconstruction*. London, New York: Hodder and Stoughton.

Pagetti, C. 2000. *Science Fiction, Dictionary of Literary Utopias*, 550–556. Paris: Honoré Champion.

Parrett, A. 2004. *The Translunar Narrative in The Western Tradition*. Aldershot & Burlington: Ashgate Publications.

Poole, W. 2003. Francis Goldwin, Henry Neville, Margaret Cavendish, H. G. Wells: some utopian debts, *ANQ 16*.

Robinson, Kim Stanley. 1992. *Red Mars*. New York: Bantam Spectra.

———. 1993. *Green Mars*. London: Harper Collins.

———. 1996. *Blue Mars*. New York: Bantam Books.

———. 2009. *Galileo's Dream*. London: Harper.

———. 2012. *2321*. London: Orbit.

———. 2015. *Aurora*. London: Orbit.

Rosset, Françoise. 2016. *Voyage, Dictionnaire Critique de l'Utopie au Temps des Lumières*, 1353–1371. Chêne-Bourg: Georg.

Russ, Joanna. 1970. *And Chaos Died*. New York: Ace.

———. 1978. *The Two of Them*. Middletown: Wesleyan.

Suvin, Darko. 2010. *Defined by a Hollow. Essays on Utopia, Science Fiction and Political Epistemology*. Oxford, Bern, Berlin: Peter Lang.

Trousson, R. 1975. *Voyages aux pays de nulle part*. Bruxelles: Ed. de l'Université.

———. 2000. *"Science", Dictionary of Literary Utopias*, 544–550. Paris: Honoré Champion.

Verne, Jules. 1997 (1865). *De la Terre à la Lune*. Project Gutenberg. https://www.gutenberg.org/ebooks/799. Accessed June 12, 2021.

———. 2004 (1866). *Robur, le Conquérant*. Project Gutenberg. https://www.gutenberg.org/ebooks/5126. Accessed June 12, 2021.

Wagner-Lawlor, Jennifer. 2013. *Postmodern Utopias and Feminist Fictions*. New York: Cambridge University Press.
Winterson, Jeanette. 2009. *The Stone Gods*. New York: Mariner Books.

Regional Imaginaries

Geographical Poetics

Liam Benison

INTRODUCTION

The Enlightenment is commonly held to mark a transition from utopias set in remote locations, such as Thomas More's (1516), to "uchronias" set in the future, as in modern science fictions (Vieira 2010, 9). However, the evocation of space is a powerful narrative tool, and many modern works of utopian speculation incorporate comparisons of different places. This raises questions about the nature of geographical representation in literary utopias, and the continuities and differences that can be observed between pre- and post-Enlightenment works. This chapter explores these questions as part of a general introduction to utopian geography. Following a brief review of some recent approaches to this subject, I explore the ideological significance of spatial representations in some important early modern utopias and the imaginative geographies of some post-Enlightenment works, including George Orwell's *Nineteen Eighty-Four* (1949) and Ursula K. Le Guin's *The Dispossessed* (1974).

Lise Leibacher-Ouvrard regards the utopian writer as "a landscape architect who lays out the structures of the other society in the space over which it extends" (Leibacher-Ouvrard 1989, 93). As a result, the ideologies that inform the utopian social imaginary can be read "engraved in the stone or revealed by the configuration of places" (93) that comprise its architectures

L. Benison (✉)
University of Porto, Porto, Portugal

P. Marks et al. (eds.), *The Palgrave Handbook of Utopian and Dystopian Literatures*, https://doi.org/10.1007/978-3-030-88654-7_42

and landscapes. A full appreciation of utopias, therefore, depends on an understanding of how imagined geography shapes utopian ideas about a better
society. The comparison of the idea of two distinct societies—the author's and
readers' and a better one—has classical models, including Aristotle's *Politics*,
Plato's *Republic*, and St. Augustine's *The City of God against the Pagans*. The
presentation of the spatial contrast differs depending on historical context.

Studies of utopianism from a spatial perspective regard geography as deter-
minative in explaining the function of both modern and early modern utopias.
Such studies focus on how utopias evoke Benedict Anderson's notion of the
imagined community: the creation of a sense of deep, historical ties that
members of nation-states typically share. Amy Boesky argues that utopian institutions are envisioned to confer a sense of identity on citizens and that utopias
demonstrate the way in which these institutions are made, and the tensions and
ambiguities involved in imagining a national space and social improvements to
it (1996, 9, 21–22).

Others draw on Fredric Jameson's idea of cognitive mapping to explain the
way in which utopias create visualizations of imaginary communities. Philip
E. Wegner sees time and space as mutually constitutive of what he refers to
as the "narrative utopia," in which description serves as the action or plot
to present a "cultural space and communal identity" before the eyes of the
reader, using Barthes' notion of semiosis. Wegner argues that the narrative
utopia "plays a crucial role in the constitution of the nation-state as an original spatial, social, and cultural form" (2002,xix). Robert T. Tally regards the
uchronia as most important in the late nineteenth century, in response to a
crisis in capitalism. He draws on the ideas of Jameson, Wegner, and Herbert
Marcuse to argue that the task of postmodern utopias is to create maps of
the world system so that alternatives can be proposed (Tally 2013, 3–4, 6–
7). Such spatial approaches are important because they evince mechanisms by
which imaginative geography signifies meaning in utopias and shed light on
utopia's role in constructing imagined communities and nation-states. They
also confront the dilemma that, in the process of presenting imaginaries of
society for critique, utopias might reinforce the status quo that they seek to
challenge.

More wrote *Utopia* in the context of a paradigmatic shift in the way that
space was experienced and known. Maps were becoming a widespread means
of understanding space as a result of new print technologies and growing
geographical knowledge created by expanding European navigation and trade.
A geometric, abstract notion of space supported the institutionalization of the
nation-state and imperial projects. It became so important that the concept
of place—an embodied knowledge of being situated locally—almost disappeared from European philosophy in the seventeenth century (Casey 1997,
133–134). Space also dominated utopias at least until the Enlightenment, even
though More's ingenious pun, which has come to define the genre, emphasizes place: *utopia* derives from the Greek *topos* for "place," with the prefixes
ou- and *eu*-signifying a place that is both nowhere and good. The fate of place

in utopia needs more attention than it has received and might be important in finding ways to address the dilemma mentioned above. That matter is beyond the scope of this chapter, but attention to the distinctive placial or spatial nature of the imaginative geographies of the utopias discussed here might point the way to future research.

The foundation of More's Utopia is an act of landscape architecture and social division. The island was a peninsula until Utopus conquered the local Abraxans and had a 15-mile-wide channel cut across "waste" ground to separate his new state from the continent. The primary purpose of this engineering feat was defense: to prevent future enemies from invading. It also "struck [the neighbors] with wonder and terror at its success" (More 2018, 44). The trope of border terror has a classical origin in the blood rites performed by Greek city-states to deter "barbarians" from the city (Gillies 1994, 5–6).

The island is the archetypal geographical setting for a utopia. Vita Fortunati has identified the island concept in utopia as emblematic of enclosure, protection, self-sufficiency, security, peace, and serenity. It has roots in ancient notions of the garden, such as the Garden of Eden, but its geography also represents utopians' "fear of contamination." Fortunati explains that "the external world represents a threat to utopian order, which can be maintained only by strict regulation" (2014, 51–61). The geography of More's utopia is thus ideal for its defense. It signifies its uniqueness through its isolation and power to maintain its ideological purity. The island has a crescent shape with a "placid and smooth" internal bay, furnishing a safe harbor for trading ships, as well as a convenient means of transport from one end of the island to the other. The bay's entrance is "perilous," with channels between half-submerged rocks known only to the Utopians (More 2018, 43). A fortress between the channels also defends the entrance. The capital city, Amaurot, is located "at the navel of the land" for maximum defensibility (More 2018, 45). The famed scholar Erasmus, a friend of More's, observed that Utopia's defensive shape was inspired by the geography of More's native England (Goodey 1970, 15–30).

The assumption of *Utopia* is that social harmony requires uniformity. Utopia has 54 major cities, which are "all spacious and magnificent, entirely identical in language, customs, institutions and laws … all of them are built on the same plan and have the same appearance" (More 2018, 45). Erasmus glossed this description with the phrase "likeness breeds concord" (More 2018, 45). Each city is equidistant so that none is further than one day's walk from the next. All have the same population and equivalent farmland, are built on the same grid plan after the model of Amaurot, have four market squares, and are surrounded by a green belt of farms. Harmony is achieved by geometrical distribution of social functions in space. In an echo of Inca and Aztec architecture, the temple, its dome, and the seven encircling walls are painted with illustrations of the knowledge of all the arts and sciences, including astronomy, mathematics, and geography. These representations present citizens with an awe-inspiring and instructive architectural emblem of the cosmos and all knowledge, which also has the political purpose of imposing the city's ideology of social harmony. The architectures of other early modern utopias propose different geometrical solutions to achieve social harmony. Tommaso Campanella's *City of the Sun* (1602), set on the island of Taprobane, invokes a cosmic analogy, which might have been inspired by Chinese urban models and Beijing's Forbidden City (Akkerman 2015, 130). The city comprises a concentric ring of seven walls, cut through by four streets that exit via a gate at each point of the compass. Its form makes an ideogram of the cosmos, but also has the purpose of making its center impregnable. In its center is a temple without walls, a focal point for seeing and being seen across the entire city.

The island geography of Francis Bacon's *New Atlantis* (1627) is elaborated with minimal detail compared with *Utopia*, but its isolation serves a similar defensive function. Bacon's aim was the design of a social and political system that would support his program for the advancement of knowledge in *The Great Instauration*. The society's central feature is Salomon's House, a scientific institution that conducts ongoing research into the natural world and creates ingenious inventions. By contrast with More's Utopians, who know nothing of Eurasian philosophy, Bensalem is a repository for knowledge of the whole world. Unlike Campanella's encyclopedic walls, however, Bacon understands the advancement of human knowledge to be an ongoing project. Bensalem's isolation not only protects its enhanced society from contamination by the vices of the outside world but it also allows the work of Salomon's House to continue over generations. Part of its system for acquiring new knowledge is to send spies, or "merchants of light," to all parts of the world to collect useful knowledge. They are trained to speak the languages of the countries they visit and dress as locals to keep their identity secret (Bacon 2008, 486–487). Bacon's innovation marks an important recognition of the limits of isolation in a society which depends on the growth of knowledge. The poetic geography of Bensalem makes a filtered isolation, which envisions intelligent control over who or what comes in and stays out.

A number of regulatory stages of quarantine need to be passed to enter Bensalem. First, the newcomers are offered assistance to depart—without visiting. Then they are asked to avow their Christianity and declare that they have not "shed blood lawfully or unlawfully within forty days past" (154). They are then permitted to leave their ship and enter the Strangers' House, where they remain under close watch for three days. Once they gain a license to stay for six weeks, they are restricted to a radius of one and a half miles from the city without special leave (Davis 2008, 14–15). The application of these rules in architectural context controls newcomers' access to and movement around utopia. Bensalem's quarantine regulations have a concentric geography through which a foreigner might pass ring by ring with the authorities' permission and under their watchful eye.

Other utopian settings share the island's characteristics of remoteness and isolation. Francis Godwin's *The Man in the Moone* (1638) draws on an ancient idea of the moon as another earth (Campbell 1999, 153). It is a visible yet unknowable adjacent world that can serve as a mirror on the author's society. Godwin's narrator Domingo Gonsales visits several worlds or islands that are compared: St. Helena, Tenerife, the moon, and China. It is on St. Helena that Gonsales builds the famous flying machine that takes him to the moon, borne aloft by 25 carnivorous swans (Godwin 2009, 77–81).

The moon is a Christian realm of giants, ruled by 699 princes, headed by the Supreme Monarch, Irdonozur. The trajectory of Gonsales's travel takes him gradually closer to its political core, the narrative evoking the concentricity of Bacon's and Campanella's imaginaries. His first princely acquaintance is Pylonas, whose name is derived from Greek *pulôn* "gateway" (Godwin 2009, 101, note 3). Pylonas provides the opportunity for Gonsales to meet Irdonozur at the end of his stay. They talk through a window reminiscent of confession. The reader is not told what is said; the moon's political heart remains a mystery (110).

The remote location of *Terra Australis Incognita*, the enormous "unknown" continent that appeared on maps in Europe's southern antipodes, a product of the Renaissance geographical imagination, made it a popular utopian setting (Ronzeaud 1982, 142). It is the site for Gabriel de Foigny's *The Southern Land Known* (1676), a utopia of hermaphrodites who avoid sexual passions, eschew eating in public and go to war with one mind. Their territory occupies much of the vast continent, yet, like Utopia, it has an "admirable uniformity of language, custom, architecture, and agriculture," so that, "[t]o know one region is to know them all" (Foigny 1993, 40). The landscape is flat. The narrator Sadeur is amazed to learn that the inhabitants had leveled all the mountains. The land's even gradient also extends under the sea for three leagues from the shore, providing a barrier to foreign ships.

On this vast, flat terrain is laid out a rectilinear geometry of social structures based on the square and the circle, the ideal forms of harmony in Leon Battista Alberti's treatise on architecture (1452). These shapes also reflect contemporary principles for the design of fortresses and city walls (Leibacher-Ouvrard 1989, 94). The landscape is divided into square *seizains* ("sixteens"), consisting of 16 quarters of 25 houses each. Each *seizain* comprises three types of buildings, all circular. At the center is the Hab ("house of elevation") for communal eating, built of transparent stone. There are four Hebs ("houses of education") at the meeting point of four quarters, and 25 Hiebs ("men's houses") for communal dwelling in each quarter. The idea of this arrangement is to create social harmony through uniformity and transparency.

The History of the Sevarambians (1675–1679) by Denis Vairasse (also Veiras) is also set in *Terra Australis*. The solar theocracy was founded by Sevarias, a Zoroastrian exile from Persia, and is later discovered by Dutch castaways led by Captain Siden. Sevarambia's geography is concentric and hierarchical, echoing Campanella's city across a wider landscape. An outer region, Sporoumbe, the first reached by the castaways, is near the coast. It has cities of regular size and fertile plains irrigated by canals. It is also the region where disabled and deformed people are sent to live. The more naturally favored inner region of Sevarambe is separated from Sporoumbe by an almost impass-able mountain range. Siden is told that in Sevarambe, "every thing is more beautiful and magnificent" (Veiras 2006, 168).

The capital city, Sevarinde, is located on a fortified island in the middle of Sevarambe. It has a square layout with rectilinear streets. The Palace of the Sun, the Viceroy's mansion, has a panoptic design, imitating Campanel-la's temple and Foigny's Hab. Twelve doors in each façade, sited exactly opposite to those on the facing wall, enable people outside to see in. Those inside can survey the entire city and its surrounding landscape. The 12 doors echo the New Jerusalem (*Revelation*, 21), making the palace a figure of the universe (Leibacher-Ouvrard 1989, 99). This architecture invests the Viceroy with the unquestionable authority of the cosmological order and is inspired by Campanella's city, the temples of Peru, the pyramids of Egypt, and Beijing's Forbidden City (Laursen and Pham 2017, 427–442).

The narrator of Hendrik Smeeks's *Description of the Mighty Kingdom of Krinke Kesmes* (1708) is a Dutch merchant Juan de Posos whose ship is blown off course in a storm en route to the Philippines from Panama; the ship's crew stranded on an island of the Southland. The visitors explore a wilder-ness region and sight a truncated tower on the horizon. While they gaze at the towers of a distant city from a mountain, they are silently surrounded by the king's soldiers and taken to the city of Taloujaël. Krinke Kesmes is a large, almost square island with a circumference of about "400 hours' walk-ing" (Smeeks 1995, 36). Travel is restricted. Attempts to leave are punishable by death. Hence, the island's geography and the rules that enforce its social isolation defend the utopia from the corruption of the outside world. As in *Sevarambians*, Krinke Kesmes's island geography and institutional architec-ture create concentric barriers of protection. The capital city Kesmes remains an inaccessible mystery in the interior. Taloujaël is located in a central plain, surrounded by densely wooded mountains. Between the mountains and the coast lies a wasteland inhabited by barbarians, who are the descendants of multilingual passengers of a Persian shipwrecked on the shore centuries earlier. The idea of these rings of mountains, wastelands, and dangerous people is to prevent outsiders from passing through, and allow space for the authorities to apprehend them before they reach utopia.

The city of Taloujaël is almost perfectly round with 13 ramparts. De Posos is given a tour of the truncated tower, which has the shape of the pyramids of Cuzco and Mexico, with external steps and a roof terrace overlooking the surrounding city. On a higher floor below the roof terrace is the Sanctuary room where asylum seekers are tried. They are asked a quarantine question also used in Bensalem: whether they have recently "committed Manslaughter or something else by accident or necessity" (Smeeks 1995, 106, 107). The acquitted go free, but the convicted are locked in a room next door without food to starve to death or commit suicide. The pyramid is an architectural symbol of the regime's power to decide who enters utopia freely and who will be annihilated. One of the first utopias set in the future, Louis-Sébastien

Mercier's *The Year 2440: A Dream If Ever There Was One* (1771) compares the unjust Paris of the eighteenth century with a more just and rational Paris in the future. The idea of Paris and its well-known places are critical to the reader's estrangement and engagement with the narrative. The description of the Palace of Versailles in ruins, for example, encodes an ideological argument.

The late nineteenth century was productive for utopian literature. Works optimistic about a socialist future such as Edward Bellamy's *Looking Backward 2000–1887* (1888) achieved great success. However, in the early twentieth century, warfare, revolutions, genocide, and the threat of nuclear annihilation shattered that optimism. Tally argues that a belief emerged that any alternative to the present "spatiopolitical configurations" will be inevitably "far worse" (Tally 2013, 3–4). Dystopias, like the post-war ecotopia provoked by the understanding of impending climate catastrophe, are typically set in a worse future, although some retain hope of a limited return to a better, simpler golden age after social and climate collapse. Their imaginative geographies are instructive of social problems that have become global and depend for their resolution on human relationships with the biosystems of the earth.

Perhaps no dystopia continues to warn with such prescience of the threat of totalitarianism as George Orwell's *Nineteen Eighty-Four* (1949). The heuristic value of Wegner's argument that utopian narrative develops a dialectic between space and time becomes clear in his discussion of Orwell's work. He shows how a variety of geographies evoke imaginaries of different temporalities that advance Orwell's democratic socialist ideology and analysis of totalitarianism. The glass paperweight "enclosing a tiny world," and the room that is "a world, a pocket of the past where extinct animals could walk" trigger Winston Smith's memory of better times (Orwell 2013, 213, 218). Wegner regards these tiny spatialities as evidence of Orwell's conservative utopian imaginary, which looks back to a time of English and individual autonomy; the irony is that Orwell knew that that "golden age" was built on the exploitation and violence of the British Empire (Wegner 2002, 217). The totalitarian forever-present is evoked by the gray, run-down streets of everyday human experience, Winston's apartment dominated by the telescreen, and the torture chambers of the Ministry of Love. Ingsoc's irrational violence, hatred, and suppression of joy, combined with Newspeak and its efficient technologies of surveillance, squeeze the individual into ever more confined spaces in which to walk, think and communicate.

Less bleak is Ursula K. Le Guin's *The Dispossessed* (1974). Its comparative geography contrasts the "fallen" lunar utopia of Anarres with three spaces of Urras, the earth, which reflect the division of global power during the Cold War. The Urrasti rivalry between A-Io and Thu resembles between the capitalist and socialist worlds, besides the "third-world" military dictatorship of poor Benebili. Anarres is an alternative earth, like Godwin's moon. Tirin expresses wonder at discovering this shift in perspective: "Our earth is their Moon; our Moon is their earth" (Le Guin 2015, 39). However, the anarcho-syndicalist society of Anarres is a more ambiguous utopia than

Godwin's moon. Its self-imposed isolation from Urras and other parts of the universe leads to a resistance to new ideas and a decline into conformity. In the moon's harsh environment, economic difficulties make daily life increasingly challenging and hunger more frequent. The trajectory of the hero Shevek's journey is reversed by comparison with early modern utopias. Unlike Gonsales, Shevek flees "utopia" in search of the freedom needed to write and publish his General Temporal Theory. He observes the customs of the readers' world, which becomes estranged through his eyes, reflected against the mirror of Anarres.

For Wegner, Le Guin's "open-ended" utopia rigorously maintains a "horizon of possibility" but offers no geography of what a better world might look like, aside from the "absent presence" of the civilization of the Hainish (Wegner 2002, xxiv–xxv, 179–180). Shevek only glimpses the reality of the world of the Hainish from the interior landscape of their spaceship, which takes him home to Anarres. There are "large and private" rooms with high ceilings and "walls wood-panelled or covered with textured weavings" (Le Guin 2015, 319). He notices that it strikes a graceful balance between the opulence of Urras and the austerity of Anarres (Le Guin 2015, 319). The reader cannot know what the world of the Hainish might be like from Shevek's experience of this place. Perhaps that is Le Guin's point: it might be better for utopists to focus on places rather than the architecture of entire societies.

The temporal setting of Italo Calvino's *The Baron in the Trees* (1957) is the French Siege of Genoa in 1800, but there are also ecotopic references to the environmental challenges of the 1950s. In both periods, economic forces exacerbated deforestation. One day, the young baron Cosimo flees from the authoritarianism of his noble family, and vows to live the rest of his life in the trees. The utopian geography of Ombrosa ("place of shade") and its extraordinary variety of life is the *frastaglio* "entanglement" of branches and leaves (Calvino, 2013, 236).

Giulia Pacini argues that this treescape forms more than a mere narrative location: the trees have a "non-conscious and yet purposive" agency to create places that "allow for special activities, feelings, and social relations" (Pacini 2014, 57–68). Cosimo learns about the varieties of plants in his region, the life they support, and how to feed, clothe, and shelter himself. He travels and nourishes his intellect and relations with his human and animal neighbors. The geography of Ombrosa is created in the performance of Cosimo's activities of living and the trajectories of his explorations. Calvino asks readers to consider a new relationship between human society and the natural world.

Even a future-set, time-traveler utopia can have the geography of a *terra incognita*. John Burnside's *Havergey* (2017) is set on an unknown island near the Scottish mainland. Refugees from "The Collapse" of the first quarter of the twenty-first century, when 90 percent of the world's population died from a wave of plagues, have established a sustainable way of life there. Havergey is discovered by John, a time traveler from the "Machine People," who shares his name with the author. John departed for the future in a Tardis not long before The Collapse. As in *New Atlantis*, John is taken into quarantine on arrival. He learns about the customs of Havergey from Ben, his Watcher.

Place is critical to Burnside's understanding of utopian sociability, and *Havergey* resists utopia's association with the spatiality of the nation-state imaginary. Ben says, "I'm not much interested in ideas like national character, but I do believe that place, if it's looked at closely enough, can say a great deal about how people behave" (Burnside 2017, 14). Burnside's utopians live sustainably from the land and sea. They have no desires to travel across time or space. As Ben says, "each of us sees this place as a gift" (18). There is no private property, and everything is shared, except for a few personal items, and their bodies. Ben explains that they have an "ability to be well, sometimes in harsh conditions" (41). Their sociability has adapted to suit the nature of the place where they live.

Havergey opens with the observation that "Utopia is not a place at all" (Burnside 2017, 1). John never experiences Havergey for himself and learns about it only through his dialog with Ben. As in *The Dispossessed*, the expected utopian imaginary is pushed to a possibility on the horizon. Ben shares no cartographical details of the island but conveys its utopian ideals through a more poetic geographical discourse. Havergey is "criss-crossed with trails: deer lanes through tall meadows and beechwoods, desire paths and old bridleways" (Burnside 2017, 48). Its western pastures are described as they look on a foggy evening when the cattle "loom large in the gathering whiteness" (50). These descriptions recall the landscape near Winston Smith's "Golden Country": "An old, close-bitten pasture, with a footpath wandering across it and a molehill here and there" (Orwell 2013, 181). Like Orwell and Le Guin, Burnside offers glimpses of utopian places, but the possibility of the characters fully experiencing utopia remains beyond the horizon.

Alexis Wright's *The Swan Book* (2013) is set in a militarized future Australian state after climate catastrophe, where millions of refugees "walked in the imagination of doomsayers and talked the language of extinction" (Wright 2013, 22). No one seems to have a place to call home. The main character, Oblivia, an Aboriginal girl, has been abandoned after a gang rape. After a long sleep in "the deep underground bowel of a giant eucalyptus tree" (23), she awakes in the future. If she has a place, it is the black swan, both imaginary and real, that inspires her efforts to escape her oppressive circumstances. Wright's evocative imagery draws on her Waanyi Aboriginal heritage. In classical Aboriginal cultures, time is cyclical, and knowledge is embodied in places in a landscape whose care is divided by totem among the living descendants of the ancestral creation spirits. There is no "golden age" tradition of a better past; past and present are combined in an ongoing connection and cycle (Dutton 2010, 247). Wright blurs category distinctions and brings human, spiritual, and imaginary worlds together in the landscape in which Oblivia heads north in search of connections with the lost timeless presence of the Dreaming.

In *Terra Nullius* (2017), Wirlomin Noongar novelist Claire G. Coleman twists Nevil Shute's trope of Australia as the last meeting place on earth into a dystopic imaginary. The book's conceit rests on the knowledge that Aboriginal people have survived and adapted to millennia of environmental and social change on the earth's second driest continent. Part ecotopia, Australia is the last island conducive to human survival on earth swamped by rising seas. It is also the last refuge of humans fleeing colonization by the Toads, amphibian invaders from another galaxy. Many have been captured and enslaved. Those still free need constantly to move to avoid air-raids and massacres. Australia's hot, dry landscapes and underground rivers are as protective to the humans as they are life-threatening to the Toads. The overarching dystopian imaginary is a spatial one: the survival of Esperance highlights that the remaining Aboriginal "desert tribes," who are "supremely adapted to this environment ... could live in the desert far better than the Toads could" (Coleman 2017, 206).

Conclusion

Utopia is fundamentally a spatial literary form that works by making contrasts between geographical imaginaries of different social formations. Descriptions of landscapes and built structures are encoded with the social ideas, ideologies, institutions, and practices of the different forms of society compared. In the works discussed here, the spatial geometry of early modern utopias is best exemplified by Foigny's *The Southern Land Known* (1676). Modern works maintain the foundational comparison of different spatial imaginaries, but complicate it, for example, by introducing additional worlds, as in *The Dispossessed* (1974). They also show greater interest in the characters' embodied experience of places. In ostensible eutopias such as *Havergey* and even in the most dystopian *Nineteen Eighty-Four* (1949), descriptions of place point to the possibility of utopia over the horizon. However, utopia remains a space estranged from its *topos*.

References

Akkerman, Abraham. 2015. *Phenomenology of the Winter-City: Myth in the Rise and Decline of Built Environments*. New York: Springer.

Bacon, Francis. 2008. New Atlantis. In *The Major Works*, ed. Brian Vickers, 457–490. Oxford: Oxford University Press.

Boesky, Amy. 1996. *Founding Fictions: Utopias in Early Modern England*. Athens: University of Georgia Press.

Burnside, John. 2017. *Havergey*. Toller Fratrum: Little Toller Books.

Calvino, Italo. 2013. *Il Barone Rampante*. Milan: Oscar Mondadori.

Campbell, Mary B. 1999. *Wonder and Science: Imagining Worlds in Early Modern Europe*. Ithaca, NY: Cornell University Press.

Casey, Edward S. 1997. *The Fate of Place: A Philosophical History*. Berkeley: University of California Press.

Coleman, Claire G. 2017. *Terra Nullius*. Sydney: Hachette Australia, iBooks.

Davis, John C. 2008. Going nowhere: Travelling to, Through, and from Utopia. *Utopian Studies* 19 (1): 1–23.

Dutton, Jacqueline. 2010. 'Non-Western' Utopian Traditions. In *The Cambridge Companion to Utopian Literature*, ed. Gregory Claeys, 223–258. Cambridge: Cambridge University Press.

Foigny, Gabriel de. 1993. *The Southern Land, Known*. Trans. David Fausett. Syracuse: Syracuse University Press.

Fortunati, Vita. 2014. L'ambiguo immaginario dell'isola nella tradizione letteraria utopica. In *Il Fascino inquieto dell'utopia: Percorsi storici e letterari in onore di Marialuisa Bignami*, ed. Giuliana Iannaccaro, Alessandro Vescovi and Lidia De Michelis, 51–61. Milano: Ledizioni.

Gillies, John. 1994. *Shakespeare and the Geography of Difference*. Cambridge: Cambridge University Press.

Godwin, Francis. 2009. *The Man in the Moone*, ed. William Poole. Peterborough, ON: Broadview Editions.

Goodey, Brian R. 1970. Mapping 'Utopia': A Comment on the Geography of Sir Thomas More. *The Geographical Review* 60 (1): 15–30. https://doi.org/10.2307/213342.

Laursen, John Christian, and Kevin Pham. 2017. Empires for Peace: Denis Veiras's Borrowings from Garcilaso de La Vega. *The European Legacy* 22 (4): 427–442.

Leibacher-Ouvrard, Lise. 1989. *Libertinage et utopies sous le règne de Louis XIV*. Genève: Librairie Droz.

Le Guin, Ursula K. 2015. *The Dispossessed*. London: Gollancz, iBooks.

More, Thomas. 2018. *Utopia*, trans. Robert M. Adams and ed. George M. Logan. 3rd ed. Cambridge: Cambridge University Press.

Orwell, George. 2013. *Nineteen Eighty-Four*. London: Penguin.

Pacini, Giulia. 2014. Arboreal and Historical Perspectives from Calvino's *Il Barone Rampante*. *Romance Studies* 32 (1): 57–68.

Ronzeaud, Pierre. 1982. *L'utopie hermaphrodite: La Terre australe connue de Gabriel de Foigny (1676)*. Marseille: C.M.R. 17.

Smeeks, Hendrik. 1995. *The Mighty Kingdom of Krinke Kesmes (1708)*, ed. David Fausett, trans. Robert H. Leek. Amsterdam: Rodopi.

Tally, Robert T. 2013. *Utopia in the Age of Globalization: Space, Representation, and the World-System*. New York: Palgrave Macmillan.

Veiras, Denis. 2006. *The History of the Sevarambians: A Utopian novel*, ed. John Christian Laursen and Cyrus Masroori. Albany: State University of New York Press.

Vieira, Fátima. 2010. The Concept of Utopia. In *The Cambridge Companion to Utopian Literature*, ed. Gregory Claeys, 3–27. Cambridge: Cambridge University Press.

Wegner, Phillip E. 2002. *Imaginary Communities: Utopia, the Nation, and the Spatial Histories of Modernity*. Berkeley: University of California Press.

Wright, Alexis. 2013. *The Swan Book*. Artarmon, NSW: Giramondo Publishing Company, iBooks.

Utopia in "Non-Western" Cultures

Jacqueline Dutton

INTRODUCTION

Over the past 20 years, our collective understanding has shifted regarding which literature can express utopias, dystopias, and various other utopianisms. Where a utopia comes from, which cultural traditions contribute to shaping the worldview it articulates are now considered important elements to be analyzed, as evidenced in this section on global utopian perspectives, ranging from African to Chinese to Latin American utopias. Polemic still intervenes, however,[1] and any utopian studies conference or general publication on the topic is largely dominated by work on western utopian literature. The increasing production of postcolonial utopian and dystopian narratives and the innovations they communicate are profoundly changing the field, disrupting the historically grounded paradigms of the past (Pordzik 2001; Ashcroft 2017). There are nevertheless significant differences between examining literary utopias and dystopias from a postcolonial perspective and studying imaginaries of the ideal from different cultural traditions. These approaches are complementary, and their convergences and divergences will be outlined in this chapter.

The principal aim here is to question whether utopias from "non-western" cultures demonstrate specific and identifiable traits that influence particular literary projections of better and worse societies. The central thesis is that

J. Dutton (✉)
University of Melbourne, Melbourne, Australia

P. Marks et al. (eds.), *The Palgrave Handbook of Utopian and Dystopian Literatures*, https://doi.org/10.1007/978-3-030-88654-7_43

"non-western" utopias draw on different worldviews to enrich their contributions to utopian literature. In order to explore this premise, I will consider some recent examples of utopian and dystopian texts from Japanese, Francophone Algerian, and Indigenous Australian literature. These narratives represent a range of worldviews that both intersect with and are distinctive from western and postcolonial utopias. Japan is clearly neither western nor postcolonial, though has some affinities with western colonial culture. Japan's colonial empire extended to Taiwan, Korea, and Manchuria in the late-nineteenth and early-twentieth centuries, and its imperial intentions were clear during World War II, but it did not have the same intergenerational influence on its colonies as western colonial powers have exercised. Algeria was a colony of France from 1830 to 1962 and is now a "non-western" Francophone postcolonial and mainly Islamic culture. Indigenous Australian cultures are highly varied, "non-western", and postcolonial, yet they require differentiation from other postcolonial Australian cultures. Each of these examples are decentered, less-studied areas for utopian enquiry, representing interesting cases to examine that complement and complete the work on utopia from other cultural traditions presented in this volume.

RECOGNIZING AND DESIGNATING
UTOPIAS FROM OTHER CULTURES

Addressing terminology to begin, I have discussed the inherent problems of referring to these utopian and dystopian narratives as "non-western" in other publications (Dutton 2010), critiquing the differentiation between the west and the "rest" as a hierarchizing process, and contesting the collapsing of so much diversity into two homogenizing binaries. I have suggested alternative formulae to designate "non-western" utopias, such as "intercultural imaginaries of the ideal" (Dutton 2010, 2020a, 2021), emphasizing the comparative, competing, and/or collaborative exchange that takes place when worldviews collide and a fictional projection of a different society results. In the special issue of *Utopian Studies* I co-edited with Lyman Tower Sargent, we adopted "utopias from other cultural traditions" as our preferred expression (Dutton and Sargent 2013), focusing attention on the difficulty of recognizing representations of ideal societies and spaces that arise from cultures founded upon different ethics and esthetics. The reference to "other" still implies an alterity based on a western viewpoint and western sameness in a utopian model, which is unsatisfactory for similar reasons to those outlined above. I have returned here to "non-western" cultures, with the same hesitations experienced previously, to maintain some kind of continuity with past papers and to work through some of the contrasts and alignments this process displays in relation to postcolonial utopian methods. I also continue to balance out the binary of "non-western" with my partiality for intercultural imaginaries of the ideal. However, as the latter is unfortunately not immediately identifiable with utopian theory, which is certainly the field in which these studies should be located, utopias from "non-western" cultures prevail.

An additional complication to recognizing utopias and dystopias is the more frequent use of "speculative fiction," especially in Asia, to describe a wider range of narratives. Understood by Marek Oziewicz as "a super category for all genres that deliberately depart from 'consensus reality'" (Oziewicz 2017, np), speculative fiction includes fantasy, science-fiction, and horror, as well as utopias and dystopias, weird fiction, alternative history, magic realism, steampunk, cli-fi, and many other variations. These texts often present utopian or dystopian projects but are not necessarily identified as such, either by the authors or in scholarship. For example, the four volume entitled *Speculative Japan* contain short stories translated and published by Kurodahan Press which were previously inaccessible to those unable to read Japanese does not ever mention utopia. The editor, Edward Lipsett, has the explicit goal to "reveal a different worldview" not just in terms of the original futures described in these stories, but also to show that these projections are fundamentally different in content and expression because they emanate from Japanese culture: "We perceive the world around us in different ways, and think about it, and talk about it, in different ways" (Lipsett 2018, 7).

JAPANESE IMAGINARIES OF THE IDEAL

Japanese narratives depicting imaginaries of the ideal developed in harmony with the country's archipelagic geography and foundational belief system, Shinto. *Tokoyo no kuni* was the indigenous designation for an ideal time and place, a kind of Golden Age that evolved into the projection of an island paradise in the East called Ise, as well as an association with the eternal divine lineage of the Emperor. Ancient literary texts mentioning *tokoyo no kuni* include the *Kojiki* and the *Nihon Shoki*, as does the *Manyoshu*. The glaring difference between representations of this Japanese imaginary of the ideal and ancient western models of Plato's *Republic* or Virgil's *Aeneid* and *Eclogues* is the inherent mutability and ambiguity of *tokoyo no kuni*—the latter can be found in either life or death, in divine or human realms, as a geographical place or in the person of the Emperor.[2] Japanese imaginaries of the ideal were obviously more influenced by neighboring Asian cultures prior to western exposure, integrating concepts from Buddhism and Confucianism, to develop a messianic notion of *miroku* as a time and place when humans are liberated from suffering. The floating world of *ukiyo* is another incarnation of Japanese ideals of ambiguity, a time and place in between the material and immaterial worlds, where happiness, pleasure, and beauty are treasured precisely because of their impermanence and mutability. Wit, charm, extravagance, hedonism, and transgression were the norms in this imagined parallel universe, as depicted in popular woodblock prints and poetry, opposing the obligations and hard work of everyday life in the repressive years of Edo period Japan under Tokugawa shogunate rule (1603–1868).

Following the "opening" of Japan to the west during the Meiji era (1868–1912), utopian-style novels began to appear, such as Akutagawa Ryunosuke's *Kappa* (1927), an allegorical satire set on an amphibious island (like *tokoyo no kuni*) that also bears some resemblance to Jonathon Swift's *Gulliver's Travels* (1726). It is a depressingly dystopian place where the critique of contemporary Japanese society is performed, but the protagonist does not appreciate the substitute society, where imperialism and productivity reign and even cannibalism is acceptable when workers are no longer needed (Moichi 1999). Many of Japan's most famous novelists have written their own ideal societies, from Yukio Mishima's *Utsukushii Hoshi* (*The Beautiful Star*,1962) to Haruki Murakami's *Sekai no Owari to Hadoboirudo Wandarando* (*Hard-Boiled Wonderland and the End of the World*, 1985) to Nobel laureates Kazuo Ishiguro's *Ukiyo no gaka* (*An Artist of the Floating World*, 1987) and Kenzaburo Oe's *Chiryoto* (*Tower of Healing*, 1990). Each of these texts follows a canonical utopian model to some extent but also features indigenous Japanese tropes such as ambiguous parallels that render unclear the divisions between utopia and dystopia, the real world and the imagined one.

There are several scholarly studies of Japanese utopian literature that support interpretations of epistemological otherness without explicitly embracing this otherness as a feature of Japanese imaginaries of the ideal. Instead, there tends to be an identification of these indigenous features as divergence or separation from the western models of utopian literature. Seiji Nuita's (1971) foundational article argued that Japanese "energy of consciousness" was not sufficiently dissociated from nature to encourage the Japanese to give birth to utopian visions prior to the introduction of the western model, and Isao Uemichi (1982) echoed this denial of Japanese indigenous utopianism. Koon-Ki Ho's (1991) more nuanced research is nevertheless still categorical in defining Japanese imaginaries of the ideal as *non*-utopian: "Unlike the Western or Chinese mythology which plays a key role in the heralding of Utopian thinking, the ancient Japanese mythology betrays a Japanese mind rather indifferent to Utopian speculation" (Ho 1991, 202). However, the very elements that he cites as demonstrating *non*-utopian thinking in the ancient *Taketori Monogatari* (late ninth or early tenth century) are ambiguity and mutability, which are precisely those qualities that can be recognized throughout literary representations of Japanese imaginaries of the ideal, from ancient times until the present. Susan Napier's work on *Amanonkoku okanki* (*Record of a Voyage to the Country of Amanon*) by Yumiko Kurahashi clearly reveals the ambiguity and mutability of the body in this feminist utopia that like most Japanese utopias, diverges from the western canonical model, though Napier refers to it as "more a deconstruction of Utopia than a vision of an actual ideal place in itself" (Napier 1996, 170). All of these caveats and lacunae that appear to separate Japanese narratives of ideal imaginary places actually serve to support the central thesis proposed here: Japanese imaginaries of the ideal are "non-western" utopias that draw on different worldviews that enrich rather than diminish their contributions to utopian literature.

Project (Keikaku) Itoh's *Hāmonī* (ハーモニー) (Harmony) (2008; trans. 2010) and Haruki Murakami's *1Q84* (2009–2010) are two recent novels from Japan that do explicitly reference utopian traditions, while demonstrating inherently Japanese interpretations of the imaginary of the ideal. The blurb on the back of *Harmony* begins "In the future, Utopia has finally been achieved thanks to medical nanotechnology and a powerful ethic of social welfare and mutual consideration." This medical utopia where all diseases and injuries can be cured or prevented is nevertheless interpreted by most readers, especially non-Japanese ones, as a dystopia, because there is no free choice or range of emotions besides wellness and harmony. Even suicide becomes almost impossible, a crime against the body and the state, which is an interesting stance given the traditional Japanese reverence for *hara-kiri* in contrast to Christian values regarding suicide as shameful. The human body as the vital site for this medical utopia is incredibly mutable. In fact, by the end of the novel, technology and moral philosophy have evolved to such an extent that the soul and consciousness are considered redundant and not essential to "humanity." The well body is all that matters; the soul and consciousness can get in the way of wellness. With the rise of mental illnesses and the psycho-social suffering they can bring, there is a hint of ambiguity to this apparently dystopian but potentially utopian proposal. The novel becomes even more ambiguous in its utopian versus dystopian qualities when one realizes that the author was editing the manuscript in hospital until he died from cancer at the age of 34. Clearly, the underpinning elements of ambiguity and mutability are present in this Japanese utopian novel.

On the English publisher's official website, *1Q84* (2011) is described as "a dystopia to rival George Orwell's".[3] The fact that the novel takes place in 1984 and in a parallel existence called 1Q84 (where Q stands for question) is an obvious and immediate intertextual figure relating to Orwell's *Nineteen Eighty-Four*. This link is completely recognizable to readers of canonical utopian literature. However, it is less evident to non-Japanese readers that *1Q84* also plays on Japanese-English sounds: the number nine in Japanese is pronounced *kew*, which is a homonym of Q in English. The ambiguity of the title, the characters, and the plot of the novel, together with the mutability of their existence across two parallel Japans, and multiple bodies, is perfectly aligned with traditional Japanese imaginaries of the ideal. There are several other allusions to Orwellian tropes, including the Sakigake cult whose members are like "mindless robots" controlled by a totalitarian state, and whose leader is all-seeing like Big Brother, but the love story at the center of Murakami's novel is very different from Orwell's doomed couple. The mention of Manchuria as a failed agrarian paradise for the male protagonist Tengo's father adds to the specificity of the Japanese colonial example, but the strongest feature of this utopia is the impermanence of the parallel floating world.

Francophone Algerian Alternative Worlds

Orwell's reach is long, across time and space, to inspire songs by David Bowie and The Jam, television programs like *Big Brother* all over the world, and rather too many comparisons with our contemporary existence.[4] There are also several novels other than Murakami's inspired by 1984, including Algerian author Boualem Sansal's bestseller *2084: La Fin du monde* (2084: The End of the World) (2015). References to Orwell are deliberate and easily recognizable in this text where history has been rewritten or suppressed, and the eternal wars against unknown enemies are constantly shifting but the fighting never ceases (see also Dutton 2020b). Sansal's perspective seems to fit with a canonical western utopian paradigm, yet distinctive traits drawn from classic Islamic imaginaries of the ideal are mobilized and inverted in this Algerian dystopia.[5]

The pilgrimage as a continually evolving, dynamic, and shared site for Islamic utopianism has been confirmed in recent scholarship (Arjana 2017; Bakhsh 2013; Dutton 2010) and is developed and exploited in *2084*. Pilgrims are the only inhabitants of Abistan, this "land of the believers," who can move around, not quite freely, but according to itineraries and calendars established by the government. They are also holders of knowledge and teach the rebel protagonist Ati to doubt what others have told him about the world he inhabits. Another key signal of indigenous Islamic utopianism is the lack of temporality and privileging of cyclical time in messianic and millennial predictions (Dutton 2010; Sachedina 1981). Though the title of the book obviously designates a year, no-one can say what it signifies—the beginning or the end of the war, the birthdate of the prophet Abi, the date of his enlightenment— but as Ati learns more about his country, he realizes that dates do not apply to Abistanis in the immense immobility of time.

The utopian and dystopian tropes in Algerian Francophone narratives are wide-ranging and diverse, including the thinly disguised post-war Alger in Mohammed Dib's post-apocalyptic novel *Qui se souvient de la mer?* (Who Remembers the Sea?) (1962), the desire for linguistic and cultural tolerance in Assia Djebar's novels *Le Blanc d'Algérie* (Algerian White) (1996) and *La Disparition de la langue française* (The Disappearance of French Language) (2003) (Schneider 2006; Dutton 2016), and the island in Azouz Begag's *L'Île des gens d'ici* (The Island of the People From Here) (2006). While these examples are classic markers of the genre infused with Algerian perspectives, there is nevertheless distinct cultural specificity in the one-man play *Un Bateau pour l'Australie* (A Boat for Australia) written and performed by Fellag (1991), which recounts the extraordinary myth that circulated in Algeria in 1987 that Australia was welcoming Algeria's unemployed, and would provide them all with a job and a kangaroo, which led to huge demands for visas at the Australian Embassy in Alger. Karim Amellal's dystopian projection of France based on Marine Le Pen's nationalist party winning the 2017 presidential election translates the postcolonial Algerian experience in *Bleu, Blanc, Noir* (Blue,

White, Black) (2016), but none of these Algerian (or Franco-Algerian) writers develop on Islamic imaginaries of the ideal to the extent that Sansal does in *2084*.

Kamel Daoud's two novels suggest a deeper engagement with Islamic imaginaries of the ideal from an Algerian cultural experience, critiquing contemporary society though he does not really present an explicit utopian or dystopian alternative. His first novel *Meursault, contre-enquête* (The Meursault Investigation) (2013) rereads and rewrites Albert Camus' *L'Etranger* (The Outsider) (1942) from the perspective of the younger brother (Haroun) of Camus' anonymous murdered "Arab" (Moussa Ould el-Assasse). By composing a counterpoint to a western canonical text, Daoud—like Sansal—offers access to a different imaginary, even if not necessarily following utopian or dystopian models. There are distinct signs that Daoud is actively and intellectually pursuing projections of a better society in Algeria through his writing. First, Daoud (and Sansal) still live in Algeria, which is unusual for successful Francophone African writers who mostly move to France, the United States, or Canada, especially if they speak out against the national regime, as these authors do against Algeria's fundamentalist Islamic government. This choice indicates hope for change in their own country.

Second, Daoud was educated in Arabic and taught himself French as a foreign language through reading and studying, unlike Sansal and the older generations of (post)colonial Francophone Algerian writers. Daoud's second novel *Zabor ou Les psaumes* (Sabor or The Psalms) (2017) introduces a semi-autobiographical narrative of a writer who learns French and through storytelling in that language is able to make sense of life in Algeria. This constructed identity and pathway demonstrates capacity for worldmaking. Third and perhaps most convincingly, Daoud's journalistic essays directly address Islamic paradigms of paradise and utopia, including one translated and published in *The New York Times* entitled "Paradise, the New Muslim Utopia, (2016)" which begins "Future writing project: a topography of paradise in the medieval Muslim imagination." He juxtaposes the vision of a democratic postcolonial utopia in Algeria against the powerful new post-mortem utopia of the Islamosphere, highlighting the absurdity of the current Islamicist paradise.[6]

Indigenous Australian Post-Apocalyptic Times

Indigenous Australian narratives of imaginaries of the ideal are grounded in such radically different paradigms to western utopian traditions that it is often difficult to identify them as germane to the genre. Origin stories are not located in the ancient past as they are in most other traditions expressing a "golden age," but rather in a dynamic continuing cycle. Early ethnographers Baldwin Spencer and F.J. Gillen (1996) erroneously translated the Arandic word *Altyerre* and related term *Alcheringa* as the "Dream*time*" imposing a western creationist ideology and linear timeline onto Indigenous Australian atemporality (306). The misreading of this concept continues today, causing

significant misunderstanding, and while "Dreaming" might be more acceptable to refer to Indigenous Australian past, present, and future stories, it
is preferable to use the Arandic *Altyerre* or Warlpiri *Tjukurpa* which are
becoming more widely recognized in general Australian usage (Green 2012).
Indigenous Australian imaginaries of the ideal can be everywhere and "everywhen" (Stanner 1979, 24), perpetuated by the songlines that criss-cross the
island-continent. These songlines reconnect the initiated traveler to Country
and reinscribe their body and beliefs in the complex system of *Alcheringa*
through singing and seeing the landmarks identified in shared stories.

In his recent article for the exhibition and catalog *Songlines: Tracking the
Seven Sisters* (National Museum of Australia, Canberra), Darren Jorgensen,
like Bruce Chatwin and Ted Strehlow before him, describes the dynamic
nature of songlines—always unfinished, and never completely comprehensible
or explained (Jorgensen 2017, 182–183). His work on Indigenous Australian
art, literature, and utopia foregrounds the post-apocalyptic element as part
of the lived experience of Australian Indigenous peoples—and many other
postcolonial peoples. Evident in novels like *Doctor Wooreddy's Prescription
for Enduring the End of the World* (1983) by Mudrooroo (Colin Johnson)
and *Land of the Golden Clouds* (1998) by Archie Weller, the projection past
the present allows for future positive interpretations of Indigenous society in
Australia.[7] Non-Indigenous Australian futuristic narratives depicting Indigenous Australian communities like Terry Dowling's Ab'O desert communities
in his *Rynosseros* series (1990, 1992, 1993, and 2007) also subscribe to the
"everywhen" concept of cyclical time.

A similar strategy is employed by Alexis Wright, Waanyi writer from the
southern Gulf of Carpentaria, in *The Swan Book* (2013) though the future
described is rather bleaker. Wright interweaves ancient beliefs and modern
issues, ranging from environmental destruction, poverty, and dispossession
to Indigenous women's self-empowerment in a place of degradation and
violence. There are clear western utopian and dystopian tropes in this post-
apocalyptic scenario enacted by global climate change, but the worldview
expressed is Indigenous, blurring temporalities, reality, and metaphor, in a
kind of dynamic, ongoing narrative that is never completely closed off. *The
Swan Book* represents hope at the end of the world (Sefton-Rowston 2016),
but not according to western markers for improvement. Instead of harmony,
oblivion rules—the female protagonist's name is Oblivia Ethyl(ene)—and the
binaries that characterize western mainstream thinking (for example, inclu-
sion/exclusion) are collapsed. It is the Apocalypse that brings change and
only place or Country is (re)generative in time. Yet so much is unresolved,
from sovereignty to self-determination, made almost impenetrable by confused
mental states that embody "both the dissonance of dystopian reality and
utopian dreaming" (Mead 2018, 528). Wright's prose displays the rupture
from western literary and utopian models of structure and clarity that is
also observable in texts by Indigenous Australian writers Kim Scott, Marie

Mundaka, Larissa Behrendt, and Bruce Pascoe (Wheeler 2013). Their narrative style and content demonstrate the fundamentally different worldview of interconnectedness, atemporality, and the primordial role of Country (Graham 1999).

Claire G. Coleman is a South Coast Noongar writer from Western Australia whose *Terra Nullius* (2017) bears the subtitle *A Novel*, as though the genre of the text may require confirmation, but there are other surprises in store for the reader. The seemingly historical narratives of Natives and Settlers are abruptly flipped to future projections halfway through the novel, cleverly destabilizing perspectives and transposing the inclusion/exclusion binary so as to encourage reader identification with the excluded. Though Coleman's style, techniques, and structures are perhaps more familiar than those employed by Wright, the temporal fluidity and evident cycles of events reveal the Indigenous Australian worldview at work in this fiction that bleeds from utopia into dystopia and back again. Like the transparent symbolism of Oblivia's name in Wright's novel, the female protagonist in Coleman's novel is called Esperance, and she does represent hope for her people. The other Native hero, Jacky Jerramungup, defines the Settlers not as "inhuman Toads," but "nonhumans." His final words in the text are "translated" as meaning that there is very little difference between the human Natives and the nonhuman Settlers—both are capable of equally bad and good deeds: "There is nothing in their hearts and minds that does not also exist in the hearts and minds of the human species" (300).

CONCLUSION

The initial question posed in this article relates to the fundamental difference between "non-western" imaginaries of the ideal and western utopian models. *Terra Nullius* adds another dimension to the question. If nonhumans do not possess any existential differences from humans, can "non-western" utopias really be that different from western utopias? Based on these recent texts from Japanese, Francophone Algerian, and Indigenous Australian cultures, which each bear the imprint of at least 150 years of western utopian influences, a range of perspectives is possible. The long Japanese tradition of imagining ideal places prior to the introduction of the western utopian model has resulted in deeply ingrained and strongly evident features of the indigenous worldview, notably ambiguity and mutability, in the Japanese utopian novel. In the case of the Francophone Algerian texts, though they do express an Islamic worldview relating pilgrimage and cyclical time to an ideal existence, the complications of colonialism and its aftermath followed by repressive Islamicist regimes have dammed the direct flow from foundational Islamic worldviews. Confusion between French colonial oppression and Islamic fundamentalism muddies the waters further, making this "non-western" utopia comprehensible only when read as a postcolonial utopia as well. The extreme incongruity between Indigenous Australian imaginaries of the ideal and western utopias in terms of atemporality and understanding of Country or place is clearly maintained despite attempted colonial eradication as the continuity of Indigenous cultures is not ideologically or politically challenging to Indigenous peoples in the same way that Islamic fundamentalism can be perceived as perverting the past. Postcolonial readings of these "non-western" utopias are therefore complementary to recognizing their debt to ancient Indigenous ideals.

"Non-western" utopias really are different from western utopias, but they are not all equally so. As Orwell has taught us, some are more "equal" than others.

NOTES

1. Krishan Kumar's statement in 1987 that "Utopia is *not* universal" in *Utopia and Anti-Utopia in Modern Times*, 19, has had lasting resonance.
2. For more detail on the roots and evolution of *tokoyo no kuni*, see Dutton, "Non-western" Utopian Traditions (2010).
3. Murakami's official English website (harukimurakami.com) lists the *IQ84* summary: http://www.harukimurakami.com/book_summary/1q84-summary.
4. Orwell's presence in contemporary popular culture is evident by the adoption of terms like *doublespeak*, current politicians' denial of history, and fake news reporting. The fact that British music reporter Dorian Lynskey has just published a new book on the topic entitled *The Ministry of Truth: The Biography of George Orwell's 1984* (2019) demonstrates both the prescience and the popularity of Orwellian paradigms.
5. Comparative critiques of Orwell's and Sansal's novels tend to emphasize continuities rather than innovations (see, for example, Regis-Pierre Fieu, De *1984* à *2084*. Mutations de la peur totalitaire dans la dystopie européenne) though Petr Vurm interprets *2084* as a critical dystopia given the hope expressed for a brighter future.
6. Lahouari Addi mounted excellent arguments for a more democratic utopian project in Algeria in his 1992 article "Islamicist Utopia and Democracy" and continues to link radical Arab nationalism of the past with political Islam as an impediment to political modernity (2017).
7. The Aboriginality of both Mudrooroo and Archie Weller has been questioned. However, their works cited here draw on the same tropes identified in other Indigenous Australian utopian texts. Please see Foley 1997 for a discussion of their Indigenous Australian identity.

REFERENCES

Addi, Lahouari. 1992. Islamicist Utopia and Democracy. *The Annals of the American Academy* 524: 120–130.

Addi, Lahouari. 2017. *Radical Arab Nationalism and Political Islam*, trans. Anthony Roberts. Georgetown, TX: Georgetown University Press.

Amellal, Karim. 2016. *Bleu, Blanc, Noir*. Avignon: Editions de l'Aube.

Arjana, S.R. 2017. *Pilgrimage in Islam: Traditional and Modern Practices*. London: Oneworld Publications.

Ashcroft, Bill. 2017. *Utopianism in Postcolonial Literatures*. Abingdon, Oxon, and New York: Routledge.

Bakhsh, Alireza Omid. 2013. The Virtuous City: The Iranian and Islamic Heritage of Utopianism. *Utopian Studies* 24 (1): 41–51.

Coleman, Claire G. 2017. *Terra Nullius: A Novel*. Sydney: Hachette.

Daoud, Kamel. 2013. *Meursault, contre-enquête*. Arles: Actes Sud.

Daoud, Kamel. 2016. Paradise: The New Muslim Utopia. *The New York Times*. https://www.nytimes.com/2016/08/02/opinion/paradise-the-new-muslim-uto pia.html. Accessed 15 June 2019.

Daoud, Kamel. 2017. *Zabor, ou Les Psaumes*. Arles: Actes Sud.

Dutton, Jacqueline. 2010. "Non-Western" Utopian Traditions. In *The Cambridge Companion to Utopian Literature*, ed. Gregory Claeys, 223–258. Cambridge: Cambridge University Press.

Dutton, Jacqueline. 2016. World Literature in French, *littérature-monde*, and the Translingual Turn. *French Studies* 70 (3): 404–418. https://doi.org/10.1093/fs/ knw131.

Dutton, Jacqueline. 2020a. Utopia, Limited. Transnational Utopianism and Intercultural Imaginaries of the Ideal. In *The Transnational in Literary Studies: Potential and Limitations of a Concept*, ed. Kai Wiegandt, 107–123. Berlin: De Gruyter.

Dutton, Jacqueline. 2020b. Writing French in the World: Transnational Identities, Transcultural Ideals. In *Francophone Literatures as World Literature*, ed. Christian Moraru, Nicole Simek, and Bertrand Westphal, 209–226. New York: Bloomsbury Academic.

Dutton, Jacqueline. 2021. Transnational Utopianism: Framing the Future in French Language Literatures. In *Transnational French Studies*, ed. Charles Forsdick and Claire Launchbury. Liverpool: Liverpool University Press.

Dutton, Jacqueline, and Lyman Tower Sargent. 2013. Introduction: Utopias in Other Cultural Traditions. *Utopian Studies* 24 (1): 1–5.

Fellag. 1991. Un Bateau pour l'Australie. https://www.youtube.com/watch?v=v-FBz8_cD8g. Accessed 15 June 2019.

Fieu, Regis-Pierre. 2017. De *1984* à *2084*. Mutations de la peur totalitaire dans la dystopie européenne. *Carnets* 11. http://journals.openedition.org/carnets/2344. Accessed 19 April 2019.

Foley, Gary. 1997. Muddy Waters: Archie, Mudrooroo & Aboriginality. http://www. kooriweb.org/foley/essays/pdf_essays/Muddy_Waters_Archie_Mudrooroo_and_ Aborig.pdf.

Graham, Mary. 1999. Some Thoughts about the Philosophical Underpinnings of Aboriginal worldviews. *Worldviews: Environment, Culture, Religion* 3: 105–118.

Green, Jennifer. 2012. The Altyerre Story—'Suffering Badly by translation.' *The Australian Journal of Anthropology* 23: 158–178.

Ho, Koon-Ki. 1991. Japanese in Search of Happiness: A Survey of the Utopian Tradition in Japan. *Oriens Extremus* 34 (1/2): 201–214.

Itoh, Project. 2010. *Harmony*, trans. Alexander O. Smith. San Francisco, CA: Haikasoru.

Jorgensen, Darren. 2017. The Last Songs of Tjapartji Bates. In *Songlines: Tracking the Seven Sisters*, ed. Margo Neale, 182–183. Canberra: National Museum of Australia Press.

Kumar, Krishan. 1987. *Utopia and Anti-Utopia in Modern Times*. Oxford: Blackwell.

Lipsett, Edward, ed. 2018. *Speculative Japan 4: "Pearls for Mia" and Other Tales, Preface*. Kumamoto: Kurodahan Press.

Lynskey, Dorian. 2019. *The Ministry of Truth: The Biography of George Orwell's 1984*. New York: Doubleday.

Mead, Philip. 2018. Unresolved Sovereignty and the Anthropocene Novel: Alexis Wright's *The Swan Book*. *Journal of Australian Studies* 42 (4): 524–538. https://doi.org/10.1080/14443058.2018.1539759.

Moichi, Yoriko. 1999. Japanese Utopian Literature from the 1870s to the Present and the Influence of Western Utopianism. *Utopian Studies* 10 (2): 89–97.

Murakami, Haruki. *1Q84* Summary. http://www.harukimurakami.com/book_summary/1q84-summary. Accessed 15 June 2019.

Murakami, Haruki. 2011. *1Q84*, trans.Jay Rubin and Philip Gabriel. London: Penguin Random House.

Napier, Susan. 1996. *The Fantastic in Modern Japanese Literature: The Subversion of Modernity*. London and New York: Routledge.

Nuita, Seiji. 1971. Traditional Utopias in Japan and the West: A Study in Contrast. In *Aware of Utopia*, ed. David Plath, 12–32. Urbana: University of Illinois Press.

Oziewicz, Marek. 2017. Speculative Fiction. *Oxford Research Encyclopedia of Literature*. http://oxfordre.com/literature/view/https://doi.org/10.1093/acrefore/9780190201098.001.0001/acrefore-9780190201098-e-78. Accessed 15 June 2019.

Pordzik, Ralph. 2001. *The Quest for Postcolonial Utopia: A Comparative Introduction to the Utopian Novel in New English Literatures*. New York: Lang.

Sachedina, Abdulaziz Abdulhussein. 1981. *Islamic Messianism: The Idea of Mahdi in Twelver Shi'ism*. Albany: SUNY Press.

Sansal, Boualem. 2015. *2084: La Fin du Monde*. Paris: Gallimard.

Schneider, Annedith. 2006. Mourning in a Minority Language: Assia Djebar's *Algerian White*. *Journal for the Study of Religion* 19 (2): 41–52.

Sefton-Rowston, Adelle L. 2016. Hope at the End of the World: Creation Stories and Apocalypse in Alexis Wright's *Carpentaria* and *The Swan Book*. *Antipodes* 30 (2): 355–368.

Songlines: Tracking the Seven Sisters. 2017. National Museum of Australia, Canberra, 15 September 2017–25 February 2018. http://songlines.nma.gov.au/. Accessed 15 June 2019.

Spencer, Baldwin, and F.J. Gillen. 1996. *The Arunta*. Oosterhout, Netherlands: Anthropological Publications.

Stanner, W.E.H. 1979. *White Man Got No Dreaming: Essays 1938–1973*. Canberra: Australian National University Press.

Uemichi, Isao. 1982. Paradise in Japanese literature. In *Proceedings of the Fourth International Symposium on Asian Studies*. Hong Kong: Asian Research Service.

Vurm, Petr. 2018. 1984–2084. Faux-semblants révélés, émotions refoulées: l'amour, la haine et l'indifférence à l'âge totalitaire chez George Orwell et Boualem Sansal. *Acta Universitatis Carolinae Philologica* 3: 193–204. https://doi.org/10.14712/24646830.2018.47.

Wheeler, Belinda. 2013. Introduction: The Emerging Canon. *A Companion to Australian Aboriginal Literature*, ed. Belinda Wheeler, 1–14. New York: Camden House.

Wright, Alexis. 2013. *The Swan Book*. Sydney: Giramondo Publishing.

Africa

Ainehi Edoro-Glines

Introduction

In *Archaeologies of the Future*, Fredric Jameson stipulates that one of the preconditions for a utopia is that "it must respond to specific dilemmas and offer to solve fundamental social problems" and that "it is the social situation which must admit of such a solution or at least its possibility" (Jameson 2007, 11–12). For African utopian thinkers, the central problem has always been and continues to be what Walter Mignolo, borrowing from Anibal Quijano, terms a "colonial matrix of power" (Mignolo 2007, 476). They have had to reimagine the African world through images that are not subject to the rule of European knowledge-making. Jameson also explains that precisely because utopias present social issues writ large, they are less about fulfilling social fantasies and more about diagnosing social problems. Utopias do not "offer visions of happy worlds." They are, instead, "diagnostic interventions" into "fundamental social problems" (11, 12). If we define utopia broadly as the political, ideological, and esthetic procedure for validating the necessity for a radically new world, then the African literary archive has a wealth of figures and conventions that can certainly enrich the understanding of the form of utopia. Thus, even though utopia in the conventional Thomas More sense is not well-represented in African literature, there is a long tradition of philosophy and fiction built on the search for new rules governing the creation of worlds.

A. Edoro-Glines (✉)
University of Wisconsin-Madison, Madison, WI, USA

P. Marks et al. (eds.), *The Palgrave Handbook of Utopian and Dystopian Literatures*, https://doi.org/10.1007/978-3-030-88654-7_44

Envisioning New Worlds

The founding of new worlds is a recurrent motif in African literature. The epic of Sundiata, for instance, tells the story of a disabled boy who transforms his small village into the center of an empire. In one seventeenth-century account, Ethiopia's Wallata Petros leaves her husband to answer Christ's call to "found communities" (Galawdewos 2018, 43). Petros's hagiography focuses on her transformation from an unhappy wife to the leader of a network of monasteries and prayer communities spread across seven cities. And, more recently, Wole Soyinka's development of the Ogun paradigm begins as the deity traverses a chthonic forest of dark, metaphysical matter in order to unite the spheres of the ancestors, the unborn, and the living (1976a). Ogun is portrayed as a visionary, an inventor, and a figure of technological advancement: through the extraction of iron, Ogun is able to clear the mythic forest separating the various spheres of existence. While these mythic stories are not strictly speaking utopian narratives, they demonstrate the preponderance in the African literary tradition of texts that seek to capture that moment when an existing structure is dismantled to allow the emergence of a new world. These stories tend to be built around maverick figures who abandon the familiar space of existence for something strange, risky, and radically other. Their actions tend to transform spaces and bodies in unrecognizable ways while founding new histories and mythologies. Working specifically with the myth of Ogun, Soyinka has made it possible to see this class of characters in the light of an African revolutionary paradigm. For example, in the poem "Ogun Abibiman" (1980), he uses the Ogun revolutionary figure to trace a genealogy that links Shaka kaSenzangakhona, Fidel Castro, and Nelson Mandela, arguing that the twentieth century is a period of black utopian imagination.

In the postcolonial context, utopian thinking is constitutively decolonial. A set of interlocking domains of economic control, knowledge production, political power, and subjective formation built on racism and patriarchy, the colonial matrix of power (or coloniality) is the enduring power-knowledge complex on which modernity is constituted and by which it continues to propel itself. Philosophers like V. Y. Mudimbe and, more recently, Achille Mbembe (2013) have dissected the epistemological dimensions of coloniality and concluded that what counts as knowledge about Africa has always been measured or validated against Western norms. Mudimbe terms this epistemological structure the "colonial library" (Mudimbe 1997, 78) while Mbembe calls it "black reason" but what both terms point to is the difficulty of assigning form and value to African worlds, objects, bodies, esthetics, and history, without first subjecting them to Western conceptual tools and categories. If we understand utopia, as Jameson does, to be a form that presents a simplified, "single-shot solution" to big, systemic problems, one place to find utopian thinking is the body of images generated as paradigms of epistemic resistance (2007, 11).

Some of the earliest criticisms by African scholars against the colonial archive took the form of utopian formulations. The solution offered in these early interventions shows that these writers knew they were up against something more pervasive than specific acts of colonial injustices. They were challenging an epistemological order, not just colonialism as a particular kind of political economy. They were asking: can we establish a new body of rules to govern the procedures of producing, evaluating, justifying, and circulating knowledge about Africa? In J.E. Casely Hayford's philosophical novel, *Ethiopia Unbound* (2003), one of the solutions proffered is the establishment of a university. Toward the end of the book, the principal character Kwamankra reflects on the implication of this institutional intervention:

> I would found in such a University a Chair for History; and the kind of history that I would teach would be universal history with particular reference to the part Ethiopia has played in the affairs of the world. I would lay stress upon the fact that while Rameses II was dedicating temples to "the God of gods and secondly to his own glory," the God of the Hebrews had not yet appeared unto Moses in the Burning Bush, that Africa was the cradle of the world's systems and philosophies, and the nursing mother of its religions. In short, that Africa has nothing to be ashamed of its place among the nations of the earth. I would make it possible for this seat of learning to be the means of revising erroneous current ideas regarding the African. (sic, 194, 195)

What Kwamankra really wants in his yearning for a "universal history" centered on Africa is a completely new ground of intelligibility for the African world— its own principle of knowledge and understanding, its own economy, politics, and ethics (Mignolo 2007, 453). What Kwamankra seeks is an "epistemic shift," breaking free of the knowledge-power matrix of a modernity erected on coloniality (Mignolo 2007, 453).

In African literature, utopia has been helpful for imagining what such a shift would look like and how it would transform the world. What would Africa as protagonist of world history look like? What kind of future does such a history imply? How would geopolitics be reconfigured to bear the imprint of an African logic of power? These questions have been explored for decades in politics and through both the realist and the futuristic esthetics literature. What Achebe's historical fiction, Nnedi Okorafor's science fiction, Pan-Africanism, and Afro-futurism have in common is a set of images of what Africa might have looked like or could look like if the colonialist framework of modernity ceased to be in force.[1] Indeed, the era of decolonization in Africa was characterized by utopian thinking of this sort. Political leaders, historians, artists, and fiction writers came up with various ideas about what an ideal African world outside Eurocentric terms of power, space, and time might look like. Breaking free from the systemic structures of colonialism implied the arrival of a radically different world. This essay traces the utopian vein within African literary

discourse by establishing a link between the utopian theories of decolonization and utopian formulations in fiction. In the African context, the discourse
on utopia cuts through two main trajectories: political power and archival
reconfiguration.

THE POLITICAL KINGDOM

The end of colonial rule promised the establishment of new political communities, however, there was not always agreement over what these communities
would look like. In the debates around the formation of the Organization
of African Unity (OAU) in the early 1960s, some "assumed that the West-
phalian conception of the sovereign state was the desirable vehicle for moving
Africa forward in the post-independence era" (Young 2010, 46). But there
were those who saw this as a doomed future, claiming it was based on the
liberal fantasy of self-governance and, thus, divorced from the realities of
global conditions. Led by Kwame Nkrumah, this group of thinkers imagined instead a united African state, inspired by Pan-Africanist values, which
could hold its ground in a highly contested geopolitical context. Nkrumah's
Africa Must Unite, published in 1963, is a key text in the formulation of this
alternative political economy, but he had been exploring similar ideas since
the late 1930s.[2] His celebrated mantra, "Seek ye first the political kingdom
and all things shall be added unto you" conveys the utopian texture of his
vision of a decolonized African world (quoted in Pierre 2012, 37). Even
though the notion of a political kingdom was originally part of his domestic
political campaign, it eventually became the central image in his vision for a
pan-Africanist future. In his address to the first OAU summit, he explains:

> African Unity is above all, a political kingdom, which can only be gained by
> political means. The social and economic development of Africa will come only
> within the political kingdom, not the other way round. The United States of
> America, the Union of Soviet Socialist Republics, were the political decisions of
> revolutionary peoples before they became mighty realities of social power and
> material wealth. (quoted in Biney 2007, 271)

The political kingdom is a utopian imaginary that anticipates the coming
of a transformed world. Scholars have drawn attention to Nkrumah's theological rhetoric, in which prophecy and biblical conventions are deployed to
evoke a messianic vision of Africa's future. He imagined a "New Africa, independent and absolutely free from imperialism, organized on a continental
scale, founded upon the conception of one and united Africa." The "New
Africa" ushered in by the political kingdom is the alternative to what was then
perceived as Africa's "sham independence" (quoted in Omari 1970, 121).
Underlying this aspiration for total freedom is Nkrumah's persistent argument that colonialism is a structural problem that runs deep into the tectonic

layers of global politics. Colonialism has to do with how the world is spatially divided, arranged, and imbued with political and economic power. The image of a political kingdom of united African states was the alternative to a future of weak states, limited sovereignties, and ultimately a fragmented continent. It evokes a radically different world order in which Africa would guarantee the grounds of its political power. The image of a political kingdom also implies an eschatology in that it evokes what comes after the end of a world configured to keep Africa outside of the corridors of power. Continental unification is not just the promise of an "economic paradise" (Biney 2007, 5). It would mean a redrawn geopolitical map that moved Africa from the peripheries of power to the center of global machinations. We can, thus, hold on to "the political kingdom" as a utopian image, first, because it evokes reconfigured geopolitics and, secondly, because it promises the true, absolute (as opposed to the sham) end of colonialism. Lastly, it underlies a restructuring of the time of modernity such that decolonization would no longer be a catching up with Europe and America. Imbued with the power to drive the course of global history, Africa is pulled out of what Dipesh Chakrabarty calls "history as a waiting room" (Chakrabarty 2000, 65).

The period of decolonization was also characterized by a search for an African origin of modernity. Kwamankra's vision of a world history centered on Ethiopia is one of the earliest formulations of a paradigm that would go on to inform later historiographical projects. A little less than a decade before *Africa Must Unite* was published, the Senegalese historian Cheikh Anta Diop published the seminal text on African world history titled *Nations Nègres et Culture* (1954). Diop's idea of history has rightfully been critiqued for being Hegelian. A form of historical naturalism, it features a black subject of history whose biographical development is the content of world history. Diop attempts a reversal in which Egypt becomes the grounds of intelligibility for a world history that chronicles the unfolding of African consciousness. In this history, Europe is given the Hegelian treatment by being relegated to a supernumerary status. In spite of all its shortcomings, there is something to be said for the scale of Diop's historical vision and its projected image of Africa.[3]

In "Archive Fever" (1995), Jacques Derrida insists that the archive is a kind of power, not simply a place where things are stored for future reference. The archive is the power to establish the founding logic by means of which signs, images, thought, truth, and the grounds of their validity are generated, consolidated, and given value. Implicit in the image of the political kingdom and an Egypt-centered world history is the yearning for a new archive or an epistemological order beyond "the colonial library" where African thought can guarantee the grounds of its validity, with colonialism relegated to, at best, a footnote in a long history that is decidedly African. Precisely because the archive is a founding logic and not simply a storehouse of documents, it is also future-oriented. Derrida writes.

> In an enigmatic sense…the question of the archive is not, we repeat, a question of the past. This is not the question of a concept dealing with the past which might already be at our disposal or not at our disposal, an archivable concept of the archive. It is a question of the future, the question of the future itself, the question of a response, of a promise and of a responsibility for tomorrow. (1995, 27)

The archive is, thus, a constitutively utopian principle in the ways it introduces new laws for governing how things come to count as knowledge. Diop's Egypt is not merely a historical "good place" where we can plant a desirable African past. Nkrumah's political kingdom is not simply an economic paradise. These are both ways of rethinking the intersection of space, history, and power in order to make a radically different African future thinkable. That is why Kodwo Eshun, in "Further Considerations on Afro-futurism," insists that, in spite of their blinkers and failures, these mid-century frameworks of utopian thinking should be recognized for their presentation of "worldviews that seek to reorient history" (Eshun 2003, 297). "By creating temporal complications and anachronistic episodes that disturb the linear time of progress," adds Eshun, "these futurisms adjust the temporal logics that condemned black subjects to prehistory" (297).

If we take Nkrumah's political kingdom and Diop's Egypt as coordinates by which an African utopian form might be located, we can assemble a cluster of African novels around the question of reorienting space and reconfiguring the archive in order to make an African logic of order visible. As noted earlier, the point of these utopias is not to present "visions of happy worlds, spaces of fulfillment and cooperation" (Jameson 2007, 12). The object is instead to get to the root causes of hegemonic structures while offering solutions.

Epistemic Utopias

Novels of decolonial utopias offer worlds built on a new logic of order by exposing the systemic erasures and distortions in colonial modes of knowing while offering ideal alternatives.[4] These texts tend to explore questions having to do with language, history, the human, and political economy. In Sofia Samatar's *A Stranger in Olondria* (2013), the organizing problem has to do with language, print technology, and imperialism. Olondria is a fictitious medieval empire with a rich literary history cobbled together from various medieval European worlds. In contrast, the Tea Islands is a non-literate community modeled after what is today South Sudan. As the main character moves between both worlds, we see his non-literate oral culture struggle to make itself knowable in an epistemological context where the capacity to exist in print is the grounds for knowability.[5] Print technology, books, and the discursive field of literature have made Olondria translatable, knowable, but also available for utopian imagination. In a sense, *A Stranger in Olondria* is a meta-commentary on utopia and the material conditions necessary for its production. It interrogates the role of books, libraries, print technology, and a literary discourse in making worlds visible as objects of desire and fantasy.

In *Things Fall Apart* (2017 [1958]), Achebe addresses the political and philosophical grounds on which a world can lay claims to form and order. This is a direct response to the specific ways in which Africa is always figured as a world without functioning instruments of order like law, the sovereign exception, and the commonwealth. Africa, as Hegel claims in *The Philosophy of History*, is a space of pure, uncodifiable violence (Hegel 2001, 113). *Things Fall Apart* is a text that some might consider the least utopian of narratives. Even though it was published in 1958 at a time when the utopian fervor of decolonization was very much in the air, the text has been categorized as historical fiction and praised for its realist representation of a pre-colonial African society. But, as Simon Gikandi argues, "Achebe's archeology of the past" attempts to erect an alternative "arrangement" of African life (1991, 21). Umuofia might not fit the liberal notion of a "desirable society" (Jameson 2007, 12), but it is a well-ordered society. Order is expressed in the near-perfect synthesis of law, violence, space, and power. Umuofia demonstrates an internal logic of order in the spheres of law, economics, politics, identity, and culture. First, Umuofia is at the center of a broader inter-clan community bound by strict rules of engagement. From the legal deliberation on Udo's wife's murder to Okonkwo's banishment, Umuofia is portrayed as built on a well-founded legal system through which violence is consistently translated through law into political power. The Earth Goddess is a form of sovereign power who guarantees the terms on which every act of violence is codified—whether it is the inadvertent murder of a teenager, the killing of twin newborns, the threat of impending war, or assaulting one's wife, every act of violence is named, its legality validated. If we can imagine a utopia inspired by Walter Benjamin's "Critique of Violence," it would be Umuofia, a world where illegitimate, uncodifiable, unmanageable violence has been abolished, in part, by setting up complex safety mechanisms that enable the community to expel what exceeds its legal bounds. However, in order for this set piece to demonstrate the systemic operation of his African world, Achebe has to render Umuofia a closed world, or what Soyinka calls a "hermetic milieu" (2017, 72), and Jameson "a commitment to closure" (2007, 4). There is an imaginary wall that separates Umuofia from the rest of the world, similar to the trench that King Utopos, in More's work, constructs around the island of Utopia. Achebe's reader is not encouraged to imagine that there is a world outside of Umuofia until the arrival of the British. The characters live their lives completely oblivious that there is a world beyond their immediate border. Everything in the text revolves tightly around Umuofia and the other clans in its orbit. In every sense, then, Umuofia, before the British, is a world unto itself. It imagines itself to be the extent of the world. This hermetically sealed universe is designed to express a classic element of utopian fiction, which Jameson describes as the "combination of closure and system in the name of autonomy and self-sufficiency" (2007, 5). Umuofia's closedness provides an artificially stable world where Achebe demonstrates, like an inventor, how an African logic of order works. It creates a mental space where the idea of an African world undefined by the colonial event can be thought. Achebe's Umuofia offers a world in which the colonial event and the archive it helped consolidate are as yet unthinkable.

Even though readers have come to embrace what they see as the novel's anthropological realism, it is the case that, at closer look, the success of the book as a powerful critique of colonialist thinking derives not from the fact that it shows us what a pre-colonial world looks like in reality, but that it shows us what a pre-colonial world could have been, might have been, without the colonial event. Umuofia is Nkrumah's political kingdom in miniature, set in the "utopian enclave" of the past (Jameson 2007, 16).[6] Lupita Nyongo, who plays Nakia in Ryan Coogler's Black Panther (2018), says in an interview that Wakanda is what Africa could have become if colonialism had not happened. "Wakanda is special because it was never colonized." It is, as such, "a reimagining of what could have been possible had Africa been allowed to realize itself for itself." Keeping Nyongo's statment in focus, we can make the claim that what separates Umuofia from Wakanda is merely scale and the temporal location of the utopian enclave. If Umuofia is what Africa could have been in the past without colonial interference, Wakanda is what Africa might have become in the future without colonial interference. If we bracketed colonialism, we can draw an unbroken line from Umuofia to Wakanda, from clan power to world power, from village utopia to geopolitical utopia. Wakanda is not the only utopia that explores the geopolitical implications of the dream of African world order. For, example, in Nisi Shawl's *Everfair* (2016), an alternative history narrative, an international group of militants establish a utopian community in the heart of the Congo to bring an end to King Leopold's brutal reign.

Nnedi Okorafor's *Lagoon* (2015) offers a particularly striking example of a utopian reorienting of global power. Set in the near future, *Lagoon* is a first-contact alien story about the end of the world as we know it. The novel's main charts are the human encounter with these aliens. The aliens are shapeshifting beings with ties to the ancestral past. In rhetoric that recalls *Things Fall Apart*, the alien governing council is referred to as "the Elders from the stars" (Okorafor 2015, 160).[7] Aliens landing in Lagos leads to widespread pandemonium. But as the story progresses, it becomes apparent that the aliens are benevolent and that they are eager to give the Nigerian government a non-fossil-based energy source that will end the destructive impact of crude oil extraction.

The notion of benevolent aliens is clearly utopian, as is their goal to initiate a transformed eco-future that is led by Africa. Toward the end of the novel, the Nigerian President declares:

For the first time since we cast off the shackles of colonialism, over a half century ago, since we rolled through decades of corruption and internal struggle, we have reached the tipping point. And here in Lagos, we have passed it. Many of you have seen the footage on the Internet or heard the news from loved ones. Last night, Lagos burned. But like a phoenix, it will rise from the ashes—a greater creature than ever before. (Okorafor 2015, 276)

The president's speech evokes the systemic transformation dreamed of in Nkrumah's political kingdom. The difference between the "sham independence" of the 1960s and finally "cast[ing] off the shackles of colonialism" is the power that is based on the control of a planetary economy. In *Lagoon*, the end of colonialism brings about two forms of reterritorializing. The first form is geopolitical in the sense that Africa is the new center of a transformed world. Apart from the fact that Nigeria is given first dibs on this new technology, the utopian epicenter of the new world is an "aquatic forest" (Okorafor 2015, 1) located somewhere in the Gulf of Guinea off the coast of Lagos. Africa's global exceptionality is also established by the mere fact that an African city is the setting for an alien first-contact narrative. Typically, the tradition of science fiction excludes third-world cities from the courtesy of alien visits; aliens tend to land in San Francisco, New York City, or Tokyo. This fact is a reflection of the latent colonialist assumption in the genre, and an acknowledgment of the supernumerary status of the Global South as far as geopolitics is concerned. Okorafor's novel breaks with this tradition.[8]

If all *Lagoon* offered were geopolitical remapping, it would simply be a reversal of the corridors of power from Anglo-America to Africa. This is where the second form of reterritorializing intervenes. The true end of colonialism involves not just the reorientation of the global order but also the reordering of the species. In this reterritorializing of the world, humans are demoted from their sovereign position on the chain of being. A truly decolonial world would be oriented toward Africa, but it would also see the end of old hierarchies between humans and animals, humans, and the physical world, and land and sea. Okorafor's aliens, in spite of their benevolence toward humans, are more attuned to animal life. They are concerned about the mass killing of sea life due to crude oil extraction. Lagos, as a coastal city and the economic epicenter of the sixth largest oil-producing country, is chosen to lead the transformation of the global economy. The end of colonialism is not a legal decision made within the framework of western political history and its terms of power. The end of colonialism is the redistribution of space in such a way that the old orientation centered on the Western world ceases to exist. It also means an end to the old orientation centered on humanity as the sovereign occupant of land, which is itself a spatial formation prioritized over the planet's watery worlds. Africa becomes the center not simply of global power but of a multispecies, ocean-oriented world.

CONCLUSION

What counts as utopia within the African context is different from what counts as utopia within the European tradition. Fredric Jameson's point that "utopias seem to be by-products of Western modernity" (2007, 11) is valid, but it does not stipulate that the form of utopia and its driving ideological and historical forces would be identical in all parts of the world. The novel was invented in Europe, but what counts as the African novel is a unique enough object to warrant its own history and ideological investment. The same goes for utopia as a concept and a literary form. Jameson might use the term utopia in his book, but the true object of his study is merely the form in which the genre emerges within the narrow contexts of Europe and its North American extension. If the historical and ideological contexts of humanism, Protestantism, Renaissance theology, and the English monarchy cannot be transported to other parts of the world, why should the specific elements of the European iteration of the utopian form be replicable in other literary traditions? Africa's relationship with modernity is different from Europe's, as are its ideological demands on literary form. Thus, the goal in this chapter has been to suggest questions, terms, and problematics through which utopian forms can be identified and analyzed within the African literary discourse.

NOTES

1. See, Anthony Appiah (1993). Appiah misses this anti-colonialist utopianism in his critique of Wole Soyinka's call for an African account of history in which the "colonial factor" (78) is merely a "catalytic incident" (78) and not the founding event. Appiah implies that Soyinka is in denial of the fact of history, and that whether he chooses to accept it or not his world is constituted by the colonial event. But it is clear from Appiah's criticism that writers like Soyinka imagined what was possible from suspending the historiographical sovereignty of the colonial event.
2. See, Kwame Nkrumah (1938).
3. There is a rich collection of theories and debates on the necessity of making Africa's past open for new forms of political, ideological, and cultural imagination. With varying degrees of utopian fervor, these texts make the claim that establishing a framework outside colonial discourse for historical analytics promises an *alternative* pathway through world history. See George G. M. Saunders' *Stolen Legacy*, Amilcar Cabral's *Return to the Source*, Martin Bernal's *Black Athena*, Wole Soyinka's *Myth Literature and the African World*, and Chinua Achebe's critique of Conrad in "An Image of Africa".
4. The publication of William M. Timlin's The Ship that Sailed to Mars and the Afrikaans novella C.J. Langenhoven's Loeloeraai in 1923 are considered to be significant moments in the history of South African speculative fiction. Timlin's book draws heavily from the tradition of fairytales and

fantasy—a Tolkien-esque story set in Mars. Langenhoven's text reads more like fantasy with its a-historical resolution of racial conflict through equality and spirituality. In both texts, as in Michael Cope's *Spiral of Fire* (1987) utopia leans more on the side of existential exploration. In Spiral of Fire, the principal character is writing a novel about a utopian planet devoid of hierarchy. But as Dierdre Byrne notes in "Science Fiction in South Africa," utopia is a form of "psychological catharsis" that aids the character in exploring "his unresolved problems in living as a white man in the strife-torn, Nationalist South Africa of the 1980s" (523). While these texts certainly enrich our understanding of utopian forms in the African literary tradition, the focus of this study is on fiction that conveys a sense of history, of space as it intersects with power, and that questions the logic behind the arrangement and the visibility of worlds.

5. For a related argument see Alena Rettova (2017).

6. See, Fredric Jameson (2007). He continues that: "Such enclaves are something of a foreign body within the social: in them, the differentiation process has momentarily been arrested, so that they remain as it were momentarily beyond the reach of the social and testify to its political powerlessness, at the same time that they offer a space in which new wish images of the social can be elaborated and experimented on" (16).

7. Okorafor certainly encourages such comparisons between her book and Achebe's *Things Fall Apart*. See, Nnedi Okorafor (2017). Here, she says: "If I had to choose one [comparison], I'd chose *Lagoon* and pair it with Chinua Achebe's *Things Fall Apart*. Both are First Contact/Alien Invasion narratives. And both are directly connected to our world".

8. *District 9* (2009), does something similar. Aliens arrive in Johannesburg. However, the film forecloses the utopian possibilities of the convention by reproducing problematic racial hierarchies.

REFERENCES

Achebe, Chinua. 2017. *Things Fall Apart*. In *The African Trilogy*. New York: Penguin Books.

Appiah, Anthony. 1993. *In My Father's House: Africa in the Philosophy of Culture*. Oxford: Oxford University Press.

Biney, Ama Barbara. 2007. *Kwame Nkrumah: An Intellectual Biography*. PhD thesis, University of London, School of Oriental and African Studies. https://eprints.soas.ac.uk/28819/1/10672987.pdf. Accessed June 6, 2021.

Black Panther. 2018. Directed by Ryan Coogler. New York: Marvel Studios.

Byrne, Dierdre. 2004. Science Fiction in South Africa. *PMLA* 119 (3): 522–525.

Caraivan, Luiza. 2014. South African Speculative Fiction. In *Reading the Fantastical Imagination: The Avatars of a Literary Genre*, 95–105. ed. Dana Perce. Newcastle upon Tyne: Cambridge Scholars Publishing.

Chakrabarty, Dipesh. 2000. *Provincializing Europe: Postcolonial Thought and Historical Difference*. Princeton: Princeton University Press.

Conrad, Joseph. 2012. *Heart of Darkness*. New York: Penguin.

Derrida, Jacques. 1995. Archive Fever: A Freudian Impression, trans. Eric Prenowitz. *Diacritics* 25 (2): 9–63.

District 9. 2009. Directed by Neill Blomkamp, QED International, Wingnut Films & TriStar Pictures Film.

Eshun, Kodwo. 2003. Further Considerations on Afro-Futurism. *The New Centennial Review* 3 (2): 9–63, 287–302.

Galawdewos. 2018. *The Life of Walatta-Petros*, trans. Wendy Laura Belcher and Michael Kleiner. Princeton, NJ: Princeton University Press. pp. 95–105.

Gikandi, Simon. 1991. *Reading Chinua Achebe: Language and Ideology in Fiction*. London: James Currey.

Hayford, Casely J. E. 1969. *Ethiopia Unbound: Studies in Race Emancipation*. London: Routledge.

Hegel, George Wilhelm. 2001. *The Philosophy of History*. Kitchener: Batoche Books.

Hunt, Kenya. 2020. Finding Black Community in the UK as a Black American Expatriate. https://lithub.com/finding-black-community-in-the-uk-as-a-black-american-expatriate/. Accessed June 6, 2021.

Jameson, Fredric. 2007. *Archaeologies of the Future: The Desire Called Utopia and Other Science Fictions*. London: Verso.

Mbembe, Achille. 2013. *Critique of Black Reason*. Durham: Duke University Press.

Mignolo, Walter D. 2007. Delinking. *Cultural Studies* 21 (2): 449–514.

More, Thomas. 2003. *Utopia*. Ed. and trans. Paul Turner. New York: Penguin.

Mudimbe, V. Y. 1997. *Tales of Faith: Religion as Political Performance in Central Africa*. London: Athlone Press.

Nkrumah, Kwame. 1938. Negro History: European Government in Africa. *The Lincolnian*, April 12, 2.

Okorafor, Nnedi. 2015. *Lagoon*. New York: Gallery/Saga Press.

———. 2017. Interview: A Conversation with Nnedi Okorafor. Interviewed by Leif Schenstead-Harris. *Weird Fiction Review*. 20 Feb. 2017. http://weirdfictionreview.com/2017/02/interview-conversation-nnedi-okorafor/. Accessed June 6, 2021.

Omari, T. Peter. 1970. *Kwame Nkrumah. The Anatomy of an African Dictatorship*. New York: Africana.

Pierre, Jemima. 2012. *The Predicament of Blackness: Postcolonial Ghana and the Politics of Race*. Chicago, IL: University of Chicago Press.

Rettova, Alena. 2017. Sci-Fi and Afrofuturism in the Afrophone Novel: Writing the Future and the Possible in Swahili and in Shona. *Research in African Literatures* 48 (1): 158–182.

Samatar, Sofia. 2013. *A Stranger in Olondria*. Northampton, MA: Small Beer Press. Kindle edition.

Schmitt, Carl. 2006. *The Nomos of the Earth in the International Law of the Jus Publicum*

Shawl, Nisi. 2016. *Everfair*. New York: Tor Books.

Soyinka, Wole. 1975. *Death and the King's Horseman*. London: Methuen.

———. 1976a. *Ogun Abibiman*. London: Methuen.

———. 1976b. Appendix: The Fourth Stage. In *Myth, Literature and the African World*, ed. Wole Soyinka. 140–160. Cambridge, MA: Cambridge University Press.

The View. 2018. Lupita Nyong'o, Danai Gurira Talk 'Black Panther' Success. *YouTube*. https://youtu.be/t-M8AgSNdFA. Accessed June 6, 2021.

Young, Kurt B. 2010. Africa Must Unite Revisited: Continuity and Change in the Case for Continental Unification. *Africa Today* 57 (1): 43–63. http://muse.jhu.edu/article/405059.

South Asia

Barnita Bagchi

INTRODUCTION

Modern South Asia, with its constitutive nation-states including Bangladesh, Bhutan, India, Nepal, Pakistan, Maldives, and Sri Lanka, is a populous, multilingual, and geopolitically influential sub-continent in the world. The region as a whole has produced much utopian literature, and this chapter can only begin to suggest the cultural richness of its offerings. As a term, "utopia" is European in its origin, a punning, perpetually ironic word, playing with the Greek eu-topia, a good place, and ou-topia, no place. There is no real equivalent of the term utopia in South Asian languages, though terms such as *svargaloka* and *svapnaprithivi*, respectively, heavenly world and dream world, Sanskrit in origin, have affinities. Utopia, in literature, is an imagined society described in some detail and located in space and time. Utopian imagination tends to proliferate in times of modernity, felt change, and crisis. With its plurality of religions, its caste system in Hinduism, its long history of cultural contact with other civilizations, and its ability to combine at any one time elements that seem to be from different, incompatible time periods, to combine "the archaic" and "the contemporary" (Patel 2000, 48), as it were, within its modernities, South Asia offers a distinctive set of trajectories for the utopian imagination.

B. Bagchi (✉)
Utrecht University, Utrecht, Netherlands

P. Marks et al. (eds.), *The Palgrave Handbook of Utopian and Dystopian Literatures*, https://doi.org/10.1007/978-3-030-88654-7_45

Modern South Asian utopian writers and actors such as Rabindranath Tagore, M.K. Gandhi, Muhammad Iqbal, Ramabai Saraswati, and Rokeya Sakhawat Hossain see utopia as contingent and in a state of dynamic change (Bagchi 2016). South Asian male and female utopian writers and activists, many of whom are also educators, reinvent tradition, show transnational influences, and take part in creating communities of utopian experimentation (Bagchi 2016). Tagore, Gandhi, Iqbal, and B.R. Ambedkar (four toweringly iconic writers and public actors from twentieth-century South Asia, whose work is influential in India, Nepal, Pakistan, and Bangladesh) each goes beyond parochial nationalism to find their own distinctive utopian visions. These can be based in the ideal of a renovated village moving in oceanic circles (Gandhi); a utopian set of educational institutions enshrining cosmopolitan esthetics and creativity (Tagore); a cosmic, pan-Islamic, utopian vision of the world (Iqbal); and the activist, socially conscientious Navayana or renovated Buddhist utopia of the here and now in which lower-castes, or Dalits, play a leading role (Bagchi 2016). The following chapter analyses utopian literature from the region in vernacular or *bhasha* literature (*bhasha* literature is a term prevalent in India) as well as in English. I pay particular attention to Tagore (1861–1941), described by the British political scientist G. Lowes Dickinson (1862–1932) as "the great utopian" (quoted in Chatterjee 1990, 72), and to his grounded utopian communities, emphasizing both esthetics and cooperative rural reconstruction. I argue that religion is in much South Asian utopian writing not written out but reinvented, and I further examine how Buddhism, with its emphasis on extirpation of suffering, as well as on social justice, has produced South Asian utopian literature. Tagore and Rokeya Sakhawat Hossain (1880–1932), influential across the sub-continent, are arguably two of the most innovative writers of utopian literature in South Asia. Hossain has been previously examined by feminist scholars (Bagchi 2009, 2012) in the context of her utopian imagination and her speculative and science fictional imagination (Chattopadhyay 2017). Tagore, however, has hardly been considered as an imaginative, innovative writer of literary pieces mingling utopian and dystopian elements. This chapter examines a dance drama, *Tasher Desh* (*Land of Cards*, 1933), and a play, *Raktakaravi* (*Red Oleanders*, 1925) by Tagore. It also deals with the far-reaching resonances of Hossain's short story "Sultana's Dream" (1905), characterizable as feminist utopia, as science fiction, and as satire, as well as utopian writing by neo-Buddhist and Marxist Rahul Sankrityanan (1893–1963) who also propagated *ghumakkarshastra* or the art of wandering. The chapter concludes with an examination of utopian elements in children's literature by Salman Rushdie. In terms of present-day nation-states, the writers examined in this chapter have affiliations with India (Tagore, Hossain, Rushdie, and Sankrityayan), Nepal (Sankrityayan), Bangladesh (Tagore, Hossain), Pakistan (Rushdie), and Sri Lanka (Sankrityayan). They also have affiliations with regions cutting across present-day national boundaries, notably Kashmir (Rushdie), Bengal (Tagore, Hossain), and northern or mountainous South Asia (Sankrityayan).

Rabindranath Tagore

Around the same time that Yevgeni Zamyatin and Aldous Huxley were writing now-celebrated and canonized dystopian texts such as *We* (1921) and *Brave New World* (1932), the Indian writers Rabindranath Tagore and Rahul Sankrityayan were publishing a range of works that resonate with the utopian mode. Tagore, the first Asian writer to win the Nobel Prize (1913), is a figure in whose oeuvre utopianism figures strongly. His rural educational and agricultural centers at Santiniketan and Sriniketan (rural Bengal in present-day India) were grounded utopian communities in which multiple civilizations, languages, and modes of arts were taught and practiced, along with cooperative work and rural reconstruction. After discussing these communities, and, in relation to this, Tagore's critique of the nation and his espousal of the world university, I discuss two works by Tagore, *Red Oleanders* (English version published in 1925) and *Land of Cards* (*Tasher Desh* in Bengali, published in Bengali in 1933, and often performed in India and abroad). Both these works are dramatic, and also musical, written for the members of the Santiniketan community, to be performed by them.

"Neither the colourless vagueness of cosmopolitanism, nor the fierce self-idolatry of nation-worship, is the goal of human history," wrote Tagore in *Nationalism* (1918, 5). In the Tagoreian grounded cosmopolitan utopia in Santiniketan, we find models of ecological sustainability, attempted harmonies between agricultural cycles and labor, on the one hand, and pedagogical cycles and work, on the other; valorization of Santhal esthetics and beauty; and an everyday routine which laid stress on the local. Santiniketan was a community, not a miniature nation. Indeed, Tagore was critical of the category of the nation: "A nation, in the sense of the political and economic union of a people, is that aspect which a whole population assumes when organized for a mechanical purpose" (Tagore 1918, 8). Idolatry of this mechanical, instrumental entity called the nation led, said Tagore, to nationalism, of which he is also severely critical. He associated the nation-state with the West and was critical when countries such as Japan began imitating the West in its strident nationalism, which then led to colonialism and imperialism. Since aggressive British nationalism and colonialism deprived the majority of South Asians of an enriching education, Tagore created a university. On a micro-scale, Tagore founded, between 1918 and 1921, Visva-Bharati in Santiniketan, where the world, *visva*, made its home in a nest, the university motto being "Yatra visva bhavati eka nidam" (where the world makes its home in a single nest). He had founded a school at Santiniketan in 1901, and also founded the Kala Bhavana, a center for Indian Modernist art, in 1919. Tagore, who expressed time and again his belief in the need to reconcile East and West, and for the one to learn and take elements from the other, created an "Eastern university," for which he speaks in *Creative Unity* (1922). Tagore's ideal of the university is both utopian and cosmopolitan. Underlying it is the belief that the earth is one country: "Now the problem before us is of one single country, which is this earth, where the races as individuals must find both their freedom of self-expression and their bond of federation" (Tagore 1922, 171).

Tagore argues that one of the best places for achieving such a federation of man is the university, where "the exploiting utilitarian spirit" (171) would not hold sway. Tagore reports that he:

> formed the nucleus of an International University in India, as one of the best means of promoting mutual understanding between the East and the West. This Institution, according to the plan I have in mind, will invite students from the West to study the different systems of Indian philosophy, literature, art and music in their proper environment, encouraging them to carry on research work in collaboration with the scholars already engaged in this task. (172)

The school, the university, cooperative agriculture, arts, and crafts—all cohabited in Tagore's utopian community of Santiniketan. A truly synthetic, multivocal education would be imparted here, which would also conform to Tagore's notion of the multicultural civilization and society of India, with strands including the Vedic, the Puranic, the Buddhist, the Jain, the Islamic, the Sikh, and the Zoroastrian (194). The Chinese, Japanese, Tibetan, Western, and other cultures would come in dialog with this civilization (194).

Tagore wrote more than 60 plays. His musical and dance dramas are still regularly performed. He was a most innovative choreographer, taking elements of Indonesian and Sri Lankan dances, of South Asian classical dance forms such as Manipuri, Kathakali, Bharat Natyam, and folkdance, such as the dance of the Santhals, the indigenous tribal people who inhabited the area around Santiniketan and Sriniketan. He was critical of elaborate, expensive European proscenium theater: "The theatres that we have set up in imitation of the West are too elaborate to be brought to the door of all and sundry. In them the creative richness of poet and player are overshadowed by the wealth of the capitalist" (Tagore 1913, 544). He proposed instead that Indian theater should follow the example of classical Sanskrit theater and Indian folk forms, using as little scenery as possible. Brilliant, minimalist designs were made by artists such as Nandalal Bose, a celebrated Modernist artist of Santiniketan, for Tagore's plays and musical and dance dramas.

Tagore's innovative works strikingly mix dystopian and utopian modes, employing idioms of musical drama in Bengali, his first language. He wrote plays with musical interludes, such as *Land of Cards* (also a dance drama) and *Red Oleanders*, in Santiniketan: both these plays have utopian and dystopian contours, but utopian hope and anticipatory consciousness dominate, even if *Red Oleanders* is grimmer than *Land of Cards*. In *Red Oleanders*, greed for wealth leads to a mechanical civilization exploiting its people. There are also utopian elements in *Red Oleanders*, in which a young woman, Nandini, leads a rebellion, and critiques a terrible brand of capitalism and totalitarianism. The dwellers of the principal setting of the play, Yakshapuri, dig incessantly for minerals, while the king of the land is powerful, but remains in isolation behind a screen. Yakshas in Indian mythology are caretakers of trea-sures hidden under the earth. Nandini, who speaks with lyricism, joy, and love, keeps dialoguing with the people and with the king, who is always shielded by a screen. The symbolic, blossoming red oleander wristlet of Nandini brings together freedom and death, rolling in the dust as it does at the end of the play, when rebellion breaks out and Nandini rushes to her death in that revolt, with the king himself also abandoning his shackled might. *Red Oleanders* was written in the mountainous north-east of India in Shillong and is said to have been inspired by seeing pieces of iron crushing a red oleander flower: the critique of accumulative industrial capitalism through a female, lyrical, Romantic figure is conveyed in a highly symbolic style and register.

In *Tasher Desh* or *Land of Cards* (Tagore 2019), the inhabitants of an island (the land of cards of the title that forms the principal backdrop of the story) are locked into four hierarchies, represented by suits of cards. A prince, tired of his palace, travels in search of adventure, accompanied by his friend, a merchant. Shipwrecked in the Land of Cards (where inhabitants, dressed like playing cards, are trained to behave mechanically, emotionlessly, and hierar-chically), the Prince, with his magnetic, charming personality, stirs up a revolt by changing the cards. The island's women, infused with rebellion and love, take the lead among the islanders, and successfully break down the barriers and hierarchies in the land. The hierarchies of British colonial, racist offi-cialdom, and the caste system of Brahminical Hinduism are criticized in this work, which Tagore dedicated to Subhash Chandra Bose (1897–1945), the prominent anti-colonial Indian politician.

Rahul Sankrityayan

The breaking down of hierarchies and barriers is also a potent theme in Rahul Sankrityayan's work, with both Buddhism and Marxism as influences. Sankrityayan (for an overview of his life and work, see Chudal 2016) trav-eled as first a Hindu and then a Buddhist monk widely, to places such as Iran, China, Ladakh in Himalayan India, Kashmir, Nepal, Sri Lanka, and the former Soviet Union.[i] From his trips to Tibet, he brought valuable artifacts, notably Pali and Sanskrit manuscripts, back to India. He was a polyglot, knowing languages such as Hindi, Sanskrit, Pali, Urdu, Persian, Arabic, Tamil, Kannada, Tibetan, Sinhalese, French, and Russian. It is unsurprising that Buddhism influenced Sankrityayan, as it also influenced the great Dalit or lower-caste politician, writer, and social activist, Ambedkar, who converted to Buddhism; that religion, with its emphasis on full understanding and then extirpation of suffering, as well as on social justice, has generated South Asian utopian imag-inaries through millennia. One of the South Asian myths that neo-Buddhist writers such as Sankrityayan reinvents is that of Uttarakuru, a mythical region of milk and honey evoked in Hindu literature such as the Vedas and the epic *Mahabharata* and in Buddhist literature such as the Nikayas (Bhattacharya 2000). The country is spoken of as being in northern South Asia. In the epic

Mahabharata, Uttarakuru is the ultimate abode of blessed souls, with free love not regarded as sinful (Bhattacharya 2000; Prakash 1986). The people who live there own no property and do not have to work for their living. Corn ripens there by itself and sweet-scented rice is found boiling on stoves (Prakash 1986). Buddhistic utopian myths, even more than the Hindu versions, stress the communistic nature of Uttarakuru. Sankrityayan sees Uttarakuru as a primitive communist utopia where hunting, gathering, and collecting honey are common, where there is no sense of private property or violence, and where everyone participates in work. His Marxism, which sees ancient South Asia as a site where social justice and communism were also experimented with, inflects this vision: in his novel, in Hindi, *Simha Senapati* (*The Lion General* 1947), Uttarakuru and the ancient republic of Lichchhavi, in what would be the Kathmandu valley in present-day Nepal, are presented as utopian, communistic worlds.

Sankrityayan also wrote the utopian narrative, in Hindi, *Baisvi Sadi* (2006, originally published in 1923–1924), a novel which is framed by a dream, and set in northern South Asia in 2124. The novel narrates a journey to the future. Visvabandhu (Friend of the World), a male, narrates the tale. He awakens after sleeping for 200 years, in a cave in Nepal, at the age of 60. In the 100th year of a global era, the world is ruled through a confederation of states. Visvabandhu is a philosopher and teacher from the ancient Buddhist Nalanda University. In a utopian world of the future, hydroelectricity, agriculture, and irrigation works have transformed society materially. In a world of educational advancement and egalitarian relations, private property is abolished. People are not repressed by religion, gender, or caste. Education is compulsory for 17 years. Children are educated in boarding schools. The working day is four hours long, five days a week. Travel is encouraged after nine months of work. Most goods are traded, only a few are produced locally. Marxism and Buddhism are synthesized, a trend visible throughout Sankrityayan's oeuvre. He was also a proponent of the art of wandering or *ghumakkarshastra* (Sankrityayan 1994). While South Asia is rich in wandering yogis and other ascetics with sites of pilgrimage important in the diverse religions of the region, Sankrityayan saw wandering as an end in itself, which gives his utopian imagination a nomadic quality.

ROKEYA SAKHAWAT HOSSAIN

Rokeya Sakhawat Hossain published most of her writings in Bengali; she also wrote one creative work in English, the now-canonical feminist utopia "Sultana's Dream." Hossain's oeuvre is full of utopian short stories and novellas (such as the novella *Padmarag* or *The Ruby* 2005, in Bengali), and parables with folk-tale and fairy-tale-like structures (Bagchi 2009). Hossain wrote as a locally cosmopolitan, South Asian, and Bengali Muslim writer. She became a much-respected educator and writer, working with men and women of all religions, while being a practicing Muslim who wrote vocally against wooden fundamentalism from all religions (Hossain 2003). Hossain is seen today, thanks largely to the work of feminist scholars such as Amin (1996), Bagchi (2009), and Ray (2002), as a major figure in the history of women's activism and education in South Asia. There were other women from the Bengali Muslim community who had written fiction before Hossain. Scholars such as Amin (1996) and Anisuzzaman (2000) have exploded the myth of the 'backward' Bengali Muslim writer, male or female: it is now evident that writing by this community had its own history and early achievements, which literary history simply forgot in its mainstream narratives, for a long time. Born into a landholding family in east Bengal, Hossain (1880–1932) did not get formal schooling or higher education. Her conservative father discouraged Hossain's hunger for learning, but a supportive elder sister and elder brother helped her pursue her study of English and Bengali, respectively. The same elder brother facilitated Hossain's marriage at the age of 16 to a much older man who respected Hossain's intelligence, hunger for education, and talent for writing. After marriage, Hossain moved to a provincial town, Bhagalpur, in what would be the present-day province of Bihar in India, where her husband was a government official. Hossain wrote "Sultana's Dream" while living in Bhagalpur, and the fable was published in a magazine called the *Indian Ladies' Magazine* in 1905. The Indian Tamil Christian writer Kamala Satthianadhan, 1879–1950, started this periodical in 1901. The magazine published major women writers such as the poet and nationalist leader Sarojini Naidu.

In "Sultana's Dream," a utopian feminist fable, women's education, in the concrete shape of all-women universities, propels social change and progress in an imagined country, Ladyland, where women rule public affairs, while men, in a tongue-in-cheek role reversal, remain confined to activities in the private sphere. Ladyland is the dream-vision of Sultana, a recognizably non-Occidental woman: the fact that the term signifies a female political ruler clearly points to how sweeping Hossain's goals for Bengali, Indian, South Asian, and non-Occidental women's education were. In Ladyland, when a queen who "liked science very much" (Hossain 2005, 7) had all the women educated, stopped the early marriage, and built two separate universities for women, strange things started happening, as any reader of "Sultana's Dream" will know. When the men's military warfare leads the country to the brink of ruin, the Lady Principal of one of the universities uses the fruits of scientific research conducted in the women's universities to scare the enemy into running away by directing rays of concentrated heat and light at them. By this time, the women have placed the men in the *mardana* or male seclusion as a pre-condition for their help in the war. The ladies "rule over the country and control all social matters, while gentlemen are kept in the *mardanas* to mind the babies, to cook, and to do all sorts of domestic work" (15). In this science and technology-loving utopian fable, agriculture, transport, and many other activities are carried on by electricity, and there are other technological schemes for efficiency. "Sultana's Dream" is a short work, but it bears the twin signatures of most literary feminist utopias across space and time: the belief that female knowledge and leadership are the keys to human development and progress, and that women do better at furthering such development if allowed to do so untrammeled by patriarchy. "Sultana's Dream" is also a major example of South Asian science fiction, or *kalpavigyan* (Chattopadhyay 2018). Chattopadhay, building on the work of Bagchi (2009) regarding the importance of utopia in Hossain's work, has called Hossain's brand of *kalpavigyan* or science fiction "speculative utopianism" (Chattopadhyay 2017).

SALMAN RUSHDIE

Utopian imagined worlds are also powerful grounding elements in children's literature and fantasy: the Hundred-Acre woods in the Pooh stories, Hogwarts School in the Harry Potter books—examples can be multiplied (Hintz and Ostry 2013, 1). The imagined worlds are sometimes better or worse than the reader's own, slanting these worlds toward utopia or dystopia. In children's literature, the child often confronts the adult world, questions about justice are asked, and tensions between individual and collective freedom are represented, as in much utopian and dystopian literature. In an interview, Salman Rushdie said, in relation to such matters in his book *Haroun and the Sea of Stories*:

> My book *Haroun and the Sea of Stories* is about a boy in a fantasised version of Bombay, the son of a storyteller called Rashid who is known as the Ocean of Notions by people who like his stuff, and as the Shah of Blah by people who don't. When his wife leaves him for the extremely boring man upstairs, he loses his ability to tell stories. Rashid has always told Haroun that the stories come from a magic sea, so Haroun goes there in an attempt to retrieve his father's talent, but discovers a plot by the forces of silence to pollute it.

> It's a childhood adventure story but also a grown-up parable about language and silence… It was written in 1990 after I promised my young son—his middle name is Haroun—that when I finished the book that turned out to be *The Satanic Verses* I would write a book for him. (1998)

Haroun, a book for children, is thus also a book for a particular child. The sea of stories in the title is an intertextual reference to *Kathasaritsagara*, a title meaning the ocean of the streams of stories, an eleventh-century collection of Indian legends, fairy tales, and folk tales in Sanskrit, consisting of 18 books of 124 chapters, in both poetry and prose. The utopia of *Haroun*, which is the world of free storytelling and fertile creativity, is also oceanic. In this context, it is resonant that Gandhi also imaged his utopian village as an oceanic circle:

> In this structure composed of innumerable villages, there will be ever-widening, never-ascending circles. Life will not be a pyramid with the apex sustained by the bottom. But it will be an oceanic circle whose centre will be the individual always ready to perish for the village, the latter ready to perish for the circle of villages, till at last the whole becomes one life composed of individuals, never aggressive in their arrogance, but ever humble, sharing the majesty of

the oceanic circle of which they are integral units. (Gandhi and Brown 2008, 158–159)

Khattam-Shud, the villain in *Haroun*, has a name signifying the end of stories: appositely, he says, "'The world, however, is not for Fun ... The world is for Controlling.' 'Your world, my world, all worlds,' came the reply. 'They are all to be Ruled. And inside every single story, inside every Stream in the Ocean, there lies a world, a story-world, that I cannot Rule at all'" (Rushdie 1991, 161). The novel refers to Kashmir, troped as an earthly paradise in South Asia, one claimed by both India and Pakistan, where a major part of the action takes place. "Dull Lake," a water body, in *Haroun* is very similar to "Dal Lake" in Kashmir, and we hear of Kashmir in the echoing words "Kosh-mar" or cauchemar, nightmare, and "Kache-mer" (40), or cache-mer, a place which hides the sea. Kashmir is a land famous for craft and art, including storytelling by fearless village clowns, whence derives the title of Rushdie's other novel set partly in Kashmir, *Shalimar the Clown* (2005). *Haroun* also intertextually references the remarkable film *Goopy Gyne Bagha Byne* (1969) directed by Satyajit Ray, which, like *Haroun*, is for children, while also being a parable of freedom and creativity, sketching a utopia of peace and esthetics. Goopy and Bagha, the two male village rustics in that film who, through a boon granted by a king of the ghosts, acquire magical powers to please people through their singing and drumming, become, in *Haroun*, two large fishes, with many mouths, who speak in rhyme, travel in pairs, mate for life, ingest story waters and create new stories. In this utopia constituted by the sea of stories, we read that to ruin a happy story, we first need to make it a sad one; to ruin an action drama, one needs to make it move too slowly, and that every story has an anti-story or shadow-self, an anti-utopia to the story-utopia (159–160).

Conclusion

This chapter, focusing on writings by Rabindranath Tagore, Rahul Sankrityayan, Rokeya Sakhawat Hossain, M.K. Gandhi, and Salman Rushdie, has argued that representative modern South Asian utopian literature breaks down different kinds of hierarchies, notably those of gender, caste, and class. Such literature can critique nationalistic ideologies, can rewrite myths of utopia found in ancient South Asian texts, and expresses itself in a variety of genres, such as musical dance drama (Tagore), science fiction (Hossain), historical novel, and travel writing (Sankrityayan), and fiction for children (Rushdie). The literary works analyzed in this chapter were written in *bhashas* or South Asian vernacular languages, and, subsidiarily, in English. Analyzing such liter-ature widens our knowledge of the literary utopia, and allows us to move toward constructing non-Eurocentric canons of utopian literature. Rushdie's *Haroun and the Sea of Stories* is an apt synecdoche for South Asian utopian literature, seeing, as it does, imagination, playfulness, and openness to many cultures, languages, and media as utopian.

References

Amin, Sonia Nishat. 1996. *The World of Muslim Women in Colonial Bengal*. Leiden: E.J. Brill.

Anisuzzaman. 2000. *Muslim Manas o Bangla Sahitya, 1757–1918*. Kolkata: Pustak Bipani.

Bagchi, Barnita. 2009. Towards Ladyland: Rokeya Sakhawat Hossain and the Movement for Women's Education in Bengal, c. 1900–c. 1932. *Paedagogica Historica* 45 (6): 743–755.

Bagchi, Barnita, ed. 2012. *The Politics of the (Im)possible: Utopia and Dystopia Reconsidered*. New Delhi: SAGE Publications India.

———. 2016. Many Modernities and Utopia: From Thomas More to South Asian Utopian Writings. In *Utopía: 500 Años*, ed. Pablo Guerra, 195–220. Bogotá: Ediciones Universidad Cooperativa de Colombia.

Bhattacharya, R. 2000. Uttarakuru: The (E)Utopia of Ancient India. *Annals of the Bhandarkar Oriental Research Institute* 81 (1–4): 191–201.

Chatterjee, Ramananda, ed. 1990. *The Golden Book of Tagore: A Homage to Rabindranath Tagore from India and the World in Celebration of His Seventieth Birthday*. Kolkata: Rammohun Library & Free Reading Room.

Chattopadhyay, Bodhisattva. 2017. Speculative Utopianism in Kalpavigyan: Mythologerm and Women's Science Fiction. *Foundation: The International Review of Science Fiction* 46 (2): 6–19.

———. 2018. Bengal. In *The Encyclopedia of Science Fiction* ed. John Clute, David Langford, Peter Nicholls and Graham Sleight. London: Gollancz. http://www.sf-encyclopedia.com/entry/bengal. Accessed 5 February 2019.

Chudal, Alaka Atreya. 2016. *A Freethinking Cultural Nationalist: A Life History of Rahul Sankrityayan*. Oxford: Oxford University Press.

Gandhi, Mohandas Karamchand, and Judith Brown. 2008. *The Essential Writings*. Oxford: Oxford University Press.

Goopy Gyne Bagha Byne. 1969. Directed by Satyajit Ray. Kolkata: Purnima Pictures.

Hintz, Carrie, and Elaine Ostry, eds. 2013. *Utopian and Dystopian Writing for Children and Young Adults*. London: Routledge.

Hossain, Rokeya Sakhawat. 2003. The Worship of Women. Trans. Barnita Bagchi. In *Talking of Power: Early Writings of Bengali Women*, ed. Malini Bhattacharya, 105–115. Kolkata: Stree Books.

Hossain, Rokeya Sakhawat. 2005. Part-trans. and ed. Barnita Bagchi. *Sultana's Dream and Padmarag: Two Feminist Utopias*. New Delhi: Penguin, 2005.

Patel, Geeta. 2000. Ghostly Appearances: Time Tales Tallied Up. *Social Text* 18 (3): 47–66.

Prakash, Buddha. 1986. Uttarakuru. *Bulletin of Tibetology* 22 (1): 27–34.

Ray, Bharati. 2002. *Early Feminists of Colonial India: Sarala Devi Chaudhurani and Rokeya Sakhawat Hossain*. New Delhi: Oxford University Press.

Rushdie, Salman. 1991. *Haroun and the Sea of Stories*. New Delhi: Penguin.

———. 1998. Salman Rushdie On... *London Evening Standard*. https://www.standard.co.uk/go/london/theatre/salman-rushdie-on-6311756.html. Accessed 18 June 2019.

Rushdie, Salman. 2005. *Shalimar the Clown*. London: Vintage.

Sankrityayan, Rahul. 1947. *Simha Senapati*. Allhabad: Kitab Mahal.

———. 1994. *Ghumakkarshastra*. Allahabad: Kitab Mahal.

———. 2006. *Baisvi Sadi*. Allahabad: Kitab Mahal.

Tagore, Rabindranath. 1913. The Stage Trans. Surendranath Tagore. *Modern Review* 14 (6): 543–545.

———. 1918. *Nationalism*. London: Macmillan.

———. 1922. *Creative Unity*. London: Macmillan.

———. 2019 [1933]. *Tasher Desh*. Tagore Reweb. Accessed 18 June 2019.https://www.tagoreweb.in/Plays/taser-desh-132/taser-desh-2548. Accessed 18 June 2019.

Latin America

Kim Beauchesne and Alessandra Santos

INTRODUCTION

How can we speak of utopia when the world we currently live in seems to be, yet again, falling apart? Climate change—the "defining issue of our time," according to the United Nations—is causing unprecedented disruption on a global scale. Many regions, such as eastern Ukraine and Syria, are being ravaged by war. According to a recent official report by the World Health Organization (2019), world hunger has increased over the last three years. In Latin America alone, examples of human and ecological disasters abound. The Amazon rainforest has been burning and is recording its highest deforestation rate in a decade after Jair Bolsonaro's first year as the president of Brazil (Sandy 2019). Puerto Rico, among other islands, is still recovering from Hurricane Maria more than two years later (Mazzei and Rosa 2019). Venezuela, Ecuador, Chile, Bolivia, and Colombia, to name but a few, are facing troubling times at the social, political, and economic levels. This list could go on. However, at the same time, we are observing countless efforts to make our world a better place. The voices of Greta Thunberg and other environmental activists have become viral. The "Ni Una Menos" ("Not One [Woman] Less") movement against gender-based violence is spreading over Latin America. Moreover, massive protests over socioeconomic conditions are currently taking place in the region. Utopia has not ceased to be extremely relevant, and probably never will.

K. Beauchesne (✉) · A. Santos
University of British Columbia, Vancouver, Canada

P. Marks et al. (eds.), *The Palgrave Handbook of Utopian and Dystopian Literatures*, https://doi.org/10.1007/978-3-030-88654-7_46

In order to make this claim, it is essential to clarify how the concept of utopia may be conceived. As the first section of this handbook demonstrates, there are many ways in which utopia—and the related notions of dystopia and hyperutopia, among others—have been defined over the centuries. Within this context, we would like to return to the theoretical perspective we emphasized in *The Utopian Impulse in Latin America* (2011). In the introduction to this co-edited volume, we insisted on the importance of the concept of a "utopian impulse," a term coined by Ernst Bloch (1986) to refer to the human drive to make ideals possible; or, in his own words, it is the "expectation, hope, intention towards possibility that has still not become: this is not only a basic feature of human consciousness but, concretely corrected and grasped, a basic determination within objective reality as a whole" (7). What stands out in this viewpoint is not only the broad scope of the utopian impulse—which has been criticized by Ruth Levitas for its universalizing dimension (1990, 7–8)—but also its potential to bring a real (that is, "objective" and concrete) transformation. In this sense, Bloch's interpretation of utopia is especially pertinent because it does not strictly dissociate it from praxis: instead, according to the German philosopher, utopia is akin to a dynamic and anticipatory urge that may be considered as a tangible "catalyst of the future" (Levitas 1990, 87). These are the aspects that we privilege in our studies on utopia—in both the above-mentioned co-edited volume and in *Performing Utopias in the Contemporary Americas* (2017)—which enable us to perceive the utopian impulse in Latin America as a subterranean current that runs through the region, often triggering actions for change at many levels.[1]

It is important to stress, however, that the goals of such actions may vary greatly. In recent scholarly works on utopia—by Rutger Bregman (2017), Martin Schoenhals (2019), and Michael Harvey (2019), for instance—this concept seems to be synonymous with "an ideal world," or even more generally, "happiness" (Schoenhals 2019, 1). There is no doubt that these abstract terms are highly subjective. On the one hand, they could be translated as the desire for equality, sustainability, justice, inclusiveness, and democracy. This standpoint would corroborate Russell Jacoby's assertion that the utopian tradition is based on the search for "peace and brotherhood" as well as "ideas about paradise, equality, and freedom" (2005, xi–xii). On the other hand, it is well known that utopia is a strikingly complex notion that may belong to different ideological positions and can easily turn into dystopia. In Latin America, since the period of the Conquest and even before, the coexistence of fantasy and monstrosity, gains and losses, and genocides and resilience, is part of the very fabric of its contradictory history. Furthermore, it is probably this set of underlying contradictions that has kept the utopian impulse alive in the region, despite its apparent demise. Although in *The Utopian Impulse in Latin America* we have already shown how utopia—never completely dissociated from dystopia—has played a central role in the Latin American cultural tradition, the aim of this essay is to summarize and expand our previous study, taking into account current debates and recent publications on this matter.

Selected Works on Utopia in Latin America[2]

Even though the term *utopia* was coined by the English Renaissance humanist Thomas More, it would be simplistic to deny that utopian thought existed long before the publication of his 1516 novel, both in England and in other parts of the world. Indeed, it seems appropriate to consider that the cosmovision of the pre-Conquest indigenous peoples from what we now call the Americas included a variety of potent utopias. The notion of a paradise lost, which was recorded in the sixteenth-century Codices Telleriano-Remensis and Vaticanus A (among other sources), originates in pre-Hispanic Central Mexico (Graulich et al. 1983, 585). Likewise, Alfred Métraux (1928), in his historical reconstruction of the large-scale migrations of the Tupi-Guarani peoples that were motivated by the search for a "land without evil" (Bethencourt 2015, 99), argues that these occurred before the arrival of European explorers. While polemical, this hypothesis has nonetheless been corroborated by Hélène Clastres (1995) and other renowned ethnologists (see Dreyfus 1976; Shapiro 1987). It is evident that pre-Columbian sociocultural traditions tend to be idealized from a contemporary perspective. For example, the Andean social organization based on the *ayllu*—"a sib or clan that constituted the basic socioeconomic unit of Inca society" ("Ayllu") that was established in pre-Inca time and persists today—has led a few scholars, such as Louis Baudin in 1961 (2011), to elaborate the representation of the Inca Empire as a kind of socialist utopia. In any case, it is crucial to acknowledge that many components of native cultures, such as the Inca Virgins of the Sun (Gandía 1946, 102; Quijano 1993, 142), did generate the main utopian topoi of the Conquest, like the ones that are related to El Dorado and the Amazons.

This view adds nuance to the commonly accepted belief that the first European explorers of America "invented" the region (see Pérez de Oliva 1991; O'Gorman 2006) and perceived it as a blank slate on which they could impose their prefabricated dreams. On the one hand, it is undeniable that Christopher Columbus's description of the New World is reminiscent of the biblical Garden of Eden, Isidore's *locus amoenus*, as well as images elaborated by Pierre d'Ailly, Pliny the Elder, Aeneas Sylvius Piccolomini, and Marco Polo (Pastor 1988, 7–13). On the other hand, as Beatriz Pastor rightly claims in *El jardín y el peregrino: ensayos sobre el pensamiento utópico latinoamericano, 1492–1695* (The garden and the pilgrim: Essays on the Latin American utopian thought, 1492–1695) (1996), the foundational utopias of the Conquest are much more complex, not only because they are a heterogeneous network of European and native myths and symbols but also because they often coexist with dystopias. Therefore, they may not be reduced to a series of unrealistic fantasies; they must rather be understood as an elaborate cognitive process of familiarization with an unknown environment.

Later works from the colonial period, such as Bartolomé de las Casas's *Brevísima relación de la destrucción de las Indias* (A Short Account of the Destruction of the Indies) (1552) or Inca Garcilaso de la Vega's *Comentarios reales de los incas* (Royal Commentaries of the Incas) (1609, 1617), have been compared to More's *Utopia*, since they seem to share the main source (Plato's *Republic*) and a similar conception of ideal places (see Menéndez Pelayo [1905–1915]; Durán Luzio [1976, 1979]; Brading [1986]; Zamora [1988]; Arias and Meléndez [2002]). However, we agree with Pastor when she states that such narrow parallelism circumscribes the concept of utopia to a single text instead of considering it more broadly as a mentality. As Bloch suggests, "to limit the utopian to the Thomas More variety … would be like trying to reduce electricity to the amber from which it gets its Greek name and in which it was first noticed" (1986, 15). In this sense, it is clearly more appropriate to interpret the utopian impulse underlying the chronicles of the New World as a hybrid imagination that departed from the European canonical models.

At the same time, the indigenous writers from the colonial period undoubtedly expressed their own multifaceted utopian thought. The famous *ladino* chronicler Felipe Guaman Poma de Ayala,[3] in his markedly dystopic denunciation of the horrors of the Conquest and colonization of Peru, created a fictional dialog between himself and the King of Spain in his *El primer nueva corónica y buen gobierno* (The First New Chronicle and Good Government) (2009, 974–999). This kind of textual strategy has led Pastor to argue that "what defines the thought of the conquered versus that of the conquerors is the recurring formulation of a particular utopia: that of a possible communication across cultural boundaries that makes a negotiation of alterity feasible" (1996, 525).[4] However, the viability of this potential discourse of reconciliation was constantly questioned by the harsh sociohistorical circumstances, in the face of which native people constructed powerful strategies of resistance, such as the ones that gave rise to Túpac Amaru II's indigenous-led rebellion against colonial rule (1780–1783).

Like the native insurgents, there is no doubt that many Creoles hoped to build a better world as well. It is important to note, however, that their utopia was rather ambiguous: as Carlos A. Jáuregui demonstrates, the brief dramatic works (or *loas*) of the seventeenth-century protofeminist writer Sor Juana Inés de la Cruz reveal that Creole intellectuals were interested in both vindicating their particular culture and maintaining their ties with the imperial order (2008, 219). It is in the first decades of the nineteenth century that this incipient Creole discourse would bring about the great utopian projects of independence. After José de San Martín, Simón Bolívar, and other *libertadores* defeated the Spaniards in key military battles, Andrés Bello, the "intellectual father of South America," undertook the task of portraying the geographic area as a potentially ideal society (Lindstrom 2004, 87). Despite his emphasis on the need for "cultural autonomy," his writings are permeated by the ambiguity we've mentioned. For instance, "Silva a la agricultura de la zona tórrida" ("Ode to Tropical Agriculture"; 1826), while praising what the region has to offer, is indebted to the traditional rhetoric of classical Antiquity (more specifically, Virgil's *Georgics* [29 BC]). Another crucial aspect of his utopian aspirations is that, as a jurist, he "proposed clear and specific goals" to lead "the way toward progress" (Rojas 2012, 70). One of them was to unite the continent, thereby reinforcing the pan-American utopia—also known as "Bolívar's dream" of a "Gran Colombia" (1819–1831)—that would later be embraced by José Martí and Pablo Neruda, among others, until the current president of Venezuela, Nicolás Maduro (Rapoza 2019). It is thus not surprising that regional unification is often considered to be one of the most constant utopias in Latin America (Santana Castillo 1999, 160).

A wide range of utopian tendencies took form in the twentieth century, such as the "rise and fall" of the "cult of *mestizaje*" (miscegenation), as Marilyn Grace Miller accurately puts it in her 2004 study, and the "search for an Inca" studied by Alberto Flores Galindo (1986)—that is, the desire to return to an idealized pre-Columbian society, allegedly deprived of poverty or vices (see Beauchesne and Santos 2011)—in addition to the utopia of modernity that had emerged much earlier. We would like to pay particular attention to the influential socialist movements of the 1960s and 1970s, which also encompass the liberation theology movement that arose in the mid-1950s. A major exponent of such socialist movements is indubitably Ernesto "Che" Guevara, whose revolutionary practice and thinking famously turned him into a T-shirt icon (Kunzle 2008). Beyond the complex debates around his controversial figure, it bears emphasizing that the ideas he put forth in his writings share many points in common with the concept of the utopian impulse. More precisely, the notion of a "new man" that he formulates in *El socialismo y el hombre en Cuba* (Socialism and Man in Cuba) (1965) is characterized by the following aspects: it is forward-looking (its "image is not yet completely finished—it will never be" [1997, 203]), its scope is collective (it leads to "the society of communist human beings" [204]), and it is geared toward social change (including "complete freedom" [213], among other objectives). It is well known that the revolutions of the 1960s and 1970s were followed by a phase of disenchantment, which is often referred to as the end of utopia (see Magris 1999; Jacoby 2005). The failure of various socialist projects and the partial collapse of left-wing ideologies have generated a widespread skepticism that Jorge G. Castañeda analyzes at great length in *Utopia Unarmed: The Latin American Left After the Cold War* (1993). While it is impossible to ignore that some social(ist) movements have lost credit, it may be argued that the utopian impulse in Latin America has never died, since it keeps manifesting itself in quotidian life (see Cerutti Guldberg 1989).

In the period immediately following the end of the Cold War, more specifically with the fall of the Berlin Wall in 1989 and the dissolution of the Soviet Union in 1991—and subsequently the end of its support to Cuba—the consequences led to the end of multiple military dictatorships that had been established in Latin America.[5] The following transition period, known as re-democratization, saw a continued disenchantment derived from the aforementioned collapse of left-wing ideologies, as well as the enduring debt that

Latin American nations faced after the so-called "economic miracle" authoritarian regimes had promoted.[6] The consolidation of neoliberal economies that ensued from the 1990s on helped influence the notion that a new economic era was in sight promising recovery from the disastrous consequences of the dictatorships (in terms of both the economy and trauma from violations of civil and human rights).

As we have previously discussed in *The Utopian Impulse in Latin America*, "the initial phase of the uncritical, 'happy globalization' that followed the fall of the Berlin Wall in 1989" ended, and the notion that neoliberalism was "utopian" also collapsed, given the tremendous inequalities that continued well into the new twenty-first century (13). Nevertheless, the 1990s and early 2000s saw a continuation of utopian projects in the region that resisted neoliberal ideologies, such as Mexico's Zapatista Movement, Brazil's Movimento dos Trabalhadores Rurais Sem Terra (Landless Workers' Movement), and the World Social Forum that was first held in Porto Alegre in 2001, to name a few of the anti-globalization tendencies aligned with North American resistance.[7] Environmentalist movements also continued or emerged, such as conservation efforts in the Brazilian Amazon after the death of activist Chico Mendes in 1988, or the creation of environmental solutions derived from the informal economies of garbage collectors, generated due to an excess in consumption and waste production.[8] These examples indicate a variety of instances in which the utopian impulse may be identified in contemporary Latin America. Recently, scholars have explored the topic in a variety of disciplines, and Sandra Brunnegger has noted how "Latin America has served variously as a terrain for the conception, planning, or implementation of utopias at varying historical moments" (2018). We will elaborate further with a few specific instances of utopian tendencies in the region.

REFLECTIONS ON RECENT UTOPIAN MANIFESTATIONS IN LATIN AMERICA

In literary history, scholars have associated utopias with science fiction (most notably, Fredric Jameson), and in some cases, have claimed that utopia belongs to the realm of fiction (see Frye 1965). In that sense, Latin Americanist scholars who have studied science fiction as a genre have established a link with the notion or proposition for a better society within science fiction stories. In its obverse, dystopia has also been explored in Latin American literature. As a genre, science fiction is part of speculative fiction, which explores both the present context in which the work is produced and future possibilities. In chronologies and compilations of Latin American science fiction (see Bell and Molina-Gavilán 2003; Molina-Gavilán et al. 2007; Ginway and Brown 2012; De Fays 2016), authors have identified utopian tendencies in literary production from a variety of Latin American countries, including Argentina, Bolivia, Brazil, Chile, Guatemala, Mexico, Peru, and Uruguay, among others. Utopia as a literary genre has reflected preoccupations with the use of technology and notions of development as progress.

Furthermore, some utopian or dystopian literary works produced in Latin America propose an inquiry into the very notion of what it entails to be human, particularly in the face of violations of human rights.[9] The proposition that Latin America is a place of magical realism is also sometimes associated with the "science fiction" qualities of the region, namely utopian (idealized) or dystopian (horrifying) realities portrayed in works of fiction. Recently, however, critical studies have showed that the genre has been part of the long literary history of the region. Rachel Haywood Ferreira claims that "science fiction has been a global genre from its earliest days and that Latin America has participated in this genre using local appropriations and local adaptations" (2011, 1). In her book on early Latin American science fiction, Haywood Ferreira highlights the relevance of utopia to early productions and dedicates one entire chapter to the place of utopia and dystopia in the region's literary productions. The author also associates early utopian literary fiction to periods of national unrest, marking the importance of turbulent contexts to the production of utopian literature that envisions a better life.[10] According to M. Elizabeth Ginway (2015), specific areas of Latin America, such as the Amazon region, may be represented as a utopian dream in literature.

Brasília, the capital of Brazil, is considered a utopian planned city, which unavoidably turned into a social dystopia of inequalities. Beyond Brasília, recent scholarship on the topic has attracted attention to the utopian dimensions and geopolitical implications of physical space, including dwelling and housing opportunities (Massidda 2018), and public health conditions (see Coelho de Amorim et al. 2019). It is pertinent to mention that recently there has been an intensifying interest in cities, geography, and architecture as utopian or dystopian spaces in Latin America (see Lejeune 2006; Heffes 2013; Carranza and Lara 2015). Freedom of movement, as well as forced and economic migrations, have also been discussed in the light of utopia and dystopia (see Pérez-Bustillo and Hernández Mares 2017). The implications of imaginary spaces associated with Latin American mythology have been analyzed from the lens of utopia and dystopia, insofar as fictional stories reflect the actual conditions of physical and political spaces (see Spires 2008). Utopian spaces of nuclear-free zones in Latin America have likewise been examined (see Musto 2018).

Moreover, it is important to emphasize that the locus of the utopian impulse in Latin America has been in social movements and in manifestations of social resistance to inequalities, oppression, violence, and exploitation (see Gogol 2015). In addition to the social movements that already have been mentioned here, we reiterate the fundamental importance of a concrete utopia in the form of resistance to the current threats to democracy facing the Latin American region. The resistance to deforestation of the Amazon is an ongoing project, particularly at the current conjuncture, in which political rulers are advocating for the further opening of the Amazon region to development and exploitation of resources (Watts 2019). The movement for indigenous rights has continued, in connection to the conservation and environmental struggle, as well as to the plight of indigenous territory, which should be preserved together with the incredible riches of indigenous cultures in Latin America.[11] Feminist and women's rights movements, as well as LGBTQ movements, also continue to thrive in the face of an ultra-conservative political turn in several Latin American countries. This turn functions as a real threat to the safety of women and members of the LGBTQ community.[12] The protest song "Un violador en tu camino" (A Rapist in Your Path), inspired by Rita Segato and first performed in Chile for the International Day for the Elimination of Violence against Women (November 25, 2019), was enacted subsequently in multiple countries as a manifestation of indignation about the numerous crimes perpetrated against women. There are multiple other significant social movements not explored here, such as the plight for reparations to descendants of enslaved Africans, or anti-racism protests for basic civil rights for Afro-descendants in Latin America.[13]

Given the ongoing enterprise for concrete utopias in the region, we must point out one of the most important aspects in discussions pertaining to Latin America. As we have previously noted (Beauchesne and Santos 2011, 2017), it is essential to stress how heterogeneous the area is. Latin America—as a geopolitical region, as the site of the largest biodiversity on Earth, and as a crucible of cultures—represents a "heterogeneous network of transcultural viewpoints" (Beauchesne and Santos 2017, 7). Therefore, single or homogenous notions of what utopia entails are not possible. One must also remember the underlying contradictions of Latin American history, which entails discrepancies surrounding the violent processes of colonization, slavery, environmental disasters, detrimental prejudices, catastrophic inequalities, and persistent human rights violations. That said, the region has historically endured. It is evident that a utopian impulse persisted within "strategies of resistance in the face of injustice" (Beauchesne and Santos 2011, 8). In that sense, we reiterate the argument we established in our previously published works on utopias in Latin America: that utopian projects respond to crisis, envision practical results in policy, and impact quotidian experiences. We believe that a discussion of the utopian should always face dystopian challenges head-on in order to enable utopian possibilities and to ensure that there is a future.

Notes

1. The choice of the term *current* is not arbitrary here, since Bloch himself uses the metaphor of electricity to refer to the utopian impulse (1986, 15), as we will see below.
2. This section is an updated and expanded version of a part of our introduction to *The Utopian Impulse in Latin America* (2011).

3. The term *ladino*, in the context of colonial Latin America, was used to refer to the foreigner—and later "all natives"—who "was so competent in Castilian that he would not be taken for a foreigner" (Adorno 2006, 38; see also Covarrubias 1611, 747).

4. Our translation of "lo que define el pensamiento de los vencidos frente al de los vencedores es la formulación recurrente de una utopía particular: la de una comunicación posible a través de fronteras culturales (*cultural boundaries*) que haga posible una negociación de la alteridad."

5. The military dictatorships ended in Argentina in 1983, Brazil in 1985, and Chile in 1990, for example.

6. The term *economic miracle* was employed during authoritarian-bureaucratic regimes in Latin America to refer to periods of economic growth in the 1970s and 1980s. These growth periods were illusions, and they came at the expense of foreign debt and sanctions from the World Bank and the International Monetary Fund, and resulted in high inflation and a period of economic austerity for countries like Brazil and Argentina.

7. For example, with mass protests against the World Trade Organization staged in Seattle, Washington, in 1999.

8. For instance, the *Eloísa Cartonera* publishing house, which emerged after the 2001 crisis in Argentina and was mentioned in *The Utopian Impulse in Latin America* (13).

9. For example, Brazilian author Ignácio de Loyola Brandão has written several novels envisioning a dystopian Brazil, reflecting the impact of historical violence and the consequences of authoritarian regimes in the country. For further information, see Ginway (2004).

10. For more details on how speculative fiction functions as a reflection of the present, see Suvin (2010), as quoted in Haywood Ferreira (2011, 16).

11. Among the multiple indigenous rights movements taking place in Latin America, we may mention indigenous resistance to land appropriation in Brazil, as well as resistance to defamation of indigenous peoples by the current Brazilian president. Sônia Guajajara, one of Brazil's main contemporary indigenous leaders, founded an association called Articulação dos Povos Indígenas do Brasil (APIB; Brazil's Indigenous People Articulation) to fight for indigenous rights. Indigenous resistance in Bolivia has been discussed in Benjamin Dangl's *The Five Hundred Year Rebellion: Indigenous Movements and the Decolonization of History in Bolivia* (2019).

12. Violence against women and LGBTQ communities has reached alarming numbers in Latin America. Violent acts against women are most predominant in Central America but are also high in Brazil and Mexico. According to the United Nations, 38% of women in Latin America have experienced domestic violence, and the rate of femicide is rising. Violence against LGBTQ communities, particularly against

transgender people, is most prominent in Brazil. According to the group Transgender Europe, 78% of transgender murders in the world occur in Latin America. More specifically, according to Reuters, 40% of transgender deaths worldwide occur in Brazil. Please refer to reports from the United Nations (http://unstats.un.org) and from the World Health Organization (http://www.paho.org).

13. According to George Reid Andrews (2004), 22% of Latin Americans are Afrodescendants.

References

Adorno, Rolena. 2006 [1996]. Cultures in Contact: Mesoamerica, the Andes, and the European Written Tradition. In *The Cambridge History of Latin American Literature*, vol. 1: Discovery to Modernism, eds. Roberto González Echevarría and Enrique Pupo-Walker, 33–57. Cambridge: Cambridge University Press.

Arias, Santa, and Mariselle Meléndez, eds. 2002. *Mapping Colonial Spanish America: Places and Commonplaces of Identity, Culture, and Experience*. Lewisburg: Bucknell University Press.

Andrews, George Reid. 2004. *Afro-Latin America, 1800–2000*. Oxford: Oxford University Press.

"Ayllu." *Merriam-Webster.com Dictionary*, Merriam-Webster. https://www.merriam-webster.com/dictionary/ayllu. Accessed 1 June 2021.

Baudin, Louis. 2011 [1961]. *A Socialist Empire: The Incas of Peru*.Trans. Katherine Woods. Eastford: Martino Fine Books.

Beauchesne, Kim, and Alessandra Santos, eds. 2011. *The Utopian Impulse in Latin America*. New York: Palgrave Macmillan.

———, eds. 2017. *Performing Utopias in the Contemporary Americas*. New York: Palgrave Macmillan.

Bell, Andrea L., and Yolanda Molina-Gavilán. 2003. *Cosmos Latinos: An Anthology of Science Fiction from Latin America and Spain*. Middletown: Wesleyan University Press.

Bethencourt, Francisco, ed. 2015. *Utopia in Portugal, Brazil and Lusophone African Countries*. New York: Peter Lang.

Bloch, Ernst. 1986 [1954–1959]. *The Principle of Hope*. 3 vols. Trans. Neville Plaice, Stephen Plaice, and Paul Knight. Cambridge: MIT Press.

Brading, David. 1986. The Incas and the Renaissance: The Royal Commentaries of Inca Garcilaso de la Vega. *Journal of Latin American Studies* 18 (1): 1–23.

Bregman, Rutger. 2017. *Utopia for Realists: How We Can Build the Ideal World*. Trans. Elizabeth Manton. New York: Back Bay Books.

Brunnegger, Sandra. 2018. Introduction. Possible Worlds: Imagining Utopia in Latin America. *Bulletin of Latin American Research* 37 (2): 127–129.

Carranza, Luis E., and Fernando Luiz Lara. 2015. *Modern Architecture in Latin America: Art, Technology, and Utopia*. Austin: University of Texas Press.

Castañeda, Jorge G. 1993. *Utopia Unarmed: The Latin American Left After the Cold War*. New York: Knopf.

Cerutti Guldberg, Horacio. 1989. *Ensayos de utopía*, vol. 3. Mexico City: Universidad Autónoma del Estado de México.

Clastres, Hélène. 1995 [1989]. *The Land-without-Evil: Tupí-Guaraní Prophetism*. Trans. Jacqueline Grenez Brovender. Urbana: University of Illinois Press.

Coelho de Amorim, Annibal, Valcler Rangel Fernandes, Juraci Vieira Sérgio, and José Paulo Vicente da Silva. 2019. Health and Equity in Latin America: Utopias and Reality. *Health Promotion International* 34. Issue Supplement 1 (March): 11–19. https://doi.org/10.1093/heapro/daz014. Accessed 1 June 2021.

Covarrubias Orozco, Sebastián de. 1611. *Tesoro de la lengua castellana o española*. Madrid: Luis Sánchez.

Dangl, Benjamin. 2019. *The Five Hundred Year Rebellion: Indigenous Movements and the Decolonization of History in Bolivia*. Chico: AK Press.

De Fays, Hélène. 2016. Pensamiento utópico/distópico en la ciencia ficción de Hispanoamérica. In *Utopía: 500 años*, ed. Pablo Guerra, 221–248. Medellín: Universidad Cooperativa de Colombia.

Dreyfus, Simone. 1976. H. Clastres, La Terre sans Mal. *L'Homme* 16 (2–3): 167–169.

Durán Luzio, Juan. 1976. Sobre Tomás Moro en el Inca Garcilaso. *Revista Iberoamericana* 42: 349–361.

———. 1979. *Creación y utopía: letras de Hispanoamérica*. Heredia: Universidad Nacional.

Flores Galindo, Alberto. 1986. *Buscando un inca: identidad y utopía en los Andes*. Havana: Casa de las Américas.

Frye, Northrop. 1965. Varieties of Literary Utopias. *Daedalus* 94 (2): 323–347.

Gandía, Enrique de. 1946. *Historia crítica de los mitos y leyendas de la conquista americana*. Buenos Aires: Centro Difusor del Libro.

Ginway, M. Elizabeth. 2004. *Brazilian Science Fiction: Cultural Myths and Nationhood in the Land of the Future*. Lewisburg: Bucknell University Press.

———. 2015. The Amazon in Brazilian Speculative Fiction: Utopia and Trauma. *Alambique. Revista académica de ciencia ficción y fantasía / Jornal académico de ficção científica e fantasia* 3 (1). https://doi.org/10.5038/2167-6577.3.1.3. Accessed 1 June 2021.

Ginway, M. Elizabeth, and J. Andrew Brown. 2012. *Latin American Science Fiction: Theory and Practice*. London: Palgrave Macmillan.

Gogol, Eugene. 2015. *Utopia and the Dialectic in Latin American Liberation*. Leiden: Brill.

Graulich, Michel, Doris Heyden, Ulrich Köhler, Berthold Riese, Jacques Soustelle, Rudolf Van Zantwijk, Charles R. Wicke, and Karl A. Wipf. 1983. Myths of Paradise Lost in Pre-Hispanic Central Mexico. *Current Anthropology* 24 (5): 575–588.

Guaman Poma de Ayala, Felipe. 2009 [c. 1615]. *The First New Chronicle and Good Government: On the History of the World and the Incas up to 1615*. Trans. and ed. Roland Hamilton. Austin: University of Texas.

Guevara, Ernesto. 1997 [1965]. Socialism and Man in Cuba. In *Che Guevara Reader: Writings By Ernesto Che Guevara on Guerrilla Strategy, Politics & Revolution*, ed. David Deutschmann, 197–214. Melbourne: Ocean Press.

Harvey, Michael. 2019. *Utopia in the Anthropocene: A Change Plan for a Sustainable and Equitable World*. New York: Routledge.

Haywood Ferreira, Rachel. 2011. *The Emergence of Latin American Science Fiction*. Middletown: Wesleyan University Press.

Heffes, Gisela, ed. 2013. *Geografías urbanas: geopolíticas del deseo en América Latina.* Madrid: Iberoamericana-Vervuert.

Jacoby, Russell. 2005. *Picture Imperfect: Utopian Thought for an Anti-Utopian Age.* New York: Columbia University Press.

Jáuregui, Carlos A. 2008. *Canibalia: canibalismo, calibanismo, antropofagia cultural y consumo en América Latina.* Madrid: Iberoamericana-Vervuert.

Kunzle, David. 2008. Chesucristo: Fusions, Myths, and Realities. *Latin American Perspectives* 35 (2): 97–115.

Lejeune, Jean-François, ed. 2006. *Cruelty and Utopia: Cities and Landscapes of Latin America.* New York: Princeton Architectural Press.

Levitas, Ruth. 1990. *The Concept of Utopia.* Syracuse: Syracuse University Press.

Lindstrom, Naomi. 2004. *Early Spanish American Narrative.* Austin: University of Texas Press.

Magris, Claudio. 1999. *Utopia e disincanto.* Milan: Garzanti Libri.

Massidda, Adriana L. 2018. Utopian Visions for Buenos Aires Shantytowns: Collective Imaginaries of Housing Rights, Upgrading and Eviction (1956–2013). *Bulletin of Latin American Research* 37: 144–159.

Mazzei, Patricia, and Alejandra Rosa. 2019. Hurricane Maria, 2 Years Later: 'We Want Another Puerto Rico.' *The New York Times.* https://www.nytimes.com/2019/09/20/us/puerto-rico-hurricane-maria.html. Accessed 1 June 2021.

Menéndez Pelayo, Marcelino. 1905–1915. *Orígenes de la novela.* 4 vols. Madrid: Bailly- Baillière.

Métraux, Alfred. 1928. *La civilisation matérielle des tribus Tupi-Guarani.* Paris: Paul Geuthner.

Miller, Marilyn Grace. 2004. *Rise and Fall of the Cosmic Race: The Cult of* Mestizaje *in Latin America.* Austin: University of Texas Press.

Molina-Gavilán, Yolanda, Andrea Bell, Miguel Ángel Fernández-Delgado, M. Elizabeth Ginway, Luis Pestarini, and Juan Carlos Toledano Redondo. 2007. Chronology of Latin American Science Fiction, 1775–2005. *Science Fiction Studies* 34 (3): 369–431.

Musto, Ryan A. 2018. 'A Desire so Close to the Hearts of All Latin Americans': Utopian Ideals and Imperfections Behind Latin America's Nuclear Weapon Free Zone. *Bulletin of Latin American Research* 37: 160–174.

O'Gorman, Edmundo. 2006 [1958]. *La invención de América: investigación acerca de la estructura histórica del Nuevo Mundo y del sentido de su devenir.* Mexico City: Fondo de Cultura Económica.

Pastor, Beatriz. 1988. *Discursos narrativos de la conquista: mitificación y emergencia.* Hanover: Ediciones del Norte.

———. 1996. *El jardín y el peregrino: el pensamiento utópico en América Latina (1492–1695).* Mexico City: UNAM.

Pérez de Oliva, Hernán. 1991 [1528]. *Historia de la invención de las Indias,* ed. José Juan Arrom. Mexico City: Siglo Veintiuno.

Pérez-Bustillo, Camilo, and Karla Hernández Mares. 2017. *Human Rights, Hegemony, and Utopia in Latin America: Poverty, Forced Migration and Resistance in Mexico and Colombia.* Chicago: Haymarket Books.

Quijano, Aníbal. 1993. Modernity, Identity, and Utopia in Latin America. Trans. John Beverley. *Boundary 2* 20 (3): 140–155.

Rapoza, Kenneth. 2019. In Venezuela, Maduro Lives His Simon Bolivar Moment. *Forbes*. https://www.forbes.com/sites/kenrapoza/2019/01/29/in-venezuela-mad uro-lives-his-simon-bolivar-moment/?sh=786c5dc334f0. Accessed 1 June 2021.

Rojas, Lourdes. 2012 [1997]. Bello, Andrés. In *Encyclopedia of the Essay*, ed. Tracy Chevalier, 70. New York: Routledge.

Sandy, Matt. 2019. 'The Amazon Is Completely Lawless': The Rainforest After Bolsonaro's First Year. *The New York Times*. https://www.nytimes.com/2019/12/ 05/world/americas/amazon-fires-bolsonaro-photos.html. Accessed 1 June 2021.

Santana Castillo, Joaquín. 1999. Utopía y realidad de la integración latinoamericana y caribeña en los albores del siglo XXI. In *Latinoamérica, encrucijada de culturas*, eds. Leopoldo Zea and Mario Magallón, 135–161. Mexico City: Fondo de Cultura Económica.

Schoenhals, Martin. 2019. *Work, Love, and Learning in Utopia: Equality Reimagined*. New York: Routledge.

Shapiro, Judith. 1987. From Tupã to the Land without Evil: The Christianization of Tupi-Guarani Cosmology. *American Ethnologist* 14 (1): 126–139.

Spires, Adam. 2008. The Utopia/Dystopia of Latin America's Margins: Writing Identity in Acadia and Aztlán. *Canadian Journal of Latin American and Caribbean Studies* 33 (65): 107–136.

Suvin, Darko. 2010. *Defined by a Hollow: Essays on Utopia, Science Fiction and Political Epistemology*. Bern: Peter Lang.

United Nations. 2021. Climate Change. *un.org*. https://www.un.org/en/global-iss ues/climate-change. Accessed 1 June 2021.

Watts, Jonathan. 2019. Activists Hold Climate Conference Deep in the Amazon Rainforest. *The Guardian*. https://www.theguardian.com/environment/2019/ nov/15/a-journey-to-the-centre-of-the-amazon-in-radical-bid-to-solve-climate-crisis. Accessed 1 June 2021.

World Health Organization. 2019. World Hunger Is Still Not Going Down After Three Years and Obesity Is Still Growing—UN Report. *WHO.int*. https://www. who.int/news/item/15-07-2019-world-hunger-is-still-not-going-down-after-three-years-and-obesity-is-still-growing-un-report. Accessed 1 June 2021.

Zamora, Margarita. 1988. *Language, Authority and Indigenous History in the Comentarios reales de los incas*. Cambridge: Cambridge University Press.

The Pacific and Australasia

Peter Marks

Introduction

More than 50,000 years ago people from South East Asia arrived, probably by boat, at the landmass that in 1901 was formally named the Commonwealth of Australia. These people, today collectively called Aboriginals, eventually formed perhaps 500 nations based on clan groupings, spreading out to inhabit the island continent that today is the world's sixth-largest nation. They are widely recognized as humanity's longest surviving culture, with a population estimated at one million by the time Europeans settled in 1788. Nor were they entirely alone through the following centuries in the vast region washed by the Pacific Ocean. Stuart Banner notes that

> Alaska natives arrived from Siberia ten to forty thousand years ago. There is evidence of human activity in British Columbia and Washington beginning around 10,000 to 8,000 B.C., and in California not long before that. Polynesian navigators are thought to have reached Tonga around 4000 B.C., Fiji around 1500 B.C., Hawaii around A.D. 500 and New Zealand only around A.D. 1200, not long before the first Europeans arrived. (2007, 6)

P. Marks (✉)
University of Sydney, Sydney, NSW, Australia

© The Author(s), under exclusive license to Springer Nature
Switzerland AG 2022
P. Marks et al. (eds.), *The Palgrave Handbook of Utopian and Dystopian Literatures*, https://doi.org/10.1007/978-3-030-88654-7_47

In contrast to these actual travels, Europeans had journeyed to the Pacific virtually for centuries in their imaginations. The ancient Greeks conceived of a zone they named the Antipodes, from the Greek meaning "opposite feet." A Great Southern Land was still an expectation for the first Europeans who actually began to explore what they called the New World from the late fifteenth century, as it was for James Cook, who led three voyages to the region in the late eighteenth century. An early fictional traveler was Raphael Hythloday, who in *Utopia* tells Thomas More that he was on the last three of Amerigo Vespucci's pioneering voyages around the end of the fifteenth century. Marooned at one point, Hythloday claims that "by strange good fortune, he got, via Ceylon to Calicut" (2002, 5). As an accompanying footnote explains, "More covers in a prepositional phrase the distance from Eastern Brazil to Ceylon, a distance of some fifteen thousand miles. Somewhere in there is Utopia" (5n, 4). We now call that "somewhere" the Pacific Ocean. But, as Banner makes plain, this enormous geographic space, nearly twice the size of the Atlantic Ocean, had long been settled by diverse groups, who experienced the arrival of Europeans as invasion. Even the last of the groups, the Maori, was in situ centuries before *Utopia* was first published. All had rich myths and belief systems that, if not technically utopias, spoke of distinctive social possibilities. Andrew Milner and Verity Burgmann record an Aboriginal "oral tradition of retrospective euchronia, dreamtimes of one kind or another, where the people belong to the land rather than the land to the people, before history and hence also before the Europeans" (2016, 201). Jacqueline Dutton explores more recent Aboriginal utopian works elsewhere in this volume. Bill Ashcroft detects an "orientation to the Not-Yet-Become" in "the island nations of Polynesia, Melanesia and to a smaller extent Micronesia—those islands described by the utopian term 'Oceania'" (2016, 164). This chapter explores how the Pacific and Australasia (the latter name designating both Australia and New Zealand) provided real and imagined spaces for social experiment, both for the region's first inhabitants and for later Europeans who claimed, erroneously, to have "discovered" it.

IMAGINING THE PACIFIC

The speculative geographical position where More locates Utopia suggestively places it at edge of sixteenth-century European knowledge. In 1516, European exploration of the far side of the Atlantic was tentative and potentially fatal, voyages beyond the tip of Tierra del Fuego into the Pacific even more so. Many died who sailed with Ferdinand Magellan in 1519 on the first recorded circumnavigation of the globe by Europeans, Magellan himself being murdered in the Philippines in 1521. At least he sailed on the ocean his chronicler, Antonio Pigafetta, would christen the "Pacific Sea" (2007, 18). The idea of Terra Australis Incognita had been long established in the European sensibility, David Fausett noting: "An early geographical concept was that of a spherical world with symmetrical hemispheres and a great southern

landmass that counter-balanced the known world (Africa, Europe, and Asia)."
Fausett adds that "the unknown world was defined on the basis of symmetry
with the known. The same logic implied that the southern continent might
be inhabited, but this idea was rejected—it was thought to be peopled if at
all by monsters" (1993, 10). Fausett underscores the conjectural nature of
this notion and its complex relationship to reality, commenting that in the
eighteenth century the myth of a southern continent "flourished as a literary
theme, an enigma that symbolized the growing contrast between mythical
and empirical knowledge" (3). Glyndwr Williams offers two literary examples
from seventeenth-century English writers John Donne and Robert Burton. In
Donne's "Hymne to God My God in My Sickness" the dying speaker cries
out "Is the Pacific Sea my home? Or are/the Eastern Riches?," while Burton
in *The Anatomy of Melancholy* (1621) proclaims: "I will yet make a Utopia of
mine own, a New Atlantis, a poetical commonwealth ... For the site of [which]
I am not fully resolved, it may be in Terra Australis Incognita" (quoted
in Williams 1997, 71). The Pacific, then, presented a huge and seemingly
empty canvas for European utopian projection. Williams observes that "juxtaposed with the actual discoveries, mostly disheartening, of the seventeenth
century navigators, was a continuing hope that somewhere in the unexplored
vastnesses of the southern oceans lay lands of unimaginable fruitfulness and
wealth" (70). It took another 150 years before extensive scientific charting of
the Pacific and its landmasses by Europeans was anything like comprehensive.
The pretense of discovery was legitimized by Europeans through mapping.
Even so, names such as "Pacific" were not universally adopted, and "Terra
Australis Incognita" accentuated the newcomers' dearth of knowledge. The
first full map of Australia, Frenchman Louis Claude de Saulces de Freycinet's
Carte générale de la Nouvelle Hollande (1811), acknowledged Dutch explo-
ration, while "Terra Australis or Australia" was not used until the first maps by
Englishman Matthew Flinders in 1814. Even there, the continent was divided
bluntly into massive, largely uncharted blocks: "New Holland" and "New
South Wales" (Gerritsen 2013, 225).

The title page of Denis Vairasse's 1675 utopia, *The History of the Sevarites*,
which registers a continent "commonly called Terra Australis Incognita," still
refers to an imagined land somewhere in the Pacific. Fausett suggests that
Vairasse draws on "the influence of seventeenth-century English utopianism"
(113), creating an extremely detailed, relatively tolerant democratic world of
sun-worshipping inhabitants, with limited elements of gender equality and
communal living. Nicole Pohl judges that Vairasse's "history"' and "Gabriel
de Foingy's *La Terre Australe connue* (*The Southern Land Known*) (1676)
document simple, virtuous and self-sufficient communities [that] offer their
own contribution to the contemporary [European] debate on luxury" (2010,
63). As imagination gave way to actuality, reports of a paradisical Pacific grew.
Louis de Bougainville in *Voyage Around the World* (1771) commented that
traveling on Tahiti was like "being transported into the Garden of Eden,"
praising Tahitians as greeting "us with signs of friendship." He adds that

"Everywhere we found hospitality, ease, innocent joy, and every appearance of happiness among them" (quoted in Carey 1999, 155–156). John Carey notes how Denis Diderot in *Supplement to Bougainville* (1796) uses his primary text to denounce "'civilised' values." But Carey suggests that "the truth was less idyllic, as Diderot knew," quoting de Bougainville, who admitted that while he had thought Tahitian society was roughly equal and prized liberty, he later found out that he "was mistaken. The distinction of ranks is very great in Tahiti, and the disproportion very tyrannical. The kings and grandees have power of life and death over their servants and slaves" (157). As Frank and Fritzie Manuel argue, though, during the eighteenth century "ideal societies multiplied in the balmy region of the Pacific—in Tahiti and on the island of Nouvelle Cythere—*rêves exotiques* [exotic dreams] bred by the real voyages of Captain James Cook and Louis Antoine de Bougainville" (1979, 22). Part of the attraction of this state of nature myth, particularly for the primarily male explorers, was what were perceived to be more relaxed sexual mores of the Pacific islanders. As Patty O'Brien explains:

> The fantasy of islands populated by classically beautiful and sensual women seeking sexual liaisons with foreign men stemmed from the early voyage accounts of British and French visits to Tahiti. These new women awakened visions of a lost classical past wherein sexuality was untouched by the corrupting hand of Christianity or other negative effects of modern civilisation. (2006, 68)

This persistent myth gets replicated across cultural forms through works such as Herman Melville's *Typee* (1846), Paul Gauguin's portraits of young French Polynesian women, or films based on the Bounty mutiny (1789), where the attractiveness and supposedly relaxed sexuality of Tahitian women provide a motive force for insurrection. John Connell proposes that something similar occurs in Margaret Mead's *Coming of Age in Samoa* (1928), and the pages of *National Geographic*, wherein a "disproportionately large number of reports from Pacific islands, found people who were picturesque and exotic, beautiful and sexually alluring" with the women "often semi-naked" (2003, 567). These portraits are reductive and obscuring, with O'Brien emphasizing that "the stereotype of sexually free women hides the persistent presence of violence in the story of Pacific sexual exchanges, and it also obscures myriad colonial anxieties" (267). O'Brien's critique emphasizes the need to advance beyond a sense of the Pacific as passive and prelapsarian.

It also requires the willingness to hear voices from the Pacific itself. Ashcroft locates a utopian response that challenges colonial views of the region and forges an interactive identity through the notion of "Oceania." A key early contribution comes from Samoan-born writer Albert Wendt's in his "Toward A New Oceania." Wendt ridicules the idealizing of the Pacific and its peoples by "papalagi" (Europeans), arguing there were "no suntanned Noble Savages existing in South Seas paradises, No Golden Age, except in Hollywood films,

in the insanely romantic literature and art by outsiders about the Pacific."
Wendt adds:

> We, in Oceania, did not, and do not, have a monopoly on God and the ideal
> life. I do not advocate a return to an imaginary pre-*papalagi* Golden Age or
> Utopian womb.... Our quest should not be for a revival of our past cultures,
> but for the creation of new cultures, which are free of the taint of colonialism
> and based firmly on our own pasts. (1982, 206)

Wendt instead celebrates the South Pacific Festival of the Arts in 1972 and
1976 as indicating liberation from Western systems:

> This artistic renaissance is enriching our cultures further, reinforcing our iden-
> tities, self-respect and pride, and taking us through a genuine decolonisation;
> it is also acting as a unifying force in our region. In their individual journeys
> into the void, these artists ... are explaining us to ourselves and creating a new
> Oceania. (215)

This self-activated notion of Oceania argues for something autochthonous,
clear-eyed, and innovative.

Australia

Daniel Hempel relates how "mythological eutopias such as the Blessed Isles,
Hesiod's Golden Age, the biblical Ophor and Marco Polo's fables kingdoms have ... been repeatedly associated with geographical regions that
roughly correspond to Australia" (2020, 13). While the generic label Terra
Australis Incognita often prevailed, the British who colonized the actual
country invoked a different term, Terra Nullius, or "Nobody's Land" for
the land eventually named "Australia." This offered them legal camouflage
for the taking of land from Aboriginals who had lived there for millennia.
Darren Jorgensen argues that the sort of utopian projections indicated by
Hempel was detrimental to established inhabitants: "from its very inception,
utopian spatialization has not been kind to Indigenous people. Anticipating
a program of colonial violence in centuries to come, Thomas More's original
utopian society is only founded after the conquest of a foreign land" (2006,
178). Jorgenson cites H.G. Wells's *The War of the Worlds* (1898), published
110 years after the First Fleet of British settlers and convicts arrived in Botany
Bay from Portsmouth: "The Tasmanians, for example, were entirely swept out
of existence in a fifty-year war of extermination waged by European immigrants. Are we such apostles of mercy to complain if the Martians warred
in the same spirit?" (179). Wells's invading Martians were only fictional, but
Penny Van Toorn underscores how the notion that Aboriginal Australians were
doomed to extermination persisted, the "eminent anthropologist WB Spencer,
Director of the National Museum of Victoria in Melbourne" asserting in 1927
that "Australia is the present home and refuge of creatures, often crude and

quaint, that have elsewhere passed away and given place to higher forms" (2006, 2). The contrast between this brutal attitude and the idealizing of Pacific peoples could scarcely be starker.

Sydney in fact was set up as a penal colony to relieve the overflow from British prisons, and life was far from idyllic for the approximately 170,000 convicts transported between 1788 and 1869. Critically, though, they could earn their freedom and prosper. One fictional success was Abel Magwitch, the escaped prisoner whom Pip helps in Charles Dicken's *Great Expectations* (1861). Sent to penal servitude in New South Wales, the subsequently freed Magwitch makes his fortune, sending money back to London to help the unsuspecting Pip become a gentleman. Magwitch's fictional accomplishment was mirrored by actual prisoners, and by assisted settlers. The land was available, attained by driving off Aboriginal inhabitants who also succumbed to European diseases such as smallpox. Social hierarchies were less established and rigid for the newcomers than in Britain, creating fresh possibilities for British settlers and freed convicts. A more egalitarian culture enabled the belief in Australia as a workingman's paradise (the gender imbalance enhanced by the predominance of men transported as criminals and by early settlement patterns). Despite these positives, Lyman Tower Sargent proposes that race is the "most common theme" in Australian utopian writing, emphasizing that historically "it is overwhelmingly racist" (2008, 115). Indeed, when the various colonies federated in the Commonwealth of Australia in 1901, the Immigration Restriction Act (commonly referred to as the "White Australia Policy") curtailed non-European immigration and strongly reflected Australia's historical racist fear of Asian invasion. The policy would remain in force until the middle of the twentieth century.

Some of these elements are present in William Lane's *The Working Man's Paradise* (1892), which envisages a socialist future for the emerging nation. Edward Bellamy's *Looking Backward* was simultaneously popular in late-nineteenth-century Australia, and Lane offers a vision of a better socialist future in a local setting. Lane's novel ends with devoted socialist and union firebrand Ned Hawkins on the run but inspired by the socialist cause, the novel exhorting its readers to throw off the shackles of slavery. These radical hopes were not fulfilled in the real world Lane inhabited and hoped to change. Disgruntled, he tried to actualize his ideals overseas, leading a group of over 200 Australians to Paraguay in an attempt to set up the utopian "New Australia Colony." Later voyages raised the population to between 500 and 600 people (Halford 2010, 127). Lane's colony was based on communist principles interlaced with sexual equality, teetotalism, and racism—it was reserved for English-speaking Whites only. The colony soon split into two groups: "New Australia" and "Cosme," the latter led by the ascetic Lane. Both failed as viable communities, most inhabitants returning to Australia; the increasingly conservative Lane emigrated to New Zealand. Sargent does not categorize *The Working Man's Paradise* as a utopia, but Milner and Burgmann argue that its coda "certainly broaches eutopian themes" (202), adding that the actual

Paraguayan colony "retained considerable hold over subsequent Australian eutopian and dystopian imagination" (203).

One drawback for utopian imagining in Australia for non-Aboriginals was their often negative response to a harsh, alienating landscape, captured by writer Marcus Clarke's insight that Australian scenery exuded a "Weird Melancholy." Yet the sheer size of the uncharted continent initially allowed the possibility that, like North America, it might approximate a new Eden. Matthew Graves and Elizabeth Rechniewski, in "Essays From an Empty Land: Australia as Political Utopia" (2010), identify three figures—William Wake-field, Thomas Maslen, and James Vetch—who, in different nineteenth-century schemes, produced utopian projections of how the center of the continent (largely unknown to Europeans) might be settled and exploited. Maslen even created a "map" that included a large river connected to an imagined great inland sea, an enduring and sometimes fatal myth for European explorers. He creates an idyll of fertile soils and pleasant climate, easy exploration, and friendly Aboriginals. Yet, as Graves and Rechniewski reveal, neither he nor Vetch ever visited Australia. An actual New Arcadia movement of the 1890s sought to set up rural communities to exploit land not used by the state (ignoring the presence of Aboriginals). But Melissa Bellanta (2002) recounts that while utopian schemes envisaged environmental miracles, the land itself could never sustain such fantasies. The romantic sense of Australia as an isolated ancient land rich with immense promise still survives, but the twentieth century integrated the nation into world politics, broader social changes, and global climate disaster. Physical distance from the centers of power and conflict can at times be an advantage, as with the post-apocalyptic survivors of Nevil Shute's *On the Beach* (1957) living on briefly in Australia as nuclear fallout envelops the globe. The same is true of characters in George Turner's *The Sea and Summer* (1987) which depicts a climate-ravaged 2041. Still, the dystopian environment conjured in the *Mad Max* film franchise (1979–2015), where the post-apocalyptic landscape brutally imposes itself on the pitiful remnants of civilization, speaks to a harsh, inescapable reality.

New Zealand

Britain established Australia as a penal colony, but its colonialization of New Zealand in the nineteenth century was more a commercial venture, given the abundant natural resources in and around the country: seals, whales, timber, and (once forests were cleared) fertile land for dairy and sheep farming. The Treaty of Waitangi (1840) between the Crown and some Maori tribes provided the prospect of relatively harmonious relations between settlers and the long-established Maori (who outnumbered the settlers until the 1860s). The reality was far more complicated and fractious, the mid-century period disturbed by land wars that deprived Maori of territory they had held for centuries. Historian James Belich notes that "regrettably, there was not one treaty, or set of treaties, but five" with different terminology and emphases that prompted different interpretations which remain contested (1996, 194). Much of the early colonization of New Zealand, such as that managed by Edward Gibbon Wakefield's New Zealand Company, presented the land as pristine and amenable to utopian development. Diane Brand suggests that "Wakefield's social manifesto was to create utopian cities which were powered by an Arcadian hinterland" (2017, 314). Robert Pemberton's *The Happy Colony* (1854), for example, proposes that an agrarian socialist utopia be constructed by "The Workmen of Great Britain," to whom the book is addressed. A "Philosopher" suggests "the beautiful island of New Zealand to be the spot for the first stone of the temple of happiness to be laid, as it may be said to be an infant state, and uncorrupted by any large collection of people" (25). The long-established Maori population of roughly 80,000 people did not factor into calculations that required taking 200,000 acres of land for ten towns based on circular ground plans. The Philosopher argues that this "first society founded upon labour and perfect education will commence the perfection and happiness of man" (71). The scheme never took root, but it reflected how New Zealand was seen to provide opportunities for relatively poor British workers to prosper.

Sargent argues that from its founding "New Zealand has been the site of a series of utopian projects designed to create a national utopia or small-scale utopias." He makes the large claim that "New Zealand appears to be unique in the way that utopian projects became part of the normal discourse of political debate" (2001, 1). Sargent and Lucy Sargisson provide an extensive account of actual utopian projects, declaring that the country has "a special place in the history of utopianism" (2004, xv). James Belich titled the second volume of his national history *Paradise Reforged: A History of the New Zealanders from the 1880s to the Year 2000*, employing the term "Better Britain" to designate the confident local belief that New Zealand was in many ways an improvement on the colonial center. Especially in the years 1890–1912, the country proudly saw itself as the "social laboratory of the world," Dominic Alessio noting that advances included allowing women to vote (1893), a process for the peaceful arbitration of industrial disputes, and the introduction of old-age pensions (1898). Alessio records that "a small invasion force" of foreign commentators including Keir Hardie, Ramsay MacDonald, George Bernard Shaw, and Sidney and Beatrice Webb "visited New Zealand with the intention of proselytizing the colony's successes" (2008, 26), the better to push their own political projections back home.

New Zealand had been the site for utopian speculation as early as *The Travels of Hildebrand Bowman* (1788), which recounted the travels of its fictitious hero supposedly lost on one of James Cook's voyages to New Zealand. Bowman journeys through various lands—including cannibalistic Carnovirria and bucolic Anditante—to the more idyllic Bonhommica, an island whose chief city has no beggars and whose citizens have a sixth sense: a moral sense. *Hildebrand Bowman* works as a satire upon late-eighteenth-century Britain, but it also leverages New Zealand's remoteness and newness to suggest possibilities for better societies. Far more famously, the country provided the catalyst for Samuel Butler's *Erewhon: or Over the Range* (1872), by far the most influential utopia associated with New Zealand. Butler emigrated from Britain in 1859, staying until 1864 and running the sheep station he depicted in *A First Year in Canterbury Settlement* (1863). These elements fed into *Erewhon* (an anagram of "nowhere") which draws initially on a New Zealand setting, before the narrator Higgs goes over the range into Erewhon itself. Names of characters such as the "native" Kahabuka, or Higgs's love, Arowhena, have Maori derivations. *Erewhon* satirizes Victorian Britain, not New Zealand, with Butler adventurously mixing utopian and dystopian elements, and employing alienating aesthetic techniques such as inversion, exaggeration, and dislocation, as well as absurdity to prompt new perspectives. Among its numerous provocations, Butler portrays the Erewhonians as more technologically advanced than their Victorian contemporaries. Yet the former have destroyed machines for fear that such entities might evolve to rule the planet. These ideas now seem remarkably prescient; that he formulated some of them in the backblocks of New Zealand underscore his quirky genius.

Julius Vogel's *Anno Domini 2000, or Women's Destiny* (2002), first published in 1889, reflects Vogel's assurance that the actual country was in the vanguard of late nineteenth-century social reform. Vogel was Premier of New Zealand twice in the 1870s (explaining his interest in political structures and systems) but though his projection of a future more than a century ahead is askew on many points, the novel's subtitle underlines how in Vogel's world of 2000 sexual equality is the norm: women hold the highest positions in government, law, and business. The American President is a woman. While the book's literary shortcomings cruelled its initial success, it was republished in 2000 when, as if in fulfillment of its predictions, New Zealand's Governor General, Prime Minister, Chief Justice, and the CEO of its largest company were indeed all women. That said, the country (like Australia) took on the mantle of working *man*'s paradise. It also claimed the title of "God's Own Country" from Thomas Bracken's 1890 poem. Bracken lauds a nation "framed by Nature in her grandest noblest mold/Land of peace and plenty, land of wool and corn and gold." This romantic, self-aggrandizing attitude was ironized somewhat in the modification of the term to "Godzone" or "Gordzone." Especially in the twentieth century the pastoral foundation myth was criticized by a range of writers as false to the nation's more brutal racial history, its cultural mundanity and uniformity, and its failure to achieve lofty social ambitions. As James K. Baxter put it in his poem "New Zealand": "These unshaped islands, on the sawyer's bench/Wait for the chisel of the mind." Baxter and others deftly deployed that chisel.

This critique of an easy-going but conformist society generated dystopian responses, including by major writers such as Janet Frame and C.K. Stead. Stead's *Smith's Dream* (1971) posits a near-future New Zealand ruled by the dictator Volkner, his name referencing Germanic nationalism and John Vorster, then-Prime Minister of South Africa's apartheid regime. Stead fused several factors behind contemporary protests in New Zealand—a controversial 1970 rugby tour of South Africa; New Zealand's involvement in the Vietnam War; the demands of feminism and Maori activism—with the classic New Zealand trope of the "man alone." The eponymous Smith attempts to find solace from a failed marriage through self-isolation in the bush, but is increasingly drawn into guerrilla war against Volkner's regime. Stead warns how New Zealand ingrained cultural complacency might slip into compliant orthodoxy. Janet Frame's more complex and inventive *Intensive Care* (1970) presents a disturbing projection, its futuristic third section imagining a post-nuclear holocaust world in which New Zealand is used for an experiment in which survivors are separated by computers into "humans" and "animals." The latter are used for work, for scientific study, or for food. The novel deals with individual and group identities as well as social organization, Gina Mercer suggesting that Frame's adolescent experience of seeing "the favorable reception of Nazi philosophy in certain sectors of New Zealand society in the late 1930s" informed *Intensive Care*'s depiction of "the atrocities her own culture might be capable of, given the right circumstances" (Mercer 1994, 154). Frame in fact had suffered electro-shock therapy as a young woman, later capturing her journey in an autobiography on which Jane Campion's award-winning film *An Angel at My Table* (1990) is based. This mixes the bucolic idyll of Frame's New Zealand childhood, her long, hellish years of medical treatment, escape to a culturally invigorating (if smug) Europe, to eventual and happy return to suburban Auckland as an acclaimed writer. If not a utopia, New Zealand is a haven.

Smith's Dream would be adapted as *Sleeping Dogs* (1977), that movie itself a rare occurrence in a nation where feature films were only ever occasional before the international breakthroughs of New Zealand-born directors Campion and Peter Jackson. (New Zealand-born Andrew Niccol wrote *The Truman Show* and wrote and directed *Gattaca*, dealt with in the chapter on utopian cinema.) New Zealand's isolation and its rural roots generally preclude highly industrialized utopias and dystopias. Geoff Murphy's film *The Quiet Earth* (1985) goes against at least part of this norm, a scientific experiment to establish a global energy grid seemingly going wrong and wiping almost of the world's population except, it appears, three New Zealanders. One of these, the scientist Zac Hobson, eventually destroys the system behind the disaster to stop it occurring again, but the ambiguous ending, where he apparently wakes on perhaps another planet, has been read as a form of symbolic resurrection for humanity and the planet. New Zealand's isolation and natural beauty play to this quasi-Edenic possibility. So too do Peter Jackson's adaptations of J.R.R. Tolkien's tales, filmed in the idyllic New Zealand landscape. While theorists such as Fredric Jameson make a compelling case for a fundamental distinction between Tolkien's fantasy and the utopian genre, the Jackson films, with their sumptuous depictions of the beautiful Shire, splice seamlessly with a New

Zealand government-sponsored tourist campaign that champions the country in utopian terms as "100% Pure New Zealand."

CONCLUSION

The notion of the Pacific and Australasia as antipodal sites of utopias and dystopias endures in a weakened sense, even as lived reality has regularly proved less than ideal. Part of the idealization derives from European wish fulfillment, as well perhaps from the northern hemisphere's sense of superiority. In Aldous Huxley's *Ape and Essence* (2005 [1948]), for example, a New Zealand Re-Discovery Expedition to North America arrives after the dangerous side effects of a nuclear holocaust subside after a century. New Zealand has survived, the narrator informs readers, "not, I need hardly say, for any humanitarian reason, but because, like Equatorial Africa, it was too remote to be worth anyone's while to obliterate" (28). More recently New Zealand has attracted the attention of the mega-rich searching for an attractive bolt-hole from the more environmentally challenged northern hemisphere. The prospect of Silicon Valley billionaires prepping of the apocalypse in New Zealand seems perverse and dystopian, an ironic reflection of the long-held European belief in the region more generally as a utopian world. While the Pacific and Australasia retain something of a romantic image, the reality of lived experience both before and after European exploration and settlement has been and continues to be far less idyllic, but also far more complex, contested and creative.

REFERENCES

Alessio, Dominic. 2008. Promoting Paradise: Utopianism, and National Identity in New Zealand, 1870–1930. *New Zealand Journal of History* 42 (1): 22–42.

Ashcroft, Bill. 2016. *Utopianism in Postcolonial Literatures*. London: Routledge.

Banner, Stuart. 2007. *Possessing the Pacific: Land, Settler and Indigenous People From Australia to Alaska*. Cambridge, MA: Harvard University Press.

Baxter, James K. New Zealand. https://www.poetryfoundation.org/poems/92732/new-zealand-58c03423619f5.

Belich, James. 1996. *Making Peoples: A History of the New Zealanders: From Polynesian Settlement to the End of the Nineteenth Century*. Honolulu: University of Hawaii Press.

———. 2001. *Paradise Reforged: A History of the New Zealanders from the 1880s to the Year 2000*. Auckland: Allen Lane.

Bellanta, Melissa. 2002. Clearing Ground for the New Arcadia: Utopian, Labour and Environment in 1890s Australia. *Journal of Australian Studies* 26 (72): 13–20.

Bowman, Hildebrand. 2016. *The Travels of Hildebrand Bowman*. Peterborough, Ontario: Broadview Press.

Bracken, Tom. God's Own Country. https://www.angelfire.com/poetry/nzheritageflag/Godsowncountry.html.

Brand, Diane. 2017. Grand Designs Down Under: Utopias and Urban Projects in Mid-Nineteenth Century New Zealand. *Journal of Urban Design* 22 (3): 308–325.

Butler, Samuel. 1970. *Erewhon*. London: Penguin.

Carey, John (ed.). 1999. *The Faber Book of Utopias*. London: Faber and Faber.

Connell, John. 2003. Island Dreaming: The Contemplation of Polynesian Paradise. *Journal of Historical Geography* 29 (4): 554–581.

Fausett, David. 1993. *Writing the New World: Imaginary Voyages and Utopias of the Great Southern Lands*. Syracuse, New York: Syracuse University Press.

Frame, Janet. 1970. *Intensive Care*. Wellington: Reed.

Gerritsen, Rupert. 2013. Terra Australis or Australia. In *Mapping Our World: Terra Incognita to Australia*, ed. Peter Barber, et al., 225. Canberra: National Library of Australia.

Graves, Matthew, and Elizabeth Rechniewski. 2010. Essays From an Empty Land: Australia as Political Utopia. *Cultures of the Commonwealth* 17: 37–51.

Halford, Richard. 2010. Reviving the Radical 1890s: Contemporary Returns to William Lane's Australian Utopian Settlements in Paraguay. *Antipodes* 24 (2): 127–133.

Hempel, Daniel. 2020. *Australia as the Antipodal Utopia: European Imaginations from Antiquity to the Nineteenth Century*. London: Anthem Press.

Huxley, Aldous. 2005. *Ape and Essence*. London: Vintage.

Jorgensen, Darren. 2006. The Utopian Imagination of Aboriginalism. *Arena* 25 (6): 178–190.

Lane, William. 2009. *The Working Man's Paradise*. Sydney: Sydney University Press.

Manuel, Frank E., and Fritzie P. Manuel. 1979. *Utopian Thought in the Western World*. Cambridge, MA: Harvard University Press.

Mercer, Gina. 1994. *Janet Frame: Subversive Fictions*. St Lucia, Qld: University of Queensland Press.

More, Thomas. 2002. *Utopia*, ed. George Logan and Robert Adams. Cambridge: Cambridge University Press.

Milner, Andrew, and Verity Burgmann. 2016. Utopia and Utopian Studies in Australia. *Utopian Studies* 27 (2): 200–209.

O'Brien, Patty. 2006. *The Pacific Muse: Exotic Femininity and the Colonial Pacific*. Seattle: University of Washington Press.

Pemberton, Robert. 1854. *The Happy Colony*. London: Saunders and Otley.

Pigafetta, Antonio. 2007. *First Voyage Around the World (1519–1522): An Account of Magellan's Expedition*. Toronto: University of Toronto Press.

Pohl, Nicole. 2010. Utopianism After More: The Renaissance and Enlightenment. In *The Cambridge Companion to Utopian Literature*, ed. Gregory Claeys, 51–78. Cambridge: Cambridge University Press.

Sargent, Lyman Tower. 2001. Utopianism and the Creation of New Zealand Identity. *Utopian Studies* 12 (1): 1–18.

———. 2008. Australia as Dystopia and Eutopia. *Arena* 231: 109–125.

Sargent, Lyman Tower, and Lucy Sargisson. 2004. *Living in Utopia: New Zealand's Intentional Communities*. London: Routledge.

Stead, C.K. 1971. *Smith's Dream*. Auckland: Longman.

Van Toorn, Penny. 2006. *Writing Never Comes Naked: Early Aboriginal Cultures of Writing in Australia*. Canberra: Aboriginal Studies Press.

Vogel, Julius. 2002. *Anno Domini 2000: Or Women's Destiny*. Honolulu: University of Hawaii Press.

Wendt, Albert. 1982. Towards a New Oceania. In *Writers in East-West Encounter: New Cultural Bearings*, ed. Guy Amirthanayagam, 202–215. London: Macmillan Press.

Williams, Glyndwr. 1997. *The Great South Sea: English Voyages and Encounters, 1570–1750*. New Haven: Yale University Press.

China

Roland Boer

INTRODUCTION

The Chinese term for "utopia" is *wutuobang*, a loan word that echoes the sound and also has the meaning of the Latinized form of the Greek original "*outopos*." Why not use one of the well-attested terms in the Chinese tradition, such as "Great Harmony [*datong*]" or "Peach Blossom Spring [*taohua yuan*]"? The reason is that the Western concept of utopia/eutopia—as a no-place that is simultaneously a good place—is ultimately foreign to Chinese culture and ways of thought. I seek to explain why this is the case. The explanation needs to be both philosophical and literary, identifying key moments in the development of philosophical and thus cultural sensibilities, as well as presenting how these assumptions emerge in some key literary texts. In more detail, I begin with the early Confucian idea of *datong*, or Great Harmony, and emphasize that it is seen as a verifiable and historical reality. In this light, I analyze in the second part two short stories from different time periods: Tao Yuanming's "Account of the Peach Blossom Spring" (c. 400) and Cai Yuanpei's "New Year's Dream" (1904). Cai's story brings us to the third part of my analysis, in which *datong* comes to be reinterpreted in light of communism. We find this development in the story by Guo Moruo, "Marx Enters a Confucian Temple" (1925), the analysis of which brings me to Mao Zedong.

R. Boer (✉)
Dalian University of Technology, Dalian, China

© The Author(s), under exclusive license to Springer Nature Switzerland AG 2022
P. Marks et al. (eds.), *The Palgrave Handbook of Utopian and Dystopian Literatures*, https://doi.org/10.1007/978-3-030-88654-7_48

617

I close with a consideration of developments since Mao, specifically in terms of Deng Xiaoping's emphasis on another Confucian term, *xiaokang*, a moderately well-off, healthy, and peaceful society that is realistically achievable. As a definition of the socialist stage before communism-*datong*, this would become core government policy.

BETWEEN EAST AND WEST: THE PROBLEM OF TRANSCENDENCE

The point that "utopia"—*wutuobang*—is a concept ultimately foreign to Chinese sensibilities may seem quite stark. One may object: what about all of the mutual interaction of concepts and cultural assumptions that span centuries? Granted, but I emphasize that it is *ultimately* foreign to Chinese culture. To explain: the key difference turns on the question of transcendence. More specifically, it is the Western tradition's legacy of ontological transcendence that shapes the way utopia is perceived. The transcendent realm—with distinct theological undertones in even its most secular forms—is both far better than the world in which we live and yet cannot be experienced or empirically known. This ontological transcendence shapes (some would suggest "distorts") Western politics, social and cultural assumptions, and so also a literary genre such as that of utopia. Thus, the empirically unknowable world of utopia is precisely a world that is seen to be both a "no-place" and a "good place," the two senses embodied in the Greek *ou/eutopia*. True, it may contain (even implicit) criticism of the status quo, but it is a place that is distant, cut off, and unattainable.[1]

How is this concept foreign to Chinese culture? There are a number of reasons, the first of which concerns the distinction between "outer transcendence [*waizaichaoyue*]" and "inner transcendence [*neizaichaoyue*]." While the former is characteristic of Western notions of transcendence (for which God, or at least a placeholder for God, is the ultimate cause), "internal transcendence" is characteristic of Chinese culture. The latter is "life-focused" and seeks to improve one's current social situation through an ethical order and by means of "self-cultivation [*xiushen*]," in which "heaven and human beings are one [*tianren heyi*]" (Ren 2012; Shen 2015; Guo 2016; Xu 2016). Importantly, this process is experientially knowable rather than unknowable. Thus, cultural and indeed religious traditions that express comparable sensibilities—Buddhism is the best example—can be "sinified [*zhongguohua*]" in the sense that they become part of Chinese culture. By contrast, those that espouse external or ontological transcendence, such as the monotheistic religions and modes of philosophical analysis, are always seen in some sense as "foreign teaching [*yangjiao*]."

The Great Harmony (*Datong*) as a Topos

A second reason for such foreignness emerges from the Confucian tradition and its concept of *datong*, which means the great unity, togetherness, or harmony. To understand why, we must follow a path from the Confucian *Book of Rites (Liji)* of the third-second centuries BCE to the important reinterpretation at the hands of the commentator He Xiu (129–182 CE).

Let us begin with the *locus classicus* of *datong* in the *Book of Rites* (*Liji*):

> When the Great Way [*dadao*] was practiced, all-under-heaven was as common [*tianxia wei gong*]. They chose men of worth and ability [for public office]; they practiced good faith and cultivated good will [*xiumu*]. Therefore, people did not single out only their parents to love, nor did they single out only their children for care. They saw to it that the aged were provided for until the end, that the able-bodied had employment, and that the young were brought up well. Compassion was shown to widows, orphans, the childless, and those disabled by disease, so that all had sufficient support. Men had their portion [of land], and women, their homes after marriage. Wealth they hated to leave unused, yet they did not necessarily store it away for their own use. Strength they hated not to exert, yet they did not necessarily exert it only for their own benefit. Thus selfish scheming was thwarted before it could develop. Bandits and thieves, rebels and traitors did not show themselves. So the outer gates [*waihu*] were left open. This was known as the period of the Great Unity [*datong*]. (translation by Nylan 2001, 196; see also Legge 1885, 364–366)

I would like to emphasize two features of this profoundly influential text. First, *datong* is a historical era. In this text, the era is of the past, as the opening phrase of the following stanza indicates: the way has "fallen into disuse and obscurity [*jiyin*]." The setting of the text is a discourse between Confucius and a certain Yan Yan. Confucius laments current conditions in the state of Lu (in Shandong province), offering his vision of what it had been like at a better time.[2] Second, the text implicitly undermines the family by focusing on the common good. The primary concern is not parents and children, but all in society—including the widowed, childless, orphans, and sick. All should have opportunities in life and appropriate care. In this situation, everything is "as common [*wei gong*]." I have emphasized these two features—the past setting and a focus on the common good at the expense of family—since they will be important in two of the short stories I will consider later.

While for Confucius *datong* is a past era, the next moment in the tradition reworks this assumption in an ascending order. This appears in the work of He Xiu (129–182 CE), who provided a commentary-on-a-commentary on the *Spring and Autumn Annals* (*Chunqiu*), which were reputedly edited by Confucius. He Xiu distinguished three ages, with one superseding the other: the "decayed and disordered [*shuailuan*]" world; one of "rising peace [*shengping*]"; and one of the "great peace [*daping*]."[3] These ages would later—through Kang Youwei (1935)—be connected with the Confucian terminology of *datong*. Thus, the "great peace [*daping*]" (later to become "the greatest peace [*taiping*]")[4] became equated with *datong*.

Nonetheless, He Xiu's important contribution lies elsewhere: the great peace is not of imagination and rumor, but of what can be seen and is verifiable. To explain: He Xiu identifies a threefold schema of words and worlds that are "rumored [*suochuanwen*]," heard of or "recorded [*suowen*]," and "seen [*suojian*]" (Li 2013, 58–59). These are then connected with the three eras.[5] Thus, what is "rumored" becomes the "decayed and disordered [*shuailuan*]" world, one of chaos in which the heart is "course and unrefined [*cucu*]," the country is broken up into small states and records non-existent. Rumors abound of skulduggery, assassination, intrigue, and inappropriate behavior in light of established rituals. By contrast, the "recorded" or reported world has records and it unites all of the Chinese people. This is the time of "rising peace [*shengping*]": although not ideal, for it still has leaders and people engaging in less than appropriate behavior, it is an improvement. The "seen" world, directly experienced, becomes the great peace and tranquillity (*daping* and later *taiping*). Here the world is one, whether distant or nearby, large or small, while the heart (*xin*) or inner being is now deep and thoroughly known (*xiang*).

With He Xiu's contribution we find the deeper philosophical reason why the Western concept of utopia is foreign to Chinese sensibilities. Note carefully: the better world for which one strives—great(est) peace or great harmony—is one that is seen directly, and so experienced and empirically verifiable. Even the lower level—rising peace—is a world in which records and thus order exist. By contrast, the unrecorded and unseen world, of which only rumors and hearsay exist, is the world of chaos and disorder. How does one achieve either "rising peace" and ultimately the greatest peace? Through careful research, planning, implementation, and reassessment, with the need to record such planning and ensure that it is empirically verifiable. Recall the earlier point concerning "inner transcendence," which is based on self-cultivation and social improvement. Clearly, this whole approach differs from the Western sense of "ou/eutopia," which is an externally transcendent world, beyond human experience, and thus can be known only through rumor and hearsay. In the tradition that developed after He Xiu, the world of hearsay would come to be seen as one of chaos and disorder—a stark contrast.

In a moment, I will examine two short stories that express such sensibilities, but I would like to ask a methodological question: can the term "utopia" be extended to the quite distinct Chinese sense of an improved and better world that is empirically verifiable and for which one plan and achieve step-by-step? I have emphasized the differences between the two approaches in light of their cultural underpinnings, mentioning earlier that the term for "utopia" in Chinese is a loan word—*wutuobang*.[6] If one does want to undertake comparisons, then the differences need to be a factor at every stage of analysis—even in light of mutual interaction and influence. In doing so, perhaps we need to speak not of "utopian" but of a "topian," in the sense that the verifiable location of Chinese stories is a distinct *topos*. It simply will not do to deploy Western categories to understand China (known as *yixi jiezhong*), for this will lead to distorted results (Andolfatto 2019). Nor will it do to assume an easy comparison without taking into account the deeper cultural differences (Fokkema 2011).

"Peach Blossom Spring" and "New Year's Dream"

Two short stories from very different time periods illustrate some of these core features. The first, "An Account of the Peach Blossom Spring [*taohua yuan ji*],"[7] was written c. 400 CE by the famous poet Tao Yuanming (365–427 CE), and it has come to be regarded as the first literary representation of such a world.[8] The story tells of a fisherman at the time of the Eastern Jin empire toward the close of the fourth century CE. His fishing boat happens upon an agricultural community, hidden behind a narrow opening. The people he meets ask him concerning his origin and the world outside, while offering wine and meals. They tell him that their ancestors had come to the place during Qin dynasty (221–207 BCE), seeking to escape the chaos and harshness of the times and that they have had no further contact with the outside world. As the fisherman readies to leave, the people ask him not to tell others of their home. He ignores them and leaves a trail, but upon returning with others he is unable to find it again.

A couple of features stand out in this key text. The first is the clear this-worldly reference, with a specific date (the Taiyuan reign of the Eastern Jin toward the end of the fourth century) and a fisherman, who finds himself at the headwaters of a stream lined with peach blossoms. As with Confucius's presentation of *datong*, the historical references too are of real dynasties, including the Qin and Han. Second, there is an understated sense that there had been a simpler and better time, before the empires that began to rule China as a whole with the Qin. Of course, there were states before then, and it not clear whether the people hankered for a time without emperors or wished for a state that genuinely took care of its people. We are reminded again of the Confucian *datong*, which was in the *Book of Rites* an earlier and ideal era, rather than the decline of the present. That the author, Tao Yuanming, had retreated from the skulduggery and corruption of the Eastern Jin court and penned this piece and much of his poetry in quiet seclusion gives the brief story an implicitly critical dimension also to be found in the account of Confucius.

The second text comes from a very different time, in the last years of the whole imperial system and from the context of a weak and humiliated China. Entitled "New Year's Dream [*xinnian meng*]," it was the only story written by Cai Yuanpei (1904; see also Liu 2010).[9] The story tells of a man named Zhongguo Yimin ("Chinese citizen") who travels abroad and learns many skills, only to return to China and realize that too much energy was devoted to national concerns, and—for those colonized countries with no actual state as such—to families. He is drawn to a conference of many people, where concrete and detailed proposals are put forward for surveys of the current situation and a more rational organization of society, professions, and the lives of the common people. However, the most pressing problem was China's colonial subjugation, weakness, and continued humiliation by those who deemed Chinese people inferior. Here too plans are drawn up, with the story making a transition to the anticipated anti-colonial struggle. Only when China achieves national liberation does it become possible to re-organize society along rational and planned lines. In the closing lines of the story, we find the development of a multi-polar world with no efforts at domination and hegemony. Inside China, terms such as "yours" and "mine" began to fade away, as did "ruler" and "subject." Education for the young, medical care for the sick, and care for the elderly came about, along with the complete infrastructure that provided the foundation for a new level of prosperity and well-being. As the story closes, the author—now 90—recounts the proposed date for a global congress that would deliberate on the next stage of human civilization.

The most obvious feature of this story is the detail of the concrete planning, not in terms of a description of the structures of a distant "utopia," but in terms of how to get from the current parlous state to the desired one. The echo of He Xiu's recordable and verifiable worlds should be obvious. Further, the story locates—like He Xiu—the proposed world in the future rather than the past (as with Confucius's *datong*). At the same time, the more direct Confucian influence emerges most strongly with criticism of the energy devoted to families (see above). The requirements of the collective good demand that the demands of families be superseded. The final image of global harmony and the desire to go even further also echoes the image of *datong* found earlier, but I would like to emphasize another feature that reflects the time of writing: the bulk of the text is taken up with planning and implementing an anti-colonial struggle for national liberation, which is seen as an inescapable prerequisite for any realization of the project. Here we touch on the role of Marxism in China, to which I will turn in a moment.[10]

"Peach Blossom Spring" and "New Year's Dream" come from very different eras, but I have put them side by side since they evince in different ways the influence of the Confucian *datong*, one in terms of an earlier time and the other in terms of the world to come. Importantly, the stories have a clear this-worldly reference point and thus little of the transcendent tone characteristic of Western thought. The detail is scarce in Tao Yuanming's story, but in that by Cai Yuanpei most of the space is given over to careful detail and planning for achieving the desired world. In this light, the observation by Andolfatto (2019, 9) in relation to "New Year's Dream" also applies to "Peach Blossom Spring": even though the text is "disguised behind overtly *fictional* modalities of narration (whose primary allegiance is therefore to the ideal), [it] operates as an ultimately *empirical* and *realistic* one."

Communism as Datong

Cai Yuanpei's "New Year's Dream" was written during a revolutionary time, as the whole imperial system was about to fall to the republican revolution in 1911. Many were the possibilities presented for China's path in philosophical, political, and literary representations. One path that turned out to be a dead-end was the Confucian-inspired liberal reformism of Kang Youwei (1858–1927) embodied especially in the posthumously published *Book of Great Harmony*, or *Datong shu* (1935; see also Ding 2008; Fang 2016). A more fruitful path would open with Communism, which we may see through two examples: a short story by Guo Moruo and with Mao Zedong.

Only four years after the founding of the CPC, the writer Guo Moruo penned a short story entitled "Marx Enters a Confucian Temple" (1925). The story begins with red sedan chair stopping in front of a Confucian temple (*wenmiao*). As Marx steps inside, he is greeted by Confucius and a number of disciples. Cultural differences are revealed in the modes of interaction, but Marx is soon prompted to speak of his ideas of communism, since some had been saying that Chinese cultural assumptions and Marxism were incompatible. Marx emphasizes that his approach is neither religious nor one of crass materialism, but that it emphasizes concrete proposals for an increase in the socio-economic well-being of the common people so as to achieve common prosperity sufficient for the sake of communism: from each according to ability, to each according to need. Confucius agrees, interjecting to quote from various Confucian Classics, and at one point clapping his hands and crying out: "Your ideal society and my world of *datong* coincide with each other." Thereupon, he quotes the text from the *Book of Rites* (see above). In reply, Marx calls Confucius an old comrade (*lao tongzhi*) and observes, "I did not know that 2,000 years ago, in the far East, we had such an old comrade as you!" (1985, 164, 166; see also Yan 2013).

I would like to emphasize a particular feature of the story: Marx points out that his proposals are not a "figment of the imagination," and are certainly not "utopian socialism." The term used for "utopian" in this case is *kongxiang*, "empty thinking." In reply, Confucius indicates the concrete reality of his approach as well. This point in the story highlights why Marxism was able to take root in China and influence the course of its history. Instead of the perpetual Western tendency to misread Marxism in terms of messianic utopianism and its associated ontological transcendence (Losurdo 2008, 2017; Boer 2011), in China, Marxism is seen as a distinctly realistic approach that takes socio-economic realities as its basis.

All of this brings us to Mao Zedong, who also saw *datong* in light of Communism. Early on, Mao already felt that "the great harmony [*datong*] is our goal" (Mao 1990a, 89), with later connections made with Sun Zhongshan (Yat-sen), the anti-colonial struggle, and self-determination by all Asian countries (Mao 1990b, 560; 1983–1986, 144; 2009b, 484).[11] The clearest connection between *datong* and Communism comes on the eve of Liberation.

Mao points out that while others had been unable to find a way to *datong*, the Communists have been able to do so by identifying the need to work toward the "conditions in which classes, state power and political parties will die out very naturally [*ziran de guiyu xiaomie*]," so that humanity can enter *datong* (Mao 2009c, 1469). The direct allusion is to Engels (1988, 535), but Mao also follows what was by then Marxist orthodoxy, distinguishing between the stages of socialism and communism. The latter may eventually entail a natural dying out of classes and the state, but socialism is a time of struggle and development, dealing with internal and external foes. This requires strengthening of the state, for only when all opposition had been overcome on a global scale could one begin to move to Communism, or *datong* (Mao 2009c, 1475–1476).

A specific point arises from Mao's reinterpretation of *datong* in light of Communism. He does not see this eventual achievement as one of perfection, of the abating of all contradictions in a state of blissful harmony. If he had done so, he would have been appropriating a Western perception of ontological transcendence. Instead, we need to keep in mind his core studies on "contradiction analysis" (2009a, d), in which he argues that contradictions are universal, and that they would continue in the context of socialism and indeed communism. But how? They would be "non-antagonistic contradictions [*feidui kangxing maodun*]." True, they would need to be managed so as to avoid antagonism, but in making this argument Mao remained true to the Chinese tradition in philosophy. As the popular saying puts it, "things that oppose each other also complement each other [*xiangfan xiangcheng*]." So also in *datong*, which entails not the abolition of all difference and contradiction, not a utopian "perfect world" characteristic of Western traditions in which difference and struggle are overcome. Instead, contradictions would be very much present in *datong*, but they will need to be managed so as to be non-antagonistic, or—as the term itself suggests—harmonious.

REALISTIC EXPECTATIONS: *XIAOKANG* SOCIETY

Mao, however, was at times somewhat impatient, launching the chaotic diversion of the Cultural Revolution as a perceived shortcut that put aside the need for careful planning and implementation. Instead, it fell to Deng Xiaoping to put China back on track. As he did so, he observed that China had perhaps bitten off more than it could chew in its effort at modernization, so "smaller mouthfuls [*xiaokou*]" were needed, a "lowering of the standard a little" (Deng 2008a, 194). The term Deng used to speak of this more realistic goal was not *datong* but another term from the Confucian tradition: *xiaokang*, with a sense of being moderately well-off, healthy, and peaceful.

We have already met this term earlier, for it forms the middle stage between chaos and the Great Harmony. A little background: in the same text from the *Book of Rites* quoted earlier, Confucius is reported to have spoken of a lesser state. It replaced "all under heaven is as common [*tianxia wei gong*]" with "all under heaven is as family [*tianxia wei jia*]." With such a focus, people look after their own and set up defenses to protect themselves. Hierarchies exists, for which appropriate codes, duties, and institutions must be established, but there is always a risk of selfish schemes and warfare (see Nylan 2001, 196; Legge 1885, 366–367). For Confucius, this *xiaokang* was clearly a step down from the earlier *datong*, but it was the reality of his own time. Another even earlier text, the *Book of Songs* (*Shiji*) from tenth century BCE speaks of *xiaokang* in more favorable terms. Here we find that people are heavily burdened by myriad evils: robbers, oppressors, the wily, the obsequious, the unconscientious, and so on. From all this, they seek at least a little easing of the burdens (Legge 1871, 495–498). Importantly, these desires are presented as a wordplay on *xiaokang*, with the first character *xiao* (小) coupled with other characters that bring out the meanings of *kang* (康): rest (*xiu*), relief (*xi*), repose (*kai*), and tranquillity (*an*). In this light, x*iaokang* is clearly an improvement over a state of chaos and disorder.

This was the sense that Deng Xiaoping wished to emphasize when he first deployed the term *xiaokang* in 1979. He spoke of achieving a "moderately well-off family [*xiaokang zhi jia*]," which was shorthand for "a moderately well-off country [*xiaokang de guojia*]" (Deng 2008b, 237–238). For Deng, *xiaokang* is an improvement—in both economic and cultural senses—from woeful conditions, especially for a country subjected too long to poverty, backwardness, and bullying by foreign powers. Clearly, Deng Xiaoping had drawn upon another Confucian term with a long pedigree, one that still evokes the three ages but emphasizes what is realistically achievable. Of course, he did so in terms of Marxism, so that *xiaokang* came to be seen as characteristic of the stage of socialism that precedes communism. So influential was Deng's move—which he repeated on many occasions after 1979—that it became by 2002 core government policy as a "moderately well-off society in an all-round way [*quanmian xiaokang shehui*]" (Jiang 2002; Hu 2012; Xi 2017). The date for such an achievement: 2021. The benchmarks: managing profound risks (think of COVID-19), poverty alleviation, and environmental health. The means: careful planning, implementation, and assessment, all of which are recorded and verifiable.

CONCLUSION

This overview of "utopia" in China has emphasized how the achievement of a better world is seen as empirical, realistic, and achievable through careful planning. Uncovering this emphasis has entailed working through philosophical, literary, and even political developments. This task took us from the Confucian notion of *datong* and its crucial reinterpretation by He Xiu in terms of what is recordable and verifiable, through the short stories by Tao Yuanming and Cai Yuanpei, until we arrived at the reinterpretation of *datong* in light of Communism with Guo Moruo and Mao Zedong. The final turn took us to Deng Xiaoping's more modest and achievable goal of a *xiaokang* society, which was once again drawn from the Confucian tradition. By now, it should be a little clearer why the ontological transcendence entailed in the Western idea of "utopia," a world that is empirically unverifiable, is ultimately foreign to Chinese sensibilities.

NOTES

1. One may object: what about the drive to immanence that is characteristic of the peculiar European history of secularization? The very assertion of radical immanence still operates within the transcendent-immanent framework.
2. The State of Lu was a vassal of the State of Zhou. Given Lu's relatively long history (c. 1042–249 BCE), Confucius could in the sixth century BCE look back on its history.
3. The text may be found on a number of websites, such as www.guoxue 123.com/jinbu/ssj/gyz/index.htm.
4. The Chinese differs only by one small point: from 大平 (*daping*) to 太平 (*taiping*).
5. As one would expect, scholarship on the development of He Xiu's "three worlds" is immense, so I cite here only some of the more notable recent works (Jiang 1995; Chen 2007; Wang 2007; Xu 2011; Gao and Chen 2014; Chen 2016).
6. Even more, Chinese does not speak of "dystopia" but "anti-utopia"—*fanwutuobang*—a rather different concept.
7. It is often shortened to "*taoyuan*."
8. The original text is brief, with only 314 characters. One may find the Chinese text on many internet sites, usually including copious notes and a vernacular translation. An English translation in the same vernacular style may be found Owen's *Anthology of Chinese Literature* (Tao 1996).
9. One may consult an English translation provided by Andolffatto (Cai 2019).
10. Cai Yuanpei (1868–1940) was primarily an educational reformer with revolutionary tendencies. He became president of Beijing University, revised its educational philosophy and structure, appointed future communist leaders such as Chen Duxiu and Li Dazhao, and set up the work-study program for Chinese students in France, a program that included Zhou Enlai and Deng Xiaoping.
11. Sun Zhongshan (Yat-sen) was also keen to reinterpret the Confucian *datong* in a socialist direction, in terms of education of the young, care of the old, and appropriate work for all (Xu 2014, 29).

REFERENCES

Andolfatto, Lorenzo. 2019. *Hundred Days' Literature: Chinese Utopian Fiction at the End of Empire, 1902–1910*. Leiden: Brill.

Boer, Roland. 2011. Marxism and Eschatology Reconsidered. *Mediations* 25 (1): 39–60.

Cai, Yuanpei. 1984 [1904]. Xinnian meng. In *Cai Yuanpei quanji*, vol. 1, 230–241. Beijing: Zhonghua shuju.

———. 2019. New Year's Dream. In Lorenzo Andolfatto, *Hundred Days Literature: Chinese Utopian Fiction at the End of Empire, 1902–1910*, trans. Lorenzo Andolfatto, 199–212.

Chen, Hui. 2016. Gongyang 'sanshishuo' de yanjin guocheng ji qi sixiang yiyi. *Zhongguo shehui kexue wang fabiao yu wenhua* 12: 1–10.

Chen, Qitai. 2007. Chunqiu gongyang 'sanshishuo': dushuyizhi de lishi zhexue. *Shixue shi yanjiu* 2: 11–13.

Deng, Xiaoping. 2008a [1979]. Guanyu jingji gongzuo de jidian yijian (1979.10.04). In *Deng Xiaoping wenxuan*, vol. 2, 194–202. Beijing: Renmin chubanshe.

———. 2008b [1979]. Zhongguo ben shiji de mubiao shi shixian xiaokang (1979.12.06). In *Deng Xiaoping wenxuan*, vol. 2, 237–238. Beijing: Renmin chubanshe.

Ding, Tao. 2008. Kang Youwei zhengzhi sixiang lilu ji jiagou zhi tantao. *Tonghua shifan xueyuan xuebao* 29 (11): 4–7.

Engels, Friedrich. 1988 [1894]. *Herrn Eugen Dührings Umwälzung der Wissenschaft. 3. Auflage*. In *Marx Engels Gesamtausgabe*, vol. I, no. 27, 485–538. Berlin: Dietz.

Fang, Ying. 2016. Deng Xiaoping xiaokang shehui sixiang de lilun yuanyuan ji dangdai jiazhi. *Lilun guancha* 10: 14–16.

Fokkema, Douwe. 2011. *Perfect Worlds: Utopian Fiction in China and the West*. Amsterdam: Amsterdam University Press.

Gao, Jiyi, and Xubo Chen. 2014. Lundong, He de 'sanshi yici' shuo. *Anhui daxue xuebao (zhexue shehui kexue ban)* 1: 36–45.

Guo, Moruo. 1985 [1925]. Makesi jin wenmiao. In *Guo Moruo quanji*, vol. 10, 161–168. Beijing: Renmin wenxue chubanshe.

Guo, Xiaojun. 2016. Lun rujia zhexue de lunli jingshen – yi "neizaichaoyue" wei shijie. *Jiangsu shehui kexue* 6: 31–36.

Hu, Jintao. 2012. *Jianding bu yi yanzhe zhongguo tese shehui zhuyi daolu, qianjin wei quanmian jiancheng xiaokang shehui er fendou (2012.11.08)*. Beijing: Renmin chubanshe.

Jiang, Qing. 1995. *Gongyangxue yinlun*. Shenyang: Liaoning jiaoyu chubanshe.

Jiang, Zemin. 2006 [2002]. Quanmian jianshe xiaokang shehui kaichuang zhongguo tese shehuizhuyi shiye xin jumian (2002.11.08). In *Jiang Zemin wenxuan*, vol. 3, 528–575. Beijing: Renmin chubanshe.

Kang, Youwei. 2010 [1935]. *Datongshu*. Beijing: Zhongguo renmin daxue chubanshe.

Legge, James. 1871. *The Chinese Classics: Vol. 4, Part 2: The She King, or The Book of Poetry*. Hong Kong: London Missionary Society.

———. 1885. *The Sacred Books of China: The Texts of Confucianism. Part III: The Li Ki, I-IX*. Oxford: Clarendon.

Li, Jing. 2013. "Chunqiu gongyangzhuan" zhi sanshi. *Chang'an daxue xuebao (shehui kexue ban)* 15 (4): 58–63.

Liu, Tao. 2010. Yi xiaoshuo wei zhongguo lifa – Cai Yuanpei "xinnian meng" jie. *Hanyu yan wenxue yanjiu* 4: 64–70.

Losurdo, Domenico. 2008. Wie der "westliche Marxismus" geboren wurde und gestorben ist. In *Die Lust am Widerspruch. Theorie der Dialektik – Dialektik der Theorie. Symposium aus Anlass des 80. Geburtstag von Hans Heinz Holz*, ed. Erich Hahn and Silvia Holz-Markun, 35–60. Berlin: Trafo.

———. 2017. *Il marxismo occidentale: Come nacque, come morì, come può rinascere.* Rome: Editori Laterza.

Mao, Zedong. 1983–1986 [1926]. Guomindang youpai fenli de yuanyin ji qi duiyu geming qiantu de yingxiang (1926.01.10). In *Mao Zedong ji, Bujuan*, vol. 2, ed. Takeuchi Minoru, 143–149. Tokyo: Sōsōsha.

———. 1990a [1917]. Zhi Li Jinxi xin (1917.08.23). In *Mao Zedong zaoqi wengao, 1912.6–1920.11*, 84–91. Changsha: Hunan chubanshe.

———. 1990b [1920]. Zhi Zhang Guoji xin (1920.11.25). In *Mao Zedong zaoqi wengao, 1912.6–1920.11*, 559–561. Changsha: Hunan chubanshe.

———. 2009a [1937a]. Maodunlun. In *Maozedong xuanji*, vol. 1, 299–340. Beijing: Renmin chubanshe.

———. 2009b [1937b]. Zhongri wenti yu Xi'an shibian – he Shimotelai tanhua. In *Mao Zedong wenji*, vol. 1, 479–494. Beijing: Renmin chubanshe.

———. 2009c [1949]. Lun renmin minzhu zhuanzheng (1949.06.30). In *Mao Zedong xuanji*, vol. 4, 1468–82. Beijing: Renmin chubanshe.

———. 2009d [1957]. Guanyu zhengque chuli renmin neibu maodun de wenti. In *Mao Zedong wenji*, vol. 7, 204–244. Beijing: Renmin Chubanshe.

Nylan, Michael. 2001. *The Five "Confucian" Classics.* New Haven: Yale University Press.

Ren, Jiantao. 2012. Neizaichaoyue yu waizaichaoyue: zongjiao xinyang, duode xinnian yu zhixu wenti. *Zhongguo shehui kexue* 7: 26–46.

Shen, Shunfu. 2015. Shengcun yu chaoyue: lun Zhongguo zhexue de jiben tedian. *Xueshujie* 1: 151–160.

Tao, Yuanming. 1996. An Account of the Peach Blossom Spring. In *An Anthology of Chinese Literature, Beginnings to 1911*, ed. and trans. by Stephen Owen, 309–310. New York: W. W. Norton.

Wang, Gaoxin. 2007. He Xiu de gongyang 'sanshi' shuo de lilun goujian. *Shaanxi shifan daxue xuebao (zhexue shehui kexue ban)* 36 (1): 21–26.

Xi, Jinping. 2017. *Juesheng quanmian jiancheng xiaokang shehui, duoqu xinshidai zhongguo tese shehuizhuyi weida shengli (2017.10.18).* Beijing: Renmin chubanshe.

Xu, Tao. 2016. Zhongxi zhexue huitong shiyu zhong de "neizaichaoyue" yu "tianren heyi." *Xueshu yuekan* 6: 166–176.

Xu, Xuetao. 2011. He Xiu gongyang sanshishuo jiqi jie jing fangfa. *Xueshu yanjiu* 4: 22–28.

Xu, Youlong. 2014. Deng Xiaoping xiaokang shehui sixiang de lishi yuanyuan jiqi quanmianxing. *Guancha yu sikao* 3: 28–31.

Yan, Lianjun. 2013. 1925, Makesi yu Kongzi duihua – yi Guo Moruo xiaoshuo "Makesi jin wenmiao" wei zhongxin. *Xiandai zhongwen xuekan* 1: 16–26.

Russia and the Soviet Union

Mikhail Suslov

INTRODUCTION

In the Russian intellectual tradition, utopia mirrors a very specific historical experience: the existence of a territorially large and hypertrophic state in the land of scarcity; the peripheral location of Russia in relation to the global centers: Byzantium, the Golden Horde, and Western Europe; and the prevalence of the Christian Orthodoxy with its emphasis on collective salvation. The country, which was stricken by deadly famines in 1891, 1921–1922, 1932–1933, and 1946–1947, was dreaming of an abundance of food, and hence utopian fantasy revolved around the simple and primordial wish to live in a land where you can eat your fill. Historically, such dreams were intertwined with hopes to find this land of plenty somewhere outside of the reach of the oppressive and repressive state. Folk tales located such lands (one of the common names of this utopia is *Belovod'e*, the "Land of White Water") in Central Asia, beyond the Urals, in Siberia, or on the shores of the Pacific. Many peasants fled their home villages in search of *Belovod'e* and similar lands even at the beginning of the twentieth century (Chistov 2003).

The legend about a distant land of freedom and abundance taps into the rich cultural heritage of Russian religious sectarianism. The seventeenth-century religious schism alienated a large portion of Russian believers from the official Church. In their turn, the "Old Believers" who kept to ancient tenets of Russian Orthodoxy, developed a sectarian and apocalyptic mindset, as well

M. Suslov (✉)
University of Copenhagen, Copenhagen, Denmark

P. Marks et al. (eds.), *The Palgrave Handbook of Utopian and Dystopian Literatures*, https://doi.org/10.1007/978-3-030-88654-7_49

as engaging in a radical repudiation of the world around them. For them, the Antichrist has already come to the world and there is nothing left to save but the souls of the brothers in faith. This milieu became a testing ground for numerous models of utopian communities. One of the primary concerns of these sectarian utopianists was the problem of sex and family life (Engelstein 1992); their experiments featured such extremes as unbounded group orgies and mass castrations (Etkind 1998; Panchenko 2002). A form of sectarianism also fed into Russian Revolution, the Bolshevik Party seeing itself as the home to the chosen few, who fought against a powerful existential enemy in order to salvage the world and deliver freedom and happiness to the dispossessed (Slezkine 2017).[1]

Russian utopianism largely drew on the religious messianism of Orthodox Christianity. The key term here is *Katechon*, meaning 'Retainer' or 'Keeper', which denotes the one who holds the world from falling into the embrace of the Antichrist.[2] This term reflects the understanding that Russia has a providential, global mission, and that this mission is somehow salvific not only for Russia but for the entire world. Nikolai Fedorov, a renowned visionary of the late imperial period, provides a perfect example. His ideas about future technologies regenerating dead people resonated with much of the Soviet utopian ideas. It is less known that he came up with a geopolitical project of constructing the universal Russian Empire, which would bring the whole world under a single command in order to unite forces and coordinate the massive task of physical resurrection (Lukashevich 1977; Young 2012). Utopianism of Russia's providential mission played a significant role in late imperial fantastic literature. Many Russian social fantasies could be called "utopias of authenticity": they outline a better Russia in which the radical Westernization of the eighteenth century was rolled back, and the country uncovered internal, authentic sources of development and perfection. The social ideal of "conservative utopias" (Walicki 1975) of this sort was traditionalist and patriarchal, portraying the pre-Petrine past as a lost idyll, and calling for isolation from the West. Conservative utopias and dystopias numerically dominated the genre at the turn of the twentieth century. Such authors as Sergei Sharapov, Nikolai Shelonskii, Ivan Romanov, Dmitrii Ilovaiskii, and Aleksandr Krasnitskii reflected on the perils of impending revolution, the ascendance of the Western liberal values, and advocated an assertive Russian imperial policy (Suslov 2009).

The socialist streak of Russian utopianism has an honorable pedigree. In 1863 Nikolai Chernyshevsky wrote his fantastic fragment "Fourth Dream of Vera Pavlovna" in the cult novel *What Is to Be Done?* In this work, Russian utopianism rises to the level of solving problems of international importance. For several generations of Russian youth this novel gave an explicit answer to the question of social justice and to the purpose of life. Hundreds of communities appeared in imitation of Chernyshevsky's musings, and both the Russian Populism (*Narodnichestvo*) and the Social-Democratic movements were greatly indebted to Chernyshevsky (Ulam 1976). Petr Tkachev, a revolutionary of the Jacobin stamp, Socialist George Plekhanov, as well as Lenin and many other future Bolshevik leaders drew extensively on Chernyshevsky's thoughts (Pereira 1975).

In the early 1900s utopian fantasy in Russia was boosted up by H. G. Wells, Camille Flammarion, and Jules Verne, whose books were translated into Russian, and made widely available. A handful of the left intellectuals tried to capitalize on the popularity of this kind of literature, which was used to propagate various just and harmonious societies, usually on Mars. The most important examples of this trend are Porfirii Infant'ev *On the Other Planet: A Story of Life of the Inhabitants of Mars* (1901), Leonid Bogoiavlenskii's *In the New World* (1904), and Aleksandr Bogdanov's *The Red Star* (1908). All three share the same admiration of simplicity, morality, naturalness, and life in harmony with nature, as opposed to the urbanism, capitalism, luxury, and artificiality of their contemporary civilization. Like conservative utopias, the communist ones were anxious about the increasing rhythm of modern life, the building of an altogether artificial environment in big cities, and the alienation of people that was increasingly making them mere appendages of the capitalist system as a whole. With the exception of socialist fantasies about a new solidarity, pre-revolutionary Russian utopias were mostly concerned with issues relating to Russia's identity and place in the world, which is why their essential attributes were their geopolitical and conservative nature. Utopianism in this period was characterized by the predominance of visions of sectarian exceptionality of the "chosen few," and popular imagination about a land of plenty.

EARLY SOVIET UTOPIAS

On the eve of the revolution 1917, the culture of experimentation, unorthodox thinking, and avant-garde arts flourished in Russia. Richard Stites argues that "utopianism … is the key to the emotional force of the Russian Revolution" (1988, 4). In spite of its strong self-colonizing and self-Orientalizing tradition,[3] Russia became the land of a living socialist utopia, the scouting party of humanity. The Russian utopian culture, therefore, stripped out most of its inferiority complexes, while the previous fixation on identity lessened. The tidal wave of innovations in means of transportation, communication, energy-production, and industry stirred up imagination, while, at the same time the drastic living conditions in the country, which had just survived the decade of the WWI, revolution, and the civil war, widened the gap between the desirable and the actual.

The sectarian tension around sexual issues persisted in experimental thinking and practice of the 1920s (Engelstein 1992; Etkind 1998), enriched by the philosophical tradition of abovementioned Nikolai Fedorov, who called for the population to limit biological procreation and to channel sexual energy into technological recreation (Young 2012; Hagemeister 1989). Konstantin

Tsiolkovsky, the foremost theoretician of space flights and an idiosyncratic philosopher (Siddiqi 2008), found sexual reproduction degrading for human's dignity and believed in future parthenogenesis (Hagemeister 2011, 31). "Bourgeois sexuality" and the privacy of marital bed were vigorously attacked by proponents of asceticism in furniture design, planners of the new communist houses, and experimenters in gender relations (Matich 1996). The first Russian feminists theorized women's liberation from the fetters of patriarchal morality and family relations (Clements 1979).

Science fiction (SF) in this period not only disseminated communist utopianism but also a dream of various technological wonders. Examples include Iakov Okunev's *Griadushchii mir* (*Future World*, 1923), a somewhat unimaginative illustration of the socialist ideals, featuring collectivism, a planned economy, and the collective education of the young generation. *Aelita* (1923) and *The Garin Death Ray* (1927) by Aleksei Tolstoi are more sophisticated examples of this kind of literature, becoming bestsellers and undisputed classics of the early Soviet SF. Two works stick out from the rest of the SF novels: Evgenii Zamiatin's renowned anti-utopia *We* (*My*, 1920), which inspired George Orwell (Claeys 2010, 114), and Aleksei Chaianov's fantasy about a peasants' paradise, *The Journey of My Brother Aleksei to the Land of Peasant Utopia* (1920).

The tightening of Stalin's regime in the 1930s and the proclamation of "Socialist Realism" as the only literary method permissible for the Soviet writers created an atmosphere that was not conducive to utopian fantasy. In opposition to the "golden age" of SF in the USA of the 1930s–1940s, Soviet SF lived through something of a dark age (Schwartz 2013). Indeed, the production of SF considerably declined. The All-Soviet Writers' Congress of 1934 pointed out that SF should not be an "arbitrary combination of already known facts," but it should "infer … necessary conclusions from the new conditions of actual life in the Soviet Union" (Pervyi 1934, 216). Emel'ian Iaroslavskii, a prominent Soviet ideologist and a leading figure of atheistic propaganda, fleshed this idea out, arguing that the present life in the country was "more fantastic" than any fantastic novel, and that builders of socialism were naturally interested to know what would happen in 15 or 20 years (Pervyi 1934, 240). Soviet SF of the 1930s put the figure of the engineer at the fore in line with these principles. Many SF novels dealt with military innovations and, sometimes, with their catastrophic consequences as, for example, in Georgy Adamov's *The Mystery of the Two Oceans* (*Taina dvukh okeanov*, 1938) and Aleksandr Kazantsev's *Burning Island* (*Pylaiushchii ostrov*, 1941). Engineers were believed to wield enormous power, and imagining them in SF involved both positive and negative connotations—the latter flourished in the atmosphere of suspicion to the "foreign specialists" (Maguire 2013, 251). Stalin-era SF, which followed these precepts and portrayed the immediate future of the Soviet Union, was dubbed "short-range SF" (*fantastika blizhnego pritsela*).

Planning and Marxist Philosophy

After the death of Stalin in 1953, the intellectual debates about (but within the limits of) Marxism became possible, and there was a partial comeback of the legacy of modernism (Howell 1994). The late 1950s-early 1980s became the "golden age" of Soviet SF. The success of this genre was spurred by Soviet breakthroughs in space (the launch of "Sputnik" in 1957 and the first manned space flight by Iurii Gagarin in 1961) and other technological and scientific achievements. SF production in this period was stimulated by the culture of planning—itself cultivated by the economic practice of five-, and later—seven-years plans—the growing popularity of cybernetics, and translations of the works of Western futurologists. In the Soviet context, an infatuation with futurology, planning, and forecasting became a special academic discipline, "scientific prognosis" (*nauchnoe prognozirovanie*), which was positioned as a step forward in comparison to the "bourgeois futurology." This step was thought possible due to the Marxist ("genuinely scientific") insight into the universal laws of development (Rindzevičiūtė 2016; Ivanenkov 1984).

The plotline of space travel served as a perfect parable for this kind of "scientific prognosis": a spaceship—a scale-model of the communist society—launched toward a distant planet. The ingredients of success include the precision of all calculations, a firm hand of the ship's captain and the courage of its crew. Similarly, in the real world, guided by the Communist Party (CPSU) and armed by the teaching of Marx, the Soviet society would inevitably land in the world of communism. By way of proof, in 1961 the Third Program of the CPSU was adopted, laying out three goals for the next 20 years: attaining an economy of abundance, reaching solidarity among the Soviet people, and cultivating a new communist person—all key staples of the Russian thought since the late nineteenth century. In the Program, the Party leaders solemnly promised that "this generation of the Soviet people will live under communism," understood as a society of "free and conscious working people" (Materialy 1961, 138, 231). Of course, the dream of a communist society had been an integral part of the Soviet everyday life and state propaganda in the previous decades, but this time, the dream was articulated, defined, codified, and rubber-stamped by the highest officials, and a specific deadline for its implementation was set up: 1980. The term 'utopia,' previously sniffed at in the official discourses and treated as a childish daydreaming, had returned to public speeches with a positive air (Vajl' and Genis 1996). Importantly, when the Third Program was being developed, the working group consisting of some 100 scholars and experts consulted utopias conceived by Henri de Saint-Simon and Charles Fourier (Fokin 2007, 34). By leaning on the utopian classics, this work program triumphantly affirmed that eternal dreams of the humanity were coming true in the Soviet Union. One of the journals publishing SF responded: "The dream of many generations of people is coming true. [This is the dream] about a society without rich and poor, in which happiness will be pouring [on us] in a full-flowing stream" (Nadezhnaia mechta 1962, 3).

In this context, SF became enormously popular and influential genre of the 1960s, targeted mostly at the upper and most educated crust of the Soviet society: the intelligentsia, which emerged from Stalin's and Khrushchev's decades of massive industrialization.[4] The "golden age" of Soviet SF resonated with the optimistic mindset of the 1960s (the "generation of the sixties," *shestidesiatniki*, who enjoyed a relative lessening of state pressure on free thinking under Khrushchev, the so called "Thaw"). It is calculated that between 1959 and 1965, 1200 titles of SF writings were published with the combined total of the print run estimated as 140 million copies (Komissarov 2010, 35). Various SF writings extended large-scale plans of transforming nature into a fantastic future. They usually depict sweeping projects, such as the drainage of seas, the leveling mountains, constructing whole floating continents in Georgy Gurevich's *We Are from the Solar System* (*My—iz Solnechnoi sistemy*, 1965), or warming up the Earth in Efremov's *Andromeda Nebula* (*Tumannost' Andromedy*, 1958). The moment of conflict was typically created by the dangerous struggle with the forces of nature, as in *Planeta bur'* (*Planet of Storms*, 1959) by Aleksandr Kazantsev,[5] *Destination: Amaltheia* (1962, originally *Put' na Amal'teiu*, 1960) and *Far Rainbow* (1967, originally *Dalekaia raduga*, 1963) by the Strugatsky brothers (Csicsery-Ronay 1986). *Ural'skii sledopyt*, one of the key literary magazines for Soviet SF, published an editorial in the genre of a SF sketch "Fairy tales of the thirtieth century," whose punchline was: "the greatest pleasure and the greatest happiness is to overcome difficulties: struggle [with elements]!" (Skazki 1960, n.p.).

ANTHROPOLOGICAL OPTIMISM AND THE PEDAGOGIC UTOPIAS

Debates about the communist future lean upon the same optimistic and teleological philosophy of human perfection. The utopian world predicted by Karl Marx and Friedrich Engels should ensure the utmost development of human capacity: perfecting elements such as creativity, work, solidarity and love, physical fitness, power of emotions, and so on. By extension, ideal communist people were seen as athletes with strong human passions but with highly developed abilities to keep them in control. They would find their joy in creative work, in studying the enigmas of the universe and in serving the common good. From the Marxist viewpoint, communism is the endpoint of human history in the sense that there could be nothing beyond communism. At the same time, communism opens up possibilities for the many stages of perfection. From this perspective, all previous history of humankind was merely a preparatory phase or a rough draft for the genuine history yet to be written. As Elana Gomel puts it, in Soviet SF "the utopian subject is both dynamic and static, both a fluid potentiality and a set goal" (Gomel 2004, 358). In the canonical *Andromeda Nebula* by Ivan Efremov, the communist history began in the twenty-first century and it passed through three stages—the Era of Reunification, the Era of Common Labor, and the era of Meeting Hands, each of which consists of a number of shorter periods (1958, 26–27).[6] This and other dynamic Soviet fantasies of the 1950s–1980s decisively break with the ideal of an eternally frozen society as portrayed in classic utopias.

Unlike utopias of the 1920s, Soviet SF in its "golden age" was less smitten with salvific promises of technology. For the utopias of 1960s, technological perfection is something implied and self-evident, and the actual focus of their interests is bringing up perfect and harmonious humans, sometimes with overtones of a classicist return to idyllic simplicity and harmonious unity with nature. The idea of spiritual perfection with some elements of occultism and interest in Oriental philosophy sounded especially loudly in Efremov's later works (Schwartz 2012). Soviet utopian narratives connect two interrelated parts of the post-Stalin anthropological vision: a classic ideal of a harmonious person, plus depictions of a community of scientists/astronauts. Indeed, "hard science" and engineering continued to play an enormous role in the 1960s, but unlike early Soviet SF, its purpose was not that much directed toward impressing the reader's imagination by daring designs and inventions, but rather to explore the role of science as a social institution. Written by the technical intelligentsia for the technical intelligentsia, SF of this period took science as a metaphor and a philosophical concept of human's ability to understand and change the world (Marsh 1986). Efremov's *Andromeda Nebula* explicitly states that in a utopian future society, the majority of the population will be scientists—a profession that condenses the Marxist understanding of human purpose: creativity, innovation, and insatiable thirst for knowledge.

Brothers Arkady and Boris Strugatsky knew Marxism well and took it seriously (Cherniakhovskaia 2013, 56). On the eve of "Perestroika" (Mikhail Gorbachev's policy of restructuring the Soviet economy in the 1980s), Arkady Strugatsky insisted that he had never doubted the truthfulness of communist ideals: "I have imbibed them from my childhood." Boris Strugatsky, who lived long enough to see the collapse of the Soviet Union in 1991, wrote in 1994 that humanity had not invented anything "more radiant, just and attractive" than communism (quoted in Volodikhin 2014, 18, 20). Their *Monday Begins on Saturday (Ponedel'nik nachinaetsia v subbotu*, 1965) subtitled "A Fairy Tale for Research Assistants of Young Age" was written with effervescent irony in defiance of the solemn canonical utopias. The narrative zooms in on the fictitious scientific institute NIICHAVO (NII is the typical abbreviation of academic institutions in Russia, meaning "Scientific-Research Institute,"— here "NIICHAVO" sounds similar to the Russian word "nothing," evoking a parallel with utopia as "nowhere"). The institute explores magic and sorcery by means of up-to-date laboratory methods. Humor is accountable for only a part of the novel's appeal; it is more important that it reconstructs an ideal social ethos for the world of the future. The slogan of the protagonists comes from earlier Strugatskys' novels: working is more interesting than taking a rest (Strugatsky and Strugatsky 1965, 114). In line with this, the book's title is *Monday Begins on Saturday*. This book represents a group of scientists completely carried away by their ideas, projects, and studies. These people are not interested in consumption, instead they spend their lives exploring and transforming the world around them. Trying to grasp the spirit of the communist utopia, the Strugatsky brothers extrapolated the atmosphere and relations inside a research institution onto society as a whole. Literature follows life; in the late 1950s a number of "scientific towns" emerged, such as Dubna and Obninsk (both 1956) near Moscow and Akademgorodok in Novosibirsk (1957).

In their "utopia for intelligentsia," the Strugatsky brothers picked up on an important theme in Soviet utopianism: the waning of interest in profits, possession, and commodities. In line with Marx and Engels, the Strugatsky brothers believed that creative labor under communism would not require such material stimuli. Here they followed the mainstream of the Soviet SF. For example, the aforementioned *Andromeda Nebula* also sketches how the main protagonist, one of the most important persons on the planet, packs his few things in order to relocate:

> Dar Veter collected his personal belongings, put magnetic tapes with voices of his closest relatives and with his own thoughts in a casket. He took... a copy of one ancient Russian painting from the wall, picked up a bronze statuette of an artist Bello Gal'... He added some clothes and put it all in an aluminum box. (Efremov 1958, 96)

Darko Suvin aptly noted that the Soviet SF is a "blending the rationalist Western European strain of utopianism and satire with the native folk longings for abundance and justice" (1979, 243). This abundance, however, implies self-discipline in order to avoid vulgarization of the communist utopia. In the spirit of free-will and asceticism, in *We Are from the Solar System* by Gurevich people have unlimited access to commodities, but they are trained to possess only those things which they need every day. The rest is loaned from the public warehouses in order not to stuff apartments with too much junk. SF writers such as Kazantsev, Gurevich, and early texts by the Strugatsky brothers carefully distanced their imaginary worlds from utopias such as the land of Cockaigne. For them, communist is not about grilled geese flying right into one's mouth, but about the cultivation of the desire to work in a creative way and overcome challenges. Their Soviet-era works visualize the allegory of a perfect communist society, populated by healthy men and women, who are kept busy by arts and sciences, and who, donning spacesuits, optimistically look into the future of life on other planets.[7]

Pedagogical projects for shaping perfect inhabitants of the perfect world remained the crux of utopianism of the 1960s–1970s, fed by two schools of mind-training, which sprouted in the intellectual milieus of Moscow in late 1950s. One of these was the circle of "methodologists" led by Marxist philosopher Georgii Shchedrovitsky (Kukulin 2011). Borrowing the term from the SF of the Strugatsky brothers, Shchedrovitsky saw himself as a "progressor," vested with the task of improving human thinking. Around the same time, Genrikh Al'tshuller (pen-name Genrikh Al'tov), a professional SF writer and inventor, developed a complex of practical methods boosting human creativity, which he called TRIZ (an abbreviation of the Russian phrase, meaning 'Theory of Solving Research Questions'). These pedagogical utopias rest on a common concept: an assumption that the communist society of the future requires a qualitative leap forward in the development of human cognition, and that such a new level of cognition is achievable by means of some specific tools and techniques.

Efremov emphatically argued that pedagogy is a "fine work, which requires analysis of the individual and a very careful approaches" (1958, 116). The time when the upbringing of new generations was chaotic and un-scientific was over, and a global system of boarding schools should come to the fore. Gurevich's *We Are from the Solar System* presents another comprehensive communist utopia, which shows the same global network of boarding schools, where children from age six or seven live permanently. In the early 1960s, the Strugatsky brothers gave this idea blood and flesh in a short story "Malefactors" (1962). The background of the story is the sunny and joyful communist utopia, filled with the heroic deeds of space explorers, scientists and doctors. The focus is, however, on teaching (Strugatsky and Strugatsky 1962, 25–29) and includes such elements as the heightened role of the teacher as not merely a specialist in her field but as a mentor who guides pupils in the world of moral choices, focusing on the practice-oriented and problem-solving education.

Conclusion

Soviet utopian SF never fully obliterated pre-revolutionary traditions, instead incorporating them with philosophical Marxism. Visions of the land of plenty transmogrified into the illustration of the communist principle "from each according to his abilities, to each according to his needs," but with an important admixture: ascetic contempt of all things materialist. Messianism as a compensatory mechanism of a peripheral empire and the sectarian belief in salvation acquired universal qualities in the framework of Marxist teleology and social philosophy, which imparted a galactic-scale mission to all humanity. SF spilled over into the genres of anti-utopia, dystopia, and "ambiguous utopia," which blossomed in late 1960s, 1970s, and 1980s and engaged the most talented writers such as the Strugatsky brothers. It is little wonder that these genres attracted some attention from the censorial authorities and even security services (Komissarov 2010; Eremina and Smirnov 2013). However, the primary interest of writers remained focused on the large philosophical issues of progress, human nature, and humanity's place in the universe. The collapse of the Soviet Union in 1991 sounded the funeral knell not only for the official communist utopia but also for optimistic and humanistic Soviet SF. It would be replaced by the new wave of identarian, conservative, imperial, and geopolitical SF, whose parochialism and pessimism serve as better means to express the current cultural atmosphere of conspiratorial thinking, revanchism, and xenophobia (Suslov and Bodin 2019).

NOTES

1. See Berdyaev, Nicolas. 1960 [1937]. *The Origin of Russian Communism.* Ann Arbor: University of Michigan Press. The émigré philosopher speculates on the parallels between the Bolsheviks' ideology and the Russian messianic religious culture.
2. See Hell, Julia. 2009. Katechon: Carl Schmitt's Imperial Theology and the Ruins of the Future. *The Germanic Review: Literature, Culture, Theory* 84 (4): 283–326. Here, she offers an overview of Carl Schmitt's political reading of the term *Katechon.*
3. Cf.: Etkind, Aleksandr. 2012. *Internal Colonization: Russia's Imperial Experience.* Cambridge: Polity.
4. In 1959 intelligentsia ("workers of intellectual labor," as they were defined officially) counted 20 million people.
5. The novel was cinematized in 1961 by Pavel Klushantsev (Barker and Skotak 1994). In the US, the film was edited and released as *Voyage to the Prehistoric Planet* (1965) and *Voyage to the Planet of Prehistoric Women* (1968) without mentioning its Soviet origin.
6. In their novels Strugasky brothers briefly mention the "Theory of Historical Sequences" and the "Vertical Progress"; we can surmise that the authors had in mind something similar to Efremov's theory of historical progress. See Cherniakhovskaia, Iuliia. 2013. *Politiko-filosofskoe osmyslenie problem obshchestvennogo razvitiia v tvorchestve A. i B. Strugatskikh.* Dissertation in political studies, Moscow, MGU, 82–86.
7. A profusion of visual material of this kind, featuring cosmonauts, scientists, and abstract images of perfect inhabitants of the communist utopia, is available at: https://back-in-ussr.com/2014/01/sovetskaya-mozaika.html.

References

Barker, Lynn, and Robert Skotak. 1994. Klushantsev: Russia's Wizard of Fantastika. *American Cinematographer* 75 (6): 76–83 and (7): 77–82.

Berdyaev, Nicolas. 1960 [1937]. *The Origin of Russian Communism.* Ann Arbor: University of Michigan Press.

Cherniakhovskaia, Iuliia. 2013. *Politiko-filosofskoe osmyslenie problem obshchestvennogo razvitiia v tvorchestve A. i B. Strugatskikh.* Dissertation in political studies, Moscow, MGU.

Chistov, Kirill. 2003. *Russkaia narodnaia utopiia.* St Petersburg: Dmitry Bulanin.

Claeys, Gregory. 2010. The Origins of Dystopia: Wells, Huxley and Orwell. In *The Cambridge Companion to Utopian Literature*, ed. Gregory Claeys, 107–134. Cambridge: Cambridge University Press.

Clements, Barbara. 1979. *Bolshevik Feminist, the Life of Aleksandra Kollontai*. Bloomington: Indiana University Press.

Csicsery-Ronay, Istvan. 1986. Towards the Last Fairy Tale: On the Fairy-Tale Paradigm in the Strugatskys' Science Fiction, 1963–72. *Science-Fiction Studies* 13 (1): 1–41.

Efremov, Ivan. 1958. *Tumannost' Andromedy*. Moscow: Molodaia gvardiia.

Engelstein, Laura. 1992. *The Keys to Happiness, Sex and the Search for Modernity in fin-de-siècle Russia*. Ithaca: Cornell University Press.

Eremina, Ol'ga, and Nikolai Smirnov. 2013. *Ivan Efremov*. Moscow: ZhZL.

Etkind, Aleksandr. 1998. *Khlyst: Sekty, literatura i revoliutsiia*. Moscow: NLO.

———. 2012. *Internal Colonization: Russia's Imperial Experience*. Cambridge: Polity.

Fokin, Aleksandr. 2007. *Obrazy kommunisticheskogo budushchego u vlasti i naseleniia SSSR na rubezhe 1950–60-kh gg. XX veka*. Dissertation in History, Cheliabinsk, ChGU.

Gomel, Elana. 2004. Gods Like Men: Soviet Science Fiction and the Utopian Self. *Science Fiction Studies* 31 (3): 358–377.

Hagemeister, Michael. 2011. The Conquest of Space and the Bliss of the Atoms: Konstantin Tsiolkovskii. In *Soviet Space Culture: Cosmic Enthusiasm in Socialist Societies*, ed. E. Maurer, J. Richers, M. Rüthers, and C. Scheide, 27–41. Basingstoke, GB: Palgrave Macmillan.

———. 1989. *Nikolaj Fedorov: Studien zu Leben, Werk und Wirkung*. Bern: Peter Lang.

Hell, Julia. 2009. Katechon: Carl Schmitt's Imperial Theology and the Ruins of the Future. *The Germanic Review: Literature, Culture, Theory* 84 (4): 283–326.

Howell, Yvonne. 1994. *Apocalyptic Realism: The Science Fiction of Arkady and Boris Strugatsky*. New York: P. Lang.

Ivanenkov, Sergei. 1984. *Metodologicheskoe problemy sotsial'nogo predvideniia v sovetskoi filosofskoi literature 1970-kh godov*. Dissertation in Philosophy, Moscow, MGU.

Komissarov, Vladimir. 2010. *Nauchno-fantasticheskaia literatura v zhizni sovetskoi intelligentsia 1940–1980-kh godov: Nekotorye sotsial'no-istoricheskie aspekty*. Ivanovo: Press-Sto.

Kukulin, Il'ia. 2011. Alternative Social Blueprinting in Soviet Society of the 1960s and the 1970s, or Why Left-Wing Political Practices Have Not Caught on in Contemporary Russia. *Russian Studies in History* 49 (4): 51–92.

Lukashevich, Stephen. 1977. *N.F. Fedorov (1828–1903): A Study in Russian Eupsychian and Utopian Thought*. Delaware: University of Delaware Press.

Maguire, Muireann. 2013. Aleksei N. Tolstoi and the Enigmatic Engineer: A Case of Vicarious Revisionism. *Slavic Review* 72 (2): 247–266.

Marsh, Rosalind. 1986. *Soviet Fiction Since Stalin: Science, Politics and Literature*. Totowa, N.J: Barnes & Noble.

Materialy XXII s"ezda KPSS. 1961. Moscow: Gospolitizdat.

Matich, Olga. 1996. Remaking the Bed: Utopia in Daily Life. In *Laboratory of Dreams, the Russian Avant-Garde and Cultural Experiment*, ed. J.E. Bowlt and O. Matich, 59–78. Stanford, CA: Stanford University Press.

Nadezhnaia mechta. 1962. *Ural'skii sledopyt: Ezhemesiachnyi zhurnal* 1. Available at: http://www.uralstalker.com/uarch/us/1962/01/2/.

Panchenko, Aleksandr. 2002. *Khristovshchina i skopchestvo: Fol'klor i traditsionnaia kul'tura russkikh misticheskikh sekt*. Moscow: OGI.

Pereira, N.G.O. 1975. *The Thought and Teachings of N. G. Černyševkij*. The Hague: Mouton.

Pervyi vsesoiuznyi s"ezd sovetskikh pisatelei. Stenograficheskii otchet. 1934. Moscow: Khudozhestvennaia literature. Available at: https://rusneb.ru/catalog/000199_000 009_006511623/.

Rindzevičiūtė, Egle. 2016. A Struggle for the Soviet Future: The Birth of Scientific Forecasting in the Soviet Union. *Slavic Review* 75 (1): 52–76.

Schwartz, Matthias. 2012. Guests from Outer Space. Occult Aspects of Soviet Science Fiction. In *The New Age of Russia: Occult and Esoteric Dimensions*, ed. M. Hagemeister, B. Menzel, and Glatzer Rosenthal, 211–237. Bern: Peter Lang.

———. 2013. How Nauchnaia Fantastika Was Made: The Debates About the Genre of Science Fiction from NEP to High Stalinism. *Slavic Review* 72 (2), 224–246.

Sharapov, Sergei. 2014 [1902]. Cherez polveka. In Sharapov. *"Delo idet o spasenii Rossii": Izbrannye sochineniia*. St Petersburg: Russkii ostrov. Available also at: https://sci.house/literatura-hudojestvennaya-scibook/cherez-polveka-fantas ticheskiy-politiko.html.

Siddiqi, Asifa. 2008. Imagining the Cosmos: Utopians, Mystics, and the Popular Culture of Spaceflight in Revolutionary Russia. *Osiris* 23 (1): 260–288.

Skazki tridtsatogo veka. 1960. *Ural'skii sledopyt: Ezhemesiachnyi zhurnal* 1. Available at: http://uralstalker.com/uarch/us/1960/01/3/.

Slezkine, Yuri. 2017. *The House of Government, a saga of the Russian Revolution*. Princeton: Princeton University Press.

Stites, Richard. 1988. *Revolutionary Dreams: Utopian Vision and Experimental Life in the Russian Revolution*. New York: Oxford University Press.

Strugatsky, Arkady, and Boris Strugatsky. 1962. Zloumyshlenniki. *Znanie-sila* 2: 25–29.

———. 1965. *Ponedel'nik nachinaetsia v subbotu*. Moscow: Detskaia Literature.

Suslov, Mikhail. 2009. *Conservative Utopia in Late Imperial Russia*. PhD dissertation, Florence, European University Institute.

Suslov, Mikhail, and Per-Arne Bodin (eds.). 2019. *The Post-Soviet Politics of Utopia: Language, Fiction and Fantasy in Modern Russia*. London: I.B. Tauris.

Suvin, Darko. 1979. *Metamorphoses of Science Fiction: On the Poetics and History of a Literary Genre*. New Haven, MA: Yale University Press.

Ulam, Adam. 1976. *Ideologies and Illusions, Revolutionary Thought from Herzen to Solzhenitsyn*. Cambridge: Harvard University Press.

Vajl', P., and A. Genis. 1996. *60-e, mir sovetskogo cheloveka*. Moskva: Novoe literaturnoe obozrenie.

Volodikhin, Dmitry. 2014. *Poklonenie kul'ture: Stat'i o brat'iakh Strugatskikh*. Sevastopol': Shiko-Sevastopol'.

Walicki, Andrzej. 1975. *The Slavophile Controversy: History of a Conservative Utopia in Nineteenth-Century Russian Thought*. Oxford: Oxford University Press.

Young, George. 2012. *The Russian Cosmists: The Esoteric Futurism of Nikolai Fedorov and His Followers*. New York: Oxford University Press.

Lives: Meanings and Endings

Psychoanalysis

Edson Luiz André de Sousa

You have to live life to the limit, not according to each day but according to its depth. One does not have to do what comes next if one feels a greater affinity with that which happens later, at a remove, even in a remote distance. One may dream while others are saviors if these dreams are more real to oneself than reality and more necessary than bread. In a word: one ought to turn the most extreme possibility inside oneself into the measure for one's life, for our life is vast and can accommodate as much future as we are able to carry.

–*Rainer Maria Rilke.*[1]

INTRODUCTION

This short excerpt from the poet Rainer Maria Rilke is in line with some of the themes explored by Ernst Bloch in his monumental trilogy published in 1959, *The Principle of Hope*, a profound reflection on the role of utopia, its history, and its impact on several other fields of study. Some of the themes that Bloch examines in his work can be read in this beautiful passage by Rilke: the purpose of hope, the enigma of desire, the tension between the world of dreams and the one we call reality, the "not yet" as one of the essential categories of hope. Psychoanalysis, as a discipline, also arises in the flow of this utopian current, inasmuch as it introduces a device that attempts to open up a unique space for dreaming for each subject, spaces for the construction

E. L. A. de Sousa (✉)
Federal University of Rio Grande do Sul, Porto Alegre, Brazil

P. Marks et al. (eds.), *The Palgrave Handbook of Utopian and Dystopian Literatures*, https://doi.org/10.1007/978-3-030-88654-7_50

of new fictions of oneself that allow for an opening to other ways of life. Sigmund Freud, in proposing the concept of the unconscious at the end of the nineteenth century—developing, until his death in 1939, a theory that could account for this experience—revealed to humanity just how strange we are, the unknown that resides within us, in this way deposing from its position of authority and control over life the subject of the conscience. Freud (1964, 285) wrote in one of his texts that the ego "is not even master in its own house." The invention of the unconscious would be, according to the founder of psychoanalysis, the third great narcissistic blow to humanity after Copernicus and Charles Darwin.

Psychoanalysis was only possible within the current of a utopian school of thought insofar as the field developed a method where each subject could have the possibility to construct, through narrative, new fictions of life, new horizons of history. Psychoanalysis is fundamentally a language experiment where we have the opportunity to narrate not only what we imagine we have experienced, but most importantly to make way for what we would like to experience. By bringing to the fore the enigma of human desire, the subject has the opportunity to question their way of life, observe their repetitive compulsions, bringing to their lives a critical dimension that may even make way for other possibilities of being in the world. In other words, psychoanalysis can open up new principles of hope. This allows psychic suffering to be approached critically, as the identification of the cause of the subject's dissatisfaction implies a radical questioning of every choice made in the past as well as those that will be made in the future. Utopia is fundamentally a narrative experience dedicated to fiction, creation, fantasy and the ethics of desire.

The unconscious is a kind of utopian fountain in which we bathe, oftentimes drowning in its deep waters. Freud was radical in demonstrating the value of bridges of language in these dangerous and unknown currents. The method is remarkably simple: narrate the story of your pain to someone else, as freely as possible. Freud proposed the concept of free association as a method of therapeutic speaking, thereby demonstrating to the subject the outline of the fiction that they have built for their life. The experience of speaking allows each subject to redesign these narratives through language, consequently allowing for a shift in position in relation to their story. We can see here just how much psychoanalysis can open up spaces to revolt, to reinvent one's life, to create.

In a way, every single act of creation has a utopian dimension. Freud was interested not only in the individual suffering of his patients, but also deeply concerned with the social bond, mass movements, political drifts, war, religious fanaticism, racism, and many more themes related to group psychology. He wrote extensively on these themes in particular: *Totem and Taboo* (1913), *Group Psychology and the Analysis of the Ego* (1921), *The Future of an Illusion* (1927), *Civilization and Its Discontents* (1930), *Why War?* (1932, correspondence between Freud and Einstein on war), *Moses and Monotheism* (1939), among others.

Psychoanalysis sought to establish critical spaces in order to make possible the building of a culture that could not only awaken us from our slumber and from common sense, but also open a field of dreams, triggering the desire to build new ways of thinking and living. Freud demonstrated that our acts fundamentally depend on the horizon points that lie before us. Still, these points are not always visible, lying as they do in the realm of the ideal. Through his theory, Freud outlined an unprecedented geography of the human psyche, working to design another grammar for interpreting our actions. In this way, he revealed that there are undersides, discontinuities, and shadow zones to our lives. These shadows definitively opened up a scar in the romantic image of Enlightenment thinking, which could no longer satisfactorily explain the reasons behind our actions. It was necessary to offer another way of thinking, one that could account for the chasm that had opened up in each subject between thinking and speaking, speaking and doing, thinking and feeling. This new practice, founded by psychoanalysis, resembles the Baroque. The Baroque would introduce, permanently, the decentring of the subject in the realm of forms. The subject can no longer be represented by a perfect spherical shape as it had been for centuries. It was the circle that served as the basis for reading the movement of the stars. This was the case at least until Kepler demonstrated that the movement of the planets orbiting the sun did not follow a circular path but rather an elliptical one. This revelation shook the foundations of scientific and religious thinking of the time; Kepler would pay a high price for the truth that he had shared with the world. In a superb essay on the Baroque, Severo Sarduy (1991) argues that it was ultimately Kepler who revolutionized the way of thinking of the age and not necessarily Copernicus. The latter could more appropriately be considered a reformist: in spite of having removed the Earth from its central position, he did not renounce the perspective as the organizing structure. The function of utopias has always been to create these spaces of decentring, therefore interrupting the repetitive compulsions of history. As Emil Cioran reminds us in *History and Utopia*, "a society incapable of generating... a utopia is threatened with sclerosis and collapse" ([1960] 2015, 81).

The utopia that the psychoanalytic experience brings to the fore is a shared construction between the person narrating their lived experiences and another who listens—in other words, what activates the narrative fiction is the desire to relate a story. Walter Benjamin provides a fundamental reflection on this point in proposing a distinction between the concepts of *Erlebnis* (the lived experience) and *Erfahrung* (experience). The *Erlebnis* (lived experience) is not sufficient for the subject to be able to connect to what they have lived through, what they feel, what they think. Crucially, for this lived experience to be *Erfahrung* (experience), conditions need to exist for recounting and narrating what is being lived. It is ultimately necessary to create mental spaces, images, and words that subjectively validate each person's capacity for understanding the world. This is why the realm of fantasy can no longer be separated from what we call reality.

Utopia as a principle continues to be a current that flows against reality. Its meaning, contrary to what common sense would dictate, would not be a movement toward reality but mainly against it. Utopia is usually thought of as an illusion, a fantasy, a delirium, as empty plans. This notion foregrounds the classical present-future vector. Its horizon would always be the pursuit of becoming real. If we become trapped in this perspective such utopian forms lose their strength. As Roger Dadoun (2000) proposes, we can reverse the direction of the vector and consider utopia as a movement that goes from the future to the past. This is what Freud considers when he demonstrates, through his method, that our past is also constantly rebuilt by means of the narrative. It is not frozen in time, but instead alive and moving. This is how utopia could fulfil the function of the counterflow, disrupting our certainties, shaking the excessive normality that we ascribe to events. Utopia suspends the false destinies to which we subscribe as a way to anesthetize our most valuable asset: our responsibility toward life and tomorrow. In this sense, utopia is a kind of hole in the image that has often been wrongly understood as prescriptive, announcing ideal forms and ultimately the secret to shared happiness.

The force of utopian images lies precisely "outside of the image," hinting at that which we have not yet been able to imagine, that is, our unpaid debt to our imagination, as Fredric Jameson (1994) reminds us. Something about this not-place is intangible, which does not mean that evoking it will not always lead us back to attempts to name it. A striking example of this notion is subtly implied in Thomas More's *Utopia*: when Hythloday is asked where exactly the island is located, a cough from another listener obscures the answer.[2] Here More metaphorically establishes the iconoclastic side to his utopia. Utopia therefore opens up, through the act of writing, a possible space for this "outside the image." Its logical function is to illustrate the misuse of all images when they purport to present the object transparently, as "natural" and indisputable. Utopian discourse acts as caesura.

None of the great utopians sought to take the place of gods. Utopian texts are simply fiction that, through the power of the imagination, seeks to open a critical wound in the landscapes of our time. What these authors intended was to critically awaken their eras, thereby opening up new frontiers for the imagination and the sense of responsibility toward history. What Ernst Bloch called critical hope we see materialized in the Utopia of More, in Tommaso Campanella's *City of the Sun*, in Francis Bacon's *Atlantis*, and in so many other utopian places brought to existence in the authors' texts, in their islands of language. In other words, whenever we want to dream forward we have to know the basics of some of the operating principles of the social machine in order to better know how to dismantle it. To dismantle a gear, we need to remove pieces. In this sense, utopia is more about removing an excess of images and meaning, in the same way that in psychoanalytic interpretation the certainties of the subject are suspended, rather than prescribing new codes of conduct or plans for happiness. Taking psychoanalysis and utopia as a revelation of the truth is a kind of rejection of the commitment that each person has to their imagination. This means that denying the utopian text implies resigning ourselves to the texts along which lines we already live, bound in typical voluntary servitude.

Therein lies the catastrophe expressed by Walter Benjamin, who ties it to the experience of repetition: "That things are 'status quo' is the catastrophe" (2006, 184). We know just how much a thirst for power has transformed some "utopias" into cruel, authoritarian, and dogmatic machinery. The utopia of interest to us is not one that anticipates what should be, but rather that which we do not yet know and that we must invent. Fredric Jameson's discussion on the utopian text as revealing a kind of negative side to reality comes to mind. Utopia would be like pouring a little water into your hand and producing an ocean and then a shore, as set forth by the Argentine poet Juan Gelman (2004)[3]:

> do not pour water into your hand
> because it will turn into the ocean
> and then the shore

It is on this shore that we will build other frontiers for life, opening up new creative spaces. For Jameson, the value of utopia lies in what it reveals about what we *owe* history. In a way the utopian text could reveal the kind of frontiers that do not allow us to cross over. This is not a matter of heralding a dream that is absent, but mainly to express the failure of the "dream" that we cultivate. According to Jameson (1994, 75):

> [T]he vocation of Utopia lies in failure; in which its epistemological value lies in the walls it allows us to feel around out minds, the invisible limits it gives us to detect by sheerest induction,... the mud of the present age in which the winged Utopian shoes stick, imagining that to be the force of gravity itself. As Louis Marin taught us in his *Utopiques*, the Utopian text really does hold out for us the vivid lesson of what we cannot imagine: only it does so not by imagining it concretely but rather by way of the holes in the text that are our own incapacity to see beyond the epoch and its ideological closures.

Utopia therefore opposes the repetition compulsion in a similar vein to the psychoanalytic proposal which relies on the power of memory to disrupt the repetitive streams of the subject's history. As we know, these automatisms for repetition destroy creative spaces of desire.

All utopias put desire center stage. Roger Dadoun (2000, 32) even suggests that we can call this the desire for utopia, each term returning continuously to the other in a fundamentally inconclusive encounter. We know that desire is only revealed to the subject when it is acted upon. It is the act that is revealing of each person's position in life. By interpreting these acts, we can infer the subject in a particular scenario. By the same token, no utopia can do without a practice and a stance in terms of a statement and authorship. This is also the focal point of psychoanalysis. Utopia, or rather, the desire for utopia, needs to offer new metaphors. More than ever, we need poetic thinking which, once established, would affect real political action in every sense of the word. We know how much poetry revives language, courageously reaching the limits of expression, outlining with determination what is formless. As we have already mentioned, it produces a counter thinking. Paul Celan describes his experience with poetry as an effort to explore what he called the *Gegenwort* (counter-word), which simultaneously announces the word that is missing and the word that is yet to come. To a certain extent, psychoanalysis is similar to the poetic process in the sense that it intends to produce a noisy silence, because, as the Brazilian poet Manoel Ricardo de Lima (2004) remarks: "there is a period of silence that is often needed to work through some [of our] inner ambiguities."[4]

And what ambiguities could these be? One of the pillars of psychoanalysis is precisely to demonstrate how we, as speaking subjects, consist of images interwoven into a complex identity tapestry. The ego is fundamentally an image. It is therefore only by tearing through this tapestry of identities that some of us can untangle ourselves from these symptoms, which are nothing more than curdled feelings stemming from a history. The analytical act aims fundamentally to destabilize the certainties of the subject, attempting to make way for new significations and images that could arise from the discursive fabric. We are well aware that this opening is not made without resistance; it is not possible to reach a new position without a critical traversing through the story that formed us. This is the only way that we can dream of a future that is not merely a repetition, but a future that can actually make way for something entirely different. Karl Marx begins a letter to his father from Berlin, November 10, 1837, with this poignant reflection that summarizes in part what I have tried to address here:

Dear Father!

There are life-moments that, like border markers, stand before an expiring time while at the same time clearly pointing out a new direction.

In such transitional moments we feel ourselves compelled to observe the past and the future with eagle-eyes of thought, in order to attain consciousness of our actual position.

We are well aware that this is not a fixed position, as each event reshapes the map that forms us and, as Freud so elegantly demonstrated, placing the subject before the truth that lies at their foundation is no easy feat. Working in this territory entails addressing the resistances which constitute the intrinsic forces of this circuit. Indeed, for Freud the resistances that oftentimes materialize in the symptoms signal the existence of something with which we must make contact. Georges Bataille is very clear on this point: "In this way the avoidance of the truth ensures, in reciprocal fashion, a recognition of the truth". ([1967] 1988, 41)

Utopia and l'objet Petit a

The French psychoanalyst Jacques Lacan makes an important contribution to this topic in proposing the concept of the *"objet petit a*,"[5] which he defines as the object cause of desire. He first elaborates on this theme in a seminar on anxiety in 1962/1963 (Lacan 2014). This object escapes any attachment, any meaning, any definition. It thus confirms what Freud had already stressed: there is no natural object in the chemistry of our desires. Our desires are not instincts and every object of desire is the unique construction of the subject. This perspective is crucial in that it not only frees the subject, but simultaneously opens up the responsibility related to the choices to be made. The *objet petit a* thus introduces a sense of disarray as it exposes the fallacy of our belief in encountering the object of desire. We must consider this object as always falling away, as something that "resists any assimilation to the function of a signifier" (Lacan 2014, 174). The *objet petit a* therefore creates an opening in the discourse, constantly pointing out the site of the lack, the hole in the text, exactly as proposed by utopian discourses.

Conclusion

We conclude with two reflections that illustrate with precision the malaise that comprises the subject. The first is a passage from Freud, who helps us to detach utopian thinking from a simplistic concept of happiness. If the pleasure principle is, to a certain extent, our principle of hope (Ernst Bloch), we cannot derive from it any assurance of happiness. In Freud's words:

> As we see, what decides the purpose of life is simply the programme of the pleasure principle. This principle dominates the operation of the mental apparatus from the start. There can be no doubt about its efficacy, and yet its programme is at loggerheads with the whole world, with the macrocosm as much as with the microcosm. There is no possibility at all of its being carried through; all the regulations of the universe run counter to it. One feels inclined to say that the intention that man should be "happy" is not included in the plan of "Creation." (Freud [1930] 1961, 23)

The second passage is a reflection on utopia from Lacan, in an excerpt from the seminar given on 23 April 1969, *From an Other to the other*. In this seminar, Lacan's focus is on questioning the relationship between form and thought. In particular, he questions how a form can be given to what eludes thought. Lacan states that thinking wrestles with the norm and the transgression of the norm; he seeks a thought that would allow him to recover this transgressive force. Indeed, this is the utopianist's eternal quest: a *counter thinking*. According to Lacan:

It is here that the function of thinking can take on some sense by introducing the notion of freedom.[6] In a word, it is by *thinking about Utopia* that, as its name states, is a place that is nowhere, no place, it is in Utopia that thinking would be free to envisage a possible reform of the norm. This indeed is how in the history of thinking from Plato to Thomas More things have been presented. With regard to the norm, the real locus in which it is established, it is only in the field of Utopia that freedom of thought can be exercised. (Lacan [1968–1969], XVII, 5; emphasis added)

The most important function of utopia and psychoanalysis alike is to activate desire without ever showing the way forward. In this way it would have the purpose of activating our responsibility in building a story that calls for action and taking a stand when faced with life's challenges. It is precisely this sentiment that underpins the final verse of Rilke's "Archaic Torso of Apollo":

would not, from all the borders of itself,

burst like a star: for here there is no place

that does not see you. You must change your life.

NOTES

1. Rilke, *The Poet's Guide to Life: The Wisdom of Rilke*, 13–14.
2. See Marin, *Utopiques: jeux d'espaces*, 116.
3. Trans. Raquel Jones.
4. Lima, *Personal Correspondence*, trans. Raquel Jones.
5. This famous Lacanian phrase is, from Lacan's point of view, untranslatable, and Lacan preferred that it remain so. According to *Oxford Reference*, "Lacan always insisted that the term remain untranslated so as to give it an algebraic status in English, and for the most part this is respected. Literally, it might be rendered as the 'object (little) a', but this is still not completely right since the 'a' stands for autre (other), so strictly speaking it should be the 'object (little) o'."
6. Lacan is referring here to the transgressive force of thought.

REFERENCES

Barbanti, Roberto (ed.). 2000. *L'art au XXe siècle et l'utopie*. Paris: L'Harmattan.
Bataille, Georges. [1967] 1988. *The Accursed Share: An Essay on General Economy*, trans. Robert Hurley. New York: Zone Books.
Benjamin, Walter. 2006. *Walter Benjamin: Selected Writings, Volume 4: 1938–1940*, trans. H. Eiland and M.W. Jennings. Cambridge, MA; London: Harvard University Press.
Cioran, Emil. 2015. *History and Utopia*, trans. Richard Howard. New York: Arcade.

Dadoun, Roger. 2000. Utopie: l'émouvante rationalité de l'inconscient. In *L'art au XXe. Siècle et l'utopie*, ed. Roberto Barbanti. Paris: L'Harmattan.

Freud, Sigmund. [1930] 1961. *Civilization and Its Discontents*, trans. James Strachey. New York: W. W. Norton.

———. 1964. *New Introductory Lectures on Psychoanalysis*, ed. James Strachey. London: Hogarth.

Gelman, Juan. 2004. A mão. In *Isso*. Brasília: Editora da UnB.

Jameson, Fredric. 1994. *The Seeds of Time*. New York: Columbia University Press.

Lacan, Jacques. 1968–1969. *The Seminar of Jacques Lacan: Book XVI: From an Other to the Other: 1968–1969*, trans. Cormac Gallagher. Retrieved from: http://hdl.han dle.net/10788/165. Accessed 17 June 2021.

———. 2014. *Anxiety: The Seminar of Jacques Lacan: Book X*, trans. A.R. Price. Malden; Cambridge: Polity Press.

Lima, Manoel Ricardo. 2004. *Personal Correspondence*, Unpublished.

Marin, Louis. 1973. *Utopiques: jeux d'espaces*. Paris: Les Éditions de Minuit.

Marx, Karl. 1837. *Letter from Marx to His Father*, trans. Paul M. Schafer. https://www.marxists.org/archive/marx/works/1837-pre/letters/letter-to-father.pdf. Accessed 17 June 2021.

Oxford Reference. https://www.oxfordreference.com/view/10.1093/oi/authority 20110803100243702. Accessed 17 June 2021.

Rilke, Rainer Maria. 2007. *The Poet's Guide to Life: The Wisdom of Rilke*, trans. Ulrich Baer. New York: Random House.

———. *Archaic Torso of Apollo*. https://poets.org/poem/archaic-torso-apollo. Accessed 15 June 2021.

Sarduy, Severo. 1991. *Barroco*. Paris: Gallimard.

Education

Darren Webb

INTRODUCTION

Education is a key utopian category. Not only is it central to some of the most powerful articulations of utopian method and politics—most notably "the education of desire" (Abensour)—but it is also the principal institution within many visions of a utopian commonwealth. Education has two Latin roots (*educere* or "to lead out" and *educare* or "to mould") and these are both at play (and sometimes in conflict) in the relationship between education and utopia. The present chapter explores this relationship from three broad and contrasting perspectives. The first discusses the nature and role of schooling within classical utopian texts; the second explores education as a mechanism for opening up utopian possibilities within the present; and the third considers the utopian dynamics of deschooling and alternative educational spaces.

The educational ideas found within utopian literature vary considerably in both depth and detail. William Morris's *News from Nowhere* (1890) says almost nothing about "education" other than that learning in this epoch of rest occurs informally, through observation and imitation, without the mediation of schools or any other institutions (Morris 1995, 33–34). In Tommaso Campanella's *City of the Sun* (1602) and Johann Valentin Andreae's *Christianopolis* (1619), on the other hand, children are handed over to state boarding schools at an early age to undertake a systematic and tightly

D. Webb (✉)
University of Sheffield, Sheffield, UK

P. Marks et al. (eds.), *The Palgrave Handbook of Utopian and Dystopian Literatures*, https://doi.org/10.1007/978-3-030-88654-7_51

prescribed curriculum, all under the governance of a single director of education, designed to produce virtuous citizens devoted to the common good.
One might differentiate within the utopian tradition between visions in which
education serves to draw out (*educere*) human potentialities—epitomized,
perhaps, by the ideas of Charles Fourier—and those in which education
serves to mould (*educare*) human character to render it fit for life in utopian
society—one thinks here, for example, of Robert Owen (Leopold 2011).

Scholarly focus on the educational ideas of utopian writers seems to have
fallen out of favor. In the 1960s one found book-length surveys of utopian
educational theory (Fisher 1963; Ozmon 1969) together with detailed studies
of the educational ideas of specific utopians (Harrison 1969; Zeldin 1969).
This aspect of the utopian tradition receives less attention today. This is partly
because contemporary utopianism is less attached to "education" conceived
as a national system of state-controlled institutions cultivating good citizens
and is more inclined to focus on the creation of alternative educational spaces
or the processes of learning embedded within everyday life. It is also because
energies have shifted from the literary to the political sphere, away from the
imaginative reconstitution of societies within which educational structures play
a principal role and toward the consideration of pedagogical strategies within,
against and beyond education-as-such.

SCHOOLING, VIRTUE AND UTOPIA

Reading the classic Renaissance utopias today is an interesting exercise. In spite
of often profound differences in political and religious outlook, there were
commonalities when it came to the structure and functioning of education in
More's *Utopia* (1516), Campanella's *City of the Sun* (1602) and Andreae's
Christianopolis (1619). In terms of formal structure, much is recognizable
today. The Renaissance utopians envisaged universal compulsory education as
a state-controlled school system directed by a department within government
and divided into elementary, secondary and tertiary levels. Within schools, one
found uniform dress, a standardized curriculum, learning organized around
age groups, extrinsic systems of rewards, mechanisms of monitoring and
surveillance and a focus on behavior management. Learning was supplemented
by physical education to train both body and mind and time was set aside for
play. Alongside formal schooling, the citizens of utopia engaged in processes
of lifelong learning (avid reading, attending public lectures, learning from
audio-visual displays). Within these utopian commonweals there existed a
professional strata of educators devoted to studying and teaching, selected on
the basis of their aptitude for learning.[1]

More interesting, perhaps, than the structure of schooling in these early
utopian texts were its two key functions. The first of these is particularly interesting given widespread dissatisfaction among educators in the global North
with the ways in which education is increasingly being tied to economic
concerns (Ball 2007).[2] The focus on employability, for example, is often

regarded as a crass economistic distortion of the true purpose of education, which is to enhance human understanding and promote human flourishing (Collini 2012). Tying education to considerations of individual future employment and national economic productivity was, however, an integral feature of utopian visions from the very outset. In both *City of the Sun* and *Christianopolis*, a key function of the educative process was the identification at an early age, through observation of manual training, of each child's natural occupational "inclination" (Andreae 1916, 210; Campanella 1981, 23). There was no issue at all with subordinating education to the economic needs of society. To serve the twin interests of individual fulfilment *and* economic productivity, children were assigned at school, at the very earliest age, a role in the division of labor to which they were best suited and for which they were duly trained.

The second function of schooling was more significant still. This was moral/virtue/character education. As More said of the Utopians, "they use with very great endeavour and diligence to put into the heads of their children, whiles they be yet tender and pliant, good opinions and profitable for the conservation of their weal-public" (1994, 125). Virtuous citizens with good character were essential to the healthy functioning of Utopia, and moral training from the early years—when children were still pliable—was the best means of cultivating good character and countering the pull of vices such as pride. More was, of course, a close friend of Erasmus and the influence of Erasmian humanism can be found not only in More but also in Campanella and Andreae. For Erasmus, moral education and the teaching of true virtue were necessary for cultivating human potential and promoting social harmony (Parrish 2010). This last point was crucial. More emphasized that teaching "virtue and good manners" is "wondrous profitable to the defence and maintenance of the state of the commonwealth" (1994, 125) and Andreae stressed that cultivating "the best and most chaste morals" is essential "to preserve the safety of the republic" (1916, 187, 210).[3]

In contemporary sociological terms, these two functions of schooling—cultivating the virtues, manners, character and modes of behavior needed to maintain the harmonious health of society and allocating individuals to the role in the social division of labor to which they are best suited—would be termed socialization and stratification. From a simple functionalist perspective, these are indeed the two key roles played by education in society (Davis and Moore 1945; Durkheim 1956). Seen from this perspective, the early utopians got it right—they knew what education was for. Campanella says at one point that "it is necessary first of all to look at the life of the whole and to then look at that of the parts" (1981, 45). Durkheim would have agreed entirely, asking how the life of the whole body of society can best be served by that part of it called education.

Bemoaning the loss of such a holistic approach to education, and drawing inspiration from Erasmian humanism and More's *Utopia*, David Parrish calls for "an education policy which seeks more aggressively to cultivate from the

earliest childhood the virtues necessary for citizenship and for individual flourishing within a good society" (2010, 602). This takes us away, then, from
considerations of the role of education within the best state of a commonwealth and toward an exploration of the *utopian potentiality* of education
within the existing order of things.

Schooling, Reproduction and Dystopia

Basing educational reform within contemporary society on the structures of
educational provision found within utopian systems of the past is fraught
with danger. Education cannot be abstracted from the wider social and
economic relations in which it is embedded and of which it is expressive. The
utopias of More, Campanella and Andreae were communist societies characterized by common ownership, the abolition of wage labor, production for
communal use and distribution according to need. The systems of education embedded within these utopias served to conserve, maintain and preserve
existing economic, social and political relations. This is, as Durkheim tells us,
the functional role of state-maintained education: to reproduce the society of
which it is part (1956, 123).

Virtue education, when transposed onto societies characterized by private
ownership, wage labor and commodity production, will serve merely to
reproduce existing relations of power, dominance, marginalization and minori-
tization. For evidence, one need only ask "whose virtues?" and then look
at the ways in which "Fundamental British Values" are being cultivated in
the UK (Crawford 2017). Similarly, while education for employability was
central to early utopian designs, this serves a more insidious function in a
society characterized by a growing surplus population. Here character education assumes importance in forming subjectivities able to endure patiently and
with "resilience" as they struggle to sell their labor power and find a foothold
amidst increasingly austere and precarious conditions (Webb 2019).

Contemporary systems of education are, in fact, increasingly characterized
as *dystopic*. In *Dystopia and Education* (Heybach and Sheffield 2013), a succession of writers—with Orwell's *Nineteen Eighty-Four* serving as a common
analytical frame—trace what they see as the dystopian aspects of schooling in
the Anglophone world: constricted curricula, mechanized learning, standardized high-stakes assessments, invasive systems of surveillance and discipline,
institutionalized bullying, the dehumanization of educational interactions,
the stifling of emotional expression and the stunting of children's potential
for human flourishing, all operating within physical environments that often
resemble crumbling prisons. One of the contributors concludes that "the
beauty of possibility has been taken from school" (Freedman 2013, 10).

While conceding its dystopian nature, David Bell characterizes the present
juncture as a *critical* dystopia, "a configuration of place (re)produced through
relations of domination" but "in which utopian modes of resistance have not
been entirely foreclosed" (2017, 10, 66). For Bell, radical experiments in

education constitute one of the utopian modes of resistance which "seek to realize alternative ways of organizing life" (66). In fact, utopian experiments in education offer a two-pronged attack. On the one hand, they seek to re-vision the common school, retrieving collective memories of past radical educational practice (Hope 2019) and offering detailed proposals for the schools of the future (e.g. Fielding and Moss 2011; Robinson and Aronica 2016). On the other, they offer strategies for working within mainstream educational institutions in order to help realize these visions. The US teacher-led movement Rethinking Schools, for example, strives to transform classrooms into "places of hope, where students and teachers gain glimpses of the kind of society we could live in and where students learn the academic and critical skills needed to make that vision a reality" (Rethinking Schools 2017). Two complementary utopian projects are thus at work: the project of *imaginatively* reconstituting the structure of schooling and the formation of utopian subjectivities capable of *materially* transforming both schooling and society.

Utopian Pedagogy

The first of these projects—re-visioning the common, public, state-maintained school as a *singular* institution—faces certain difficulties (Webb 2016). How does one abstract "schooling" from the social totality and isolate it as the site for the operation of the utopian imagination? The results will tend toward recuperated visions barely discernible from the present (Halpin 2003) or will elide questions of how the "utopian" school articulates with a state-maintained education sector complicit in reproducing inequalities, exclusion and marginalization (Fielding and Moss 2011). Ahlberg and Brighouse (2014) remark that any utopian design confined to a specific sector or institution will be limited in its effect on the overall social structure and relations of power. Like others (e.g. Papastephanou 2009), they argue that any utopian vision for education needs to be embedded within a wider vision of the social totality.

The second project—the project of utopian pedagogy—attempts to forge a link between vision and reality. In answer to the age-old question of "can education change society?" Michael Apple says "it depends. And it depends on a lot of hard and continued efforts by many people" (Apple 2013, 2). The figure of Paulo Freire looms large here. Not only did he coin the term "utopian pedagogy" (Freire 1972a) but his seminal *Pedagogy of the Oppressed* (Freire 1972b) is the touchstone for those engaged in the concerted utopian efforts to which Apple refers (Kirylo 2020). Freire's educational praxis has given rise to an industry of exegesis and analysis which space precludes from summarizing here (see Webb 2012). The important thing to stress is that Freirean pedagogy, and its refraction through the critical lens of feminist educators such as bell hooks and Antonia Darder (hooks 1994; Darder 2001), locates transgressive and transformative utopian possibilities within the sphere of education even in its current dystopic state (Giroux 2020).

In very broad terms, utopian pedagogy is a counter-hegemonic project that strives to shatter contemporary common sense and challenge the ideology of "there is no alternative." It is concerned with creating spaces for the exploration of desires, longings and hopes, and for drawing out utopian possibilities within concrete experience. It is a pedagogy of transformative hope; a pedagogy aimed at liberating the imagination as to the possibilities for systemic change. Utopian pedagogy is underpinned by a profound confidence in the capacity of human beings to construct (both imaginatively and materially) new ways of organizing life. It seeks to cultivate an awareness that human beings are self-organizing and self-determining historical agents and a confident belief in the transformative power of collective action (Webb 2013).

The (re)education of desire is one of the fundamental aims of utopian pedagogy (Papastephanou 2009). Some of the seminal texts in the field define utopia in terms of desire—"the desire for a better way of being" in Levitas' oft-cited words (Levitas 1990, 8)—and the role of utopian pedagogy is "to teach desire to desire, to desire better, to desire more, and above all to desire in a different way," to borrow Abensour's famous characterization of William Morris' project (Thompson 1977, 791). Not content merely with stimulating the desire *for* a new society, utopian pedagogy—utopia as a pedagogical project—is concerned with developing subjects equipped to *create* and *inhabit* this new world. The overall aim is nothing less than "human emancipation" through "a transformation in the ways in which subjectivities are created and desires are produced" (Giroux 2014, 81).

A number of texts explore the theory and practice of utopian pedagogy from varying political, disciplinary and national perspectives (e.g. Coté, Day and de Peuter 2007; Hammond 2017; Rodriguez 2015; Rodriguez and Magill 2017; Webb 2017a). In terms of daily classroom practice, Rethinking Schools publishes a vast array of resources designed *by* teachers *for* teachers seeking to work within, against and beyond: *within* the constraints of managerial structures and prescribed curricula but *against* the oppressive, alienating, degrading, exploitative social system within which education is embedded and pointing *beyond* society-as-it-is toward society as-it-could-be.[4] An important point to note—and here we link back to the history of utopian literature and forward toward a different utopian approach—is that an effective utopian pedagogy cannot operate within the confines of formal education alone (Webb 2017a, 2018).[5]

DE-SCHOOLING, ANARCHISM AND PREFIGURATION

The discussion thus far has focused primarily on education understood as a system of schooling funded by the state—its structure and function within classical utopian literature and the possibilities of a utopian pedagogy operating within the dystopian realities of the sector today. Of course, schools and colleges are not society's only educational spaces; trade unions, political parties, community groups and faith organizations are all important educational institutions. Growing attention too is being paid to "public pedagogy" (the ways in which film, literature, museums, galleries, art, the media and cultural practices more generally perform key pedagogical functions) and to "social movement learning" (the informal learning that takes place through movement participation and in particular the counter-hegemonic understandings that emerge as actors learn in and through struggle) (Choudry 2015; Sandlin et al. 2010). Any effective utopian pedagogy needs to operate in, through and across all these different educational sites. The focus of this section of the chapter, however, is on schooling *beyond* the remit of the state and on *de*-schooling as a utopian project.

Schools outside and beyond the sphere of the state have a history long pre-dating state provision and have regularly served as sites for utopian experimentation. Robert Owen's school at New Lanark, the Institute for the Formation of Character (established 1816), was presented as the platform for engineering a race of "superior beings" fit to create and inhabit the "new moral world" (Owen 1970, 146). Given the perfect plasticity of children, Owen declared, with the correct educational methods they could be "moulded" to the shape of "any human character" (110). All it took was for a man such as he to understand the significance of this truth and to put it into practice. A century later in Barcelona, Francisco Ferrer founded the *Escuela Moderna* (established 1901), a school explicitly aimed at prefiguring a new world to come, realizing in its practices alternative ways of being, relating and learning (Bray and Haworth 2019; Suissa 2006, 78–82). Ferrer's example has subsequently inspired countless anarchist free schools, instances of what Ruth Kinna (2016) terms here-and-now utopianism.

Freed from the restrictions and controls imposed by public funding regimes, anarchist free schools are heralded as sites for the education of desire and the formation of utopian subjectivities. Shantz (2012) sees them as liminal spaces which offer glimpses of the new world in the shell of the old. One interesting feature of anarchist free schools, and a theme which runs through most of this chapter, is the focus on moral education. As Suissa puts it, "an implicit or explicit form of moral education underpins all aspects of the anarchist educational process and curriculum" (2006, 81). Anarchist schooling seeks to promote a particular set of values (co-operation, solidarity, mutual aid, care, autonomy) which enable the schools to act, here and now, as microcosms of the new society (Shantz 2012; Suissa 2001). Indeed, A.S. Neil's Summerhill school—a school that has attained almost legendary status as a utopian space that makes it possible for children to find themselves, to realize the kind of person they were becoming (Cooper 2014)—has been widely criticized for its laissez-faire pedagogy and *lack* of moral directiveness (e.g. Mueller 2012; Suissa 2006).

Approaching the question of education and utopia from a slightly different angle, Ivan Illich (1970) took issue with those who located emancipatory hope in the institution of the school. Rather than establishing *alternative* schools, the key to a here-and-now utopianism for Illich lay in *de*-schooling society. Offering a dystopian reading of schooling as a system of servitude, Illich envisaged a society in which learning and teaching took place without schools or teachers as both children and adults learnt casually, incidentally, informally, in the workplace and through participation in all spheres of community life, or purposefully, with intent, through a network of learning exchanges. Channelling the messianic spirit of the nineteenth-century utopian socialists, Illich proclaimed an educational revolution that would free humanity from the enslavement in which schooling places it and facilitate the rebirth of Epimethean Man.

In fact, Illich's ideas have a long history, stretching at least as far back as Fourier. In what he termed "associative education," Fourier tells us that there would be no schools or teachers (Fourier 1971, 74). Each individual's manifold dispositions would freely develop through learning taking place in the wider community—in the orchards, the gardens, the workshops and through self-motivated book-learning and the exchange of ideas. This Fourierist vision has had widespread influence, not only on Illich but also on Morris's description of education in *News from Nowhere* (1890), on John Dewey's brief utopian excursus on education (1933), on Marge Piercy's vision of Mattapoisett in *Woman on the Edge of Time* (1976) and on David Harvey's depiction of education in *Edilia* (2000). As Dewey put it: "The most utopian thing in Utopia is that there are no schools" (1933).

CONCLUSION

The relationship between education and utopia is a dialectical one. The radical transformation of society requires a radically transformed educational practice but a radically transformed educational practice requires a radically transformed society. This presents certain problems but also highlights two significant points. The first is that any utopian vision of "education" must be embedded within a vision of an imaginatively reconstituted social totality. The second is that the utopian potentiality of educational practice depends on the extent to which it is linked to wider social and political struggles. A key question, of course, to paraphrase Marx, is who is to educate the educator? We cannot (surely) appeal to a Utopos figure to establish the best state of a commonwealth and an education system befitting it. The dialectic of education and utopia must be a collective process. It must also be a dialectic of both/and: working both within schools and against schools, both within the state and beyond it.

Utopian and dystopian literature has an invaluable pedagogical role to play in the project of transformative education. Critical dystopias serve as a forewarning underpinned by critical hope, extrapolating from society's darkest tendencies (Baccolini and Moylan 2003). Utopian visions inspire, mobilize and give direction to struggle. They provide a critical viewpoint from which the inadequacies of the present become starkly visible. They call into question the existing order of things and render the present mutable and open to change. They liberate the imagination and make it clear that alternatives can be thought of and fought for. They provide a goal and a spur to action and act as a catalyst for change in a way that social criticism on its own cannot. They are powerful pedagogical tools (Webb 2017b).

By way of conclusion, and returning to its double Latin roots, I quote Papastephanou's suggestion that:

> To cast education in a transformative rather than apologetic-reproductive role regarding social life we may need to synchronize educare and educere. Possibly, as educere, education can bring out precisely what educare in its modern historical specification has moulded us to overlook: that we are, at least anthropologically, free and able to demand the impossible. (2014, 14)

NOTES

1. One notable feature of the classical utopias, which resonates powerfully still, is the profound disjuncture between nominal equality of opportunity for men and women founded on equal access to compulsory education and the subjugation of women within patriarchal economic, social and political structures. Although women could in theory attain the highest offices in these utopias, few in fact did and the primary role of women was childbirth and cooking. Within Campanella's eugenic mating regime, for example, a woman who, after having been "mated" with several men, was unable to conceive, was "made available for communal use."

2. I make reference here to the global North because I am acutely aware of the whiteness of the literature discussed in the chapter together with its focus on the western utopian tradition and (largely) on education as experienced in the global North.

3. Campanella lists the virtues to be cultivated in children as, *inter alia*, generosity, magnanimity, chastity, fortitude, justice, diligence, truth, beneficence, gratitude and compassion (1981, 22). Within these utopias one can see the tense interplay of both educere *and* educare—drawing out each individual's particular inclinations while *also* moulding them with good character and virtue. The primary function of education, however, was the preservation of the state.

4. For the full list of publications, see www.rethinkingschools.org. As a concrete example, Cervantes-Soon (2017) offers a powerful account of the experiences of working-class girls in Preparatoria Altavista, a school in Cuidad Juárez utilising Freirean pedagogy with truly transformative effects.

5. Savannah Shange (2019) offers an important corrective to the exalted claims sometimes made on behalf of "teachers as transformative intellectuals" (a phrase coined by Giroux 1985, which often serves as Freirean pedagogy's rallying cry), tracing the carceral logics at play in even the most well-intentioned utopian endeavours of radical educators working in progressive schools.

REFERENCES

Abensour, Miguel. 2017. *Utopia from Thomas More to Walter Benjamin.* Univocal Publishing.

Ahlberg, J., and H. Brighouse. 2014. Education: Not a Real Utopian Design. *Politics and Society* 42 (1): 51–72.

Andreae, J.V. 1916. *Christianopolis.* New York: Oxford University Press.

Apple, M. 2013. *Can Education Change Society?* Abingdon: Routledge.

Baccolini, R., and T. Moylan (eds.). 2003. *Dark Horizons: Science Fiction and the Dystopian Imagination.* London: Routledge.

Ball, S. 2007. *Education plc.* Abingdon, Oxon: Routledge.

Bell, D. 2017. *Rethinking Utopia: Place, Power, Affect.* New York: Routledge.

Bray, M., and R. Haworth (eds.). 2019. *Anarchist Education and the Modern School.* Oakland, CA: PM Press.

Campanella, T. 1981. *City of the Sun.* London: Journeyman Press.

Cervantes-Soon, C. 2017. *Juárez Girls Rising: Transformative Education in Times of Dystopia.* London: University of Minnesota Press.

Choudry, A. 2015. *Learning Activism.* Toronto: University of Toronto Press.

Collini, S. 2012. *What Are Universities For?* London: Penguin.

Cooper, D. 2014. *Everyday Utopias: The Conceptual Life of Promising Places.* London: Duke University Press.

Coté, M., R. Day, and G. de Peuter (eds.). 2007. *Utopian Pedagogy: Radical Experiments Against Neoliberal Globalization.* Toronto: University of Toronto Press.

Crawford, C. 2017. Promoting 'Fundamental British Values' in Schools: A Critical Race Perspective. *Curriculum Perspectives* 37 (2): 197–204.

Darder, A. 2001. *Reinventing Paulo Freire: A Pedagogy of Love.* Boulder, CO: Westview.

Davis, K., and W. Moore. 1945. Some Principles of Stratification. *American Sociological Review* 10: 242–249.

Dewey, J. 1933. Dewey Outlines Utopian Schools. *New York Times,* April 23 1933. Sec. 4:7, cols. 3–5.

Durkheim, E. 1956. *Education and Sociology.* New York: Free Press.

Fielding, M., and P. Moss. 2011. *Radical Education and the Common School.* London: Routledge.

Fisher, R.T. 1963. *Classical Utopian Theories of Education.* New York: Bookman Associates.

Fourier, C. 1971. *Design for Utopia: Selected Writings of Charles Fourier.* New York: Schocken Books.

Freedman, K. 2013. An Aesthetic of Horror in Education: Schools as Dystopian Environments. In *Dystopia and Education*, ed. J. Heybach and E. Sheffield, 3–14. Charlotte, NC: IAP.

Freire, P. 1972a. *Cultural Action for Freedom*. Harmondsworth: Penguin.

———. 1972b. *Pedagogy of the Oppressed*. Harmondsworth: Penguin.

Giroux, H. 1985. Teachers as Transformative Intellectuals. *Social Education* 49 (5): 376–379.

———. 2014. *The Violence of Organized Forgetting: Thinking Beyond America's Disimagination Machine*. San Francisco: City Lights Books.

———. 2020. *On Critical Pedagogy*. London: Bloomsbury.

Halpin, D. 2003. *Hope and Education: The Role of the Utopian Imagination*. London: RoutledgeFalmer.

Hammond, C. 2017. *Hope, Utopia and Creativity in Higher Education*. London: Bloomsbury.

Harrison, J.F.C. 1969. *Utopianism and Education: Robert Owen and the Owenites*. New York: Teachers College Press.

Harvey, D. 2000. *Spaces of Hope*. Edinburgh: Edinburgh University Press.

Heybach, J., and E. Sheffield (eds.). 2013. *Dystopia and Education*. Charlotte, NC: IAP.

hooks, b. 1994. *Teaching to Transgress*. London: Routledge.

Hope, M. 2019. *Reclaiming Freedom in Education*. London: Routledge.

Illich, I. 1970. *Deschooling Society*. London: Marion Boyars.

Kinna, R. 2016. Utopianism and Prefiguration. In *Political Uses of Utopia*, ed. S. Chrostowska and J. Ingram, 198–215. New York: Columbia University Press.

Kirylo, J. (ed.). 2020. *Reinventing Pedagogy of the Oppressed*. London: Bloomsbury.

Leopold, D. 2011. Education and Utopia: Robert Owen and Charles Fourier. *Oxford Review of Education* 37 (5): 619–635. https://doi.org/10.1080/03054985.2011.621679.

Levitas, R. 1990. *The Concept of Utopia*. London: Allen Lane.

More, T. 1994. *Utopia*. London: J. M. Dent.

Morris, W. 1995. *News From Nowhere*. Cambridge: Cambridge University Press.

Mueller, J. 2012. Anarchism, the State, and the Role of Education. In *Anarchist Pedagogies*, ed. R. Haworth, 14–31. Oakland, CA: PM Press.

Owen, R. 1970. *A New View of Society*. Harmondsworth: Penguin.

Ozmon, H. 1969. *Utopias and Education*. Minneapolis: Burgess.

Papastephanou, M. 2009. *Educated Fear and Educated Hope*. Rotterdam: Sense Publishers.

———. 2013. Utopian Education and Anti-Utopian Anthropology. *International Education Studies* 6 (2): 22–32.

———. 2014. To Mould or to Bring Out? Human Nature, Anthropology and Educational Utopianism. *Ethics and Education* 9 (2): 157–175.

Parrish, J. 2010. Education, Erasmian Humanism and More's *Utopia*. *Oxford Review of Education* 36 (5): 589–605.

Piercy, M. 1976. *Woman on the Edge of Time*. New York: Alfred Knopf.

Rethinking Schools. 2017. *About Rethinking Schools*. www.rethinkingschools.org/about/index.shtml. Accessed 1 September 2017.

Robinson, K., and L. Aronica. 2016. *Creative Schools: Revolutionizing Education from the Ground Up*. London: Penguin.

Rodriguez, E. (ed.). 2015. *Pedagogies and Curriculums To (Re)imagine Public Education: Transnational Tales of Hope and Resistance.* Singapore: Springer.

Rodriguez, A., and K. McGill (eds.). 2017. *Imagining Education: Beyond the Logic of Global Neoliberal Capitalism.* Charlotte, NC: IAP.

Sandlin, J., B. Schultz, and J. Burdick (eds.). 2010. *Handbook of Public Pedagogy.* Abingdon: Routledge.

Shange, S. 2019. *Progressive Dystopia: Abolition, Antiblackness, and Schooling in San Francisco.* London: Duke University Press.

Shantz, J. 2012. Spaces of Learning: The Anarchist Free Skool. In *Anarchist Pedagogies*, ed. R. Haworth, 122–144. Oakland, CA: PM Press.

Suissa, J. 2001. Anarchism, Utopias and Philosophy of Education. *Journal of Philosophy of Education* 35 (4): 627–646.

———. 2006. *Anarchism and Education.* Abingdon: Routledge.

Thompson, E.P. 1977. *William Morris: Romantic to Revolutionary.* London: Merlin Press.

Webb, D. 2012. Process, Orientation, and System: The Pedagogical Operation of Utopia in the Work of Paulo Freire. *Educational Theory* 62 (5): 593–608.

———. 2013. Pedagogies of Hope. *Studies in the Philosophy of Education* 32 (4): 397–414. https://doi.org/10.1007/s11217-012-9336-1.

———. 2016. Educational Studies and the Domestication of Utopia. *British Journal of Educational Studies* 64 (4): 431–448.

———. 2017a. Educational Archaeology and the Practice of Utopian Pedagogy. *Pedagogy, Culture & Society* 25 (4): 551–566.

———. 2017b. Utopia in Sheffield? We Have to Start Somewhere. *openDemocracy,* June 28. https://www.opendemocracy.net/en/transformation/utopia-in-sheffield-we-have-to-start-somewhere/.

———. 2018. Bolt-Holes and Breathing Spaces in the System: On Forms of Academic Resistance (or, Can the University Be a Site of Utopian Possibility?). *Review of Education, Pedagogy and Cultural Studies* 40 (2): 96–118.

———. 2019. Education and the Construction of Hope. In *Theories of Hope*, ed. R. Green, 131–154. Lanham, MD: Lexington.

Zeldin, D. 1969. *The Educational Ideas of Charles Fourier.* London: Frank Cass.

Religion

José Eduardo Franco

Introduction

The emergence of the religious idea and its underlying religious feeling results from a perception of the human environment in a given space and time as imperfect, fragile, and in need of harmony. It is seen as a primordial downfall or loss of paradise, an expulsion, a sin that has broken the harmony between God, Nature and mankind. The fall from a perfect world, from an absolute communion with the divine, creates a world of pain, drama, frailty and incompleteness. The history of Culture only truly begins with the invention of mythical narratives about the origins of humanity, after a process of expulsion from a paradise or a perfect initial state, both idyllic and divine. This initial state is similar to the maternal womb, where everything is provided without effort, without need of transforming any conditions. In this early stage there is perfect symbiosis, an ideal equilibrium; therefore, there is only nature. Culture is "born" through the process of making the land habitable and hospitable. It is what makes a human fully human, marking the constant struggle for recovering the lost paradise. This suggests a particular sense of utopia, resembling a mythical or archetypal model. Culture is all the creative and transforming action that man adds to nature.

This notion of Culture allows us to understand the creative and transformative sense of the founding and transforming dynamics of human history, as being marked by a chain of expulsions. The maternal womb metaphor is a

J. E. Franco (✉)
Aberta University, Lisbon, Portugal

P. Marks et al. (eds.), *The Palgrave Handbook of Utopian and Dystopian Literatures*, https://doi.org/10.1007/978-3-030-88654-7_52

good one, as it also places the biological phases of human life within a chain of expulsions marking the history of human cultures and civilizations. That is, life in the maternal womb would metaphorically represent paradise, the first primordial phase of non-culture and nature. Culture begins with the expulsion of the human baby from the maternal womb and its process of adaptation to the human world during childhood, which then follows an actual chain of expulsions; from childhood to adolescence and youth, from youth into adult working life, with family and social responsibilities, from adult life to old age, with retirement and facing the frailties arising from physical decay. The last experience of expulsion is death, a great and mysterious passage, of eternity or metempsychosis for believers, or nothing for non-believers in life beyond the grave.

Similarly, the succession of empires, civilizations, settlements and migrations imply complex chains of expulsions, whether they are hetero-expulsions or self-expulsions, and always carry the displacement of a comfort space to some other reality. This is especially evident in the migratory movements that have always marked human history. It is said to have happened with the archetypal migrations narrated in the first book of the Bible, when Patriarch Abraham is invited by God to leave his land and begins a long migration with his descendants toward the Promised Land, where he would establish a new religion and the basis of new civilizations. It is also the case now with contemporary migration, whether to escape poverty and to seek a better life or to find peace away from war.

This displacement, often marked by violence, typically inspires a process of metamorphosis or cultural recreation, either by substitution and/or symbiosis leading to acculturation through cultural exchanges and mutual influences. This can result in inculturation, that is, a hybrid blend of cultures that leads to the formation of new ones. If this notion of culture and cultural formation necessarily implies an experience of violence, it also implies the concept of hospitality, even though it is an artificial construct. Only when the conditions for hospitality are realized does the highest, even sacred, function of culture come to pass.

In short, there is always a utopian drive for a "promised land" at the end of the expulsion. Indeed, as Thomas de Koninck concludes in his book on the problem of Culture:

> we are made of the same matter as dreams, and our small life is shrouded in slumber. A total awakening would probably kill us. But a progressive awakening allows us to live and give meaning to life, which is the meaning of culture. (Koninck 2003: 159)

Here we find another level above the material dimension resulting from the experience of expulsion, the quest for the meaning of existence as hospitality, in the deepest sense, where the genesis of culture is intimately associated with a utopian appeal. This chapter traces conceptual and textual links between religion in the broad sense (incorporating a sense of the sacred and notions of hospitality) and the history of utopian writing.

SACRED PLACE: MYTH AND UTOPIA

Ultimately, human culture arises through the distinction between the sacred and the profane. Art, science and wisdom are developed from the awareness that the humanization of nature implies a process of distinction, of defining the boundaries of time and space by referencing an ideal of transfiguration, of overcoming the animal condition, elevating it to a meaning that justifies its difference from the natural realm. It is not by chance that the terms "culture" and "cult" share the same etymological origin. The sacralization of certain natural spaces is present in the early stages of high culture and human civilization. In turn, this is related to the primitive manifestations of artistic and literary creation and thought over the cosmos. These early expressions of human culture reveal a fundamental drive that establishes the exercise of the memory of the sacred, related to the possibility of imagining a better and fulfilled future. Awareness of the sacred is closely linked to the understanding of the human condition as something distinct from nature. Sacred places conceived by the various religions end up constructing a utopian haven, where utopia can be developed, as a sort of performative exercise for a larger, more comprehensive, global and complete experience. Just like the sacred space, utopia is associated with the notion of uchronia, involving a transformation or transfiguration of space and time, but always within these structuring coordinates and never outside them.

The theosacred concept of sacred place is connected to a historical-cultural concept, the *place of memory*, both civil and political, explored by the French historian Pierre Nora. He explains that in places chosen to erect the collective memory, nothing is done spontaneously, but always artificially with all the limits implied by the intention of representation: "The places of memory are born and live from feelings that are not generated in spontaneous memory, but from the need to create Archives, keep birthdays, organize celebrations, elegies, register actions, because these operations are not natural" (Nora, xxiv). In turn, this typology is different from another one that has been studied by authors such as Alberto Manger and Umberto Eco: imaginary lands and places. While these authors share common ideas regarding the power of imagining as the motor of the so-called material history, they speak to different aims and methods. This differentiated typology of places presents a simultaneously mythical and utopian dimension. It is mythical because it refers to an explanation of the origin of things. It is utopian in the sense that it idealizes places of fulfilment or the possibility of extraordinary conditions for existence. Every sacred place breaks the logic of human places and times wherein the normality of everyday life exists. It breaks the logic of chronological time to provide *kairos*, which means the synthesis of time, a unified and sacred time, an opening to the experience of eternity to uchronia and utopia.

As a utopian time–space, the sacred place creates a contrast between the imperfectability of the profane and its painful human experience, and the striving for perfectibility. The concept of religion emerges from here: "religo" means "to reconnect," to recover the lost link between the natural and the spiritual or transcendent realms, to restore a lost harmony for individual and collective human life. In this sense, sacred places are themselves a small-scale utopia, a possibility for greater achievement. We could say that religion and the sacred are the raw material and a template for utopia. The sacred place is inextricably associated with the demand for a sense of hospitality, and the reconnection with a divine or transcendent realm that may provide it. The underlying reason for utopian creation is the perception of the present reality as the experience of expulsion, decay, crisis, insufficient hospitality, both material, psychological, moral and, especially, spiritual. Utopian creation would restore this lost harmony experienced in ordinary life.

HOSPITALITY AND SACREDNESS IN PARADIGMATIC UTOPIAN TEXTS

Ultimately, a utopia is a project for the future to overcome disenchantment with the world and with its evident desecration. Utopian projects aim to recover a lost hospitality and provide the resacralization of the human realm, whether in the form of a stronghold or in a broad perspective extending to the entire Earth. Some essential utopian texts can be used to evidence these elements, as they try to overcome the dramatic expulsion from a comfort zone, whether political, social or even civilizational.

The City of God [*De Civitate Dei*] by Augustine of Hippo (354–430) is a remarkable Christian religious work with a fruitful utopian objective, aimed at the goal of including all humanity in the economy of salvation offered by the biblical God. Written in response to the period of uncertainty that marked the fall of the Western Roman Empire, the text proposes that the historical journey of humanity is marked by a struggle between two cities, the heavenly and the earthly. They are understood to be interconnected and both fulfill the divine plan for an historical progression toward consummation in an otherworldly realm. This work's global reading of the path of humanity across time starts from a protology, or the study of origins and "first things," and moves toward an eschatology, the study of "last things." In other words, *The City of God* plots history from the creation of the world, when everything was good, passing through the experience of decline or decadence, and the need for redemption; in the fullness of time will arrive the opening of eternity for men with goodwill.

Augustine establishes a systematic reflection on the philosophy and theology of history, elaborating on the idea of progress and utopia as a process of actual concretization in history. Utopia is realized in a progressive way through a complex relationship with the experience of entropy, between sacred and profane, between grace and sin, that accompanies that progress. The Augustinian utopia in *The City of God* is never fully realized on Earth as a project of perfect hospitality, but as an ongoing project coexisting with inhospitality and with the antithesis of the sacred. Utopia is always something not yet accomplished, and only fully realized in another dimension, in eternity, where the limits of time and space would be removed.

During the medieval period, the figure of the Calabrian abbot, Joachim de Fiore (c.1135–1202) emerges in Western thought, with his influential theological elaboration of what we may call the utopia of the Third Age of the Holy Spirit. This monk, a reformist of the monastic life of Cistercian tradition, conceived a peculiar theology of history that would influence the Western utopian thought until today. His prophetic-utopian exegesis stems from his acute perception of the life of the Church and the society of his time, which he considered to be fallen, morally and religiously corrupt. The Church had become worldly and had lost its sacral efficacy. The basis of his theological reflection is a biblical exegesis that seeks to reconcile the Old and New Testaments based on a particular interpretation of Trinitarian theology in its influence on human history. God's economy of salvation marks the human journey through time in an ascending evolutionary line, tending to greater perfection that would be consummated in a last earthly epoch by special grace of the Third Person of the Divine Trinity.

Joachim de Fiore imagined the world in this final age of history as a great monastery, a sacred global space, in which all men would live in prayer and full communion with the divine world, recovering the loss of sacredness due to the excesses of the present world. The Utopia of the Third Age would meet an evangelical ideal of peace, justice, fraternity, holiness, hospitality, a closer relationship with God, and parity among races, nations and social statutes. It shaped popular rituals like the Festivities of the Holy Spirit in Europe, later recreated in modernity in several continents with the same promise of the new era of resacralization of the world prophesied by Joachim.

After a proto-utopian era, there was a new utopian era during the sixteenth century, inaugurated by the publication in 1516 of *Utopia* by Thomas More, the Chancellor of Henry VII who was disgraced and sentenced to death. More's title is responsible for the classification of a new literary genre that, as this Handbook attests, has proved itself remarkably resilient. *Utopia* originally was written in Latin, with the full title, *Libellus vere aureus, nec minus salutaris quam festivus, de optimo rei publicae statu deque nova insula Utopia*. Intended for his humanist friends Erasmus, Pierre Gilles, Guillaume Budé and Jérôme Buisleden, the treatise shared the concerns of Renaissance Christian intellectuals with the moral degeneration of their present societies, marked by the intensification of divisions and wars between Christian states and by the difficulty in finding a social model of just and peaceful coexistence. Christianity, the religion that should realize full hospitality for humanity, was becoming instead a territory for conflict, disharmony and exclusion, closing doors to those who chose different ways of believing and living the religious experience.

In line with the ideal *polis* imagined by Greek philosophers, More coined the neologism *Utopia*, which can mean *good place* (*eu-topos*) and *no place* (*ou-topos*) or *not-yet-existent place*, if we follow the hope of a possible future achievement. Raphael Hythloday, the narrator, tells of an ideal politically organized community on an island somewhere (location undisclosed) called Utopia, an ideal peaceful society with its own laws and language, and featuring religious freedom, elected representatives who create the statutes, and an equal distribution of resources. Organizational principles were based on living virtue as a pleasure and not as an arduous duty, and the experience of the sacred was a factor of unity and not of dissension. In creating textually this social laboratory that would restore lost unity and hospitality, *Utopia* also presented a strong critique of the type of political organization of the emerging centralist, and increasingly authoritarian, modern states such as England.

Further south, on the Italian peninsula, we find a well-known work of modern utopian literature, *The City of the Sun* [*La Città del Sole*, 1602]. Its author, Tommaso Campanella (1568–1639), presents an ideal society that contrasts with his disappointments with the social political models of his time. Campanella was a revolutionary Dominican friar who led an insurrection in Calabria against the Spanish Empire. *The City of the Sun* belongs to the utopian literary genre, placing the possible perfect society in a city on the island of Taprobana (Ceylon in southern India), discovered by a Genovese navigator from Colombo. This anti-imperialist utopia reproduces the theological structure of Divinity and deploys the Greek trope of a society ruled by philosophers. The government is led by a metaphysical monarch called Sun, assisted by three princes allegorically representing Power, Knowledge and Love, reflecting the structure of the Universe. The text sketches out an idealized astrological society that follows the benign influence of the stars to ensure effective seasons of sowing, harvesting and mating. Human life too is attuned to the astrological, guided by priests expert in all of the astrological conjunctions. Thus, the exercise of power and social organization is to be built and legitimized in close relationship with the rhythms of nature, reproducing the motions of the cosmos. Life would be lived smoothly, restoring the lost harmony between the human, natural and divine realms, in perfect material and meaningful hospitality for human beings belonging to this solar city.

Another representative work that must be mentioned is the utopia of scientific progress authored by Francis Bacon (1561–1626). He was unhappy with the status quo of the university of his time and the way knowledge was produced, still marked by the weight of authority and restrictive protocols. In his *The Great Instauration* (1620), Francis Bacon proposed a new method of inductive knowledge, generating a new epistemology free of the tutelage of the theological and the sacred. Sensory faculties should be made operative by reason, thus creating new knowledge. He defended the idea of ending the boundaries between the traditional disciplines and proposed revising notions reinforced by scholasticism, based on an alliance between reason and the sensory faculties. A worldview emerging from the opening up of a global world might lead to a revolution in and an expansion of science, and the results should be placed at the service of improving human societies. The social responsibility of science is supported by the responsibility of the secular powers to promote scientific knowledge in increasingly diverse disciplines, highlighting the role of science in the improvement of human societies. Bacon's scientific utopianism is evident in his works *Of Proficience and Advancement of Learning Divine and Human* (1605) and *The New Atlantis* (1623). Although religion and the experience of the sacred still have important places as unifying factors of social life, and in the projection of an ideal future, Bacon's utopian vision foreshadows the elaboration of more radically secularized utopian perspectives such as positivism and nineteenth-century scientism.

Also in the seventeenth century, further to the west in Europe, we find another type of utopia that would impact the cultural heritage of several countries: the teleology of the so-called Fifth Empire. A suggestive example of this concept is found in the prophetic texts of the Jesuit priest António Vieira (1608–1697). His most relevant works are *History of the Future* and *Clavis Prophetarum*. The French scholar Raymond Cantel asserts that Vieira left us one of the most generous utopias in the history of universal thought. In his prophetic work, Vieira envisions the arrival of an era of peace and happiness on Earth as the realization of the Kingdom of Christ, founded on Love among men, and assisted by the grace of God and in harmony with nature. In this final historic era of "the Fifth Empire," the world would be governed by two rulers, an angelic pope in the spiritual realm and the King of Portugal in the secular realm. Both rulers would receive divine assistance, through the divine intermediary of Christ's coming in spirit to reform human societies on Earth. This empire would fulfill of the prophet Daniel's anticipation of the Empire of the Saints of the Most High, and the millenarian prophecy of the thousand years of happy life to be enjoyed by Christians in the last era of the history of salvation.

The Fifth Empire of Vieira has the peculiarity of not being an empire of domination, but one of harmony and of inclusion of diverse peoples and cultures, including Jews and Indians. For this reason, Cantel and others consider this utopia a precursor for models of global organizations such as the contemporary United Nations, for establishing peace among nations. The utopian vision at the heart of the Fifth Empire contrasts with the diagnosis of crisis on a planetary scale arising from social and religious conflicts during the seventeenth century. The Earth becomes a global territory for the restoration of the hospitality fundamental to the lost primordial harmony. Like the Third Age of Joachim of Fiore, the Fifth Empire would bring about the resacralization of the entire globe, offering humanity a time of grace, peace and justice in a perfect religious relationship with the natural and divine realms.

It is important to note that this more universal perspective of Western utopian thought has undergone many metamorphoses through reworkings in different countries and in different cultural, literary and ideological currents through the twentieth century. One of its most surprising metamorphoses is the work of a writer born in the Archipelago of the Azores, Natália Correia (1923–1993). She updated old utopian legacies of a better world, such as Joachim of Fiore's and Vieira's, which were successively recreated by poets and philosophers, including Fernando Pessoa and Agostinho da Silva. Correia studied and wrote in support of the Fifth Empire notion, believing that its symbolic starting point in the first islands of the Azores, with their sacred names (São Miguel and Santa Maria), affirmed its sacral programmatic foundation. Correia assigned the utopia of the Fifth Empire a feminine identity, in its origin and expression: at its origin because it would be instilled with the Holy Spirit, which she saw as the feminine face of the divine Trinity. According to Correia, the full expression of this global utopia would be marked by what she considered to be "feminine" traits, such as tenderness, sensitivity, equity, caring for the most vulnerable, affection, harmony and intimacy. She understood that only the feminine values could counteract the long history of humanity's deeply belligerent character, inspired by masculine ideals of strength, conquest and domination. For this reason, Natália Correia advocates that the old devotion to the *Patria* should give way to a full compromise with an original motherland or *matria*, guiding everyone toward the transfiguration of humanity in a universal *fratria*, an era of fraternity on Earth, with a universal hospitality directed toward all of humanity.

Finally, there is the exemplary utopianism in the thought of Immanuel Kant (1724–1804). In the context of the historical proclamation of human rights during the French Revolution, this German philosopher conceives his famous irenic utopia in the iconic *Perpetual Peace* (1795). Concerned with finding a way to solve the problem of achieving civil peace using universal law, Kant argues that a lasting peace for humanity will only be achieved with a constitution and a cosmopolitan State. He considers the construction of universal peace as an imperative stemming from the full exercise of human reason. Kant combines the categorical imperative with a practical vision to establish a global and definitive peace through three juridical levels: civil law; human rights; and cosmopolitan law. The ethical duty to build peace in harmony with reason will be possible with a federation of republican states that abide by the universal law that establishes a global citizenship, hospitable to all humanity.

It is important to emphasize that these authors and works conceive of utopia as reflecting two aspects of human life: the desire for a radical break with the present model of societies; and a preference for the category of possibility over the category of necessity. Utopian thought thus can inspire two different and even antagonistic dynamics for human improvement: one, that engages a sensibility respecting pluralism, freedom, and the fair sharing of resources necessary for human life, in all its diversity; and another, in the creation of projects for segregation and exclusion. Using this approach we can identify two major types of utopias: exclusive utopias and inclusive utopias. Utopian projects such as More's or Campanella's present the possibility of an ideal society, as long as it is separated through the education and selection of humans capable of meeting the requirements of the perfect yet restrictive societies they envision. These and other alternative models are exclusive utopias, not unrelated to the dangerous inspiration of eugenic and segregationist projects on the basis of building an "ideal" world—which is taken to mean eliminating the differences in and variations of humanity. Inclusive utopian projects, in contrast, permit, and admit, the various types of human distinctiveness, the great diversity of races, colors, religions, in the idealization of a future of peace and harmony on Earth. This of course is a vision that embodies Kant's important concept of *cosmopolitanism.*

CONCLUSION

Ultimately, utopian thought advocates a return of the world and humanity to itself, to a self-reconciliation, with nature and the divine realms according to an idea of transcendence. In this sense, utopian thought shares the same profound idea of the sacred place, a religious and cultural utopia of reconversion of the world entails its temporal understanding in a three-dimensional perspective. The painful experience of the immediate present meets with more remote calm of the divine, creating a nostalgic longing both for an idealized a lost paradise of the past; and for an ideal future seen as an extension into the not-yet of that idealized, perfect past. Somehow, despite considering the different religious, and mythic, mystical or spiritual traditions, returning to or remaking a sacred place is like experiencing a return to the maternal womb from which we were expelled, a return to the cosmic primordial origins, and at the same time, is like delving into a projection of the future. The sacred place is not a mere interval in the vastness of space and time, but rather functions as the possibility of fullness of space and time, as a sacred and necessary interruption that brings about the *renovatio temporum* (renewal of time) and the *renovatio mundi* (renewal of the world). The sacred place is a utopian project in the making. Perhaps the metaphor of the sacred place as *oasis* in the arid desert of life may have relevance: such a place offers a replenishment from the banality and frailty of ordinary life, where everything "looks like new."

It is important to emphasize that sacred places considered in this way are sources of life. They are places for redoing primordial gestures with mimetic theatricality according to performative power; that is, gestures that seek realization through associated liturgies. As places of palingenesis, or regeneration and inner fortification, they can evoke silence or festivity, modest prayer or exhilarating joy. Here we can find the possibility of understanding the sacred place as a utopian haven, and, in some cases, the utopian reconfiguration of the whole world with the recovery of its enchantment as a global lost paradise. The utopian dimension of sacred place entails the realization *hic et nunc* (here and now) and in a reduced rehearsed version, the envisioning of a better place, *eutopia*, to be one day expanded to all mankind and the whole Earth. Sacred places function as "centres," or places of recentering, where people nourish themselves with the ever-renewed fascination of origins, and where the undefined longings for the future or for the eternal return to an original source, are realized. The sacred places and the religious experience that they enable are the earliest sources of utopia, which is constantly actualized in successive elaborations.

References

Agostinho, Santo. 1991–1995. *A Cidade de Deus* [The City of God], 3 Vols. Lisboa: Fundação Calouste Gulbenkian.

Bacon, Francis. 2008. *Nova Atlântida e a grande restauração* [The New Atlantic and the Grand Restauration]. Lisboa: Edições 70.

Campanella, Tomás. 1990. *A Cidade do Sol* [The City of the Sun]. Lisboa: Ed. Guimarães.

Cantel, Raymond. 1960. *Prophétisme et Messianisme dans l'Oeuvre de Antonio Vieira* [Prophetism and Messianism in the Work of Antonio Vieira]. Paris: Hispano-Americanas.

De Koninck, Thomas. 2003. *A Nova Ignorância e o Problema da Cultura* [The New Ignorance and the Problem of Culture]. Lisboa: Edições 70.

Eco, Umberto. 2015. *História das Terras e dos Lugares Lendários* [History of Lands and Legendary Places]. Lisboa: Gradiva.

More, Thomas. 1960. *A Utopia* [Utopia]. Lisboa: Ed. Guimarães.

Nora, Pierre. 1984. *Les Lieux de Memoire* [Places of Memory], vol. 1. Paris: Gallimard.

Vieira, António. 2013. "História do Futuro" and "A Chave dos Profetas." In *Obra Completa* [Complete Works], ed. José Eduardo Franco and Pedro Calafate, Tomo III, vols. I, V and VI. Lisboa: Círculo de Leitores.

Hospitality

Gonçalo Marcelo

Introduction

It might seem odd to include an entry on hospitality in a handbook dedicated to utopian and dystopian literature. After all, is not the *u* in the *u-topos* of utopias supposed to indicate that such a place—or object, or practice— does not exist anywhere? And, in contrast to this, is not hospitality present in everyday life? And if so, shouldn't we just acknowledge it as a daily, almost effortless routine engrained in common cultural practices, embedded in many societies? Should this be the case, then any "utopia of hospitality" would be nonsensical, insofar as it makes no sense to posit as a utopian horizon something that is already here among us. And yet, while we can recognize in small tokens or gestures what we take to be expressions of hospitality, whether "real," "absolute" hospitality ever takes place, and whether it is even possible that it does, are different questions entirely.

Taking a look at philosophical debates on hospitality, its status turns out to be problematic, involving many difficulties and perhaps an intrinsic tension and paradox. In what follows, I intend to briefly explore this tension by drawing on three philosophical accounts of hospitality, those put forward by Jacques Derrida, Paul Ricœur and Richard Kearney. However, this philosophical exploration of hospitality, which emphasizes its mildly utopian register, is anchored in literary imagination. This should not come as a surprise. Indeed, fiction is sometimes the best method to unveil some phenomenological traits

G. Marcelo (✉)
University of Coimbra, Coimbra, Portugal

675

P. Marks et al. (eds.), *The Palgrave Handbook of Utopian and Dystopian Literatures*, https://doi.org/10.1007/978-3-030-88654-7_53

of daily experience or to depict, albeit in an idealized manner, what is at stake in a given situation or choice.[1] These three philosophers therefore begin with literary texts and the questions of language, including translation, in order to analyze the conceptual and ethical implications of hospitality. Derrida draws from Sophocles; Kearney often cites biblical examples; and Ricoeur develops a notion of "linguistic" hospitality from the notion of literary translation. What is at stake here is to discuss whether hospitality is even *possible*. If an analysis of what it would take for us to be truly hospitable reveals that hospitality is not something that we can really achieve, would this make it a delusion? And if we conclude from this that hospitality has the status of a "utopia," are we suggesting that we should let it go or, to the contrary, that we should let it inspire and edify us? These will be some of the key questions guiding us.

In this first section of the chapter, I present Derrida's, Ricœur's and Kearney's depictions of hospitality: from "im-possible" to "difficult" and to "radical" hospitality. I suggest that hospitality is both impossible and possible, or rather, following Kearney, that it involves a "wager" and a "leap" from the impossible to the possible. In this main section of the chapter, I show some of the ways in which these philosophical explorations are themselves grounded in literary examples, and namely in Greek tragedy and the Bible. It goes without saying that the Greek and Hebraic sources do not exactly count as utopian or dystopian literature. But I would like to argue that for the definition of hospitality I will be adopting here, and following in the footsteps of Kearney, these sources are indeed good examples of such a difficult (albeit not entirely impossible) utopia of hospitality.

In the brief second section, I will further specify what is meant by utopia here, mainly by drawing from Ricœur's own definition of constitutive, non-pathological utopias. In that section I will argue that utopias need not be unreal or escapist; but rather, that they can aim at changing reality and influencing action. This, indeed, is the case of a utopia of hospitality. Finally, in my third section, I draw on other literary examples in which this elusive utopia of hospitality appears and what they can teach us. My first example is drawn from a purely utopian text—none other than More's own *Utopia*, accompanied by Rabelais' satirical counterpart—and the second from a recent, almost dystopian work, Behrouz Boochani's *No Friend But the Mountains*. The examples are radically different and yet they can both be illuminating, in distinctive ways.

Allow me to start from a basic description of the initial encounter. What happens when two strangers meet and one of them is the foreigner, the one who does not belong? The possibility of hospitality arises from an intersubjective situation in which, in its first moment, there is no symmetry or reciprocity. Instead, if we place ourselves in the position of the host—who is often in a position of superiority, insofar as the newcomer is perhaps dispossessed, far from home, wandering—what should we make of the new arrival? How are we to react? When we find descriptions of hospitality as being impossible or difficult, the inner difficulty that we face has to do not only with the challenge of being up to the ethical demands of a scene of hospitality, but also of overcoming the temptation to react to the arrival with suspicion, rejection or hostility. Part of the drama of hospitality is thus the following: when faced with such an encounter we can never neglect the possibility that the host becomes hostile. Indeed, both Derrida and Kearney insist on the ambiguity of hospitality in its relation with hostility, pointing to the etymology of the concept.

Surprising as it might seem, etymology is here important for several reasons. The first reason is indirect, having to do with the role of language in the practice and "process" of hospitality. Indeed, the one whom we encounter and who comes from elsewhere might sound strange precisely by virtue of the fact that they might not speak our language. This is why hospitality also involves something like a linguistic mediation or a translation; importantly, Ricœur theorizes the notion of "linguistic hospitality" (Ricœur 2006). The second reason has to do with the etymology of the word *hospitality* itself, as it reveals the inherent tension between *hostility* and hospitality. Derrida and Kearney invoke Émile Benveniste's work *Indo-European Language and Society* (1973) in which he spells out the double meaning contained in the Latin *hostis* (which is the root-word of hospitality): guest *and* enemy. Benveniste explains:

> 2) The primitive notion conveyed by *hostis* is that of equality by compensation: a *hostis* is one who repays my gift with a counter-gift. Thus, like its Gothic counterpart, *gasts*, Latin *hostis* at one period denoted the guest. The classical meaning "enemy" must have developed when reciprocal relations between clans were succeeded by the exclusive relations of *civitas* to *civitas*. (cf. Gr. *xénos* 'guest' > 'stranger')
>
> 3) Because of this Latin coined a new name for "guest": **hosti-pet-*, which may perhaps be interpreted as arising from an abstract noun *hosti* "hospitality" and consequently meaning "he who predominantly personifies hospitality, the one who is hospitality itself." (Benveniste, n.p.)

Kearney (2015, 177) suggests that this original meaning indicates a relationship demanding trust, "a laying down of one's weapons" and thus a conversion of hostility into hospitality. But then, argues Benveniste, when interpersonal relations of trust (between clans) are over time evolved into political relationships (*civitas* to *civitas*), the *hostis* also comes to signify an enemy. As such, Kearney states, the link between hospitality and hostility "became a drama of choice and decision" (Kearney 2015, 177).

Kearney also notes that, according to Benveniste, through other words *hospes* and *hospites*, also possible roots of *hospitality*, one finds the same tension, as they both "contain the root word *pet, potestas*—power. So the host served as a sort of guest-master who had the capacity and authority to welcome or refuse foreigners into his home. In other words, the guest-master had the power to include or exclude whomever he wishes" (Kearney 2015, 178). As such, Kearney explains, in Indo-European societies we witness the ambivalence of the favorable stranger (the guest) and the hostile stranger (the enemy) which means that hospitality is a "wager" (Kearney 2015, 173). Given that the host gives rise both to hospitality and hostility, "one can turn into the other, and back again. Hospitality is never a given; it always a challenge and a choice" (178).

Derrida names this ambiguity by coining the term "hostpitality" [*hostip-italité*] (Dufourmantelle and Derrida 2000, 45). In his approach, Derrida conceives of hospitality as absolute. He holds that there is a dilemma between *the* Law of hospitality—"unconditional hospitality that dispenses with law, duty or even politics"—and the laws of hospitality, "circumscribed by law and duty" (Dufourmantelle and Derrida 2000, 135). This is to say that for Derrida hospitality only exists if it is unconditional, hyperbolical. It is the gift without reservation whereby the host does not even ask the guest for their name, where they come from or where they are going (135). Accordingly, for Derrida, there are two regimes of the law of hospitality: the unconditional/hyperbolical regime; and the conditional/juridico-political regime. Between them is an irreducible tension that is always at risk of perversion (85). It is thus almost as if the host were, as in Levinasian hyperbolical ethics, a "hostage" of the stranger (109, 123). Absolute hospitality supersedes concrete laws of hospitality, somehow requiring that these laws exist, but also necessarily transgressing them and any notion of duty.

It is not surprising, then, that if asked to give concrete empirical examples of absolute hospitality, we would be hard-pressed to find them. But that is not the point, given that Derrida himself emphasizes its impossibility. This is not to say that a meditation on literary examples cannot be of use, however. Indeed, Derrida comes back to Attic tragedy, and specifically to the Theban trilogy, commenting on Oedipus' relation with Antigone. In *Oedipus at Colonus*, we find the wandering father and daughter, Oedipus the blind old man seeking hospitality, and Antigone guiding him and becoming his eyes. They speak as foreigners to foreigners. Antigone represents a hyperbolical and paradoxical example of hospitality because, according to Derrida, she is at the same time appealing to "the" law of absolute hospitality, and transgressing the laws of her own land: she asks foreigners for hospitality, but has crossed the border illegally. More importantly, in *Antigone* she disobeys a civil law (laid down by her uncle, Creon) in order to obey divine law (Ricœur 1991), offering her brother, the "traitor" Polynices, hospitality in the form of a proper burial (Dufourmantelle and Derrida 2000, 85). This comes at the expense of Antigone's own life.

For Derrida, hospitality has a supra-ethical status, and this involves a questioning of language itself in its relation with selfhood. Derrida emphasizes that language is not only a site of belonging (such as the experience of the mother tongue) but also an experience of expropriation (ibid., 89), a paradoxical experience of the stranger within ourselves. Ricœur, on the other hand, ties together the linguistic and the ethical dimensions through the paradigm of translation. A translation is an answer to the foreign, the stranger. And this is why it can be a model for hospitality: "it seems to me that translation sets us not only intellectual work, theoretical or practical, but also an ethical problem. Bringing the reader to the author, bringing the author to the reader, at the risk of serving and of betraying two masters: this is to practice what I like to call linguistic hospitality. It is this which serves as a model for other forms of hospitality that I think resemble it" (Ricœur 2006, 23). As Kearney has emphasized, the Ricœurian ethics of translation involves a process of inter-linguistic hospitality, because it calls for taking responsibility for the stories put forward by others and "invite empathy with strangers and adversaries by allowing for a plurality of narrative perspectives" (Kearney 2007, 155).

For Ricœur hospitality, like other ethical gestures, is not properly impossible but difficult, and this is also Richard Kearney's interpretation. Kearney builds on Ricœur's hermeneutic philosophy, and namely on his theory of narrative and imagination, to put forward his own account of radical hospitality, which has a theoretical background but also meaningful practical applications. In the recent *Radical Hospitality* (2021), written with Melissa Fitzpatrick, Kearney explores four dimensions (or faces, as he calls them) of hospitality: linguistic, narrative, confessional and carnal. He is closer to Ricœur than to Derrida insofar as he shies away from pure hospitality and wagers on hermeneutical hospitality, i.e., in a model more rooted in conversation and exchange. Kearney and Fitzpatrick explore the linguistic face of hospitality to demonstrate how hospitality and the threat of hostility are, as we have seen, rooted in language. They examine the confessional face in terms of religious hospitality, through the conceptual angle of translation. The carnal dimension is shown through concrete examples of hospitality in which the embodied nature of the hospitable act is of the utmost importance. It is, however, the narrative face that contributes most to our argument, because in this dimension we are shown, in very concrete terms, practical examples of mediations from the theory to the practice of hospitality, by means of narrative imagination.

Taking Ricœur's paper "Reflections on a new Ethos for Europe" (Ricœur 1996) as a starting point, Kearney makes a first attempt at extending the model of linguistic hospitality to encompass narrative hospitality. He does so by distinguishing three traits of narrative hospitality: narrative plurality (every story can be told from a variety of perspectives); narrative transformation (the historical past can have its unexplored possibilities revisited); and narrative pardon (through narrative exchange one can develop empathy with others and work through the wounds of the past) (Kearney and Fitzpatrick 2021, 24–25). Kearney then describes a ten-year engagement in series of practical projects that have allowed him to explore the three traits abovementioned, and how they foster narrative hospitality. I will focus on just one such project: the Guestbook Project.[2]

The Guestbook Project embraces the motto "Exchanging Stories Changing Histories." It gathers a team encouraging young people from divided communities to come together and exchange their stories (ibid., 26) thus forming an empathetic bond that wagers on the impossible transition from hostility to hospitality. The process is as follows. First, the wound must be acknowledged.

It might be that the participants have no direct experience of hostility toward each other's community, but that this hostility is ingrained in their community's history, and passed down through the life stories of their families. Perhaps their parents, grandparents or siblings were victims. The story of how hostility is experienced and/or anticipated is a part of the process of potential healing. As participants are exchanging stories they are invited to take up one another's perspective. As a final step, they are encouraged to compose a new story together, in which they incorporate what they have learned from seeing the world through each other's eyes. Hopefully, they now understand that there is no real reason why hostility cannot be transformed into hospitality.

This, of course, is the "im-possible" leap of hospitality. It is not to be taken for granted, for behind hospitality there always looms the threat of hostility. But the wager is that if an act of reconciliation is possible through narrative exchange—if, that is, through the "work" of the imagination they together can tell a new story wherein hostility is overcome—then the leap from hostility to hospitality is possible in reality too. And if this can be done at the "micro" level of an interpersonal exchange, who knows if it cannot be done at the "macro" level of communities. The whole process of narrative exchange between the two youngsters as they find ways to share each other's viewpoint is recorded in a short video that is uploaded to Guestbook's webpage. It is likely many of these attempted exchanges will fail, because hospitality is indeed difficult. But the point is that when they do *not* fail, they can become inspirational, as models for influencing others through the power of example. Herein lies the potentially utopian character of these experiments in hospitality, and reconciliation.

For Derrida, literature provides striking examples of such a process, the recovery of hospitality. And Kearney often points to the biblical stories of Abraham and Sarah hosting the strangers under the Mamre tree (Genesis 18:1–15), and of Jesus hosting the strangers on the road to Emmaus (Luke 24:13–35) (Kearney and Fitzpatrick 2021, 2). He cites Homeric scenes of hospitality such as the recognition of Odysseus by Eurycleia and even the old dog Argos, upon returning to Ithaca (Marcelo 2017, 6). But how, then, can we frame hospitality as a utopia?

Hospitality as a Utopia

It might just be that hospitality is not the more "natural" or common reaction to the foreign, even though it is evidently the right thing to do, and examples of hostility unfortunately abound. It might be instead in the tension between empirical reality and imagined potentiality that we find the utopian function. To grasp the effect of this conceptualization of hospitality upon reality, it is worth coming back to Ricœur's philosophy of imagination.

In the *Lectures on Ideology and Utopia* Ricœur distinguishes between two basic forms of utopia as an expression of the social imaginary: constitutive and pathological utopias. Whereas ideology legitimates existing social orders and practices, utopia questions them. It is an "exploration of the possible" (Ricœur 1986, 311), distancing itself from empirical reality in order to criticize it and to envision different possibilities. Utopia is somehow an antidote to all naturalization of social relations. Just because a given structure of power relations or web of social practices is instituted, as a result of given traditions or as an imposition of a de facto authority, this does not mean that they are the sole possibilities for human action. This is part of utopia's constitutive function: as a figment of productive imagination, it is meant to act as an imaginative variant of, or alternative to, reality.

This means that utopia's relation with reality is dialectical; it might not be meant to reproduce reality as it is. But neither is it supposed to be so far-fetched as to be completely detached from reality. If it were, that is, if this alternate reality contained no element of familiarity, then its potential utopian status might eventually be lost. Pathological utopias, then, *would* be "escapist," in that they present worlds so distant from reality that no critical purchase can take place; there can be no effect on the very reality they wish to question. But non-pathological utopias do have effects on reality. The view from "nowhere" (Ricoer 1986, 17) can serve to alter something somewhere, regardless of whether or not it was meant to do so.

According to Ricœur, utopias are not meant to be static, they do not correspond to a fully defined picture of (an alternative) reality, neither are they supposed to formulate a blueprint or a program for political action (Ricoeur 1986, 290), even if they are indeed written with the goal of political transformation. When they do show us different, perhaps more meaningful ways of living together, they implicitly contain an invitation, a suggestion for us to change our normal habits. In a word: utopias can be inspiring. And this, I believe, is also what happens with utopian scenes of hospitality. Not because hospitality (even though not in its "absolute" form as defined by Derrida) doesn't happen in everyday life. But because it remains, to borrow from Ricœur's and Kearney's vocabulary, a task, a challenge and a wager. Hospitality is often the least likely and the most difficult answer when it comes to facing the stranger. It does imply the impossible leap of overcoming hostility. This is why it is utopian. But its utopian character doesn't mean, as critics of utopia might argue, that it will never happen. To the contrary, hospitality does take place. The utopia here lies elsewhere: in the hope that in a world plagued by war and incomprehension, the inspiring character of the gestures and scenes of hospitality, edifying and inspirational as they are, can make hospitality more widespread, and less conditional.

In the past, I have argued that Ricœur's approach of recognition had the status of a utopia and that it could be edifying and inspirational (Marcelo 2011). I am now arguing the same for the case of hospitality, the utopia of hospitality, such as it can be interpreted in the footsteps of Ricœur and Kearney. Hospitality can happen anywhere and in the most unlikely places. But the fact that it is often the exception makes us wonder. Should it be trivial and it would lose its utopian character altogether—and perhaps, from a normative standpoint, that should be the goal: to make hospitality so widespread that it wouldn't even be a question. But given that this is not the case, its mildly utopian status remains intact. In the brief section that follows I provide some different examples of scenes of hospitality such as they appear in different literary examples.

From More to the *Mountain*

It is not uncommon for utopian and dystopian narratives to have travelling as a central element. This is trivial, almost a trope, for it makes perfect sense, from a narrative standpoint, to identify the reader with a familiar viewpoint, that of a protagonist, that is then confronted with the exotic or fantastic experiences taking place in nowhere of utopian imagination. Take More's *Utopia* or Swift's *Gulliver's Travels* as classic examples of the experience of the recounting of one's experience while travelling as quintessential examples.

But if this is so, then it comes as no surprise that hospitality can also be a topic of importance from the utopian standpoint. Thus the importance of hospitality in More's narrative *Utopia*, which would not been possible had the traveler Hythloday not enjoyed almost an Homeric type of hospitality at the places he visited.[3] As Cameron comments "both Hythloday and Odysseus represent the figure of the traveler offering personal narratives in exchange for hospitality" (Cameron 2015, 15). And this hospitality is extended to "Morus" (the figure of More himself in the narrative), who hosts Hythloday: besides lending an ear and being open to discussion, Morus also offers food, in what can be read as a classic scene of hospitality. Parallels between More's endeavor and ancient Greek culture can also be extended, as they suggest a comparison between More's scenario, and that of Plato's dialogues (Cameron 2015, 15). It is obvious that both Plato and More, contrary to escapist pathological utopias as defined by Ricœur, imagine alternative ways of organizing society (Vieira 2010, 5).

In light of Ricœur's and Kearney's philosophies of hospitality, these examples can be read as covering two basic elements of narrative hospitality, containing both the conversational—albeit argumentative—aspect and the material, carnal aspect. Hythloday is offered food and hospitality in exchange for the narratives of his own exotic experiences. Read in this light, hospitality thus appears as an enabler of utopia itself for without predisposition to listen to these odd views from nowhere brought by this unusual messenger, there could not even be any hermeneutic possibility for the utopian content. Without hospitality, therefore, the message conveyed by the productive imagination would be blocked. These scenes of hospitality to the utopian traveler become only more significant when we understand hospitality to be decisive trait of the *Utopia* scenario.

It also goes without saying that the utopian element comes in many forms; besides hopeful utopias, we can find other forms of utopian and dystopian forms. In her delineation of the concept of utopia, Fátima Vieira lists satirical utopias, anti-utopias and dystopias as darker sides of the utopian imagination

(Vieira 2010, 15 ff.). These can amount to depictions of downright horrific societies, or of utopian efforts gone wrong. What happens to language in these texts is critical: sometimes a deceitful play of language justifies pathological ideologies, as in Huxley's and Orwell's explorations of the subtle manipulation of language by oppressive regimes. Other times, the texts display humor and irony to undergird satiric forms of social (or philosophical, or literary) criticism. And if narratives are just trying to imaginatively convey autobiographical experiences, without intending to be called "utopias" or "dystopias," they can be traversed by utopian or dystopian elements that take our imagination elsewhere, and in that process somehow *do* reconfigure our perception of reality. Allow me to very briefly provide two examples of these two latter forms in connection with the utopia of hospitality.

In his examples of hospitality in Western literature Richard Kearney mentions in passing Rabelais' the feasts of Rabelais as classic examples of scenes of hospitality. And we have already seen how the material, carnal aspect of hospitality is for Kearney of the utmost importance. The sharing of food, and the feast of the senses are strong features of a carnal hermeneutics of hospitality. But these of course acquire hyperbolical, exaggerated features in satirical prose. Rabelais clearly puts forward (anti-)utopian elements, namely in the sections of the text on the Abbey of Thélème. But elsewhere in *Gargantua and Pantagruel* Rabelais' mordant accounts of the feasting on food, drink and all the sensuous pleasures are certainly a poignant counterexample, scenes of hospitality taken too far, to the point of frenzy. Here, again, laughter is a good companion, and corrective, of idealization.

Finally, we find a striking example in Behrouz Boochani's *No Friend but the Mountains* (2018), which was not meant to be either utopian or dystopian, but nonetheless draws together the threads of my argument on utopia and hospitality. Boochani is a Kurdish migrant who escaped Iran attempting to reach Australia, who almost died in the sea and was then trapped at Manus Island's illegal detention center in Papua New Guinea, controlled by the Australian government. The narrative is a pointed tale of a migrant in a quasi-utopian search for hospitality, but who meets instead circumstances so dire and absurd that his narrative account deserves to be qualified as dystopian.[4] The narrative's genre is almost impossible to determine, as autobiographical narrative is suffused with philosophical and poetic elements, as well as reflections of Kurdish culture. In a way, every forced migrant leaves for a promised land, facing an ordeal in the attempt to reach it. In other words, every forced migrant is moved by a personal vision of a utopia of hospitality, in the hope of reaching safer ground, and a better life. Boochani's case, then, is no different from many others, except that in this case the narrative is written in a unique way.

And what is striking, besides the depiction of the "Kyriarchal system"[5] of Manus prison and its dreadful dystopian register, is the fact that amid the toils of the migration and imprisonment experiences, there are improbable and seemingly impossible scenes of hospitality among strangers, foreigners welcoming foreigners in a hostile land, attempting to make that leap from the impossible to the possible. This is the case in Boochani's interactions with several characters: Hamid, with whom he establishes some sort of silent, tacit communication in a space outside of the compound; or Reza, "the gentle giant," who tragically meets the looming shadow of hostility, of inhospitableness, in one of the sourest turns of the book. Yet we see also the same tacit tokens of hospitality, almost undetectable but still effective, exemplified in some of the detainees' interactions with the native Papuans hired by the Australian government.

These brief examples are meant to illustrate the range of the various modes in which a utopia of hospitality, as well as dystopias of hostility, can appear in the literary imagination. Through the critique of social reality that they implicitly or explicitly mobilize, they can serve as inspiration, or else as cautionary tales. Either way, in them the utopian and dystopian elements are in tension with reality, once again showing that imagination and reality are not opposing extremes, rather a dialectical pair, always in tension.

Acknowledgements This text benefited from the postdoctoral scholarship granted by the Foundation for Science and Technology, FCT, I.P. (SFRH/BPD/102949/2014) and the contract signed under the D.L. 57/2016 "norma transitória." The paper is also financed by national funds through the Foundation for Science and Technology, FCT, I.P., in the framework of the CECH-UC project: UIDB/00196/2020.

NOTES

1. Thought experiments are one way to put forward such imaginative explorations. Consider, for instance, Rawls' original position or the trolley problem. But literary fiction of course provides thicker accounts and so it is no wonder that some philosophers use it abundantly.
2. https://guestbookproject.org.
3. See Cameron (2015, 5); Heffernan (2014, 14); cit. by Cameron (2015, 5).
4. Here the question of whether the account is really "utopian" given that this is an account of something that allegedly really happened is not of paramount importance. The vivid details that Boochani provides of the Manus prison are mediated by figments of his imagination and self-interpretation, as well as by the narrative reconstruction of the translator, who was actually a co-editor of the book, given that he wrote and discussed the book trough exchanges via text messages with Boochani himself, while he was in Manus. As such, what matters in the description of the dystopian element in this narrative is, to reiterate, the oppressive environment of the prison (which is described as if it had agency, as if it was the arbitrary oppressor itself).
5. This is the concept coined by Boochani and Tofighian to depict the oppression exerted by Manus prison.

References

Benveniste, Émile. 1973. *Indo-European Language and Society*, trans. E. Palmer. Coral Gables: University of Miami Press. Online edition has been revised and updated by Jeremy Lin, Jacqueline Lewandowski, and Vergil Parson. Published here [https://chs.harvard.edu/read/benveniste-emile-indo-european-lan guage-and-society/] by permission of the University of Miami. Accessed June 16, 2021.

Boochani, Behrouz. 2018. *No Friend But the Mountains: Writing from Manus Prison*, trans. O.Tofighian. Sydney: Picador.

Cameron, Scott M. 2015. Interdependencies of Idea and Practice in More's Utopia. *Liberated Arts: A Journal for Undergraduate Research* 1(1), article 2: 1–7.

Derrida, Jacques. 2000. *Of Hospitality*. Anne Dufourmantelle Invites Jacques Derrida to Respond, trans. R. Bowlby. Stanford: Stanford University Press.

Heffernan, James A.W. 2014. *Hospitality and Treachery in Western Literature*. New Haven: Yale University Press.

Homer. 2017. *The Odyssey*, trans. E. Wilson. London: W. W. Norton & Company.

Kearney, Richard. 2007. Paul Ricoeur and the Hermeneutics of Translation. *Research in Phenomenology* 37: 147–159.

———. 2015. Hospitality: Possible or Impossible? *Hospitality and Society* 5 (2 and 3): 173–184.

Kearney, Richard, and Melissa Fitzpatrick. 2021. *Radical Hospitality: From Thought to Action*. New York: Fordham University Press.

Marcelo, Gonçalo. 2011. Paul Ricœur and the Utopia of Mutual Recognition. *Études Ricœuriennes / Ricœur Studies* 2 (1): 110–133.

———. 2017. Narrative and Recognition in the Flesh: An Interview with Richard Kearney. *Philosophy & Social Criticism* 43 (8): 777–792.

More, Thomas. 2016. *Utopia*, trans. R.M. Adams, ed. M. George Logan. Cambridge: Cambridge University Press.

Rabelais, François. 2006. *Gargantua and Pantagruel*, ed. M.A. Screech. London: Penguin.

Ricœur, Paul. 1986. *Lectures on Ideology and Utopia*, ed. George H. Taylor. New York: Columbia University Press.

———. 1991. *Oneself as Another*, trans. K. Blamey. Chicago: The University of Chicago Press.

———. 1996. Reflections on a New Ethos for Europe. In *The Hermeneutics of Action by Paul Ricœur*, ed. Richard Kearney, 3–14. London: Sage.

———. 2006. *On Translation*, trans. E. Brennan, intro. R. Kearney. London and New York: Routledge.

Sophocles. 1992. *Antigone and Oedipus at Colonus* in *Sophoclis Fabulae*, trans. H. Lloyd-Jones and N.G. Wilson. Oxford: Clarendon University Press.

Vieira, Fátima. The Concept of Utopia. 2010. In *The Cambridge Companion to Utopian Literature*, ed. Gregory Claeys, 3–27. Cambridge: Cambridge University Press.

Sexualities

Quitterie de Beauregard

Introduction

Pitting third-wave feminism and now emerging queer theory and practices against persistent conservative backlash, the culture wars of recent decades have undeniably cultivated an ideological ground for a renewed dystopian imaginary. It is only a single step from there for gender minorities to argue that, as it stands, contemporary society's extreme(-ist) defense of normative sex and gender norms (often disciplined with violence) constitutes not a fictional, but a real-life dystopia. In the wake of Donald Trump's electoral success and the "Women's March" movement, for example, protesters sported the white bonnet and crimson cape described in Margaret Atwood's classic feminist dystopia *The Handmaid's Tale* (1986) to challenge the attacks on women's bodily autonomy. Blurring the lines between fiction and reality, readers of Atwood seemed to become the watchful wardens of phrase commonly attributed to Simone de Beauvoir: "Never forget that a political, economic or religious crisis will be enough to cast doubt on women's rights. These rights will never be vested. You'll have to stay vigilant your whole life."[1]

However, it could hardly be said that successful cautionary tales of gender oppression and coercive regulations of sexual practices are enough to justify what some critics have identified as a global shift toward gender issues in the utopian imagination. In their situatedness, but also inherent and perpetual self-redefinition, contemporary representations of gender expression and sexuality

Q. de Beauregard (✉)
Sorbonne Université, Paris, France

P. Marks et al. (eds.), *The Palgrave Handbook of Utopian and Dystopian Literatures*, https://doi.org/10.1007/978-3-030-88654-7_54

suggest their own incompatibility with the unambiguous and steadfast social features of Utopia. It is precisely through their resistance to the rigidity of fictional societies that representations of gender and sexuality have produced valuable and powerful dystopias. Though written primarily from an androcentric standpoint, George Orwell's *Nineteen Eighty-Four* (1949) still portrays sexual freedom as resistance to the loss of individuality and agency. Julia, who is part of the fanatical "Anti-Sex League," unexpectedly initiates an affair with Winston. The main female character is famously described as a "rebel from the waist down" (Orwell [1949] 1983, 147). While acting on a rebellious impulse that would make her a "sex criminal" in Ingsoc, she contrasts with Winston through her relative political apathy and hopelessness regarding the regime (Patai 1982). Julia is still "othered" and remains a catalyst through which Winston's political and sexual frustration ripens into revolutionary ideals.

Yet to relegate the question of gender and sexuality to a subgenre of contemporary dystopias is to dismiss an overdue analysis of an essential feature of utopias: the formation of the individual identity through the lens of gender and sexuality—and perhaps most prevalently, through family dynamics and the question of posterity. To articulate a history and analysis of queerness and sexuality in utopian fantasies, it is essential to approach this paradox. This chapter asks, how does one write a society in which the Other, the marginal individuality and its sexual ambiguity become the center of this radical thought-experiment? Does the situatedness of gender expression and sexuality forbid the formation of a utopian society?

When looking at the prototype of all contemporary utopias (and dystopias), More's *Utopia* (1516), contemporary readers can be befuddled by the lacunae regarding the fundamental questions with which more recent dystopias concern themselves. These lacunae include the status of reproductive rights, the role of women and the representation of sexuality.[2] Though More establishes the structure of communal child-rearing (encouraging selfless qualities within the community and future generations), the subjection of women is still a component of Utopia. On feast days, wives bow down to their husbands and children to their parents and ask for forgiveness for any fault. Women are also mostly confined to household tasks. What can be inferred is that gender roles, as opposed to rules concerning gender, are not subject to utopian refashioning, as are rules concerning slaves, wealth and community life. Normative patriarchal rules still apply, and the revolutionary potential of the utopian imagination stops. As utopia/science-fiction theorist Fredric Jameson points out, the irreducibility of "the family unit" in More seems already to resist the utopian re-imagination (Jameson 2005, 207) of a more just social contract.

By the beginning of the twentieth century, the coincidence of the Suffragette Movement with the appearance of the first modern feminist literary utopias is unmistakable. Touching on issues of marriage, financial independence and the inherent virtue of women, explorations of fictional matriarchal societies begin to introduce gender as a relevant and persistent feature of the utopian thought experiment. Delving into key issues of women's rights at the time, author and economist Charlotte Perkins Gilman published *Herland* in 1915 as a serial in the radical *Forerunner*. The novel presented contemporary readers with a revolutionary society where women live collectively in harmony, produce children through parthenogenesis, and flourish well outside the war-ridden androcentric world of the novel's four male visitors from "ourland." Rediscovered in the so-called golden age of feminist utopias in the 1970s, the matriarchal world designed by Gilman enjoyed a revival of interest when it was republished as a standalone novel by Pantheon Books. Indeed, the tradition of the gynocentric utopia heralded by Gilman and other late-nineteenth- and early-twentieth-century writers was enhanced by second-wave feminists' new definitions of gender and revised expectations of sexual freedom. The early feminists' literary legacy is seen in novels such as *The Female Man* by Joanna Russ (1975) or *Women on the Edge of Time* by Marge Piercy (1976). These follow a utopian plot pattern, whereby a central character travels through space or time (or both) and is guided through a hidden or unknown world alternative to their own, which is free of the social ills that plague their home. In Russ's story, four "splinter versions" of the author—Joanna herself, Jeannine (from the past), Janet (from one future) and Jael Reasoner (from a more distant future) ("the four Js"), learn about a matriarchal utopia called "Whileaway" (Janet's home), where a gender-specific plague wiped men out centuries ago, leading to the development of a (mostly) pacifist, classless, women-only world where, as in *Herland*, parthenogenic births necessarily made possible the survival of the race after the plague.

Marge Piercy's *Woman on the Edge of Time* delineates the utopian, future world of the city of Mattapoisett which is in some ways reminiscent of Russ's utopia. The novel's protagonist, Connie Ramos, is a down-and-out working-class Latina with one child and a history of drug abuse, stints of incarceration and psychiatric care. Under the influence of reality-altering drugs, first at home and then at the psychiatric institute where she is committed, Connie is "transported" to Mattapoisett. In this world, norms of gender, sexual orientation and monogamy are irrelevant: the values of community and humanist dialectics prevail. Language itself is radically altered: the gender-neutral pronoun "per" (short for "person") is universally employed, anticipating recent efforts to introduce inclusivity for gender non-conforming individuals. Though they have reached the status of "classics" in feminist circles, other critics tended to downplay their achievements, raising instead utopian and dystopian texts that disregard gender in favor of class oppression, for example, as an essential feature to be developed. Fredric Jameson describes "the gender turn" (2005, 140) as symptom of a deviation from materialist critiques of labor, wealth production and class hierarchy; but the idea of a divorce between gender and class struggle has also been addressed by feminist theorists (and utopians). Disengaging from the essentialist idea that equality and pacifism are inherently womanly characteristics—an argument commonly found in first-wave feminism—Monique Wittig has been instrumental in presenting gender oppression as a class struggle in need of radical, utopian revolutions. In her collection *The*

Straight Mind and Other Essays (2002), she leans on the idea that women constitute an unspoken, marginalized class within the class system itself. The author of *Les Guérillères* (1969)—a classic example of feminist utopia—advocates for the acknowledgment of this category, but also articulates the dual response to this challenge which, as we will see, permeates distinctive strands of gender utopias:

> What does "feminist" mean? Feminist is formed with the word "femme," "woman," and means: someone who fights for women. For many of us it means someone who fights for women as a class and for the disappearance of this class. For many others it means someone who fights for woman and her defence—for the myth, then, and its reinforcement. (Wittig 2002, 14)

In her essay "One Is Not Born a Woman" ([1981] 2002), Wittig identifies the source of gender-based oppression with materialist, historical facts and not with a natural, biological division between sexes (even when it is presented advantageously for women). Opposing the argument according to which subjectivism is detrimental to class struggle, she presents sexual violence and oppression as social institutions.

As utopian imaginaries center around the integrity of the private body, in resistance to the primacy of a normative public or social habitus, sexuality and gender have progressively become integral to radical stories of change, propelled by pivotal steps in the elaboration of feminist and queer theory. Yet one still must acknowledge the overpowering literary weight of dystopias in discourses about gender and sexuality, a continual locus of violence and oppression. The drive to uniformity of some utopias, denounced by Emil Cioran in *History and Utopia* (2015), characterizes the one feature that resists most fervently the very idea of gender diversity and subjectivism in general: "Hostile to anomaly, to deformity, to irregularity, [the utopia] tends to the affirmation of the homogeneous, of the typical, of repetition and orthodoxy. But life is rupture, heresy, derogation from the norms of matter" (77). To understand the deconstruction of gender and sexual categories pursued by more recent feminist and queer utopias we must examine the rationalization of gendered and sexual practices in utopian and dystopian imaginaries.

THE RATIONALIZATION OF SEXUALITY

One dominant feature of traditional utopias is the moral necessity of free will and agency, even as the mind/body dualism perpetuated by the Judaeo-Christian dialectic informs the idea that sexuality is an obstacle to the exercise of reason and temperance. According to Michel Foucault, the "protracted Christian asceticism" (1978, 158) and generalized shaming of all things fleshly ultimately leads to a fascination with, and a discursive upsurge in, sexuality and its "deviances" beginning in the eighteenth century. More importantly, the implementation of forms of "biopower" means the political harnessing and disciplining of the body and/as the political body as key matters of power and discourse. This biopolitical secularization and instrumentalization of sexuality, far from relating to eroticism, underpins the majority of discourses found in utopias and dystopias alike.

Indeed, the rationalization of sexuality was pertinent to the question of carnal pleasure in the tradition of imagining harmonious societies. The far-reaching Platonic principle of balance and harmony against dangerous excesses of passion requires the classical, humanist utopia to think of sexuality in terms of procreative monogamy and the exercise of restraint. To cement the ruling class's virtues, purity and unity in his fictional *Republic*, Plato goes as far as proposing a eugenic selection of female and male guardians:

The best men must have sex with the best women as frequently as possible, while the opposite is true of the most inferior men and women, and, second, that if our herd is to be of the highest possible quality, the former's offspring must be reared (as guardians) but not the latter's. And this must all be brought about without being noticed by anyone except the rulers, so that our herd of guardians remains as free from dissension as possible. (Plato and Bloom 1968, V: 454d-e).

Although Plato does not exclude women from the ruling guardian class, the crafting of his utopian republic illustrates what Foucault would call "a male ethics" (Foucault 1990). Chosen for their reproductive capacities, women are not so much a receptacle of the virtuous temperance of philosopher-kings as they are subjects under the purview of the ideal of communal goods and the elimination of private property: "women figured only as objects or, at most, as partners that one had best train, educate, and watch over when one had them under one's power, but stay away from when they were under the power of someone else (father, husband, tutor)" (Foucault 1978, 22). This androcentric and passionless representation of utopian sexuality thus anticipates the Foucauldian "attention to the processes of life, characterized [by] a power whose highest function was perhaps no longer to kill, but to invest life through and through" (Foucault 1978, 139). The development of the modern concept of "population" and the institutionalization of bodies, infamously formalized by Malthusianism and social Darwinism, is decipherable in the representation of state-regulated, ritualized sexuality.

The ideal of heteronormative (yet supposedly egalitarian) complementarity is presented in several male-authored utopian texts. Beyond the (relative) equity between spouses, More's utopians undress in front of each other once before marriage to ensure their complementarity and the reasonable choices of partners. In a more contemporary setting, More's ideal of complete complementarity is evoked in René Barjavel's utopian science-fiction description of Gondawa in *The Ice People* ([1968] 1971). Barjavel's novel presents the contemporary scientific with an outstanding discovery: humanity was already there 900,000 years ago in the shape of an unimaginably advanced civilization induced by the conquering of a universal equation giving way to an endless source of energy. In a ritual "designation" ceremony, prepubescent

Gondas were selected to be mated together for life in such a perfect way that they recognize each other. This mixture of supernaturality and advanced technology is also translated through the description of procreation: when "designated," Gondas receive a ring, which they episodically remove in order to have children. In Barjavel's fictional world, the civilization of Gondawa is heavily contrasted with their rival empire: Enisoraï. The Enisors are described as a capitalistic, nefarious empire that disregards the utopian ideal of balance by proliferating in terms of population, wealth and power-seeking. This caricature of an industrial-capitalist United States, a counterpart to the wisdom displayed in Barjavel's utopia, ultimately destroys the latter with nuclear weapons, a blunt symbol for their hypertrophied passion and sexuality.

The depiction of rationalized sexuality, based on the ancient value of temperance and seldom compatible with genuine affection, is transmogrified into a key feature of contemporary dystopias, in which state ideology replaces a humanist emphasis on individual agency, in favor of a uniform common purpose. One example is Aldous Huxley's *Brave New World* ([1932] 2006), in which organic pregnancy and birth are deemed disgraceful and taboo, and the body is a mere vessel for ideological conditioning and passionless conformity. Controlled by inventions such as "the Malthusian belt" and the enervating drug "Soma," this brave new world engineers a deeply unjust caste system. Despite Huxley's implicit critique, however, Caitriona Dhuill argues in *Sex in Imagined Spaces* (2010) that Huxley's portrayal of his female characters still does focus on sexual attractiveness and grooming: "the heterosexual sex act is still figured as the 'having' of the woman by the man; the highest accolade a woman can have in this culture is to be described as 'pneumatic,' a term for which Huxley does not deem it necessary to invent a male equivalent" (56). Again, the dystopian (or utopian) rationalization of sexuality does not allow women (and gender non-conforming individuals) to become actual subjects with agency and irregularities.

In Margaret Atwood's *The Handmaid's Tale* (1986), on the other hand, the "reason" for sex is justified through a fundamentalist reading of the Bible that is itself instrumentalized by the theocratical commanders of "Gilead," a dystopic, near-future vision of a splintered United States. Plagued by environmental deterioration and a far-reaching fertility crisis, sexual relations are confined to ritual rapes of so-called handmaids, who are at once considered fallen women and receptacles of "sacred duty." Reinforcing the dualism between sacred motherhood and the sin of the flesh, the Commanders continue to enjoy the "services" provided by *Jezebel's*, an aptlyname brothel "employing" recalcitrant handmaids. In the first season of Bruce Miller's television adaptation of Atwood's novel (2017), the repression of "deviant" sexuality goes so far as to punish one rebellious lesbian handmaid with female genital mutilation, underscoring the dystopic Manicheism of same-sex female pleasure and a punitively normative definition of sex as heterosexual and procreative.

"Mother the Machine": The Canonization of Maternalism in Feminist Utopias

The legacy of the rationalization of sexuality in utopian imaginaries is the separation of sexuality and pleasure from procreation. The dystopian counterpart to this ideal is encompassed in *1984*'s "Ingsoc" word "goodsex" (Orwell [1949] 1983), which limits sexual intercourse limited to married couples desiring to procreate, without any sexual pleasure on the part of the woman. This sort of focus on generating children as a form of ideological reproduction is paradoxically shared by both traditional and feminist utopias. Even while demonstrating the need for sexual freedom and equality, a presumption in many utopian novels is the need to establish motherhood and child-rearing as central if not sacred pillars of social organization, civilization and citizenship.

In Gilman's *Herland* as well as in Gerhart Hauptmann's *The Island of the Great Mother* (1925), motherhood achieves religious status, and both birthing and caring for children are exercised as essential duties (Dhuill 2010, 79). Celebrating the ideal of the Mother Goddess, matriarchal communities estrange themselves from the debasing influences of androcentric civilization, in order to ensure the upbringing of peaceful, selfless generations of children. If Gilman's *Herland* could be read as an inspirational thought experiment about women's "essentially" caring nature, that novel's sequel offers a more nuanced take. *With Her in Ourland* ([1916] 1997) follows the "Herlander" Ellador, now married to one of the male explorers who sought out that promised land of "girls, girls, girls!" Gilman's conclusions, disappointingly for many contemporary readers, converge at the ideal of sexual complementarity. The revelation in *Herland* that "Ourland" is ridden with misogyny and sexual injustice prompts Ellador to seek the perfect equilibrium of the sexes, by accompanying her husband back to his land and attempting a true collaboration there between man and woman.

Both Gilman's and Hauptmann's maternalist utopias eventually combine the ideal of *caritas* and motherly bond as empowering qualities in essentialist arguments about sexual complementarity and biological destiny, anticipating the renaissance of feminist maternalist utopias in the 1970s. The publications of Mary Daly's *Beyond the God Father* (1973) and Merlin Stone's *When God Was a Woman* (1976), also known as *The Paradise Papers: The Suppression of Women's Rites*, underline the phallogocentrist historical erasure of the symbols of the "Sacred Feminine" in favor of a patriarchal figure. Daly's central theory in *Gyn/Ecology* (1978) states that "God represents the necrophilia of patriarchy, whereas Goddess affirms the life-loving being of women and nature" (xi). The fashioning of this immutable sacred feminine nature anchored in gynocentric myths, not unlike Jung's conception of a collective unconscious (Tonkin 2012) also ties into the nascent ecofeminism of the decade. Identifying the image of the life-giving womb with the matrix of planet Earth, feminist maternalist utopias restructure society around the fundamental value of equity and equilibrium. Akin to the Amazon myth, the worlds imagined by these authors are often on the margin of the civilized or known world, either temporally (Russ's *The Female Man*) or spatially (Gilman's *Herland*).

Utopian dreams of parthenogenesis, however, do not always entail an immutable representation of gender expression. In Angela Carter's apocalyptic novel *The Passion of New Eve* (1977), the deification of motherhood is heavily parodied in a sequence where the protagonist, Evelyn, is kidnapped in a gynocentric cult ruled by a surgically enhanced, grotesquely mythological "Mother" of overblown proportions and multiple breasts. In this microsociety, the utopian dream is to give birth to a new Eve, who in turn will produce a parthenogenic offspring: "Myth is more instructive than history, Evelyn; Mother proposes to reactivate the pathenogenesis archetype, utilising a new formula. She's going to castrate you, Evelyn, and then excavate what we call the 'fructifying female space' inside you and make you a perfect specimen of womanhood" (65). Following the evocation of iconic female figures and goddesses in an ecstatic litany of names,[3] the scene clearly targets the excesses of essentialist and exclusionary rhetoric of second-wave feminism.

In *Women on the Edge of Time*, Piercy delivers a similar conclusion, though she does rely on more classical utopian tropes, such as the portrayal of the ethical gap between the befuddled, foreign protagonist and the utopian natives to whom the structure of their society seems only natural. Indeed, Connie's preconception about the overwhelming influence and relevancy of gender standards is thwarted by the Mattapoisett's revolutionary stance on gender and sexuality: "All coupling, all befriending goes on between biological males, biological females, or both. That's not a useful set of categories. We tend to divvy up people by what they're good at and bad at, strengths and weaknesses, gifts and failings" (203). In addition to the irrelevancy of heteronormative labels of sexuality and the use of the gender-neutral pronoun "per," the bemused Connie witnesses how citizens of Piercy's utopia are all artificially born in a machine: "all in a sluggish row, babies bobbed. Mother the machine. Like fish in the aquarium at Coney Island" (96). However, Piercy goes further than the dystopian trope of technological, eugenic birth-giving and envisions a society where each child is raised by three "mothers," in addition to the communal mothering task taken on by "kidbinders." Reshaping the family unit while trying to scrap all traces of heteronormativity or essentialism, Piercy's utopian scope also incorporates restructured version of romantic partnerships. Citizens of Mattapoisett can indeed have multiple partners, the love between them corresponding to the ancient categories of *agape* ("hand-friend") or *eros* ("pillowfriend"). Despite those differences and regardless of gender, both versions of relationships appear as binding.

This encompassing redefinition of sexuality and gender also anticipates the recent inclusion of intersectional racial concerns (Crenshaw 1989) within feminist struggles. At first, Connie Ramos expresses disgust with Mattapoisett's post-racial egalitarianism: "she hated them, the bland bottleborn monsters of the future, born without pain, multicolored like a litter of puppies without the stigmata of race and sex" (Piercy 1976, 102). It takes time for Connie to recognize and accept that the very concept of "Woman" has becoming irrelevant. Piercy's reimagining of gender and race in her utopia remarkably forecasts queer and feminist theorists who seek to recast women and gender minorities as social as well as sexual beings. Echoing in fact the words of Charlotte Perkins Gilman, radical feminist Monique Wittig argues that "the category of sex is the category that sticks to women, for only they cannot be conceived of outside of it. Only they are sex, the sex, and sex they have been made in their minds, bodies, acts, gestures; even their murders and beatings are sexual. Indeed, the category of sex tightly holds women" (Wittig 2002, 8). The deconstructionist core of utopian reimagination of tightly enforced gender categories brings to the surface two distinct strands of feminist fictions and prefigures the fundamental challenge to the essentialist notion of femininity we now see in contemporary critical theory and current academic discourse regarding identity politics.

THE QUEER BODY AS UTOPIA

Contemporary feminism's critique of earlier feminists' attachment to (essentialist) matriarchal visions is increasingly indebted to the emergence of queer theory in recent decades. A radically inclusive utopian imaginary abolishes the relevancy of gender norms and archetypes altogether. The possibility of thinking "outside gender" logically connects with the definitional sense of utopia as a place that is beyond reach or does not exist. In many ways, the unintelligibility of the queer body makes it very existence utopian. This radicality subtly permeates fictional depictions of same-sex communities where lesbianism becomes the norm; being removed from any relation to man, homosexual woman escapes the heterosexist gaze and patriarchal objectification. Donna Haraway's famous "Cyborg Manifesto" (1985) presents an ironic "post-gender" utopia that centers itself around the conceptual body of the posthuman cyborg: "It means both building and destroying machines, identities, categories, relationships, space stories. Though both are bound in the spiral dance, I would rather be a cyborg than a goddess" (181). Anchored in materialist feminism, Haraway's rhetoric hinges around the denunciation of gender, class or race as the artificial product of historically harmful discourses that seek to restrain and pigeonhole identities. Sketching utopian queer spaces would thus require extracting oneself from historical categories, which may be why readers often turn to science-fiction writers to find relevant models for such endeavors. Indeed, Haraway herself singles out novels such as Russ's *Female Man* as an example.

Ursula K. Le Guin is of course another such science-fiction author, giving us numerous radical "thought experiments," including the stunning *The Left Hand of Darkness* (1969). Descriptive rather than predictive, according to the author, her works frequently flirt with utopian themes. The protagonist of this novel, a Genly Ai, is sent from Earth to the planet Gethen to convince their leaders to join a confederation of planets seeking peace and harmony. Ai is struck with "cognitive estrangement" at the organization of the "ambisexual" world of Gethen, where even the idea of gender neutrality does not define accurately the gender category of its population: "Yet you cannot think of a Gethenian as 'it.' They are not neuters. They are potentials, or integrals. ... I must say 'he,' for the same reasons as we used the masculine pronoun in referring to a transcendent god: it is less defined, less specific, than the neuter or the feminine" (94). Though this foreign planet is hardly portrayed as entirely meliorative, the depiction of gender and the criteria used to define identity and individuality features a utopian rhetoric which challenges the human species' shortcomings.

The extrapolation of gender indeterminacy onto extra-terrestrial creatures can also be found in the fiction of another prominent female science-fiction writer, Octavia Butler. Her *Lilith's Brood*, or *Xenogenesis*, trilogy (1987–1989) is premised on the extinction of the human race and the foundation of a new, hybrid species. Lilith, Adam's rebellious first wife (and/or she-demon, according to several Jewish legends) lends her name to the protagonist at the origin of a new genesis, marked by hybridity and miscegenation. After a near-apocalypse, Lilith is introduced to the Oankali race, aliens who offer a new life on Earth in exchange for the right to interbreed with humans, which they describe as a biological imperative for their survival. The last novel, *Imago* (2012), focuses on the "oloii," an Oankali subdivision of creatures: chameleon-like and gender indeterminate, this hybrid species allows for humans and aliens to create "constructs." Butler's invention defies gender binarism and its alternative—the in-betweenness of gender neutrality: "There were still some Humans who insisted on seeing the *ooloi* as some kind of male–female combination, but the *ooloi* were no such thing. They were themselves—a different sex altogether" (7). The gender indeterminacy of *oolo*i challenges human norms and the abjection for creatures at the margins of intelligibility (Kristeva 1982). Indeed, translated by phrases such as "bridge," "weaver" or "magnet," the *ooloi* are characterized by their organic, irreversible and indisputable attraction that binds them with humans, a need akin to a matter of life and death. Most importantly, the novel intertwines the concepts of hybridity with that of adaptability and posterity.

Conclusion

While the most influential feminist representations of gender prejudice have been articulated in contemporary dystopias, it is necessary to recognize the literary legacy of maternalist utopias that have accompanied both the first and second wave of feminism. Centering a sanctified version of motherhood and femininity, the depiction of these fictional matriarchal societies relied on the revaluation of supposedly intrinsically feminine values and virtues that have been erased by a phallocentric writing of history. The emergence of a renewed take on gender, coinciding with queer theory and the criticism of essentialism, has undermined the relevance of gender norms and categories altogether.

Nonetheless, specifically queer narratives are still at the margins, though that is changing fast. If the healing powers of the posthuman alien–human constructs reflect Haraway's cyborg feminism, the casting of identity minorities in the roles of aliens or monsters underlines the restraints of science-fiction regarding the elaboration of a gender utopia. Though useful in its utopian structuration—producing identities and bodies that are beyond the limited perceptions of our prejudiced society—the collusion of the idea of queerness and non-humanity does put into question the place given to gender non-conformity in the utopian imaginary; which raises the question: Is critical theory the only "good place" for the full expression of utopian sexualities and gender identities?

Notes

1. 1Though the sentence is routinely credited as part of de Beauvoir's *The Second Sex* (1949) and has been massively used during recent feminist protests, there is no certainty as to its origin.
2. In this short diachronic perspective, I am disregarding the mention of same-sex sexuality or gender minorities as anachronistic labels that would have been ignored in *Utopia* and almost any other literary representation alike.
3. The paratactic evocation of a collective pantheon of womanhood in Carter's parody, including Kali, Maria, and Aphrodite, is a conspicuous jab at Monique Wittig's *Les Guérillères*, where the right page confronts the reader with a similar psalmody of iconic women (fictional or real) such as Lysistrata, Io, Iseut, or Judith.

References

Atwood, Margaret. 1986. *The Handmaid's Tale*. New York: Houghton Mifflin Harcourt.

Bachofen, Johann Jakob. 2005. *An English Translation of Bachofen's Mutterrecht (Mother Right): Lycia, Crete, and Athens*. New York: Edwin Mellen Press.

Barjavel, René. (1968) 1971. *The Ice People*, trans. Charles Lam Markmann. New York: William Morrow.

Butler, Octavia E. 2012. *Imago*. New York: Open Road Media.

Carter, Angela. 1977. *The Passion of New Eve*. London: Virago.

Cioran, E.M. 2015. *History and Utopia*, trans Richard Howard, ed. Eugene Thacker. Reprint. New York: Arcade Publishing.

Crenshaw, Kimberlé. 1989. *Demarginalizing the Intersection of Race and Sex: A Black Feminist Critique of Antidiscrimination Doctrine*, 139. Feminist Theory and Antiracist Politics: University of Chicago Legal Forum.

Daly, Mary. 1978. *Gyn/Ecology: The Metaehtics of Radical Feminism*. Boston: Beacon's Press.

———. 1985. *Beyond God the Father: Toward a Philosophy of Women's Liberation*. Boston: Beacon Press.

Dhuill, Caitriona. 2010. *Sex in Imagined Spaces: Gender and Utopia from More to Bloch*. Milton Park: Taylor and Francis.

Foucault, Michel. 1978. *History of Sexuality Volume 1: An Introduction*, trans. Robert Huxley. New York: Pantheon Books.

———. 1990. *History of Sexuality Volume 2: The Use of Pleasure*, trans. Robert Huxley. New York: Vintage Books.

Gilman, Charlotte Perkins. (1915) 1999. *Herland*. In *Herland, The Yellow Wall-paper, and Selected Writings*. New York: Penguin.

———. (1916) 1997. *With Her in Ourland*, ed. Mary Jo Deegan and Michael R. Hill. Westport: Greenwood Press.

Haraway, Donna J. 1991. A Cyborg Manifesto: Science, Technology, and Socialist-Feminism in the Late Twentieth Century. In *Simians, Cyborgs and Women: The Reinvention of Nature*, 149–181. New York: Routledge.

Hauptmann, Gerhart. 1925. *The Island of the Great Mother, Or, The Miracle of Île Des Dames: A Story from the Utopian Archipelago*. New York: B.W. Huebsch and the Viking Press.

Huxley, Aldous. (1932) 2006. *Brave New World*. New York: Harper Perennial.

Jameson, Fredric. 2005. *Archaeologies of the Future: The Desire Called Utopia and Other Science Fictions*. London: Verso.

Kristeva, Julia. 1982. *Powers of Horror: An Essay on Abjection*. New York: Columbia University Press.

Le Guin, Ursula K. 2000. *The Left Hand of Darkness: 50th Anniversary Edition*. New York: Penguin.

Miller, Bruce (Writer), Morano, Reed (Director). 2017. Too Late. *The Handmaid's Tale* (season 1, episode 3). Hulu.

Orwell, George. (1949) 1983. *1984*. New York: Houghton Mifflin Harcourt.

Patai, Daphne. 1982. Gamesmanship and Androcentrism in Orwell's 1984. *PMLA* 97: 856–870. https://doi.org/10.2307/462176. Accessed 1 June 2021.

Piercy, Marge. 1976. *Women on the Edge of Time*. New York: Alfred A. Knopf.

Plato, and Allan Bloom. 1968. *The Republic*. New York: Basic Books.

Russ, Joanna. 1975. *The Female Man*. London: Women's Press.

Tonkin, Maggie. 2012. *Angela Carter and Decadence: Critical Fictions / Fictional Critiques*. New York: Palgrave Macmillan.

Wittig, Monique. (1981) 2002. One Is not Born a Woman. In *The Straight Mind and Other Essays*, 9–20. Boston: Beacon Press.

———. 2002. *The Straight Mind and Other Essays*. Boston: Beacon Press.

Death

Paola Spinozzi

[Vita], ut scis, non semper retinenda est; non enim vivere bonum est, sed bene vivere. Itaque sapiens vivet quantum debet, non quantum potest. ... Cogitat semper qualis vita, non quanta sit.

Seneca, *Ad Lucilium Epistularum Moralium*, Liber octavus, LXX, c. 65 AD.

INTRODUCTION

Death is an event that involves aging, pain and suffering, illness and the deterioration of the body, the right to die, the act of dying, the expression of grief and mourning, funeral rites, and the cult of the dead. Death is also a biological process defined by human intervention through institutionalized health care, treatments for incurable and terminal diseases, therapeutic persistence, and palliative care. The control of mortality and illness through medical research and surgery has changed the meaning humans attribute to suffering. The biblical and eschatological, or secular and stoic meaning of suffering has been challenged by the idea that suffering is a human limit, no longer inscribed in a spiritual or transcendent system. The free choice of death thus expresses the will to reject pain, but also denounces the impossibility of attributing meaning to it. Theories, categorizations, and representations of death encompass medicine, biotechnologies, psychology, ethics and metaphysics, religion,

P. Spinozzi (✉)
University of Ferrara, Ferrara, Italy

P. Marks et al. (eds.), *The Palgrave Handbook of Utopian and Dystopian Literatures*, https://doi.org/10.1007/978-3-030-88654-7_55

and the law. And yet the countless contingencies of living and dying call for constant redefinitions of the concept of life and death.

The history of utopia as a genre is marked by the contrast between nature and norm. Because human beings are all too inclined to follow their instincts and passions, utopian writers envision societies regulated by rational and homogeneous principles. The utopian imagery originates from the conflict between a sharp perception of the here and now and a sense of estrangement that generates an external point of view. This oscillation places the end of life at the intersection between the givenness of reality and the openness of an imagined elsewhere where human beings can be perfected. However, perfectibility clashes with ontological finitude. As the vision of an alternative society cannot overcome the finite nature of human life, the utopian thinker attempts to mitigate, neutralize, or ignore the human limit par excellence. Death, escaping regulation, is the ultimate aporia of utopia. Knowing that evil cannot be eradicated, utopian writers adopt dirigiste practices. Knowing that death cannot be eluded, they seek to neutralize its inevitability. Not only living well, but also learning to die well, taking leave of life with dignity, choosing to abandon it if necessary, are the highest expressions of freedom, exemplified by the death of Socrates. While finitude poses an insuperable challenge, utopian writers question institutionalized death, rationalize fear, and regulate mourning. Death in utopia can be understood as a sustained reflection on end-of-life decisions and codification of funerary practices.

PERSPECTIVES ON DEATH

Attitudes toward death can be seen in the historical perspective adopted by Philippe Ariès, Michel Vovelle, and Alberto Tenenti, and in the culturalist perspective developed by Jonathan Dollimore and Jan Assam. The assumption that shifts of attitudes are slow or occur between long periods of immobility supports Ariès' wide-ranging diachronic approach to the study of death. To gain insight, scholars must extend their enquiry to a longer period than that which separates two major successive changes. If they focus on a narrow chronology, they risk attributing original characteristics to phenomena that are much older. As Ariès writes:

> The historian of death must not be afraid to embrace the centuries until they run into a millennium. The errors he will not be able to avoid are less serious than the anachronisms to which he would be exposed by too short a chronology. Let us, therefore, regard a period of a thousand years as acceptable. (1981, xvi–xvii)

Tenenti (2000) underlines the dangers of sectoral research and the limits of ethno-anthropological studies that dwell too much on the external aspects of funerary events, disconnecting death from the ordinary rhythm of existence and its possibilities, and transforming it into a sort of gateway of uncertain nature toward other superhuman or non-historical realities.

In Dollimore's view, the discourse on death elaborated by the historians is affected by an ethical value judgment about the decline of Western civilizations. The historicization supported by Ariès or Zygmunt Bauman is instrumental in supporting the argument that the decline of the West is due to the propagation of a morbid and perverse connection between sexuality and death. The desire to historicize phenomena that Dollimore considers transhistorical reveals, in his opinion, an ideological goal. The link between Eros and Thanatos is not only an integral part of human existence, but it also functions as an extreme and privileged mode of knowledge. Drawing upon Nietzsche, Freud, and Bataille, he considers this link as one of the primary categories of the Western world. While reaching its most intense expression in the Renaissance, the relationship between desire and death has not worsened in the contemporary era. In fact, it is a relationship endemic to Western cultures in a broad sense (Dollimore 1998, XI).

The history of death as the history of culture is supported by Jan Assmann, who reads the entire human culture as the response of different societies to the event of death. Culture originates from the awareness of being mortal and creates a space and a time in which human beings can think beyond their limited horizon of life. The ability to extend their work, experience, and projects toward broader horizons and dimensions of fulfilment allows them to make life meaningful and mitigate the intolerable awareness of finitude (Assmann 2000).

On the one hand, Ariès, Vovelle, and Tenenti adopt a wide historical approach to identify the slow transformation of attitudes toward death, while on the other Dollimore and Assmann emphasize the importance of culture in determining behaviors and rituals. Death in utopia will thus be explored through both a historical and a cultural perspective: ways of dying, ideas of the afterlife and immortality, funerary customs, iconography, and monuments will be connected to specific periods but also will be conceived as structural components of utopia as a genre.

The Art of Dying in Early Modern Utopias

The passage from the medieval to the early modern age reveals the syncretic characteristics of Western cultures toward death. In *De arte bene moriendi* (1620) Cardinal Bellarmine warns that we should be concerned about eternal life during our existence, rather than in the moment of agony, when we have lost discernment, implying that life on earth is a preparation for eternal life. The problem he addresses is still unsolved today: how do we master ourselves in the moment of death? The concept of voluntary death in antiquity stems from the need or will to protect honor, escape from poverty, or free oneself from serious illness caused by aging. Dignity of life, developed by the humanists between the sixteenth and seventeenth centuries, defines voluntary death as a personal choice, free from moral blame or dishonor, in contrast with the medieval conception of suicide, unacceptable in theological terms.

The Catholic condemnation of suicide, corroborated by common morals and validated by canonical and civil law, is deconstructed through the rereading of classical ethics.

The Stoic tradition, recontextualized in the conception of serene death by humanists such as Thomas More, Erasmus of Rotterdam, and Pico della Mirandola, develops in parallel with the views of the Roman Catholic Church during the Counter-Reformation. While in the Middle Ages disease, old age, and death were seen primarily in terms of decay and putrefaction, early modern utopian writers sought to enhance the sense of dominion over death by neutralizing the body. They contributed to overcoming medieval conceptions of death through a rationalization process that stood at a distance from the macabre topoi of iconography and literature in order to enhance dignity and composure in the act of dying. It is the ideal of a Christian death free from agitation and terror, pervaded by sweetness and serenity because the end has been rationalized. Tenenti clarifies that the ethical-religious dream of a peaceful death is an ideal outlined since the fifteenth century, although it is difficult to assess its collective resonance. The idea of dying peacefully is also part of utopia as an ethically self-sufficient conception of the European individual between 1400 and 1600 (Tenenti 1957).

In Great Britain, the art of dying flourished in the writings of popular preachers who investigate death as the moment of truth. *The Craft of Dying*, published anonymously in 1450, attests to the tradition of *ars moriendi*. It focuses on the material aspect of death, on the process of dying, and on iconographic and literary representations from the fourteenth and fifteenth centuries, when life was constantly threatened by the bubonic plague and other diseases, wars, and famine. Thanks to the activity of printers such as William Caxton, *The Craft of Dying*, which merges German, French, and Anglo-Saxon sources, had wide circulation. The topos of *ars moriendi* resonated through the seventeenth century in the books of Christian devotion by Jeremy Taylor, a cleric in the Church of England. The poetic style of expression he adopted in *The Rules and Exercises of Holy Living* and *The Rules and Exercises of Holy Dying*, published in 1650 and 1651, earned him fame during the Protectorate of Oliver Cromwell.

The will to intervene in the existence of finite creatures is an aporia that the utopian project overcomes by drawing inspiration from *ars moriendi*. Knowing how to take leave of life can transform an event in which the dying feel subjugated into a noble final test of emotions and pain: utopian thinkers seek to dominate death, instead of being dominated. The will to legitimize voluntary death without contradicting religious tenets is one of the most complex problems that the Catholic humanist Thomas More faced in a Tudor England divided by the schism, something he tries to resolve in the society described in *Utopia*. Raphael Hythloday's explanation about assisted dying on the island of Utopia reveals a twofold perspective: the social acceptance of the practice requires religious and ethical validation, while the importance attributed to economic and material benefits underlies utilitarian motivations. Spiritual and philosophical legitimation on the one side and social and economic advantage on the other invite close inspection, not least because the Catholic More opposed the Church of England and was beheaded for that opposition. More attempts to rationalize the event of death by emphasizing the value of human intervention: patients affected by terminal illness and constant pain ought to realize that they have outlived their existence. Choosing to die willingly, serenely, and with hopes of resurrection, is an honorable way of facing finitude (Spinozzi 2016).

Utopian travellers, in learning the habits and customs of the foreign country, often learn that the practice of burial has been rejected in favor of cremation. Public health, religious beliefs, and symbolic motivations in Tommaso Campanella's *Civitas Solis* (*City of the Sun*, 1602) dictate that dead bodies should not be buried but instead should be burnt to be purified and turned into fire, which is noble, alive, and generated by the sun. Campanella rescues the dead from the process of decay by elevating the body to a symbolic domain, in which the lifeless limbs become one with a vital entity. From Campanella's utopia onwards, cremation becomes a thematic feature of the genre. Numerous utopias present cremation as the main funerary rite, even in times when the Church had a total monopoly, which determined that burial was the only possibility. The choice of burning the dead, a complex topic in the western history of funerary customs, has a sustained place in utopias, partly on the wave of classical suggestions and partly thanks to the possibility of imagining otherness.

The elaboration of mourning offers an insight into the conceptualization of death in utopia. According to Ariès, mourning marks a profound change in mentality after the sixteenth century and until the middle of the nineteenth century. Personal demonstrations of grief would not be tolerated after the period of mourning:

> The man who was too afflicted to return to a normal life after the short period of time allowed by custom had no alternative than to retire to a monastery, or to the country, outside the world where he was known. At least among the upper classes and in the towns, mourning had become too highly ritualized and socialized to play the role it had once filled, that of emotional release. It had become impersonal and cold. Instead of allowing people to express what they felt about death, it prevented them from doing so. Mourning acted as a screen between man and death. (Ariès 1981, 327)

The emphasis on essential rites acquires a distinctive symbolic value in the utopian genre. Absence of pomp and moderate manifestations of mourning mitigate the fear of nothingness after death and shift the focus of the event from eschatological speculation to a commemoration of the deceased as an exemplum for the community. In utopia, therefore, meditation associated with mourning creates an intense bond between the living and the dead, neutralizing the uncertainty of the afterlife and strengthening the confidence that survival will be granted by remembrance.

DEATH AND MEMORY IN THE SEVENTEENTH AND EIGHTEENTH CENTURY

The distinction between religion and ethics is at the core of the debate on death as a choice in the seventeenth and eighteenth centuries. Between 1607 and 1608, John Donne wrote the first English work in defense of suicide, *Biathanatos*, published posthumously between 1644 and 1647. Donne makes a distinction between selfish suicide, committed exclusively for personal purposes, and suicide that imitates the sacrifice of Christ: while the former must be forbidden, the latter should be sanctioned. His view is developed by David Hume in the essay *On Suicide*, published posthumously in 1777: suicide does not disturb the order of Divine Providence, it is indeed admissible as are all the actions that man has the power to perform daily, without violating the law of God. The positions of More, Donne, and Hume attest to the continuity in British culture of the investigation of death understood as a voluntary event that can arise from a personal choice, conscious and meditated. While claiming that death freely chosen according to rational principles does not subvert the divine order, such positions suggest that ethics and religion should be entwined.

In the seventeenth- and eighteenth-century utopias, the elaboration of death reveals the different philosophical-religious orientations of utopian thinkers: Christian, in *Reipublicae Christianopolitanae descriptio* (1619) by Johann V. Andreä; materialistic, in *L'Autre Monde. Les États et Empires de la Lune* (1657, posthumous) by Cyrano de Bergerac; deistic, in *L'an deux mille quatre cent quarante. Rêve s'il en fut jamais* (1771) by Louis-Sébastien Mercier; atheistic, in *Histoire des Ajaoïens* (1768, written in 1682) by Bernard de Fontenelle. Philosophical and religious conceptions explaining the afterlife reveal how partial the effort to build a secular utopian society is in the face of man's unchangeable mortality (Trousson 2004). In the decade of 1789–1800, the Revolution inherited from the Enlightenment the desire to exorcise superstitions fuelled by fear of death and uncertainty about the existence of eternal life. The new institutions foster concepts of death as eternal sleep and civic immortality. While examining the period between 1790 and 1815, Vovelle notices that few eras have left more utopias about death. Already in 1770 or 1771 Sébastien Mercier, in *L'An deux mille quatre cent quarante*, consecrates four chapters to what a funeral should be in Paris: an event freed from macabre pomp and presented as a testament to life, dedicated to the construction of collective memory. Mercier's meticulous description takes visual shape in architectural projects: while planning the ideal city, the representatives of French revolutionary architecture, Étienne-Louis Boullée, Claude-Nicolas Ledoux, and Jean-Jacques Lequeu, lay emphasis on the place of the dead (Vovelle

2004). Boullée's cenotaphs are spatial expressions of his utopian mentality. They are at the core of a secular rite celebrating collective memory, a fundamental way of understanding death in utopia. Faced with doubts about the existence of the afterlife, the utopian architect transforms the mortal remains of great men into emblematic memories by erecting a grandiose monument that invites worship. The cenotaph also contains Masonic symbolism linked to the rites of cremation, something that will be developed in the nineteenth-century debate on funerary practices.

Death, Progress, and Eugenics in Nineteenth-Century Utopias

Utopianism in France gained momentum in the early 1800s in the projects elaborated by Saint-Simon, Proudhon, and Fourier, whose theories resonate in the following decades. After that, literary utopia undergoes a metamorphosis. While the crisis of utopian beliefs generates an endogenous process of disintegration, Gabriel Tarde, Jules Verne, Paul Adam, Anatole France, Maurice Spronck, and Daniel Halévy all draw inspiration from the possibilities inherent in the utopian genre to imagine their societies. Paul Adam's *Lettres de Malaisie* (1898) offers a reflection on civil life, in which the ideal of a healthy and honest existence, followed by a peaceful death, should sound reassuring. And yet the pacifying view of physical health, moral harmony, and serene end hides the unsolved enigma of death, attempting to alleviate angst by reabsorbing human life into collective or cosmic existence. When the artificiality of utopian harmony becomes apparent, ancestral fears and violent death re-emerge. Utopias between the nineteenth and twentieth centuries highlight death as physical or aesthetic intoxication. Giving death, as the sadist Schultze does in Verne's *Les Cinq Cents Millions de la Bégum* (1879), and giving oneself death, as happens in Halévy's *Histoire de Quatre Ans* (1903), produce thrills of pleasure.

In the second half of the nineteenth century, in response to the crisis of the myth of progress and the devastating effects of industrialization in Great Britain and France, the utopian genre expresses fin-de-siecle catastrophism and prophecies of the apocalypse. The pervasiveness of death indicates the crisis of the genre: the end of humankind, civilization, and the planet encapsulate in metaphorical terms a critique of the utopian elsewhere, a place in which inhuman perfection suppresses individuality. Finitude intersects with the debate on the end of the species, arising from Charles Darwin's theories of evolution and chance as the generating principle of life and death. In Victorian Britain, with technocracy replacing teleology, death becomes the disruptive, deviant event to manage through an apparatus of medical practices and behavioral norms. Victorian views of death validate in scientific terms the idea that a human being, although individually finite, survives in the continuation of his/her own species. On a material level, the production of goods and the attribution of intrinsic value to things and possessions attempt to dispel the anguish of death, but also increase the terror of relinquishment and loss. Industrialization and capitalism, the control of mortality through the evolution of science and technology, and sophisticated forms of mourning and funerary rituals shape the mentality of Victorian utopian writers.

Euthanasia and cremation reflect the productivity paradigm and the hygiene issues that arose during the nineteenth century. Anthony Trollope's dystopia *The Fixed Period* (1882) constructs, with ambiguous modes of representation, a discourse around the pedagogy of euthanasia and cremation, playing on the paradox between knowing that one must die and knowing how one must die. The extreme idea of euthanasia attached to a "fixed period" for all is a parody of the retirement age established by the British government as well as of the notion of physical and mental decay associated with old age. Protagonist John Neverbend's utopia revolves around a didactic program aimed at instructing citizens to accept the fixed period of death as a conscious, rational choice. It is a hyperbolic reading of Stoic ethics, since voluntary death is based on a predetermined and binding parameter, not on the freedom of choice motivating Stoic death. *The Fixed Period* can be read as a parody of *ars moriendi*, based on the concept that human beings live well if they perform their role in society and contribute to its functioning. They die well if they choose to disappear when they become socially useless or expensive. Trollope's island of Britannula is More's island of Utopia observed through a distorting lens: the argument of the incurable disease, through which the Utopians may choose to embrace voluntary death, is replaced by Neverbend's a priori position, according to which old age is the most terrible disease, to be eradicated with death. Trollope suggests that the emphasis on the unemployment, and therefore uselessness, of elderly people makes compassionate euthanasia instrumental to an economic conception of death, supported by a social system that establishes the lifespan of individuals according to their market value. While the "good death" incorporated pious motivations, economic interests, and eugenic requirements, the proposal for the institutionalization of cremation highlighted three advantages: improvement of hygiene, rationalization of cemetery spaces, and reduction of pomp. Trollope actively participated in the cremationist movement, signing with the pre-Raphaelite painter John Everett Millais a document in favor of the Cremation Society of England, established in 1874 under the aegis of the Queen's physician, Sir Henry Thompson. When Trollope wrote *The Fixed Period*, cremation was not legal, and it became so only in 1884, two years after his death (Spinozzi 2004).

Cremation generates an intertextual dialogue among *The Fixed Period*, *The Coming Race* (1871) by Edward Bulwer-Lytton, and *Erewhon: or, Over the Range* (1872) by Samuel Butler. *The Coming Race* reveals that cremation can heal the gap between the materiality of the ceremonies and the need for spirituality. Bulwer-Lytton reacts to the ostentation of the burial by attributing a sacred meaning to the ceremony of cremation, which evokes the bas-reliefs of a classical sarcophagus, where the hieratic postures of the bystanders enhance the solemn and composed atmosphere of the funeral. As in Campanella's *Civitas*

Solis, cremation mitigates the loss of the body because its transformation acquires a high symbolic value: the ashes are linked to the cycle of existence, they remind of the life infused into the person by the Creator. Bulwer-Lytton rewrites the classical funeral rite, softening the emotional impact and focusing on stylized gestures. Like Trollope, Butler resorts to irony to criticize the exterior display of grief in Victorian culture. Mourning, which in the Victorian code involves public visibility, becomes a collective ritual showcasing tangible things in Erewhon. Butler ridicules exteriority by showing how tears become objects of exchange. The three writers reveal how the conceptualization of death is marked by a complex mixture of realism, satire, irony, and autobiography.

DEATH AND ACCEPTANCE IN TWENTIETH-CENTURY UTOPIAS

In the 1900s, dystopia and science fiction explore the myth of the apocalypse in the dual meaning of the ultimate end of the world or regeneration. The invasion of aliens, such as the Martians who in Herbert G. Wells's *The War of the Worlds* (1898) want to exterminate humanity, shows that the death of the single individual is insignificant in the face of the vastness of death-generating events on a planetary scale. The apocalypse can destroy human civilization and cause the end of human dominance on earth or can mark the origin of a new social organization. From a palingenetic perspective, death, rather than being perceived as a final event, is a phase of transition, which involves a mental, biological, psychological metamorphosis, and a rebirth of humanity. In *Last and First Men* (1930) Olaf Stapledon focuses on death, rebirth, and transformation. The Last Man, in telepathic contact with the barbarians of the twentieth century, reconstructs the history of humanity over the course of billions of years. The immensely powerful Last Men, similar to Egyptian gods, serenely await the explosion of the sun and their own end.

Daniela Guardamagna (2004) notes that it is necessary to distinguish between political dystopias, where death is swift and the focus is on the pervasive presence of pain, and existential dystopias, in which the sense of finitude is overarching. In George Orwell's political dystopia *Nineteen Eighty-Four* (1949), death manifests itself in absence: extreme physical pain and torture are followed by the vaporization of individuals punished by the regime. Aldous Huxley's existential dystopia *Brave New World* (1932), on the contrary, exemplifies the utopian desire to build a static world that guarantees the absence of suffering. However, the removal of a common human destiny declares the failure of the pseudo utopia. The final dialogue between John Savage and Mustapha Mond, the Resident World Controller of Western Europe, reaffirms the right to live life as it was lived before the advent of the new world. To John Savage, the romantic components of suffering and death appear vital, despite the pain. And in Franz Werfel's *Stern der Ungeborenen. Ein Reiseroman* (*Star of the Unborn* 1946), the horrendous spectacle of decrepit beings wailing like babies, or other monstrous, semi-human creatures, cursing death and life, shows the reader that to reject good old normal death is a crime against nature. The ability to accept death thus becomes the dividing line between a dystopian world and the human alternative. Achieving utopia means spending life in conscious expectation of death.

Conclusion: Death and the Limit

Utopia as a genre allows the author to express subversive ideas about the dominant system by evoking an alternative elsewhere. Yet, when utopia tries to face and neutralize death, it fails, since the perfectibility of man, on which the utopian design is based, cannot be expanded beyond the limits of human life. It is a structural failure that reaches the essence of utopia. The theme of death in utopia sheds light on the contradictions and antinomies on which the utopian construction is based. While pursuing harmony, well-being, and happiness, utopia cannot solve the problem of finitude. Strategies of control and normalization reveal that the event of death undermines the idea of perfectibility on which each utopian project is founded. In the impossibility of expunging the end, utopia chooses to organize it. Utopian writers reflect on the art of dying, examine the possibility of voluntary death, exhibit ceremonies attended by all members of society to make death acceptable. They adopt cremation, a practice that removes the material aspect of death because utopia cannot accept the corpse just as it cannot accept the aspects of reality that elude control. They describe funeral rites characterized by the absence of grief, because rationalization and social function absorb the affective and emotional dimension in utopia. Preparing for death, embracing the uncertainty of an afterlife, and building collective memories of the dead are powerful secular attempts to cope with the fear of individual death. Narrativizing death involves inserting it in a plot that allows utopian writers to negotiate taboos and censorship inherent in the topic. Utopian narratives interrogate and offer alternatives to attitudes toward death in their own time and simultaneously address issues of trans-historical and trans-national scope, exploring when to die, how to die, and what it is that dies.

References

Adam, Paul. 1898. *Lettres de Malaisie: Roman*. Paris: Éd. de la Revue blanche.
Andreä, Johann V. 1619. *Reipublicae Christianopolitanae descriptio*. Argentorati [Strasbourg]: Sumptibus hæredum Lazari Zetzneri.
Ariès, Philippe. 1949. Attitudes devant la Vie et devant la Mort du XVIIe au XIXe Siècle. *Population* 3: 463–470.
———. 1974. *Western Attitudes Toward Death from the Middle Ages to the Present*, trans. Patricia M. Ranum. Baltimore: Johns Hopkins University Press. French edition: Ariès, Philippe. 1975. *Essais sur l'Histoire de la Mort en Occident du Moyen Âge à nos Jours*. Paris: Seuil.
———. 1977. *L'Homme devant la Mort*. Paris: Seuil. English edition: Ariès, Philippe. 1981. *The Hour of Our Death*, trans. Helen Weaver. New York: Alfred A. Knopf.

Assmann, Jan. 2000. *Der Tod als Thema der Kulturtheorie: Todesbilder und Totenriten im alten Ägypten*. Frankfurt am Main: Suhrkamp.

———. 2001. *Tod und Jenseits im Alten Ägypten*. München: C.H. Beck Verlag. English edition: Assmann, Jan. 2005. *Death and Salvation in Ancient Egypt*, trans. David Lorton. Ithaca: Cornell University Press.

Bauman, Zygmunt. 1992. *Mortality, Immortality and Other Life Strategies*. Stanford: Stanford University Press.

Bellarmino, Roberto. 1620. *De arte bene moriendi*. Roma: Zanetti.

Bulwer-Lytton, Edward. 1871. *The Coming Race*. Edinburgh and London: William Blackwood and Sons.

Butler, Samuel. 1872. *Erewhon: Or, Over the Range*. London: Trübner & Co.

Campanella, Tommaso. 2008. *La città del sole - Civitas solis: il manoscritto della prima redazione italiana (1602) e l'ultima edizione a stampa (1637)*, ed. Tonino Tornitore. Torino: N. Aragno.

Comper, Frances M.M., ed. 1917. *The Book of the Craft of Dying and other Early English Tracts Concerning Death: Taken from Manuscripts and Printed in the British Museum and Bodleian Libraries*. London: Longmans, Green & Co.

Cyrano de Bergerac, Savinien de. 1657. *Histoire comique: Contenant les États et Empires de la Lune*, ed. Henri Le Bret. Paris: Charles de Sercy.

Dollimore, Jonathan. 1998. Introduction. In *Death, Desire and Loss in Western Culture*, ix–xxxii. London: Penguin.

Donne, John. 1644. *Biathanatos: A Declaration of That Paradoxe or Thesis, That Selfe-homicide is not so Naturally Sinne, that it may never be otherwise*. London: John Dawson.

Guardamagna, Daniela. 2004. L'accettazione del dolore: presenza della morte nella distopia novecentesca. In *Perfezione e finitudine. La concezione della morte nell'utopia in età moderna e contemporanea*, ed. Vita Fortunati, Marina Sozzi, Paola Spinozzi, 255–265. Torino: Lindau.

Fontenelle, Bernard LeBovier de. 1998 (1768). *Histoire des Ajaoïens*, ed. Hans-Günter Funcke. Oxford: Voltaire Foundation.

Hume, David. 1783. *Essays on Suicide, and the Immortality of the Soul*. London: M. Smith.

Huxley, Aldous. 1932. *Brave New World*. London: Chatto & Windus.

Mercier, Louis-Sébastien. 1771. *L'An deux mille quatre cent quarante. Rêve s'il en fût jamais*. A Londres [Dresden?]: [Walther].

More, Thomas. 1516. *Libellus vere aureus nec minus salutaris quam festiuus de optimo reip. Statu*. Louvain: Arte Theodorici Martini.

Orwell, George. 1949. *Nineteen Eighty-Four*. London: Secker & Warburg.

Spinozzi, Paola. 2004. *The Fixed Period* di Anthony Trollope e la pedagogia del 'giusto' morire nelle utopie della seconda metà dell'Ottocento inglese. In *Perfezione e finitudine. La concezione della morte nell'utopia in età moderna e contemporanea*, ed. Vita Fortunati, Marina Sozzi, and Paola Spinozzi, 227–254. Torino: Lindau.

Spinozzi, Paola. 2016. Acerba illa vita velut carcere atque aculeo. Health or Death in More's *Libellus vere aureus*, Early Modern Thought and Contemporary Debate. *Utopian Studies* 27: 586–600.

Stapledon, Olaf. 1930. *Last and First Men: A Story of the Near and Far Future*. London: Methuen & Co.

Taylor, Jeremy. 1650. *The Rules and Exercises of Holy Living*. London: R. Royston.

———. 1651. *The Rules and Exercises of Holy Dying*. London: R. Royston.

Tenenti, Alberto. 1957. *Il senso della morte e l'amore della vita nel Rinascimento*. Torino: Giulio Einaudi Editore.

———. 2000. Introduzione. Un fenomeno europeo. In *Humana fragilitas. I temi della morte in Europa tra Duecento e Settecento*, ed. Alberto Tenenti, 9–24. Clusone: Ferrari Editrice.

Trollope, Anthony. 1882. *The Fixed Period: A Novel*. Edinburgh and London: W. Blackwood & Sons.

Trousson, Raymond. 2004. Dalla morte atea alla morte deista in utopia nei secoli XVII e XVIII. In *Perfezione e finitudine. La concezione della morte nell'utopia in età moderna e contemporanea*, ed. Vita Fortunati, Marina Sozzi, and Paola Spinozzi, 157–181. Torino: Lindau.

Vovelle, Michel. 1974. *Mourir autrefois: Attitudes collectives devant la Mort aux XVII et XVIII Siècles*. Paris: Gallimard.

———. 1983. *La Mort et l'Occident de 1300 à nos Jours*. Paris: Gallimard.

———. 1993. *L'Heure du grand Passage. Chronique de la Mort*. Paris: Gallimard.

———. 1996. *Les Âmes du Purgatoire ou Le Travail du Deuil*. Paris: Gallimard.

———. 2004. Morte, mortalità, utopia di fronte alla Rivoluzione Francese. In *Perfezione e finitudine. La concezione della morte nell'utopia in età moderna e contemporanea*, ed. Vita Fortunati, Marina Sozzi, and Paola Spinozzi, 183–196. Torino: Lindau.

Wells, H.G. 1898. *The War of the Worlds*. London: W. Heinemann.

Werfel, Franz. 1946. *Stern der Ungeborenen. Ein Reiseroman*. Stockholm: Bermann-Fischer Verlag.

The Posthuman

Naomi Jacobs

Introduction

In contemporary discourse, "the posthuman" refers to what will succeed "the human" as we know it: specifically, the new state of being resulting from the convergence of human and machine. In the utopian vision of the transhumanists, human enhancement through new technologies will bring godlike powers. Techno-skeptics foresee a more dystopian future, fearing that we will modify ourselves to the point of losing our humanity. With different concerns and assumptions, critical posthumanists affirm the utopian potential of the posthuman as a figure for more inclusive and flexible subjectivities, politics, and social formations, while rejecting the transhumanist "erasure of embodiment" (Hayles 1999, xi) and the construct of "the human" as the crown of creation. The tension between a desire to improve humankind and a fear of losing what is unique and valuable in the human species remains at the heart of utopian and dystopian fictions exploring the concept of the posthuman.

This chapter offers an overview of approaches to the posthuman and then sketches a pre-history of the posthuman in selected utopian texts. The shift to greater acceptance of human enhancement in the late twentieth century will be traced in the speculative fictions of Marge Piercy. Finally, the issue of transgenic guided evolution will be addressed in two dystopian trilogies from recent decades: Octavia Butler's *Xenogenesis / Lilith's Brood* (1987–1989), and Margaret Atwood's *MaddAddam* (2003–2013). In Butler, the

N. Jacobs (✉)
University of Maine, Orono, ME, USA

P. Marks et al. (eds.), *The Palgrave Handbook of Utopian and Dystopian Literatures*, https://doi.org/10.1007/978-3-030-88654-7_56

hybridization of humans with alien beings serves as a metaphor for transgenic engineering. In Atwood, a genetic engineer attempts to replace humankind with an "improved" posthuman species. Both authors see humankind in its current state as dangerously flawed; they interrogate the value of "the human" as well as the desirability of a posthuman future.

Defining the Posthuman

The first recorded use of the term "post-human," according to the OED, appeared in criminologist Maurice Parmelee's *Poverty and Social Progress* (1916). Speaking of eugenic measures to eradicate "socially undesirable types," Parmelee observed that to change human nature to such an extent "would bring into being an animal no longer human, or for that matter mammalian... a post-human animal" (319). As used today, the term goes well beyond the development of a new animal.[1]

For the optimistic futurists who take the name of transhumanists, the posthuman will be a being with abilities and strengths vastly superior to our own, whether a genetically or technologically enhanced version of *homo sapiens sapiens*, or an artificial being—a robot, android, cyborg, or artificial intelligence.[2] A transhuman is in a transitional state between human and posthuman; in the broadest sense, the category includes anyone with an artificial joint, a cochlear implant, or a cardiac pacemaker. The transhumanist project is grounded in humanist values such as faith in reason and science, and the primacy of the free and self-defining individual. According to transhumanist philosopher Max More, "our own expansion and progress without end... [is a] true humanist goal." However, this version of humanism regards the human species as merely a "temporary stage along the evolutionary pathway" (1994, n.p.).[3]

Transhumanists forecast a utopian future in which genetic engineering, biomedicine, information science, nanotechnology, and neuroscience will enable greatly enhanced strength, intelligence, and sensorium, as well as perfect health, unimaginable pleasure, extreme longevity, and even immortality. Nick Bostrom's much-cited "Letter from Utopia" is a message to present-day humanity from "Your Possible Future Self." Readers are urged to escape the "deathtrap" of the body and "move your mind to more durable media" (Bostrom 2008, 3); to "[e]xpand cognition... beyond any genius of humankind" (4), and to aspire to a state of unending bliss "greater" than human life in its moments of greatest ecstasy (7). Once uploaded in digital form to "synthetic brains" (More, n.p.), identity and consciousness will be liberated from the confines of the body and the limitations of space and time. The values here are power, speed, intensity—at the command of an independent "self." Posthumans will have been so dramatically modified as to be "no longer... usefully classified with Homo sapiens" (More, n.p.).

Some critics of technophilic posthumanism might be described as techno-skeptics, seeing transhumanism as ceding "to technology a determinism over human affairs that it does not, cannot, and should not enjoy" (Bendle 2002, 60). They consider such faith in the beneficence of technology to be politically naïve. Further, some regard technological enhancement of human bodies and/or consciousness as inherently problematic. To the extent that we become like machines or leave behind our physical natures, they fear we will lose virtues seen as unique to the human, such as free agency, creativity, and relations of love, compassion, and justice.[2]

The variously termed "cultural" or "critical" posthumanists offer a middle way between the technophilic and technoskeptic accounts. While acknowledging accomplishments of classical humanism, such as principles of universal rights, they reject the humanist notion of Man as the "measure of all things" (Braidotti 2013, 50). Feminist, post-colonialist, and new materialist thinkers argue that "the human" as a rational, untrammeled, self-defining agent, wholly distinct from and superior to non-human animals and machines, has never been more than an exclusionary construct that has served to justify domination and exploitation. In their view, we have never been human, and are already posthuman (Hayles 1999). Critical posthumanists reject the transhumanist desire for omnipotence and immortality, while embracing the utopian potential of the cyborg as an "ironic political myth" (Haraway 1991, 149) that might break down old hierarchies. Against the transhumanists' desire to become like gods, Donna Haraway has famously declared, "I'd rather be a cyborg than a goddess" (176)—rather an embodied, intersectional, fluid being than an omnipotent, disembodied consciousness. In a similar vein, Rosi Braidotti calls for "A posthuman ethics for a non-unitary subject," grounded in "an enlarged sense of inter-connection between self and others, including the non-human or 'earth' others, by removing the obstacle of self-centred individualism" (Braidotti 2013, 49–50). If we are to live in harmony with each other and with the planet, we must relinquish the exceptionalist claim to unique human value, acknowledging our common plight and common cause with all living beings.

BETTER HUMANS THROUGH UTOPIA

A pre-history of the posthuman, in the sense of an enhanced human being, can be traced in early modern utopias. Literary utopia arose as a humanist endeavor, confident that a better human being is attainable through human thought and effort. Thomas More's *Utopia* (1516) takes human nature as a given. His ideal society accommodates this fixed nature by satisfying needs of the body, mind, and spirit, while instituting strict surveillance and severe punishments to discourage negative tendencies. New laws, customs, and institutions would produce better-behaved human beings, motivated by reason rather than passion. But the Utopian citizens are still human in their limitations. To aspire to perfection would be to seek a place higher than the one divinely assigned, just a little lower than the angels.

Utopian socialists of the nineteenth century such as Edward Bellamy and William Morris argue that a changed environment and institutions could produce not just a better social order, but an enhanced human organism. Good nutrition, healthy work, freedom of mind, congenial company, pleasant surroundings, and an equitable economic system would produce a perfected human type: happy, beautiful, healthy, and strong both mentally and physically. Some works of this period, such as Mary E. Bradley Lane's *Mizora: A Prophecy* (1880–81) and Charlotte Perkins Gilman's *Herland* (1915), do advocate selective breeding. The science-minded citizens of Mizora have bred out supposedly atavistic qualities including maleness, sexual desire, aggression, and the dark skin associated with the "elements of evil" (Bradley 2000, 92). Residents of Herland who manifest inferior character traits voluntarily refrain from reproducing. Thus, the citizens of each generation are more intelligent, attractive, strong, and balanced in temperament. But once again, though improved, they have no superhuman powers and seemingly aspire to none.

In the early decades of the twentieth century, scientists identified RNA and DNA and began to understand the role of DNA in heredity. DNA's double helix structure was described in 1953. At the same time, machines were being developed with power to perform computational feats at superhuman speed. The brain began to be conceptualized as an information processing machine, and the self as an array of data, blurring the distinction between machine and human. The insight that heredity is "written" or "coded" in our cells stimulated speculation about how that code might be edited or rewritten. Accordingly, the prospect that genetic engineering and other technology could directly modify both individuals and the species became a common theme in utopian and dystopian texts, and in science fiction more generally.

The critical utopias of the 1970s tend to be skeptical of bodily enhancement and wary of the use of genetic engineering to gain posthuman powers. In Samuel R. Delany's *Trouble on Triton: An Ambiguous Heterotopia* (1976), for instance, any individual may acquire a new gender, race, sexual orientation, or physical type through outpatient procedures; but such changes often seem mere novelties, like a new wardrobe, and do not necessarily bring happiness, health, or success. Joanna Russ's *The Female Man* (1975) features the terrifying assassin Jael, whose teeth have been replaced by "one fused ribbon of steel" (158), a "steely, crocodilian grin" (210). With her metallic fangs, retractable claws, "unnatural" silver eyes (159), silver hair and fingernails, and joy in killing, she is figured as both a machine and an animal—both superhuman and other than human. She certainly offers no model for the future.

In Marge Piercy's *Woman on the Edge of Time* (1976), time-traveling protagonist Connie Ramos encounters human enhancement in both utopian and dystopian settings. Genetic engineering is seen in a positive light when used to eliminate disease or reduce social inequality. Reproductive policy in the utopian future assures a higher proportion of dark-skinned people in the population and a rich racial mix in every community. Lab-generated fetuses are

gestated in a "brooder," in order to free women from the burdens of pregnancy. Men are able to breastfeed to assure equality in infant care. But there
has been little attempt to enhance other human abilities or to radically extend
the lifespan. While some community members do advocate more extensive
genetic engineering, others (including the character who serves as Connie's
guide) ask "Why try to control everything?" (109) and prefer to leave genetic
mixing to chance.

Piercy dramatizes the dystopian potential of technological "enhancement"
in two worlds, both permeated with greed, racism, and sexism. In Connie's
own time and place, in the 1970s in New York, scientists use brain implants to
control people who have been institutionalized as mentally ill. The chief scientist sees this as an enhancement. He boasts of his ability to "electrically trigger
almost every mood and emotion—the fight-or-flight reaction, euphoria, calm,
pleasure, pain, terror!... we can control [the patient's] violent attacks and
maintain her in a balanced mental state" (196). But these mechanically generated emotions are depicted as obscene, and the patient's loss of free will as a
humiliation. She becomes nothing more than a puppet for the scientist's entertainment. Furthermore, the social conditions that produced her rebellious and
supposedly "insane" behaviors will remain unchanged.

Connie also glimpses a dystopian future where the genetically engineered
wealthy enjoy 200-year life spans up in space. Unaltered "woolies" who are
"still animal tissue" (291) live on the toxic earth, grow old by 40, and are
relegated to the organ bank once having outlived their usefulness. The sex
worker Gildina is a caricature of femininity, so thoroughly altered through
implants, hormones, and surgical "enhancements" that she can hardly walk.
Gildina's current "owner" Cash, a corresponding caricature of masculinity, is
seven feet tall, with a deep voice "beyond the human range" (292). Gildina
explains that Cash "turns off fear and pain and fatigue and sleep, like he's
got a switch... He can control the fibers in his spinal cord, control his body
temperature... He has those superneurotransmitters ready to be released in his
brain that turn him into just about an Assassin" (291–292). Wealthy families and corporations have "armies of genetically engineered fighters" (292)
like Cash, some with "No animal tissue. Entirely improved" (292). Both
Gildina and Cash have become less than human as a direct result of having
been "improved." Although the scene is played for comedy, this vision of
a posthuman future warns of the dangers of unchecked modification of the
human body, the potential for abuse, and the likelihood that any benefits
would be very unevenly distributed.

Fifteen years later, Piercy put forth a more positive account of human
enhancement, as well as a challenge to the distinction between human and
machine, in the cyberpunk dystopia *He, She and It*, published in England as
Body of Glass (1991). The intervening years had seen significant advances in
genetic technology, biomedicine, and neuroscience; more sympathetic representations of cyborgs in popular culture, such as Ridley Scott's 1984 film *Blade
Runner*; and critical interventions including Haraway's "A Cyborg Manifesto"

(1991 [1985]), which directly influenced Piercy's thinking. Accordingly, Piercy's second work is more open to human enhancement and even makes the case that an android can be "thoroughly a person, though not a human one" (Piercy 1991, 421).

In a dystopian 2059, nuclear war and global warming have rendered much of the earth uninhabitable except under protective domes. The prosperous minority live in exclusive communities; the impoverished majority inhabit the Glop, a lawless, poisoned urban sprawl. A few resisters have set up utopian enclaves, constantly under threat from ruling corporations. Human enhancement is common. One corporate boss is "reputed to be absolutely loaded with circuitry, including an artificial heart, pancreas, eyes and additional sensors. Indeed his eyes... were too perfect to be real" (Piercy 1991, 389). After listing her own enhancements, including retinal implants, a corneal implant, and a "plug set into my skull to interface with a computer," protagonist Shira reassures the android Yod that "We're all cyborgs... You're just a purer form of what we're all tending toward" (150).

The most notable example of human enhancement is the warrior Nili, daughter of an all-woman community built in Israel, which has been rendered toxic by nuclear exchange. The women of the Black Zone have mastered cloning, genetic engineering, and body augmentation. Nili, who describes herself as "well-equipped" (198), has superhuman strength and speed, and can tolerate high levels of radiation. Shira is told that it's only "a matter of definition" whether Nili is "a machine or human" (191), but this is not meant as a criticism. Indeed, Shira thinks that Nili looks "more artificial" than Yod, whose ontological status is a central concern of the book: "[Nili's] hair, her eyes were unnaturally vivid and her musculature was far more pronounced" (222). As the novel concludes, the wise woman Malkah is on her way to Israel with Nili to be "augmented"; she thinks with pleasure that she will have "eyes like a great cat" and a new heart (417). To make people into "partial machines" is seen as the "right path" (412) to a posthuman future. The contrast with Russ's treatment of Jael, or Piercy's of Gildina and Cash in her earlier work, is striking.

THE TRANSGENIC POSTHUMAN IN OCTAVIA BUTLER AND MARGARET ATWOOD

Human beings have long guided the evolution of plants and animals. In the 1970s, geneticists began to directly manipulate DNA to create genetically modified organisms (GMOs), beginning with bacteria and progressing to plants. By the 1990s, they were achieving some success with mammals, from mice to pigs. In transgenesis, genes from one species are introduced into a quite different species. Thus are created fluorescent rabbits containing jellyfish DNA, or goats whose milk contains spider silk. Scientists today are working on human-pig chimeras for purposes of "incubating" human organs for transplant.

These developments open wholly new possibilities for transformation of the human body: not merely the editing of human DNA, but the incorporation of genes from the entire range of creation. Taken to the extreme, human DNA could become just one ingredient of new, transgenic organisms, spliced together from multiple sources. While such a prospect may feel disturbing to the extent that it threatens human distinctiveness, it also allows for new alliances across species boundaries. This focus on new species is taken up in major speculative trilogies by Octavia Butler and Margaret Atwood.

Both trilogies depict unaltered humanity as inherently self-destructive. In Butler's *Xenogenesis* trilogy (1987–89), the few humans to have survived a nuclear holocaust are often cruel and violent. Even the best among them are resistant to change. The pre-plague world of Atwood's *MaddAddam* (2003–2013) is similarly horrific, supporting the view of some characters that "Human society... [is] a sort of monster" (Atwood 2003, 243). Humanity's very survival is threatened by the ecological effects of our own greed, violence, exploitation, and mindless consumption. Both authors suggest the necessity and perhaps the inevitability of a posthuman future; but their vision is far from the apotheosis of the human promised by transhumanists.

Dawn, the first volume of Butler's trilogy, is narrated by a woman named Lilith, one of a small group of humans to survive a nuclear holocaust. They have been kept in suspended animation for 250 years by their captors/saviors, an alien race called the Oankali who have traveled through the universe for millennia. As the Oankali engage in genetic "trade" with other beings they encounter, they are constantly transformed. Each iteration is morphologically new, a hybrid being that mixes DNA of the current stage of Oankali evolution with that of their latest partners. Certainly, they select new traits with an eye to gaining new powers; for instance, they harness the human "talent for cancer" (Butler 2000, 547) to enable the growth of new limbs. Over their long history, they have gained enormous sophistication in technology, as well as in social exchange.[4] As a group they are able to meld minds, to communicate without speaking; with sensory filaments, they can read another being's DNA as we would read a written text. They can also edit DNA; for instance, Lilith is given greater physical strength and resistance to disease when she is chosen to bear hybrid children. But their goal is renewal, and they feel no grief for the losses that come from merging with other beings. Indeed, the longing for encounter with the unfamiliar is an irresistible need, a felt hunger; they "taste" genetic variation as we might relish a delectable new food. The Oankali have no investment in a species identity; the ability to trade is the only trait they "never trade away" (441).

The humans, by contrast, cling desperately to their species identity, even though they were nearly brought to extinction by what the Oankali diagnose as the fatal contradiction in human nature: a combination of intelligence and hierarchical behavior. Repulsed and terrified by the strangeness of their tenta-cled hosts, they resent the irresistible seductions that lure them into coupling with an Oankali mate and thus participating in the trade. Oankali genetic engineering is a sensual and sexual endeavor. A male and a female are linked by a third gender called the "ooloi" in a connection bringing unspeakable pleasure. This is no laboratory experiment, but a deeply intimate exchange which forges a lifelong bond. When a new being is to be generated, the ooloi mates with a male and a female human, combining human DNA with that of its Oankali mates. The resulting "construct" child may look more or less human, but the particular form it will take cannot be known until after its birth. While the Oankali are untroubled by these uncertainties, humans attempt to force reality to fit their preconceived ideals, even threatening to amputate the tentacles of construct children in order to make them look more human. In her exploration of the potential of transgenesis, Butler uses the metaphor of alien encounter to anatomize the psychology of metamorphosis. She paints an emotional landscape of the posthuman far more complex than the unproblematic bliss and power promised by transhumanists, acknowledging the terror and peril of the posthuman, as well as its fascination and promise.

Where Butler's narrative remains firmly in the realm of science fiction, Atwood grounds her *MaddAddam* trilogy in contemporary genetic science. The three volumes deploy crisscrossing timelines and multiple narrators to tell how the brilliant geneticist Crake set out to "re-boot" humanity (Atwood 2003, 334) by replacing it with a posthuman "Paradice model" designed to minimize impact on the planet. In addition to Crake and his lover Oryx, the characters include Crake's friend Jimmy; the new race of "Crakers" that Jimmy has been charged to care for; members of an ecological cult called God's Gardeners and of an ecoterrorist group called MaddAddam; and finally, a herd of transgenic pigs who join with surviving Gardeners, Maddaddamites, and the Crakers to defeat the vicious Painballers. All of this plays out in a world already tending toward human extinction, due to anthropogenic climate change and ecological devastation. With her characteristic blend of mordant humor and gruesome violence, Atwood asks us to consider both the necessity of a transformed humanity and the dangers of any project to engineer a new being.

Crake is a posthumanist in the most extreme sense, setting out to "take a set of givens, namely the nature of human nature, and steer these givens in a more beneficial direction" (Atwood 2003, 293). In order to eliminate war, cruelty, exploitation, unhappiness, and even industrial civilization, he designs a version of humanity incapable of repeating the horrors of the past. To clear the way for this new race, he must eradicate *homo sapiens* through an engineered plague. Not even his friend Jimmy is sure whether Crake is "a lunatic or an intellectually honorable man who'd thought things through to their logical conclusion" (343).

Crake's goal is a transgenic Eden peopled by peaceful, naked beings, innocent of malice, fear, and even curiosity. Beautiful in form and feature, they come in all colors to eliminate racism. With built-in insect repellent, UV protection, luminescent eyes, and disease resistance, they are "[p]erfectly adjusted to their habitat" (Atwood 2003, 305), needing no clothing or shelter in a world heated by global warming. They mate infrequently and only for reproduction, thus eliminating over-population and sexual competition. They are herbivores, able to digest grass, kudzu, and even their own droppings, so they need not grow food or kill to eat. The "ancient primate brain" has been altered (305) to eliminate jealousy, possessiveness, tribalism, and hierarchy. Their peacefulness leaves them incapable of "shooting and killing people...not being human as such" (207).

But this improved model of humanity is far from the godlike posthuman of the transhumanists. They grow to adulthood in seven years, maintain a child-like innocence and credulity, and are programmed to die in perfect health at the age of 30, without knowing this is their fate (Atwood 2003, 303)—thus to be spared the infirmities of age and the fear of death. Eliminating aggression, Crake also eliminates a sense of humor. Because he believes that "Symbolic thinking of any kind would signal downfall" (361), he attempts to "edit out" (311) dreams, stories, religion, imagination, and song. However, Crake and his team are unable to control every detail. The Crakers' brains are "more malleable than Crake intended" (273). Though designed to be like "blank pages" (347), they begin to acquire literacy and culture. They are full of curiosity, and on the basis of Jimmy's improvised answers to their incessant questions, they develop a ritual-based religion with Crake as creator-god. Furthermore, they manifest unexpected powers, such as intuiting the thoughts of a sleeping or depressed person, and a Craker child is able to serve as interpreter between the humans and the transgenic "pigoons" (hybridized pig and racoon creatures). By the end of the final volume, it has become clear that Crakers can interbreed with humans—a prospect not envisioned by Crake, who assumed all humans would have died in the plague. If these hybrid offspring prove fertile, edited-out traits will reappear and the purity of Crake's "master race" will quickly be diluted. Indeed, the Crakers might even benefit by regaining the human capacity for violence, for unknown numbers of humans have survived the plague, and some are hostile.

The failure of Crake's grand plan shows the hubris of any attempt to re-engineer humanity from scratch. At the same time, Atwood suggests that certain human traits that fuel the worst of our behaviors may also be funda-mental to the brilliance and beauty of our achievements. The culminating battle, in which humans, Crakers, and pigoons form an alliance to defeat their murderous enemies, presents a vision of a future in which the human, the posthuman, and the nonhuman can cooperate to forge a new beginning for living beings on a damaged planet.

CONCLUSION

Utopian speculators have long imagined ways to improve human beings. But only in the twentieth century have visions of a dramatically improved species become more than fantasy. These same advances aroused fears that such technology could be misused, that something precious would be lost if humankind were significantly altered, or that the pursuit of godlike powers for a few fortunate individuals will only hasten a truly posthuman future: one entirely without humankind. When humanity is gone, nature might very well flourish; new species will certainly arise as they have done after every great extinction of the planet's history. Even without biological life, the planet will have its own future on an unimaginable scale of time. Eventually stars will flicker out, black holes consume each other, and, to paraphrase Hamlet, the rest will be silence. But for now, writers like Butler and Atwood help us to think through the utopian and dystopian implications of posthuman futures.

NOTES

1. The secondary literature on the posthuman is extensive. See, in addition to others cited above: Michael Hauskeller, 2013, Utopia in Trans- and Posthumanism, in *Post- and Transhumanism: An Introduction*, ed. Robert Ranish and Stefan Sorgner, Peter Lang, 101–108; Andy Miah, 2008, A Critical History of Posthumanism, in *Medical Enhancement and Posthumanity,* ed. B. Gordijn and R. Chadwick, 71–94, New York: Springer; Cary Wolfe, 2009, *What is Posthumanism?* Minneapolis: University of Minnesota Press.
2. The scope of this essay does not allow discussion of those tales of posthuman anxiety, such as Karel Capek's R.U.R., in which artificial beings created to serve humanity overthrow their masters. Such works express in an indirect way our fears that artificially enhanced humans might displace the "natural" human.
3. For a qualified defense of transhumanism, see Andrew Pilsch, 2017, *Transhumanism: Evolutionary Futurism and the Human Technologies of Utopia*, Minneapolis: University of Minnesota Press.
4. On posthuman subjectivities in Butler, see Naomi Jacobs, 2003, Posthuman Bodies and Agency in Octavia Butler's *Xenogenesis*, in *Dark Horizons: Science Fiction and the Dystopian Imagination*, ed. Raffaella Baccolini and Tom Moylan, 91–112, New York: Routledge.

REFERENCES

Atwood, Margaret. 2003. *Oryx and Crake*. New York: Nan A. Talese/Doubleday.
———. 2009. *The Year of the Flood*. New York: Nan A. Talese / Doubleday.
———. 2013. *MaddAddam*. New York: Anchor Books/Random House.
Bendle, Mervyn F. 2002. Teleportation, Cyborgs and the Posthuman Ideology. *Social Semiotics* 12 (1): 45–62.
Bostrom, Nick. 2008. Letter from Utopia. *Studies in Ethics, Law, and Technology* 2 (1): 1–7.

Bradley, Mary E. 2000. *Mizora: A Prophecy,* ed. Pfaelzer. Syracuse: Syracuse University Press.

Braidotti, Rosi. 2013. *The Posthuman.* Cambridge, UK: Polity.

Butler, Octavia. 2000. *Lilith's Brood.* Omnibus edition of *Dawn* (1987), *Adulthood Rites* (1988) and *Imago* (1989). Previously collected as *Xenogenesis.* New York: Warner.

Delany, Samuel R. 1976. *Trouble on Triton: An Ambiguous Heterotopia.* New York: Bantam Books.

Haraway, Donna J. 1991. A Cyborg Manifesto: Science, Technology, and Socialist-Feminism in the Late Twentieth Century. In *Simians, Cyborgs, and Women: The Reinvention of Nature,* ed. Cyborgs Simians, 149–182. New York: Routledge.

Hayles, N. Katherine. 1999. *How We Became Posthuman: Virtual Bodies in Cybernetics, Literature, and Informatics.* Chicago and London: The University of Chicago Press.

Lane, Mary E. Bradley. 2000 [1890]. *Mizora: A Prophecy.* Edited and with a Critical Introduction by Jean Pfaelzer. Syracuse: Syracuse University Press.

More, Max. 1994. On becoming posthuman. *Free Inquiry* 14 (4) (Fall): 38–41.

Parmelee, Maurice. 1916. *Poverty and Social Progress.* New York: Macmillan.

Piercy, Marge. 1976. *Woman on the Edge of Time.* New York: Fawcett Crest.

———. 1991. *He, She, and It.* New York: Fawcett Crest.

Russ, Joanna. 1975. *The Female Man.* Boston: Beacon Press.

Index

Printed in the United States
by Baker & Taylor Publisher Services